P9-DNJ-949
R02028 56174

Chicago Public Library
C
P
L
REFERENCE
Form 178 rev. 11-00

ENCYCLOPEDIA OF AMERICAN HISTORY

Colonization and Settlement 1608 to 1760

VOLUME II

ENCYCLOPEDIA OF AMERICAN HISTORY

Volume I
THREE WORLDS MEET
Beginnings to 1607

Volume II
COLONIZATION AND SETTLEMENT
1608 to 1760

Volume III
REVOLUTION AND NEW NATION
1761 to 1812

Volume IV
EXPANSION AND REFORM
1813 to 1855

Volume V
CIVIL WAR AND RECONSTRUCTION
1856 to 1869

Volume VI
THE DEVELOPMENT OF THE INDUSTRIAL UNITED STATES
1870 to 1899

Volume VII
THE EMERGENCE OF MODERN AMERICA
1900 to 1928

Volume VIII
THE GREAT DEPRESSION AND WORLD WAR II
1929 to 1945

Volume IX
POSTWAR UNITED STATES
1946 to 1968

Volume X
CONTEMPORARY UNITED STATES
1969 to the Present

Volume XI
COMPREHENSIVE INDEX

ENCYCLOPEDIA OF AMERICAN HISTORY

Colonization and Settlement
1608 to 1760

VOLUME II

Billy G. Smith, Editor
Gary B. Nash, General Editor

Facts On File, Inc.

Encyclopedia of American History:
Colonization and Settlement (1608 to 1760)

Editorial Director: Laurie E. Likoff
Editor in Chief: Owen Lancer
Chief Copy Editor: Michael G. Laraque
Associate Editor: Dorothy Cummings
Production Director: Olivia McKean
Production Manager: Rachel L. Berlin
Production Associate: Theresa Montoya
Art Director: Cathy Rincon
Interior Designer: Joan M. Toro
Desktop Designers: Erika K. Arroyo and David C. Strelecky
Maps and Illustrations: Dale E. Williams and Jeremy Eagle

Facts On File, Inc.
132 West 31st Street
New York NY 10001

Library of Congress Cataloging-in-Publication Data

Encyclopedia of American history / Gary B. Nash, general editor.
p. cm.
Includes bibliographical references and indexes.
Contents: v. 1. Three worlds meet — v. 2. Colonization and settlement — v. 3. Revolution and new nation — v. 4. Expansion and reform — v. 5. Civil War and Reconstruction — v. 6. The development of the industrial United States — v. 7. The emergence of modern America — v. 8. The Great Depression and World War II — v. 9. Postwar United States — v. 10. Contemporary United States. — v. 11 Comprehensive index.
ISBN 0-8160-4371-X (set) ISBN 0-8160-4362-0 (v. 2)
1. United States—History—Encyclopedias. I. Nash, Gary B.
E174 .E53 2002
973′.03—dc21 2001051278

Facts On File books are available at special discounts when purchased in bulk quantities for businesses, associations, institutions, or sales promotions. Please call our Special Sales Department in New York at (212) 967-8800 or (800) 322-8755.

You can find Facts On File on the World Wide Web at http://www.factsonfile.com

Printed in the United States of America

VB FOF 10 9 8 7 6 5 4 3 2 1

This book is printed on acid-free paper.

Contents

To Sage Adrienne Smith
and the children of all of the contributors
to this encyclopedia

List of Entries

About the Editors

General Editor: Gary B. Nash received a Ph.D from Princeton University. He is currently director of the National Center for History in the Schools at the University of California, Los Angeles, where he teaches American history of the colonial and Revolutionary era. He is a published author of college and precollegiate history texts. Among his best-selling works is *The American People: Creating a Nation and Society* (Addison Wesley, Longman), now in its fifth edition.

Nash is an elected member of the Society of American Historians, American Academy of Arts and Sciences, and the American Philosophical Society. He has served as past president of the Organization of American Historians, 1994–95, and was a founding member of the National Council for History Education, 1990.

Volume Editor: Billy G. Smith, Montana State University, received a Ph.D. from the University of California, Los Angeles. He is a published author of several books, including *The "Lower Sort": Philadelphia's Laboring People, 1750–1800* (Cornell University Press) and the forthcoming *Down and Out in Early America* (Penn State University Press).

Acknowledgments

I thank the contributors to this volume for giving so much time and energy to researching and writing the entries, as well as for being so pleasurable to work with: James F. Adomanis, Maryland Center for the Study of History; Richard A. Bailey, University of Kentucky; Doug Baker, Oklahoma State University–Oklahoma City; Daniel P. Barr, Kent State University; Michael C. Batinski, Southern Illinois University; Marshall Joseph Becker, West Chester University; Rosalind J. Beiler, University of Central Florida; Michael A. Bellesiles, Emory University; Troy O. Bickham, Southeast Missouri State University; Wayne Bodle, Indiana University of Pennsylvania; George W. Boudreau, Penn State–Harrisburg; Monique Bourque, Swarthmore College; Catherine A. Brekus, The University of Chicago; James Bruggeman, Principal, Irving School; Jane E. Calvert, University of Chicago; Jeffrey D. Carlisle, University of North Texas; Paula Wheeler Carlo, Nassau Community College; Roger Carpenter, State University of New York–Oswego; Nicki Walker Carroll, Mississippi State University; Michael S. Casey, Graceland University; Joseph J. Casino, Philadelphia Archdiocesan Historical Research Center; Charles L. Cohen, University of Wisconsin–Madison; Anthony Connors, Clark University; Maia Conrad, Christopher Newport University; Jane P. Currie, independent scholar; Gail D. Danvers, King's College, London; Alexander Dawson, Montana State University–Bozeman; Anita DeClue, Montana State University–Bozeman; Kenneth A. Deitreich, West Virginia University; Brian DeLay, Harvard University; James Delbourgo, Columbia University; Mary Sudman Donovan, Hunter College; James D. Drake, Metropolitan State College of Denver; Donald Duhadaway, Wesleyan University; Kathleen DuVal, McNeil Center for Early American Studies; Katherine Carté Engel, University of Wisconsin–Madison; Lisa A. Ennis, Georgia College & State University; Ellen Fernandez-Sacco, University of California–Berkeley; Walter Fleming, Montana State University–Bozeman; Dan Flory, Montana State University–Bozeman; John B. Frantz, The Pennsylvania State University; Darcy R. Fryer, Yale University; David A. Geier, MedCon, Inc.; Mark R. Geier, The Genetic Centers of America; Donald F. M. Gerardi, Brooklyn College, City University of New York; Peter S. Genovese, Jr., Bowling Green State University; Lorri Glover, University of Tennessee; Catherine Goetz, independent scholar; Larry Gragg, University of Missouri–Rolla; Allen C. Guelzo, Templeton Honors College, Eastern University; Karen Guenther, Mansfield University; George W. Harper, Asia Graduate School of Theology–Philippines; Emma Hart, University of St Andrews; Donald E. Heidenreich, Jr., Lindenwood University; Alison Duncan Hirsch, Penn College of Technology; Thomas J. Humphrey, Cleveland State University; Brooke Hunter, University of Delaware; Thomas N. Ingersoll, Ohio State University; Michael J. Jarvis, University of Rochester; Virginia Jelatis, Western Illinois University; James Jenks, Historian, Garcia and Associates; Richard R. Johnson, University of Washington; Linda Kneeland, Montana State University–Bozeman; Susan Kollin, Montana State University–Bozeman; Margo Krager, Bozeman, Montana; Andrew C. Lannen, Louisiana State University; Thomas J. Lappas, Indiana University; Emma Lapsansky, Haverford College; Timothy James Lockley, University of Warwick; Paul Mapp, Harvard University (Ph.D. candidate); Dale Martin, Montana State University–Bozeman; Michelle Maskiell, Montana State University–Bozeman; Brian McKnight, Mississippi State University; James E. McWilliams, Southwest Texas State University; Jonathan Mercantini, University of Miami; Jane T. Merritt, Old Dominion University; Randall M. Miller, Saint Joseph's University; Stephanie Muntone, Philadelphia, Pennsylvania; Mary Murphy, Montana State University–Bozeman; Keat Murray, Lehigh University; Caryn E. Neumann, Ohio State University; Greg O'Brien,

University of Southern Mississippi; Stephen C. O'Neill, Weymouth, Massachusetts; J. M. Opal, Brandeis University; Leslie Patrick, Bucknell University; Kenneth Pearl, Queensborough Community College; William Pencak, Pennsylvania State University; Melanie Perreault, Salisbury State University; Carla Gardina Pestana, Ohio State University; Matthew Taylor Raffety, Columbia University; Peter Rainow, San Mateo, California; Ty M. Reese, University of North Dakota; Victoria C. H. Resnick, Indiana University–Bloomington; Christopher Rodi, Montana State University–Bozeman; Shane Runyon, University of Florida; Sharon V. Salinger, University of California–Riverside; Steven Sarson, University of Wales–Swansea; Margaret Sankey, Auburn University; Elizabeth D. Schafer, Loachapoka, Alabama; Bradley Scott Schrager, Miami University; Ronald Schultz, University of Wyoming; Susan Sleeper-Smith, Michigan State University; Paul Smith-Hawkins, Pima Community College; Jean R. Soderlund, Lehigh University; Deborah C. Taylor, Montana State University–Bozeman; Gavin J. Taylor, Bucknell University; Joseph S. Tiedemann, Loyola Marymount University; Tristan Traviolia, U.C.L.A.; Jenny Turner, New York City, New York; Judy VanBuskirk, SUNY–Cortland; Eugene VanSickle, West Virginia University; C. B. Waldrip, University of Alabama; Brett L. Walker, Montana State University–Bozeman; Grant Weller, Air Force Academy; Kate Werner, Montana State University–Bozeman; Thomas R. Wessel, Montana State University–Bozeman; Jonathan Wright, independent scholar; Yolonda Youngs, Montana State University–Bozeman; Serena Zabin, Carleton College.

I much appreciate the editor, Owen Lancer, for his hard work, patience, and, mostly, for his keen sense of humor. Trinette Ross served as a wonderful and diligent research assistant, detecting and correcting numerous errors. My colleagues at MSU have always provided a stimulating and enjoyable environment in which to work and live. And my partner, Michelle Maskiell, and daughter, Sage Adrienne Smith, are the joys of my life.

Foreword

The Encyclopedia of American History series is designed as a handy reference to the most important individuals, events, and topics in U.S. history. In 10 volumes, the encyclopedia covers the period from the 15th century, when European explorers first made their way across the Atlantic Ocean to the Americas, to the present day. The encyclopedia is written for precollegiate as well as college students, for parents of young learners in the schools, and for the general public. The volume editors are distinguished historians of American history. In writing individual entries, each editor has drawn upon the expertise of scores of specialists. Articles contributed by the various volume editors are uncredited. This ensures the scholarly quality of the entire series.

This 10-volume encyclopedia of "American history" is broadly conceived to include the historical experience of the various peoples of North America. Thus, in the first volume, many essays treat the history of a great range of indigenous people before contact with Europeans. In the same vein, readers will find essays in the first several volumes that sketch Spanish, Dutch, and French explorers and colonizers who opened up territories for European settlement that later would become part of the United States. The venues and cast of characters in the American historical drama are thus widened beyond traditional encyclopedias.

In creating the eras of American history that define the chronological limits of each volume, and in addressing major topics in each era, the encyclopedia follows the architecture of *The National Standards for United States History, Revised Edition* (Los Angeles: National Center for History in the Schools, 1996). Mandated by the U.S. Congress, the national standards for U.S. history have been widely used by states and school districts in organizing curricular frameworks and have been followed by many other curriculum-building efforts.

Entries are cross-referenced, when appropriate, with *See also* citations at the end of articles. At the end of most entries, a listing of articles and books allows readers to turn to specialized sources and historical accounts. In each volume, an array of maps provide geographical context, while numerous illustrations help vivify the material covered in the text. A time line is included to provide students with a chronological reference to major events occurring in the given era. The selection of historical documents in the back of each volume gives students experience with the raw documents that historians use when researching history. A comprehensive index to each volume also facilitates the reader's access to particular information.

In each volume, long entries are provided for major categories of American historical experience. These categories may include: African Americans, agriculture, art and architecture, business, economy, education, family life, foreign policy, immigration, labor, Native Americans, politics, population, religion, urbanization, and women. By following these essays from volume to volume, the reader can access what might be called a mini-history of each broad topic, for example, family life, immigration, or religion.

— Gary B. Nash
University of California, Los Angeles

Introduction

Colonization and Settlement focuses on the era from 1607, when Jamestown was founded as the first permanent English colony in North America, to 1760, as the Seven Years' War ended and Great Britain became the supreme European power on the continent. The volume concentrates on a century and a half during which the interaction among Native Americans, Europeans, and Africans created a host of new and continually changing cultures and societies. During this period, Europeans struggled to establish colonies (which subsequently evolved in unexpected and complex ways); Indians struggled to maintain their cultures, lands, and independence; and black men, women, and children struggled against the barbarity of slavery. The remarkable societies and unresolved problems thereby left a legacy that Americans still confront today.

While the encyclopedia's geographic spotlight shines most brightly on the eastern portion of the continent that would become the new United States, people and events in other parts of the North American mainland are also illuminated. Readers will find topics ranging from Spanish Florida to Russian Alaska, from Puritan Massachusetts to French New Orleans, and from Virginia's Powhatan Confederacy to California Indians. The entries reflect a major trend in historical interpretation during the past few decades by including not only the rich and politically powerful but also poorer people, immigrants, women, Native Americans, and African Americans. Thus, John Winthrop, John Smith, and Jonathan Edwards appear alongside Anthony and Mary Johnson, William Moraley, Cornstalk, and Squanto. In addition, important environmental issues are treated, as humans, other animals, and plants transformed the North American physical landscape in ways that remain with us in the modern United States.

ENTRIES A TO Z

abolitionism

Before 1763 abolitionists in British North America expressed their opposition to SLAVERY in a variety of ways, including slaves risking their lives through escape and the publication of antislavery tracts. Thousands of enslaved Africans and NATIVE AMERICANS challenged their oppression through daily resistance and flight. Their efforts helped destabilize the institution, particularly in the northern colonies, where no staple crop required huge amounts of LABOR and, therefore, large numbers of slaves. A few slave-owning colonists demonstrated their ambivalence toward slavery by manumitting their slaves, although often only in their wills. The BOSTON judge SAMUEL SEWALL argued in *The Selling of Joseph* (1700) that "all Men, as they are the Sons of Adam, are Coheirs; and have equal Right unto Liberty." Additionally, an initially small but growing number of QUAKERS published tracts and lobbied within their religion for a ban on purchasing, selling, and owning slaves. These Friends based their opposition to involuntary bondage on the belief that God's spirit, or the "inner light," could enter anyone who sought to live without sin, regardless of ethnic background, GENDER, EDUCATION, or social CLASS.

Quakers of the PHILADELPHIA Yearly Meeting, encompassing primarily PENNSYLVANIA and NEW JERSEY, developed the most sustained abolitionist movement among Euro-Americans. The English founder of Quakerism, George Fox, in 1657 reminded Friends to treat their Indian and black slaves well, and he later suggested emancipation after a term of years. In 1688 four members of the Germantown, Pennsylvania, meeting petitioned the Philadelphia Yearly Meeting against slavery. They wrote, "to bring men hither, or to rob and sell them against their will, we stand against. In Europe there are many oppressed for conscience sake; and here there are those oppressed wh[o] are of a black colour." During the early 18th century, as slave imports rose in Pennsylvania and other colonies, individual Friends continued to speak out and publish, including William Southeby, who petitioned the Pennsylvania legislature in 1712 to emancipate all slaves within the colony. In New Jersey John Hepburn published *The American Defence of the Christian Golden Rule, or An Essay to prove the Unlawfulness of making Slaves of Men* (1715). Benjamin Lay took direct action in the 1730s to dramatize the injustice of slavery, "kidnapping" the child of a Quaker couple for several hours to demonstrate the emotional distress of African families who lost their daughters and sons to the SLAVE TRADE. At the 1738 Philadelphia Yearly Meeting, he appeared in military dress, plunging a sword into a hollowed-out book disguised as a Bible and filled with red juice, sprinkling "blood" on Friends seated nearby. The Quaker leaders, many of them slaveholders, escorted Lay from the meeting.

The Philadelphia Yearly Meeting moved more actively against slavery in the 1750s, when a new group of leaders

The Selling
OF
JOSEPH
A Memorial.

FORASMUCH as Liberty is in real value next unto Life: None ought to part with it themselves, or deprive others of it, but upon most mature Consideration.

The Numerousness of Slaves at this day in the Province, and the Uneasiness of them under their Slavery, hath put many upon thinking whether the Foundation of it be firmly and well laid; so as to sustain the Vast Weight that is built upon it. It is most certain that all Men, as they are the Sons of *Adam*, are Coheirs; and have equal Right unto Liberty, and all other outward Comforts of Life. *GOD hath given the Earth* [with all its Commodities] *unto the Sons of* Adam, *Psal* 115. 16. *And hath made of One Blood, all Nations of Men, for to dwell on all the face of the Earth, and hath determined the Times before appointed, and the bounds of their habitation: That they should seek the Lord. Forasmuch then as we are the Offspring of* GOD &c. *Act* 17.26,27,29.

Shown here is the first page from "The Selling of Joseph," a tract by Samuel Sewall. *(New York Public Library)*

took control. Most important were abolitionists JOHN WOOLMAN and ANTHONY BENEZET, who linked their effort to end slaveholding to a broader Quaker reform movement. The Yearly Meeting issued its first denunciation of slavery, *An Epistle of Caution and Advice* (1754), warning slave owners that "to live in Ease and Plenty by the Toil of those whom Violence and Cruelty have put in our power, is neither consistent with Christianity, nor common Justice." Gradually, over the next 20 years, the Philadelphia Yearly Meeting moved toward a stronger position, first in 1758 by excluding from leadership men who imported, bought, or sold slaves, then in 1776 prohibiting slaveholding outright. Yearly meetings elsewhere likewise moved against black bondage. The London Yearly Meeting recommended expulsion of slave traders, for example, and in 1773 the New England Yearly Meeting banned slavery. Many Quaker owners freed enslaved men, women, and children, while more obstinate Friends chose to be disowned.

The white abolitionist movement outside the Society of Friends (Quakers) gained steam only during the American Revolution, an era during which many black Americans fought, took flight, and filed petitions for freedom.

Further reading: Gary B. Nash and Jean R. Soderlund, *Freedom By Degrees: Emancipation in Pennsylvania and Its Aftermath* (New York: Oxford University Press, 1991).

—Jean R. Soderlund

Acadians

In April 1604 Pierre du Gua, sieur de Monts, established about 100 French settlers on Saint Croix Island, in Passamaquoddy Bay, an inlet of the Bay of Fundy in what is now Canada. European fishermen had frequented the area since 1497. When conditions on the island proved unsatisfactory, the remnant of the colony was moved across the bay to Port Royal the following summer. The colony, which became known as Acadie (either from 16th-century mapmakers' Arcadia and/or from a Micmac word), developed a unique culture with a distinctive language, dress, and customs. Although MORTALITY was high in the early years, by 1750 the population had spread throughout the region and had grown to nearly 10,000, due in part to a high birth rate and large families. The ECONOMY centered on AGRICULTURE and FISHING. Major crops included wheat, oats, barley, rye, peas, corn, flax, and hemp, while colonists ate pork rather than beef, reserving their cattle for milk, TRADE, and as work ANIMALS. They also brewed spruce beer and fir beer. Community life centered on their Roman Catholic faith and was cemented by the constant and long-term labor required for claiming fertile farmland from the waters of the Bay of Fundy by the use of a dyke system.

In the international wars among France, England, and the Netherlands over control of North America, the Acadians remained largely neutral, although the area changed hands among European nations many times throughout the 17th century. In 1713 the Treaty of Utrecht awarded the British all of Acadia except Île Royal (Cape Breton) and Île St. Jean (Prince Edward Island). Fourteen years later the Acadians agreed that in return for being allowed to retain their religion, customs, and firearms, they would profess conditional allegiance to England and would not provide aid to the French or their Indian allies.

However, in the aftermath of KING GEORGE'S WAR, Governor Edward Cornwallis insisted that they take an oath of unconditional loyalty to the British Crown. The Acadians refused. Although the British relented, many Acadians fled to French Quebec and swore oaths of unqualified allegiance to the French monarch. Some residents who remained in Acadia sent supplies of grain and cattle to the French garrisons at Louisbourg, Beauséjour, and Gaspereau. The British believed the Acadians presented a potential internal security threat at the onset of the SEVEN YEARS' WAR. Soon after Fort Beauséjour fell to the British in the spring of 1755, British soldiers seized the property of Acadians and arrested their Catholic priests. Lieutenant Governor Charles Lawrence also ordered many Acadians to be moved to various distant destinations. Conditions on board the transport ships were very inadequate, and perhaps 20 percent of the 6,500 deportees died en route. The refugees were dropped off in groups all along the North American seaboard as well as in the CARIBBEAN and South America. Many ports refused to accept sick and starving strangers, and as many as half of these died on the trans-Atlantic voyage to England. Many who survived eventually made their way to France and to the French colony of LOUISIANA. Deportations from Canada continued for several more years until there were few left in their homeland.

The TREATY OF PARIS (1763) permitted Acadians to return to their former homeland if they pledged loyalty to Britain, but many had already adapted to new homes elsewhere. Those who did return frequently found their old farms occupied by migrants from New England.

Further reading: Charles D. Mahaffie, Jr., *A Land of Discord Always: Acadia from its Beginnings to the Expulsion of its People, 1604–1755* (Camden, Me.: Down East Books, 1995).

—Joseph J. Casino

Acts of Trade and Navigation (Navigation Acts)

Between 1651 and 1733 Parliament passed a series of acts designed to regulate trade in colonial America. These policies reflected the evolving principles of MERCANTILISM:

that colonies existed to strengthen the ECONOMY of the mother country. Although not always strictly enforced, these policies did bring additional wealth to the British economy by controlling American trade and protecting the interests of British MERCHANTS and manufacturers. The policies also had unexpected consequences: They stimulated the economic development of colonial North America, especially before the mid-18th century.

England hoped to strengthen its economy and saw its colonies as a means to this end. The colonies would serve as a source of raw materials and a market for finished goods. English manufacturers would process the raw materials, the country would export more than it imported, and it would consequently rely less on resources from competing European nations. The Trade and Navigation Acts were designed to facilitate these goals.

The Navigation Acts of 1651 focused on shipping and were designed to challenge Dutch competition in overseas trade. The law required that most American goods be carried in English or colonial ships and that at least one half of the crew be citizens of the empire (including colonists). This encouraged the growth of England's merchant marines. It also kept revenue "in the family," rather than paying the Dutch to transport colonial goods.

In 1660 Parliament passed a second navigation act that amended the earlier policy. Now, all colonial trade would be carried in English or colonial ships, with the master and three-fourths of the crew being British. In addition, the act gave England greater control over colonial exports and increased the ease of levying taxes on the products. Certain commodities of great value to the mother country (TOBACCO, sugar, INDIGO, and cotton, for example) were to be shipped only to England or to other British ports. They would then be sold within the empire or reexported to other European ports. In later years rice, molasses, furs, and naval stores were added to this list of "enumerated" goods. The law added intermediaries to the transport process, thereby increasing the cost but also providing income to English coffers. In the 1660s the import duties on tobacco from MARYLAND and VIRGINIA amounted to 25 percent of English customs revenue.

In 1663 Parliament passed the Staples Act, specifying that all European exports to British colonial America must be shipped to England first. Prices on these reexported goods were thereby increased, making many British products the cheapest alternative for American consumers.

Colonists reacted to these policies in a variety of ways. Tobacco planters argued that paying customs duties significantly lowered their profit. Small planters, especially, were affected by these higher costs. New England merchants and shippers often ignored the acts; many continued to trade with the Dutch or find other ways, like SMUGGLING, to avoid the new policies.

To further tighten imperial control, Parliament passed the Revenues Act of 1663, requiring that ship captains transporting certain colonial goods pay a "plantation duty" on any enumerated items not delivered to England. In addition, a staff of customs officials was assigned to colonial port cities. These measures were only marginally successful, however, as there were too few customs officials to adequately supervise all of the trade. Parliament tried again in 1696 to close loopholes in earlier acts and established vice-admiralty courts to try cases of smuggling and other trade offenses.

Between 1699 and 1733 Parliament passed other legislation to protect the interests of British merchants and manufacturers from colonial competition. The 1699 Woolen Act and the 1732 Hat Act prohibited the exporting and intercolonial sales of certain textiles and colonial-made hats. The 1733 Molasses Act, designed to protect planters and merchants in the West Indies, levied a high tax on molasses imported to the colonies from non-British ports. New England merchants and distillers largely ignored the policy, however, often bribing customs officials to escape the tariff.

In general, these policies did accomplish their mercantilist goals. England achieved a favorable balance of trade and grew less dependent on foreign markets. The British treasury grew richer from customs duties paid by colonists. The acts also had significant consequences for the American colonies. Although mercantilist theory stressed the economic development of the mother country at the expense of its colonies, these acts actually promoted the development of the colonial economy. The colonists benefited from guaranteed markets and from incentives paid for producing certain commodities. Some acts stimulated New England SHIPBUILDING. Other acts were virtually ignored, as colonial merchants freely traded rum, molasses, and sugar with little interference from customs officials. These trade regulations proved mutually beneficial, at least until the mid-18th century, after which some colonists began to feel the limitations of some of the restrictions.

See also TRADE AND SHIPPING.

Further reading: John McCusker and Kenneth Morgan, eds., *The Early Modern Atlantic Economy: Essays on Transatlantic Enterprise* (Cambridge, U.K.: Cambridge University Press, 2001).

—Virginia Jelatis

Africa

As the ancestral homeland of many early Americans, Africa was vital in shaping American culture. From the 16th to the 18th century, African societies were neither more monolithic nor static than European ones; they differed greatly and changed over time. The huge continent of Africa consisted of diverse populations with rich histories, practices, and institutions that constituted various cultures. European traders encountered complex and varying forms of government, economies, religions, and arts that had characterized Africans' lives for many centuries. Contrary to the belief that developed among many Europeans to justify SLAVERY, Africa was not "inferior" to Europe in any of these ways.

Nearly all the African peoples brought to British North America came from the coast and interior of western and west-central Africa. English slavers frequented the ports north of the Congo, bringing many slaves to North America during the early years. Later in the 18th century more slaves came to English colonies from the Portuguese ports of Luanda and Benguela. Approximately one-quarter of the captured population came from the coast of what is now southeastern Nigeria. About 15 percent each came from Senegambia (the land between and around the Senegal and Gambia rivers), the Gold Coast, and the coast between and including current day Sierra Leone and the Ivory Coast. The peoples inhabiting these areas spoke several hundred mutually unintelligible languages and practiced social customs that, in some extremes, were as different from one another as they were from those of Europeans.

African societies also differed politically from one another. Governance ranged from highly militaristic and hierarchical empires, such as Ghana, Mali, and Songhai, to village states, to relatively stateless societies. In many places local identity, customs, and language differences militated against any widespread unity. Individual allegiances were normally to the extended family and the village. Sometimes the allegiances extended more broadly to a kinship group or a clan; sometimes they spread beyond to a larger political unit—a state or an empire. Relations did, however, traverse political and language boundaries. Long-distance traders moved across political boundaries, religions and secret societies spread and provided a commonality in larger areas, and historical events occasionally united groups. However, most frequently, people from western and west-central Africa possessed a worldview idiosyncratic to their own group.

African economic interests varied, revolving around AGRICULTURE, industry, and commerce. Diverse occupations of Africans captured and sold in the SLAVE TRADE reveal the variety of economic activities that existed before Europeans arrived. Farmers, the largest group captured, grew rice, millet, maize, yams, and manioc or harvested bananas, plantains, and palm products. Other early African captives came from long traditions as blacksmiths; weavers; potters; workers in bronze, copper and gold; and traders who had wide-ranging movements over the continent. Others had been herders and fishermen. Even musicians, priests, and the nobility numbered among the captives.

The variety of Africans' artistic expressions flourished long before Europeans' arrival, and they continued, albeit transformed, despite the trans-Atlantic slave trade. MUSIC, DANCE, song, sculpture, and carving flourished throughout the continent, and these ART forms traveled to the New World with the captives. Africans spoke many languages, only a few of which were written. Instead, a vibrant oral literature preserved communities' traditions and stories. Proverbs played important roles in greetings, songs, and folktales.

Indigenous religions commonly involved ancestor veneration, consistent with the family or kinship group as the fundamental unit of social organization. The spirits of ancestors exercised the principal religious influence upon most groups. Indigenous religions continued often side by side with religions that later appeared. Initially some rulers reluctantly accepted Islam, which appeared in sub-Saharan Africa at Bornu around the late 11th century. Although quite different from indigenous religions, Islam was embraced more readily than Christianity. That Christianity did not establish a foothold until the Portuguese established MISSIONS in the 16th century should not come as a surprise, for it preached human unity while simultaneously enslaving Africans.

Slavery had long existed as an economic and social institution among many of the agrarian societies of western and west-central Africa. However, slavery varied considerably among African societies and through time. Some western Africans sold slaves along with gold and spices in commerce that led across the Sahara to North Africa. By the 17th century some Africans had become partners with Europeans in the maritime slave trade, but bondage in Africa exhibited fundamentally different characteristics from slavery in the New World. Unlike European and American bondage, African slavery frequently was characterized by personal relationships between masters and slaves and by a chance for slaves to obtain their freedom and be accepted as equals. Moreover, African slavery was neither hereditary nor racially based.

As in most places where slavery existed, African societies usually obtained slaves by violent means, warfare being the most common method. Another technique involved condemning people to slavery through judicial or religious proceedings for civil crimes or religious offenses. Frequent and severe droughts and famines also forced some Africans to sell themselves or their relatives into slavery so that families might survive. Finally, while many slaves in sub-Saharan Africa were women, western traders primarily sought men as laborers in the colonies.

Africans were the largest group of immigrants, albeit involuntary, to British North America in the 18th century, and the labor of these slaves and their descendants accounted for much of the prosperity of the southern colonies and of America itself. Their African heritage, which many maintained in the New World, shaped the nature of slave communities as well as the culture of early America.

See also SLAVE RESISTANCE; SLAVE TRADE.

Further reading: John Thornton, *Africa and Africans in the Making of the Atlantic World, 1400–1680* (Cambridge, U.K.: Cambridge University Press, 1992).

—Leslie Patrick

African Americans

The people referred to today as African Americans were neither African nor American in the colonies. They had been involuntarily captured and transported from AFRICA to colonies throughout the Western Hemisphere for purposes of enslavement, or they were descended from those people. They were not Americans because—slave, servant, or free—with very few exceptions, they had virtually no positive standing before English law, especially as it was interpreted in the North American colonies. Although among the oldest American-born populations, they tragically no longer had a true home.

Historians' myopia has largely contributed to the fact that we know less about the quality of their lives than we might. Scholars once complacently accepted Africans' subservient status in the colonies. By the end of the 19th century, black historians, followed by their white counterparts, began to reverse that perspective by examining the emergence of SLAVERY and the conditions in which enslaved people found themselves. Many historians now seek to demonstrate the ways that people of African ancestry negotiated both with whites and among themselves for a few freedoms. Despite this recent trend in scholarship, it remains important to recognize the severe restrictions under which the vast majority of black people lived.

Although a few African men likely had visited the North American continent before it was colonized by the British, permanent black presence in North America did not begin until 1619, with the arrival of "twenty Negars" at JAMESTOWN, VIRGINIA. Significantly, the first 20 people were not slaves; they occupied a status resembling that of white indentured servants, yet after completing their servitude, neither were they entirely free. As their numbers grew, their status diminished, so that by the beginning of the 18th century enslavement was reserved exclusively for these descendants of the African continent, yet some gained freedom after having completed their term of INDENTURED SERVITUDE. Despite nominal freedom, servants and free blacks encountered monumental restrictions while living in a society that came to expect the status of the black person to be that of the slave.

Initially, the period of servitude was limited for the black involuntary immigrant, and a modest free black population emerged during the 17th century. This small free black population prospered relative to those who would arrive later. For instance, MARY JOHNSON and ANTHONY JOHNSON of Virginia gained their freedom after completion of their servitude, married, and acquired 250 acres on which they built an estate before 1653. They continued to prosper for much of the 17th century. By 1660, however, the prospect of freedom had evaporated for most people of African descent. Those Africans who arrived or their descendants born after the 1660s did not fare so well. Enslavement and strictly drawn racial lines would be finalized by the 18th century.

How and why did the small population that could achieve a certain sort of freedom grow to one for whom slavery became their "natural" and legal status? While enslavement had already begun in the CARIBBEAN, on the North American continent the institution's inception would be in Virginia in the 1660s. Every British mainland colony eventually followed suit, establishing complex SLAVE CODES that declared and justified slavery as the heritable condition for persons of African ancestry.

Despite their shared experiences of capture in the slave trade, the Middle Passage, and restrictions upon them, the African-born populace was no more monolithic than any other group in North America. They arrived with widely differing languages and other cultural attributes. They developed various cultural forms that reflected their adaptation to the conditions in which they lived. One important distinction was that African-born people differed from the American-born (CREOLES) populace. Over time, the Creole population also developed distinct cultures that depended largely upon the region and circumstances in which they lived.

Initially, Africans joined NATIVE AMERICANS and white indentured servants who labored involuntarily in the Chesapeake Bay region, although none of the white workers were slaves. The population of Africans grew slowly at first; at the outset, white servants outnumbered them. Until 1660 most unfree labor in the region was white, but, as the supply of English servants diminished and as Virginia elites were disturbed by the unrest of ex-servants, the labor force changed its color. By 1680 unfree labor was 80 percent black.

By 1750 black people in all the British mainland colonies numbered 236,395, constituting one of every five inhabitants of the colonies. Their numbers grew initially because of the SLAVE TRADE and subsequently as the result of declining mortality and increasing reproduction among slaves. The slave trade delivered more men than women of

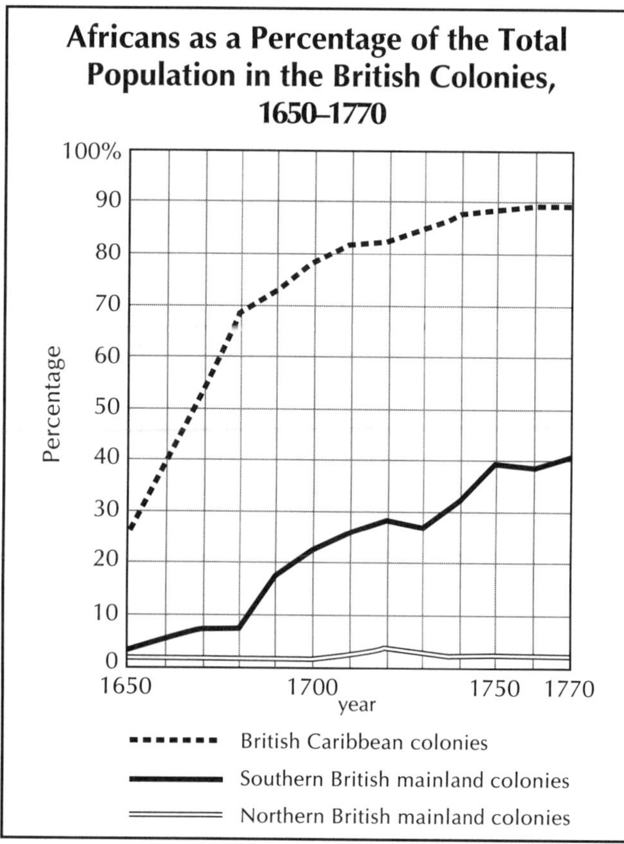

African ancestry to North America. The early settlers relied primarily on the labor of men, and, therefore, women were not imported in large numbers at the outset. British ideas about a sexual division of labor did not last long, however. As planters abandoned their reluctance to use female labor, the imbalance between men and women narrowed. The trauma of the Middle Passage and the introduction to the new environment of North America caused the first generation of black women to be largely infertile. Over time, a more balanced sex ratio developed, resulting in a higher birth rate; by 1720 more black people were born in the colonies than were imported. Two decades later the majority of black people had been born in the British colonies.

Black people were widely dispersed throughout the colonies, and they were, in their work and lives, immensely diverse. Those enslaved in southern colonies primarily toiled in TOBACCO, rice, INDIGO, and other crops that required a great deal of physical labor for a long time each year. Slave labor made sense to the economic calculations of the white colonists, and they also believed that people descended from Africa were better suited than white or Native American laborers for such arduous work. The northern colonies relied less on a slave labor force, in part because wheat and other crops required less intensive labor. Consequently, a much smaller population of black men worked in a wider variety of tasks than their southern counterparts. Northern male slaves toiled primarily as field hands in stock and dairy farming in rural areas, in the ironworks, as assistants to artisans, and in the maritime trades of the port cities. Black women commonly worked in the fields as well as in homes.

The cultural characteristics of African Americans and the rate of their acculturation varied from region to region and over time. Historian Ira Berlin has usefully designated three different regions determined largely by the numbers and types of labor that black people performed. In the farming Mid-Atlantic and New England colonies, slaves were outnumbered by whites, and their culture reflected much white influence. In the Chesapeake region, increasing numbers of Africans were imported after 1680 to join black people who had been born in North America. These two groups, however, remained somewhat separate from each other. Newly arrived African men were "sent . . . to the distant, upland quarters where the slaves did the dull, backbreaking work of clearing the land and tending tobacco." Many, though not all, Creoles, on the other hand, worked as artisans and in households. GEORGIA and SOUTH CAROLINA created yet another cultural context. Although originally illegal in Georgia, slavery had begun on a large scale by 1750. South Carolina was the most distinct colony in British North America, with a larger black than white population. Many slaves were transported directly from the African continent to these colonies of the Lower South, and they "remained physically separated and psychologically estranged from the Anglo-American world and culturally closer to Africa than any other blacks on continental North America," writes Ira Berlin.

The extent of the SLAVE TRADE was one major determinant of acculturation. Acculturation occurred most rapidly among American-born blacks who lived in areas where the slave trade imported few, if any, Africans directly from the continent. However, regardless of where and among whom they lived, as historian Donald R. Wright observed, "blacks in America first had to have extensive social contacts with a substantial number of other blacks—they had to exist in black communities—before there could be a real development of group values, ways, and beliefs." The nature of these interactions, however, changed over time and varied according to location. In colonies such as South Carolina, where there were large numbers of imported Africans, slaves remained somewhat separate from whites and retained more of their traditional ways. Where they resided and worked among an overwhelmingly white population, black people could be isolated and lonely.

Formal education was virtually nonexistent, especially for those who were enslaved in the southern colonies. The SOCIETY FOR THE PROPAGATION OF THE GOSPEL IN FOREIGN PARTS was among the handful of groups that endeavored to introduce literacy and Christianity to blacks. Its efforts were more successful in the northern colonies than in the southern. A few white colonists, like Elias Neau and Quaker ANTHONY BENEZET, worked to provide education for black New Yorkers and Pennsylvanians. Despite these efforts, few black men and women enjoyed literacy, and even fewer published their writing. Not surprisingly, the best-known black authors resided in the North. Lucy Terry Prince (1730–1821) of Massachusetts was probably the first person of African ancestry to publish a poem, "Bars Fight" (1746), in the colonies. In 1760 Jupiter Hammon (1720–1806?) published a poem, "An Evening Thought: Salvation by Christ, with Penitential Cries." While Phillis Wheatley is the most renowned descendant of Africa to publish poetry and a book in early America, she did not do so until 1773. There is an apparent absence of militancy about slavery in all of these writings, in part because these authors likely were primarily concerned to write black people into existence and in part because severe criticism of slavery was unlikely to have been published.

Although most people of African descent did not produce written texts, other evidence reveals that they did not easily accept their subordinate status, whether slave, servant, or free. Some historians have argued that their conversion to Christianity and appropriation of such beliefs was one form of resistance. Unfortunately, little is known about the religious beliefs that they brought with them across the Middle Passage. Still, many resisted from the moment of their capture, and slaves occasionally mutinied while on board slave ships. Daily individual acts of resistance, including theft, arson, breaking tools, working slowly, and even assault and murder were among the most common ways that slaves demonstrated their resistance. Escape, though more frequent among men than women and often only temporary, was another avenue to a hoped for freedom. Newspapers, including Benjamin Franklin's *Gazette,* advertised for fugitive slaves during the era, revealing how frequently slaves "stole themselves." Finally, some organized revolts with the express desire to overthrow the institution that kept them in bondage. The bloodiest of these was the STONO REBELLION in South Carolina in 1739. Revolts and insurrections were not limited to the South, as the NEGRO PLOT OF 1741 took place in New York.

Regardless of where and when they lived during the colonial era, all black people suffered one disability in common—the laws defining criminal activity were much harsher toward them. Every colony legislated codes to regulate the behavior of both slaves and free blacks. Black people were punished more harshly for crimes against property, people, and the moral and religious order of society. Ironically, slaves were more likely to be protected from the ultimate punishment, execution, because they were a valuable investment to their owners. If a slave was executed, his or her owner was entitled to petition the government for reimbursement of lost property.

Despite temporal and regional differences as well as different conditions—free, servant, or slave—all African Americans were vulnerable because of their racial heritage. After a few generations on the North American continent, Africans and their descendants were neither Africans, nor Americans, nor were they truly African Americans.

Further reading: Carol Berkin, *First Generations: Women in Colonial America* (New York: Hill & Wang, 1996); Ira Berlin, *Many Thousands Gone: The First Two Centuries of Slavery in North America* (Cambridge, Mass.: Harvard University Press, 1998); Michael L. Conniff and Thomas J. Davis, *Africans in the Americas: A History of the Black Diaspora* (New York: St. Martin's Press, 1994); A. Leon Higginbotham, *In The Matter of Color, Race & The American Legal Process: The Colonial Period* (New York: Oxford, 1978); Kenneth Morgan, *Slavery and Servitude in Colonial North America: A Short History* (New York: New York University Press, 2000); Gary B. Nash, *Red, White & Black: The Peoples of Early North America* (Upper Saddle River, N.J.: Prentice Hall, 1974, 2000); Donald R. Wright, *African Americans in the Colonial Era: From African Origins Through the American Revolution* (Arlington Heights, Ill.: Harlan Davidson, 1990).

—Leslie Patrick

agriculture

Colonial agriculture was a mix of European, Native American, and African influences. Europeans brought some seed, cultivation techniques, metal tools, and a zeal for material accumulation to the enterprise. NATIVE AMERICANS provided a wealth of new plants and cultivation techniques. Africans contributed significantly to the seed pool, applied skills learned in their homelands, and provided much of the labor that eventually created an agricultural base sufficient to feed a growing population and to accumulate export surpluses. Agriculture was the foundation of the colonial ECONOMY, molded colonial society, and identified political power.

Native Americans practiced agriculture on the North American continent for at least 2,000 years before the arrival of Europeans. By the 16th century extensive Native American agriculture existed from the St. Lawrence River to FLORIDA and west to the Mississippi Valley. Native American agriculture thrived along the river valleys of the Great Plains and reached a level of technological sophistication in the Southwest not seen again until late in the 19th century. Native Americans grew several varieties of maize (corn), beans, squash, pumpkins, TOBACCO, and cotton in fields that in some places extended for miles. Contrary to popular images of Indians as hunters, agriculture provided many tribes with more than half of their FOOD requirements and with important trade items for exchange among the tribes and, later, with Europeans. Maize, or Indian corn, was their most important crop. Maize does not grow naturally; it is the product of at least three different grasses that required generations of cross-breeding and continuous cultivation. By the 16th century it was already the most productive seed grain in the world.

New World agriculture began in present-day Mexico, worked its way to the Southwest and across the Gulf of Mexico to the Mississippi Valley in the Midwest, then spread across the continent. In the Southwest Native Americans created elaborate irrigation systems that diverted stream flow and captured runoff. In the Salt River Valley of Arizona extensive canals carried water as far as two miles from the river. Southwest farmers developed ingenious methods of diverting runoff by building systems of check dams at the mouths of arroyos that spread the water across their fields.

Southwestern Native American farmers planted at least three varieties of maize, three different kinds of beans, and four varieties of squash and pumpkins. In the moisture-deficient Southwest these crops were planted in separate fields. Native farmers in wetter climates planted their crops in the same field, with cornstalks used to support bean vines and squash and pumpkins used as ground cover to retard weeds. Southwestern farmers also cultivated cotton and tobacco. Until Spanish sheep became available, cotton provided the principal fiber for CLOTHING and blankets.

Native farmers in the East planted maize on well-spaced hills; using a digging stick, they cultivated the ground around the plants, and when the maize was well established they planted beans, pumpkins, orache, and sunflowers between the cornstalks. Farmers in the Carolinas planted three varieties of maize with different maturing rates, allowing for ample time to plant and an extended harvest after about three months of growth. Generally, native agriculturalists also planted large gardens that produced abundant supplies of vegetables until the maize, beans, and other field crops were mature. In the 16th century and earlier these farmers planted large fields of tobacco (*Nicotiana rustica*). Later they adopted a tobacco from the Orinoco region of South America (*Nicotiana tabacum*) that JOHN ROLFE had acquired. Captain JOHN SMITH recorded that natives in the region girdled trees and then pulled out the upper roots to prepare fields for cultivation. Women did the work of agriculture after the fields were prepared, planting maize and beans on hills from May through June and harvesting the crops from August until October. Carolina and VIRGINIA native farmers husked their maize after drying it in the sun and then stored the seed in woven baskets.

In the 18th century Virginia Native American farmers were observed growing popcorn that ripened by midsummer, watermelon acquired from the English, and peaches probably obtained from the Spanish or from Florida natives. CHEROKEE, CHOCTAW, Creek, and CHICKASAW farmers in the interior raised large crops of maize, beans, and squash. Families maintained individual gardens near their houses, but all participated in preparing and planting communal fields. Individual families then harvested their allotted portion of the crops. Although men among these "civilized tribes" participated in all phases of their agriculture, women did most of the work of planting, cultivating, and harvesting. The civilized tribes eventually adopted many European farming methods, including fencing their fields, but, one authority insists, they refused to adopt the plow, perhaps because it was too efficient and might have led to lack of farmwork for older members of the tribes.

Early in the 17th century French explorers in the St. Lawrence Valley area observed extensive native farming. Native farmers raised large crops of maize, both for their own CONSUMPTION and for trade to the hunting Indians in the interior. HURON men participated in the agricultural enterprise by burning trees and removing brush from fields, although women did most of the work preparing the fields around the dead trees and removing rotting tree roots. The Huron and others in the region raised crops of flint corn and maize as well as sunflowers, squash, and beans. One branch of the Huron raised so much tobacco they became known as the Tobacco Nation. Huron and other native farmers tried to raise sufficient maize and other crops to last for two or more years as a guard against famine. One authority estimates that Huron fields produced nearly 40 bushels per acre. When the crop fell significantly below that level, the Hurons abandoned the field for several years. Agricultural products probably accounted for more than 60 percent of Huron food needs.

South of the Huron in interior NEW YORK, the Five Nations of the IROQUOIS Confederation engaged in a sophisticated agriculture that yielded food for consumption and an important trade item. Particularly in the 17th century, the Iroquois carried on an aggressive campaign against the Huron that extended to the destruction of smaller agricultural tribes north of Lake Erie in pursuit of dominance in the FUR TRADE. Food stuffs, which the Iroquois had in abundance, were a key trade item with the hunting Indians of Canada. Iroquois men generally participated in burning trees and underbrush to prepare fields while the women performed the work of cultivation and harvesting. The products of the field were the property of the women and added to their unusual influence in the business of the Five Nations. The Iroquois also constructed platforms from

This mold-board plow was the type often used by Anglo American farmers. *(National Museum of American History, Smithsonian Institution)*

which the young and women guarded the crops. In addition, they encircled their fields with snares to trap small ANIMALS, soaked their seed corn in hellebore to poison raiding birds, and hung captured crows by their feet around the fields to discourage other raiders. About every 10 years, when soil fertility declined, the Iroquois abandoned one area for another nearby that previously had been prepared. In the 18th century the Iroquois incorporated cattle, swine, and poultry into their agricultural mix.

When Europeans ventured to the Atlantic coast and later into the interior, they discovered a relatively large, generally sedentary native population that subsisted on an abundance of agricultural products. Although Europeans often thought Indian agriculture "primitive," Indian TECHNOLOGY, including wood, shell, flint, and bone hoes, digging sticks, and mattocks, was efficient and tended to preserve soil conditions at a high level of fertility for relatively long periods of time. Indeed, early explorers and later colonists from MAINE to GEORGIA benefited and often owed their survival to Indian agriculture.

Agriculture dominated economic activity in the North American colonies, rivaled only by the fur trade in economic importance. By the time English settlers were permanently implanted in the New World, Spanish settlers were already well underway appropriating and exploiting Native American fields and irrigation systems in the Rio Grande Valley of NEW MEXICO, rapidly moving into the Salt River Valley and its extensive irrigation works, and introducing cattle, sheep, horses, and fruit trees to the Southwest. From their entry into the Southwest in the late 16th century until the PUEBLO REVOLT of 1680, Spanish settlers stole LAND and virtually enslaved the native population for agricultural labor. The Pueblo Revolt in New Mexico and Comanche activity in Texas forced the Spanish back to the lower Rio Grande for more than a decade. Early in the 18th century the Spanish returned to Texas, where they established large cattle ranches that produced for the market in NEW ORLEANS, and to the upper Rio Grande, where they established more cattle ranches and introduced irrigated wheat farming to the PUEBLO. The Spanish brought a wealth of new crops to the Southwest, including wheat, oats, onions, peas, watermelons, peaches, and apples, as well as sheep, horses, and cattle. Spanish invasions of the Southwest profoundly affected civil government among the native population and the agriculture they practiced.

Agriculture was always part of the program the VIRGINIA COMPANY OF LONDON intended for the first successful English colony. Colonists at JAMESTOWN were expected to raise their own food as well as produce items for trade with the mother country. Colonists soon learned from local native farmers how to plant and cultivate maize themselves, but without maize acquired by theft, barter, or gift from natives, the colony probably would not have survived. Not until Governor SIR THOMAS DALE allotted each settler three acres of fee simple land on which to cultivate his own crops and abandoned communal farming did the colony begin to produce sufficient food to feed itself. Maize became the salvation for many new colonies. It could be cultivated in fields already prepared by native farmers and harvested late or early with simple hand tools. By contrast, European small grains, such as wheat, required well-prepared fields and threshing and milling machines to produce sufficient supplies. Maize essentially solved the problem of survival for the Jamestown colony, but it did not provide a product that produced a profit.

In 1612 John Rolfe introduced a tobacco variety that had a milder taste than the locally grown types; the colonists then had their money crop. Within a few years tobacco dominated Virginia agriculture and spread throughout the Chesapeake region. Within a decade Virginia farmers exported more than half a million pounds of tobacco each year. With the exception of relatively small food crops, Virginia farmers planted tobacco exclusively. A crop that quickly depleted soil fertility, tobacco forced constant expansion of fields and rapid movement into the interior, initiating conflict with natives that twice between 1620 and 1650 led to the near destruction of the colony. By the end of the colonial era Virginia had increased tobacco production to more than 18 million pounds a year.

Tobacco agriculture initiated a system of production that dominated the social, political, and economic life of Virginia and, ultimately, MARYLAND, the Carolinas, and Georgia. Those who could acquire large tracts of land farmed their acreage intensely, then allowed it to lie fallow for as long as 20 years while new acres came into production. Those who could not obtain large tracts were forced to abandon their land and move farther into the interior. Large plantations became the norm in the southern colonies near the coast. Large planters dominated colonial legislatures and sponsored numerous laws to control the production and quality of the tobacco crop. Nevertheless, overproduction plagued the region. Declining prices, as low as a penny per pound by the end of the 17th century, encouraged further legislative efforts to control production and quality. Most small farmers ignored planting restrictions for as long as they could. Then, in 1730, Virginia enacted a comprehensive Inspection Act that established mandated grading of tobacco and required the crop to be sold only through warehouses where government-appointed inspectors ensured the quality of the product. Tobacco that did not meet the standard was destroyed. Large planters benefited from the destruction of tobacco that did not meet quality standards, while smaller farmers were hastened off the land.

South of the Chesapeake Bay in the Carolinas, settlers first produced Indian maize but quickly turned to rice as a staple crop. Early rice planting was only moderately successful, but with a rice variety from AFRICA cultivation expanded rapidly. By the end of the 17th century SOUTH CAROLINA planters exported nearly 400,000 pounds; by 1730 rice exports reached more than 9 million pounds. Exports continued to increase until 1770, when planters exported more than 80 million pounds, primarily to the West Indies. In the early years of cultivation, planters generally sowed their rice on upland fields and presumed that sufficient rain would nourish the crop. By the mid-18th century, however, planters employed irrigation or planted in swampy areas near the coast. Rice became for South Carolina what tobacco had become for Virginia. Large planters accumulated land, slaves, and wealth that one author noted "provided the economic basis for the most extensive plantation system in colonial America."

By the middle of the 18th century, rice culture had spread to the Savannah River region of Georgia. There, one enterprising planter developed a method for capturing tidal flow through a series of dikes that held the freshwater on his fields. The method allowed much larger fields, planting farther inland, and the reduction of the time spent eliminating competing weeds. Using the tidal flow along South Carolina and Georgia rivers quickly became the common method for raising rice. At the time of the American Revolution, rice was exceeded only by tobacco and flour in the value of agricultural exports from British North America.

From 40 years before the American Revolution, INDIGO also became an important crop in South Carolina. During KING GEORGE'S WAR shipping became difficult for bulky products like rice, and some planters turned to indigo, which had a high price and relatively small bulk. In 1748 Parliament established a bounty on all indigo grown in the American colonies, which lasted until the revolution. In 1770 South Carolina planters exported more than 150,000 pounds of indigo. Although the cropping of indigo lasted only three or four decades before the end of the British bounty made it unprofitable, profits from its cultivation allowed many planters to accumulate land and slaves that, in turn, permitted them a relatively easy transition to cotton agriculture. Coastal planters in South Carolina and Georgia possessed the land, slave labor, and capital to begin large-scale production of sea island cotton.

While rice remained preeminent in the Deep South, it was generally confined to the coastal regions or limited by tidal flow to relatively few miles inland. New migrants to the region were shut out of the rice culture and turned to livestock instead of planting. Many rice planters also raised extensive herds of cattle. Cattle were already important in North and South Carolina by the end of the 17th century, and this expanded in the half century that followed. Cattle roamed freely, grazing on the public, or "King's," lands. Fall cow hunts (round-ups) separated marketable cattle and marked calves. The West Indies provided a ready market for hides, tallow, and dried beef. By the early 18th century South Carolinians grazed nearly 100,000 head of cattle. The cattle industry thrived in the Carolinas and Georgia until midcentury, when deteriorating ranges and disease diminished their numbers. The cattle industry moved west along the Gulf Coast and continued to supply the West Indies market, but most shipping by the end of the 18th century was through Mobile and New Orleans rather than CHARLESTON and SAVANNAH.

While staple crops like tobacco and rice continued to dominate southern colonial agriculture, the 18th century witnessed some diversification. Large planters had always planted corn and wheat in fields where tobacco had depleted fertility. A growing domestic population and periodic crop failures in Europe created demand for American-grown small grains and some maize. Western Virginia farmers in the Shenandoah Valley raised wheat for milling and substantial maize that they used for their own consumption and to fatten cattle and hogs. The growth of Baltimore and PHILADELPHIA provided a market outlet for western farmers in Virginia and Maryland. Tobacco planters on Maryland's eastern shore found it more and more difficult to acquire sufficient land to allow worn-out tobacco fields to lie fallow for extended periods. Many consequently switched to wheat and maize in the mid-18th century. Sugar plantations in the CARIBBEAN, with their large slave populations, proved a profitable market for Maryland wheat and maize.

Staple crop production in the southern colonies required extensive land use and intensive labor. Land distribution in the colonies varied according to the status of the colony as either royal (such as Virginia after 1624), proprietary (like PENNSYLVANIA), or corporate (MASSACHUSETTS). English land holding was heavily encumbered by a host of feudal remnants in the form of rents, services, and homage. Whether royal, corporate, or proprietary, attempts to replicate the English system generally failed in the American colonies. Even when quitrents or other services were attached to land, colonial farmers tended to see their land as fee simple, unencumbered by any obligations but to pay local taxes, and then only when they could not be avoided. Inheritance laws in England such as entail and primogeniture, meant to preserve a stable hierarchical society, existed in most colonies but were generally ignored. Farmers and speculators easily transferred land titles by simply registering the fact of the transfer with a local magistrate. The ease of transfer allowed for land accumulation and encouraged white settlement.

Virginia established the pattern of land acquisition that prevailed in the southern colonies as well as Pennsylvania, New Jersey, DELAWARE, and New York. To attract settlers, Virginia in 1618 offered a "headright" of 50 acres to anyone who could pay their own cost of transportation and an additional 50 acres for each family member whose transportation was paid. Although the proprietary colonies preferred to sell land, all eventually employed some variation on the headright system to attract settlers. Early in the 18th century the British government offered Crown lands for purchase. Wealthy Englishmen such as ROBERT "KING" CARTER and WILLIAM BYRD II acquired tens of thousands of acres by purchase from the Crown. Virginia required no survey before the sale of lands, and farmers frequently found they had purchased or squatted on land that belonged to someone else. Conflicting land claims dominated the Virginia courts until well into the 19th century. Nevertheless, land passed into the hands of farmers who quickly placed as much as they could into commercial crops.

Squatting became nearly institutionalized from Pennsylvania to NORTH CAROLINA in the interior. Scots-Irish settlers with little regard for English law insisted that the abundance of land was a gift from God. During the Revolutionary War, at least in part as a way of retaining the loyalty of back-country farmers, Virginia enacted a preemption act that allowed squatters the first right to purchase land on which they settled or, if someone else purchased the land, to be paid for improvements they had made. In any event, Crown and proprietor efforts to install a land system that replicated the deferential domain of England largely failed. If farmers could not purchase land, they rented with the intent to buy in the future. When all else failed, they moved farther into the interior and squatted on the land until forced to leave.

Some of the agricultural LABOR in the Middle Colonies and most of it in the South was performed by bound laborers. In the 17th and early 18th centuries approximately half the European immigrants to the British colonies came as indentured servants. Mostly young men, servants sold their labor for a period of years, usually four to seven, in return for passage to the colonies. The indenture contract was a negotiable instrument that could be bought and sold along with the indenture. Purchasers of indenture contracts generally agreed to provide food, shelter, and clothing for the term of labor and pay "freedom dues" of clothing, food, tools, and occasionally land at the end of the term if, indeed, the servant survived. Life for a servant was one of work and brutal conditions. They had little recourse from abusive masters while being subject to severe punishment or added years to their servitude for the most trivial crimes. One authority estimates that nearly 40 percent of indentured servants did not survive their term of indenture and that many of those who survived still were unable to obtain land. Nevertheless, some became middling farmers or took advantage of other commercial opportunities in the growing colonies. In the southern colonies beginning in the late 17th century, INDENTURED SERVITUDE largely came to an end, and black SLAVERY became the dominant form of forced labor.

Slaves of African descent accounted for the largest single group of migrants, albeit forced, to British America in the 18th century. Slaves faced a life as harsh as that of servants, but without the saving promise of eventual freedom. Some scholars argue that many of the first slaves who arrived in Jamestown in 1619 were granted freedom after a term of service, but by the late 17th century slavery became the norm for laborers brought from Africa. Nevertheless, during the 17th century some slaves gained their freedom, established thriving communities, and sometimes even purchased slaves of their own.

Slave labor became more extensively used and more restrictive in the 18th century. In 17th-century South Carolina slaves often raised food for themselves and for sale, enjoyed some freedom to TRAVEL for hunting and FISHING, and, by law, had Sundays free of labor. The development of rice agriculture initially curtailed those freedoms. Rice was labor intense; mastering of tidal pools greatly increased the acres planted and the demand for slave labor. Large plantations bought slaves directly from Africa, kept them relatively isolated during their first months, then placed them under close supervision. Later in the 18th century, as masters began to rely on the "task system," slaves were assigned a certain amount of work, or task, to accomplish each day. Many slaves managed to use this system to their own advantage to carve out extra time that they controlled.

The restrictions on slaves and their increase coincided with the flowering of the PLANTATION SYSTEM in the 18th century. Wealth produced from tobacco and rice provided planters the opportunity to emulate the country gentlemen of England. Large plantation houses sprang up throughout the South, a command structure of slave overseers and task work systems became the norm, and the master and his family grew more remote from the daily lives of their slaves. Whites seldom joined their black slaves in the fields, and fears of slave rebellion, real and imagined, became more common. Slaves, indeed, did rebel, sometimes by destroying equipment, engaging in work slowdowns, and running away. Violent rebellions occurred in 1710 in Maryland, in New York in 1712 and 1741, and, most well known, in the STONO REBELLION of South Carolina in 1739. Individual and organized resistance occurred among relatively new arrivals and among slaves relatively acculturated to British ways. As slaves successfully created families and communities, kinship ties may have influenced a decline in organized rebellion, although individual acts of resistance continued.

By the end of the first quarter of the 18th century, the pattern of agricultural development around staple crops and cattle raising within a plantation system dominated by slave labor was well established and could not have existed without the continual arrival of African bondpeople. Africans brought agricultural skills from their homelands that were critical to the success of the southern cattle industry. Rice culture clearly would have been seriously retarded in South Carolina and Georgia without rice varieties from Africa and the knowledge of slaves about how to grow the crop. The large-scale production of tobacco could not have occurred had not black slaves provided the intense labor necessary to produce a crop. Southern agriculture was black agriculture, with the profits going to whites.

While staple-crop agriculture developed through the 17th century south of the Chesapeake, a wholly different agriculture dominated the colonies north of the Chesapeake. European farming began in New England in 1620 with the arrival of the PILGRIMS at PLYMOUTH, Massachusetts. The Plymouth dissenters came to free their souls from the corruption of the ANGLICAN CHURCH but needed to feed their stomachs as well. Stolen caches of corn fed the Pilgrims their first winter, but in spring 1621 Pilgrims began to plant maize in the manner that local Native Americans taught them and in fields that native farmers had used for generations. Later in the decade Puritan immigrants north of Plymouth brought large numbers of cattle, goats, and swine, and in 1635 Dutch MERCHANTS introduced sheep to the colony.

The Pilgrims had intended to farm communally, but disputes within the congregation soon ended cooperative ventures; by 1627 Plymouth had allotted 20 acres of farmland to each family for their individual use. Individuals were intent on raising surplus crops for profit, and farms quickly expanded production to include wheat, rye, and oats, along with sheep and cattle. Generally, sheep were confined while cattle and hogs grazed freely in the forest. The British West Indies provided a ready market for New England agricultural products. BOSTON and New London, CONNECTICUT, became thriving markets for beef from Massachusetts, Connecticut, and RHODE ISLAND. As one author put it, "if New England had staple crops, they were annual crops of beef, pork and wool." Until surpassed by South Carolina late in the 17th century, Massachusetts was the largest livestock producing colony in North America. The rapid expansion of English settlements in New England in the 17th century and encroachments on Indian land led to bloody confrontations with natives in 1636 and 1675. New England farmers praised God, but mammon competed quite well for their affection.

New England farmers also produced quantities of maize and wheat in the 17th century along with tobacco, particularly in the Connecticut Valley. Connecticut tobacco was a different variety from that found in Virginia and had been acquired from Native American farmers. Although never grown in the quantities found in the southern colonies, it still was sold profitably to England in the 18th century. Black stem rust and insects began to seriously deplete wheat culture in New England by the latter part of the 17th century. Farmers consequently increased their production of maize and rye. Wheat cultivation migrated west and south to New York, Pennsylvania, and western Maryland. There, wheat production increased dramatically in the 18th century and encouraged the development of a flour milling industry centered around the Chesapeake and Philadelphia. The West Indies again provided the principal market for milled wheat.

Farmers in New York, Pennsylvania, and Maryland also raised "neat" cattle intended for beef and milk. Generally, production was low, and farm women converted most milk to cheese and butter for home or local consumption. In the late 18th century better breeding habits and importation of improved livestock led to cattle intended specifically to produce milk. Increased production meant a surplus of cheese and butter. By 1769 Philadelphia had become a center for marketing butter intended for the West Indies trade. Cheese and butter production, nevertheless, tended to remain the work of farm women, and the products sometimes became a principal source of family income.

New England and Middle Colony farms remained comparatively small by the standards of Virginia and the southern colonies. Livestock, wheat, maize, and other small grain cultivation was not as labor intensive as tobacco and rice. Nevertheless, northern farmers were also in need of labor beyond that provided by family members. Slavery entered the northern colonies within a few years after the first slaves arrived in Virginia and spread to every colony north of Maryland. In the northern colonies slaves often lived in towns and worked in the growing SHIPBUILDING industry, in construction, or as assistants to ARTISANS. Most, however, worked on the farms of the countryside, often alongside their owners. Few northern farmers owned more than one or two slaves, who sometimes lived in the master's house and ate at his table. The largest concentration of slaves in the North was in Rhode Island, near Narragansett Bay, where immigrant planters from the West Indies tried to replicate the plantation system of their former homes. They built manor houses that rivaled those in the South, often owned more than fifteen slaves, bred race horses, and practiced the ways of country gentlemen. The tobacco farms of the Connecticut Valley became the home of another concentration of slaves in New England. Control of slave labor was always more lax in the North, and slaves often were hired out and occasionally were allowed to retain some portion of their earnings. Still, they remained slaves.

By the time of the American Revolution, colonial agriculture had developed into a profitable enterprise. The production of staple crops supported a plantation economy in the southern colonies. Food stuffs, primarily wheat and other small grains, dominated the Middle Colonies, and a mixed agriculture of livestock, wool, and maize characterized most of New England. The enterprise was sufficient to support a rapidly growing population that doubled in size about every 25 years. It provided surpluses for export that supported merchant concentrations in several cities and a host of auxiliary occupations like MARINERS, teamsters, blacksmiths, land agents, lawyers, doctors, and the like. None would have been possible without land the Indians had long cultivated; crops, particularly maize, that Native American farmers had bred to high levels of return; varieties of crops such as sorghum grains, rice, and indigo brought to North America by slaves; the forced labor of thousands of displaced black Africans; and the insatiable material demands of Europeans. All joined in the mix that produced American agriculture in the colonial era.

Further reading: R. Douglas Hurt, *Indian Agriculture in America: Prehistory to the Present* (Lawrence, Kans.: University of Kansas Press, 1987); Howard S. Russell, *A Long Deep Furrow: Three Centuries of Farming in New England* (Hanover, N.H.: University Press of New England, 1982); Allan Kulikoff, *Tobacco and Slaves: The Development of Southern Cultures in the Chesapeake, 1680–1800* (Chapel Hill: University of North Carolina Press, 1986); Judith A. Carney, *Black Rice: The African Origins of Rice Cultivation in the Americas* (Cambridge, Mass.: Harvard University Press, 2001).

—Thomas R. Wessel

Alaska, Russia in

Until the mid-18th century only local ALEUT and INUIT Indians knew of Alaska. In 1741 Russian explorers VITUS JONASSEN BERING and Aleksei Chirikov sailed from Kamchatka aboard two ships as part of Russia's Great Northern Expeditions of 1733 to 1743. Bering had concluded during earlier expeditions that Siberia and Alaska were not connected by land, and together the two explorers sought to map the Alaskan coast and investigate fur trading possibilities. Although a storm separated the two ships, each reached the Alaskan coast. On the return voyage Bering was shipwrecked and died on the island that was later named after him, but Chirikov reached Russia in late 1741, bringing news of excellent trading possibilities.

By the late 1740s Russian maritime routes to the Alaskan peninsula had been expanded, and fur traders competed for sea otter pelts for trade in Asia. The Russians established their first outpost in 1784 at Three Saints Bay on Kodiac Island. They used considerable violence toward indigenous populations, at times enslaving entire villages. By 1799 control of the lucrative FUR TRADE fell under the control of a single monopoly, the Russian American Company, which had strong connections to the Russian royal family. Later that year the company established the larger outpost of Novoarkhangelsk, or Sitka. A Russian Orthodox mission was also established. With a large port secured, American sea captains and the Russian American Company entered into an exclusive pact under which Aleut Indians were forced to hunt sea otters and the Americans transported the pelts to Asia for trade.

Although trade flourished, the sea otter population slowly declined, forcing the Russians to colonize farther south. The harsh climate and difficult agricultural conditions made supplying the Russian outposts difficult. By the 1830s sea otters along the West Coast of North America were virtually wiped out, which led to the Russian sale of Alaska to the United States in 1867.

Further reading: James R. Gibson, *Imperial Russia in Frontier America: The Changing Geography of Supply of Russian America, 1784 to 1867* (New York: Oxford University Press, 1976); Hubert H. Bancroft, *History of Alaska 1730–1885* (San Francisco: University of California Press, 1986).

—James Jenks

Albany Congress (1754)

In June–July 1754 representatives from the Six Nations of the IROQUOIS and seven English colonies—NEW YORK, NEW HAMPSHIRE, MASSACHUSETTS, RHODE ISLAND, CONNECTICUT, PENNSYLVANIA, and MARYLAND—met at Albany to try to resolve differences over trade and land policies and to develop a plan to confront French expansion from Canada into the Ohio Valley. Although the Board of Trade in England had ordered the congress, the disparate and conflicting interests present prevented it from achieving its main goals. Each of the colonies pursued its own self-interest. Outside of the formal proceedings, for example, Pennsylvania managed a huge purchase of Indian land. Rather than peace, the various dealings eventually led to a deadly conflict among New Englanders, Pennsylvanians, and the Indians over the Wyoming Valley in Pennsylvania.

Chief Hendrick presented the Iroquois grievances to the congress, which included the taking of Mohawk land, the provision of too much rum, encroachments by Virginia and Pennsylvania on Iroquois lands in the west, and continued trade by Albany with the French. The delegates denied all of these grievances, and, not surprisingly, they did not come to an agreement concerning their relationship with the Iroquois.

Benjamin Franklin drew this famous cartoon in an unsuccessful effort to promote colonial unity. *(Hulton/Archive)*

The colonies did agree on some matters at the congress: They recommended fortifications against the French, the establishment of a single superintendent of Indian affairs, and royal control of future Indian land acquisitions. The most famous, although arguably unimportant, legacy of the congress was a proposal, spearheaded by Benjamin Franklin of Pennsylvania, for a colonial union. Under this plan the colonies' external affairs, particularly matters of defense, would be controlled by a council of representatives who were to be elected by the colonial assemblies and a president appointed by the Crown. Known as the Albany Plan of Union, not one colonial assembly ratified it. Some have pointed to the plan as a precedent for subsequent American union under the Constitution. Others have suggested that the Iroquois Confederation shaped thinking about the plan and hence indirectly had a role in the writing of the Constitution. Evidence on such matters is not conclusive. Most scholars question this connection on two grounds. First, they are not convinced that Benjamin Franklin and others were influenced by the Iroquois. Second, many scholars do not believe that the Albany plan had an impact on the forms of government that came out of the American Revolution.

Further reading: Francis Jennings, *Empire of Fortune: Crowns, Colonies, and Tribes in the Seven Years' War in America* (New York: W. W. Norton, 1988).

—James D. Drake

alcohol

At a time when it was believed that drinking water endangered one's health, colonists of every rank, age, race, and size drank alcoholic beverages often and in considerable quantity. Governor WILLIAM BRADFORD of PLYMOUTH, like his contemporaries, distrusted water. When asked why so many men lived such long lives in Plymouth, Bradford listed the enemies to health and the origins of disease: "chaing of aeir, famine, or unholsome foode, much drinking of water, sorrows & troubls, etc." More than a century later the *Pennsylvania Gazette* reported on various disasters experienced by individuals as a result of drinking water. On one occasion a laborer "would have died, had not a Person present forced a Quantity of rum down his Throat, by which Means he soon recovered." Colonists regarded water as "lowly and common," a drink better suited to barnyard ANIMALS than humans. As a result, colonists avoided water as much as possible and quenched their thirst with a variety of alcoholic beverages.

Alcoholic refreshments did not simply substitute for water, however. They fulfilled a number of specific functions. In the 17th and 18th centuries Americans, along with their counterparts in England and Europe, believed that spiritous liquors were nutritious and healthful. Rum, gin, and brandy did not merely accompany a meal but belonged to the same group as FOOD and, as such, supplemented "limited and monotonous diets." Ardent spirits had medicinal faculties as well and could cure "colds, fevers, snakebites, frosted toes, and broken legs and as relaxants . . . would relive depression, reduce tension, and enable hard-working laborers to enjoy a moment of happy, frivolous, camaraderie." A traveler through Virginia witnessed "the vile Practice of giving children, as well as those of all other ages, Rum in the morning as soon as they rise . . . & the Parents encourage it reckoning it wholesome." MIDWIVES prepared a "caudle" for women in labor, a drink made with ale or wine mixed with spices. The PURITANS believed so deeply in the health benefits derived from strong drink that they permitted imbibing on the Lord's day "in the case of nesseitie for the releife of those that are sicke or faint or the like for theire refreshing."

By the early decades of the 18th century, the beverages of choice were varieties of distilled liquors, referred to as spirits—whiskey, rum, gin, and brandy. The alcohol content averaged 45 percent, or, in distillers' terms, 90 proof. During the colonial period, according to one authority, the "annual per capita CONSUMPTION of hard liquor alone, mostly rum, approached four gallons." If the drinking public had had to rely only on spiritous liquors, the supplies would have been ample, but these beverages constituted only one form of the alcoholic beverages consumed. Colonists also drank fermented brews, beer, wine, and most often cider. With an alcoholic content of 10 percent, it is likely that most of the alcohol coursing through colonists' veins came from cider. Colonists rarely imbibed wine or beer, with the exception of "small beer," a home brew containing 1 percent alcohol. In the period just before the revolution, Americans consumed an average of only one-tenth gallon of wine per year.

Early Americans did not have equal access to alcoholic beverages. White adult men drank the greatest share, consuming two-thirds of the total. Free laborers' wages often included a pint of beer or some other alcoholic beverage. While women did not abstain, it was improper for them to drink in public or to get drunk. Unfree laborers, servants, and slaves had limited opportunity for and circumscribed access to alcoholic beverages. Laws in every colony prohibited tavern keepers from serving them without the express permission of their masters, and because of their status they were unlikely to have the money necessary to pay for drinks. On some occasions masters promised slaves alcoholic beverages as an incentive, but these drinks were often watered.

See also RUM TRADE.

—Sharon V. Salinger

Alden, John (1599?–1687)

John Alden was 21 years old when he was hired in Southampton, England, as a cooper (barrel maker) for the *Mayflower* voyage of the PILGRIMS in 1620. Presumably a member of the Church of England and a common laborer with no previous connection to the Pilgrims, Alden chose to remain in the small settlement of PLYMOUTH after surviving the first winter. Alden was listed among the signers of the MAYFLOWER COMPACT. He married fellow *Mayflower* passenger Priscilla Mullins sometime before 1623. The couple moved across Plymouth Bay to help settle the town of Duxbury in the 1630s. There they farmed, raised a large family of 10 children, and remained for the rest of their lives. Alden served as a magistrate and as treasurer for the Plymouth Colony and occasionally presided as deputy governor. He died in 1687, the last surviving signer of the Mayflower Compact, and was buried in Duxbury.

Henry Wadsworth Longfellow, a descendant, used the historical Alden as a character in his *Courtship of Myles Standish*. This popular romantic poem, published in 1858, portrayed Alden as the good friend chosen by the rough soldier MYLES STANDISH to woo young Priscilla Mullins. Alden attempted to win Priscilla for Standish but instead fell in love with her himself. Priscilla realized this and asked "Why don't you speak for yourself, John?" There is no historical evidence for the rivalry among the suitors. The story was probably based on oral family tradition.

—Stephen C. O'Neill

Alden, Priscilla (1602–1686?)

Priscilla Mullins was born in Dorking, Surrey, England, to William and Alice Mullins. The Mullins family were dissenters from the Church of England and joined the congregation of Separatists, commonly known to history as the PILGRIMS, who journeyed aboard the *Mayflower* in 1620 to New England. William and Alice brought the younger two, Priscilla and Joseph, of their four children. Priscilla, barely 18, was one of only four adult women in the entire company to survive the first winter in PLYMOUTH. Both her parents and her brother died during the "general sickness" of the first winter. Sometime between 1621 and 1623, Priscilla married JOHN ALDEN, a fellow passenger aboard the *Mayflower*, who had been hired as a cooper for the voyage and chose to remain in Plymouth. Priscilla and John moved across Plymouth Bay to Duxbury around 1631, where they farmed and raised a family of 10 children. Priscilla died sometime before her husband's death in 1687, although the exact date is not recorded.

In the 19th century Priscilla Mullins Alden became the romantic heroine of Henry Wadsworth Longfellow's dramatic poem *The Courtship of Myles Standish,* published in 1858. The story is based on oral family tradition and was first printed in Rev. Timothy Alden's 1814 *Collection of American Epitaphs and Inscriptions.* Longfellow's *Courtship* portrays Priscilla as a perceptive young woman courted by both Captain MYLES STANDISH, Plymouth's military leader, and his friend Alden. Priscilla immediately sees through Alden as he attempts to woo her for Standish but falls in love with her himself. There is little evidence for the story's authenticity, but Longfellow's poem became an instant bestseller and remained an American classic for generations.

—Stephen C. O'Neill

Aleut

The people known as the Aleut are the aboriginal inhabitants of the 1,100-mile Aleutian Island chain stretching southwest from mainland Alaska. The earliest of these people, the Paleo-Aleuts, migrated to North America over the Siberian land bridge, most likely between 5,000 and 3,000 B.C.E.

Although first called *Aleut* by Russian maritime explorers, the tribe refers to themselves as *Unangan*, or "the people." Ethnically related to the INUIT (Eskimo), the Aleut maintain their own dialects and culture. Before contact with Russians in 1741, the Aleut lived in scattered villages usually composed of related families. A chief or head man might govern several small villages, but no single leader reigned over all the Aleut. These villages consisted of semisubterranean dwellings and had a CLASS-based social system that included slaves taken in raids against other indigenous bands. Aleut villages were located near freshwater and in positions safe from attacks from neighboring tribes. Village sites near rivers also provided an abundance of salmon.

Local SACHEMS practiced MEDICINE, led spiritual activities, and enforced hunting rites and taboos. The Aleut were adept at harvesting the resources of the sea, and bands survived by hunting sea lions, seals, whales, and fish from bidarkas, the small, highly maneuverable vessels used by Aleut hunters. In some areas men hunted caribou, bears, and birds while also collecting eggs and edible plants. Women wove intricately detailed grass baskets and worked stone and bone for decorative and utilitarian uses. Bidarkas also provided an effective vehicle for intertribal trade between islands.

Russian fur traders who came to the Aleutian Islands in the 1740s in search of sea otter pelts exploited Aleut hunting skills. The Russians often held Aleut women and children hostage to force Aleut men to hunt sea otters. As the sea otter population declined near the Aleut home waters, Russians took Aleut men to new hunting grounds, some as far away as southern Alta California. Beginning in 1761 the Aleut rebelled, killing Russian traders and destroying Russian vessels. The Russians struck back in 1766, crushing the rebellion and instituting a policy of genocide against the Aleut. The Aleut population declined dramatically under Russian rule, from a precontact population of approximately 25,000 to only 2,000 by the end of the 19th century. Today approximately 8,000 Aleut live in Alaska.

See also ALASKA, RUSSIA IN.

Further reading: William C. Sturtevant, ed., *Handbook of North American Indians: Subartics,* vol. 6 (Washington, D.C.: Smithsonian Institution Press, 1982).

—James Jenks

Alexander, Mary Spratt Provoost (1693–1760)

An important merchant, Alexander was born on April 17, 1693, in NEW YORK CITY, the daughter of John and Maria (DePeyster) Schrick Spratt. In 1697 Alexander's father died, and her mother married the smuggler David Provoost, whose surname the Spratt children adopted. Three years later Maria Provoost died, and Alexander moved into her maternal grandmother's home.

Marrying her stepfather's brother, Samuel Provoost, in 1711, Alexander invested monies gained from her mother's estate into her husband's importing ventures and served as his financial partner. Giving birth to three children before her husband died in either 1719 or 1720, Alexander gained sole control of her husband's business. She wed James Alexander, an influential NEW YORK politician and attorney, in 1721, and they had seven children together. Alexander was kin to Scottish aristocracy, and the couple's son William appropriated the title "Lord Stirling" during his military career in the SEVEN YEARS' WAR.

A major New York City importer, Alexander expanded her mercantile pursuits originally obtained from her first husband, selling her own merchandise as well as items her husband received from clients bartering for legal work. According to tradition, she also provided goods for military campaigns, stocking the Fort Niagara expedition led by General William Shirley.

The Alexanders' mansion was considered a nurturing environment for the city's leading citizens to meet and discuss political and business concerns. Alexander was significant for the amount of power and influence she possessed as a businessperson in one of the colonies' major seaports, representing the financial autonomy that the Dutch community encouraged women to obtain. She affected New York colonial political decisions and was credited, probably incorrectly, with advising ANDREW HAMILTON regarding legal proceedings for newspaper editor JOHN PETER ZENGER, acquitted of libel in 1735. Alexander died on April 18, 1760, and was interred in a vault at Manhattan's Trinity Church.

Further reading: May King Van Rensselaer, *The Goede Vrouw of Mana-ha-ta: At Home and in Society, 1609–1760* (New York: Charles Scribner's Sons, 1898).

—Elizabeth D. Schafer

Algonquin

The term *Algonquin Indians,* also spelled *Algonquian* and *Algonkin,* is used to describe both a specific group of Indians and an entire language group. During the colonial period Algonquin-speaking Indians lived from the Atlantic coast to the Colorado Rockies and from northern Canada to SOUTH CAROLINA. Among the major groups who spoke Algonquin languages were the NARRAGANSETT, Wampanoag, POWHATAN, and Ojibwa Indians. When English boats landed at Roanoke, JAMESTOWN, and PLYMOUTH, Indians belonging to the Algonquin language group met them in each case. The specific group of Indians called Algonquin, the subject of this entry, lived in the Ottawa Valley in southern Canada.

Before Europeans arrived in North America, Algonquin Indians engaged in a wide range of social and economic activities, guided in part by the ENVIRONMENT in which they lived. During the warm summer months, the Algonquin gathered into a large community and focused their activities around FISHING and AGRICULTURE. Although the cool temperatures and marginal soil of the Ottawa Valley made it difficult to rely on farming as a significant subsistence activity, the Algonquin in southern areas grew corn, beans, and squash. During the winter the communities dispersed into smaller hunting groups. Contrary to the popular image of Indian societies as egalitarian utopias, various forms of stratification marked Algonquin society. A strict GENDER division of LABOR determined the activities of men and women. Men typically hunted, fished, and cleared agricultural fields, while women planted and tended the crops, gathered roots and nuts, and looked after the children. The right to use specific hunting lands was passed patrilineally, from father to son, although in some Algonquin tribes kinship was traced matrilineally.

During the early 17th century the Algonquin expertise in hunting made them ideal allies in the burgeoning FUR TRADE, and they became an important trading partner with the French. Economic competition between the IROQUOIS Indians and the Algonquin exacerbated preexisting tensions and escalated into full-scale war. When the Iroquois virtually shut down the St. Lawrence River as a trade route into the interior of Canada, the Algonquin acted as brokers between the French and the HURON Indians. At first the strategy worked well, and the Algonquin prospered under the new arrangement by exchanging French trade goods for Huron corn. Soon, however, they were caught up in the complex diplomatic and military struggles that marked the fur trade around the Great Lakes. Eliminated as brokers when the French began to trade directly with the Huron, the Algonquin attempted to maintain their economic prominence by negotiating with Dutch traders in the 1620s. This maneuver upset the Mohawk Indians, an Iroquois tribe that had established a trade relationship with the Dutch upon their arrival in the Hudson River Valley in 1609.

War broke out once again as each side sought to defend their access to the European goods they had increasingly come to see as vital to their very existence. In 1645 the French convened a peace conference that temporarily eased the violence, but sporadic fighting continued throughout the 17th century. When England and France engaged in a series of imperial wars in the 18th century, the Algonquin fought alongside the French. After the French loss of Canada in the SEVEN YEARS' WAR, the Algonquin signed a peace treaty with the British in 1760. During the American Revolution the Algonquin fought with the British against the rebellious colonists and once again found themselves on the losing side. Eventually, the Algonquin, like other native groups, were relegated to reservations.

Further reading: Richard White, *The Middle Ground: Indians, Empires, and Republics in the Great Lakes Region, 1650–1815* (New York: Cambridge University Press, 1991); Bruce Trigger, ed., *Handbook of North American Indians,* Vol. 15, *Northeast* (Washington, D.C.: Smithsonian Institution, 1978).

—Melanie Perreault

almshouses

Established in the colonies as early as 1685 in BOSTON and the 1730s in NEW YORK CITY and PHILADELPHIA, almshouses (also called poorhouses) were originally intended as temporary residential institutions to shelter members of a community who were unfortunate in a variety of ways and who had no family able or willing to care for them: the poor, the elderly, abandoned or illegitimate children, the injured, and the mentally ill or defective. The earliest almshouses were small and supported primarily by poor taxes. Almshouses only partially replaced the "outdoor" relief system, which was based on payments of cash or goods directly to the needy, their families, or an overseer of the poor or member of the community for distribution to the applicants. Many communities combined outdoor relief to applicants considered most worthy of assistance with renting or purchasing a house and supporting paupers within it. Private aid from individuals and organizations continued to provide aid for the "virtuous" poor, but by the mid-18th century larger cities such as Boston, New York, and Philadelphia began to move to institutions as the primary way to provide effective aid to the needy while most efficiently spending public funds. Overseers of the poor remained responsible for assessing and collecting the poor taxes but did so as administrators of the institutions.

Within the poorhouse inmates were expected to work around the institution at tasks such as cleaning, cooking, nursing the sick, gardening and husbandry, and some manufacturing. The labor of inmates supposedly accomplished two purposes: to help offset the cost of residents' room and board and to teach the inmates orderly and virtuous habits so that when they left the institution they would be more likely to support themselves.

Poorhouses were important parts of the local ECONOMY whether they were located in urban or rural areas: They provided employment for area residents and conducted business with local MERCHANTS as well as providing relief to the destitute. By the 1760s poorhouses were important in the political economy of urban areas as well, as local tensions over immigration, expenditure of public funds, increasing numbers of poor folk, and responses to epidemic disease were reflected in elections and appointments of public officials.

In the increasingly unstable colonial economy it was vital for the working classes to have almost continuous employment in order to avoid having to seek assistance from the authorities. Most unskilled labor was seasonal, so poor relief was a part of the survival strategy for many poor families.

Further reading: John K. Alexander, *Render Them Submissive: Responses to Poverty in Philadelphia, 1760–1800* (Amherst: University of Massachusetts Press, 1980); Robert E. Cray, Jr., *Paupers and Poor Relief in New York City and its Environs, 1700–1830* (Philadelphia: Temple University Press, 1988).

—Monique Bourque

American Philosophical Society

The American Philosophical Society was founded in 1743, modeled on the Royal Society in London as an intercolonial organization for the exchange of "useful knowledge." Like so many of the organizations that Benjamin Franklin created, the society was intended to draw men into correspondence and conversations that would prove beneficial both to their own lives and to the community as a whole.

JOHN BARTRAM, a Quaker farmer and botanist, outlined the first plan for the organization in 1739. Writing to London merchant and natural philosopher Peter Collinson, Bartram envisioned a club where the "most ingenious & Curious men" could study "natural secrets arts & sciences." He thought the group could secure a meeting house, sponsor lectures, and promote other avenues of inquiry.

Bartram, a brilliant student of natural SCIENCE, had little background or ability in organizing public plans. His friend Benjamin Franklin, however, had both that ability as well as a growing interest in expanding the intellectual lives of his fellow colonists, having already created the Junto, a social and study club for PHILADELPHIA ARTISANS, and the Library Company of Philadelphia in 1731. In 1743 Franklin published the plan for the American Philosophical Society that he and Bartram had worked out in "A Proposal for Promoting Useful Knowledge among the British Plantations in America." With colonies now established, Franklin wrote, "there are many in every Province in Circumstances that set them at Ease, and afford Leisure to cultivate the finer Arts, and improve the common Stock of Knowledge."

From 1743 to 1746 the society welcomed members, including Franklin, Bartram, physician THOMAS BOND; fellow Junto members THOMAS GODFREY, William Coleman, and William Parsons; and colonial notables such as CADWALLADER COLDEN, Robert Hunter Morris, and James Delancey. Despite an impressive membership list, however, interest in the organization soon faltered. Franklin described the members as "very idle Gentlemen" in 1745, and plans for regular meetings or a publication came to nothing. By 1746 the organization was no longer meeting.

The American Philosophical Society was revived in the 1760s, shortly after the American Society for Promoting and Propagating Useful Knowledge was founded in 1766. On January 2, 1769, the two organizations merged to become the American Philosophical Society, held at Philadelphia, for Promoting Useful Knowledge.

Further reading: Whitfield J. Bell, Jr., *Patriot Improvers: Biographical Sketches of Members of the American Philosophical Society,* Vols. 1 & 2 (Philadelphia: American Philosophical Society, 1999).

—George W. Boudreau

Andros, Sir Edmund (1637–1714)

Edmund Andros was born in London into a family of ardent royalists and professional soldiers long resident in the Channel Island of Guernsey. Andros began his own military training in Dutch service and then, after the 1660 restoration of the Stuart monarchy, in the Grenadier Guards and as a major in an English regiment stationed in the CARIBBEAN. In 1674 the patronage of James, Duke of York, secured him the governorship of the duke's province of NEW YORK, recently conquered from the Dutch. Andros proved a capable although autocratic executive in establishing English forms of government and forging an enduring alliance, the famous Covenant Chain, with the IROQUOIS Indians. Recalled to London in 1681 to answer charges of misconduct pressed by a faction of New York's merchants, he was replaced as governor in 1683 but then commissioned royal governor of the newly formed DOMINION OF NEW ENGLAND in 1686 with a lavish annual salary of £1,200.

In BOSTON Andros lost no time in implementing his instructions to curb illegal trade, favor the ANGLICAN CHURCH, and govern without a representative assembly, all measures that flew in the face of the colonists' cherished liberties. Dissent grew, heightened by war with the eastern Indians and Andros's determination to rule through a clique of officials brought from England and New York. On April 16, 1689, as news of England's GLORIOUS REVOLUTION reached Boston, a popular uprising overthrew the Dominion government and held Andros and his subordinates prisoners until they could be returned to England. There, charges of misrule were again dismissed, and Andros was sent back to North America in 1692 as royal governor of VIRGINIA.

Andros initially worked effectively with Virginia's assembly to reorganize its government and defend its frontiers. By 1696, however, powerful local interests led by James Blair, the Bishop of London's commissary in the colony, began campaigning in London for his removal. In declining health, Andros returned to England and in 1698 surrendered his post. Since 1674 he had held absentee office as bailiff of Guernsey, and he now served briefly as its lieutenant governor. Thrice married, Andros died childless in London in 1714.

Edmund Andros has passed into American history as a legendary tool of Stuart tyranny, with the Boston revolt celebrated as the forerunner to the events of 1776. More obedient soldier than pliant politician, he scorned to conciliate either his colonial subjects or his London superiors, bringing each of his three colonial governorships to a contentious end. Even so, he was plainly an able, honest, and steadfast servant of the Crown. The very qualities that made him suspect to his English Protestant subjects—his cosmopolitan background, brusque militancy, and skill in dealing with such as Indians, French, and Dutch—also made him an effective, if ill-fated, executive during a time of war and internal strife, the most troubled years of American colonial history.

See also DUDLEY, JOSEPH; RANDOLPH, EDWARD.

Further reading: Stephen S. Webb, *1676: The End of American Independence* (New York: Knopf, 1984); Robert C. Ritchie, *The Duke's Province* (Chapel Hill: University of North Carolina Press, 1977).

—Richard R. Johnson

Anglican Church (Church of England)

Seventy-three years before the first permanent English colony was founded in VIRGINIA in 1607, Parliament proclaimed King Henry VIII (1509–47) "the only supreme head in earth of the Church of England." This Act of Supremacy (1534) was the first step leading the Anglican Church into the Protestant Reformation. The road was long and troubled because the church retained features of its Catholic tradition (like bishops) while incorporating Protestant ideas and principles into its *Book of Common Prayer.* PURITANS in the early 17th century, eager to make the church more thoroughly Protestant, clashed with the authorities of both church and state. The conflict led to civil war (1642–49), the execution of the king, the abolition of bishops and the *Book of Common Prayer,* and a period of Puritan rule under Oliver Cromwell. The exiled Anglican Church returned with the restored BRITISH MONARCHY in 1660.

This religious and civil turmoil, coinciding with the first phase of English settlement in North America, was mirrored in colonial religious geography. The Anglican Church was established in the Chesapeake area, and the Puritan reformers created their own "Bible Commonwealth" in New England. Although Virginia's system of parishes, vestries (parish governing boards), and *Book of Common Prayer* worship established the English pattern, by the 1660s only a handful of clergy served the Virginia church.

The real Anglican growth in North America began toward the end of the 17th century, when Henry Compton, bishop of London (1675–1713), took direction of the fledgling colonial church. On his initiative, instructions to colonial governors included public support for Anglican parishes. In 1689 he compensated for the lack of colonial bishops by appointing James Blair, a minister serving in Virginia, as his commissary (bishop's representative) to provide a modicum of clerical leadership. By the 1740s the commissary system had become a feature of the Anglican Church in nine colonies. The most pressing problem, however, was the shortage of colonial clergy. In 1701 Compton collaborated with Thomas Bray in setting up the SOCIETY FOR THE PROPAGATION OF THE GOSPEL IN FOREIGN PARTS (SPG) to recruit and support missionaries and teachers. Providing stipends for missionary clergy and schoolmasters, books for parish libraries, and funds and materials for work among NATIVE AMERICANS and slaves, this innovative quasi-public philanthropy became the major vehicle for the expansion of the Anglican Church throughout the colonies until the American Revolution.

By the time GEORGIA, the last colony, was founded in the 1730s, the Anglican Church was the religious establishment in all the southern colonies. Except in NEW YORK CITY, it would never gain legal establishment anywhere in the North, but with SPG aid there was vigorous expansion there. Some northern parishes (King's Chapel, BOSTON; Christ Church, PHILADELPHIA; Trinity Church, New York) became important centers for growth. New Anglican churches of graceful neoclassical design in imitation of the work of Christopher Wren and James Gibbs in England attracted widening attention, particularly among the urban elite. SPG charity schools opened for slaves, free AFRICAN AMERICANS, and the poor. In New York City throughout the 18th century, SPG schoolmasters worked with the city's slave population in the face of fears about the danger of educating slaves. SPG missionaries to Native American tribes in the North and South had only mixed results, although there were notable successes among the New York Mohawk, some of whom became schoolmasters and Anglican lay readers (nonordained leaders of worship).

This northern growth was particularly controversial in New England, where the Puritan founders had built a tightly knit society with its own religious establishment (the Congregational Church). New Englanders looked upon the Anglican Church, with its twin traditions of episcopacy (the system of church leadership by bishops) and prescribed worship by the *Book of Common Prayer*, as a threat to their way of life. In 1722 the alarm was raised when seven faculty and recent Yale graduates, themselves clergy of CONNECTICUT's Congregational establishment, declared for episcopacy. SAMUEL JOHNSON was among those who went to England for ordination. For decades after his return as an SPG missionary, he planted other Anglican churches in Connecticut and trained a generation of missionary priests to work in New England and the Middle Colonies.

By 1763 the colonial Anglican Church was on firm footing, with parishes, Native American MISSIONS, and charity schools in both North and South. It also sponsored two colleges, the COLLEGE OF WILLIAM AND MARY in Virginia (1693) and KING'S COLLEGE (now Columbia University) in New York (1754). One serious problem remained, the absence of colonial bishops to complete its polity. From time to time Anglican leaders had petitioned for a bishop, but in the 1760s they made a concerted effort. Opposition was strong, particularly from New England's leaders like Boston's Jonathan Mayhew, who denounced episcopacy as a tool of oppression: "Is it not enough, that they persecuted us out of the Old World? Will they pursue us into the New to convert us here?" When such strong religious emotions combined with rising discontent over unpopular imperial policies in the 1760s, the ground was laid for the American Revolution. The Anglican Church, closely identified with Crown and empire, faced its most difficult challenge in the years ahead.

Further reading: John Frederick Woolverton, *Colonial Anglicanism in North America* (Detroit: Wayne State University Press, 1984); Patricia U. Bonomi, *Under the Cope of Heaven: Religion, Society, and Politics in Colonial America* (New York: Oxford University Press, 1986).

—Donald F. M. Gerardi

animals

Indigenous animals proved beneficial to NATIVE AMERICANS and to immigrants to the North American colonies. Animals imported to the colonies affected the native peoples and ENVIRONMENT both usefully and detrimentally. Animals served as sources of labor, FOOD, CLOTHING, and wealth. Wildlife native to the Americas consisted primarily of small mammals, birds, fish, reptiles, and amphibians.

Many Native Americans considered animals sacred. Some ceremonial mounds were formed in symbolic animal shapes. Animals were worshipped, sacrificed, and slaughtered to meet specific religious and dietary needs. Native Americans sometimes believed that specific animals such as eagles were spiritually powerful, appropriating animals for clan names and rituals.

Fur trading was a major colonial economic enterprise, and it served as a catalyst for European immigration, settlement, expansion, and industrialization. Alliances were formed between Europeans and Native Americans based on fur trading. Deer and beaver were especially valued by fur traders for their skins and pelts. Beaver fur was pressed into felt used to make hats and was in high demand in Europe. In addition, fur from foxes, minks, and otters was prized.

FISHING and whaling were also animal-related economic endeavors along the Atlantic coast. The English Parliament began passing the Navigation Acts in 1651, restricting colonial exports of fur, among other items, solely to England and English colonies. Native Americans began to rely on trading furs and hides for European goods, and, instead of only killing animals necessary to meet individual and tribal survival needs, they trapped and hunted with commercial motivations. Consequently, wildlife populations decreased significantly. Tribes competed to supply furs to European traders, even migrating westward to seek new animal resources.

Because hunting was limited to privileged aristocrats in Europe, colonial settlers of all social classes savored the opportunity to hunt for both personal needs and commercial profit. Squirrels and rabbits provided a local source of meat and skins and were not widely exported. Other wild animals, ranging from raccoons to bears, were targeted by fur traders for their skins, claws, and organs.

The abundance of deer provided additional economic opportunities. Native Americans frequently wore deerskins, known as brain tan, traditionally worn only by the European elite. Natives taught the colonists how to tan skins with brains and smoke. Deerskins proved durable, weather resistant, and stronger than homespun cloth made from cotton and wool, and this leather was sewn to produce shirts, breeches, and moccasins. Colonists quickly developed buckskin trading, selling both raw and tanned skins to domestic and foreign markets.

Exporting deer hides was consistently commercially profitable and a reliable income source for colonists. Skins could be processed at colonists' homes and were shipped from numerous ports, such as SAVANNAH, GEORGIA, which sent 2.6 million pounds of deerskins to England during a 20-year period in the mid-18th century. In 18th-century Europe deerskins were considered both fashionable and functional. Because of its colonial origins, buckskin came to symbolize patriotism, and militiamen wore it in combat against British troops.

Europeans reintroduced large animals, such as oxen, cattle, and horses, that had become extinct in North America thousands of years earlier. Horses fulfilled labor needs by transporting heavy loads. They were swift hunting steeds, which enabled Indians to pursue big game animals, especially bison. They also strengthened the military might of the Plains Indians, helping them maintain their independence against the European onslaught. Cattle allowed Indians to pursue dairy husbandry, processing butter and cheeses to supplement their diets. However, the introduction of dairy farming encouraged the Cherokee to accrue large herds and to institute SLAVERY to meet the resulting LABOR demands.

Other Old World animals new to the Americas included cats and donkeys. Bees immigrated with settlers and proved valuable for producing honey to sweeten bland foods. Hernando de Soto first brought pigs to North America in 1539, and colonists eventually drove hogs to market over trails that ultimately became major railroad transportation routes. Europeans discovered unfamiliar animals in North America, such as the turkey, which soon supplemented colonial diets. Flocks of turkeys were driven to market similarly to hogs, resting overnight at appointed coop stops. Some naturalists, such as JOHN BARTRAM, studied the variety of colonial animals, both indigenous species and amalgams of imported and native stock.

Most animals imported from Europe adjusted quickly to their new settings and competed with native animals for food and habitats. Many of the new arrivals destroyed vegetation and contaminated water sources that indigenous animals relied on for sustenance, and some species consequently became extinct. Rodents arriving on ships introduced and spread European diseases that killed indigenous animals with no immunity. Some diseases and parasites were also transmitted to humans. Contagious animal diseases included brucellosis, hog cholera, tuberculosis, and rabies.

European immigrants often established agricultural lives dependent on animals. In addition to raising livestock to meet familial needs and to sell locally, some colonial farmers tended animals commercially, shipping meat and milk to colonial and global markets. New England villages often specified a common area for residents' animals to graze. During the early years animals occasionally were accepted to pay taxes to colonial governments. Smaller mammals, such as swine, goats, and sheep, also provided new sources of protein-rich meat. Poultry were vital for meat and eggs, while chickens provided entertainment in the form of cock fighting. European livestock were bred to create new breeds for specific colonial conditions. The Dominique chicken was one of the first chicken breeds developed in the colonies. Colonists also hunted native ducks and geese.

Animals influenced all colonists' daily lives and colonial economies. African-American slaves and white indentured servants, both male and female, interacted with animals as part of their chores and learned how to control these creatures to perform tasks. Contemporary documents reveal how animals were used in the colonies. For example, recipes included entire pigs' heads. Beef altered dietary habits, enriching nutrition with proteins necessary to sustain a higher quality of life and longer life spans and fertile periods, resulting in larger populations. Archaeological evidence also shows that the distribution of meat from rural to urban areas was based on rural surpluses and cyclical agricultural patterns, with evidence of home butchering predominating in both the country and city in the colonial era.

While many animals were domesticated, nearly all were expected to work, and few fulfilled the modern Western role as pets. In addition to performing labor and protecting villages, many Native American dogs were castrated and fattened for food. The Spanish and British used horses and dogs to subdue native peoples. Christopher Columbus introduced European dogs—greyhounds and mastiffs—to the New World on his second voyage in 1493. Militarily, dogs served as sentries, scouts, and attackers. Some colonists, like George Washington, carefully bred dogs, specifically hounds, to develop breeds with desirable qualities unique to colonial concerns, such as hunting in new conditions. Often, imported dogs mated with wild WOLVES and coyotes, creating hybrids.

See also AGRICULTURE; DISEASE; FUR TRADE.

Further reading: Kathryn E. Holland Braund, *Deerskins & Duffels: Creek Indian Trade with Anglo-America, 1685–1815* (Lincoln and London: University of Nebraska Press, 1993); Alfred W. Crosby, *Germs, Seeds & Animals: Studies in Ecological History* (Armonk, N.Y.: M. E. Sharpe, 1994).

—Elizabeth D. Schafer

architecture

Both NATIVE AMERICANS and European colonists designed and constructed a vast array of structures in North America. In the early 17th century, for example, the HURON and IROQUOIS Indians typically lived in longhouses, which they built by stretching mats or bark over a wooden frame. Some houses were as large as 100 feet in length and sheltered multiple families. The ALGONQUIN inhabitants of much of the East Coast often lived in wigwams, which they made by lashing saplings together into circular or rectangular frames and sheathing them with grasses, reeds, or woven mats. Meanwhile, the native residents of the desert Southwest and the Pacific Northwest designed considerably different dwellings and meeting houses.

White colonists brought designs and techniques from Europe that they adapted to the climate, topography, available building materials, and skills of local artisans in North America. The earliest colonial buildings in the New World often were crudely and quickly constructed while lands

Shown here is an 18th-century two-story log cabin, with less than 900 square feet of living space. *(Library of Congress)*

were cleared for cultivation. Coarse "earthfast" structures appeared in all regions. They lacked foundations, chimneys, or window glass, and, like some native analogues, were built of posts driven into the ground and covered in mud plaster, roughly split boards, bark, or thatched mats. Indeed, in New England some of the first colonial houses were described by the Algonquin word *wigwam,* and in Manhattan as late as the 1620s shelters were characterized as square cellars covered with sod roofs. The earliest Quaker settlers in PENNSYLVANIA initially lived in caves.

Between 1650 and 1700 these very rudimentary structures gave way to more substantial building types that generally paralleled the traditional forms of the colonists' ethnic origins. English vernacular models appeared most frequently in New England and VIRGINIA. Houses typically were one- or two-room "open plan" buildings with a central entry, built of timber frames, and covered with rough clapboards and shingles. Variations, including such embellishments as glass windows, interior chimneys, and second stories, reflected not only local material and labor availability but economic stability and social status. While architectural form followed the English vernacular in both the Chesapeake area and New England, building standards did not. Buildings in New England were substantially constructed and progressively expanded to include upper floors and appurtenant wings. Early on in the Chesapeake area, however, houses were often shoddily built and had to be replaced every few years. This crude construction in the Chesapeake area reflects various factors: a hot, humid climate; a significant gender imbalance, with men significantly outnumbering women, which was not conducive to a settled family life; the heavy investment of capital in a labor force of bound workers rather than in an enduringly built environment; and a pervasive psychological sense of impermanence brought about by high mortality and economic uncertainty.

By the third decade of the 18th century, substantial medieval vernacular Dutch style houses and public buildings dominated the built environment in NEW YORK and NEW JERSEY. Framed of timber with masonry facades and parapet gables with either a step- or spout-shaped front gable, these buildings emulated aesthetic conventions, if not construction techniques and materials, commonly found in the Netherlands. Urban Dutch style houses most often were two-room, side-hall plan buildings, designed for both domestic and public functions, with the family residence situated at the back and a shop on the street front.

French and Spanish influences also distinguished buildings in areas of corresponding ethnic settlement. New Orleans, with its French architects and engineers, produced buildings reminiscent of those in France, if on a much more modest scale. The Spanish domination of Florida resulted in very complex structures, like the ST. AUGUSTINE fort. The Spanish left a longer-lasting impression in the Southwest, where colonists employed local Indian techniques of adobe construction.

Native American longhouses on Manhattan Island before the Dutch settlement of New Amsterdam [New York]
(The Granger Collection)

By the beginning of the 18th century, British culture influenced architecture throughout the British colonies. House and public building design emulated late baroque architecture then in fashion in England. Referred to as Georgian after the reigning monarchs, these structures were based on a one- or two-story box plan with window and door openings arranged in strict symmetry. The typical double-pile Georgian "closed plan" house, with its central passage from which separate rooms were entered, allowed for greater privacy and the division of domestic functions, such as cooking, washing, and sleeping. In all regions throughout the 18th century, Georgian house design was primarily the province of the elite.

Public buildings, the majority of which were churches and government structures, also observed a neoclassical paradigm that adhered to strict symmetry and restrained ornamentation. Consciously symbolizing American stability, variations in size, facade embellishments, and appurtenances generally remained within the design standard. American master-builders, who were, in effect, architects as well as artisans, increasingly drew upon scores of English and European design publications for their inspiration. Most notable among these were James Gibbs's *A Book of Architecture* (1728), Abraham Swan's *The British Architect* (1745), and Andrea Palladio's *Four Books of Architecture* (1570). Thus, Peter Harrison planned the Redwood Library (1748–50) in NEWPORT, RHODE ISLAND, using Edward Hoppus's *Fourth Book of Palladio* (1736). ANDREW HAMILTON designed the Pennsylvania State House (1730–41), now Independence Hall, in PHILADELPHIA, based on typical large English brick houses. Many Protestant churches, like Christ Church (begun 1727) in Philadelphia, were simplified from models designed by such British architects as Christopher Wren and James Gibbs. BOSTON's Christ Church (1723–41), now Old North Church, reflects much of Wren's designs for churches in London after 1666, while many other colonial churches were modeled on Gibbs's St. Martin-in-the-Fields (1721–26) in London. Many of the largest structures built at the end of the colonial era were ALMSHOUSES and jails, reflecting growing social and economic problems, especially in urban areas.

Further reading: Fiske Kimball, *Domestic Architecture of the American Colonies and of the Early Republic* (New York: Charles Scribner's Sons, 1922; reprint, New York: Dover, 1966); William H. Pierson, *American Buildings and Their Architects* (New York: Oxford University Press, 1971); Leland M. Roth, *A Concise History of American Architecture* (New York: Harper & Row, 1979).

—Catherine Goetz

art

During the early colonial period diverse art forms were present throughout North America. NATIVE AMERICANS and European colonists creatively expressed themselves through many mediums, using styles borrowed from earlier generations and other cultures and developed within diverse landscapes.

Native Americans combined utilitarian and aesthetic properties through the decoration of everyday items. The medium and style of these products varied regionally. Wood was a common medium for carving objects such as totem poles in the Northwest and for constructing "false face" masks among the IROQUOIS. Native Americans created symbols and pictures by chipping away rock surfaces (petroglyphs) or by painting on rock with dyes (pictographs). Painted animal skins decorated shields and tepee covers in the Plains region. Painting (common in the Southwest) or incisions (typical in eastern North America) decorated pottery. Artists used bone awls and sinew thread for appliqué on tanned hides (eastern North America regions). The WAMPUM belt was an example of appliqué that was widely used in negotiating protocol with Europeans. The creation of visual arts was GENDER specific. Women generally performed basket-making and needlework, while men engaged in weaving and embroidery.

MUSIC and DANCE were also well-developed art forms among Native Americans; these were interwoven into public and private ceremonies alike. Musical instruments included ceramic, wooden, or cane flutes, gourd rattles, and rawhide or water drums. Music was largely vocal and included various types of song forms. Songs were short and arranged in cycles with many repetitions. Long performances often surrounded these songs. There were many

This painting, known as *A Young Dutch American Girl,* 1730, was the work of the "Gansevoort Limner," an unknown Dutch portrait painter. *(National Gallery of Art)*

differences in regional styles of music and dance: Eastern Woodlands ceremonies included hand-held rattles and water drums with dances and songs performed by women and men; pulsating vocals accompanied by rawhide rattles and drums were common art forms of Plains groups.

Europeans also expressed a diverse array of art forms. Early explorers from Europe created maps, drawings, and watercolors of the inhabitants, flora, and fauna of North America. In the British colonies imported European art provided models for engravings, mezzotints (a method of engraving that produced effects of lighting and shading), and painting styles. Common art forms produced in the British colonies during this early period included decorated household furniture, carved gravestones, and portrait prints.

By the mid-18th century British colonial wealth and stability increased, as did commissions for artists to paint portraits of wealthy patrons and their families. Art and its production developed into a source of national pride. With this shift in social prominence, artists moved from their former craftsperson status into a new professionalism. This rise in artistic status also witnessed a shift from Puritan austerity to a more provincial style. With this new style artists integrated iconographic symbols, landscapes, and material possessions into portraits and prints. An elite CLASS of magistrates, military leaders, naval captains, and MERCHANTS were among those who commissioned artists. Prints were an inexpensive and popular art form that included portraits, maps, and topographic views. Important British colonial painters included Henrietta Deering Johnston, JUSTUS ENGELHARDT KUHN, JEREMIAH THEUS, JOHN HESSELIUS, ROBERT FEKE, John Singleton Copley, and John Smibert. Prominent British colonial engravers of the period included JEREMIAH DUMMER, PETER PELHAM, and WILLIAM BURGIS. Dutch painters in the British colonies included Sir Anthony Van Dyck, Henri Coutourier, and Pieter Vanderlyn.

American colonial art integrated cosmopolitan art forms from Europe with provincial perspectives. Without the presence of established academies or apprentice masters, artists in British, French, and SPANISH COLONIES combined and created art forms that reflected a diversity of European artistic traditions. French colonial art forms included altar screens, votive paintings, and portraits. Pierre-Noël Levasseur worked in Canada and created intricate altar screens. NEW ORLEANS painter José Francisco Xavier de Salazar y Mendoza incorporated Spanish and Mexican traditions to create portraits of prominent citizens. LOUISIANA art forms also included watercolors of geographic features of North America and propaganda pieces to lure settlers to the area.

Paintings and sculpture from the Spanish BORDERLANDS of NEW MEXICO and Texas were primarily religious and intended for church mission decoration. Roman Catholic missionaries came to convert Native Americans and used painting and sculpture in this process. Church mission decorations initially consisted of frescos, later replaced by altar screens. Altar screens combined the work of several artists and included painting, ARCHITECTURE, and sculpture. In the 17th century Spanish colonists' religious ceremonies included figural sculptures of Mary, Jesus, and various saints. These images provided processional figures in reenactments and tools for conversion of Native Americans to Christianity.

Further reading: Milton W. Brown, *American Art to 1900: Painting, Sculpture, Architecture* (New York: H. N. Abrams, 1977); Christian F. Feest, *Native Arts of North America* (London: Thames & Hudson, 1980).

—Yolonda Youngs

artisans

The artisan was a ubiquitous and pivotal figure in colonial America. Whether crafting such simple and commonplace items as shoes, coats, and nails or producing more complex commodities such as homes, furniture, and transatlantic sailing vessels, early American SOCIETY depended on the labor of the skilled craftsperson. Together with commerce and AGRICULTURE, artisan production lay at the heart of the North American colonial ECONOMY.

Within a generation of their founding, each of the major European-American settlements supported thriving craft economies. In rural areas farmer-artisans supplied the local milling, blacksmithing, and construction needs of their communities, while in the 17th- and 18th-century cities contemporaries pointed to the fact that American artisans produced virtually any article available in England or continental Europe.

At any time during the colonial era, the surest way to define an artisan was by reference to his or her possession of a skill. It was the knowledge of materials, tools, techniques, production processes, and marketing strategies that set artisans apart from those whose incomes depended on their brawn alone. In a world already divided into those who worked with their heads and others who worked with their hands, artisans occupied a middle ground, combining in their trade a degree of manual labor with the intellectual refinement of rigorous training, thought, and planning.

Artisans purchased this skill through a long period of apprenticeship to their craft. As potential artisans reached the age of 13 or 14, their parents sought to secure their future by placing them with a master craftsperson in whose shop they would learn the "mysteries of the trade" that would make them full-fledged craftsmen and craftswomen. Most apprenticeships involved written contracts negotiated between parents and masters that stipulated that the apprentice live in the home of the master until adulthood, learn the skills of the craft as well as fundamentals of reading, writing, and basic mathematics, and receive a gift of CLOTHING and often tools at the expiration of their term.

Apprenticeships lasted through the adolescent years and generally ended by the age of 21. The average period of apprenticeship thus lasted about seven years. Trades requiring less skill often ended earlier, while those that required highly refined skills, such as instrument making and engraving, generally lasted a year or two longer. By the time they approached the end of their service, apprentices were well versed in the everyday operations of their CRAFTS and possessed most of the skills necessary for the practice of their trades. With their "freedom dues" in hand, young craftspersons were ready to embark on the next stage of their training.

In the journeyman phase of their careers, young American artisans who possessed skills but few funds spent the years immediately after their apprenticeships saving the money that would allow them to marry and enter their trade as full-fledged masters. In English America this meant working for a few years on a piecework basis for an established artisan in one of the seaport cities or larger country towns. When the journeymen had accumulated the savings and credit necessary to rent a shop, buy tools and materials, and set up a home, they were ready to join the ranks of the community's master craftsmen. This was the path followed successfully by most young craftspeople before the turn of the 18th century. However, after 1700, especially in urban centers, growing numbers of journeymen found it difficult and often impossible to procure sufficient capital or skills to become independent masters.

Before the end of the 18th century, most masters operated as independent producers, owning their own tools, purchasing their own materials, and relying on the help of their families, journeymen, apprentices, and, less frequently, free or bound laborers to fashion their goods. Most worked in small shops (often attached to their homes) that in urban areas they rented and in rural areas they generally owned. The workday, which typically ran from 10 to 12 hours in winter and 14 to 16 hours in summer, was regulated by the available hours of sunlight, candles being too expensive for nighttime work. Most artisans worked five and a half days during the week, reserving Sundays for rest, recreation, and worship. The artisan's tools were hand-held, and machinery was primitive, usually nothing more elaborate than a foot-driven potter's wheel or a hand-cranked wood lathe. Power thus came from the exercise of human muscle, and the pace of work was governed as much by the strength and endurance of the producers as by the nature of the work itself.

While most colonial products came directly from the shops of small masters, some were too large, complex, or expensive to be produced by a single artisan. In some of the more capital-intensive enterprises, such as shipyards, individual artisans worked as subcontractors to the owners of the concern, providing their own tools and hiring their own journeymen and apprentices to work beside them. In others, such as iron foundries, ropewalks, and tanneries, artisans simply hired their time for an agreed-upon amount. In both cases, however, artisans retained the personal and work autonomy that marked the life of skilled craftspeople everywhere in colonial America.

Defined in these ways, artisans were found throughout colonial America. Craftspeople were located in the countryside as well as the city, in the South as well as the North, and on the high seas as well as on terra firma. In short, artisans were present wherever more than a small handful of colonists congregated for trade and settlement.

Colonial artisans shared with their European counterparts a body of moral precepts and a distinctive view of the world. The cornerstone of the artisan moral tradition was labor, and from this foundation flowed related notions of democracy, competency, independence, and community. Given the critical services rendered by early American artisans, it is easy to understand why they thought of their skilled labor as a central element in the smooth functioning of colonial society. The time spent in apprenticeship, the skills laboriously learned and honed through years of practice, and the lifelong contribution to the well-being of the community gave the artisan a deep-seated feeling of pride, purpose, and social respectability. In practicing their trades, artisans saw themselves as performing a service not only to their families and customers but also to the larger community in which they lived. Colonial artisans thus viewed skilled labor as at once a social, moral, and economic act. To work was to employ their skills in service equally to self, family, and the community at large.

Further reading: Gary B. Nash, *The Urban Crucible: Social Change, Political Consciousness, and the Origins of the American Revolution* (Cambridge, Mass.: Harvard University Press, 1979); Billy G. Smith, *The Lower Sort: Philadelphia's Laboring People, 1750–1800* (Ithaca, N.Y.: Cornell University Press, 1990); Ronald Schultz, *The Republic of Labor: Philadelphia Artisans and the Politics of Class, 1720–1830* (New York: Oxford University Press, 1993).

—Ronald Schultz

B

Bacon's Rebellion (1676–1677)

In 1676 one of the most important rebellions in early North America erupted in VIRGINIA. Settlers had long chafed under their royal governor, SIR WILLIAM BERKELEY. They had many complaints, but it was Berkeley's Indian policy that proved most volatile. Amid a storm of criticism, the governor had earlier conceded the land north of the York River to POWHATAN tribes. To be sure, Berkeley wanted his colony to expand but without creating a conflict with neighboring NATIVE AMERICANS. Mindful of Indian opposition, especially since the powerful Susquehannah had migrated from PENNSYLVANIA to the Virginia backcountry in the 1660s, Berkeley genuinely feared a full-scale war.

Although many settlers shared Berkeley's concern, those fears did not deter land hunger, especially among poorer and western colonists. By 1660 the colony's population had mushroomed as newcomers joined freedmen (former indentured servants) in demanding land. Eastern established planters had acquired most of the acreage in the tidewater counties, leaving the landless with two alternatives: renting permanently from landowners or moving inland. Newcomers and freedmen soon envisioned the Indians, who possessed the land they coveted, as the source of Virginia's growing pains.

This mixture of fear and jealousy produced violent conflict in 1675. It all started, strangely enough, over hogs, when traders from the Doeg tribe confiscated Thomas Mathew's livestock as collateral for unpaid goods. Mathew and his friends gave chase, recovered the hogs, and attacked the traders. The Doeg retaliated, and soon a series of skirmishes and raids swept across the frontier.

Fearing their enemies, settlers expected decisive action from Berkeley, but again he disappointed. In March 1676 Berkeley and the assembly decided to build FORTS, but at locations far from the actual conflict. For settlers, the defensive plan appeared more like a plan for profit, allowing assemblymen the opportunity to monopolize Indian trade. Having lost faith in their government, the frontiersmen looked for other alternatives.

They found one in a newcomer to the colony, Nathaniel Bacon. Unlike most newcomers, Bacon—a favorite of Berkeley, a council member, and a wealthy landowner—had enjoyed a prosperous start in Virginia. Like most newcomers, Bacon was disdainful of Indians. Assuming that Berkeley would eventually grant him a commission for his actions, Bacon and the western colonists waged war on the Indians. Having earlier sensed the rebellious mood of the frontiersmen, Bacon now realized that hatred of Indians diverted anger away from the government. When he wrote Berkeley for a commission, Bacon informed the governor of the potential for rebellion and how best to avoid it. Under his leadership, Bacon argued, frontiersmen would project their frustrations onto Indians. Racial hatred would thus ease CLASS tensions and unify white people against Indians.

Berkeley refused. He did not want to alienate Indian allies, in part to protect the valuable trade with them, nor did he trust the men whom he considered frontier "rabble." Indeed, the governor thought it more dangerous to sanction Bacon's men than to rebuke them. Berkeley had another solution for defusing rebellion: He called for a new assembly, removed voting restrictions on landless men, and welcomed criticisms of his leadership, but his plan backfired. The new assembly passed reforms that empowered the common folk, and it legalized the enslavement of Indians.

Meanwhile, Bacon's men proceeded to attack Indians without a commission. Upon hearing the news that Berkeley had labeled them rebels, Bacon and his followers lived up to the label, directing hostility not only toward Indians but the government as well. On June 22, 1676, Bacon entered JAMESTOWN with 500 men and at gunpoint forced Berkeley to grant the commission. Bacon was declared "General of Virginia," while a "Manifesto and Declaration of the People" called for all Indians to be killed or removed

During Bacon's Rebellion the farmers marched to Jamestown in September 1676, took over the House of Burgesses (shown here), and passed laws for reform. *(Library of Congress)*

and for the rule of elite "parasites" to end. Bacon's men now returned to the frontier to wage war against Indians. However, they soon turned back toward Jamestown when Berkeley nullified the commission and tried to raise troops to fight the rebels. Berkeley fled across the CHESAPEAKE BAY as Bacon reentered the city.

The next months proved among the most chaotic in Virginia's colonial history, as the exile and the rebel vied for control of the colony. The rebel appeared to be winning. As Bacon paraded captured Indians through the countryside, flocks of freedmen and newcomers joined his ranks. Even established planters, who had always opposed the "Bacon rabble," gravitated toward rebel leadership to prevent the plunder of their estates. Berkeley responded by sailing back to Jamestown with guarantees of freedom to loyal slaves and servants, but Bacon made similar promises before the governor could dock. Never getting off his ship, Berkeley watched as Bacon razed Jamestown.

Bacon's Rebellion officially ended when English troops arrived to secure peace in January 1677, but it unofficially ended when Bacon died of dysentery in October 1676. After the dynamic leader's death, the rebellious spirit expired. Having crushed the Indians, frontiersmen turned their attention to the October harvest.

What began as a crusade against NATIVE AMERICANS nearly became a social revolution. Frontiersmen initially blamed Indians for their problems but later included the upper-class leadership. Although the rebellion never achieved its logical conclusion of political revolution, the threat was enough to initiate change. Unlike Berkeley, who had been dismissed from his duties, the remaining elite followed Bacon's advice. By almost exclusively importing African slaves rather than indentured servants after the rebellion, the elite apparently hoped that racial hatred of black people would unify white people and thus soothe future class conflict.

See also BERKELEY, LADY FRANCES; POWHATAN CONFEDERACY.

Further reading: Edmund S. Morgan, *American Slavery, American Freedom: The Ordeal of Colonial Virginia* (New York: Norton, 1975).

—C. B. Waldrip

banking and credit

The banking and credit systems of British North America were very different from the financial institutions of today and were even less developed by 17th-century English standards as well. Commercial banks did not exist in Britain's North American colonies, nor were the colonists disposed to create centralized political or financial establishments. However, a system emerged that adequately satisfied the needs of the growing and developing ECONOMY of the colonies. Personal financial networks and government policies initiated by colonial legislatures to solve the colonies' shortage of currency and investment capital were the main institutions of banking and credit in early America.

Mercantile credit was the foundation of this system in the colonies. English and Scottish merchant houses would extend credit to their intermediaries or colonial MERCHANTS in eastern seaports on the promise of future goods. These "merchant bankers" would then distribute credit to their connections in the countryside. The system functioned along an avenue of credit and debt that ran from the rural farmer to urban mercantile firms to London or Glasgow. This credit was usually short-term and was to be remitted with the next harvest. Outside the mercantile sector access to credit was extremely limited. Merchants or wealthy landowners loaned money locally for the purchase of land or other enterprises. These individuals or firms provided many of the financial services of modern banks.

This system of mercantile credit was generally more beneficial to wealthy individuals than poorer ones. Although certainly an important part of the system, poorer members of SOCIETY were not extended as much credit as were the wealthy. The latter were viewed as better risks because they usually possessed greater assets in land or slaves. This belief also generated a regional disparity in access to British credit. The cultivation of TOBACCO, rice, and INDIGO in the South for the English market made that region a more attractive investment. In this period the South received nearly 80 percent of the British credit lent to the American colonies.

The extension of personal credit played an important role in the formation of colonial society because it helped community leaders garner political support. By manipulating the creditor/debtor relationship, the early gentry created a patriarchal social order based on hierarchies of dependence in which political power (based on personal loyalty and social rank) rested with those who possessed access to foreign markets and credit.

Colonial governments were important actors in the banking and credit systems of early America. Through loan offices (or "land banks") colonial legislatures provided loans to white male heads of households with land as collateral. Borrowers usually received currency worth up to half the value of the property being mortgaged and were free to spend the money in any manner they wished. The legislatures placed limits on how much currency one person could receive from the loan office in order to guarantee wide access and to prevent the depreciation of the currency already emitted. The repayment schedule extended over long periods, usually up to 12 years. Interest rates on the loans varied from colony to colony, but they were generally low, ranging from 5 to 6 percent in the Middle Colonies to 12.5 percent in SOUTH CAROLINA. The majority of colonies charged interest either at or slightly below 8 percent, the legally established limit for private transactions. In general, the land banks were successful. They dispensed funds broadly, raised revenues for the colonies through interest, enjoyed widespread support because they provided legal tender to country farmers who lacked gold or silver, and enabled large landowners to turn land into liquid capital.

Further reading: Edwin J. Perkins, *American Public Finance and Financial Services, 1700–1815* (Columbus: Ohio State University Press, 1994).

—Peter S. Genovese, Jr.

Baptists

Although they identified closely with the English PURITANS, Baptists parted ways with their fellow dissenters over the issues of infant baptism and the civil government's role in matters of religion. Convinced that the New World offered greater opportunities for religious freedom, many Baptists made the voyage to North America. Because of the intolerance these so-called Anabaptists experienced, many of them assimilated into the establishment churches, whether Congregational or Anglican. However, upon the arrival of ROGER WILLIAMS in 1631, Baptists had their much-needed champion for liberty of conscience. Even though his tenure as a Baptist was brief, Williams aided in founding the first Baptist church in North America in Providence, RHODE ISLAND, in 1638. A second church soon followed (1641) under the leadership of John Clarke, who provided stability to the growing denomination.

Following the establishment of their first two churches, Baptists grew slowly in the New England Colonies. The Middle and Southern Colonies, however, provided a more conducive environment for growth, most of which occurred in the latter part of the 18th century. This growth multiplied after the formation of the PHILADELPHIA Association in 1707, which provided an example of church cooperation that would foster the phenomenal expansion of Baptists in the late 1700s. In 1707 about 50 Baptist churches existed; in 1763 there were about 250.

Three major issues arose in Baptist life during this period. The first was the concern for religious liberty, or soul liberty. Under the leadership of figures such as Roger Williams and Isaac Backus, Baptists struggled to avoid granting the government undue authority in matters of religion. For instance, they opposed mandatory church attendance and taxation on behalf of the established church. Second, Baptists expressed great concern for the purity, or regenerate nature, of the visible church. Thus, they sought to secure the conversion of every member through such practices as the administration of church discipline. The third matter Baptists dealt with into the early 19th century was the division between Separate Baptists, who emphasized the continued work of the Holy Spirit, and Regular Baptists, who were wary of much of the enthusiasm prominent in the revivals known as the First GREAT AWAKENING.

During the First Great Awakening some Baptist women assumed new roles. Although most continued in the traditional roles of wives and mothers, some Separate Baptists permitted women to pray aloud during religious meetings. They also defended the practice of female exhorting—the public calling of others to repent. Examples include Martha Stearns Marshall, a Separate Baptist known for her public prayers and exhortations, and Margaret Meuse Clay. Although certainly not the rule, women served as deacons and elders in some churches. They were not always allowed to speak publicly in these capacities, but their congregations still recognized such women as spiritual leaders.

Baptists also welcomed both Native American and African-American converts more warmly than did the established churches. However, most Baptists still shared the common racial prejudices of this period. Thus, they distinguished between Christian fellowship on the one hand and social and racial equality on the other hand. New England Baptists may have relinquished some of these prejudices before their southern counterparts, but Baptists of the South still undertook MISSIONS work to both NATIVE AMERICANS and slaves.

Further reading: William G. McLoughlin, *New England Dissent, 1630–1833: The Baptists and the Separation of Church and State,* 2 vols. (Cambridge, Mass.: Harvard University Press, 1971); Carla Gardina Pestana, *Quakers and Baptists in Colonial Massachusetts* (New York: Cambridge University Press, 1991).

—Richard A. Bailey

Bartram, John (1699–1777)

An important scientist and naturalist and known as the originator of American botany, John Bartram was born in Marple, PENNSYLVANIA, the eldest son of farmer William Bartram and his wife, Elizabeth Hunt. After the death of John's mother in 1701, his father remarried in 1707 and took his second wife and their children in 1711 to live in NORTH CAROLINA. John and his younger brother, James, remained behind, living with their grandmother. John married Mary Maris on April 25, 1723, and three months later inherited his grandmother's farm near PHILADELPHIA. They had two children, only one of whom reached adulthood. Two years after Mary's death in 1727, Bartram married Ann Mendenahall. They had nine children, including William Bartram, who followed in his father's role as a scientist.

Despite being raised in a devout Quaker household, John Bartram struggled with his faith. By the mid-1750s he was critical of Quaker pacifism and the divinity of Jesus, prompting the Society of Friends (Quakers) to disown him in 1757. Nevertheless, he was active in his local Quaker community and was buried in the Darby Friends burial ground.

As a child Bartram received only a basic formal EDUCATION, studying for about four years at the Darby Quaker School, yet he was fascinated with SCIENCE, taking a special interest in botany. He produced the American colonies' first botanical garden and worked with Joseph Breintnall to collect and identify specimens of North American trees. Through Breintnall Bartram gained access to the scientific circles of Britain, corresponding with various members of the Royal Society and developing a friendship and 35-year correspondence with one of its leading figures and fellow Quaker, Peter Collinson. Through Collinson Bartram published seven papers in the *Philosophical Transactions of the Royal Society* and the results of a series of plant experiments in the popular *Gentleman's Magazine.*

Bartram was also an avid explorer, regularly traveling in the North American interior. His expeditions included journeys to the sources of the Schuylkill River in Pennsylvania, the Blue Ridge Mountains of VIRGINIA, the Catskill Mountains, the swamps of DELAWARE, the backcountries of the Carolinas, and FLORIDA. By the 1740s Bartram's reputation had spread, resulting in a steady stream of special requests for North American specimens from scientists throughout the Atlantic world. During his expeditions he collected plants, ANIMALS, and American Indian artifacts, keeping some specimens for his own collections but sending a great deal to his associates. Several artifacts were sent to Sir Hans Sloane, who founded the British Museum, where a number of Bartram's contributions remain on display to this day.

Bartram's achievement as a naturalist led to international recognition. He was a founding member of the AMERICAN PHILOSOPHICAL SOCIETY, was elected to the Veteuskapsakademie (Sweden's Royal Academy of Sciences), and received a medal from the Society of Gentlemen in Edinburgh. In 1765 Bartram was appointed the botanist to King George III (1760–1820), which carried an annual stipend of £50. He died at home on his Kingsessing farm.

Further reading: E. Berkeley and D.S. Berkeley, *The Life and Travels of John Bartram: From Lake Ontario to the River St. John* (Tallahassee: University Presses of Florida, 1982); Thomas P. Slaughter, *The Natures of John and William Bartram, 1734–1777* (New York: Knopf, 1996).

—Troy O. Bickham

Batts, Thomas (flourished 1671)

Explorer Thomas Batts was one of the first known Englishmen to cross the Appalachian Mountains, in 1671. Major General Abraham Wood, commander of Fort Henry, obtained a commission from Governor Berkeley of VIRGINIA charging Batts with investigating the territory west of the mountains in search of the "South Sea." The original group included Robert Fallam, Penecute (an Indian guide), Thomas Woods, and Jack Weason. General Wood sent seven additional Indian guides to join the expedition three days later. The arrival of the seven Apomatack was fortunate because Penecute became ill several days later. Fallam's detailed journal of the expedition provides an important resource for scholars today.

The group traveled along the Roanoke River to the Blue Ridge Mountains, where they discovered a west-flowing stream they called Wood's River (later renamed New River). After following the river to Peter's Fall (near the present-day Virginia–West Virginia border), they were forced to turn back due to threatening weather. Along the way Fallam recorded trees with carvings etched into their trunks, presumably by earlier white explorers.

On the return trip they met WILLIAM BYRD, accompanied by a larger group of men conducting their own EXPLORATION of the area. Batts returned to Fort Henry after traveling 23 days and 720 miles. Significantly, Batts and Fallam's claim to the New River strengthened England's claim to the Ohio Valley and most of the Allegheny territory.

Further reading: Robert D. Mitchell, *Appalachian Frontiers: Settlement, Society Development in the Preindustrial Era* (Lexington, University of Kentucky Press, 1991).

—Lisa A. Ennis

Beaver Wars

The Beaver Wars of the mid-17th century are associated with the rise to power of the IROQUOIS Confederation of NEW YORK. In a series of attacks between 1649 and 1654, Mohawk and Seneca warriors decimated the HURON, Erie, Petun, and Neutral Indian nations and established themselves as the dominant Indian power from New England to Wisconsin. Later in the century attacks against the Illinois tribes and the Susquehannah in Pennsylvania stretched Iroquois influence to the Ohio Valley and as far south as VIRGINIA.

By 1630 the Huron of Canada had established a lucrative trade in beaver and other animal skins with French traders in Montreal. Their trading empire skirted the north shore of Lakes Huron and Erie into the Michigan peninsula, then north as far as Lake Nippissing. Each year dozens of Huron cargo canoes brought skins down the Ottawa River to Montreal. The Iroquois had established their own beaver trade with the Dutch at Fort Orange (Albany). The Iroquois, however, quickly depleted the fur-bearing animals in New York and attempted to gain access to plentiful supplies in Canada. Failing to reach agreement with the Huron, the Iroquois turned to raiding Huron canoe trains on the Ottawa River. Then, in a daring raid, the Iroquois attacked the principal Huron towns in March 1649, scattering survivors, and brought to an end Huron hegemony over the Canadian fur trade.

The Huron trading system had relied on the agricultural production of the Petun, Erie, and Neutral nations in the area north of Lake Erie. In the absence of the Huron, the Ottawa of Michigan entered the fray, trading with the Erie, Petun, and Neutral nations for foodstuffs and tobacco to carry into the Canadian interior in exchange for furs. Late in 1649 the Iroquois attacked and effectively destroyed the Petun. In 1651 the Neutral nation scattered before an Iroquois attack, and in 1654 the same fate befell the Erie. Continued rivalry with the Ottawa and the movement of the FUR TRADE toward the western Great Lakes encouraged Iroquois ventures to the west. The contest for dominance of the fur trade renewed old rivalries with the Susquehannah in Pennsylvania, ending only in 1675 when the Iroquois drove them south.

Intermixed with efforts to dominate the fur trade was the Iroquois need to recover population lost to battle and disease. The Iroquois tradition of adopting captives to replace lost sons, brothers, and husbands (mourning wars) undoubtedly helped fuel the Beaver Wars. The Iroquois may also have been intent on extending "The Tree of Peace," the symbol of their confederation, by bringing other tribes under its protection. Whether to dominate the fur trade, replace lost relatives, or to follow imperialist aims by extending their social and political system, the Beaver Wars propelled the Iroquois to a dominant position among Northeast Indians in the 17th century.

—Thomas R. Wessel

Benezet, Anthony (1713–1784)

Anthony Benezet, an important colonial reform leader, was born in France to Huguenot parents who, in 1715, fled first to Rotterdam, then to England, where the family stayed until immigrating to PHILADELPHIA in 1731. Anthony became a Quaker and considered following his father's mercantile business but became a schoolteacher instead. That decision limited his income significantly, which suited his goal to adhere strictly to the Quaker doctrine of plainness. The basis of all his efforts—for abolition of SLAVERY, justice for NATIVE AMERICANS and the poor, pacifism, temperance, and EDUCATION—was aversion to greed. He wrote, "The great rock against which our society has dashed" is "the love of the world & the deceitfulness of riches, the desire of amassing wealth." He taught first in Germantown, then in 1742 became an instructor at the Friends' English School in Philadelphia.

In 1750 Benezet started free classes for African-American students at his home in the evening while continuing to teach white children during the day. He also established a school for girls in 1755. He considered black students equal to white students and continued the informal classes until 1770, when he convinced the Philadelphia Monthly Meeting to open an "Africans' School." Among Benezet's African-American pupils were former slaves Absalom Jones and Richard Allen, who became ministers and leaders of the Philadelphia black community. Another student was James Forten, who became an abolitionist and wealthy manufacturer. Benezet wrote in 1781 that he had "for many years, had the opportunity of knowing the temper and genius of the Africans; particularly those under his tuition, who have been many, of different ages; and he can with truth and sincerity declare, that he has found among them as great variety of talents, equally capable of improvement, as among a like number of whites."

Benezet was JOHN WOOLMAN's chief collaborator in convincing the Philadelphia Yearly Meeting to ban slaveholding. He served as one of the overseers of the press who approved Woolman's 1754 essay and wrote the initial draft of the Philadelphia Yearly Meeting's first denunciation of slavery, *An Epistle of Caution and Advice* (1754). Benezet worked within the Society of Friends (QUAKERS) to strengthen its testimony against slavery, published numerous articles and pamphlets, and corresponded extensively with abolitionists abroad. His most influential writings include *Observations on the Inslaving, importing and purchasing of Negroes* (1759) and *A Caution and Warning to Great Britain and Her Colonies* (1766). After 1776, when the Philadelphia Yearly Meeting banned slaveholding among its members, anti-slavery Friends sought to abolish slavery among non-Quakers as well. Anthony Benezet played a major role in this transition, urging enactment of the Pennsylvania gradual abolition law (1780), the first in the United States. Although disappointed that a more liberal law was not passed, he lobbied every Pennsylvania legislator for approval.

See also ABOLITIONISM.

Further reading: Gary B. Nash and Jean R. Soderlund, *Freedom By Degrees: Emancipation in Pennsylvania and Its Aftermath* (New York: Oxford University Press, 1991).

—Jean R. Soderlund

Bering, Vitus Jonassen (1681–1741)

Jonassen Bering was a Danish-born Russian naval officer and navigator who led the first expedition that reached America from the West. Bering supervised the large-scale EXPLORATION program initiated by the emperor Peter the Great to expand Russia's Asiatic possessions and to discover if Asia and America were physically united. In 1728 Bering initially examined the water passage between Kamchatka and America. On June 15, 1741, two ships, the *St. Peter* and *St. Paul,* commanded by Bering and Aleksei Chirikov, respectively, sailed from Kamchatka. After two weeks the ships became separated in fog. On July 26 a German naturalist, Georg Steller, on board *St. Peter* sighted land, and five days later he spent a few hours on Kayak Island. Bering discovered several more islands near Alaska. He lost nearly half of his crew to scurvy and other hardships. Bering died on December 17, 1741, on an uninhabited island that now bears his name. The rest of Bering's men managed to return to Kamchatka, with Chirikov having discovered several of the Aleutian Islands.

Later, the British explorer Captain James Cook proposed to name the strait that separates Asia and America after Bering. The results of the Bering expedition led to the Russian colonization of the shores of Alaska several decades later.

See also ALASKA, RUSSIA IN.

Further reading: Gerhard F. Muller, *Bering's Voyages* (Fairbanks: University of Alaska Press, 1986).

—Peter Rainow

Berkeley, Lady Frances (1634–1695?)

Lady Frances Berkeley was married to three colonial governors, and she wielded political power in her own right. In the 17th century aristocratic women rarely exercised overt political influence. They occasionally engaged in political discussions in parlors and surely swayed influential dinner guests but almost never debated with assemblymen. These political boundaries, however, did not apply to Lady Frances Berkeley. Although she earned a reputation as a gracious hostess, welcoming royalist exiles during the ENGLISH CIVIL WAR, Lady Berkeley formed the "Green Spring faction" that became a dominant political force in VIRGINIA.

Frances Culpeper arrived in Virginia with her aristocratic parents around 1650. Two years later she married Samuel Stephens, governor of Albemarle. Six months following Stephens's death in 1669, the widow became the mistress of Green Spring by marrying Virginia governor SIR WILLIAM BERKELEY. Lady Berkeley obviously garnered the respect of her husband and his peers. During BACON'S REBELLION Lord Berkeley sent his wife to England as his agent. She defended her husband ably, casting her cousin Nathaniel Bacon as an ungrateful traitor. Despite her efforts, however, Lady Berkeley could not prevent the dismissal of her husband at the rebellion's end.

Although Lord Berkeley died in 1677, his wife continued to engage in politics. Determined to empower her husband's coterie, she organized the Green Spring faction. Her political activism brought Lady Berkeley close to Philip Ludwell, the future governor of the Carolinas. They married in 1680 and lived out their days at Green Spring.

Further reading: Wesley Frank Craven, *The Southern Colonies in the Seventeenth Century, 1607–1689* (Baton Rouge: Louisiana State University, 1986).

—C. B. Waldrip

Berkeley, Sir William (1606–1677)

Knighted in 1639, Sir William Berkeley was appointed governor of VIRGINIA in 1641. He arrived in the colony the following year to announce the termination of the VIRGINIA COMPANY OF LONDON. Berkeley early looked and acted the part of royal governor. His fancy dress and comfortable home contrasted with the rugged background of the developing colony, and his words carried the weight of regal authority. For colonists accustomed to the Virginia Company, life under Berkeley became burdensome. Rich and poor colonists alike grumbled over the governor's high taxes, his centralizing tendencies, and especially his Indian policy. Considering Berkeley's unpopularity, it is remarkable that he governed more than three decades, from 1642 to 1677, with only a brief break during the ENGLISH CIVIL WAR (1652–60).

In 1676 BACON'S REBELLION erupted in the colony. After land hungry colonists clashed with Indians on Virginia's frontier, Berkeley failed to satisfy discontented Virginians despite the advice of frontier leader Nathaniel Bacon. Bacon had implored the governor to wage war against Indians to avoid rebellion, but Berkeley refused, eventually choosing to battle Bacon rather than Indians.

Bacon's Rebellion highlights Berkeley's ineptitude as a leader. Time and again, the gentleman-governor proved incapable of understanding the men he considered "rabble." Berkeley was shocked, for example, when a new assembly, which he fostered, supported Bacon and legalized the enslavement of Indians, nor did Berkeley exercise the decisiveness his words so often implied. He once captured Bacon, but rather than execute the rebel, Berkeley forced a public apology to embarrass him. Bacon did not blush long, however, for he again rallied his men and sent the governor into exile.

After nearly a year of plunder and indiscriminate killing of Indians, Bacon's Rebellion ended. A royal investigative committee laid partial blame on faulty leadership and suggested the governor's removal. Berkeley's harsh program of retaliation cinched the matter, and in May 1677 he grudgingly conceded and returned to England.

See also BERKELEY, LADY FRANCES.

Further reading: Wesley Frank Craven, *The Southern Colonies in the Seventeenth Century, 1607–1689* (Baton Rouge: Louisiana State University Press, 1986); Edmund S. Morgan, *American Slavery, American Freedom: The Ordeal of Colonial Virginia* (New York: Norton, 1975).

—C. B. Waldrip

Beverley, Robert (1673?–1722)

Born in Virginia and educated in England, Beverley was born a member of high society. His father was a politician and married into one of the oldest VIRGINIA families. By the time the elder Beverley died in 1887, the family owned nearly 50,000 acres on the Appalachian frontier. The couple had three sons, but Robert's brothers died young, making him the sole heir.

At 19 Beverley finished school in England and returned to Virginia, where he began his political career. He served in a number of judicial, administrative, and legislative posts, including in the House of Burgesses. However, like his father, Beverley's outspokenness hindered his career. In 1703 he wrote numerous letters criticizing Virginia's governor. When the letters were made public, the governor blocked Beverley's every political move, and he soon thereafter retired from public life.

Beverley is best remembered for his book *History and Present State of Virginia* (1705). On a trip to England Beverley was asked to review a work on the BRITISH EMPIRE in America. Finding the section on Virginia full of errors, he offered to correct the work. Instead, he wrote a new history of the colony, full of observations about southern planters. In 1722 he published *The Abridgement of the Public Laws of Virginia.*

In 1696 Beverley married Ursala Byrd, William Byrd's daughter. Within a year the 16-year-old Ursala died in childbirth. Beverley spent the rest of his "retirement" involved in land speculation, hunting, FISHING, gardening, and writing; he even reentered public life on a limited scale.

—Lisa A. Ennis

blacks See African Americans

Bond, Thomas (1712–1784)

Significant in the development of early American MEDICINE, Thomas Bond was born in Calvert County, MARYLAND, on June 3, 1712, the son of Richard Bond (a planter) and Elizabeth Benson Chew (widow of Benjamin Chew). Bond was a birthright Quaker who drifted away from the Society of Friends (QUAKERS) until disowned around 1742. After studying medicine in Annapolis, he went to Europe for further studies, spending two years in Paris, though not receiving an M.D. Upon returning in 1734 Bond settled in PHILADELPHIA and began practicing medicine. While interested in hygiene and epidemiology, he was also a skilled surgeon—especially successful at removing stones from the bladder. Bond also advocated SMALLPOX inoculation, publicly recommending the practice in 1737. He was also appointed one of the port physicians in 1741. Two years later Bond entered into a medical partnership with his physician brother Phineas (1717–73) that lasted 40 years.

Like other educated and enlightened citizens of the times, Bond contributed to society in nonmedical ways as well. As a member of Benjamin Franklin's circle, Bond joined the Junto and served as a Franklin family physician. He became a member of the Library Company of Philadelphia in 1741 and a founding member of the AMERICAN PHILOSOPHICAL SOCIETY in 1743, he was elected to the Philadelphia Common Council in 1745, and he conceived the PENNSYLVANIA Hospital, which opened in 1752 with the active support of Franklin. It was the first American institution established explicitly to treat the sick, injured, and mentally troubled. As a frequent board of trustees member for the University of Pennsylvania, Bond supported the establishment of a medical department in 1765.

In 1766 Bond resigned from the board to become an attending physician at both the hospital and the almshouse, where he formalized his earlier practice of taking students on rounds. Strongly believing in the efficacy of clinical instruction, Bond offered the first course of clinical lectures in the colonies, giving students the opportunity to study patients in a hospital setting. As a clinical physician Bond preferred using his observations and experience when treating patients rather than relying on the various systems of medicine advocated by others. Bond also believed in using mild healing measures, such as limited bleeding and a variety of baths. He died in Philadelphia on June 9, 1784.

—Anita DeClue

Bonnet, Stede (unknown–1718)

Born to a wealthy family, Stede Bonnet became a notorious pirate. He served in the royal army and retired with the rank of major. He became a plantation owner on the island of Barbados in the CARIBBEAN. According to some sources, Bonnet could no longer stand living with his constantly nagging wife, although the reality probably was quite different. In 1717 he purchased a sloop, outfitted it with 10 guns, recruited a crew of 70 men, and named his ship *Revenge.* Bonnet then headed off with the express purpose of becoming a pirate. Although the crew bordered on mutiny because of his frowning on the MARINERS' usual drinking, swearing, and debauchery, Bonnet's training as a military officer enabled him to discipline the crew, despite his apparent seasickness. He took two ships as "prizes" along the VIRGINIA coast, sold some of the pirated goods, then came upon the ship of notorious pirate EDWARD TEACH (Blackbeard). Bonnet's and Blackbeard's ships sailed in consort for some time, as Bonnet remained a virtual prisoner aboard Blackbeard's ship. Bonnet was dismissed by Blackbeard and sailed off on his own, with Blackbeard keeping most of the jointly acquired spoils. Bonnet headed to NORTH CAROLINA, where he received a pardon from Governor Charles Eden.

Bonnet sailed for the Caribbean hoping to secure a privateer's commission against the Spanish but instead pursued his old nemesis Blackbeard. Outsmarted by Blackbeard, Bonnet returned to PIRACY, taking the alias of "Captain Thomas" and naming his sloop the *Royal James.* He soon captured several prizes off Virginia and in DELAWARE Bay. William Rhett received a commission to capture Bonnet and surprised the pirate in the Cape Fear River, North Carolina. After a fierce battle Bonnet and crew were taken to CHARLESTON, where Bonnet's light guard and the possible cooperation of Governor Robert Johnson made it possible for Bonnet to escape. Rhett recaptured Bonnet, who was placed under heavy guard. Twenty-five of Bonnet's crew were found guilty, and on November 8, 1718, 22 of them were hanged. Bonnet was found guilty two days later and hanged.

Further reading: Daniel Defoe, *A General History of the Pyrates,* ed. Manuel Schonhorn (Mineola, N.Y.: Dover, 1999).

—Stephen C. O'Neill

borderlands

Borderlands are places between colonies or nation-states. They are usually areas contested by several peoples. For example, in the colonial period the present-day southeastern United States was a borderland, contested by the British, the Spanish, the French, and numerous native peoples, including the CHEROKEE, the CHOCTAW, and the CHICKASAW.

The historiographic concept of the borderlands has a contested history itself. Historians have long argued over whether we should see the expansion of European peoples onto the lands of NATIVE AMERICANS as a frontier or as many borderlands at specific times and places. Frederick Jackson Turner's "frontier thesis," developed in the late 19th century, described a process of white Americans moving west onto new lands. According to Turner, as the frontier spread west, it brought new economic and social stages. Places where Indians had hunted for their livelihoods became populated by traders, then ranchers, farmers, and eventually industrial city dwellers.

Recognizing that Turner's model omitted both non-British colonizers and a substantial phase of co-occupation, his student Herbert Eugene Bolton pioneered the concept of borderlands to study Spanish North America. In the borderlands that Bolton described, Spanish officials, soldiers, and friars coexisted with Indians for centuries on the same land, in contrast to Turner's advancing line.

Nearly a century after Turner and Bolton formulated their models, historians still struggle with the question of which concept is more useful for studying Indian-white interactions. Historians following in Turner's footsteps see white expansion as a process that gradually enveloped native peoples. They have improved Turner's deficient attention to the Indian side of the frontier. In Turner's work Indians appeared only in the first short stage of supposed progress to civilization. His successors have recognized the continuing Indian presence and have tended to see the process as one of the increasing power of white people to control the land rather than Turner's normative process of "civilization." However, more recent frontier studies still tend to center on white processes. Indians are present, but usually only react to white actions. Another criticism is that the term *frontier* may be too weighted by its connection with the glorification of European settlement to be of much analytical use.

The concept of borderlands is appealing to many historians who want to study the interactions of various peoples—Native American, European, and African—in colonial America. Because the borderlands school generally recognized a longer and more important Native American role than did Turner, the New Western and New Indian schools of historians have tended to follow a borderlands approach. They see borderlands as places where different peoples came together and had to figure out how to coexist.

By studying borderlands, historians have reached several important general insights. The European conquest of the Americas was not inevitable. In fact, in many places and times, Native Americans converted Europeans to their diplomatic, economic, social, and cultural ways. Colonial power had its limits. Even regions that European powers claimed to rule were often, on the ground, ruled by native peoples. As places of cross-cultural contact, borderlands are ideal for comparative cultural history. For example, many Europeans who observed Native Americans in the colonial period noted that women did the farming, in contrast to GENDER roles in Europe. Europeans tended to believe that Native American men forced the women in their societies into the "drudgery" of agricultural work. This misconception reveals much about the gender systems and beliefs of European and Native American societies. Finally, by studying a wide variety of Indian-white reactions, borderlands studies have helped to destroy the myth that Indians were (or are) monolithic and powerless.

See also CORNSTALK; HENDRICK; LA DEMOISELLE.

Further reading: Jeremy Adelman and Stephen Aron, "From Borderlands to Borders: Empires, Nation-States, and the Peoples in Between in North American History" (*American Historical Review,* 104 [June 1999], 814–41).

—Kathleen DuVal

Boston

Boston's location on the Shawmut Peninsula, with three lofty hills (the Tremont or Tri-mountain), natural springs, and a deep and protected harbor, was a natural choice for the first wave of Puritan settlers to MASSACHUSETTS, who arrived in 1630. The PURITANS envisioned themselves as establishing a "city on a hill," and here was the hill. They were invited from Charleston by the Reverend William Blackstone, a hermit who had been living on the peninsula since 1625.

The town of Boston was founded in September 1630 as the capital of the Massachusetts Bay Colony. Its form of government was created in 1633 as the town meeting with elected selectmen, and it lasted until Boston was incorporated as a city in 1822. Early Massachusetts governors JOHN WINTHROP and Henry Vane and the leading Puritan ministers John Wilson and JOHN COTTON resided in Boston. The Boston Common was established as the common pasturage in 1632, and the town market was created in 1634. Harvard College was established in neighboring Cambridge across the Charles River in 1636. Boston's population swelled quickly to nearly 1,700 in the first decade, then slowed as immigration declined.

Trade dramatically affected Boston's character after the disruption of the ENGLISH CIVIL WAR of the 1640s, transforming the town into one of the most important shipping ports in the BRITISH EMPIRE. Shipping was based heavily on the export of timber, cod, and rum and the import of wine, wheat, molasses, and finished materials. SHIPBUILDING flourished as the need for ships grew. The city's MERCHANTS diversified their operations, taking a lead in the African slave trade and dealing directly with smugglers and privateers. Merchants largely ignored the Navigation Acts, resulting in Boston, profiting as a commercial center.

An entrenched elite of several families developed, they provided leadership to the town and the colony from Boston. Leaders from among the Winthrop, Saltonstall, and Sewall families, with popular support, were responsible for arresting Royal Governor SIR EDMUND ANDROS and his associates in 1688, imprisoning him on an island in Boston Harbor. They hoped for the return of the godly Puritan Commonwealth, but the Second Charter of 1691, a compromise achieved by INCREASE MATHER, extended SUFFRAGE to non-Puritans by eliminating church membership as a requirement for franchise status and created a royal governor appointed by the king.

A series of fires, especially the major ones in 1676 and 1711, consumed large portions of the town's center. Boston quickly recovered each time, aided by legislation requiring brick for new structures in town. This spurred construction of some of the most impressive buildings in the colonies: the Old Brick Church and Old State House between 1711 and 1713, Christ Church (the Old North Church) in 1723, and the Old South Meetinghouse in 1729 (all of which, except for the Old Brick, are still standing). Roads were graded for drainage, paved with cobblestones, and routinely cleaned. Subterranean drainage was created in 420 sections between 1708 and 1720. The most important construction project was Long Wharf in 1711. It extended from King Street nearly a mile into Boston Harbor, making it one of the largest in the world.

By 1720 Boston was the largest British port in North America, with a population close to 12,000. It exerted its cultural and stylistic influence across New England and to the other colonies. Printing and book selling, painting and engraving, goldsmithing and cabinet making were just some of the advanced, specialized trades that flourished in Boston. The bustling town was the home of leading theologians, political aspirants, and a mercantile elite, as well as laborers, mechanics, housewives, prostitutes, slaves, transient seamen, and even the young Benjamin Franklin.

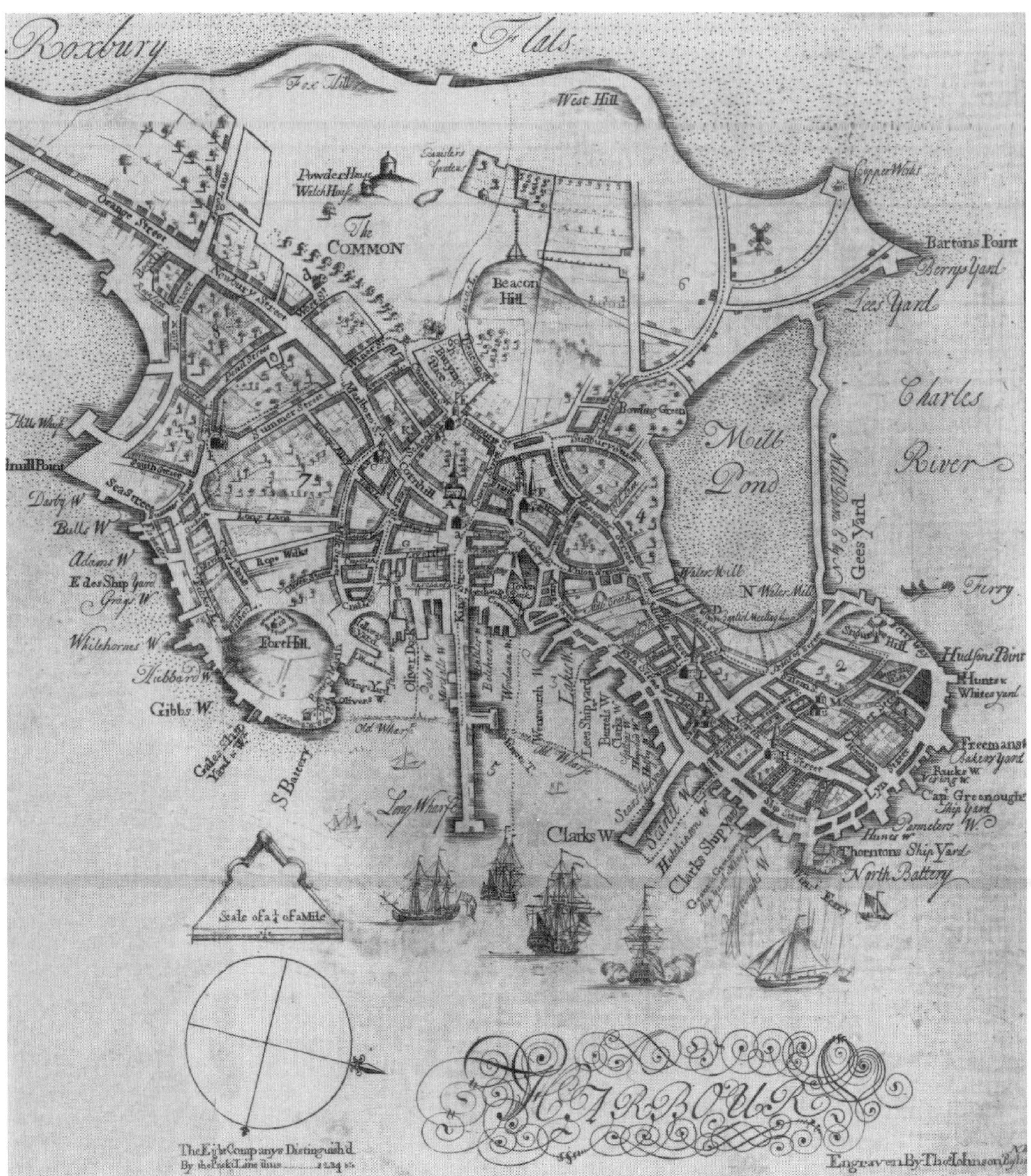

This 1728 map shows Boston when it was still the largest city in the thirteen colonies. *(Library of Congress)*

As Boston approached its highest pre-Revolutionary population, more than 16,000, a major economic depression in the 1740s combined with increasing poverty, SMALLPOX epidemics, and deaths resulting from the continual warfare with France. Boston entered a period of declining shipping, decreasing population, and civil unrest. Wealth inequalities increased dramatically. Crowds of people often took to the streets to advocate their own political agendas. The vocally political nature of Bostonians of all classes from the 1740s to the 1770s gave rise to various discontents and was a vital ingredient to the start of the American Revolution.

Throughout the colonial period, Boston was preeminent as a political, commercial, educational, theological, and cultural center, rivaled only by PHILADELPHIA and NEW YORK CITY.

See also ENDECOTT, JOHN; KNIGHT, SARAH KEMBLE; MATHER, COTTON; SEWALL, SAMUEL.

Further reading: Gary B. Nash, *The Urban Crucible: Social Change, Political Consciousness, and the Origins of the American Revolution* (Cambridge, Mass.: Harvard University Press, 1979); Walter Muir Whitehill, *Boston: Topographical History,* 3rd ed. (Cambridge, Mass.: Belknap Press of Harvard University Press, 2000).

—Stephen C. O'Neill

Boston Philosophical Society

The Boston Philosophical Society was perhaps the first organization founded in the American colonies for the pursuit of the study of experimental and natural philosophy. Established in April 1683 by the father-son team of INCREASE MATHER and COTTON MATHER, the society was patterned after the Royal Society of London, which had been established in Restoration London in 1660 and chartered by Charles II in 1662. In his autobiography, INCREASE MATHER wrote "I promoted a design for a private philosophical society in Boston, which I hope may have laid the foundation for that which will be our future edification." The two Mathers, as well as their colleagues in the society, saw no contradiction between the study of the natural world and the belief in an all-powerful, active deity. The members, including the Mathers, the Reverend SAMUEL WILLARD, and others sent correspondence to England and presented papers to the periodic meetings of the group.

The society was short lived, however. Dissatisfaction with the Crown's revocation of the Massachusetts Charter in 1684, the subsequent arrival of EDMUND ANDROS as governor in December 1686, and the declaration of the DOMINION OF NEW ENGLAND took the members' attention away from natural philosophy. Although few records survive, we may surmise that the society lasted only two to five years.

—George W. Boudreau

Boylston, Zabdiel (1680–1766)

Zabdiel Boylston, a surgeon and physician born at Muddy River (now Brookline), MASSACHUSETTS, introduced SMALLPOX inoculation in America. After an apprenticeship to his physician father, Boylston became a successful surgeon and apothecary shop owner, developing new medications as well as medical procedures. Although his practice was lucrative, little is known about him until 1721, when a smallpox epidemic erupted in BOSTON.

Reverend COTTON MATHER had twice appealed to the Boston medical community to consider inoculation—the little-known method by which a healthy person is deliberately given a mild case of smallpox in order to produce lifetime immunity. Many people and physicians feared that inoculation would only spread the DISEASE because infected people were contagious. Religious opposition was based on the belief that only God could inflict such maladies. Only a letter from Mather in June 1721 spurred Boylston to action. Mather had included a publication of the Royal Society of London describing the ancient practice of inoculation in Constantinople. Remembering the smallpox epidemic of 1702 and "how narrowly I then escap'd with my Life," Boylston responded by inoculating his six-year-old son Thomas and two servants. Angry mobs threatened Boylston's life, and a bomb was thrown through Reverend Mather's window. However, most of the clergy supported Mather and Boylston, as eventually did Boston's physicians when they examined Boylston's record. Of the 241 people he inoculated (known as "variolated") between July 1721 and February 1722, only six (2 percent) died; among those not inoculated, smallpox killed 844 (14 percent) of the 5,889 Bostonians who contracted the disease.

Noting that more people had been inoculated in Boston than in England, British supporters of inoculation invited Boylston to London, where in 1726 he published *An Historical Account of the Small-pox Inoculated in New England,* a detailed clinical account of his experiments. He was the first American-born physician to be inducted into the prestigious Royal Society of London. After returning to Boston, Boylston resumed his practice and promoted inoculation when smallpox struck again in 1730. In 1740 he sold his shop and retired to the family farm in Brookline, where he engaged in local politics, bred horses, and conducted scientific experiments until his death in 1766.

Further reading: Zabdiel Boylston, *An Historical Account of the Small-pox Inoculated in New England* (London: S. Chandler, 1726. Reprint, New York: Arno Press, 1977); John Duffy, *Epidemics in Colonial America* (Baton Rouge, Louisiana State University Press, 1953, 1971).

—Anthony Connors

Braddock, Edward (1695–1755)

Edward Braddock was born in 1695 in Perthshire, Scotland, the son of Major General Edward Braddock (d. 1725). He joined the Coldstream Guards in 1710 and had 45 years' experience with the European style of warfare when he was appointed commander of all British forces in North America.

When he arrived in VIRGINIA in the spring of 1755, his main task was to drive the French away from Fort Duquesne (later Pittsburgh), at the strategic confluence of the Allegheny, Ohio, and Monongahela Rivers. Earlier attempts by militia and volunteers to capture the fort had failed. Braddock possessed little knowledge of wilderness fighting and a considerable disdain for Indians and colonial troops. Because the British regiments were under strength, half the force of 2,000 men was colonial recruits. Indian scouts, carpenters, sailors, and a siege train completed the army. Because of his experience with the abortive expedition the preceding year, George Washington was invited to sign on as an aide, although he had little respect for Braddock's military skills.

Provision and transportation problems plagued the expedition from the beginning. The column experienced hard going, hampered by excess baggage and wagons. In the heat of June, plagued by insects, the engineers had to widen an old Indian trail through the dense forest and then surface it to accommodate both wagons and cannon. Braddock finally decided to rush ahead with 1,500 of his best troops with only bare necessities carried by packhorses. Progress was methodical and by the book, with flankers out and scouts vigilant.

When the advance guard began to cross the Monongahela 10 miles from Fort Duquesne on July 9, a numerically inferior force of 900 French and Indians ambushed them. Exhorting his men to fight like Englishmen, Braddock refused to allow them to shoot from behind cover, as did the provincials. After Braddock was wounded the British began a chaotic retreat to the river, hotly pursued by the enemy. Washington placed Braddock in a cart and took him to safety while the British organized a rear guard defense. They suffered 977 casualties out 1,459 troops. Braddock suffered greatly for four days before dying, and he was buried in the middle of the trail so that his grave would be protected from desecration by the Indians. Washington's organization of the retreat earned him a military reputation.

Further reading: Lee McCardell, *Ill-Starred General: Braddock of the Coldstream Guards* (Pittsburgh, Pa.: University of Pittsburgh Press, 1986).

—Joseph J. Casino

Bradford, Cornelia Smith (unknown–1755)

Cornelia Smith married Andrew Bradford (1686–1742), a prominent printer in PHILADELPHIA, in 1740. Already the publisher of the *American Weekly Mercury*, her husband produced the first *American Magazine* in 1741, beating Benjamin Franklin in publishing the first magazine in the colonies by less than a week. After Andrew's adopted nephew and successor WILLIAM BRADFORD spurned a marriage to Cornelia Smith Bradford's adopted niece, causing great awkwardness in the household, Andrew rewrote his will, leaving the press to his wife. When Andrew died childless in 1742, his widow took over publication in partnership with two men. She dissolved the arrangement in 1744 and operated the press independently until her retirement in 1746, after which the publication of both the magazine and newspaper ceased. Cornelia Smith Bradford died in 1755, having become the first woman independently to operate a newspaper in America.

—Margaret Sankey

Bradford, William (1590–1657)

William Bradford, governor of PLYMOUTH Colony, was born in England to a family of prosperous yeoman farmers. Raised by uncles after his father's death, Bradford became literate and read Erasmus and Foxe's *Book of Martyrs* avidly. Hearing the preaching of Richard Clifton, Bradford broke with the Church of England and embraced the idea of Protestant Separatism, much to the horror of his family. Under government pressure, the Separatist community at Scrooby, led by Bradford and William Brewster, moved to the Netherlands, joining other dissident Protestant communities. While there Bradford worked in the textile industry and, in 1613, married Dorothy May, by whom he had a son, John. Cultural differences with the Dutch and the prospect of renewed war with Spain led the group to plan a move across the Atlantic to lands held by the London Adventurers company in New England.

In 1619 the group set out in two vessels, the *Speedwell* and the *Mayflower*, but only the *Mayflower* was able to complete the crossing. Arriving in New England, Bradford helped to scout the site of the settlement, returning to the ship only to find that his wife had fallen overboard and drowned. Bradford concentrated his energies on holding the colony together as a signatory of the MAYFLOWER COMPACT and as the chief liaison with SQUANTO. When Governor Carver died, Bradford stepped in as the governor of the colony until his death in 1647. Bradford's administration survived constant crises, including sickness, famine, encroachment by squatters on the lands of natives, and threats from the London investors, whom the colony eventually bought out at great sacrifice. Bradford also maintained good relations with JOHN WINTHROP, whose rival colony in BOSTON began to sap the strength of Plymouth.

Bradford and his second wife, Alice Southworth, adopted many of the colony's orphans. In his later years Bradford wrote the *History of Plymouth Plantation,* a valuable source on the early settlement, as well as poetry and commentary on classical works.

—Margaret Sankey

Bradford, William (1663–1752)

The founder of a large family of printers, William Bradford came to PENNSYLVANIA in 1685 as a distributor of Quaker books published by his master, Andrew Sowle. Bradford married Sowle's daughter Elizabeth and embraced the Quaker faith. Bradford returned to England, then traveled back to Pennsylvania, where he established a printing press. He was called before Pennsylvania's Council for printing an unauthorized version of the colonial charter, an act that won him the support of the QUAKERS, who committed to buy his books and gave him a 40-pound-per-year salary. To ensure materials for printing, Bradford was instrumental in the establishment of America's first paper mill with the help of a Dutchman, William Rittenhouse.

Bradford lost favor with the Quakers when he printed an address of the discredited George Keith. Tried for this offense, the case went unresolved when the jury, handling the actual printing type, accidentally spilled the tray and destroyed the evidence. Governor Benjamin Fletcher of NEW YORK invited him to New York, where he became Royal Printer of New York and New Jersey. He continued to distribute books from his wife's family, including her sister Tace Sowle Raylton. Bradford joined the Church of England in 1703 and received support from them. In 1725 he established the first New York newspaper, the *New York Gazette.* Retiring in 1744, he died in 1752 in NEW YORK CITY, leaving behind a dynasty of American printers.

—Margaret Sankey

Bradstreet, Anne Dudley (1612–1672)

America's first published poet was born in 1612 on the estate of the earl of Lincoln, where her father, THOMAS DUDLEY, was steward. Raised on the estate, she was educated by her mother, Dorothy Yorke Dudley, using the earl's great library, including works by Philip Sidney, Walter Raleigh, and the French Calvinist poet du Bartas. Stricken with SMALLPOX at age 16, Anne recovered and in 1628 married Simon Bradstreet, the Cambridge-educated assistant to her father. The family, which had embraced nonconformist PROTESTANTISM, chose to follow JOHN WINTHROP and his party to MASSACHUSETTS in 1630 on board the *Arbella.* Settling at Cambridge, Ipswich, and finally Andover, the family established themselves as part of the intellectual and political elite, with Thomas Dudley serving as judge and governor.

Many members of the family wrote poetry, shared among themselves, and Anne began writing poems as well as prose meditations and autobiographical material for family consumption. Many of her short poems dealt with the experience of living in the New World, including fear for her often-absent husband, grief at the death of grandchildren, anxiety in childbirth (she bore eight children), and the loss of her house and 800-volume library to fire in 1666. The longer poems are marked by her Puritan faith and a keen interest in and understanding of SCIENCE, astronomy, and nature. These works show a neglected side of Puritan life, especially in the poems written to celebrate her passionate physical relationship with her husband and her admiration for Queen Elizabeth I (1558–1603) as a Protestant and powerful woman leader.

In 1647 Anne's brother-in-law, Reverend John Woodbridge, returned to England, taking a copy of Anne's long poems, which he had published anonymously in London in 1650 as *The Tenth Muse, Lately Sprung Up in America* and which identified its author as a respectable and esteemed woman from America. The volume met with praise on both sides of the Atlantic and won the admiration of COTTON MATHER, who declared her work "statelier than marble." Anne revised and improved the poems beginning in 1666, and a second edition appeared in 1678, six years after her death. Her shorter works were collected and published by the family after her death.

Further reading: Douglas Wilson, *Beyond Stateliest Marble: The Passionate Femininity of Anne Bradstreet* (Nashville, Tenn.: Highland Books, 2001).

—Margaret Sankey

Brainerd, David (1718–1747)

A Christian missionary to NATIVE AMERICANS and the author of important personal journals, David Brainerd was born in Haddam, CONNECTICUT. He attended Yale College from 1739 to 1742. He became a New Light during the GREAT AWAKENING and was expelled from Yale for claiming that a tutor had "no more grace than a chair." At the invitation of Ebenezer Pemberton, a Presbyterian clergyman in NEW YORK CITY, Brainerd became a missionary to the Mahican Indians in NEW YORK, then in 1744 accepted an assignment among the DELAWARE of PENNSYLVANIA and

NEW JERSEY. The Society in Scotland for Propagating Christian Knowledge sponsored his work.

While Brainerd met an unenthusiastic response among Delaware who had migrated west to the Susquehanna Valley, he achieved greater success in 1745 at Crossweeksung, an Indian town on Crosswicks Creek in Burlington County, New Jersey. Brainerd and his interpreter, Moses (Tunda) Tatamy, a Delaware and recent convert, inspired a revival, converting scores of people within just a few months. When the crowds overflowed Crossweeksung, some moved to better lands at Cranbury, in Middlesex County, where Brainerd tried to create an agricultural mission—essentially a New England–style "praying town." After David Brainerd died of tuberculosis in 1747, his brother John succeeded him as minister. In 1758 the combined missionary efforts of the brothers contributed to the Delaware loss of traditional New Jersey lands. David Brainerd's deeply introspective journals went through many editions, including one by Jonathan Edwards. Brainerd's religious meditations were particularly influential among 19th-century evangelists.

Further reading: Richard W. Pointer, "'Poor Indians' and the 'Poor in Spirit': The Indian Impact on David Brainerd" (*New England Quarterly*, 67 (1994), 403–26).

—Jean R. Soderlund

Brattle, Thomas (1658–1713)

Born in BOSTON, MASSACHUSETTS, to a wealthy merchant family, Brattle attended Harvard College, focusing on mathematics and science. After receiving his B.A. in 1676, he continued his study of these subjects, in 1680 collaborating on observations of a comet that drew the notice of Sir Isaac Newton and earned Brattle membership in the Royal Society, Britain's oldest, most prestigious scientific organization. Moving to London in 1682, he studied with the chemist Robert Boyle and the astronomer John Flamsteed. He returned to Boston in 1689, after his parents' death, and lived off his considerable inheritance while furthering his research.

During the Salem witch trials of 1692, Brattle joined INCREASE MATHER and most other local ministers in rejecting the evidential basis for the many convictions and executions. Brattle's letter attacking the court's rulings helped motivate Governor William Phips to halt the proceedings. Brattle and his younger brother William, a tutor at Harvard College, later parted company with these same ministers in establishing the Brattle Street Church as a haven for religious liberalism and in helping to oust Mather from Harvard's presidency. These actions helped to prepare the way for the rise of American Unitarianism.

—George W. Harper

Brent, Margaret Reed (1601?–1671)

Margaret Reed Brent is often inaccurately described as the first female lawyer who practiced in the colonies. Born at Gloucestershire, England, Brent belonged to a prestigious and powerful Catholic gentry family. Concerned about potential civil and economic restrictions enforced by PURITANS against ROMAN CATHOLICS, Brent and several of her siblings migrated to MARYLAND in 1638. Lord Baltimore, a distant relative and founder of the colony, insisted that the Brents receive favorable land grants. The Brent women secured 70 acres, known as "Sisters Freehold," in the colony's capitol, ST. MARY'S CITY. They also bought 50 acres, and Brent's brother later deeded her 1,000 more. Most Maryland colonists, including the Brents, invested in TOBACCO.

As a single woman landowner, Margaret Brent was permitted certain legal rights and often filed claims independently in the provincial court against debtors. She also addressed the court as her brother's and citizens' legal representative; other unmarried and widowed women acted similarly. The dying Governor LEONARD CALVERT regarded Brent's business acumen so highly that he named her executrix of his personal estate. Brent enacted Calvert's power of attorney as Lord Baltimore's representative to sell his cattle and used the funds to pay mercenary soldiers from VIRGINIA who had quelled a Protestant uprising. Although she defused a potentially volatile situation, Brent's efforts displeased colonial leaders.

In January 1648 Brent insisted that she be given two votes in the assembly, one as a landowner and another as Calvert's attorney, so that she could directly participate in government, making her the first Euro-American woman to demand to vote. The provincial court refused her request because she was a woman. Lord Baltimore criticized her for squandering and usurping his estate, but the colonial assembly recommended that Brent retain her role as executrix based on her peaceful dealings with the soldiers. After losing favor with Lord Baltimore, Brent settled in Virginia on the plantation Peace, which she populated with British migrants to secure large land grants.

Sometimes described as a pioneering feminist, the never-married Brent, unusual for that era and place, where there were six men per woman, is also depicted as an assertive adventurer who protected her personal and property interests, retaining her lifelong affiliation with the upper class. In historical context Brent acted from a sense of entitlement and responsibility rather than as a proponent of changing patriarchal legal traditions restricting the rights of married women. Brent died on her plantation in 1671.

Further reading: Karen Berger Morello, *The Invisible Bar: The Woman Lawyer in America 1638 to the Present* (New York: Random House, 1986).

—Elizabeth D. Schafer

Brims (flourished 1700–1730)

"Emperor" Brims of Coweta, one of the founding towns of the Creek Indian Confederacy, was a dominant force in Creek diplomacy during the early 18th century. Brims had the unenviable task of trying to maintain peaceful relations with the English, the French, and the Spanish—all of whom wanted an alliance with the Creek to the exclusion of the others—as well as dealing with neighboring Native tribes.

Early in his career Brims favored the English because of the greater abundance of trade goods they could offer. The alliance was short lived, however, when dishonest English traders caused the Creek to search out the French and Spanish for trade goods. Additionally, the CHEROKEE and Yamasee put strains on the Creek–English alliance. The Cherokee were allies of the English but bitter enemies of the Creek. The Yamasee were related to the Creek but warred on the English.

Brims quickly learned that each of the powers placed demands on the Creek that, if accepted, would cause friction with the other powers. Rather than commit to any single alliance, Brims played one group off against another, seeking benefits from each while using their fear of one another to extract concessions from them and to protect Creek independence. Brims's policies were not always successful, and at times portions of the Creek nation went against his wishes, but during his rule the Creek Confederacy remained key to the balance of power in the region. He died between 1730 and 1733.

Further reading: David H. Corkran, *The Creek Frontier, 1540–1783* (Norman, University of Oklahoma Press, 1967).

—Jeffrey D. Carlisle

British Empire

The British Empire, whereby the British spread throughout and controlled much of the globe, evolved in several stages. Historians have conventionally dated a first phase of the British Empire from King Henry VII's (1485–1509) support of the voyages of John and Sebastian Cabot in 1497–98, through its rapid growth after the English defeated the Spanish Armada in 1588, to its maturity in 1763 at the end of the SEVEN YEARS' WAR. Properly called the British Empire after the 1707 merger of England and Scotland into the single kingdom of Great Britain, it developed during the period when European colonization and competition was based on theories collectively known as the mercantile system. MERCANTILISM sought to concentrate the profits from world commerce primarily in Europe. Starting in 1651, the English Parliament passed various ACTS OF TRADE AND NAVIGATION that implemented duties, prohibitions, and bounties all meant to stimulate trade. Although these were often evaded through SMUGGLING and never effectively enforced, the Navigation Acts attempted to ensure that English colonies would participate in a system of economic exchange geared to enrich England by providing it with both raw materials and a market for its finished products.

Before 1700 English authors addressing empire and/or English national pride in colonial expansion focused almost exclusively on the Americas and the West Indies. The English presence in India, for example, was dismissed as merely the commercial interests of London MERCHANTS, yet the commercial relationships of this "first" British Empire were arguably primary throughout. By historian Linda Colley's estimate, one of every five families in 18th-century Britain drew its livelihood from trade and distribution, not including the farmers and manufacturers who profited from domestic and external trading networks. While overseas merchants could not succeed without naval protection, almost all of those engaged in trade benefited in some way from Britain's single-minded and violent pursuit of colonial markets. Furthermore, the great trading companies such as the East India Company, the Levant Company, and the Russia Company, along with London's mercantile community in general, supplied the government's long-term loans that underwrote Britain's imperial wars. Domestic and foreign trade furnished the majority of governmental tax revenues; until the end of the 18th century, customs and excise levies together supplied between 60 and 70 percent of governmental revenue.

International war characterized the expansion of the British Empire in the 17th and 18th centuries. Commercial rivalry with the equally mercantilist Dutch led to three wars between the Netherlands and England between 1652 and 1674. The Dutch colony of NEW NETHERLAND in the Hudson River Valley was one arena for conflict, but contention over trade with India and the lucrative slave trading in AFRICA and the CARIBBEAN were equally important. After the 1688 GLORIOUS REVOLUTION King William III (1689–1702) fanned the well-established antagonism between the English and French governments; their ministers added competition for empire to their continental and commercial rivalries. From 1689 until 1713 Britain and France were almost continuously at war. In North America these French and British conflicts were known as KING WILLIAM'S WAR (1689–97), QUEEN ANNE'S WAR (1702–13), the WAR OF JENKINS' EAR (1739), KING GEORGE'S WAR (1743–48), and, finally, the French and Indian War (1754–63), which was known in Europe as the Seven Years' War.

The TREATY OF PARIS (1763), which ended the latter war, gave Britain a vital victory over France and its allies in North America, the West Indies, Africa, and India. France withdrew from the mainland of North America, ceding its

British Colonies in America, 1607–1763
Quebec
St. Lawrence R.
Lake Huron
Lake Ontario
Lake Erie
Ohio R.
Hudson R.
Maine District (Massachusetts) 1622
New Hampshire 1623
Massachusetts 1620
Plymouth Colony (1620–1691)
New Netherland (1624–1664)
New York 1664
Rhode Island, 1636
Connecticut, 1635
New Haven Colony (1638–1643)
Pennsylvania 1682
New Sweden (1638–1655)
East Jersey (1664–1702)
New Jersey, 1664
West Jersey (1676–1702)
Maryland 1634
Delaware, 1664
Virginia 1607
ATLANTIC OCEAN
North Carolina 1653
Carolina (1663–1729)
South Carolina 1670
Georgia 1733
N
Area of former colonies
Colonial borders
Proclamation Line of 1763
Quebec boundary, 1763
1607 Date of English settlement
Plymouth Colony (1620–1691) Colonies defunct before 1730
0 150 Miles
0 150 Kms

claims to Canada and the Ohio and Mississippi Valley regions. Britain also gained control of east and west FLORIDA, Cape Breton Island, the remainder of Nova Scotia, several Caribbean islands (Grenada, St. Vincent, Dominica, and Tobago), Senegal in Africa (a slaving post), and the Mediterranean island of Minorca. Britain also realized a greatly increased military and commercial position in India. At this point the British Empire could be said to be a truly worldwide empire, with the original 13 North American colonies temporarily at its core.

Ominously for the consolidation of this worldwide enterprise, London officials had been unable to establish strong institutions of imperial control in North America comparable to those constructed by the Spanish in their Latin American empire. Although interested in exerting royal control in the North American colonies, the 17th-century British Stuart monarchs experienced great difficulty controlling the North American colonies. British attempts to bring the American colonies under the direct control of the king or to strengthen the program of mercantilist laws (restricting colonial manufactures, prohibiting paper currency, and regulating trade) were fitful in the early 18th century. The day-to-day administration of colonial affairs was decentralized and inefficient. A Board of Trade and Plantations had been established in 1696 to advise the government, but real colonial authority rested in the Privy Council (the central administrative agency for the government as a whole), the admiralty, and the treasury. None of these concentrated exclusively on colonial affairs because they also were responsible for administering laws at home; all faced a confusion of authority. Both the Crown and Parliament sent their own appointees to administer British interests in the colonies rather than to enlist influential and talented Americans. They thus offered few incentives to local men to join the imperial enterprise, thereby ignoring the successful precedents of incorporating native Scots into the administration of the empire in Scotland. If anything, the North American colonies experienced a period of "benign neglect" from the British Empire, allowing the colonies to enjoy a good deal of self-rule.

The various American colonial legislatures generally resisted attempts to exert imperial authority well before the American Revolution. By the 1750s colonial assemblies had established the right to levy taxes, make appropriations, approve appointments, and pass laws for their respective colonies. Although such laws were subject to veto by the royal governor or the Privy Council in London, governors found themselves unable to resist the assemblies' control of the colonial budget. Moreover, the Privy Council could be circumvented by repassing disallowed laws in slightly altered form. Furthermore, any theoretical distinction that the American colonists wanted to make between royal authority, on the one hand, and parliamentary authority, on the other, made absolutely no sense in London, because the British monarchs had long been unable to function without the consent of Parliament. After 1763 the British government enacted a new set of policies for the American colonies, policies that were dictated by changing international realities and a new set of political circumstances within Britain itself. These new policies were among the decisions that highlighted British Eurocentrism and contributed to American disillusionment with the imperial relationship.

In the 17th- and 18th-century struggles over colonial control in the Americas, a rapidly growing population was one of Britain's strong advantages. By 1700 approximately 250,000 settlers and slaves lived in England's mainland colonies, and the population was doubling every 25 years. New France matched that pace, but with only 14,000 people in 1700, it could not close the gap. By contrast, the population of the Spanish MISSIONS was in continual decline. Of course, native peoples greatly outnumbered settlers except in eastern New England and the Virginia tidewater.

The ENGLISH CIVIL WAR of the 1640s had given Indians an opportunity to resist European imperialism more effectively, but the Indians of the Eastern Woodlands did not unite into an effective anti-English league at least until KING PHILIP'S WAR (1675–76). By the 1670s most of the coastal natives had already been devastated by disease or soon would be. In each of the four colonial wars between Britain and France, Indians played substantial roles, whether they helped the Spanish and French colonists to survive or aided the British colonists to expand their territory. The histories of NATIVE AMERICANS, until recently structured by narratives of decline and cultural loss, are now being restructured as narratives of mutual influence and hybridity, as in the case of the CATAWBA.

English-language historiography of the British Empire long focused on European influences on the Americas; this has now expanded to trace colonial influences on England and Scotland. Raw materials from the American colonies and Asian textiles and tea transformed the material cultures of Britain. Addictive colonial foods, such as sugar, TOBACCO, tea, coffee, and chocolate, along with exotic goods like silk, rice, cotton textiles and dyestuffs, all changed the social and dietary patterns of British society. Perhaps even more important, imperial trade provided a changed context for British conceptions of commerce and empire. The fruits of empire, especially tea and sugar, became so widely available, for example, that by the 1740s English moralists could exaggerate that even haymakers and chambermaids wasted their time drinking tea. Beyond the new social relations and civil society developed in coffee shops and around the tea table, by the 1750s colonial imports into Britain were reexported, mostly to other European markets. The imperial sector was by far the most dynamic in British commerce; its trading outposts in India, crucial to the China tea trade, and its colonies in North America and the West Indies provided what seemed like limitless expansion. Imports from North America increased almost fourfold in value in the first half of the century, while West Indian imports more than doubled in the same period. Despite widespread and very profitable smuggling, the value of tea brought to London by the East India Company grew more than 40-fold in the same period. Exports to the colonies also boomed, especially compared to a relatively stagnant inter-European trade. The booty in territory and commodities that had accompanied imperial wars in the Americas, Africa, and India, climaxing in the huge gains of the Seven Years' War, seemed to confirm that British imperial power and commercial profit would continue to go hand in hand into the foreseeable future.

Further reading: Linda Colley, *Britons: Forging the Nation 1707–1837* (New Haven, Conn.: Yale University Press, 1992).

—Michelle Maskiell

Brulé, Étienne (1592?–1633)

Étienne Brulé was the first recorded *truchement,* or interpreter, between the French and the HURON Indians—France's allies and trading partners in the Great Lakes region. He was the first European to see, or at least provide descriptions of, the Ottawa Valley, the Susquehanna Valley, Georgian Bay, and four of the Great Lakes. Details about his life are sketchy because he left no written record of his own; the only traces of him are accounts by French officials and missionaries. He lived most of his life among the Huron and probably had a Huron wife and children, which French missionaries thought immoral.

Brulé probably was born near Paris and came to Quebec in 1608. Two years later he volunteered to winter with the ALGONQUIN and Huron in order to learn the Huron language and find out more about them and their land. By the next spring Brulé was dressed Huron style and knew enough of the language to interpret for SAMUEL DE CHAMPLAIN. In 1615 and 1616 Brulé spent some time with an IROQUOIS Indian group, probably Seneca. He later claimed that he had only barely and miraculously escaped death at their hands, but at his departure he agreed to explore trading possibilities for them. By 1620 he was living with the Huron at Toanché and was employed as an agent for the French trading company. He probably helped teach the Huron language to missionary Gabriel Sagard, who compiled the first dictionary of that language.

In 1626 Brulé sailed for France as interpreter for Amantacha, the son of a Huron leader. After his return to New France, he worked for the English, who briefly took control of the colony between 1629 and 1632. Brulé was murdered at Toanché in 1633. The reasons for his death are unclear, but it was likely a byproduct of the FUR TRADE wars; perhaps his dealings with the Seneca threatened Huron dominance in the fur trade. His death fractured Toanché. The Huron abandoned the village and established two new villages at Wenrio and Ihonatiria. Sagard wrote that the Huron killed and ate him; this is unlikely but has led one historian to call him "the first Frenchman, but by no means the last, to be completely assimilated by the Indians."

Further reading: Bruce G. Trigger, *The Children of Aataentsic: A History of the Huron People to 1600* (Montreal: McGill-Queens University Press, 1987).

—Alison Duncan Hirsch

Burgesses, House of (1619–1775)

For the first decade of English settlement in VIRGINIA, the colony and its parent organization, the Virginia Company, concentrated on the daily survival of the settlers and the establishment of a viable cash crop. By 1619 the military-style government that had been in place for nearly 10 years was replaced by a more representative system that included the House of Burgesses.

When Sir Edwin Sandys gained control of the foundering Virginia Company in 1618, he ordered the colony's newly appointed governor, SIR GEORGE YEARDLEY, to establish a representative governmental body in the hope that it would make Virginia more appealing to potential settlers. This new legislature would meet annually with the governor and the council to address important issues. Once in session, the full assembly could adopt laws that would then be sent to England, where the Virginia Company held veto power. Although its stated powers were limited, the House of Burgesses was the first representative government in the New World and grew to a position of primary importance in Virginia by the time of the American Revolution.

The first meeting of the assembly took place in JAMESTOWN in August 1619. There, 22 burgesses reported from their individual plantations and towns. In this first session the assembly endorsed the system of INDENTURED SERVITUDE in which impoverished Europeans would work for a number of years as servants in exchange for their transport to Virginia. Once freed, they would normally receive some land and possibly tools or money in order to begin farming.

In its early years the House of Burgesses operated under the sometimes oppressive control of the royal governor. In 1661, after the Restoration in England, new burgesses were elected, and SIR WILLIAM BERKELEY was

The first meeting of the House of Burgesses in Jamestown, Virginia, the first elected legislative assembly in America *(Library of Congress)*

reinstated as governor. This new royalist legislature pleased Berkeley, and he refused to call a general election until BACON'S REBELLION 15 years later. After Bacon's Rebellion the Crown unsuccessfully attempted to rescind the House of Burgesses' ability to initiate legislation.

By the early 18th century the House of Burgesses and the system of government in Virginia was changing. A 1699 law forbade candidates to give FOOD or drink to potential voters. Although seldom enforced, the law illustrates the fear that only wealthy men could afford to "campaign" properly and win a seat in the assembly. Most important to the rise of the House of Burgesses was the close proximity of its members to Virginia's farmers. Through their community ties burgesses often gauged issues far more effectively and could react to them quicker than could the governor or the council.

As the colony moved through the turbulent years after the beginning of the SEVEN YEARS' WAR, the House of Burgesses gained even more importance in the eyes of Virginians. With England's abandonment of the policy of "salutary neglect," the House of Burgesses appeared to be the sole institution standing between full English domination and colonial serfdom. As a result, eligible voters in Virginia paid close attention to the men they sent to Williamsburg to defend what they perceived as their rights as Englishmen in America. After playing an important role in the coming of the American Revolution in Virginia, the House of Burgesses faded out of existence. The final entry in the *Journal of the House of Burgesses* reads: "Monday, the 6th of May, 16 Geo. III. 1776. Several members met, but did neither proceed to business, nor adjourn, as a House of Burgesses. FINIS."

Further reading: Edmund S. Morgan, *American Slavery, American Freedom: The Ordeal of Colonial Virginia* (New York: Norton, 1975); Lucille Griffith, *The Virginia House of Burgesses, 1750–1774* (Tuscaloosa: University of Alabama Press, 1968).

—Brian McKnight

Burgis, William (flourished 1715–1731)

One of colonial America's first artists, Burgis's date and place of birth are unknown. He immigrated from London to NEW YORK CITY in the mid-1710s and soon began publishing illustrations by subscription. Detailed pictures of New York cityscapes, particularly the harbor, were very popular at this time, and Burgis met with great success.

In 1722 Burgis moved to BOSTON, where for the next eight years he published similar pictures, including the first cityscapes of Boston. The popularity of his work reflected the increasing secularism of Boston as the Puritan influence over the city slowly waned and popular ART became more acceptable. Typically, these illustrations were purchased by subscription. Burgis then engraved and printed them; he occasionally sent his drawings to London to be engraved there, after which they would be delivered to his customers. Burgis is known to have drawn, or at least published, pictures of HARVARD COLLEGE, Boston, and several area churches. These probably were framed, glazed, and hung on the walls of people's homes.

When his landlord died in 1728, Burgis married his wealthy widow, Mehitable Selby, thus acquiring her husband's property. Mehitable also owned property in her own right, unusual for a married woman at this time. Clearly, this improved Burgis's economic standing, for over the next two years he was described not only as an artist and property owner but also a "gentleman." By 1731 Burgis placed all of his wife's property in his name and fled town, because he was being sued in civil court. Five and a half years later, his wife petitioned for divorce on the grounds that, having taken all of her estate, he had not been seen or heard from since.

Divorce by desertion was not uncommon during this time. The law did not recognize a wife's property as separate from her husband's, and so Burgis's actions were legal. It is unclear whether her divorce petition was granted, though possibly she had him declared legally dead so that she could escape the debts he had left behind.

—Victoria C. H. Resnick

Burr, Esther Edwards (1732–1758)

Daughter of the great theologian and Congregational minister JONATHAN EDWARDS, wife of the president of the College of New Jersey (later PRINCETON COLLEGE), and mother of a daughter, Sally, and son, Aaron, Jr. (who subsequently became the third vice president of the United States), Esther Edwards Burr's experience is extraordinary not only because of the men who surrounded her but also because of the journal she exchanged with confidante Sally Prince of BOSTON between 1754 and 1757. Burr and Prince, like many Puritan women, developed a close friendship in youth that they maintained in adulthood.

Puritan women frequently kept journals to assist in their efforts toward self-understanding and improvement, but Burr's practice of exchanging journals with Prince was unusual. In her writing Burr expressed the challenges of marriage, homemaking, and motherhood. Burr wrote, for example, of the burden of having many children, already feeling overwhelmed with just two. Her death at an early age cut the journal short, but her observations create a rare and rich firsthand account of the daily life and values of an elite woman in colonial America.

Further reading: Carol F. Karlsen and Laurie Crumpacker, eds., *The Journal of Esther Edwards Burr, 1754–1757* (New Haven, Conn.: Yale University Press, 1984).

—Jane P. Currie

Butterworth, Mary Peck (1686–1775)

A suspected counterfeiter, Mary Peck Butterworth was born on July 27, 1686, at Rehoboth, PLYMOUTH Colony (MASSACHUSETTS), the daughter of Joseph and Elizabeth (Smith) Peck. She married John Butterworth, Jr., about 1710. Soon after RHODE ISLAND distributed notes of credit valued at five pounds, Butterworth, collaborating with relatives and residents of Rehoboth, initiated a counterfeiting scheme. During the colonial era counterfeiting was a common practice when greedy individuals took advantage of both the unsophisticated printing processes used to produce money and MERCHANTS' unfamiliarity with the diverse domestic and foreign monies circulated throughout America. Colonial counterfeiters represented a myriad of socioeconomic classes and ethnicities. Both men and women were notorious counterfeiters.

Butterworth devised a method to manufacture fake currency without leaving evidence of her crime. She placed a piece of currency underneath a piece of starched muslin and rubbed a heated iron over the surface. The currency's pattern was imprinted on the cloth, which she used to transfer the image to pieces of paper with an iron. Butterworth improved each note by inking them with quill pens. Afterwards, she burned the cloth, thereby destroying the evidence. Most counterfeiters used copper plates to achieve an image transfer, but such templates were difficult to demolish and provided evidence for prosecutors to cite in court.

By 1722 Butterworth's prosperity attracted attention. Her husband built an elaborate house, and relatives and townspeople were caught trying to pass fraudulent bills. Officials began investigating the Butterworths' activities and arrested several of her conspirators. Butterworth's brother and sister-in-law, who has participated in the counterfeiting scheme, told authorities how Butterworth created her fake currency. She was subsequently exonerated when the charges against her were dismissed because of lack of proof, and none of her associates was convicted. Ceasing her counterfeiting career, Butterworth lived with her husband and seven children in their extravagant home. Butterworth died on February 7, 1775, at Rehoboth.

Further reading: Richard LeBaron Bowen, *Rhode Island Colonial Money and Its Counterfeiting, 1647–1726* (Concord, N.H.: Rumford Press, 1942).

—Elizabeth D. Schafer

Byrd, William, II (1674–1744)

An important colonial literary figure, William Byrd II was born near Richmond, VIRGINIA, the son and sole heir of William Byrd and Mary Horsmanden Filmer. At the age of seven he was sent to be educated in England and the Netherlands, becoming a licensed attorney in 1695. Unsuccessful as an attorney, Byrd was elected a burgess for Henrico County in 1696 and represented the Virginia colony in London in 1698. As Virginia's representative, Byrd protested the use of the colony's taxes to fund military operations in northern colonies. He was removed from this position when he alienated the Board of Trade by presenting an address from the king to the Virginia Council and HOUSE OF BURGESSES, a function of the governor. After his removal Byrd spent most of his time in England and was active in England's scientific community. He was made a member of the Royal Society in 1697. When his father died in 1705, he claimed his inheritance and his father's posts of receiver general and auditor of the colony, from which he received between 3 and 5 percent of Virginia's tax receipts as a salary. In 1709 he took his father's seat on the Virginia Council.

In addition to his political activities, Byrd was a prolific writer, publishing several books about Virginia, poetry, as well as theatricals. Byrd was also one of Virginia's largest land speculators, acquiring over 100,000 acres along the Roanoke River. Selling little of the land, he amassed 179,400 acres by his death. Byrd engaged in many economic endeavors, including trade with American Indians, surveying boundaries between Virginia and the Carolinas, and prospecting for raw materials like coal, iron, and copper. Byrd experimented with mixed AGRICULTURE on his plantations; nevertheless, TOBACCO remained his primary cash crop produced by slaves. Despite his outspokenness against the institution of SLAVERY, Byrd participated in the trafficking of slaves and supervised the day-to-day administration of his black laborers to ensure successful yields. He died at his mansion in Charles City County in 1744.

Further reading: Kenneth A. Lockridge, *The Diary, and Life, of William Byrd II of Virginia, 1674–1744* (Chapel Hill: University of North Carolina Press, 1987).

—Eugene VanSickle

Byrd family

The history of the Byrd family epitomizes the experience of the "distressed cavaliers" who settled VIRGINIA. By the 17th century this family of London goldsmiths had married its way into England's aristocracy. In 1670 William Byrd I (1652–1704) moved to Virginia at the invitation of his dying uncle and inherited 1,800 acres, but the estate hardly satisfied him. When Governor WILLIAM BERKELEY sought to raise western settlements to insulate Virginia from Indian attacks, Byrd saw an opportunity. He agreed to settle 250 tithables, and Virginia's Royal Council rewarded him with more lands. Byrd also married Mary Horsmanden Filmer, a wealthy widow connected to an ancient family from Kent.

WILLIAM BYRD II (1674–1744) left Virginia for England at the age of seven. There, he trained as a lawyer and imbibed the glittering social milieu of London. Returning to Virginia upon his father's death, William found himself with both 25,000 acres and boundless marriage prospects. He selected Lucy Parke, daughter of a rakish English gentlemen. The course of this stormy marriage—immortalized in the diary Byrd kept from 1709 to 1712—reveals plantation life in gritty detail. Lucy frequently abused their many slaves and berated her often unfaithful husband, yet the couple also indulged in passionate fits of lovemaking. Like his father, William sought higher offices and more lands. In 1727 he explored Virginia's BORDERLANDS on behalf of the Royal Council. After agreeing to settle families in the lands he surveyed, William received 105,000 acres. At his death Byrd owned some 179,000 acres and a plantation known as Westover.

The Byrd family's patriarchs did much to settle the Old Dominion, while its matriarchs helped to raise an interconnected set of ruling families, but their achievements came at the expense of indentured and enslaved labor. By the time William Byrd III (1728–77) came of age, Virginia's gentry had become an insular, powerful aristocracy with the means and will to defy the mother country. In 1775 every member of the Royal Council was descended from a 1660 councilor, and many traced their lines to William Byrd I and Mary Horsmanden Filmer Byrd.

Further reading: Kenneth A. Lockridge, *The Diary, and Life, of William Byrd II of Virginia, 1674–1744* (Chapel Hill: University of North Carolina Press, 1987); David Hackett Fischer and James C. Kelly, *Bound Away: Virginia and the Westward Movement* (Charlottesville: University of Virginia Press, 2000).

—J. M. Opal

California Indians

After migrating from Asia across the Bering Strait land bridge and traveling south through Alaska and western Canada, indigenous peoples began the human occupation of the lands now known as California, a habitation that dates back approximately 12,000 years. In about 9,000 B.C.E. California Indians began to change their ECONOMY from primarily hunting to mostly collecting seeds. By 2000 B.C.E. indigenous peoples had developed varied subsistence patterns that included hunting, FISHING, and gathering, with acorn as the main staple. Although none engaged in horticulture, this diversification brought impressive population growth, estimated at a maximum precontact number of 320,000 living in more than 500 villages and speaking more than 100 languages and 300 different dialects. A more complex sociopolitical village network also emerged, known as a tribelet. Under this system tribes were divided into small, family-based villages and governed by a single chief. While villages were generally communitarian in nature, especially regarding FOOD gathering responsibilities, individual wealth and property were recognized. Men owned hunting and fishing equipment, for example, while women owned baskets and acorn grinding implements. Many tribes also valued shells, which may have represented a form of currency or a highly sought-after trade item. Intertribal trade was common, while organized warfare was rare.

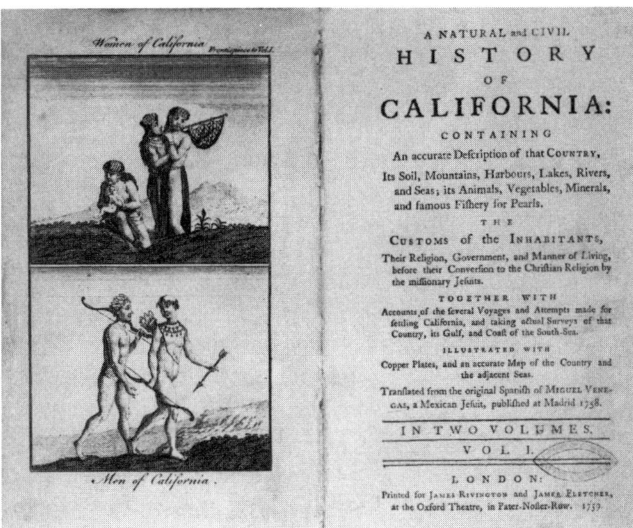

A NATURAL and CIVIL
HISTORY
OF
CALIFORNIA:
CONTAINING
An accurate Defcription of that COUNTRY,
Its Soil, Mountains, Harbours, Lakes, Rivers, and Seas; its Animals, Vegetables, Minerals, and famous Fifhery for Pearls.
THE
CUSTOMS of the INHABITANTS,
Their Religion, Government, and Manner of Living, before their Converfion to the Chriftian Religion by the miffionary Jefuits.
TOGETHER WITH
Accounts of the feveral Voyages and Attempts made for fettling California, and taking actual Surveys of that Country, its Gulf, and Coaft of the South-Sea.
ILLUSTRATED WITH
Copper Plates, and an accurate Map of the Country and the adjacent Seas.
Tranflated from the original Spanifh of MIGUEL VENEGAS, a Mexican Jefuit, publifhed at Madrid 1758.
IN TWO VOLUMES.
VOL. I.
LONDON:
Printed for JAMES RIVINGTON and JAMES FLETCHER, at the Oxford Theatre, in Pater-Nofter-Row. 1759.

The title page of "A Natural and Civil History of California," an English translation of an account by Miguel Venegas, a Mexican Jesuit. The book describes the land, resources, and people of the region. The illustrations depict the native inhabitants, women (top) and men (bottom). *(Hulton/Archive)*

Until the Spanish expedition led by Gaspar de Portolá in 1769, contact between California Indians and Europeans had been fleeting. The establishment of a string of MISSIONS along the California coast ended indigenous isolation, as coastal Indians were forced into missions and compelled to convert to Catholicism. Traditional life patterns were lost, and the population of the coastal tribes dropped by 35 percent within the first 40 years of Spanish occupation. Resistance by California Indians to Spanish rule included individual flight to the interior, the murder of missionaries, local rebellions at single missions, and even infanticide to preserve children from life in a mission. With mission secularization by the Mexican government in 1834 and the Anglo invasion beginning with the discovery of gold in 1849, California Indians were forced off mission and traditional lands and forced to participate in a capitalistic economy for which they were unprepared. The Indian MORTALITY rate remained astronomical, and only 15,000 survivors remained at the close of the 19th century.

Further reading: Alfred Kroeber, *Handbook of the Indians of California* (New York: Dover, 1976); Robert F. Heizer, *The Destruction of California Indians* (Lincoln: University of Nebraska Press, 1974).

—James Jenks

calumet

The calumet is the term given by the French to the pipe used by the native peoples of North America for ritual smoking. The pipe consists of a bowl, often elaborately carved, and a stem, typically decorated with feathers, beadwork, or quill work. Such pipes were regarded as sacred objects and used to communicate with supernatural powers. They were considered to be "transmitters;" the smoke carried prayers to the creative forces. Mistakenly called "peace pipes," calumets were used during many solemn occasions when circumstances demanded the presence of the supernatural, including the conclusion of peace agreements, the declaration of war, adoption, and as tribal ritual or daily prayer. The calumet is a source of great power and one cannot be deceitful or insincere while holding a medicine pipe. According to Cheyenne lore, George Custer knocked TOBACCO from a bowl while smoking with the Cheyenne chiefs, a major breech of respect and an act the Cheyenne believe cost him his life.

The pipes are most closely identified with the Plains Indians (particularly the Siouan and ALGONQUIN peoples), although also commonly used by tribes in the Southeast and Northeast of the present-day United States. On the Plains pipe bowls carved from catlinite, or pipestone, and soapstone are distinctive of tribes such as the Lakota and Blackfeet.

—Walter Fleming

Calvert, George (Lord Baltimore) (1580?–1632)

George Calvert was the founder of a colony he never lived to see. He was born in 1580 in Yorkshire, England, to the Catholic family of LEONARD CALVERT and Alicia Crossland. Having finished his studies at All Saints' College, Oxford, he was appointed Keeper of Writs, Bills, Records, and Rolls during the reign of James I in 1606. As secretary to Sir Robert Cecil, Calvert advanced in the service of the king and was eventually made clerk of the Privy Council as well as Keeper of the King's Signet (1619–25).

In 1619 Sir George Calvert succeeded Sir Thomas Lake as one of the king's secretaries of state and continued advancing in positions and securing the confidence of his sovereign by his fidelity and accurate knowledge of business. On February 20, 1624, King James (1603–25), who described Calvert as "right trusty and well-loved," bestowed on him the title "Lord Baron of Baltimore" in the kingdom of Ireland.

While secretary of state, Calvert obtained a charter from King James granting him the province of Avalon in Newfoundland in 1620. After an unsuccessful attempt at colonization there in 1623, Calvert petitioned the king and received a land grant in the northern Chesapeake region (present-day MARYLAND). Although he dreamed of a colony in the New World as a haven for persecuted ROMAN CATHOLICS, he opened his colony to all religious creeds. He drew up a charter for the colony and named it Terra Mariae, or Mary's Land, for Queen Henrietta Maria. The charter contained his vision of political and religious freedom, which permitted both Roman Catholics and Protestants to settle Maryland—the first colony to grant religious freedom. Calvert died before the charter was granted, and the task of colonization fell to his oldest son, Cecilius. After months of delay, on November 22, 1633, Cecil Calvert sent what he called "a hopeful colony into Maryland with a fair and probable expectation of good success."

Further reading: Luca Codignola, *The Coldest Harbor of the Land: Simon Stock and Lord Baltimore's Colony in Newfoundland, 1621–1649* (Kingston, Ont.: McGill-Queen's University Press, 1988).

—James F. Adomanis

Calvert, Leonard (Lord Baltimore) (1606–1647)

Leonard Calvert, the third lord Baltimore, was born in England in 1606 to GEORGE CALVERT (the first lord Baltimore) and Anne Mynne. His brother Cecilius (the second lord Baltimore), selected Leonard Calvert to lead 300 mostly Catholic settlers to establish the colony of MARYLAND in 1633. Leonard followed his brother's instructions "to preserve unity and peace among all the passengers." After a perilous four-month voyage on two small ships, the *Ark* and *Dove,* the colonists arrived at JAMESTOWN. Calvert notified William Claiborne, who had settled Kent Island in the CHESAPEAKE BAY in 1631, that Claiborne was now a member of the Maryland plantation and must relinquish his relations with the VIRGINIA colony. Claiborne protested this demand to the Virginia Council, and when they rejected it, Lord Calvert momentarily ended his challenge.

Leaving Virginia, the Maryland colonists sailed up the Chesapeake Bay to the Potomac River and landed at St. Clement's (now Blackiston's) Island on March 25, 1634. New challenges awaited Leonard Calvert, however. He bargained successfully for land, HOUSING, and trade with the Piscataway Indians, who gave up part of their village for immediate use by the colonists and agreed to evacuate the town completely after the harvest. A fort and town were built, named ST. MARY'S CITY. Conditions were primitive, and settlers were threatened with harsh winters, illness, and Protestant enemies.

In April 1635 a conflict ensued between the Maryland colonists of St. Mary's and the Kent Island settlers led by William Claiborne; he was a formidable foe over the next decade, and he tried to drive Calvert from office in 1645. Calvert was formally commissioned governor in 1637, and he exercised considerable power. A Protestant rebellion in 1644 forced him to flee to Virginia, after which William Claiborne assumed control. Returning with an army from both colonies in 1646, Calvert routed Claiborne and restored his office. Calvert died a few months later on June 9, 1647.

See also NATIVE AMERICANS.

Further reading: Gloria L. Main, *Tobacco Colony: Life in Early Maryland, 1650–1720* (Princeton, N.J.: Princeton University Press, 1982).

—James F. Adomanis

Canada See French colonies

Canonicus (unknown–1647)

Canonicus was the sachem (or chief) of the NARRAGANSETT Indians at the time of the English invasion of America. Canonicus's exact origins are unknown, but he was rumored to be a direct descendent of Tashtasick, legendary founder of the Narragansett tribe. Canonicus is perhaps best known for having sold ROGER WILLIAMS, with whom he maintained a lifelong friendship, the land on which Williams founded the city of Providence, RHODE ISLAND. Canonicus regarded the English with deep suspicion, rightly seeing them as a threat to the Narragansett traditional dominance of neighboring tribes. Despite his suspicions, Canonicus allied the Narragansett with the English against their traditional enemies, the PEQUOT, in the PEQUOT WAR of 1636.

After helping defeat the Pequot, the English turned against Canonicus and sided with the Mohegan in a series of brutal military campaigns. This betrayal, together with the formation of the New England Confederation in 1643, marked the beginning of the end for the Narragansett, who, in an attempt to avoid annihilation, declared their allegiance to the English Crown. Nevertheless, a power struggle following Canonicus's death in 1647 served to further weaken the Narragansett and they were eventually decimated during KING PHILIP'S WAR of 1675–76.

Further reading: L. Raymond Camp, *Roger Williams, God's Apostle of Advocacy* (Lewiston, N.Y.: E. Melon Press, 1989).

—Kenneth A. Deitreich

captivity

The first cross-cultural captives in early North America were actually Indians taken by Europeans during the first decades of EXPLORATION and colonization. We know that Columbus captured Arawaks for export to Spain as slaves and exotic symbols of the New World, but even the English in VIRGINIA and New England took Indians hostage during the 17th century to train them as interpreters. Few went willingly. One of the most famous of these Indian captives, SQUANTO, was a Patuxet seized on the New England coast by seafarers in 1614 and sold into SLAVERY in Spain. He escaped and returned to his home, only to find his people ravaged by DISEASE and a group of English Separatists (PILGRIMS) living at PLYMOUTH. The same year settlers in JAMESTOWN, Virginia, kidnapped POCAHONTAS, the daughter of the ALGONQUIN werowance POWHATAN. Acting as diplomat for her father and a bridge between cultures, Pocahontas agreed to marry JOHN ROLFE and returned with him to England, where she died in 1616.

Nevertheless, popular notions about captivity usually come from the harrowing narratives of white colonists taken by Indian warriors during times of crisis. Indeed, Jamestown more often evokes memories of Captain JOHN SMITH's tale of his own capture and trial before Powhatan, than Pocahontas's captivity. MARY WHITE ROWLANDSON dictated one of the first published accounts of captivity after spending nearly 12 weeks with Narragansett and Wampanoag Indians in 1675 and 1676. Taken from her frontier home in Lancaster, MASSACHUSETTS, at the onset of KING PHILIP'S WAR, Mary described her experience as a test of her faith in God. Demoted from mistress of her own household to the servant of an Indian "Master," Mary struggled with privation and hunger as she tried to make sense of her captors' motives. Although she condemned their actions, Mary's narrative also revealed a familiarity that existed between NATIVE AMERICANS and English colonists even outside of captivity.

For Native Americans, captivity had a variety of purposes. Traditionally, native groups adopted Indian captives to strengthen political ties and replenish populations decimated by war and disease. Sometimes individuals were taken to replace specific members of a clan. The IROQUOIS, for instance, took captives during mourning-war campaigns against customary enemies and revenged the death of a family member by either killing or adopting a captive. Women and children were most often adopted. By the mid-18th century non-Iroquois people made up as much as two-thirds of the Iroquois population.

Contrary to prevalent fears among colonists, Indians tortured or killed white captives only under specific circumstances. They sometimes killed white people during their initial attack or as an example to force obedience from other captives. More often, Indians kept prisoners alive to exchange for ransom or to adopt them into their households. Once in a native community, captives were adopted through a series of sometimes dangerous rituals. They might be required to run a gauntlet of villagers wielding sticks and other weapons. Native Americans also symbolically washed and reclothed adopted captives to mark their rebirth as Indians. Although captives sometimes became servants, as did Mary Rowlandson, many white people found themselves equal members of native families. Some adapted well to Indian life and, especially if taken as children, even rejected Euro-American society. To her family's horror, Eunice Williams, the daughter of minister John Williams, repeatedly refused to return to Puritan society after her capture from Deerfield, Massachusetts, in 1704 by Catholic Mohawk. Like Eunice, MARY JEMISON, captured at age 15 by Shawnee in western PENNSYLVANIA, stayed with her native family, eventually marrying a DELAWARE and then a Seneca man. During the SEVEN YEARS' WAR Delaware and Shawnee took many white people captive from frontier plantations in Pennsylvania. When peace came after 1763, Col. Henry Bouquet oversaw the return of more than 200 captives. He found that many of those who had been adopted into Indian families as children could no longer speak the language of their birth and proved difficult to repatriate. Some ran away to rejoin Native American kin but were recaptured by Bouquet's men and forcibly returned to the English. Euro-Americans equated kinship or cultural identity with biology and one's national origins. Native Americans, on the other hand, had more flexible definitions of kin that allowed them to absorb others into their communities more easily, whether by capture or choice.

Further reading: John Demos, *The Unredeemed Captive: A Family Story from Early America* (New York: Knopf, 1994); June Namias, *White Captives: Gender and Ethnicity on the American Frontier* (Chapel Hill: University of North Carolina Press, 1993).

—Jane T. Merritt

Caribbean

A brief overview of the European practices instituted by nations economically dependent on the raw materials and LABOR extracted from the Americas allows some understanding of the multiple and interlocking histories of Caribbean colonization and settlement. This trade escalated as the CONSUMPTION of precious metals, sugar, and other substances increased in continental Europe. In the 1580s European explorers found a series of islands in a small sea, bounded on the west by the Gulf of Mexico and by the Atlantic Ocean on the east. Between 1585 and 1763 the overlay of different cultures combined with the application of new European technologies to alter the ENVIRONMENT (with the introduction of new plants, seeds, and ANIMALS) to shape colonial culture and the function of various Caribbean islands into colonies, FORTS, markets, and ports.

Indigenous Peoples of the Caribbean

The islands were originally the homelands of indigenous peoples who most likely migrated north from South America. The Arawak and Taino inhabited many of the 700 small islands of the Bahamanian Archipelago and the larger islands of the Greater Antilles, Cuba, Jamaica, Hispaniola, Puerto Rico, and Trinidad. Among their immediate neighbors were the Guanahatabey at the west end of Cuba and the Island-Carib, who occupied the Windward Islands, Guadeloupe, and Martinique. At the time of initial European contact, large permanent villages on the Greater Antilles typically contained 1,000 to 2,000 people governed by a chief, or cacique, a position held by either men or women. Over time their organized systems of religion, government, and AGRICULTURE blended with African and European cultural traditions. At times NATIVE AMERICANS were also brought from the North American mainland and sold into slave labor on the islands. The exploitation of indigenous peoples as slaves and, despite their resistance, the combination of overwork, war, and disease decimated the population, which dwindled from precontact estimates of more than 3 million into the tens of thousands. As the population of Native Americans diminished, the trade in indentured European servants and enslaved Africans increased as colonizers sought laborers.

For the Spanish, followed by the English, French, Dutch, and Danes, Caribbean ports provided a central hub of communication for enterprises that established trade and settlement. Spain maintained its commercial monopoly in precious metals, TOBACCO, slaves, and sugar (1530–1570) by legally closing its empire to foreign trade. In so doing, Spanish commerce in the Antilles stagnated for the next half century. Beginning in 1625, European mercantile companies began investing in a "triangular trade" that carried manufactured goods to the West African coast that were then exchanged for slaves to bring to the Caribbean. In the West Indies ship captains received cargoes of refined sugar, coffee, and INDIGO to sell in Europe. By 1700 Spain had lost considerable power in the Caribbean, and their trade declined as they were challenged by the expansion of Dutch, English, and French involvement in continental shipping. Spain retained parts of Cuba, Puerto Rico, and eastern Hispaniola as haciendas (rancher societies) that raised cattle for hides. Each European monarchy claimed areas of the Caribbean for conquest and settlement. Despite the hiatus in warfare instituted by treaties signed by colonizing powers, the imperial regimes sought control over the white, black, and mixed-race populations that increased with emigrating settlers and the enslaved.

The Rise of Sugar

In the mid-1600s small-scale cultivation of tobacco that used indentured European servants as its labor force changed. The possibility of earning enormous profits transformed agricultural production with the development of large sugar plantations, which relied on African slave labor for cultivation and manufacture. The colonial ARCHITECTURE of forts, fields, plantation "big house," slave quarters, ports, and cities was designed with segregated spaces intended for masters, slaves, and a few free blacks. Responding to European demand for sugar, rum, and molasses, the sugar industry flourished in British Jamaica and French Saint-Domingue. Between 1741 and 1745 Saint Domingue and Jamaica exported more than 42,000 and 15,600 tons of sugar, respectively. Cuba, tightly controlled by Spain, also began to develop sugar estates. The tropical PLANTATION SYSTEM extended across the Caribbean, and the rising ECONOMY of the sugar trade connected the islands. Both the Danish Virgin Islands and the Dutch Leeward Islands operated as "free ports" for the sale of slaves to supply plantation labor.

As the demand for labor intensified, millions of slaves endured the horrors of the Middle Passage as they were shipped from AFRICA to the Caribbean. By the 1750s nearly 90 percent of the population of the sugar islands were slaves. During the 350 years of slavery in the Americas, more than 10 million Africans became bound laborers on French, British, Danish, Dutch, and American tobacco, sugar, coffee, and indigo plantations. In the Caribbean the very small population of white planters freely used violence to control the large number of black slaves. European nations shared in the success of international investors of the trading companies as profits from the SLAVE TRADE and the sugar islands helped finance European economic development.

Society and Daily Life

Planter society was highly stratified, and its castes were determined by segregated racial hierarchies. Each island legally defined a myriad of racial differences and the terms of slave ownership, such as the French *Code Noir,* issued in 1685 and continuously amended until the late 1700s. Other colonial governments passed similar codes to restrict social privileges for people of color.

Before the arrival of European women, Spanish soldiers frequently took native or African women as sexual partners, whether they were willing or not. In the 17th and 18th centuries MERCHANTS and planters frequently engaged in the practice of concubinage, claiming multiple black women for their partners. Many enslaved women working as domestics, nurses, cooks, and field hands were exploited sexually, yet some relationships were consensual, providing a degree of legal recognition to the children thereby produced and creating a small population of free black people uncommon in mainland North America. As the percentage of people of mixed ancestry increased, colonial governments even more clearly specified privileges for those classified as white, black, or colored by identifying European, Indian, or African descent by degrees.

The system of racial bondage was perhaps physically more brutal in the Caribbean than in any other area of the Americas. At times the average life expectancy of a recently arrived African slave was a mere seven years. Masters found it profitable to work slaves to death, then replace them with newly purchased bondpeople from Africa. Because of the continual importation of Africans, slave culture maintained stronger African roots in the Caribbean than in most areas of mainland North America. Finally, Caribbean slaves suffered from a severe demographic imbalance as men outnumbered women (except in Barbados), making lasting relationships difficult to establish. These conditions created a population that failed to reproduce itself and enslaved communities that struggled to retain their West African cultural heritage.

Further reading: Richard Dunn, *Sugar and Slaves: The Rise of the Planter Class in the English West Indies, 1624–1713* (Chapel Hill: University of North Carolina Press, 1973, 2000); Barbara Bush, *Slave Women in Caribbean Society, 1650–1838* (Bloomington: Indiana University Press, 1990).

—Ellen Fernandez-Sacco

Carter, Landon (1710–1778)

Plantation owner, diarist, politician, scientist, and revolutionary, Colonel Landon Carter was in many ways the quintessential gentleman of colonial VIRGINIA. The second son and heir to the estates of powerful plantation owner ROBERT "KING" CARTER, Landon Carter was a man of great ability and accomplishment but of even greater expectations. Carter proved an energetic amateur scientist, using his plantation, Sabine Hall, in Richmond County as a laboratory for experimentation. He published many of his findings on animal husbandry, pest control, and management techniques. Additionally, he worked as an amateur physician, practicing on his family, friends, and slaves. Carter also kept a diary from 1752 until 1755 that is a rich historical source about genteel life in early Virginia.

Despite his powerful family background, it took him four tries to gain election to the HOUSE OF BURGESSES in 1752, in part because of his firm belief in his own superiority. He demanded deference from "lesser" men and objected to the way his son, Robert Wormley Carter, courted political office, saying he had "kissed the arse of the people." Once in office, Landon Carter became a leading figure in the legislature, acting as spokesperson in the "Pistole Fee Dispute" between Lieutenant Governor Robert Dinwiddle and the burgesses in 1753.

Carter remained in the House until 1768, and, between his political and scientific writings, he became, according to one historian, "the most published author of his generation in Virginia." Nevertheless, his dour personality and dark view of human nature won him far less acclaim and success than he felt was due the son of a "King."

Carter spent his later years in attempts to build his legacy, primarily by promoting his assertion that he, not Patrick Henry, as had been widely reported, had been the first Virginian to speak out for American independence. He died at Sabine Hall in 1778.

Further reading: Jack P. Greene, ed., *The Diary of Colonel Landon Carter of Sabine Hall* (Richmond: University of Virginia Press, 1965).

—Matthew Taylor Raffety

Carter, Robert "King" (1663–1732)

Robert "King" Carter became by all accounts the richest man in colonial America. As such, he set the style and tone of the emerging planter CLASS in Colonial VIRGINIA. His domineering style and assurance of his position as a gentleman earned him the appellation "King" from both enemies and admirers. From his great hall at Carter's Grove in Lancaster County, Carter ruled a far-flung empire of TOBACCO plantations throughout Virginia. Carter became the ideal for the aspiring Virginia elite, from the opulence of his great hall to his personal arrogance to his conspicuous gambling and CONSUMPTION.

Carter's father, John Carter, immigrated to Virginia in 1649 and rapidly ascended to become one of the leading landholders and tobacco planters of the young colony. Robert Carter, John's second son, was born to John and his fourth wife, Sarah Ludlow, in 1663. Robert spent several of his early years studying in England, but on the death of his elder brother, John Carter, Jr., he returned to manage his father's holdings.

Robert Carter served as a vestryman at Christ's Church and as a justice of the peace before being elected to represent Lancaster County in the HOUSE OF BURGESSES in 1691, where he served as Speaker of the House in 1696 and again in 1699 and sat on the powerful Committee of Propositions and Grievances. His position as agent to Lord Fairfax, proprietor of substantial holdings along the Rappahannock River, enabled Carter to expand his own vast holdings, adding nearly 90,000 acres to his family's already substantial lands. He was quick to discover the toll that tobacco production took on the soil, and he continually sought fresh lands to purchase, or, in the case of the North Neck, lease from Lord Fairfax. By the mid-1720s Carter had begun dividing his holdings among his heirs, most notably his son LANDON CARTER, for more efficient operation. By the end of his life Carter had amassed more than 300,000 acres, 1,000 slaves, 2,000 head of cattle, and 100 horses. Carter died in 1732, having secured the Carter family's position of prominence in the Old Dominion for generations to come.

—Matthew Taylor Raffety

Carteret, Philip (1639–1682)

Philip Carteret became deputy governor of the colony of NEW JERSEY in 1665 at the age of 26. Born on the island of Jersey, Carteret was a cousin of Sir George Carteret, who had received the proprietorship of the colony from the duke of York after the English seized it from the Dutch in 1664. Accompanied by 30 colonists from Jersey, Philip Carteret arrived in a colony with a diverse population of Dutch, Swedes, PURITANS from CONNECTICUT and Long Island, a small number of Africans (slave and free), and a few remaining Lenape Indians. Carteret established the new government under a version of Concessions and Agreements largely copied from those of SOUTH CAROLINA.

Carteret faced problems immediately. The New Englanders defied him when he tried to collect taxes and quitrents, and by 1672 their resistance had become a colonywide revolt. Once that was successfully quelled, the Dutch reasserted their authority when they briefly retook NEW YORK from the English in 1673–74. By the time Carteret took charge again, half of the proprietorship had been sold to a group of QUAKERS. The colony was split in two, with Sir George Carteret retaining the proprietorship of East New Jersey. Philip Carteret served as governor of that colony until 1680, when his cousin died and SIR EDMUND ANDROS asserted jurisdiction over New Jersey. After Andros's recall to England, Carteret served as governor for another year until Sir George's widow sold the proprietorship to a group of 24 proprietors and the new governor, Thomas Rudyard, arrived.

Further reading: John E. Pomfret, *The Province of East New Jersey: The Rebellious Proprietary* (Princeton, N.J.: Princeton University Press, 1962).

—Alison Duncan Hirsch

Castillo, Diego del (flourished 1650)

Along with Captain Hernán Martin, Diego del Castillo led an expedition from Santa Fe in 1650 charged by General Hernando de la Concha, governor of NEW MEXICO, with exploring north and central Texas. Their 600-mile expedition included a six-month period with the Jumano on the Nueces River, a group that, as well as playing a role in colonial trade, had long inspired a great deal of fascination and cultural analysis among the Spanish colonists. Del Castillo's expedition returned with report of pearl-yielding mussels on the Nueces that led, four years later, to the profit-motivated, although unsuccessful, expedition of Diego de Guadalajara.

—Jonathan Wright

Catawba

In 1585 the Catawba Indians were one of many tribes who inhabited the Piedmont region of the American Southeast in the present-day states of NORTH CAROLINA, SOUTH CAROLINA, and VIRGINIA. Related groups, such as the Saponi, Sugaree, Shuteree, Pedee, Waxhaw, and Wateree, occupied the region between the coastal plain and the Appalachian Mountains. Like many other NATIVE AMERICANS, these groups suffered tremendous losses from European diseases in the late 17th and 18th centuries. As once independent tribes and villages lost massive portions of their populations, they became more susceptible to attacks by enemies. Economic life became difficult, as both male and female providers succumbed to disease. Men were unable to hunt; women were unable to farm.

In addition to decimation by disease, the Catawba also suffered from a growing dependence on English trade goods like guns, metal cooking implements, and metal tips for arrows. Such objects not only made daily life easier but made them more effective in warfare against their enemies, primarily the IROQUOIS Indians to the north and the neighboring TUSCARORA. To acquire these metal objects, the Catawba and other southern Indians engaged in the deerskin trade. The new dynamics of trade altered traditional subsistence patterns for the Catawba, who now ranged farther from home villages for longer periods than in the era before contact with Europeans. Furthermore, their new economic position in the trade made them more vulnerable to changes in the British market. These new realities affected many of the tribes in the South, causing great movement and consolidation among them. Because the Catawba had secured a position as "middlemen" in the deerskin trade and gained a reputation among the English settlers as adept and fierce warriors, they remained somewhat protected from the fiercest of frontier violence with the colonists. Many of their neighbors were not so lucky. Decimated by DISEASE and warfare and threatened economically, remnants of smaller tribes sought refuge among the Catawba, who adopted them into the tribe to replenish their own losses.

By the 1750s Catawba villages contained a generation of refugees from surrounding tribes who all went under the name Catawba, according to British sources. The mid-18th century was a time of hardship as well for the Catawbas, who suffered great losses again from SMALLPOX epidemics in the 1740s and 1750s. Coupled with a declining deerskin trade, these events undermined the Catawba strength in the Southeast. In the 1760s (and to the present) the Catawba continued to exist as a nation, albeit one that had been replenished by many nearby tribes.

Further reading: James Merrell, *The Indians' New World: The Catawbas and their Neighbors from European Contact through the Era of Removal* (New York: Norton, 1989).

—Thomas J. Lappas

Catesby, Mark (1682–1749)

Mark Catesby was a naturalist, illustrator, the author of the first major illustrated work on the natural history of the British colonies in the Americas, and one of the first artists to illustrate birds and ANIMALS in their natural surroundings. He was born in Essex, England. Catesby developed an interest in botany as a child and in his young adulthood developed relationships with other collectors and botanists. Catesby accompanied his sister to Williamsburg, VIRGINIA, in 1712; there he became acquainted with a number of prominent residents interested in horticulture, including Governor William Byrd III. Between 1712 and 1714 Catesby traveled to the Appalachians, the Bahamas, and Jamaica, collecting plant specimens and observing birds and animals. He became interested in the interrelationships between animals and their ENVIRONMENT. Catesby went back to England in 1719 but returned to the New World in 1722, backed by a group of British plant collectors and enthusiasts including Samuel Dale and William Sherard, physician Sir Hans Sloane, and Francis Nicholson, the new governor of SOUTH CAROLINA. Catesby traveled in South Carolina and GEORGIA between 1723 and 1725, returning to the Bahamas in 1725. Already known as a watercolor painter of merit, Catesby learned to etch his own plates for the engravings for his subscription-supported *Natural History of Carolina, Florida, and the Bahama Islands*, published between 1731 and 1743, with an appendix in 1747. He was elected a member of the Royal Society in 1733. A notable figure in the international scientific community, Catesby corresponded with a wide circle of European and colonial artists and collectors. His *Natural History* remained an important reference book well into the 18th century.

Further reading: Amy R. W. Meyers and Margaret Beck Pritchard, eds., *Empire's Nature: Mark Catesby's New*

World Vision (Chapel Hill and London: University of North Carolina Press, 1998).

—Monique Bourque

Champlain, Samuel de (1567–1635)

Perhaps more than any other individual, Samuel de Champlain was responsible for the establishment of permanent French settlement in New France, modern-day Canada. Faced with the competing interests of fur traders, religious leaders, government officials, and, of course, various Native American groups, Champlain remained a tireless advocate for the French colony. Often celebrated in heroic histories as the "Father of New France," Champlain's legacy was somewhat more ambiguous, particularly his relationship with the native peoples he encountered.

Champlain began his career as an explorer in 1599, when he joined an expedition to the West Indies. In 1603 Champlain served as the cartographer on a voyage to New France and the following year began his long association with the effort to colonize the New World. After a series of exploratory missions during which he produced several extraordinarily accurate maps of the region as far south as Cape Cod, Champlain established Quebec as the base for French colonial endeavors. By 1613 he was named a vice regal official in New France and was given the authority to administer the colony as he saw fit. Champlain believed this power to extend over the NATIVE AMERICANS living in lands claimed by the French, and he made numerous attempts to interfere in the affairs of the nearby Montagnais Indians. These efforts only served to exacerbate the relationship between the French and the native peoples, especially as competition in the FUR TRADE intensified preexisting animosities among various native groups.

In 1617 Champlain presented his plan for colonization to the Chamber of Commerce in Paris. Like many such plans, Champlain's was a rather optimistic appraisal of the potential for a mixed ECONOMY based on the exploitation of fish, timber, AGRICULTURE, and livestock, as well as the already established fur trade. His report also emphasized that a strong colony in New France was necessary to prevent competing European interests, such as the English and Dutch, from overtaking the lands. Despite the reluctance of some MERCHANTS to get involved in any activities that might detract from the lucrative fur trade, Champlain eventually was confirmed as commander of New France and returned in 1620.

Convinced that a sedentary lifestyle based primarily on agriculture was a key component of "civilized" living, Champlain attempted to convince the Montagnais to abandon their culture, convert to Christianity, speak French, and adopt a new way of life as farmers, much to the dismay of Europeans interested in the fur trade. In 1629 the English captured Quebec and held the settlement until 1632. In the intervening years Champlain continued to act as chief advocate for French colonization, publishing his most ambitious work, *Les Voyages de la Nouvelle France,* just after the English returned the colony to France. Champlain returned to the colony and acted as chief administrator until his death there in 1635.

Further reading: William J. Eccles, *The Canadian Frontier, 1534–1760* (Albuquerque: University of New Mexico Press, 1983).

—Melanie Perreault

Charleston

Founded in 1680 and known as Charles Town throughout the colonial period, this city on the coast of SOUTH CAROLINA was named after English king Charles II (1660–85). English proprietors secured the land grant for their colony from Charles II and laid out this planned city, including streets with a grid pattern, on land taken from Indian nations, including the Yamasee and the CHEROKEE. Aided by immigrants from the West Indies, particularly Barbados, the proprietors succeeded in building a profitable city and colony in the late 17th century despite widespread epidemics and exceedingly high death rates. Located between the Ashley and Cooper Rivers and on the Atlantic Ocean, Charles Town became a thriving port city in the early 18th century and the focus of economic life in the colony. In 1719 Charles Town elites overthrew the proprietary government, and the colony came under royal control. Throughout the royal period (1720–76), Charles Town served as the political center of the colony, and wealthy residents of the city monopolized provincial government.

The only city in the southern colonies, Charles Town attracted a very diverse population. Migrants from Barbados and England were joined by JEWS, French Huguenots (Protestants), and other Europeans. Indian traders, free blacks, and a large slave population added to the cultural mix of Charles Town. Power in the colony, however, remained firmly in the hands of Charles Town white elites. Local merchants involves themselves in elaborate and lucrative international markets. INDIGO (introduced by 17-year-old ELIZABETH LUCAS PINCKNEY in the early 18th century), rice (cultivated through the labor and knowledge of African slaves), and deerskins (acquired through Indian trading) produced huge profits for the planters and merchants of Charles Town. By 1763 the town was home to the wealthiest citizens of British North America. Absentee planters—who resided only occasionally on their plantations—maintained residences in Charles Town, living alongside and socializing with wealthy merchants. City elites built some of the grandest homes in North America and made Charles Town a center of cosmopolitan life. THEATER, horse racing, private clubs, balls, and the first musical society in North America (St. Cecilia, 1762) made Charles Town one of the most culturally sophisticated cities in colonial America.

Most of the wealth that city residents enjoyed came from SLAVERY. The SLAVE TRADE was by far the largest part of Charles Town's commercial interests, and slaves produced highly profitable crops on plantations outside the city. Slavery played a larger role in the economic life of South Carolina than in any other mainland North American colony. South Carolina had the highest percentage of blacks, most of whom toiled in a brutal system of bondage and whose work paid for the lavish lifestyles of local elites. Despite the exploitative nature of slavery, Charles Town also offered AFRICAN AMERICANS a unique opportunity for autonomy and for crafting a vibrant culture. By 1750 more than 40 percent of the city's nearly 7,500 residents were black. Slaves hired for day labor, free sailors and dock hands, and free black women workers enjoyed greater mobility than plantation slaves, and their presence made controlling urban slaves more difficult. Not surprisingly, free black people and slaves sometimes forcibly resisted their abuse by white Charlestonians. In 1739 just 15 miles southwest of Charles Town, African Americans organized the largest revolt against slavery in British North America, the STONO REBELLION.

See also CITIES AND URBAN LIFE.

Further reading: Robert Weir, *Colonial South Carolina: A History* (New York: KTO Press, 1983); Peter H. Wood, *Black Majority: Negroes in Colonial South Carolina from 1670 through the Stono Rebellion* (New York: Norton, 1974).

—Lorri Glover

Chauncy, Charles (1705–1787)

Chauncy was a leading opponent of the GREAT AWAKENING and supporter of the American Revolution. After receiving his B.A. from HARVARD COLLEGE in 1721 and an M.A. in 1724, he became pastor at BOSTON's First Church ("Old Brick") in 1727 and served its congregation for the rest of his life. Chauncy reflected his wealthy, liberal congregation in opposing the "New Lights" headed by Northampton's JONATHAN EDWARDS. Chauncy's "Enthusiasm Described and Caution'd Against" (1742) criticized those who he claimed confused their emotional ravings with the workings of the Holy Spirit. Chauncy insisted that an educated clergy, settled congregations, and reasoned judgment were essential if people were to become genuine Christians. Chauncy also came to believe that all people would be saved, in contrast to his adversaries who insisted humans were miserable sinners and only a cataclysmic infusion of grace could redeem them. Until his old age he refrained from publishing such ideas, which subsequently became the foundation of Universalism, one of America's most popular elite religions in the 19th century. However, he genuinely believed that he had discovered universal salvation to be "The Mystery Hid from Ages and Generations," as he entitled a pamphlet of 1784.

Chauncy was also one of the strongest supporters of the resistance to British policy in Boston after 1760. He detested the ANGLICAN CHURCH's hierarchy and feared that the possible arrival of bishops and what he considered an Anglican effort to undermine New England's Congregational churches went hand in hand with the British campaign to reduce North America to political "bondage." He was such a prominent patriot leader that he fled Boston in 1744 when the British army occupied the town. Ironically, Chauncy's support of the revolution was every bit as "enthusiastic" as the religious doctrines of those he denounced.

See also RELIGION, EURO-AMERICAN.

Further reading: Alan Heimert, *Religion and the American Mind from the Great Awakening to the Revolution* (Cambridge, Mass.: Harvard University Press, 1966).

—William Pencak

Cherokee

In 1650 the Cherokee people of North America consisted of some 22,000 NATIVE AMERICANS, probably related to the IROQUOIS nations of the Great Lakes region. Relocated to the southeast area of the Appalachian Mountains (present-day VIRGINIA, NORTH CAROLINA, Tennessee, Kentucky, GEORGIA, and Alabama), they organized three clusters of small towns in what is now North Carolina, SOUTH CAROLINA, and Georgia. From European visitors' reports it would appear that each site consisted of some 40 log cabins. The town chose a leader, men and women shared authority in their agriculture and hunter/gatherer livelihood, and there was a clear division of labor between chiefs who brought peacetime leadership (symbolized by the color white) and those with lesser status who led in wartime (symbolized by red). Peacetime leadership was characterized by careful reasoning and restrained oratory; wartime leaders were expected to raise passions and excite warriors to battle. A good chief might expect to pass on his position to the child of his oldest sister—usually, but not always, a male child. Women played a variety of influential roles in governing Cherokee affairs.

Except for the early presence of Spanish flintlock muskets, little evidence exists of the merging of Cherokee culture with that of the Spanish explorers whom they had encountered before 1600. By the early 18th century, however, there was intermarriage between Cherokee women and the English as well as trade relationships involving exchanges of Indian foodstuffs for European guns, knives, brass kettles, and other manufactured goods. By 1684 two South Carolina Cherokee towns had signed a treaty with the English; over the next five decades they joined forces against the TUSCARORA, Creek, and French. This alliance even involved several Cherokee representatives traveling to England, in 1729, for an audience with King George II (1727–60). They signed a treaty against the French, who had made a similar compact with the Cherokee towns in present-day Tennessee. One result of this collaboration was a significant change in Cherokee CONSUMPTION patterns, making them dependent on a steady supply of European goods and ultimately eroding their culture. Guns and the supplies to use them were a central focus of this trade, but Cherokee women also sought cloth, sewing tools, cookware, lace, ribbons, buckles, and other manufactured items.

From the beginning of collaboration with Europeans, many of the Cherokee people were wary of the provisions for land divisions set out in the series of treaties and of what might be required of them to maintain these agreements. Between 1730 and 1756 the Cherokee were embroiled in the treacherous politics of the British-American settlers (who promised to build a fort to protect Cherokee families while the men went to war against the French), of the French (to whom some Cherokee towns had sworn loyalty), and of their own communities (where Cherokee leaders often bore the blame for broken European promises). During these years Cherokee leaders ceded to white settlers a large tract of land in what is now western South Carolina.

When hostilities between the French and British escalated during the SEVEN YEARS' WAR (1756–63), Cherokee leaders were hard-pressed to distinguish acts of hostility by the French from those perpetrated by the English, who claimed to mistake Cherokee warriors for the enemy. Many Cherokee wished to withdraw from European politics entirely. Still, some of their leaders, remaining loyal to Britain, ceded more land in Tennessee and Virginia. They were rewarded by another trip to England, where George III reiterated his friendship.

In part to meet their rising debt for consumer goods between 1770 and 1775, Cherokee leaders ceded millions of acres of land to American settlers, including areas of North Carolina and Kentucky. During the War for Independence the Cherokee sided with the British against American settlers in hopes that, in return for military support, the Crown would return some of their land. With the American forces victorious in the Southwest, however, the Cherokee were forced to surrender even more land in North and South Carolina. In the 1781 Treaty of Long Island of Holston, the Cherokee nation became completely subordinated to the American government, and Cherokee consumption and cultural patterns became increasingly overwhelmed by European styles.

—Emma Lapsansky

Chesapeake Bay

Countless generations of NATIVE AMERICANS and European colonists used the resources of the Chesapeake Bay for transportation, FISHING, and hunting. About 11,000 years ago melting glaciers formed the bay. Native Americans settled around the Chesapeake Bay, which they called Chesepioc, meaning "great shellfish bay." The bay served as the nucleus of Native Americans' lives, providing a stable FOOD source. Stunned by the bay's size and resources, the Spanish considered the Chesapeake Bay as a superior port for vessels, calling it Bahía de Santa María. The English referred to it as the Great Bay of the Chesapeakes.

Native peoples built villages and hunting camps along the coast of the bay. Deer and wildlife were attracted to the bay, providing pelts to trade and meat to eat. The ALGONQUIN formed the majority of the Indians around the bay; they tried to retain isolation from the Susquehannock of the IROQUOIS nation. Some tribes entered into alliances, such as the POWHATAN CONFEDERACY. As more tribes settled in the bay area and as European adventurers arrived seeking land and trade, the indigenous people of the region engaged in cultural and other conflicts. Although some transactions were amicable, hostilities between the Algonquin and Europeans often resulted in abductions and murders. In 1570 a group of Spanish JESUITS established a settlement near the York River, intending to convert Native Americans to Catholicism, but the Algonquin resisted. The English planned to settle the Chesapeake Bay region as early as the 1580s, but three attempts to settle Roanoke Island failed. However, John White, an artist, returned to England with his drawings and maps, which became very well known.

The original JAMESTOWN settlers arrived at the Chesapeake Bay in April 1607, sailing up the James River. This colony suffered from starvation and exposure to the elements. Governor JOHN SMITH ordered men to harvest oysters and sturgeon from the Chesapeake to feed the settlers. The Algonquin taught the English how to grow TOBACCO, which was the catalyst for a massive shipping and economic system depending on the waterways of the colonial Chesapeake Bay. English ROMAN CATHOLICS settled ST. MARY'S CITY, MARYLAND, in 1634, taking advantage of the Chesapeake Bay to develop major SHIPBUILDING and tobacco industries. The early LABOR force was multiracial, including European indentured servants, a few Indian slaves, and

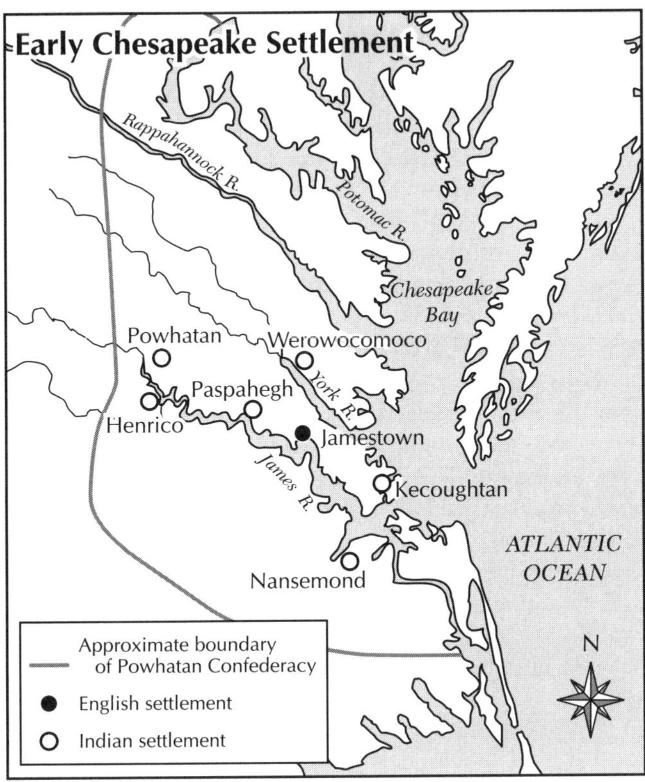

a handful of black servants and slaves. More land was cleared as soil became depleted by the demands of tobacco plants. As the supply of English indentured servants lessened and the Africans became more easily available, a system of racial bondage evolved at the end of the 17th century. The Chesapeake Bay enabled permanent settlements to thrive, and its tributaries were crucial as settlers migrated west. Pirates flourished, and shipwrecks littered the Chesapeake Bay.

Further reading: Arthur Pierce Middleton, *Tobacco Coast: A Maritime History of Chesapeake Bay in the Colonial Era* (Baltimore: Johns Hopkins University Press and the Maryland State Archives, 1984).

—Elizabeth D. Schafer

Chickasaw

The Chickasaw Indians resided in present-day northern Mississippi and western Tennessee. Their population declined from about 5,000 in 1700 to around 3,000 by mid-century, then rebounded. Their language and culture closely resembled the CHOCTAW Indians to their south, with whom they shared a similar history of their origins in a region west of the Mississippi River. Their first contact with Europeans most likely occurred in 1541, when Spaniard Hernando de Soto's military expedition encamped near their villages, sparking conflict and unleashing deadly diseases. Contact with the British and French began in the late 1600s, and the Chickasaw established a fruitful trade relationship and alliance with Britain centered around exchanging deerskins for guns and other manufactured items. Chickasaw warriors raided Choctaw villages to obtain captives for the Carolina slave market until the Choctaw also acquired guns from the French in the early 1700s.

France sought to sway Chickasaw allegiance away from Britain, but they could never supply enough trade goods to appease the Chickasaw, so they chose to wage war on them instead. France encouraged their Choctaw allies to attack the Chickasaw nearly constantly in the 18th century and even mounted two full-scale military expeditions of their own against the Chickasaw in 1736 and 1739, but both invasions failed. Despite consistent Chickasaw victory and a reputation for fierce and powerful warriors, this constant warfare threatened Chickasaw survival by unduly stressing their population numbers. They compensated by absorbing other peoples into their society. After the French war against the Natchez Indians in the late 1720s, hundreds of Natchez people fled to live among the Chickasaw. In addition, the Chickasaw readily adopted British fur traders into their families and villages. These traders ensured ready access to European trade goods, and they brought new ideas and skills as well as new bicultural children into the nation.

Although their alliance with Britain remained strong throughout the 18th century, the Chickasaw essentially used the British to obtain access to the guns and other supplies that ensured their continuing independence amidst tremendous outside pressure to succumb to foreign domination or migrate from their homeland.

Further reading: Mary Ann Wells, *Native Land: Mississippi 1540–1798* (Jackson: University Press of Mississippi, 1994); Arrell M. Gibson, *The Chickasaws* (Norman: University of Oklahoma Press, 1971).

—Greg O'Brien

childhood

Parents and guardians in early North America loved and raised their children with the cultural values and skills required by their various societies. Because of high MORTALITY rates, European colonists considered infancy a dangerous state to be endured, and babies were admired more for their progress toward adulthood than for their innate capabilities. Early marriages and large families were common, and members of extended families and kinship groups helped raise children when either the death of parents or forced separation disrupted nuclear families.

Children were a crucial part of the labor force in this preindustrial agrarian ECONOMY. They began to contribute to the family welfare at a young age, whether belonging to Puritan or Chesapeake farm families, as members of Indian tribes, or when coerced into the workforce on slave plantations.

In 17th-century New England Puritan families were large, nuclear, and stable, characterized by early marriages and high birth rates. In contrast, in the mid-Atlantic region later marriages and shorter life expectancies created orphans and instability, resulting in more extended and stepfamilies. The family structure of white people in both regions converged during the 18th century. Euro-Americans believed that a parent's duty was to ensure that babies grew straight and erect with the ability to speak, reason, and walk upright, which separated them from wild beasts. The use of swaddling bands and narrow cradles that inhibited movement, walking stools that held babies upright, and CLOTHING that gave the illusion of an adult posture indicate that infants were considered "innately depraved" and in need of shaping. Babies were thus hurried through infancy to physical independence.

Childhood ended at about age seven, when children were given household responsibilities and began lessons in religion and reading. Girls typically learned domestic skills from their mothers, and boys followed their fathers' chores in this predominantly patriarchal world. Clothing indicated age and status—children of both GENDERS wore petticoats and caps until boys were considered mature enough to wear trousers. Most children were apprenticed out of the home at the age of 12 or 13. To "break the will" of uncooperative youngsters, PURITANS and other Europeans often used physical force in the 17th century. Corporal punishment declined in the later 18th century, when parents began to develop a view of childhood as a time of joy and innocence rather than of danger and depravity.

Slave children matured under the very difficult conditions of bondage. Slave owners sometimes hindered family formation, separating children and parents, and harshly punished young slaves. Still, AFRICAN AMERICANS enjoyed some success in creating close family relationships. Following African kinship patterns, slaves formed extended family networks often comprised of friends who became "fictive" kin to raise orphans and maintain family bonds. Community "aunties" and "uncles" looked after girls and boys in the absence of other family members. Because slave owners envisioned infants as future workers, pregnant and nursing mothers usually received brief respite from field labor. Mothers carried babies on their backs into plantation fields, in the manner of their ancestors. At age six or seven some slave children began work as domestics while others began doing small chores around the farm. At nine or 10, most entered fieldwork. Some were apprenticed to skilled ARTISANS at age 14 or 15, also the age at which slaves (called "woman girl" and "man boy") were most often sold.

Slave parents passed on a blended African and European culture, using religion, storytelling, MUSIC, and DANCE to create a sense of group identity. Masters usually forbade reading, but literate adults occasionally were able to educate girls and boys. Parents also taught children methods of resistance, from daily survival skills to acts of resistance and rebellion, as ways to cope with oppression. Runaway slave women very rarely left their children, often risking capture by taking them along.

Although Native American children grew up in diverse, autonomous tribes, some common themes of childhood emerge. Families were enmeshed in a network of extended family, clan, and tribal relationships. Unlike white children, Indian children often enjoyed close ties with numerous adults. Infants were valued as links to the supernatural world and were often nursed until the age of five. Parents used cradleboards, like the Euro-American swaddle method, to give security and create discipline in babies while they grew. Europeans were often astonished at the freedom that Indian parents afforded their offspring. Children learned skills required for membership in their adult society in the areas of survival, religion, and ethics through play, imitation, and storytelling. Spiritual quests for a personal "guardian spirit" were common rites of passage into adulthood. Informal apprentice relationships trained youth for storytelling and other leadership roles in the community. Adults educated children by using incentives, ridicule, fear of supernatural beings, and, rarely, physical punishment. Because pain tolerance was generally a cultural ideal, children were trained in physical endurance. As contact with Euro-Americans increased, deadly diseases, loss of land, and physical relocation required Native American parents to adapt their methods of child rearing to a changing world.

Further reading: Karin Calvert, *Children in the House: The Material Culture of Early Childhood, 1600–1900* (Boston: Northeastern University Press, 1992).

—Deborah C. Taylor

Choctaw

The Choctaw Indians resided in present-day central and eastern Mississippi and claimed rights over territory extending to the Mississippi River, the Gulf Coast, and into present-day Alabama. Their population numbered about 20,000 in 1700, dropped to about 14,000 in the middle of the 18th century, and began to grow again in the latter half of the century. There existed among the Choctaw three principal geographic and political divisions: the western, eastern, and Six Towns (or southern) divisions that reflected the diverse ethnic origins of the Choctaw people. Sometime between Spaniard Hernando de Soto's military expedition through the Southeast in the 1540s and 1699, when the French arrived on the Gulf Coast, distinct groups of southeastern Indians had joined together to form the historically known Choctaw. The most likely reason for this migration is that SMALLPOX unleashed by de Soto's campaign ravaged southeastern Indian populations, encouraging the refugees to join culturally similar peoples for safety in numbers.

The Choctaw welcomed the new French presence on the Gulf Coast and along the Mississippi River in the early decades of the 18th century because they needed a counterweight to British-sponsored slave raids into their villages. Armed with British guns, the Creek Indians and other groups residing close to British settlements in Carolina seized upwards of 1,000 Choctaw in the late 1600s for sale to the West Indies. Once the French arrived in the area, the Choctaw acquired their own guns and successfully countered the slave-catching attacks. Because of this aid from France, the Choctaw remained closely allied to that country until France's defeat in the SEVEN YEARS' WAR in 1763. In the 1720s and 1730s the Choctaw assisted France in attacking and driving out the Natchez Indians from the Mississippi River area after the Natchez had rebelled against the French presence. Similarly, the Choctaw waged intermittent war against another French enemy, the CHICKASAW Indians, throughout the 18th century until 1763.

Not all Choctaw approved of an alliance solely with France. In the late 1740s a civil war broke out among the Choctaw divisions, in part over whether to form a trade alliance with Britain. Certain western division warriors, such as RED SHOES, attacked French traders and officials in their towns, thus igniting the civil war (1746–50) that caused the deaths of hundreds of Choctaw. Nevertheless, the Choctaw continued to seek a British trade alliance after 1750, and they stubbornly resisted being dependent on only one European power.

Further reading: Patricia Galloway, *Choctaw Genesis, 1500–1700* (Lincoln: University of Nebraska Press, 1995); James Taylor Carson, *Searching for the Bright Path: The Mississippi Choctaws from Prehistory to Removal* (Lincoln: University of Nebraska Press, 1999).

—Greg O'Brien

cities and urban life

By 1690 five important urban centers in the present-day United States had acquired both similar and unique characteristics. BOSTON, NEWPORT, NEW YORK, PHILADELPHIA, and CHARLESTON, all located on rivers, were positioned to maximize the trade and military advantages of the Atlantic rim communities. Through these centers flowed manufactured goods, money, produce, and—significantly—information. By the 1740s each town had at least a skeleton of municipal government; a weekly newspaper; a variety of skilled craftspeople; a diversity of cultures and religions; well-developed commercial, consumer, and credit systems; and at least rudimentary city services (e.g., mail, markets, TAVERNS, inns, theaters, constables, poverty relief programs, prisons, and some educational institutions). Although most of the cities were in areas controlled by Britain, other small urban nodes of a few hundred people also had appeared by 1700 and would take shape as cities by the end of the century. NEW ORLEANS and Chicago developed as a result of French-Indian trade. ST. AUGUSTINE (FLORIDA), Tucson (Arizona), and San Antonio (Texas) grew out of Spanish Catholic MISSIONS. By 1775 Spanish explorers had established a beachhead on what would become San Francisco (California).

The urban areas represented economic and social opportunities and challenges. Each had an adjoining agricultural region from which to draw produce for CONSUMPTION and international trade. Each had international political and economic influence disproportionate to its small size; by 1750 Philadelphia—with only about 15,000 residents—was considered to be the second most important city in the BRITISH EMPIRE. Beginning as early as the 1690s, publishing operations in every city began gaining momentum, turning out thousands of books, pamphlets, broadsides, and magazines, including 4,000 titles between 1740 and 1760. Although Boston remained the largest (approximately 7,000 in 1690 and 16,000 in the 1740s), New York and Philadelphia became the most vigorous urban centers after 1740, growing rapidly in both population and independence for women, a significant number of whom chose to remain single in order to control their own assets. Each urban center struggled with municipal administrative challenges: road maintenance, waste disposal and pollution, HOUSING codes, fires, and petty crime.

Regional, religious, economic, and cultural variations helped define unique characteristics of cities. The few urban areas in the South were very small, shaped by a PLANTATION SYSTEM where many plantations were the equivalent of self-sufficient villages containing their own craftspeople, agricultural produce, and private docks. Although Charleston—with only 7,000 residents by 1750—contained furniture-makers and printers who were the equal of those in other cities, it lagged behind with other services. For example, whereas Boston, Philadelphia, and New York all had colleges by the time of the Revolution, Charleston did not. The percentage of slave labor and free black residents in some of the cities also influenced urban culture. New York and Charleston, where slaves accounted for more than 20 percent of the population, both experienced slave uprisings in the 18th century. Philadelphia, under the influence of Quaker values, had a smaller slave population. Quaker influence also caused Philadelphia to lag behind the other cities in the development of THEATER.

As the 18th century progressed, cities also developed a hierarchical CLASS structure, which by 1760 was defined by a dramatically unequal distribution of wealth. Whereas in 1690 the poorest 50 percent of free urban people controlled about 10 percent of the cities' assets, their economic share had declined to less than 5 percent by 1760. This disparity, evident everywhere, was most pronounced in Philadelphia, where the poorest half of the population owned only 3 percent of the city's assets, while the richest 5 percent had more than half of the city's wealth—almost double the percentage they had controlled in 1690. Affluent urbanites strutted their wealth, importing wines, cheeses, books, and ART from abroad and erecting public buildings and private residences copied from opulent British designs.

Easy availability of information, the display of wealth, and wartime booms followed by recessions left urbanites restless and discontent, a factor that fed the desire for reform and led to the Revolution. Frequent communication among urban areas also facilitated the publicizing of revolutionary ideas, such as those espoused by JOHN LOCKE and Thomas Paine. This combined with social class tensions and a growing appetite for consumer goods to highlight the English colonists' concerns about "fairness," "equality," and "freedom"—concepts that appear frequently in Revolutionary rhetoric.

By 1770 the combined population of Boston, Newport, New York, Philadelphia, and Charleston was only about 60,000, less than 3 percent of the 1.5 million inhabitants in Anglo-America, yet American leadership emerged from these urban areas, and the cities continued to lead the nation for decades to come.

Further reading: Gary B. Nash, *The Urban Crucible: Social Change, Political Consciousness, and the Origins of the American Revolution* (Cambridge, Mass.: Harvard University Press, 1979); Nash, *Forging Freedom: The Formation of Philadelphia's Black Community, 1720–1840* (Cambridge, Mass.: Harvard University Press, 1988).

—Emma Lapsansky

class

Class was an integral and ever-present part of early American life, although its presence was never felt completely or uniformly. Like much of early American life, the nature of class relations depended to a great extent on region. In the early years of European settlement, colonial societies bore the heavy imprint of cultural and social dislocation, flux, and recomposition as the first generations of conquerors and settlers attempted to impose their European conceptions of social order on an ever-changing world of multicultural interchange. Before the 17th century in Spanish America and the 18th century in the other Euro-American colonies, they seldom succeeded. The sheer complexity of establishing footholds in the New World, of treating with the indigenous inhabitants, of establishing viable economic connections with the home countries—coupled with the fact that all European colonization efforts excluded whole classes of people—made for a cluster of colonial societies in which social hierarchies were more often chimerical than real. As hard as they may have tried to reconstruct the Old World in the New, Euro-Americans perforce created unique social systems that were, for a time, remarkably fluid and open. Only after several generations of established settlement did CREOLE societies begin to resemble their transatlantic counterparts.

This fluidity is most clearly evident in the two regions of English settlement. In the northeastern arc of English settlements, small family farms predominated. Within these units of agrarian production, male household heads exercised formal legal and public power over family members, although in practice power in families flowed from many sources: men made decisions about fields and livestock; women made decisions about the household and its gardens, about the farmyard, and about the family orchard; older children directed the upbringing and tasks of younger siblings; adults directed the lives of servants and, sometimes, slaves. Family farm communities lacked a center of power. Composed, for the most part, of economically equal members, family farm communities formed one-class societies of small producers that provided little basis for focused, centralized power. Even though often engineered, consensual politics generally obtained in these communities, and age, more than any other factor, formed the locus of local power. This was especially true of New England villages, where several studies have demonstrated the persistence of "town fathers"—older men who guided formal and informal community decision making—in positions of local authority. These decentralized communities realized a degree of centralization only occasionally, whenever the outside world of colonial magistrates and contending armies intruded in local affairs.

In the CONNECTICUT and Hudson River Valleys and the countryside surrounding NEW YORK CITY and PHILADELPHIA, AGRICULTURE took on a larger-scale, commercial aspect. In these areas clientage and asymmetrical class relationships made power much more centralized.

Wealthy landholders claimed economic, social, and political power throughout these commercial regions by lending money, renting and leasing land, hiring temporary labor, and helping in hard times. More often than not, these landowners turned their economic power as a rentier class into political power, calling in the suffrages of their clients and lessees as a condition of their obliging paternalism.

If power was more centralized around class relationships in commercial farming areas, it was most concentrated in the northern seaport cities. As Gary B. Nash has shown, from the very beginning of settlement in BOSTON, New York City, and Philadelphia, cities were the most unequal places in the Northeast. Dominated economically by a class of wealthy import/export MERCHANTS, the northern seaport cities supported a diverse SOCIETY made up of independent ARTISANS, retail merchants, laborers, MARINERS, indentured and hired servants, and slaves. In these, the most stratified locales in northern society, a rudimentary class system linked merchant to retailer, retailer to artisan, artisan to journeyman and apprentice, and everyone to the cities' bound laborers and mariners. The nature of this class system is often distorted and misunderstood—indeed it is occasionally even denied—by those who see class existing only in its centralized, industrial form. For although centralized in comparison with its rural counterparts, the commercial ECONOMY of the seaport cities supported class relations that were remarkably decentralized compared with those that would exist in the 19th century. These seaport societies revolved around trade, and this made merchants one center of urban society. Merchants employed mariners for their vessels, bought the time of indentured servants, and purchased slaves as personal and household servants. However, at the same time, they also contracted with independent artisans for goods and farmers for produce. For their part, master artisans hired journeymen and trained apprentices, but they also bought the time and persons of indentured servants and slaves as the supply of dependent LABOR and the size of their purses dictated. Even the position of laborers and mariners (together composing the largest group of working people in the seaport cities) was ambiguous. Servants typically hired themselves on an annual basis and mariners for the duration of a voyage. This brought them under the direct personal supervision of their temporary owners, who controlled not only their working but their personal lives as well. Although they possessed some legal rights and protections, the position of servants and mariners was closer to that of slaves than free wage laborers, at least during the term of their respective indentures. The overlapping diversity of these class relations was typical of mercantile communities throughout the New World and, indeed, characteristic of similar communities in Europe, Asia, and AFRICA as well. Class relations remained diffuse in these communities, and, while in some respects they might prefigure the world of industrial capitalism, they mostly represented a semicentralized world of independence and dependence, of clientage and custom, of freedom and bondage.

It is only when we turn to the English plantation complex that we encounter a well-articulated and centralized class system in early America. From their inception the English CARIBBEAN and southern mainland colonies were designed as colonies of exploitation. Unable to find significant mineral wealth or to exploit Native American labor effectively, as had their Spanish predecessors in the New World, the English were able to follow their Iberian counterparts in establishing lucrative staple-producing societies. Relying first on English indentured servants, the southern mainland colonies quickly evolved into societies in which class was the dominant form of inequality. In colonies to which few women came before the mid-17th century, the near absence of family life focused colonial life on the economic nexus. Developing from the English institution of year-long contracts struck between landlords and agricultural servants, the indenture system of MARYLAND and VIRGINIA quickly became a system of quasi SLAVERY. Servants could be bought and sold or their persons and labor gambled away. For those found guilty of increasingly minor infractions, their time in "service" could be extended two-, three-, or four-fold as punishment and as a means of enhancing the wealth and power of the region's planter class. The lines of class were thus clear in the early Chesapeake: the bulk of the work of planting TOBACCO—the region's staple crop—was performed by indentured servants who labored for an increasingly wealthy and powerful class of plantation owners.

If the indenture system represented the most class-centered form of inequality in early British American society, the slave system that supplanted it after 1680 was even more so. Slavery in the Chesapeake was in many respects a direct result of the indenture system of the early and middle 17th century. After 1660 slave prices fell as servant prices rose, making the purchase of slaves increasingly the norm. BACON'S REBELLION, which pitted ex-indentured servants against their former masters, accelerated the purchase of slaves, who by 1650 were already considered a class unto themselves: servants for life. By 1710 the Chesapeake colonies had become fully committed slave societies, with African slaves constituting 42 percent of Virginia's and 23 percent of Maryland's total population. The same held true farther south in the Carolinas, where slavery and its attendant class system arrived with the first white immigrants. Comprised of displaced settlers from the sugar island of Barbados, there was little question about the status of the African slaves they brought with them. Once SOUTH CAROLINA planters had mastered the techniques of rice growing—learned, ironically, from their African bondpeople—they quickly turned the fledgling province into the most prosperous of the British mainland colonies. By the early 18th century South Carolina had become the mainland's only black-majority colony.

Thus, by the turn of the 18th century, the basic pattern of class relations that would come to dominate the plantation complex was in place in the mainland colonies. It involved the domination of southern society by a small class of very wealthy and powerful planters whose wealth derived from the exploitation of a subaltern class of slaves. That dominance encompassed the white, small-farming population as well. Interspersed throughout the plantation complex were other white people, most of whom were family farmers much like their northern counterparts, although they competed directly with large planters by growing small quantities of the local staple in addition to producing their own FOOD and fodder. The financial power of the plantation grandees coupled with the virtual control they exercised over colonial legislatures and county court systems made the class system of the plantation regions, along with those of New Spain, the most centralized in pre–19th-century America.

Early North America was thus a concatenation of systems of power and inequality. Working outward from colonial families to local communities and on to colonial society as a whole, inequalities of power in all of its aspects took on many forms, but despite the existence of rudimentary forms of capitalism and several configurations of class, outside the plantation complex class was never the central organizing institution of early American society. In fact, within the northeastern arc of the British mainland colonies—except, perhaps, in the large seaport cities—it is difficult to find any stable centers of power at all. That would begin to change as rapid population growth in the 18th and early 19th centuries, repudiation of colonial status, the creation of independent nationhood, and the infusion of capital into productive relationships began to transform early North America into an industrial nation. However, while the impact of commercial expansion and early industrial capitalism on the structure of power and inequality in the new nation was profound, the question of class in early 19th-century American society admitted no unequivocal answer.

Further reading: Gary B. Nash, *The Urban Crucible: Social Change, Political Consciousness, and the Origins of the American Revolution* (Cambridge, Mass.: Harvard University Press, 1979); Edmund S. Morgan, *American Slavery, American Freedom: The Ordeal of Colonial Virginia* (New York: Norton, 1975); Robert A. Gross, *The Minutemen and Their World* (New York: Hill & Wang, 1976).

—Ronald Schultz

clothing

Dress in early North America indicated peoples' CLASS and status, religious beliefs, and, at times, the impulse to escape these social categories. Europeans were used to a system of elaborate social meaning in dress, which was not lost on NATIVE AMERICANS, to whom adornments signified importance. Insensitive to indigenous cultures, the English viewed Indians, who wore "skins of beasts" when not naked, as wild and subhuman. African slaves, who often arrived in North America with virtually nothing on their backs, were allotted the roughest cloth as a mark of their inferior status. In time, Europeans on the frontier adopted pieces of Indian dress, New England women ignored sumptuary laws, Native Americans fashioned clothing out

Iroquois women and warrior. The latter carries a wooden shield on his back. The illustration is by Samuel de Champlain. *(Hulton/Archive)*

of European cloth, and slaves acquired dyes and tailoring skills to express individuality in dress.

Wealthy MERCHANTS imported most of their cloth from England and considered local homespun coarse and suited only for workers and servants. English sumptuary laws prohibited the use of fancy laces, ruffles, and embroidered cloth by any but the upper classes. PURITANS, QUAKERS, and many Dutch, Swedish, and French Protestants believed that simplicity and order in dress reflected order in one's relationship to God. Still, they adhered to the laws' purpose of class differentiation and reserved the best materials for prosperous merchants. After a time colonial women refused to obey English dress laws, which were abolished in the 1680s, opening the way for Americans to imitate the wealthy in their attire. VIRGINIA elites surpassed even the English in their fashionable dress styles, which they wore to display their wealth and power and to rebel against the Protestant clothing ethic.

Native Americans dressed in various styles according to tribal customs. In general, they wore clothing made from animal skins: boots, dresses, shirts, leggings, a fur cloak in winter, and hats. Ceremonial outfits were decorated with dyes, feathers, quills, and beadwork. Contact with Europeans introduced cloth that Indians adapted to their own styles and items of clothing, such as shirts and hats, that expressed their cross-cultural mobility. Frontiersmen similarly emulated native dress, whether for practical reasons (leggings and moccasins worked better in the backcountry) or to show their adaptive ability and "American" identity. Colonial militia, for example, wore fringed hunting shirts as a mark of patriotism when fighting the British "redcoats."

The Euro-American workingman's costume consisted of loose breeches, canvas jerkin, woolen hose, and felt or straw hats. Poorer women wore simple short gowns, which allowed for physical labor, and modest linen caps, although farm wives used vegetable dyes to create "Sunday best" outfits from homespun. Prosperous American men dressed in breeches of fine cloth, waistcoats, silk stockings, broadcloth coats with silver buttons, silver buckled shoes, heavy cloaks, and wool or beaver hats. Affluent women wore long broadcloth gowns with lace decorated petticoats in the latest European fashion. In the 18th century, when a greater variety of fabric and styles became available from the East India Company, a loose nightgown dress, turbans, and Spanish capes became fashionable.

Slaves made inexpensive "negro cloth" into shirts and pants for men, dresses for women, and long shirts for children. Many abandoned their poorly fitting shoes in favor of bare feet. Women patched discarded items and sewed dressier clothes, dyed bright colors, for special occasions. Slaves often followed African customs of dress, such as breechcloths, wrap-around skirts, and a variety of headwear to express their individuality and origins. Runaway slave advertisements often described the missing person's clothing in detail, suggesting that dress was an important identifier as well as a mark of personal identity.

Woodcut of a Puritan couple in daily dress *(Hulton/Archive)*

Further reading: Diana de Marly, *Dress in North America,* vol. 1 (New York: Holmes & Meier, 1990); Shane White and Graham J. White, *Stylin: African American Expressive Culture from Its Beginnings to the Zoot Suit* (Ithaca, N.Y.: Cornell University Press, 1998); Richard L. Bushman, *The Refinement of America: Persons, Houses, Cities* (New York: Vintage Books, 1992).

—Deborah C. Taylor

Coddington, William (1601–1678)

William Coddington was born in Boston, England, in 1601. An assistant director in the MASSACHUSETTS BAY COMPANY, he arrived in BOSTON as part of the great migration to the Massachusetts Bay Colony in 1630. For a few years he prospered in a variety of posts, including company treasurer (1634–6) and deputy in the colonial legislature (1636–7). Allying himself with the antinomian religious leader ANNE MARBURY HUTCHINSON, Coddington left Massachusetts Bay and went to Aquidneck Island (the largest island in Narragansett Bay in eastern RHODE ISLAND) in 1638, where he helped found Portsmouth (then called Pocasset). After a dispute with Hutchinson, he moved to the south of the island and founded the settlement of NEWPORT in 1639. The following year he managed to unite Portsmouth and Newport under his leadership, hoping to build an aristocratic fiefdom under his control. However, the British Parliament united Aquidneck with ROGER WILLIAMS's Providence in 1644. When a temporary victory undoing that decision (1651) was rescinded in 1652, Coddington returned to Boston for several years. He served as governor of the united colony of Rhode Island in 1674–75 and again in 1678, before he died on November 1, 1678.

—Doug Baker

Colden, Cadwallader (1688–1776)

An important doctor and scientist, Cadwallader Colden was born in Ireland and raised in Scotland, where his father, the Reverend Alexander Colden of the Church of Scotland, had a church in Duns. Although meant by his father to follow religion, Colden instead studied MEDICINE in London after graduating from the University of Edinburgh in 1705. He moved to PHILADELPHIA in 1710. Like other educated gentlemen of the day, he was also interested in a variety of sciences, aspiring to achievements primarily in botany. He corresponded with Benjamin Franklin, Alexander Garden (namesake for the gardenia), and Carolus Linnaeus in Sweden. Colden also joined an international group that studied natural history, helping introduce new species and genera of plants found in America. In 1727 he wrote the *History of the Five Indian Nations* along with other treatises, including several on YELLOW FEVER.

His medical career gave way to one in politics and government when Colden moved to NEW YORK in 1718. In 1720 he became surveyor general for the colony, while the following year found him a member of the governor's council. He rose to lieutenant governor in 1761 and served several times as acting governor. In the turbulent years leading up to the American Revolution, Colden continued to be a strong force in New York, repeatedly earning the enmity of patriots as he steadfastly remained loyal to the British Crown. After the Declaration of Independence, Colden retired to his Spring Hill estate in Flushing, New York, where he died on September 20, 1776.

—Anita DeClue

Colden, Jane (1724–1766)

Botanist and illustrator, Jane Colden was born in NEW YORK CITY to physician and scientist CADWALLADER COLDEN and Alice Christie. Educated at home, Colden's interest in botany was fostered and supported by her father, and she handled much of her father's botanical correspondence. An early proponent of the Linnaean system of plant classification, she corresponded with and/or met many of the most prominent naturalists of her time, including Carolus Linnaeus, Peter Collinson, William and JOHN BARTRAM, and Alexander Garden. An active participant in the growing colonial scientific community, she exchanged plant specimens with other collectors and compiled a substantial catalog of plants from the lower Hudson River Valley. Colden's only publication appears to have been a description of the gardenia in the *Edinburgh Essays and Observations*, but she was widely known and respected in scientific circles for her skill in illustration. She developed a technique for making ink impressions of leaves and drew and painted plants.

Like many women of her period, Colden's participation in the burgeoning of colonial SCIENCE was limited primarily to assisting in the researches of a male family member. She resolved the tension between running a household and maintaining scientific activity by abandoning science when she married physician William Farqhuar in 1759.

Further reading: Marica Bonta, *Women in the Field: America's Pioneering Women Naturalists* (College Station, Tex.: Texas A&M Press, 1991).

—Monique Bourque

College of Philadelphia

The College of Philadelphia began in 1749, when Benjamin Franklin published the anonymous pamphlet *Proposals Relating to the Education of Youth in Pensilvania* that called for the creation of a public academy along a model unique in Anglo-American educational history. Practicality was Franklin's goal in the academy: "As to their Studies, it would be well if they could be taught every Thing which is useful, and every Thing which is ornamental: But Art is long, and their Time is short." Instead of the "ornamental" classical curriculum that dominated the educations of wealthy young white Americans, students at Franklin's proposed academy would be trained in modern subjects to prepare them for future careers. His educational plan was firmly grounded in his own practical self-education, his grasp of Enlightenment ideas, and the needs of the ethnically and religiously diverse population of PHILADELPHIA.

The academy quickly became an institution far different from what Franklin had envisioned. Much of that transformation was due to the Anglican priest William Smith (1727–1803), whom the trustees hired as a professor in 1754. The following year, under Smith's influence and leadership, the board applied for a new charter that would allow them to grant college degrees, but Smith's personal habits and politics repelled as many as they enticed. He had little interest in forming a coalition with QUAKERS, LUTHERANS, or PRESBYTERIANS in the religiously diverse city. His personal interests were in teaching and befriending the sons of wealthy Anglican MERCHANTS, not in providing charity EDUCATION for ARTISANS' children. Franklin eventually came to consider Smith one of his most bitter enemies, and the College and Academy of Philadelphia became a hotly contested issue in the increasingly divisive PENNSYLVANIA politics, having serious repercussions for the school during the late colonial period and during and immediately after the Revolution.

—George W. Boudreau

College of William and Mary

Chartered on February 8, 1693, the College of William and Mary in VIRGINIA is the second oldest institution of higher EDUCATION in British America. A college was planned as early as 1618, but the 1622 POWHATAN uprising decimated the planned site. Reverend James Blair secured the 1693 royal charter, which endowed the school with 10,000 acres, nearly £2,000, a steady income from TOBACCO duties, and named the college for William III and Mary II, the ruling English monarchs. The original brick main building, attributed to Sir Christopher Wren, was completed in 1699, and the college's elegant structures inspired the colony's gentry to construct mansions in Wren's architectural style.

Initially, the college's academic standards were minimal, although they improved over time. Blair departed from the traditional English curriculum, adding DANCE in 1715 and mathematics the following year. In his will physicist Robert Boyle endowed an Indian school with land and funds to support a master to teach "reading, writing, and vulgar arithmetick." Established in 1706 as part of the College of William and Mary, the Indian school served as many as 20 NATIVE AMERICANS, but their numbers dwindled to nothing by the 1770s. In 1729 the college completed its faculty of six masters teaching moral and natural philosophy, mathematics, divinity, and grammar and enrolled around 60 students. Distinguished alumni include Thomas Jefferson, James Monroe, and Edmund Randolph.

—Michael J. Jarvis

colleges See education; specific colleges

Conestoga (1690–1763)

The Conestoga were descendants of Susquehannock Indians who lived in eastern PENNSYLVANIA during the 17th century and struggled against domination by IROQUOIS Indians to the north. The Susquehannock hunted, fished, and planted corn, beans, and squash for their subsistence and competed with Delaware River tribes to monopolize intercommunity trade along the Susquehanna River. Fearful of Iroquois attack, the Susquehannock sought refuge in MARYLAND in the 1660s, but by 1675 and 1676 VIRGINIA and Maryland colonial militias drove them back north during the crisis of BACON'S REBELLION. The Susquehannock population, which may have reached as high as 6,500, subsequently decreased due to disease and warfare, and the Iroquois and Delaware River Indian communities absorbed some survivors.

A small band also resettled at the confluence of the Susquehanna River and Conestoga Creek some time around 1690 at a town they called Quanistagua (or sometimes Caristauga). Members of Seneca, Oneida, Cayuga, and TUSCARORA bands joined them, and the inhabitants eventually became known simply as the Conestoga Indians. After his first official visit to the town in 1700, WILLIAM PENN signed a treaty of "Peace and Amity" with the Conestoga, promising to protect them. In 1717 Penn set aside 415 acres of land on his 16,000-acre Conestoga Manor for Indian use with the stipulation that they obey all British laws and become subjects to the king. During its heyday in the early 18th century, Conestoga was a major trade town in Pennsylvania with a highly mobile population of 100 to 150 Indians. Conestoga warriors joined the Iroquois in war against their southern enemies. Their leader, aptly named Civility, cultivated a close relationship with William Penn and his appointed colonial governor and, until their demise in 1763, Conestoga offered gifts whenever a new governor arrived in the colony. In return they expected reciprocity and often asked the governor for gifts of leather or clothing as recognition of their loyalty (a gesture that white settlers too often interpreted as "begging").

Civility worked hard to regulate the ALCOHOL trade at Conestoga. In 1734 he insisted that the governor limit the number of trade licenses issued and make the sale of liquor illegal. Because of their close contact with white Pennsylvanians, however, by midcentury the Conestoga had adopted many of the cultural practices of their Euro-American neighbors. Some became Christian. All became involved in the market ECONOMY, especially manufacturing and selling brooms and bowls to nearby white settlers. In December 1763 the PAXTON BOYS attacked and killed the 20 Conestoga who still lived on the manor.

Further reading: Paul A. W. Wallace, *Indians in Pennsylvania* (Harrisburg, Pa.: Pennsylvania Historical and Museum Commission, 1981; originally 1961).

—Jane T. Merritt

Congregationalists

Congregationalists are Protestants whose congregations govern themselves directly rather than submitting to the government of elected elders or appointed priests and bishops. Congregationalists reject the imposition of more than minimal restraints on a local church's actions by higher ecclesiastical authorities or on an individual member's beliefs by prescriptive creeds. Congregationalists have occasionally drafted descriptive creeds, including most notably the Savoy Declaration (1658), a counterpart to the PRESBYTERIANS' Westminster Confession.

English Congregationalism drew its initial impetus from Robert Browne's book *A Treatise of Reformation without Tarrying for Anie* (1582). Brown and other radicals organized independent underground congregations, with one in the town of Scrooby eventually coming under the leadership of Puritan cleric John Robinson. In 1608 Robinson and lay elder William Brewster oversaw their flock's flight to the Netherlands; in 1620 Brewster and much of the congregation migrated again, planting PLYMOUTH Colony in North America. Plymouth's PILGRIMS stressed their autonomy from the Church of England. Within a decade the Massachusetts Bay Colony had been established north of Plymouth by more moderate PURITANS who denied any such autonomy. Nevertheless, Massachusetts Bay's Puritans followed Plymouth's Pilgrims in choosing Congregational church government. Migrants from Massachusetts carried Congregationalism with them as they settled the rest of New England.

In 1648 New England's Congregational churches adopted the Cambridge Platform defining their common polity. Beginning in the latter part of the century, as these churches endured a prolonged period of perceived decline, their ministers responded by modifying that polity in order to give themselves greater leverage over both their lukewarm churches and their secularizing communities. The crisis of "declension" continued until the GREAT AWAKENING, when a surge of conversions brought fresh vitality to churches led by New Light clergy like JONATHAN EDWARDS. At the same time, the Awakening's excesses triggered resistance on the part of churches led by Old Light clergy like CHARLES CHAUNCY. Tensions between these two blocs anticipated Congregationalism's eventual division into distinct Trinitarian and Unitarian denominations.

Further reading: Williston Walker, *The Creeds and Platforms of Congregationalism* (New York: Scribner's, 1893; reprint, Philadelphia-Pilgrim Press, 1960).

—George W. Harper

Connecticut

In the early 17th century approximately 6,000 to 7,000 NATIVE AMERICANS belonging to several different tribes of the ALGONQUIN confederation lived in present-day Connecticut. The region was less densely settled by Native Americans than the region to the east (present-day RHODE ISLAND), and most of the Algonquin communities cooperated with early European settlers. The Dutch explored the Connecticut River Valley before the English reached it. Adriaen Block, a Dutch explorer, sailed up the Connecticut River as far as present-day Windsor in 1614, and in 1633 the Dutch built a fort on the site of present-day Hartford. In the same year, however, PLYMOUTH colonist William Holmes started a trading post at Windsor, and English settlement soon superseded Dutch claims to the region.

There were two distinct waves of English settlement in the 1630s: the first, from 1633–36, focused on the Connecticut River towns of Windsor (1633), Wethersfield (1635–36), and Hartford (1636); the second, from late 1635 to 1638, included the coastal towns of Saybrook (1635) and Quinnipiac (New Haven, 1638). Most settlers were disaffected Massachusetts Bay colonists who moved south in search of good farmland and more congenial religious and political leadership. In spite of the close similarities between the two settlements, they were governed separately until 1665: the Connecticut River towns as the Colony of Connecticut under the leadership of John Winthrop, Jr. (the first governor), Zion Gardiner (builder of the English fort at Saybrook), and George Fenwick; and the Quinnipiac region as the Colony of New Haven, under the spiritual leadership of Reverend John Davenport and the secular leadership of merchant Theophilus Eaton.

The first clash between Native Americans and English settlers in Connecticut came in 1636, when the PEQUOT, a powerful Connecticut River Valley tribe, attacked the fort at Saybrook. The English settlers, mustered under Captain JOHN MASON, retaliated in 1637 by launching a surprise nighttime attack on the Pequot fort at Mystic. The English set fire to the fort, killed most of the captured Pequot, and enslaved others, distributing the captives to their Indian allies as war prizes. This brief but intense military episode, the PEQUOT WAR, effectively ended Native American opposition to English settlement in the Connecticut River Valley. Algonquin tribes other than Pequot generally sold land to English settlers and coexisted peacefully with them. Nevertheless, both the Connecticut and New Haven colonies joined the New England Confederation (1643–84), a regional defense league, and Connecticut sent several hundred men to MASSACHUSETTS and Rhode Island to fight in KING PHILIP'S WAR (1675–76).

Before the Restoration Connecticut's political structure was loose and simple. Initially eight magistrates appointed by the Massachusetts General Court governed the region, but the Connecticut settlers, dissatisfied with the Massachusetts leadership, soon asserted their independence from the mother colony. In 1639 they adopted the Fundamental Orders of Government, a civil covenant that resembled a Puritan church covenant and was, in fact, based on a 1638 sermon by THOMAS HOOKER. The Fundamental Orders provided only a rough outline of the colony's government, however, and settlers were anxious to secure their claims to the land and to self-government. Governor John Winthrop, Jr., traveled to England in 1661–62 and obtained a charter that legally established the Connecticut colony, licensed it to absorb New Haven (which it did in 1665), defined its boundaries (theoretically extending west to the Pacific Ocean), and granted it generous privileges of self-government. The charter called for annual elections of a governor, deputy governor, and 12 assistants; these men formed the upper house of the colonial legislature. In addition, each town was permitted to send two representatives to the lower house. The upper and lower houses of the legislature together formed the General Assembly, which met twice annually and was empowered to pass laws that did not conflict with English law.

Connecticut, like the other New England colonies, faced a severe threat to self-government when James II attempted to annul the colonial charters and unite all of the northern British-American colonies in the DOMINION OF NEW ENGLAND under Governor SIR EDMUND ANDROS. Connecticut was subject to the dominion from the fall of 1683 until the spring of 1689, when news of the GLORIOUS REVOLUTION reached America. The freemen then voted to reinstate the predominion magistrates and appealed to the new monarchs, William and Mary, to restore Connecticut's charter. The restored charter, confirmed in 1693, served as the basis of Connecticut's government until 1818.

After the political struggles of the first two generations of settlement, Connecticut residents turned their attention to trade, EDUCATION, and religious life. The English population grew rapidly, reaching 130,000 by the census of 1766; meanwhile, the black slave population remained small (3,000 in 1766, slightly more than 2 percent of the colony's population), and the Indian population declined from a high of 6,000 or more in the early 17th century to a mere 600 by the mid-18th century. In the 17th century both Indians and Africans were held as slaves, but they constituted only a tiny fraction of the population. In 1715 the General Assembly, frightened by news of the recent Indian wars in the Carolinas, forbade the importation of Indian slaves; Indian SLAVERY died out gradually in the early to mid-18th century. In contrast, the number of Africans and AFRICAN AMERICANS held as slaves in Connecticut tripled between the 1740s and 1760s. Most slaves worked as domestic servants or labored beside their owners on farms and in small craft shops. In the late colonial period it became increasingly common for slaveholders to manumit their slaves, although freedmen's former masters were required to support them if they seemed likely to become charges on the community.

Both free black people and the few Indians who remained in the colony had difficulty supporting themselves. Indians, in particular, were subject to debilitating commercial restrictions. They could not legally purchase arms, iron, steel, horses, boats, or other goods that would enable them to launch a military challenge to English rule. Their movements within the colony were restricted. Connecticut officials viewed Indians as a corrupting influence on English colonial society. They encouraged them to convert to Christianity but, at the same time, discouraged ordinary English settlers from associating with Indians and imposed stiff penalties on English folk who chose to live in Native American communities. The General Assembly did not condone wanton behavior toward local Indians, however; it also enacted legislation to protect Indian goods from seizure and Indians accused of crimes from summary punishment.

Until the mid-18th century Connecticut's ECONOMY was overwhelmingly agricultural. Capital was scarce, farmers depended on family LABOR supplemented (in wealthier households) by a few servants or slaves, and most families focused their energy on subsistence AGRICULTURE. Maize (Indian corn) was the principal crop; it was even used as money in the 17th century. Farmers also grew wheat, rye, peas, oats, barley, flax, and hemp and raised a wide variety of livestock, including cattle, sheep, and swine. Connecticut farmers exported surplus grain, meat, and livestock to other parts of New England, Newfoundland, and the West Indies. In the 18th century the growth of trade and the expansion of British markets in the West Indies led many Connecticut farmers to specialize in the production of livestock for export. Small industries, such as clock-making, iron-making, and SHIPBUILDING, developed in the colony's principal towns. Although the volume of the colony's trade increased rapidly, its focus remained provincial; BOSTON, NEW YORK, and the British West Indies were Connecticut's most important trading partners.

The growth of commerce and manufacturing fomented economic and political conflict within the colony. MERCHANTS residing in the eastern coastal towns called upon the General Assembly to issue more currency, which would enable them to pay off their debts (debt was a perennial problem for colonial merchants) and purchase more British imports. Residents of agriculturally oriented western Connecticut feared that economic growth in the coastal regions, combined with coastal merchants' land speculation in the Susquehanna River Valley (in present-day PENNSYLVANIA), would drive down property values in western Connecticut, and they succeeded in destroying the New London Society for Trade and Commerce, the merchants' power base. The western residents' ultimate triumph reflects the continuing importance of farming and rural life in late colonial Connecticut. As late as 1766 90 percent of the colony's population was still engaged in agriculture.

Connecticut was a vigorous, generally conservative center of religious and intellectual life almost from the period of its founding. Religious enthusiasm animated the region's first English settlers, and the colony's founding documents reflect its Puritan mission. From 1644 colonial law obligated every resident to contribute to the support of the Congregational Church. Although QUAKERS, BAPTISTS, and Anglicans frequently challenged this law, the General Assembly repeatedly upheld it. The Code of 1650 mirrored another overriding Puritan goal, widespread literacy. Every town of 50 or more families was required to employ a teacher of reading and writing, while every town of 100 or more families was required to found a grammar school as well. Many 17th-century New England schools were fleeting and unstable operations, but Connecticut repeatedly reaffirmed its educational mission. A grammar school was founded in New Haven as early as 1660, and in 1700 the General Assembly ordered the maintenance of a grammar school in each of the four county seats.

In the early 18th century Connecticut colonists, like other Puritan New Englanders, struggled with a sense of "declension," of having fallen away from the spiritual mission of their forebears. Connecticut's clerical and intellectual elite responded by expanding educational opportunities for young men and reforming church government. The colony's Collegiate School (later YALE COLLEGE) was incorporated by the General Assembly in 1701 and opened in Killingworth in 1702. It moved several times before settling permanently in New Haven in 1717. Yale College, created as an alternative to HARVARD COLLEGE, was the third institution of higher EDUCATION in British colonial America. For the first half century of its existence, it functioned primarily as a theological seminary, although it also trained men for political leadership. The college was plunged into controversy in 1722, when rector Timothy Cutler and tutor SAMUEL JOHNSON converted to Anglicanism. Their defection to the ANGLICAN CHURCH provoked a conservative reaction at Yale. In the following decades the college adhered strictly to the orthodox tenets of New England Congregationalism and the traditional classical curriculum.

Meanwhile, the Congregational Church attempted to shore up its power through the Saybrook Platform of 1708, which called for greater coordination of religious life through associations of pastors and consociations of autonomous town churches. The Saybrook Platform failed to resolve the underlying weaknesses in Connecticut's religious life, however, leaving the colony ripe territory for the religious revivals of the 1730s and 1740s. Itinerant preachers converted thousands of Connecticut men and women to evangelical Christianity, leaving a bitter divide between revivalist "New Lights" and antirevivalist "Old Lights." The religious divide duplicated, to some extent, the emerging economic divide between commercially oriented, New Light, eastern Connecticut and agriculturally oriented, Old Light, western Connecticut. Many churches, however, were split down the middle; in some cases New Lights seceded and formed autonomous congregations. The Old Lights marshaled their political strength to pass legislation restricting the activities of evangelical preachers. Some New Light judges were thrown off the bench, while New Light assemblymen were denied their seats in the legislature. In the 1760s the New Lights organized a political counterattack and drove the Old Lights from office. These New Light politicians ultimately provided Connecticut's Revolutionary political leadership.

As Connecticut's economy and religious life evolved, so, too, did its social life and legal culture. In the 17th century Puritan culture emphasized social order and consensus. The colony's laws were based on the legal code of the Old Testament. There was relatively little violent crime or sexual misconduct, and most debt and property disputes were resolved through arbitration rather than litigation. By the early 18th century, however, the courts were becoming much busier. Civil litigants increasingly relied on professional lawyers to plead their cases, and the courts gradually instituted a gendered double standard in adjudicating both fornication and slander suits. Divorce suits became more frequent. Evangelical religion, long-distance trade, and the passage of generations gradually eroded the influence of town meetings, village churches, and local gentlefolk, creating a more complex and individualistic society.

Further reading: Richard L. Bushman, *From Puritan to Yankee: Character and the Social Order in Connecticut, 1690–1765* (Cambridge, Mass.: Harvard University Press, 1967); Cornelia Hughes Dayton, *Women Before the Bar: Gender, Law, and Society in Connecticut, 1639–1789* (Chapel Hill: University of North Carolina Press, 1995).

—Darcy R. Fryer

consumption

Eighteenth-century North America witnessed a marked increase in the purchase and use of imported objects among white colonists. The previous century had seen basic improvements in standards of diet, dress, shelter, and furnishings for the wealthy. However, by the end of the 17th century these improvements started to move further down the social scale. Items of FOOD, drink, and CLOTHING that had been considered "luxuries" or even "decencies" started to become "necessities." Consumer objects had little productive or explicitly practical value; their purpose was cultural. Elites and nonelites alike spent ever-increasing amounts on goods that could indicate high social status. By midcentury even prisoners in a PHILADELPHIA poorhouse may have drunk "Bohea tea."

The most common consumer item was cloth. The wide variety of available dry goods made fashionable clothing, and the ability to appear fashionable, accessible even to society's middle and lower ranks. The second most popular consumer goods were groceries and related items: chocolate, sugar, and, most of all, tea and its accoutrements. Tea rapidly replaced coffee as the nonintoxicating drink of choice among all CLASSes. Moreover, most colonists aspired to turn tea-drinking into a social ritual through the use of specialized objects such as tea tables, cups, saucers, teapots, and silver spoons. By the middle of the 18th century almost every household in North America had at least part of a tea equipage, and in some urban counties even the poorest households had full sets. Even more than clothing, tea became a symbol of the colonists' connection to the BRITISH EMPIRE and its markets.

White women, who had long been responsible for the purchase of household goods, found increased cultural authority in consumerism. Women's purchasing allowed them to imitate London styles, thereby creating new standards of polite fashion and behavior. Tea tables became known as female spaces, and fashionable dress became women's prerogative.

One reason for this flood of goods into 18th-century North America was the contemporaneous increase in migration. The enormous mobility of the 18th-century Atlantic world had put new demands on social stratification. As so many people moved beyond the worlds in which they were known, other markers of elite status besides reputation had to be pressed into service. Consumer goods became new indicators of status hierarchies.

Social critics commented on the confusion between classes caused by the array of colorful clothing options and chinaware. Other critics feared the onset of an enervating luxury that might sap the strength of the colonies. They criticized fashionable women and men for their attention to goods and dependence on the consumer market. Their particular concern was the confusion of class hierarchies that consumer goods might provoke. Because so many people could don a fashionable dress, it seemed difficult to separate the elites from their social inferiors.

Eighteenth-century consumption differed from older status systems in its emphasis on the proper use of specific goods. Merely to own teacups or silver spoons was not enough; it became necessary to use them in specific gentrified spaces, such as parlors or assembly rooms. Carriage and demeanor likewise determined the acceptability of fashionable dress. Thus, behavior itself changed as a result of consumption.

Women and men of all classes participated in the consumer market. Those who could not afford to purchase newly imported cloth bought used clothes. Even criminals became consumers, stealing fashionable clothes, tea sets, and punch bowls. Taverns and pawnshops ran thriving businesses in secondhand consumer goods.

Consumerism was not limited to European immigrants. In Europe, for example, fashionable young men wore beaver hats made of pelts trapped by NATIVE AMERICANS. Native Americans, conversely, had been consuming European items since they met the first European traders. Indians often chose goods for other reasons than European fashions, such as ceremonial uses. They thus participated in the consumer market on their own terms. Many tribes became dependent on European metal goods, which eventually placed them at a disadvantage in their interaction with white people. However, Indians also recognized the social uses that colonists made of consumer goods, and by the 18th century some Indian diplomats, wearing laced hats and ruffled shirts, had become as fashionable as any colonial governor.

Further reading: Richard L. Bushman, *The Refinement of America: Persons, Houses, Cities* (New York: Vintage Books, 1992); Cary Carson, Ronald Hoffman, and Peter J. Albert, eds., *Of Consuming Interests: The Style of Life in the Eighteenth Century* (Charlottesville and London: University Press of Virginia for the United States Capital Historical Society, 1994).

—Serena Zabin

convict labor

The English government compelled some convicts to emigrate to the colonies to labor as indentured servants. The system of banishing convicts emerged in 1597, when English magistrates were given the power to exile rogues and vagabonds. Beginning in 1718, they used this discretion to transport convicted felons to the New World. Leaders in England considered their ability to exile convicts to be a major innovation in the administration of justice, and the system operated as an intermediate option between capital punishment and lesser sanctions, such as whipping and branding.

The system benefited Great Britain most. Shipping convicts to the colonies provided one means of ridding its society of its unwanted. Convict transportation spared Britain from having to build and maintain a massive prison system. British leaders paid little attention to the servants themselves. As one authority on the topic noted, they consigned them to a merchant and assumed no further responsibility. It is estimated that 50,000 convicts were transported to the colonies during the colonial period.

Colonial leaders reacted angrily when they realized that they were expected to receive convict servants. Chesapeake area residents accused Britain of dumping its "Scum and Dregs" on colonial shores. They assumed that convicts carried communicable diseases contracted in jail. More troublesome, though, was the potential for unrest from these servants. It seemed unlikely that convict servants would work hard, and colonists assumed that their presence would corrupt the very foundation of society, setting a bad example for honest people. A few colonies took steps to prevent convicts from landing on their shores. Some Caribbean colonies set firm population ratios between white and black residents. They refused convict servants because they were "not considered among the Whites." Jamaica passed a law to encourage white immigration and specifically excluded convicts. Transporting Britain's felons to the colonies engendered some of the most heated antiimperial debate before the American Revolution.

The majority of the convict servants worked in the colonies with the greatest demand for cheap labor, VIRGINIA and MARYLAND. Convicts arrived after the time when the labor system in the Chesapeake area had transformed from white indentured servants to black slaves. Convicts were shipped primarily to regions that were expanding economically and where planters were unable to obtain sufficient numbers of slaves. In Virginia they worked the TOBACCO and grain fields in the region north of the York River. In Maryland convicts landed in four of 14 counties, where they constituted about 7 percent of all labor. The economies of these four counties, Baltimore, Charles, Queen Anne, and Anne Arundel, relied primarily on tobacco production along with smaller quantities of grain and corn. Just before the Revolution, convicts appeared in the Virginia and Maryland backcountry. These more newly settled regions experienced intense labor shortages, and although planters preferred the labor of slaves, they purchased convicts if left with no other options. Western Maryland contained approximately 14,000 inhabitants, including fewer than 150 convict servants.

Further reading: A. Roger Ekirch, *Bound for America: The Transportation of British Convicts to the Colonies, 1718–1775* (New York: Oxford University Press, 1987).

—Sharon V. Salinger

Cooke, Elisha, Jr. (1678–1737)

Elisha Cooke, Jr., succeeded his father and namesake as leader of the opposition party in MASSACHUSETTS upon the latter's death in 1715. Cooke's party won control of the assembly beginning in 1720, in part because he and his followers created America's first political machine, the BOSTON Caucus. Thereafter, slates of caucus candidates were usually elected almost unanimously until Cooke's death. A wealthy physician, real estate owner, and hospitable fellow who was always ready for a drink, he was easily able to stand election expenses. Cooke served as Massachusetts's agent to England from 1723 to 1726 in an unsuccessful effort to convince the British government that Massachusetts was right in standing up to its governors. He continued to defend colonial rights and plague British governors until his death. His personal importance appears in the fact that after his death, the caucus went into eclipse as government supporters led by Thomas Hutchinson came to power. However, it came back in the 1760s, and thus Cooke is considered the forerunner of Revolutionary politicians such as Samuel Adams and James Otis.

Further reading: William Pencak, *War, Politics, and Revolution in Provincial Massachusetts* (Boston: Northeastern University Press, 1981).

—William Pencak

Cornbury, Lord See Hyde, Edward, Viscount Cornbury

Cornstalk (1720?–1777)

Cornstalk was an important leader among the Shawnee Indians for almost 25 years during the mid-18th century. He was born in central PENNSYLVANIA but as a child migrated with his people to eastern Ohio to escape the pressures of English colonization. Deeply influenced by the recurring migrations of native peoples, Cornstalk became a strong proponent of Indian land rights. During the SEVEN YEARS' WAR his Shawnee warriors attacked white settlements along the Pennsylvania and VIRGINIA frontiers. In 1763–64 Cornstalk supported a unified Indian resistance to British land encroachment and unpopular trade policies. Over the next decade he repeatedly struck Virginia settlements in the Shawnee-claimed hunting grounds along the Greenbriar River. His militant opposition to white encroachment made Cornstalk the principal target of Virginia governor Dunmore's military invasion of the Ohio country in 1774. Despite inflicting heavy losses on the Virginia militia at the Battle of Point Pleasant in September, Cornstalk was forced to surrender vast amounts of territory in what is now the state of West Virginia. Afterwards military reverses and the seemingly endless tide of colonial settlers induced Cornstalk to abandon military opposition in favor of peaceful interaction with the white settlers. In 1777, while trying to ameliorate escalating tensions between Indians and settlers, Cornstalk and his son were murdered by a mob of angry settlers at Fort Randolph, Virginia. His death triggered decades of conflict between the Shawnee and the United States, which did not conclude until the death of Tecumseh in 1813.

Further reading: Gregory Evans Dowd, *A Spirited Resistance: The North American Indian Struggle for Unity, 1745–1815* (Baltimore: John Hopkins University Press, 1992).

—Daniel P. Barr

Cotton, John (1585–1652)

John Cotton was the architect of Congregationalism in New England. Born in Derby, in the English midlands, Cotton attended Trinity College, Cambridge, receiving his B.A. in 1602 and his M.A. in 1606. At Trinity he heard William Perkins, whose sermons stressed the role of God's law in showing sinners their helplessness to save themselves, thus driving them to prepare for conversion; unfortunately, Cotton himself was only driven to dread Perkins's preaching. Later, after Cotton had joined the faculty of Emmanuel College, Cambridge, he heard Richard Sibbes, whose sermons stressed not the law and human preparation but the Gospel and divine initiative. In 1612 Cotton experienced that initiative in his own conversion.

Later the same year, Cotton took a pastorate in Boston, on England's Lincolnshire seacoast. There he spent the next 20 years evangelizing his community, catechizing his congregation, and coming to exercise great influence over English Puritanism's rising generation. After an early run-in with his bishop, he enjoyed at least a measure of peace until 1632, when the ANGLICAN CHURCH's Court of High Commission finally moved against him. He responded by donning a disguise, fleeing to London, hiding for several months, and then in 1633 sailing for MASSACHUSETTS, arriving in BOSTON on the same ship that carried THOMAS HOOKER.

Cotton was soon chosen to be the "teacher" of Boston's First (Congregational) Church, of which John Wilson was the pastor. While Cotton followed Sibbes in stressing the dissimilarities potentially differentiating one conversion experience from another and the convert's essential passivity in the face of God's irresistible grace, Wilson, instead, followed Perkins in stressing the fundamental similarity of all such experiences and the convert's active role of preparation. ANNE MARBURY HUTCHINSON, one of Cotton's English parishioners who had followed him across the Atlantic, responded that Wilson, Hooker, and other preparationist ministers were preaching salvation by works rather than faith. The result was the Antinomian Controversy of 1637–38, whose resolution left preparationist ministers in control and cast a cloud over Cotton's reputation.

If Cotton swam against New England's prevailing current with his understanding of conversion, he used his understanding of church government to help define that current's main channel. His most important publication on this topic was *The Keyes of the Kingdom of Heaven* (1644). He also helped to draft the Cambridge Platform of 1648, which gave New England Congregationalism its definitive form.

John Cotton *(Boston Public Library)*

Further reading: Kenneth Silverman, *The Life and Times of Cotton Mather* (New York: Harper & Row, 1984).

—George W. Harper

crafts

Through sheer necessity, colonial Americans engaged in a large variety of crafts. Initially, only the most basic craft services were available, with ARTISANS such as blacksmiths, wheelwrights, and house carpenters providing the products essential to everyday life. As the colonies expanded, so did the variety of trades followed by settlers. At the time of the Revolution, PHILADELPHIA, NEW YORK, BOSTON, and CHARLESTON contained a substantial number of artisans offering manufactures from silver sauceboats to schooners. Fewer artisans lived in the countryside, and backcountry settlers relied more heavily on home manufactures. Many of the poorer farmers were unable to afford the more expensive products of urban artisans, including mahogany furniture and jewelry that were purchased mostly by wealthy MERCHANTS and planters.

America's artisans were as diverse as their wares. Ranging from affluent master artisans with 10 or more employees to impoverished journeyman workers who roamed the country in search of a job, New World "mechanics" belonged to different CLASSES. They also came from different races. Thousands of enslaved artisans, or "handicraft slaves," lived in the southern colonies working as carpenters, tailors, shoemakers, wheelwrights, and blacksmiths, and laboring either on the properties of their planter owners or in the workshops of their mechanic masters. Slaves also fashioned common items like pottery and grass baskets for their own use, incorporating African traditions into their products.

NATIVE AMERICANS constituted a third significant group of artisans in colonial America. The pottery, mats, weapons, and CLOTHING produced by America's first peoples reflected the distinct cultures and customs of their various societies. Because Native Americans rarely left written records of their lives, these crafts have become tremendously important, as occasionally they are all that remain of the precontact and early settlement eras.

Further reading: Carl Bridenbaugh, *The Colonial Craftsman* (Mineola, N.Y.: Dover Press, 1990).

—Emma Hart

Creole

The term *Creole* has assumed several meanings and conjured as many images. Meaning "home-grown," the Latin word originally referred to any person of French or Spanish descent born in the colonies of the CARIBBEAN Basin. The Acadian exiles who settled in southern LOUISIANA represent the sole exception; they were called Cajuns. Thus, the original usage of *Creole* not only accounted for millions of inhabitants in the West Indies, the Gulf Coast, Mexico, and Central America, but also encompassed numerous ethnic combinations of Europeans, Africans, and Indians. Even in Louisiana, where the term has persisted to the present, scholars and inhabitants have disagreed on the exact meaning. At different times *Creole* has been applied to the white aristocracy, to residents of NEW ORLEANS and Baton Rouge, or to all of southern Louisiana's populace.

According to the inclusive definition, colonial Creoles of Louisiana represented a heterogeneous cultural and racial milieu. France hoped to establish Louisiana as a productive, slave-based, commercial colony—a larger version of Haiti. Toward this goal French officials offered attractive land grants to encourage planters to bring slaves into Louisiana, and they garrisoned their American empire with soldiers and criminals. French settlement of Louisiana, then, represented a multiclass and multiracial endeavor. The French slave societies of AFRICA and the West Indies directly influenced the culture of this new settlement. In Senegal, Saint-Domingue (Haiti), Martinique, and Guadeloupe a scarcity of European women and intimate daily contact between white and black people nurtured a general acceptance of racial mixing. This established colonial tradition of MISCEGENATION likewise took root in Louisiana.

Miscegenation lent a distinctive quality to Louisiana race relations. Masters manumitted thousands of their enslaved relatives. This liberated class formed the *gens de couleur libre* ("free people of color") and they continued to mix among themselves as well as with other black and white people and with Native Americans. As the races mixed, French, African, and Indian customs combined to create a unique culture. An ethnic fusion of language, MUSIC, DANCE, religion, and cuisine marked Creoles with a distinct cultural character that still exists. Not surprisingly, scholars employ the term creolization to describe the process of creating a distinctive, native culture from disparate cultural elements.

See also MULATTOES.

Further reading: Gwendolyn Midlo Hall, *Africans in Colonial Louisiana: The Development of Afro-Creole Culture in the Eighteenth Century* (Baton Rouge: Louisiana State University Press, 1992); Gary B. Mills, *The Forgotten People: Cane River's Creoles of Color* (Baton Rouge: Louisiana State University Press, 1977).

—C. B. Waldrip

crime and punishment

Crime and punishment run deep in the grain of colonial America. The Salem WITCHCRAFT Trials (1692) are the most well-known case of crime and punishment in the North American English colonies, symbolizing the centrality of religious beliefs in the 17th century and emblematic of the threats to order and stability, yet this spectacular instance of crime and punishment obscures a much more pervasive, if mundane, reality. Crime and punishment permeated the English colonies, grew in number and changed in nature from the 17th to the 18th century, and differed from colony to colony. Although certain groups were more likely to be found guilty and were punished more harshly, members of all classes engaged in some form of criminal activity.

During the 17th century powerful ideas about religion and social order overshadowed other explanations for crime and punishment. Small and scattered settlements may have fostered a neighborly environment for some, but people from outside a particular community were often viewed with suspicion and treated as criminals. Historians once believed that sailors, slaves, and NATIVE AMERICANS committed most crimes during the 17th century. Sailors were suspect because of their imprudent morality and slaves because, despite all pronouncements to the contrary, it was well understood that they had reason to rebel. Indians posed the principal threat to the colonists' claims to the land.

However, recent studies have shown that people from all racial and ethnic groups and age cohorts engaged in some type of criminal activity. Ministers and MERCHANTS were rarely disciplined for committing crimes. The most helpless Americans, in both early and modern times, suffered punishments disproportionately.

Crimes of the 17th century, dominated by religious concerns, included breaking the Sabbath, idolatry, blasphemy, and, of course, witchcraft. While MASSACHUSETTS led the way in this regard, VIRGINIA, perhaps the least religiously oriented of colonies, punished similar crimes. Public drunkenness, fighting, and swearing also incurred authorities' retributive justice.

In the 17th century punishments did not aim to rehabilitate. Jails were used primarily to hold suspects awaiting trial. Punishments were physical, publicly inflicted, and intended to make an example of the offender. Shaming penalties such as branding, displaying symbols (as in *The Scarlet Letter*), ducking, and sitting in the stocks and pillory were not used as frequently as were whips and fines. The lash of the whip fell overwhelmingly upon the backs of slaves, servants, apprentices, and the laboring and dependent classes. Fines were reserved for those who had committed infractions and were able to make restitution. This penalty, of course, ruled out servants and slaves, because they did not possess the resources to pay. Thieves paid extra damages in addition to restoring the stolen property. The more times an individual committed a crime, the harsher the penalty.

Punishments fell most heavily upon disobedient children, male and female slaves, single women (especially maidservants), Native Americans, and impoverished white males. In the 17th and 18th centuries men more frequently than women were accused and found guilty of crimes. The worst physical punishments were reserved for the enslaved population, although executions of slaves did not often occur because the slaves were expensive investments and therefore somewhat protected by the property-owning class.

Publicly executing an offender was, in many respects, the most dramatic punishment. The death penalty, although used less frequently than in England, could be visited upon rebellious sons as well as people who committed murder, infanticide, sexual offenses (fornication, bastardy, and sodomy), witchcraft, defying the ban on QUAKERS and JESUITS in Massachusetts, and rape (except when committed against black women). Under the court's sentence to be "hanged 'til you be dead," the condemned

This engraving shows a criminal being hanged in public. *(Hulton/Archive)*

offender marched from the jail to the gallows at an appointed time, a solemn affair calculated to leave an indelible impression upon the assembled crowd of spectators of the consequences of transgressions.

By the 18th century many small settlements had become established towns where there was considerable growth in wealth and population; the protection of property became central to defining the nature of crime and punishment. Prostitution, public drunkenness, and scandalous public behavior joined Sabbath breaking as the variety of crimes expanded. However, theft of property, including burglary and robbery, became the most prevalent offense. One form of theft was peculiar to slaves; they could steal themselves by escaping. Burning residences, crops, and other buildings of value to a landowner was a crime defined as endangering persons and property. In cities forgery, counterfeiting currency, picking pockets, and other forms of petty theft were among the crimes for which the poor most frequently endured punishment. The wealthy, although they lived off the backs of the laboring classes and slaves, did not often suffer for their economic crimes, just as elite criminals in the modern United States frequently escape harsh penalties.

Although prosecutions could only be private, the court system was public and became more complex as time progressed. Few early Americans were knowledgeable about the law, and, in general, free white men of property sat on juries and acted as judges. Courts did not function, however, to allow all colonists access. While white women and men had access to the courts, black people and Native Americans rarely were entitled to the legal "rights of Englishmen."

See also AFRICAN AMERICANS; SLAVE RESISTANCE; SLAVE TRADE.

Further reading: A. Leon Higginbotham, *In The Matter of Color: Race and the American Legal Process in the Colonial Period* (New York: Oxford University Press, 1978); Lawrence Meir Friedman, *Crime and Punishment in American History* (New York: Basic Books, 1994); Eric H. Monkkonen, ed., *Crime & Justice in American History: Historical Articles on the Origins and Evolution of American Criminal Justice,* 2 vols. (Westport, Conn.: Meckler, 1991).

—Leslie Patrick

Croghan, George (unknown–1782)

Of Scots-Irish origin, George Croghan began his long career as an "Indian trader" in PENNSYLVANIA around 1741 and developed tremendous influence over English trade because of his extensive lines of credit with British and colonial merchants and his close relations with the native population. He settled on the Aughwick Creek, west of the Susquehanna River, which became a way station for Ohio Indians traveling to PHILADELPHIA. There, he married the daughter of Mohawk chief Nickas, with whom he had a child, Catherine, who later married Joseph Brant. From 1752 to 1756 Croghan acted as a provincial agent to the Ohio Indians, including DELAWARE, IROQUOIS, Shawnee, Wyandot, and Twightwees at Logg's Town near present-day Pittsburgh. In exchange for gifts and promises of protection, he implored the Ohio Indians to reject their French alliances. Croghan's diplomatic efforts entailed more self-interest than self-sacrifice. Deeply in debt, he wanted to make sure that English traders, and his own firm in particular, maintained exclusive economic control over the Ohio Valley.

In 1756, as the SEVEN YEARS' WAR heated up, SIR WILLIAM JOHNSON, the newly appointed superintendent of Indian affairs in the northern colonies, made Croghan his deputy and representative. Croghan used his influence with Ohio Indians to negotiate an end to frontier violence. In the 1760s Croghan, still wearing two hats, conducted trade with Indians at Fort Pitt while acting as deputy superintendent of Indian affairs. He did not always succeed in either venture. Croghan failed to stop Ohio Indians from joining compatriots in the Great Lakes region against the English during PONTIAC'S REBELLION. He also suffered economic losses during the Seven Years' War and repeatedly petitioned the Pennsylvania government for compensation. After the Treaty of Fort Stanwix in 1768, Croghan speculated on land opened to settlement in the Ohio Valley. Ironically, his own economic interests further eroded peaceful relations with Indians along the frontier, which Croghan had been paramount in creating.

Further reading: Richard White, *The Middle Ground: Indians, Empires, and Republics in the Great Lake Region, 1650–1815* (New York: Cambridge University Press, 1991); James H. Merrell, *Into the American Woods: Negotiators on the Pennsylvania Frontier* (New York: Norton, 1999).

—Jane T. Merritt

Crow

The Crow Indians are a Native American tribe of the Siouan language family of the northern Plains culture area. Originally from the country around Lake Winnipeg in Manitoba, Canada, the Crow gradually began to move onto the prairie beginning in approximately 1500, before finally settling in the Yellowstone and Big Horn River Valleys of Montana and Wyoming some time before 1700. The Crow name for themselves is "Absarokee" or "Apsaruke," translated as "Children of the Large-beaked Bird." It is unknown to what bird this might refer, but early interpreters mistranslated this to mean the "Crow."

Initially a northeast woodlands tribe, the ancestral Crow were horticulturalists, cultivating maize (corn), several types of beans, and squash. According to tribal history, a severe drought forced the Crow to move westward onto the Plains. By about 1550 the Crow were part-time farmers and part-time bison hunters who settled near Devil's Lake in present-day northeastern North Dakota. Here, two chiefs, No Vitals and Red Scout, were each gifted by a great vision from the "One Above." Red Scout received an ear of corn and was told to settle down and plant that seed for their subsistence. No Vitals received a pod of TOBACCO seeds and was told to go west to the high mountains and plant the sacred seeds there. Using a woman's quarrel over meat as an excuse, some time between 1600 and 1625 No Vitals and his followers split away from Red Scout and began a journey that lasted a century. Red Scout's people remained behind, planted their corn, and became the Hidatsa tribe. No Vitals and his people eventually became the people now known as the Crow. During this century of wandering the Crow traveled north to Cardston, Alberta, then south to the Great Salt Lake, still farther south to the Canadian River in Texas and Oklahoma, and, finally, north, following either the Arkansas River or the Missouri River, eventually entering into what is now northern Wyoming and southern Montana before 1700.

As with many of the northern plains tribes, the Crow lived on the plains for perhaps as long as 100 years before acquiring horses. According to Crow folklore, around 1725 a Crow war party journeyed to the Green River area in present-day Wyoming and either purchased or stole a stallion from another tribe, probably the Shoshone. A more mystical story tells of a Crow man who saw strange ANIMALS in a dream. He later set out to find these animals and finally saw several emerge from a lake. He captured them and brought them to the Crow village. The Crow named this new animal Ichilay, which means "to search with," perhaps referring to its usefulness for searching for game and enemies. Soon the Crow became rich in horses and thus the target of raiding parties from other tribes.

The Crow culture was, in character, northern plains. Within their territory the Crow hunted, lived in hide tepees, fought with their neighbors, and, generally, built a life around the buffalo (bison). They were regarded as superb warriors and buffalo hunters easily recognized by their magnificently decorated CLOTHING. They were called Beaux Hommes ("Handsome Men") by the early French. The Crow social structure is rooted in their clan system, kinship established through matrilineal lines of descent, although still highly respectful of paternal kin. Deeply religious, the Crow practiced the Sun Dance and the Tobacco Society Ceremony, a uniquely Crow ritual of adoption.

Today, the majority of 9,155 Crow people live on the Crow Reservation in south-central Montana, south and east of Billings. The total area of the reservation is 2,235,093 acres, mostly grazing land and farmland.

Further reading: Peter Nabokov and William Wildschut, *Two Leggings: The Making of a Crow Warrior* (Lincoln: University of Nebraska Press, 1982).

—Walter Fleming

crowd actions

Throughout Europe in the early modern age, crowds frequently gathered to effect some common and specific end. Such crowds acted without official sanction but often enjoyed the informal support of rulers. Unlike today's "mobs," which sometimes are considered (rightly or wrongly) maniacally violent and inherently illegal, early modern crowds acted with a certain decorum and possessed some claim to legitimacy with authority figures. French and British crowds protested FOOD shortages, tax burdens, and price hikes by employing limited and symbolic violence. If bread prices soared, for example, English laborers might impale a loaf of bread on a staff and march to a bakeshop, demanding "fair" prices that would allow poorer people to purchase a basic necessity and permit bakers to earn a decent income. When crowds did resort to violence, they usually targeted property instead of persons. Women often participated in or even led European crowds, particularly those inspired by food shortages.

Material and political peculiarities in colonial North America altered patterns of crowd action. As in Europe, crowds in North America defended the prerogatives of ordinary people, and women often joined in crowd activities. However, the comparative abundance of food in the New World obviated the need for many bread riots, while the relative weakness of state authority encouraged some crowds to move beyond traditional demands. BACON'S REBELLION and LEISLER'S REBELLION, in particular, signified direct challenges to constituted power. In the 1670s thousands of ex-servants who had successfully worked off their indenture to pay off their passage to North America roamed colonial Virginia. They had few prospects of obtaining scarce land other than by seizing it from NATIVE AMERICANS. When a young gentleman named Nathaniel Bacon accused the colony's rulers of pandering to Indians and monopolizing all the arable lands, many of the discontented freedmen rallied behind him. For three months in 1676, Bacon's forces defied royal officials, plundered loyalists, and murdered Indians. They even burned JAMESTOWN on September 19. Only Bacon's death and the arrival of troops from England restored order.

In 1689 the governor of NEW YORK capitulated when the GLORIOUS REVOLUTION across the Atlantic dethroned his sovereign, James II. Into the resulting power vacuum stepped Jacob Leisler, a small merchant of German lineage. Leisler drew support from New York's laboring people and from Dutch inhabitants wearied of English domination. Leislerian crowds ransacked merchants' mansions during the summer of 1689, while their leaders freed imprisoned debtors and called for the popular election of justices of the peace and militia captains. In 1691 a new governor backed by the new monarchs, William and Mary, arrived to resume power. Recognizing the threat that the Leislerians posed, the governor had Leisler and his chief adjutant hanged and then, for good measure, decapitated.

Most crowds in colonial North America, however, concerned themselves with more pedestrian ends. They defended their presumed right to sell wares, settle land, and obtain subsistence. The typical crowd aimed not to topple rulers but to correct their abuses; not to overturn the social order but to return it to an imagined equilibrium. After Bacon's Rebellion Virginians resumed less dramatic crowd actions. In 1682 TOBACCO planters sought to stem the flow of their product to Europe. The transatlantic trade, they believed, mainly benefited royal officials and wholesalers. Thus, planters large and small cut down whole swaths of tobacco groves to deprive merchants of merchandise. Fifty years later a Tobacco Inspection Act threatened small planters who grew crops of marginal quality. In response inspection warehouses were torched across the Potomac region, often with the tacit approval of wealthy planters. These planters-turned-arsonists supplemented direct action with humble petitions to the Virginia Assembly. In upstate New York tension between TENANTS and Dutch patroons occasionally sparked serious riots as poorer people protested high rents. Crowds freed fellow tenants from prison—often by getting the sentries drunk—and refused to pay rents during lean years, but they rarely demanded redistribution of land or political power.

In BOSTON a midnight crowd dressed in clergymen's robes tore down a new public market in 1736 to preserve the old method of open food marketing. Such symbolic, limited crowd actions persisted above all in frontier regions. In Revolutionary MAINE squatters sometimes dressed like Indians to intimidate proprietors who sought to impose rents. These "White Indians" placed wood chips in their mouths while confronting proprietors, consciously cultivating a savage image in order to face down their opponents. Yet again, the rioters almost never injured anyone and aimed only to preserve the autonomy they enjoyed on their rude settlements.

Crowd actions reflected attitudes toward work and authority in colonial SOCIETY. The plebeian sense of fairness so evident in crowds' demeanor stemmed from a distinctly preindustrial work ethic. Ordinary people considered LABOR an inevitable burden with limited but absolute rewards. Few thought in terms of a career with graded advancements up the social scale. Rather, those who tilled their fields or tended their shops expected little more than a "decent competency" but demanded nothing else. The elites whom crowds faced generally agreed that diligent commoners deserved basic necessities. This shared sense of entitlement gave crowd actions their moderate, negotiated character and distinguished them from slave revolts.

Crowd actions frequently climaxed with a standoff between an assembly and a single gentleman. Sometimes the crowd intimidated the grandee and gained its demands, while other times the gentleman shamed the many into sheepish submission. Crowds thus exhibited the intensely personal and contingent nature of authority in early America, and the actions of crowds anticipated the popular resistance to Great Britain in the decade preceding the American Revolution.

Euro-Americans accorded scant legitimacy to the demands of AFRICAN AMERICANS and NATIVE AMERICANS. Slave revolts occasioned considerable violence and dread. In 1712 about 20 slaves, many still bearing their African names and tribal markings, may have set fire to a number of buildings in NEW YORK CITY. They had covered themselves with a sacred powder endowed with protective properties, but nothing could defend them from the savage response of the white authorities. Thirteen slaves were hanged on the gallows, three were burned at the stake, one starved in CAPTIVITY, and another was broken upon the wheel. A rash of mysterious fires and thefts in the same city in 1741 and 1742 inspired a similar round of arrests and tortures. The STONO REBELLION in SOUTH CAROLINA in 1739 constituted the largest slave revolt in early America. When the Spanish offered freedom to runaway slaves in FLORIDA, between 75 and 100 slaves rose up along the Stono River in 1739, killed some 30 white people, and headed toward Florida. However, the militia caught them first, and the rebellion ended in bloody repression. Native Americans likewise engaged not only in warfare against white people in British America but also in numerous revolts in the SPANISH COLONIES and FRENCH COLONIES, including the PUEBLO REVOLT in 1680, the NATCHEZ REVOLT between 1729 and 1731, and the PIMA REVOLT in 1751.

See also NEGRO PLOT OF 1741; SLAVE RESISTANCE.

Further reading: Paul A. Gilje, *Rioting in America* (Bloomington: University of Indiana Press, 1996).

—J. M. Opal

Culpeper, Thomas, Lord (1635–1689)
Son of Lord John and Judith Culpeper, Thomas inherited his father's title, estate, and a share of a 5.7 million-acre proprietorship in VIRGINIA. In 1673 Thomas and the earl of Arlington, Henry Bennett, were granted the quitrents of Virginia for 31 years. Lord Culpeper was commissioned governor of Virginia for life in 1675 but not sworn in until the death of Governor SIR WILLIAM BERKELEY.

Culpeper governed from London and went to Virginia only after Charles II forced him to go in 1680. Thomas was instantly popular as he pardoned offenses committed during BACON'S REBELLION, expanded the powers of the governor, and returned to England. In 1682 civil unrest forced Culpeper back to Virginia to implement royal prerogative and increase revenues at the expense of the planting CLASS. Despised by Virginians and out of favor with King Charles II (1660–85), Culpeper was tried for leaving his post. He died in London in 1689.

Further reading: Stephen Saunders Webb, *The Governors-General: The English Army and the Definition of the Empire, 1569–1681* (Chapel Hill: University of North Carolina Press, 1979).

—Eugene VanSickle

D

Dale, Sir Thomas (unknown–1619)

From 1610 to 1616 Thomas Dale served intermittently as the high marshal and deputy governor of the VIRGINIA colony. Dale began his career, like some of the officials who ruled Virginia in its first decades, as a mercenary in the army of the Dutch Estates General, in which he rose to a captaincy. In the Dutch service (1588–98, 1603–11) and with the earl of Essex's Irish expedition (1599–1600), Dale became acquainted with SIR THOMAS GATES, Sir Thomas West (subsequently Lord De La Warre), and Sir Robert Cecil, all of whom played major roles in the foundation of the Virginia colony. In 1611, just before his departure for Virginia, Dale married Elizabeth Throckmorton, daughter of Sir Thomas Throckmorton and Elizabeth Berkley, who was related to Sir Walter Raleigh. Dale's military service, powerful friends, and marriage are emblematic of the alliances of blood, marriage, and common service that tied together the upper CLASS males who led the English colonization of Gaelic Ireland and the Americas.

Knighted by James I in 1606 as "Sir Thomas Dale of Surrey," Dale won his appointment to the VIRGINIA COMPANY OF LONDON based on his reputation for bravery and discipline, two qualities necessary to bring order, health, and prosperity to a colony that had won the well-deserved enmity of its POWHATAN neighbors and had fallen into civil disorder, disease, and starvation. As deputy governor and later as governor when Gates departed in 1614, Dale labored mightily to insure the colony's survival.

The colony's central problem was its inability to raise FOOD and resulting dependency on corn traded or, just as often, pillaged from the Powhatan. This scarcity of foodstuffs was exacerbated by the work habits of the colony's laborers, who, in the eyes of gentlemen soldiers such as Dale, were of the "vulgar and viler sort," "roarers" and "loyterers" unwilling to work unless compelled by hunger or harsh discipline. Rather than allow the irregular, casual work habits of the preindustrial English, Gates and Dale imposed the military discipline of their Netherlands campaigns, forcing the plantation hands to work steady, regular hours, and accounting for their work against provisions disbursed to them by the company storehouse. Under their military regime codified in the *Lawes Divine, Morall and Martiall,* Virginia laborers were tortured and executed for crimes ranging from poor workmanship to seeking refuge with the Powhatan Indians. Dale's treatment of his subordinates was consistent with his belief in the correctional virtues of martial discipline and with genteel Europe's "bestialization" of the "lower orders"—the peasantry and vagrant laborers—who were traditionally likened to oxen, cattle, or swine and whose station in life was to serve the "better sort."

The new work regime alleviated but did not eliminate the colony's dependence on Indian foodstuffs. Dale also improved the health of the colonists somewhat by creating "particular plantations"—Henrico, Rochdale Hundred, and Bermuda City—away from the unhealthful lowlands surrounding JAMESTOWN. He granted independent farmers private allotments of land within these small, palisaded settlements where they could grow their crops and pasture their livestock in return for an annual "Rent of Corn" to the company. Dale's expansion of the settlements further complicated relationships with the POWHATAN CONFEDERACY. Both sides conducted a cruel guerrilla war against each other, a war that tipped in favor of Governor Dale when, in 1613, Captain Samuel Argall's expedition captured Powhatan's beloved daughter Matoaka (POCAHONTAS). Dale "laboured along time" to successfully induce Pocahontas to renounce "publickly her countrey Idolatry" and embrace Christianity. From this conversion and her subsequent marriage to colonist JOHN ROLFE sprang a nine-year truce with the Powhatan.

Dale left for England in 1616, leaving the Virginia Colony with an uneasy peace and prosperity greater than when he first landed on its shores. In 1617 Dale was appointed commander of an East India Company fleet that sailed for the East Indies to challenge the Dutch domination of the eastern trade. His forces clashed with a Dutch fleet in 1619 in a "cruel bloody fight" near Java. While provisioning his fleet in India, Dale fell ill and died "after twenty days of languishing sickness and many testimonies of good Christianity, contempt of death, and singular zeal and affection towards the Company's service."

Further reading: Darrett B. Rutman, "The Historian and the Marshal: A Note on the Background of Sir Thomas Dale" (*Virginia Magazine of History and Biography*, LXVII [1960], 284–94).

—James Bruggeman

dance

In the 17th and 18th centuries colonial dance featured a variety of forms, origins, and purposes. Colonial dance contained significant CLASS and ethnic divisions, as the wealthy European gentry (or landed aristocracy), poorer colonial laborers, enslaved Africans, and NATIVE AMERICANS each danced according to the rhythms of their unique cultural and ethnic heritages.

Wealthy white colonists enjoyed emulating distinctly European dance forms, often hiring formal dance instructors knowledgeable about popular European dances and purchasing elaborate musical instruments with which to accompany their dances. Despite a burgeoning colonial culture of dance—often developed through the integration of ethnic and distinctly colonial techniques—it nevertheless remained fashionable for wealthier colonists to dance in strictly European forms. The colonial gentry danced in their opulent homes for smaller audiences; most often women and young girls danced to demonstrate skills befitting their social and economic class. Outside the private sphere the colonial elite enjoyed formal public dances (such as dances following theater performances), where elite couples would perform their well-practiced formal dances before an audience. Wealthy colonists attempted to maintain their social standing in part through their solitary claim on formal European dance forms.

Poorer European colonists enjoyed dancing without the strict form and structure often followed by their "betters." Unable to purchase expensive instruments, the less well-to-do colonists danced to the accompaniment of "Jew's harps" and homemade instruments, such as flutelike wind instruments. The average colonist enjoyed community dances that avoided the strict formality of traditional dance, instead opting to dance in free-form jigs, hornpipes, and reels. The latter involved a blend of individual dancing interspersed with individual dancers weaving figure eights around other solitary and stationary dancers.

Nevertheless, these sharp class divisions did not endure indefinitely. The early 18th century welcomed the advent of dance writing, such as John Essex's *The Dancing-Master: or the Art of Dancing Explained* (London, 1725). This new writing technique allowed authors to record specific dance steps. Although dance writing did not immediately integrate the upper- and lower-class colonial dance experience, it loosened a portion of the colonial elite's stranglehold on the knowledge of fashionable European dance.

For slaves, 17th- and 18th-century dances enhanced African cultural identity and provided an expressive outlet for an oppressed segment of colonial society. Enslaved Africans used dance to celebrate, socialize, worship, pray, and relax. African dances often conjoined the spiritual and secular experience. African culture manifested through unique dances thrived in the American colonies. One African dance, the "Ring Dance," featured barefoot men and women encircled, dancing rhythmically to the sound of their shuffling feet, clapping hands, and collective voice. In a concrete manner, African dance fostered a vibrant culture of resistance fueled by dance's capacity to nurture unique cultural and ethnic heritages.

Similar to the African-American dance experience, Native American dance sustained indigenous culture. Archaeological evidence and Native American oral history demonstrate that dance was an integral component in virtually all Native American tribes long before the European arrival. During colonial times Native American dance continued to have widespread spiritual and cultural significance, including celebration, religious prayer, courting rituals, and controlling or harmonizing with nature. These dances featured a vast array of forms, as NATIVE AMERICANS danced to the sounds of their unique regional and tribal voices, drums, and rattles. By retaining important cultural and spiritual practices, dance sustained a vibrant Native American culture throughout the colonial period.

—Christopher Rodi

Dare, Virginia (1587–unknown)

Virginia Dare was the first English child born in North America. Daughter of Ananias Dare, a bricklayer, and Eleanor Dare, daughter of John White, the governor of the fledgling Roanoke colony, Virginia was born in August 1587. The presence of women and children in the 1587 Roanoke colony signaled a fundamental shift in English strategy to populate the island, moving from a military PRIVATEERING base to an effort to establish a more permanent colony with families as a stabilizing force. Unfortunately, the 1587 group was destined to become the famous "Lost Colony" of Roanoke. When Governor White left the colony to return to England for supplies shortly after Virginia's birth, the arrival of the Spanish Armada off the English coast delayed his return until 1590. When he finally reached the site of the settlement, White discovered an abandoned fort and indications that the settlers had moved to a nearby island. The colonists were never found, however, and their fate remains a mystery.

Further reading: Karen Ordahl Kupperman, *Roanoke: The Abandoned Colony* (Totowa, N.J.: Rowman & Allanheld, 1984).

—Melanie Perreault

Dartmouth College

Dartmouth College had its roots, like several other colonial educational initiatives, in the preachings of GEORGE WHITEFIELD and the enthusiasm of the GREAT AWAKENING. ELEAZAR WHEELOCK, a Yale graduate and Congregational minister in Lebanon, CONNECTICUT, was inspired by Whitefield and turned that inspiration into a desire to educate Native American boys who could then return to their people to serve as missionaries. Wheelock carried out his teaching from his own house at first, but in 1754 he gained the support of Colonel Joshua Moor, a local landowner. The result was Moor's Indian Charity School.

Wheelock attempted to gain a formal charter for his academy in the early 1760s but was turned down by the upper house of the Connecticut Assembly, perhaps out of fear that the school at Lebanon might compete for admissions with Yale College. The years that immediately followed proved difficult ones for Wheelock and the Indian school. Although he had educated 29 Indian boys and 10 Indian girls as well as eight white students, the number of NATIVE AMERICANS seeking admission declined significantly. Competition was one factor in that decline: KING'S COLLEGE in NEW YORK, under the direction of President Myles Cooper, was attempting to draw in Indian students to the Anglican EDUCATION being provided there. SIR WILLIAM JOHNSON, the commissioner of Indian affairs, let it be known that he preferred missionaries of the established church among native peoples. Wheelock realized that his plans to train missionaries to Native Americans would require that he train white students to carry out that work. Rather than face the competition of Yale and opposition from Connecticut's leaders, Wheelock accepted the offer of land and a collegiate charter from NEW HAMPSHIRE governor John Wentworth in 1769.

Further reading: Jurgen Herbst, *From Crisis to Crisis: American College Government, 1636–1819* (Cambridge, Mass.: Harvard University Press, 1982).

—George W. Boudreau

Founding of Dartmouth College *(Billy Graham Center)*

Davenport, James (1716–1757)

A significant preacher during the GREAT AWAKENING, James Davenport received his B.A. from Yale College in 1732 and was ordained a Presbyterian minister in 1738. In 1740, while serving as a pastor on Long Island, he heard the Anglican itinerant preacher GEORGE WHITEFIELD, then on his first tour of America. During this initial surge of the Great Awakening, Davenport determined to follow Whitefield's example, abandoning his pastorate and preaching his way across New England. His campaign culminated in 1741 with a visit to New Haven, CONNECTICUT. He warned Yale's students against their president, cautioned the townspeople against their pastor, and even established a separatist congregation for those residents he considered truly regenerate. Connecticut's legislature responded by banning itinerancy. When he returned in 1742, he was convicted of disturbing the peace and deported to NEW YORK.

Davenport next visited BOSTON, MASSACHUSETTS, but most local ministers, even the awakening's supporters, closed their churches' doors to him. He consigned these critics to hell, preaching in the open streets and finding an audience among the urban poor. As before, the authorities took action, this time declaring him insane and again deporting him to New York. In 1743 he made one last foray, visiting New London, Connecticut, where he persuaded his listeners that in order to be saved they must destroy their "idols." They responded by burning books and then building a bonfire for much of their CLOTHING, including Davenport's own trousers. To the awakening's defenders, such actions were an aberration; to its detractors, though, they were the norm. In 1744 Davenport published an apology, *Confessions and Retractions.* He continued in the ministry until his death, serving as moderator of the Presbyterian Synod of New York in 1754.

Further reading: Edwin Scott Gaustad, *The Great Awakening in New England* (New York: Harper & Row, 1957).

—George W. Harper

Davies, Samuel (1723–1761)

Presbyterian minister and college president, Samuel Davies was born on November 3, 1723, in New Castle County, DELAWARE. He was the first son of Welsh parents David Davies, a farmer, and his second wife, Martha Thomas. He was educated at local elementary schools and prepared for the ministry at the Fagg's Manor school in Chester County, PENNSYLVANIA. There, he was influenced by the school's founder, Samuel Blair, a "New Light" Presbyterian minister. Upon completion of his studies in 1746, he was licensed to preach by the New Castle Presbytery. In 1747 he was ordained and assigned to vacant congregations in Hanover and surrounding counties in southeastern VIRGINIA. Because the Church of England was legally established in the colony, he had to contend for the right of Dissenters to preach and worship in the colony.

So many Anglicans joined Davies's congregations that the Synod of New York formed the Hanover Presbytery in 1755. Davies was its first moderator. The synod sent him with GILBERT TENNENT, JR., in 1753 to Great Britain to collect donations for the College of New Jersey. In 1759 he was appointed its president. Davies was a prolific writer whose sermons, hymns, and poems were published and distributed widely in North America and Great Britain.

Davies's first wife, Sarah Kirkpatrick, whom he married in 1746, died in childbirth. A year later he married Jane Holt, with whom he had six children, five of whom survived him. His health, never strong, was weakened by overwork and tuberculosis, and he died on February 4, 1761.

Further reading: George W. Pilcher, *Samuel Davies: Apostle of Dissent in Colonial Virginia* (Knoxville: University of Tennessee Press, 1971).

—John B. Frantz

Day, Stephen (1594?–1668)

Stephen Day (sometimes spelled Daye) is often credited as being the first printer in the American colonies, a claim buttressed by the decision in 1641 of the General Court of MASSACHUSETTS to grant him 300 acres for being "the first that set upon printing." There are, however, serious doubts concerning the validity of this claim, just as there are doubts on most of the details concerning his life.

Born in England, Day arrived in New England in 1638 with Reverend Jose Glover, a wealthy dissenting minister who intended on establishing a printing press in Cambridge, Massachusetts. Day, listed in legal documents as a locksmith, possibly was hired by Glover to put together the cumbersome press upon its arrival in Cambridge. When Glover died from a fever during the voyage, his widow, Elizabeth, maintained ownership of the press and retained Day to do the printing. Six months later the first item to come off the Cambridge press was *The Oath of a Free-Man,* a broadsheet containing an oath that every adult householder had to sign in order to become a legal citizen. Perhaps Stephen's son, Matthew, was responsible for this publication, because he may have served a four-year apprenticeship to a printer in England, while Stephen was barely literate. Day's press printed the first book in the American colonies, the *Bay Psalm Book* (1639). Day's career as a printer ended in 1648, when Henry Dunster, the president of Harvard College and the second husband of Elizabeth, forced him out and sold the press to the college, where it served as the foundation for Harvard University Press.

Further reading: Benjamin Franklin V., *Boston Printers, Publishers, and Booksellers, 1640–1800* (Boston: G.K. Hall, 1980).

—Kenneth Pearl

Deerfield Massacre (1704)

This gruesome episode in QUEEN ANNE'S WAR became famous among English Americans as a case study in the nature of frontier warfare. Deerfield, a small community of nearly 300 at the confluence of the Connecticut and Deerfield Rivers (just south of present-day VERMONT), stood at the edge of the New England frontier. In February 1704 a force of French regular soldiers, *coureurs de bois,* and their Native American allies descended upon the town, killing 44 men, women, and children and capturing another 109. Twenty-one captives died on the journey north to Canada.

After nearly three years of CAPTIVITY, John Williams, the town's minister, returned home to write *The Redeemed Captive Returning to Zion* (1707), which became a best-seller and was republished in several editions. Williams recounted his experiences as a captive, the killing of two of his children and his wife, and his struggles against the Catholic priests who worked to convert him and his children. In the end, he and his sons returned with their faith secure. His daughter Eunice, however, chose to remain in Canada. Like 29 other captives, principally young children, she made her life with her father's enemies.

Further reading: Richard I. Melvoin, *New England Outpost: War and Society in Colonial Deerfield* (New York: Norton, 1989); John Demos, *The Unredeemed Captive: A Family Story from Early America* (New York: Knopf, 1994).

—Michael C. Batinski

Dekanawideh (Deganawideh, Dekanahwidah) (1550?–1600?)

Dekanawideh, the "Peacemaker," was a legendary Haudenosaunee ("People of the Longhouse," or IROQUOIS) who introduced the Law of Great Peace to the warring Haudenosaunee tribes and prompted the confederation of the Five Nations—Mohawk, Oneida, Onondaga, Cayuga, and Seneca (the TUSCARORA joined about 1722). The name Dekanawideh (Deganawidah) is variously translated as "setting his teeth together" and "two river currents flowing together." Little about this legendary figure is certain. Concurrent but not clearly fixed, the dates of the Iroquois confederation and Dekanawideh range from the mid-14th century to the early 17th century. Likewise, Dekanawideh's origin and heritage are variously explained: He was a HURON, an Onondaga adopted by the Mohawk, a healing spirit, a holy man born of a virgin mother, or the reincarnated Good Twin of Iroquois creation myth.

Apart from these differences, Dekanawideh is a crucial figure in Iroquois history and in U.S. history as well. Surviving versions of Dekanawideh's story share a basic narrative in which the visionary consoles Hiawatha (Hayonhwatha), a noble Mohawk who mourns the losses caused by interminable warfare. After teaching Hiawatha the Rituals of Condolence, Dekanawideh communicates his vision of Great Peace (Ka-yah-ne-renh-ko-wah) and presents the great white WAMPUM belt (Ska-no-dah-ken-rah-ko-wah) and the eagle feather (Ska-weh-yeh-seh-ko-wah). Dekanawideh and Hiawatha pacify the war despot Tadodahoh by combing snakes from his hair and initiate him as the first Firekeeper of the Confederacy. Hiawatha travels from tribe to tribe professing Dekanawideh's plan, which includes the Tree of Great Peace (Ska-renj-heh-se-go-wah) and detailed procedures for the annual Confederate Council meeting around the council fire. The council consists of fifty chiefs (Rodiyaner), each appointed by female clan leaders of his respective tribe. Today, the League of Six Nations continues to function according to Dekanawideh's code. Some recent scholarship argues for a direct Iroquois influence in shaping U.S. democracy and constitutional government.

Further reading: Colin G. Calloway, *First Peoples: A Documentary Survey of American Indian History* (Boston: Bedford, 1999); Bruce E. Johansen, *Native America and the Evolution of Democracy.* (Westport, Conn.: Greenwood, 1999).

—Keat Murray

De Lancey, James (1703–1760)

An important NEW YORK politician and judge, James De Lancey, whose family were French Huguenots who immigrated to New York after the 1685 revocation of the Edict of Nantes, inherited a great merchant fortune from his father. He attended law school in England before returning to New York to practice law. Named to the New York Supreme Court in 1731, he was elevated to chief justice by Governor William Cosby, who needed De Lancey's political support to use the Supreme Court as a court of exchequer for the colony. In that position De Lancey presided over the JOHN PETER ZENGER case, in which he attempted to protect the governor by disqualifying Zenger's attorneys until faced with the impeccable ANDREW HAMILTON. As leader of the free-trade political faction, De Lancey supported currency expansion and the primacy of the colonial legislature over the governor, a position that led to problems with Governor William Clinton's plans for defending the colony in 1743. Clinton's plans would have alienated MERCHANTS key to De Lancey's faction by replacing them with government commissioners.

Despite this, De Lancey presided over the ALBANY CONGRESS in 1754, promising the IROQUOIS Indians that their land would never be seized without compensation. In 1755 he parted with his own political faction over a land tax and the colony's policies in the SEVEN YEARS' WAR. Instead, he allied himself to William Johnson, the powerful Clinton-appointed agent to the Iroquois. So displeased was De Lancey with MASSACHUSETTS governor William Shirley's prosecution of the war that he successfully petitioned the government in London to have him removed. During the war De Lancey also spearheaded the establishment of KING'S COLLEGE (now Columbia University) as a publicly supported but officially Church of England institution, defying the powerful Presbyterian Livingston faction.

De Lancey continued to serve as chief justice until his death in 1760. His son, James De Lancey, continued his political policies and was a prominent Loyalist during the American Revolution, leading to the confiscation and forfeiture of the De Lanceys' substantial estates and fortune.

Further reading: D. A. Story, *The De Lanceys: A Romance of a Great Family* (London: T. Nelson, 1931).

—Margaret Sankey

De Lancey family (1686–1763)

The De Lancey family was one of the foremost in 18th-century NEW YORK. It built its preeminence through trade, real estate investments, strategic marriage alliances, and the steady accretion of political power. Étienne (Stephen) De Lancey (1663–1741), the founder of this aristocratic New York clan, descended from a wealthy Huguenot family. He fled Normandy, France, following the Edict of Nantes (1685) and, in 1686, arrived in NEW YORK CITY, where he established a leading mercantile house that specialized in supplying the goods that Albany merchants bartered for furs. Stephen served as New York City alderman (1691–93) and member of the New York Assembly (1702–09; 1710–15; 1725–37). In 1700 he married Anne Van Cortlandt, daughter of Stephanus (1643–1700), a Dutch landowning aristocrat who at his death was chief justice of the New York Supreme Court.

Five of Stephen's 10 children survived into adulthood. James (1703–60), an English-educated attorney, in 1728 married Anne, daughter of CALEB HEATHCOTE, one of the province's wealthiest men. The family's most gifted politician, James became a member of the Governor's Council (1729–53), chair of the commission appointed to draft the Montgomery Charter for New York City (1730), justice of the colony's Supreme Court (1731–33); and chief justice (1733–60). Appointed lieutenant governor in 1747, he served twice as acting governor (1753–55; 1757–60). He died suddenly on July 30, 1760. Peter (1705–70) represented the Borough of Westchester in the Assembly from 1750 to 1768, at which time he stepped aside for his son John. In 1737 Peter married Elizabeth, daughter of CADWALLADER COLDEN, New York's lieutenant governor from 1761 to 1776. Oliver (1718–85) attained his EDUCATION in his father's trading house before becoming a successful merchant in his own right. Though he could be belligerent and lacked James's urbanity, he still had a notable political career: alderman (1754–57), assemblyman (1759–60), and councillor to the governor (1760–83). A loyalist in the Revolution, he died in Yorkshire, England, in 1785. Susannah (1707–91) married Sir Peter Warren, hero of Louisbourg (1745) and member of Parliament (1747–52), who shrewdly advanced the De Lancey interests in London. In 1742 Anne (1723–75) married John Watts, Oliver's business partner, assemblyman (1752–57), and councillor to the governor (1758–76).

Because many De Lanceys became Loyalists in the American Revolution and refugees by the war's end, the family's power declined rapidly with Britain's defeat.

Further reading: William Smith, Jr., *History of the Province of New York*, ed. Michael Kammen, 2 vols. (Cambridge, Mass.: Harvard University Press, 1972).

—Joseph S. Tiedemann

Delaware

Delaware was the second smallest of the 13 original colonies. The boundaries of colonial Delaware contained just 1,982 square miles, divided among three counties: New Castle (the northernmost county), Sussex (the southernmost and largest county), and Kent (situated between Sussex and New Castle). The southern portion of colonial Delaware rested squarely on broad Atlantic coastal plains and contained approximately 190 square miles of wetlands. The northwestern portion of the colony yielded to gently undulating foothills, most prominent in New Castle County. The Delaware River and Delaware Bay dominated the landscape, as the river flowed from north to south, past the towns of New Castle and Wilmington and into the Delaware Bay, ultimately emptying into the Atlantic Ocean. In part due to the trade advantages associated with the region's proximity to a navigable river and the Atlantic Ocean, European powers competed for control of the region.

Original Inhabitants

Archaeological evidence suggests that as early as 6500 B.C.E. nomadic hunters and gatherers subsisted within the Delmarva Peninsula. Between 1000 and 1300 C.E. indigenous populations began developing less nomadic methods of hunting and gathering as they increasingly relied on local FISHING spots and rudimentary agricultural production methods. Thus, by the time Europeans arrived in the region, Native American communities had enjoyed thousands of years of uninterrupted use of the Delmarva Peninsula's FORESTS, streams, wetlands, and bays.

When the first European colonists arrived in the early 17th century, three indigenous tribes considered the Delmarva Peninsula their homeland. The two most prevalent Native American tribes, the Lenope and the Lenape, shared a common, although slightly varied, ALGONQUIN language. The Lenope and Lenape became distinct tribes in about 1300 C.E. The two tribes migrated seasonally, relied on the fishing resources of seasonal fish migrations and the hunting resources of Delaware's virgin forests, and lived adjacent to the Delaware River and the Delaware Bay. The third Native American tribe, the Nanticoke, lived in the southwest portion of the Delmarva Peninsula in what would later be known as Sussex County. The European colonists referred to these three culturally and ethnically distinct Native American tribes as Delaware Indians.

The relationship between the Lenape and the European colonists is emblematic of the overall relationship between Delaware Indians and the colonists. Beginning in the early 17th century, the Lenape enjoyed more than 50 years of cordial trading with Dutch and Swedish colonists. This often mutually beneficial relationship continued while Quaker-dominated PENNSYLVANIA ruled the Delaware colony.

Yet, the story of European encroachment on native lands does not involve simply peaceful trading relationships. By the mid-18th century a combination of European settlement of native hunting grounds, European diseases (to which the Native American population lacked immunity), and a growing European population forced the NATIVE AMERICANS from the lands of their ancestors. This involuntary diaspora resulted in the Lenape's mid-18th-century migration, first to western Pennsylvania (to profit from the lucrative FUR TRADE), and subsequently to Ohio, Canada, and, in some cases, past the Mississippi River to present-day Oklahoma. Despite the Lenape's forced eviction from land their ancestors had roamed for more than 1,000 years, the Lenape language and culture survive to this day.

European Control of Delaware

The European control of the Delaware colony often resembled an imperial game of musical chairs; many major European powers—including England, the Netherlands, and Sweden—competed for an opportunity to sit in Delaware's chair. It would not be until England wrested control of Delaware from the Dutch in 1664 that the music would finally stop, with England in sole control of Delaware.

Attempting to locate a northwestern water route to Asia, Dutch explorer HENRY HUDSON voyaged into the Delaware River (what he called "South River") in 1609, marking the initial European foray into the Delmarva Peninsula. The Dutch did not attempt a permanent settlement until 1631, when they established a 28-man settlement at Cape Henlopen on Lewes Creek named Zwaanendeal. Ostensibly aimed at harvesting and selling the lucrative whale oil evident in Delaware Bay's abundant whale population, the settlement lasted less than a year before an unknown band of local Indians killed the colonial settlers, purportedly due to a misunderstanding resulting from an Indian "theft" of a Dutch tin coat of arms. The Dutch did not attempt to resettle in the Delaware region for another 24 years.

In 1638 the New Sweden Company established a permanent settlement on Minquan Kil (eventually renamed Christiana River to honor the queen of Sweden). As the Thirty Years' War (1618–48) raged on the European continent, Sweden aimed to become a strong colonial power, yet from 1648 to 1654 the Swedish settlement did not receive any supply shipments from Sweden. The initial settlement did not number more than 200 Swedes and Finns and ultimately failed to create Swedish hegemony in the Delmarva Peninsula.

By 1655 disputes over the control of the Delaware River and the fur trade that relied on the river's transportation caused the Dutch to reassert control of the Delmarva Peninsula. In that year the Dutch captured the Swedish Fort Christiana and incorporated Delaware into the preexisting NEW NETHERLAND. Dutch colonial successes, however, were short lived, as their appetite for colonial power collided with a more robust and powerful English appetite for colonial supremacy.

In 1664 a British naval force commanded by James, duke of York (who in 1685 became King James II of England), captured NEW AMSTERDAM. A smaller group of warships commanded by Sir Robert Carr subsequently attacked the Dutch stronghold at New Amstel. The British renamed this northern Delaware town New Castle. From 1664 to 1682 a deputy of the duke of York governed the Delaware region as a portion of the English colonial possession.

In 1682 European possession of the colony again changed hands, although this time not between countries but rather between citizens of the same country. Maintaining ultimate English control of Delaware, WILLIAM PENN, proprietor of PENNSYLVANIA, requested and obtained control of the Delaware region from the duke of York. Penn allowed the northernmost of the three counties to remain named New Castle, but he renamed the two southernmost counties Kent and Sussex.

The Delaware colony was not yet independent, as Delaware remained a collection of counties belonging to Pennsylvania, alternately known as the "Government of the Counties of New Castle, Kent, and Sussex on Delaware" or simply as the "Lower Counties." William Penn's Act of Union in 1682 ensured that residents of the Lower Counties received an equal voice in Pennsylvania's General Assembly. Despite Penn's attempts to maintain union among Pennsylvania and the Lower Counties—including having the General Assembly meet in New Castle in 1684, 1690, and 1700, away from its traditional seat of power in PHILADELPHIA—Quaker-dominated Pennsylvania and the more heterogeneous Lower Counties were unable to coexist in the same legislature.

In 1701 William Penn allowed the divided legislative assembly to meet separately. In 1704 Delaware's assembly met independently for the first time in New Castle. Although meeting in a separate assembly, the Penn family's proprietary relationship to Delaware would continue until the Revolutionary War.

Slavery and the Delaware Economy

Beginning in the mid-17th century, enslaved African labor provided the backbone of Delaware's ECONOMY. Swedish control of Delaware (1638–55) brought a limited number of African slaves to the region due in part to the limited maritime assets of the New Sweden Company, yet after only nine years of Dutch control (and colonial access to the DUTCH WEST INDIA COMPANY's thriving slave trade), in 1664 slaves already represented approximately 20 percent of the Lower County population. Whereas European indentured labor provided the impetus to successful economies in early VIRGINIA and MARYLAND (later to be shifted to slave labor), Delaware's economy lacked sufficient indentured servants; as a result, slave labor almost exclusively developed Delaware's economy.

The late-17th and early-18th century agricultural economy encountered fluctuating (although often high) prices for domestically produced TOBACCO, corn, and wheat. By the mid-18th century tobacco ceased to be a lucrative crop in Delaware, and large planters increasingly used slave labor to produce wheat and corn.

Delaware on the Eve of Revolution

On the eve of the American Revolution, Delaware had attained its status as one of America's 13 original colonies. European settlement, westward expansion, and DISEASE had caused the death or migration of the vast majority of the colony's Native American population. In 1770 between 20 and 25 percent of Delaware's population was of African descent, and more than 95 percent of the African population continued their enslaved toil in the fields, homes, and parlors of the affluent members of Delaware's white society. Although initially hesitant to sign the Articles of Confederation, Delaware became the first state to ratify the United States Constitution.

Further reading: John A. Munroe, *History of Delaware* (Newark: University of Delaware Press, 1993); William H. Williams, *Slavery and Freedom in Delaware 1639–1865* (Wilmington, Del.: Scholarly Resources Books, 1996).

—Christopher Rodi

Delaware (Lenape, Lenni Lenape)

When the Europeans arrived in the early 17th century, three cultures—the Lenape, Munsee, and Lenope—lived along the Delaware River, then known to Europeans as the "South" river. These Algonquin speakers initially were called "River Indians" by the colonists, but after renaming the river the Delaware Europeans called them "Delaware Indians" or simply "Delaware." A fourth culture in that area, sometimes included with the "Delaware," was the Ciconicin (Sikonese), first identified as the "Bay Indians" due to their location on Delaware Bay and because their horticultural lifestyle differed from the River Indians.

In the 19th century some observers adopted the "Heckewelder equation" to describe the three cultures, linking the Turtle clan with the Lenape, the Wolf with the Munsee, and the Turkey with the Lenope. The histories of these three cultures differ somewhat. Before 1000 C.E. the ancestors of all three cultures were among the small, wide-ranging bands that foraged throughout the Middle Atlantic region of the Eastern Woodland zone. Between 1000 and 1200 these foragers developed strategies that were specific to smaller areas. Archaeologically, this is evident in the transition from the Middle Woodland Period (ca. 0 to A.D. 1000) to the Late Woodland Period (ca. 1000 to ca. 1750), when the bow and arrow were developed. By 1300 each group had developed an intensive foraging lifestyle (involving FISHING, hunting, and gathering of foodstuffs) adapted to a specific territory. These cultural patterns were in operation when Europeans first made records of these peoples in the early 17th century.

The best known of the three cultures is the Lenape. Their long and cordial relations with WILLIAM PENN and the QUAKERS in PENNSYLVANIA followed more than 50 years of peaceful trade and land sales with Dutch and Swedish colonists. These were among the longest peaceful relations between NATIVE AMERICANS and European colonists. The Lenape occupied the west side of the lower Delaware River from Old Duck Creek (now the Leipsig River) in northern Delaware to Tohiccon Creek, just south of the Lehigh River. The Lenape were organized into 13 matrilineal bands, each of which used one of the drainage streams that fed the Delaware River. The principal FOOD of the Lenape was the eight species of anadromous fish (including shad, alewives, and striped bass) that spawned in their territory. Other foods were abundant in this region, particularly in the rich swamps and marshes associated with the river system. Migratory waterfowl, their eggs and chicks, and a rich supply of plants provided the Lenape with an extensive and varied diet while at their "summer" fishing stations.

Each Lenape band established a warm weather fishing station in late winter to take advantage of the huge fish migrations that lasted into November. The women of the lineage gathered fish from these overlapping spawning runs. These fishing stations, used seasonally for between five and 15 years, occupied vaguely defined areas within which the individual families of the band could set up their wickiups near those of their immediate kin. In the fall, with fish and nuts still plentiful and wild ANIMALS fattened for winter, the Lenape held their "annual renewal ceremonies." All Lenape from every band gathered at one of the fishing stations to feast, arrange marriages, and carry out other family matters.

Like most Native Americans in the area, the Lenape migrated seasonally. At the beginning of winter, when the fish runs had ended and gathering of resources became more difficult, the several Lenape families in each band abandoned their fishing station to begin cold weather foraging in the interior. Before dispersing the families decided whether to return to the same fishing station the following spring. If the resources in that area had become too depleted, they might resolve to establish a new station, usually within a few miles distance and always near the mouth of their principal stream. The general location would be noted before the families in the band broke camp to go on their winter hunt. This winter dispersal took the more agile families to the distant parts of their territory, near the sources of their river and often beyond. The less mobile families, limited by infirm or elderly members, stayed closer to their fishing areas. Families might not see one another for months, but as soon as the first warming days of spring were felt each Lenape family would head downstream to the designated fishing station.

The Munsee occupied the territory east of the upper Delaware River and retained a general foraging lifestyle after 1000 C.E. Only four species of anadromous fish, the subset termed "long-run," spawned beyond Tohickon Creek, into the Lehigh and upper Delaware drainages. Therefore, the Munsee had access to only half the species that made Lenape fishing a viable way to focus their gathering lifestyle. The Munsee consequently combined hunting and gathering with fishing, and they also grew and stored maize (corn) as an emergency crop. The location of the Munsee homeland, close to New Amsterdam, led to many traditions and details of their lives being recorded by Dutch colonists and traders.

The Lenope occupied southern NEW JERSEY up to, but not including, the Raritan Valley. The similarity between the names Lenape and Lenope led the colonists to call the latter "Jerseys" to avoid confusion. They separated from the Lenape by 1300, but remained related to them both culturally and linguistically. While several of the Lenope bands had access to the Delaware River, most were located along the Delaware Bay and the Atlantic shore, where they had developed their culture to use the specific ecology of southern New Jersey. These bands thus concentrated more heavily on gathering maritime resources.

By 1750 many members of these three cultures had moved out of their homeland. While members of all three native cultures migrated, the size and patterns of each group differed considerably. The Lenape moved directly west beginning before 1661 to take advantage of and ultimately to control the western Pennsylvania fur trade. The Munsee generally moved north, although many bands moved west along the NEW YORK border and beyond Pennsylvania. Most of the Lenape never left New Jersey, although a few moved into the Forks of Delaware at the Lehigh River, then north and west. The descendants of all three cultures retained their identities into the 20th century. The continuities were so strong that the Lenape language still survives among a few descendants of this native culture.

See also TEEDYUSCUNG.

Further reading: Paul A. W. Wallace, *Indians in Pennsylvania.* (Harrisburg, Pa.: Pennsylvania Historical and Museum Commission, 1981).

—Marshall Joseph Becker

De Vargas, Diego (1643–1704)

Spanish colonial governor of NEW MEXICO, Diego De Vargas (Diego de Vargas Zapata y Lújan Ponce de León) was chosen to retake New Mexico after a successful rebellion by NATIVE AMERICANS. In 1680 the PUEBLO Indians revolted after decades of forced religious conversion, mandatory labor, and the destruction of traditional life patterns. They drove the Spanish south to El Paso, Texas, and killed more than 100 Spaniards. Two factors, to establish defensible territory against Native American attack and to recolonize through mission-building, especially in the face of European competition, were the essential elements that led to De Vargas's reconquest of New Mexico. De Vargas himself was eager to retake the lands he had been driven from a decade earlier.

De Vargas's first duty was to quash rebellious Pueblo Indian tribes in the area of El Paso. The Pueblo tribes pledged their loyalty to the returning Spanish governor and his forces, who then marched on to reconquer Santa Fe, New Mexico. Pueblo Indians in the Santa Fe area were surprised by the return of the Spanish and submitted to De Vargas's return. He was also able to convince the Indians of his intent to reestablish Spanish rule peacefully, and he gave pardons to all the Pueblo involved in the revolt.

De Vargas's initial return to New Mexico was to secure reconquest. With a semblance of security reestablished, he began to focus on colonization. He returned to New Mexico in 1693, bringing settlers, friars, and more soldiers with him. Many Pueblo Indians rose up against Spanish rule, forcing De Vargas again to capture Santa Fe. Despite this and other small-scale confrontations in 1696, De Vargas was able to maintain the Spanish hold on New Mexico. Apache Indians killed De Vargas during a campaign in 1704.

—James Jenks

disease

Diseases took an incredible toll on human life in early North America in part because people from three continents came together carrying and introducing diseases indigenous to their own societies. NATIVE AMERICANS suffered the worst, and their MORTALITY tragically was higher than perhaps any in human history. When they initially encountered such common European diseases as SMALLPOX, measles, and dysentery, millions died. In extreme cases 90 percent of some Indian groups perished as entire villages were destroyed. In their sexual interaction with Indians, Europeans sometimes contracted a new disease, syphilis (or at least a strain previously unknown to them), and spread it throughout Europe. Most immigrants to the New World experienced a dangerous "seasoning" period during which they likely would catch various new diseases. Africans also endured a seasoning process that cost many lives. In addition, they introduced various tropical diseases like YELLOW FEVER and malaria to the New World.

The best estimates are that more than 400,000 Native Americans lived in the territory east of the Appalachian Mountains by 1600, including about 105,000 Indians in New England, 150,000 in the Mid-Atlantic region, and 150,000 in the Southeast. The arrival of English and Dutch colonists caused a very sudden and dramatic rise in the death rate among natives due to "virgin-soil" epidemics (outbreaks of disease to which a population has had no previous exposure) of plague, smallpox, chickenpox, mumps, measles, and influenza. The initial exposure of indigenous peoples to these deadly viral diseases often afflicted nearly all of the population. From 1616 to 1619 a mysterious plague, probably either bubonic or pneumonic, contracted from Europeans sailing along the coast of MAINE killed perhaps 90 percent of the seacoast Algonquins. The Great Lakes native inhabitants, including the HURON, IROQUOIS, and Mohawk, experienced an epidemic of smallpox that killed at least 50 percent of the inhabitants during the 1630s and 1640s. In 1759 an epidemic of smallpox killed half the CHEROKEE and CATAWBA. The native populations were often so destabilized by these virgin-soil epidemics that their losses occasionally reached 90 percent or higher.

The virulence of European epidemics in combination with the physical aggressiveness of the settlers eventually depopulated most of the eastern seaboard region of its native inhabitants as they either died or moved westward. VIRGINIA's Indian people declined so rapidly in the nine decades after the colony was established that only about 1,800 survived in 1700. The native population of New England fell to about 10,000 by 1675 and only a few hundred by 1750. This depopulation proceeded so rapidly that natives likely were a minority east of the Appalachians during the late 1680s, and by the 1760s only 150,000 Indians lived east of the Mississippi River.

Virginia was deadly for early colonists as well. During the initial two decades of English settlement, mortality was incredibly high. Conditions on board European ships included the absence of sanitary equipment, overcrowding, insufficient FOOD and MEDICINE, and passengers with contagious diseases, all of which caused colonists to arrive in such a poor state of health that they fell easy victims to typhoid, typhus, and chronic dysentery. Because of their long voyage and poor living conditions in the early settlements, colonists sometimes suffered from scurvy, caused by severe prolonged dietary deprivation of vitamin C. With the advent of long sea voyages, scurvy ranked first among the causes of disability and mortality among sailors. Even on land, scurvy sometimes occurred in early America.

JAMESTOWN and the surrounding communities were ideal sites to maximize the transmission of human pathogens. These early settlements were along a section of the James River where tides carried and mixed saltwater with the freshwater flowing down the river. In the summer, when the river current slowed, the salt tide reached its maximum extent inland and created water levels containing six times the salinity present in normal freshwater. Additionally, the opposing forces of the current from the stream and the tide produced a large stretch of river that was virtually stagnant and polluted with human waste that entered the water by runoff from the shore. The result was that every summer an ENVIRONMENT was produced in which typhus and dysentery flourished. The vulnerability of the settlers was particularly high because of their weakened state from insufficient food, the location of their settlements on the riverbank, and their use of the James River rather than wells as their main source of drinking water. Between 1618 and 1624 as many as two-thirds of the deaths of colonists resulted from disease. The diseases declined only as the English moved inland, where wells provided drinking water and they could obtain healthier freshwater from the James River.

Malaria, introduced after 1650, became the Chesapeake's most virulent pathogen. Slaves carrying the most lethal variants of malaria came from AFRICA to the New World, and mosquitoes spread it to the European and Native American population. Once established, malaria was impossible to eradicate without draining the mosquito-infested swamps, although colonists were unaware of the mode of transmission of the disease in any case. Malaria profoundly affected public health in the southern tidewater region, and it was a primary reason colonists in the CHESAPEAKE BAY region lived shorter lives than did New Englanders. Malaria also encouraged wealthy white people to live in CHARLESTON during the unhealthy summers, leaving their rice plantations to be run by overseers. The disease rarely killed its victims directly because American settlers used cinchona bark, which contained quinine to limit the ravages of the disease. Still, it weakened the immunity of its victims, who faced recurring bouts of fever, and minor infections sometimes proved fatal in chronic malaria sufferers. Indeed, for every direct malaria fatality, five died of its indirect effects. Pregnant women and new mothers were particularly vulnerable to the disease. The movement inland of southern populations decreased the impact of malaria because the disease is limited to swampy or marshy areas where mosquitoes breed. Therefore, the disease existed almost entirely in the southern tidewater (although it also afflicted a few northern locations). As colonists moved into the Piedmont, the population at risk for acquiring malaria declined.

The rapid increase in slaves in the region in the early 18th century also limited malaria-induced deaths. People of African descent, although not immune to the disease, tolerated attacks better and enjoyed a higher survival rate than did whites. This is partly because many of them carry a single mutation in their hemoglobin gene that results in the production of hemoglobin S instead of hemoglobin A. Individuals who carry the S mutation from one parent and the hemoglobin A gene from the other parent are carriers of the sickle-cell trait. When an individual has hemoglobin S genes from both parents, they have sickle-cell disease. In areas where malaria is endemic, individuals with the sickle-cell trait have a significant advantage because it confers significant resistance to malarial infection, which is less able to attack the red blood cells that contain the altered form of hemoglobin. However, this advantage comes with a high price. If both parents carry the sickle-cell trait, 25 percent of their children will have sickle-cell disease, which is devastating.

Most Euro-American colonists outside the tidewater South enjoyed longer, healthier lives than their European contemporaries because of the generally benign disease environment. Euro-Americans suffered from fewer diseases because the low population density reduced the transmission of fatal illnesses among individuals. The winter season, when people were weakest because of the lack of fresh food, was safer because a poor transportation system limited transmission of diseases. Other months generally gave the typical family a better source of nutrients to help ward off sickness and to recover from infectious disease.

Most public health crises occurred in cities, where only a fraction of the population lived. Between 1638 and 1763 more than half the major smallpox outbreaks happened in urban communities; 38 percent occurred in the four largest colonial cities of Charleston, BOSTON, NEW YORK CITY, and PHILADELPHIA. Yellow fever was almost exclusively limited to port cities. The most serious epidemics in the countryside were outbreaks of diphtheria. However, by 1730 in the more densely populated regions of New England and the Delaware Valley, the spread of infectious disease through agricultural regions increased significantly. These regions were struck especially hard during wars, when soldiers were exposed to various diseases while on a campaign, and, returning home, they sometimes spread them to their families and neighbors.

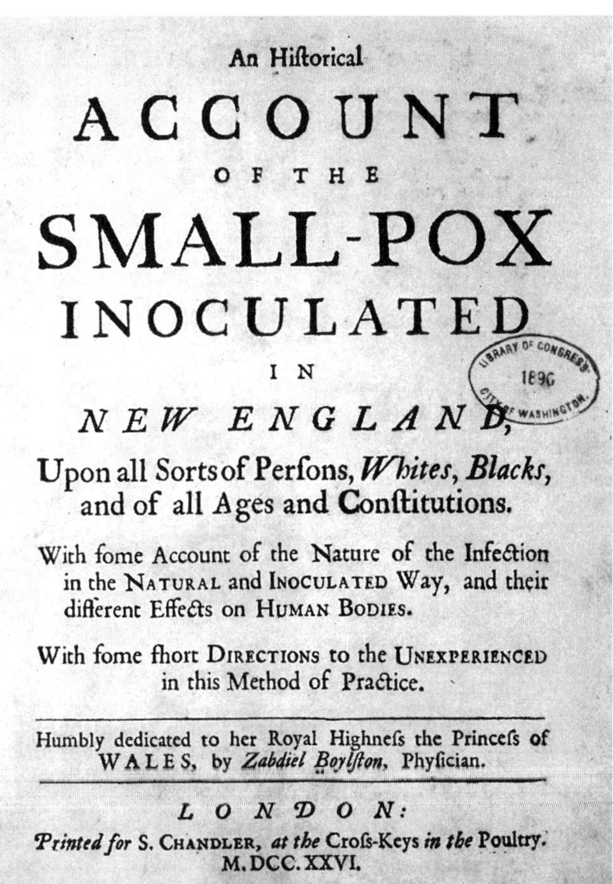

An Hiſtorical
ACCOUNT
OF THE
SMALL-POX
INOCULATED
IN
NEW ENGLAND,
Upon all Sorts of Perſons, *Whites*, *Blacks*, and of all Ages and Conſtitutions.

With ſome Account of the Nature of the Infection in the NATURAL and INOCULATED Way, and their different Effects on HUMAN BODIES.

With ſome ſhort DIRECTIONS to the UNEXPERIENCED in this Method of Practice.

Humbly dedicated to her Royal Highneſs the Princeſs of WALES, by *Zabdiel Boylſton*, Phyſician.

LONDON:
Printed for S. CHANDLER, *at the* Croſs-Keys *in the* Poultry.
M.DCC.XXVI.

A publication describing the administration and results of inoculation against the smallpox epidemic, 1726 *(Hulton/Archive)*

Smallpox (or variola) was the most dangerous disease in North America and eventually became endemic in the major cities. It is a highly communicable febrile viral disease characterized by three or four days of high fevers and rapid pulse followed by the development of widely disseminated vascular, then pustular, skin eruptions. Smallpox is usually transmitted from person to person, but the virus may contaminate CLOTHING, bedding, dust, or inanimate objects and remain infectious for months. Exposure to the disease resulted in almost universal contagion among people who had never been previously exposed to the disease. The occurrence of a large-scale epidemic usually resulted from the absence of the disease from a population for a significant time; when smallpox returned, most inhabitants had no natural defense against the virus. European migrants carried smallpox to the colonies. Indeed, outbreaks of smallpox onboard ships were so common that seaports sometimes mandated that passengers be quarantined before being allowed to land in the city.

American colonials feared smallpox for good reason, because few other diseases had the capacity for infecting and killing a greater portion of people. In 1721 smallpox struck Boston, infecting as many as half the inhabitants and killing perhaps 15 percent of the afflicted. In 1731, during a three-month epidemic in New York City, more than half the inhabitants were infected and 7 percent of the afflicted died. Charleston in 1738 was struck by an epidemic of smallpox that infected half the city, and 18 percent of the infected died.

Once contracted, no cure was available then (or now) for smallpox. However, inoculation to provide immunity was gradually introduced in the colonies in the mid-18th century. ZABDIEL BOYLSTON, a surgeon and physician born in MASSACHUSETTS, introduced variolation in America. This procedure called for transferring a small amount of pustular matter from an infected individual to a healthy person in the hopes of bringing on a less virulent case of smallpox. This procedure was dangerous because perhaps 3 percent of its recipients died. In addition, because the variolated person was contagious, many early Americans resisted the procedure, fearing that it would cause widespread epidemics. Both COTTON MATHER and Benjamin Franklin (after losing a son to smallpox) helped popularize the procedure, which accounted for a general decline in smallpox deaths during the 18th century.

After smallpox, the most lethal disease in colonial North America was diphtheria, a communicable disease caused by *Corynebacterium diphtheria,* which produces a powerful exotoxin that inhibits protein synthesis when the bacterium is infected by a bacterial virus called beta. In this disease the throat swells and then becomes congested with a thick membrane over the larynx and trachea. In extreme cases death due to respiratory obstruction, heart failure, or overwhelming toxemia and shock occurs. No age is immune to the disease, but it most commonly affects children younger than five.

The earliest outbreaks may have been recorded in 1659, although it was often confused with scarlet fever before 1730. In the 1730s this pathogen mutated into its current highly virulent form and wreaked havoc among a population that had no acquired immunity against the disease. In 1737 at Kingston, NEW HAMPSHIRE, the first major attack of diphtheria occurred; it was reported that every one of its first 40 victims died. In Hampton Falls, New Hampshire, in 13 months 20 families lost every one of their children, and 210 people (95 percent of them children) out of a population of 1,200 perished, a death rate equal to that caused by smallpox. Half the children younger than 15 died in Haverhill, Massachusetts. This epidemic, unlike others that usually dissipated in less than a year, infested New England, spread to the Delaware Valley, and by 1741 may have claimed 20,000 lives, including a 10th of all children living north of MARYLAND. The occurrence of localized epidemics of diphtheria continued throughout the colonial period, but by 1745 so many children had been exposed to the disease that the immune population was large enough to prevent another major epidemic on this scale. The epidemics of the 1730s and 1740s set a background for the GREAT AWAKENING, as many people sought spiritual understanding in the midst of an incredible tragedy.

The third most spectacular pestilence during the colonial period was yellow fever, a tropical disease brought because of the SLAVE TRADE from Africa to the West Indies to North America. High fever, hemorrhagic diathesis, and signs of renal and liver damage characterize the disease. The fulminating forms of this disease are highly fatal. Death is usually due to renal failure, overwhelming toxemia, liver failure, or intercurrent infection. The transmission of the disease is facilitated by a particular mosquito (*Aëdes egypti*) that was not originally native to North America. These insects breed well in water barrels, and they were often carried on ships trading with the CARIBBEAN. They then spread infection to dockworkers and people living near the wharves. Charleston, Philadelphia and New York felt the brunt of yellow fever. In 1699 the first epidemic struck North America and killed many residents of Charleston and one out of every three Philadelphians. Severe epidemics returned in the 1740s and early 1760s but did not occur again until the 1790s, when a major epidemic of yellow fever afflicted all the American port cities.

Other illnesses prevalent in the colonies included many still common today: measles, mumps, and chickenpox. Overall, children easily survive these illnesses with good care, but adults are at great risk. Because of the isolation of many colonial settlements, many previously unexposed adults contracted the diseases and died. For example, measles was the leading cause of death in Boston in 1729. Respiratory illnesses also proved dangerous because of the absence of fresh food during the winter months. In 1699 flu struck Fairfield, CONNECTICUT, where 7 percent of the residents died in just three months. In the winter of 1753–4, pneumonia struck Holliston, Massachusetts, killing 13 percent of the inhabitants. These cases were exceptions to the general rule that a low population density and adequate diet spared most Euro-Americans from the severe ravages of infectious diseases, at least outside the major port cities.

In conclusion, colonial Americans fared quite well with regard to infectious diseases when compared with their European counterparts, although the health of the Euro-American population depended partly on its geographic location. AFRICAN AMERICANS enjoyed some limited protection from malaria but suffered from common European diseases to which they had few immunities. Native Americans died in unprecedented numbers because of diseases introduced by Europeans, both inadvertently and occasionally on purpose.

Further reading: John Duffy, *Epidemics in Colonial America* (Baton Rouge: Louisiana State University Press, 1953, 1971).

—Mark R. Geier and David A. Geier

domesticity

A component of the English patriarchal system that evolved in response to the Protestant Reformation, domesticity describes the female role in the GENDER division of LABOR within the family. PURITANS in particular empowered the family patriarch as the unquestioned authority and established rigid roles for women that they hoped would provide stability, continuity, and order to their lives. Although wives were considered a "necessary good," women were thought to be inferior to men and given a diminished social position that limited their influence to the private sphere of the home. English colonists, seeking comfort and familiarity, attempted to bring "civilization" to the "wilderness" by replicating their Old World duties and lives in the New World. Circumstances in the colonies, however, led to a broader definition of domestic life in many regions, as colonists were obliged to adapt their values to new conditions. Consequently, colonial domesticity differed significantly from either the English model or the more narrowly defined 19th-century "domestic feminism."

Enforced by law and reinforced by religion, domesticity was the main institution in a woman's life, and the home was a refuge of English custom. Married women had no independent legal rights and were subordinate to their husbands. In the family they were expected to perform both productive and reproductive domestic duties. Their household responsibilities included cooking, cleaning, sewing, weaving, candle-making, butchering, tending a kitchen garden, caring for poultry, and performing dairy work. They spent much of their adult lives in the cycle of pregnancy, birth, and nursing while simultaneously raising older children and executing domestic duties. Mothers passed on "huswife" skills to their daughters, creating strong mother-daughter bonds. Wealthy women also managed servants and slaves.

Because of the scarcity of utensils and tools such as washtubs and candlemolds, housework was more difficult for American than for English women. For the first few generations in the New World, the domestic sphere was often more broadly defined than it had been in England. Domestic products contributed significantly to family welfare and prosperity, and thus many housewives were able to ply their managerial and technical skills and had a relationship with the working world. In New England Puritan "goodwives" submitted both to God's and their husbands' wills. The model housewife was compared to a tortoise confined to her shell—a secure and stable domestic world. Seventeenth-century Chesapeake families, on the other hand, were often disrupted by a shortage of women, death, remarriage, and divided loyalties. Patriarchal power was, to a greater extent, shared with widows' inherited power, and labor was too scarce to maintain the English gendered division of labor. Women worked the fields rarely but when necessary, and they frequently turned a profit from household production, such as spinning, weaving, and churning. Chesapeake women were probably less submissive than their Puritan counterparts, although their family futures and fortunes were less secure.

By the early 18th century the evolution of a colonial aristocracy with inherited land and power strengthened domestic patriarchalism among the affluent. White women, equating their domestic lifestyle with civilization and prosperity, believed they were elevated above both slave women, who were employed alongside men, and Native American women, whom they considered to be overworked. Euro-Americans viewed domestic patriarchy as the only civilized family arrangement and perpetuated the system by imposing it on slave and Native American families.

Further reading: Mary Beth Norton, *Founding Mothers & Fathers: Gendered Power and the Forming of American Society* (New York: Vintage Books, 1997).

—Deborah C. Taylor

Dominicans

The Dominicans, a preaching order founded in the 13th century, quickly became associated with the Inquisition. Because of this and the behavior of highly visible Dominicans like Johan Tetzel, the order was in disrepute by the 16th century. However, because of their association with the family of Christopher Columbus, they were included in the voyages of Spanish EXPLORATION from 1509, establishing MISSIONS in Mexico, Peru, Macao, and the Philippines, as well as in other Spanish and Portuguese colonies. Perhaps the most influential Dominican in the history of colonization was Bartolomé de Las Casas, who protested the Spanish treatment of natives and demanded reform of the *encomienda* (a system in which NATIVE AMERICANS were required to work for and pay tribute to Spanish colonists).

The Dominicans suffered a number of martyrdoms through their dangerous and far-flung mission activity, including six at Guadalupe in 1604. Because of the need for recruitment and new Dominicans, the order pressed for the ordination of native and mixed-race priests and nuns, which in turn gave the Dominicans a number of saints, including St. Rose of Lima, St. Martin de Porres, and St. Juan Masias, all of whom were Latin Americans of mixed-race ethnicity. Dominican nuns were influential in the Spanish school systems of the Americas and in a continuing mission of charitable activity with the displaced natives begun by de Las Casas, who set up workshops and protected agricultural estates. Having lost their reputation through the excesses of the Inquisition and the accusations of the Protestant Reformation, the Dominicans subsequently regained their power and influence as the premier order in the Spanish and Portuguese Americas.

—Margaret Sankey

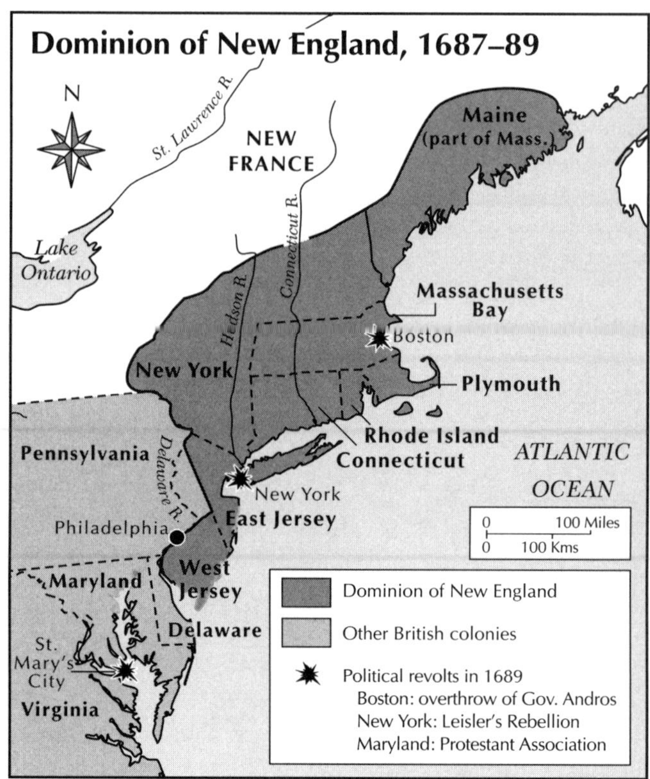

Dominion of New England (1686–1689)

The Dominion of New England was a consolidation of the northern English colonies imposed by the British Crown that stood for three years until overthrown by armed revolt in the aftermath of the GLORIOUS REVOLUTION. At its greatest extent, between 1688 and 1689, the dominion stretched from the MAINE frontier to the northern boundary of PENNSYLVANIA. As early as the 1630s, the Crown had sought—unsuccessfully—to send a governor general to rule New England colonies already considered dangerously independent. These colonies, in turn, save for RHODE ISLAND, formed their own loosely knit alliance, the New England Confederation, for purposes of defense and mutual advice. Following the 1660 restoration of the Stuart MONARCHY, complaints of the colonists' illegal trading and, particularly, of MASSACHUSETTS's encroachment on its neighbors and persecution of religious dissidents brought renewed pressure to conform to Crown authority. In 1676 royal messenger EDWARD RANDOLPH brought back information that led London officials to demand that Massachusetts accept a revision of the charter that formed the basis of its government. NEW HAMPSHIRE, hitherto governed from BOSTON, was set off as the region's first royally governed colony in 1679. Massachusetts's stubborn refusal to compromise delayed a settlement until 1684, by which time the Crown had begun a concerted campaign to remodel charters both in England and North America to establish more direct and autocratic rule. Not only was the charter of Massachusetts now formally annulled, but the colony was gathered with neighboring New Hampshire, PLYMOUTH Colony, and Rhode Island's Narragansett region into a single unit, the Dominion of New England, to be governed directly by the Crown without any of the customary locally elected officials or assemblies. A further argument favoring union was to provide for more coherent defense against French and Indian attack. In September JOSEPH DUDLEY, one of a handful of dissident colonists who had collaborated with Randolph in planning the new government, was commissioned president of the dominion. Dudley presided with a royally appointed council from May until December 1686, when English army officer SIR EDMUND ANDROS arrived as governor, backed by two companies of English soldiers. Legal proceedings had now annulled the charters of Rhode Island and CONNECTICUT, and Andros incorporated them under his control. In 1688, responding to a growing French threat to the colonists' northern border, NEW YORK and East and West Jersey were likewise added to the dominion.

Andros soon alienated his unwieldy province. Sullen submission became open opposition as the governor pressed his instructions to raise taxes without representative consent, review all land titles, and provide for religious toleration while favoring the ANGLICAN CHURCH—all policies that struck at the cornerstones of Puritan life in New England. Andros scorned to conciliate his subjects, ruling through English officials such as Randolph and a group of intimates brought from his former government of New

York, some of them ROMAN CATHOLICS. Town meetings were restricted, juries packed, and dissidents jailed. "Either you are Subjects," the governor bluntly informed one protesting group, "or you are Rebels."

His subjects made their choice. In the spring of 1689, as Andros was on the frontier defending against Indian raids, news arrived from England of the overthrow of his patron, James II, by William of Orange. Andros sped back to Boston only to be caught up in a popular uprising in the city on April 18 that imprisoned him and his subordinates, later sending them back to London. The dominion dissolved into its component parts, restoring charter government. In New York a coup headed by Jacob Leisler took power, expelling Andros's lieutenant governor, Francis Nicholson.

As an experiment in royal autocracy and consolidation, the dominion failed. London made no further attempt to emulate the French and Spanish practice of ruling established colonies without the forms of representative government. New Englanders cherished memories of their part in its overthrow, which they would recall in the 1770s. More immediately, however, the dominion represented the formation of a more uniform, London-directed English empire in America. In the settlement that followed its fall, King William (1689–1702) restored both elected assemblies and Crown-appointed governors to Massachusetts and New York, a turning point in defining the constitutional balance subsequently established in the great majority of 18th-century English colonial governments in America.

See also GOVERNMENT, BRITISH AMERICAN.

Further reading: Viola F. Barnes, *The Dominion of New England* (New Haven, Conn.: Yale University Press, 1923); Richard R. Johnson, *Adjustment to Empire: The New England Colonies, 1675–1715* (New Brunswick, N.J.: Rutgers University Press, 1981).

—Richard R. Johnson

Dudley, Joseph (1647–1720)

Joseph Dudley was born in Roxbury, the son of a former MASSACHUSETTS governor. From Harvard and training for the ministry he turned to politics, as deputy and then, in 1676, assistant (ruling magistrate) in the Massachusetts General Court. A turning point followed in 1682, when he was sent to London to defend the colony against charges of illegal trading and abusing its charter powers. There he perceived the reality of growing royal power and the opportunities it offered, and he began to work with EDWARD RANDOLPH and other British officials to undermine the colonists' stubborn resistance to London's regulation of New England. In May 1686, following the annulment of the Massachusetts charter, Dudley accepted the Crown-appointed presidency of a provisional government, the DOMINION OF NEW ENGLAND, uniting Massachusetts with its neighboring colonies, but Dudley and his allies had scarcely begun to organize the new regime (and advance their own interests in land speculation) when he was superseded, in December 1686, by royal governor SIR EDMUND ANDROS.

Dudley continued in office as chief justice of the dominion, and in April 1689 he shared in the dominion's overthrow by popular revolt. Imprisoned in Boston and reviled as a traitor to his native land, Dudley was sent back to England early in 1690. There, with other dominion officials, he was exonerated from charges of misrule and in 1691 returned to the colonies as NEW YORK's chief justice, where he presided over the treason trial of Jacob Leisler. By 1694, however, he was back in England seeking the governorship of Massachusetts. He served as lieutenant governor of the Isle of Wight and, briefly, as a member of Parliament. His prolonged solicitation of both English policy makers and former New England opponents finally bore fruit, and in June 1702 Dudley took office as governor of both Massachusetts and NEW HAMPSHIRE.

Dudley's governorships reflected the conflicting promises he had made to obtain them. He worked hard to protect his northern and eastern frontiers from French and Indian attack, mounting expeditions that finally captured French Port Royal in 1710. He showed skill in dealing with suspicious assemblies, but he wavered between advancing Anglicanism and defending Congregationalism, arousing the fierce opposition of INCREASE MATHER and COTTON MATHER. He also became embroiled in several politically embarrassing episodes involving his associates' involvement in illegal trading and schemes for a private bank. He was replaced as governor in 1715 and died five years later.

Dudley, noted his obituary, was "visibly form'd for Government." To his enemies, he was a slippery politician willing to betray his Puritan upbringing for his own advancement. However, he is better assessed as one among a generation of able colonial leaders who chose to hew closer to English imperial models of social behavior and political loyalty.

Further reading: Richard R. Johnson, *Adjustment to Empire: The New England Colonies, 1675–1715* (New Brunswick, N.J.: Rutgers University Press, 1981).

—Richard R. Johnson

Dudley, Thomas (1576–1653)

Thomas Dudley served four times as governor and 13 times as deputy governor of the MASSACHUSETTS Bay Colony. Born most likely near Northampton, England, his father and mother both died during his youth, and he was raised by family and friends. He married Dorothy Yorke in 1603, and she eventually bore six children. Between 1616 and 1629 he prospered as a very capable steward for the earl of Lincoln Dudley. Meanwhile, he committed himself to the reform of the ANGLICAN CHURCH and became involved with other PURITANS, joining JOHN COTTON's congregation in England and helping to plan the Massachusetts Bay Colony.

He sailed to North America on the *Arabella* as the deputy governor of JOHN WINTHROP in 1630. The next decade was characterized by difficulties between the two men as they struggled for power and to define the political structure of the new colony. The problems were gradually resolved, in part because of the marriage of Dudley's son Samuel to Mary, the daughter of Winthrop. As governor and deputy governor Dudley staunchly defended Puritan orthodoxy against both ROGER WILLIAMS and ANNE MARBURY HUTCHINSON. While governor in 1650, he signed the charter for Harvard College.

When his first wife died in 1643, Dudley married Katherine Deighton Haghorne, and they had three children. His son Joseph became Massachusetts's governor in 1692. His daughter ANNE DUDLEY BRADSTREET became a talented poet.

dueling

In colonial North America and early modern Europe gentlemen sometimes settled disputes through ritualized combat. The practice began in 16th-century Italy, then moved to Bourbon France, where it proved immensely popular. Some 4,000 French nobles perished in duels from 1589 to 1607; the carnage continued until Louis XIV resolved to stop it. From the Continent, the *code duello* traveled to the United Kingdom, and by the early 18th century English gentlemen regularly faced off in small-scale battles. The contestants followed an unspoken set of rules. Each man fired only when facing his opponent, and participants often intentionally missed if the adversary displayed requisite bravery. Juries rarely convicted either of the duelers—unless one of the combatants broke the rules. Clergymen and Scottish philosophers railed against the practice as impious bloodlust, but duels remained popular until the middle of the 19th century. Indeed, from 1779 to 1846 six of 14 prime ministers participated in at least one duel.

In North America the *code duello* remained a genteel affair, but ordinary sorts occasionally joined in. Commoners wrestled or brawled in plebeian imitation of their better-armed superiors. Although scattered duels took place in the northern colonies, Puritan and Quaker asceticism clashed with such worldly affairs, but the practice thrived below the Potomac, especially as a southern gentry crystallized in the 18th century. These ritualized battles became part of an aggressively competitive and hypermasculine culture of cockfighting, hunting, and horse racing. Duels also frequently broke out on college campuses, where young gentlemen mixed in combustible intimacy. Southern duels were public affairs. The combatants typically had courtiers, or "seconds," and invited crowds of supporters. If challenged, a man might decline on the grounds that his opponent was socially inferior; duels ideally involved only equals. Refusing a duel, however, was usually taken as a sign of cowardice.

These confrontations reflected a society built around "honor." A man's honor depended on the moral and physical courage he displayed to his peers. Honor also connoted a family's reputation. In emulation of the British gentry they so admired, southern gentlemen felt enormous pride in their lineage and responded savagely if aspersions fell upon the family name. If sullied, honor had to be redeemed, for without it a man sank into ignominy and disgrace. Southerners typically fought in response to certain keywords, such as "liar," "poltroon," or "coward." As in Great Britain, duels survived well into the 19th century. The culture of honor and the contests that reified it inhibited the growth of regular channels of grievance mediation characteristic of "modern" societies.

Further reading: Bertram-Wyatt Brown, *Southern Honor: Ethics and Behavior in the Old South* (New York: Oxford University Press, 1982).

—J. M. Opal

Dummer, Jeremiah (1645–1718)

Born in MASSACHUSETTS, the son of a farmer and large landowner, Dummer was a first cousin of SAMUEL SEWALL and an important figure in New England. Apprenticed at age 14, Dummer established his own shop when his indenture ended assisted by a loan from his master. Dummer prospered and eventually took in apprentices, influencing the ARTISANS of the next generation. In 1672 he married Anna (or Hannah) Atwater, daughter of a prominent New Haven merchant, and they had seven children. They included William Dummer, who became lieutenant and acting governor of Massachusetts, and Jeremiah Dummer, Jr., a political writer and agent in London who helped raise funds for founding YALE COLLEGE.

The first American-born silversmith to practice engraving, Dummer produced much work that remains in churches; he also engraved the plates for CONNECTICUT's paper money. Dummer is the first identifiable portrait painter in New England, and at least four canvases still exist. With the success of his shop and merchant ventures, Dummer became one of the wealthiest men in BOSTON. He entered trade in 1685, soon became the part owner of several ships, and by 1708 was able to abandon silversmithing to devote his time to shipping. Dummer's wealth facilitated his rise to social prominence. His career began in the local militia in 1671, and Dummer served in government from the 1670s onward in a variety of prominent roles, from treasurer to justice of the peace. Dummer and his sons are examples of the role money, ability, and connections played in the creation of a colonial elite.

—Victoria C. H. Resnick

Duston, Hannah Emerson (1657–1736?)

Hannah Emerson Duston, the first American woman honored with a permanent statue, is considered a heroine by some historians and a villainess by others. Born at Haverhill, MASSACHUSETTS, on December 23, 1657, Duston was the daughter of Michael and Hannah (Webster) Emerson. She married Thomas Duston in 1677. Members of the Abenaki tribe abducted her on March 15, 1697. These NATIVE AMERICANS raided British settlements such as Haverhill during KING WILLIAM'S WAR, in part for British prisoners and scalps. Duston was taken prisoner along with her week-old daughter and her nurse, Mary Neff. Thomas Duston eluded capture, rescuing the couple's other seven children.

Duston watched as her abductors killed other captives, including her baby. Over a period of 15 days, she walked approximately 100 miles to the north through snow and mud. On March 30 the Native Americans divided the captives into two groups, and Duston and Neff were kept together on an island (later called Dustin Island) where the Merrimack and Contoocook Rivers intersect. They learned that their captors, a group consisting of two men, three women, and seven children, planned to take them to St. Francis, Canada, where they would be forced to run a gauntlet.

On the evening of March 30 Duston directed Neff and Samuel Leonardson, a teenaged boy, to attack their captors with hatchets that she had stolen. Duston killed nine Indians, and Leonardson slew one; a woman and child, whom Duston had planned to spare, escaped. Duston scalped the victims as evidence to collect a bounty. The trio returned to Haverhill on April 21. Several weeks later Duston narrated her ordeal to the General Court seated in BOSTON. Because she was married, her 25-pound bounty went to her husband. However, Hannah Duston became a heroine throughout the colonies.

Preachers incorporated interpretations of Duston's heroism in sermons that stressed that her spirituality strengthened her to overcome her captors. In 1702 COTTON MATHER wrote about Duston's abduction in *Magnalia Christi Americana,* declaring that she acted in self-defense and should be praised for killing Native Americans who had been converted to Catholicism by the French. Duston died about 1736. She was mostly forgotten until 1861, when the people of Haverhill erected a statue in her honor. Some scholars denounce Duston's actions as unjustifiably murderous.

Further reading: Laurel Thatcher Ulrich, *Good Wives: Image and Reality in the Lives of Women in Northern New England 1650–1750* (New York: Knopf, 1982).

—Elizabeth D. Schafer

Dutch Reformed Church

The Dutch Reformed Church was a Calvinist branch of the Christian faith stemming from the Reformation. Because of its role in the Dutch Revolt against Spain, it was an important facet of Dutch identity and was carefully exported on the ships of the Dutch East and West India Companies. The first congregation in North America was formed in 1626 in NEW AMSTERDAM, following a pattern set by earlier congregations in Dutch Guinea and Brazil: a hierarchy of consistories, classis, provincial and national synods, and adherence to the Heidelberg Confession and the canons of the Synod of Dordrecht. The first congregation, meeting in a specially constructed room over a mill, merited only a "comforter of the sick," a lay prayer leader and counselor, but by 1628 it merited an ordained minister, Jonas Michaelius, from the Netherlands. These early church workers were recruited by the company and by individual patroons and were expected to act not only as ministers but also as schoolteachers and community spokespeople. As the Dutch settlements expanded to Brooklyn and Flatbush, so did the church, hiring ministers, most of whom had had earlier experience in other Dutch colonies, and building new churches, frequently financed by the selling of pews and private subscriptions.

In lands of the DUTCH WEST INDIA COMPANY, the Reformed Church was the only legal religious establishment, although the company encouraged toleration of Lutheranism to promote emigration. While making an exception for the Swedish settlers conquered by the Dutch, who were allowed to have their own Lutheran minister, the church dealt harshly with QUAKERS, JEWS, and ROMAN CATHOLICS. However, the Palatine, Swiss, Puritan, and Huguenot settlers, many of whom had come to North America via the Netherlands, fit neatly into the Dutch Reformed Church. The 1664 change to English rule did not disturb the church's monopoly on public funding, because it remained the majority, although it was now required to tolerate the Church of England. The church officially supported SLAVERY but encouraged its members to educate their servants and slaves. Church missionary efforts to the NATIVE AMERICANS, especially the neighboring Mohawk, yielded important ethnographic information but could not compete with the work of the JESUITS. Ministers' plans to seize and educate Native American children were discouraged by the company, which saw it as a provocation of the tribes.

Increasing diversity in the colony created problems in the late 17th century. The government of Peter Leisler, opposed by the church clergy, persecuted the Dutch Reformed Church, as did the English governor, EDWARD HYDE, VISCOUNT CORNBURY, who attempted to place Anglican ministers in Dutch congregations. The church opposed the foundation of KING'S COLLEGE (now Columbia University) as a Church of England institution but was mollified by the foundation of Queen's College (now Rutgers University) in New Jersey as an alternative. Eventually, problems of ordaining ministers trained in the colonies, local religious questions that the hierarchy in the Netherlands was unsuited to answer, and the decline of the Dutch language led to a formal declaration of separation of the colonial church from the Dutch establishment in 1771. The denomination continued to call itself the Dutch Reformed Church until 1867, when it became the Reformed Church in America.

Further reading: Gerald F. De Jong, *The Dutch Reformed Church in the American Colonies* (Grand Rapids, Mich.: Erdmans, 1978).

—Margaret Sankey

Dutch West India Company (1621–1791)

Modeled on the 1602 Dutch East India Company, the joint-stock Dutch West India Company (*Westindische Compagnie*) was chartered on June 3, 1621, to undertake the settlement and colonial development of AFRICA and the Americas. Willem Usselinx had proposed such a company in 1591 to spread PROTESTANTISM, expand Dutch trade and influence, and strike against Spain's American possessions. A few military and commercial outposts were established in the early 17th century, but colonization remained uncoordinated before 1621. The company blended trade, warfare, and colonization in four principal areas: Brazil and the Wild Coast (modern-day Suriname and Guiana), the CARIBBEAN, NEW NETHERLAND, and West and Central AFRICA. Its earliest efforts were aimed at PRIVATEERING against Spain. Between 1621 and 1637 company vessels captured more than 600 Iberian ships worth 118 million guilders. The company also pursued salt-raking in Aruba, Bonaire, Curaçao, and St. Martin to support the Dutch dairy and FISHING industries, trade with VIRGINIA, Santo Domingo, and Brazil for TOBACCO and sugar, and fur trading at New Amsterdam and Fort Orange in New Netherland.

The capture of Pernambuco in 1630 inaugurated the company's disastrous colony in Dutch Brazil. The need for LABOR on the large-scale sugar plantations established by Dutch settlers spurred the company to expand into the SLAVE TRADE and to capture various African slaving factories from the Portuguese in the 1630s and 1640s. Heavy capital and military expenditures and a planter rebellion forced the company to abandon Brazil with catastrophic losses in 1654, from which the company never recovered. Three wars with England plunged the company into further debt and resulted in the loss of New Netherland in 1664; meanwhile, English and French mercantile exclusion of Dutch shipping further reduced revenue. In 1674 the States General liquidated the insolvent company and chartered a new one more tightly focused on trade.

The second Dutch West India Company concentrated its efforts in developing Curaçao and St. Eustatius as free-port entrepots where goods from Spanish, French, and British colonies were exchanged for Dutch manufactures. Sugar and tropical staples production continued, but contraband trade with colonial neighbors was far more profitable, especially during war, when Dutch neutrality made them desirable shippers for European-bound Caribbean produce. With nearly 3,000 annual shipping entries and clearances, St. Eustatius was one of the busiest ports in the Americas in the 1770s. The company was finally abolished in 1791 by the States General and the company's former colonies transferred to the Council of the Colonies.

Further reading: Wim Klooster, *Illicit Riches: Dutch Trade in the Caribbean, 1648–1795* (Leiden, Netherlands: KITLV Press, 1998); Johannes Postma, *The Dutch in the Atlantic Slave Trade, 1600–1815* (Cambridge, U.K.: Cambridge University Press, 1990).

—Michael J. Jarvis

Dutch-Indian Wars

The Dutch–Indian Wars were a series of armed conflicts between the Dutch colony of NEW NETHERLAND and neighboring Indian peoples, mostly ALGONQUIN. The clashes developed for a number of reasons, primarily because the growing number of Dutch farmers created land disputes. The Dutch colonial administration widened the rift between settlers and natives. The DUTCH WEST INDIA COMPANY maintained friendly relations and traded (including selling of firearms) with the formidable IROQUOIS confederacy—a long-standing enemy of the Algonquin tribes. However, due to security concerns, the Dutch refused to sell arms to their neighbors, the Algonquin. In addition, colonial authorities tried to impose various regulations and restrictions on the Indians.

The Dutch and Indians engaged in three major wars: the Algonquin (Kieft) War, the Peach Tree War, and the Esopus Wars. The Algonquin (Kieft) War (1641–5) began with Indian attacks on Dutch settlers in the summer of 1641. The attacks were provoked both by the mounting mutual accusations over a succession of interracial murders, and by the efforts of the director general (governor) of New Netherland, WILLEM KIEFT, to impose a tax (payable in corn) on nearby tribes.

The campaign in Manhattan and Staten Island went badly for the Dutch, and a truce was arranged in March 1642. The war resumed in February 1643 when the Mohawk from the Iroquois confederacy attacked the Algonquin living along the lower Hudson River. Kieft sought to improve his shattered reputation as a military commander by attacking the Algonquin; Dutch soldiers subsequently massacred 80 people at the encampment at Pavonia. This outrage united 11 Algonquin tribes in common straggle against the Dutch and sparked off a new round of war that devastated the entire colony except New Amsterdam and Fort Orange (Albany). The plantations of the English settlers in nearby Westchester and Long Island were also ruined.

In 1644 the Dutch fortified New Amsterdam with a stone wall—present-day Wall Street takes its name from this wall—and strengthened the garrison with reinforcements from Dutch colonies in Brazil and the West Indies. Additionally, the Dutch hired the experienced English captain John Underhill, who had participated in the PEQUOT WAR in New England. In March 1644 150 soldiers under the new commander attacked the fortified Indian village north of Stamford. Of 700 Indian warriors, only eight escaped; the Anglo–Dutch force lost only 15 men. This appalling blow on the Indian stronghold destroyed the Algonquin alliance. Confronted with the successful European advance from the south and Iroquois pressure from the north, the Algonquin tribes accepted peace in August 1645.

The Peach Tree War of 1655 ended the temporary policy of coexistence that had been implemented by the Dutch governor PETER STUYVESANT. In the atmosphere of mutual suspicion, one violent episode led to war. On September 6, 1655, a Dutch farmer killed an Indian woman who was stealing peaches. Nine days later, while Dutch soldiers commanded by Stuyvesant attempted to secure the colony of New Sweden, approximately 2,000 Indians raided Manhattan. Within three days natives killed 100 settlers, captured 150 others, and destroyed the homes of 300 other Dutch people. The Dutch conducted a series of punitive raids in Manhattan and Long Island. Using military force and diplomacy, Peter Stuyvesant ransomed some hostages. While the resulting peace was fragile and short-lived, Manhattan was never again subjected to Indian attacks.

The Esopus Wars (1658–64) resulted from Indian resistance to Dutch encroachments on their lands in the Esopus Valley. In May 1658 natives killed a Dutch farmer and burned two houses. The Dutch demanded that the Indians deliver the murderers. The Dutch also attempted to fortify their settlements in the valley. This led to increasingly hostile Indian response. The Dutch, supported again by the Mohawk, defeated the Indians. In July 1660 a peace preserving Dutch settlement in the Esopus Valley was concluded. Nevertheless, the Algonquin resentment over the peace terms led to the resumption of hostilities in June 1663. Despite several harsh blows on the Dutch (two villages were annihilated), the Indians were defeated and, by a treaty concluded in May 1664, forced to relinquish most of their lands and to accept Dutch control over the Esopus Valley.

The Dutch–Indian wars brought about political changes in New Netherland when military failures, particularly Kieft's incompetence, led to the introduction of a representative consultative body. Additionally, while the wars finished with Dutch victory, the state of almost permanent struggle exhausted the colony, making it an easier prize for their English neighbors.

Further reading: Joyce D. Goodfriend, *Before the Melting Pot* (Princeton, N.J.: Princeton University Press, 1994).

—Peter Rainow

Dyer, Mary (1610?–1660)

A Quaker martyred for her faith, Mary Dyer was born in England. By 1635, when she migrated to MASSACHUSETTS Bay, Dyer had married London milliner William Dyer. In Massachusetts she resided in BOSTON, joined the church there, and associated with religious leader ANNE MARBURY HUTCHINSON. A "monster birth," a deformed fetus born to Dyer while Hutchinson attended her as midwife, was used by anti-Hutchinson propagandists as evidence of the monstrosity of Hutchinson's group's religious views and its defiance of authority. When Hutchinson walked out of the Boston church at her excommunication in March 1638, Dyer demonstrated her support by accompanying her. Dyer's husband, William, a magistrate and merchant, was disarmed and disfranchised for supporting Hutchinson. The Dyer family moved with the Hutchinsons and others in 1638 to NEWPORT, RHODE ISLAND. On a return visit to England in the 1650s Dyer converted to Quakerism. She returned to New England in 1657, after Quaker missionaries had begun to proselytize in the region, and she quickly became prominent in the local movement. Like many other QUAKERS, Dyer heard a divine call to "witness to the truth" in Massachusetts, and she traveled there as a missionary. On September 12, 1659, she was banished on pain of death. Upon her return later that year she was sentenced to die along with some of her coreligionists. At the intervention of her family, the court reprieved her. Letters written by her son on her behalf indicate that although he did not share her new faith, he did not want to see her die for it. She was made to accompany two condemned men and watch them die before being released. In spite of the importuning of family members, Dyer returned to Massachusetts on May 21, 1660. Executed on June 1, she was the only female Quaker missionary so treated anywhere. Quaker publicists jumped to eulogize her and the other martyrs, and she became a symbol of the religious intolerance of Massachusetts and the strength of the early Quaker faith. Her case offers the best example in support of an argument that links the early supporters of Hutchinson to the later Quaker successes in Rhode Island.

Further reading: Marilyn J. Westerkamp, *Women and Religion in Early America, 1600–1850: The Puritan and Evangelical Traditions* (New York: Routledge, 1999).

—Carla Gardina Pestana

E

economy

The economy of colonial North America was shaped by a number of factors. Because it was part of England's imperial empire, the colonies were subject to the controls and policies dictated by Parliament. Within this broad framework, however, the economy of each colony responded to regional factors such as geography, climate, and resources available to the local population.

England believed that its outposts existed to benefit the empire, and it established policies based on the theory of MERCANTILISM to regulate colonial economies accordingly. The colonies, for example, would serve as both a source of raw materials and a market for English finished goods. Each region would produce commodities that did not compete with England or with one another. Moreover, unless otherwise stipulated, these commodities would be shipped only to England, where they would be sold or then shipped to other European ports. Although this system did limit economic options, colonists generally benefited from England's oversight, especially before the mid-18th century. The colonists had a guaranteed market for their products and British ships to protect their cargo during transport. On occasion, England even paid incentives to planters and MERCHANTS, encouraging them to produce certain commodities. Thus, each colony found exports that fulfilled England's mercantilist policies while also capitalizing on the system's protections.

TOBACCO was the cash crop of the Chesapeake colonies and the single most important commodity produced in colonial America. During the colonial period it accounted for more than one-quarter of the value of all exports. Employing the LABOR initially of indentured servants from England and, later, of slaves from AFRICA, VIRGINIA settlers grew tobacco on farms and plantations. A few subsidiary industries, such as wagon and barrel making, developed to support tobacco production. MARYLAND also exported tobacco, but by the early 1700s, because of overproduction and decreasing tobacco prices, settlers in both Maryland and Virginia began to diversify their economy. They cultivated wheat, hemp, and flax and developed local industries to produce iron and textiles. Although most of Virginia's early settlers were men, women also lived and worked in the colony. Female indentured servants worked as domestics and in tobacco fields. Because MORTALITY rates among men were high, many women were widowed and left alone to oversee farms and plantations.

Farming was an important part of the New England economy, as settlers cultivated corn and wheat for local CONSUMPTION and for export. Much of this work was performed by wage and family labor, including women and children. The rocky soil and cooler climate encouraged settlers to diversify, and colonists also engaged in FISHING, LUMBERING, and SHIPBUILDING. For much of the 17th century, New Englanders also participated in the FUR TRADE, buying and exporting pelts from their Indian neighbors.

The Middle Colonies of PENNSYLVANIA, NEW YORK, DELAWARE, and NEW JERSEY were rich in farmland, and their economy was based primarily on AGRICULTURE. Settlers grew wheat and flax, raised livestock, and processed lumber for export. Early in the colonial era most of their surplus was sold to the West Indies to support planters and their slaves, because planters there focused on the production of sugar rather than foodstuffs. After the mid-18th century the Middle Colonies also shipped flour to Britain.

In the Lower South, Carolina's economy was diverse in the late 17th century when settlers helped supply the West Indies with corn, peas, livestock, lumber, and naval stores. In addition, Carolina traders purchased and exported deerskins from the local Indians. Traders also engaged in a SLAVE TRADE of Indians until tensions with neighboring tribes made this enterprise imprudent.

By the early 1700s the economy of SOUTH CAROLINA and later GEORGIA shifted to plantation agriculture. Rice and INDIGO dominated the economic landscape. Rice tended to be a "rich man's" crop, as it required large investments of land and labor. Many rice planters also grew indigo as a second staple. Small farmers grew indigo on less expensive upcountry land.

The success of these staple crops was due largely to the talents and labor of African slaves, who worked the farms and plantations. Rice and indigo were grown in West Africa, and many of the slaves imported from there already possessed the knowledge and skill needed to cultivate these crops. White planters took advantage of that knowledge in their workforce.

By the 1750s the southern backcountry was also growing and developing its own regional economy. Located approximately 100 miles inland and stretching from Pennsylvania south to Georgia, the backcountry attracted German and Scots-Irish immigrants who were looking for inexpensive land. Most were subsistence farmers, but by the 1760s small commercial towns, such as Camden, South Carolina, and Winchester, Virginia, grew to support a developing commercial economy.

As the colonies matured, merchant, artisan, and professional classes grew to support local industries. Merchants coordinated long-distance ocean trade, including the buying and selling of black slaves. An artisan CLASS emerged, working as shoemakers, tailors, coopers, blacksmiths, weavers, and potters. Women worked on family farms and businesses and also as domestic servants. A professional class, including doctors and lawyers, also developed, especially in the cities.

By the mid-1700s the colonial economy had matured and developed under England's protective policies. Rice, livestock, and dairy products were not among Parliament's enumerated commodities, and thus they could be sold to areas outside England. Ships made in New England carried these foodstuffs to the Lower South, the West Indies, and across the Atlantic. Tobacco production continued as the demand in Europe increased 10-fold during the 18th century. The success of plantation staples encouraged the demand for labor, bringing increased wealth to merchants and traders involved in the slave trade.

As the population grew, more of the farm output was sold locally. The growth in local consumption stimulated demand for other goods and services. The economy of the colonies was thereby becoming integrated. For example, between 1700 and 1770, the volume of trade between CHARLESTON and England doubled, but it increased sevenfold between Charleston and the northern colonies.

The developing economy also brought greater social inequality. Most middle- and upper-class colonists enjoyed improved standards of living, but there was also a growing lower class. In the port city of PHILADELPHIA, for example, the rich were getting richer while the poor got poorer. During the course of the 18th century, the wealthiest 10 percent saw their share of taxable property increase from 40 to 70 percent. The poorest third of the population, however, saw their share drop from 5 to 1 percent.

By the 1760s, although the colonies were still part of Britain's empire, they were no longer simply a source of raw material and a market for finished goods. The colonies had developed a growing internal market and constituted an important component of the Atlantic economy. Many colonies also came to believe that the increasing economic restrictions imposed by Parliament were beginning to limit their economic growth.

See also TRADE AND SHIPPING.

Further reading: John J. McCusker and Russell R. Menard, *The Economy of British America, 1607–1789* (Chapel Hill: University of North Carolina Press, 1985).

—Virginia Jelatis

education

Of all the cultural institutions transplanted to the New World by colonists, education has received the least attention from historians. This historiographical fact is likely the result of the vast differences that separate the realities of colonial education from the expectations of later generations of Americans. None of the British colonies created a free, mandatory, public education system that would dominate the lives of the young for a decade or more, as their descendants created in the mid-19th century, but this is not to say, as historians have often misconstrued, that early Americans cared nothing about education. Instead, they transplanted some pedagogical customs to the New World, created others once there, and developed learning methods that supported their central beliefs and adapted them for the lives they would lead.

When the leaders of the MASSACHUSETTS BAY COMPANY chose as their corporate seal a scantily clad Native American saying "Come over and help us," they were making no idyllic statement. The "help" that this idealized Indian was requesting was a religious education in the Protestant faith. The company's supporters held the proselytizing of NATIVE AMERICANS to be among the religious and nationalistic goals that they could carry to the New World. By the late 16th century Native Americans were already viewed as enviable prizes in the Protestant–Catholic battle in Europe. JESUITS in New France had been in the New World for decades already, and their annual reports detailed the catechizing and conversion of thousands of Native Americans to the Catholic faith. Those conversions, as well as the ones carried out by Spanish friars in New Spain, left English Protestants both envious and fearful.

England's earliest discussions of colonization noted teaching and converting Native Americans as a central impetus for settlement in the New World. However, by the time these plans became realities, little effort was actually put into mass conversion of Indians. The struggle for establishing settler colonies, the serious strife that quickly developed between natives and English settlers, the resistance of natives to proselytizing, and the general difficulty of drawing natives to the abstractions of Calvinist theology all limited the number of Indian converts to English PROTESTANTISM. Similarly, the 1622 plan for Henrico College in VIRGINIA included a proposal for the instruction of Indians, but the scheme failed because of the Indian uprising that year and the takeover of the colony by the royal government. Where success did occur in teaching and converting Indians, it was on a scale much smaller than that carried out by the Jesuits to the north. Still, there were notable successes enjoyed by Puritan clergyman JOHN ELIOT and the Mayhew family in Massachusetts Bay, ROGER WILLIAMS in RHODE ISLAND, and later by Moravian and Lutheran missionaries in PENNSYLVANIA and ELEAZAR WHEELOCK, the founder of DARTMOUTH COLLEGE in NEW HAMPSHIRE.

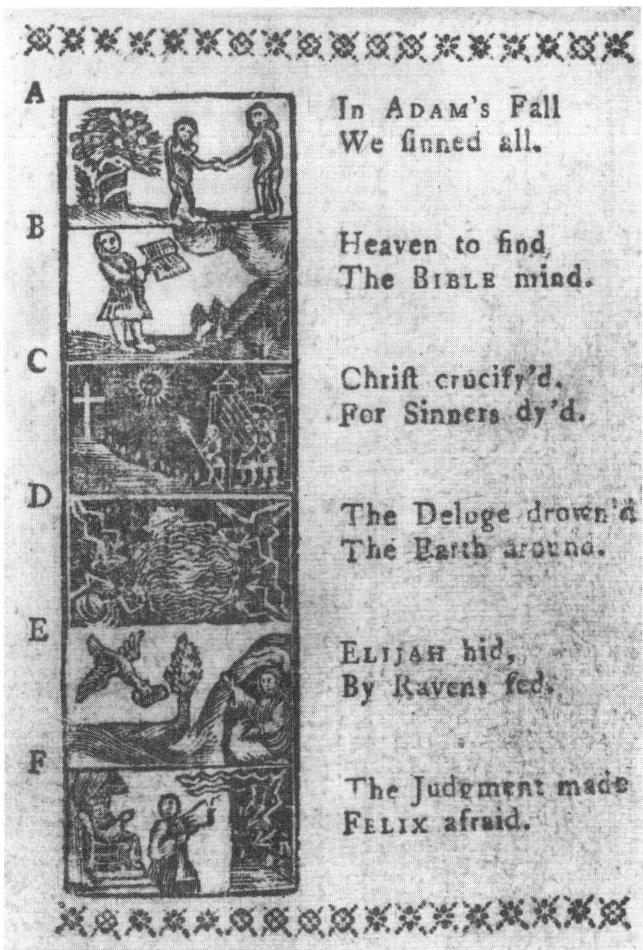

A In ADAM's Fall
We ſinned all.

B Heaven to find,
The BIBLE mind.

C Chriſt crucify'd,
For Sinners dy'd.

D The Deluge drown'd
The Earth around.

E ELIJAH hid,
By Ravens fed.

F The Judgment made
FELIX afraid.

A page of the New England Primer, used by colonists to educate their children and mix Bible lessons with the alphabet *(Hulton/Archive)*

Education was closely tied to the cultural backgrounds of the groups settling each of the colonies, and each colony developed a unique educational pattern. Religion was the foremost of these characteristics affecting educational culture. For example, the Calvinist beliefs of the people who settled New England in the 1630s strongly emphasized a personal interpretation of the Bible. PURITANS therefore stressed literacy and established community schools that would teach as well as help shape individual lives. Within the first decade of settlement, the Puritans established grammar schools and HARVARD COLLEGE, and by 1642 passed legislation demanding that families and masters be responsible for providing basic literacy to youths. Within the ensuing decades laws required each New England village of 50 or more families to have a schoolmaster and that towns with more than 200 inhabitants be able to train young men in a grammar school to prepare them for college.

None of the colonies outside New England displayed a similar zeal for formally mandated levels of education, in part because other colonies did not demand the same level of church-state social control that New Englanders required. The different religions' varying perspectives on CHILDHOOD and the family strongly affected the way colonies developed educational patterns for children. In Quaker Pennsylvania, for example, the Society of Friends' early emphasis on the importance of nurturing families and the "special" nature of childhood led the colony's Quaker-led leadership to defer questions of child training to individual families. WILLIAM PENN's admonition to "have but few books" often led historians of education to misunderstand colonial Quaker educational beliefs. Penn advocated reading good books rather than limiting literacy; QUAKERS were not antiintellectual in their policies, but they believed that childhood was a pivotal moment that required careful nurturing overseen by loving parents and guardians. Pennsylvania's educational culture therefore developed in a pattern as unique as the colony's population. Quakers created public academies, including the Friends school established in 1683, in which schoolmaster Enoch Flower taught pupils reading, writing, and basic ciphering. In addition, other religious denominations, including Anglicans, German and Swedish LUTHERANS, Moravians, BAPTISTS, and German Reformed sects all established educational institutions to teach their children in curricula that reflected their beliefs.

Beyond the religiously based schools, few colonists studied classical language or mathematics. As historian Bernard Bailyn observed, to fully understand the educational patterns of colonial America, one must examine the entire process by which people hoped to transmit their cultures from one generation to the next. For a large part of the white population, education entailed a formal period of vocational training when students would learn the "art and mystery" of a specific craft. Apprenticeship, whose customs were rooted in the Middle Ages, was the most common form of education for the "middling sort" of colonists. An apprenticeship agreement, negotiated between the youth's parents and the master, usually prescribed the level of schooling that the child should receive during his or her apprenticeship. The schoolmasters and mistresses whose advertisements filled the columns of newspapers offered instruction in reading, writing, ciphering, and a few other subjects, often in day schools for one set of children and night schools for those required in craft shops during the day. Indeed, it was the differing pedagogical methods of the 17th and 18th centuries that often led historians to misunderstand the educational achievements of colonists. Scholars sometimes tallied the number of people who signed documents as indicative of the literacy of early Americans. However, white colonists usually learned "passive literacy" (reading) rather than "active literacy" (writing). Considering these educational backgrounds, we can estimate that as many as 85 or 90 percent of adults in some areas could read.

One group excluded from formal education in colonial America were those who came to the New World in chains. Some attempts were made to educate AFRICAN AMERICANS, including allowing black New Englanders to attend classes with their white neighbors or teaching segregated classes like those COTTON MATHER offered for black and Indian children in 1717. Religious groups—including NEW YORK missionaries of the SOCIETY FOR THE PROPAGATION OF THE GOSPEL IN FOREIGN PARTS, the ANGLICAN CHURCH, and Philadelphia's Quaker Yearly Meeting—established some schools for black pupils. Thomas Bray's Associates, an England-based philanthropic organization, was also instrumental in creating schools for African Americans, including schools in Philadelphia and Williamsburg. Men like Philadelphia Quaker ANTHONY BENEZET, who taught black students for four decades, helped educate leaders for African Americans in urban areas, yet only a tiny portion of African Americans received any formal schooling, and their literacy rates consequently were extremely low. Indeed, masters often prohibited the education of their slaves, fearing that literate bondpeople would write passes to aid in their own escape.

As each of the colonies matured and developed a more stratified social hierarchy, education increasingly became a central determinant of where one fit into society. While struggling planters in the 17th-century Chesapeake area put little energy into creating permanent schools, their more prosperous 18th-century descendants used education—as they used material goods, ARCHITECTURE, and leisure practices—to establish themselves at the pinnacle of their colony's society. Much of this gentry education took place on the plantations themselves, with private tutors hired to teach the children residing there. Philip Fithian, who taught the children of planter ROBERT "KING" CARTER in the early 1770s, instructed the five daughters, two sons, and a nephew in various topics. The eldest son, 18-year-old Benjamin Tasker Carter, was "reading Salust; Grammatical Exercises, and Latin Grammar," subjects obviously preparing him for college and, eventually, for the refined behavior expected of a Virginia gentleman. His younger kinsfolk followed in his footsteps, studying English grammar, writing, and mathematics. Eldest daughter Priscilla Carter, preparing for her role as a planter's wife, studied Addison and Steele's *Spectator,* writing, and was "beginning to Cypher" at age 15, while her younger sister was "beginning to write" at 13. Other subjects, such as fencing and dancing, completed the children's education. The lessons learned by the elites were designed to connect them with other gentry children, and no one else. When on January 30, 1774, Fithian found two of his young charges dancing in the schoolroom with a group of slaves, he "dispersed them . . . immediately."

In other colonies creating educational patterns unique to the society's gentry was repeated. Each of the colonial colleges established by the early 1740s—HARVARD COLLEGE, the COLLEGE OF WILLIAM AND MARY, YALE COLLEGE, the College of New Jersey—were centers of genteel identity as well as places where the young elite could prepare to identify themselves as leaders and to learn classical curricula. Benjamin Franklin reacted against that aspect of college life in the 1720s, when he characterized Harvard students as "fops" and "blockheads." He echoed the charge in 1749, when he himself called for the creation of a public academy in Philadelphia, the school that would eventually become the College and Academy of Philadelphia and then the University of Pennsylvania. "Art is long, but their time is short," Franklin wrote, explaining why the students who would attend the school he proposed would learn practical subjects as well as some classical studies. Still, understanding the political realities, he solicited support from the colony's wealthy Anglican elite and altered his curricular plans to include subjects that they desired for their sons. In the end, the COLLEGE OF PHILADELPHIA held little of the pedagogical uniqueness that Franklin had proposed. It was essentially one more school training a colony's gentry for leadership.

Franklin's creation of the College of Philadelphia was just one such founding in the mid-18th century that reflected the changing beliefs and structures of colonial societies. The GREAT AWAKENING was the leading force in creating new schools. As GEORGE WHITEFIELD and his fellow itinerants crisscrossed the colonies, they spread new religious fervor and called into question the old social order. The new order that arose, as well as the growing prosperity of the various colonies, brought about the creation of the College of New Jersey (PRINCETON COLLEGE), KING'S COLLEGE (Columbia), the College of Rhode Island (Brown), Queen's College (Rutgers), and DARTMOUTH COLLEGE. By the end of the 1760s, the American colonies were served by nine institutions of higher learning, each drawing from different theological backgrounds, based on local traditions of support, and each closely tied to their colonies' leadership and elite.

Further reading: Lawrence A. Cremin, *American Education: The Colonial Experience, 1607–1783* (New York: Harper & Row, 1970).

—George W. Boudreau

Edwards, Jonathan (1703–1758)

Perhaps the greatest minister and theologian in early America, Jonathan Edwards was born on October 5, 1703. He was the fifth child and only son of the Reverend Timothy Edwards, the pastor of the Congregational church of East Windsor (then within the jurisdiction of MASSACHUSETTS) and Esther Stoddard, the daughter of the Reverend Solomon Stoddard, the influential pastor of the Congregational church in Northampton, Massachusetts. Schooled by his father, Edwards was entered in 1716 at the new Collegiate School chartered by the CONNECTICUT colony, renamed YALE COLLEGE in 1718.

The curriculum Edwards encountered at Yale was based on the staples of classical Protestant scholasticism. This "old logic," which "mightily pleased" him, inclined Edwards to look to the Puritan past for the substance of his theology, yet the generosity of Yale's British friends had also endowed the college with a library containing some of the newest scientific and philosophical texts, especially those of JOHN LOCKE and Isaac Newton. From these, Edwards acquired, alongside a very traditional Calvinist theology, a sharp curiosity over the scientific revolution of the 1600s and how it might be bent toward serving Calvinist ends. His notebooks, especially on "The Mind" and "Natural Science," show that Edwards was particularly attracted to the immaterialism usually associated with Bishop George Berkeley and Father Nicholas Malebranche. "That which truly is the substance of all bodies is the infinitely exact and precise and perfectly stable idea in God's mind," Edwards concluded in one early notebook entry, "together with his stable will that the same shall gradually be communicated to us and to other minds according to certain fixed and exact established methods and laws." This did not mean that physical realities did not exist, but

Jonathan Edwards *(Library of Congress)*

it did mean that whatever existence physical realities did have was entirely dependent on God's will and had "no proper being of their own."

Edwards graduated from Yale in 1720, served briefly as minister to a Presbyterian congregation in NEW YORK CITY, and in 1724 returned to Yale as a junior instructor. In November 1726 the Northampton church invited him to become the associate of his aging grandfather, Solomon Stoddard, and he was ordained by the Northampton church on February 22, 1727. Five months later he married Sarah Pierrepont of New Haven. After Stoddard's death in 1729, Edwards succeeded him as pastor of the Northampton church.

Edwards's preaching in his first years in the Northampton pastorate show him as cautious and conventional, but in the winter of 1734–35, as a result of series of sermons that Edwards aimed against the decay of Calvinist orthodoxy, "a Concern about the Great things of Religion began . . . to prevail abundantly in the Town," in which "more than 300 souls were savingly brought home to Christ." Edwards published an account of the revival and a justification of his own encouragement of it in 1737 as *A Faithful Narrative of the Surprising Work of God.* However, a second and far more dramatic revival of religious concern occurred in 1740 in the wake of the New England preaching tour of the celebrated Anglican itinerant GEORGE WHITEFIELD. At the height of this "awakening," in July 1741, Edwards preached (at Enfield, Connecticut) his most famous sermon, *Sinners in the Hands of an Angry God.*

Unhappily, Edwards soon found that the passionate emphasis on divine sovereignty and personal religious conversion that he demanded aroused suspicion and opposition from the elite pastors of BOSTON's wealthy Congregational churches. He published a series of defenses of revivalism beginning in 1741 with *The Distinguishing Marks of a Work of the Spirit of God* and rising in 1746 to his most important work on religious experience, *A Treatise Concerning Religious Affections.* Edwards also discovered another form of opposition within his own congregation when in 1744 he proposed to change Northampton's practice of open admission to communion and instead begin restricting access to only the demonstrably converted. The congregation resented the criticism of their own sincerity implied by this change, and at the end of a six-year struggle they dismissed Edwards from the Northampton church.

Edwards assumed the post of missionary to the Indian congregation at Stockbridge, Massachusetts, where he was able to turn his time and thinking back to the philosophical problems that had dominated his youth. In 1754 he published *Freedom of the Will,* a rigorously logical defense of the compatibility of human responsibility with absolute divine determination of human choice and followed that in 1758 with *The Great Christian Doctrine of Original Sin Defended.* In 1757 the College of New Jersey (later PRINCETON COLLEGE) invited him to become its third president. However, after only two months in office, Edwards died on March 22, 1758, because of complications arising from a SMALLPOX inoculation. His two "dissertations" on ethics and ontology, *The Nature of True Virtue* and *Concerning the End For Which God Created the World,* were published in 1765.

Further reading: A. C. Guelzo, *Edwards on the Will: A Century of American Theological Debate* (Middletown, Conn.: Wesleyan University Press, 1989); John E. Smith, *Jonathan Edwards: Puritan, Preacher, Philosopher* (South Bend, Ind.: University of Notre Dame Press, 1992).

—Allen C. Guelzo

Edwards, Sarah Pierpont (1710–1758)

Sara Pierpont Edwards was the wife of JONATHAN EDWARDS, an architect of the GREAT AWAKENING. She wrote an account of her religious conversion during the revival, noting that she was "swallowed up, in the light and joy of the love of God." She was among many women who began to realize that women's and men's souls might be equal before God and that therefore women might also claim a portion of equality in social and political ways as well.

Sarah Pierpont was the daughter of Rev. James Pierpont, one of the founders of Yale, and Mary Hooker, the daughter of the founder of Hartford, CONNECTICUT. Jonathan Edwards, who would become one of early America's greatest theologians, began a four-year courtship of Sarah Pierpont when she was only 13. After marriage they settled in Northampton, MASSACHUSETTS, where her husband had his first ministry. As the minister's wife, she set an example of hospitality to traveling preachers, friends, and relatives, while raising 11 children, all of whom, unusually for the time, survived CHILDHOOD. Impressed with his wife's management of their home and her participation as his intellectual partner, Jonathan Edwards used his family as the model in his writings. Sarah frequently used her tact to extract her husband's salary from reluctant taxpayers as well as to write kind letters discouraging her daughters' many suitors.

The pressures of public life, combined with the death of her sister and recurring postpartum depression, plunged Sarah into mental breakdown in January 1742, when she was beset with hallucinations and fainting spells. Jonathan, who asked Sarah to recount the entire experience to him, interpreted the episode as a spiritual breakthrough after which she could be assured of salvation. This assurance was crucial, and her husband used her experience as a model for *Some Thoughts Concerning . . . Revival of Religion* (1742). When her husband was dismissed by the Northampton congregation in 1750, the family moved to the mission settlement at Stockbridge, where Sarah aided both her husband's writing and his ministry to NATIVE AMERICANS. In 1752 she accompanied their daughter Esther to Newark to marry Aaron Burr, the president of PRINCETON COLLEGE. Burr died in 1757, followed a year later by Jonathan Edwards, who had gone to New Jersey to replace him as president and was weakened by a SMALLPOX inoculation. When Esther died, Sarah journeyed to retrieve her orphaned grandchildren but contracted dysentery on the return trip and died in PHILADELPHIA in 1758.

—Margaret Sankey

Eliot, John (1604–1690)

John Eliot was a Christian missionary to NATIVE AMERICANS and a translator of the Bible into Algonquin. Born in Widford, Hertfordshire, England, Eliot graduated from Jesus College, Cambridge, in 1622. Later, while working as a schoolteacher, he came under the influence of THOMAS HOOKER, embraced Puritan tenets, experienced conversion, and felt a call to the ministry. Forced to flee to MASSACHUSETTS in 1631, a year later he was installed as pastor of the Congregational church in Roxbury, a position he held until his death.

Eventually Eliot became concerned for the evangelization of the Native Americans of eastern Massachusetts, whose numbers were in serious decline. The foundation for his work among them was laid by a series of laws the Massachusetts legislature enacted in 1646 making it illegal for Native Americans to maintain their traditional worship and setting aside land for their settlement in communities. That same year Eliot preached his first sermon in Algonquin without an interpreter. By 1674 he had organized his converts into 14 villages of "Praying Indians" with a total population of about 3,600. Because it was taken for granted that their Christianization required their "civilization," tribal customs were supplanted by a theocratic code derived from the Bible by Eliot himself, with oversight exercised by a Native American magistrate under an English superintendent.

A gifted linguist, Eliot prepared an Algonquin catechism (1654) and grammar (1666), as well as translations of the Westminster Larger Catechism (1654) and both Old (1663) and New (1661) Testaments. The latter constituted the first edition of the Bible printed in the Western Hemisphere. His belief that Native Americans might be descendants of the "Ten Lost Tribes" of Israel animated his own activity, while his recognition as "Apostle to the Indians" energized the efforts of others and inspired the establishment in 1649 of the Society for the Propagation of the Gospel in New England. Although KING PHILIP'S WAR (Metacom's Rebellion, 1675–6) dealt a near-fatal blow to his settlements, they maintained a tenuous hold on life as late as the early decades of the 18th century.

Eliot's other published works include the *Bay Psalm Book* (1640), a metrical edition of the Psalter prepared in conjunction with Richard Mather and Thomas Welde that was the first book printed in New England, and *The Christian Commonwealth* (1659), a political treatise suppressed by the government of Massachusetts for its ardent republicanism at a time when the Stuarts were poised to retake the throne of England.

Further reading: Richard W. Cogley, *John Eliot's Mission to the Indians before King Philip's War* (Cambridge, Mass.: Harvard University Press, 1999); Ola Elizabeth Winslow, *John Eliot: "Apostle to the Indians"* (Boston: Houghton Mifflin, 1968).

—George W. Harper

Endecott, John (1599?–1665)

A devout Puritan and hard-line conservative, John Endecott (later generations spelled the name Endicott) was the most formidable of the early MASSACHUSETTS Bay Colony leaders. His first wife, Anne Gower, was the cousin of Matthew Craddock, the first governor of the MASSACHUSETTS BAY COMPANY. Endecott was sent to Massachusetts in 1628 as the first governor of the colony with the specific purpose of preparing the small settlement for the arrival of the PURITANS in the Great Migration of the 1630s. Endecott arrived at Salem and assumed command of the settlement from Roger Conant. He quickly arrested THOMAS MORTON of Merry Mount across Massachusetts Bay for selling GUNS to the native tribes, cutting down Morton's festive Maypole as well. When JOHN WINTHROP and the Puritan fleet arrived in 1630, Endecott recognized and submitted to their authority, serving as governor, deputy governor, or assistant for the rest of his life.

Endecott was censured by the Massachusetts General Court in 1634 for cutting the cross out of the British flag, calling it too "Popish." Endecott soon afterward commanded an expedition against the PEQUOT in CONNECTICUT in 1636, ostensibly for the killing of two Massachusetts traders after a quarrel. His expedition destroyed a Pequot village on Block Island. In retaliation the Pequot attacked the English frontier settlement at Saybrook, Connecticut. The resulting escalation of hostilities on both sides led to the destruction of an entire Pequot village of 600 people in 1637. Endecott's blunt handling of the first situation was a direct cause of the brutal PEQUOT WAR of 1637, which virtually exterminated the Pequot. Endecott later proved equally harsh to the QUAKERS in Massachusetts. As governor of Massachusetts from 1655 to 1665, he persecuted them relentlessly. Among the Quakers was MARY DYER, a recent convert to the Society of Friends (Quakers). When offered her life if she would accept permanent exile, Dyer refused and was hanged as a martyr to her faith in 1660.

John Endecott helped improve EDUCATION by helping to found a free school in Salem and serving as a HARVARD COLLEGE overseer. He died and was buried in BOSTON in 1665 while serving as governor.

Further reading: Lawrence Mayo, *John Endecott: A Biography* (Cambridge, Mass.: Harvard University Press, 1936).

—Stephen C. O'Neill

England

See British Empire

English Civil War

The causes of the English Civil War (1642–1649) were complex. These included the swelling ranks and rising aspirations of the urban middle CLASS within English society and the Puritan party within the English church; the growing frustration felt by both these groups as well as the rural gentry at the Elizabethan and Stuart monarchies' repeated frustration of their aspirations; and the Stuarts's aggressive defense of a type of civil and ecclesiastical government and eventually of a theology that threatened these groups' legitimacy and even the lives of many of their members. War loomed when the politically dexterous King James I (1603–25) was succeeded by the maladroit King Charles I (1625–49), who drove these disparate groups into each other's arms.

Relations between Charles and Parliament's House of Commons were poor from the start. When war with Scotland forced Charles to ask the Commons for a military appropriation, it refused; consequently, Charles dissolved this so-called Short Parliament (1640) after just three weeks. Further setbacks at the hands of the Scots compelled him to call for new elections, though, convening what came to be known as the Long Parliament (1640–53). Relations between king and Commons steadily worsened until finally both sides took up arms. After several inconclusive battles during 1642 and 1643, Parliamentarian Oliver Cromwell led his New Model Army to triumph at Marston Moor (July 2, 1644), Naseby (June 14, 1645), and Preston (August 17–19, 1648). Charles was executed for treason on January 30, 1649, the monarchy was abolished, and a commonwealth was proclaimed. Cromwell served as lord protector from 1653 until his death five years later, maintaining a measure of order during a time of great social ferment. Eventually, moderates engineered the restoration of the monarchy and the coronation of Charles's eldest son as King Charles II (1660–85).

The war's impact on England's American colonies was significant. VIRGINIA's leaders, siding with the Crown, worked to eradicate Puritan influence in the South. New England's leaders, siding with Parliament, worried that London rather than BOSTON would be the model for the coming universal reform of church and state. The PURITANS' Great Migration of the 1630s halted and even reversed itself as men of action returned to England in order to fight on Parliament's behalf. With the monarchy's restoration, New England became a haven for three of the "regicides" who had signed Charles I's death warrant.

Further reading: C. V. Wedgwood, *The Great Rebellion: The King's Peace, 1637–1641* (London: Collins, 1955).

—George W. Harper

English immigrants

Most immigrants to British North America in the 17th century were of English extraction. English immigration to North America began with the founding of JAMESTOWN in 1607 and accelerated after the founding of MASSACHUSETTS Bay Colony in 1629. In the Great Migration, which lasted from 1629 until the onset of the ENGLISH CIVIL WAR in 1649, approximately 20,000 English men, women, and children migrated to New England and as many as 40,000 to other English colonies, particularly MARYLAND and VIRGINIA. Most of the New England settlers were PURITANS (many from East Anglia, the center of English Puritanism), most were people of modest means—farmers, craftspeople, or lesser gentry—and most immigrated in family groups. The Chesapeake region drew a much larger percentage of single adults (mostly men), moneyed investors, and servants.

Immigration patterns changed markedly after 1649. During the English Civil War, some Puritan settlers returned to England. Relatively few English immigrants settled in New England after 1649; later 17th- and 18th-century immigration focused on the South and, above all, PENNSYLVANIA and the Middle Colonies. The population of the Delaware Valley (Pennsylvania, NEW JERSEY, and DELAWARE) escalated from about 3,000 settlers in 1680 to 24,000 in 1700 and 170,000 by 1750. Initially, QUAKERS from Wales and the English midlands dominated the region's culture. They sought to escape religious persecution and to create a society that reflected Quaker ideals. After 1715, however, many non-Quaker English immigrants also settled in these colonies, so that by 1760 Quakers were a minority in the region. The Quaker leadership's liberal social policy quickly made the Delaware Valley one of the most ethnically and religiously diverse regions of British America.

A large percentage of English immigrants to the Delaware Valley and the South were indentured servants, teenagers and young adults who obtained free passage to the New World by bartering their LABOR for a period of years (typically four to seven years, although children were sometimes bound for much longer terms). All the British colonies imported indentured servants, but they were most numerous in Virginia and Maryland in the 17th century, where an average of 2,000 servants arrived each year from the 1630s until 1700. INDENTURED SERVITUDE declined in the southern colonies in the late 17th century as economic conditions in England improved and the cost of importing slaves declined. During the 18th century most indentured servants went to the Middle Colonies. English convicts (and occasionally prisoners of war) were transported to North America in a slow but steady stream throughout the colonial period. Convicts were bound for even longer terms than indentured servants were, typically seven to 14 years. Most went to the southern colonies. The transportation of convicts to the American colonies was controversial, however, and colonists generally discouraged it.

In 1690 90 percent of the colonists in British America were of British descent. In the 18th century, however, a large percentage of immigrants to the British colonies were German, Scottish, Scots-Irish, and African. Between 1715 and 1775 250,000 people fled famine and poverty in northern Britain—the north of England, the Scottish lowlands, and northern Ireland—and sought economic refuge in British America. The movement began as a trickle but accelerated rapidly in the 1760s. Both families and young, single adults tried their fortunes in the New World. Many came as indentured servants. They faced horrific conditions aboard immigrant ships and often encountered ethnic prejudice from other British Americans. As the richest land along the eastern seaboard had long since been claimed and cultivated, most of the new northern British immigrants moved west to backcountry regions of Pennsylvania, Virginia, the Carolinas, and GEORGIA, where they established small farms. The northern British and Scots-Irish influence is still evident in Appalachia today. Still, the largest group of new arrivals in 18th-century British America were Africans forcibly brought to the New World as slaves.

Further reading: Bernard Bailyn, *The Peopling of British North America: An Introduction* (New York: Knopf, 1986); David Hackett Fischer, *Albion's Seed: Four British Folkways in America* (New York: Oxford University Press, 1989).

—Darcy R. Fryer

Enlightenment, American

Scholars have most often identified the writings of Francis Bacon, Isaac Newton, and JOHN LOCKE on SCIENCE, philosophy, and government as the wellsprings of the Enlightenment in both Britain and British America, their greatest influence occurring roughly between the 1680s and the era of the French Revolution (1789). Immanuel Kant summarized the aims of "enlightenment" in the phrase *sapere aude*—dare to know for oneself. Traditionally conceived, to be enlightened was to throw off slavish adherence to tradition and insist on one's own critical ability to make judgments about nature, religion, politics, and society. These new freedoms prioritized individual religious conscience and the separation of church and state, the replacement of superstition and merely textual authority by experimental science to investigate nature, the replacement of monarchies and absolutist regimes by representative and constitutional forms of government, and the freedom to attempt a wide range of practical reforms for the good of society.

As a result of increasing transatlantic trade, the British American provinces became culturally more sophisticated during the 18th century and, looking to Britain for models, gradually developed similar social institutions for the exchange of ideas and information within the "public sphere." These included newspapers and magazines, coffee houses, Masonic lodges, social clubs, public libraries, and the establishment of new colleges, all of which were knit together by extensive correspondence networks and the circulation of printed books (mostly imported from London), known collectively as the "republic of letters."

The colonists appropriated some elements of European Enlightenment culture but rejected others. For example, Benjamin Franklin's leading role in creating the Library Company of PHILADELPHIA, the AMERICAN PHILOSOPHICAL SOCIETY, the Pennsylvania Hospital, and other institutions reflected continuity with British traditions of civic-minded improvement and the use of science and TECHNOLOGY to achieve practical benefits in areas like AGRICULTURE and navigation. By contrast, the unabashed anticlericalism of *philosophes* like Voltaire did not resonate as deeply with Americans, whose societies, unlike Catholic France, had never known a socially dominating established church.

Some features of the American Enlightenment were conscious departures from European models. The one stronghold of American anticlericalism was, unsurprisingly, the colony where Anglicanism (the established Religion of England) was also strongest: VIRGINIA. Deism (the view that God constructed the universe as a self-running machine, from which he then withdrew) enjoyed a rare institutional base at the COLLEGE OF WILLIAM AND MARY, where Thomas Jefferson was a student. In 1786 Jefferson helped legalize the separation of church and state in Virginia. WILLIAM PENN, the Quaker proprietor of Pennsylvania, had made religious toleration the law in his colony a century earlier, but the pluralistic character of American religious life ultimately owed more to the sheer diversity of denominations in the colonies rather than any one program of toleration.

The teachings of liberal English Anglicans like Samuel Clarke and John Tillotson and moderate Scots Episcopalians like Francis Hutcheson found important venues at colleges and churches, promoting enlightened ideas about individual moral and intellectual capacities. Like Quakerism, these traditions sought to reconcile spiritual and commercial free will with benevolent and unifying social activity. Scottish "moral sense" writers argued for the existence of innate benevolence and social sympathy in human beings, while "common sense" philosophers insisted on the trustworthiness of individual sensory knowledge as a basis for making judgments about nature and morality. These ideas became especially dominant after the 1790s as an antidote to the threats of philosophical skepticism and atheism many perceived in the French Revolution and as a way of doing science without contradicting Protestant doctrine.

British American attitudes to nature took shape within an immensely flexible intellectual framework that emphasized that the universe was a divine and rational work whose structure was intelligible through human reason. There was no decisive conflict between science and religion in this era. All colonial science, or rather "natural philosophy" (later physics and chemistry) and "natural history" (later biology), existed within Protestant thought, never outside it. This framework was often referred to as "physico-theology," or "natural theology," both of which indicate that ideas relating to the physical structure of nature were generally considered a branch of religious devotion. American thinkers were eclectic in combining biblical and philosophical views of natural phenomena. COTTON MATHER believed that SMALLPOX was caused both by atomic effluviae *and* sinful behavior, while JONATHAN EDWARDS, despite his serious interest in Newtonian natural philosophy, retained the orthodox Calvinist view that humans did not possess free will and that their spiritual fate was predetermined.

The greatest impact of the Enlightenment in North America has most often been thought to be political. The revolution against British rule, from the Declaration of Independence's affirmation of universal natural rights to the federal Constitution's system of republican representation, safeguarded by checks and balances between the people and their government, remains the transcendent achievement of the American Enlightenment. More recently, however, scholars have focused on the social groups deliberately excluded from this revolution. Despite their literacy and despite a famous request from Abigail to John Adams to "remember the ladies" in constructing a new polity, British American culture continued to insist that women's roles as wives and mothers were incompatible with political activity. QUAKERS JOHN WOOLMAN and ANTHONY BENEZET were early antislavery leaders who succeeded in banning the SLAVE TRADE among the Quakers by 1758, but financial self-interest and fear of reprisal on the part of southern slaveholders prevented the extension of the Declaration's principles to AFRICAN AMERICANS in 1776. NATIVE AMERICANS suffered directly as a consequence of American independence, because the expulsion of the British removed a major obstacle to the settlement of western lands.

See also BOSTON PHILOSOPHICAL SOCIETY; MEDICINE; PHILADELPHIA.

Further reading: Ned C. Landsman, *From Colonials to Provincials: American Thought and Culture, 1680–1760* (New York: Twayne, 1997); Henry F. May, *The Enlightenment in America* (New York: Oxford University Press, 1976).

—James Delbourgo

environment

It is nearly impossible to understand early American history, ECONOMY, and culture without factoring in the environment. At its most basic level the environment provided Indians, Europeans, and Africans in America with the necessities of life: FOOD, shelter, and CLOTHING. The environment placed broad limits on what peoples in early America could do, but it also provided opportunities to form new societies. For a topic as large as the early American environment, a case study approach is best, so this short essay examines early New England and VIRGINIA as well as Indian uses and concepts of the environment.

Indian peoples did not think of nature as a category separate from their own existence; they were part of nature, lived within its annual cycles, and incorporated it into their religious and social rituals. Indian peoples performed ceremonies to ensure bountiful harvests and efficacy in hunting. Around the time of the first summer harvest, a festival brought people together to renew community ties. Hunters usually performed a brief rite at the death of their prey and gave some sort of offering for the spirit of the animal. Such commemorations enabled people to give thanks for nature's bounty as well as to ensure that a sort of harmony and balance with nature was maintained so as to maintain future abundance. Indians used the natural environment in diverse ways depending on the particular environmental constraints or prospects in their local area. For this reason, HOUSING styles varied tremendously across the North American continent. Almost every Indian group practiced some farming, and those living east of the Mississippi River depended overwhelmingly on crops of corn, beans, squash, and other cultivated plants. Despite a goal of harmony within nature, Indians altered local environments to support their lifestyles, sometimes to the point of straining certain natural resources to the limit. Such tensions became particularly obvious when Indians entered into the FUR TRADE with Europeans. Whether it was beaver in the North or deer in the South, Indians depleted certain animal populations rapidly by 1763 in order to acquire European manufactured goods that they depended upon. They consequently gradually abandoned many of the rituals that had so intimately tied them to the environment. Europeans contributed to this depletion of natural resources by Indians, but they went much farther than Indians in altering the natural environment.

In early New England settlements, FORESTS, fish, farms, and furs dominated everyday life. Fish supplied the initial attraction for Europeans to New England and then developed into a worldwide industry before 1600. The primary fish resources were codfish (from which Cape Cod received its name), sea bass, haddock, herring, Atlantic salmon, lobster, mullet, crab, oysters, clams, and mussels. A large SHIPBUILDING industry developed by the 1650s. New

This sketch shows how early settlers altered the landscape, often by clearing away forests to make way for farming. *(Library of Congress)*

Englanders constructed sawmills, shipped white pines to England for ship's masts, sold wood to the West Indies, and extracted potash, tar, pitch, and turpentine for naval stores.

Wood frame homes fixed New England Puritan society in place. Nature around the house was forced to adapt, and PURITANS made the environment fit human needs rather than fitting themselves into the environment. Women maintained vegetable and herb gardens, and men farmed cash crops like wheat and corn. New Englanders practiced row-crop AGRICULTURE and created a tame world of fields and fences rather than forests. English colonists initially used Indian-cleared land and then began clearing their own acreage for farms and towns. In addition, livestock (cattle, horses, hogs) required fencing in or out, and they competed with and drove away native animal species. The cooperage industry (barrel-making) and the trees that supplied it were essential to the transportation of farm products and other goods. Plank roads further consumed forests.

Big business in early New England was spelled beaver. In high demand throughout Europe by the late 1500s, beaver pelts supplied material for hats, winter coats, and castoreum oil that served as a base for perfumes. Everybody who was anybody had to have a beaver hat. The beaver fur trade often established the first connection between English and Indians in New England as well as between the French and Indians in the Great Lakes area. As the fur trade grew, the beaver skin became the primary unit of financial measure. During the peak of the fur trade era, some 200,000 pelts a year were sold to the European market, with a large adult beaver skin yielding enough fur for 18 hats. The fur trade severely depleted beaver numbers by the early to mid-18th century, and it altered the New England landscape by eliminating beaver ponds and the related meadows around them. Thus, New England's rich supplies of forests, fish, and furs allowed the Puritans to create an enduring existence based on family farms and small towns, along with ports and merchant centers like BOSTON.

Environmental history is also crucial to understanding colonial Virginia, although the story is much different than in New England. The VIRGINIA COMPANY OF LONDON established the colony in 1607 as a business venture. From the beginning it sought a profit-making product that could be extracted from Virginia and sold in England. Before that happened the unfamiliar environment of Virginia nearly killed the JAMESTOWN colony with salt poisoning and an unavoidable dependence on Indians for food. In order to make a profit, the Jamestown colonists tried a range of products, such as deerskins, timber, sassafras, silk (with imported silk worms), glassmaking, iron, fruit trees, flax, and hemp, but none worked. Beginning experiments in 1612, JOHN ROLFE demonstrated that TOBACCO could produce profits.

Although the Virginia climate and soils provided ideal conditions for cultivating tobacco, attempting to grow the plant in large quantities ran into environmental constraints and contributed significantly to the type of SOCIETY and culture that developed in colonial Virginia. Tobacco leached minerals out of the soil very quickly and was therefore a land-intensive business venture. This feature of tobacco farming encouraged settlement in the river valleys of Virginia, with the aim to own hundreds and even thousands of acres so that worn-out land could remain fallow while tobacco planting moved onto virgin soil. Naturally, conflicts with Indians arose, and the POWHATAN Indians revolted against English land grabbing with deadly attacks in 1622 and 1644. In addition to being land intensive, tobacco was also labor intensive. The Virginia Company enacted the headright system in the 1610s to encourage immigration. Initially, indentured servants supplied the necessary labor, but Virginia planters switched to African slave labor in the latter half of the 17th century as that labor source became more cost effective.

This need for large landholdings and labor crews produced an almost feudal society in colonial Virginia. Virginia remained overwhelmingly rural, with large plantations and a captive labor force, few towns, a dispersed population living along river banks, and government based in counties rather than in towns. Landed aristocrats in Virginia promoted social cohesion among their ranks and denied competitors access to prime tobacco lands through the ending of INDENTURED SERVITUDE, passing of tobacco quality laws, and institution of government regulation of the industry in 1730. Those who produced high-quality tobacco gained the designation "crop masters" and more easily acquired credit from English and Scottish MERCHANTS than did other tobacco farmers. In Virginia, thanks to the environment and human ingenuity, tobacco turned into money and molded colonial society.

Further reading: William Cronon, *Changes in the Land: Indians, Colonists, and the Ecology of New England* (New York: Hill & Wang, 1983); John Opie, *Nature's Nation: An Environmental History of the United States* (New York: Harcourt Brace, 1998); Timothy Silver, *A New Face on the Countryside: Indians, Colonists, and Slaves in South Atlantic Forests, 1500–1800* (New York: Cambridge University Press, 1990).

—Greg O'Brien

epidemics See disease

ethnocentrism

"Monsters shaped and faced like men;" "a fanatical, self-conceited sort of people;" "near beasts;" "ignorant, mean, worthless, beggarly Irish Presbyterians;" "devilish Satyr apes;" "wild and beggarly Irish;" "heathens;" "savages." These derogatory expressions (ethnophaulisms) are but a small sample of the descriptive terms used by early Americans to classify individuals from cultures and classes unlike their own.

Ethnocentrism is the tendency to judge others in terms of the norms of one's own group, culture, or class and to assert the alleged superiority of one's own group. Ethnocentric beliefs can predispose one ethnic group or social class to derogate, segregate, or commit violence against other people. Ethnocentrism intensified in the 17th-century Atlantic world as immigrants and natives both confronted other groups of people and often reshaped their own ethnic identities. Indians, Africans, and Europeans initially understood "strangers" through cultural categories and caricatures arising both from their sense of their own superiority and from their anxiety about the sufficiency of their own folkways in comparison to those of "others." As Europeans increasingly encountered other peoples during the 16th and 17th centuries, their ethnocentrism often intensified. Economic change stimulated a growing material and cultural disparity between the wealthy and the poor in Europe, and the former often regarded the latter as "the brutish part of Mankind." Simultaneously, growing domestic migration brought wandering "strangers" to cities like London. As the Reformation shattered Christianity into a myriad of competing ethnoreligious sects, each touted its superiority over others. When Europeans began overseas expansion, they encountered a bewildering variety of exotic cultures that challenged them not only to interpret the alien cultures but also to define themselves as exceptional imperial peoples. The systematic conquest and subjugation by the Tudor and Stuart dynasties of their Celtic peripheries—Scotland, Ireland, and Wales—confirmed and reinforced the assumptions held by the ruling elite of southeastern England that their culture was superior because it combined the benefits of English Christianity with those of classical civility, as defined by the Renaissance humanists. They believed the Celtic groups, especially the "barbarously savage" Catholic Irish, were stuck in an earlier stage of human development and would therefore benefit from English colonization. The English elite subsequently applied this ideological cant to the native peoples of North America, AFRICA, and the CARIBBEAN.

Similarly, Spanish and Portuguese Christians came to accept invidious associations of Africans with paganism, bestiality, and cultural depravity, and, ultimately, slavery. Influenced by the biblical legend of Ham and religious imagery contrasting white "purity" with black "depravity,"

Elizabethan elites, like their Iberian counterparts, ranked black people as a "special category of mankind," considerably behind the cultural evolution of NATIVE AMERICANS. Aversion to African racial and cultural characteristics, when coupled with the imperatives of the SLAVE TRADE, eventually made Africans vulnerable to exploitation deemed unacceptable for white people.

Still, English intellectuals examined alien cultures for signs of similarities that would answer their own questions about whether English society corresponded to universal, God-given principles of social organization. Many thought of Indians, like the Irish and the English, as springing from a common human stock, and they attributed shared similarities and differences in skin color and physiognomy to be "accidental" or the result of environmental factors. In addition to adherence to English Christianity, English writers judged the "civility" of other cultures according to the degree to which they demarcated CLASS and GENDER distinctions, possessed a hereditary hierarchy, maintained nuclear families, and practiced settled agriculture. Social class was at the heart of the European literati's definition of civilization. French officials identified "savagery" in ALGONQUIN societies in the weakness of political authority, the absence of clear class divisions, and the lack of subordination of commoners to native elites. Indeed, English explorers and colonizers were eager to identify native chiefs, SACHEMS, and werowances as equivalent to European "kings," "queens," and even "emperors," and the English frequently approved of visible distinctions between "betters" and "commoners" among natives. The superficial congruence of some European and Indian cultural and political practices fostered the illusion among metropolitan elites that Indians could be rapidly and easily assimilated into New World Christian empires.

European elites also categorized the lower classes as "savage." The wandering rural poor of Europe bore many cultural traits of an alien, "uncivil," and ungoverned people whose peripatetic ways and fitful work habits were regarded contemptuously by their "betters" as requiring reform by means of involuntary servitude. The metropolitan merchant elite and rural gentry equated "civilization" with a stable, hierarchal social order that "superior" aristocracies imposed on the bestial and depraved lower classes of their respective realms. Early modern elites, thereby, fused race, culture, authority, and class.

Indian and African peoples were also ethnocentric, often contemptuous of European colonists who, despite superior ships and metallurgy, could barely feed themselves without native help. As ROGER WILLIAMS reported, if "the Europeans are always wrangling and uneasy," Indians wondered, why do they "not go out of this World, since they are so uneasy and discontented by it." Nevertheless, native peoples thought that, perhaps with regular bathing and disciplined education in native ways, Europeans might become productive and contributing members of their respective clans, villages, and tribes. Convinced of the superiority of their cultures, Indians often encouraged individual Europeans to seek adoption by families in their communities and used persuasion, bribery, and force to incorporate entire European settlements into their polities. Unlike their xenophobic leaders, many lower-class white men and women took up the natives' offer.

In the *Pay d'en haut* of the Great Lakes region, the *coureurs des bois* (French fur traders of peasant origins) intermarried extensively with the Algonquin to gain access to trade networks and the protection that native kinship offered. Frequent interracial unions along the English, French, and Spanish frontiers laid the foundation for the mixed raced "new" peoples of North America—the MÉTIS and the Mestizo. Similarly, many white indentured servants did not always share the aversion that their "betters" displayed toward Africans. White and black servants frequently fraternized, engaged in sexual liaisons, and even ran away together, sometimes seeking protection in neighboring Indian villages. Only gradually, through legally enforced segregation, the social construction of race and white skin privileges, and the effects of intercultural competition and conflict, did European commoners in the Americas come to assimilate the xenophobia and, eventually, racism that their upper class "betters" displayed towards Africans and native peoples.

Because the power of European states was weak on the peripheries, frontier communities fostered cultural negotiation and accommodation and a degree of acceptance, or at least coexistence, of European and native cultural traditions. Indians, Europeans, and, to a lesser extent, Africans in the BORDERLANDS were mutually dependent and symbiotic. To realize their religious, imperial, and commercial aspirations, metropolitan elites and their colonial administrators struggled to obtain orderly frontiers by regulating settlement, protecting tributary tribes and their lands from European settlers, and controlling how Europeans, Indians, and Africans interacted. The metropolitan English eventually failed to pacify their frontiers because of resistance to their visions of imperial comity by not just Indians but also by the burgeoning European communities who competed with Indians for control of frontier resources.

When expanding their ethnic communities sparked hostile confrontations with Indians, white colonists were often better able than Indians to overcome some of their ethnic differences. Indians did not see themselves as one people. Throughout the 17th century Algonquin–Iroquoian intercultural conflicts were as bloody and genocidal as many English–Indian clashes. Imperial authorities supported and exploited these Indian rivalries to their advantage, just as the Indians played off competing imperial powers to further their own interests. Despite differences among their vernacular ethnic cultures, Euro-Americans were able to generate a more intense feeling of pan-European ethnic identity because they were predominantly Protestant peoples and shared a common political allegiance to Crown and commonwealth. In contrast, Indian efforts to build pan-Indian ethnic unity were more halting, as in KING PHILIP'S WAR, and did not really bear fruit in the Ohio and Great Lakes region until NEOLIN and Pontiac in the 1760s.

Racism, unlike ethnocentrism, seemingly did not exist widely among European colonists until the late 17th century. The earliest African slaves in VIRGINIA, for instance, may not have been treated significantly differently than white indentured servants. Meanwhile, New Englanders interpreted individual Indian behavior and individual adherence to European cultural norms and religious traditions as standards to distinguish between "good" and "bad" Indians. Protoracist fulminations against the "savages," therefore, could alternate with claims that the English and Indians were "of one blood."

OPECHANCANOUGH's uprisings against the Virginia colonists in 1622 and 1642 were understood by the colonists as an affront to their attempts to transform the POWHATAN into ethnic English people. The conflicts thereby exacerbated ethnocentric feelings. The intercultural conflicts of King Philip's War, KING WILLIAM'S WAR, and QUEEN ANNE'S WAR intensified distrust of Indian "incivility" and "savagery," undermined distinctions between "civilized" Christian Indians and those they regarded as pagan savages, and led to demands that they be made separate and subordinate to the Anglo-European colonists. Colonial authorities and elites thus became convinced that the solution to the "Indian problem" was their segregation into reservations and PRAYING TOWNS, not integration or amalgamation into European communities. Protracted intercultural warfare encouraged colonial lawmakers to levy increasingly harsh restrictions on all Indians, thereby fusing Christian and non-Christian Indians together into a single category because, as one New Englander claimed, "tis very difficult, unless upon long knowledge, to distinguish Indians from one another." This shift in the way white people distinguished themselves from alien "others" on the basis of religion and culture would blossom into what is best defined as "racism."

The slow evolution from ethnocentrism and group prejudice to segregation and racism was driven by competition among Indians and Europeans for resources, the breakdown of local and regional accommodations among diverse peoples, intercultural warfare, and a growing self-confidence among Europeans in their ability to survive and prosper in the new environment without the assistance of its native peoples.

See also RACE AND RACIAL CONFLICT.

Further readings: Bernard Bailyn and Philip D. Morgan, eds., *Strangers within the Realm: Cultural Margins of the First British Empire* (Chapel Hill: University of North Carolina Press, 1991); Colin G. Calloway, *New Worlds for All: Indians, Europeans, and the Remaking of Early America* (Boston: Bedford/St. Martin's, 1994); Winthrop Jordan, *White Over Black: American Attitudes toward the Negro, 1550–1812* (Chapel Hill: University of North Carolina Press, 1968); Karen Ordahl Kuppermann, *Indians and English: Facing Off in Early America* (Ithaca, N.Y.: Cornell University Press, 2000); Neal Salisbury, *Manitou and Providence: Indians, Europeans, and the Making of New England, 1500–1643* (New York: Oxford University Press, 1982); Richard White, *The Middle Ground: Indians, Empires, and Republics in the Great Lakes Region, 1650–1815* (New York: Cambridge University Press, 1991).

—James Bruggeman

exploration

The first people to explore North America most probably were northeastern Asians who, thousands of years ago, crossed the land bridge that once linked Asia and North America. When European explorers began arriving in the late 15th century, Indians had no maps to offer them nor any description of the continent as a whole. The Indians had, however, thoroughly settled and explored the Americas, and they had created a system of trails in North America that guided European adventurers and colonists in their attempts to explore and map the continent. In the 16th century Spanish and Spanish-sponsored expeditions began exploring the eastern portion of North America.

The earliest serious French push toward exploration began in 1603 with SAMUEL DE CHAMPLAIN, the geographer with a party of fur traders. The FUR TRADE remained the main motive for French exploration of North America. Champlain's responsibility was to make maps of the New World, specifically the St. Lawrence River and the Atlantic coast from Nova Scotia to Martha's Vineyard. Champlain took the lead in French settlement of Canada, founding Port Royal and Quebec. His cooperative attitude toward the ALGONQUIN and HURON Indians eased French colonization and eventually brought Champlain far enough west to see the lake that now bears his name. In 1609 Champlain explored VERMONT, naming it "Les Monts Verts"; later the Green Mountains were settled by English colonists from CONNECTICUT and NEW YORK. In 1615 he became the first European to see the Great Lakes.

Champlain's successors ÉTIENNE BRULÉ and JEAN NICOLET laid claim to this area. It became a center for the French fur trading industry. At the same time, the French began pushing south into Ohio and down the Mississippi River. During the 1670s Pierre Esprit Radisson and Médard Chouart, sieur des Groseilliers explored Hudson Bay and sparked the founding of the HUDSON'S BAY COMPANY. In 1673 the Jesuit father Marquette discovered the junction of the Wisconsin and Mississippi Rivers and, with Louis Jolliet, sailed south as far as the Arkansas River. In 1682 RENÉ-ROBERT CAVELIER, SIEUR DE LA SALLE sailed all the way to the Gulf of Mexico. He claimed the fertile area at the mouth of the gulf for France, naming it Louisiana in honor of Louis XIV. La Salle and his party were also the first Europeans to see Niagara Falls (1678).

The French opened up the fur trade in the west with explorations down the Missouri River (1712–17) and the Red River (1713). During the 1730s and 1740s Pierre de la Verendrye and his sons penetrated the interior of North America to the Black Hills of South Dakota, opening the Grand Portage from Lake Superior to the Lake of the Woods and extending the water route to Lake Winnipeg. Because their interest was in the fur trade and not in permanently settling the land, the French did not build towns or establish governments, nor did they try to drive away the Indians on whose harvesting of pelts their fur trade depended. Instead, they constructed FORTS and trading posts along the river systems. The conflict between the French and English over claims to the Ohio Valley was the cause of the French and Indian War (SEVEN YEARS' WAR). The English emerged victorious, poised to expand their exploration and settlements toward the west.

Early English exploration of North America was directed toward finding the elusive (and nonexistent) Northwest Passage—a water route across North America to Asia. In 1607 HENRY HUDSON sailed up the Atlantic coast from VIRGINIA following maps made by JOHN SMITH. Hudson's party found the mouth of the Hudson River and followed its course, hoping this might be the way to the west. As they sailed north, however, the river became shallower, and soon after they passed the site on which Albany was later built they gave up the search. A year later, on his last voyage through the icy waters north of Canada, Hudson was set adrift by a rebellious crew.

During the early 1600s the English continued to sail north and eventually planted long-lasting settlements all along the Atlantic coast. Between 1607 and 1638 the British founded seven colonies and thoroughly explored and mapped the rivers and bays of New England. The royal charters of the colonies granted them the authority to expand their territory throughout the land, as far as they were able. As the population grew and the colonists needed more living space, they began gradually to carry out this command. They were attracted by Indian rumors of great waters beyond the mountains, but the Appalachians were a formidable barrier not breached until late in the century.

Gradually, colonists penetrated the interior of the continent seeking living space and fertile farmland rather than mineral treasures. In 1650 Edward Bland and Abraham Wood penetrated the interior of Virginia, reaching the fork of the Dan and Roanoke Rivers and returning with the news that the interior land was richer and more fertile than the land on the coast. In 1671 Wood commissioned THOMAS BATTS and Robert Fallam to cross the Appalachians in search of the South Sea. They followed the Roanoke River through the Blue Ridge Mountains to the present-day border between Virginia and West Virginia. In 1698 Thomas Welch became the first English person to cross the Mississippi. In 1699 John Lederer reached the summit of the Blue Ridge Mountains. In 1716 Alexander Spotswood blazed a trail to the Shenandoah Valley; many immigrant families in search of farmland would TRAVEL this trail, and by midcentury they had settled the valley. In the 1770s Daniel Boone opened the final gateway into the interior of North America with his Wilderness Road to Kentucky. The Lewis and Clark Expedition of 1804 would nearly complete the task of mapping the continent.

Beginning in the 1570s, Spain's desire to convert the inhabitants of the Americas to Catholicism and to bring the natives under Spanish control led to missionary explorations. Between 1687 and 1711 Jesuit priest Father Eusebio Kino founded MISSIONS throughout southern California, NEW MEXICO, and southern Arizona. In 1741 Russian fur traders began exploring the West in their attempts to extend the fur trade to the Alaskan coast. Danish-born VITUS JONASSEN BERING first sighted the strait that bears his name in that year.

Further reading: Richard E. Bohlander, ed., *World Explorers and Discoverers* (New York: Macmillan, 1992); David J. Weber, *The Spanish Frontier in North America* (New Haven, Conn.: Yale University Press, 1992).

—Stephanie Muntone

F

family life See marriage and family life

Feke, Robert (1707?–1752?)

The son of a Baptist preacher, Robert Feke, a notable colonial painter, was born in Oyster Bay, NEW YORK. Only one painting remains from his time there, and it is not until Feke's move to BOSTON in 1741 that he enters the historical record. His early portraits were seen as provocative, although his color choices were considered a bit stiff and rigid. Feke may have studied in England or Europe in the early 1740s, because his style became less staid after these years, and his preference for strong, bright colors, luxurious fabrics, and background landscape settings began to emerge. Many of Feke's younger patrons, tired of the somber tones of artists from earlier generations, found his preference for silver and bright pastels appealing. Feke's career peaked in 1748, when he painted many large-scale single and group portraits of Boston's leading families. About 60 of Feke's works survive, most from this time.

After his success in Boston, Feke moved to PHILADELPHIA, where he did several additional portraits and influenced the early work of JOHN HESSELIUS. The last record of him is on August 26, 1751; he probably died in Bermuda or Barbados.

Feke had an important influence on the development of painting in the colonies. Because there were few professional painters, Feke's innovations attracted particular attention. Having one's likeness captured by such a man was a luxury available to only a very few.

—Victoria C. H. Resnick

fertility

Childbearing was an activity that defined women's lives in early America. Reproduction was essential to the survival of the colonies, and most women repeated the two- or three-year cycle of pregnancy, birth, and nursing an average of eight to 10 times between marriage and menopause. Perhaps one in five women died from causes associated with childbirth, and newborns died at a rate of one in 10. The birth rate was very high: approximately 50 births per 1,000 people (compared to fewer than 15 per 1,000 in the United States today). This rate of reproduction was key to the success of the English colonies.

In the 17th-century Chesapeake region and in New England, native-born women typically married at age 16, younger than did their immigrant mothers. Women generally bore their last children at about age 37, which allowed for two decades of childbearing and led to a completed fertility rate of eight children per family. As the ratio of women to men equalized and as infant MORTALITY rates decreased in the late 17th century, the Euro-American population began to increase naturally.

The growth of the slave population was a factor in the evolution of American SLAVERY. The first few generations of slaves in British mainland America suffered a natural decrease in population as their deaths outnumbered their births. However, by the 1730s the establishment of slave families produced a rapid natural increase in births. This, in turn, contributed to the growth of a native-born, self-reproducing slave CLASS by the end of the colonial period. American-born slaves had higher birth rates and lower death rates than did African-born slaves. The result was an increasingly CREOLE (native-born) slave population and a more balanced male–female ratio. Because the population increase was unusual in a New World slave society, it has been argued that the evolution of a mature slave society consisting of AFRICAN AMERICANS several generations removed from their African origins led to the uniquely American system of slavery.

Compared to Euro-Americans, Native American and African weaning customs generally caused wider intervals between births, because nursing in preindustrial societies tended to inhibit the new mother's fertility. Slaves commonly nursed their babies for up to 30 months, while

Indian mothers sometimes weaned children at age five or six. Both groups sometimes abstained from sex for several years in order to control the spacing of births. Toward the end of the 18th century fertility among Euro-Americans declined sharply to a completed rate of five or six children per family, nearer that of England and France. Increased efforts to limit family size, such as withdrawal during intercourse and prolonged nursing, suggest the advent of a new idea that fertility could, and perhaps should, be controlled.

Among white people less than 3 percent of babies were born outside of marriage. There was little understanding of fertility, and therefore attempts at contraception were often ineffective. Folk MEDICINE prescribed herbal teas and female douches to prevent unsanctioned pregnancies, although coitus interruptus was probably the most commonly used method of contraception. Because of inexact medical methods for determining pregnancy, quickening, or the first perception of fetal movement that occurred during the fourth or early in the fifth month, was considered proof of the existence of life. Before quickening, abortion was common, legal, and culturally accepted; it was used primarily to terminate illegitimate pregnancies rather than to limit family size. After the fetus showed signs of life, abortion without due cause was considered a crime. The most common technique used to abort an unwanted fetus was the ingestion of an abortifacient, an herbal potion that induced miscarriage. Arbortifacient brews contained aloe, pennyroyal, or savin, an extract from juniper bushes. Less common and more dangerous was the use of instruments to mechanically abort a pregnancy.

The birthing process in early North America was the domain of women. Facing an often dangerous and dispiriting experience, women gathered to share in and help with birth, led by experienced MIDWIVES. Men were allowed only if no women were available, and the community ritual created female solidarity and spiritual closeness as well as control over a primary rite of passage. Because medical knowledge was limited, midwifery skills were considered as much spiritual as medical, and a supportive group of experienced and caring women must have been reassuring and empowering.

For many in early North America, children were a gift from God and not to be questioned or planned. Childbirth was also God's trial, and deformed or unusual babies or births could be proof of either spiritual worth or failure. The inevitability of fertility and birth, their attendant dangers, as well as the exhausting work of caring for a seemingly endless stream of babies made life difficult for women.

Further reading: Robert V. Wells, *Revolutions in Americans' Lives: A Demographic Perspective on the History of Americans, Their Families, and Their Society* (Westport, Conn.: Greenwood Press, 1982).

—Deborah C. Taylor

fishing

Fishing was of great importance in early America. For both NATIVE AMERICANS and European settlers, fish provided a relatively easily assessable FOOD source. Commercial fishing, already important to the ECONOMY of Europe, was also essential to the development of the New England economy.

For Native Americans in the Eastern Woodlands, Great Lakes, and Pacific Northwest, fish were an important source of nutrition and protein. Native peoples took fish with nets, spears, and lines. Along the Atlantic coast they built complex fishing weirs (fish traps) that consisted of stakes driven into shallow water with brush placed between the stakes. Some of these weirs covered areas as large as two acres. The natives of the Pacific Northwest depended on fish more heavily than people in other regions, from both the ocean and the rivers that interlaced the area. Some peoples of the region, using large dugout canoes, harpoons, and sealskin floats, engaged in whaling.

The fishing methods used by Europeans sometimes determined who made first contact with Native Americans. It is possible that the French, British, and Basques were fishing off the Grand Banks of Newfoundland a decade before Columbus's first voyage. Commercial fishing was a competitive industry, so those who knew of these excellent fishing grounds were not about to share the secret with others. European commercial anglers used two general methods of fishing. In "wet," or "green," fishing, fish were salted immediately after being caught and placed in the ship's hold. "Dry" fishing, usually used by the English, necessitated going ashore and setting up drying stations. The presence of English MARINERS on shore permitted the early development of trade between the English and natives. It also likely promoted the spread of European diseases among native peoples.

In the earliest descriptions of the New World, Europeans commented on the abundance and size of fish. A Dutch minister claimed that one could "catch in one hour as many as ten or twelve [people] can eat," and the English who extolled the virtues of the New World in colonization tracts also noted the abundance of fish. Fish also served as fertilizer for crops in New England, probably learned from Native Americans.

Fishing became a major component of the New England economy. Indeed, in the early years of settlement, PLYMOUTH and MASSACHUSETTS Bay sought to protect the fishing industry by protesting competition from English

Scenes of the French colonial fishing industry in New England and Canada. Fishermen bring in the catch, then salt and dry the fish before shipping it to Europe. *(Library of Congress)*

commercial anglers. Fishing comprised one-third of New England's exports to the mother country between the 1680s and the American Revolution.

—Roger Carpenter

Flashman, Edward (1733?–1806)

One of the most charismatic and enigmatic figures in early America, Edward Flashman was a soldier, merchant, and adventurer, perhaps matched in his experiences only by JOHN SMITH. Sketchy accounts of his life are recorded in two sets of personal papers (many since lost) that he supposedly deposited with Benjamin Franklin and Thomas Jefferson. Flashman probably was born in the English Midlands ca. 1733, the youngest son of a merchant. By the early 1750s he moved to London to seek his fortune. With a combination of luck, charm, and opportunism, he won the favor of and then became embroiled in a scandal with the duchess and duke of Tarryington. Perhaps wanting to remove him from Britain, the duke subsequently purchased Flashman's commission in a regiment serving in North America.

In PENNSYLVANIA in the mid-1750s, Flashman met George Washington and Benjamin Franklin as they were organizing the colonial defense from the perceived French threat. Exhibiting the condescending attitude typical of British officers toward their counterparts in the colonial militia, Flashman offended Colonel Washington by treating him with disdain (perhaps one reason Washington eventually supported the American Revolution). Flashman accompanied Washington on two military expeditions into the West. In July 1754 he was captured when Washington surrendered FORT NECESSITY. Misinterpreting the terms of surrender written in French, Flashman persuaded Washington to sign the document in which Washington admitted personal responsibility for the execution of a French diplomat—an admission that subsequently caused Washington great embarrassment. Relations between the two men never recovered, and the mere mention of Flashman's name brought uncharacteristic ranting from Washington. Flashman was a staff officer when NATIVE AMERICANS and their French allies ambushed British and colonial troops commanded by EDWARD BRADDOCK in July 1755. By some accounts, in the chaos of the retreat Flashman saved Washington's life.

In disreputable circumstances Flashman fled America. By June 1756 he was in Calcutta, India, where he survived confinement in the "Black Hole" (June 20–21, 1756). The following year he served under Robert Clive at Plassey (June 23, 1757), from which Flashman emerged in possession of three elephants carrying much of a nawab's treasury. He lived briefly in Europe and then, apparently pressured by William Pitt, returned to North America during the SEVEN YEARS' WAR. In 1759 Flashman served with JAMES WOLFE and was present at the battle for Quebec (September 13, 1759); he may be portrayed in Benjamin West's famous painting *The Death of Wolfe.* Flashman retired from the British military in 1761 and used the substantial prize money from India to expand on his father's position in the African SLAVE TRADE.

The final decades of his life are nebulous at best. He may have been involved in several important events that led to the American Revolution, because he lived in both BOSTON and PHILADELPHIA and apparently befriended Thomas Paine. He claims to have fought on the side of the Revolutionaries during the war, although his declarations are not substantiated. After the Revolution Flashman contracted with the English government to carry prisoners from London to Australia. The Crown originally paid him based on the number of passengers leaving England, but many did not survive the journey. When the government changed the contract so that pay was fixed according to the number of prisoners who actually arrived in Australia, an irate Flashman retired briefly to an estate in Leicestershire, England. As he wrote Adam Smith, "Damme, Sir, if the halfwit Crown and its crawling Servants will tell me how to sail my ships." Flashman apparently died of apoplexy in 1806 during an argument with Meriwether Lewis ("you're totally insane" reportedly were Flashman's final words).

Further reading: George MacDonald Fraser, *Black Ajax* (London: HarperCollins, 1997).

—Dale Martin and Billy G. Smith

Florida

On September 8, 1565, Don Pedro Menéndez de Avilés and a landing party of nearly 600 settlers and soldiers claimed possession of Florida for Spain. Located just south of the small French colony founded in 1762, ST. AUGUSTINE was named by Menéndez after the Bishop of Hippo. Almost immediately the Spanish admiral and his soldiers attacked and killed many of the French settlers, and within three months they had eliminated all of the French colonists. However, the Europeans had to contend with the peninsula's original residents.

Before the Spanish and French arrived Florida was home to many indigenous groups. Nearly 10,000 years ago the first NATIVE AMERICANS entered the peninsula. Among the many tribes Europeans encountered were the Timucua and Guale in the northeast, the Apalachee in the Panhandle, and the Calusa and Tequesta across Florida's southern half. Although these peoples spoke different languages, embraced various spiritual beliefs, and maintained distinct cultural traits, many of their experiences were similar. Because most tribes lived near or along the water, fish and shellfish provided a reliable source of their protein. In addition, they cultivated corn, beans, and squash. For most Florida tribes the land allowed for permanent settlement and seasonal migrations were not necessary. Beyond Florida's contemporary boundaries native peoples traded with tribes as far away as the Great Lakes region. Trade goods included copper, soapstone, and quartz crystals, but the most significant exchanges came with the arrival of the Europeans.

Florida's first European settlers lived in a region occupied by the Timucuan tribes. Although speaking a similar language, they were not united as a confederacy, and intertribal warfare was common. Each tribe was usually led by a male chief, or cacique, while a lesser chief headed each village. Both the great and lesser chiefs inherited the power of authority. However, unlike in Europe, power came through the female line of kinship. When the Spaniards first encountered the Timucuans, they determined to alter this route to power. The Spaniards, like other Europeans, accepted their system of MONARCHY but took issue with the idea of matrilineal inheritance. This was only one among many areas in which the Spanish attempted to change the traditions of indigenous peoples.

Conflicts frequently arose when Spaniards tried to use force or coercion to transform natives. While the Spanish challenged certain aspects of all tribal life and often treated natives as potential threats, the colonists were deeply concerned with the state of the natives' souls. Wherever the Spanish established a colony, they took great pains to convert Indians to Catholicism. To meet this goal the Spanish built a significant chain of MISSIONS across the southeastern frontier.

Among the first Europeans to settle Florida were a group of Jesuit missionaries, whose efforts marked the first Jesuit missionary work in all of Spanish America. They also helped solidify Spanish claims to additional lands beyond St. Augustine. After being chased from Florida by natives in 1572, Spanish missionaries returned in 1595. Instead of JESUITS, Franciscans were selected to manage the natives' souls. Unlike the Jesuits, the Franciscans started close to St. Augustine and worked their way throughout the interior of Florida and along the coast. Their missions were often placed inside existing villages, and they normally did not attempt to create new towns, as the Jesuits had. By 1655 Franciscan activities reached their peak in Florida, when more than 70 missionaries managed more than 20,000 Indians. Although the Franciscans enjoyed greater success converting Indians, this was not accomplished without conflict. Periodically, missionaries were forcibly removed from their assigned tribes. Nevertheless, the missionaries' success enlarged Spain's sphere of influence across the region. This influence, while valuable, did not guarantee the Spanish expansion of Florida's boundaries.

When the British settled JAMESTOWN in 1607, the Spanish had ample reason to be concerned. As Virginia slowly became a viable colony, colonial Florida consisted of little more than St. Augustine, several small military installations, and scattered Catholic missions. Spanish Florida did not truly expand until 1698, when Pensacola was founded along the western Panhandle. The creation of Pensacola came as a response to French attempts at colonization along the Gulf region. In other words, Pensacola was established as a defensive move and was not part of a calculated expansion. This began a pattern the Spanish would repeat throughout the 17th and 18th centuries. When forced, the Spanish tried to expand, but, generally, the Spanish could only watch as their claims were taken by other European powers. Although Spain wanted to maintain its presence in the region, Florida's lack of material wealth constantly undermined its efforts.

The absences of mines, extensive infrastructure, or an economic base limited Florida's settlers. To most outsiders Florida was a wasteland of swamps, mosquitoes, and hostile natives. Ironically, other Europeans were even more threatening than were Indians. British forces frequently attacked St. Augustine, pirates burned and looted the city numerous times in the 17th and 18th centuries, and its policies on accepting runaway slaves often provoked military attacks. Thus, Florida was a region the Spanish held but could not populate, while the British thought the peninsula a logical extension of their own coastal empire. However, while Florida could not expand, Spanish officials deemed it important enough to defend.

As attacks by privateers proved St. Augustine a vulnerable outpost, Spanish officials decided that substantial defenses were necessary for the colony's survival. Beginning in 1672, the Spanish started building a masonry fort called Castillo de San Marcos. This large coquina fort promised the Spaniards that passing ships carrying specie from other colonies would be protected as they followed the Gulf Stream on the way to Spain. Furthermore, the fort posed a considerable challenge to would-be attackers, but never so threatening as to guarantee peace in Florida. The basic conflict between Spain's inadequate settlement and British desires created considerable fear and anxiety along the southeastern frontier.

Throughout the 17th century British settlers continually moved south, along with a few French traders and colonists, ignoring Spanish claims of sovereignty and moving across West Florida. When the British founded GEORGIA in 1733, Spain's loss of Florida appeared inevitable. Still, Spain exerted some influence on frontier politics. The Spanish policy on offering runaway slaves asylum in St. Augustine encouraged Georgia to maintain its own ban on SLAVERY until 1755. Ultimately, the Spanish lost Florida because of the SEVEN YEARS' WAR rather than from an attack by a British colony.

In the 1763 TREATY OF PARIS, which ended the war, Spain's holdings on the continent drastically changed. The Spanish gained French lands west of the Mississippi, but the British took possession of East Florida and completed their control of the Atlantic Coast. For the British who surveyed their new possession, Florida offered little potential because its few towns were abandoned and, according to one observer, the area lay in a "state of Nature . . . not an acre of land planted in the country and nobody to work or at work." Still, St. Augustine's fort provided additional military support for Britain's coastal communities, and the fertile inland had the potential for agricultural wealth. The British were never able to realize such riches, however, because in 1784 Florida was returned to the Spanish Empire. When the American Revolution began, the Spanish in LOUISIANA saw an opportunity to recover their former territory. Although the Spanish successfully fought the British in West Florida in 1799, they regained Florida through diplomacy, not military action. In the 1783 Treaty of Paris, Britain lost all the land they received from their victories in the Seven Years' War, and Florida reverted to Spanish ownership.

See also FORT MOSE; SPANISH COLONIES; SPANISH IMMIGRATION.

Further reading: David J. Weber, *The Spanish Frontier in North America* (New Haven, Conn.: Yale University Press, 1992).

—Shane Runyon

food

Survival in the New World for all people depended on their ability to adapt their diets to new foods. Europeans, NATIVE AMERICANS, and Africans encountered one another on a basic level, borrowing food growing and gathering techniques, recipes, and tastes. In fact, contact between Europe and the Americas fundamentally changed diet and nutrition worldwide, as the so-called Columbian Exchange carried new foods both ways across the Atlantic and around the world.

The first Europeans to visit the Americas often exaggerated the easy abundance of food compared to conditions on their crowded continent. After a period of adjustment to new tastes and techniques of procurement, colonists generally enjoyed a healthier diet and longer lifespan than did their contemporaries in Europe. Native Americans had developed more than 200 varieties of maize, or Indian corn, a crop high in yield and nutrition, especially when planted the traditional way, together with squash and beans. Maize became the colonial staple once the newcomers learned how to cultivate and prepare the grain. Europeans were astonished by the bounty of the woods, from which native peoples harvested nuts, berries (some "2 inches around!"), root vegetables, herbs, birds, and game. The sea seethed with hundreds of varieties of fish and shellfish, including lobsters said to be five feet long. Europeans learned a host of skills from Indians, including methods of hunting and FISHING, tapping maple trees and preparing syrup, stewing beans, and parching and grinding corn for meal.

Along with maize, beans, and squash, Europeans exported other Native American foods that enriched and transformed diets around the world, including peanuts, manioc, pumpkin, chile peppers, pineapples, cocoa, and turkeys. Other food, such as tomatoes and potatoes, did not enter the colonial diet until they first became accepted in England. New World crop cultivation in Europe, Asia, and AFRICA improved health, lengthened lives, and resulted in a population boom in northern Europe that, ironically, provided waves of immigrants to the Americas in later centuries.

Native Americans farmed their staple crops, gathered plants, hunted game, and fished in a seasonal cycle that depended on the diversity and balance of their ENVIRONMENT. Some Europeans misunderstood the Indian way of gearing their diet to seasonal products and considered them "paupers in the land of plenty." Eventually, Native Americans adapted their diets and lifestyles to include imported Old World foods, such as wheat, barley, carrots, peas, apples, and grapes, and used new technologies like iron cooking pots and hunting rifles. European livestock made an even greater impact on the American landscape and diet. Colonists, who preferred a diet heavy in meat and who harnessed animal power, imported and bred cows, horses, sheep, goats, chickens, and hogs. These hoofed creatures and fowl reproduced rapidly, reshaping Indian lands and lifestyles. Indeed, pigs became so plentiful in VIRGINIA that, according to a European correspondent of the time, Virginians themselves became "hoggish in their temper . . and prone to grunt." Honeybees, called "English flies," added a new sweetener to the American diet. European settlers, unused to the water, brewed homemade ale, "small beer," and cider as a daily beverage. They made rum from molasses and bourbon from corn and rye, which they drank and traded with native people.

Euro-American housewives used spices liberally (in part to mask food spoilage) in their stews, hashes, and soups and cooked in large iron pots over the hearth fire. They preserved foods by pickling, salting, smoking, and drying. Meals were plain and simple in farm kitchens and more elaborate in wealthier homes. Colonial style for all classes favored tables groaning with large quantities of meat and fish dishes. Milk, cheese, and beef were not common on colonial tables until the early 18th century. Cooks adapted recipes from their home countries, such as the NEW HAMPSHIRE housewife who created English mince pies from bear meat, dried pumpkin, maple sugar, and a corn crust. A traditional English pudding became "Indian pudding," made with ground corn, maple syrup, and eggs. Affluent colonists appreciated the quantity of food available, but some bemoaned the quality of American foods, longing for their accustomed (and, they thought, superior) European fare.

Although they possessed few cookbooks, southern plantation families may have enjoyed a more varied diet than northerners. African slaves did much of the cooking in plantation kitchens and introduced new foods, especially vegetables, into the American diet. Slave owners provided a high starch, low protein diet barely adequate to sustain black field workers, but the impressive natural increase in the slave population suggests supplemental nourishment. African customs as well as their meager rations caused slaves to be frugal and innovative in their cooking, making use, for example, of many parts of an animal or vegetable. Africans brought rice, kidney and lima beans, nuts, okra, yams, sesame, sorghum, and watermelons (called August ham) to the Americas and cultivated these when possible to enhance their diets. Some slaves raised chickens, caught fish, and used the leftover parts of their masters' pigs, frying the small intestines into chitlins. They introduced traditional African dishes, such as barbecue, cooked nutritious vegetable greens in "pot likker," and invented dishes from corn, such as hominy grits and hush puppies.

Further reading: Alice Morse Earle, *Home Life in Colonial Days* (Stockbridge, Mass.: Berkshire House, 1926, 1992).

—Deborah C. Taylor

forests

One of the first things that Europeans arriving in North America noticed were the seemingly inexhaustible forests. If eastern North America had been prairie instead of extended forests, European settlement would have occurred in a much different fashion, yet early reports about American forests can be misleading. True, huge specimens of trees had been found and the number of trees seemed infinite, but American forests were subject to damage and alteration by severe weather, natural decay, and human intervention. Moreover, American forests were not as dense as was first reported.

The first Europeans in North America generally failed to realize that Indians had dramatically shaped the appearance and composition of forests. Indians burned forests regularly in order to clear out underbrush and promote the growth of berry-producing plants and shrubs, and they used fire as a hunting tool to force game ANIMALS into small, easily surrounded zones. Periodic burning produced an open, parklike forest in much of eastern North America that provided rich foraging area for deer and other animals. Europeans marveled constantly at the savannahlike forests where horses could be ridden at full speed with little chance of running into limbs or undergrowth. In addition, Indians harvested trees for a wide range of purposes, including building construction, weapons, canoes, footwear, tools, and firewood.

For Europeans trees provided energy and resources. Europeans recognized many tree species in the 360 million acres of forest in the eastern third of the continent. Varieties of oak, beech, maple, ash, poplar, walnut, chestnut, persimmon, cherry, mulberry, willow, and pine seemed familiar to Europeans, and they knew many potential uses for those trees. Furthermore, the seemingly endless American forests seemed like a vast wilderness, a dangerous place that was home to mysterious creatures such as WOLVES, bobcats, mountain lions, bears, and rattlesnakes. A major goal became to remove these "pests" by eliminating their homes, made all the easier because money could be made through the exploitation of forest resources.

Trees provided material in early America for ships, naval stores, buildings (including wood shingles), and various containers such as barrels and hogsheads, as well as fencing and plank roads. The British and various colonial governments tried to limit the numbers and types of trees that could be cut, but such restrictions generally proved ineffective. By 1700 half a million acres of forest had been cleared, resulting in drier air, stronger winds, erosion, the disappearance of small streams, and a decline in wildlife. A world of "fields and fences" was being created to replace the "wild" forests.

See also ENVIRONMENT; LUMBERING.

Further reading: William Cronon, *Changes in the Land: Indians, Colonists, and the Ecology of New England* (New York: Hill & Wang, 1983); Michael Williams, *Americans and Their Forests: A Historical Geography* (New York: Cambridge University Press, 1989).

—Greg O'Brien

Fort Mose (1738–1763)

Located two miles north of ST. AUGUSTINE, Florida, Gracia Real de Santa Teresa de Mose, or Fort Mose, housed the first free African-American community in the present-day United States. Established and sanctioned by Florida governor Manuel de Montiano in 1738, Fort Mose was a sanctuary for slaves who successfully escaped their bondage in British colonies. After entering Florida, escaped slaves earned their freedom if they converted to Catholicism and promised to defend the Spanish territory. Once accepted into the Spanish colony, these African-American slaves were settled in Fort Mose, where they were required to join or support the black militia. Led by former slaves, the militia served as St. Augustine's first line of defense.

The Spanish policy of offering asylum to runaway bondpeople did not reflect an enlightened policy on slave labor. The Spanish in Florida were not against SLAVERY but instead felt the threat of a growing BRITISH EMPIRE. As SOUTH CAROLINA's power grew and British settlers moved into GEORGIA, the Spanish used the British dependence on slavery as a weapon. By offering runaway slaves freedom, the Spanish hoped to inspire massive slave revolts in the British colonies and thus eliminate the growing British threat. This goal nearly became a reality in 1739 when slaves revolted at Stono, South Carolina. After successfully defeating their white owners, the slave leaders of the STONO REBELLION planned to flee to Florida and freedom. In part, this rebellion precipitated a British retaliatory attack on St. Augustine in 1740. One of the first areas to be attacked was Fort Mose. When the fort fell to British forces, the African militia moved into the city and joined the larger garrison; by all accounts, they fought bravely.

For those who gained their freedom in Florida, life at Fort Mose was difficult. Wetlands and a constructed moat isolated the fort from the rest of the community. Consequently, Fort Mose was one of the first segregated communities. While its primary purpose was the maintenance of a militia, it was also home to the soldiers' families. For women and other noncombatants, employment was possible in St. Augustine. However, a constantly weak ECONOMY forced most to remain inside the fort. Although survival was often difficult, residents at least were not in bondage.

For many British slaves Fort Mose was a symbol of freedom. Although the policy of asylum increased tension along the Florida frontier, Spanish officials typically favored the rights of escaped slaves. In 1759 a census of Mose found the fort housed only 67 residents. While few in number, its influence on the region's political climate was considerable. When the British took possession of Florida in 1763, the residents of the fort were evacuated, and the former slaves were moved to Cuba as free Spaniards.

See also SPANISH COLONIES; SPANISH IMMIGRATION.

Further reading: Jane Landers, *Black Society in Spanish Florida* (Urbana: University of Illinois Press, 1999); Shane Runyon, "Fort Mose: The Free African Community and Militia of Spanish St. Augustine" (M.A. Thesis, Montana State University, 1999).

—Shane Runyon

Fort Necessity

Fort Necessity was an aptly named structure erected in 1754 by VIRGINIA provincial soldiers under the command of an inexperienced George Washington. The Virginians were the vanguard of a larger provincial army that intended to oppose the French occupation of the Ohio River forks (present-day Pittsburgh). Originally built as a storehouse, the small stockade at Fort Necessity became a makeshift military fort on July 3, 1754, when Washington and his 400 Virginians retreated to the site after attacking and killing a small French detachment in the forest at nearby Jumonville Glenn. A significantly larger force of French and Indians from Fort Duquesne reached the area during the early morning hours and laid siege to Fort Necessity throughout the day. The result was disaster. The fort occupied a shallow valley surrounded by wooded hills, which allowed the French and Indians to fire downhill into the small palisade with little obstruction. After an eight-hour firefight in a raging thunderstorm, during which time Fort Necessity began to fill with water, Washington surrendered. In exchange for the freedom of his troops, Washington signed a surrender agreement written in French, which he could not read. The document blamed Washington for the battle at Fort Necessity and provided much of the impetus for the British decision to send an army under General EDWARD BRADDOCK to the Ohio forks the following year, which in turn marked the beginning of the SEVEN YEARS' WAR in North America.

Further reading: Fred Anderson, *Crucible of War: The Seven Years' War and the Fate of Empire in British North America, 1754–1766* (New York: Knopf, 2000).

—Daniel P. Barr

forts

Forts were central to all colonization efforts in North America because organized violence against Europeans by other Europeans and by Indians was common in the New World. Indeed, a fort was usually the first building constructed by a new colony. NATIVE AMERICANS like the PEQUOT, although lacking European engineering skills, also produced palisades and forts for defense against both other tribes and European invaders.

While the North American colonial era coincided with the great age of fortification in Europe, colonial forts rarely approached the great masonry piles that dominated the European landscape and mindset. Instead, colonial forts tended to be more rudimentary, constructed most often of wood or earth. Because forts provided protection from cannon bombardment, one major reason colonial forts never achieved the size and strength of their European counterparts was that they did not face comparable threats. Artillery pieces of the power routinely used in Europe could not be transported through the North American wilderness. The largest colonial forts, like the massive fortifications of Louisbourg protecting the Gulf of Saint Lawrence, were on the coasts because they might encounter heavy guns mounted on ships.

Forts provided both tactical and operational advantages. The most common weapons included the bow and arrow and various personal gunpowder firearms. Loading, aiming, and firing these weapons generally required a person to stand upright, thus exposing himself to enemy fire. A shooter with protection, such as that provided by the walls of a fort, enjoyed a considerable advantage over his opponent. Forts provided secure depots for supplies, protected places for military forces to rest and recover, and a place for a defeated force to retreat. An advancing enemy encountering a fort had to either detail sufficient forces to besiege the garrison, thus weakening the advance, or else bypass the fort, risking an enemy sally in their rear. Forts also provided safety for noncombatants during raids.

Many forts, especially those of the French, served economic as well as military purposes. Trading posts were established within forts, and the garrison of a fort could ensure the safety of nearby traders. The security provided by a fort attracted settlers and traders to the area, and villages, towns, and finally cities often developed on the sites of forts.

Finally, forts served a political purpose, which was sometimes more important than their military usefulness. Establishing a fort legitimized a claim to the surrounding area far more strongly than any other method except populating the region. The English and French disputed ownership of the Ohio River Valley and associated regions for years, but when the French began establishing forts in the region, the English demanded their immediate removal. Fighting broke out shortly thereafter, setting the stage for the SEVEN YEARS' WAR. One particular location exemplifies the political and economic powers of forts. One English aim in the war was to eliminate the French Fort Duquesne, built on a point in western PENNSYLVANIA where the Allegheny and Monongahela Rivers meet to form the Ohio River, a strategically valuable spot. The legitimizing effect forts had on a territorial claim demanded an immediate response from the English if they hoped to prevent the French from consolidating their hold on the region. Once the British forced the French to abandon Fort Duquesne, they built Fort Pitt on the same spot, which eventually became the city of Pittsburgh, Pennsylvania.

From the earliest efforts at colonization, through the end of the Seven Years' War, and into the Revolutionary Era, forts were central to the lives of colonists. Forts provided economic and political benefits to their possessor as well as operational and tactical military advantages.

See also FORT NECESSITY.

Further reading: Fred Anderson, *Crucible of War: The Seven Years' War and the Fate of Empire in British North America, 1754–1766* (New York: Knopf, 2000).

—Grant Weller

Fort William Henry Massacre (1757)

The British built Fort William Henry in 1755 at the foot of Lake George, where it blocked French access to the Hudson River Valley and posed a threat to the French settlements of Montreal and Quebec. On August 6, 1757, during the SEVEN YEARS' WAR, 8,500 French and Indians under Louis Joseph, marquis de Montcalm, laid siege to the fort and its 2,000 military and civilian inhabitants. Within three days the garrison surrendered. According to the terms offered to Lt. Col. George Monro, the French took most of the military stores, but the troops were permitted to depart with the honors of war, carrying their muskets and their baggage.

Many NATIVE AMERICANS with Montcalm felt betrayed by these terms, because they had canoed long distances to join the assault; their only pay was to be in the form of martial trophies because plunder (a customary spoil of war) was now denied to them. On August 9 some Indians invaded the fort's rum stores, then went to the hospital, where they killed and scalped a number of patients. Scalps were also taken from corpses in the cemetery, thus spreading SMALLPOX among the Indians.

The following morning the anxious English departed without waiting for the promised French escort. Within a short time Indians attacked them, murdering between 69 and 184 people, seizing the property of others, and holding still others for future ransom. Montcalm and a detachment of French regulars eventually rescued about 400 people and took them to safety at Fort Edward. The massacre became a rallying cry for the British during the Seven Years' War.

Further reading: Ian K. Steele, *Betrayals: Fort William Henry and the "Massacre"* (New York: Oxford University Press, 1990).

—Joseph J. Casino

Franklin, Ann Smith (1696–1763)

Native Bostonian Ann Smith married James Franklin in 1723 during his struggle for freedom of the press. In 1727 the Franklins moved their family to NEWPORT, RHODE ISLAND, where James became the first printer in the colony. When James died in 1735, Ann took over the business. Presumably her children assisted, as both her daughters were adept typesetters. Typesetting requires dexterity rather than strength, so this could be done by women without risk to their femininity. Although her son James (trained by his uncle Benjamin Franklin) assumed control after reaching his maturity in 1748, mother and son billed jointly for the next 10 years. After her son's death in 1762, Ann returned to work. Clearly a skilled craftswoman in addition to her newspaper and many other works, Franklin also did much of the official printing for the Rhode Island General Assembly, including the *Acts and Laws of 1745*. The loss of a husband usually meant economic hardship for the family. By becoming the first female printer in New England, Ann Franklin safeguarded her family's assets and security.

Further reading: Elaine Forman Crane, *Ebb Tide in New England: Women, Seaports, and Social Change, 1630–1800* (Boston: Northeastern University Press, 1998).

—Victoria C. H. Resnick

Franklin, Deborah Read (1705–1774)

Born in Pennsylvania in 1705, Deborah Read lived the typical life of a colonial girl in the Middle Colonies. She is remembered primarily as the common-law wife of Benjamin Franklin and the mother of prominent PHILADELPHIA patriot Sarah Franklin Bache, who garnered support for the Revolutionary cause and nursed Continental troops in Philadelphia during the American Revolution.

Benjamin Franklin's private life was very complicated. Benjamin and Deborah met briefly when he arrived in Philadelphia, but their relationship faltered when Franklin moved temporarily to London. Deborah married, but her husband abandoned her. Meanwhile, Benjamin had an illegitimate child, William. Benjamin and Deborah became married by common law on September 1, 1730, in part because Deborah technically was still married to her first husband. In addition, because Benjamin was a Deist (that is, he believed in a divine Creator but did not subscribe to an established religion), their marriage was recognized as a common law marriage—English custom recognized the union if the couple lived together for a number of years and treated each other as husband and wife. Their marriage lasted until Deborah's death in 1774. Deborah bore the burden of Franklin's long absences from home and often ran his Philadelphia stationary business while he was away tending to the affairs of the emerging nation. Besides raising William, Deborah had two children, a son who died at age four and Sarah, who survived both her parents. Deborah's portrait was painted by artist Benjamin Wilson in 1758 and now hangs in the AMERICAN PHILOSOPHICAL SOCIETY in Philadelphia.

—Paula Smith-Hawkins

Frelinghuysen, Theodorus Jacobus (1691–1747?)

A leader of the GREAT AWAKENING in NEW JERSEY and born in present-day Germany near the Dutch border, Frelinghuysen studied at the University of Lingen. The university, a hotbed of pietism, emphasized godly living and fervor over scholasticism. Frelinghuysen would remain a pietist for the rest of his life.

Ordained in 1715, Frelinghuysen served locally before accepting a call to become pastor to five congregations of Dutch Reformed churches in New Jersey under the mistaken impression that they were located in Germany. He immigrated in 1719 with his schoolteacher and friend, Jacobus Schuurman. Frelinghuysen immediately challenged the local clergy. He opposed the Lord's Prayer for being too formal, restricted Communion to those who showed visible signs of spiritual rebirth, and upset the rich by sermonizing that the most faithful people often were poor and unimportant. When Frelinghuysen excommunicated his opponents, he initiated a struggle between orthodoxy and pietism. In 1725 Frelinghuysen's opponents issued a long *Klagte* (complaint) and tried to enlist the aid of traditionalist Dutch Reformed clergy in silencing him. Frelinghuysen, supported by his congregations, invoked the principle of congregational polity, which places all authority in the individual church. His more traditional colleagues resisted his advocacy of greater parish autonomy, although the pietists eventually prevailed.

Frelinghuysen was accused of having a homosexual relationship with Schuurman, and the two men eventually married sisters, in part to end criticism. Frelinghuysen's date of death is unknown; some theorize that he died during one of his struggles with mental illness. Frelinghuysen's evangelical fervor and itinerancy contributed significantly to the Great Awakening in the Middle Colonies. GILBERT TENNENT often shared Frelinghuysen's pulpit, JONATHAN EDWARDS admired him, and GEORGE WHITEFIELD asserted that Frelinghuysen inspired the movement.

—Victoria C. H. Resnick

French and Indian War

See Seven Years' War

French colonies

During the period 1585–1763, the French established colonies in North America stretching from the Maritime Provinces of present-day Canada, up the St. Lawrence River, through the Great Lakes region, and down the Mississippi to its mouth in LOUISIANA. Although the French settlers were never as populous as their British counterparts, they made up for their limited numbers by establishing alliances with many Indian nations. They realized that through trade and diplomacy they could maintain their influence among NATIVE AMERICANS who lived in the interior of the country. In addition to establishing strong trading relations and military alliances, the French also relied on missionaries, notably the JESUITS, to convert Indians to the Catholic faith. In this way, the French government maintained good relations with Indian people, but at the expense of the missionary societies rather than the French Crown. This three-part strategy of trade, alliance, and conversion allowed the French to maintain their position in North America until the early 1760s, when the British defeated the French and their Indian allies in the SEVEN YEARS' WAR. By 1763 the French gave up their claims to North America in the TREATY OF PARIS.

Fish, Fur, and Exploration

The French initially arrived in North America in the 16th century when French and Basque fishermen began to fish off the Grand Banks, an area rich in cod southeast of Newfoundland. Some vessels landed on the shore to dry their fish, and Europeans interacted with Indians in the region for the first time. These meetings were characterized by brief trading sessions in which Europeans exchanged copper or iron tools for furs. In the 1530s and 1540s Jacques Cartier made three voyages between Europe and Canada, hoping to find a lucrative gold or silver mine in the woods of Canada. After a series of conflicts with the Indians (often referred to as the St. Lawrence Iroquoian), who lived on the St. Lawrence River, Cartier ceased exploring the river, and French attempts to inhabit the region ground to a halt.

Tadoussac and the First Settlements

For the next 60 years there were no serious French attempts to occupy North America. This hiatus ended in 1598, when Mesgouez de la Roche, a nobleman from Breton, received a renewed commission from King Henry IV as lieutenant general in New France. The title allowed La Roche to build FORTS, grant lands, and make laws. In addition, his position gave him monopoly power over the lucrative FUR TRADE. The following year, partly due to some resentment of La Roche's monopoly by French MERCHANTS, other traders were granted licenses as well. Pierre Chauvin was given a 10-year license to build a fur trading post at Tadoussac, a traditional ALGONQUIN and Montagnais trading area at the confluence of the Saguenay and St. Lawrence Rivers. The post represented one of the first attempts at permanent French settlement in the New World, but it would not last long as a year-round post. The harsh weather on the exposed point compelled the would-be settlers to return to France after the first winter. In the ensuing years the French returned to the region seasonally to trade with Native Americans in the area rather than inhabiting the area all year. In 1603 Pierre de Gua, sieur de Monts, received the title of vice-admiral in Acadia, consisting of most of the Canadian Maritimes and the coast of MAINE. He established Port Royal in Nova Scotia, although it, too, was an early failure, abandoned by 1607.

Era of Champlain

One of the first French officials to realize the importance of fostering good relations with Native Americans was SAMUEL DE CHAMPLAIN. Although he initially believed that settlement on the islands was superior to colonizing the interior of Canada, he began to envision the development of the interior as the most promising prospect for the French. Champlain allied himself in 1608 with the Montagnais and Algonquin inhabitants of the St. Lawrence area and thereby gained better access to the mainland fur trade. An experienced cartographer and explorer, Champlain knew the region as well as any European, and he chose a strategically located point where the St. Lawrence River narrows to establish a fort. From this site French cannons and firearms could intercept either IROQUOIS or European competitors in the lucrative beaver fur trade. Here, Champlain established Quebec, which would become the center of French political, economic, and religious life. With two strategic positions, at Tadoussac and Quebec, and with the promise of good trading relations with local Indians, the French seemed poised to maintain a successful colony.

Cementing his alliance with the Montagnais, HURON, and Algonquin, Champlain joined them on a raid against the Iroquois, their long-time enemy who inhabited most of what is now NEW YORK State. On July 30, 1609, Champlain and his allies defeated a group of Iroquois on the shores of the lake that bears Champlain's name. The move helped solidify the French relationship with the Indians living north of Iroquois territory, but it caused much resentment among the Iroquois themselves. Furthermore, the northern tribes were receiving French firearms, metal for arrow points, copper kettles, and other trade goods. As the Iroquois became excluded from trading in European goods (especially firearms and arrows), their animosity toward the French grew. Although Iroquois–French relations would vacillate throughout the colonial period, the Iroquois often adopted an anti-French position, caused in part by their exclusion from French trade.

Although there were very few French settlers along the St. Lawrence River, France had established a trade network and military alliances with the northern Indians in addition to securing Tadoussac and Quebec, crucial economic and military positions. Despite these alliances, the French colonies were precarious through the 1630s. King Louis XIII lacked the capital and interest to fund adequately the remote colonies, so the Crown attempted to use private corporations to support the migration of French Catholic settlers to the New World. The most prominent of these was the Company of One Hundred Associates, which was given large land grants in exchange for agreeing to move 4,000 French settlers to the New World. Although these land grants were designed to attract farmers to New France, the difficulty of farming, the lack of a cash crop, and the harsh winters tended to stifle immigration from France.

The company struggled from the outset. In 1629 the English captured Quebec but eventually returned it to the French in 1632 in the Treaty of St-Germain-en-Laye. Upon its return, Champlain was appointed governor of New France. At the time the population numbered only about 100 permanent settlers, the vast majority of whom lived in or around Quebec. By 1640 the population had grown only slightly, with approximately 300 settlers in addition to 29 Jesuit priests and 53 soldiers. In the same year the Isle of Montreal was granted to the Compagnie du Saint Sacrament, a mission settlement greatly influenced by the Jesuits, which was designed to be a more religiously oriented village than commercial Quebec. One conflict that divided Montreal and Quebec was their perception of the ALCOHOL trade with the Indians. Traders often used alcohol to get Indian trading partners drunk and thereby negotiate favorable trading terms, yet the more religiously minded settlers, and especially the Catholic missionaries, vehemently opposed trading alcohol to Indians. This issue helped hasten the founding of Montreal. Part of their intention in making the village a beacon of Catholic piety was to attract western Indians. For its part, Montreal (or Ville-Marie, as it was originally called) maintained its religious orientation, and its population grew to more than 600 by the 1660s.

Missionaries

One of the most important aspects of the French settlement of North America was the use of missionary societies both to maintain relations with Native Americans and to fund the colonies. The most influential of the missionaries were the Jesuits, a relatively wealthy and well-organized society that had the financial resources and abilities to spread Christianity among the Indians. The French Crown lacked the capital to support expensive TRAVEL into the interior and the giving of gifts to Indians, according to the norms of woodland diplomacy. In exchange for land grants to build colleges, schools, and hospitals and the right to convert Indians to Christianity, the Jesuits acted on behalf of the Crown among Indian peoples, tying the tribes to France by means of religious alliances. Although this was effective, often the Jesuits' perspective on the best interests of their Indian converts overshadowed the demands of French governmental officials, causing conflict between the secular leaders of the colony and the priests.

Of all the French, the Jesuits had some of the most profound effects on Indian peoples. In the 1630s Father Paul Le Jeune formulated the idea to establish permanent, sedentary MISSIONS. Because the Algonquin and Montagnais led a seminomadic lifestyle, they were often hunting, FISHING, or moving between villages, making it difficult for the Jesuits to instruct them in the Catholic faith. Before the 1630s missionaries traveled with Indian peoples and attempted to win converts while following Indian subsistence patterns. Le Jeune believed that if the Indians adopted European-style HOUSING and an agricultural ECONOMY, they would be more accepting of Catholicism as well. Although most Montagnais initially resisted Le Jeune's efforts, the increasing threat of Iroquois raids, which grew more frequent in the late 1630s and 1640s, convinced some Indians that living near the French would be a wise economic and military move.

The sedentary mission of Sillery became the model for other mission villages throughout Canada. The migration to the missions precipitated numerous conflicts within the Montagnais and Algonquin communities. Those who accepted Christianity were favored by the Jesuits and French officials, while traditional Indians were often excluded from positions of power in the missionary governments established by the priests. Not surprisingly, this led to numerous conflicts between the two factions. This pattern of Christian and traditional factions was mirrored in many of the other mission villages as well. The Sillery mission, like many traditional Indian villages, was decimated by epidemics of European diseases. The Indian population of Sillery gradually gave way to French settlers, and by 1663 the village was no longer an active mission. Similar Jesuit missions emerged at Odanak, Kahnawake, St.

The Territory of New France
Lake Superior
Sault Ste. Marie
St. Lawrence R.
Chippewa
Ft. La Pointe
Ft. Michilimackinac
St. Ignace
Menominee
Lake Huron
Lake Ontario
Ft. St. Antoine
Baie Verte
Ft. Niagara
St. Michael the Archangel
Mississippi R.
Wisconsin R.
Winnebago
Lake Michigan
Ottawa
Wyandot
Iroquois
Fox
Detroit
Lake Erie
Ft. Le Boeuf
Pays d'en Haut
Sauk
Assumption
Ft. Venango
Guardian Angel
Ft. Miami
Ft. Duquesne
Missouri R.
Ft. Crevecoeur
St. Joseph
Illinois R.
Illinois
Ft. Ouiatenon
Miami
Shawnee
Vincennes
Ohio R.
Des Peres
Cahokia
Kaskaskia
Illinois Country
Ste. Genevieve
Osage
Tennessee R.
Ft. Assumption
Arkansas R.
Quapaw
Chickasaw
Creek
Arkansas Post
Ft. Toulouse
Mississippi R.
NATCHEZ
Wichita
Ft. Tombeche
Tunica
Caddo
Ft. St. Pierre
Red R.
Ft. Rosalie
Choctaw
Natchitoches
Mobile
Baton Rouge
Louisiana
New Orleans
CHITIMACHA
ATLANTIC OCEAN
Gulf of Mexico
British territory
French territory
Spanish territory
Mission
Fort
Settlement
French internal migration
Miami Native American tribe
NATCHEZ Tribe decimated by disease, warfare, or enslavement
N
0 200 Miles
0 200 Kms

François de Sales, and other locations that lasted into the 18th century, and some continue to exist as native villages today. Missions not only altered subsistence patterns by increasing Indian dependence on European trade goods, but they also undermined native religions, which were directly attacked in the mission villages.

Colbert and New France

Political changes in Europe greatly affected the colonial effort in the Americas. By the 1660s young King Louis XIV accepted his full regal duties and began a reign characterized by a consolidation of power in the Crown and increased control over his kingdom. His agent of centralization in the colonies was Minister of the Marine Jean-Baptiste Colbert, who fulfilled the mercantilist goals of the king. Colbert sought to open markets in BOSTON to French trade, make peace with the Iroquois, who had been a constant threat to French habitants, and rein in the Jesuits and make them subservient to the Crown. Although good relations with the English were never developed, Colbert succeeded in making a temporary peace with the Iroquois between 1665 and 1685, and he limited the power of the Jesuits in the New World. Moreover, the number of French colonists in Canada increased to 10,000 by 1670.

Exploration and Expansion: La Salle and Tonti

Another example of Louis XIV's expansionist policies was the successful enlargement of French influence past Montreal into the Great Lakes region and down the Mississippi River. Supported by Intendant Jean Talon and Governor Frontenac, westward expansion would not only provide the French with further influence among the western tribes but also provide new sources of furs. During Colbert's tenure the French established Michilimackinac, an important fort and trading post located between Lake Huron and Lake Michigan. This strategic center gave the French a centralized location in the western fur trade. Contrary to Colbert's wishes, the Crown granted 25 licenses to individual fur traders, who became known as *coureurs de bois*, or "runners of the woods." These French frontiersmen did a tremendous business with the western Indians and often married into the tribes. Such economic and social ties to tribes further aided the relationship of France with western Native Americans.

French influence in the American interior took an important turn in April 1682, when RENÉ-ROBERT CAVELIER, SIEUR DE LA SALLE and Henri Tonti completed their journey down the Mississippi and arrived at its mouth, which they named Louisiana. In 1700 the French established NEW ORLEANS and formed relations with the tribes near the Mississippi Delta. As in the north, the French allied themselves with neighboring tribes like the CHOCTAW but angered the more distant tribes like the CHICKASAW, who were excluded from the trade, leading to the Chickasaw War of 1736. Also as in the North, French alliances with many tribes solidified their position along the St. Lawrence, Great Lakes, and Mississippi waterways. With the British in control of the East Coast and the French with a tenuous but extensive grasp on the interior, the stage was set for a battle for the continent. Conflict erupted when the French attempted to extend up the Ohio River into lands claimed by the British.

Seven Years' War

The river valleys that had opened the west to the French became the center of conflict with the British in the middle of the 18th century. When the governor general at Quebec, Roland-Michel Barrin, comte La Galissonière, suggested that the French build forts in the Ohio and Mississippi River Valleys, the British settlers in VIRGINIA became alarmed. Between the Illinois country and New Orleans, only 2,000 French troops staffed the posts, although the posts were buttressed by alliances with neighboring tribes. The British thus were fearful of even minor threats to their territory. When the French established Fort Duquesne at the confluence of the Ohio, Allegheny, and Monongahela Rivers in PENNSYLVANIA, the British retaliated.

A young George Washington, at the head of Virginia militiamen, rode west to inform the French that they were encroaching on English soil. After a few skirmishes, Washington was defeated at Great Meadows and sent back to Virginia with embarrassing terms of surrender. Following this, the English sent General EDWARD BRADDOCK to the west, who was defeated as well. The French settlers in Acadia, who had been living under English rule for a few decades, bore the initial brunt of this conflict. Forced to move from their farms in the Maritimes, many sought refuge in Louisiana, where they became known as Cajuns. Although war was not officially declared in Europe until 1756, the American theater had been the scene of conflict for two years. In 1759, on the Plains of Abraham near Quebec, the young British major general JAMES WOLFE defeated Louis-Joseph Montcalm in a battle that lasted less than half an hour. Although the rest of French Canada fell in 1760, the French did not officially give up their claims to Canada until 1763. In the Treaty of Paris the British received control over Canada, and the French presence in the New World was relegated to the CARIBBEAN.

Further reading: William J. Eccles, *The French in North America, 1500–1783* (East Lansing: Michigan State University Press, 1998); Bruce Trigger, *Natives and Newcomers: Canada's "Heroic Age" Reconsidered* (Montreal: McGill-Queen's University Press, 1985).

—Thomas J. Lappas

French immigrants

Most of the French immigrants to the Americas went to French colonies in Canada, Louisiana, the Caribbean, the Great Lakes region, and the Mississippi River Valley. From 1608, with the founding of the first permanent French settlement at Quebec, French interests on the North American continent were both economic, centered on the fur and deerskin trade, and religious, with Jesuit and Recollet missionaries and Ursuline nuns working to convert the native population to Catholicism. A few French Protestants (Huguenots) also migrated to French settlements but never established separate churches there. Many more immigrated to English colonies, particularly after 1685, when Louis XIV revoked the Edict of Nantes, which had guaranteed Huguenots limited freedom of worship. They constituted the largest group of religious refugees to seek haven in America since the PURITANS' Great Migration of the 1630s.

In the 1660s a few French Protestant families settled in New England and New York, forming small communities in Salem, MASSACHUSETTS, and on Staten Island. In 1678 one group, which had first migrated from France to the German Palatine, founded the town of New Paltz, New York. In the 1680s and 1690s tens of thousands of Huguenots fled France for England and the Protestant nations of continental Europe. Perhaps 2,000 of these eventually made their way to English America, settling primarily in the cities of BOSTON, NEW YORK CITY, and CHARLESTON and in rural SOUTH CAROLINA.

Most Huguenot immigrants were young and unskilled, but many families—the Manigaults of South Carolina, the DeLanceys of New York, the Faneuils of Boston—achieved remarkable economic and political success. WILLIAM PENN made a concerted effort to attract French refugees to PENNSYLVANIA, but only a handful went there, including André Doz, who worked for Penn as gardener and vintner, and Anne and Jacques Le Tort, who traded with the Indians on Pennsylvania's frontiers. Other French traders who migrated from Canada to the Susquehanna Valley were ROMAN CATHOLICS. The Pennsylvania government suspected men like Martin Chartier and Pierre Bizaillon of being French spies.

Most French immigrants who came to English America became fully assimilated, and their separate cultural identity had disappeared before 1800. Small in numbers and with religious doctrines close to those of the English churches, especially the PRESBYTERIANS, the Huguenots intermarried with the English and the Dutch, and their congregations merged with English ones.

Further reading: Jon Butler, *The Huguenots in America: A Refugee People in New World Society* (Cambridge, Mass.: Harvard University Press, 1983).

—Alison Duncan Hirsch

frontier

See borderlands

Fuca, Juan de (active 1590s)

Juan de Fuca was a Greek-born sea pilot and the reputed discoverer in 1592 of a Northwest Passage from the northwest coast of North America to the Arctic or Atlantic Ocean. According to an account written by Michael Lok, a prominent English promoter of the search for a Northwest Passage, de Fuca claimed to have led two Spanish ships into an inlet on the Pacific coast between 47° and 48° N. Passing through the inlet, de Fuca's ships sailed for 20 days to a "North Sea" and to lands "rich of gold." While no Northwest Passage extends from the Pacific coast to the Arctic or Atlantic Ocean, and while there is no Pacific inlet lying at the precise latitude indicated by de Fuca, there is a strait on the Pacific coast between 48° and 49° N that leads to Puget Sound and to the Inside Passage between Vancouver Island and the North American mainland. This strait was named after Juan de Fuca in 1787. It remains uncertain whether de Fuca or Lok invented the tale of de Fuca's 1592 voyage, or whether they misinterpreted or embellished the story of a real, possibly undocumented Spanish expedition.

Further reading: William H. Goetzmann and Glyndwr Williams, *The Atlas of North American Exploration* (New York: Prentice Hall General Reference, 1992).

—Paul Mapp

fur trade

The fur trade was initiated by indigenous people, initially controlled by Indian middlemen, and began almost 100 years before JAMESTOWN, PLYMOUTH, and BOSTON were founded. The first Europeans came to North America to fish, not to collect furs or to establish communities. The fur trade grew slowly and sporadically and eventually emerged as a commercial enterprise in the Saint Lawrence Gulf during the 1580s. Because of the resource-rich FISHING banks and the repeated yearly sojourns of Europe's fishermen, the Indian desire to entice the Europeans into trade was eventually successful. It was the quantity and quality of the furs offered by NATIVE AMERICANS that helped transform Europeans into fur traders. Furs were a scarce commodity in Europe because most fur-bearing ANIMALS had become extinct on that continent by the late Middle Ages. North America was not only rich in furs but had an Indian labor force that trapped, processed, and transported pelts along established indigenous trade routes.

The earliest Indian traders likely were Tarrentine from Nova Scotia and the Gulf of Maine. They were fur trade middlemen, skilled sailors who used European-style shallops to collect furs from coastal Indian villages. The JESUITS referred to them as "courageous and active sailors." Their shallops weighed up to 12 tons, were often 12 meters long, and had multiple masts. Jesuit observations about the presence and daring of Indian traders are confirmed by the written accounts of explorers like HENRY HUDSON. In 1609 Hudson, at or near Penobscot Bay, noted that "two French Shallops full of the country people came into the Harbour. . . . They brought many Beaver skinnes and other fine Furres, which they would have changed for redde Gownes. For the French trade with them, for red Caccockes, Knives, Hatchetts, Copper, Kettles, Trevits, Beades, and other trifles." Indian traders plied the North Atlantic coastline, collecting and storing furs till the summer months, when Europeans arrived. In 1580 an unscrupulous English explorer described his theft of 300 moose hides, "the most part of them . . . eighteen foot by the square," from an unguarded building.

In addition to the coastal MAINE trade, there were indigenous trading villages where native people and foreigners gathered during the summer months to exchange furs and agricultural produce for European trade goods. The most populous of these sites was Tadoussac, controlled by the Montagnais. Their territory included the Saguenay River, a crucial outlet from the vast fur-rich hinterland. Tadoussac was in close proximity to indigenous and European fishing grounds, and as many as 20,000 people gathered here during the summer months.

The holocaust of DISEASE disrupted Indian control over the early trade, and the French, Dutch, and British became directly involved in the exchange process. Through an alliance with the HURON and the founding of Quebec (1608), the French gained control of the St. Lawrence River Valley, the only inland river route from the Atlantic seaboard to the continental interior. The French had access to vast quantities of prized peltry, but their ability to harvest those furs depended on Indians. A small French population coupled with the vastness of the North American landscape over which France claimed sovereignty created high rates of intermarriage between French men and Indian women. By 1680 French traders traveled in Minnesota, Hudson Bay, and in the Mississippi Delta.

The fur trade became an arena of cultural interaction, often referred to as the "middle ground," where French and Indians participated equally in the exchange process and where French men lived in an Indian world in which indigenous custom held sway. The fur trade encompassed far more than economic gain, and the French proved willing to forego profits to foster their political and diplomatic objectives. Both licensed traders (*voyageurs*) and coureurs de bois married Indian women. Some descendants remained part of native communities; others founded societies of people of mixed ancestry (MÉTIS) at such places as Detroit, Mackinac, Green Bay, and Chicago.

For the Dutch furs were a lucrative commodity, and by the early 1600s as many as 40,000 pelts per year were shipped from Fort Orange (now Albany) to Amsterdam. The Dutch also relied on intermarriage to improve their access to peltry and on many illegal traders (*Bosch Loopers*), who produced higher volumes of peltry than NEW AMSTERDAM's licensed traders.

By 1650 the English displaced the Dutch. English traders were less enthusiastic about intermarriage, often brought their families, and usually worked near trading posts. For the English the fur trade, like the acquisition of Indian lands, was primarily an economic rather than a cultural form of exchange. The fur trade fostered the economic independence of the English colonies. SQUANTO introduced the trade to the PILGRIMS, who traded on both Cape Cod and the Kennebec River in Maine and used the profits to repay the colony's debts. MASSACHUSETTS Bay Company also engaged in the fur trade along the Merrimack River and established Springfield to obtain furs from the CONNECTICUT River Valley.

By the 18th century the establishment of towns, the transformation of beaver ponds into farms and pastureland, and the depletion of fur-bearing animals dramatically reduced the New England fur trade. France dominated the beaver trade, and Britain vigorously contested that hegemony. The 18th-century French trade was both viable and profitable; Great Lakes furs grossed as much as 1 million livres per year. France had established furs as a viable commercial enterprise, and the beaver, transformed into the felt hat, remained a fashion staple for more than 300 years. Even when beaver hats were replaced by silk ones in the 1840s, beaver skins remained a high-volume export, used primarily for coats. Eventually the fur trade moved from the Great Lakes into the Northwest, where furs were more plentiful and less expensive to harvest.

While the beaver trade was synonymous with northern regions, deerskins shaped the history of the southern fur trade. By the mid-18th century, the CATAWBA, CHEROKEE, Creek, CHICKASAW, and CHOCTAW annually harvested as many as 400,000 deerskins for shipment to England. French and later Spanish LOUISIANA controlled the exports of this southeastern trade. The demand for deerskins continued to increase throughout the 18th century because of the repeated disease outbreaks that crippled European livestock herds. Indian-processed deerskins were a welcome substitute and produced high quality breeches, gloves, harnesses, saddles, and book bindings. Increased demand caused overhunting, and by 1800 the deer population had precipitously declined.

England and France repeatedly challenged each other's access to furs. The fur trade exacerbated national rivalries and intensified colonial conflicts. By 1721 England successfully wrested control of Hudson Bay from the French. In the 1760s the Franco-Anglo fur trade rivalry in the Ohio River Valley helped to trigger the SEVEN YEARS' WAR. Following the conquest of Canada, England dominated the trade. By the time of American Revolution, England imported 95 percent of all its furs from North America; almost 80 percent of pelts came

An illustration showing Native Americans swapping their furs for rifles with French colonists *(Hulton/Archive)*

from recently acquired lands previously claimed by the French, and beaver displaced deerskin as the more valuable import.

The fur trade is often negatively portrayed as contributing to the demise of indigenous peoples by intensifying their materialism, undermining the spiritual connections they shared with animals, and spreading ALCOHOL and firearms. Recent research suggests alternative scenarios. The trade offered Indians the opportunity to participate in an emerging global marketplace, and they were not uniformly corrupted by that involvement. The fur trade did not, by itself, produce material acquisitiveness, nor were profits from the trade used to create individual wealth among Indians. Instead, goods and wealth were often distributed according to indigenous custom. Native Americans did not reflexively and unconsciously respond to market forces. Frequently, Indians angered traders by failing to hunt, thereby refusing to provide the quantity of furs that traders demanded. Moreover, the Indian desire for cloth and CLOTHING rather than GUNS and alcohol fostered trade. At both 18th-century Detroit and Michilimackinac, for example, cloth constituted 70 to 75 percent of the goods traded. The remaining trade goods included iron implements for cultivating fields, cooking foods, and carving wood, as well as hunting tools, TOBACCO, silver ornaments, mirrors, musical instruments, and luxury items such as English china and eating utensils. During the 18th century firearms and alcohol constituted less than 1 percent of the trade goods carried from Montreal to Detroit and Michilimackinac.

The fur trade was more extensive, long-lived, and familiar to Indians than historians generally envision. In precontact North America the exchange of furs and other items was both intracontinental and intercontinental. Before Europeans arrived buffalo robes from GREAT PLAINS INDIANS were traded at southwestern markets, and deerskins were carried along rivers to Cahokia and into Mexico as tribute. The trade in furs included a variety of animals, not simply the beaver and the white-tailed deer desired by Europeans. European arrival transformed the fur trade into a global enterprise. It included not only the French, British, Dutch, and Spanish but also the Russians, who traded among the INUIT for sealskins, and the Swedes, who traded among the DELAWARE Indians. Eventually, even something as common as black raccoon from Indiana's Kankakee River Valley became part of John Jacob Astor's fur-trading empire with the 19th-century Chinese.

Further reading: Susan Sleeper-Smith, *Indian Women and French Men* (Amherst: University of Massachusetts Press, 2001); Richard White, *The Middle Ground: Indians, Empires, and Republics in the Great Lakes Region, 1650–1815* (New York: Cambridge University Press, 1991).

—Susan Sleeper-Smith

G

Gates, Sir Thomas (unknown–1621)
From 1611 to 1614 Thomas Gates served as acting governor of the VIRGINIA Colony. Born in Colyford, Devonshire, Gates was a "West Countryman," a member of a closely knit alliance of aristocrats from western England and the Welsh borderlands—men such as Humphrey, Raleigh, Somers, Grenville, and their friends—who in the final decades of Elizabethan England intensely promoted the colonization of Ireland and America and the Protestant cause on both sides of the English Channel. Accordingly, Gates sailed with the Sir Francis Drake expedition of 1585, which captured Cartegena, burned ST. AUGUSTINE, and carried back to England some of the Roanoke colonists. Knighted for bravery after his attack on Cádiz, Gates fought the Spanish in Normandy and the Azores and participated in the English occupation and colonization of Gaelic Ireland. By 1600 Gates and his company were in the Netherlands, where he made acquaintance with SIR THOMAS DALE and other gentlemen who late figured prominently in the Virginia Colony.

Gates and other West Countrymen petitioned James I for a patent to plant a colony in Virginia, and he was prominent among the gentry grantees mentioned in the charter of 1606, which established the Virginia and PLYMOUTH Company. Gates invested heavily in the Virginia Company, reflecting a trend among many gentry—who held more than a third of company stock—to channel rents from their TENANTS or profits from other sources into entrepreneurial activities such as colonial settlement and overseas trading ventures.

Sailing to Virginia with Governor Lord De La Warr in 1609 with 500 men and women, the now Lieutenant General Gates and the crew of the pinnace *Sea Adventurer* were shipwrecked in Bermuda. Poet and fellow castaway William Strachey's chronicle of this event later inspired William Shakespeare's *The Tempest.* Escaping Bermuda on two pinnaces built on the island, Gates arrived in JAMESTOWN to find the colony nearly extinguished after the "starving time" of the previous winter. He began the evacuation of the surviving colonists back to England, only to be turned back at the mouth of the James River by Governor De La Warr, who had just arrived from England. De La Warr resurrected Jamestown and sent Gates back to England for supplies. Gates returned in 1611 with livestock and 280 men, mostly ARTISANS and laborers, but also a few "gallants to escape their evil destinies" and 80 women (most of whom were sold as wives to the settlers), including Lady Gates and their two daughters. Lady Gates died in passage, and, arriving in the colony, Gates sent his daughters back to England. De La Warr, too, had returned to England in ill health, and the colony's government devolved first upon George Percy, then upon Thomas Dale, and finally upon Gates. As acting governor, he struggled with the inability or unwillingness of the English to raise enough food to feed themselves and their consequent dependence on Indian corn.

Gates's implementation of the company's instructions to subjugate the neighboring tribes and force them to pay tribute in foodstuffs inflamed relationships with the POWHATAN, already rubbed raw by George Percy's earlier butchery of the Powhatan Queen of Paspahegh and her children. Displaying the arrogant and hot-tempered mentality of Elizabethan male aristocrats, Gates, Percy, and Dale were quick to take offense at any perceived threats by the Powhatan and countered with massive retaliation to any challenge—real or perceived—from that quarter in the belief that he who struck first and inspired fear would survive. They seized and killed even those Indians coming to the settlements to trade food, in Percy's words "for a Terrour to the Reste to cawse them to desiste from their subtell practyses." Between 1609 and 1614 several hundred English musketeers, under the command of High Marshall Sir Thomas Gates and other veteran captains of the Netherlands campaigns, burned the Powhatan's villages and fields, wrestling from them control of the James River basin. This first Powhatan war raged until the capture of

Powhatan's daughter, POCAHONTAS, and her marriage to JOHN ROLFE.

Gates established fortified settlements and populated them with independent farming families, who profited fabulously from the later TOBACCO boom. He also imposed the same harsh military rule that governed the English troops in the Netherlands, enforcing it mercilessly on those laborers who tilled the company plantation. As retribution for running away to the Indians, "Some he appointed to be hanged Some burned Some broken upon wheles, others to be staked and some shott to death." As punishment for shoddy seamstress work, Ann Leyden and June Write "were whipt, and An Leyden beinge then with childe (the same night thereof miscarried)." Fear, Gates thought, was necessary to keep both intractable Indians and unmanageable laborers in line. Despite the fearful discipline of work gangs, the colony was unable to grow enough to feed itself and continued to beg, buy, and bully food from the Indians throughout its first two decades.

The Gates-Dale administrations secured a tenuous but stable foothold for the colony on the James River from the CHESAPEAKE BAY to the Fall Line, but at the expense of the Indians and the colony's laborers. In 1614 Gates returned to England to take an active role in Virginia Company affairs, but by 1620 he had sold his stock and returned to service in the Netherlands, where he died in 1621, a year before his work in Virginia was nearly undone by the Powhatan uprising of 1622.

Further reading: Karen Ordhal Kupperman, *Indians and English: Facing Off in Early America* (Ithaca, N.Y.: Cornell University Press, 2000).

—James Bruggeman

gender

Originally a term used to describe a grammatical form, scholars now use the term *gender* to refer to sex roles of men and women in a given society. *Gender* differs from the term *sex*, which distinguishes whether a person is male or female. Therefore, sex involves biological and physiological differences. In discussing gender, scholars examine what is masculine or feminine. What any given society views as manly or womanly concerns gender. For social scientists gender is a category of analysis—a way of examining any given culture by focusing on a specific group of people. Some social scientists argue that gender is revealed through language; we understand our gender roles through the words and phrases that define our identity. Others feel that gender roles reflect essential natures found in one's sex. Another group of scholars argues that gender is a function of our material world; without possessions to pass on to progeny, prehistoric peoples did not have such rigid gender roles as they did once humans became agricultural, settled down, and were able to pass on their goods to their children. Discussions of gender involve values, norms, and the social roles of men and women.

Different cultures and societies have different understandings of what gender roles are appropriate for their peoples. For example, in 1680 the people of the Taos Pueblo in the Southwest rebelled against the Spanish conquistadores. Part of the conflict arose over conflicting gender roles. In Spain, as in most Western cultures, men did most of the construction on homes and buildings. For the people of the pueblo, the making of the mud and straw adobe bricks was the work of women. This conflict over gender roles contributed to the revolt. Pueblo men felt emasculated by the work and refused to make the bricks. This example of a conflict of gender roles shows how concepts of gender, ideas about what a given society views as masculine or feminine, shape the everyday lives of people.

Ideas of what is manly or womanly vary in specific historical and cultural ways. For example, colonial men and women in North America had sharp LABOR divisions based on gender. Plowing, carpentry, masonry, and animal husbandry were "men's work," whereas cooking, brewing beer, making soap or candles, and sewing served as "women's work." Early Americans lived in a patriarchal society, that is, one in which men had more power than women. Even the Quaker leader WILLIAM PENN (whose religious sect advocated gender equality) organized the first PENNSYLVANIA government providing a special category for "women, children, and idiots." Thus, gender also helps one understand power relations in a given society.

As historians concentrate on change over time, the changing gender roles of men and women in American society over the past four centuries serve as a mechanism for understanding the lives of people in the past. In examining the various cultures that existed in early American society, including English, French, Dutch, Native American, Jewish, and African, we can learn much about gender in early America.

Gender roles and definitions varied regionally among European settlers in early America. In the 17th-century southern colonies, English men greatly outnumbered women. There was considerable pressure on girls to marry or engage in sex at a young age, although many women had to wait until their INDENTURED SERVITUDE ended before they wed. If they were widowed (not uncommon in an era of high MORTALITY), women often inherited their husband's property and bargained for marriages to wealthy plantation owners. Some women, like ELIZABETH LUCAS PINCKNEY, managed plantations in the 18th-century South, regardless of the rigidly prescribed gender roles. As part of their masculine identity, men prided themselves on their dancing (a well-turned calf meant a man was a good dancer) and loved to drink whisky, gamble, race, and ride horses. Women in early New England more frequently migrated as part of family groups, and they usually functioned within narrowly defined gender roles. On her husband's death a New England woman received "the widow's third." That is, a portion of her marital property was given to her while the rest was distributed among her children. New England inheritance patterns favored men, because gender roles prohibited women from managing their own legal affairs. Meanwhile, Quaker women in the Middle Colonies usually took a more active role, often preaching their religion.

Nearly all African-American men and women came involuntarily to the New World as slaves. Although some lived as free people—for example, large groups of free black people lived in NEW ORLEANS—most did not. For these men and women, their traditional gender roles were often compromised by SLAVERY. Both men and women worked in the fields doing heavy labor. Within the plantation household women often took on the burden of raising not only their own children but the children of the plantation owners.

NATIVE AMERICANS also had clearly differentiated gender roles, although women often exercised considerably more social, economic, and political power than did European women. Among the IROQUOIS, for example, women grew most of the FOOD and exercised considerable political power, as older women selected chiefs. In addition, women could easily divorce their husbands by placing his property outside their longhouse door.

Further reading: Kathleen M. Brown, *Good Wives, Nasty Wenches, and Anxious Patriarchs: Gender, Race, and Power in Colonial Virginia* (Chapel Hill: University of North Carolina Press, 1996).

—Paula Smith-Hawkins

Georgia

Georgia was the last of the original 13 colonies to be settled by the British. The idea of a new colony south of SOUTH CAROLINA had been discussed in London during the late 1720s, and it eventually came to fruition due to the happy confluence of philanthropic ideals and imperial concerns. Leading British parliamentarians had become concerned about the plight of the poor, and those serving on the Parliamentary Gaols Committee saw at firsthand the treatment of criminals, many of whom had been jailed for debt. In an attempt to break the vicious circle of poverty, debt, and jail, the idea of a new American colony, one that would serve as a safe haven for the poor, became popular. At the same time, British government ministers were acutely aware of the vulnerability of their southern colonies in North America, with both the French in the Mississippi Valley and the Spanish in FLORIDA capable of posing a threat to one of the most profitable parts of the empire. This threat was brought home during the Yamasee War of 1715, which caused great damage to many Carolina plantations. The new colony, it was thought, would be able to act as a buffer state and would enhance British territorial claims in the Southeast.

The job of creating the new colony was delegated to a group of 21 trustees, many of whom sat in Parliament and had access to the highest levels of government. Almost uniquely for a new colony, the British Parliament provided a substantial portion of the initial funding, ultimately amounting to several hundred thousand pounds. This was partly because Prime Minister Walpole often relied on the block votes of the trustees to pass important legislation in Parliament, but it was also confirmation that Georgia was not intended to be a commercial colony.

With a solid financial base the trustees chartered a ship, the *Anne,* and recruited 114 men, women, and children who, together with Trustee General JAMES EDWARD OGLETHORPE, would be entrusted with founding the new colony. The *Anne* sailed in November 1732 and arrived at the future site of SAVANNAH in February 1733. After obtaining a formal cession of lands from local Indian leader TOMOCHICHI, Oglethorpe had virgin forest cleared in order to lay out the new town of Savannah.

The first settlers in Georgia were a mixed group. Unlike many other southern colonies, whose initial populations consisted almost entirely of young white men, early Georgians were mixed in age, sex, CLASS, and ethnicity. In the first decade of settlement, most arrived "on the charity," meaning that the trustees paid their passage to the New World. These people were supposed to be the "worthy poor," who merited the chance of a new beginning. Only after 1742, when parliamentary money began to dry up, did the number of free settlers paying their own passage begin to rise.

All early settlers shared the color of their skin: They were white. Because of the belief that SLAVERY would make Georgia more difficult to defend from Spanish attacks and that it would not provide the working opportunities for ordinary poor white settlers that the trustees believed were vital, racial bondage was prohibited in Georgia in 1735. This experiment with free labor was unique in British North America, and it was an abject failure. From the outset settlers complained that the heat made work impossible for white people, that Georgia would not be able to compete with South Carolina for settlers due to the existence of slaves there, and that they were unable to exploit the natural resources fully because of a shortage of workers. A vocal group of malcontents emerged in Georgia consisting mainly of English and Lowland Scottish settlers who repeatedly pressed the trustees to permit slavery, but Highland Scots in the small town of Darien and the Salzburgers in Ebenezer urged the trustees to maintain the ban on racial bondage so that poor white people would not be economically disadvantaged. The malcontents then enlisted the help of Thomas Stephens, son of William Stephens, the trustees' secretary in Georgia. He argued the proslavery case directly to those in power in London, forcing the trustees to publish several defenses of the colony.

The trustees could not escape the fact, however, that Georgia was not an economic success. Experiments with silk production, intended to make the colony self-financing, were constantly set back by poor weather and inexperienced workers. Indentured servants frequently fled to South Carolina, where they were welcomed and released from their remaining years of servitude. Many settlers who had paid their own passage also left for Carolina, knowing it offered better economic opportunities. After nearly 20 years of trustee control, Georgia remained a backwater. Its population was small, its contribution to the imperial economic system was negligible, and it remained a financial burden on the British government.

The decision to permit slavery, made effectively in the late 1740s but not enacted until 1751, was a major turning point in the history of Georgia. Planters from South Carolina, aware of the rice-producing potential of Georgia's sea islands, invested in the colony. As the population grew, so did the demand for goods and services provided by ordinary people. When the trustees surrendered their charter to the British Crown in 1752, they passed on a colony that had a rosy future. By the time the first royal governor, John Reynolds, arrived in 1754, Georgia's population had swelled to 7,000, with 2,000 slaves providing the backbone of the labor force.

Georgia's population, unlike its neighbor South Carolina, retained a white majority, but Euro-Americans were concentrated in the backcountry. In the coastal parishes containing rice plantations, there were often nine slaves for every white person, many of whom were imported directly from AFRICA. Consequently, African elements of culture, language, religion, and familial relationships lingered in the sea islands far longer than elsewhere in British America. The planters who owned these slaves became the principal men in Georgia. Men such as James Habersham, Jonathan Bryan, and Noble Jones made their fortunes in Georgia and were able to dominate the colony socially, politically, and economically through the number of offices they held. Each justice of the peace, assembly member, and juror tended to be chosen from the same small group of elite white men.

Nevertheless, Georgia continued to be attractive to ordinary poor white families, especially in the later colonial years. The prospect of free lands enticed many from the Chesapeake area and PENNSYLVANIA to move south. Nonslaveholding white people therefore constituted the largest social group in the colony, with some enjoying a comfortable sufficiency. Poverty still existed, however, especially for widows with children, and, lacking widespread public or private charitable help, many poor white people eked out a bare subsistence in conditions of terrible hardship.

Away from the coast the settlement of backcountry areas relied on the Indian trade. Unlike in other southern colonies, few Native American tribes in Georgia lived near the coast. The small and scattered native groups that had settled in the low country, the most notable being the Yamacraw ruled by Tomochichi, did not possess sufficient trade goods to interest many traders. In order to access the true wealth of the Indian trade, the town of Augusta was founded in 1736, and traders from Georgia and South Carolina both used the town as the starting point for expeditions deep into Creek, CHEROKEE, and other Native American lands. Augusta occupied a strategic position on the Indian trails but also provided the highest point to which boats could navigate up the Savannah River. Despite being more than 130 miles from Savannah, MERCHANTS arriving at Augusta with furs and other goods could ship them easily to the coast; this, above all else, secured the economic future of the backcountry.

Discouraged by the struggling economy and by continuing conflict with the Spanish in Florida, the trustees gave Georgia to Parliament in 1752, a year before the charter was due to expire, and it became a royal colony. The first royal governor, John Reynolds (1754–7) proved inept in dealing with his own council and with Indians. He was replaced in 1757 by Henry Ellis, who maintained an important alliance with the Creek Indians, who rescued the colonists from the Cherokee Indians during the SEVEN YEARS' WAR.

From the 1750s until the Revolution, Georgia developed steadily. Economic output rose phenomenally, from 500 barrels of rice in 1752 to 10,000 by 1756. The colony's human population continued to grow, reaching 33,000 by 1773, including 15,000 slaves. Georgia also increased in size. Land cessions amounting to 5 million acres from the Creek in 1763 and 1773 saw Georgia expand south to the St. Marys River and northwest to the headwaters of the Savannah River. Of all the new colonies that Britain founded or conquered in the 18th century—a list that includes Nova Scotia, Newfoundland, Quebec, and west and east Florida—only Georgia became fully integrated into the imperial mercantilist system, with a flourishing ECONOMY based on African slave labor. By the time of the Revolution, most visitors would have been hard pressed to identify a difference between Georgia and South Carolina.

Further reading: Betty Wood, *Slavery In Colonial Georgia* (Athens: University of Georgia Press, 1983); Harold E. Davis, *The Fledgling Province: Social and Cultural Life in Colonial Georgia, 1733–1776* (Chapel Hill: University of North Carolina Press, 1976).

—Timothy James Lockley

German immigrants

Immigrants from the area that eventually became Germany constituted the largest non-British European population in the British colonies. Approximately 100,000 German speakers came to British North America during the colonial period; in 1775 they and their descendants accounted for nearly 10 percent of the American population. Drawn by many of the same factors as their British counterparts, German migrants sought economic opportunity and religious freedom in the New World, and they were often pushed out of Europe by material difficulties, wars, and the threat of conscription into the military. Also mirroring broader colonial trends, German migrants included a combination of free individuals and families as well as unfree indentured servants.

A handful of German speakers were among the original settlers of JAMESTOWN, VIRGINIA, in 1607. German Mennonites arrived in PENNSYLVANIA soon after that colony's founding, establishing Germantown near PHILADELPHIA in 1683. German immigration to colonial North America was primarily an 18th-century phenomenon, however. In 1709 3,000 Protestant refugees from the Palatinate came to North America via England, most settling in NEW YORK's Hudson River Valley. Beginning around 1720 a much larger and more continuous stream of German immigrants began to journey across the Atlantic. They typically landed in Philadelphia, then spread west into Pennsylvania, south through the Shenandoah Valley, and into the piedmont and hill country of the Carolinas. Between 1730 and 1770 nearly 75,000 German immigrants made this trip. Most came from the areas surrounding the Rhine and Neckar Rivers in southwestern Germany and Switzerland. This region saw tremendous out-migration between 1709 and 1800 due to decades of war followed by increasing population growth. Although somewhat less than a third of the more than 500,000 people who left Germany in this period looked for greener pastures in British North America (the majority moving eastward into central Europe and Russia), these were huge numbers from the American perspective. At the peak of this immigration, 29,100 Germans disembarked in the decade between 1750 and 1759, most before 1754, when the SEVEN YEARS' WAR stemmed the flow.

German immigrants came to North America both individually and with their families as free people and as unfree laborers. Families were more common in the earlier decades of the 18th century; young single men dominated the immigrant stream after it peaked at mid-century. Those who arrived earlier were more likely to have money to establish themselves in their new homes, but as the number of immigrants grew, so, too, did the number who sold their future labor in order to pay for their passage. Overall, about 45 percent of German immigrants indentured themselves as servants. Ship captains either negotiated contracts in Europe or advanced immigrants the cost of passage and received payment in North America when the individual was sold at auction. Periods of servitude typically lasted three or four years. Women received slightly shorter indentures than men; children sometimes served longer terms. Over time the business of immigrant transport and labor became increasingly exploitative, causing Germans on both continents to protest conditions.

A small but important portion of German migrants to British America came for religious refuge and freedom. These groups tended to cross the Atlantic in organized migrations and to settle together in the New World. The Salzburgers, Protestant refugees from Catholic Austria, established Ebenezer, GEORGIA, in the 1730s. Large numbers of Mennonites and Moravians, along with smaller groups of Amish, Schwenkfelders, and Dunkers, also arrived. This religious migration occurred primarily before 1755, and most of these immigrants remained in Pennsylvania. The vast majority of German migrants, however, belonged to the dominant German Protestant churches, Lutheran and German Reformed, and moved for economic rather than religious reasons. The European state churches were slow to send ministers to North America, and consequently many Germans, like numerous others in 18th-century North America, lacked religious leadership. Ministers such as the Lutheran HENRY MELCHIOR MUHLENBERG and the Reformed preachers Johann Phillip Boehm and Michael Schlatter worked to organize churches and to funnel resources from Europe, enjoying increasing success by the end of the colonial period.

German immigrants formed strong ethnic communities in British America, retaining many of their customs even as they embraced many British political ideas. Because they settled near family, friends, and fellow immigrants, some regions, particularly in Pennsylvania, took on a decidedly German character. Moravian and German Reformed churches supported German schools, while printers like Christopher Saur of Germantown offered German-language almanacs, grammars, and newspapers. Indeed, Benjamin Franklin and other Pennsylvanians occasionally complained that Germans maintained their own traditions too successfully.

The Penn family's attempts to revise land policy and the colony's defense of its western frontier from Indian attacks helped spur naturalizations and politicize German immigrants in Pennsylvania, where they became a significant political force. By 1763 Germans were active in many aspects of colonial government while retaining their ethnic identity.

See also GOTTLIEB MITTELBERGER.

Further reading: Aaron Spencer Fogleman, *Hopeful Journeys: German Immigration, Settlement, and Political Culture in Colonial America, 1717–1775* (Philadelphia: University of Pennsylvania Press, 1996); A. G. Roeber, *Palatines, Liberty and Property: German Lutherans in Colonial British America* (Baltimore: Johns Hopkins University Press, 1993); Marianne Wokeck, *Trade in Strangers: The Beginnings of Mass Migration to North America* (University Park: Pennsylvania State University Press, 1999).

—Katherine Carté Engel

German Reformed Church

The German Reformed Church was founded as a result of religious changes evolving from the Protestant Reformation. Ulrich Zwingli and John Calvin supported the principles of justification by faith alone and the sole authority of the Bible, but they differed from Martin Luther on other points, especially on the meaning of the Eucharist. Calvin advocated Christ's spiritual presence in the bread and wine, while Zwingli believed that the elements were mere symbols and that the celebration was a memorial service of Christ's life and death. The German Reformed Church came to encompass the teachings of both Zwingli and Calvin, with some contributions from Luther's colleague Philipp Melanchthon.

The German Reformed Church was established in the British colonies by German and Swiss pioneers who migrated to PENNSYLVANIA and other colonies in the early 18th century. Their congregations were mostly widely scattered along the frontier, where most Germans settled because earlier migrants had occupied eastern lands. Because of the scarcity of clergy, the German Reformed Church, like other established denominations, faced difficulties throughout the colonial era; schoolteachers or men who possessed a modicum of religious training often performed the tasks of a minister. Scarce financial resources forced rural congregations to share facilities with other denominations, most commonly LUTHERANS.

Throughout the colonial period the German Reformed Church had a close relationship with the Dutch Reformed synods of Holland. The GREAT AWAKENING that swept the colonies in the 1740s spurred Holland church officials to support their German counterparts by supplying Bibles and catechisms to the people along with additional ministers. When German Reformed ministers formed a denominational organization in 1747, they reported to Reformed Church authorities in Holland and, in return, received financial support from them.

Two pastors, John Philip Boehm and Michael Schlatter, were instrumental in organizing the "Coetus of the German Reformed Congregations in Pennsylvania." Boehm immigrated from the region of modern-day Germany to the Perkiomen Valley of southeastern Pennsylvania as a schoolteacher in 1720. Soon the Reformed settlers in the area asked him to lead worship services. By 1725 he began to perform pastoral duties, and in 1729 the Classis of Amsterdam ordained him at the request of his congregations. The classis dispatched Swiss-born Michael Schlatter to the British colonies in 1746 expressly to oversee the German Reformed congregations in the colonies. They chose Schlatter because of his knowledge of both Dutch and German.

Boehm and Schlatter, along with four other German Reformed ministers and elders from the various Pennsylvania congregations, met in PHILADELPHIA to organize the coetus. The group formally adopted the Heidelberg Catechism as the doctrinal standard of their denomination. This synod remained under the supervision of the Holland synods until 1793. At the time of the separation, the coetus supervised more than 230 congregations and more than 15,000 communicants nationwide.

Further reading: Charles H. Gladfelter, *Pastors and People: German Lutheran and Reformed Churches in the Pennsylvania Field, 1717–1793*, vol. 2: *The History* (Breinigsville, Pa.: Pennsylvania German Society, 1981).

—Karen Guenther

Glorious Revolution (1688–1689)

The Glorious Revolution, also known as the Bloodless Revolution, was the abdication of the English throne by Catholic King James II (1685–88) in late 1688 and the subsequent accession of his eldest child, Mary, and her Dutch husband, William of Orange, both Protestants. A major constitutional consequence was the Bill of Rights (1689), which asserted the supremacy of Parliament over William and Mary and all future monarchs. It destroyed the concept of divine-right MONARCHY and automatic hereditary succession, and it limited the monarch's power over law, taxation, and the military. News of the Glorious Revolution and the Bill of Rights was received enthusiastically in the colonies. The revolution ultimately influenced American justifications for independence, the Constitution, and the Bill of Rights.

Numerous factors worked in concert before 1688 to set the stage. King James II and his elder brother, Charles

II (1660–85), both enthralled by the power of the French king, advanced absolute monarchy in England and the colonies. Fears of Catholicism were rife in England and North America, especially after 1685, when Louis XIV revoked the religious liberties of French Protestants and invaded the Protestant Palatinate. With the birth of James's only son in 1688, a Catholic succession for England and loss of Protestant freedoms seemed imminent. Social unrest was further exacerbated by economic stagnation and propagandistic LITERATURE. Women participated with men in popular protests and served as petitioners and fundraisers. Women were also among the most vocal skeptics of the legitimacy of the elderly king's infant son. In response to these developments, Parliament encouraged William of Orange to raise an invading army to depose the king. James, however, abdicated and fled to France along with his wife and son.

Rebellions ensued in several colonies. As in England, economic stagnation and hatred of Catholicism were the common denominators. In the Chesapeake area the ongoing social, economic, and political discontents of indentured servants and tenant farmers were further inflamed by depressed TOBACCO prices and fears of Indian raids. Although VIRGINIA experienced violent disturbances before the Glorious Revolution, all but the northernmost counties remained relatively tranquil in its aftermath. The situation was more volatile in neighboring MARYLAND, where most inhabitants were Protestant but most political appointees were Catholic. Despite earlier complaints by the assembly, the Catholic proprietor, Lord Baltimore, who had been absent from the colony since 1684, continued to act arbitrarily. Baltimore issued an order to proclaim the new monarchs, but his messenger died en route to Maryland, and local officials neglected to recognize the change of government. Reacting to rumors of a French-Indian-Catholic plot to take over Maryland and slaughter Protestants, a newly created Protestant Association led by militia officer John Coode successfully removed the Catholic proprietors from power and requested that Maryland be made a royal colony.

Popular discontent surfaced in the Northeast following James II's dissolution of the MASSACHUSETTS charter and consolidation of the New England colonies, NEW YORK, and NEW JERSEY into the DOMINION OF NEW ENGLAND. In 1689 the dominion's governor, SIR EDMUND ANDROS, who had enforced unpopular laws and taxes, was seized and imprisoned by a BOSTON crowd. King William and Queen Mary dissolved the dominion and granted Massachusetts a new charter that safeguarded personal liberties. In New York the incarceration of Andros and the flight of Lieutenant Governor Nicholson prompted Jacob Leisler, a prominent merchant, to proclaim himself lieutenant governor in the names of the new monarchs. Dutch women were especially supportive of Leisler because their economic, religious, and inheritance rights were being eroded under the English, and they felt that he was more sympathetic and responsive to their concerns. But Leisler's backing was not universal, and he and his son-in-law, Jacob Milborne, were executed for treason in 1691. Determined efforts by their supporters facilitated their posthumous exoneration in 1695.

Further reading: Lois G. Schwoerer, ed., *The Revolution of 1688–89: Changing Perspectives* (New York: Cambridge University Press, 1992).

—Paula Wheeler Carlo

Godfrey, Thomas (1704–1749)

The son of a PHILADELPHIA farmer, Thomas Godfrey was a year old when his father died. Upon his mother's remarriage, Godfrey was apprenticed to a glazier, for whom he glazed the windows of present-day Independence Hall. While an apprentice, Godfrey discovered a natural aptitude for mathematics, teaching himself with borrowed books. When Benjamin Franklin started his Philadelphia business in 1728, he rented a first-floor shop and living quarters to Godfrey and invited him to join the Junto. Godfrey soon left the group; Franklin complained that he was too focused on the precision and exactitude of details. They continued to collaborate on public projects, such as the Library Company, the PENNSYLVANIA Hospital, and an insurance company.

Although his work as a glazier provided little firsthand contact with the sea, Godfrey is rumored to have spent many hours in waterfront taverns, where he learned of the problems associated with navigational TECHNOLOGY. After observing the double reflection of a piece of fallen glass, he realized that by the use of a similar reflection it would be possible to draw the image of the sun down to the horizon. By this means one could establish a ship's latitude. First tested in 1730, the quadrant was used on runs to Newfoundland and Jamaica and then sold commercially in New York.

An active astronomer, Godfrey observed Jupiter's moons and predicted an eclipse of the sun. He died in 1749 survived by a wife and two sons.

—Victoria C. H. Resnick

Gorton, Samuel (1592?–1677)

A radical religious leader, Samuel Gorton was born in Gorton, Lancashire, and lived in the Newgate area of London (a center of radical religious activity) from 1622, where he was employed as a clothier. In 1636 he migrated to New England, residing briefly in BOSTON, PLYMOUTH, and various RHODE ISLAND towns before establishing a settlement at Shawomet (later Warwick, Rhode Island) in 1642. His radical religious views and tendency to challenge colonial civil authority that was not firmly based in English law and a royal charter embroiled him in controversies. In 1643 Gorton and six supporters were seized and carried to trial in MASSACHUSETTS for blasphemy. The magistrates and deputies split over whether to execute him as a heretic, and he and his followers were instead put to hard labor in various towns. When it became clear that Gortonist preaching was influencing some residents, the magistrates reconsidered and banished the seven on pain of death. In a move calculated to forestall further intervention by Massachusetts in the Shawomet area, Gorton arranged the submission of some Narragansett Indians to King Charles I (1625–49). Gorton went to England to lay his case before the parliamentary commission on foreign plantations. He published an attack on Massachusetts, *Simplicities Defence against Seven-Headed Policy* (1646). He won the protection of the English authorities and, in 1648, returned to Shawomet, which he renamed after his new patron, the earl of Warwick. Gorton published other tracts, generally religious polemics. He continued as a religious leader and a magistrate until his death in 1677.

Gorton's faith was mystical, influenced by Baptist views on baptism, atonement, and lay prophecy and countered much Puritan orthodox doctrine. He enjoyed complicated scriptural exegesis, priding himself that his abilities exceeded those of eminent minister JOHN COTTON. He supported religious toleration for QUAKERS. His sect apparently continued after his death, for in 1777 Ezra Stiles reportedly met an elderly man who followed the teachings of Gorton.

Further reading: Raymond Dye Irwin, "Saints, Sinners, and Subjects: Rhode Island and Providence Plantations in Transatlantic Perspective, 1636–1665" (Ph.D. dissertation, Ohio State University, 1996).

—Carla Gardina Pestana

government, British American

According to a BOSTON doctor writing in the early 1750s, colonial government consisted of "three separate negatives":

> thus, by the governor, representing the King, the colonies are monarchical; by the Council, they are aristocratical; by house of representatives, or the delegates from the people, they are democratical: these are distinct and independent of one another, and the colonies enjoy the conveniences of each of these forms of government without their inconveniences, the several negatives being checks upon one another.

His opinion at the time was entrenched. English adherence to a mixed government gained momentum throughout the 16th century, hinging on the idea that a balanced government indefinitely preserved liberty by juxtaposing society's basic socioconstitutional elements: king, lords, and commons. This fundamental precept, later popularized by Montesquieu's *Spirit of the Laws* (1748), structured the theoretical framework within which the earliest settlers established governments throughout colonial America.

1607–1660: Foundings

Within this shared framework, British America's first colonial governments adopted numerous forms. The Crown placed its first successful settlement, VIRGINIA, under the VIRGINIA COMPANY OF LONDON, granting it a charter whose only limitation required the joint-stock company to render laws "agreeable to the laws, statutes, government, and policy of our realm." Under Governor Edwin Sandys, Virginia convened America's first representative assembly, composed of the governor, his appointed council, and two elected burgesses from every parish. The assembly met annually, and all laws it passed were subject to the governor's veto and, ultimately, that of the Virginia Company. The enfranchisement of all landowning white male inhabitants made the assembly a model for future representative institutions that eventually characterized governments throughout British America. When the Privy Council annulled the Virginia Company's charter in 1624, Charles I turned Virginia into a royal colony. The assembly, despite this shift in authority, remained intact.

A different governmental structure materialized in New England. The MASSACHUSETTS BAY COMPANY followed a charter that called for a governor and a council of 18 assistants to be elected annually by the colony's freemen. A general court maintained power to render laws consistent with the laws of England. Although the charter was a secular document, a powerful group of Calvinist investors moved to establish the colony as a Bible commonwealth. An opportunity presented itself when the investors discovered that the charter failed to require the company to remain in England. Thus, in 1630 JOHN WINTHROP, charter in hand, led a fleet to the Massachusetts Bay Colony, where—relatively free from the Crown's oversight—he established a semitheocratic society. Clergy were denied power to wield secular authority, but the colony's government demonstrated its theocratic tendencies through the religious mindset of its secular leaders, who, among other decisions, based the colony's moral codes on biblical rather than common law. In 1648 the colony countered its theo-

Different Types of Colonial Government, 1763
Hudson's Bay Company
St. Lawrence R.
Nova Scotia
Province of Quebec
Lake Huron
Lake Ontario
Lake Erie
Maine District (Massachusetts)
Hudson R.
New Hampshire 1679
Massachusetts 1691
New York 1664
Rhode Island, 1663
Connecticut 1662
Pennsylvania 1681
New Jersey 1702
Maryland 1632
Delaware 1682
ATLANTIC OCEAN
Ohio R.
Virginia 1624
Indian Reserve
North Carolina 1729
South Carolina 1729
Georgia 1732
West Florida
East Florida
N
0 150 Miles
0 150 Kms
Corporate or self-governing colonies
Proprietary colonies
Royal colonies
Other British territory
Proclamation Line of 1763
Colony borders
1729 Date of royal charter or grant

cratic bias with the adaptation of "The Book of General Laws and Libertyes," which defined more clearly the functions of the magistrates, the "liberties" of the people, and due process.

In 1632 GEORGE CALVERT, the first lord Baltimore and a Catholic convert, received a proprietary charter to MARYLAND. Although Calvert was dead when the charter's status became official, the document granted his heirs the privilege to govern as "absolute Lords and Proprietors." With respect to legislation the proprietor could make laws subject to "the Advice, Assent, and Approbation of the free men of the same Province . . . or of their Delegates or Deputies." When Baltimore's son, the second lord Cecilius, organized a venture to the colony in March 1634, he sent his younger brother LEONARD CALVERT to manage the colony according to the charter's stipulations. Calvert, while stressing religious tolerance, granted large manors to an elite Catholic gentry and in 1638 mediated this manorial control with the establishment of Maryland's first representative assembly—a body that was to reflect "the like power . . . as in the House of Commons." The ascendancy of Parliament in 1640 pushed Baltimore to appoint a Protestant governor and present a bill of religious toleration called the Act Concerning Religion. As the long Parliament became established, however, Calvert's proprietary status came under fire, and, by 1651, a group of Maryland PURITANS, who rejected the act, had placed themselves in power. Not until 1657, after Oliver Cromwell's ascent, was Baltimore reinstated, and the Protestants relented, accepting the Act of Toleration and, in turn, a precarious stability.

1660–1681: New Foundings

After the restoration the 17th-century colonial governments of Virginia, Massachusetts Bay, and Maryland were joined by Carolina (1663), NEW YORK (1664), and PENNSYLVANIA (1681). The "restoration colonies" were all proprietary governments, but each one took on unique characteristics, further complicating the diverse patchwork that constituted colonial American government.

In 1663 Charles II granted eight proprietors rights to establish a colony in the Carolina region. The earl of Shaftsbury, with the help of JOHN LOCKE, outlined the colony's government in the Fundamental Constitutions of Carolina. To "avoid erecting a numerous democracy," the Fundamental Constitutions instituted a palatinate court, which called for a "parliament," prepared legislation, appointed officers, and dispersed funds. The parliament consisted of the proprietors, landed nobility, and deputies representing the colony's freeholders. Carolina's government distinguished itself from other colonies through its pyramidal landholding structure, whereby proprietors, nobles, yeomen, serfs, and freeholders owned land according to their rigidly defined status. Locke, ironically, later became known for ideologies supporting representative government, propertied individualism, and the political upheavals that ushered these ideas into reality. The Fundamental Constitutions, however, not only failed to foreshadow such republican developments but quickly proved hopelessly inappropriate as Carolina's governing structure. Under the burdens of slow population growth, the refusal to ratify the Fundamental Constitutions, and the popularity of fur trading over farming, Locke's proposed hierarchical blueprint was routinely ignored. Few manors developed, settlers surveyed the land independently, and the proprietors, many of whom were absentee, remained politically weak. The decentralized political authority that subsequently prevailed in Carolina until the 1720s easily accommodated the hundreds of planters from Barbados who arrived to settle large plantations along the Ashley and Cooper Rivers with slaves, rice, and the quest for profit.

New York initiated a form of government especially sensitive to its background. England, which conquered NEW NETHERLAND in 1664, established a chartered government under the leadership of Richard Nicholls that aimed to integrate English laws and Dutch customs. Nicholls immediately instituted the Duke's Laws, named after James, duke of York, which created a governmental structure of overseers elected by the colony's freeholders. New York's lack of an assembly, however, became a conspicuous point of contention. Throughout Governor SIR EDMUND ANDROS's tenure, 1674 to 1683, towns pushed vehemently for an assembly to legitimate the taxation schemes that Charles II wanted imposed. When financial problems became unbearable, James replaced Andros with Thomas Dongan and reluctantly decreed an assembly. New York's assembly, which effectively balanced the interests of the Dutch and English, conferred power on the governor, council, and "the people in general assembly" while granting the vote to all freeholders.

The pressure placed on Nicholls to initiate an assembly was largely in response to the founding of NEW JERSEY in 1665. The duke of York's grant to Sir George Carteret and John, Lord Berkley resulted in a colony in which New Jerseyans could elect an assembly. The establishment of the most democratic system in the BRITISH EMPIRE not only intensified opposition to New York's lack of an assembly but attracted a large number of Puritans and Dutch Protestants to settle in New Jersey. These religious dissenters, however, posed a problem for Carteret and Berkley when they resisted the ruling and taxation authority of the Restorationists. Faced with this dilemma, Berkley sold his grant to two QUAKERS in 1674, who subsequently turned the grant over to three other trustees, one of whom was WILLIAM PENN. After a division of the colony into East and West Jersey in 1676, Carteret (who owned East Jersey) sold his grant to yet another group of proprietors, one of whom was also William Penn. In 1702 a growing and diverse group of settlers from many backgrounds as well as an emerging Quaker elite united to become the royal colony of New Jersey.

Like Baltimore, William Penn also exploited his royal connections to seek a haven for a religiously persecuted group. Obtaining a charter from Charles II in 1681, Penn secured for his Quaker brothers and sisters the right to grant land on the terms of his choosing, create manors, and make all laws subject to "the approbation of the Freemen of the said Country." He established an assembly, called for religious toleration, and labeled his venture a "holy experiment." Penn articulated his governing vision in a document called the Frame of Government of 1681. It stipulated that all Christians could vote and hold office, that settlers would not be taxed to support a church, that the upper and lower houses of assembly were to be elected by the enfranchised male property holders, and that the governor lacked a veto. To keep Penn's proprietary power in check, the Crown ordered that all laws be reviewed by the king for inspection. In return, the Crown agreed to levy no taxes without the consent of the assembly, Parliament, or the colony's proprietor. Penn settled his colony with the help of an organization of wealthy Quakers called the Free Society of Traders, who funded the arrival of thousands of settlers and worked under Penn's belief that "Governments rather depend on men than men upon governments."

1660–1760: The Emergence of Political Stability

Despite differences in their specific governmental structures, these colonies—linked as they all were to the same metropolitan political culture—followed a similar trajectory of development throughout the colonial period. After several decades of chronic political disorder, most colonies experienced an era of extraordinary stability lasting into the 1760s.

After a rare period of stability between 1660 and BACON'S REBELLION (1676), Virginia succumbed to conflicts arising from the Crown's effort to control the colony's political and economic mechanisms. These tensions divided Virginia's gentry and led to 50 years of constant political instability, with one governor rapidly succeeding another. Starting in the late 1710s, however, in the context of Robert Walpole's emphasis on political harmony among all governmental branches and with an increasingly profitable TOBACCO ECONOMY, Virginia benefited from a series of governors who capably managed the interests of the elite planters while tending to those of yeomen and their legislators. During the terms of Hugh Drysdale and Sir William Gooch, voting Virginians continually placed a ruling elite in positions of legislative authority, assumed a position of deferential adherence to its decisions, and ushered in a period of unprecedented political stability.

SOUTH CAROLINA experienced its share of factionalism into the 1720s. Battles between MERCHANTS and planters, West Indian immigrants and ENGLISH IMMIGRANTS, and town and country ripped through the colony and resulted in the overthrow of the weakened proprietors in 1719. Throughout the 1720s the demand for increased paper currency and a severe depression intensified political infighting. With the permanent implementation of a royal government in 1730, however, the political situation began to improve. Disparate groups began to share in the colony's increasing economic prosperity, the common pursuit of profit united the interests of the yeomen, merchants, and planting elite, and the growing slave majority unified whites in a single, if broad, interest group.

Pennsylvania's political turmoil initially centered on the antiauthoritarianism of the Quaker elite and the proprietary interests of William Penn. Later, it flared up between the Quaker elites who secured power and a "country party" led by DAVID LLOYD. Throughout the contentious tenures of Charles Gookin and Sir William Keith, Pennsylvania foundered on the issues of land tenure, paper currency, and proprietary power. As in Virginia and South Carolina, however, stability soon followed. A tight coalition of Quaker elites consolidated economic power, permanently diminished proprietary privilege, and gained control of the assembly. By the 1730s a tightly knit group of wealthy merchants and landholders forged a steady consensus among the colony's traditional warring factions, and, in turn, a stable political environment evolved.

MASSACHUSETTS followed the same basic course. Metropolitan authorities undermined Puritan leadership throughout the late 17th century and, in so doing, created an opportunity for the region's rising merchant CLASS to make a successful power grab, a development that initiated a country–town rift. Fifty years of conflict ensued, with royal governors, including Sir Edmund Andros, attempting to assert power, the Crown claiming monopoly over large trees used for the masts of ships, and merchants trying to bend the assembly to their economic wishes. The contest over royal prerogative had diminished by the 1730s, however, and with it so did the rural–urban tension that had plagued the colony for so many years. As in the other colonies, a prominent elite—in this case a group of maritime merchants—consolidated political power on the basis of a strong rural–urban consensus. Aside from the land bank controversy in 1740–41, Massachusetts government reached a level of stability on par with governments throughout British America.

New York's path to political stability was the least successful. The Leislerian conflict, the commercial-gentry rivalry of the 1720s, and the Morris–Cosby dispute, among many other factors, precluded the kind of governmental stability that prevailed elsewhere. Nevertheless, by the 1730s New York began to practice a form of politics that one historian has described as "a model of tension within a broad framework of consent." Routine, almost ritualistic, rivalries yielded to loosely organized parties whose very presence minimized the possibility of violent civil disorder. Ironically, New York's constant factionalism may have been the basis for the region's eventual political stability.

Underlying Agents of Change

These remarkable parallels toward political consensus throughout colonial British America speak to a convergence of several underlying factors. Historians have duly noted the emergence of a colonial elite, institutional development, and the rise of the public sphere as factors contributing to the strength of colonial governments in the 18th century, but the glue giving collective shape to these individual factors involved the differences among colonial governments and the political ideology that those differences nurtured.

With royal governors, assemblies, and councils, colonial governments seemed to mirror the ideal English constitution. Beneath the surface, however, the American governments were quite different. In England royal patronage ensured that Parliament remained loyal to the Crown, with often as many as half the Members of Parliament holding Crown offices. The electorate, for its part, was too weak to maintain vigilance over these corrupt arrangements, because only about one-quarter of adult males could vote. One outcome of this concentration of political power was the emergence of a vocal opposition group of "radical Whigs," also known as "commonwealthmen," who drew upon classical republicanism to argue that human beings, who were naturally inclined to abuse power, required a truly representative government to safeguard liberty. In light of England's patronage system, they claimed that corruption had overtaken virtue and that English liberty was falling prey to a sinister executive conspiracy.

The commonwealthmen remained on the fringe in England. In America, however, their message resonated deeply. Not only did royal governors lack patronage power, but the assemblies had achieved a defining voice within colonial governments. With their allegiance not being swayed by patronage appointments, assemblies in America responded more directly to the will of their constituents, who constituted about 70 percent of the adult white male population. (The land required to vote generally was the same in England and America, but land was much more readily available in America). By the mid-18th century it had become clear to many Americans that their own governments reflected the ideal English constitution more accurately than did England's system. Thus, when England, after the SEVEN YEARS' WAR, abandoned its period of "benign neglect" of the American colonies and started to impose new, restrictive measures on the colonies, Americans eagerly embraced the radical Whig ideology and used it to solidify their opposition to what they perceived as arbitrary rule. It was on this point that the diversity of colonial governments ultimately converged.

Further reading: Jack P. Greene, *Negotiated Authorities: Essays in Colonial Political and Constitutional History* (Charlottesville and London: University of Virginia Press, 1994); Bernard Bailyn, *Origins of American Politics* (New York: Knopf, 1970).

—James E. McWilliams

Graffenried, Christopher, baron de (1661–1743)

Swiss colonizer Christopher Graffenried, hoping to restore his family's fortunes in North America, immigrated from Switzerland to London, where he formed a partnership in 1707 with Louis Mitchell to organize a Swiss colony in the Proprietorship of Carolina. Mitchell had been appointed by the canton of Bern to find a suitable site to resettle Protestant refugees who were flooding into Switzerland because of Louis XIV's wars. A great favorite of Queen Anne (1702–14), Graffenried used his influence at court to gain royal approval for the project, which also offered the British government a solution for their own resettlement of Protestant refugees from the Palatinate. With the plan subsidized by the Crown and Graffenried created a baron, the settlement seemed viable, and the first boatload of colonists sailed in January 1710.

Unfortunately, more than half the colonists died en route, either onboard ship or during the TRAVEL overland through Virginia. When Graffenried arrived months later, he found the settlers sick and desperate and the government of Carolina in chaos after the death of the governor, who had been too busy with politics to provide the promised support. Struggling to found their settlement, the Swiss and Palatine colonists were caught in the 1711 outbreak of the TUSCARORA WAR and survived only because Graffenried promised neutrality in the fight between the local Indians and Carolina settlers. Even so, the new settlement was battered by the war. Graffenried attempted to secure mining concessions to provide his people with an income, but this scheme failed. Selling his interests in the land, he returned to Switzerland. Eventually, New Bern's location made it successful as a trading post, and it survived to attract further Swiss and Palatine immigration.

—Margaret Sankey

Great Awakening

A manifestation of philosophical, political, economic, institutional, and demographic changes, the Great Awakening was a multifaceted religious movement that swept through American PROTESTANTISM beginning in the 1720s the repercussions of which shaped the religious outlook of America's founding generation. The movement's ideological impetus had its beginnings in Europe in the late 1600s, when visionaries like Sir Isaac Newton and JOHN LOCKE began to describe a universe different from the one previously conceived by religious theorists. This new concept involved a rational rather than capricious order to the universe, one in which, as New England Great Awakening preacher JONATHAN EDWARDS proclaimed, God's overpowering goodness was "irresistible."

Out of the philosophical position of rationalism, residents of western Europe and the American colonies gained increasing understanding of and control over their world. Navigation instruments, printing presses, vaccinations against epidemics, and botanical innovations were among the discoveries and inventions that convinced these innovators that the world was subject to predictable laws. The result was erosion of the general belief in a vengeful God who would arbitrarily choose to save some souls and damn others. A forgiving God gained ascendancy, one who would grant "grace" (forgiveness and salvation) to anyone who would profess faith and dedication. These new ideas had had their origins in Europe, but they acquired special power in the North America colonies, where increasing ideological independence was bolstered by the growing number of people in whom profitable exports and plentiful, inexpensive land bred optimism. For many American yeoman farmers, MERCHANTS, and ARTISANS, increasing economic independence convinced them that they could master and improve their own fate, with or without divine assistance. By 1720 church attendance had declined in all the American colonies.

At the same time American religion faced new institutional challenges. English colonists had been accustomed to a national church sanctioned by the government and supported by taxes levied on members and nonmembers alike. New Englanders had replicated this system, but with a Congregational instead of an ANGLICAN CHURCH. In the South and in parts of NEW YORK, the Anglican Church reigned, but in most of the colonies there were also vigorous alternative sects—QUAKERS, Mennonites, and Dutch Reformed, with a few ROMAN CATHOLICS and JEWS added to the mix. Traditional Native American—and even African—religious practices also attracted some English followers. Only in PENNSYLVANIA were citizens free to join the church of their choice without also being taxed in support of the established denomination. Because there were few educational institutions to train ministers and no Anglican bishops in the colonies, there were not enough educated and credentialed religious officials to maintain theological discipline and consistency in American churches. American clergy had to return to England to be ordained, and often their congregations viewed them as incompetent, aloof, and uninspiring. The result by the 1720s was a restless mixture of institutions and individuals ripe for dramatic remodeling.

Transformation came in the form of "revivals" begun by local ministers in NEW JERSEY, Pennsylvania, and MASSACHUSETTS as early as the 1720s. In the Raritan Valley region of New Jersey, much of the ideological leadership came from THEODORUS JACOBUS FRELINGHUYSEN, a Dutch Protestant immigrant of the pietist tradition who, worried that American Christians had grown too lax in the practice of their faith, preached stirring sermons differentiating between the "broad way" and the "narrow way." The broad way was easier and more attractive, Frelinghuysen argued, but only the narrow way would result in "Eternal Life, everlasting Glory and everlasting Joy and Salvation." Frelinghuysen's emotionally stirring sermons prepared the way for Presbyterian evangelical preacher WILLIAM TENNENT, SR., and his three sons to echo a similar message in Pennsylvania and in the western mountains of VIRGINIA. Convinced that individual and community salvation required that community members dedicate themselves to serving the Lord, preachers like Frelinghuysen, the Tennents, and their followers stressed the importance of biblical scripture.

Their revival movement, which gathered momentum during the 1730s, followed a format similar to that of British minister JOHN WESLEY's. He traveled through England and the colonial South preaching a religion that stressed social service to prisoners, slaves, and other oppressed people and a disdain for the liturgy of traditional Protestant churches. Wesley also emphasized a personal conversion experience frequently involving a dramatic and emotional public confession of sins and embracing of renewed faith, which one observer described as "bitter shrieking and screaming" and "convulsionlike tremblings." The final spark of America's Great Awakening was lit by rebel Anglican minister GEORGE WHITEFIELD, who arrived from England, almost single-handedly coalesced a movement, and then left its expansion in the hands of an equally charismatic New Englander, Jonathan Edwards. Edwards and other itinerant preachers responded to invitations that helped build a network of revivalist communities in New Jersey, Pennsylvania, DELAWARE, and a few outposts in

NEW YORK, MARYLAND, western Virginia, and CHARLESTON, SOUTH CAROLINA.

Wesley had worked with Whitefield in England, and the two had developed a compelling preaching style that drew thousands to hear them wherever they spoke. By 1741 Whitefield had become the first person who almost everyone in all the colonies had seen or heard of. Many men who had abandoned the boredom of church services turned out to hear Whitefield, and tens of thousands of women were drawn to carry out their own evangelizing. Jonathan Edwards's wife, SARAH PIERPONT EDWARDS, wrote a detailed account of her experience of being "swallowed up, in the light and joy of the love of God." She was but one of many women who began to see that women's souls might be equal before God and that therefore women might also claim equality in social and political ways as well. Whitefield, an itinerant preacher who modeled himself after him, regularly preached to mixed audiences of men and women, black and white. Through such gatherings many African Americans had their first compelling experience with Christianity. Several noted black religious leaders were recruited in these gatherings. Richard Allen, converted in a Wilmington, Delaware, meeting, later founded the African Methodist Episcopal Church—the world's first black Christian denomination. Following an emotional conversion, John Marrant of Charleston, South Carolina, began to "read the scripture very much," and he preached to maritime black communities in Massachusetts and Nova Scotia before settling in England.

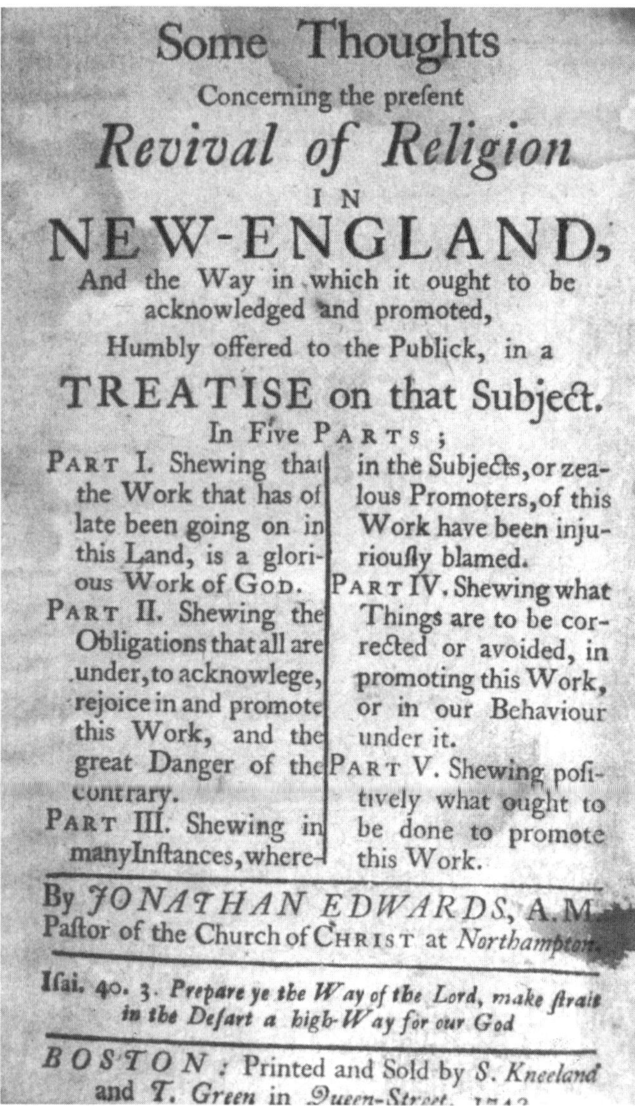

Some Thoughts
Concerning the prefent
Revival of Religion
IN
NEW-ENGLAND,
And the Way in which it ought to be acknowledged and promoted,
Humbly offered to the Publick, in a
TREATISE on that Subject.
In Five PARTS;

PART I. Shewing that the Work that has of late been going on in this Land, is a glorious Work of GOD.
PART II. Shewing the Obligations that all are under, to acknowlege, rejoice in and promote this Work, and the great Danger of the contrary.
PART III. Shewing in many Inftances, wherein the Subjects, or zealous Promoters, of this Work have been injurioufly blamed.
PART IV. Shewing what Things are to be corrected or avoided, in promoting this Work, or in our Behaviour under it.
PART V. Shewing pofitively what ought to be done to promote this Work.

By *JONATHAN EDWARDS*, A.M.
Paftor of the Church of CHRIST at *Northampton*.

Ifai. 40. 3. *Prepare ye the Way of the Lord, make ftrait in the Defart a high-Way for our God*

BOSTON: Printed and Sold by *S. Kneeland* and *T. Green* in *Queen-Street*.

Title page of . . . *Revival of Religion in New-England* by Jonathan Edwards *(Billy Graham Center)*

English followers of Whitefield and Wesley swept across the American countryside, especially in New England and the South, deputizing lay preachers, distributing FOOD and medical care to the needy, opening some schools for orphans, stirring consciences against SLAVERY, and gathering converts among both free black people and slaves, who would in large numbers adopt the religion of these advocates. Many Methodists, BAPTISTS, and Quakers adopted the idea that all souls were equal before God, and, although they did not openly advocate abolition, they became identified with justice for the dispossessed—including poor white people and AFRICAN AMERICANS. Itinerant ministers and revival meetings were a perfect match for isolated rural communities, and in such areas their impact was phenomenal. Poor white farmers—men, women, and children—found the social aspect of revival meetings compelling and reassuring. Black people—both slave and free—joined in revival meetings and took note of these new ideas, and in subsequent plots for slave insurrections their code of behavior called for leniency for practitioners of these liberal religions. Methodists and Baptists often went beyond Quakers in incorporating black members into their congregations and in appointing black preachers.

The Great Awakening created fissures in the old church communities, with members taking sides and realigning power and authority. "Old Lights," who tended to be of the upper CLASS, sought to hold on to an educated ministry and a prescribed service, decrying what they viewed as the undignified worship behavior of the revivalists. For their part, "New Lights" viewed their rivals as stodgy, boring, snobbish, "frigid," and lacking in true religious commitment. Specialized knowledge of the Scriptures and intellectual debate about theology were less important, argued the New Lights, than was a deep and heartfelt connection to God. In New England, some New Light CONGREGATIONALISTS split off to found Baptist churches; in the South PRESBYTERIANS as well as Baptists made inroads into the traditionally Anglican countryside. In each case establishing congregations offered more immediate and emotional religious experience to artisans, yeoman farmers, and small shopkeepers. These more accessible religions eventually became the religions of the frontier. Despite divisions among themselves, however, the liturgy of American Protestants remained remarkably similar. American Protestants remained unified in their distrust of Roman Catholics and Jews, and most church members felt a new sense of empowerment to examine, question, and judge their leaders. Never again in North America would clergy be imposed upon a congregation; American congregations controlled their ministers, not the other way around.

Despite its apparent antiintellectualism, the Great Awakening also spawned educational institutions designed to train ministers. Presbyterians established PRINCETON COLLEGE and DUTCH REFORMED CHURCH leaders started Rutgers, both in New Jersey. Baptists founded Brown University in Rhode Island, and Congregationalists opened DARTMOUTH COLLEGE in NEW HAMPSHIRE. Soon, other minister-training schools would dot the countryside. Thus, this religious revival movement became the impetus for a burgeoning national EDUCATION system.

Two more enduring legacies of the Great Awakening are its effects on American political leaders and its influence in leading American citizens toward a separation of church and state. The rumblings within traditional religious structure gave permission for thoughtful Americans to embrace the Enlightenment—that European extension of rational thought that encouraged scientists to investigate and test the behavior of the universe and to attempt to explain and harness that behavior in new machines, models of the heavens, and complex studies of flora and fauna. Benjamin Franklin and Thomas Jefferson are among the best-known of the advocates of Deism, but many intellectuals subscribed to the idea that the universe might be a system set in motion by a God who then left it for humans to manage. The shaping of the documents that underpin American political life—the Declaration of Independence and the Constitution—are flavored with the idea that religious freedom is the "natural" result of the assumption that "all men are created equal."

In responding to a mélange of class, race, GENDER, regional, and philosophical tensions, the Great Awakening can be described as the first truly unifying event of the British colonies in America. In some ways it was a rehearsal for the unity that would be called upon by white Americans during the Revolution and for the religious themes that would undergird the black communities' struggles for their freedom.

Further reading: Edwin Scott Gaustad, *The Great Awakening in New England* (New York: Harper & Row, 1957); Alan Heimert, *Religion and the American Mind from the Great Awakening to the Revolution* (Cambridge, Mass.: Harvard University Press, 1966).

—Emma Lapsansky

Great Plains Indians

The Great Plains, also known as the Great American Desert, are a wide swath of land in the center of North America defined partly by scant rainfall. They extend from the Rio Grande in the south to the Arctic Ocean in the north, from the Rocky Mountains in the west to approximately the 100th meridian in the east. People have lived on the Great Plains for millennia—for between 10,000 and 40,000 years. Archaeologists divide Plains Indian history into several periods: the era of Paleo-Indians (before 6000 B.C.): the Archaic Period (6000 to 0 B.C.); the Plains-Woodland period (500 B.C. to A.D. 1000); the Transitional period, Plains-Woodland to Plains Culture (A.D. 900 to 1500); and Historic Plains Indian Culture, rather arbitrarily declared finished 200 years ago.

The Indian population of the plains was never fixed. The plains have always been subject to a drought cycle, causing peoples and ANIMALS to advance onto the plains only to retreat decades or centuries later when a new period of drought occurred. These cycles were unpredictable and of uneven duration.

Many NATIVE AMERICANS who would become the Plains Indians lived in villages on the prairie fringes of the plains or along plains rivers and engaged in AGRICULTURE, supplementing their diets with hunting. Before contact with Europeans, Great Plains people often used dogs to assist them in travel, depending on them to pull travois, a sort of sled made of poles that could carry either goods or children. Indian peoples began to resettle the Great Plains just before the European presence made itself felt in the 17th century. Natives brought and developed elaborate systems of religious and secular art, predominantly quilling and painting.

Plains peoples did not share a single unified culture. Centuries of moving on and off the plains had changed cultural groups considerably. For example, there were six different language groups represented on the plains: Algonquian, Siouan, Caddoan, Uto-Aztecan, Athabascan, and Kiowa-Tanoan. Groups speaking these languages did not necessarily live near one another. Although belief systems, artistic practices, and technologies often were similar, they differed from group to group. These people also did not live in peace, as rivalries for the best hunting and territory affected them before European contact intensified intertribal conflict and violence.

In the late 17th century, Plains people began to feel the first ripples of European influence from the Northeast and Southwest, influences that led to the gradual modification of traditional Plains cultures and interactions. Plains Indians also encountered tribes fleeing westward away from European expansion. As contact increased, cultures changed. Some tribes, for instance, incorporated beads and metal obtained from European traders and fashioned new designs influenced by Eastern Woodlands tribes.

Indians struggled to control the flow of European goods onto the Plains. French traders from Upper Canada exposed Plains peoples to the gun, which provided some Indian people's technological and economic power over their rivals. In the late 17th and early 18th centuries the western Sioux gained a monopoly over access to French trade and guns. About the same time Plains Indians in the Spanish Southwest, through trade and raids, acquired their first horses. Despite Spanish attempts to subdue the PUEBLO Indians of the region, the Pueblo managed to remove the Spanish briefly from NEW MEXICO in 1680. After the PUEBLO REVOLT the Comanche traded with the newly liberated Pueblo peoples, obtained horses previously owned by the Spanish, and controlled their spread through intertribal trade north and east onto the Great Plains. The Comanche tried to maintain a monopoly on horses, as the Sioux did on guns. Despite these efforts, both goods spread gradually across the Plains through trade and capture.

The gun and horse revolutionized plains societies. They made TRAVEL easier and nomadism on the dry plains feasible. They also increased violence among Indian peoples as tribes competed for dominance in the 18th century. For example, the Comanche used their control of horses to challenge Apache power on the southern plains, replacing it with their own. The Sioux, meanwhile, used guns to subdue river tribes and to win control of the northern plains. Guns were not the only TECHNOLOGY of violence adopted by natives to use against one another; Indian peoples in the Southwest adopted Spanish cavalry techniques and leather armor. This change is documented by hide paintings that show unmounted tribes accustomed to infantry fighting facing mounted, armored tribes on the plains. The introduction of the gun and the horse allowed for the creation of tribal "superpowers" on the plains, a state of affairs that lasted into the 19th century.

The Sioux exemplify how guns and horses transformed power on the plains. As the Plains headed into a wet cycle for most of the 18th century, they abounded in wildlife, useful for both survival and trade. Initially the beaver and then, by the early 19th century, the bison provided ready sources of profit for natives and, therefore, access to European trade goods. In the north the quest for beaver led the Sioux to abandon horticultural life and to attack and dominate such tribes as the Mandan, Hidatsa, and Arikara along the Missouri River. The Sioux's guns later allowed them to demand tribute from these villages. Agricultural tribute from other tribes enabled the Sioux to farm less and hunt more, thereby increasing their wealth. Another European import, DISEASE, helped the Sioux expansion because diseases struck settled and more populous villages harder than they struck nomadic peoples. This dominance of the Sioux and other groups helps explain why some less powerful and exploited Indians subsequently aided Euro-American expansion onto the Plains. Many Plains tribes who lost power and lands in the mid-18th century hoped that new white allies might make better neighbors than strong Indian enemies.

See also EXPLORATION; POPÉ.

Further reading: Colin F. Taylor, *The Plains Indians: A Cultural and Historical View of the North American Plains Tribes of the Pre-Reservation Period* (London: Salamander Books, 1994); Richard White, "The Winning of the West: The Expansion of the Western Sioux in the Eighteenth and Nineteenth Centuries" (*Journal of American History*, 65, 1978: 319–43).

—Jenny Turner

Grenville, Sir Richard (1541?–1591)

Richard Grenville was the admiral of a fleet and general of two expeditions that founded Roanoke, the first English colony in North America. Grenville was born at Buckland Abbey, Devon, into a wealthy and powerful West Country gentry family. Their friends, neighbors, and relations included such energetic promoters of PRIVATEERING, PROTESTANTISM, and Irish and American colonization as the Raleighs, Gilberts, Hawkins, and Arundells. Apprenticing to power, Grenville studied law in 1559 and was elected to Parliament in 1563, but his hot temper and forceful personality found its true outlet when he and companions, including JOHN SMITH and William Gorges, took part in the emperor Maximillian II's campaign against the Turks in 1567. Shortly thereafter, in 1568–69, he joined his relative Sir Humphrey Gilbert to suppress Fitzmaurice's uprising in Munster, thereby initiating his lifelong involvement in subjugating the "wild" Irish and colonizing their lands with English settlers. English colonization of Ireland thereby became the forerunner and competitor to English colonization of North America.

Political difficulties frustrated Grenville's plans to search for the Northwest Passage, but Sir Francis Drake adopted the plan for his circumnavigation voyage of 1577–80. Although an inexperienced seafarer, Grenville's social status and family connections led his cousin Sir

Walter Raleigh to appoint him commander of two voyages, in 1585 and 1587, to establish a colony and privateering base on Roanoke Island. Grenville and his lieutenant Ralph Lane's reprisals against the Roanoke Indians, and Grenville and Raleigh's failure to resupply the colony because of their involvement in naval action in 1588 against the Spanish Armada, contributed to the colony's disappearance.

Diverted by the Armada and discouraged by the failure of the Roanoke colony, both Grenville and Raleigh turned back to Ireland, where between 1589 and 1591 they worked to establish a plantation in Munster. The lure of Spanish gold tempted Grenville back to sea as vice admiral of a naval force that lay in wait in the Azores for the homebound Spanish treasure fleet. Surprised by a powerful Spanish naval escort, Grenville was mortally wounded, and his ship, the *Revenge,* was fatally damaged in a fierce battle celebrated in Tennyson's epic poem "The Last Fight of the Revenge." Grenville died three days later aboard the Spanish flagship, cursing the refusal of his men to blow up the *Revenge* and themselves rather than accept capture. To the end, Grenville was an aristocrat who regarded "the meaner sort" as mere instruments for realizing his grand schemes for wealth and fame.

—James Bruggeman

Guadalajara

Less densely populated than the major Native American areas to the south, the Guadalajara region was home to the Nahua Indians, who lived in scattered sedentary agricultural villages. These NATIVE AMERICANS were conquered by Captain Nuño de Guzmán between 1530 and 1532. Guzmán founded the first city of Guadalajara in 1532. The settlement moved several times before finding its permanent home in 1542, after which Guadalajara became one of the dominant cities of western Mexico. By 1550 the bishop of New Galicia had relocated to Guadalajara, and by 1560 Guadalajara had become the administrative center for all of western Mexico and the capital of New Galicia under the authority of the viceroy of New Spain.

Guadalajara grew slowly, containing approximately 1,500 people in 1600, when, according to one scholar, the inhabitants "ran hares through the streets with their hunting dogs." In the early years more than half the Spaniards living in the city were administrative, although MERCHANTS and livestock traders quickly became important as well. Because the climate was arid, AGRICULTURE was relatively inconsequential, but livestock raising was central. Guadalajarans consequently often lacked wheat and maize but never wanted for inexpensive meat.

By the 18th century Guadalajara became a major, if isolated, urban center comprising 350 city blocks and a large suburban area. Impressive buildings, including a cathedral (consecrated in 1618) and the Government Palace (1643), graced the city by the end of the colonial period.

Further reading: Eric Van Young, *Hacienda and Market in Eighteenth-Century Mexico: The Rural Economy of the Guadalajara Region, 1675–1820* (Berkeley: University of California Press, 1981).

–Donald Duhadaway

Gullah

Technically, Gullah encompasses only the distinct black culture found near the southern coast of SOUTH CAROLINA, but historians, folklorists, and anthropologists traditionally link it to the Geechee culture of the GEORGIA Sea Islands. Throughout southern slave societies successive generations of slaves maintained many of their African traditions, influencing white and black culture alike. In a process described as creolization, African and European cultural inheritances fused together to produce distinctive African American cultures. Over time the unending process of cultural fusion often concealed cultural roots, yet the relative isolation of Gullah facilitated the retention of African characteristics that remain highly visible today.

Gullah retained many of its Africanisms through language. The first slaves brought to South Carolina came from the CARIBBEAN, where many had gained familiarity with British culture. Initially, most had constant, intimate contact with white people in South Carolina, and most acquired the English language of their masters. As the colony expanded, based increasingly on rice cultivation, planters obtained more slaves directly from AFRICA, and they revivified African culture in their new homes. The development of large rice plantations combined with the rising fear of malaria, which drove planters to absentee ownership during the summer and fall, limited contact with white people and allowed slaves to form a new mode of oral expression.

As a dialect, Gullah largely combined English vocabulary with African grammar. African slaves usually spoke mutually unintelligible languages, but the English of American-born slaves provided a unifying vocabulary. African slaves simply appropriated English words and applied them to familiar speech patterns. Thus, an English-based "pidgin" language developed. The transformation of pidgin—which by definition has no native speakers—into a CREOLE language occurred as African-American children inherited Gullah from their African parents.

The creolization of Gullah included not only the creation of a distinct language but the use of that language as well. Gullah-speaking slaves, for example, often followed the African tradition of "basket-naming," bestowing names of social significance or personal circumstance on their children. One practice involved giving temporal names to children to denote time or day of birth; many slaves shared the names Monday, Friday, March, August, Christmas, and Midday. Speaking in parable was another common African feature of Gullah. Indirect and ambiguous language conveyed subtleties to black people while it disguised hidden meanings from whites. Indeed, the notorious trickster, Brer Rabbit, may have first surfaced in Gullah parables.

Further reading: Peter H. Wood, *Black Majority: Negroes in Colonial South Carolina from 1670 through the Stono Rebellion* (New York: Norton, 1974); Margaret Washington Creel, *A Peculiar People: Slave Religion and Community Culture Among the Gullah* (New York: New York University Press, 1988).

—C. B. Waldrip

H

Hamilton, Andrew (1676–1741)

Andrew Hamilton was born and educated in Scotland, but for unknown reasons he was forced to immigrate to America, most likely because of political troubles during the reign of King William (1689–1702). He assumed the name Trent and lived in VIRGINIA and MARYLAND, where he managed an estate and ran a classical school. By the time of Queen Anne's rule (1702–14), he was using the name Hamilton again. He married the wealthy widow Anne Brown and entered the upper ranks of colonial society. Hamilton made a return trip to England in 1712 and was admitted to Gray's Inn in London, being called to the English Bar only two weeks later. Returning to his plantation in Maryland, Hamilton's legal career gained wide notice. His legal services for WILLIAM PENN and his agents brought about Hamilton's removal to PHILADELPHIA in 1717. There he continued his legal work for the proprietors, who granted him a 153-acre estate; he held several public offices, including recorder of the city, prothonotary of the supreme court, and representative and Speaker of the Assembly. He was known as a political independent but retained his connections with the proprietary family. Hamilton was responsible for designing the State House, which later became known as Independence Hall. He was appointed judge of the vice admiralty court in 1737, just a few years before his death in Philadelphia.

Hamilton's biggest claim to fame, which made his reputation as the greatest colonial lawyer, was his successful defense of NEW YORK printer JOHN PETER ZENGER in 1735. New York's royal governor, William Cosby, had dismissed Chief Justice LEWIS MORRIS in favor of a political crony. Morris and attorneys James Alexander and William Smith attacked the governor's high-handedness in a series of unsigned articles printed in the new *Weekly Journal,* which they had persuaded Zenger to begin publishing. Zenger was arrested on charges of seditious libel. He retained Alexander and Smith to represent him, but the royal judges disbarred them for questioning the validity of the judges' commissions from Governor Cosby. Zenger's friends invited Hamilton to undertake his defense. The law limited the jury to determining the fact of publication, leaving the question of libel to the judges. Hamilton, taking the case for no fee, masterfully argued for the jury to deliver a "general verdict" on both the law and the facts, concluding that freedom of the press "is the best cause; it is the cause of liberty." It is not libel, he argued, if the statements Zenger printed about public figures were true. Zenger was found not guilty. The trial set a precedent for the independence of juries and was a major victory for the freedom of the press throughout the colonies.

Further reading: James A. Alexander, *A Brief Narrative of the Case and Trial of John Peter Zenger* (Cambridge, Mass.: Harvard University Press, 1969); Robert R. Bell, *The Philadelphia Lawyer: A History, 1735–1945* (London: Associated University Press, 1992).

—Stephen C. O'Neill

Hammon, Jupiter (1711–1800?)

According to his master's ledger, Jupiter Hammon was born to slave parents on October 17, 1711, at the Lloyd plantation located near Oyster Bay, Long Island, NEW YORK. Hammon enjoyed extraordinary privileges that were denied to most colonial slaves. His master, Henry Lloyd, permitted him to read theological books in his library and attend schools on the plantation. Lloyd sold Hammon a Bible in 1733, which enhanced his literacy and influenced his religious beliefs. Lloyd trusted Hammon as the family's bookkeeper, including maintaining slave-trading records.

Religion was a pivotal force in Hammon's life. He attended the Lloyds' church and became aware of abolitionists because Oyster Bay was the nucleus of New York's antislavery Quaker movement. Hammon listened to abolitionist speakers and major religious figures, including GEORGE WHITEFIELD during the GREAT AWAKENING.

Hammon experienced an epiphany in which he became devoutly religious and determined that his purpose in life was to protest slavery subtly through preaching to slaves on the Lloyd estate.

Hammon incorporated biblical themes in poetry and essays, using hymns as his pattern for rhythm. His 1760 debut poem, "An Evening Thought," expressed the idea that slaves would ultimately be freed through the salvation of Jesus. Hammon was the first American slave to publish antislavery writings that were read by a diverse audience, although many white colonists dismissed him.

After Henry Lloyd's death in 1763, Hammon served his son Joseph. When Lloyd fled to Hartford, CONNECTICUT, in 1776 to evade invading British troops, Hammon accompanied him. In that literary-minded city Hammon published more writings that expressed his antislavery Calvinist views. His first poem published in Hartford addressed the slave poet Phillis Wheatley, suggesting that she should write about religious subjects. His evangelical writing reiterated his main theme that God used slavery to test AFRICAN AMERICANS' faith in heavenly freedom. Hammon urged black people to support one another spiritually while remaining obedient to their masters. Although Hammon did not believe that he would ever be freed on this earth, he tried to improve conditions for younger generations of slaves.

After Joseph Lloyd committed suicide in 1780, John Lloyd inherited Hammon, who continued writing in Hartford until 1783, when Lloyd returned to Oyster Bay. In that year Hammon published "A Dialogue Entitled the Kind Master and the Dutiful Servant," stressing that sin was what divided slaves and masters. Hammon's final short book was *An Address to the Negroes of the State of New York,* printed in 1787. concerned about slaves' suffering economic misfortunes if they were suddenly freed and forced to compete for employment, Hammon argued that gradual emancipation was the best solution. Although a pioneering African-American literary figure, Hammon has often been ignored because Wheatley overshadowed him.

Further reading: Philip M. Richard, *Nationalist Themes in the Preaching of Jupiter Hammon* (Chapel Hill: University of North Carolina Press, 1990).

—Elizabeth D. Schafer

Harris, Benjamin (unknown–1716)

Benjamin Harris, the first individual to start a newspaper in the American colonies, began his career in the book trade in his native London in 1673 with the publication of an anti-Catholic tract. When the Catholic James II ascended the English throne in 1685, Harris fled to BOSTON, where he resumed publishing and bookselling. His most famous publication, the *New England Primer* (1690), was a spelling text for children that sold for two centuries; it is known as the Little Bible of New England. Harris became the richest bookseller in Boston in part due to innovative practices such as selling coffee and tea along with his publications. His establishment became known as the city's only coffeehouse suitable for respectable women.

Harris recognized that Boston's commercial activity provided advertising possibilities to support a newspaper. In September 1690 he published *Publick Occurences Both Foreign and Domestick,* the first American newspaper. The newspaper contained three printed pages and one blank page, because the custom was for the first reader to write a letter on the blank page and send it to a friend. While Harris meant for his newspaper to appear regularly, his criticism of the colony's Indian allies and reports on the sexual peccadilloes of the French king led to the newspaper being banned; the official reason was that Harris had printed without a license. In the following years Harris continued to run his coffee shop and publish books, and for a year he served as the governor's official printer. Harris returned to London in 1695 and spent his last years in the publishing trade and in selling quack medicines.

Further reading: William David Sloan and Julie Hedgepeth Williams, *The Early American Press, 1690–1783* (Westport, Conn.: Greenwood Press, 1994).

—Kenneth Pearl

Harrison, Peter (1716–1775)

Born in England and raised a Quaker, Peter Harrison became one of the colonies' premier architects. He converted to Anglicanism when he immigrated to America, settling in NEWPORT, RHODE ISLAND about 1740. Following his immigration and conversion, Harrison ran a successful business and married a wealthy woman, Elizabeth Pelham, who brought a dowry of more than £20,000. These actions catapulted Harrison to the top of Newport society. Harrison, his wife, and their four children had their portrait painted by JOHN SMIBERT.

Although his early architectural designs were for ships and lighthouses, Harrison soon moved on to larger projects, such as country homes for the wealthy. In 1748 he designed the Redwood Library, basing his work on Greek classical images, which made him well known throughout New England, although he was never paid for this project. Harrison designed several religious structures, including King's Chapel in BOSTON, which was the first stone church in America, and the first Jewish temple built in New England. This last project was especially difficult, because Harrison was ignorant of Jewish ritual and he had no model upon which to base his plans. Harrison also plotted the Brick Market in Newport and many homes for prominent families. Not until the 20th century was Harrison acknowledged as America's "first architect," although he would not have described himself in those terms. Harrison always considered himself a gentleman and his ARCHITECTURE the work of an amateur.

—Victoria C. H. Resnick

Harvard College

North America's oldest institution of higher EDUCATION, Harvard College (now Harvard University) was founded in 1636 and officially chartered in 1650. Its patrons used Cambridge University, a Puritan stronghold in England, as an archetype. Throughout the 17th century Harvard's leaders explicitly designed the school to produce Congregational ministers. PURITANS believed that faith had both spiritual and intellectual dimensions. Thus, they considered the education of ministers a matter of first importance. Harvard's early presidents, Henry Dunster and CHARLES CHAUNCY, also sought to train certain "hopefull Indian youthes" as Protestant ministers in order to deliver native peoples from "paganism." An Indian College appeared in 1654, but only a handful of pupils attended, and the neglected enterprise vanished by the 1690s. Most of Harvard's students hailed from the upper echelons of New England society. A sizable number of farmers' and ARTISANS' sons also attended, however, making the school a vehicle for a limited kind of social mobility. Students imbibed the classical curriculum of Greek, Latin, and mathematics that had characterized higher learning in the Western world since the late medieval period. In the 18th century the curriculum broadened to include more philosophy and SCIENCE, while the graduates turned increasingly to law, MEDICINE, and politics.

See also COLLEGE OF PHILADELPHIA; COLLEGE OF WILLIAM AND MARY; DARTMOUTH COLLEGE; KING'S COLLEGE; JOHN LEVERETT; PRINCETON COLLEGE; YALE COLLEGE.

Further reading: Samuel Eliot Morison, *Harvard College in the Seventeenth Century* (Cambridge, Mass.: Harvard University Press, 1936); James Axtell, *The School Upon a Hill: Education and Society in Colonial New England* (New Haven, Conn.: Yale University Press, 1974).

—J. M. Opal

Heathcote, Caleb (1666–1721)

Land speculator, farmer, contractor, merchant, politician, and churchman Caleb Heathcote was an early builder of the NEW YORK colony. Born in Derbyshire, England, to a family actively involved in trade through the British East India Company, he migrated to New York in 1692, bringing a share of the family wealth and extensive trading connections. He married Martha Smith in 1699. The couple had six children, four of whom died in CHILDHOOD. He settled his family on land he purchased north of Mamaroneck and in 1701 was granted the Manor of Scarsdale (the last manor granted in British North America). A commercial entrepreneur, he built MILLS for sawing wood and grinding corn and linseed, and he urged the British authorities to develop New York naval and textile products for export to the West Indies.

His political activity included service on the governor's council (1692–98, 1702–66) and serving as mayor of NEW YORK CITY (1711–13), colonel of the Westchester militia, and judge of several Westchester county courts. The imperial administration rejected his proposal for a conference of colonial administrators to formulate strategy for dealing with the Indians, yet he was appointed surveyor general of customs for the northern department, where he worked to improve customs administration and collection.

A devoted churchman, Heathcote served as vestryman of Trinity Parish (1697–99, 1711–14) and chaired the committee that built the first church. He corresponded regularly with the SOCIETY FOR THE PROPAGATION OF THE GOSPEL, of which he was a member, and helped establish Anglican congregations in Westchester, Rye, New Rochelle, Eastchester, and Yonkers. He started a day school and a Sunday school in Rye and as mayor of New York City promoted the development of schools.

Further reading: Dixon Ryan Fox, *Caleb Heathcote: Gentleman Colonist* (New York: Scribner's, 1926).

—Mary Sudman Donovan

Hendrick (1680?–1755)

Hendrick (Teoniahigarawe, Theyanoquin) was a leader in the IROQUOIS League and the primary negotiator between the league and the British from 1710 until 1755. Born a Mohican, Hendrick was adopted into the Mohawk tribe as a child. A Protestant convert, he believed that the interests of the Iroquois lay in alliance with the British. In 1710 Hendrick traveled to London as one of the "Four Indian Kings" to rally support for an invasion of New France. The Iroquois League did not always support Hendrick's policies. In 1747 he led the Mohawk against the French without the league's support. When land-hungry New Yorkers seized Mohawk land in the 1740s and 1750s, Hendrick told New York governor George Clinton that the British had broken their alliance. Hendrick's threat prompted the ALBANY CONGRESS of 1754, in which representatives of various British colonies promised to respect Indian land rights.

Hendrick died leading a Mohawk force against the French in 1775.

Further reading: Daniel K. Richter, *The Ordeal of the Longhouse: The Peoples of the Iroquois League in the Era of European Colonization* (Chapel Hill: University of North Carolina Press, 1922).

—Kathleen DuVal

Herrman, Augustine (1605–1686)

A native of Prague in Bohemia, Augustine Herrman was a surveyor and merchant who moved to the Dutch colony of NEW NETHERLAND, where he became a member of PETER STUYVESANT's nine-man advisory council in 1647. He also served as arbitrator, power of attorney, and recorder of judicial cases in the struggling colony. Skilled in the graphic arts, Herrman sketched a view of NEW AMSTERDAM in 1656 that appeared at the bottom of Van der Donck's map of New Netherland.

In 1659 Governor Stuyvesant entrusted Herrman with an embassy to the governor of MARYLAND, whose proprietor, Lord Baltimore, claimed Dutch territory as part of his grant from the king of England. Herrman's mission was threefold: to arrange a future meeting concerning the boundary question; to retrieve servants, slaves, and debtors, who had fled from Dutch to English territory; and to ascertain whether Maryland would stop sending agents into the Delaware Valley to bestir the inhabitants against Dutch rule. Herrman kept a journal of his embassy in which he appears as a formidable debater against Maryland's governor and council. However heated the arguments, Herrman succeeded in exacting no promises or resolutions on any of the disputed issues. Shortly after his embassy Herrman moved to Maryland, where he later used his graphics and surveying skills to produce the first map that accurately showed the waterways of Maryland. Impressed with Herrman's map, Lord Baltimore granted him a large tract of land in present-day Cecil County that Herrman named "Bohemia Manor" in honor of his native land. He died there in 1686.

Further reading: Augustine Herrman, *Journal of the Dutch Embassy to Maryland,* in Charles T. Gehring, ed., *New York Historical Manuscripts: Dutch* (Baltimore: Genealogical Publishing Company, 1981).

—Judy VanBuskirk

Hesselius, John (1728?–1778)

Born in PHILADELPHIA to a Swedish immigrant family, John Hesselius became a painter like his father, Gustavus Hesselius. Hesselius first appears in the historical record buying paper at Benjamin Franklin's shop, and later he painted a portrait of Franklin's daughter Sarah. Hesselius learned painting from his father, and he quickly became a popular artist, specializing in original portraits and copies of other likenesses. A prolific artist, Hesselius composed at least 100 portraits, many of influential families such as the Calverts.

His early work is known for the dark shading of flesh typical of his father, but mostly for the influence of ROBERT FEKE, whom he meet during one of Feke's visits to Philadelphia. Like Feke, Hesselius emphasized bright colors, lush fabrics, and landscape settings in his backgrounds. His style changed in the late 1750s, about the time he married a wealthy widow and moved to her plantation in MARYLAND. Under the influence of the English painter John Willaston, Hesselius began to include elegant composition and sophisticated modeling while maintaining Feke's emphasis on color and landscape. Hesselius is known for pictorial honesty in capturing the personality of his sitters and for providing documentation on the reverse side of his paintings.

Hesselius's clients demonstrate the interconnected nature of the upper classes in the Middle Colonies. As many of his sitters were related and there are no records of advertisements, it appears that Hesselius's business relied primarily on word of mouth.

—Victoria C. H. Resnick

Hooker, Thomas (1586–1647)

The founder of CONNECTICUT, Thomas Hooker was born in Marfield, Leicestershire, England, to poor but devout Puritan parents. He won a scholarship to Emmanuel College, Cambridge, the premier Puritan educational establishment. While there he experienced conversion according to the common Puritan pattern, passing through profound anguish to equally profound assurance of salvation. After receiving his B.A. in 1608 and his M.A. in 1611, he joined Emmanuel's faculty.

In 1618 Hooker left Emmanuel, serving as Anglican pastor in Esher, Surrey, and later in Chelmsford, Essex. His bold, conversion-centered preaching, which won many followers, attracted the notice of church officials. In 1629 they suspended him from Anglican orders, and the next year they summoned him before the ANGLICAN CHURCH's Court of High Commission. Initially he fled to Holland, but he later returned to England and finally opted for immigration to MASSACHUSETTS, arriving in BOSTON in 1633 on the same ship that carried JOHN COTTON.

In 1634 Hooker became pastor of the Congregational church in Newtown (present-day Cambridge). His insistence on a sharp distinction between the national (religious) covenant and all civil (political) covenants brought him into immediate conflict with the government of Massachusetts, which had made SUFFRAGE dependent on church membership. For this and other reasons, in 1636 he led his congregation in an exodus to the banks of the Connecticut River, founding the town of Hartford and helping to establish the colony of Connecticut. The new colony's Fundamental Orders, adopted in 1639, reflected Hooker's influence in that they opened the franchise to non–church members.

Hooker was the leading theoretician of New England preparationism, a school of thought that saw conversion as a long, arduous process through which the seeker must pass before attaining salvation. On this point he clashed with Cotton, whose telescoped understanding of the process stressed God's gracious initiative. Their dispute came to a head in the Antinomian Controversy of 1637–38, which revolved around the informal, inflammatory ministry of Cotton's disciple ANNE MARBURY HUTCHINSON. Hooker's views on conversion found expression in a number of publications, including *The Soules Preparation for Christ* (1632) and *The Sinners Salvation* (1638). He expounded his perspective on ecclesiastical polity in the enormously influential *Survey of the Summe of Church Discipline* (1648).

Further reading: John H. Ball III, *Chronicling the Soul's Windings: Thomas Hooker and His Morphology of Conversion* (Lanham, Md.: University Press of America, 1992); Sargent Bush, Jr., *The Writings of Thomas Hooker: Spiritual Adventure in Two Worlds* (Madison: University of Wisconsin Press, 1980).

—George W. Harper

housing

The types of shelters constructed in early America varied widely as humans adopted styles that reflected the environment and the function of the housing as well as their ethnic affiliation and their social and economic status. Housing among North American natives also varied widely when the English first landed in Roanoke. From multistory and multiroom buildings in the Southwest to "longhouses" in the Northeast, Indians constructed a myriad of dwellings. Many of these were uncomplicated structures that satisfied basic requirements for shelter and community assembly. In the Ohio Valley, for example, houses ranged from small, domed, single-family buildings to some more than 100 feet in length. These native dwellings were made of saplings lashed together into frames covered with grasses or woven mats.

Similarly, most houses of the earliest colonists in the late 16th and early 17th centuries were "earthfast" structures constructed of poles driven into the ground and covered in reeds, rough boards, or "wattle and daub" mud plaster. Some were primitive cellars with sod or thatched coverings or were "wigwams," a term describing the ALGONQUIN house. These rudimentary one-room buildings accommodated families and their laborers while lands were cleared for cultivation.

After the middle of the 17th century, more substantial dwellings paralleled the traditional house forms of the colonists' ethnic origins. By the third decade of the 17th century, Dutch vernacular style houses appeared throughout NEW YORK and NEW JERSEY. These timber frame buildings, many having brick masonry facades and distinctive stepped front gables, emulated the design and interior organization of houses found in the Netherlands. In New England and the Chesapeake area, where British settlers were most numerous, the English vernacular house type dominated. These open plan, square or rectangular buildings were timber framed and covered with clapboards and shingles.

Throughout the colonies the "typical" house was a single room of approximately 350 square feet. The finish of interior space depended not only on ethnic difference but on local construction techniques, LABOR and material availability, and social class. Some houses had masonry chimneys, window glass, and plaster walls, while others had dirt floors, open hearths, and wooden shutters.

House construction standards varied across regions. In general, in New England dwellings were substantial and constructed of heavy timbers or masonry. In the Chesapeake area houses of all sizes were often shoddily built and had to be replaced every few years. Climate, GENDER imbalance, and economic considerations, as well as a pervasive psychology of impermanency, accounted for inferior home construction in VIRGINIA and MARYLAND. CLASS differences became acutely apparent in this region after the middle of the 17th century, when the number of bonded workers increased dramatically. Slaves were removed from planter households to dwellings that mirrored the earliest colonial shelters—small, often windowless one-room buildings. The placement of slave houses on plantations, however, approximated village settings found in their African homelands.

While the one-room house was most common in North America throughout the colonial period, two- and three-room houses also emerged. These hall-and-parlor dwellings allowed for greater separation of domestic activities, such as cooking, washing, sleeping, and receiving visitors. Such segregation of private and more public activities often defined social class and economic status. Some two- and three-room house plans were expanded to include more elaborate hearths, second stories, and appurtenant wings. Urban two-room houses frequently accommodated both domestic and commercial requirements, with the streetside parlor functioning as a shop while the back hall served as cooking and sleeping quarters.

By the beginning of the 18th century, neoclassical, or Georgian, ARCHITECTURE influenced the houses of urban and rural elites in the North American colonies. Georgian house designs were one- or two-story box plans with window and door openings arranged in strict symmetry. The typical "closed plan" Georgian house had an unheated central passage, or hallway, from which separate rooms were entered. Restricted access into living and work areas allowed not only greater privacy and further division of domestic functions but encouraged the creation of social hierarchies within the house and community.

Further reading: William H. Pierson, *American Buildings and Their Architects* (New York: Oxford University Press, 1971); Leland M. Roth, *A Concise History of American Architecture* (New York: Harper & Row, 1979); Robert Blair St. George, ed., *Material Life in America 1600–1860* (Boston: Northeastern University Press, 1988).

—Catherine Goetz

Howe, George Augustus, Viscount (1724?–1758)

George, Lord Howe was a talented young British officer who was killed during the SEVEN YEARS' WAR. His death ended hopes of success in 1758 and deprived the English of a capable officer noted for his ability to work with colonial troops.

Howe was chosen as second in command to the administratively capable and well connected but uninspiring Major General James Abercromby. Howe gained the respect of colonial troops through his personal bravery and willingness to disregard the trappings of rank. He shocked his staff officers by washing his own linen and eating with camp utensils. He was one of the few British officers who believed colonial troops could be capable soldiers if properly led and did not dismiss colonial officers as social inferiors. He trained with Captain Robert Rogers's rangers and insisted his regular troops learn the same woodcraft and combat skills.

In a skirmish with French forces while advancing toward Canada through NEW YORK, Howe moved forward with the advance guard of English troops, landing by boat on the west coast of Lake George. He was killed by a musket ball to the chest during a confused woodland battle with a small detachment of French forces sent to harass and slow the English advance. When Howe died, the troops, especially the colonials, lost heart. French forces under the Marquis De Montcalm defeated Abercromby, and the advance failed. The MASSACHUSETTS Assembly appropriated £250 for a testimonial plaque placed in Westminster Abbey, a mark of the respect in which the colonials held him.

See also WAR AND WARFARE.

Further reading: Fred Anderson, *A People's Army: Massachusetts Soldiers and Society in the Seven Years' War* (Chapel Hill: University of North Carolina Press, 1984).

—Grant Weller

Hudson, Henry (1565?–1611?)

Henry Hudson was an English navigator and explorer who sailed for Holland and England looking first for a northeast and then a Northwest Passage to Asia. Little is known about Hudson's early life, but he must have been a competent navigator because three financial backers hired him to make several dangerous voyages.

The Muscovy Company, an English trading company, initially sponsored Hudson's search for a northeast passage from Europe to the Far East in 1607. That spring Hudson and a small crew sailed on the *Hopewell,* first to Greenland and then the Svalbard (Spitzbergen) islands on their way through the Arctic Ocean. However, he was forced to turn back, as he did again the following year on a similar mission for the same company. In 1609 the Dutch East India Company financed Hudson's third voyage, which he undertook on the *Half Moon* with a crew of fewer than 20 men. Dangerous icebergs and bad weather helped produce tensions that threatened mutiny among his mixed crew of English and Dutch sailors. Therefore, Hudson abandoned the search for a northeast passage and headed the *Half Moon* south along the east coast of North America in search of a Northwest Passage he had heard about while in Holland. Entering present-day NEW YORK harbor, Hudson sailed north for 150 miles on what was later named the Hudson River. North of present-day Albany Hudson became convinced that the river did not lead to the passage, so the expedition returned to England. In England the government seized the ship and forbade him to sail on behalf of any foreign nation.

His final voyage was underwritten by a variety of sponsors, including the British East India Company. In 1610 he set out on the ship *Discovery* to look for a Northwest Passage. By early August he passed through what was later called Hudson Strait and entered into a large "sea" now known as Hudson Bay in northern Canada. Hudson was uncharacteristically timid in his decisions in the bay; he headed south along the east shore of the bay instead of heading due west across it. By the time he had determined that this, too, was a false lead, winter had arrived and froze in the ship. Trouble among the crew finally reached a climax the next June, when Hudson, his son John, and seven other sailors were seized and placed in a small boat. The

English navigator Henry Hudson *(Hulton/Archive)*

Discovery returned to England, and no more was heard from Hudson and the others.

Although the Northwest Passage did not exist, Henry Hudson's explorations provided the foundation for English claims to Canada and the Dutch settlement of NEW NETHERLAND, which eventually became New York.

Further reading: Barbara Saffer, *Henry Hudson: Ill-fated Explorer of North America's Coast* (Philadelphia: Chelsea House Publishers, 2001).

—Doug Baker

Hudson's Bay Company (1668)

The Hudson's Bay Company was a successful trading enterprise in North America. It began when Pierre Esprit Radisson and Médard Chouart, sieur des Groseilliers, two French adventurers, came up with a plan to reach the great beaver country and the South Seas by way of Hudson Bay and the rivers that flowed into it from the west. Unable to attract any French interest, they offered their ideas to the English, and in 1668 their backers organized a company. Its purpose was to acquire and transport furs and skins from North America to the London market. Groseilliers and his party traveled to the Hudson Bay area, and in 1670 the company was granted the right of sole trade and commerce for all the rivers of Canada east of the Continental Divide that did not flow into the Atlantic, the Arctic, the St. Lawrence, or the Great Lakes and for all the land that they drained.

The company relied on NATIVE AMERICANS to provide furs of bear, beaver, buffalo, deer, elk, fisher, fox, martin, seal, squirrel, and wolf, plus feathers, quills, swan skins, and pemmican. Furs were made into bales and shipped to England each August, where they were sold by auction in London. Most were then shipped to other European countries. The royal charter blocked the company from developing new European markets, placing a severe strain on it whenever demand slowed in Britain. The territory around Hudson Bay was divided into six main areas, with the trade in each area conducted from a post. For the century of its existence, the company did not seek out traders but waited for Native Americans to come to the post. The two French founders, despised as foreigners and suspected of treachery, were unable to persuade the company to penetrate deeper into the West to acquire more customers and circumvent the traders of New France. This trade policy led to the development of tribes, mostly HURON and Assiniboine, who acted as brokers to other tribes who could not easily reach Hudson Bay. In the 1770s the company's traders started to penetrate the inland.

Further reading: Ann M. Carlos, *The North American Fur Trade, 1804–1821: A Study in the Life Cycle of a Duopoly* (New York: Garland, 1986).

—Caryn E. Neumann

Hume, Sophia Wigington (1702–1774)

Sophia Wigington Hume was born in 1702 in CHARLESTON, SOUTH CAROLINA. Her parents, Henry and Susanna (Bayley) Wigington, were prominent members of South Carolina society. Hume's father was an official for the colony, and his riches assured that she enjoyed privileges, such as EDUCATION, considered appropriate for upper-CLASS girls. Her maternal grandmother, Mary Fisher, was a Quaker minister, and Hume often argued with her restrictive mother, who followed Fisher's teachings about moral conduct.

Sophia Wigington married Robert Hume, a wealthy lawyer, in 1721, and they had two children. She enjoyed indulging in CLOTHING and jewelry as well as entertainment, such as operas and masquerades. After her husband died in 1737, she endured illnesses and underwent a religious conversion experience. She joined the Society of Friends (QUAKERS) in 1741, selling her material possessions to seek religious salvation. Hume relocated to London, England, where she focused on Quaker teachings. After six years she returned to her hometown and began preaching about her spiritual epiphany.

Hume published *An Exhortation to the Inhabitants of the Province of South Carolina* in 1748, urging others to forsake luxuries, repent, and abandon their pride and vanity. Hume's ideas were not initially well received. She persisted, speaking to both Quakers and non-Quakers in Charleston and traveling to PHILADELPHIA and London, where she wrote *A Caution to Such as Observe Days and Times* in 1763, criticizing formal religious festivals and emphasizing social and spiritual accountability. Hume promoted reform to curb worldliness in *Extracts from Divers Antient Testimonies* in 1766, which reiterated texts by George Fox and WILLIAM PENN. While in England, she was designated a minister and eventually became one of the most prominent female Quaker preachers.

Returning to Charleston in 1767, Hume devoted her energy to distributing her texts and preaching about her beliefs, which included that women should focus on their home, family, and church and not solicit public attention, somewhat paradoxically in view of her own notoriety. A year later, frustrated by the decline of Quakerism in Charleston, Hume sailed for London, where she died on January 26, 1774.

Further reading: Sharon M. Harris, ed., *Oxford American Women Writers to 1800* (New York: Oxford University Press, 1996).

—Elizabeth D. Schafer

Huron

Four IROQUOIS-speaking tribes, known as the Wendat ("island people" or "dwellers on a peninsula"), but called Huron ("ruffian") by the French, inhabited the region between Georgian Bay and Lake Simcoe (in central Ontario today). Between 1440 and 1610 they formed a confederacy to prevent blood feuds and fighting among themselves. The confederacy council considered issues of peace, war, and trade with outsiders and strove to resolve internal disputes; tribal and village councils decided other matters.

In 1614, when the French had first official contact with the Huron, approximately 25,000 Huron lived in about 20 palisaded villages consisting of bark-covered longhouses, each housing about six families. The Huron traced their origins back to the first woman, Aataentsic, and organized themselves into matrilineal clans that controlled the farmland. Each clan claimed descent from a common female ancestor, and marriages united most villages. Women cooked, sewed, tanned leather, cared for children, gathered food, made baskets, wove mats and FISHING nets, and raised swidden. Men hunted and fished, cleared new fields, grew TOBACCO, and fashioned tools. They also carried on trade and made war and peace. With the development of the European FUR TRADE, as happened in many indigenous societies, male economic and social power in Huron society increased. Huron children were free and undisciplined, at least by European standards. Sexual freedom was the norm, although marriage generally was monogamous and could be terminated easily by either partner.

Huron religion taught that all things in nature possessed spirits, or *oki*. The afterlife was a reunion of family, and there was no last judgment or hell. Dreams were very important and had to be acted on in either real or symbolic terms, otherwise serious illness would result. SHAMANS often deciphered dreams.

In 1614 the Huron entered a formal trading alliance with the French, becoming the chief purveyors of furs to Quebec. They continued to act as intermediaries in the European–Indian trade between the Great Lakes and the St. Lawrence River Valley.

After unsuccessful attempts by the French Recollects, the JESUITS (called "Black Robes") established a mission at Ihonatiria in 1634, and other MISSIONS soon followed. Conversions were slow until 1634, when major epidemics of European DISEASES killed half the population during the next five years. The conversion of some Huron to Christianity and their consequent separation from the rest of the community helped undermine the unity of Huron villages.

During the BEAVER WARS the NEW YORK Iroquois, who were allied to the Dutch rivals of the French for control of the fur trade, began attacking Huronia. Because the Dutch provided the Iroquois with firearms, the Huron were at a disadvantage. In 1647, after years of merely intercepting Huron shipments of furs to Montreal, the Iroquois began to destroy Huron villages and Jesuit missions and kill people. Many Huron fled to New France in 1650, some settling north of Quebec at Lorette. Many Huron captives were also adopted into Iroquois tribes.

Some of the Huron refugees, now called Wyandot, subsequently migrated westward to the Great Lakes region. Pursued there by the Iroquois, they joined with Great Lakes ALGONQUIN to drive their enemies back to New York. By 1701 the Wyandot had moved to the Ohio Valley, where they remained until forced by the United States government to move to Kansas in the 1840s.

Further reading: Denys Delâge, *Bitter Feast: Amerindians and Europeans in Northeastern North America, 1600–64* (Vancouver: University of British Columbia Press, 1993).

—Joseph J. Casino

Hutchinson, Anne Marbury (1591–1643)

Born in Alford, England, to an unorthodox minister, Anne Marbury grew up exposed to her father's radical religious notions, inspiring her deep commitment to religious faith and theological debate that eventually landed her at the center of the Antinomian Controversy in BOSTON between 1636 and 1638. After marrying a merchant and giving birth to a number of children, Hutchinson and her family migrated to MASSACHUSETTS Bay Colony in 1634, primarily to follow JOHN COTTON, a Puritan minister they regarded highly. In Massachusetts Bay it was not uncommon for groups of women to meet in homes during the week to discuss scripture and theology. Hutchinson began holding these meetings at her home soon after her arrival. In addition, JOHN WHEELWRIGHT, Hutchinson's brother-in-law, began preaching at her Boston home when colonial officials, disturbed by his controversial views, denied him the opportunity to establish his own church. Wheelwright's preaching, in spite of his failure to receive official consent, constituted a formidable challenge to religious authority. Hutchinson was implicated in this dispute because she provided Wheelwright with a meeting place and because she organized theological discussions among women, an activity suspicious to many male magistrates and ministers.

Concurrently, Massachusetts Bay leaders struggled with what they perceived as a threat from Antinomians—people who embraced a "Covenant of Faith," believing that only faith is needed for salvation regardless of devotion to the laws of the Bible, church, or state. Although Hutchinson and Wheelwright probably were not Antinomians, their accusations that many Puritan ministers taught a "Covenant of Works" by emphasizing outward behavior rather than inward faith threatened the legitimacy of the clergy. Further complicating matters was a concomitant struggle for political power, especially the authority of the state to regulate the ECONOMY. Questioning that authority, many MERCHANTS and ARTISANS supported Hutchinson, Wheelwright, and Cotton. Adding to the tensions, the PURITANS were engaged in the PEQUOT WAR, which threatened the existence of the colony.

Perhaps most threatened by Anne Hutchinson was Governor JOHN WINTHROP, who served as both prosecutor and judge at Hutchinson's trial. Winthrop called her before the court in 1637 to answer charges of her alliance with Wheelwright, who had been banished from the colony for sedition, and of holding meetings of women in her home. Hutchinson defended her religious views very ably. She argued further that no law prevented private meetings in homes, and that even if she had committed wrongdoing in allowing those with different theological views to speak, that was a matter of religion rather than an issue to be condemned by a civil court. Thus, she claimed, her trial was without cause. Winthrop ultimately condemned Hutchinson for behaving inappropriately by transcending the confines of her GENDER.

Anne Hutchinson preaching in her house in Boston *(Library of Congress)*

In an almost forgone conclusion the civil trial and the church trial that followed led to Hutchinson's banishment from the church and the colony. She and some of her followers fled to RHODE ISLAND, where her family had resettled, but they soon felt threatened there by a growing influence of Massachusetts Bay leaders and relocated to Dutch-controlled Long Island. In 1643 Hutchinson was killed in an Indian raid, and some Puritans interpreted her death as evidence of God's justice.

Hutchinson's experience is telling of the interconnection between church and state that existed in Massachusetts Bay and the strong response that followed any threat, whether theological or secular, to the colony's stability. Colonial leaders used the power of the state to suppress religious dissent, challenges to the authority of magistrates, and resistance to socially prescribed gender roles.

Further reading: Selma R. Williams, *Divine Rebel: The Life of Anne Marbury Hutchinson* (New York: Holt, Rinehart & Winston, 1981).

—Jane P. Currie

Hyde, Edward, Viscount Cornbury (1661–1723)
Edward Hyde served as a member of the British Parliament, but, heavily in debt, he requested and received an appointment as governor of NEW YORK and NEW JERSEY in 1702, where he hoped to gain a fortune. As governor, Hyde stole funds, took bribes, and prosecuted people who did not belong to the ANGLICAN CHURCH. His American enemies accused him, apparently falsely, of scandalous behavior by routinely dressing in women's CLOTHING. His administration of both colonies proved calamitous. Recalled to England in 1708 but threatened with arrest for unpaid debts, Hyde refused to return. Upon inheriting his father's title of earl of Clarendon, Hyde returned to England, but, save for brief service on the Privy Council in 1711, he held no other important posts.

Further reading: Patricia U. Bonomi, *The Lord Cornbury Scandal: The Politics of Reputation in British America* (Chapel Hill: University of North Carolina Press, 2001).

—James Jenks

I

indentured servitude

Indentured servitude was a form of bound labor. The most common type of indenture, or contract, in the British colonies required that the servant serve a master "well and faithfully [in] such employments as the master might assign" for a specified period of time, usually three to four years, and in a particular location. In return, the master promised to pay the passage of the servant to the colonies, provide FOOD, CLOTHING, and HOUSING during the term of indenture, and, depending on the particular transaction, provide the servant "freedom dues" upon completion of service.

The indenture referred to a document, a form that contained the terms of the servitude. It recorded the beginning and ending dates of service and the provisions of freedom dues. At the end of the term, the contract was the only proof the individual had that she or he was free. An English pamphleteer, John Hammond, strongly urged servants to take special care to guard the document in order to avoid any problems when the term of service was completed.

The precise terms of the indenture ranged widely, depending on where the servant was located and the type of LABOR performed. Skilled servants occasionally received wages, or clauses were included in their contracts to permit them to work outside the master's domain at times when the master had insufficient tasks for the servant. German servants sometimes asked that they be taught English as part of the agreement. Freedom dues varied widely as well and included anything from money and land to tools, clothes, ANIMALS, or seeds. One historian of the Chesapeake area described how masters extended the length of servants' contracts for minor infractions in order to keep them from attaining their freedom. If they did successfully fulfill their contracts, servants often had a difficult time collecting their freedom dues. In one case a master literally fled before he paid the servant his dues.

The origins of indentured labor remain somewhat hazy. In the early 1580s the Englishman Sir George Peckham wrote a pamphlet intended to secure subscriptions from individuals who wished to colonize Newfoundland. A portion of the pamphlet analyzed why North American colonies were important for the British, and the concluding section argued that peopling these colonies need not be difficult. Peckham outlined the principle upon which indentured labor was based. English men and women would voluntarily exchange the cost of their passage to the New World for a fixed period of labor servitude.

Historians credit the VIRGINIA COMPANY OF LONDON, the joint-stock company authorized to settle and develop Virginia, with inventing the form of indentured servitude used throughout the colonies. A broadside issued by the company in 1609 referred to indentured labor, suggesting that servants arrived in the British North American colonies in the early settling of JAMESTOWN. This one-page advertisement announced that wealthy and noble persons had agreed to emigrate to the new colony in the CHESAPEAKE BAY and that all those who wished to make the voyage, no matter what their occupation or skill, were to appear at Sir Thomas Smith's house in Philpot Lane, London, to enroll. The "Adventures," or masters who agreed to take the servants, received an additional allotment of land for each servant they procured. The servants were promised their transportation and freedom after seven years of labor.

The use of a contract to bind laborers did not originate with English colonization. However, indentured servitude included a series of innovations. The terms of the contract involved a stricter set of obligations than did other labor contracts and provided ways to enforce the provisions if the work was not performed. The practice of "selling" servants was new. The Virginia Company arranged the transportation to the colony for hundreds of servants and then sold them to resident planters. In addition, contracts were standardized, replacing what in England tended to be verbal rather than written agreements. Finally, English servants frequently left home at the age of 10, often moved annually from household to household, and labored primarily in AGRICULTURE. Although colonial indentured servants worked in the agricultural sector, especially in the Chesapeake area, they also served masters in the cities and towns. While many labored under highly unstable and exploitative circumstances, they commonly served their entire indenture with just one or two masters.

In the 17th century most servants immigrated to the colonies from England. By the 18th century the English were joined by Germans, Irish, and Scots. White indentured servants from England performed most of the labor in the earliest British settlements in the New World, and their successors in the 17th and 18th centuries continued to play key roles. Some estimates claim that between one-half and two-thirds of all of the white immigrants to colonial North America arrived as indentured laborers.

In the early decades of the 18th century a new form of indentured servitude appeared—the redemptioner system. Thousands of German and Swiss families began their passage to the New World only to find that they had insufficient resources to finance the entire voyage. Ship captains took whatever money the passengers possessed and, upon arrival in the colonies, gave the passengers a period of time, usually 14 days, to secure the balance of payment. If the immigrants were unable to raise the additional money, the captain sold them into servitude to satisfy the debt.

Who were the indentured servants? They came from a broad segment of English society, usually were about 15 to 25 years of age, were comprised of a mixture of skilled and unskilled laborers, and were predominantly male. In the 17th century these people often became victims of shady emigrant agents, the English "spirits." Some spirits were hired by merchants to gather a servant cargo; others worked independently and sold individuals to ship masters. Armed with sweets and liquor, spirits roamed the streets and docks of London and lured unsuspecting children and adults on board ships bound for the colonies, where they were sold into servitude. In 1664, in an attempt to control the activities of the spirits and to ensure that no one was forced into servitude, the British Parliament authorized an official registry office.

What motivated individuals to TRAVEL to the New World and to sign away four or five years of their labor to work for an unknown master? By exchanging their labor for a period of time for the costs of transportation to the New World, some servants dreamed of prosperous futures while others fled Europe out of desperation. WILLIAM MORALEY, for example, left a journal describing his route to indentured servitude. His father was a successful watchmaker in London until 1720, when his fortunes collapsed along with the stock of the South Sea Company. The family moved from London not long after Moraley's father died. He took his small inheritance and ventured back to London to "seek my fortune." London offered him no prospects for his future; indeed, he was imprisoned briefly for debt and released in 1729. Faced with a bleak economic future, Moraley sold himself into servitude, bound for five years.

Other servants left similar though less detailed accounts about what motivated them to leave their homelands to labor in the colonies. Servants embarking from London longed to "procure a better livelihood." Some attributed their move to a "want of employ," to better "pursue ones calling," or to "better their fortune." Two Irish men opted to emigrate as servants because they thought they could "live much better and with more ease in the country to which they are going than they could in their country." After they completed their terms of indenture, their economic futures hopefully would brighten. They likely had no realistic notion of what awaited them, but thousands still moved to North America.

Once individuals decided to make the journey, they boarded ships destined for the colonies. Although most 17th-century servants signed indentures before embarking, by the 18th century an increasing number of them arrived in the colonies without contracts. When a ship docked in port, advertisements would appear in the local newspaper announcing the arrival of servants for sale. Potential masters would appear at the dock, examine the human cargo, pay the captain or merchant, record the indenture on an official listing, and take the servant home.

Indentured labor flourished because free laborers were scarce. "Help is not to be had at any rate" came the cry from North America throughout most of the colonial period. Employers could not find free laborers, and when they could, they were extremely costly. As Governor Leete of CONNECTICUT wrote in 1680, "there is seldom any want relief; because labor is deare." The surveyor general of NEW YORK explained in 1723 why workers were in short supply. "Every one is able to procure a piece of land at an inconsiderable rate and therefore is fond to set up for himself rather than work for hire." Without a sufficient number of free laborers, employers turned to unfree workers.

Indentured servants helped relieve the colonial labor shortage. They were, in the words of one historian, the machines that grew TOBACCO in the 17th-century Chesapeake area and carried the burden of labor in the sugar plantations of the West Indies as well. Rates of MORTALITY for these servants were extremely high; most did not live long enough to finish their terms of service. Gradually, over the course of the 17th century, indentured servitude declined in importance as planters turned increasingly to slave labor. The shift in unfree labor occurred in part because the supply of indentured servants from England diminished. In addition, rates of mortality declined, making the investment in slaves for life more profitable. Some collected their own lands and began to grow tobacco. Others were displaced and fomented uprisings. Established Chesapeake area planters did not like the added competition from these former servants and feared their unrest, especially their participation in BACON'S REBELLION. Slaves offered planters certain advantages. Because they served for life, slaves would never become competitive in the tobacco market. A carefully designed and repressive legal system would work to prevent slave rebellion.

In contrast to the plantation economies of the Chesapeake area, Lower South, and West Indies, New England colonies relied only minimally on indentured labor. Although land was plentiful in the Northeast, no profitable staple crop, like tobacco or sugar, dominated. Economic organization was based on the family farm, and when additional labor was required, employers hired on a casual basis. Indentured servitude played a more active role in the Middle Colonies. Initially, during the founding years of PENNSYLVANIA, unfree laborers worked in the agricultural sector but not in a staple-crop ECONOMY. Pennsylvania farmers produced primarily wheat and other commodities for local CONSUMPTION, which did not require as much labor as southern crops. By the second decade of the 18th century, servitude shifted from the rural to the urban sector. Servants labored in the homes of wealthy MERCHANTS and the shops of successful ARTISANS.

Servants' experiences differed depending on where they lived and the type of tasks performed. Those who worked in the steamy, inhospitable climates of plantation colonies in the labor intense industries of sugar and tobacco production suffered from hard labor conditions and high death rates. Planters also found it difficult to motivate servants to work. They were, as one historian of the Chesapeake area notes, essentially prepaid by the costs of transportation and thus they lacked incentives. As a result, masters threatened servants with extending the length of their service or withholding their freedom dues if they did not perform adequately or if they attempted to run away. In contrast, working for a Quaker family in Pennsylvania in an artisan's shop or as a domestic servant usually meant not only humane treatment but also a better possibility for social and economic success after the term of service ended.

Indentured labor gradually died out over the course of the late 18th century. Its demise was not due to a concerted effort to end the system. Rather, transatlantic fares became more affordable, enabling more immigrants to buy their own tickets. Also, the mid-Atlantic states depended less and less on unfree labor because of a steady increase in the number of free workers.

Further reading: Sharon V. Salinger, *"To Serve Well and Faithfully": Labor and Indentured Servants in Pennsylvania, 1682–1800* (Bowie, Maryland: Heritage Books, 2000); David Galenson, *White Servitude in Colonial America* (New York: Cambridge University Press, 1984).

—Sharon V. Salinger

Indians See Native Americans; specific tribes

Indians of the desert Southwest

The desert Southwest, extending from the Rio Grande in present-day NEW MEXICO to the California border, was the home of settled Pueblos and mobile raiders. The Pueblo and other settled peoples developed sophisticated forms of agriculture that efficiently used the limited water resources of the region. Some created extensive irrigation canals, while others relied entirely on scarce rainfall, diverting run-off onto planted fields. Nomadic Athabascan people entered the Southwest from the north in the mid-15th century, eventually splitting into the Apache, who remained nomadic raiders well after the 18th century, and the NAVAHO, who combined raiding with agricultural practices learned from their settled neighbors. All were profoundly influenced by the arrival of the Spanish in the 16th century.

While representing several language groups, Pueblo people were organized in a similar fashion. They all lived in multistory adobe dwellings built around a central plaza. Each Pueblo possessed one or more round or square kivas, part of which was built below ground. It was entered by a ladder from the top. Within the kiva priests performed a variety of rituals generally associated with prayers for rain and successful crops. Pueblo society practiced a form of dual leadership that made some priests responsible for civil and internal matters while a second group was responsible for military and external affairs. Agriculture was both individual and communal. Individual families controlled the use of planting grounds, while the entire community worked to repair and clean irrigation ditches. Before the arrival of the Spanish, crops consisted primarily of maize, beans, and squash.

The Akimel Au Authm (Pima) constructed a large elaborate irrigation system in the Salt River Valley in and around present-day Phoenix. This system, developed over several hundred years, consisted of miles of main canals and diversion ditches. Others in the Arizona region relied on a type of flood irrigation that took advantage of run-off from thunderstorms by building numerous small temporary dams to spread the water across a field located at the mouth of an arroyo. The Tohono O'odham (Papago) used such methods in the Gila River Valley, planting numerous fields to ensure that some produced a crop.

The Spanish arrival altered both farming and governance among the sedentary people of the Southwest. Spanish explorers and Catholic priests introduced wheat, fruit trees, and livestock (primarily sheep) to the region. They also imposed a civil government on the Pueblo. While native priests remained important and powerful within Pueblo societies, an appointed and later elected governor acted as a mediator between the Spanish and the Catholic Church. Over time rivalries between secular leaders and traditional priests created serious factionalism within Pueblo society. By far the most important Spanish introduction altering Southwest native life, however, was the horse.

Spanish rule was harsh, leading to confiscation of native land and enslavement of native people. Several unsuccessful rebellions preceded a major revolt in 1680, led by a warrior priest from San Juan Pueblo named POPÉ. The Rio Grande pueblos, supported by those as far west as Zuni and Hopi, pushed the Spanish out of the region for nearly 12 years, although the Spanish returned and reasserted their control. While the settled people of New Mexico eventually learned to live with their Spanish overseers, the Spanish were never successful in bringing the Apache and Navajo under their control.

Undoubtedly, Spanish horses found their way into native hands before 1680, but the revolt probably increased the number of horses available to the Apache and Navajo. Horses had few predators to limit their numbers and consequently multiplied rapidly. By the time the Spanish returned to the upper Rio Grande in New Mexico and initiated their invasion of the homeland of the Akimel Au Authm and Tohono O'odham in Arizona after 1690, they confronted skillful, horse-mounted, mobile warriors. The Apache and to a lesser extent the Navajo resisted and terrorized both the Spanish and native farmers for the next 175 years.

Further reading: Ramón A. Gutiérrez, *When Jesus Came the Corn Mothers Went Away: Marriage, Sexuality, and Power in New Mexico, 1500–1846* (Palo Alto, Calif.: Stanford University Press, 1991).

—Thomas R. Wessel

indigo

A blue dye, indigo is obtained from more than 40 different varieties of perennial shrubs of the genus *Indigofera* within the pea family. Indigo-producing plants are native to tropical and subtropical regions throughout the world, including the Americas, AFRICA, India, and Asia. Indigo has been used as a pigment for inks and paint as well as a dyestuff for cloth and yarns. The dye's affinity for a variety of natural fibers, such as wool, linen, and cotton, and its colorfastness to both washing and sunlight have made it popular with textile manufacturers for thousands of years.

Traditionally, the leaves of indigo plants had been harvested and fermented to produce a dye paste, which was used regionally in tropical and subtropical areas of the world, especially India. Later, the addition of a final drying step gave producers a concentrated dye ideal for long-distance trade. Indigo dyes were introduced to western Europe by 16th-century Portuguese and Spanish traders returning from India and the East Indies and soon became an important trade commodity. By the 1700s there was a strong European demand for large quantities of indigo dye for garments and furnishing fabrics as well as for linen for flags and woolens for military uniforms.

Early in the 17th century European colonists in North America and the CARIBBEAN experimented with indigo cultivation. However, by 1650 most West Indian plantations had shifted to hugely profitable sugar production, and SOUTH CAROLINA planters were concentrating on rice cultivation. English textile manufactures, unable to obtain the dye from a British colony, turned to the French West Indies for their indigo supplies.

A young colonial woman, ELIZABETH LUCAS PINCKNEY, worked to hybridize indigo plants to suit the growing conditions of South Carolina. By 1744, aided by slaves and a West Indian overseer knowledgeable about indigo, she was successful and devoted much of that initial crop to seed production. She and her new husband, Charles Pinckney, gave the seeds to their neighbors. As further encouragement to new indigo planters, the South Carolina legislature offered a bounty on the exported dyestuffs. Shortly afterward, Britain, anxious for a source of indigo dye for its growing textile industry, added an additional bounty to the crop. Indigo was a very profitable colonial export commodity for the next 30 years. On the eve of the American Revolution, annual exports from South Carolina's ports were more than 1 million pounds, second only to rice in its importance to the colony. Indigo production complemented rice production very well because the two crops had different growing seasons, and indigo required high ground while rice was grown in the lowlands.

Further reading: Jenny Balfour-Paul, *Indigo* (London: British Museum Press, 1998).

—Margo Krager

Inuit

The Inuit, sometimes referred to as "Eskimo," are the original inhabitants of the Arctic and Subarctic region extending eastward from the Aleutian Islands, through northwestern Alaska, through northern Canada, and to Greenland. The Inuit and ALEUT arrived in North America during a much later migration from Asia than did the ancestors of the Indians who inhabit the regions from Subarctic Canada through Tierra del Fuego at the southern tip of South America. By the late 16th century the Inuit had developed into many distinct cultural groups. These include the Yup'ik Eskimo of western Alaska, the Inupiat of northern Alaska, the Mackenzie Delta Eskimo, and the Netsilik of northern Canada. Additionally, there are diverse Inuit in the current territory of Nunavut, the province of Quebec, the Atlantic Provinces, as well as Greenland.

This tremendously diverse geographic area led to the development of equally diverse cultures among the Inuit. While Inuit from the coastal and polar regions focused on sea mammals for their economy, other inland subarctic groups hunted caribou or other game. Additionally, each group developed technologies, whether the kayak, igloo, bow and arrow, or toboggan, that were appropriate to the particular region in which they lived.

During the colonial period, from 1585–1763, Inuit people did not experience the massive cultural changes and upheavals experienced by Indians to the south. English explorer Martin Frobisher sailed into the Arctic in the 1570s and supposedly brought back a captive to England, but there was no prolonged contact between cultures. When the Old World began making more significant contact with the Inuit, it was the Russians who did so rather than western Europeans. Traversing the Bering Strait (named for VITUS JONASSEN BERING, a Russian who sailed through the Strait in 1728), the Russians arrived rather late on the colonial stage, although they had few imperial competitors in the Northwest. The Russians introduced iron tools and Old World diseases to the Yup'ik of the Bering Strait region. Similar patterns emerged, with the Inuit adopting iron tools and suffering from DISEASE in ways similar to the Indians to the south. But unlike the Indian populations of the United States, many Inuit did not come into significant contact with white people until the 19th and sometimes 20th century.

Further reading: Olive Patricia Dickason, *Canada's First Nations: A History of Founding Peoples from Earliest Times* (Norman: University of Oklahoma Press, 1992).

—Thomas J. Lappas

Iron Acts (1750, 1757)

The purpose of the Iron Acts passed by the British Parliament was to regulate the erection of slitting MILLS, plating mills, and steel furnaces in the colonies. The legislation, passed in 1750, particularly affected London manufacturers, who could import bar iron from the colonies duty free and sell the manufactured iron products in the colonies. Over time merchants from Bristol, Birmingham, and Liverpool objected to these discriminatory provisions that benefited only London merchants. In 1757 Parliament passed a second Iron Act, this time permitting the importation of colonial bar iron into all British ports duty free.

These acts were part of the system of MERCANTILISM by which Great Britain attempted to protect its own iron industries from competition in its colonies and to maintain a supply of raw iron ore from the colonies. The passage of the two Iron Acts provided colonial ironmasters with a guaranteed market for their product but limited their growth potential. Although imperial authorities failed to enforce the Iron Acts effectively, colonial ironmasters joined the rebellion against Britain in part because they perceived their livelihoods threatened by these restrictive policies.

See also IRON MANUFACTURING.

Further reading: Arthur C. Bining, *British Regulation of the Colonial Iron Industry* (Philadelphia: University of Pennsylvania Press, 1933).

—Karen Guenther

iron manufacturing

Iron manufacturing in colonial North America had its origins in the promotional tracts of Thomas Harriot during the 16th century. Harriot noted that iron manufacturing in the New World would be of great benefit to England because of the abundance of natural resources, particularly iron ore, limestone, and timber. Early attempts were made to develop iron plantations at JAMESTOWN, but the glow from the furnace stacks alerted NATIVE AMERICANS, who demolished the facilities and killed the workers. The scarcity of capital limited the opportunities for future development in the Chesapeake area throughout most of the 17th century.

New Englanders erected the first successful venture at Saugus, MASSACHUSETTS, in 1646. To promote iron making, workers were exempted from military service and the furnace from taxation. The availability of creeks and streams, along with ore and wood, dictated the success or failure of the operations at Saugus and other locations throughout New England. Not all of the ventures prospered, and fewer than a dozen ironworks existed in New England at the end of the 17th century.

The colonial iron industry began to thrive in the 18th century. After QUEEN ANNE'S WAR iron production boomed in MARYLAND, NEW JERSEY, PENNSYLVANIA, and VIRGINIA. The Pennsylvania enterprises were the most successful; by the time of the Revolution, more than 70 furnaces, forges, and other ironworks were in operation throughout the colony. "Iron plantations" developed in the interior, located close to water for power, iron mines for ore, and forests for fuel. These plantations were as self-sufficient as their counterparts in the Chesapeake area, providing HOUSING for the owner and workers as well as other outbuildings to service their needs. In addition to the furnace complex, a typical iron plantation included a general store, blacksmith shop, gristmill, barns, grain fields, orchards, and bake ovens. The workforce was comprised of skilled and unskilled settlers, indentured servants, and slaves. Ironmasters were the largest slaveholders in colonial Pennsylvania.

By the time of the Revolution, more furnaces were in operation in the colonies than in the entire British Isles. The production at these facilities prompted Parliament to pass restrictive legislation beginning in 1750. Like other imperial regulations of the era, the IRON ACTS had little effect on eliminating competition from the colonies. At the time of the Revolution, the iron produced in the colonies exceeded 30,000 tons annually, approximately one-seventh of the world's production.

Further reading: Arthur C. Bining, *Pennsylvania Iron Manufacture in the Eighteenth Century,* 2nd ed. (Harrisburg, Pa.: Pennsylvania Historical and Museum Commission, 1971).

—Karen Guenther

Iroquois

Iroquois technically refers to a large language group of Indian people in the Northeast and mid-Atlantic area that in the 17th century included confederations such as the HURON of Canada, the Susquehannah of PENNSYLVANIA, and the CHEROKEE of the Carolinas, as well as numerous smaller tribes such as the Petun, Erie, and Neutral Nation north of Lake Erie, in addition to the TUSCARORA in NORTH CAROLINA. Generally, however, *Iroquois* applied to the Five Nations of the Iroquois Confederation of NEW YORK, consisting of the Seneca, Cayuga, Onondaga, Oneida, and Mohawk in the 17th century and joined by the Tuscarora early in the 18th century. This confederation eventually dominated a region extending from New England to Wisconsin and the St. Lawrence River to Virginia.

The source of the Iroquois Confederation of New York is lost in time. Iroquois oral tradition placed its origins well before the 14th century, while others date the confederation from late in the 15th century. In any event, all agree that the confederation was the work of a Huron prophet, DEKANAWIDEH, who, with his Onondoga or Mohawk disciple, Hiawatha, preached a message of unity among the Iroquois and laid the foundation for a political system that generally sustained internal peace and created a working relationship among its principal members. Most Native American origin stories, including those of the Iroquois, generally involve personages with superhuman attributes. However, Dekanawideh and Hiawatha are described as having very human skills and faults. Dekanawideh is physically deformed but shrewd and politically perceptive. Hiawatha is often insufferable but eloquent. These descriptions suggest that Iroquois memories are of actual people from a real past time.

The Iroquois called their confederation the League of the Ho-dee-nau-sau-nee, or People of the Longhouse. The Seneca acted as the keepers of the western door, while the Mohawk occupied this role in the east. Seneca and Mohawk were the elder brothers of the confederation, while the Oneida and Cayuga were younger brothers. The Onondaga were Keepers of the Flame and hosted meetings of the confederation. The addition of the Tuscarora in 1722, when they fled white aggressors in North Carolina, added a third younger brother and sixth nation to the confederation. Fifty SACHEMS represented the nations at council meetings of the confederation. As elder brothers, the Seneca and Mohawk gave first consideration to issues before the confederation council. The matter was then taken up by the Cayuga and Oneida. If a consensus existed, the Onondaga confirmed the decision; if not, the Onondaga broke the impasse.

The Iroquois were predominantly farming people who also hunted. The elder women controlled the fields and their produce. Women exercised considerable political power, selecting each nation's representatives at the confederation council and even, at times, deciding questions of war and peace. Women also enjoyed substantial social authority. Lineage descended through the female line, for example, and women could divorce their husbands by placing his goods outside the door of their longhouse. The rough equality between men and women reflected the Iroquois's generally egalitarian social order.

When French explorers first entered the St. Lawrence region in 1609, the Huron had already driven the Iroquois south into central New York. Enmity with the Huron continued to midcentury and with the French until 1701. In the three decades after French arrival, the Huron established an extensive fur-trading system that took their cargo canoes as far west as Lake Michigan and as far north as Hudson Bay. Each summer the Huron transported beaver skins down the Ottawa River to Montreal. The New York Iroquois established a smaller fur-trading system with the Dutch at Fort Orange (Albany), while the Susquehannah made profitable contact with Swedish settlements in DELAWARE.

The depletion of fur-bearing ANIMALS in New York moved members of the Iroquois Confederation to approach the Huron and persuade them to share in their northern trading empire. However, Huron refusal initiated aggressive Iroquois raiding on Huron canoe trains on the Ottawa River. Finally, in a midwinter campaign in 1649, warriors from the Seneca and Mohawk nations attacked several Huron towns, scattering the survivors and ending

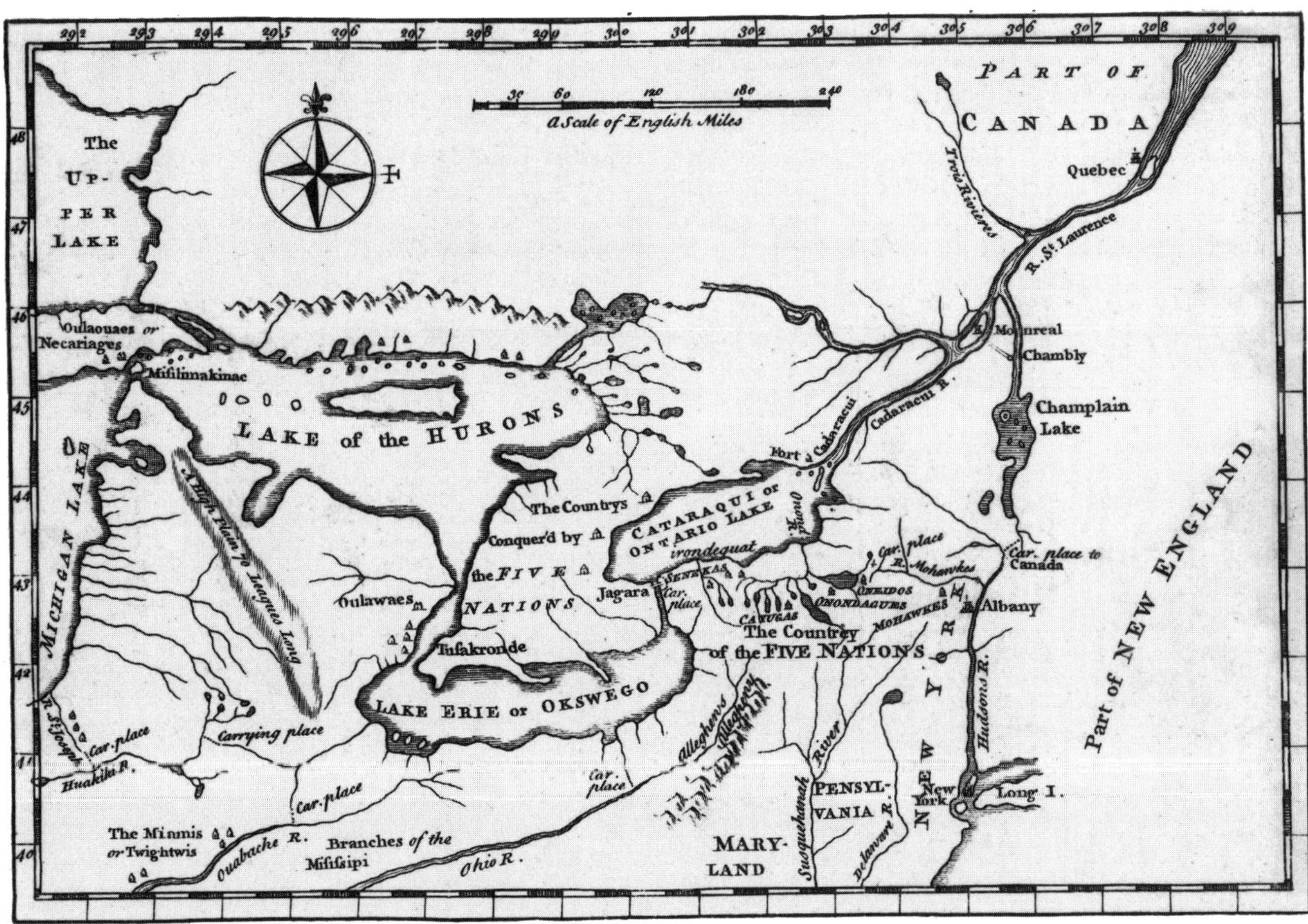

This historical map shows the locations of the tribes that formed the Iroquois Confederacy. *(Hulton/Archive)*

Huron control of the northern fur trade. Over the next five years confederation warriors decimated the Petun, Erie, and Neutral Nations, who had provided much of the foodstuffs that Huron traders transported into the interior. These BEAVER WARS propelled the Iroquois on a half-century campaign to control the FUR TRADE, gain captives for adoption to replace their depleted numbers, and, possibly, to extend the concepts of the Confederation's "Tree of Peace" to surrounding tribes. Whatever their motivation, the Iroquois's successful campaigns against the Susquehannah and the Illinois tribes placed the confederation in a powerful position between the French in Canada and the expanding English colonies on the Atlantic coast. The process was punctuated by periodic conflict with the French and closer contact with the English, who had replaced the Dutch at Albany. The confederation signed treaties of peace with MASSACHUSETTS and CONNECTICUT in 1677 and with VIRGINIA in 1679. In 1658, 1665, 1684, and more or less continuously thereafter until 1701, French military forces fought the Iroquois in the St. Lawrence Valley and along the Hudson River in an unsuccessful bid to subdue the Iroquois. Constant war with the French and other tribes, however, left the confederation in a weakened condition by the end of the century. The Five Nations apparently understood that their past military successes would be difficult to sustain and that their reputation far exceeded their physical ability to play the role of military arbiter. Consequently, the confederation sought and obtained a treaty with the French in 1701 and chose to remain neutral in the clash between the English and French.

Although the Five Nations often acted independently of one another, the confederation's neutrality remained generally intact through the SEVEN YEARS' WAR. Individual members participated in the fighting: Mohawk under the influence of SIR WILLIAM JOHNSON fought alongside the English in 1762, and some Seneca joined Pontiac in his fight against English authority in Detroit. Nevertheless, the Iroquois Confederation chose diplomacy over war until the eve of the American Revolution. In the 18th century the internal cohesion of the confederation gradually eroded.

English missionaries converted many Mohawk and Oneida Iroquois to the Church of England or the Puritan Church of Massachusetts. The French had earlier converted other Mohawk to Catholicism and moved an entire village to the St. Lawrence Valley. When the French ceded Canada to Great Britain in 1763, the Iroquois found it harder to maintain neutrality or "play off" one European power against another, as they had in the past. The weakness of the bonds that had held the nations together became evident when Mohawk leaders opted to join the English during the American Revolution while the confederation officially remained neutral. Eventually, the Oneida allied with the Revolutionaries, an event that for all practical purposes ended the confederation.

Further reading: Francis Jennings, *The Ambiguous Iroquois Empire* (New York: Norton, 1984); Daniel K. Richter, *The Ordeal of the Longhouse: The Peoples of the Iroquois League in the Era of European Colonization* (Chapel Hill: University of North Carolina Press, 1992).

—Thomas R. Wessel

J

Jamestown

Called "James City" by its English settlers, Jamestown was settled under the auspices of the VIRGINIA COMPANY OF LONDON in 1607 on James Island, a deep-water anchorage 60 miles up the James River from where it empties into CHESAPEAKE BAY. To English eyes the north bank of the James west to its confluence with the Chickahominy may have appeared to be "unused" wilderness, but it actually was the domain of the Paspiheigh tribe of the POWHATAN CONFEDERACY, a people who actively occupied and exploited it, but not in the ways to which the English were accustomed. The Paspiheigh immediately contested the English claims to "ownership through use," sending clouds of arrows over the palisaded walls surrounding James City's wattle-and-daub huts. To defend themselves against the Paspiheigh and possible incursions of Spanish warships, the English built James Fort on high ground away from the river, and it become the core around which James City and the colony expanded.

The Virginia Company founded James City at an inauspicious time. The Chesapeake region and its Powhatan inhabitants were suffering under the most severe drought in seven centuries, sparking an agricultural crisis that limited the amount of FOOD the Powhatan could willingly trade for the copper jewelry, glass beads, and other goods manufactured by James City ARTISANS. The English settlers hoped the exchange of these manufactured goods for food would sustain them until they could become self-sufficient producers of their own foodstuffs. When the Powhatan judged trade to be disadvantageous or dishonorable and withheld their foodstuffs, the desperate English under JOHN SMITH bullied and browbeat corn from them and sacked and burned their villages, which unleashed a decades-long guerrilla war punctuated by brief periods of uneasy peace.

James City's neighbors, the Paspiheigh, were the immediate victims of the warfare. In February 1610 the English killed the Paspiheigh werowance Wowinchopunk. After the starving winter of 1609–10, George Percy sallied forth from James City, burned the Paspiheigh village, and put the captured Paspiheigh queen to the sword after executing her children by "Throweinge them overboard and shoteinge owtt their Braynes." Between 1616 and 1669 the Paspiheigh disappeared from the Virginia census, yet by 1612 there were Indians living in James Fort and working for the colonists. A number of intermarriages occurred between English working men and Indian women, a practice strenuously denounced by the upper-CLASS clergy of James City as "uncivilized."

Drought also increased the James River's deadly salinity, thereby contributing to the extreme MORTALITY in the early years. Only 38 of the original 104 settlers survived the first year of settlement, causing the premature evacuation of James City itself. Between 1607 and 1625 nearly 5,000 of the 6,000 European immigrants died from diseases like typhoid as well as malnutrition and conflict with natives. Virginia became a "death trap," and were it not for JOHN ROLFE's successful experiments with TOBACCO, mortality may have outpaced immigration for most of the century. Tobacco quickly became VIRGINIA's chief and most profitable export. Tobacco exports rose from 20,000 pounds in 1617 to more than 40 million pounds by 1727, overwhelming European competitors. James City became a boomtown, with tobacco cultivated even in its streets.

English MERCHANTS supplied planters with manufactured goods and indentured servants, predominantly young men; merchants returned home with profitable cargoes of the "stinking leafe." Many servants were from the lower classes—the poor, vagrant, and imprisoned—judged by the English and Virginians to be "the vile and brutish part of mankind," fit only for forced labor. Others came from respectable artisan and yeoman families, but once in Virginia were worked hard, often mistreated, bought, sold, and even gambled away by their masters. Before 1670 these bonded laborers came from the lower and "middling" classes of southern and western England but were quickly replaced by slaves from AFRICA and the CARIBBEAN.

In 1619 John Rolfe, the father of the tobacco boom, reported that "there came in a Dutch man-of-warre that sold us 20 negars," an addition to the 31 Africans already there "in the service of all planters." Within a generation of their arrival, lifetime bondage for African servants became an established custom, although not yet recognized in law. In the same year James City witnessed the arrival of "Young maids to make wives for so many of the former Tenants," to be sold by the Virginia Company for not less than "one hundredth and fiftie [pounds] of the best leafe Tobacco." The importation of European and African laborers to toil in households and on tobacco fields swelled the colony's population from a few hundred English colonists in 1618 to 13,000 by 1674, 800 of whom lived in James City.

Under its 1618 charter the Virginia Company hoped to concentrate settlers in four boroughs—James City, Charles City, Henrico, and Kecoughtan—in which life and government would be that of a municipality rather than that of an English county. The tobacco boom, however, sparked a "plantation revolution" that by the 1620s spread the settlement into 49 tobacco plantations up the James River all the way to the fall line. By the 1620s James City experienced its own suburban sprawl marked by small satellite settlements spreading out farther into Paspiheigh lands. As planters fanned out along rivers and bays, English tobacco merchants were able sail their ships right to the plantations' wharves, thereby diminishing the commercial importance of the four boroughs; they were soon supplanted by organization of local government by counties. "[T]he Advantage of the many Rivers which afforded a commodious Road for Shipping at eveery Man's Door," ROBERT BEVERLEY noted in 1705, [resulted in] "not any one Place of Cohabitation among them, that may reasonably bear the Name of a Town." The unceasing intrusion of European settlement into Indian lands also ignited the Powhatan resistances of 1622, 1644, and 1676, resulting in the deaths of substantial numbers of English settlers whose distance from towns made them highly vulnerable to attack. Settlers would scurry to the protection of James Fort during these outbreaks but just as quickly return to their wide-flung estates when hostilities cooled.

After the demise of the Virginia Company, James City developed in "fits and starts" in three waves: in the 1620s and 1630s, in the 1660s, and in the 1680s. James City's development was planned and implemented not according to the dispersed settlement patterns dictated by the new maritime tobacco trade but according to a model of what Virginia speculators saw to be the lucrative possibilities of the emerging English manufacturing towns, specifically, developing urban industries and constructing and renting quarters for workers attracted to such enterprises. In the 1630s Governor John Harvey encouraged the commercial development of James City by declaring it Virginia's sole port of entry. He also encouraged the immigration of skilled artisans, particularly brickmakers and bricklayers, to build up the town and manufacture items for sale at home and abroad. Harvey's industrial schemes failed, but they were revived after 1660 by speculators such as Philip Ludwell, who invested heavily in James City land, built brick row houses to quarter artisans and workers, and otherwise attempted to create a James City that was more than a statehouse and "a collection of taverns serving those coming to the capital on official business." The Town Act of 1662 required each of the 19 counties to construct a substantial brick building in James City, and it reimbursed individuals who undertook similar construction. James City's fire-prone wooden frame buildings thereby were gradually replaced by brick structures that conformed more closely to the fire and building codes of an English town.

Widespread settlement also shifted political, social, and ecclesiastical control from the governor and his council in James City to the county courts, which were dominated by local elites comprised of the largest planters in the county. These men were not the high-born sons of the English aristocracy who sat on the governor's council during the company period or who constituted the first General Assembly that met in the choir of the James City church in 1619. They were the tough, ambitious, land-grabbing, Indian-hating, self-made men who preempted lands of the Virginia Company after its dissolution and who ousted Governor Harvey in 1635 for his commercial schemes and conservative Indian policies. They in turn died away and were replaced from the 1640s onward by the immigration of a third generation of leaders—Bland, Byrd, Carter, Culpeper, Digges, Burwell, Ludwell, and Mason—the well-connected younger sons of English merchant families long associated with Virginia. Based on family land in the colony, inherited wealth, or family shares of original Virginia Company stock, they built up substantial plantations from lands already cleared and cultivated by the first and second generations of Virginians. They gradually assumed places of power and authority in the county courts, the assembly, and the governor's council and founded the great 18th-century Virginia ruling dynasties.

The transition to a stable, country aristocracy married to the maritime tobacco trade ultimately spelled the demise of James City. It lost its status as the mandatory port of entry for Virginia in 1662, at a time in which tobacco production and, therefore, political power was beginning to shift northward. Conflict between jealous local magnates and Governor Berkeley and his "Green Spring Faction" over their monopoly of provincial offices and patronage ignited BACON'S REBELLION. In 1676

Nathaniel Bacon burned down James City to deny its use to Governor Berkeley.

The final wave of development in James City in the 1680s consisted of its rebuilding after Bacon's conflagration, but rebuilding on a modest scale without the grandeur of earlier years. Jamestown, thereafter, became little more than the seat of provincial government, although surrounding James City County tripled in population from 1674 to 1699. In 1698 James City's statehouse again burned to the ground. The growing power held by residents of York County, men such as James Page of Middle Plantation, made that settlement the logical successor to James City as the colony's new capital. The following year the capital of Virginia was moved to the new town site of Williamsburg, formerly Middle Plantation. James City gradually disappeared, and the old town site on James Island was taken over by the Ambler and Travis plantations, on which the bicentennial of Jamestown was celebrated in 1807.

Further reading: Edmund S. Morgan, *American Slavery; American Freedom: The Ordeal of Colonial Virginia* (New York: Norton, 1975); Ivor Noel Hume, *The Virginia Adventure: Roanoke to James Towne: An Archaeological and Historical Odyssey* (Charlottesville: University Press of Virginia, 1997); Bernard Bailyn, *Voyagers to the West: A Passage in the Peopling of America on the Eve of the Revolution* (New York: Knopf, 1986).

—James Bruggeman

Jemison, Mary (1743–1833)

Mary Jemison was born at sea when her parents, Thomas and Jane Erwin Jemison, were en route from Belfast to PHILADELPHIA. Shawnee Indians and French soldiers attacked their farm near present-day Gettysburg on April 5, 1758, capturing Mary, her parents, three other Jemison children, and several neighbors. While her captors killed most of the prisoners, Mary was adopted by two Shawnee sisters and given the name Dehgewanus.

During the third year of Jemison's captivity, while living in the Ohio country, her sisters arranged a marriage to a Delaware warrior, Sheninjee, with whom she had two children. In 1762 she moved with her Indian relatives to Little Beard's town on the Genesee River in NEW YORK. After Sheninjee's death, Jemison married Hiokatoo, a tribal leader some 50 years older than she, by whom she had six children. She remained his wife until his death in 1811 at the age of 103.

General John Sullivan destroyed Little Beard's town in 1779, and Jemison moved to the Gardeau Flats along the Genesee River. On several occasions Jemison had the opportunity to return to the white community, but she refused and chose to stay with her Indian family. The knowledge that white society would ostracize her children was a determining factor in her decision. In her narrative Jemison spoke firsthand of the destructive effects of ALCOHOL on the Seneca. Her son John killed his brothers Thomas and Jesse in drunken rages before he himself was murdered.

Jemison had acquired land under the Treaty of Big Tree (1797), and her claim was acknowledged by the New York legislature in 1817. For several years Mary supported a white man, calling himself George Jemison, who purported to be her cousin. He eventually cheated her out of several hundred acres of land. In 1831 Jemison moved to the Buffalo Creek Reservation, where she died in 1833.

A figure of great curiosity, Jemison had become known as "the White Woman of the Genesee," and in 1823 she agreed to meet with Dr. James Everett Seaver for three days to record her life story. The resulting book, *The Narrative of the Life of Mrs. Mary Jemison* (1824), was an overnight bestseller. At the time of her meeting with Seaver, she had three living children, 39 grandchildren, and 14 great-grandchildren. In 1874 William Pryor Letchworth moved her remains and her home to his estate, now Letchworth Park, and commissioned H. K. Bush-Brown to sculpt a bronze statue of her, which was erected in 1910. While Seaver and subsequent white male editors couched Jemison's story as that of a woman who retained her whiteness despite a life among the Indians, her narrative can also be read as the autobiography of a Seneca woman.

Further reading: June Namias, *White Captives: Gender and Ethnicity on the American Frontier* (Chapel Hill: University of North Carolina Press, 1993).

—Mary Murphy

jeremiads

Named for the Old Testament prophet Jeremiah, whose spiritual and political leadership helped his countrymen survive disasters, jeremiads were political sermons delivered by Puritan ministers that assessed the state of the community's covenant with God. Considered the first distinctively American literary genre, these ritualistic and formulaic sermons were intended to guide an imperiled people toward their divine destiny. They were denunciations, usually delivered in thunderous tones, of moral corruption and spiritual degradation that reinforced the conception of a divine plan for the community, described the consequences of transgressions from the terms of the covenant, and advocated a reformed relationship with God on the part of the individual and the community.

Sermons of this type had been used for centuries in Europe to elicit good behavior from the people through threats of divine punishment. But American PURITANS adapted the message of the jeremiad to their unique situation as God's servants in the New World. In the generations after the original colonization of New England, when the society seemed to be falling away from God, Puritan ministers used jeremiads to denounce the colonists for their sins and bemoan their loss of piety, yet they still promised that God would renew the covenant with them if they repented. Instead of being simply prophesies of doom, Puritan jeremiads were decidedly optimistic, reinterpreting divine punishment as a sign of favor from God. As with a strict but loving father, God's punishments were an indication to Puritans that they were indeed God's chosen people and attested to the promise of success in their endeavor to establish a city of God. In the 17th and early 18th centuries jeremiads were delivered to commemorate important public occasions, such as days of prayer, fasts, or elections. Among the earliest and best known of these is JOHN WINTHROP's *A Model of Christian Charity*, delivered in 1630. They served an important function in early New England by establishing behavioral norms and delineating the contours of the community. Later, in the 18th and 19th centuries, the genre continued to flourish. The influence of jeremiads expanded beyond New England and contributed significantly to early conceptions of American national structure and identity as they were used to define national purpose and garner public support at such critical junctures in the country's history as the American Revolution and the Civil War.

Further reading: Sacvan Bercovitch, *The American Jeremiad* (Madison: University of Wisconsin Press, 1978).

—Jane E. Calvert

Jesuits

Founded by St. Ignatius of Loyola in the 16th century, the Society of Jesus, or Jesuits, played a significant role in the colonization of the Portuguese, Spanish, and French empires. Intended as a bulwark against the Protestant Reformation, Jesuits were used primarily to establish institutions of learning to serve the children of Europe's ruling class and to provide confessors and advisers to the elite. Owing special obedience to the Pope and exempted from the strictures of the Council of Trent, the Jesuits were a special task force meant to reestablish Catholicism during the Counter-Reformation in Europe. As a result, fewer than one in 10 Jesuits served outside the continent in mission work.

Those who left Europe, however, followed the explorations and contacts made by their governments, joining Spanish parties in Mexico and Portuguese settlements in Macao and Goa and following their mission to attach themselves to the European and native rulers of these areas. Jesuits quickly founded schools to serve the European community and educate natives. Men like St. Francis Xavier and Matteo Ricci worked to learn and translate Chinese and Japanese, producing dictionaries for European use. The French dispatched Jesuits to their possessions in New France, beginning with the 1611 mission to Arcadia. Quebec had a Jesuit College by 1635, while other Jesuit fathers labored among the HURON, Ottawa, Miami, and Illinois, working to learn their languages as well as to maintain good relations for France. In Canada the Jesuits became known as the "Black Robes" and won the respect of some natives because of their willingness and ability to withstand ritual torture. In British North America Jesuits entered MARYLAND in 1634 at the behest of its proprietor, Cecil Calvert, serving the Catholic population as circuit riders; their routes extended into western PENNSYLVANIA.

Jesuits were expelled from Canada in 1763 by the British, but their influence lingered among French Canadians and helped poison the relationship between the older British colonies and their new possession. Fear of Jesuit influence was part of the negative reaction of the colonists to the Quebec Act, which seemed to promise Catholic privileges. Additionally, the Jesuits played a role in the destruction of the Huron, interfering in their animosity with the IROQUOIS, who in 1649 defeated the Huron. Despite these failures, the Jesuits took part in the establishment of French culture and dominion in Canada and the Mississippi River Valley and served as advisers and supporters of the Spanish and Portuguese imperial elite in the Americas.

—Margaret Sankey

Jews

Jews have been a part of the American story as long as any other European group. Indeed, even if the speculation that Christopher Columbus himself claimed Jewish ancestry is incorrect, it is certain that six Jewish MARINERS accompanied him on his famous voyage to the Americas in 1492. Jews remained on the vanguard of European settlement in the New World throughout the 16th century as Sephardic Jews from Spain and Portugal came to new colonial outposts. Most of these were *maranos*, who, because of religious persecution, outwardly professed the official Catholicism of their nations but secretly maintained their Jewish belief and practice. Others of Jewish ancestry who did convert permanently were known as Conversos. Always tenuous, the *maranos*' situation became untenable both in the New World and in the Old as the Inquisition proclaimed a series of autos-da-fé to root out and put to death false converts. Fearing for their lives, Latin American Jews

An 18th-century Jewish synagogue *(Library of Congress)*

fled to the relatively tolerant Holland and to Dutch possessions in the Americas.

North America's first Jewish population arrived as 23 people fleeing from the Portuguese reconquest of Brazil from the Dutch. They came ashore at NEW AMSTERDAM on September 7, 1654. Owing to influential friends in Holland, the DUTCH WEST INDIA COMPANY ordered that the refugees be granted asylum over the strong objections of Governor PETER STUYVESANT. By the time England took control of New Amsterdam in 1664, renaming it NEW YORK CITY, the Jewish community had become an integral part of the small city's commercial and social life. The beginning of the 18th century saw the community grown to 100, and other developing trading centers in British North America began to develop small Jewish communities of their own, particularly in NEWPORT, CHARLESTON, PHILADELPHIA, Montreal, and SAVANNAH.

Although the majority of Jews in colonial North America were Sephardic (of Iberian origin), a small but increasing number of Ashkenazic Jews began to trickle in from the Germanic and Slavic parts of Europe. Strife developed between newcomers and the more established Sephardim over the form of religious services and the control of community organizations, although it was not until the 19th century that the Sephardic Jews would lose control over the American Jewish community.

American Jews remained a highly mobile and cosmopolitan minority in the 18th century, and, with strong family and business contacts in both the British and Dutch spheres, they played an important role in the mercantile life of the early Americas. Although Jews generally were not allowed to vote or participate in the political process, anti-Semitism was relatively tame in the wide-open social environment of the colonies. Influential Jews like Aaron Levy of Philadelphia and Gershom Sexias of New York traveled in the most elite of colonial circles.

Further reading: Eli Farber, *A Time for Planting: The First Migration, 1654–1820* (Baltimore: Johns Hopkins University Press, 1992).

—Matthew Taylor Raffety

Johnson, Anthony (unknown–1670)

One of the first African people in British North America, Anthony Johnson took advantage of the somewhat ambiguous legal condition of African people in the early colonies to become a successful planter. Before 1660 most black people in VIRGINIA apparently were considered servants for a limited number of years rather than slaves in perpetuity. Details of his early life are sketchy, but he arrived in Virginia in 1621, was purchased as a bound laborer for a fixed number of years, and worked producing TOBACCO.

Fortunately surviving the 1622 Indian rebellion, Johnson received additional good luck when "Mary a Negro Woman" arrived on the Bennett plantation where he worked. In 1625 Mary was the only woman living on the plantation; at some point she and Anthony married. Sometime between 1625 and 1650, both Anthony and Mary gained their freedom and assumed the surname "Johnson." By 1653 the Johnsons were living at Pungoteague Creek in Northampton County on Virginia's Eastern Shore. They had built a small estate consisting of at least 250 acres and numerous cattle and hogs.

Beginning in 1653 Anthony Johnson appears more often in official records. That year a fire destroyed a large part of his plantation. Anthony and Mary, who by this time had two sons and two daughters, sought relief from the county court. The court agreed that the fire was devastating and exempted Mary and the two daughters from taxation for life. Significantly, their race did not factor into the court's decision, and it appears that the court considered Mary and the daughters the equals of white women in the country. Later in 1653 Anthony reappeared in court in a dispute over a cow. He challenged John Neale, an important planter, for ownership, and although the disposition of the case is not known, the court did order an investigation rather than finding for Neale based on his word as a white man.

Shortly after the Neale incident, Johnson again found himself in a legal conflict. John Casor, one of Johnson's black laborers, claimed that he was being held against his will, although actually he had entered the colony as an indentured servant. Another local planter, Robert Parker, took up Casor's cause and, through the threat of legal action, convinced Johnson and his family that Casor should be free. Johnson subsequently freed Casor, who immediately went to work on Parker's farm. A few months later Johnson, obviously still troubled over Parker's interference in the matter, sued in the Northampton County court. The court found for Johnson in this matter and returned Casor to the Johnson farm, presumably for the remainder of his life. Sometime in the middle 1660s the Johnson family moved northward to Somerset County, MARYLAND.

Anthony Johnson died in 1670, but his family remained successful. Mary negotiated a 99-year lease on their farm, and the family remained close. Little else is known about the Johnson clan except that several of his sons married white women and that one son, John, died in 1706 leaving no heir.

During the last decades of the 17th century, Virginia and other southern colonies passed laws that redefined the status of AFRICAN AMERICANS, making them and their offspring slaves for life. White racism increased accordingly. Anthony Johnson had lived most of his life in an era when racism was less harsh and opportunities for black people were greater.

See also JOHNSON, MARY.

Further reading: T. H. Breen and Stephen Innes, *"Myne Owne Ground": Race and Freedom on Virginia's Eastern Shore, 1640–1676* (New York: Oxford University Press, 1980).

—Brian McKnight

Johnson, Mary (unknown–1672?)

An African immigrant to VIRGINIA, Mary Johnson experienced bondage in the 17th century before racism hardened in British America. Little information about Mary's early years has survived, but probably she had been forced by slave traders to march to the Atlantic coast of AFRICA while chained with other captives. She was branded and forced to endure the brutal Middle Passage across the Atlantic aboard the *Margrett and John.* Brought against her will to Virginia in the spring of 1622, Mary's age upon arrival is unknown. She was taken to Richard Bennett's large TOBACCO plantation on the James River.

Although Africans were scarce in the colonies, Mary met Anthony and married him, in fact if not by English law. The couple enjoyed a 40-year relationship and raised four children, whom they baptized in the Christian faith. It is not known how the couple made the transition from bondage to freedom, but they left Bennett's plantation seeking land of their own. The Johnsons settled on Pungoteague Creek in a small farming community that included black and white families. By 1650 the Johnsons had accumulated an estate of more than 250 acres, on which they raised cattle and pigs, but in 1653 fire ravaged the plantation. Local authorities helped by granting the Johnsons' petition that Mary and her two daughters be exempt during their lifetimes from local taxes levied on people who worked in AGRICULTURE. The wives and daughters of planters had traditionally been granted this exemption, but race was beginning to become a factor and black women were normally denied this privilege. In the 1660s the Johnsons moved to MARYLAND in search of fresh land. Anthony found work as a tenant on a 300-acre farm that he named Tonies Vineyard in Somerset County, but he died shortly after the move. Mary wrote her will in 1672, and she then disappears from the historical record. Mary Johnson lived at a time when white racism was more benign, and African Americans enjoyed a better opportunity to exercise personal rights, such as individual freedom and property ownership.

See also AFRICAN AMERICANS; JOHNSON, ANTHONY; WOMEN'S STATUS AND RIGHTS.

Further reading: Carol J. Berkin, *First Generations: Women in Colonial America* (New York: Hill & Wang, 1996).

—Caryn E. Neumann

Johnson, Samuel (1696–1772)

Anglican priest, philosopher, and educator, Samuel Johnson was born on October 14, 1696, in Guilford, CONNECTICUT, the second child of Mary Sage and Samuel Johnson, Sr., a farmer and operator of a mill. By age five Johnson was studying Hebrew, and at the local grammar school he learned Greek and Latin. He graduated from the Collegiate School at Saybrook in 1714 and became a tutor at his alma mater that moved in 1716 to New Haven, where it is now Yale University. He received the Master of Arts degree in 1717. Three years later Johnson was ordained and installed by the Connecticut Congregational Association as minister of the nearby West Haven Church. In 1722 he and several ministerial associates created excitement at Yale's commencement by announcing their conversion to the Church of England. After Johnson's Episcopal ordination, he was assigned to the Stratford parish. He organized a regional convention of Anglican clergy, campaigned for the appointment of an Anglican bishop, and established a rectory school where he prepared numerous young men to study for the priesthood.

Simultaneously, Johnson continued his scholarly activities. He was especially interested in encyclopedias. His publications reflected the ideas of the enlightenment. Johnson's scholarship won him an honorary doctorate from Oxford in 1743 and the presidency of KING'S COLLEGE (later Columbia) in NEW YORK CITY in 1754. He implemented an unusually broad curriculum and initiated a building program. He resigned the presidency in 1763 and returned to Stratford, where he again became the rector of its ANGLICAN CHURCH.

His family life was often tragic. In 1725 he married Charity Floyd Nicoll, a New York widow with two sons and a daughter, and they had two sons. After she died in 1756, he married Sara Beach in 1761. During the next two years he lost through death his second wife, a son, two stepchildren, and a grandson. He died in Stratford in 1772.

Further reading: Joseph J. Ellis, *The New England Mind in Transition: Samuel Johnson of Connecticut, 1696–1772* (New Haven, Conn.: Yale University Press, 1973).

—John B. Frantz

Johnson, Sir William (1715–1774)

As superintendent of northern Indian affairs, Sir William Johnson served as the main linchpin between the Six Nations of the IROQUOIS Indians and the BRITISH EMPIRE during the middle decades of the 18th century. Soon after migrating to North America from Ireland in 1738, Johnson cultivated relations with the Mohawk, the eastern nation of the Iroquois, through involvement in the local Indian trade. Johnson proved an extremely effective middleman: He appropriated Indian dress and mastered their political etiquette. After the death of his first wife, a German indentured servant, he became intimately involved with two tribal women, with whom he had two sets of children. He took Molly Brant, the sister of Chief Joseph Brant, as his common-law wife. His ease at adopting Indian customs won him friendship and respect. He received the Indian name Warraghiyagey ("one who does much business") as a mark of esteem, yet Johnson was first and foremost an agent of empire whose political and cultural loyalties remained firmly rooted in Anglo-American society. Throughout his career Johnson fashioned a British–Iroquois alliance that served imperial interests: namely, to promote a cost-effective FUR TRADE, to facilitate colonial accumulation of Indian lands, and to enlist Indian political and military support against the French.

Johnson came to prominence during KING GEORGE'S WAR (1774–78) when the NEW YORK governor employed him to enlist the services of Mohawk warriors. Johnson's success raised his profile among imperial officials and facilitated his appointment to the newly created office of superintendent of Indian affairs in 1754. During the SEVEN YEARS' WAR (1754–63) he employed intercultural skills to prevent the Iroquois from siding with the French. His manorial estate, Fort Johnson, functioned as the diplomatic headquarters of the Anglo-Iroquois alliance. In addition, Johnson recruited warriors from all Six Nations to participate in the war and led a number of campaigns, including the Battle of Lake George in 1755 and the defeat of Fort Niagara in 1759. Military success earned him the title of baronet.

Following the war Johnson participated in strenuous efforts to create a system of regulations for the Indian trade. Financial constraints coupled with a new political climate prevented successful implementation. Johnson also convened peace negotiations with Indian nations who had taken up arms during Pontiac's Rebellion (1763–5). The climax of Johnson's career came with the Fort Stanwix Treaty (1768), when he renegotiated a boundary line with the Six Nations, separating Indian country from white settlement. Johnson spent the remaining years of his life consolidating his position as a major New York land baron. Close ties with the Mohawk enabled him to become the largest landowner in the Mohawk Valley, and he settled hundreds of tenant families on his estate. In 1763 Johnson built an even larger home, Johnson Hall, and by the time of his death in 1774 he had founded his own community named Johnstown.

Further reading: Gail D. Danvers, "Gendered Encounters: Warriors, Women and William Johnson" (*Journal of American Studies*, 35:2, 2001); Milton W. Hamilton, *Sir William Johnson: Colonial American, 1715–1763*. Port Washington, N.Y.: Kennikat Press, 1976); Timothy J. Shannon, "Dressing for Success on the Mohawk Frontier: Hendrick, William Johnson, and the Indian Fashion" (*William & Mary Quarterly*, 3rd ser., 53:1, 1996, 13–42).

—Gail D. Danvers

Johnston, Henrietta Deering (1670?–1729)

Henrietta Deering became Gideon Johnston's (1668–1716) second wife in 1705 in Dublin, inheriting four stepchildren. Her new husband was a Trinity-educated clergyman deeply in debt who decided to immigrate to North America with the assistance of the SOCIETY FOR THE PROPAGATION OF THE GOSPEL. Arriving in CHARLESTON, SOUTH CAROLINA, in 1708, they found that a rival clergyman had taken the position Gideon had been promised. Although the family received assistance from Governor Nathaniel Johnson, they kept afloat because Henrietta Johnston was an accomplished, self-taught portrait artist. She quickly attracted the patronage of leading families, who valued her eye for their rich and elegant CLOTHING and possessions. Unusually, she worked in pastels, which were rare in England and unknown in America.

Through these years her husband, who eventually regained his church living, was frequently ill, and the couple lost their only child, Charles, to a CHILDHOOD fever. Often mocked for being Irish, they formed close ties to the powerful French Huguenot community in South Carolina. In 1711 Henrietta Johnston returned to England to buy ART supplies and to successfully petition the society for more support. She also carried samples of Carolina rice to buyers in London. As she returned to North America, her husband traveled to England to enroll his sons and Prince George of the Yamasee Indians in school. While he was gone, Henrietta weathered two hurricanes and the Yamasee War, during which she harbored numerous refugees in the parsonage. Gideon Johnston died in 1716, when his sloop overturned while he was seeing Governor Charles Craven off to England.

As sole support of the family, Henrietta continued to produce portraits, in 1725 following John Moore to New York to answer the commissions of leading families. Significantly, Johnston's sketches of elite members of Charleston society are frequently their only existing likenesses.

—Margaret Sankey

Jolliet, Louis (1645–1700)

Louis Jolliet is best known for exploring the upper Mississippi River with JACQUES MARQUETTE. At age 10 Jolliet entered the Jesuit college at Quebec to prepare for the priesthood. Attracted by the economic opportunities and adventures of the FUR TRADE, he ceased his clerical training and focused on becoming a COUREUR DE BOIS. For several years Louis Jolliet engaged in trade, EXPLORATION, and diplomatic activities. On June 4, 1671, he signed a declaration at Sault Ste. Marie when Simon Daumont de Saint-Lusson secured formal possession of a vast area of land extending from Hudson Bay to the Pacific Ocean east to west and south to the Gulf of Mexico for French king Louis XIV.

Learning that a great river, perhaps a route to China, existed, Marquette wanted to explore it. In October 1672 Jolliet became partners with six coureurs de bois and traveled to the St. Ignace mission at Michillimakinac to join Marquette. By May 1673 the adventurers began canoeing in the headwaters of the river. Within a month they reached the Mississippi River. Heading south, they occasionally stopped at Native American villages along the shores. In July, worried about possible capture by the Spanish in FLORIDA, the group turned around at the modern-day border of Arkansas and LOUISIANA after determining that the river flowed into the Gulf of Mexico. This journey secured long-standing Native American–French alliances in the Mississippi Valley.

En route, Jolliet's diary and maps charting the tributaries of the river were ruined when rapids overturned his canoe, so he recreated both from memory. In New France Jolliet secured grants to pursue fur trading, establishing a company on the St. Lawrence. He also undertook an overland journey to Hudson Bay in April 1679 to assess the threat of English traders to French interests. Refusing the English invitation to join their venture, Jolliet determined that the Hudson Bay area was Canada's best fur-producing region and speculated that the English consequently would dominate Canadian trade. Jolliet drew maps of the St. Lawrence River and kept an elaborate journal of his trip to Labrador in 1694. Three years later Jolliet was named a hydrography professor at the College of Quebec.

Further reading: Jean Delanglez, *Life and Voyages of Louis Jolliet, 1645–1700* (Chicago: Institute of Jesuit History, 1948).

—Elizabeth D. Schafer

journalism

Although the first newspaper published in the American colonies began in BOSTON in 1690, it proved to be a short-lived experience because government authorities suppressed it immediately. It was not until April 24, 1704, when *The Boston News-Letter* appeared, that the public could enjoy a regularly published newspaper, although only on a weekly basis. Other rival newspapers appeared in Boston quickly, and other cities followed suit as PHILADELPHIA, NEW YORK CITY, Annapolis, CHARLESTON, NEWPORT, and Williamsburg began publishing weeklies.

In 1727 the *Maryland Gazette,* the first newspaper in the province of Maryland and the oldest continuous surviving newspaper, was established at Annapolis by William Parks. At this time there were but six other newspapers published in America. The *Gazette* was discontinued in 1736 but revived again in 1745 under the management of Jonas Green. It is still published today and has been called the "flourishing patriarch of American journals."

By 1775 37 weekly newspapers existed in 11 colonies. These newspapers were similar in structure, usually a small weekly folio, four pages in length, with the following format: Page one contained foreign news; page two, domestic news; page three, local news; and page four, advertisements. Political news and the proceedings of legislative bodies aroused lively interest. Issues including ABOLITIONISM, religion, women's rights, EDUCATION, and medical discoveries highlighted the news. Specific events, such as the trial of JOHN PETER ZENGER, the GREAT AWAKENING, the STONO REBELLION, the SEVEN YEARS' WAR, the

Stamp Act Crisis, and the Boston Tea Party appeared in colonial weeklies.

Rather than articles penned by reporters, important letters and documents were often quoted at length. This became particularly critical when issues welded people together in their resistance to Britain beginning in 1763. Although local news was sometimes negligible, advertisements told the story of the ECONOMY, society, and cultural events of a particular town or region. Essays and poetry sometimes filled a considerable portion of newspapers, especially in Benjamin Franklin's *Pennsylvania Gazette*. The use of an occasional editorial cartoon, such as Franklin's famous "Join or Die" woodcut advocating uniting of the colonies during the Seven Years' War, also appeared.

Besides newspapers, early Americans wrote autobiographies, journals, and political pamphlets. These authors sometimes described their own experiences, meditating on their lives, seeking to attract settlers to the colonies, defending a particular religious view, or attacking specific governmental policies. Examples of 17th-century chroniclers include JOHN SMITH, WILLIAM BRADFORD, JOHN WINTHROP, and COTTON MATHER, while 18th-century examples include ROBERT BEVERLEY and WILLIAM BYRD II.

A second phase of American journalism after 1750 was greatly influenced by the Enlightenment. By the middle of the 18th century, the colonists became more aware of the efforts of Sir Isaac Newton and others to explain the mechanical laws of the universe and the philosophy of natural law. Writers began to emphasize rational thought, to think of history as possibly revealing the meaning of life, and to see institutions such as the law as having a life of their own. The works of Benjamin Franklin, Alexander Hamilton, Thomas Hutchinson, and David Ramsey are typical of the approach.

Except for what appeared in newspapers, secular LITERATURE was limited to the wealthy. Theological books did abound, but outside of the Bible and almanacs, the newspaper was the only printed medium found in most colonial family homes.

Further reading: David A. Copeland, *Debating the Issues in Colonial Newspapers: Primary Documents on the Events of the Period* (Westport, Conn.: Greenwood Press, 2000).

—James F. Adomanis

K

Kalm, Peter (1716–1779)

Peter (Pehr) Kalm was one of dozens of European travelers in North America who recorded their attempts to understand what the 18th-century North American landscape could teach them about the New World and what solutions it might provide for problems in AGRICULTURE and ecology in the Old World. A student of Swedish naturalist Carolus Linnaeus, who is best known for creating a hierarchical ranking of animal species, Kalm visited Norway, Finland, Russia, and North America on behalf of the Swedish Academy of Sciences, investigating what vegetation might be profitably transplanted to European soil. Traveling through Canada, NEW YORK, NEW JERSEY, and PENNSYLVANIA in the late 1740s, he compiled an extensive botanical diary. He also made contact with Americans who shared his interests, especially in PHILADELPHIA, where the scientific community surrounding the inquisitive Benjamin Franklin and the naturalist JOHN BARTRAM made him welcome. They encouraged his study of many aspects of American society, from ARCHITECTURE to Indian languages, geography, animal husbandry, and economics, as well as insects, agriculture, and plant experimentation. Kalm was especially fascinated with medicinal uses of plants, with vineyards, and with the possibilities for silk farming. Many Philadelphia QUAKERS, whose connections with men of similar interests in England gave them a rich knowledge of these subjects, willingly exchanged notes with him.

Kalm is best remembered for his insightful reports of his travels, including some early observations on the American national character, which he theorized was born out of the colonists' interactions with their ENVIRONMENT. He assessed their farming techniques as wasteful—"the easy method of getting a rich crop has spoiled [them]." He noted that the abundance of land in North America encouraged his profligacy by supporting mindless population growth, because no one need fear poverty and "a new-married man can, without difficulty, get a spot of ground, where he may sufficiently subsist with his wife and children." The result, said Kalm, was that the colonists had no incentive to learn efficient farming, hence their knowledge of agriculture was "imperfect." Kalm's observations, published in Sweden in 1753, were republished in English in 1770 as *Travels into North America, Containing its Natural History and a Circumstantial Account of its Plantations and Agriculture.* He is credited with being the first observer not only to catalog American flora and fauna but also to explore the dangers of Americans' thoughtless use of natural resources.

—Emma Lapsansky

Keith, William (1680–1749)

William Keith was one of the most competent and popular colonial governors in the 18th century. The son of Jean Smith and William Keith, a baronet, he was born in Scotland. As a young man he supported the return of the Stuart monarchy, for which he was jailed briefly in 1704. Keith won an appointment as surveyor general of the southern colonies in 1714, and three years later was appointed lieutenant governor of PENNSYLVANIA.

Keith wrote several important and influential reports to the British government, warning in particular about the threat of the French encircling the British colonies. He also advocated establishing a stamp tax to raise funds to pay for a standing army on the frontier. As governor, Keith was enormously popular among PHILADELPHIA ARTISANS, whom he courted to the disgruntlement of the city's wealthy MERCHANTS. When replaced as governor by Patrick Gordon, he was never able to regain his power.

Keith returned to Britain in 1728, where he was a Board of Trade adviser. However, he fell into considerable debt, and in 1734 he was sent to debtors' prison.

Further reading: Gary B. Nash, *Quakers and Politics, Pennsylvania 1681–1726* (Princeton, N.J.: Princeton University Press, 1968).

Kieft, Willem (1597–1647)

Willem Kieft became the third director general of New Netherland in 1638. Determined to impose order and discipline in the raucous polyglot colony, he imposed tough new penalties for those illegally involved in the FUR TRADE, restricted liquor licenses, regulated TOBACCO production, and instituted stringent punishments for those engaged in "adulterous intercourse with heathens, blacks and other persons." Shouldering out local men from decision making, Kieft ruled in an autocratic manner throughout his nine-year tenure.

Kieft's headaches only began with his unruly colonists. The English claimed title to all of New Netherland, prompting Kieft in his first years in office to purchase most of present-day Queens and Kings Counties from local Indians. Still, Kieft could not stem the flow of English colonists, expelled for heresy by the Calvinist colonies of PLYMOUTH and MASSACHUSETTS Bay, to various settlements on Long Island, nor could he do more than protest against the Swedish settlement on the DELAWARE River.

Kieft himself exhibited little of the self-control and moderation he expected from his subjects, particularly with respect to the native peoples in the region. In 1640 he levied taxes on the ALGONQUIN to support soldiers' salaries and the construction of FORTS under the pretense that the Dutch were protecting the local Indians from their enemies. When a band of Raritan resisted, Kieft falsely charged them with theft and authorized a raid that resulted in slaughter and plunder. The Raritan struck back, and so began an escalating conflict that plunged most of the native people around Fort Amsterdam into bloody confrontation with the Dutch for four years. Kieft's tactics included bounties on Indian heads, surprise night attacks, and raids on friendly Indians. Kieft's predicament became so grave that he armed the enslaved population, appealed to the English for help, and assembled committees of prominent men to advise him. Instead of rubber-stamping Kieft's actions, these committees clamored for more local control and eventually condemned the director general for the Indian wars that had decimated the colony. Their complaints resulted in Kieft's recall. After greeting his successor, PETER STUYVESANT, Willem Kieft boarded a ship that sank off the coast of Wales in September 1647.

Kieft's Indian policy effectively counterbalanced developments that attracted settlers, such as the loss of the DUTCH WEST INDIA COMPANY's trade monopoly and new land policies. By the end of Kieft's administration, New Netherland lay desolate and NEW AMSTERDAM's population had dwindled to 250 souls.

Further reading: Oliver A. Rink, *Holland on the Hudson: An Economic and Social History of Dutch New York* (Ithaca, N.Y.: Cornell University Press, 1986).

—Judy VanBuskirk

King George's War (1744–1748)

King George's War was the American conflict between France and England that paralleled the War of the Austrian Succession (1740–48) in Europe. The northern colonies were not expected to take a major part, but Governor William Shirley of MASSACHUSETTS persuaded his colony's assembly to approve a force of more than 4,000 volunteers to capture the French base at Louisbourg on Cape Breton Island. Motivated by anti-Catholic sermons and the promise of plunder, the province rallied enthusiastically. Assisted by a fleet under Sir Peter Warren that bombarded the fort, Louisbourg surrendered on June 27, 1745. The following spring a French fleet with 7,000 troops under the duc D'Anville headed to attack the British colonies, but it was decimated by SMALLPOX, scurvy, and storms.

Thereafter, the tide turned. An enthusiastic Shirley raised 7,500 New Englanders in hopes of conquering Canada in 1746. However, a promised British fleet never arrived, and NEW YORK, anxious to preserve its profitable and illegal trade with the French and Indians, refused to help. During the winter 900 of the 3,000 provincials who waited at Louisbourg for a British garrison to relieve them died of disease.

British naval vessels also impressed sailors in the colonies into the British navy, somewhat justifiably because American MERCHANTS encouraged deserters to operate their lucrative PRIVATEERING vessels. Two Louisbourg veterans were killed by a press gang in 1745, and in November 1747 the impressment of between 46 and 300 sailors in BOSTON harbor caused the inhabitants to form a crowd, take hostage British officers on shore, and provoke Captain Charles Knowles to threaten to blow up the town. America's first antiwar newspaper, *The Independent Advertiser,* founded by a young Samuel Adams and others, protested the expense of Shirley's expeditions in lives and money. For the first time in North America, the newspaper also used the doctrine of British philosopher JOHN LOCKE—that a government that failed to protect life, liberty, and property deserved to be resisted—to justify crowds (or "assemblies of the people") defending such rights.

At the Peace of Aix-la-Chapelle Britain exchanged Louisbourg for Madras in India, leaving unsettled the frontier between Canada and New England. Although Britain reimbursed Massachusetts 183,000 British pounds for war expenses, the colony was bitter that its conquest was so lightly disregarded by a mother country whose sea captains had also proven insensitive to the monumental efforts of the province.

Further reading: Douglas E. Leach, *Roots of Conflict: British Armed Forces and Colonial Americans, 1677–1763* (Chapel Hill: University of North Carolina Press, 1986).

—William Pencak

King Philip's War (1675–1676)

King Philip's War saw Indians in southern New England desperately and violently try to preserve their autonomy in the face of English encroachment. Before 1675 different Indian groups had pursued different strategies to cope with English expansion. For example, many of the surviving members of the Massachusetts tribe accommodated the English by converting, outwardly at least, to Christianity; other Indians had submitted to colonies, as when the Wampanoag swore their loyalty to PLYMOUTH in return for the promise of protection; finally, some, such as the Mohegan and NARRAGANSETT, formed strong alliances with colonies, going so far as to support the English in the PEQUOT WAR. The effectiveness of all these strategies was limited, but they had led to a delicate balance of power in the region. Nevertheless, the Indian population declined steadily in the face of dramatic English growth. Making matters worse, the economic position of Indians had been weakened by the decline of the FUR TRADE and decreased demand for WAMPUM.

In 1675 the Wampanoag, led by METACOM, or, as the English knew him, King Philip, opted to sever their ties of loyalty to Plymouth when that colony executed three Wampanoag for the death of John Sassamon, a Christian Indian. Wampanoag attacked the settlement of Swansea, killing a handful of settlers. Whether they intended to start a large war is unclear, but the English colonies quickly united in an effort to suppress what they perceived to be a rebellion. Even so, English efforts failed, and their poor treatment of nonhostile Indians forced many, including the Narragansett, Nipmuc, and those of the CONNECTICUT River Valley north of Springfield, into alliance with the Wampanoag. More disturbing, in an action that was analogous to the internment of Japanese citizens by the United States in World War II, the English herded up loyal Christian Indians and confined them to a windswept island in BOSTON harbor.

The Wampanoag and their allies initially prosecuted the war effectively, forcing the English to abandon many settlements in western MASSACHUSETTS. They relied on quick surprise attacks wherein fire was their most effective weapon. They were also aided by the internal squabbles of the English, as old disputes over colonial borders and new arguments over the morality of the war surfaced among the colonists. However, their success proved short lived. The English learned to rely more heavily on their

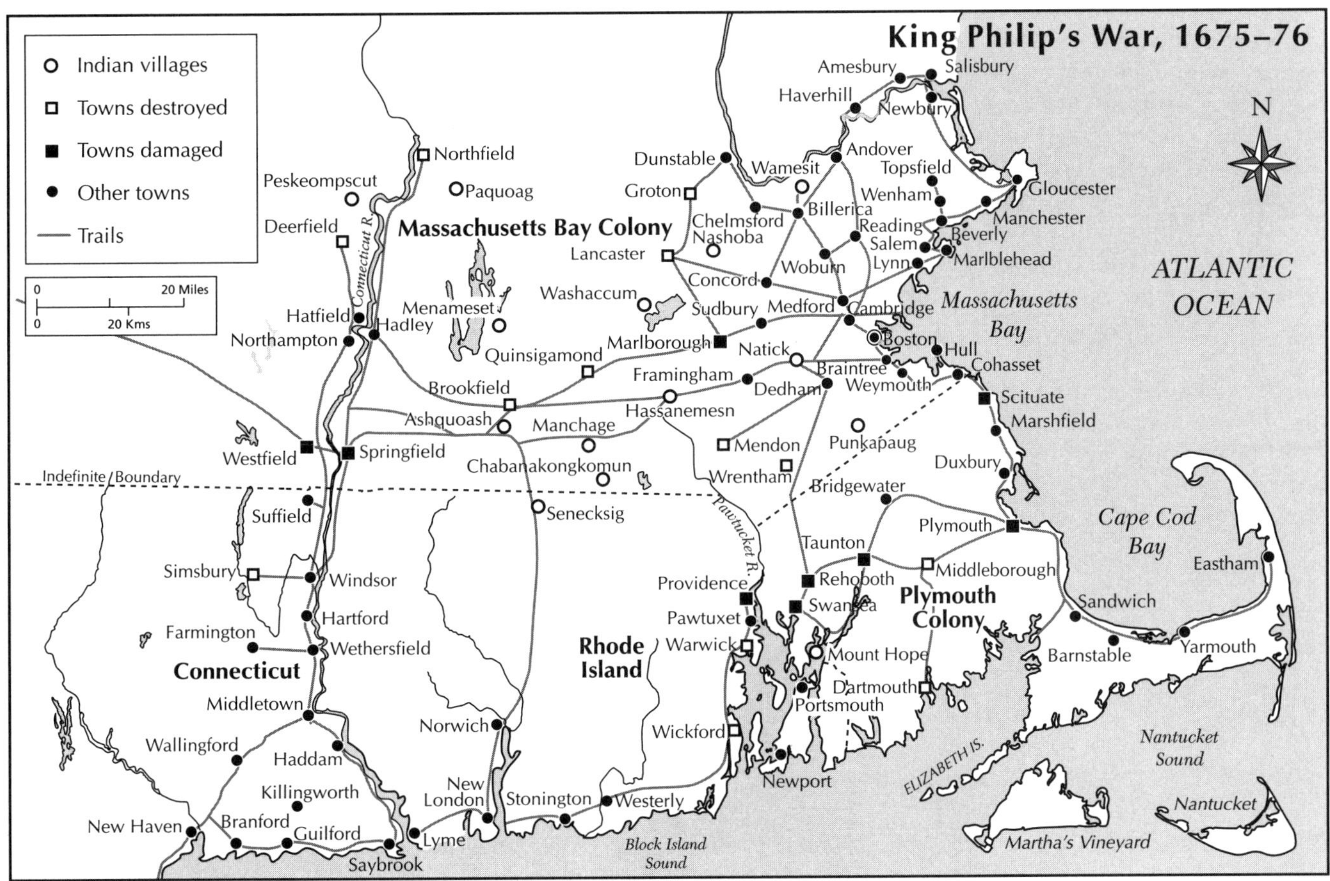

Indian allies, including the Mohegan and those Christian Indians earlier confined in Boston harbor. Equally important, during the winter of 1675–76, Metacom's forces sought safety in NEW YORK, only to be attacked by the Mohawk. By spring and summer of 1676 large numbers of Indians were surrendering to the English, and those who continued to fight saw themselves pursued by English troops invigorated by Indian allies. In August 1676 an Indian loyal to the English killed Philip, and the conflict bearing his name ended.

The war destroyed the possibility of a biracial society and intensified hatreds associated with a latent frontier mentality. Indians had suffered the most in the war, and the depletion of their population significantly reduced their influence in the region. The percentage of NATIVE AMERICANS in the region declined from one-fourth to one-tenth. Indians died not only from combat wounds and disease, but the English sold many of their Indian captives into SLAVERY. The removal of so many Indians from New England destabilized the region as colonists disputed the morality of the war and their entitlement to Indian land. These disputes eventually contributed to the establishment of the DOMINION OF NEW ENGLAND in 1686 and the temporary loss of colonial autonomy. Those Indians who survived the war and remained in New England followed a wide variety of paths, but all found their actions more tightly restricted. Many found themselves working as servants for the English and unable to recreate their past community ties. Outside of New England the results of King Philip's War favored the Mohawk. They forged an alliance with New York that proved to be the seeds of the Covenant Chain, a series of English-Indian alliances that shaped relations in the Northeast well into the next century. The memory of King Philip's War and the way that contemporaries wrote about it helped determine relations between Indians and Anglo-Americans into the 19th century.

Further reading: James D. Drake, *King Philip's War: Civil War in New England, 1675–1676* (Amherst: University of Massachusetts Press, 1999); Jill Lepore, *The Name of War: King Philip's War and the Origins of American Identity* (New York: Knopf, 1998).

—James D. Drake

King's College (Columbia University)

The founding of King's College reflected the ethnic, religious, and cultural controversies that had shaped colonial NEW YORK's society for almost a century before the college opened its doors. The issues of Dutch versus English leadership, of how Anglicized the colony's culture should become, about battles between locating the center of the colony's culture in NEW YORK CITY or elsewhere, and about the transformations brought by the GREAT AWAKENING all influenced the creation of the school that would one day be Columbia University.

The first mention of a college for the colony of New York was made by LEWIS MORRIS, who described the location as "the center of English American [and] . . . a proper place for a college" in a 1704 letter to the SOCIETY FOR THE PROPAGATION OF THE GOSPEL IN FOREIGN PARTS, but it was not until 1746 that the colony's governor, assembly, and council approved a lottery to raise £2,250 for that purpose. The school immediately became the subject of controversy. First, location was the issue. Advocates of a rural setting, among them CADWALLADER COLDEN, railed against the corruption of New York City, its tippling houses, and other base entertainments, but supporters of an urban college overcame that opposition. They raised £13,000 and secured land from Trinity Church in 1752 for the college's location.

The location controversy paled by comparison to the debate over religion at the College of New York. The Rev. SAMUEL JOHNSON, a former tutor at YALE COLLEGE who, like President Timothy Cutler, had converted from Congregationalism to the Church of England, led the charge for New York's college to be an Anglican institution. Cutler was both enthusiastic for his chosen faith and frightened at the widespread support for the GREAT AWAKENING and the colleges it inspired. In 1747 Johnson called the College of New Jersey (Princeton) "a fountain of Nonsense" and was angered that this "dissenting" institution, close to New York, would draw support away from the Anglican school he hoped to found.

William Livingston emerged as the leader of non-Anglicans in the college controversy. Raised in the DUTCH REFORMED CHURCH in Albany, Livingston was a 1741 graduate of Yale who had grown weary both of the religious revivalism going on around him and Thomas Clap's extreme orthodoxy at the college. Livingston and his supporters called for an enlightened, liberal arts curriculum that left theological study to the private hours of the students.

In November 1751 the New York legislature established a board of trustees comprised largely of Anglicans to oversee the school's lottery funds. Two years later that board chose Samuel Johnson as the first president of the college. In May 1754 the controversy flared up again, when Trinity Church repeated its offer of land for the college, but now required that its president always be an Anglican and that its religious services always be conducted in the forms of the Church of England. Livingston again led a vociferous opposition, stating that the church was not established in New York, that using lottery funds to support an Anglican institution was an insult to dissenters, that Trinity's first offer had no such requirements, and that the charter should be submitted to the assembly, not the governor. The trustees ignored the protests by Livingston and others, and on May 20 petitioned the governor and council for a charter. On June 4 Lieutenant Governor James DeLancey ordered the colony's attorney general to prepare a royal charter. Livingston and his supporters continued their dissent, waging a newspaper war and sending numerous petitions to the colonial assembly. On November 2 the governor signed the charter of the school, now to be known as King's College. The Anglican-dissenter controversy continued until December 1756, when the assembly agreed to allot half the funds raised by the lottery to the city of New York and half to the college.

Samuel Johnson served as president from 1754 to 1763 and established a curriculum that included the standard liberal arts, languages, and sciences as well as husbandry, surveying and navigation, history, geography, government, and commerce. Johnson's repeated goal as master of the college was educating and training New York's future elite in ideas that conformed with the Church of England. He showed little interest in educating pupils outside that goal, including the Society for the Propagation of the Gospel's plan during the SEVEN YEARS' WAR to send Indian students to the college.

Further reading: David C. Humphrey, *From King's College to Columbia, 1746–1800* (New York: Columbia University Press, 1976).

—George W. Boudreau

King William's War (1689–1697)

King William's War was the American equivalent of the War of the League of Augsburg in Europe, which began when King James II (1685–88) of England was overthrown by his son-in-law William III, stadtholder (chief executive officer) of the Netherlands, at the invitation of Parliament. James fled to the court of a fellow Catholic, Louis XIV of France, and warfare between French and English possessions began wherever common boundaries made it possible. In North America the English colonies failed to cooperate against the French. They were severely divided among themselves over the legitimacy of Jacob LEISLER'S REBELLION in NEW YORK and the ability of William Phips of MASSACHUSETTS to direct an intercolonial effort. As a result, for most of the war the mobile NATIVE AMERICANS allied with the French Canadians to raid upstate New York and the MAINE (then part of Massachusetts) frontier, more or less at will. The pro-English IROQUOIS in New York and Massachusetts's settlements in Maine, of which only three survived, endured most of the fighting.

The war's major effort was an expedition to conquer Canada undertaken in 1690 by Massachusetts. Commanded by Phips, it succeeded in capturing Port Royal in Acadia (Nova Scotia), but after reaching the walls of Quebec was forced to withdraw on October 25 as winter and a frozen St. Lawrence River loomed. Although only 30 of 1,300 Massachusetts men died in combat, perhaps 500 others perished from DISEASE and shipwrecks as the fleet of 32 ships was scattered by storms from Canada to the CARIBBEAN. The expedition put Massachusetts some 40,000 pounds in debt, forced it to adopt a depreciated paper currency, and led to the abandonment of many frontier towns. The early disastrous years of the war were undoubtedly one cause of the Salem WITCHCRAFT episode of 1692, because important people throughout Massachusetts believed Satan was the cause of their troubles. The only positive result of the Quebec Campaign was that it showed the loyalty of the province to Britain and may have won a more liberal royal charter for Massachusetts, with Phips as governor. The Peace of Ryswyck, signed in 1697, settled nothing in North America.

Further reading: Richard R. Johnson, *Adjustment to Empire: The New England Colonies, 1675–1715* (New Brunswick, N.J.: Rutgers University Press, 1981).

—William Pencak

Knight, Sarah Kemble (1666–1727)

Madam Knight, as she is often called, made a journey in the fall of 1704 from BOSTON to New Haven and NEW YORK CITY. Along the way she kept a journal that recorded not only the progress of her trip, but also her thoughts and observations, providing a detailed glimpse of daily life in colonial New England. Sarah Kemble was raised in Boston, where she married Richard Knight by 1689. She kept a writing school, hence her title of "Madam," supposedly with young Benjamin Franklin as a pupil. She also possibly kept a stationery store in her large house. Several boarders lodged in her house, and, unusually for a woman, she involved herself in a variety of legal matters on their behalf and her own.

Madam Knight made her 1704 trip to settle the estate of her cousin Caleb Trowbridge on behalf of his young widow. Filled with an urbane Bostonian snobbishness, Knight's journal presents the rustic, rural, and difficult nature of people and travel. Sarah Knight's personal journal was left in manuscript form until 1825 when it was published under the title *The Journals of Madam Knight, and Rev. Mr. Buckingham.* Her journal distinguishes her as one of the rare women, and also one of the few secular, authors of the colonial period. Her journal is a travelogue liberally sprinkled with occasional verses and filled with picaresque characters like the country "bumpkin," chewing TOBACCO, spitting, and staring around "like a Catt let out of a Baskett." She viewed local native "Indians of the Country" as "savages" because of their failure to become more like the

English settlers. She describes the dark and hazardous roads of the time, the fording of streams, and the rustic lodgings along the way. One amusing episode finds Madam Knight being kept awake all night by several other lodgers loudly drinking rum in the room next to hers.

Madam Knight left no other writings. She followed her daughter to the New London/Norwich area of CONNECTICUT, where she continued her small business dealings until her death, leaving a sizable estate of £1,800.

Further reading: Malcolm Freiberg, ed., *The Journal of Madam Knight* (Boston: D. R. Godine, 1972).

—Stephen C. O'Neill

Kuhn, Justus Engelhardt (unknown–1717)

A German émigré, Kuhn arrived in MARYLAND in 1706 and painted for a time in Annapolis, where he specialized in portraits of several interrelated Catholic families, the Carrolls, the Digges, and the Darnalls. Rather than focusing on the personal character or physical attributes of his subjects, Kuhn's work illustrated the abundance of their estates. His portrait *Eleanor Darnall*, painted about 1710, is remarkable for its depiction of a vast plantation of large gardens replete with multiple buildings, fountains, and colonnades. In this portrait the sitter Eleanor, daughter of Maryland aristocrats, stands before an elegant balustrade in diminished proportion to an elaborately decorated vase nearby. Framing her are heavy draperies and flowers, and beyond the balustrade, a seemingly un-attenuated formal landscape. Kuhn also painted a portrait of Eleanor's brother. The setting for *Henry Darnall III* was similar and contains what is thought to be the first American depiction of a black person, one of the family servants. Undoubtedly, Kuhn's patrons appreciated the artistic magnification of their assets. According to his contemporaries, Kuhn held aristocratic pretensions. It was noted that his accouterments were so fine that one would not suspect he was a painter.

Kuhn is the earliest documented portrait painter in the American South. Only one of his 10 known works was signed, his portrait *Ignatius Digges* in 1710. Kuhn was buried in Anne Arundel County, Maryland.

—Catherine Goetz

L

labor

The history of labor in colonial America covers more than 200 years, spans a vast geography, and includes important regional diversity. Adding to the complexity, laborers themselves often left little written record, making it difficult to piece together the experiences and stories of their lives. A common theme, however, does appear. Until well into the 18th century, scarcity describes labor everywhere. Potential employers complained that even if laborers were available, wages were too high. This lament came from TOBACCO producers in the Chesapeake area as well as ARTISANS in the port cities. Labor shortages were the result of the rich natural resources found in the colonies, primarily land. Colonists had less need to work for someone when they could own land.

Colonists turned to a variety of solutions to solve some of the problems created by labor scarcity. The three major port cities, BOSTON, PHILADELPHIA, and NEW YORK CITY, and the Middle Colonies blended bound with free workers. The plantation owners in the southern, Chesapeake, and West Indian colonies responded to the shortage of workers by depending primarily on unfree laborers.

Colonial America contained three distinct types of unfree labor—apprentices, indentured servants, and slaves. Each form was used in varying degrees in every colony. However, the nature of each system varied. Apprentices combined EDUCATION with labor. Apprentices were bound to a master for a period of years, and in exchange for obedience and work the master provided FOOD, CLOTHING, lodging, and training in the "art and mysteries" of a trade. The colonial system of apprenticeship came from England, where it was intended to supply society with skilled labor and at the same time to reduce the burden of supporting orphaned and other poor children.

Apprenticeship did little to relieve the labor shortage in the colonies. Unlike servants and slaves, apprentices came primarily from the native-born population. More important, because they started their service at a very young age, they contributed little in terms of labor, often being relegated to running errands, sweeping floors, lighting and tending fires, and other odd jobs. Older apprentices gained the skills that enabled them to participate more fully in the labor force. Apprentices served artisans most often, although masters who also taught skills ranged from doctors to lawyers, seamstresses to domestic service.

INDENTURED SERVITUDE contributed greatly to easing the labor shortage in the colonies. Between one-half and two-thirds of white immigrants from Great Britain and continental Europe immigrated as indentured servants. The vast majority of colonial servants labored in the agricultural sector. Most entered into servitude because they were too poor to finance their own passage to the colonies and were willing to exchange service for a specified period of time, usually three to four years, for the price of their transportation.

African SLAVERY provided the bulk of workers in the southern colonies, especially after 1700. The brutal system reduced human beings to property. In the early 17th century little distinction apparently existed between servants and slaves. Gradually, white colonists passed laws that bound African slaves for life and passed this condition on to the slaves' children.

The Chesapeake Area and Lower South

Although the economies of the Chesapeake area and the Lower South developed differently, both regions relied on staple crops that required intensive labor. In the Chesapeake area planters grew primarily tobacco; in the Lower South they focused their energies on rice and INDIGO. The first JAMESTOWN settlers in 1607 worried very little about labor. Many assumed that they could grow rich in Virginia on its natural abundance. They were so confident that they would not have to work that the first ships transported a large percentage of gentlemen (who would not work because of their status) and skilled craftsmen, like silversmiths and jewelers, who could extract precious metals and stones. If they did need labor, the colonists fully expected to mold the local Indians into a labor force.

Nothing went according to plan. Death stalked the colonists, and gold and silver were nowhere to be found. In addition, the Indians understandably refused to work for them. JOHN ROLFE introduced the one ray of hope for Jamestown beginning in 1612, when he discovered that the lands of Virginia were well suited for the cultivation of tobacco. At that time the English smoked tobacco for its medicinal qualities. This changed, however, when regular shipments of the weed arrived from the New World. People increasingly smoked for pleasure, and the demand for the "jovial weed" rose dramatically. Tobacco helped solve the colony's financial problems, but it had a hidden difficulty. The cultivation of tobacco was labor intensive—it required many workers over a long planting, growing, and harvesting season.

The VIRGINIA COMPANY OF LONDON, the joint-stock company in charge of promoting and developing Virginia, indentured young English people to solve their immediate labor needs. These servants entered into servitude for the company by exchanging the cost of their transportation to VIRGINIA and food, shelter, and clothing for seven years of service. The company promised this first group of servants a share in the profits from the colony. The company, however, struggled financially and devised another system to entice people to sign on as servants. Instead of buying and shipping the servants, the company encouraged anyone who planned to immigrate to Virginia to pay the costs of their own servants' travel. For each servant transported, the master received 50 acres of land. The company also promised land to the servants as part of their freedom dues. According to the first population census in 1625, more than 40 percent of Virginia's residents were indentured servants; almost all of them had emigrated from England.

About three-quarters of the 75,000 whites who immigrated to the Chesapeake colonies from Britain between 1630 and 1680 came as indentured servants. Masters struggled with how to force servants to labor under harsh, inhospitable conditions when they lacked economic motivation. In a sense, servants were prepaid by their transportation to the colonies. They did not earn any additional benefit from their labor. Gradually, legislators devised a legal system that devoted a great deal of attention to controlling servants' behavior. If servants ran away, masters could add time to their contracts, whip them, crop their hair, or, if they absconded habitually, brand them. The laws licensed masters to use "reasonable" force if they needed to exert control over their servants.

For the first 50 years of Virginia's existence, servants were the machines that grew tobacco. Gradually, toward the end of the 17th century, slaves began to replace servants. This transformation occurred for a number of reasons. As economic conditions and workers' incomes improved in England, the supply of servants dwindled while the demand for labor continued to increase. Simultaneously, the availability and relative costs of slaves decreased. During the early 17th century high MORTALITY rates made it more cost effective to invest in the short-term service of a servant than in the more expensive slave for life. As the risk of early death diminished and when the Royal African Company's monopoly on the SLAVE TRADE ended in 1698, the costs of Africans decreased, and planters turned to slaves. The decline in mortality also meant that more servants survived their servitude and collected their land. In addition, Chesapeake area planters feared that they would compete in the tobacco market. Because slaves served for life, they posed no risk of competition.

The cycle of tobacco production extended over an entire calendar year. The heaviest labor occurred during the late summer and early fall, but the crop demanded almost daily attention. Because tobacco required so much care, it was well suited for gang labor, small units of about eight to 10 workers. This allowed the tobacco master or overseer to command close supervision of the workers; one member of the gang often set the pace for the group. The slaves who labored in the tobacco fields worked from sunup to sundown, and because their workday was organized around time rather than output, they had little incentive to work quickly. Although masters adhered to strict GENDER division of labor regarding white women and would not place female servants in the fields, they had no reservations about black women. Through the 18th century black women outnumbered men as field workers, and they were often joined by black children.

The story of staple crop development and labor unfolded differently in the Lower South. SOUTH CAROLINA's settlers came primarily from the West Indies and arrived with their slaves. The system of labor did not evolve from one dependent on white servitude to one dependent on black slavery. Rather, slaves were present in the colony from its inception. In the early decades of the colony, no single crop dominated production. By the second generation planters focused their energies on rice. Rice was not part of the English diet, but planters recognized its potential value because it was an important dietary staple in southern Europe. Even though the boggy soils of the Carolinas were perfectly suited for rice cultivation, the first attempts failed because planters did not know enough about what they were doing. Successful rice cultivation coincided with the arrival of a large number of West Africans who were familiar with rice production. They introduced the style of planting, cultivating, cooking, and even singing work songs that provided the rhythms of production. The key role they played did not soften the effects of slavery. Ironically, the slaves' ability to grow rice moved the colony more quickly toward a heavy reliance on slave labor.

The cycle of rice cultivation lasted for more than a year, with the most intense activity at midsummer and midwinter. Unlike tobacco, rice growing featured slack periods, and slaves often ended their day before sunset. Nevertheless, rice demanded heavy work, and it was grown near swamplands and stagnant waters that bred DISEASE.

During the mid-18th century Carolina planters developed an additional export crop, indigo. The best varieties of indigo also came from the West Indies, and West African skills contributed to its successful cultivation. Indigo plantations reeked from the smells of fermenting plants, and the odors attracted swarms of flies and other insects.

Both rice and indigo required large labor forces, and planters turned to a number of sources. As in the Chesapeake area, local Indians refused to work for them or often died from European diseases if they were enslaved. Planters imported some indentured servants but never in sufficient numbers to satisfy their labor needs. They relied most heavily on African slaves, who provided more than just their labor. West African expertise allowed for the successful production of rice and indigo. By the third decade of the 18th century, blacks constituted a majority of the South Carolina population.

Caribbean

The history of labor in the Anglo-CARIBBEAN mirrored that of the Chesapeake area in that the labor force shifted from white indentured workers to African slaves. However, this transformation of labor occurred far earlier than in MARYLAND and Virginia. During the first four decades of the 17th century, the majority of laborers were indentured servants from England, Wales, Scotland, and Ireland. During the 1640s Barbados planters began to realize the advantages of slave labor. Unlike servants, slaves served for life and could be treated far more harshly. As the island's sugar industry developed, planters increasingly invested in slave labor. Although the smaller islands followed a similar labor pattern, they did so a bit later.

Planters preferred that slave cargoes include a balanced gender ratio, and in the early years of the slave trade an almost equal number of men and women were shipped to the Caribbean. Over time the slave trade consisted almost exclusively of men. Because women played essential roles in agricultural production, African societies could ill afford to lose them; they considered men to be more expendable.

Middle Colonies and New England

No staple crop dominated agricultural production in the Middle Colonies and New England, and the demand for labor consequently was less intense. Most farmers in these regions practiced a mixed AGRICULTURE and depended on family members for labor. Immigrants to New England settled in townships and divided the lands among the household units. PENNSYLVANIA families gathered in villages, and land was distributed to families based on their status. NEW YORK developed the most unusual organization. In some regions originally settled by the Dutch, patroons controlled vast amounts of land worked by tenant farmers; in newer regions families cultivated smaller acreages.

Immigrants to New England in the 1630s often brought servants with them. They realized how much labor was involved in creating new settlements. However, once these servants achieved their freedom, they were not replaced. Indentured labor never played a significant role in the labor force. Perhaps one-quarter of all MASSACHUSETTS families owned servants. New England farm families did require additional labor, especially during harvesting, building, and birthing. They preferred to rely on their children or, if necessary, exchange or hire labor for specific days and tasks.

Pennsylvania's founding generation predicted that labor would be scarce. The Free Society of Traders, the joint-stock company in charge of the colony's development, planned to import servants and slaves. As in the colonies to the north, unfree laborers did play an important role in establishing the first farms. Approximately 271 servants and between 400 and 500 slaves resided in Pennsylvania in the early decades. By the early 18th century the demand for unfree labor shifted from the rural to the urban sector. By the 18th century Philadelphia accounted for a disproportionate number of unfree laborers. Throughout the history of the colony, servants and slaves were members of interchangeable labor forces. Residents preferred the labor of white servants, but when they were in short supply they bought slaves.

Gendered Division of Labor

Households everywhere participated in a gendered division of labor. Women had primary responsibility for the house and children, and among middling and poorer families they also cultivated gardens. Men were relegated to the fields. During periods of peak labor demand, this structure altered somewhat. For example, in Pennsylvania when wheat and hay were harvested, men and women formed teams. Women operated slightly lighter scythes and helped reap and pile the grain. Haying followed, and because the scythes for this were considerably heavier, women trailed the men and spread the grass to dry. Both men and women loaded the hay onto the wagons.

This engraving shows a colonial carpenter at work. *(Library of Congress)*

Households participated in a range of activities in which the roles of men and women were interdependent. In textile production, for example, men assumed the primary responsibility for growing the flax. Women might do some weeding, but their most important contribution was turning the flax into cloth and then making items of clothing. The economic status of the household dictated to a large extent the ways in which women spent their time. Women in middling families devoted a large percentage of their labor to food preparation and preservation. They performed the labor themselves or with the assistance of their daughters. Upper-CLASS women were responsible for the same range of tasks but were more likely to supervise servants than to perform the work themselves. Women in poorer families maintained their households and took care of their children. They also supplemented their families' incomes in various ways. In the cities they took in washing or sewing for a small fee or scavenged in the streets for discarded items; in rural areas they might weed gardens or gather vegetables in exchange for food.

Women contributed to the economic well-being of their families beyond their household tasks. They were involved in an often hidden but essential network that exchanged goods and services. These rarely involved cash but constituted an important part of their families' incomes. Women who made cheese, for example, might trade with a neighbor for candles or preserves. Women also tended the sick, pulled flax together, and assisted at a birth. New England PURITANS demonstrated how they valued women's work by attaching a symbolic value to their labor. For each man who arrived in the colonies without his family, the Massachusetts Court of Assistance offered him cash to be used to hire the services usually performed by a wife.

The value of women's labor eroded in the 18th century. Key to this shift was the transformation of the ECONOMY. Although women were always subservient to men, this position did not affect their essential contributions to the household economy. During the 18th century money played an increasingly larger role, and market consciousness expanded. Consequently, the value of labor came to be measured more in terms of cash. While women's work remained virtually unchanged and they continued to labor in the home, they received little external cash value. Women were no longer considered to be part of the "real economy," as domestic labor had become marginalized.

See also CONVICT LABOR.

Further reading: Philip Morgan, *Slave Counterpoint: Black Culture in the Eighteenth-Century Chesapeake and Lowcountry* (Chapel Hill: University of North Carolina Press, 1998); Gary B. Nash, *The Urban Crucible: Social Change, Political Consciousness, and the Origins of the American Revolution* (Cambridge, Mass.: Harvard University Press, 1979).

—Sharon V. Salinger

La Demoiselle ("Old Briton") (?–1752)

La Demoiselle, known among the British as "Old Briton," was an anti-French leader among the Miami Indians of Ohio during the mid-1740s. A Piankashaw by birth, La Demoiselle married into the tribe and became an influential war leader among the Miamis inhabiting the town of Kekionga on the Maumee River. Around 1745, he became involved in an emerging political dispute that centered upon the Miamis' wavering economic and military attachment to the French. Increasing trade prices had driven many Miami leaders, including La Demoiselle, to support a rebellion against the French-supported alliance chiefs who dominated the tribe's political leadership. In opposition to Piedfroid, the headman of Kekionga and a staunch supporter of the French alliance, La Demoiselle and his supporters attacked the French trading post at the town in 1747. Following this attack, La Demoiselle removed his followers to a new village along the Miami River, Pickawillany, where he forged union among anti-French Indian elements in the Ohio country and created a new trade relationship with the English. However, a smallpox epidemic and continued political factionalism among his supporters seriously undermined La Demoiselle's efforts. His rebellion came to a sudden halt in June 1752, when a French-led force of Ottawas and Chippewas sacked Pickawillany. La Demoiselle, who vowed never to return to the French alliance, was killed and most of his followers, unwilling to emulate his example, returned to the old alliance with the French.

Further reading: Richard White, *The Middle-Ground: Indians, Empires, and Republics in the Great Lakes Regions, 1650–1815* (New York: Cambridge University Press, 1991).

—Daniel P. Barr

land

The study of land policies in colonial North America falls into two general categories. One category examines England's efforts to claim title to North American territory. Another focuses on the transfer of land from the Crown to specific groups or individuals. In general, while England followed European customs, its land policies were not carefully conceived or uniformly applied.

Before England could claim possession of its "New World" territory, it had to establish the basis for those claims. The Crown based its original title on the commonly accepted right of discovery doctrine. This theory argued that any new territory not already under the dominion of a Christian or Muslim ruler was the property of those who "discovered" it. John Cabot's voyages to North America in 1497 and 1498 provided justification for English possession.

Spain also claimed North America, but England countered that Spain had not settled the territory, thus it forfeited any claims. This theory of *vacuum domicilium* (that people had a right to inhabit "unsettled land") was also used to justify usurping Native American land rights. Because the native population did not develop the land according to European models, England declared the land "vacant" and claimed title.

Although England did not recognize land ownership by NATIVE AMERICANS, it did hope to maintain peaceful relations with local Indians. For this reason officials sometimes negotiated treaties and made token payments to secure large tracts of lands. In PENNSYLVANIA, for example, land treaties between founder WILLIAM PENN and the Lenape Indians led to few tensions and a generally peaceful transfer of land. More often, however, officials obtained land through coercion, deception, or warfare. The PEQUOT Indians, for example, lost all their CONNECTICUT lands after a conflict with New England settlers in 1637. In the WALKING PURCHASE OF 1737 the Lenape Indians of Pennsylvania lost more than 1,000 acres due to British manipulation of treaty language. Indians were also forced to cede land when unable to pay debts to colonial MERCHANTS.

To minimize confusion and conflict, British officials discouraged individual land purchases between colonists and Indians. According to English interpretation, the land was the property of the king and only the Crown could authorize such transactions. Land transfer from the Crown to groups or individuals could occur in a number of ways, including grants, individual purchase, church or corporate group purchase, or by renting or squatting.

VIRGINIA, for example, began as a business venture organized by English stockholders. The company received a land grant, and each member who paid his own way to the colony was given a portion to settle plus a headright of 50 additional acres for each individual whom that member was paid to transport. In exchange for transport, these poor migrants worked as indentured servants for a fixed period of time (usually four to seven years). At the end of their term, many received a small tract of land as part of their "freedom dues." This system promoted the accumulation of large landholdings by original settlers and smaller holdings on less desirable land by poor laborers.

Other colonies, such as SOUTH CAROLINA and Pennsylvania, were settled through proprietary grants. These land grants were given by the king to reward friends or political supporters. The proprietors would then sell or rent the land and collect fees for its use. These fees, or quitrents, were generally between two and three shillings per acre and were used to help finance local governments. Land for the MASSACHUSETTS Colony was granted to a group of individuals who planned to establish religious communities. Plots of land were distributed to families for private settlement, with some held in reserve for public use.

As the colonial population grew, land was transferred through individual sales and inheritances as well as by sales through land companies. Land speculators like Benjamin Franklin and George Washington often grew rich by purchasing western lands and then reselling them to new settlers a few years later.

While most property owners were men, single women could buy and sell property and married women might inherit a portion of land from their husbands' estates. When women married, their land became the property of their husbands unless a premarital agreement had been reached. Although it varied by colony, free black people could hold property. In 17th-century Virginia, for example, some black indentured servants received small plots of land when their terms of service concluded. However, these rights were curtailed by legislation in the final decades of the 17th century.

As the population increased, settlement spread westward. Many new settlers were squatters who claimed land ownership simply by their presence. Local officials, hoping to use backcountry settlements as a buffer between coastal communities and Native Americans, sometimes gave immigrants land. Officials also granted thousands of acres to land speculators. By the mid-18th century as many as two-thirds of white colonial families owned land.

Further reading: Allan Kulikoff, *From British Peasants to Colonial American Farmers* (Chapel Hill: University of North Carolina Press, 2001).

—Virginia Jelatis

La Salle, René-Robert Cavelier, sieur de (1643–1687)

Robert de La Salle, a nobleman from Rouen, France, arrived in Canada in 1667 determined to achieve fame as an explorer. He is best known for his voyages to the lower Mississippi River and Gulf Coast. La Salle departed Canada in 1682 and made his way down the Mississippi River, establishing peaceful contact with several major Native American groups in the region. On April 9, 1682, near the mouth of the Mississippi, La Salle formally claimed for France all lands drained by the great river. He named the area LOUISIANA in honor of King Louis XIV.

La Salle returned to France and gained the king's permission to plant a colony. Four ships containing nearly 300 soldiers, sailors, and settlers (including seven women) left France in 1684 bound for Louisiana. Instead of taking the familiar route by river from Canada, La Salle decided to approach Louisiana from the sea. Navigational errors caused the flotilla to miss the Mississippi River and instead make landfall in modern-day Texas. La Salle and the settlers were off-loaded and left with one ship, the *Belle,* which foundered and sank in 1686.

Discontent soon began to grow. When a crude fort was hastily constructed, living space in it was reserved for those of wealth and high rank. The common workingmen who built it slept outside, exposed to the elements. Disease, desertion, and occasional Indian raids steadily reduced their numbers and sapped their morale.

Mistakenly believing the Mississippi River to be nearby, La Salle made several fruitless attempts to locate it. Finally realizing his predicament, in 1687 La Salle departed with 17 men on an overland trek to Canada in search of assistance. Unhappy with La Salle's leadership, several of the men staged a mutiny and killed him. A few survivors escaped to finish the journey, but for those left at the settlement help came too late. Most of the settlers that embarked from France with La Salle perished in the New World. Although La Salle's colonization attempt was a spectacular failure, his exploration successfully established France's claim to the Louisiana territory and helped spur Spanish, French, and English interest in exploring the Gulf Coast region.

Further reading: Anka Muhlstein, *La Salle: Explorer of the North American Frontier* (New York: Arcade Publishing, 1994).

—Andrew C. Lannen

Leisler's Rebellion (1689–1691)

Leisler's Rebellion occurred when the predominantly Dutch population of New York ousted royal officials during rumors of political troubles in England. The uprising has been attributed to the threat posed to the Dutch community by English rule, fears of a Catholic plot, and CLASS conflict between rich and poor. Its leader, Jacob Leisler (b. 1641), was a German native who came to NEW NETHERLAND in 1660 as a soldier for the DUTCH WEST INDIA COMPANY; he joined the DUTCH REFORMED CHURCH in Manhattan a year later. He married the widow of a rich merchant, thus becoming one of the wealthiest men in the colony, and became a trader. Leisler gradually lost both money and influence in the 1680s as trading became more expensive and the English established political dominance.

When the GLORIOUS REVOLUTION (1688) took place, confusion reigned in New York, and Leisler seized the chance to restore his power. In June 1689 he gained military control of NEW YORK CITY by taking over Fort James and exploited the population's fear of French attack by sending his armed followers to search and detain all suspicious people. Leisler and other militia captains formed a committee of safety, with representatives from Westchester, Kings, Queens, Staten Island, and Manhattan Counties, and the committee proclaimed William of Orange to be king. In December 1689 Leisler assumed the roles of lieutenant governor and commander in chief of New York, while England appointed a new governor who did not set sail for the colony until the end of 1690. The uprising ended on March 20, 1691, when regular troops under the control of the governor marched to the fort to demand its surrender. Most militiamen who relinquished their arms were granted pardons. Leisler and his principal supporters were jailed for treason and murder resulting from a skirmish in which two English soldiers died. By May 32 Leislerians had been arrested, and eight were sentenced to death, including Leisler, who was hanged on May 16, 1691. The rebellion failed because Leisler misread the nature of the revolution, failed to comprehend the complexities of English court politics, and did not understand that New York was relatively insignificant on the English schedule of priorities.

Further reading: Charles Howard McCormick, *Leisler's Rebellion* (New York: Garland, 1989).

—Caryn E. Neumann

Le Moyne, Jean-Baptiste, sieur de Bienville (1680–1767)

A capable official in French LOUISIANA, Jean-Baptiste Le Moyne was born in Montreal and raised by his brothers, all of whom served in the navy with distinction. After a 1697 injury, Bienville visited France and, a year later, moved to Louisiana. In 1698 Bienville explored the Mississippi River, then became second in command of forces near present-day Biloxi, defending France's river claims. In this capacity he led diplomatic expeditions to native tribes. In 1700 Bienville took command of the new Fort de Mississippi, becoming the highest-ranking government official. An excellent planner and an able governor, over the next decade Bienville battled French neglect, famine, immoral clergy, and the hostility of local tribes.

Demoted in 1712, Bienville was forced to serve under the new leader, Antoine Lamothe, sieur de Cadillac, who advanced due to his finances and connections. Bienville joined the factionalism that paralyzed the government. During the feud Cadillac sent Bienville and 34 men to battle 800 Natchez, but Bienville defeated them through subterfuge. After Cadillac's recall Bienville again became governor, establishing NEW ORLEANS as an administrative center. Recognizing the need for a stable ECONOMY, Bienville encouraged the cultivation of sugar, cotton, TOBACCO, and rice and oversaw the importation of slaves. In 1724 he enacted the slave laws called the Code Noir. Humane for the time, the Code Noir was designed to completely regulate slave life.

Bienville tended to create conflict, and the leadership recalled him in 1724, although he returned as governor in 1732. He led two disastrous campaigns against the CHICKASAW and retired to France in 1739.

—Victoria C. H. Resnick

Lennox, Charlotte Ramsay (1720?–1804)

Heralded as the first American novelist, Charlotte Lennox (birth name Ramsay) was born sometime in the 1720s, although details of her early life are uncertain. Early biographical accounts indicate that she was born in 1720 in NEW YORK, the daughter of that colony's lieutenant governor; however, more recent accounts suggest that she was probably born several years later in Gibraltar, the daughter of James Ramsay, an officer in the British army who was later stationed in America. She lived in North America for only a brief time, probably from 1739 to 1743. She left New York for England in 1743, perhaps because her father died and she became the ward of her aunt, whom Charlotte Ramsay found to be insane on her arrival. Forced to fend for herself, she married Alexander Lennox, a printer, in October 1747. They had two children before separating in 1792.

Lennox turned to professional writing shortly after her marriage, first publishing poetry in *Poems on Several Occasions, Written by a Young Lady* (1747), and then producing novels. Her first celebrated work was *The Life and Times of Harriot Stuart* (1750), a semiautobiographical account of a young struggling woman. Together with *Euphemia* (1790), Lennox offers detailed descriptions of colonial New York life and relationships among the British, Dutch, and American Indians in the colony. In 1752 she produced *The Female Quixote,* which twists Cervantes's classic story to create a female heroine, Arabella, whose "madness" is that the romance fiction of the day was an accurate portrayal of society. Once unleashed, Arabella has a series of adventures that mix comedy with astute social criticism. The work was a tremendous success, winning the praise of SAMUEL JOHNSON, Henry Fielding, and Horace Walpole. Lennox continued to write, but none of her subsequent publications matched the success of *The Female Quixote.* She produced translations of French works and a collection of Shakespeare's plays, and she edited a women's magazine, *The Lady's Museum.* She also tried her hand at the THEATER, where she met with less success. Her rapid decline in literary circles after the production of her *Old City Manners* (1775) meant that she was impoverished by the time of her death.

Further reading: Miriam Rossiter Small, *Charlotte Ramsay Lennox: An Eighteenth-Century Lady of Letters* (New Haven, Conn.: Yale University Press, 1935).

—Troy O. Bickham

Leverett, John (1662–1724)

John Leverett was the first nonministerial president of HARVARD COLLEGE (1707–24). In his youth he attended Harvard College, receiving his B.A. in 1680 and his M.A. in 1683. In 1685 he and William Brattle were hired to serve as resident tutors at Harvard under absentee president INCREASE MATHER. The latitudinarian theological perspective they embraced began Harvard's shift away from the traditional Calvinism of its early years, through the rationalistic moralism of the 18th century, to the overt Unitarianism of the 19th century. Leverett's promotion of liturgical worship motivated the entry of many of his students into the Church of England and even the Anglican priesthood. In 1692 Harvard awarded honorary doctorates to both Leverett and Mather, but within a few years Mather had forced Leverett out.

Leverett subsequently developed a legal practice, entering politics, serving a term in the MASSACHUSETTS legislature, and winning appointment as a judge. In 1699 he joined with William and THOMAS BRATTLE as well as other progressives to establish the Brattle Street Church as a haven for religious liberalism. In 1707, after Mather and his allies had finally lost control of Harvard' governing board, Leverett was elected Harvard's president, serving in that capacity until his death. Under his leadership Harvard continued to broaden its theological perspective. For example, a lavish bequest from Thomas Hollis, an English Baptist merchant, funded the creation in 1721 of a chair of divinity bearing the benefactor's name and requiring of its occupant no explicit affirmation of orthodoxy.

—George W. Harper

limners

Limners were untrained and semiskilled artists, usually anonymous to us, who worked during the 18th and early 19th centuries in America. Typical examples of their paintings and sketches depict flat, awkward, front-facing individuals in richly detailed costumes or landscape settings copied from European prints. The word *limner* was first used in the medieval era to refer to the illuminations of manuscripts but came to be used for many 16th-century European artists, particularly portrait painters.

The work of limners rose to popularity in the American colonies during the 1720s, particularly in NEW YORK and New England. During the 18th century Puritan standards in cities such as BOSTON relaxed and a larger percentage of the inhabitants in other areas had sufficient time, income, and interest to support the inexpensive work of artists. Many limners were immigrants from England seeking a less competitive environment in which to work.

Successful and established artists of the 18th century would demonstrate their work in their studios, with viewings available for a small fee, but because they traveled extensively most limners used engravings of royalty and other popular figures as models for common people's portraits. American portraits tended to be less idealized than did European, with the subjects portrayed in more honest and unflinching realism.

Illustrations of prominent people, such as clergy and governors, were often available by subscription. Also very popular were detailed cityscapes, such as WILLIAM BURGIS's 1722 depictions of BOSTON and PETER PELHAM's illustrations of Louisbourg. Prints would be framed and glazed before being used to decorate the home. Nearly all of these ARTISANS had to be itinerant to find enough clients and customers; most also had to diversify into other trades for economic survival. While most limners worked in supplemental fields such as selling paint or carpentry, others worked as DANCE instructors and farmers.

—Victoria C. H. Resnick

Lining, John (1708–1760)

Born in Scotland in 1708, where he received excellent medical training, John Lining moved to America in 1730 at the age of 22. He settled in CHARLESTON, SOUTH CAROLINA, where he earned a distinguished reputation as a physician. He was also one of many educated men of the time who demonstrated the inquisitiveness and scientific interest indicative of the American Enlightenment.

In his role as a physician, Lining saw many cases of YELLOW FEVER, especially during the 1732 and 1748 epidemics. After making a thorough study, he sent an account of the DISEASE pathology to Dr. Robert Whytt, professor of MEDICINE at the University of Edinburgh. An Edinburgh medical journal published it in 1753.

As a scientist, Lining wondered about how different weather conditions influenced human metabolism—growing up in the harsh climate of Scotland, for example, and then moving to the semitropical conditions of South Carolina. To satisfy his curiosity, Lining made daily meteorological observations: air temperature, humidity, levels of cloud cover, rainfall amounts, and wind speed. To track weight loss or gain, Lining carefully recorded the weights of everything he ate and drank, in addition to all bodily elimination: perspiration, urine, and feces. His findings appeared in the *Transactions of the Royal Society of London* in 1743. His were the first published accounts of weather conditions in British North America. Lining was also curious about electricity, repeating Franklin's famous kite experiment. He died on September 21, 1760.

—Anita DeClue

literature

From the songs, stories, and speeches that form the oral cultures of Native North America to the European EXPLORATION narratives, colonization tracts, Puritan sermons, and African slave narratives, literature in the colonial period encompassed a diverse range of texts. Whether it functioned as a means of strengthening tribal identities or as a way to communicate wonder and apprehension at encountering new lands and new peoples, colonial American literature reveals the responses different cultures expressed toward their natural and social worlds.

The earliest narratives produced in North America predate the colonial period. American Indians, who peopled the continent long before Europeans arrived, created a body of oral literature that evolved over a long period of time and in numerous languages. The oral traditions of American Indians offer a complex picture of life in the colonial era and express a worldview that differs markedly from the worldview the colonizers brought with them. European settlers often commented on the Indians' highly developed oratory skills, which were demonstrated in ceremonial songs, chants, prayers, and incantations as well as speeches and treaties. POWHATAN's famous 1609 speech to Captain JOHN SMITH, for instance, testifies to the ways Indians often produced eloquent and pointed responses to the invasion of their homelands. Difficulties arise, however, in studying Native American oral traditions today. This literature has notably diminished from the moment of contact, and the narratives that do remain are often distorted by European translations. Intended to be transmitted orally and communally, this literature may be further misconstrued when removed from its original context. Nevertheless, the oral cultures of American Indians function as a central aspect of colonial North America and serve as a reminder that literary traditions thrived on the continent long before the appearance of European colonizers.

European literature in the colonial period begins with the exploration narratives written by Spanish, French, English, Dutch, and Russian travelers. Accounts such as Thomas Harriot's 1590 *Brief and True Report . . . of Virginia,* SAMUEL DE CHAMPLAIN's 1613 *Voyages,* and the reports from VITUS JONASSEN BERING's 1728 journey to present-day Alaska often used European literary conventions to describe their experiences in a new terrain. Drawing on the belief systems of their own lands, these explorers typically portrayed the worlds they encountered in terms that served the social and political needs of their own cultures. Their accounts were often influenced by fables that had long circulated in Europe that told of previously unheard of plants and ANIMALS, unusual geographical formations, and strange people who inhabited the land. This literature frequently borrowed classical imagery from the Greeks and Romans to tell of Golden Age encounters in an Arcadian land. Because the literature typically expressed what explorers hoped to see rather than what they actually encountered, the reliability of these accounts is often questionable. European narratives of exploration are nevertheless valuable documents for what they tell us about the expectations, drives, and desires of the cultures that created them.

Like the accounts penned by explorers, the writings produced by European settler communities were also influenced by imagery that predated settlement. PILGRIMS and PURITANS, for instance, used biblical allegory to make sense of their condition and justify their presence in North America. As indicated by the writings of WILLIAM BRADFORD, JOHN WINTHROP, MICHAEL WIGGLESWORTH, ANNE DUDLEY BRADSTREET, and others, these settlers understood their mission as an "errand into the wilderness," a journey much like the exodus of the Israelites from Egypt. The settlers understood the land as a blank slate on which they could create a new civilization, "a city on a hill" illustrating God's will to the world. Puritan CAPTIVITY narratives, such as MARY WHITE ROWLANDSON's 1682 account of her capture during an Indian attack and sermons such as JONATHAN EDWARDS's *Sinners in the Hands of an Angry God* (1741), further developed the idea of settlement as a divine test. With its clear division between hero and enemy, Rowlandson's captivity narrative developed into a literary form that told of the spiritual trial and eventual restoration of the Christian believer. Meanwhile, sermons such as those written by Edwards and others built on the imagery of captivity as a way of addressing personal and communal salvation, countering unruliness and division among settlers, and alleviating Puritan fears of the Indians.

Finally, many of the Africans who were captured and brought to North America as slaves also produced a body of writing. The earliest known literary work created by an African American is Lucy Terry's "Bars Fight," a poem written in the 1740s and preserved orally until its publication in 1855. The piece tells of an Indian ambush of two white settler families in 1746 in MASSACHUSETTS. The first known work of African American prose, *A Narrative of the Uncommon Sufferings and Surprising Deliverance of Briton Hammon, a Negro Man,* was published in 1760. Like the hundreds of slave narratives following it, Hammon's account asserted the humanity of the Africans who were enslaved and justified the black struggle for freedom.

Further reading: Colin Calloway, ed., *The World Turned Upside Down: Indian Voices from Early America* (Boston: Bedford/St. Martin's Press, 1994); Richard Slotkin, *Regeneration Through Violence: The Mythology of the American Frontier, 1600–1860* (Middletown, Conn.: Wesleyan University Press, 1973).

—Susan Kollin

Livingston, Philip (1716–1778)

Grandson of ROBERT LIVINGSTON (the founder of Livingston Manor on the Hudson River), Philip was, like his grandfather, a NEW YORK merchant and politician. He attended YALE COLLEGE with his brothers Peter and John and then used his entrepreneurial skills and social connections to profit from trade during the SEVEN YEARS' WAR.

Unlike his grandfather, who was known for his parsimony, Philip donated some of his wealth for the public good. He contributed funds to civic projects, such as KING'S COLLEGE (Columbia University), New York Hospital, the St. Andrew's Benevolent Society, and the New York Society Library, and established a professorship of divinity at Yale in 1746.

In 1754 Livingston began his political career as a NEW YORK CITY alderman, then entered the assembly in 1758, where he represented Livingston Manor with his brother William Livingston and cousin ROBERT R. LIVINGSTON. He was a delegate to the Stamp Act Congress of 1765. Philip was chosen speaker of the assembly in 1768, but, under pressure from the DeLancey faction, he and other family members were voted out of office the following year. Known as "Philip the Signer," he represented New York at the First and Second Continental Congresses, where he signed the Declaration of Independence. At first reluctant to oppose Britain and hoping for reconciliation, Philip and other Livingston family conservatives ultimately yielded to pressure and committed themselves to independence. In preparation for war, the Livingstons built two MILLS that year—one to grind grain and the other for gunpowder. Philip died in 1778 while active in the Continental Congress and the New York Senate, having helped frame the New York State Constitution.

Further reading: Clare Brandt, *An American Aristocracy: The Livingstons* (Garden City, N.Y.: Doubleday, 1986).

—Deborah C. Taylor

Livingston, Robert (1654–1728)

Robert Livingston, the "Proprietor of Livingston Manor" and speaker of the provincial assembly, was one of NEW YORK's richest men when he died in 1728. The son of a Scottish Presbyterian minister, Robert arrived in Albany in 1674 from Rotterdam, Holland, fluent in Dutch and experienced in commercial shipping. He entered the Dutch-controlled FUR TRADE as an agent of a MASSACHUSETTS fur company, where his knowledge of the Dutch and friendly relations with the IROQUOIS contributed to his economic success. Within a year he entered local politics as the secretary to the board of Indian commissioners. Livingston built important social and political connections when he married Alida Schuyler Van Rensselaer in 1679. The daughter of future mayor Peter Schuyler and recent widow of wealthy patroon Nicholas Van Rensselaer, Alida was a socially prominent upper Hudson heir. She was also a hard-working, intelligent Dutch woman who bore and raised 10 children (six grew to adulthood) while active in the family business. Robert relied on her good sense in politics and business throughout their long marriage.

Livingston began building his landholdings in 1684 by purchasing a 2,000-acre tract from his trading partners, the Iroquois, for "three hundred guilders" and a variety of trade goods. Two years later he expanded his holdings to 160,000 acres when he was awarded a royal patent in the form of an English baronial grant. "Livingston Manor," encompassing parts of today's Dutchess and Columbia Counties, grew under the next generation to nearly a million acres.

Livingston was well positioned both geographically along the Hudson, a bustling commercial and military waterway, and socially through close alliances with prominent politicians. He profited from political favors and government contracts from his lucrative fur trade as well as from his vast landholdings. Robert was a member of the provincial assembly from 1709 to 1725 and served as speaker from 1718. Called "the Founder," he was patriarch to a social and political dynasty of Livingstons who influenced the growth of New York and the nation through the 18th century. Many of his sons and grandsons expanded the social, political, and financial territory that Robert Livingston pioneered.

Further reading: Clare Brandt, *An American Aristocracy: The Livingstons* (Garden City, N.Y.: Doubleday, 1986).

—Deborah C. Taylor

Livingston, Robert R. (1718–1775)

Grandson of ROBERT LIVINGSTON, "the Founder," and son of Robert Livingston of Clermont, Robert R. Livingston was a NEW YORK judge and politician. With his wife, the former Margaret Beekman, he was proprietor of one of New York's largest estates and succeeded his father at Clermont. Margaret and Robert had 10 children, in whom they encouraged a love of learning; even their daughters were offered secondary EDUCATION in the humanities. Called "the Judge," Robert was known as an erudite, distinguished, and temperate man and a devoted husband.

Representing Dutchess County, Robert was elected to the New York provincial assembly in 1758 with his cousins PHILIP LIVINGSTON, representing NEW YORK CITY, and William Livingston, who spoke for Livingston Manor. Together, these members of New York's landed elite challenged the DeLancey merchant faction. Continuing in the assembly, he was appointed judge of the Admiralty Court the next year. He became associate justice of the New York Supreme Court in 1763. As chair of New York's Committee of Correspondence, he supported resistance to the Stamp Act. In 1765 Robert R. Livingston is said to have written an address to King George III (1760–1820) that landed him at the top of the king's list of colonial traitors. Although some in his family were reluctant revolutionaries, in 1775 he built a gunpowder mill on Clermont grounds to aid in the defense of the colonies. An aggressive protector of colonial rights, he, along with other members of the state's landed gentry, lost his seat in the assembly in 1768 to the merchant faction, or "popular party," and never regained the position.

Further reading: Clare Brandt, *An American Aristocracy: The Livingstons* (Garden City, N.Y.: Doubleday, 1986).

—Deborah C. Taylor

Lloyd, David (1656–1731)

David Lloyd served an important role in the political and legal development of PENNSYLVANIA. A native of Wales, he was practicing law in England when his skills attracted the attention of WILLIAM PENN. Lloyd was granted a commission by Penn in 1686 to be the attorney general of Pennsylvania. Lloyd moved with his family to PHILADELPHIA, where he soon held the appointed posts of clerk of the county court, clerk of the provincial court, and deputy master of the rolls. He was first elected to the assembly in 1693, often serving as speaker after 1694, and he served on the provincial council between 1695 and 1696 and again from 1698 to 1700.

A political quarrel arose between Lloyd and Robert Quarry, the judge of the new vice admiralty court in 1698. Lloyd was accused of interfering with the enforcement of the Navigation Acts and with having the magistrates take goods from the king's warehouse at Newcastle. Quarry complained to Penn, who subsequently rebuked Lloyd, removed him as attorney general, and dismissed him from the council. Lloyd thereafter became a staunch adversary of the proprietary family and its interests in Pennsylvania.

Lloyd's antiproprietary politics soon made him leader of the Popular Party, consisting mostly of QUAKERS from the countryside. He was elected to several more terms in the assembly. In 1717 he was chosen chief justice of Pennsylvania, an office he held until his death in 1731. As leader of the Popular Party, Lloyd worked to strengthen the power of the assembly, including its right to meet and adjourn at its own discretion. He fought to secure the right of affirmation and opposed the creation of a military force, all of which gained favor with Pennsylvania's Quakers. Lloyd authored the list of grievances addressed to William Penn in 1704 and led the attempt to impeach JAMES LOGAN, the secretary of the province, in 1707. His long efforts against proprietary interests made him one of the most influential early exponents of expanded representative government in the colonies.

Further reading: Roy Norman Lokken, *David Lloyd, a Colonial Lawmaker* (Seattle: University of Washington Press, 1959).

—Stephen C. O'Neill

Locke, John (1632–1704)

Although British philosopher John Locke never set foot in North America, he deeply influenced its political institutions. As one of the foremost theorists of human freedom and sovereignty, Locke's *Two Treatises of Government* (1689) set out the principles of liberal democracy that underlay the U.S. Constitution. Locke based the legitimacy and authority of government on "social contract" theory—that is, the idea that all those who would be governed must freely consent to the rules of civil society. He hypothesized that humans originally lived in a "state of nature," a kind of perfect freedom and equality under which all individuals enjoyed such "natural rights" as "life, liberty, and estate" (i.e., property), yet nothing protected these rights; in order to safeguard them, individuals came together and agreed upon mutually advantageous rules by which all would abide. These rules, which aimed to preserve humanity's natural rights, formed the basis for a communal or "civil government" by providing the principles for liberal democracy (as opposed to those for absolute monarchy, which Locke opposed). Among these principles were that all people should be considered equally free, that the liberty to do as one wished *within reason* should be preserved, that the property and persons of other people should be respected, and that those who violated these principles could be punished. By remaining in a society governed by such principles, Locke maintained, one agreed to live by them; the only freedoms one relinquished in exchange were those of legislative and executive decision making (that is, making laws and executing them), which were accorded to civil government.

Related to these principles of liberal democracy were Locke's recommendations about EDUCATION. Having been trained under the harsh discipline and memory-based curriculum typical of English schools at that time, he proposed instead that education be guided by freedom, tolerance, and truth. Rather than absolute standards, a child's individual talents and capacities should guide its learning. Parents and educators should teach by example; while children need to learn self-discipline, their natural desire for freedom and play should also be respected. More broadly, Locke maintained that playfulness and humor should be incorporated into learning whenever possible. Even if these ideas appear obvious or unremarkable today, Locke was among the first to offer such recommendations, and they tremendously influenced modern education.

One element of Locke's political theory was that only men had natural rights. Locke was perfectly comfortable with only men enjoying the rights of citizenship. Also necessary was that the politically enfranchised be property owners. One of the state's primary responsibilities, according to Locke, was to protect personal property. To have an original right to property, a person needed to take material not owned by others and to mix one's own LABOR with it. This property could then be sold or bequeathed to others through contracts. However, Locke argued, NATIVE AMERICANS and Africans did not adequately work their lands in order truly to own them. Instead, they merely occupied the land and could legitimately be pushed aside by those, like "industrious" Europeans, who would mix their labor with it. This belief permitted various forms of colonization and conquest, such as of those "inland vacant places in America" that were allegedly uncultivated by Native Americans and therefore open to ownership by more hard-working colonists. Indeed, Locke claimed that "in the beginning, all the world was America," by which he meant that all the earth was open for ownership until men began mixing their labor and acquiring it as personal property.

Locke was deeply ambivalent about SLAVERY. On the one hand, he condemned it as a "vile and miserable" estate contrary to a "gentleman's" generosity; on the other, he invested heavily in the SLAVE TRADE and profited handsomely from the buying and selling of human beings. He was a charter member of the ROYAL AFRICAN COMPANY, whose main business was the purchase, transport, and sale of African slaves for the British colonies in the Americas, and he bought into other companies whose purpose was to develop the profitability of New World plantations using slave labor. From 1668 to 1683 and from 1696 to 1700, Locke also helped to administer the North American colonies for the British government. He contributed to the *Fundamental Constitution for the Government of Carolina* (copies exist in his handwriting), which states that "every freeman . . . shall have absolute power and authority over his negro slave."

However, 17th-century slavery was not entirely coded by skin color, that is, racist. The British, for example, quite willingly sold into servitude the Irish, their own countrymen who were poor or in debt, as well as such believers in "nonconformist" forms of Christianity as Roman Catholics and PURITANS. Thus, it would be a mistake to think that Locke was necessarily a racist, although many of his beliefs and actions contributed to what would later become racist thinking. At the same time, he profited eagerly from the unpaid labor of those who lacked what was, for him, the supreme ingredient of human life—liberty. The legacy of Locke's contradictory impulses continue to plague American thinking today.

Further reading: John Locke, *Two Treatises of Government,* ed. Peter Laslett (Cambridge, U.K.: Cambridge University Press, 1988).

—Dan Flory

Logan, James (1674–1751)

James Logan was born in Ulster into the family of a Scottish schoolteacher. He was educated by his father and replaced him as the teacher of a QUAKERS' school in Bristol. There he met WILLIAM PENN, who took him to North America in 1699 as his personal secretary. After Penn left PENNSYLVANIA for good in 1701, Logan emerged as his real surrogate there, advising proprietary deputy governors for half a century. He accepted many provincial and proprietary offices, in which he tried to defend Penn's prerogatives and interests against the claims of an assertive Quaker elite who controlled the powerful legislative assembly. Logan was largely unsuccessful in checking these provincial infringements. His most creative political years were his first two decades in the colony. He adapted and elaborated Penn's methods of protecting Pennsylvania against a territorially aggressive MARYLAND and the expansive designs of imperial agents in NEW YORK. Between 1710 and 1718 he worked closely with his fellow Scot Robert Hunter, the royal governor of New York and NEW JERSEY, and their cooperation helped to stabilize political life in the Middle Colonies.

After 1725 Logan's political career became more routinized. His energy was increasingly devoted to his own commercial interests, especially in the FUR TRADE. This enterprise facilitated Logan's involvement in proprietary and imperial Indian diplomacy, which spanned the transition between William Penn's efforts to deal fairly with tribes in the DELAWARE Valley and the cynical designs of Penn's sons to expel Indians and profit from their father's landed empire. Logan, with his friend CADWALLADER COLDEN, saw the IROQUOIS confederation as the key to stable Anglo-Indian relations, and he worked to make Pennsylvania's ALGONQUIN-speaking tribes accept Iroquois dominance.

In 1726 Logan moved from PHILADELPHIA to the stone mansion near Germantown that he called "Stenton." He subscribed to the enlightenment ideal of gentlemanly "retirement" from the bustle of commerce. He increasingly tended to his library, his astronomical instruments, and his scientific experiments. Some of his botanical and astronomical observations appeared in the *Philosophical Transactions of the Royal Society of London,* and he corresponded with European scientists while mentoring Americans like JOHN BARTRAM and Benjamin Franklin. Logan's successors in proprietary office did not have his synoptic vision of Pennsylvania's place in the natural, economic, and imperial worlds, but many of them had somewhat more pragmatic understandings of the possibilities of Anglo-American politics. Logan died before his adopted country began its long slide into Revolutionary crisis. In many ways, his career in Pennsylvania typified the "Anglicizing" era in colonial life, after the rough edges of frontier society were rubbed off in the Atlantic coastal settlements but before a distinctively "American" cultural identity emerged in tension with a new British imperialism.

Further reading: Frederick B. Tolles, *James Logan and the Culture of Provincial America* (Boston: Little Brown, 1957); Edwin Wolf II, *The Library of James Logan of Philadelphia, 1674–1771* (Philadelphia: Library Company of Philadelphia, 1974).

—Wayne Bodle

lotteries

Lotteries have a long history, beginning as early as 1612 in JAMESTOWN, when the VIRGINIA COMPANY OF LONDON attempted to raise money for additional colonization efforts in North America. This lottery was conducted in England, with prizes that probably included land in VIRGINIA. The idea succeeded because nearly half of the operating expenses of the Virginia Company likely came from the proceeds of lotteries.

By 1699 lotteries had proliferated in the colonies so much that some officials denounced them as "a cheat." MASSACHUSETTS outlawed lotteries in 1719 because they had become so rampant; lottery agents were labeled "pillagers of the people." In 1733 Massachusetts fined people 500 pounds for operating illegal lotteries and 100 pounds for even publicizing them.

Despite these early objections, many colonies used them to raise funds for public projects, including the construction of schools, hospitals, roads, and bridges. Although PHILADELPHIA became the principal center of lotteries in the 18th century, BOSTON and the Massachusetts colony were close behind, endorsing more than 22 government-sponsored lotteries from 1749 to 1765. Harvard, Dartmouth, Yale, Columbia, and Williams Colleges replenished their building funds using lotteries.

Further reading: George Sullivan, *By Chance a Winner: The History of Lotteries* (New York: George Mead, 1972).

—James F. Adomanis

Louisiana

Explorers commanded by the French-born Canadian seigneur RENÉ-ROBERT CAVELIER, SIEUR DE LA SALLE, sailed from Canada by interior navigation to the mouth of the Mississippi River, where they claimed for France the Mississippi Valley, naming the region after Louis XIV on April 6, 1682. By subsequent EXPLORATIONS the claim was enlarged to encompass the Mobile and Missouri River systems. A Province of Louisiana was established in 1699, when Jacques and JEAN-BAPTISTE LE MOYNE, Canadian sieurs of Iberville and Bienville, respectively, established the first permanent colony between the mouths of the Mississippi and Mobile Rivers. This remained a small military outpost of a few hundred people, mostly Canadians, until 1718, when NEW ORLEANS was founded by one of the largest single immigrant waves from the Old World, sponsored by the Company of the Indies between 1718 and 1731. In 1763 Louisiana produced INDIGO and other provisions for export, for the region was rich in natural resources, but it still had a remarkably small population of 11,496 whites and 5,552 black slaves, plus an unknown number of Indians, in a census of 1766. Few immigrants arrived from France after 1731, and few slaves were carried from AFRICA to the remote seaport of New Orleans. Then, in 1763, the TREATY OF PARIS awarded the English the territory east of the Mississippi, except for the "Isle" of New Orleans, which lies primarily on the east bank. At that time Louis XV gave the remaining huge province, extending west of the Mississippi to the Rocky Mountains, to his Bourbon relation in Madrid, Charles III. Spain administered it until 1803, when Charles IV yielded it back to France, which sold it to the United States.

When the French colonized the region, they encountered powerful NATIVE AMERICANS, including the CHOCTAW, CHICKASAW, and Natchez, living in highly organized societies and producing most of their food by AGRICULTURE. The Crown attached the Illinois region to Louisiana in 1718, inhabited by the Fox, Sauk, Potawatomi, Menominee, Winnebago, and other peoples. Most soon became involved in the FUR TRADE, bartering deerskins and animal furs for European goods.

Most Europeans in Louisiana in 1763 were the descendants of migrants from western France who had arrived in New Orleans between 1718 and 1731, although Canadians from New France were a second important source of the population, but this was predominantly a multiracial society. White Louisianians faced two primary challenges: defending their claims to the province from both Indians and English and keeping their African slaves subordinated. The French generally allied with the Choctaw in chronic imperial warfare with the British and their Chickasaw allies until 1763. In 1729 the Natchez and a few black slaves attacked the French in one of the most dramatic moments of North American colonial history; the colonists rallied and brutally suppressed the Natchez. Their principal antagonists in the upper Mississippi Valley were the Fox Indians.

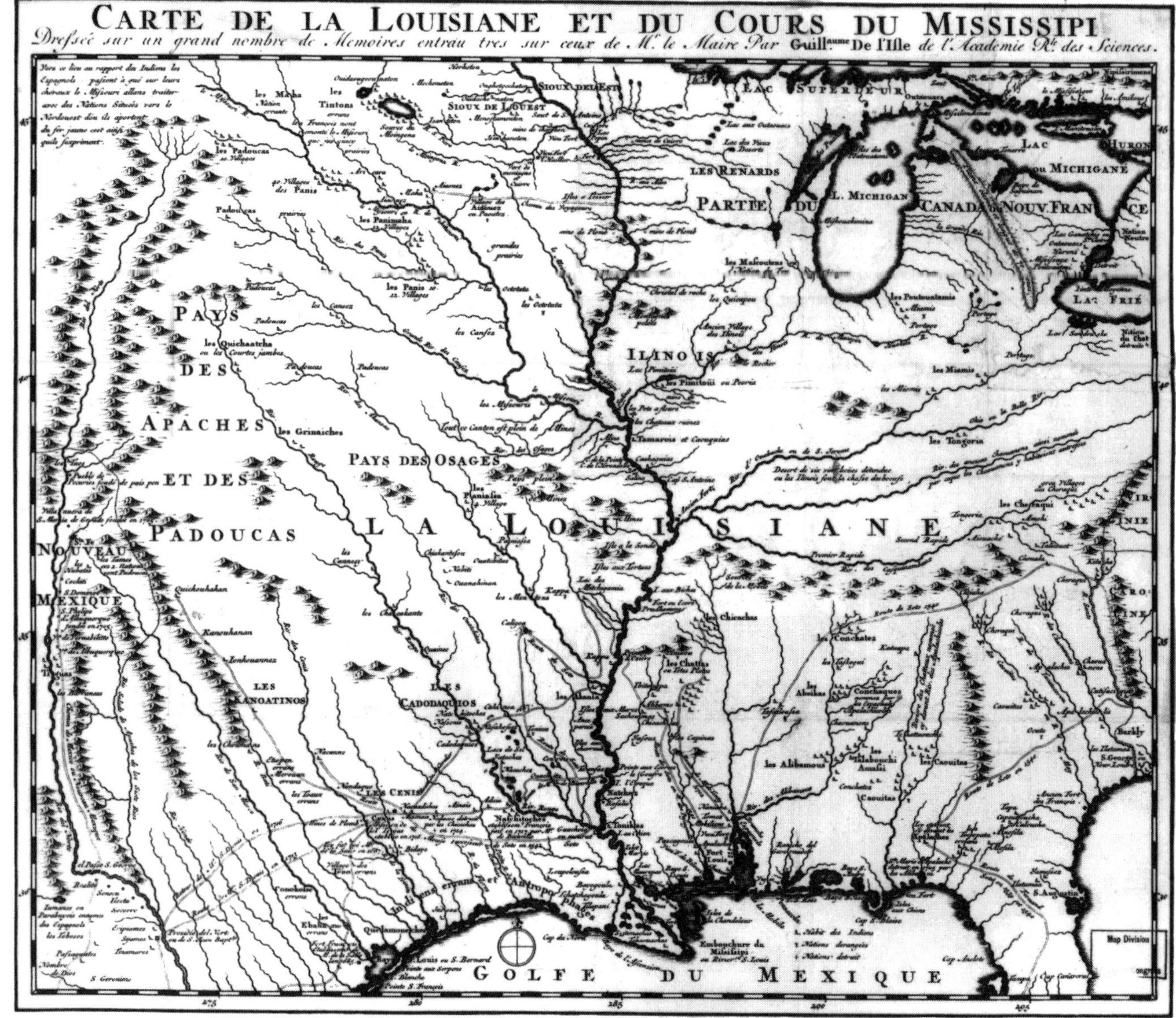

This map shows French settlements and expansion in Louisiana. *(Library of Congress)*

About 5,400 Africans were brought to New Orleans between 1718 and 1731, most coming from present-day Senegal and neighboring regions. Local planters purchased the great majority of them, so New Orleans Parish became a slave society where blacks formed a large majority. Slaves produced indigo, rice, TOBACCO, wood products, and other items exported to France and the West Indies. Treated much like the slaves in other North American colonies, they formed a comparatively tight-knit and stable community in part because slave imports were so limited between the 1730s and the 1760s. During the war years between 1754 and 1763, however, several large estate sales disrupted the family and social lives of many slaves. A tiny number of AFRICAN AMERICANS were free, most of whom were men who fought the Natchez in 1729 and thereby earned their freedom.

See also FRENCH COLONIES; FRENCH IMMIGRANTS.

Further reading: Thomas N. Ingersoll, *Mamon and Manon in Early New Orleans: The First Slave Society in the Deep South, 1718–1819* (Knoxville: University of Tennessee Press, 1999).

—Thomas N. Ingersoll

lumbering

The abundant FORESTS of eastern North America provided British colonists with one of their most valuable commodities. Although every mainland colony exported a wide variety of timber products, the lumber trade was concentrated in two regions, each with its distinctive assets and LABOR arrangements. New England was the first region to develop timber exports as a mainstay of its ECONOMY. While MASSACHUSETTS and CONNECTICUT also exported wood products, by the early 18th century the lumbering industry was concentrated in NEW HAMPSHIRE and MAINE. Typically, sawmill owners in these colonies hired wage laborers to fell a parcel of trees and then drag the logs through the snow to a sawmill or harbor. Sawmill workers drew the timber through the blades of a mechanical saw, processing as much as 3,000 feet of lumber a day from March through December. A portion of this lumber was reworked by skilled artisans such as coopers, carpenters, and shipwrights. Most of the unfinished lumber was sent abroad for sale in the West Indies, with the bulk of the profits accruing to MERCHANTS who owned the sawmills and sailing vessels.

Coastal NORTH CAROLINA also developed a flourishing timber economy in the 18th century based primarily on the production of naval stores—the pitch, tar, and turpentine used to waterproof the hulls and decks of sailing ships. By the 1760s North Carolina accounted for seven-tenths of the tar and three-fifths of all the naval stores exported from the colonies. As in New England, the production of naval stores depended on the toil of seasonal workers, but in Carolina this labor was performed by African slaves. The manufacture of tar was a tedious and time-consuming process. Slaves piled logs into conical piles, which they covered with dirt and set afire. As the tar oozed out from beneath their makeshift kilns, slaves collected it into barrels, which they rolled to harbor. The sale of tar and other naval stores earned spectacular profits for the owners of slaves and wooded land.

Further reading: Michael Williams, *Americans and Their Forests: A Historical Geography* (Cambridge, U.K.: Cambridge University Press, 1989).

—Gavin J. Taylor

Lutherans

Lutherans are the followers of a denomination founded by Martin Luther following the promulgation of his Ninety-five Theses in 1517 in Saxony. Among their beliefs is the doctrine of salvation by faith alone: God provides salvation regardless of man's good works because of his love and mercy. Luther contended that the Bible was the sole authority for faith. In addition, he rejected all of the sacraments of the Roman Catholic Church except for baptism and the Eucharist, and even his view of the latter differed from the traditional Roman Catholic interpretation. Other beliefs that contributed to the schism included the denial of the validity of indulgences, purgatory, and papal power.

Lutheranism came to the British colonies mainly from Germany and Scandinavia. The first Lutherans to settle permanently in the New World arrived from Holland in 1623. Although colonists established a congregation in NEW AMSTERDAM in 1649, Lutherans in the region did not experience freedom of worship until the English took over NEW YORK in 1664. In the meantime, Swedish Lutherans established the colony of New Sweden in present-day DELAWARE.

While Lutherans settled throughout the Middle and Southern colonies, PENNSYLVANIA was the focal point of their settlement. The first churches established by GERMAN IMMIGRANTS were small and poor, often without pastors. Because the German settlers were unfamiliar with the responsibilities of voluntarism (in which congregation members voluntarily provided funds rather than depending on taxes), they often confronted problems with obtaining ordained clergy and supporting individual church buildings.

The lack of clergy sometimes resulted in schoolmasters performing the duties of a minister, ultimately contributing to provincial and continental religious officials expressing concern for the conditions of the parishioners. In the early 1730s several Pennsylvania congregations began requesting regular pastors from the Lutheran court preacher in London. The lack of a response to these queries by 1740 forced German Lutherans to ask the king of Sweden for assistance. These requests were finally heeded when HENRY MELCHIOR MUHLENBERG accepted the call.

Muhlenberg's arrival guaranteed the success of the Lutheran denomination in the colonies, as his presence preserved many of the rural congregations in Pennsylvania from succumbing to the overtures of the Moravian leader Count Nicholas Ludwig von Zinzendorf. In 1748 Muhlenberg organized the pastors and congregations of the Middle Colonies into the Evangelical Lutheran Ministerium of Pennsylvania, the first Lutheran synod in America. By the end of the colonial period, almost 250 Lutheran congregations were established in the British colonies, 11 of which were Swedish. Four-fifths of the adherents were German. Many of the Swedish Lutheran congregations eventually were assimilated into the ANGLICAN CHURCH. The German Lutherans became the antecedents of the varied Lutheran synods of modern times.

Further reading: A. G. Roeber, *Palatines, Liberty, and Property: German Lutherans in Colonial British America* (Baltimore: Johns Hopkins University Press, 1993).

—Karen Guenther

M

Maine

The territory lying between the Piscataqua and St. Croix Rivers, the present-day boundaries of the state of Maine, was one of the earliest and most contested sites of European settlement in North America. Its original inhabitants were the Wabanaki, who practiced corn-based AGRICULTURE in villages from the Saco River westward and subsisted by hunting, FISHING, and gathering along the rivers and estuaries farther east. In 1604 a party of French settlers established a short-lived colony on an island at the headwaters of the St. Croix River; three years later the English followed suit with an aborted attempt to establish a settlement at the mouth of the Kennebec River. In 1629 the English Crown granted the territory between the Kennebec and the Piscataqua to Sir Ferdinando Gorges as a proprietary colony named the Province of Maine. This territory was annexed by MASSACHUSETTS from 1652 to 1658 and renamed York County.

By the late 17th century Maine was divided into three distinctive cultural zones. Along the coast as far east as the Kennebec River was a strip of English settlement, characterized by dispersed farms and town government. Small-scale agriculture in this area was supplemented by lumbering and SHIPBUILDING. Although descendants of the original inhabitants of Gorges's colony remained, they were increasingly swamped by migrants from Massachusetts, Scotland, Ireland, and Germany. In port towns and on the islands dotting the coast were small communities of fishermen plying their trade in the North Atlantic. By the 1670s Maine's fisheries fell into a prolonged period of decline, failing to keep pace with the better-capitalized fleets of northern Massachusetts. Farther in the interior was a frontier area characterized by conflict and cultural exchange among Wabanaki, French soldiers and missionaries, and English settlers. The English and Wabanaki fought six wars between 1676 and 1763, with the French lending substantial aid and encouragement to the Indians in all but the first. In peacetime there was considerable interaction between the Wabanaki and colonists, chiefly through missionary work and the FUR TRADE. Several French settlers established trading posts in western Acadia and married native women; the English had less success in bridging the cultural divide between Natives and newcomers.

Further reading: Roger F. Duncan, *Coastal Maine: A Maritime History* (New York: Norton, 1992); Richard W. Judd, Edwin A. Churchill, and Joel W. Eastman, eds., *Maine: The Pine Tree State from Prehistory to the Present* (Orono: University of Maine Press, 1995).

—Gavin J. Taylor

manufacturing and industry

The slow development of industry in North America was due primarily to the relative scarcity of capital and LABOR and the abundance of land in the colonies. For this reason most British Americans preferred the safer and cheaper investment, land. Furthermore, the economic policy of the BRITISH EMPIRE protected industries in Britain and imposed limitations on colonial manufactures. The colonies were thought of as markets for British products, not centers of production. Therefore, Parliament restricted the development of colonial industry that might compete with British goods. The Iron Act, for example, prohibited the construction of new iron MILLS or the production of iron hardware in the colonies. Earlier, the Woolens (1699) and Hat (1732) Acts had similarly been aimed at preventing colonial export, and therefore large-scale production, of these goods. However, the vast natural resources, the cycle of the agricultural seasons—which usually did not require year-round work in northern colonies—and the British demand for certain products all combined to produce some industrial development. The most notable colonial industries were milling, distilling, and SHIPBUILDING.

Most manufacturing was not centralized but rather performed within the household. Women played a central role in these home-based industries. Labor was usually performed without power by simple hand tools, and it consisted primarily of made-to-order goods for customers located in the immediate vicinity.

In SOUTH CAROLINA slaves dominated craft positions to the exclusion of white people in many instances. In the Chesapeake region slaves also played an active role in craft production, although in fewer numbers then in the Lower South. Although principally woodworkers, slaves also worked in shipyards and in the ironworks in Baltimore and elsewhere in the Chesapeake area.

The demand for manufactured goods in the colonies increased steadily throughout the colonial era, which encouraged both imports of British goods and domestic production. Generally, colonial consumers preferred British manufactures to the usually less-refined colonial products. Although the quality of colonial-produced goods improved throughout the 18th century, many colonists, guided more by taste and fashion than by necessity in their purchases, continued to import goods from Britain.

One of the most important finished goods exported from the colonies was rum. Taking advantage of existing trade networks, the New England colonies in particular imported West Indian molasses and distilled it into rum. Similar to shipbuilding and other domestic products, American rum served as a less expensive replacement for West Indian rum and brandy. Although colonists drank much of the rum, a good deal was exported to AFRICA in exchange for slaves. In this and all colonial production, the mercantilist theory of the empire was undermined, because colonies were supposed to serve primarily as consumers rather than producers of manufactured goods.

Further reading: John J. McCusker and Russell R. Menard, *The Economy of British America, 1607–1789* (Chapel Hill: University of North Carolina Press, 1985).

—Jonathan Mercantini

mariners

Throughout the age of European global expansion, the oceans of the world were the highways that linked continents in webs of trade, communication, and migration. In the 15th century improvements in vessel design, cartography, and navigation (the astrolabe and cross-staff) aided the EXPLORATION of the African coast and culminated in Christopher Columbus's momentous 1492 voyage. Mariners and seamen made first contact with the native peoples of West Africa, the CARIBBEAN, and the Americas and were thus Europe's first cultural ambassadors.

During the early 16th century Spain and Portugal dominated expansion into AFRICA and the Americas, but the development of the North Atlantic fishery and increased European trade caused English, Dutch, and French ship tonnage to rise sharply by century's end. As exploration gave way to colonization, ships and the men who manned them shuttled emigrants and equipment to settlements on the Atlantic rim and returned with gold, silver, and staple exports. National navies expanded to defend overseas settlements and trade from both European rivals and pirates. The demand for labor in the Americas fueled the African SLAVE TRADE, which carried an estimated 11.6 million slaves through the Middle Passage. Commercial FISHING and whaling, PRIVATEERING during wartime, and PIRACY during peace complemented the naval deployments and coastal short- and long-distance trading voyages that employed the bulk of European and colonial mariners. In 1762 an estimated 300,000 men manned the navies and merchant marines of Europe throughout the globe.

The crews of sailing vessels varied in size, but all were hierarchically ordered. *Mariner* usually denoted knowledge of navigation and implied command, while seamen generally had not yet learned or lacked navigational skills. Merchant mariners and seamen were paid monthly wages or by the voyage. Fishermen, privateersmen, whalers, and pirates earned shares of the profits of the voyages they undertook. The Royal Navy paid low wages but awarded "prize" money from captured vessels. There were often regional shortages of maritime labor, which prompted involuntary recruitment, naval impressment during wartime, and "crimping" and "spiriting" (kidnaping) in times of peace.

The 18th-century maritime population was young, mobile, well traveled, multiracial, and multiethnic. A high turnover rate kept crews young as death, infirmity, hardships associated with the work, and opportunities on land took older seamen and mariners away from the sea; the average age of British mariners in the mid-18th century was 26. In their intercolonial and international travels mariners grew familiar with many cultures and languages, traveling farther in a single year than most landsmen did in a lifetime. Africans and AFRICAN AMERICANS were disproportionately represented among the crews of British (including American) vessels. Escaped slaves and free black people found economic opportunity at sea, escaped some elements of racism, and informally linked black communities along the Atlantic rim; indeed, the first five printed slave narratives were penned by black seafarers. NATIVE AMERICANS were also employed on fishing, whaling, and trading vessels, especially in New England.

Many sailors were quick to participate in civil protests and riots, had a reputation for violence and rootlessness, and have been characterized as a resistant early proletarian group. Many others, however, remained closely tied to home port communities, supported families, and advanced throughout their careers. Regardless of disposition, the mariners and sailors drawn from coastal nations and races throughout the early modern world powered the ships that fostered and sustained global geographic and economic integration.

Further reading: Marcus Rediker, *Between the Devil and the Deep Blue Sea: Merchant Seamen, Pirates, and the Anglo-American Maritime World, 1700–1750* (Cambridge, U.K.: Cambridge University Press, 1987); W. Jeffrey Bolster, *Black Jacks: African American Seamen in the Age of Sail* (Cambridge, Mass.: Harvard University Press, 1997).

—Michael J. Jarvis

Marquette, Jacques (1637–1675)

Jacques Marquette served as a Jesuit missionary to NATIVE AMERICANS, and his EXPLORATION enabled the French to claim NEW ORLEANS and to establish domination of the Mississippi River until the mid-18th century. Marquette was born in Laon, France, to the prosperous merchant family of Nicholas Marquette and Rose de La Salle. From an early age Marquette dreamed of mission work. He attended schools tailored to prepare him for entry into the Catholic Church, learning Latin, Greek, and theology before entering the Jesuit college at Reims and the Jesuit seminary at Nancy in 1654. In preparation for taking vows, Marquette learned such practical skills as cooking, nursing, and housekeeping, which would serve him well on his mission. Between 1656 and 1666 Marquette taught at the Jesuit school at Auxerre and finalized his own studies in philosophy before being chosen for the Jesuit mission in Canada.

Arriving in Quebec in 1666, Marquette began to learn the Montagnais language and wilderness skills like carpentry and handling a canoe. He was then sent to the Ottawa, charged with building a mission, which he named Sainte-Marie-du-Sault. Having made contact with numerous other tribes, Marquette took advantage of his contacts to continue the Jesuit practice of mapmaking and collecting information through a journey to found another mission at Saint Esprit in 1669–71. Rumors abounded of a great river in

This engraving shows Marquette and Jolliet exploring the Mississippi River. *(Library of Congress)*

Illinois lands, and Marquette became determined to find it, especially after establishing a third mission at Saint Ignace, on the upper peninsula of Michigan. In 1673, accompanied by LOUIS JOLLIET, a Jesuit-trained French-Canadian fur trader, Marquette mapped the northern shore of Lake Michigan to Green Bay, then traveled down the lower Fox River to Lake Winnebago. Using the Wisconsin River to access the Mississippi River, the men met several tribes, including the Peoria and the Arkansas, with whom they established friendly relations.

Passing the mouths of the Missouri and the Ohio Rivers, Marquette determined that the Mississippi drained to the south rather than to the west. He broke off the exploration 1,700 miles from Saint-Ignace. Although seriously ill after returning to Saint-Ignace, Marquette completed his maps, which Jolliet used in subsequent trips. During a mission to the Illinois in 1674, Marquette fell critically ill and died near Ludington, Michigan.

Further reading: Joseph P. Donnelly, *Jacques Marquette, S.J., 1637–1675* (Chicago: Loyola University Press, 1968).

—Margaret Sankey

marriage and family life

In all societies the family fills a number of functions, including the primary locus of the rites of passage (birth, mating, and death); the fulfillment of primary physical, economic, and emotional needs; and the transmission of culture. Nowhere was that reality more starkly demonstrated than in colonial North America, where vast wilderness, sparse population, and the intersection of European, African, and Native American cultures helped shape distinctive family dynamics. The nature of families varied greatly over time and region as well as among racial groups.

Family structures and functions varied much more among NATIVE AMERICANS than among Euro-Americans. Among the IROQUOIS, for example, three or four families lived in a longhouse, with elder women exercising a good deal of control over the household. Husbands and wives engaged in an economic as well as emotional partnership, with women tending to AGRICULTURE and men engaging in hunting. Women exercised considerable power within families, including the authority to divorce their husbands by setting their belongings outside the longhouse entrance. Parents provided their children with a great deal of freedom. Although other Indians defined their families quite differently, Europeans were impressed and sometimes shocked by some aspects of family life among natives, especially the power exercised by women.

The "typical" 17th-century Euro-American family in the Upper South was large and complex; premature deaths of spouses engendered multiple marriages, and households were often comprised of half-siblings, step-siblings, and miscellaneous orphans in addition to extended family members, servants, apprentices, and slaves. Hence, a colonial child might well be part of a nuclear family in which death and remarriage meant that neither "parent" was biologically related to the child. The rare divorce, the binding out of children to learn a trade, and the frequent relocation of family units also contributed to many changes in a "household" and "family." On the other hand, all these variables also contributed to a strong community fabric, as cousins, friends, siblings, and step-siblings were often closely related through many different blood lines and shared experiences. White families in New England and the Middle Colonies, where MORTALITY was lower, usually were not broken as often by the death of one of the spouses, and many children consequently grew up in households containing both parents and even grandparents. As death rates declined in the Chesapeake region during the 18th century, white families there began to resemble those in the northern colonies.

Throughout the colonial period, although region, race, CLASS, and culture defined the specifics, Euro-American households shared these and other general characteristics. The predominant pattern was a patriarchal, hierarchical, nuclear family in which one primary focus was subsistence. As the time-consuming tasks of providing fuel, tending livestock and gardens, and providing FOOD and CLOTHING required a team effort, practically no one lived alone. Women were mostly responsible for domestic work—most clothing and food were made at home—and they were answerable to their husbands or fathers, who oversaw agricultural production and hunting. Thus, the household constituted a unit in which production and CONSUMPTION were self-contained.

While white family units were mostly under the authority of men, many Native American women wielded considerable influence in their families and communities. This contrasted sharply with married white women, who had almost no access to the political process or to the courts, except through their male protectors or, perhaps, through the intervention of their churches. Widowed or single women sometimes exercised slightly greater control over their economic lives, and servant women could occasionally get a hearing in the courts, but slave women had no access to power (or control over their children) except through the intervention of a sympathetic master.

Daily life was strenuous. In the temperate mid-Atlantic climate, for example, it is estimated that simply providing household fuel required the equivalent of the full-time LABOR of one adult man. Because existence in solitude was so difficult, the few people who did live alone aroused the suspicion of their neighbors, and community

This illustration shows an entire colonial family working together to prepare flax to be spun into thread for clothing or twine. *(Library of Congress)*

persecution—such as witch hunts—fell unequally upon people (especially woman) who lived by themselves. As houses were small and privacy and hygiene haphazard, households were constantly coping with illness—either individual or epidemic—and a fair amount of the family energies went into planning for these events or into actually caring for the sick. ALCOHOL was a staple of the MEDICINE cabinet, and some historians have theorized that most colonial Americans, adults and children, consumed some alcohol nearly every day, partly to compensate for polluted water and unbalanced nutrition. Infant mortality was high, and the average adult life span was less than 45 years. However, this average obscures the fact that it was not uncommon for an affluent colonial, who had survived CHILDHOOD epidemics and who might avoid the hazards of hard physical labor, to live more than eight or nine decades. In general, however, the colonial American population was healthier, better housed, better fed, and longer-lived than in Europe.

In New England, where European men migrated along with their families, births began to outnumber deaths before 1700. An affluent woman usually married before the age of 20, and, during the next few decades, she bore a child every two or three years, for a total of seven or eight children. Her husband was usually seven or eight years older, because he needed to wait to inherit land or otherwise to procure an economic foundation. A servant woman, however, who could not legally marry until her term of service ended, might be in her late 20s before she could take a mate—who was likely to be marrying late for the same reason.

By contrast, in the South, where white men greatly outnumbered women in the 17th century, population growth by natural increase (the difference between births and deaths) did not begin until the 18th century. Although the PLANTATION SYSTEM promoted young marriages for both men and women, slave and free, the population remained smaller because mortality and morbidity were higher in the southern than in the northern colonies. The shortage of white women in the South also promoted limited intermarriage among Europeans, Native Americans, and AFRICAN AMERICANS. In addition, the rape of slave women by white owners produced children of mixed race. By 1700 the South had a significant population of multiracial residents. In New England and the mid-Atlantic colonies the few free black families sometimes intermarried with local Native Americans.

Child rearing, a central part of white family life, was likewise affected by many factors. As many as half of newborns died before their fifth birthday, mostly from illnesses, accidents, and diseases. Birth (attended by MIDWIVES until the mid-18th century, when male doctors gradually assumed this role) was often an event for which family members traveled long distances to be with the expectant mother. While there is some indication that families discouraged emotional attachment to young children until they had survived infant diseases, it is still unclear how much colonial Americans differentiated between adult human nature and child culture. Although a typical household contained some toys and playthings, children often were viewed simply as small adults, as suggested by such diverse evidence as the lack of differentiation in children's clothing and the expectation that they would assume responsibility for household tasks at a very young age. Religion was also important in shaping how children were raised. New England Puritan LITERATURE instructed parents that their role was to break the will of their children to make them obedient to God. However, Quaker assessment of human nature called for protecting the child—assumed to be born innocent—from the decadent influence of the adult world until the child's conscience was strong enough to withstand temptation.

What we now think of as violence was a common part of white family life. Infanticide, although forbidden, was not uncommon. Children, wives, servants, and slaves were routinely thrashed for misbehavior. Public punishments, such as pillorying and hanging, helped reinforce the idea that corporal punishment, often prescribed by the churches, was the best way to maintain discipline.

Among the propertied classes, especially in New England, patriarchs held title to land, while sons waited, sometimes with unveiled hostility, for their fathers to die and leave them the wherewithal to marry. Lacking a system for "retirement," the old could relinquish the burden of economic responsibilities and the young could not take it up. The resulting resentment of the old sometimes erupted into violence or neglect.

EDUCATION, at least teaching sufficient literacy to read the Bible, frequently was carried out in the homes of the affluent but was more erratic for poorer people. New England soon established schools to teach young people to read the Bible. Even so, reading and writing were often taught separately, and a person might be able to read but unable to write. Southern planters sometimes imported northern teachers to educate their households, and a handful of slaves sometimes managed to acquire some literacy by surreptitiously listening to the lessons. Masters also sometimes taught their apprentices to read and to count. Hence, as with HOUSING, food, and health, typical colonial Americans had better access to information and skills than their European counterparts.

By the mid-18th century home life among affluent white people began to reflect growing leisure. Houses became larger and furnishings more conducive to entertaining because some now contained coffee and tea services, elaborate dishware, and matched seating arrangements. Moreover, white women's roles and authority expanded in both the economic and religious sphere, while technological, social, and political changes encouraged the growth of the nuclear household that would become more common in succeeding generations.

Slaves struggled to create viable and meaningful families, and their physical circumstances often shaped their success in those endeavors. Because more black men than women were imported in the 17th century, the resulting GENDER imbalance and the wide spread of slaves over vast areas often limited the ability of African Americans to form long-lasting families. As white Americans purchased large numbers of slaves to work on TOBACCO and rice plantations in the late 17th and 18th centuries, the possibilities for slaves to establish families increased. Consequently, in the upper south slaves began to reproduce their population by the third decade of the 18th century. Family connection was vitally important in providing meaningful lives for many blacks, in part because it allowed black people to fulfill various human roles that owners tried to discourage. Spouses expressed their love for one another as well as their children. Slave families and their extended kin raised and, as far as possible, protected their offspring, teaching them how to cope with the difficulties of life in bondage. Families also formed the core of the slave community, which was often strongest on large plantations. The success of African Americans in fashioning families is testimony to the human determination to overcome incredible obstacles.

Further reading: Robert V. Wells, *Revolutions in Americans' Lives: A Demographic Perspective on the History of Americans, Their Families, and Their Society* (Westport, Conn.: Greenwood Press, 1982); Daniel Blake Smith, *Inside the Great House: Planter Family Life in Eighteenth-Century Chesapeake Society* (Ithaca, N.Y.: Cornell University Press, 1980).

—Emma Lapsansky

Maryland

Maryland was a proprietary colony ruled by the lords Baltimore except during a period of royal government from 1689 to 1715. When GEORGE CALVERT, scion of Yorkshire landowners, withdrew from public life, announcing his Catholicism and inability to take the Oath of Supremacy in 1625, James I rewarded his loyal service with the title baron Baltimore (Ireland). Already an East India Company shareholder and member of the VIRGINIA COMPANY OF LONDON board of governors, Calvert was granted "Avalon" (Newfoundland) in 1620. A disappointing 1627 visit convinced him to petition Charles I for land in northern VIRGINIA, and two months after his death in April 1632 a colonial charter was granted his son, Cecilius. The ships *Ark* and *Dove* and around 140 settlers reached Maryland (named after Queen Henrietta Maria) in May 1634.

Maryland's 8,000 to 10,000 mostly ALGONQUIN Indians (40 tribes formed into the Piscataway and Nanticoke federations on the lower western and eastern shores, respectively) offered little resistance to settlement. Seeing European settlers as potential allies after attacks by Virginian and northern Susquehannock, the Yaocomico sold the new arrivals land and helped them grow FOOD. The descendants of Indians who survived European diseases subsequently moved northward out of Maryland in the 18th century. A greater threat to Maryland settlers came from the roughly 100 Virginians under William Claiborne on Kent and Popely's Islands. After a naval encounter in CHESAPEAKE BAY in April 1635, the fur-trading William Clobbery and Company replaced Claiborne with George Evelin and sued for peace.

Long-term threats to the Calverts came through objections to proprietorial despotism and Catholicism. Maryland's charter gave Baltimore palatine powers, including the right to grant lordships and land, to collect quitrents, and to hold manorial courts over TENANTS (payment to the king was two Indian arrows per year and one-fifth of all precious metals). However, the charter was otherwise vague, giving Baltimore "absolute power . . . to ordain, make laws, with the advice, assent, & approbation of the free men," and referring to "delegates . . . called together for the framing of laws." Governor LEONARD CALVERT (Baltimore's brother) initially vetoed all acts of the early assemblies because they were legislative rather than executive initiatives but eventually accepted assembly legislation in 1638.

Conflict over the structure of government and power of assemblies continued, however, and became entwined with English political and religious convulsions during Maryland's mid-century "time of troubles." Maryland was never actually a Catholic colony. Most settlers were Protestant, and Baltimore required "Acts of Romane Catholique Religion to be done as privately as may be and . . . Romane Catholiques to be silent upon all occasions of discourse concerning matters of Religion." Still, political and sectarian conflict were inseparable. The ENGLISH CIVIL WAR reached Maryland with Richard Ingle's arrival in ST. MARY'S CITY in 1644; he proclaimed "the King was no King" and claimed armed ships for Parliament. He fled to England after his arrest but returned with parliamentary letters of marque to raid royalist homes in Maryland in 1645 and 1646 (the "plundering time" during which Claiborne tried to retake his trading post). After Leonard Calvert's death in 1647, Baltimore appointed Protestant William Stone governor. Stone granted refuge to 300 Virginia PURITANS under Richard Bennett in Ann Arundel County and confirmed acceptance of all Christians with the 1649 Toleration Act. With news of the execution of Charles I, however, acting governor Thomas Greene declared Charles II king. Despite Stone's retraction, enemies persuaded Oliver Cromwell of Maryland's rebelliousness, and the Protector appointed a commission headed by Bennett and Claiborne to govern Maryland.

The 1654 assembly, after excluding Roman Catholics from voting, forbade public Mass and abolished oaths of allegiance to Lord Baltimore. Baltimore ordered Stone to reestablish his authority in Maryland, inaugurating Maryland's Civil War. The commission's forces routed Stone's 130 men at the Battle of the Severn on March 25, 1655, but by 1657 Baltimore's rule and religious toleration were restored, with amnesty given to rebels. New governor Josias Kendall, however, resigned his commission in 1660, accepting one instead from assembly delegates proclaiming themselves "a lawfull Assembly without dependence on any other power." This "Pygmie rebellion" ended after two months with the Restoration of Charles II.

Calvert's authority was tested in the Restoration era as well. Baltimore insisted that "What Privileges and Powers I have by my Charter are from the King, & that of Calling of Assemblies in any such manner & way as I think fit being an undeniable one among the rest, I cannot Deem it Honorable Nor safe to Lodge it in the Freemen." In 1669 Reverend Charles Nicholette urged the assembly to claim "a Liberty equal to the people of England." Although the council extracted a fine and apology from Nicholette, delegates subsequently complained that "our laws, whereby our Liberty and Property subsists, are subject to Arbitrary Disposition." Concurrent with BACON'S REBELLION in 1676, rebels in Charles County led by Fendall and John Coode bemoaned Calvert vainglory, despotism, nepotism, corrupting of assembly members, and the lack of an established ANGLICAN CHURCH in *Complaint from Heaven with Huy and Crye & a petition out of Maryland and Virginia.* In 1681 the provincial court found Coode guilty of plotting to kidnap Baltimore, fined him 40,000 pounds of TOBACCO, and banished him from Maryland. Proprietorial attempts to stifle discontent by limiting votes to men with a 50-acre freehold or £40 estate in 1670 and by reducing the number of delegates from four to two per county in 1681 added to grievances. After learning of James II's overthrow in the GLORIOUS REVOLUTION of 1688, Coode and others formed the Protestant Association that listed antiproprietary grievances, declared William and Mary king and queen (1689–1702), and captured St. Mary's City without resistance.

Although Baltimore kept his land and quitrents, Maryland became a royal colony. The new assembly passed acts of establishment and endowment (40 pounds of tobacco per taxable inhabitant annually for ministers' salaries) for the Anglican Church, banned QUAKERS from sitting in the assembly, and banned ROMAN CATHOLICS from public office holding and worship. Maryland returned to proprietary rule in 1715 following Charles Calvert's death and the conversion of Benedict Leonard Calvert, fourth Lord Baltimore, to Anglicanism. Royal rule witnessed a governmental revolution as well. In 1694 Governor Francis Nicholson moved the capitol to Annapolis. The assembly established standing committees to expedite business, gained greater control over money bills, reformed the courts, revised laws, and began holding executive officials to account. Royal Governor John Seymour called the assemblymen a "restless and pernicious Crew." During the second proprietary period the Calverts and their Court Party supporters regularly fought the Country Party opposition over paper money, control of public officials' and clergy salaries and fees, and, as indicated in the title of Daniel Dulany, Sr.'s, pamphlet, *The Right of the Inhabitants of Maryland to the Benefit of English Laws* (1728).

As with politics, Maryland's ECONOMY and society developed greater stability over time. Learning from Virginia, Marylanders established tobacco staple AGRICULTURE, producing 100,000 pounds as early as 1639. Assemblymen indicated tobacco's importance during price depressions in the 1660s and 1680s, agreeing with Virginians to a "stint" limiting production to raise prices and enacting town loading laws to cut transport costs and raise profits, although the Calverts vetoed both measures. In 1747 Maryland enacted tobacco inspection, whereby substandard tobacco was burned at county warehouses, keeping quality and prices high (to the detriment of smaller farmers, who cut and burned planters' tobacco in response). In 1723 first minister Robert Walpole exempted tobacco from reexport fees under the Navigation Acts, and Maryland exports rose from 30,000 pounds to 100,000,000 between the 1720s and 1770s. Maryland's economy nevertheless diversified. Wheat dominated agriculture in the west, north, and lower eastern shore by the late 18th century. Ironworks appeared in Cecil County in 1715 and Baltimore Town in 1731. Baltimore's population was only 200 in 1755 but grew rapidly with the proliferation of wheat milling and the development of SHIPBUILDING in the later 18th century. These developments encouraged a diverse urban and rural artisan and service economy.

Economic growth and development was reflected in rapidly expanding population, area of settlement, and socioeconomic differentiation. Settler population remained less than 400 in 1642, many dying of "agues and fevers" (primarily malaria) and the "bloody flux" (dysentery). The very high MORTALITY of the 17th century prevented population increase by natural means. It also undermined the nuclear family but intensified the development of extended kinship networks. Elevated mortality rates among men led to extensive property ownership by women as they inherited wealth from their husbands and provided women with greater bargaining power in the marriage market. Subsequent generations were less susceptible to "seasoning" and, with natural increase superseding immigration and a CREOLE majority before 1700, population rose to 8,426 in 1660, 42,741 in 1710, and 162,267 in 1760. Tobacco planting led to scattered settlement, with planters settling riverfront land and smaller farmers living inland. Much of the lower western shore was settled by the mid-17th century, the north and lower eastern shore after the Susquehannah treaty of 1652, and the western and piedmont areas in the 18th century.

The spread of settlement and population growth forced the provincial council and manor courts to relinquish governmental burdens to local institutions, and proliferating landownership further diminished Calvert power. From the 1660s county courts gained jurisdiction in criminal cases not involving life or limb, civil litigation, tax-raising powers, and responsibility for building and maintaining roads and public buildings, licensing taverns, policing weights and measures, overseeing orphans, directing poor relief, appointing county officials, and supervising elections. To encourage settlement, in 1634–35 Baltimore established a headright system in which free settlers received 100 acres for themselves plus 2,000 acres for every five family members or servants brought with them. Between 1635 and 1683 new arrivals received 100 acres plus 50 acres for each child under 16, after which settlers could purchase land. Landowners paid annual quitrents, and if they died intestate, their title reverted to the Calverts. Even so, the widespread availability of land undermined the Calverts' vision of a manorial society of proprietors, lesser landowners, and tenants, creating instead a powerful planter elite and a large population of smaller independent farmers—at least among whites.

LABOR requirements, always intense in a tobacco-producing economy, were initially met by indentured servants, with SLAVERY developing slowly. Thirteen slaves appeared in St. Mary's City in 1642. These early black laborers were sometimes treated similarly to indentured servants, many being freed and given an allowance of CLOTHING and FOOD after four to seven years of service. Servant migration from England declined in the late 17th century. As the prices of white servants increased and of African slaves declined, Maryland planters, many of whom had amassed greater capital, began to invest heavily in slaves. In 1663 and 1664 the assembly legally established slavery, legislating enslavement for life and declaring that baptism gave no entitlement to freedom. Slaves numbered only 750 in 1660 but rose to 8,000 in 1710 and near 50,000 in 1760. By 1763 slaves represented almost a third of Maryland's total population. Slaves were more heavily concentrated in the predominantly tobacco-growing lower western shore, where they exceeded half the population. In the increasingly wheat-growing remainder of the colony, they formed less than 15 percent of the inhabitants. The growth of slave communities, creolization of most of the slave population, and development of a thriving African-American culture and tradition of resistance by the mid-18th century enabled slaves to carve out a meaningful existence even while suffering brutal conditions.

A planter elite established itself by the end of the 17th century. As well as gaining wealth in slaves (and greater tobacco production), their land values doubled between 1680 and 1700. Wealthy planters enhanced their authority through dynastic alliances and through control of the assembly, the increasingly powerful courts, and the church vestries. They distinguished themselves through a cult of gentility, building brick Georgian mansions, filling them with genteel accoutrements, appearing in more refined clothing and carriages, and pursuing exclusive leisure activities. Increasing inequality also entailed diminished economic opportunity for poorer people. Seventy percent of white Maryland householders (many originally indentured servants) owned land in the 1660s. That figure declined to 50 percent over the next century, and by the 1760s only 15 percent enjoyed all the rights of freemen; even fewer could exercise the vote. Although slavery increased material inequality in white society, it also aided social stability through imposing disciplinary imperatives and creating notions of racial supremacy. Also, British MERCHANTS in the Chesapeake area from the 1730s enhanced access to credit and to slaves (half of southern Marylanders were slaveholders by the 1760s) and other goods so that standards of living generally rose. Not until the Revolution was Maryland's elite significantly challenged.

Further reading: Gloria L. Main, *Tobacco Colony: Life in Early Maryland, 1650–1720* (Princeton, N.J.: Princeton University Press, 1982); Russell R. Menard, *Economy and Society in Early Colonial Maryland* (New York: Garland, 1985); Lois Green Carr, Russell R. Menard, and Lorena S. Walsh, *Robert Cole's World: Agriculture and Society in Early Maryland* (Chapel Hill: University of North Carolina Press, 1991).

—Steven Sarson

Mason, John (1600?–1672)

A distinguished English magistrate and soldier, John Mason declined a commission in Oliver Cromwell's parliamentary army and immigrated to North America around 1630. When Mason arrived in MASSACHUSETTS, he was hired to plan and build defenses along BOSTON harbor and to protect the coast from pirates. He also served as captain of the Dorchester militia and helped to found Windsor, CONNECTICUT.

During the PEQUOT WAR Mason and his men, including the Mohegan leader Uncas and 70 of his warriors, set fire to Mystic Fort, killing more than 600 Pequot men, women, and children, including the revered leader Sassacus. The loss of such a leader had a great psychological impact on the NATIVE AMERICANS, as they objected to the brutality of this type of warfare. Many Indians attributed supernatural powers to Mason, and most refused to fight with him again. Mason chronicled this victory in *A Relation of the Troubles that have Happened in New England* (1677).

After the Pequot War Mason held a number of government offices in Connecticut, including chief military officer, magistrate, and deputy governor, but again became most known for his dealings in Indian affairs. Forming an apparently equal partnership, Mason and Uncas significantly increased each other's power and influence. Mason used his military strength to force the PEQUOT to accept Uncas's power. Uncas then was able to break from the Pequot Confederation, thereby increasing his power and authority. Becoming the Mohegan's protector likewise benefited Mason. Uncas reported the activities of other Indian groups to Mason and supplied warriors on occasion. The men seemed truly to be fond of one another, Mason described Uncas as a "great" friend. Uncas even granted Mason permission to establish Norwich, Connecticut, in 1660 in Mohegan territory, although land ownership issues between the English and Indians later complicated the relationship.

After his first wife died, Mason fathered seven children by his second wife, Anne Peck. They lived on a farm in Norwich until Mason's death.

Further reading: Wendy B. St. Jean, "Inventing Guardianship: The Mohegan Indians and Their 'Protector'" *(New England Quarterly,* 1999, 72[3], 362–87).

—Lisa A. Ennis

Massachusetts

The name *Massachusetts,* meaning "near the Great Hill," referred to the ALGONQUIN-speaking natives living in the general vicinity of the Blue Hills near the Charles and Neponset Rivers on Massachusetts Bay in the 16th century. Also inhabiting the land were the Nipmuc, Pennacook, Mahican, NARRAGANSETT, and Pocumtuck. The coast was explored by European MARINERS throughout the 16th century, but no permanent colony was attempted. FISHING fleets from Europe were frequent visitors to Massachusetts coastal waters by the early 1600s. Coastal trade soon developed between the natives and the Europeans, especially in fur. An epidemic transmitted from one of the visiting European ships took a heavy toll among the native population along the entire New England coast around 1617. When English settlers began to arrive within the next 10 years, they found cleared lands and little opposition from the devastated natives.

Early Settlement and Growth

The PILGRIMS, a small group of radical Protestants called Separatists, successfully founded the town and colony of PLYMOUTH along the interior western side of Cape Cod Bay in 1620. They established relations with the Wampanoag and Nauset. The Pilgrims were followed by several other small settlements around Massachusetts Bay, including Merrymount, Wessagusset, and Winnisimmet within a few years. The most important of these was the small seasonal fishing village at Cape Ann. The abundance of fish, notably cod, attracted numerous fishermen, and their need for a permanent base led to the establishment of Naumkeag (Salem) in 1624 under the leadership of Roger Conant. JOHN ENDECOTT, with a group of followers, became the first governor of the small settlement in 1628. Salem's inhabitants were just the vanguard of the "Great Migration" of English colonists to Massachusetts that followed.

The PURITANS who immigrated were Protestant reformers, dissenters from the ANGLICAN CHURCH who followed the teachings of John Calvin. The MASSACHUSETTS BAY COMPANY, hoping for great profits and looking for settlers, was granted a charter from King Charles I (1625–49) in 1629. Facing increasing persecution in England, an estimated 30,000 Puritans joined the Great Migration to the Massachusetts Bay Colony in the decade from 1630 to 1640. Their stated goal was to build a new Jerusalem in the wilderness, to be a "city upon a hill" in the words of JOHN WINTHROP, which would serve as a model for the rest of the world. Towns were established clustering around the capital of BOSTON on Massachusetts Bay and along the Connecticut River Valley 80 miles to the west, like the frontier outpost of Springfield. The few interior settlements were located along old Indian trails that soon became rough colonial roads. Each town was governed by a town meeting where "freemen" could vote. "Freeman" status was limited to church members who were adult males who owned at least £20 worth of property or its equivalent. The Congregational church, with a simple, or "plain style," of service, was firmly established as the central focus of every Massachusetts town.

Local magistrates sought close control over their Puritan commonwealth. Religious minds that differed from the expressed tenets would not be allowed to practice or even live in Massachusetts. ANNE MARBURY HUTCHINSON was banished in 1636 for her Antinomian views, despite sympathetic allies Governor Henry Vane and Reverend JOHN COTTON. Minister ROGER WILLIAMS, a talented but, to Massachusetts minds, too independent theologian, was banished after unsuccessfully trying to preach at Boston, Salem, and Plymouth; he founded RHODE ISLAND on Narragansett Bay.

Massachusetts Puritans quickly put their faith into action, especially by emphasizing EDUCATION. HARVARD COLLEGE, the first English college in the colonies, was founded in 1636 in Cambridge as the training ground for a future Puritan ministry. A printing press, the first in North America, also was set up in Cambridge in 1639. Among its first published works was *The Bay Psalm Book,* a translation of the psalms into English. In 1647 Massachusetts became the first civil society in the world to require compulsory primary education by passing a law called the Old Deluder Satan Act because keeping people ignorant of the Bible supposedly was a tactic of Satan. Massachusetts undertook minting its own currency in 1652, which it continued for many years afterwards, always printing the date 1652 to deceive royal officials. The first codification of laws in the modern world was created with passage of *The Laws and Liberties of 1648,* detailing the rights and responsibilities of individuals in the commonwealth.

Massachusetts took an early theological and political lead in the North American colonies because of its large population and, some would argue, arrogant attitude. A large group from Massachusetts, including Governor John Haynes and Reverend THOMAS HOOKER, traveled inland in 1635 and 1636 to found the Colony of CONNECTICUT. This close relation between Massachusetts and Connecticut, and the smaller colonies of Plymouth and New Haven, led to the formation of the New England Confederation in 1643 for the mutual defense and security of all four colonies. The alliance was formed in the wake of the PEQUOT WAR of 1636 against any more possible threats from Indians or the nearby Dutch and FRENCH COLONIES.

English settlement continued encroaching inland until several events precipitated KING PHILIP'S WAR (1675–76), one of the most devastating wars in American history. One out of every three English settlements in New England was attacked by a combination of several native tribes, notably

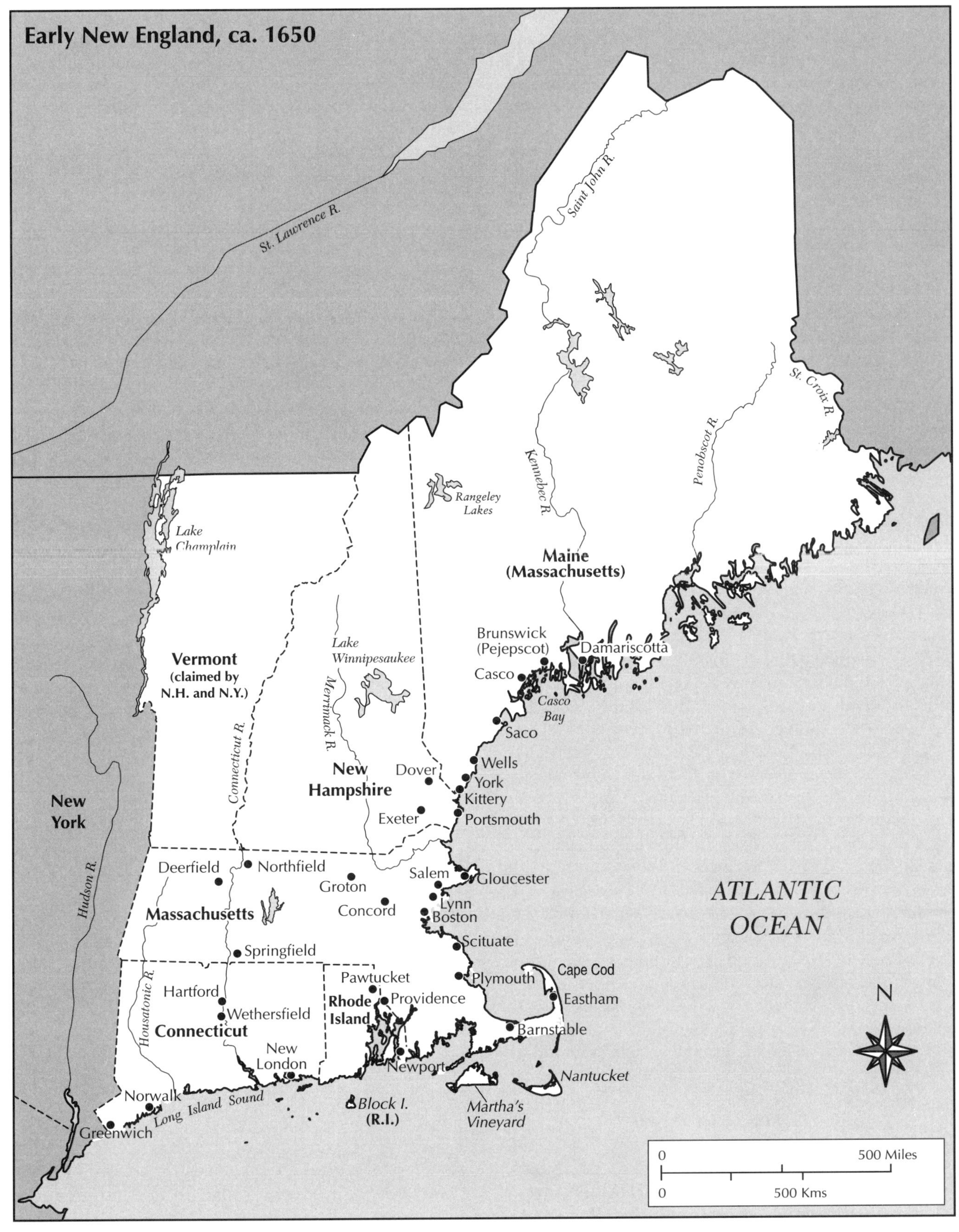
Early New England, ca. 1650
St. Lawrence R.
Saint John R.
St. Croix R.
Penobscot R.
Kennebec R.
Rangeley Lakes
Lake Champlain
Maine (Massachusetts)
Brunswick (Pejepscot)
Damariscotta
Casco
Casco Bay
Saco
Wells
York
Kittery
Portsmouth
Dover
Exeter
Lake Winnipesaukee
Merrimack R.
New Hampshire
Vermont (claimed by N.H. and N.Y.)
Connecticut R.
New York
Hudson R.
Deerfield
Northfield
Groton
Salem
Gloucester
Lynn
Boston
Concord
Massachusetts
Springfield
Scituate
Plymouth
Cape Cod
Eastham
Barnstable
Pawtucket
Providence
Rhode Island
Hartford
Wethersfield
Connecticut
Housatonic R.
New London
Newport
Nantucket
Martha's Vineyard
Block I. (R.I.)
Norwalk
Long Island Sound
Greenwich
ATLANTIC OCEAN
N
0
500 Miles
0
500 Kms

the Wampanoag led by MASSASOIT's son Philip (METACOM). Attacks on English towns ranged from Deerfield in the west to Plymouth in the east. Half of all the towns in New England suffered raids; 12 towns were completely destroyed. The war proved devastating for New England's natives—Philip was ambushed and killed, his captains executed, his villages destroyed, and the natives in nearly three colonies virtually eliminated. Even the "Praying Indians," those natives converted by the Reverend JOHN ELIOT, who had translated and published the Bible in Algonquin in 1663, were incarcerated and left to starve on an island in Boston Harbor. Many natives, including King Philip's son, were sold into SLAVERY in the West Indies. The war left the colonies with large debts and one of every 15 men of fighting age dead. The fighting continued off and on in MAINE for some dozen years more. There were later periodic attacks by natives in Massachusetts following King Philip's War, notably Haverhill in 1695 and Deerfield in 1704, but these were associated with the shifting allegiances of the natives among colonists of the continually warring nations of England and France.

With the threat of native warfare effectively reduced, the English colonists of Massachusetts looked to restoring their colony as the Puritan commonwealth, but times had moved past them. In 1684 the charter was revoked by King James II (1685–8) and the Royal DOMINION OF NEW ENGLAND was established, headed by the autocratic and tyrannical Governor SIR EDMUND ANDROS. The Massachusetts Puritans watched with horror as an Anglican Church was forcefully established in Boston, as their annual election of officials was terminated, and as political favor was doled out to Andros's close circle of cronies. Reverend COTTON MATHER called this "Decennium Luctuosum," the lamentable decade. When they had finally had enough and heard the news of the overthrow of James II by William of Orange during the GLORIOUS REVOLUTION of 1688, leading Puritans in Boston had Andros and his associates arrested and sent back to England. Reverend INCREASE MATHER was sent to London to secure the return of the charter, but compromise was necessary. After several years of lobbying, Mather was able to secure a new charter for the Province of Massachusetts Bay in 1691, which restored many of the earlier rights but also required many changes. Among the changes were a royally appointed governor, the annexation of the Territory of Maine and Plymouth Colony, and the extension of SUFFRAGE to inhabitants who were not members of the Congregational churches.

The Provincial Period

Increase Mather returned to Massachusetts in May 1692 with the new charter and the new royal governor, Massachusetts resident Sir William Phips. They immediately found the entire colony consumed by the WITCHCRAFT hysteria that was occurring in Salem. Governor Phips created a Court of Oyer and Terminer to try the hundreds of people imprisoned on suspicion of witchcraft, hoping to quickly end the whole affair. The hysteria resulted in the deaths of 20 people, the incarceration of hundreds more, and the effective end of Puritan supremacy in Massachusetts. The colony became the royal Province of Massachusetts Bay and soon found itself involved in the politics of the worldwide BRITISH EMPIRE.

As an indication of Massachusetts's new role in the empire, shipping increased dramatically. The port of Boston led the way with a new emphasis on SHIPBUILDING, importing and exporting, and serving as a hub of military activity for the English colonies in North America. Military expeditions were launched from Boston's Long Wharf, which extended nearly half a mile into the harbor. The new emphasis on mercantile affairs also brought about the creation of a bureaucracy of customs officials and a vice admiralty court (1696) based in Boston to administer a close watch on colonial affairs. Several smaller ports, Salem, Marblehead, and Newburyport, grew in population, shipping, and importance as well. The mercantile policies of the Crown were not always followed by the Massachusetts MERCHANTS who, despite the Navigation Acts, were willing to risk breaking the official policies for a profit.

Massachusetts's role in the 18th-century wars for empire was one of supplying soldiers, ships, and goods during the struggles of KING WILLIAM'S WAR, QUEEN ANNE'S WAR, KING GEORGE'S WAR, and the SEVEN YEARS' WAR, as well as defending itself and its interests. In 1745 Governor William Shirley and Sir William Pepperell planned and orchestrated the successful siege of the fortified French town of Louisbourg on the coast of Nova Scotia. This stunning victory was reversed, however, when the fortress was returned to France at the end of King George's War, much to the annoyance of all New Englanders. Massachusetts provided many of the soldiers and sailors necessary for these costly imperial wars. There was also the continual need for defense along the frontier, where the shifting allegiances of the remaining native tribes and their resistance to encroachment on their lands meant there was always the possibility of hostilities. By the mid-18th century the toll had become apparent as the number of poor rose drastically, particularly with an increase of widows and orphaned children.

Political factionalism during the 1700s took the place of the religious controversies of the 1600s. Career politicians like Governors JOSEPH DUDLEY and William Shirley held the province's highest offices during the next several decades, trying to court favor with both their patrons in England and the general Massachusetts population. Loosely organized political parties developed: a "court" party usually comprised of the governor, his cronies and political appointees, and several of the wealthier, more powerful families, and a "country" party, generally consisting of Massachusetts's artisan and laboring classes and the rural population.

Political divisions carried over in the Land Bank versus Silver Bank controversy, with the Land Bank providing a temporary boost to the local ECONOMY but creating high inflation, causing its repeal by Parliament in 1741. Party politics, never formally organized, would evolve into the Whig and Tory factionalism of the Revolutionary era. This division was clearly visible in the political feud between the Hutchinson and Otis families, in which the Hutchinson faction was the court party, holding numerous Crown offices, and the Otis faction held many of the popularly elected offices and tirelessly stressed the rights of Massachusetts citizens. James Otis, Jr., brilliantly argued the case against the Writs of Assistance in 1761 and inspired two decades of radical unrest and political fighting by the likes of Samuel Adams and John Hancock against the Hutchinson-dominated government.

Culture and Society

The inhabitants of Massachusetts were far from the typical Puritan caricature of black clothes and grim faces. Probate inventories show people wore many different types of clothes in many colors, followed London fashions, and bought imported fabrics, despite the "sumptuary laws" passed during the 1600s, which attempted to prohibit poorer citizens from wearing expensive CLOTHING. Laws like these were designed to maintain the structure of Massachusetts society, a hierarchy in each family, each church, and each town. CLASS differences, although less drastic than in England, were preserved in Massachusetts. Most people lived in small, modest houses of two or three rooms and a loft, which developed from typical English models. The wide availability of wood encouraged its use instead of brick, even for the grander homes of merchants. Houses of the mid-18th century had assumed the standard layouts of the Cape and the Saltbox, both often constructed around a large, central hearth for warmth. Birth rates were high, causing the population to grow at a rapid pace.

Life in Massachusetts during the colonial period was often difficult. Farms dominated the countryside, as subsistence farming was the most common occupation. The rocky soil of New England meant they could never produce much surplus for export. Small manufacturing and trades developed to supplement farming, including rum distilleries, iron ore forges and foundries, and lumber MILLS. The ports that dotted the coasts provided the more profitable but usually more dangerous enterprises of shipbuilding, fishing, and ocean-going trade. Imports increased as the population grew, until by the 1750s Massachusetts was importing not only manufactured and luxury goods from England but also raw materials and food like molasses for rum production and grain to feed itself. The Massachusetts merchants exploited the business opportunities afforded in the empire using their own ships to engage in the "Triangle Trade," bringing Africans as slaves to the West Indies and the southern colonies in return for raw materials to exchange for goods in Europe, some merchants making fortunes in the process.

There were diversions in colonial life. Massachusetts boasted a generally literate population who often read. Favorites included the Bible, works of Milton and Bunyan, Foxe's *Book of Martyrs*, almanacs, newspapers (after 1704), and especially religious tracts like sermons published in pamphlet form. Among the most popular texts were MICHAEL WIGGLESWORTH's long poem *The Day of Doom* and historical works by Cotton Mather and Thomas Prince. The value of education resulted in many local schools, wide readership of various printed materials, and even a knowledge of SCIENCE. SMALLPOX inoculations in the 1720s in Boston, although protested by many, were supported among the clergy, resulting in positive results and many lives saved. Local taverns, or ordinaries, which were licensed by the counties, provided a social gathering place outside the ever-present meetinghouse, where much of the town business was conducted. Rum, hard cider, and punch were favorite drinks and consumed in great quantities. TOBACCO was also commonly smoked. Roads were difficult to travel but were better than in many of the other colonies thanks to a system of post roads used by travelers. The journal kept by SARAH KEMBLE KNIGHT on a trip in 1704 provides one of the best pictures of the hazards of TRAVEL. While the local ministers may not have liked the ideas of travel or other diversions, they grew more accepting with the passing years. Increase Mather preached against dancing, and SAMUEL SEWALL railed indignantly against the fashion of wearing wigs among the young men in the early 1700s, yet Massachusetts grew ever more cosmopolitan and fashionable. Card playing, dice, and games were common, if not always approved.

Luxury trades flourished in the larger towns. Massachusetts gold and silversmiths, like Paul Revere, were recognized master ARTISANS. Furniture makers known as joiners and turners in the 1600s were replaced by professional cabinetmakers in the 1700s, producing some of the finest examples of American colonial furniture. Gravestones, all hand-carved like furniture, started out as a luxury item in the 1670s, but carving workshops could be found across the colony within 50 years. MUSIC developed far more slowly, being limited mostly to Psalm singing, but with the arrival of PETER PELHAM in Boston in the 1730s, it started to be widely enjoyed. Pelham not only played and taught music but was also a dancing master and a skilled engraver who produced quality portraits. His son-in-law, John Singleton Copley, would carry the ART of portraiture to its greatest form in the colonies. Copley engaged in the one form of fine art, portrait painting, that had been approved of and respected among the Massachusetts Puritans because it preserved images of "visible saints." By the time of his most famous paintings, the portraits of Paul Revere and Samuel Adams, he was building on nearly a century of portraiture by John Smibert, ROBERT FEKE, Joseph Blackburn, and a number of anonymous artists.

The size of the population of Massachusetts remained second only to VIRGINIA throughout the colonial period, yet it was always foremost in importance in shipping, publishing, culture, political agitation, and independence, the last of which would prove the most troublesome for Parliament and Crown as events in Massachusetts precipitated the start of the American Revolution.

Further reading: David Grayson Allen, *In English Ways* (Chapel Hill: University of North Carolina Press, 1981); Richard L. Bushman, *King and People in Provincial Massachusetts* (Chapel Hill: University of North Carolina Press, 1985); Benjamin W. Labaree, *Colonial Massachusetts: A History* (New York: KTO Press, 1979); Alden T. Vaughan, *New England Frontier: Puritans and Indians 1620–1675* (Boston: Little, Brown, 1995).

—Stephen C. O'Neill

Massachusetts Bay Company (1628–1629)

Begun as a trading venture, the MASSACHUSETTS Bay Company soon took on a spiritual mission as PURITANS used it to emigrate from England to BOSTON. Issued in May 1628 at the instigation of Sir Richard Saltonstall and Issac Johnson, the company received a charter, which, for a limited time of seven years, allowed it to ship people and provisions to establish a "plantation" in New England. If the company had the land surveyed, then the short indenture could be changed to a patent. The company's subscribers elected a governor, Mathew Cradock, who served with the aid of six associates. The first company ship was sent out under the command of JOHN ENDECOTT to take possession of the Dorchester settlement at Salem. In the following April the company sent out a further five ships carrying an additional 200 passengers, many of them poor.

In England disagreements soon emerged between those who wanted the company to be primarily a trading enterprise and those, like JOHN WINTHROP, who had a more spiritual end in view. The non-Puritan elements sold their interests to the religious men on August 26, 1629, and Winthrop became the new governor. While the company remained headquartered in England, Anglican bishops could easily spy on its operations and anyone could threaten the control of the Puritans by buying into the company. Fortunately for the Puritans, the company's charter did not specify that it had to remain in the mother country. It was hoped that the members of the company could slip away unnoticed and that the distance of North America would make English interference impossible. The Puritans took the charter and set sail in March 1630 in a fleet of 11 ships with the aim of joining the substantial base of people already established in New England. The Salem location did not prove satisfactory, so the company chose to establish itself in Boston, a thin neck of land protruding into the sea. When the government transferred to North America, the Massachusetts Bay Company became the New England Company.

Further reading: Frances Rose-Troup, *The Massachusetts Bay Company and Its Predecessors* (New York: Grafton Press, 1930).

—Caryn E. Neumann

Massachusetts School Act (1647)

The first law in MASSACHUSETTS calling for public education, this act required that all towns of 50 or more families "appoint one within their own town to teach all such children as shall resort to him to write and read." Towns with 100 households or more were also to hire a master to run a grammar school that would teach youths in a classical curriculum to prepare them to attend HARVARD COLLEGE.

Known also as the Old Deluder Satan Act, the 1647 law followed five years after Massachusetts's first educational legislation, the 1642 law that required that all families or masters of apprentices take responsibility for teaching basic reading and writing to the children in their charge. The 1647 law, then, marked a shift of responsibility for education from the family to the community, although children being taught at home were still not required to attend public schools. The style of the act had wide-ranging effects on New England's educational culture: By 1677 it had been copied by the legal codes of CONNECTICUT, New Haven, and PLYMOUTH.

The 1647 act had many restrictions, though. Its educational provisions were only for boys, as girls were not permitted to attend the grammar schools it created and could only hope for an education in basic literacy at home or in a "dame school." Although it provided for education, the law did not necessarily create public schools, as teaching was often carried out in private homes. Funding was tenuous, with costs being paid through annual taxation, not through endowments of land or money like most European schools of the period. And the wars of the late 17th century also affected children's school lives. During KING PHILIP'S WAR outlying towns petitioned the assembly for relief from requiring children to attend schools out of fear of capture by NATIVE AMERICANS. The fear continued into the next century. In March 1703 the Massachusetts House passed a law exempting towns from penalties for not enforcing the 1647 act because "Diverse of the frontier Towns which are by Law Obliged to Maintain a Grammar School, are in such Hazard of the Enemy, that it is unsafe for the children to Passe to and from the Schools."

Further reading: James Axtell, *The School Upon a Hill: Education and Society in Colonial New England* (New Haven, Conn.: Yale University Press, 1974).

—George W. Boudreau

Massasoit (1580?–1662?)

Massasoit, meaning "Great Leader," was the sachem of the Pokanocket Wampanoag Indians and an early ally of the PILGRIMS in PLYMOUTH. He was also called Ousamequin, meaning "Yellow Feather." The English labeled him "king" of some 6,000 Wampanoag people living in more than 20 villages. The Wampanoag were a loose confederation of ALGONQUIN-speaking natives in southeastern MASSACHUSETTS and eastern RHODE ISLAND. Massasoit's home village of Pokanocket, also known as Mount Hope, was located 60 miles west of Plymouth on Narragansett Bay, in present-day Bristol and Warren, Rhode Island.

Massasoit visited the Pilgrim settlers in Plymouth in March 1621 with his brother Quadequina and 60 warriors to establish relations with the English settlers. Massasoit and Governor John Carver agreed to a treaty of alliance and mutual respect. For the English in Plymouth, this treaty meant they were free from the fear of an attack by the Wampanoag surrounding them. For the Wampanoag the treaty meant gaining a new ally against their traditional rivals, the powerful Narragansett Indians to the west. Massasoit's treaty would keep the English settlers of Plymouth Colony and the Wampanoag at peace for more than 50 years. As an indication of their friendly relations, sometime in the fall of 1621 Massasoit accompanied 90 of his fellow Wampanoag to join the Pilgrims in Plymouth for several days of feasting and celebrating, known popularly as the first Thanksgiving. Intelligent, diplomatic, and respected by both English and native populations, Massasoit died around 1662 and was succeeded by his sons Alexander (Wamsutta) and Philip (METACOM), who later led a war against the settlers.

Further reading: Alden T. Vaughan, *New England Frontier: Puritans and Indians, 1620–1675* (Boston: Little, Brown, 1995); Neal Salisbury, *Manitou and Providence: Indians, Europeans, and the Making of New England, 1500–1643* (New York: Oxford University Press, 1982).

—Stephen C. O'Neill

Mather, Cotton (1663–1728)

Cotton, the son of INCREASE MATHER, joined him as pastor of the Second (Old North) Church of BOSTON in 1683 and remained there until his death. A child prodigy who graduated from HARVARD COLLEGE at age 15, he was more liberal than his father in favoring the controversial Half-Way Covenant (the baptism of the children of "half-way" church members who had been baptized but had not yet experienced salvation). Otherwise, he shared Increase's strict religious beliefs: Cotton opposed the right of nearby ministers to veto congregations' choices of their preachers, and he fought the admission of any person of good character to Communion, as favored by Northampton's Solomon Stoddard. Mather wrote incessantly. His masterpiece, *Magnalia Christi Americana,* published in 1702, related the history of New England as the work of divinely inspired institutions and men who, like JOHN WINTHROP and his own grandfather JOHN COTTON, ranked equally with biblical figures such as Moses and Nehemiah.

Mather was also involved in politics. A key actor in the GLORIOUS REVOLUTION in MASSACHUSETTS, in 1689 he was among those who imprisoned SIR EDMUND ANDROS, the royally appointed governor general of New England, when he learned that King James II (1685–8) had been overthrown in Britain. He welcomed the new governor, Sir William Phips, to Boston and baptized him. At the same time, Mather staunchly defended the proceedings against the supposed witches at Salem, most famously in his book *Wonders of the Invisible World* (1692), which led many to ridicule him once the crisis passed. Mather's intense spirituality appears in his diary, in which he claimed to receive visits from angels, predicted the end of the world, and considered such minor ailments as toothaches to have divine importance.

Mather remained active in Massachusetts politics throughout his adult life. He switched allegiance frequently, sometimes opposing and sometimes supporting the governor, before settling down as a partisan of Governor Samuel Shute and Lieutenant Governor William Dummer from 1716 until his death. Two reasons explain this: His father negotiated the new charter under which they served, and a fellow agent and his son, Elisha Cooke, Sr., and Jr., led the opposition that charged that the Mathers had sold their countrymen out by acquiescing to royal government.

Despite his traditional religious ways, Mather was a strong advocate of Newtonian SCIENCE and the method of SMALLPOX inoculation introduced in Boston by Dr. ZABDIEL BOYLSTON in 1721. Mather's tract *The Angel of Bethesda,* although not published until 1976, showed him at his best, as a learned man, aware that religion and science were compatible and contributed to human "progress." However, he is still best remembered for his belief in witchcraft and some of the extreme statements in his diary, which can all too easily be used to make the New England Puritans look ridiculous.

Further reading: Kenneth Silverman, *The Life and Times of Cotton Mather* (New York: Harper & Row, 1984).

—William Pencak

Mather, Increase (1639–1723)

Increase Mather was the foremost Puritan minister of his times. Son of another prominent minister, Richard Mather, he received a B.A. from HARVARD COLLEGE in 1656 and then went to England to study, earning an M.A. at Trinity College, Dublin, in 1658. Returning to MASSACHUSETTS in 1661, he married Maria Cotton, daughter of John, the most famous minister of the first generation of PURITANS in New England. Their first son, COTTON MATHER, became in time as influential as his father.

Throughout his life Increase staunchly supported traditional Puritanism, in which the male members of the congregation chose ministers and fellow church members. In the 1660s he opposed the Half-Way Covenant, whose supporters hoped to increase church membership by permitting the children of "half-way" members who had been baptized but had not yet experienced salvation to be baptized themselves. Here he conflicted with his more liberal father, who died during this controversy that plagued Massachusetts for a decade. At its height in 1664, Increase became the pastor of the Old North, or Second, Church of Boston, a position he held until his death 59 years later.

For six decades Mather stuck to his rigorous path, preaching and publishing dozens of books and sermons. He considered the Indian uprising of 1675 (KING PHILIP'S WAR), a Boston fire of 1677, and a SMALLPOX epidemic as divine punishment for the people's religious laxity. In 1679 he vigorously opposed Northampton's Solomon Stoddard, who argued that the only way to keep the church alive was to admit those who had not experienced salvation. Mather persuaded a synod of ministers to do likewise. He became president of Harvard College in 1685, reintroducing Greek and Hebrew studies and requiring students to reside at the college and attend their classes. He held this position until 1701, when his political enemies forced him to resign.

Mather began to play an active role in Massachusetts's politics in the 1680s. He at first staunchly defended the Old Charter of 1629 against the British government, for it, in effect, left Massachusetts completely independent. Upon sailing for England as the province agent in 1688, however, he realized its preservation was impossible. Deftly switching allegiance from King James II (1685–8) to William III (1689–1702) during England's GLORIOUS REVOLUTION, he was able to obtain a very good deal for Massachusetts: an

Increase Mather *(Library of Congress)*

elected council and a New England sea captain, Sir William Phips, as the first royally appointed governor. However, those of his allies who had remained in New England believed Mather had betrayed them and the Old Charter; throughout the 1690s he defended Phips and his successors, which led to his removal as college president.

Mather changed his political tune and went to the opposition after 1702, when JOSEPH DUDLEY assumed the governorship. He tried to oust this staunch supporter of royal power by supporting charges of corruption against him, but Dudley survived and his enemies faded, given the need to mobilize forces in QUEEN ANNE'S WAR (1702–13). Dudley, like most of the leading ministers in the colony by this time, was more lax on church membership and discipline than was Mather. Dudley wanted the ministers to establish a quasi-Presbyterian government that permitted them to reject pastors chosen by congregations, in general for being too reactionary. Mather successfully fought off this move in 1705. Shortly thereafter he retired from politics, although he continued to write extensively until the end of his life, urging the inhabitants of Massachusetts to renounce their sinful ways and to revert to their God-given status as a "chosen people."

Further reading: Michael G. Hall, *The Last American Puritan: The Life of Increase Mather* (Middletown, Conn.: Wesleyan University Press, 1988).

—William Pencak

Mayflower Compact

Passengers aboard the *Mayflower,* known as the PILGRIMS, sailed across the Atlantic in 1620 with a patent to establish a religious settlement in northern VIRGINIA. When they found themselves along the MASSACHUSETTS coast, outside the jurisdiction of Virginia, and unable to go any farther, they realized that any settlement they built would be without any legal authority. Governor WILLIAM BRADFORD wrote that there were soon "discontented and mutinous speeches" from some of the "Strangers" on board the ship, those passengers who were not members of the Separatist Church (the "Saints"). The "Strangers" (mostly members of the Church of England) threatened to "use their own liberty" and go their own way. Bradford realized cooperation was necessary for their common survival.

All the passengers then agreed to form a "civil body politic" that would bind the Separatists and the "Strangers" in a self-governing unit. It was signed by 41 passengers, all the free adult males, in the cabin of the *Mayflower* on November 11 (November 21, new style calendar), 1620, while the ship was anchored in Provincetown Harbor at the tip of Cape Cod. The covenant agreed to was specifically for their "better ordering and preservation." They agreed to "enact, constitute, and frame such just and equal laws . . . as shall be thought most meet and convenient for the general good of the Colony." It was a covenant similar to ones used in the Protestant churches of the time providing for those who agreed to the covenant to be bound by "all due submission and obedience." What the Mayflower Compact created was a secular covenant consented to by its signatories providing for a voluntary government, but one that would still be agreeable to the laws of England.

This painting shows the Pilgrims signing the compact in one of the *Mayflower*'s cabins. *(Library of Congress)*

Later historians, especially John Quincy Adams, viewed the Mayflower Compact as one of the progenitors of American democracy and a forerunner of the idea of self-government. The Mayflower Compact was superseded by the Patent of 1621, which was sent to the PLYMOUTH colony by John Pierce, one of the merchant adventurers in England who had helped finance the voyage. The original document of the Mayflower Compact has never been found.

Further reading: George D. Langdon, Jr., *Pilgrim Colony: A History of New Plymouth, 1620–1691* (New Haven, Conn.: Yale University Press, 1966).

—Stephen C. O'Neill

medicine

Medical beliefs and practices were eclectic in colonial North America. Their foundation was the ancient teachings of Hippocrates and Galen, a tradition known as "humoralism" because it explained human health and illness in terms of internal bodily balances and imbalances among the four "humors": blood (sanguine), phlegm, yellow bile (choler), and black bile (melancholy). Illness was explained as a result of five types of external cause: invisible, particulate effluvia; contagion (direct physical contact with disease); changes in air temperature; earthquakes, comets and other extraordinary natural phenomena; and divine punishment for sin. Diagnoses according to the Galenic tradition were made on the basis of relations between heat and cold and dryness and moisture in the patient. Treatments (known together as "heroic medicine") included bleeding, sweating, purges, and emetics of various kinds to restore an equilibrium of the humors.

Other important theories and practices, like "iatrochemistry" (*iatros* is Greek for "physician"), overlapped and combined with Galenic traditions. According to the 16th-century philosopher Paracelsus, illness could be explained by chemical imbalances in human bodily fluids and could therefore be treated by the use of chemical remedies, minerals, and classical botanical drugs. An innovation of the late 17th century, known as "solidism," located the essential physical imbalance not in bodily fluids but in the body's solid conducting tubes, like blood vessels and nerves. Solidism laid the basis for the development of theories explaining illness as the result of excessive or deficient activity in the nervous system. Among elite practitioners there was a direct continuity between European and American physiology, culminating in the centrality of Scottish nervous theory to the program of the first American medical school at the COLLEGE OF PHILADELPHIA (1765).

Another tradition in colonial medicine was arguably one of the most popular: astrology. English works, imported and reprinted in the colonies, offered advice on how to use astral "sympathies" and "antipathies" to aid healing by performing medical treatments under specific star signs. Anatomical texts served simultaneously as guides to midwifery, sex manuals, and handbooks of astrological physiognomy (the interpretation of facial characteristics). Almanacs, which reached a wide readership, retained astrological advice throughout the 18th century; for many, knowledge of the heavens remained a valuable medical strategy. For example, in the early 1760s Dr. James Greenhill of VIRGINIA noted that one of his patients, an epileptic slave, suffered fits only when the moon was in Capricorn. Greenhill used vomiting, purges, electric shocks, blisters, and internal medicine on his patient in search of a cure. A second striking example of overlapping medical traditions is COTTON MATHER's support of SMALLPOX inoculation in 1721. Mather evidently saw no inconsistency between championing the cause of inoculation and retaining the moral view that DISEASE was ultimately caused by sin.

The scarcity of physicians and the cost of consulting them meant that the burden of healing often fell to men and women in the home. They treated their families, servants, and slaves; women were particularly important as MIDWIVES. Home healers were largely self-taught, learning from British texts on home medicine and by experience. They bought herbal remedies from apothecaries and also mixed their own. The major remedies included cathartics, diuretics and diaphoretics (to expel foul humors), and tonics (to stimulate the nerves). Other important healers included ministers and their wives. Slaveowners and African-American doctors both treated slaves. NATIVE AMERICANS recognized four main causes of illness—sorcery, spiritual aggression, taboo transgression, and natural causes—and relied on the healing powers of SHAMANS.

Unlike New Spain and New France, British American medical practice lacked centralized organization. As a result, British colonial medicine was probably more individualistic and the traditionally elite CLASS of physicians more open and varied, embracing as it did surgical and apothecarial duties. Decentralization had disadvantages, however. Unlike their Spanish and French counterparts, American physicians were unlicensed, unsalaried, and instead charged fees. Consequently, it was difficult to distinguish legitimate physicians from illegitimate "quacks." Moreover, institutions for the care of the sick were slow to emerge. By 1650 Spain and France had established a number of New World hospitals, while British America's first, the PENNSYLVANIA Hospital, was founded only in 1751.

See also ENVIRONMENT; SCIENCE; YELLOW FEVER.

Further reading: Richard Harrison Shryock, *Medicine and Society in America, 1660–1860* (New York: New York University Press, 1960).

—James Delbourgo

mercantilism

Mercantilism refers to the economic theories followed by western European nations during the American colonial era. This economic theory rationalized the construction of powerful states in western Europe and provided a justification for establishing colonies in the New World.

Mercantilism was an economic system in which trade among nations was seen as a "zero-sum game"—one nation's gain was another one's loss. National wealth was measured by the amount of gold and silver bullion a country possessed. If France's import of British goods increased, for example, then Britain benefited because France had to pay for the balance of trade in precious specie. Thus, not only did increasing exports strengthen a country by adding bullion to the national treasury, it did so at the expense of its trading partner (and occasional adversary). Mercantilism dictated that economic growth and development should be orchestrated by the state. Central governments played a key role in regulating the ECONOMY and seeking to maximize the economic benefits of trade in order to strengthen the nation. Governments also set the prices of certain essential products, like bread, in an effort to minimize economic exploitation of poorer people.

The term *mercantilism* was not used in the 17th and 18th centuries but rather was coined by later generations to better explain the theory that had guided much of the economic development of British America. The first person to define mercantilism was Adam Smith in his pathbreaking book about capitalism, *Inquiry into Nature and Causes of the Wealth of Nations* (1776). As historians John J. McCusker and Russell Menard have argued, "mercantilism was little more than a shared perception among those who controlled northern and western Europe that foreign trade could be made to serve the interests of government—and vice versa." Nevertheless, the perception was a powerful one.

Mercantilism provided the rationale for establishing colonies because they would produce goods required by the mother country and thereby reduce its dependence on other European nations. Having its own colonial source for the production of raw materials enabled a nation to increase its balance of trade and retain more bullion at home, making it wealthier and stronger. This is evident in the expansion of sugar and TOBACCO production in Britain's American colonies. During the 17th century the BRITISH EMPIRE became an importer rather than an exporter of both of these valuable products. British officials encouraged the production of commodities that otherwise could not be profitably produced in the colonies; in 1748, for example, Parliament offered a subsidy for the production of INDIGO in SOUTH CAROLINA. By purchasing indigo grown in the British rather than the FRENCH COLONIES, Britain would keep the money in its own empire as well as reduce imports from the French. Colonies also served as markets that would stimulate manufacturing and production in the mother country. Moreover, on both sides of the Atlantic the increase in production would generate job opportunities and perhaps produce a surplus that would be available for export to other nations, further improving the balance of trade and the wealth of the empire.

Britain legislated mercantilist theory into government policy. The Navigation Acts were a series of laws—initially passed in 1651, expanded in 1660, and extended by Parliament in the 18th century—that established guidelines and restrictions for colonial trade. These laws required that trade goods within the British Empire be transported on British ships manned by British MARINERS (which included the American colonists). Moreover, the most valuable colonial products—sugar, tobacco, rice, molasses, and naval stores—could be exported solely to Britain or to other British colonies; American colonists could not ship these items directly to other European nations. Parliament also discouraged the colonial manufacture of finished products, like hats, iron, and woolen goods, and restricted the emission of paper currency in the colonies.

The British colonies benefited from some mercantilist policies, especially from the protection of shipping afforded by the British navy, the restriction of foreign competition, and the easy availability of inexpensive British goods, but Parliament's restrictions on American trade and economic development took a greater toll after 1750, contributing to the rift between Britain and the American colonies that culminated in the War for Independence.

Further reading: John J. McCusker and Russell R. Menard, *The Economy of British America, 1607–1789* (Chapel Hill: University of North Carolina Press, 1985).

—Jonathan Mercantini

merchants

Merchants played a key role in the development of the American colonies because trade was essential to their economic growth and well-being. Merchants operated on scales, from the largest (and wealthiest) who served as factors for the major British trading firms to small peddlers who traveled through the backcountry providing small necessities to men and women who lived far from towns and cities. Although initially few, the number of merchants increased as the colonies began to produce a surplus. Most merchants who engaged in transatlantic trade lived in the major port cities.

Merchants were expected to be cautious, reliable, and especially trustworthy, because they transacted most of their business on credit and their personal word. The lack of currency and near total absence of bullion in the colonies meant that money changed hands less regularly than in Europe; goods and services were more often bartered or purchased with bills of exchange. Merchants also served as the chief monetary lenders in many communities. Thus, they often functioned like bankers, at the center of a sizable network of both credit and debt. Merchants frequently used their considerable economic resources to wield political power as well, and they were well represented in most colonial assemblies.

Merchants served as a crucial link between NATIVE AMERICANS, the colonists, and European markets. Many of the earliest merchants made their livelihood from trade with Indians. They exchanged metal tools, blankets, firearms, and ALCOHOL for furs and animal skins prized in Europe. Other merchants were involved in exporting the colonies' staple goods, such as rice, TOBACCO, wheat, INDIGO, and naval stores.

Among the wealthiest American merchants were those involved in the SLAVE TRADE. In SOUTH CAROLINA men like Henry Laurens made their fortunes by importing slaves. Laurens used his wealth to become one of the colony's largest landholders, a member of the South Carolina legislature, and, later, president of the Continental Congress during America's War of Independence.

Less wealthy merchants followed settlers into the backcountry, providing necessary goods like gunpowder, iron nails, tools, and rum that could not be easily produced in homes. Even tiny settlements usually contained a small store to provide farm families with essentials in exchange for their surplus produce. For small merchants in particular, women were an essential market, and women occasionally functioned as merchants and storeowners as well.

Further reading: Bernard Bailyn, *New England Merchants in the Seventeenth Century* (Cambridge, Mass.: Harvard University Press, 1980).

—Jonathan Mercantini

Wampanoag chief Metacom *(Library of Congress)*

Metacom (King Philip, Metacomet)
(ca. 1642–1676)

Metacom was the youngest son of MASSASOIT, leader of the most powerful Indian group in the area around PLYMOUTH, the Wampanoag. Metacom was also known as King Philip, a name the English bestowed on him and that he readily accepted. When Massasoit died in 1662, his eldest son, Wamsutta, assumed the leadership of the tribe, but he died later that year, making Metacom the new leader. Like his father, Metacom tried to maintain close and peaceful relations with the Plymouth colonists. One of his first acts as leader in 1662 was to renew the Wampanoag's covenant with the colony, but a growing British population and the resulting pressures on native lands made keeping peace increasingly difficult. The 1667 settlement of Swansea on Wampanoag land increased tensions. Worsening matters, the English feared that Metacom was planning a general Indian uprising. In 1667 and 1671 Plymouth summoned him before its general court to confront him about his plans. On both occasions Metacom denied preparing for war, but the colony nevertheless charged him with humiliating fines and confiscated some of his followers' weapons. As the colonists pressed him to submit to their authority, Metacom nevertheless renewed oaths of loyalty to the colony.

Not only the English, but other Indians, especially those who had converted to Christianity, began to challenge Metacom's authority. In particular, John Sassamon, a Christian Indian from MASSACHUSETTS who had once served as Metacom's secretary, attempted to establish a ministry within Plymouth. Soon thereafter, Sassamon was found dead in a pond. Plymouth tried and executed three of Philip's followers for the murder of Sassamon. It is unknown if Philip had a role in Sassamon's murder, or even if Sassamon was murdered rather than accidentally drowned. Whatever the case, the resulting executions prompted some Wampanoag to attack Plymouth settlements in 1675, beginning what has come to be known as KING PHILIP'S WAR.

Metacom's role in the war that bears his name is unclear. Nevertheless, he was a marked man. Philip and the Wampanoag fled Plymouth, pursued by British forces. The war expanded to include most, if not all, English and Indian groups within New England, and the conflict involved one of the first widespread alliances among many Indians groups against the colonists. The Wampanoag and their allies enjoyed dramatic success for several months. Beginning in spring 1676, however, the English and their Indian allies turned the tide in their favor and began a campaign of mopping up the remnants of a listless enemy. On August 12, 1676, an Indian fighting for the English managed to kill Metacom near his home in Plymouth. The English posthumously carried out the punishment reserved for traitors by quartering and beheading Metacom's body and mounting his head on a stake. The English also managed to capture Metacom's wife and son. The fate of his wife is uncertain; like many Native American captives, his son was sold into Caribbean slavery.

Further reading: James D. Drake, *King Philip's War: Civil War in New England, 1675–1676* (Amherst: University of Massachusetts Press, 1999); Douglas Edward Leach, *Flintlock and Tomahawk: New England in King Philip's War* (New York: Macmillan, 1958).

—James D. Drake

métis

In the 17th and 18th centuries *métis* referred to people of mixed French and Indian ancestry. The children of English colonists and NATIVE AMERICANS were generally known as "half-breeds," while those of Spanish and Indian parents were called "mestizos." Because *half-breed* has come to be considered a derogatory term, scholars now use *métis* to refer to any people of mixed Indian and white ancestry.

Métis people most commonly resided in areas of the French FUR TRADE along the St. Lawrence and Mississippi-Missouri waterways, where sexual unions between Indian and French peoples offered benefits to both groups. In general, the French, more interested in trade than in the conquest and acquisition of land, used unions with native peoples to integrate into native societies. Marrying into an Indian community and establishing local ties helped the French (most often men) to be effective traders. Indian women, on the other hand, may have found marriage to French traders attractive because it gave them, as the source of European goods, higher status and more options within their own communities.

Métis peoples—the offspring of these European-Indian unions—played a special role in fur-trading communities, acting as cultural go-betweens for white and Indian worlds. European traders, for example, found métis women to be particularly attractive marriage partners, as they had knowledge of languages and cultures that could help European men interact with native societies. Métis men and women who lived within their native tribes, on the other hand, often became an important, and sometimes divisive, political force within their communities, because generally they were more accepting of European ECONOMY and culture than were Indians who emphasized maintaining traditional ways.

While some métis benefited from their status, it often led to hardship. Some métis, most often men, attained positions of power and even wealth due to their connections in both white and Indian communities. More often, however, the métis were distrusted by both Europeans and Indians, marginalized in native communities and overlooked by white governments. Some métis lived in communities of their own, developing their own ART, customs, and even linguistic dialects, such as Mischif, spoken today in North Dakota. Many became quite impoverished, and their 20th-century descendants often refer to themselves as "landless Indians."

The size of the métis population, from the 17th century until today, is difficult to measure. Métis communities have always tended to be relatively isolated, and their peoples can identify themselves (or be identified) as either white or Indian rather than métis. There likely were many more people of mixed ancestry than are generally recognized, but they found it to their advantage to join either white or Indian communities in order to gain "safety in numbers" and greater acceptance.

See also ANDREW MONTOUR; MADAME MONTOUR; MARY BOSOMWORTH MUSGROVE.

Further reading: Jacqueline Peterson and Jennifer S. H. Brown, eds. *The New Peoples: Being and Becoming Métis in North America* (Lincoln: University of Nebraska Press, 1995).

—Jenny Turner

Miantonomo (1600?–1643)

Miantonomo led the NARRAGANSETT, a group of Indians living in what is now RHODE ISLAND, during the early years of English colonization. Like most SACHEMS in New England, Miantonomo's power hinged largely on consensus and persuasion. He had to demonstrate an ability to cope with the changes wrought by colonization. With his uncle CANONICUS, Miantonomo skillfully helped the Narragansett become an economic power. The Narragansett benefited from their access to the shells needed to make WAMPUM, strings of beads viewed as sacred and valued throughout the Northeast as a form of currency in the FUR TRADE. They also avoided a major epidemic that devastated NATIVE AMERICANS in southern New England from 1616 to 1619.

The most immediate challenge to Narragansett power was the neighboring PEQUOT's involvement in the wampum trade with the Dutch. Partially in an effort to counter Pequot power, Miantonomo agreed to ROGER WILLIAMS's settlement in what became Rhode Island. Under Miantonomo's leadership the Narragansett allied with the English in the PEQUOT WAR, although they were horrified by the war's carnage.

In the long run these strategies proved inadequate. Although the Narragansett still vastly outnumbered English settlers in the early 1640s, the English presence threatened Narragansett subsistence. In a 1642 speech to the leaders of the Wyandanch and Montauk Indians of Long Island, Miantonomo lamented the environmental changes caused by the English, raising the prospect of pan-Indian military action against them.

Word of Miantonomo's plan leaked to the English, and they summoned him to BOSTON, forcing him to sign a treaty. The next year Mohegan attacked the Narragansett and captured Miantonomo, sending him to Boston to be tried for the murder of an Indian he had allegedly hired to assassinate the Mohegan leader, Uncas. The colony found him guilty and returned him to the Mohegan, who executed him.

Further reading: Neal Salisbury, *Manitou and Providence: Indians, Europeans, and the Making of New England, 1500–1643* New York: Oxford University Press, 1982).

—James D. Drake

Middleton, Arthur (1681–1737)

Arthur Middleton's family fled Barbados in the wake of slave revolts, establishing themselves outside CHARLESTON, SOUTH CAROLINA, on a 1,680-acre tract, a plantation enlarged by a further purchase of 3,130 acres from Middleton's uncle. On his father's death in 1685, Middleton inherited the plantation, named "The Oaks," and its large workforce of slaves, some of whom were NATIVE AMERICANS. Using the knowledge of the African slaves, Middleton turned to rice cultivation and had made the plantation profitable by 1699. An ambitious young man, he traveled to London in 1710 to petition the Board of Trade on behalf of South Carolina and, returning, joined the governing council, only to lead the opposition to proprietary government in 1719.

Under the Crown-appointed governor Middleton remained active on the council, pushing for a middle ground in the currency dispute that would allow limited local currency with protections against depreciation. In 1725, when Governor William Nicholson returned to England, Middleton became acting governor. His tenure of office was marred by charges of selling offices and by an economic depression in 1727 caused by the currency problems and the end of naval store bounties. Faced with an assembly unwilling to pass a tax bill without currency reform, a tax revolt led by small farmers, and Thomas Smith (who claimed that his seniority in age entitled him to the acting governorship), Middleton called on British ships and troops to keep order. Taking advantage of the crisis, the Yamasee and Creek attacked the colony. Middleton then crossed party lines to appoint his political rival, Colonel John Parker, to lead the colony's forces. Parker defeated the tribes, won a lasting peace treaty, and discredited the Spanish with their Native American allies, a point of particular concern to Middleton and other influential slave owners because their slaves frequently sought asylum in Spanish ST. AUGUSTINE. On the death of William Nicholson in 1728, the Privy Council in London named former governor Robert Johnson to replace Middleton, who retired to his estates upon Johnson's arrival in 1730 and died in 1737.

Further reading: Marion Eugene Siemans, *Colonial South Carolina: A Political History 1663–1763* (Chapel Hill: University of North Carolina Press, 1966).

—Margaret Sankey

midwives

Midwifery was a highly valued woman's profession in a time when approximately one in five women and one in 10 newborns died from causes associated with childbirth. The cycle of pregnancy, birth, and nursing was an integral part of most women's lives from their late teens to menopause, and the birth process was an important ritual during which women shared knowledge and spiritual closeness. The midwife cared for a woman's medical and spiritual needs while presiding over labor and birth aided by a gathered group. Women gave birth while supported on other women's arms or seated on the midwife's low, open-seated stool.

Midwives learned through apprenticeships and their own birth experiences and practiced herbal MEDICINE. A skilled midwife was able to turn a fetus in utero and facilitate a breech birth as well as attend to problems with a newborn. She was often responsible for baptizing babies as well as burying stillborns. Her reputation rested on the exceptional birth experiences she attended. Many of the women accused of WITCHCRAFT in New England were midwives or healers suspected of affecting either curses or good fortunes on births. ANNE MARBURY HUTCHINSON, whose activities threatened the male-dominated Puritan structure in early BOSTON, was a noted midwife and spiritual teacher. Native American and slave women also gave birth with the assistance of women healers or SHAMANS. Black midwives were called "grannies" and delivered babies for slave women as well as the wives of plantation owners.

Over the course of the 17th century, the Church of England tried to regulate midwifery, and, as scientific knowledge of birthing grew, "man-midwives" began to enter the profession. In the 18th century upper-CLASS women increasingly chose physicians with obstetric tools to manage their births, hoping for easier and safer deliveries, and midwives eventually became associated with the lower classes. The result was a gradual move away from childbirth as a social ritual controlled by women to an interventive medical process dominated by men.

See also FERTILITY.

Further reading: Paula A. Treckel, *To Comfort the Heart: Women in Seventeenth-Century America* (New York: Twayne Publishers, 1996).

—Deborah C. Taylor

mills

Mills were among the first buildings constructed in colonial North America and became the foundation for mechanical and industrial development. Sawmills were required to cut the lumber necessary for houses, barns, and stores and to produce an important commodity for foreign trade. Sawmills appeared in NEW YORK and MASSACHUSETTS by 1633, RHODE ISLAND by 1639, CONNECTICUT by 1654, NEW HAMPSHIRE by 1659, and PENNSYLVANIA by 1662. In 1671 New Hampshire alone shipped 20,000 tons of boards and exported 10 shiploads of masts. Meanwhile, gristmills were needed to grind grain into flour to feed settlers. Although saw and flour mills were the most widespread types, paper, oil, and fulling mills also dotted the rivers of North America. A fulling mill operated in Roxbury, Massachusetts, as early as 1657, and by 1700 at least 17 more compacted material into uniform cloth. VIRGINIA's first fulling mill was built in 1692, and one appeared in Pennsylvania in 1698. These mills paved the way for the expansion of textile manufacturing in the 19th century.

Powered by water, mills were among the greatest technologies in the early modern world. Waterfalls provided ideal locations for mills, but in places where falls did not exist, millers used dams and races to create the necessary power. A race paralleled the river bank like a canal, about 10 feet wide and nearly as deep. It created power by descending at a slightly shallower angle than the river itself, which over a distance raised the surface of the water in the race higher than that of the river. A mill was placed at the spot where the vertical difference between the race and the river was large enough to turn a waterwheel. Millers improved their waterpower by using dams to ensure a more constant flow of water into the race, which pooled an important supply of reserve water that helped to limit the impact of droughts and floods. Most dams were shallow, constructed from wooden planks and stones. Wooden gates were placed at the dam and above the waterwheel to control the level and quantity of water. These water systems—a dam, a race, and a waterwheel—required considerable initial capital investment by developers and depended on the expertise of ARTISANS and the brawn of laborers to build them.

Although saw, oil, fulling, and paper mills were commercial enterprises, nearly half of flour mills worked mostly on custom for local neighborhoods. Custom flour millers ground grain for local farmers for a toll, often paid by an exchange of goods or services. Flour millers operated on a larger scale in the "bread colonies" of the mid-Atlantic region as many merchant mills manufactured flour not only for consumers in cities such as PHILADELPHIA, BOSTON, and CHARLESTON but also for export, especially to the West Indies to feed slaves and planters. Around 1750 a combination of political upheaval and crop failures in southern Europe opened up new markets for mid-Atlantic grain farmers and flour producers. This expansion in trade led to several important developments in milling, encouraging millers not only to produce more flour but also to seek better ways of manufacturing it.

Among the most important improvements made in milling around the mid-18th century were the importation of French millstones and Dutch bolting cloth. Before the French burr stone, the "cullin" stone quarried near Cologne, Germany, had been the most popular. The freshwater quartz quarried in the Marne Valley in northern France was found only in small pieces, called "burrs," that were assembled into a single millstone, usually after shipment. Less abrasive than other stones, French burr stones produced the whitest flour, which fetched the highest market price. Improvements in bolting cloth also helped millers to make finer flour. Until the introduction of silk by Dutch MERCHANTS, bolting cloth had been made with wool, linen, and even horsehair. The standard quality of silk

Water mills like this one were often used to grind corn kernels into grist for cornmeal. *(Library of Congress)*

cloth allowed millers to regulate more closely the grades of flour they produced. When flour markets expanded around 1750, millers in the Middle Colonies gained a competitive edge by capitalizing on these improvements, their natural advantages, and their abundant wheat supply.

All types of mills served as important points of exchange in colonial communities. They provided goods, services, and employment opportunities for a combination of wage laborers, servants, and slaves. They also functioned as meeting places and cultural centers. The operator of a sawmill or a gristmill brokered information along with lumber and flour. Mills thus stood at the intersection of colonial life and economic development.

Further reading: Carroll Pursell, *The Machine in America: A Social History of Technology* (Baltimore: Johns Hopkins University Press, 1994); Martha Zimiles and Murray Zimiles, *Early American Mills* (New York: C. N. Potter, 1973).

—Brooke Hunter

Minuit, Peter (1580–1638)

Peter Minuit's career as a mercenary and adventurer is a clear example of the transnational character of early European EXPLORATION and settlement. Born of French Protestant parents in a German principality in 1590, Minuit eventually worked for both Dutch and Swedish exploration companies. In 1626 the 36-year-old Minuit arrived in the fledgling Dutch colony of NEW NETHERLAND when that colony's commander was under house arrest. Shortly thereafter, Minuit assumed the leadership of New Netherland's 300 colonists, split equally between Dutch- and French-speaking people.

Minuit found daunting challenges when he came to power, including deplorable conditions on Manhattan island, disarray in the company's account books, deteriorating relations with the area's native population, and low morale among the European colonists, many of whom wanted to return home. Minuit began by consolidating the Dutch settlement. In the spring of 1626 Minuit bought Manhattan island from local Indians for 60 guilders in trade goods while he moved the tiny settlements from the banks of the CONNECTICUT and DELAWARE Rivers to Manhattan. His building program for this influx of new workers resulted, in the fall of 1626, in 30 log houses, a new blockhouse surrounded by palisades of wood and sod, a solid stone counting house thatched with reed, and a mill whose second level accommodated church services. During Minuit's tenure this tiny European enclave was second in size only to the English settlement of PLYMOUTH in New England.

Beyond basic survival, Minuit's main concern was to send profits back to the DUTCH WEST INDIA COMPANY, whose board was split over whether to continue sending settlers to New Netherland or to limit Dutch interest in North America to a series of trading posts like that of Fort Orange on the Hudson. Minuit worked tirelessly to promote economic development, even extending feelers to the English colony of Plymouth. In 1630 Minuit extended his base on Manhattan by purchasing another island from the area's native people for "some duffels, kettles, axes, hoes, wampum, drilling awls, jew's harps and divers other small wares." The new acquisition was named Staten Island in honor of the governing body of the Netherlands. Minuit ruled in a continually precarious situation as disgruntled settlers clamored to go home and as authorities in Europe devised various ill-fated land schemes (patroonships) to promote private investment. Although Minuit's colony sent approximately 63,000 animal pelts home, this windfall may not have been enough to cover the enormous costs of settlement.

In 1631 the company recalled Minuit, who had to defend himself against charges of extravagance and mismanagement. Despite such disgrace, Minuit managed to interest Swedish investors in the New World. He cofounded the Swedish West India Company and in 1638 led an expedition to a site near present-day Wilmington, Delaware. Having settled 50 colonists on land claimed by his former Dutch employers, Minuit headed south to the CARIBBEAN, where he perished in a hurricane off the island of St. Christopher.

Further reading: Oliver A. Rink, *Holland on the Hudson: An Economic and Social History of Dutch New York* (Ithaca: N.Y.: Cornell University Press, 1986).

—Judy VanBuskirk

Dutch colonial officer Peter Minuit purchased Manhattan Island from the local Indians for trinkets valued at $24. *(Hulton/Archive)*

miscegenation

The definition of miscegenation (racial mixing) encompasses all races and includes a broad range of intimate contact. Although the term had not yet entered European lexicons (the word was invented in 1863), miscegenation played a key role in the development of the early Americas. Beginning with Christopher Columbus's crew, the Spanish engaged in sexual relations with Native American women. As these treasure hunters sought gold to satisfy their material desires, they discovered indigenous women to satiate their physical desires. When such conquests produced progeny, conquistadores identified them as mestizos. Imported African women also provided suitable sexual outlets in the CARIBBEAN. Spaniards applied the label *mustee* to designate the children of indigenous and African heritage, and they called their Iberian-African offspring MULATTOES, then a Spanish word for mule. Although never correcting the pejorative term, Spaniards later recognized *mulatto* as a misnomer, as successive generations of mulattoes proved that, unlike mules, they could reproduce. Throughout Spain's colonial dominion Spaniards, indigenous peoples, Africans, mestizos, mustees, and mulattoes continued to mingle sexually, creating a heterogeneous cultural and racial milieu.

Most historians perceive the blurred racial boundaries in the Caribbean Basin as evidence suggesting that Spanish colonizers harbored a more liberal attitude toward miscegenation than did their English counterparts. This generalization, however, can imply that racial ideologies were rooted primarily in ethnic or national origin, and it obscures the various patterns of demographic and economic development in the various American colonies. Still, almost all British colonies gradually erected legal obstructions to prevent miscegenation. Even in the northern colonies, where SLAVERY affected a considerably smaller number of people than in the southern colonies, legislators attempted to curb racial mixing. In 1726, for example, PENNSYLVANIA enacted legislation prohibiting all interracial unions, but officials found creating the law much easier than enforcing it. Despite the prohibition, observers often recalled the sight of an interracial couple walking arm-in-arm through the streets of PHILADELPHIA.

Miscegenation proved even more problematic for the TOBACCO colonies of VIRGINIA, MARYLAND, and NORTH CAROLINA. The first generation of settlers of this region often accepted racial mixing between Europeans and NATIVE AMERICANS, in part because white women were so few in number. Before deciding on a policy of Indian eradication, for example, the men of JAMESTOWN occasionally forged loving bonds with women of the POWHATAN CONFEDERACY, and, unlike the legendary marriage of POCAHONTAS and JOHN ROLFE, these relationships were not primarily political arrangements.

Initially, few settlers of these upper southern colonies expressed apprehension about mixing sexually with Africans and their African-American descendants. Rather quickly, however, miscegenation began to involve discussions of not only race but also CLASS in the tobacco colonies. After the introduction of SLAVERY in 1619, slaves and indentured servants worked together in the tobacco fields during the day and sometimes frolicked together in their beds at night. Usually performing menial or labor-intensive tasks, indentured servants constituted the bulk of the Upper South's white population until 1675. These white conscripts had more in common with slaves than with masters, and they sometimes chose their lovers from the pool of black laborers who could sympathize with their plight. In addition, wealthy white men frequently claimed the attention of the few European women in the area.

As unions between servants and slaves increased, the rulers of the tobacco colonies recognized the precariousness of their hierarchical structure and moved inexorably toward proscribing miscegenation. Deemed "fornication," the first laws prohibiting miscegenation in the tobacco colonies had no standard format: Some restrictions applied to white people only, others applied to both races; some violators paid public penance for their offenses, others felt the sting of the lash. The growth of the mulatto class—evidently the most disturbing manifestation of interracial sex—encouraged the 1662 Virginia assembly to outlaw miscegenation and to relegate mulattoes to an inferior status. Because a majority of mulattoes had white fathers, the legislators reversed an age-old English tradition and began associating the status of children by their mother rather than their father. From that point forward, mulatto children born as slaves usually remained in bondage throughout their lives.

Often beyond the geographic and customary reach of the assembly lived the tobacco planters. Perhaps more frequently than historians can discern, white masters in the Upper South engaged in sexual dalliances with enslaved females. Most relationships undoubtedly were nonconsensual. Although hardly the retainers of absolute power, many planters claimed sexual rights to their slaves and exercised this privilege. Far fewer relationships resulted from mutual affection, but the children of such a bond occasionally enjoyed manumission and an inheritance of land and slaves.

The mulattoes in SOUTH CAROLINA gained freedom more frequently and easily than mulattoes in the CHESAPEAKE BAY region, although it was still a rare occurrence. Indeed, compared to the tobacco farmers of Maryland, Virginia, and North Carolina, white people in the rice and INDIGO cultures of the Low Country maintained a liberal attitude toward miscegenation throughout the colonial period. The first settlers of South Carolina migrated from the island of Barbados, where the scarcity of white women had aided in creating a tradition of miscegenation. The sugar magnates who sailed to South Carolina in the 1670s carried with them an acceptance of interracial sex, and although later migrants hoped to curb "sexual congress" between the races, they hardly threatened traditional practices. White and black people continued to bed in private quarters and cavort in public spaces. Hundreds of mulattoes soon peopled CHARLESTON; thousands more populated the lowland plantations. Overwhelmed by the black majority, planters perceived mulattoes as intermediaries: neither white nor black, but a distinct class deserving of certain rights and privileges.

A similar, albeit significantly larger, class of mulattoes lived in French LOUISIANA. Even more than South Carolina, Louisiana attracted white people from colonies where miscegenation had been widely accepted. French migrants from Senegal and Haiti settled throughout southern Louisiana, bringing with them slaves ranging in hue from black to visibly white. Whites, blacks, and mulattoes continued to mix in the colony, and a distinctive and complex racial system developed. Colonial records abound with six terms designating specific racial categories: *Negro* applied to one with full African heritage; *sacatra,* 7/8 Negro; *griffe,* 3/4 Negro; *mulatto,* 1/2 Negro; *quadroon,* 1/4 Negro; *octoroon,* 1/8 Negro. Although the degree of advantage or degradation sometimes depended on this system of classification, thousands of these people formed the *gens de couleur libre,* the "free people of color." White planters sometimes freed their own sons and daughters, and these manumitted people enjoyed a privileged status unlike biracial persons in any other colony.

See also CREOLE.

Further reading: Gary B. Mills, *The Forgotten People: Cane River's Creoles of Color* (Baton Rouge: Louisiana State University Press, 1977); Joel Williamson, *New People: Miscegenation and Mulattoes in the United States* (Baton Rouge: Louisiana State University Press, 1995).

—C. B. Waldrip

missions

Situated along Spain's frontiers in the Americas, the Catholic missions served as crucial civil, military, and religious institutions within the empire. Beginning in the late 16th century, they worked in conjunction with the presidios and military colonies to form the first line of imperial defense in areas that remained mostly outside of European control. Most often established in regions with little mineral wealth and separated by long distances from the centers of colonial life, many missions would fail, others would struggle to survive year in and out, but a few would prosper, bringing considerable wealth to the orders under whose tutelage they were founded.

The clergy who made their homes in these settlements were charged with a series of daunting tasks. They were to relocate indigenous populations into their orbit, creating self-contained Christian settlements that could be used to control local populations and spread the Christian gospel. They were also given the right to demand labor, tribute, and taxes, which would be used to make the missions a buffer to the more "barbarous" groups that remained outside Spanish control. The missions were also charged with teaching artisanal skills, animal husbandry, and AGRICULTURE to the local indigenous populations. Together, it was hoped, these activities would "Hispanize" these new colonial subjects. Individual missions also often held vast land grants and worked the land with indigenous labor, both for the CONSUMPTION needs of the friars and as money-making enterprises that would supply other regions with foodstuffs and consumer goods.

The missions sometimes thrived when established among already densely settled peasant populations, where sedentary agriculturalists had little means of relocating and reproducing their communities elsewhere. This was the case among Pueblo, Pima, and Opata in modern-day Sonora, Arizona, NEW MEXICO, and Texas. The Pueblo in particular were restricted by conflicts with their neighbors, making widespread flight very difficult. However, the most successful missions were the Jesuit settlements established in the region around modern Paraguay. The JESUITS founded 11 missions in Paraguay, seven in Brazil, and 13 in Argentina, with some having as many as 1,000 families at their peak. Enjoying considerable agricultural surpluses, many of these missions were quite profitable.

On the other hand, in most regions the missions struggled to function effectively during the three centuries of Spanish colonialism. Finding flight easy and actively hostile to the imperial system that the missions represented, many less sedentary indigenous cultures—the Apache and Comanche of Texas and Arizona, the population of the Gran Chichimeca of Mexico, and the Araucanians of Chile—ultimately ignored, abandoned, or attacked these colonial institutions.

These acts of resistance were common because the missions often created a difficult life for those indigenous peoples who relocated to within their orbits. The friars were typically authoritarian and responded to perceived transgressions with corporal punishment and use of the stocks. Torture was not unknown as punishment in the missions. These practices also contributed to the low birthrate among the Indians in the missions, which meant that constant recruitment (often forcible) was needed to keep these institutions functioning. Such practices ultimately came to

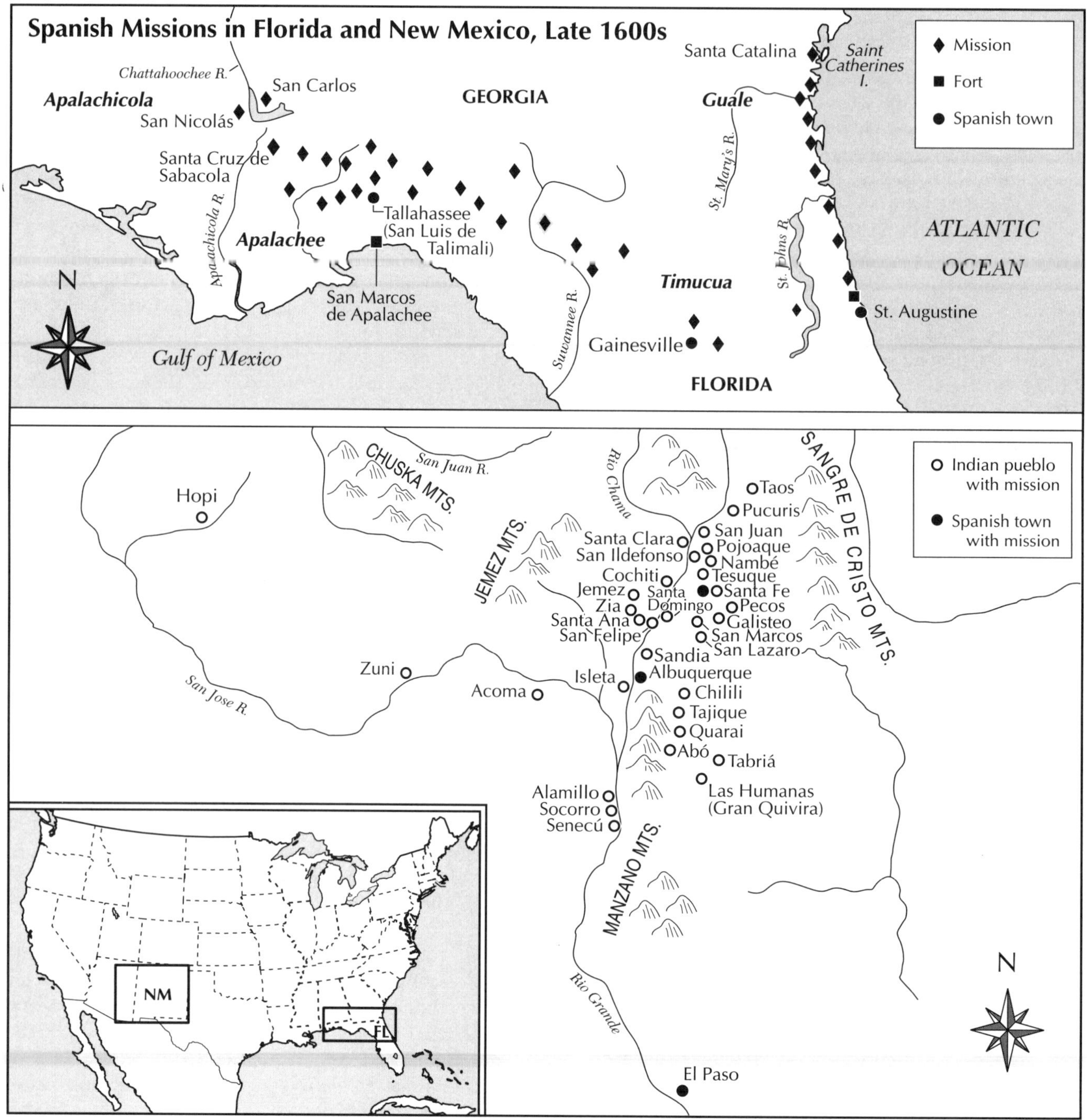

haunt some of the missions, as in the Franciscan settlements in New Mexico. In 1680, in the PUEBLO REVOLT, PUEBLO Indians rose up against the missions in the area, killing 21 of the region's 33 Franciscans and driving the Spanish out of the region for 12 years

As in New Mexico, in much of the empire Franciscans and Jesuits, typically European in origin and often European-born, acted as the principal missionaries. By the 18th century Franciscans established missions as far north as FLORIDA and GEORGIA, and for much of the colonial period the Jesuits exercised exclusive control of California, where the missions acted as the only sources of imperial authority. As the Catholic Church in Latin America became increasingly corrupt during the 17th and 18th centuries, these missions remained one of the few aggressive sites of evangelization.

They also became increasingly central to imperial defense. In response to the threats from both migrating indigenous peoples and competition from other European powers, the Crown expanded the number of missions along the northern frontier. By the mid-18th century 125 Franciscan friars worked in northern missions in Texas, Coahuila, Chihuahua, and New Mexico. These numbers expanded significantly after 1767, when the Jesuits were expelled from the empire and Franciscans took over the responsibility for regions they had formerly controlled. Moving in rapidly, Franciscan missionaries established the missions in San Diego in 1769 and San Francisco in 1776 and assumed control over other Jesuit settlements.

Further reading: David Block, *Mission Culture on the Upper Amazon: Native Tradition, Jesuit Enterprise, and Secular Policy in Moxos, 1660–1880* (Lincoln: University of Nebraska Press, 1994).

—Alexander Dawson

Mittelberger, Gottlieb (1715–1779?)

Gottlieb Mittelberger's 1756 work *Journey to the Pennsylvania in the Year 1750 and Return to Pennsylvania in 1754* publicized the horrors of the trade in German immigrant indentured servants in the 18th century. Mittelberger, a native of Württemberg in southwestern Germany, immigrated to PENNSYLVANIA in 1750 and worked as an organist and schoolteacher in a Lutheran church run by HENRY MELCHIOR MUHLENBERG. He returned to Germany in 1754, where he penned his treatise for a German audience. Mittelberger cautioned his compatriots to "carefully avoid this long and difficult voyage and the misfortunes connected with it." He saved his most venomous words for the Newlanders—the middlemen who earned commissions by finding Germans who would migrate to North America and sell themselves as servants to pay for the passage. Mittelberger railed against these "thieves of human beings" and "man-stealing" representatives of the "commerce in human beings." He also described the costs of the journey to the New World and the filthy conditions migrants endured during the passage. If they survived this arduous journey, an unpleasant fate of hard LABOR awaited those who were sold into INDENTURED SERVITUDE. "However hard one may have had to work in his native land, conditions are bound to be equally tough or even tougher in the new country," he observed.

Mittelberger is best remembered for his indictment of the conditions German migrants experienced, but ironically his work also contained a positive description of life in Pennsylvania. Although he condemned the religious and moral chaos that resulted "from the excessive freedom in that country," he noted that people were "amply fed," that "all trades and professions bring in good money," and that it was "possible to obtain all the things one can get in Europe in Pennsylvania." His description of Pennsylvania's natural ENVIRONMENT, its culture and legal traditions, and the area's NATIVE AMERICANS was widely read in Europe and incorporated into other works on the topic. The *Journey to Pennsylvania* was Mittelberger's only published writing; he lived out his days quietly in his homeland. Although his scathing record of the immigrant trade left a lasting impact in historical memory, it had little contemporary effect, as the SEVEN YEARS' WAR interrupted the large-scale migration of Germans at the time the book was published, and that migratory stream never again reached the levels it had during the early 1750s.

See also GERMAN IMMIGRANTS.

Further reading: Oscar Handlin and John Clive, eds., *Journey to Pennsylvania By Gottlieb Mittelberger* (Cambridge, Mass.: Belknap Press of Harvard University Press, 1960); Marianne Wokeck, *Trade in Strangers: The Beginnings of Mass Migration to North America* (University Park: Pennsylvania State University Press, 1999).

—Katherine Carté Engel

mobs See crowd actions

monarchy, British

Kings and queens ruled England and Scotland during the British American colonial period.

Tudor Monarchs

The first British monarch to sponsor EXPLORATION of the New World was the first Tudor king, Henry VII. In 1497 John Cabot received Henry's support for his voyage across the Atlantic and his exploration of the northern coastline. Henry VIII continued his father's policy of consolidation of the monarch's power, which helped expand Britain into an empire. Henry's wars against Spain greatly strengthened the British navy and thus the SHIPBUILDING industry necessary for overseas expansion. Henry VIII was also responsible for England's break with the Roman Catholic Church and the founding of the Church of England. This royal act helped fuel the rise of PROTESTANTISM that would send so many thousands of religious dissenters to the New World.

In 1558 Elizabeth I (1558–1603) was crowned queen. The wars against Spain continued under her rule, as did the building up of the navy and the British defeat of the Spanish Armada in 1588. In 1578 she granted Sir Humphrey

Gilbert the first royal charter to settle an American colony. When Gilbert failed to establish a colony in Newfoundland, Elizabeth offered a royal charter to Sir Walter Raleigh. This led to the founding of VIRGINIA (named for Elizabeth, the "Virgin Queen") and the settlement of Roanoke. This colony was established in 1585, evacuated in 1586, and resettled in 1587. By 1590, however, Roanoke had mysteriously vanished; no one has established what became of the colonists. Elizabeth also sponsored the voyage around the world of Sir Francis Drake (1577–80), which attracted enormous attention when he returned with a cargo worth a fortune.

Stuart Monarchs

James I (1601–25) granted a charter to the VIRGINIA COMPANY OF LONDON. His reign oversaw the beginning of successful British colonization of North America with the founding of JAMESTOWN in 1607. Partly to help the Virginia Company investors and partly for the revenue from import duties, James made it illegal to grow TOBACCO in England; by granting North America a monopoly on tobacco sales, he helped establish the colonial ECONOMY on a firm footing. In 1624, after the colony floundered, James revoked the charter and took personal control over the colony.

The great westward flow of PURITANS to North America began in the 1630s under the reign of the strict Catholic Charles I (1625–49). When Charles recalled Parliament in 1640, Puritan migration declined, but Charles was out of temper with his times and could not lead the country effectively. He was executed by the Puritan opposition in 1649. The British monarchy came to a temporary end with the king's death; the interregnum lasted until 1660. Many royalists fled Britain and settled in Virginia during the rule of the Puritan commoner Oliver Cromwell.

The monarchy was restored in 1660 in the person of the easygoing, permissive Charles II (1660–85). As a result of his anti-Dutch policies, the English seized the Dutch colony of NEW AMSTERDAM in 1664. In 1681 Charles granted WILLIAM PENN the land that would become PENNSYLVANIA. Charles immediately insisted on strict enforcement of the Navigation Act of 1651, attempting to bring efficiency and control to the badly mismanaged colonial system of trade. Further Navigation Acts were passed in 1663. Charles unwittingly sowed some of the seeds of the American Revolution when he granted self-governing charters to RHODE ISLAND and CONNECTICUT. In 1685, the final year of Charles's reign, MASSACHUSETTS's charter was revoked for noncompliance with the Navigation Acts. This combination of self-government and nonenforcement of the Navigation Acts accustomed the colonists to certain freedoms and explains the colonial outrage when later monarchs tried to achieve greater control over their unruly dominions.

James II (1685–88) abolished the local colonial assemblies and consolidated them into the DOMINION OF NEW ENGLAND. In 1689 the GLORIOUS REVOLUTION brought William III and Mary (1689–1702) to the throne. William restored the individual colonial governments, although most of them reverted to royal control in a 1696 reorganization. KING WILLIAM'S WAR, beginning in 1689, marked the beginning of the North American conflict between the British and French colonists. The British and their IROQUOIS allies attacked Montreal. The French and their Indian allies attacked towns in NEW YORK, NEW HAMPSHIRE, and MAINE. The war soon faded into a series of border skirmishes.

Queen Anne (1702–14) declared war on France in 1702. British colonists in the South attacked Spanish MISSIONS in FLORIDA to prevent the French from conquering them, and northern colonies attacked the French settlements in Canada. The war ended in 1713 with Britain the victor. Meanwhile, in 1707 the Act of Union unified Scotland and England into Great Britain.

Hanoverian Monarchs

During the reigns of George I (1714–27) and George II (1727–60) the British government was largely controlled by Parliament and the Whigs. George III, however, was not content to be a figurehead. His insistence on wielding the full power of a monarch meant constant tussles with Parliament. George III made heavy-handed attempts to govern the colonies; he acquired the reputation of a threat to American liberties. Thanks in part to Thomas Paine's *Common Sense,* George III became the focus of the colonists' grievances against England.

Further reading: T. O. Lloyd, *The British Empire 1558–1983* (New York: Oxford University Press, 1984).

—Stephanie Muntone

Monckton, Robert (1726?–1782)

A leading figure in the SEVEN YEARS' WAR, Robert Monckton achieved considerable military success. He later served as the nonresident governor of NEW YORK.

Colonel Monckton's first success in the war was the conquest of Acadia. In 1755 he captured Fort Beauséjour while a subordinate took Fort Gaspereau. With their fall all of Nova Scotia was in English hands, and Louisbourg, the great French base on Cape Breton Island, was cut off from land communications with the rest of New France. Monckton later participated in the eviction and dispersal of the French ACADIANS following their refusal to swear loyalty to Britain. Tragically, a great many of the 6,500 deportees died on transport ships as they were dispersed among other colonies.

Monckton was also not beloved by British colonists. He recruited 2,000 of them to serve in the Acadian campaign, but his colonial subordinates later accused him of attempting to deny their troops credit and even of personally humiliating colonial officers. This animosity belonged to a larger pattern of distrust and resentment between British regulars and colonials, as even George Washington felt slighted by British officers during the Seven Years' War.

Brigadier General Monckton served as second in command of the 1759 Quebec expedition under General JAMES WOLFE. During the campaign Monckton captured Point Lévis, a bluff across the Saint Lawrence River from Quebec, from which English artillery could batter the city and fortifications. Monckton had a falling out with Wolfe and was not consulted in Wolfe's decision to land troops north of the city, although Monckton and his fellow brigadiers had advocated such a course. Following Wolfe's mortal wounding, Monckton would have assumed command, except he himself was also shot. After his recovery Major General Monckton led troops in the CARIBBEAN, capturing Martinique after a tough fight and participating in the seizure of Havana, among the final actions of the war.

See also FORTS; WAR AND WARFARE.

Further reading: Fred Anderson, *A People's Army: Massachusetts Soldiers and Society in the Seven Years' War* (Chapel Hill.: University of North Carolina Press, 1984).

—Grant Weller

Montour, Andrew (Henry Montour, French Andrew, Andreas Sattelihu) (1710–1772)

Like his mother, MADAME MONTOUR, Andrew Montour acted as interpreter and cultural broker for the British during a 30-year period of tension and conflict in the mid-Atlantic region. He worked initially as a guide to Moravian missionaries in 1742 and then as translator and message-bearer for the PENNSYLVANIA colonial government from 1744 to 1754. Montour later gained the confidence of SIR WILLIAM JOHNSON, the superintendent of Indian affairs for Great Britain between 1755 and 1765. His remarkably diverse personal background allowed Andrew Montour to become an effective negotiator between cultures. From an ethnically mixed family, Andrew Montour could speak IROQUOIS, French, and English. The Susquehanna River region around Shamokin where he grew up also provided life lessons in multiculturalism. During the first half of the 18th century, the Susquehanna became home to Tutelo, Nanticoke, DELAWARE, Mahican, Iroquois, Shawnee, as well as Scots-Irish, German, French, and English settlers. Because he was able to translate across cultures, colonial officials hired Montour to perform diplomatic missions for them in NEW YORK and the Ohio Valley. However, his status as go-between also proved difficult because many Euro-Americans distrusted him as much as they relied on his services. Even those who counted the Montour family as friends had a hard time "reading" Andrew Montour's motives once the SEVEN YEARS' WAR began. Despite his assistance in tracking down Delaware and Shawnee who had attacked frontier communities in 1755 and 1756, the English suspected Montour of betrayal because of his French and Iroquois heritage. Unlike New France, Pennsylvania did not have a community of MÉTIS people. Consequently, some historians characterize Montour as an isolated individual who found no place to call his own. This might explain why he struggled with ALCOHOL abuse and insolvency even while he remained an active interpreter at Fort Pitt from 1763 to 1772. In 1772 a Seneca murdered Montour over an unknown offense.

Further reading: James H. Merrell, *Into the American Woods: Negotiators on the Pennsylvania Frontier* (New York: Norton, 1999).

—Jane T. Merritt

Montour, Madame (Elizabeth Couc, La Chenette) (1684?–1752?)

Working for the French briefly and then for the colonial governor of New York, Madame Montour became one of the most important Native American interpreters during the first half of the 18th century. Although her background is often disputed, most probably she was born in Canada of a French father and HURON mother but was taken captive at 10 years of age by IROQUOIS in NEW YORK. There, she grew up and married an Oneida warrior, Currundawanah (known as Robert Hunter by the English), who became a local hero in the CATAWBA wars. Beginning in 1711 Madame Montour acted as interpreter for New York at a treaty conference in Albany between the chiefs of the Iroquois Five Nations and the colonial governor, Robert Hunter (her husband's namesake). She was very active in diplomacy during the 1720s but became less publicly prominent as the center of Indian diplomacy moved south into PENNSYLVANIA, where her son, ANDREW MONTOUR, emerged as a cultural go-between by the 1740s. Madame Montour continued to attend treaty conferences, such as the Lancaster conference of 1744, and to host traveling diplomats in her home at Ostonwakin (French Town), on the west branch of the Susquehanna River. Among her visitors and acquaintances she counted Conrad Weiser, Pennsylvania proprietary secretary JAMES LOGAN, and several German Moravian missionaries who preached among Indian communities along the Susquehanna River. In turn, colonial governors in New York and

Pennsylvania and the commissioners of Indian affairs rewarded her well for her services.

Further reading: James H. Merrell, *Into the American Woods: Negotiators on the Pennsylvania Frontier* (New York: Norton, 1999).

—Jane T. Merritt

Moraley, William (1699–1762)

One of the few people of his status to leave a written record of his life, William Moraley wrote *The Infortunate,* an autobiographical account of INDENTURED SERVITUDE in the colonies between 1729 and 1734. *The Infortunate* illuminates the desperate circumstances that forced some Europeans to sell themselves into servitude for a few years in return for passage to North America as well as the difficulties encountered by servants in achieving success in the New World.

Moraley admits having "neglected to improve" his talents when his father apprenticed him at age 15 as a clerk to an attorney in London. Two years later his father decided against the profession and urged him to learn the "trade of watch-making." Moraley's family faced financial ruin when his father lost his investments when the "South Sea Bubble" burst in 1720. When his father died in 1725, Moraley inherited a mere 20 shillings and few prospects.

In 1729 Moraley contracted to indenture himself in "the American Plantations" for five years. After 13 weeks at sea, he landed at PHILADELPHIA. A clockmaker, Isaac Pearson, purchased Moraley's time. Like many servants, Moraley never achieved economic security after his servitude, but despite his various misfortunes he remained buoyant. An adventurous spirit, Moraley journeyed to contiguous colonies, telling entertaining tales, eluding creditors, and begging for charity.

Moraley's travels brought him into contact with people who seldom appear in contemporary accounts. He commiserated with white people in circumstances similar to his, sympathized with slaves, and greatly respected NATIVE AMERICANS' knowledge of their land. Moreover, Moraley candidly described his encounters and liaisons with women, although his behavior toward them in some instances was less than respectable. An economic failure in America, Moraley returned to England in 1734, where he lived until his death in 1762.

Further reading: Susan E. Klepp and Billy G. Smith, eds., *The Infortunate: The Voyage and Adventures of William Moraley, an Indentured Servant* (University Park: Pennsylvania State University, 1992).

—Leslie Patrick

Morris, Lewis (1671–1746)

Lewis Morris was born in NEW YORK CITY to a Welsh merchant and sugar planter from Barbados. His father soon died and his Quaker uncle came to New York to adopt him. In 1691 Morris inherited a large landed estate in NEW YORK and NEW JERSEY. He led the opposition to East New Jersey's proprietary government, and he went to London in 1701 to broker the sale of that government to the Crown. In 1710 Morris shifted his political base to New York, where he became the legislative adjutant to Governor Robert Hunter, who presided over the stabilization of that colony after a generation of political polarization. When Hunter returned to England in 1719, Morris remained the chief adviser to his successor, Governor William Burnet. In the 1730s Morris led his supporters in an unsuccessful effort to regain power by resisting New York's governor, William Cosby. He went to London to seek Cosby's recall while his allies in New York used JOHN PETER ZENGER's press to subvert Cosby's regime. In 1738 Morris became the royal governor of New Jersey. He ended a turbulent career battling with the New Jersey assembly, often defending "prerogative" positions explicitly contrary to the ones he had long advocated in New York.

Morris has been viewed as a hypocrite, a "trimmer," or an ideological chameleon. It may be fairer to say that he was best suited by talent and temperament to serving under strong leaders, mobilizing secure legislative majorities, and executing detailed programmatic instructions. When he had to take personal command or to improvise politically, he often displayed a rash and volatile spirit. Morris was also a self-tutored scholar, author, and ardent Anglophile, who worked as hard to enact the role of the English country gentleman in cultural and social life as he did in politics.

Further reading: Eugene R. Sheridan, *Lewis Morris, 1671–1746: A Study in Early American Politics* (Syracuse, N.Y.: Syracuse University Press, 1981).

—Wayne Bodle

mortality

Overall, European settlers found the climate of mainland North America healthier than that of early modern Europe. Early New England colonists, in particular, enjoyed exceptionally favorable demographic conditions. In the 17th century a New England man who reached the age of 21 could expect to live to 69, on average, while a woman could expect to live to 62. (The GENDER difference resulted largely from the risks of childbirth.) The infant mortality rate in colonial New England was about 10 percent, quite modest by early modern standards. In the malarial regions of the Chesapeake and the Lower South, life was more precarious. In 17th-century VIRGINIA a typical man who reached adulthood could expect to live to 49, while women were slightly less vulnerable to DISEASE but faced the additional risk of childbirth. Estimates of the child mortality rate in the southern colonies range between 25 and 40 percent, with 33 percent being perhaps the most likely figure. While these numbers are shocking by contemporary standards, the demographic regime of 17th-century North America was better than that of early modern England, where the life expectancy of a 20-year-old man was only 52 and urban child mortality rates ran as high as 50 percent.

North American colonists succumbed to a wide variety of diseases, some regionally specific, some nearly universal. The most disease-ridden region was the South, and the most virulent diseases were malaria and YELLOW FEVER, both transmitted by mosquitoes. Yellow fever, endemic in the South, struck the port cities of PHILADELPHIA and NEW YORK CITY periodically as well; it carried off 5 percent of Philadelphia's population in 1699 and 10 percent of New York's population in 1702. Other common diseases, such as typhus, dysentery, influenza, diphtheria, and SMALLPOX, erupted in towns throughout mainland North America, even in relatively healthy New England. European physicians began to develop a technique for smallpox inoculation in the early 18th century, and by the late colonial period many affluent British colonists chose to have themselves and their children inoculated (sometimes after trying it out on their slaves). Non–disease-related causes of death included maternal mortality for women (in New England possibly as many as one woman in six died in childbirth) and maritime and agricultural accidents for men. Health conditions in New England and the Middle Colonies were generally good, however, and most settlers (with the exception of some slaves) throughout North America enjoyed an ample and varied diet.

For new immigrants the most dangerous period was the journey to the New World and the first year or two within it. Enslaved Africans, shackled, despondent, and poorly fed, suffered most severely from the transatlantic passage; 15 to 20 percent of slaves bound from AFRICA to North America died en route. Many European immigrants, crammed in tight quarters and weakened by a monotonous diet, also succumbed to diseases aboard ship. Conditions were particularly bad in the 18th-century servant trade, and passengers occasionally even mutinied. Upon arrival in North America immigrants passed through the "seasoning time," a period of a year or so in which their immune systems adjusted to the unfamiliar disease climate. Seasoning was particularly strenuous in the South, where many settlers died of malaria, dysentery, and other diseases during their first summer in North America. In 17th-century Virginia only about 60 percent of indentured servants survived

Pre-1700 New England gravestones often depicted death as a frightening skull, warning sinners to repent of their sins. After 1700 a smiling cherub adorned many gravestones, such as the one depicted here, suggesting a more optimistic view of the afterlife. *(Library of Congress)*

their terms of service. High mortality rates contributed to social and economic instability. The Chesapeake area's demographic regime also shaped planters' LABOR preferences; they did not shift from servant to slave labor until the late 17th century, when declining mortality rates made it advantageous for planters to purchase slaves.

African and African-American slaves, concentrated in the southern colonies, faced the same epidemiological "seasoning," but their immune systems, shaped by the West African disease environment, responded somewhat differently. As many Africans had already been exposed to yellow fever and malaria, they succumbed to these diseases less frequently than did Europeans (although many Africans did die of them). On the other hand, they were particularly susceptible to respiratory complaints such as pneumonia and tuberculosis. Between a quarter and a third of slaves imported to the southern colonies died within a year. African and African-American slaves also faced some status-specific health threats, including depression (newly enslaved men and women sometimes committed suicide), exhaustion, and exposure. (These problems also manifested themselves among European settlers living in exceptionally harsh conditions; some of the first Virginia settlers appear to have suffered from debilitating depression.) In the southern colonies a third or more of children born into SLAVERY died in infancy.

While European and African immigrants struggled with the unfamiliar American epidemiological environment, countless NATIVE AMERICANS succumbed to diseases that were endemic to Europe and Africa but unknown in precontact North America. Until the 16th century Native Americans lived in dispersed communities isolated from the rest of the world's human population and enjoyed a relatively disease-free environment. After 1492, however, European explorers and settlers inadvertently (and sometimes purposefully) introduced a host of virulent diseases from the Old World, including smallpox, measles, and pneumonia. These unfamiliar diseases, combined with famine and warfare, decimated the Native American population. On the eve of European colonization the most widely accepted estimates are that between 7 million and 10 million Native Americans populated the North American continent north of Mexico; four centuries later, less than 1 million Native Americans remained. This extreme depopulation caused recurring political conflict and led to the reconfiguration of many Native American communities and political alliances in the 17th and 18th centuries.

Further reading: Robert V. Wells, *Revolutions in Americans' Lives: A Demographic Perspective on the History of Americans, Their Families, and Their Society* (Westport, Conn.: Greenwood Press, 1982).

—Darcy R. Fryer

Morton, Thomas (1597?–1647)

A London lawyer turned New England trader, Thomas Morton (a.k.a. Morton of Merrymount) first traveled to New England with Captain Wollaston in 1624. The company landed and settled at what the MASSACHUSETTS tribes called Passonagessit (now Quincy Bay) and established Mount Wollaston, a trading post and plantation. After Wollaston departed for VIRGINIA, Morton renamed the post "Ma-re Mount," where he continued trade and raised a maypole, around which he introduced his neighbors to the festive customs associated with the English May Day. However, what Morton called "revels and merriment," WILLIAM BRADFORD, the leader of the Separatist PLYMOUTH Plantation 30 miles south, termed "lasciviousness" and "a School of Atheism"; Bradford reviled Morton's "beastly practices" (drinking, dancing, and consorting sexually with Indian women), thinking this behavior would undermine the Puritan cause. Morton was arrested for trading guns to the Nauset Indians and was shipped back to England in 1628. Acquitted, he returned to Ma-re Mount in 1629 to find the Maypole demolished and his trading claims challenged. He was again arrested in 1630, tried in CHARLESTON, and then shipped back to England, where he attempted to persuade Crown authorities to reassign the claims of the New England PURITANS. During this campaign in the early 1630s Morton wrote his only book, *New English Canaan* (1637).

More of a promotional tract than a historical account, *New English Canaan* presents a compelling view of a promising new land: "the bewty of the place . . . I did not think that in all the knowne world it could be paralel'd." Divided into three parts, the volume outlines the manners and customs of the friendly natives, describes the natural endowments of a lush land, and satirizes the Separatists at Plymouth. In contrast to the civil natives who led "the more happy and freer life," who "are not delighted in baubles," and who are "full of humanity," the uncivil Puritans massacred natives at Wessaguscus, practiced life-denying austerity, and "make a great shew of Religion, but no humanity." The sardonic assault culminates when Morton chronicles how in 1628 Captain Shrimpe (MYLES STANDISH) and his "nine worthies" raid Ma-re Mount and take Morton prisoner. Blending Renaissance masque, satire, myth, prose, and poetry, Morton's literary production contests the dominance of Bradford's Separatists, substituting Arcadian imagery for Biblical typology and privileging secular colonization over a schismatic settlement. Morton's gesture toward cultural amalgamation challenged Puritan exclusionary politics and values.

Despite his condemnation of Plymouth, his advocacy of the ANGLICAN CHURCH, and his portraits of benevolent NATIVE AMERICANS, Morton failed to effect a change of policy. His book sold few copies, and, except for the many first edition copies burned as subversive, it was largely ignored for 350 years. Today, for its literary quality, *New English Canaan* remains secondary to hegemonic Puritan history. Only recently has Morton managed to escape the pejorative title William Bradford bestowed on him: the bacchanalian "Lord of Misrule" from "Merrymount."

Morton's last journey to New England in 1643 included, like the first two, a period of imprisonment (1644). This time, however, he was released. After a short stay in BOSTON in 1645, Morton trekked to MAINE, where he reportedly died two years later.

Further reading: Donald F. Connors, *Thomas Morton* (New York: Twayne, 1969); Richard Slotkin, *Regeneration Through Violence: The Mythology of the American Frontier, 1600–1860* (Middletown, Conn.: Wesleyan University Press, 1973).

—Keat Murray

Mount Vernon

Mount Vernon, the plantation home of George Washington, initially came into the Washington family's hands in 1674 as Little Hunting Creek Plantation. It remained an unimportant part of Washington family holdings until Lawrence, George's oldest half-brother, inherited the land upon his father's death in 1743. Soon afterward Lawrence built a two-story house with four rooms on each floor, and he named the house and property Mount Vernon after his former commander, Admiral Edward Vernon of the Royal Navy. Upon Lawrence's death in 1752, George leased Mount Vernon with the intentions of becoming a prosperous planter. He inherited the plantation in 1761, when his brother's widow died and control returned to the Washington family.

Washington lived at Mount Vernon for more than 45 years. While under his control, the plantation became highly profitable mostly through its economic diversity. Along with TOBACCO and wheat, Mount Vernon became the base of a thriving FISHING fleet that plied the waters of the Potomac River and CHESAPEAKE BAY. At its height the estate encompassed nearly 8,000 acres and served as home to George and Martha's small family and a large slave community. By Washington's death in 1799, nearly 300 slaves lived there. Washington willed Martha the use of Mount Vernon for the duration of her lifetime, stipulating that his slaves would become free when Martha died, which caused her great anxiety. Fearing that the slaves might expedite her demise, she freed her husband's bondpeople at the end of 1800.

Further reading: James Thomas Flexner, *Washington: The Indispensable Man* (Boston: Little, Brown, 1969).

—Brian McKnight

Muhlenberg, Henry Melchior (1711–1787)

Henry Melchior Muhlenberg was one of the primary architects of American Lutheranism. He was born September 6, 1711, at Einbeck, Hannover. He matriculated at Goettingen University in 1735 and became a teacher at the Halle Orphan House three years later. By this time Halle had become a leading center of pietism on the continent, and its ecclesiastical and theological views would greatly influence Muhlenberg throughout his career. The Leipzig Consistory ordained him as a Lutheran pastor in 1739, with his first parish at Grosshennersdorf. On Muhlenberg's 30th birthday Gotthilf August Francke informed him that three PENNSYLVANIA congregations had extended a call for a pastor in 1734 that still had not been filled. Francke recommended that Muhlenberg accept this call, and after careful consideration Muhlenberg agreed.

His first destination in the British colonies was GEORGIA, where he met two other German Lutheran pastors. When Muhlenberg arrived in PHILADELPHIA in November 1742, the three congregations that had requested a pastor were not expecting him and in the meantime had hired unordained clergy to minister to the congregations. Swedish Lutheran Church officials in the Philadelphia area supported his claim to the charge, and soon most of the officers and members of the congregations accepted him as their regular pastor. Between 1742 and his retirement in 1779 Muhlenberg served Lutheran congregations in Philadelphia, New Hanover, Providence (Trappe), and Germantown.

By the time of Muhlenberg's arrival in Pennsylvania, the province had emerged as a focal point of German immigration and of Lutheran activity. The colony's religious diversity was something that Muhlenberg constantly confronted, and he often commented in his reports to Halle that the religious environment in Pennsylvania presented difficulties that did not exist in Europe. Within a few years of his arrival, Muhlenberg had to deal with the influence of Moravian leader Count Nicholas Ludwig von Zinzendorf along with the actions of unordained men who were performing the services of clergy along the frontier. Through Muhlenberg's efforts the Evangelical Lutheran Ministerium of Pennsylvania was organized in 1748. Under his leadership this synod attempted to control the quality of clergy throughout the German-speaking areas of the colonies while maintaining lay participation in the selection process.

Further reading: Leonard R. Riforgiato, *Missionary of Moderation: Henry Melchior Muhlenberg and the Lutheran Church in English America* (Lewisburg, Pa.: Bucknell University Press, 1980); Theodore G. Tappert and John W. Doberstein, eds., *The Journals of Henry Melchior Muhlenberg*, 3 vols. (Philadelphia: The Muhlenberg Press, 1942–1958).

—Karen Guenther

mulattoes

Translated roughly, the Latin-rooted word *mulatto* means "mule." The Spanish initially applied the term to persons possessing both European and African ancestry, and the Portuguese, French, and English soon adopted the word to describe racially mixed people. Appearing first along the western coast of AFRICA, mulattoes literally belied definition; unlike their mule namesakes, mulatto women bore children to Iberian slave traders. Although these children had more Iberian ancestry than did their mothers, their fathers ignored this distinction, classifying all biracial people as mulattoes.

The French did distinguish mulatto mothers from their generally lighter-skinned children. According to a primitive form of French ethnography, the amount of "white blood" determined a person's racial category. Colonial records in LOUISIANA cite Negros (black African), *sacatras* (7/8 Negro), *griffes* (3/4 Negro), mulattoes (1/2 Negro), quadroons (1/4 Negro), and octoroons (1/8 Negro). These castes marked the degree of privilege or degradation. Beyond polite society, however, even a hint of white ancestry presented opportunities unimaginable for blacks.

When considering manumission, for example, masters usually preferred to free their biracial relatives. These emancipated thousands formed the *gens de couleur libre*—the "free people of color"—an exclusive society of mixed-race people who populated the interior of southern Louisiana.

British colonizers employed the simpler Iberian classification system rather than the more complex system that characterized French America. In the British colonies a person of mixed ancestry, no matter the amount, was a mulatto; very few of them enjoyed the lifestyle of the *gens de couleur libre*. The experience for mulattoes, however, was hardly uniform. The Lower South, the Upper South, and the North developed differently, and white attitudes toward MISCEGENATION and mulattoes generally had a distinctive regional character.

Only in the Lower South did an appreciable number of mulattoes gain their freedom. Thousands of mulattoes populated SOUTH CAROLINA, most living on lowland plantations and in CHARLESTON. Mulattoes took pride in their biracial heritage, and they came to represent an intermediate CLASS. Although white people valued mulattoes more than blacks, mulattoes possessed few of the rights afforded to whites.

In the TOBACCO colonies of NORTH CAROLINA, VIRGINIA, and MARYLAND miscegenation became publicly stigmatized as an increasing number of unions between indentured servants and slaves threatened the white aristocracy. Sometimes masters privately gave special attention to their enslaved relatives. Other times, however, masters responded to the conspicuous presence of mulattoes by meting out especially harsh punishment.

Some mulattoes hoped to escape slavery by fleeing to northern colonies, even though slavery was legal and white racism against mulattoes was deeply ingrained in those societies. Urban centers, however, provided mulattoes with some degree of anonymity and the opportunity to improve their lives. As a result, mulatto populations in PHILADELPHIA, NEW YORK CITY, and BOSTON grew slowly throughout the colonial period.

See also CREOLE; MÉTIS.

Further reading: Gary B. Mills, *The Forgotten People: Cane River's Creoles of Color* (Baton Rouge: Louisiana State University Press, 1977); Joel Williamson, *New People: Miscegenation and Mulattoes in the United States* (Baton Rouge: Louisiana State University Press, 1995).

—C. B. Waldrip

Musgrove, Mary Bosomworth (1700?–1763?)

Throughout her life Mary Musgrove existed in the "middle ground" between white and Native American society. The child of a Creek Indian woman and a white trader from Carolina, Musgrove initially lived among the Creek under the name Coosaponakeesa but was educated by white people in SOUTH CAROLINA and christened as Mary. As the wife of John Musgrove, an Indian trader, she was intimately involved in the political and economic relationships that tied Europeans and NATIVE AMERICANS together in the Southeast. By the time of the colonial settlement of GEORGIA, the Musgroves operated a trading post on the south bank of the Savannah River. Mary Musgrove made herself invaluable to General JAMES EDWARD OGLETHORPE by acting as his translator, and she used her connections among native tribes to secure the first land cessions for the new colony. When John Musgrove died about 1734, Mary married his indentured servant, Jacob Matthews. After Matthews died in 1742, Mary married Thomas Bosomworth, a dissenting Anglican minister who subsequently tried his hand as a soldier, merchant, and entrepreneur.

Mary Musgrove was the most influential woman in early colonial Georgia, being fully involved in the meetings between Oglethorpe and local Indian tribal leaders like TOMOCHICHI. While powerful women were hardly unusual in Native American societies, Europeans found Musgrove's role somewhat anomalous. Oglethorpe's departure from Georgia in 1743 allowed European racial and GENDER prejudices to reassert themselves, and Musgrove was increasingly marginalized. However, she remained in Georgia in order to get disputed land claims recognized by the colonial government. In 1759 she received title to St. Catherine's Island, the largest land grant ever given to a woman in Georgia. Mary Musgrove died in 1763.

Further reading: Michele Gillespie, "The Sexual Politics of Race and Gender: Mary Musgrove and the Georgia Trustees," in Michele Gillespie and Catherine Clinton, eds., *The Devil's Lane: Sex and Race in the Early South* (New York: Oxford University Press, 1997, pp. 187–201).

—Timothy James Lockley

music

Music took many forms across the colonies of British North America. European migrants to the New World brought many different varieties of music, both sacred and secular. Ballads crossed the ocean with immigrants and were taught by parents to children, with many regional variations on both sides of the ocean.

The PILGRIMS brought the *Ainsworth Psalter* for use in worship, with tunes edited and composed by the English scholar Henry Ainsworth. The book provided 39 tunes to be used interchangeably. Some congregations, as in Salem, found the music too hard and soon discontinued the

Psalter's use, while others used it until 1692, when the Pilgrims merged with MASSACHUSETTS Bay.

The Puritans objected to musical instruments in church; they sang liturgy but not psalms. The simplicity of their music may be attributed to their lack of musical training rather than their disapproval of the art. Their 1640 *Bay Psalm Book* was the first book printed in the North American colonies. Though it did not provide tunes, the book gave instructions about meter, and it offered advice about selecting appropriate music. Only the ninth edition of 1698 gave music, and that in just two parts.

Two styles of singing soon developed. Followers of "Regular Singing," common in urban areas, strictly adhered to the rules given in the psalters. "Irregular Singing" followed rural customs and folkways, in which each congregation had its own rules and each person had their own variation on the tune. In the 1720s reformers like THOMAS WALTER began to lecture on the importance of the "Regular" style, and by 1750 liturgical music had been standardized throughout New England.

Many colonists owned musical instruments. People of all classes owned virginals (keyboards), citterns (early guitars), violins, and wind instruments. Fiddles (broadly defined as a violin played anywhere but in the home) commonly were found in taverns. A few performers and composers flourished during the 18th century, most notably William Billings and Francis Hopkinson. Such artists always needed supplemental income, whether through manual LABOR (Billings worked as a tanner) or operating music schools. By the mid-18th century a few organs appeared in Anglican churches.

Attempting to attract more colonists to religious services, Governor JAMES EDWARD OGLETHORPE invited the Methodist minister JOHN WESLEY to visit GEORGIA in 1735. Two years later, influenced by the hymn singing of Moravian immigrants, Wesley published a collection of hymns and Psalms in CHARLESTON. Wesley's emphasis on music during church services spread, in part due to the GREAT AWAKENING. The Methodists published several hymnals in this period, some to compete with other collections of "popular spiritual songs." John Newton (1725–1807) published three volumes of hymns of his own composing, the best known being "Amazing Grace."

The Moravians were a particularly musical sect, and their singing inspired many others. They settled primarily in PENNSYLVANIA and NORTH CAROLINA, where they emphasized choral, organ, and brass music (especially trombones) and the works of J. S. Bach. They translated many of their hymns into local Indian dialects for missionary purposes and also used them to outreach to slaves.

The diversity of African cultures makes it difficult to generalize about slave music. However, song was a principal music expression in Africa, used on most major occasion. An alternation between solo and chorus, called "call and response," is common in West AFRICA and was frequently used in America as well. Moreover, performers placed special emphasis on rhythm and improvisation. A song leader might improvise on the main theme while the chorus, sung by everyone else, remained constant. Masters sometimes encouraged slaves to sing work songs, believing that it would improve morale and lower MORTALITY rates.

Slaves brought an early version of the banjo with them from Africa, incorporating it into traditional and new songs. Because it could be constructed in a variety of ways and with different materials, the banjo was well suited to the uncertainties of slave life. Drums were important in Africa and probably would have played a larger role in slave music except that their use was sometimes forbidden in British North America except in time of war.

Most slave music of this era did not include Christian themes. Slave owners sometimes discouraged evangelizing in the slave quarters, and it was not until the second half of the 18th century that efforts were made to teach the singing of psalms.

Further reading: Gilbert Chase, *America's Music: From the Pilgrims to the Present* (Urbana: University of Illinois Press, 1987).

—Victoria C. H. Resnick

N

Narragansett

At the time of contact with Europeans, these Indians inhabited the area around Narragansett Bay in what is now RHODE ISLAND. They relied on the plant and animal life of the bay's diverse estuarial ecosystem for their subsistence. When the English settled in Rhode Island in 1636, the Narragansett had achieved a measure of dominance over many neighboring Indian communities. Their status stemmed partly from their perceived ability to avoid European diseases. From 1616 to 1619 an epidemic had decimated many of the peoples in the eastern bay but spared the Narragansett, who lived primarily along its western side. In subsequent decades the Narragansett enhanced their power through their control of a major part of the WAMPUM trade. People throughout the Northeast coveted wampum—purple and white beads manufactured from shells found along the southern coast of New England—for its economic and spiritual value. Although the Narragansett dominated much of the region, their power was limited by the authority of their leaders, or SACHEMS, who had to rule by consensus. The Narragansett also faced threats from the nearby PEQUOT's increasing participation in the wampum ECONOMY. In 1637 some Narragansett allied with the English in the PEQUOT WAR.

Horrified by the casualties inflicted by their English allies in that war and fearful of the colonists' rapidly growing population, relations with the English soured. Moreover, Narragansett control over some Native American communities had weakened. In 1642 the Narragansett sachem MIANTONOMO conferred with other tribal leaders about resisting the English militarily. Word of the plot leaked, and the English forced Miantonomo to sign a treaty. The next year rival Mohegan captured Miantonomo in battle and handed him over to the English. The English found him guilty of murder and had the Mohegan execute him.

After Miantonomo's death the Narragansett struggled to maintain an uneasy peace in their diplomatic relations. They tried to stay out of KING PHILIP'S WAR, but in November 1675 the English and their Indian allies assaulted a Narragansett fort, killing several hundred, mostly women and children. After the war many Narragansett found refuge in southwestern Rhode Island under the Niantic leader Ninigret, creating the largest Indian community in southern New England. In 1709 an agreement between the colony of Rhode Island and Ninigret II declared this community the Narragansett. The Ninigret family ruled, to the consternation of many Narragansett, until 1770, when a tribal council was formed. Despite efforts of Rhode Island to destroy the tribe in the 19th century, today the Narragansett are a federally recognized tribe with a population of approximately 2,500.

See also CANONICUS.

Further reading: Ethel Boissevain, *The Narragansett People* (Phoenix: Indian Tribal Series, 1975).

—James D. Drake

Natchez Revolt (1729–1731)

The Natchez Indians lived near the Mississippi River in modern-day LOUISIANA and Mississippi. The establishment of a permanent French colony on the Gulf Coast in 1699 brought with it new mutual sexual and economic ties that bound the Natchez and French together and helped the new French colony survive its early years. As the French increased their importation of African slave labor, though, their economic ties with the Natchez grew less vital. The relationship between the two groups rapidly deteriorated as the French pressured the NATIVE AMERICANS for their lands, leading to outbreaks of violence in the 1710s and 1720s.

In 1729 Sieur De Chepart, commander of Fort Rosalie, ordered the Natchez to vacate their town of White Apple so that he could build a plantation. Outraged at De Chepart's demand, Natchez chiefs and elders compared their plight to that of slaves. Every Natchez village agreed to make war against the French.

On November 28, 1729, Natchez warriors entered Fort Rosalie pretending to offer gifts from a hunting expedition. At a prearranged signal the Indians opened fire, taking the French by complete surprise. The attack on the French fort and surrounding settlement killed 145 men, including De Chepart, plus 36 women and 56 children. The Natchez took hostage 50 white women and children plus 300 black slaves, several of whom joined the Natchez in their fight against the French. In a single day most of the white population in the area had been killed, captured, or driven from their homes.

In early 1730 a force of CHOCTAW Indians, allies of the French, inflicted heavy casualties on the Natchez and recaptured many of the hostages. A smaller French force soon arrived and forced the Natchez to hand over the remainder of the captives. A large punitive expedition mounted over the winter of 1730–31 resulted in the capture of nearly 500 Natchez prisoners, mostly women and children, who were sold into SLAVERY in the CARIBBEAN. The remaining Natchez became refugees. Many joined the CHICKASAW, Creek, and other Indian groups in the area. The rebellion begun by the Natchez in defense of their lands ended in the virtual destruction of their society.

Further reading: Daniel H. Usner, *Indians, Settlers, & Slaves in a Frontier Exchange Economy: The Lower Mississippi Valley Before 1783* (Chapel Hill: University of North Carolina Press, 1992).

—Andrew C. Lannen

Native Americans

When Europeans began arriving in North America in large numbers during the late 16th and 17th centuries, they landed in a world inhabited by hundreds of distinct tribes who had developed a variety of cultures independent of the Old World. Because of European diseases, increased warfare, and the introduction of new technologies, the period 1585–1763 witnessed massive changes in the lives of Native Americans throughout the continent. One of the most important characteristics of this transition was the variety of ways in which Indians responded to European encroachment on their lands. Tribes responded to Europeans based on their preexisting worldviews, religious beliefs, and political alliances. Equally important, different European groups arriving in the New World dealt with Indian peoples according to their own imperialist goals and cultural dispositions. Thus, settlers, furtraders, and missionaries all had different perspectives on how to deal with Native Americans. The developments in Indian-European relations that occurred in the 17th and 18th centuries had their roots in the first contacts between Indians and Europeans and in European intellectual constructs.

Population, Economies, and Cultures

Native American populations stretched from Tierra del Fuego at the southernmost tip of South America through the Arctic of Canada. The diversity of cultures, political organizations, and languages was tremendous. From village-oriented tribes to small nomadic bands and hierarchical empires to confederacies of allied tribes, Native Americans developed organizations that fit their ecological, social, and political needs. As in every region of the world, these organizations changed over time, and the location of an empire could become the location of a loosely organized set of villages a few hundred years later. The rise and fall of empires, changes in political organization, and other adaptations occurred throughout the Americas before Europeans ever set foot in the Western Hemisphere. Although most Native Americans did not have written languages, scholars have been able to create a picture of the Americas before Europeans arrived. Using linguistic evidence, archaeology, and oral traditions of native peoples, we have been able to learn a great deal about what the Americas were like before European arrival.

Despite these methods, scholars are unable to answer all the questions they ask. Scholars have had a particularly difficult time trying to gauge population sizes in the Americas prior to European arrival. Population estimates for the Western Hemisphere range from 40 million to nearly 100 million people in the late 15th century. The East Coast of North America, from Canada to FLORIDA, probably contained about 250,000 people at the time of European contact. Although we do not have exact population numbers, historians know that contact with Europeans caused a precipitous decline in the native population due to imported diseases. Before the arrival of the PILGRIMS, for example, European diseases ravaged the New England Indian population during the epidemic of 1616–17. Without the exact population, precise death rates will never be known, but even with imperfect precontact estimates, scholars estimate that some tribes on the East Coast lost between 70 and 90 percent of their people during the early colonial period.

The East was one of the earliest regions to come into contact with white people, but the tribes who lived there were far from being one homogeneous group. The East Coast of the present-day United States was populated by politically and socially diverse groups of ALGONQUIN, Iroquoian, and Siouan speakers. The POWHATAN CONFEDERACY and the Five Nations IROQUOIS consisted of villages organized in a complex political system, with accompanying rules and traditions of diplomacy among its member villages. These large, relatively sedentary groups relied primarily on a mixed economy of hunting and AGRICULTURE, in which women often did the farming while men hunted deer and small game. In northern New England groups like the Abenaki and Montagnais tended to be semisedentary, traveling during part of the year to hunt and residing in a village during the other seasons to fish or trade. These migration patterns varied from tribe to tribe according to tradition and ecological limitations. In southern New England tribes like the NARRAGANSETT, PEQUOT, and Massachusett tended to be larger and more sedentary then their northern neighbors. When the French, Spanish, and English began arriving in what is now the United States, they encountered this diverse array of civilizations.

European Contacts

Although many of the tribes on the East Coast encountered early explorers in the early 1500s, significant interaction truly began in the 17th century. In the St. Lawrence River Valley, northern New England, and the Canadian Maritime provinces the Micmac, Abenaki, Maliseet, Passamaquoddy, and Penobscot had been in contact with Basque and French fishermen by the close of the 16th century. When these Europeans made short trips to the shores to dry fish before their voyage home, they began a small-scale FUR TRADE with the local Indians. This marked the origins of the French-Indian fur trade that would help shape their relationship and the colonial experience for the next centuries. The French who followed sought deerskins, muskrats, and other pelts. However, most valuable was the beaver, whose fur was turned into felt for a type of hat fashionable among French aristocrats. Because the French needed Indians to hunt and trap beavers and other fur-bearing ANIMALS in the interior, they established peaceful alliances with their trading partners. The Indians benefited from the fur trade initially by receiving copper kettles, glass beads, and, most important, firearms and metal with which to tip their arrows. While the French developed amicable relations with the HURON, Montagnais, Algonquin, and other tribes, the new alliances caused sour relationships with the IROQUOIS, long-time enemies of the Indian allies of the French. With firearms and metal-tipped arrows, the Iroquois's enemies were more deadly than ever. Because the French excluded the Iroquois from being trading partners, the Iroquois found themselves at a technological disadvantage to their enemies.

The Iroquois Confederacy, made up of the Seneca, Cayuga, Onondaga, Oneida, and Mohawk, were a powerful force who lived in what is now upstate NEW YORK and southern Canada, yet their influence spread across much of the land east of the Mississippi. From the St. Lawrence River, through the American South, and west to the Mississippi River, the Iroquois sought to carve out a place in the trade with Europeans to acquire goods by peaceful exchange, if possible, or by raiding if necessary. The Montagnais, Algonquin, and Huron had been at war with the Iroquois before the French arrival, but the French presence affected the balance of power. In 1609 the French explorer and founder of Quebec, SAMUEL DE CHAMPLAIN, allied himself with a group of northern Indians in a raid against the Iroquois, whom they routed near the lake that bears Champlain's name. Throughout the 17th century the French were frequently at war with the powerful confederacy during the colonial period, yet the Iroquois remained relatively autonomous through the first part of the 18th century, trading with the French, English, and Dutch when it served their interests and raiding European settlements when necessary.

The English, who began to colonize the area from southern New England through VIRGINIA, initially enjoyed somewhat peaceful relations with Indians because they often depended on natives for FOOD, trade, and TECHNOLOGY. However, English invaders eventually established settlement patterns that were more destructive to Native Americans. While the French economic and social patterns tended to foster more amicable relations with Indian people, the British desire for land led to conflicts with Indians. Whether seeking religious community in New England or staple crop agriculture in Virginia, the British required land for towns and farmland for both crops and livestock. This vision of the land assumed that it was largely unoccupied, and both in New England and Virginia war consequently broke out.

In the 1630s the MASSACHUSETTS Bay Colony began to spread into the CONNECTICUT River Valley. The Pequot Indians controlled the mouth of the Connecticut River and directed the WAMPUM trade between the coastal and the interior tribes. DISEASE, which always accompanied Indian-European contact, had been particularly difficult for the Pequot. From 1616 to 1618 an epidemic swept through southern New England, wiping out entire villages. The Pequot were hard hit by this scourge and lost much of their population. In addition to disease, the Pequot suffered from very poor relations with the British. The Puritan settlers conceived of the surrounding Indians as "savages," attached to the wilderness and ignorant of God. Some thought that Indians might represent malevolent forces of the devil—a perspective that hardly allowed for calm diplomatic relations. Accusing the Pequot of having killed some Englishmen, the colonists sent a military force, which in 1637 massacred women and children as well as Pequot warriors at Fort Mystic. After selling many of the survivors into SLAVERY in the West Indies, the settlers forced those who remained to sign the Treaty of Hartford in 1638, which declared that the

Pequot no longer existed as a political entity. The treaty all but eradicated the Pequot. Nevertheless, the few remaining Pequot managed to cling to a tribal identity through the colonial period and to the present day.

In the South English settlers and native people generally coexisted peacefully for a brief period because both groups desired trade, technological exchange, and allies. However, a series of wars eventually erupted in Virginia between colonists and the powerful POWHATAN CONFEDERACY. When the English settlers landed in Virginia and settled the precarious colony of JAMESTOWN in 1607, they inhabited land controlled by a powerful chief named POWHATAN, who maintained a great deal of influence and received tribute from neighboring villages. By 1609 conflicts had erupted between the Powhatan Confederacy and the English. Skirmishes continued through 1617, when Powhatan's daughter POCAHONTAS married JOHN ROLFE, cementing through marriage an alliance between the two groups. Relations soured when Pocahontas died in Britain and Powhatan's successor, OPECHANCANOUGH, inherited the chiefdom. The English hunger for land increased greatly with their adoption of TOBACCO as a staple crop. After the 1620s settlers and indentured servants began to arrive in greater numbers. Angered by the British encroachment onto Indian lands, the Powhatan Confederacy launched a number of attacks against Virginia settlers beginning in 1622. By 1632 peace was officially declared, but English farmers continued to invade lands claimed by Native Americans. In 1644 an aged Opechancanough led a final attack against Virginia. However, the English, allied with some Indians who resented the confederacy's power, defeated Opechancanough. Although the Treaty of 1646 prohibited further British expansion, settlers continually violated it, and by 1670 the entire coast of Virginia was in English hands.

The Spanish, who by the 17th century had conquered the Aztecs and decimated or subjugated numerous Native Americans in the CARIBBEAN and Mexico, also made inroads into North America in the 16th century, particularly in the American South. Lucas Vasquez de Allyón, Alvar Nuñez Cabeza de Vaca, and Hernando de Soto all made voyages to the Southeast in the mid-16th century. Long-term Spanish influence was much greater in the American Southwest, particularly in what is now NEW MEXICO among the PUEBLO Indians. After the Spanish introduced missionaries who worked to eradicate native religions and cultures, the Pueblo attempted to drive the Spanish out of their area in the PUEBLO REVOLT of 1680. Led by a Pueblo leader named POPÉ, the revolt united a diverse group of Pueblo and killed more than 400 Europeans. In the 1690s Spanish military leader Diego de Vargas, allied with other Pueblo, suppressed the rebels, reaffirming Spanish control over New Mexico.

Disease

One of the most disastrous imports from Europe was disease. Measles, SMALLPOX, influenza, and other afflictions destroyed Indian populations, who had no natural immunities to these European diseases. The resulting depopulation weakened Indian military forces, disrupted social and economic life, and challenged Indian MEDICINE men to cure these new illnesses. Disease killed many more natives than warfare. Entire villages sometimes were wiped out from disease, and the survivors were forced to seek shelter with neighboring Indians. Repeated throughout the Americas, these types of realignments resulted in significant reordering and eradication of tribes and cultures. In the Carolinas the CATAWBA, one of many tribes in the Piedmont region, began to absorb remnants of the surrounding tribes. By 1750 Catawba villages contained people speaking 20 different languages, all called Catawba by the surrounding English settlers.

To replenish their populations, decimated by both disease and war, many eastern tribes participated in "mourning warfare" to capture members from enemy tribes, preferably young children or adolescents, who were then ritually adopted into the tribe. While such activity was common throughout eastern North America, each tribe had its own particular set of rituals of adoption. After the correct rituals were performed, the captive became a member of the tribe and even was said to have become one of the people who had been killed in war or had died by disease.

Missionaries

The French, Spanish, and English participated in significant efforts to convert Indian peoples to their brand of Christianity. For the French and Spanish this meant Catholicism, and for the British, PROTESTANTISM. Although all three nations supported and used missionaries, the French and Spanish incorporated mission societies most deeply into their colonial policy. Because the expenses of maintaining colonial outposts were too much for some French kings to bear in the 17th century, they gave generous land grants to the Society of Jesus (JESUITS) to establish colleges, hospitals, and mission villages for converting Indian peoples. In these villages the Jesuits sought to transform Indian peoples into European-style farmers, even those who lived in regions that did not support agriculture. They reasoned that urging them to accept European social forms would make them more accepting of European religions. Some of these mission villages, notably Sillery Kahnawake, Odanak, and St. François de Sales, attracted both converts and traditional Indians. While many people were interested in accepting Catholicism, others simply wanted to form alliances with the French. While some Indians accepted baptism as a means to demonstrate their alliance

Native American Population Loss, 1500–1700
Asia
ARCTIC OCEAN
GREENLAND
Baffin Bay
Baffin Island
Labrador Sea
Hudson Bay
ARCTIC
SUBARCTIC
NORTHWEST COAST
PLATEAU
GREAT BASIN
CALIFORNIA
PLAINS
NORTHEAST
SOUTHEAST
SOUTHWEST
PACIFIC OCEAN
ATLANTIC OCEAN
Gulf of Mexico
Caribbean Sea
South America
Lake Winnipeg
Columbia R.
Snake R.
Colorado R.
Rio Grande
Arkansas R.
Mississippi R.
St. Lawrence R.
Quebec
Sault Ste. Marie
Trois Rivières
Montreal
Ft. La Pointe
Ft. Orange
Ft. Good Hope
New York
Ft. Casimir
Ft. Christina
St. Mary's
Jamestown
Roanoke
Edenton
Charles Town
San Mateo
St. Augustine
Ft. Pentagoet
Portsmouth
Boston
Plymouth
Providence
New Haven
Ft. Crevecoeur
Taos
San Juan
Santa Fe
El Paso del Norte
San Pedro de Lagunas
San Miguel del Aguayo
Extent of European settlement, 1700
Major trading centers and settlements
Native American cultural areas
Indigenous population Loss by 1700
Areas of minimal population loss
More than 40%
More than 50%
More than 60%
N
0 500 Miles
0 500 Kms

with the French, others believed it a means of salvation. One factor that accelerated conversion was the presence of epidemic disease. In villages decimated by disease, where faith in their own SHAMANS faltered, missionaries were often successful in presenting Christianity as an alternative religion.

The English attempts at converting Indian peoples were more short-lived and generally less effective. The British established a series of PRAYING TOWNS set apart from the English settlers' towns. Although the Massachusetts Bay Colony's charter required the settlers to convert Indians to Christianity, they did not make serious missionary efforts until the 1640s. Thomas Mayhew and JOHN ELIOT were two of the pioneers of these praying towns. Unlike the Jesuits, these ministers were Protestant, not from a monastic order, and were paid in salaries supported by the English nobility. Like the Jesuits, they served a religious and social function. To teach Indians about Christianity, they translated the Bible and prayer books into Indian languages. They also required that Indians abandon their non-Christian relatives, live in European-style homes, and give up traditional hunting and farming techniques in favor of European-style agriculture. The English missionary effort suffered a severe blow in the wake of KING PHILIP'S WAR in 1676. Although the English eventually defeated their Wampanoag enemies with the help of praying town Indians, the event triggered a fear and resentment of Indians among the British, and they dismantled most of the mission villages in New England.

Both the French mission villages and English praying towns copied Spanish models. Although numerous religious orders participated in the conversion of Native Americans in Mexico and the Caribbean, the introduction of Christianity in the American Southwest began with Juan de Oñate, a Franciscan, in 1598. Like the French Jesuits, the Franciscans performed the duties of the Crown while converting souls. Moving through New Mexico along the Rio Grande and its tributaries, the Franciscans attacked native religions, attempting to win over souls by undermining traditional practices and beliefs. In Florida Franciscans made significant inroads among Native Americans like the Guale from the 1670s through the turn of the century. In the early 1700s war erupted between Spain and England, precipitating attacks by the English and their Indian allies from the North. Under constant fear of attack, most of the Spanish MISSIONS in Florida had collapsed by the opening decades of the 18th century.

Expansion of the Colonies and Their Role in International Politics

As the British colonies grew in size through the 17th century, they pushed farther into lands occupied by Indian peoples. In western Massachusetts, PENNSYLVANIA, and the Piedmont region of Virginia and the Carolinas, the growth of the colonies led to further conflicts. Neither the French nor the British were blind to the fact that Indian allies could help them in their conflicts with other European countries. While the Iroquois were one of the most frequently courted Indian people because of their military power, France's geopolitical position continued to exclude the Iroquois from their trade while simultaneously supplying their enemies with trade goods.

When the French explorers RENÉ-ROBERT CAVELIER, SIEUR DE LA SALLE and Henri Tonti reached the mouth of the Mississippi in 1682, they established a fur trading post in LOUISIANA that incorporated many of the southern tribes into their sphere. In 1699, at present-day Biloxi, Pierre Le Moyne, sieur d'Iberville established a post and allied himself with the neighboring CHOCTAW, Biloxi, Pascgoula, Moctoli, and Capira, who had been at war with the Creek and CHICKASAW. The British had hired the Chickasaw to capture their old enemies, who were then sold into slavery in the West Indies. In 1709 the British and their Indian allies attacked the French fort at Biloxi. The French Crown, realizing that the only way to secure Louisiana was to develop strong ties with Indian allies, funded a system of FORTS so that they could provide gifts and trade items to Indian allies. The lower Mississippi became an arena of conflict between the French and their Indian allies and pro-British Natchez and Chickasaw in the 1730s. To a certain extent, French Indian policy took on a more genocidal tone in the Chickasaw War, in which they attempted to eradicate their enemies, somewhat similar to the British in the Pequot War.

The increased French presence in the Mississippi and Ohio Valleys angered the British, who also claimed much of this area. Although the British could offer higher quality trade goods and lower prices to Indians, the French followed Indian protocols of trade to a greater extent, and in doing so secured allies through the west. In addition, the French policy of trade rather than land acquisition was understandably perceived by natives as less threatening to their own autonomy. When warfare broke out between England and France in Pennsylvania in the 1750s, the French were able to muster a large number of Potawatomi, Ottawa, and Chippewa allies, without which the French might easily have been overrun by the stronger British force. The conflict over the continent endured from 1754 through 1759, when the British took Quebec. When peace was officially declared between France and England in 1763, the French relinquished their claims to North America. France's loss was a disaster for many Native Americans, too. The presence of multiple European powers had allowed tribes to negotiate for better prices in trade and to realign themselves militarily when the situation demanded it, that is, to "play off" the British against the French. Lacking a choice of European allies, Native Americans in the

North, led by Pontiac, mounted a campaign of resistance against the British at the end of the SEVEN YEARS' WAR. Indians in the South continued to play off the Spanish against the British whenever possible.

Further reading: James Axtell, *The Invasion Within: The Contest of Cultures in Colonial North America* (New York: Oxford University Press, 1985); William Cronon, *Changes in the Land: Indians, Colonists, and the Ecology of New England* (New York: Hill & Wang, 1983); Daniel K. Richter, *The Ordeal of the Longhouse: The Peoples of the Iroquois League in the Era of European Colonization* (Chapel Hill: University of North Carolina Press, 1992); Daniel Usner, *Indians, Settlers, and Slaves in a Frontier Exchange Economy: The Lower Mississippi Valley before 1783* (Chapel Hill: University of North Carolina Press, 1992); David J. Weber, *The Spanish Frontier in North America* (New Haven, Conn.: Yale University Press, 1992); Richard White, *The Middle Ground: Indians, Empires and Republics in the Great Lakes Region, 1650–1815* (New York: Cambridge University Press, 1991).

—Thomas J. Lappas

Navajo

The ancestors of the Navajo and their linguistic relatives, the Apache, appeared in what is now the American Southwest after a long and gradual migration from central Canada. They were probably present in the Southwest by the late 15th century. The Navajo established themselves west of the Rio Grande Valley and began trading the products of their hunting and gathering ECONOMY—principally meat, hides, salt, and alum—for agricultural goods produced by sedentary PUEBLO Indians to their east. The Navajo soon began growing corn themselves, an early step in a process of cultural and economic transformation that would distinguish them from their Apache cousins.

Spanish colonizers settled among the Rio Grande Pueblo in 1598 and apparently came into early conflict with the Navajo. Territorial disputes, the Spanish practice of enslaving "barbarian" Indians, and Navajo raiding of Spanish goods and horses all contributed to a pattern of conflict that characterized the 17th century. Some Navajo seemingly participated in the 1680 PUEBLO REVOLT and helped Pueblo resist the Spanish reconquest of the 1690s. When that resistance failed, Navajo welcomed thousands of Pueblo refugees. Conflicts with the Spanish continued until 1716, when both sides became preoccupied with other enemies, principally the Ute and Comanche.

Pueblo refugees inspired profound changes in Navajo life. In the decades following the rebellion Navajo adapted much of the rich ceremonialism of Pueblo tradition to their own religion. Navajo pottery became more sophisticated and distinctive, while weaving constituted an increasingly important component of the economy. Pueblo irrigation techniques helped produce greater harvests, and Navajo families started cultivating Spanish-introduced plants such as cotton and orchard fruits. Most significantly, the Navajo economy began to reorient itself around horses, cattle, sheep, and goatherding.

By the middle of the 18th century, the Navajo people had incorporated major changes into their lives, and their territory was expanding vigorously. They increasingly fought with the western Pueblo of Hopi and Zuni, certain eastern Pueblo, and the Ute. In 1774 nearly 60 years of peace between Navajo and Spaniards ended, and the next century would be one of nearly perpetual conflict over territory, slaving, and raids.

See also SPANISH COLONIES.

Further reading: David M. Brugge, "Navajo Prehistory and History to 1850," in Alfonzo Ortiz, ed., *Handbook of North American Indians*, vol. 10: *Southwest* (Washington D.C.: Smithsonian Institution, 1983); Frank McNitt, *Navajo Wars: Military Campaigns, Slave Raids, and Reprisals* (Albuquerque: University of New Mexico Press, 1990).

—Brian DeLay

Negro Plot of 1741

Throughout the colonial era people of African descent expressed outrage at their enslavement and the conditions to which they were subjected. Those who lived in the northern colonies were no exception. In 1741 fear of a slave uprising came to a head when rumor of an insurrection spread through NEW YORK CITY, which had one of the highest percentages of slaves in British North America; about one in every five of the 11,000 residents was black, nearly all of whom were slaves. Whites remembered the insurrection of 1712, when slaves set a building ablaze and killed nearly 25 people. Nineteen slaves were executed for the arson. Moreover, tension was palpable in the spring of 1741 as fear of KING GEORGE'S WAR with Spain (1740–48) and the potential of a growing black population aiding the Spanish combined to create fear in the minds of whites.

What began with a petty burglary became a rumor of revolt. One night in late February, merchant Robert Hogg's shop was robbed of a sack of coins, two silver candlesticks, and some linen. Two slaves, Caesar and Prince, were suspected and arrested. They were not alone, however. A white husband and wife, John and Sarah Hughson, were accused of receiving the stolen goods. Authorities investigating the crime discovered as much only when they questioned the Hughson's indentured servant, Mary Burton, who informed them that she knew about the robbery. The authorities promised Burton that she would be released from indenture, enough of an incentive for her to accuse the Hughsons of receiving the stolen goods. Her accusation proved correct—the purloined goods were found on their premises.

On March 18 new fears erupted when a series of fires broke out in the city. Initially, slaves were not suspected. By raising the possibility that a conspiracy was afoot, however, the city council fueled suspicions that slaves had set the fires. When the fires burned again on April 6, the black populace was suspected. Panic gripped the town and a rumor quickly circulated that blacks and poor whites were conspiring to destroy law and order and to seize control of the city. Suspicions were quickly translated into actions: "The Negroes are rising!" cried many whites. White crowds rounded up black people, taking nearly 100 to the jail.

Officials and townspeople believed that slaves, "silly unthinking creatures," were led by whites. Daniel Horsmanden, a dedicated and ambitious attorney, rose to prominence in overseeing the prosecutions. When Horsmanden took over the case, matters changed dramatically. Using "money to loosen tongues," he cast the net wider so that between April 13 and August 29 a number of confessions were secured; more people were arrested, jailed, and executed. Horsmanden, supporting Burton's allegations, declared that the fires were a conspiracy among the black inhabitants to seize control of the city. Burton's initial accusations were aided by the confessions of black people sentenced to execution.

Mary Burton achieved freedom by cooperating with the authorities and promoting the belief that the fires resulted from a conspiracy that seemed to grow larger each time she testified. After her first appearance before the grand jury, Burton returned and accused yet more people, both black and white, of conspiring to burn the city. Burton further fueled the general xenophobia that targeted outsiders and newcomers. The ROMAN CATHOLICS and Irish were particularly suspect, according to one scholar, because "a belief persisted that a constant Catholic conspiracy was afoot to subvert the crown and the Church of England; and with war raging in the West Indies and Spanish attacks on the Georgia–Florida borderlands and sorties as close as Charleston, South Carolina." A dancing master and his indentured servant, two soldiers, and a schoolteacher fell under the suspicion of Judge Horsmanden.

In the end, 21 people were hanged, including 17 black men, two white men, and two white women. Additionally, 13 black men were burned at the stake. Seventy-two black men were pardoned but banished.

Further reading: T. J. Davis, *A Rumor of Revolt: The "Great Negro Plot" in Colonial New York* (New York: Free Press, 1985); Edgar J. McManus, *A History of Negro Slavery in New York* (Syracuse, N.Y.: Syracuse University Press, 1966); Peter Linebaugh and Marcus Rediker, *The Many-Headed Hydra: Sailors, Slaves, Commoners, and the Hidden History of the Revolutionary Atlantic* (Boston: Beacon Press, 2000).

—Leslie Patrick

Neolin (Delaware Prophet) (1725?–1775?)

Neolin was an important Indian religious leader in the 1750s and early 1760s. Near the end of the SEVEN YEARS' WAR, various native communities living in western PENNSYLVANIA and the Ohio territory experienced a crisis in their efforts to maintain their cultural traditions and territorial integrity. Many of these communities previously had profited from being able to command relatively high prices trading their pelts for European goods because the IROQUOIS were able to maintain competition between the French and the British. The French defeat in the war ended this balance and led to the decline of the economic leverage of the Iroquois. Continuing cultural stress brought about by the attractiveness of colonial goods, particularly ALCOHOL, laid the foundation for a series of messianic native leaders who urged a return to traditional ways.

One of the best-known native messiahs of this period was the DELAWARE (Lenape) Indian Neolin, whose name means "the enlightened one." His specific cultural origin is unknown, but he was probably born in the Lake Erie region, and he was active primarily in the Ohio territory during the era of Pontiac's Rebellion. Neolin experienced a series of visions, including a trip to heaven, in which the Creator provided a code of laws. These detailed instructions would enable his Indian followers both to negotiate a more direct path to heaven and to vanquish Europeans.

"Enlightened" by his visions, Neolin called for the faithful to give up the evils of European culture, including all items not produced in the old Indian ways, such as alcohol, metal tools, and guns. Neolin also urged purging the inside of the body by taking emetics as part of rituals of purification. Of note was Neolin's call for the abandonment of a number of traditional native behaviors such as polygyny, rituals involving war, and native "medicine songs." Christian elements were also incorporated into his message, reflecting the deep impact of European ideas on native societies.

Neolin could not read or write, but he drew a small "map" on deerskin that purported to trace the journey of the soul in this world and in heaven. This "map," called the Great Book of Writing, was copied and sold in great numbers by Neolin as he traveled among the native communities preaching his message. A notable feature of Neolin's oratory was his continuous weeping.

Many natives, including Pontiac, accepted Neolin's teachings. When Pontiac's Rebellion failed in 1763, Neolin vanished from the historical record. Most likely he simply died a natural death, but his "map" to heaven forms a lasting record of his activities.

Further reading: Gregory Evans Dowd, *A Spirited Resistance: The North American Indian Struggle for Unity, 1745–1815* (Baltimore: Johns Hopkins University Press, 1991).

—Marshall Joseph Becker

New Amsterdam

The island of Manhattan, which was to become the site of Dutch New Amsterdam, was first recorded by Europeans during the voyages of HENRY HUDSON, an English explorer in the employ of the Dutch East India Company, in 1609. Before European contact, Manhattan had been a swampy outpost and hunting territory of NATIVE AMERICANS, including the Canarsie and the Manhattan, who were concentrated on nearby Long Island. The first, impermanent European settlement came in 1613, when Dutch explorer Adriaen Block encamped while making repairs to his ship. On the strength of both Hudson's and Block's voyages, the Netherlands laid claim to the entire Hudson River Valley, and in order to oversee the area's economic exploitation, the DUTCH WEST INDIA COMPANY was formed in 1621.

Permanent settlement did not come to New Amsterdam until 1621, when a group of 30 Protestant Walloons settled on neighboring Nutten Island (now Governors Island). This group, along with soldiers and traders in the employ of the Dutch West India Company who were fleeing Indian attacks near Fort Orange (now Albany), settled on Manhattan in 1625. The following year PETER MINUIT, a company official, "purchased" the island from the Canarsie for 60 guilders (about $28), although it is clear that the Indians understood this transaction quite differently than did the Europeans. Fort Orange, at the northern navigable end of the Hudson River, was the

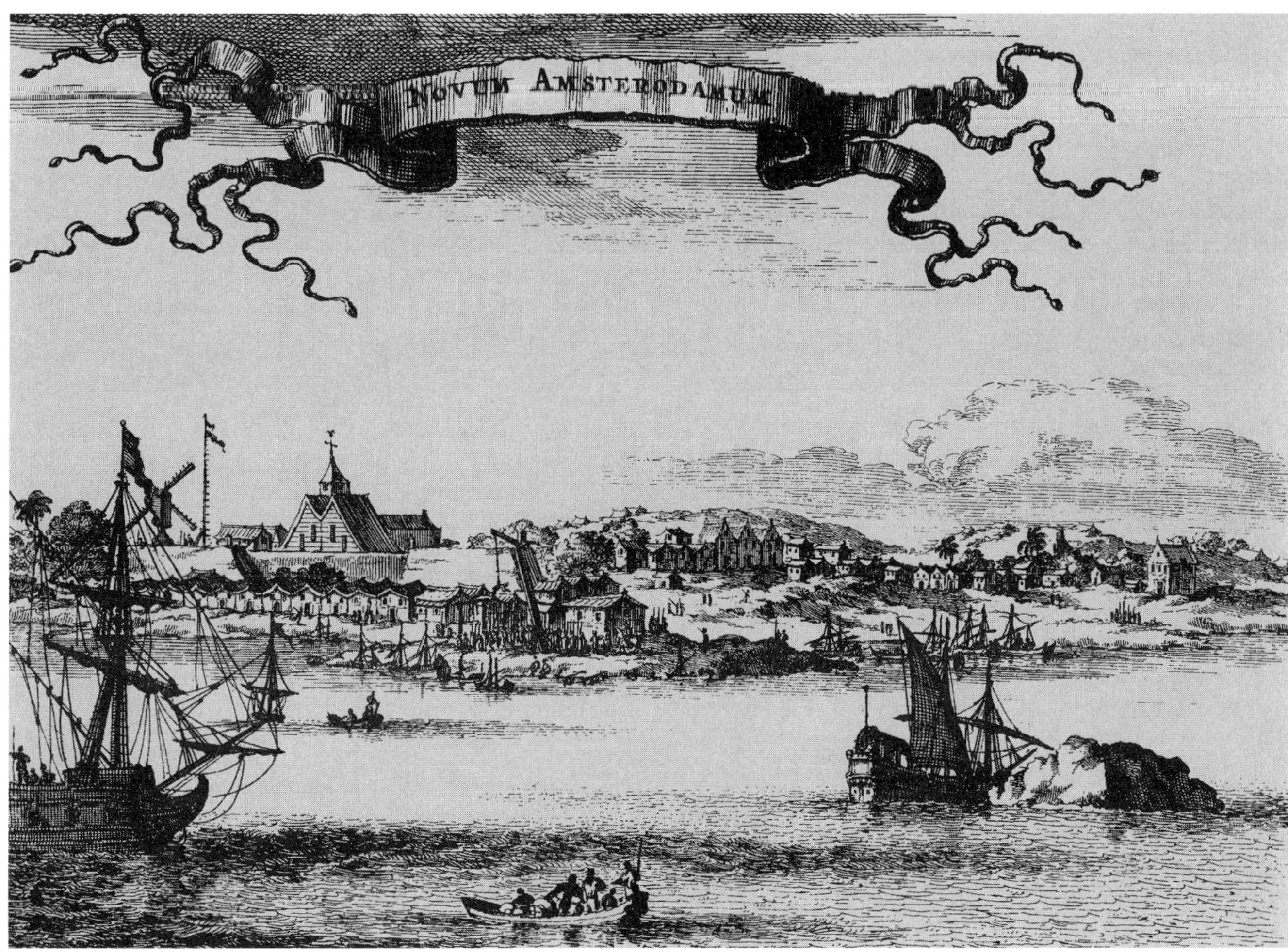

This print shows New Amsterdam's fine natural harbor, which helped make it a commercial center. *(Library of Congress)*

centerpiece of the dispersed Dutch fur trading empire called NEW NETHERLAND. However, Minuit's small settlement became an important transshipment point for goods to and from Europe due to its excellent natural deep-water harbor. Despite remaining clustered on the southern tip of Manhattan, the settlement quickly developed into one of the most important and diverse towns in the New World. Dozens of languages were spoken in New Amsterdam as seamen and traders from throughout Europe, slaves and free black people from Africa, Jewish refugees from Portuguese Brazil, and Indians mingled on the dirt streets. The Common Council, guided by PETER STUYVESANT, governor of New Amsterdam from 1647 to 1664, sought to bring order to this cosmopolitan colonial outpost, establishing building codes, setting market days, and dictating standard weights and measures to be used in trade.

English officials were concerned about the increasing wealth and size of the Dutch colony, but even more troubling was its strategic location on the Hudson, which bisected the English settlements in VIRGINIA and New England. The English sought to wrest control of the Netherlands' North American holdings; a fleet sent by the duke of York arrived off the coast in 1664 demanding that Stuyvesant turn the colony over to the British. Stuyvesant remained defiant, but commercial interests in the council recognized that the benefits of continued peace outweighed fighting for Dutch sovereignty. Both the colony of New Netherland and the town of New Amsterdam were renamed NEW YORK. Despite a brief reoccupation by Dutch forces in late 1673, New York remained in British hands and continued to grow in both size and importance as a commercial center.

Further reading: Oliver A. Rink, *Holland on the Hudson: An Economic and Social History of Dutch New York* (Ithaca, N.Y.: Cornell University Press, 1986); Joyce D. Goodfriend, *Before the Melting Pot* (Princeton, N. J.: Princeton University Press, 1994).

—Matthew Taylor Raffety

New Hampshire

One of the New England colonies, New Hampshire was among the smallest British colonies in both population and area. The future colony of New Hampshire was inhabited for at least 10,000 years. When Europeans first arrived, approximately 4,000 ALGONQUIN-speaking people of the western Abenaki Indians lived in the region. These groups subsisted by hunting and FISHING as well as by cultivating corn and beans. Besides maintaining semipermanent villages, they sent out hunting parties and, at times, migrated seasonally. Politically, western Abenaki tribes had a chief, a council, and regular meetings of all adult tribal members to discuss and decide serious matters.

French and English fishermen probably were among the first Europeans to visit New Hampshire as they stopped to dry their catch or to trade with natives. The English captain Martin Pring sailed his two ships, the *Speedwell* and *Discoverer*, up the Piscataqua River in June 1603, and the founder of the FRENCH COLONIES in North America, SAMUEL DE CHAMPLAIN, arrived in July 1605. In 1614 the well known English explorer JOHN SMITH charted the coast of the region, discovered the Isles of Shoals, and publicized its rich natural resources, particularly forests, fur, and fish in his description of future New England.

The colonization of New Hampshire began in the 1620s, when the Council for New England granted several land patents to establish settlements and trade posts in the area. On August 10, 1622, the former governor of Newfoundland, Captain JOHN MASON, and Sir Ferdinando Gorges received from the council a grant of the territory between the Merrimack and Kennebec Rivers. In 1629, when the new owners divided the territory between themselves, John Mason received the lands between the Merrimack and Piscataqua Rivers. The proprietor called his domain New Hampshire after his home county in England. In 1623 David Thompson founded the first English settlement in New Hampshire near the mouth of the Piscataqua River, which existed for several years. MERCHANTS from London, including Edward and William Hilton, established a new settlement in 1628 several miles northward that became Dover. In 1631 Mason initiated a settlement at the mouth of the Piscataqua named Strawberry Banke.

Another impetus for the colonization of New Hampshire came from its southern neighbor—the MASSACHUSETTS Bay Colony. While the Puritan dissenters from Massachusetts under the Reverend JOHN WHEELWRIGHT established the town of Exeter in 1638, the BOSTON authorities also supported a settlement in the region in 1639 that became the town of Hampton.

The natural resources of the region shaped the development of the ECONOMY and the primary occupations of the settlers (farming, fishing, fish and fur trading, LUMBERING, and SHIPBUILDING) and propelled the colony into the lucrative transatlantic trade with the CARIBBEAN and European markets. New Hampshire also supplied fish products to Massachusetts and VIRGINIA as well as to Spain, Madeira, and the Canary Islands. Most important, wood and wood products of New Hampshire (clapboards, oak barrels, and casks) were in great demand in the West Indies and southern Europe, primarily for the shipping of rum, molasses, and sugar, and as fuel for sugar processing. By 1671 New Hampshire was exporting 20,000 tons of boards and staves yearly.

The white pine forests of New Hampshire made it a source of ship masts, timber, and naval stores for the Royal Navy. The export of masts from the colony grew from 56 in 1695 to 500 in 1742. The mast trade also gave rise to a protest movement in the Exeter area. In the 1734 Mast Free Riot, colonists registered their opposition to the practice of marking the best trees in the FORESTS for the Royal Navy. With the rapidly expanding settlement of New Hampshire from the 1690s to the 1760s, the economy of the colony grew more diverse. In 1719, for example, Presbyterian colonists from northern Ireland and Scotland founded the town of Londonderry and initiated the cultivation of potatoes.

The expansion of white settlements heightened tensions with local Indians. From 1675 to 1756 there were several wars and numerous clashes between the English and the Abenaki tribes. These conflicts were interconnected with the Anglo-French struggle over North America and the long-standing enmity between the Abenaki and the IROQUOIS, who lived west of Abenaki lands. Because they frequently fought the pro-British Iroquois, the Abenaki sought French military support and trade, and they established a formidable alliance with the French during a long series of ferocious conflicts in the region. New Hampshire played an active role in this monumental struggle as a theater of military operations, as a recruitment and supply base, and as a communication route for British forces. By 1759 nearly 1,000 men from New Hampshire were enlisted to serve in the army outside the colony. During KING WILLIAM'S WAR (1689–97) the Abenaki tribes raided Dover, Salmon Falls, Exeter, Durham, and other New Hampshire settlements. Large-scale Indian raids resumed during KING GEORGE'S WAR (1744–48). During the SEVEN YEARS' WAR (1756–63) the colonial militia, led by Captain Robert Rogers, and British troops, drove the Abenaki tribes northward.

The politics of New Hampshire were dominated by disputes with the neighboring colonies of Massachusetts and NEW YORK. The widespread confusions, false claims, and misinformation about the region's geography led to overlapping land grants, ambiguous borders, and continuous territorial disputes on the southern and western frontiers of New Hampshire. Additionally, developments in the early history of New Hampshire favored claims of the Massachusetts Bay Colony on the entire territory of New Hampshire.

After the sudden death of John Mason, the small colony of only several hundred white inhabitants was left without a central government and existed as a conglomerate of semi-independent settlements. The situation was further complicated by the influx of Puritan settlers from Massachusetts, driven out of that colony by religious disputes. By 1640 these Puritan dissidents constituted more than half of the nearly 1,000 white residents of New Hampshire. There were numerous quarrels between the new Puritan settlements (Exeter, Hampton) and the traditional Anglican Strawberry Banke area; Hilton Point (the future Dover) often fluctuated in its loyalty between the two. The religious and political disputes and instability as well as the consent of local PURITANS invited interference from Boston. Wealthy landowners and merchants of New Hampshire allied themselves with the Massachusetts Puritans to resist John Mason's heirs, who attempted to confirm their land rights in New Hampshire. Additionally, the continuous menace of Indian attacks forced the New Hampshire colonists to turn to Massachusetts and its strong militia for defense. During the 1640s England, involved in its own civil war, was unable to control the territorial ambitions of the Massachusetts Bay Colony.

By 1637 Massachusetts laid claim to all of New Hampshire, and within five years nearly all settlements in the colony conceded to the authority of Boston. Strawberry Banke was incorporated by Massachusetts in 1653 and renamed Portsmouth. Because of the religious and political concessions Boston made to New Hampshire, the colony did not experience large-scale religious persecutions except for a brief repression of the QUAKERS in 1659–60.

In 1679 the Crown, to strengthen its control over New England and in response to continuous appeals from the Mason family, reversed the Massachusetts territorial gains and in September 1680 created the separate royal province of New Hampshire. Nevertheless, there were other periods when New Hampshire rejoined Massachusetts for political, economic, and security reasons. The two colonies were joined officially in the DOMINION OF NEW ENGLAND from 1686 to 1689, and between 1690 and 1692 they cooperated against the military threat of the French and Indians. From 1698 to 1741 New Hampshire and Massachusetts shared the same governor, with New Hampshire being ruled by the lieutenant governor. After 1741 New Hampshire had its own governor.

After 1749 New Hampshire struggled with New York over the lands between the Connecticut River and Lake Champlain. Before 1769 New Hampshire's governors granted land to more than 130 towns in the region. Although the Crown settled the boundary line between the two colonies in 1764 in favor of New York, the dispute continued until the American Revolution.

In 1680 the Crown established a government for New Hampshire that consisted of a president of the province (later a governor), a council of governor's appointees, and an elected assembly. Voting rights were limited to affluent males by the 50-pound property qualification. By the end of the 17th century the assembly had used its financial prerogatives to broaden its political power. This created numerous conflicts between the executive and the assembly. Governor Edward Cranfield (1682–84), whose commission was finally revoked by the Crown for numerous illegalities and abuse of power, ruled for several years without the assembly, which refused to pass his revenue bills. By 1699 the assembly had established its own leadership, a set of formal rules, and its printed organ—*The House Journal.* Even one of the most effective and pragmatic royal governors in British America—New Hampshire's Benning Wentworth (1741–67)—experienced several rounds of tough confrontation with the assembly, although the situation of the colony stabilized considerably during his tenure.

Several powerful Puritan families of wealthy merchants, landowners, and fish traders (the Cutts, Vaughans, and Waldrons) dominated politics in New Hampshire from 1640 to 1715. After 1715, with the growing importance of the mast trade, the Wentworth dynasty of mast traders came to the center of New Hampshire's political life. The family produced two governors and one lieutenant governor of the colony.

The political stabilization and economic development of the colony led to the growth of its white population (from some 10,000 in 1700 to 25,000 in the mid-1730s). The majority lived in more than 140 towns and villages, and most were of British ancestry. In 1756 the first newspaper in the colony, *The New Hampshire Gazette,* was established.

Further reading: Jere R. Daniell, *Colonial New Hampshire: A History* (Millwood, N.Y.: KTO Press, 1981); David E. Van Deventer, *The Emergence of Provincial New Hampshire, 1623–1741* (Baltimore: The Johns Hopkins University Press, 1976).

—Peter Rainow

New Jersey

Although one of the smaller colonies in physical terms, New Jersey contained a variety of ethnic and racial groups, produced a considerable amount of wheat and other foodstuffs, and had a complex and contentious political history. Italian traveler Giovanni da Verrazzano explored the New Jersey coast in 1524, and in 1609 HENRY HUDSON, an English mariner employed by the Dutch East India Company, sent a party to explore Sandy Hook Bay. Until the mid-17th century, however, the DELAWARE, or Lenape, Indians dominated present-day New Jersey. They numbered between 2,000 and 3,000 people and subsisted mainly by hunting and FISHING. There was little friction between the Lenape and the first European explorers; the Dutch and Swedish colonists were more interested in establishing trading partnerships than in acquiring land, and the Lenape valued the trade for European goods.

In the 1640s Dutch settlers began to move southward from NEW NETHERLAND (present-day NEW YORK), while Swedish settlers moved northward from New Sweden (present-day DELAWARE). As European settlements expanded and colonists sought to appropriate valuable farmland, their relations with the Lenni Lenape deteriorated. Two Indian wars, Governor Kieft's War (1641–45) and the Peach War (1655), weakened the Dutch settlements, but in 1655 the Dutch nevertheless forced the outnumbered and militarily weak Swedish population to submit to Dutch government. The region's European population remained tiny, however: about 200 Dutch, 100 Swedish, and an undetermined number of English settlers from New England.

When England conquered New Netherland in 1664, it also laid claim to the area that would become New Jersey. King Charles II (1660–85) patented the region to his brother James, who deeded it to two friends, John, Lord Berkley and Sir George Carteret. The result was a colony where New Jerseyans could elect an assembly. The establishment of the most democratic system in the English empire attracted a large number of PURITANS and Dutch Protestants to settle in New Jersey. These religious dissenters, however, posed a problem for Carteret and Berkley when they resisted the ruling and taxation authority of the Restorationists. Faced with this dilemma, Berkley later sold his half-share in the colony to two QUAKERS, John Fenwick and George Billing. In 1676 the colony was divided in half. Fenwick and Billing established West Jersey, while East Jersey was settled slightly later by a group of two dozen proprietors who had purchased shares from Carteret. West Jersey was more religious and egalitarian in tone than East Jersey, while East Jersey was more hierarchical and commercially oriented, but they resembled each other as much as they differed. A mixture of Quaker enthusiasm and economic ambition propelled both settlements.

West Jersey's early decades were stormy. Fenwick and Billing soon quarreled over the terms of their partnership. They submitted the dispute to a Quaker arbitration team, which determined that Fenwick owned 10 shares in the colony while Billing owned 90. WILLIAM PENN, one of the arbitrators, became Billing's trustee; the territorial dispute marked Penn's first involvement in American colonization. Fenwick founded Salem, the first English town in New Jersey, in November 1675. Billing subdivided and sold most of his shares, expanding the proprietary group from two to about 120 investors. Approximately half of these investors immigrated to New Jersey, and by 1682 perhaps 2,000 English Quakers had settled there. The colony's government remained highly unstable, however. Fenwick had initially tried to exercise gubernatorial powers, but his right to do so was disputed by Billing, the other West Jersey proprietors, and the royal governor of New York. Further rifts soon developed within the large and unwieldy group of proprietors; they worsened after 1685, when some shares in the colony's government passed out of Quaker hands. In 1687 Dr. Daniel Coxe, an English speculator, purchased title to the West Jersey government from Billing, and in 1693 Coxe sold it to the West Jersey Society, a corporation that speculated in lands and political interests in the Jersey colonies and PENNSYLVANIA.

The first European settlers in East Jersey were Dutch and English families from New England, Long Island, and New Netherland. When England acquired New York and New Jersey in 1664, there were already 33 families of European immigrants living in Bergen, opposite Manhattan Island. Between 1664 and 1666 English Quakers and Puritans streamed into East Jersey and founded several more towns. In 1681 Carteret's widow sold title to the colony to a group of 12 proprietors (later expanded to 24) who were predominantly Scottish and Quaker and included William Penn. The new proprietors encouraged emigration from Scotland to East Jersey and in 1683 established the town of Perth Amboy. There was continual friction between the proprietors and the English settlers, however; the proprietors challenged the settlers' land titles, while the settlers resented the proprietors' attempts to collect quitrents and dominate the colony's government. Simmering social and political tensions erupted in a wave of riots between 1698 and 1701.

In 1702 the West Jersey Society and the defeated proprietary government of East Jersey ceded political power to the Crown. The Crown united West and East Jersey as a single colony, New Jersey. Although subject to the royal governor of New York, New Jersey elected its own legislature, which met alternately in Burlington and Perth Amboy. In spite of the Crown's hopes, the unification of New Jersey did little to stabilize its government. Lingering tensions between the original sections, between various religious denominations, and between resident and nonresident proprietors continued to haunt the colony. In 1738 the Crown appointed LEWIS MORRIS, a hotheaded and opportunistic New York politician, to be the first separate governor of New Jersey. Political autonomy did not bring New Jersey peace, however; Morris was unpopular and, like the New York governors who preceded him, fought bitterly with the colonial legislature over the division of political power. Basic disputes about land titles, the supply of paper money, and the location of boundary lines between East and West Jersey and between New Jersey and New York complicated daily life in the colony until the American Revolution. In contrast, local government, based on a combination of town meetings and county courts, was fairly placid.

New Jersey was one of the less populous English colonies in North America. Its non-Indian population numbered about 14,000 in 1702; by then, few Native Americans remained in the colony. New Jersey's European population, however, was exceptionally diverse, including English, Scottish, Irish, Dutch, Swedish, and German settlers, as well as Anglicans, PRESBYTERIANS, CONGREGATIONALISTS, and Quakers. Most colonists farmed, producing grain, vegetables, hemp, flax, livestock, and lumber for export. Coastal residents fished as well. Although some of the Scottish proprietors created large estates and attempted to introduce tenant farming, family farms of 100–200 acres were the rule. New Jersey was overwhelmingly rural; even its twin market and political centers, Burlington and Perth Amboy, numbered only about 500 people each in the 18th century. Puritans from New England and Dutch settlers from New York founded primary schools in several East Jersey towns, but there were few schools in West Jersey until the 19th century.

By 1760 New Jersey's population had grown to 93,800, but its rural townships were still overshadowed by the emerging cities of NEW YORK CITY and PHILADELPHIA. Elizabethtown, Trenton, and New Brunswick gradually overtook Burlington and Perth Amboy as the colony's internal commercial centers. Trenton, founded in 1709 at the head of the Delaware River, was particularly important as a transshipment point for exports from New Jersey's agricultural hinterland; it also attracted skilled ARTISANS. Iron mining, which had begun on a small scale in the 17th century, became a more important industry after 1750, when Britain lifted the import duty on iron. In the late colonial period some affluent New York and Philadelphia families built country estates in New Jersey, beginning the region's long tradition as a suburban retreat.

By 1750 African and African-American slaves made up about 7 percent of New Jersey's population; in 1775, approximately 10,000 African Americans (mostly slaves) lived in New Jersey. NEW AMSTERDAM (New York City), as a port, was an early center of the slave trade, and Dutch farmers and other immigrants from New York brought slaves with them when they settled in New Jersey. The colony's slave population was concentrated in East Jersey, especially along the New York border. Most New Jersey slaves labored on large farms; in southern New Jersey some affluent settlers established estates that resembled Chesapeake area plantations. Quaker West Jersey, on the other hand, generally frowned on SLAVERY. In the 1740s West Jersey and Pennsylvania Quakers began to debate the morality of slavery, and in 1754 JOHN WOOLMAN published a pamphlet, *Some Consideration on the Keeping of Negroes*, in which he argued that slavery harmed both master and slave.

New Jersey's religious life was complex. West Jersey was originally founded as a refuge for English Quakers, and Scottish Quakers played a prominent role in the settlement of East Jersey. However, Quaker influence diminished over time as non-Quakers purchased proprietary shares and a flood of immigrants from New England, Britain, and Germany diluted the Quaker population. The GREAT AWAKENING, a series of religious revivals that swept through the American colonies in the late 1730s and early 1740s, affected New Jersey's Presbyterian congregations profoundly and influenced the Congregationalists, BAPTISTS, and Dutch Reformed to a lesser extent. In New Jersey as in New England, the Great Awakening divided many congregations and communities; these rifts were gradually healed as the most committed Old Light leaders passed away and were succeeded by more accommodating clergy. The Great Awakening also led to the founding of the College of New Jersey (later PRINCETON COLLEGE), a successor to the New Light Log College, in 1746. The college's innovative curriculum, which included an expanded emphasis on natural and moral philosophy, drew many students from other colonies by the 1760s. By the eve of the Revolution, the Presbyterians had displaced the Quakers as the dominant religious denomination in New Jersey.

Further reading: Graham Russell Hodges, *Root and Branch: African Americans in New York and East Jersey, 1613–1863* (Chapel Hill: University of North Carolina Press, 1999); Ned C. Landsman, *Scotland and Its First American Colony, 1683–1765* (Princeton, N.J.: Princeton University Press, 1985); John E. Pomfret, *Colonial New Jersey: A History* (New York: Scribner, 1973).

—Darcy R. Fryer

New Mexico

Situated on the northern frontier of Spain's American empire, the Kingdom of New Mexico was an essential military outpost and center of missionary activity. Early attempts to conquer and settle the region by gold-seeking conquistadores in 1540 were dismal failures, but after a series of expeditions by Franciscan missionaries in 1581–82 mapped out the region and its peoples, the Spanish were able to conquer New Mexico in 1598. It was then that a small army of 129 soldiers led by Juan de Oñate, and joined by a group of friars, established a permanent outpost in the mesa and canyon country of northern New Mexico. The Roman Catholic friars immediately began proselytizing PUEBLO Indians in Taos, San Juan, and other settled communities, while de Oñate's soldiers dealt severely with natives who resisted. This military and religious conquest was facilitated by a long history of internal conflict in the region, which undermined efforts to resist Spanish colonization. European hegemony became clear in the burning of the Pueblo of Acoma in 1598, along with the brutal punishments meted out to its inhabitants. After this demonstration of Spanish ruthlessness, most communities chose to cooperate with the Spaniards rather than fight. In the aftermath of Acoma, the Spanish began demanding tribute, while the friars established MISSIONS and insisted that the Pueblo abandon their traditions in favor of Christianity.

From its creation the colony of New Mexico was charged with producing wealth for the Crown through mines, Indian tribute, and other revenue generating activities. It was also seen as a forum for evangelization, an ideal source of souls for the Franciscan missionaries who accompanied Oñate's military force. Perhaps most important, New Mexico was meant to serve as a buffer to the more "barbarous" indigenous groups to the north, a first line of defense for the rich and vulnerable mining districts of north-central New Spain. To these ends, the friars established mission pueblos designed to congregate Indians around a single urban setting. After 1598 many Indian communities were forcibly moved to the missions and taught European forms of AGRICULTURE. Many resisted these disruptions and either fought, fled immediately, or ultimately abandoned the missions after a few seasons.

The colony faced serious problems from the start. Little mineral wealth was found in the region, and in 1605 the viceroy, 2,000 miles away in Mexico City, recommended withdrawal from New Mexico. The Franciscans, however, refused to leave because they did not want to abandon their successes; by the early 1600s they had baptized thousands of Pueblo Indians. In compromise, the Crown allowed the Franciscans to remain in New Mexico, which became a Crown colony in 1608. Santa Fe was made its capital the following year. From this date missionary activity became central to the colony. Even so, the colony retained significant numbers of soldiers and settlers who competed for Indian LABOR with the missionaries. By the early 17th century approximately 3,000 colonists and friars resided in New Mexico, and they depended almost entirely on a harsh labor regime forced on Indians for agriculture, ranching, tanning, and other activities. These early decades were also characterized by struggles between civil and religious authorities over who controlled the Indian population and who could demand labor and tribute, a complex conflict in which the friars even excommunicated a governor.

Conflicts between the friars and indigenous peoples generated Indian revolts as early as the 1640s. In the late 1670s, as a population decimated by European viruses and alienated by harsh demands by the colonizers grew increasingly desperate, a diverse group of Indian pueblos came together to plan a concerted uprising against their colonizers. The PUEBLO REVOLT, which began on August 10, 1680, drove the Spanish out of the region for 12 years. Returning to the region in the early 1690s, the Spanish once again took advantage of internal divisions to subdue most of New Mexico by 1694, failing to reconquer only the Hopi of Arizona.

After the reconquest New Mexico became increasingly important as a line of defense against attacks both by other European powers and by Indians. The presence of the French on the edges of the Great Plains in the early 18th century pushed groups like the Comanche and Pawnee southward into areas of the Apache, who, in turn, raided Spanish settlements frequently. In response the Spanish built a string of presidios running from Arizona to Texas. Santa Fe's presidio, with 100 soldiers, was beyond the line of defense.

The population of the colony grew slowly, from 14,000 in 1693 to 16,500 in 1760. Notably, this growth occurred almost entirely among inhabitants of European ancestry, who increased from 3,000 in 1693 to 7,700 in 1760. Simultaneously, the number of Indians living in the colony actually declined. European settlers concentrated in Santa Fe, Albuquerque, Santa Cruz, and farming settlements along the Rio Grande. These regions also included large numbers of mestizos and detribalized Indians (*genízaro* slaves) as well as a great many tribute- and labor-paying Pueblo Indians who lived beyond the settlements. During the 18th century the Pueblo increasingly abandoned their villages, transformed their traditional ways to more closely approximate European customs (including a change from matrilineal to patrilineal kinship), and reorganized their religious rituals under an increasingly synthetic series of religious practices.

Further reading: Ramón A. Gutiérrez, *When Jesus Came the Corn Mothers Went Away: Marriage, Sexuality, and Power in New Mexico, 1500–1846* (Palo Alto, Calif.: Stanford University Press, 1991).

—Alexander Dawson

New Netherland

New Netherland, a colony that stretched along the Hudson River from Manhattan Island to present-day Albany, was the principal Dutch outpost in 17th-century North America. The Netherlands was a major commercial power in the 17th century; Dutch MERCHANTS ruled plantations and trading posts around the world, from Brazil to Indonesia, China, and India, and they were eager to gain a foothold in North America as well. In 1609 HENRY HUDSON, an English explorer employed by the Dutch East India Company to seek a Northwest Passage to the East Indies, crossed the Atlantic in the ship *De Halve Maen (Half Moon)* and claimed the territory around the mouth of the Hudson River for the Dutch. The English, who were trading rivals of the Dutch, seized *De Halve Maen* from Hudson and contested Dutch claims to the area, initiating a pattern of Anglo-Dutch friction that would be a recurring motif throughout the half-century of New Netherland's existence. While political negotiations faltered, Dutch merchants financed private voyages to the Hudson River Valley and competed to gain control of the regional FUR TRADE.

Historians generally date the Dutch settlement in New Netherland from 1614, the year in which the States-General (Dutch parliament) granted exclusive trading privileges in the region to a group of Dutch merchants incorporated as the New Netherland Company. In the company's charter the settlement was officially named New Netherland. Although the New Netherland Company sponsored annual voyages to its possession and built a trading center, Fort Nassau, on Castle Island near Albany, it failed to establish a permanent settlement in the Hudson River Valley. The company's grant of exclusive trade expired in 1618, and it was superseded by a national joint-stock company, the DUTCH WEST INDIA COMPANY, which in 1621 assumed responsibility for overseeing Dutch trade and settlement in North America.

Early Dutch settlement efforts were divided between Fort Orange (Albany) and NEW AMSTERDAM (Manhattan). Ironically, the first European settlers in New Netherland were not Dutch but Walloon (French-speaking Belgians); 30 Walloon families settled at Fort Orange under the sponsorship of the West India Company in 1624. The Dutch settlement at New Amsterdam was established in 1625. In fact, the West India Company was too deeply absorbed in the fur trade to devote much attention to settlement. It forged an alliance with the IROQUOIS Confederacy and persuaded the Iroquois to channel the fur trade through Dutch (rather than French or English) settlements. West India Company administrators looked disapprovingly on colonists who attempted to break the company's fur trade monopoly rather than breaking farmland.

New Netherland's early years were stormy, but in 1626 PETER MINUIT arrived in New Amsterdam and assumed leadership of the colony. In five brief years (1626–31) Minuit reorganized the colony and put its economic life and military defenses on a firmer footing. Minuit's predecessor, Willem Verhulst, had paid local Indians 60 Dutch guilders (in commercial goods) for Manhattan Island, thereby strengthening Dutch claims to the territory. Minuit followed suit by purchasing Staten Island as well. These land purchases set a precedent for New Netherland colonists' acquisition of land from local Indians by purchase or treaty rather than seizure; this policy, observed in the early settlement years, was abandoned in the 1640s with disastrous results. As New Netherland was still a tiny settlement of about 270 souls, Minuit evacuated most of the soldiers and settlers at Fort Orange, recalled other settlers from the CONNECTICUT and DELAWARE River Valleys, and consolidated settlement on Manhattan Island for mutual

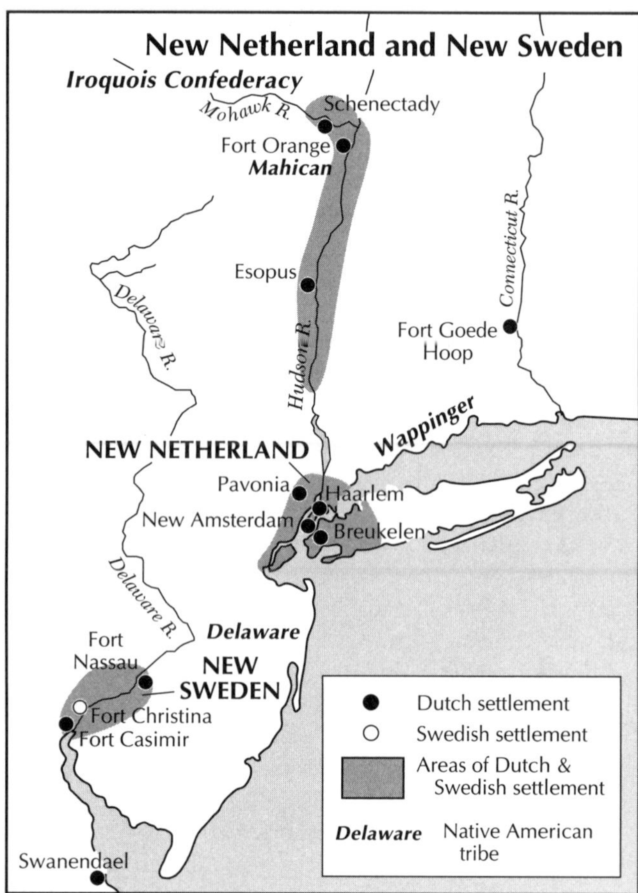

security. He also opened diplomatic relations with the English colony at PLYMOUTH. The West India Company dismissed Minuit from office in 1631, but he returned to the Delaware Valley several years later as the governor of New Sweden.

Beginning in the 1620s the Dutch experimented with several plans to lure settlers to America. The most famous of these was the patroonship system, established during Minuit's administration. In 1629 the West India Company invited Dutch citizens to apply for patroonships. Each patroon (literally, patron) who sponsored 50 immigrants to New Netherland would be granted a semifeudal domain along the Hudson River in which to create an agricultural village and manor. Patroons would exercise administrative and judicial powers within their territory, and they were also granted trading privileges, including limited access to the fur trade. Several patroonships were laid out, but only one, RENSSELAERSWYCK, proved successful; the rest were abandoned and resold to the West India Company, which abandoned the patroonship system by the mid-1630s. In 1639 the company addressed settlers' economic needs more directly by revising the company's settlement rules to permit settlers to trade freely in all commodities, including furs. In later years the company also offered free land to all comers, but New Netherland remained a mercantile colony, in contrast to the predominantly agricultural colonies of New England. Settlement proceeded slowly; the political and religious stability and economic prosperity of the 17th-century Netherlands discouraged Dutch families from removing to America.

The 1630s and 1640s were marked by internal conflict between settlers and a series of unpopular governors and by territorial conflict between New Netherland and neighboring English and Native American settlements. From the 1620s on the West India Company had periodically laid claim to parts of present-day Connecticut and had even built a small trading post, the House of Good Hope, on the Connecticut River. However, in the 1630s and 1640s English settlers from MASSACHUSETTS established several flourishing towns in the region, and in 1650 the Dutch were obliged to cede their claims to the Connecticut River Valley to the English in the Treaty of Hartford. That treaty was not the diplomatic defeat it appeared to be, however, for it secured all the territory actually occupied by Dutch settlers and forced the English to recognize Dutch claims to New Netherland. Meanwhile, the Dutch achieved another diplomatic coup on the border with Quebec. The Iroquois, armed by the Dutch, attacked the HURON, a powerful Great Lakes tribe that cooperated with the French to channel the fur trade through Montreal. The Iroquois overwhelmed the Huron and thereby drew a vast inland fur-trading region into the Dutch sphere of influence.

Even as the Dutch cooperated with the Iroquois, however, their relations with Indians in the lower Hudson Valley and coastal region deteriorated. Two principal groups of NATIVE AMERICANS lived in present-day NEW YORK before the arrival of the Dutch: the Iroquois Confederacy, formed about 1570 from five constituent tribes, the Mohawk, Oneida, Onondaga, Cayuga, and Seneca; and the ALGONQUIN tribes, chiefly the Mahican and Munsee. In the Albany region, where the Iroquois Confederacy was a major diplomatic power and Dutch settlers favored fur trading over farming, colonial administrators worked to preserve the peace, but in the lower Hudson River Valley land-hungry Dutch settlers clashed bitterly with the Mahican and Munsee. Director General WILLEM KIEFT, appointed by the West India Company in 1638, pursued an aggressive policy of land acquisition and Indian taxation. In the summer of 1641 Indian raids on outlying Dutch settlements touched off an exceptionally violent war that, in spite of brief truces in 1642 and 1643, was not concluded until August 1645. Kieft's war decimated the coastal Indian population—nearly 1,000 Indians died in the war—but it failed to eliminate Native American opposition to Dutch settlement. On the contrary, embittered Algonquin continued to harass Dutch towns for decades.

The arrival of Kieft's successor, PETER STUYVESANT, in 1647 marked a turning point for the colony. In contrast to New Netherland's earlier, mostly transient directors general, Stuyvesant governed the colony for 17 years (1647–64). He guided New Netherland through administrative reform, territorial expansion, and a fresh wave of settlement. Some of his victories were military: In 1655 Stuyvesant led an expedition that captured New Sweden and reabsorbed it into New Netherland under the name New Amstel. Upon his return Stuyvesant discovered that the Mahican and several allied tribes had made a surprise attack on New Amsterdam. He acted quickly to shore up the city's defenses: He forbade Indians to enter the city armed or remain there overnight, imprisoned those who were drunk, and punished white settlers who sold them liquor. New Amsterdam never suffered another Indian attack, although Indians laid siege to Esopus (Kingston) in 1659; hostilities dragged on until 1664, when the Dutch decisively broke the Native American power base in the lower Hudson Valley.

Stuyvesant also granted town governments greater autonomy. By the 1650s English colonists had established several villages on western Long Island, within the Dutch sphere of influence. The English colonists brought with them a vigorous tradition of self-government, and they demanded the same political autonomy that New England settlers enjoyed. Nearby Dutch communities followed suit, requesting local powers patterned on the liberal governmental structures of the English settlements. Under Stuyvesant's administration town officials, particularly the *schout* (selectman / justice of the peace) and *schepens* (sheriff / district attorney), acquired considerable power. SUFFRAGE remained far more restricted than in New England, however; New Netherland retained the Dutch system of closed corporation government, under which incumbents nominated their successors.

As New Netherland became a more stable and viable settlement, the English viewed it with increasingly covetous eyes. The English and Dutch were long-standing commercial rivals, and New Netherland became a choice prize in the Anglo-Dutch wars. When an English war fleet commanded by Colonel Richard Nicholls sailed into New Amsterdam's harbor in September 1664, Stuyvesant surrendered without a fight. As the Dutch knew from earlier skirmishes with the English in Connecticut, they could not hope to win a military victory over the far more numerous English forces. The English capture of New Netherland in 1664 was not decisive; English and Dutch forces continued to dispute control of the region for several years, and the Dutch recaptured New Amsterdam briefly in the Third Anglo-Dutch War in 1673. New Netherland was restored to the English in the peace treaty of 1674, ending the Dutch colonization project in North America.

Of all the European colonies in North America, New Netherland was the most ethnically and religiously diverse in the 17th century. The first immigrants to the colony were French-speaking Walloons; company officials and patroons also recruited settlers from England, Germany, and Norway. By midcentury scarcely half of New Netherland's European population was ethnically Dutch, and a clergyman reported that 18 languages were spoken in the port city. Numerous religious groups were represented, including LUTHERANS, English CONGREGATIONALISTS, QUAKERS, and JEWS, as well as Dutch Reformed Protestants.

New Netherland also had a substantial African-American slave population. The West India Company began importing slaves in 1626 in response to the colony's more or less permanent LABOR shortage; many were brought from the Dutch plantation colony at Curaçao rather than directly from Africa. Growing demand for slaves among private citizens forced the company to renounce its monopoly on the SLAVE TRADE in 1648. Around the same time the company created a distinctive status called "half-freedom"; "half-free" blacks, imported and owned by the West India Company, were rented out to settlers, an arrangement that saved settlers the cost of purchasing slaves and allowed the "half-free" a modest degree of personal autonomy. New Netherland's enslaved and "half-free" black colonists worked primarily in AGRICULTURE and construction; by 1664 they numbered about 700 out of a total colonial population of 8,000.

New Netherland's ECONOMY, unlike that of most of the British American colonies, was founded on trade rather than agriculture. Dutch law accorded women much more extensive legal rights than English law did, and women played an active role in commerce in the Dutch settlements. Men and women alike struggled with the West India Company's labyrinthine economic regulations, which extended not only to the lucrative fur trade but also to baking, brewing, butchering, and a host of other basic occupations. Agricultural output was low. Although the West India Company sent several hundred livestock to New Netherland in the 1620s, it ceased to provision the colony in 1626, and immigrants devoted little attention to agriculture. The colony's real strength lay in its cosmopolitan fur-trading centers. The English conquerors were reluctant to disrupt the lucrative fur-trading network established by the Dutch, and Dutch culture and customs continued to flavor New York (as the English renamed New Netherland) long after the English conquest.

Further reading: Michael Kammen, *Colonial New York: A History* (New York: Oxford University Press, 1975); Oliver A. Rink, *Holland on the Hudson: An Economic and Social History of Dutch New York* (Ithaca, N.Y.: Cornell University Press, 1986).

—Darcy R. Fryer

New Orleans

France founded New Orleans in 1718 under the regency of the duke of Orleans, from whom it received its name. A government-sponsored company undertook the rapid peopling of the LOUISIANA seaport 100 miles up the Mississippi River from the Gulf of Mexico. The colonizing effort was designed to protect French interests on the lower Mississippi. It was also linked to a massive reform of France's financial system, and when that project failed, the huge scale of its vision mocked the weak result in New Orleans. Except for the ACADIANS who arrived in 1755, few immigrants were attracted to the settlement after that, and New Orleans Parish contained only about 4,200 inhabitants in 1766.

The choice to locate the parish at many bends in the river was calculated: It was the site of an ancient Indian portage between the Mississippi River and Lake Pontchartrain, a portage that was the nexus of trade in the lower Mississippi Valley before the French arrived. This trail commanded the traffic of the river at easily policed narrows and served as the only "backdoor" route into the delta region and to the Gulf of Mexico. Diseases and out-migration had decimated local Indians, leaving only remnant tribes by 1718, but the area still functioned as the commercial nodal point of the North American interior between the Appalachian-Allegheny and Rocky Mountain chains. At this particular bend in the river, moreover, the natural levee was developed, containing rich alluvial deposits and forming an embankment that protected fields from river flooding.

By 1763 New Orleans was a lively port because virtually all of Louisiana's commerce was brokered there. Its town center was still a small urban space but studded with a few substantial public and church buildings. Plantations adjoined the geometrically plotted streets of the town center on both sides and formed a continuous strip for miles on the Mississippi's left bank and along a small portion of the opposing right bank. This town, or parish, was fundamentally a slave society: Its social organization was based on exports, particularly INDIGO and wood products produced by African labor. The town was destined to become much more populous and one of the most legendary of all southern communities.

See also FRENCH COLONIES.

Further reading: Thomas N. Ingersoll, *Mamon and Manon in Early New Orleans: The First Slave Society in the Deep South, 1718–1819* (Knoxville: University of Tennessee Press, 1999).

—Thomas N. Ingersoll

Newport

Newport was the third English settlement in RHODE ISLAND. Its founder, WILLIAM CODDINGTON, was a follower of clergyman ROGER WILLIAMS, who left MASSACHUSETTS Bay Colony in 1636 in order to create a community that permitted greater religious freedom. Coddington settled at Portsmouth, Rhode Island, in 1638, but in 1639 a dispute with other Portsmouth settlers led him and his adherents to move to the southern tip of Aquidneck Island, where they built the town of Newport. Like other 17th-century Rhode Island communities, Newport was a haven for religious dissenters. A Quaker meeting was established in Newport in 1657 and a Jewish congregation in 1658.

Newport was an important seaport and commercial center throughout the colonial era. SHIPBUILDING thrived, and merchants exported horses, salt fish, and wood products to the West Indies. In the 18th century Newport also became a center of the infamous "triangle trade." New England merchants shipped rum to AFRICA and exchanged it for slaves, sold the slaves in the West Indies in exchange for molasses, and carried the molasses back to Newport, where it was distilled into rum. Triangle traders also brought some slaves to Newport, where in 1696 they outnumbered white servants 11 to one. Many urban MERCHANTS and ARTISANS relied on slave labor, as did cattle ranchers and dairy farmers in the surrounding countryside. By 1760 AFRICAN AMERICANS made up nearly 20 percent of Newport's population, perhaps the highest concentration of slaves in the northern colonies.

The combination of long-distance trade and religious liberty made Newport an unusually cosmopolitan community. The town competed with Providence for cultural dominance of the colony. James Franklin, Jr., started printing Rhode Island's first newspaper, the *Mercury*, in Newport in 1758. By the mid-18th century Newport had also begun to attract summer visitors fleeing the malarial climates of SOUTH CAROLINA and the British West Indies. In spite of its diverse population, however, Newport remained a hierarchical society in which a small number of wealthy merchants and shipmasters monopolized political offices and other public leadership roles.

Further reading: Elaine Forman Crane, *A Dependent People: Newport, Rhode Island in the Revolutionary Era* (New York: Fordham University Press, 1985).

—Darcy R. Fryer

Newport, Christopher (1561–1617)

Christopher Newport was born near Harwich, England, around December 1561 and went to sea at an early age. During hostilities with Spain in the 1580s, Newport turned to PRIVATEERING. He participated in the capture of numerous vessels and the assault on Cádiz, losing his right arm in battle. Newport found fame and fortune by capturing a Spanish treasure ship, investing his winnings in privateers of his own.

In 1606 the VIRGINIA COMPANY OF LONDON selected Newport to command the sea-borne phase of its upcoming expedition. The fleet sailed in December for VIRGINIA. Arriving at CHESAPEAKE BAY, Newport named the capes at its mouth for the monarch's sons, Charles and Henry. The expedition proceeded to the site of JAMESTOWN. Newport retained naval command, but a council, of which he was a member, ruled ashore. As settlement building and gold mining commenced, Newport scouted the James River. Upon returning he found a colony under attack from local tribes. Newport recommended conciliation; others demanded retaliation. This debate, fed by personality clashes, polarized the council.

Newport soon sailed for London with news and "gold." Although the gold was identified as base metals, Newport obtained continued funding. In the following years Newport made several round trips, becoming enmeshed in the colony's domestic politics at every turn. Despite poor relations with key council members, Newport became vice admiral of a larger fleet in 1610 and was rewarded with additional shares in the enterprise. He was also given an honorary commission in the Royal Navy. In 1612 Newport transferred his loyalties to the East India Company. After undertaking several cruises he died in those regions, probably in August 1617.

See also JOHN SMITH.

Further reading: Ivor Noel Hume, *The Virginia Adventure: Roanoke to James Towne: An Archaeological and Historical Odyssey* (Charlottesville: University Press of Virginia, 1997).

—Michael S. Casey

newspapers See journalism; printing and publishing

New York

New York's early history was tied to the Hudson River. Navigable for 150 miles from Long Island Sound, it connects with lakes to form a water route to Canada. Most European settlement and trade happened between the two poles of Albany at the northern end and NEW YORK CITY at the southern. Despite easy water access to the interior via lakes and the Mohawk River, powerful NATIVE AMERICANS and hostile French kept the Dutch and English settlements close to the Hudson and the easternmost parts of the Mohawk. Long Island, reaching northeast from the Hudson along the New England coast, was also heavily settled.

First Inhabitants

The earliest evidence of human activity in the region comes from 9,000-year-old flint spear tips; settlements have been dated to 4500 B.C. Between these first Paleo-Indian cultures and the emergence of Iroquoian and ALGONQUIN cultures about A.D 1100., tools and agriculture became increasingly sophisticated to support an increasing population. By 1500 15,000 people lived on Manhattan Island.

Algonquin-speaking people dominated the eastern regions, Iroquoian the western. Long Island, New York City, and surrounding areas were settled by a people who called themselves Lenape. The Lenape lived in small, mobile communities. Iroquoian societies, by contrast, were more firmly rooted in large palisaded towns, the major structure of which was the longhouse. These extended-family homes were the foundations of a matrilineal and, to some degree, matriarchal society. In the 16th century, just as European explorers and traders began to enter the Hudson Valley, five bands of communities, the Mohawk, Oneida, Onondago, Cayuga, and Seneca, joined together to form the Iroquois League. The league was intended to promote peace, but in practice the confederation more often exercised their power in war.

Exploration

The first documented European explorer of New York was Giovanni da Verrazzano, commissioned by the king of France to find a northern route to China. In 1524 Verrazzano anchored between Staten Island and Brooklyn, but a storm forced him to leave without further EXPLORATION. The next year a black Portuguese pilot named Esteban Gomez sailed some distance up the Hudson before he decided that it would not lead him to China. Although other Europeans traded for furs in the area throughout the century, significant exploration and contact did not come until 1609, when HENRY HUDSON, also seeking a northern route to the Indies, sailed 90 miles up the Hudson River. Hudson's voyage had been underwritten by the Dutch East India Company; although they did not take advantage of his discovery, other Dutch MERCHANTS did. By 1614 Dutch merchants had organized a trading post for furs, and in 1621 the DUTCH WEST INDIA COMPANY was established with a monopoly over all Dutch trade with West AFRICA and the Americas.

Dutch Settlement

In 1624 the Dutch West India Company sent 30 families to settle NEW NETHERLAND. Nearly all were Walloons (French-speaking Protestants from the southern Netherlands, now Belgium). Most went north up the Hudson; others were sent to New Netherland's eastern and western borders. Not until the next year did the company send people to settle on Manhattan Island, named NEW AMSTERDAM. The company planned New Netherland as a self-sufficient community whose primary purpose was to advance the Dutch FUR TRADE with local natives. Compared to its holdings in the CARIBBEAN and in South America, the North American trading post was a disappointment, and the directors gave it little financial support.

Because the colony grew far more slowly than the company had hoped, the directors in Amsterdam offered enormous grants of land—up to 18 miles along the banks of the Hudson, but with unlimited lateral expansion—to any entrepreneur who could bring 50 people to New Netherland and stay there. The landlord, known as a patroon, had nearly complete judicial and economic powers. One of the original investors in the company, Kiliaen van Rensselaer, had one of the few profitable Dutch patroonships, which he called RENSSELAERSWYCK. Because of the company monopoly on the thriving fur trade, however, other potential investors were closed out of the colony, and the patroon system was not an overall success.

The relative peace and prosperity of the Netherlands in the 17th century made many Dutch unwilling to emigrate. The company was forced, therefore, to recruit settlers and laborers from all over northern and western Europe. One visitor claimed that 18 different languages were spoken in the colony. From the beginning fewer than half the colonists were Dutch; the rest were primarily Belgian, Swiss, English, German, and Scandinavian, and most were single young men. Religious diversity was nearly as widespread. Although the DUTCH REFORMED CHURCH was the official religious establishment of New Netherland, LUTHERANS, JEWS, and even QUAKERS won some tolerance. Over the opposition of the colony's director, the Dutch West India Company pragmatically decided that religious tolerance was necessary for settlement and trade. This practical approach to diversity would characterize the region for most of the colonial period.

New Netherland could not supply its demand for LABOR with Europeans alone. African slaves first arrived in 1626. By the 1640s slave shipments became larger and more frequent, and the proportion of Africans to Europeans rose to 10 percent of the population. As with whites, men far outnumbered women. Under Dutch rule possibilities for slaves were relatively extensive. Slaves had the same religious, economic, and legal rights as whites. In 1644, when some of the first slaves petitioned for their freedom, the company granted them "half-freedom," an arrangement by which slaves received their liberty and some land but were forced to work for the company, for wages, whenever necessary. Their descendants, free black families, owned farms in the countryside outside New Amsterdam.

The European population of English colonies in North America was increasing far more rapidly than New Netherland's. Rapid growth in New England encouraged some PURITANS to move south to Long Island. In 1640 a group from MASSACHUSETTS established the first English settlement in New York. These English settlers shared few cultural ideals with their Dutch neighbors. The contrast between New Netherland's tolerant pluralism and the New Englanders' desire for homogeneous communities quickly led to conflict.

More violent, however, were the DUTCH–INDIAN WARS in the lower Hudson Valley. Although the Dutch carefully maintained peace with the Iroquois Confederacy for the sake of the northern fur trade, tensions over land hampered relations with southern Algonquin. From 1641 to 1645 company director Willem Kieft led a savage war that killed nearly 1,600 Indians, a demographic loss from which the Lenape never fully recovered. Dozens of communities on Long Island and Staten Island were destroyed. Shorter conflicts persisted throughout the Dutch period. The company immediately recalled Kieft to the Netherlands and replaced him with PETER STUYVESANT, the last and among the most competent of the company's directors.

By the middle of the century it seemed clear that New Netherland had not been a profitable investment for the Dutch West India Company. Half the company's debt of 1 million guilders came from the North American colony alone. The English continued to encroach on Long Island, and New Netherland had not yet acquired enough white settlers of its own to hold them off. In 1640 the company tried to turn the tide. First and most significantly, it gave up its monopoly over the lucrative fur trade. Other merchants could now invest in the colony, revitalizing trade in fur and slaves and sparking other economic activity in the production of TOBACCO and timber. Second, recognizing that land was the most attractive commodity to potential settlers, they revised the patroon system to give 200 acres of land to any colonist who brought along five other settlers.

Stuyvesant transformed New Amsterdam from a struggling trading post into a bustling port city. Immigration brought thousands of new settlers, most as members of healthy families. Stuyvesant negotiated a treaty with New England to curb Puritan settlement on Long Island in 1650. Algonquin-speaking Indians lost several more conflicts in the 1650s and 1660s and ceased to be a threat to Dutch settlement along the lower valley.

English Conquest

Despite the gains in peace and population, however, New Netherland became caught up in the struggle between England and the United Provinces for commercial and naval dominance. As a pawn in the Anglo-Dutch wars, it earned the dubious honor of being the only English colony in North America acquired by conquest.

In 1664 King Charles II (1660–85) granted his brother James, duke of York, a charter for a colony that included all the land between the DELAWARE and CONNECTICUT Rivers. James immediately sent a fleet to Manhattan. Stuyvesant was more reluctant than his officials to surrender, but in the end he gave up the colony without a fight. The English immediately renamed both the city and the colony New York, in James's honor. Dutch influence in the colony persisted, however, and the process of Anglicization continued for more than a generation. Ethnic and religious heterogeneity were too deeply embedded to be eradicated, and diversity continued to be the colony's most salient characteristic.

Both as duke of York and later as king, James attempted to impose an absolute government on the colony. In 1665 Governor Nicholls drew up a law code (the Duke's Laws), drawn mainly from New England statutes but that did not allow for any elected assembly. The English on Long Island were more opposed to the new government than were the Dutch, who had never adopted representative government in New Netherland. The restrictive laws made it difficult to attract English settlers to New York, especially after the governments in NEW JERSEY implemented elected legislatures. In the first nine years after the conquest, the colony remained more Dutch than English. Thus, when a Dutch fleet sailed into Manhattan in 1673, the city again surrendered without a struggle. New York City was renamed New Orange in honor of the new Dutch military leader, William, prince of Orange. The Dutch held the colony for only 15 months, however. When the third Anglo-Dutch War ended in 1674, they returned the colony to the English as part of the peace negotiations. Although the duke granted a charter that guaranteed a legislature and personal freedoms (the Charter of Liberties) in 1683, the colony remained a Dutch society ruled by English conquerors. Settlements along the Hudson retained Dutch language and culture well into the 18th century.

Dutch women were particularly resistant to Anglicization. Under the Roman-Dutch law of New Netherland, women had many more legal and economic rights than under English common law. Dutch culture considered marriage an economic partnership; English culture set men at the head of the household. In churches and at home women continued to write and speak Dutch far longer than their male counterparts.

When James II assumed the throne in 1685, he extended his experiments in absolutism by revoking the colony's charter and dissolving its assembly. The next year he established the DOMINION OF NEW ENGLAND, an unpopular new government that included New England, the Jerseys, and New York. Even before the news reached North America in 1689 of William and Mary's victory over James in the GLORIOUS REVOLUTION, colonists had overthrown the dominion.

The New York militia, under the command of Captain Jacob Leisler, took over Fort James in Manhattan and held it in William's name. Leisler, a German-born immigrant who had married a wealthy Dutch widow, feared that a rumored French invasion would turn the colony over to dreaded Papists. Despite summoning an elective assembly, he instituted an absolute government of his own, frequently flouting English legal and economic rights. The supporters of LEISLER'S REBELLION were primarily Dutch and had few English contacts. Despite a Dutch king on the English throne, Leisler was convicted of treason. He and his son-in-law were hanged, drawn, and quartered in 1691. It would take nearly a generation before the ethnic tensions created by Leisler's execution dissipated. The economic, cultural, and geographic schisms that underlay the rebellion would characterize New York politics for the rest of the colonial period.

After 1691 New York became a royal colony with an assembly, English courts, and traditional English liberties. Anglicization proceeded slowly, however, and certain holdovers from the Dutch period continued to characterize the colony, including tenant farming on enormous manorial estates, political power consolidated in the hands of a few families, conflicts between New York City and the settlements farther up the Hudson, an economic orientation toward Atlantic trade, and, most of all, extensive ethnic and religious diversity.

British Settlement

The factional politics of the Leislerians and anti-Leislerians in the 18th century turned into a conflict between competing "mercantile" and "landed" interests. The legislature acquired more privileges as the royal governor continually sought increased revenues. Governors were rarely able to keep themselves out of the local struggles for political power, which were determined more by family alliances and ethnic differences than by particular political agendas. Political factions often formed around individual personalities. CLASS interests were rarely part of the picture; both sides of any conflict had elite leadership that claimed popular support.

In the mid-1730s political factionalism came to a head. *The New York Weekly Journal*, bankrolled by the antigovernor faction and edited by the printer JOHN PETER ZENGER, printed criticism of Governor William Cosby. Cosby's supporters arrested Zenger for libel, a charge from which he was acquitted. The Zenger case made the press an important component in 18th-century politics and forced factions to broaden their appeal.

In the 1750s and 1760s New Englanders again began to move into New York, putting pressure on the large landholders. Immigrants from western Europe, particularly Palatine Germans but including French Huguenots, Scots,

Scots-Irish, and other Germans, also began to settle the area. Some of these farmers, led by New Englanders who had been accustomed to outright land ownership, confronted the owners of manors in the Hudson Valley in violent confrontations. British troops were called in to subdue the rioters.

Increasing numbers of slaves in New York City, Albany, and the surrounding countryside also created tension. In 1712 African slaves burned down a house and killed at least nine people who came to put out the fire. Twenty-five slaves were convicted of revolt; 18 were executed, some by torture. Rumors of other slave rebellions persisted throughout the 1720s and 1730s, culminating in a 1741 investigation of a slave conspiracy to set fire to New York City, murder its white population, and hand the port over to the Spanish, with whom Britain was at war. A year-long series of trials into the NEGRO PLOT OF 1741 ended in the execution by burning and hanging of 31 people, including four whites, and the banishment of more than 70 others.

New York's ECONOMY was heavily geared toward trade, particularly the export of foodstuffs from the Hudson Valley to the West Indies and of furs to Europe. New York's economic culture was characterized by the active participation of women in trade. Drawing on older Dutch models of female traders and on newer demands of an Atlantic market, women in New York and Albany acted as MERCHANTS and shopkeepers.

The fur trade was entirely dependent on New York's alliance with the Iroquois. Albany and the trading post Oswego became places of exchange among the French, Indians, and British. New York's most important commerce was closely tied to international conflicts over North America.

War

The increasing struggles between Britain and France for North America often played out along the New York–New France frontier. Both European empires attempted to gain the support of the Iroquois Confederation (now the Six Nations), but the Iroquois in turn set the Europeans against each other for their own purposes. Because the confederation controlled most of western New York and all access to the fur trade, they were essential participants in North American diplomacy.

Although the first three Anglo-French conflicts (KING WILLIAM'S WAR, 1689–97; QUEEN ANNE'S WAR, 1702–13; and KING GEORGE'S WAR, 1744–48) were essentially inconclusive, they all destroyed frontier settlements, disrupted the fur trade, and made New York increasingly pivotal in the attempt to drive France from the continent. As English settlers encroached on Iroquois land, the Six Nations were increasingly alienated from their former allies. In 1754 British officials held a major conference in Albany to woo Iroquois loyalty. As a result of the Albany conference, when the SEVEN YEARS' WAR (1754–63) erupted that year, the Iroquois fought for the British. Most of the mainland battles were fought north of Albany, and from there the final invasion of Canada was launched. Albany itself became the center of mainland operations. In 1763 the French were driven from North America.

See also AFRICAN AMERICANS; GENDER.

Further reading: Michael Kammen, *Colonial New York: A History* (New York: Oxford University Press, 1975); Robert C. Ritchie, *The Duke's Province* (Chapel Hill: University of North Carolina Press, 1977); Joyce D. Goodfriend, *Before the Melting Pot* (Princeton, N.J.: Princeton University Press, 1994).

—Serena Zabin

New York City

In 1626 the Dutch West India Company's director, PETER MINUIT, "purchased" Manhattan from local Indians in exchange for 60 guilders worth of European goods. He named the new settlement NEW AMSTERDAM. In the first year New Amsterdam was a small settlement on the southern tip of Manhattan with 270 inhabitants, 30 houses, a mill, and a countinghouse.

Ten years later New Amsterdam had hardly expanded in size or population, but its inhabitants had become remarkably diverse. The mayor claimed that 18 different languages were spoken in the city. Most of the inhabitants were men working for the DUTCH WEST INDIA COMPANY, which had financed the settlement and owned most of the property.

In 1626 the company bought 11 male slaves and three more in 1628. Initially, slaves had many of the same legal, military, and religious privileges as whites, although MISCEGENATION was later forbidden. In 1644, when some of the first slaves petitioned for their freedom, the company granted them "half-freedom," an arrangement by which slaves received their liberty and some land but were forced to work for the company, for wages, whenever necessary.

Although New Amsterdam had begun as a rough trading post—fully one-fourth of the buildings in 1638 were taverns—by the middle of the 17th century it had developed into a bustling seaport. By 1660 the population had increased to 1,500, including many more families. The inhabitants were still a heterogeneous mix of Europeans and Africans. In 1664 the 300 slaves in New Amsterdam constituted 20 percent of the city's population. That same year James, the duke of York, sent a war fleet to New Amsterdam. The locals surrendered without resistance. The Dutch recaptured the city in 1673 and named it New Orange, but when it was ceded back to England 15 months later, it permanently gained the name New York City.

In the decades after the British reconquest of New York, the city became increasingly Anglicized and connected to the BRITISH EMPIRE. Trade increased to England and the West Indies, and English MERCHANTS owned an ever larger percentage of the city's wealth. During the wars against France and Spain, New York sent out more privateers to harass foreign shipping than any other port in North America. In the early part of the century, pirates, including Captain Kidd, received economic and social support from the governor. Sailors, soldiers, and other transients contributed to the fluidity of New York's culture.

Despite the decline of Dutch culture, which had encouraged women's economic activity, women remained practicing traders in the Atlantic world. Coverture and the exclusion of women from economic life were not characteristic of British New York City. Numerous female merchants and shopkeepers contributed to the city's role as an entrepôt for the British Empire.

The city retained the ethnic diversity that had characterized it in the Dutch era. As late as 1750 the English still did not represent a majority of the people. At midcentury the city was roughly 45 percent English, 21 percent German and Dutch, 15 percent Scots, Scots-Irish, and Irish, and 14 percent African American and African. New York City had the largest urban black population north of MARYLAND.

The British established a more rigorous slave code than had the Dutch, but it was nearly impossible to enforce. Slaves socialized with whites and each other in taverns and on the streets. In 1712 roughly 25 newly imported African slaves revolted, burning buildings and killing nine whites. In 1741 authorities suspected another plot, though on little evidence. More than 30 people, including four whites, were executed in the NEGRO PLOT OF 1741, and another 70 were banished from the colony.

See also CITIES AND URBAN LIFE.

Further reading: Michael Kammen, *Colonial New York: A History* (New York: Oxford University Press, 1975); Edwin G. Burrows and Mike Wallace, *Gotham: A History of New York City to 1898* (New York: Oxford University Press, 1999).

—Serena Zabin

Nicolet, Jean (1598–1642)

Jean Nicolet explored westward from the Atlantic Ocean, extending New France to the Mississippi River. Born in France, Nicolet came to the New World in the late 1620s and learned the ALGONQUIN and HURON-IROQUOIS languages. In the belief that China lay just beyond the Sault, the passage between Lake Huron and Lake Superior, the French decided to explore the region. With his knowledge of Native American languages, Nicolet was the best choice. The explorer and his party traveled to Georgian Bay in 1634 and then, accompanied by seven Huron, retraced Étienne Brulé's line to the Sault. He turned southward at this point, found the Strait of Mackinac, and discovered Lake Michigan for France. On the far shore of the lake, Nicolet entered Green Bay and, having donned a Chinese silk robe for the occasion, met, much to his surprise, the Winnebago instead of the Chinese. The Winnebago informed Nicolet that the "Big Water" was three days' journey away. The NATIVE AMERICANS were referring to the Mississippi, but the Frenchman believed that he had reached the Pacific Ocean, and he returned home. His discoveries were not followed up because of the hostility of the Iroquois and a lack of interest among the French. Nicolet spent the remainder of his life at Three Rivers, working as a commissary and interpreter. In 1637 Nicolet married Marguerite Couillard in Quebec, and the couple subsequently produced one child, a daughter. In October 1642 Nicolet was returning to Three Rivers when his boat sank in rough seas on the St. Lawrence River, and the explorer, who had never learned to swim, drowned.

Further reading: C. W. Butterfield, *History of the Discovery of the Northwest by John Nicolet in 1634 With a Sketch of His Life* (Port Washington, N.Y.: Kennikat Press, 1969).

—Caryn E. Neumann

North Carolina

The colony of North Carolina was among the least prominent of the original thirteen colonies, in part because of its geographic semi-isolation. The Outer Banks provided a long, rugged coastline, which blocked most of the colony from easy access to the ocean; the Cape Fear River furnished the sole deep-water port.

Original Inhabitants

When the first English colonists arrived at Roanoke in 1585 in present-day North Carolina, the CATAWBA, CHEROKEE, TUSCARORA, and various other Indian peoples occupied the area. The Tuscarora lived in the Piedmont in western North Carolina. In their society, both genders carried out essential economic roles, with men hunting and women planting corn and beans and gathering berries and other foods. Related linguistically to the IROQUOIS (of NEW YORK), the Tuscarora sometimes allied with them in raids against their common enemy, the Catawba. Like most NATIVE AMERICANS along the East Coast, the Tuscarora became dependent on European trade goods, which created struggles with neighboring

Indians to control hunting grounds and commerce with Europeans. In addition, North Carolina's colonists encroached on the land of the Tuscarora and paid their enemies to capture the Tuscarora and to sell them into slavery. In 1711, the Tuscarora retaliated by killing a British trader and then attacking colonial plantations, thereby setting off the TUSCARORA WAR (1711–13). The North and South Carolinians defeated the Tuscarora, who then moved north to become the final group in the Six Nations of the Iroquois.

Like many other Native Americans, the Catawba sustained huge population losses from European diseases, became dependent on English metal goods, and suffered attacks on their culture and independence. The Catawba acted as brokers in the trade between other Natives and the English, which helped them to maintain their autonomy. As the political structures of neighboring Indians disintegrated, the Catawba adopted many of them into their society, simultaneously creating new cultural groups. Severe SMALLPOX epidemics and the diminishing deerskin trade undermined the power of the Catawba in the mid-18th century.

The Cherokee dominated the Appalachian Mountains in present-day Georgia, Alabama, Tennessee, and North and South Carolina. Although decimated by diseases contracted from 16th-century Spanish explorers, they were able to recover their population before sustained contact and trade with the English in the 17th century. In 1650, the Iroquoian-speaking Cherokee probably numbered about 22,000. Typically, their villages consisted of a small number of log cabins, where women and men shared political and social power. Women engaged in agriculture while men hunted. Selected by each town, chiefs had a division of responsibilities between wartime and peacetime leaders. During the late 17th and early 18th centuries, select Cherokee villages signed peace treaties with Carolina's settlers, and a number of Cherokee women married Europeans, especially traders. The Cherokee's excessive reliance on European manufactured goods weakened their political bargaining power and caused them to cede large tracts of lands to white colonists to pay their debts. During the SEVEN YEARS' WAR, some Cherokee towns supported the French and launched sustained attacks on the Carolina backcountry. Generally siding with the British during the American Revolution, the Cherokee eventually lost even more land and became subordinate to the new United States government.

The "Lost Colony"

The French and Spanish explored and claimed the area in the 16th century. They were especially interested in Pamlico Sound, which they hoped to be a gateway to an ocean route to China.

In 1583, Queen Elizabeth I conferred the exclusive license to discover and colonize "remote heathen and barbarous lands" upon Walter Raleigh, who was already intensely involved in colonizing Ireland and heavily invested in lucrative PRIVATEERING forays against Spanish shipping. Planning his American colony as a base for privateering, Raleigh dispatched Philip Amadas and Arthur Barlowe in 1584 to reconnoiter a settlement site close to the West Indies and the homeward route of the Spanish treasure fleet. They found Roanoke Island, sheltered between the Outer Banks and the mainland of present-day North Carolina, to be a plausible site for a covert naval base. Amadas and Barlowe were warmly welcomed and entertained by Granganimeo, the werowance who ruled Roanoke at the pleasure of his brother WINGINA, the paramount chief of an alliance of local ALGONQUIN villages. Wingina was eager for English allies in intracultural rivalries with his neighbors. He also hoped to enhance his power and prestige by becoming an intermediary in the trade with the English.

On their return to England in September 1584, Amadas and Barlowe brought glowing reports of the New World's potential along with Wingina's advisers, Manteo and Wanchese, who learned English and taught Thomas Harriot the Roanoke Algonquian dialect. Elizabeth knighted Raleigh for his efforts, but forbade him to go to sea. Instead, Sir RICHARD GRENVILLE was named admiral of the fleet and general of the expedition. Grenville's expedition reached Wococon Island on June 29, 1585, and he planted the colony on the north end of Roanoke Island, close to Wingina's principal village, Dasamonquepeuc.

The presence of Raleigh's colony profoundly unsettled regional Algonquin life. English demands for corn threatened the Indians' surplus already made meager by several years of drought. The English also spread deadly diseases, which undermined the Algonquins' confidence in their native RELIGION. Wingina eventually adopted a policy of resistance. He changed his name to Pemisapan ("One who watches"), withdrew from the English, refused to provide them with food, and eventually hatched a plot eradicate the colony. The colonists responded by raiding Dasamonquepeuc and killing Wingina and his advisers, thereby making most Roanoke implacable enemies of the English.

The Indian embargo on trading foodstuffs, Grenville's delay in resupplying the colony, and the unexpected arrival of Sir Francis Drake and his privateering fleet in June 1586 induced the colonists to take up Drake on his offer to transport them back to England. Shortly thereafter, Grenville arrived with three ships. Finding the colony abandoned, he left 15 men on Roanoke with provisions for two years, "being unwilling to loose the possession of the country which Englishmen had so long held." The failure to find precious metals or even a suitable harbor for refitting privateers quickly soured enthusiasm among wealthy investors for the VIRGINIA enterprise. Raleigh, however, held fast to his dreams of empire and backed JOHN WHITE, the painter, in gathering support for another expedition. After his appointment as governor, White led 14 English families to Roanoke Island in May 1587. In August, White went to England to secure additional supplies and support. White's return was delayed by English naval engagements with the Spanish Armada, and when he arrived in Roanoke in 1590, he found that the colonists had vanished, leaving only clues that they might have tried to relocate the colony inland or to Chesapeake Bay.

Colonization

King Charles I claimed Carolina (the Latin name for "Charles") in 1629 by granting the region to Sir Robert Heath, but he failed to establish any settlements. King Charles II granted the area to eight supporters whom he named the Lords Proprietors over Carolina. Their charter provided them with extensive power over the colony, and they promised political and religious freedom as well as land to settlers. When these promises failed to attract many colonists, Lord Anthony Ashley Cooper (subsequently earl of Shaftesbury) and the philosopher JOHN LOCKE wrote the Fundamental Constitutions of Carolina in 1669, which maintained feudal privileges but also provided some popular rights. However, settlers did not adopt the Fundamental Constitutions, and the colony developed along considerably different lines than envisioned by the authors of that document.

The colonization of North Carolina proceeded slowly in the 17th century. Virginians established the first permanent settlement around Albermarle Sound in the early 1650s, and migration from Virginia continued, especially after BACON'S REBELLION in 1676. In 1689, the Virginia proprietors appointed a governor for the province of Albermarle, which gradually became known as North Carolina. The pace of migration increased after the English Parliament's 1705 passage of the Naval Stores Act, which encouraged the production of turpentine, tar, and pitch, all of which were possible in the area's vast pine forests. Freeholders also relied on indentured servants and black and Indian slaves to produce corn, TOBACCO, and livestock. As Native Americans were pushed west of the Appalachian Mountains, German and Scots-Irish migrants flowed into the Piedmont. Scots and smaller contingents of Swiss and French migrants settled along the Cape Fear River.

The early 18th century was a time of difficulty. The Tuscarora raided white settlements in 1711, and the Yamasee attacked the Carolinas in 1715. Pirate activity near the Outer Banks contributed to the unrest. Dissatisfied Carolinians complained about the proprietors' failure to protect them or to provide additional lands. In 1712, North Carolina was made a separate colony. The boundary between North Carolina and Virginia was surveyed in 1728, and in 1729, North Carolina became a royal colony.

At the end of the colonial era, the colony was deeply divided along regional, class, and racial lines. Small family farmers with few slaves came into conflict with more affluent eastern owners of slaves and larger estates. Western farmers, perpetually in debt, paid high fees and taxes and exercised little power in the colony's general assembly. They organized the Regulators to "regulate" their communities in a more honest and equitable fashion.

Further reading: A. Roger Ekirch, *"Poor Carolina": Politics and Society in Colonial North Carolina, 1729–1776* (Chapel Hill: University of North Carolina Press, 1981); Karen Ordahl Kupperman, *Roanoke: The Abandoned Colony* (Totowa, N.J.: Rowman & Allanheld, 1984); James Merrell, *The Indians' New World: The Catawbas and their Neighbors from European Contact through the Era of Removal* (New York: W. W. Norton, 1989); Daniel Richter, *The Ordeal of the Longhouse: The Peoples of the Iroquois League in the Era of European Colonization* (Chapel Hill: University of North Carolina Press, 1992).

—James Bruggeman and Billy G. Smith

Northwest Coast Indians

Living on a narrow strip of land along the Pacific coast that runs from present-day southern Alaska to northern California, the natives of the Northwest Coast developed one of the most materially rich cultures in North America, in part because they lived in a land of abundance. The climate of the Northwest Coast is mild, yet high in precipitation. The heavy rainfall—sometimes up to 100 inches per year—and the constant mist from the ocean created dense, verdant coniferous forests. Added to this are waters that melt off the mountain snow packs and feed the region's numerous rivers.

Northwest Coast peoples developed a materially rich culture by exploiting the naturally abundant FOOD resources of their ENVIRONMENT. Fish, particularly salmon, constituted the staple food of their diet. Whaling, game ANIMALS, and edibles from wild plants supplemented this. Other than the cultivation of small amounts of TOBACCO for ceremonial purposes, these peoples did not engage in AGRICULTURE. They generally lived in villages composed of extended kinship groups. They usually divided their year into two parts. They spent winters in villages constructed of roomy plank houses, where they occupied themselves with ceremonial and trade activities. During the summer, however, they lived at FISHING camps, catching and preserving their catch.

Northwest Indians evolved a highly complex society that stressed first accumulating, then giving away material goods. This usually took the form of the potlatch, in which a wealthy man would provide a feast for his neighbors and kin during which he would disperse CLOTHING, food, blankets, and other goods. By providing generously for others in the community, the individual acquired increased status. Trade was important, with copper plates, blankets, wood and horn utensils, and dugout canoes being exchanged. The Chinook, located on the Columbia River, served as intermediaries for much of the trade in the Northwest.

Compared with Indians on the East Coast, Northwest natives encountered Europeans far later and had fewer interactions. While Europeans conducted sporadic EXPLORATIONS of the northern Pacific coast in the 16th and 17th centuries, they did not interact with the native peoples. In the northern part of the region, the Tlingit had their first contacts with Russian fur traders in the 1740s. Farther south, the Spanish ship *Santiago* traded with Hadia in 1774. In 1778 Captain James Cook traded furs with the Nookta during his circumnavigation of the globe. When word spread of the rich furs available in the area, American, English, and Russian fur trading companies began competing in the region in the 1790s and continued to do so throughout the first half of the 19th century.

—Roger Carpenter

Nurse, Rebecca (1621–1692)

On March 13, 1692, Ann Putnam claimed to have been visited by the apparition of Rebecca Nurse, an elderly woman living in Salem Village, MASSACHUSETTS. Soon, other accusers stepped forward and described spectral visitations during which Rebecca physically attacked them and attempted to recruit the victims to join in league with the devil. Ten days after the first complaints, Nurse was arrested and faced trial in the notorious Salem WITCHCRAFT trials. Born in England in 1621, Nurse moved to New England in 1640 and married Francis Nurse in 1645. By the time she faced trial in June 1692, Nurse was one of the most unlikely suspects of the witch hunt. At 71 years old, a mother of eight, and with a reputation for piety, Nurse seemed to be unassailable. Indeed, after a public trial the jury initially returned with a verdict of not guilty, despite the testimony of expert witnesses who claimed to have examined Nurse's body and discovered physical evidence of bewitchment. After her alleged victims loudly protested and the judge asked the jury to reconsider their decision, Nurse was convicted and sentenced to death. On July 19 Nurse stood with four other convicted women at the town gallows. While Sarah Good loudly denounced the men and women responsible for the trials, Nurse reportedly went to her death quietly, a silent rebuke to the community that had once embraced her as a role model only to turn against her in the fear and confusion of the witch hunt craze. Nurse's hanging provoked an outcry in Salem, causing many residents to question the legitimacy of the process. After 19 executions, including that of Nurse's sister Mary Esty, the trials came to an end in October 1692. In 1711 the government compensated the Nurse family for what it finally acknowledged was a wrongful death.

Further reading: Carol F. Karlsen, *The Devil in the Shape of a Woman: Witchcraft in Colonial New England* (New York: Norton, 1987).

—Melanie Perreault

Oglethorpe, James Edward (1696–1785)
James Oglethorpe was a central figure behind the founding of GEORGIA in 1733. Born on December 22, 1696, the youngest of seven children of a former Jacobite family, Oglethorpe had a privileged upbringing, being educated at Eton and Oxford. At age 21 Oglethorpe gained military experience in the army of Prince Eugene of Savoy before becoming a Tory member of Parliament for Haselmere in Surrey in 1722. Gradually, Oglethorpe became concerned with the social and moral reform of the nation. As chairman of the Parliamentary Gaols Committee, Oglethorpe had observed the plight of the poor firsthand, and he agreed with those who believed that a new American colony in the disputed BORDERLANDS south of SOUTH CAROLINA would provide an excellent opportunity for the "worthy poor." Subsequently, Oglethorpe became one of the founder trustees for the new colony of Georgia and personally accompanied the first shipload of settlers to the colony.

Once in Georgia, Oglethorpe assumed the position of benevolent paternalist, resolving disputes and dispensing justice and supplies, although he lacked any official jurisdiction. While he officially reported to the trustees, Oglethorpe, in effect, ruled Georgia. On several occasions he ignored or overrode his colleagues to suit his personal whim or when circumstances demanded. For example, a shipload of 40 JEWS who arrived in Georgia in 1733 should have been sent back across the Atlantic, per the instructions of the other trustees. However, Oglethorpe believed these settlers could be a valuable addition to the colony, especially Jacob Nunez, a doctor, the only one in Georgia. Ultimately, Oglethorpe's view prevailed, and SAVANNAH eventually became home to one of the most vibrant Jewish communities in British America.

During his three visits to Georgia, Oglethorpe made essential alliances with local NATIVE AMERICANS that ensured the survival of the infant colony, and he was intimately involved in designing Georgia's first settlements, including Savannah, Augusta, Federica, Ebenezer, and Darien. He was also at the forefront of the defense of the "Georgia plan," especially the prohibition of SLAVERY, from the attacks of so-called malcontents. He not only wrote repeated letters to his fellow trustees urging them to stand firm, he also persuaded certain groups of settlers such as the Scottish Highlanders in Darien and the Salzburgers in Ebenezer to support him. While his defense of the ban was ultimately in vain, Oglethorpe formulated some of the first antislavery sentiments heard in the American colonies.

In addition to his other roles, Oglethorpe took personal charge of Georgia's defense against the Spanish in FLORIDA and the French in the Mississippi Valley. On his final visit to Georgia between 1738 and 1743, Oglethorpe was almost entirely concerned with military matters—partly because his fellow trustees had appointed William Stephens to run the civil government of the colony. Oglethorpe supervised the construction of a network of defensive FORTS and staffed them with the Georgia regiment, the first garrison permanently stationed in America. He led the regiment, together with local militias, in a failed attempt to capture ST. AUGUSTINE in Florida in 1740, but he successfully defeated a Spanish invasion in the Battle of Bloody Marsh in 1742.

After his final return from Georgia in 1743, Oglethorpe gradually lost interest in the colony. In 1745 he was detailed to repel the invasion of England from Scotland, but his half-hearted pursuit of the rebels, together with his family's own sympathies with the rebels, earned Oglethorpe a court-martial, although ultimately he was acquitted.

Oglethorpe's last 35 years were not as star-studded as his first 50. He lost his parliamentary seat in 1752, and although he returned to military service incognito for the king of Prussia for a short time, Oglethorpe eventually became a renowned London literary figure and a friend of Samuel Johnson and James Boswell. He died in July 1785 at the venerable age of 88.

Further reading: Phinizy Spalding and Harvey H. Jackson, eds., *Oglethorpe in Perspective: Georgia's Founder after Two Hundred Years* (Athens: University of Georgia Press, 1989).

—Timothy James Lockley

Opechancanough (1545?–1646)

Opechancanough, or Mangapeesomon, was kin and successor of POWHATAN and became the "great general of the Savages" who engineered the Powhatan's political, military, and cultural renaissance after their defeat by the English in the first Anglo-Powhatan War (1609–14). Opechancanough led an unremitting resistance to English conquest and colonization of Tidewater VIRGINIA until his murder in English CAPTIVITY in 1646.

Although his origins are shrouded in mystery, Opechancanough first appears in 1607 as the *werowance* of the Pamunkey, the largest tribal group in Powhatan's domain. In December 1607 Powhatan dispatched the Pamunkey leader to capture JOHN SMITH. After Smith's release Opechancanough chafed under Powhatan's conciliatory and assimilationist policies toward the English but, out of deference to his overlord, stoically suffered English aggression and insults to his dignity, including manhandling by Smith himself. Opechancanough took a leading role in the first Anglo-Powhatan War, and it was only after a fierce attack by English musketeers on his Pamunkey villages near present-day West Point, Virginia, that Powhatan reluctantly sued for a humiliating peace in 1614.

Even before Powhatan's death in 1618, Opechancanough seized effective leadership of the remnants of Powhatan's once powerful chiefdom and began a process of political consolidation and military rejuvenation. He focused on acquiring English firearms and spiritual revitalization in alliance with his principal adviser, Nemattanew, or "Jack of Feathers," a charismatic prophet intent on preserving Powhatan religious beliefs as well as a powerful warrior skilled in the use of English muskets. Convinced that there could be no Anglo-Powhatan relationship based on peace, Opechancanough prepared for war, masking Powhatan rearmament and lulling the English into complacency by disingenuous promises of Christian conversion and surrender of Powhatan land. The murder of Nemattanew by the English in March 1622 galvanized Opechancanough into launching a surprise attack on English settlements, almost eradicating the colony and killing 320 colonists before a defense could be mounted. The ensuing second Anglo-Powhatan War ground on for a decade, resulting in a qualified victory for the Powhatan. They temporarily preserved their way of life, even though their resistance tipped even sympathetic English authorities toward what would become a long-standing policy in British America of expelling Indians from lands coveted by whites and segregating them from white colonists.

English settlers, hungry for land on which to grow highly lucrative TOBACCO, continued to encroach on Powhatan territory, causing Opechancanough to lead yet another desperate attack on the English plantations in 1644, killing some 500 colonists. Then more than 80 years old, so infirm he had to be carried into battle on a litter, the great Pamunkey werowance, after two years of brutal warfare, was captured by forces under the command of Governor SIR GEORGE YEARDLEY, put on public display, and murdered by his English guards in 1646.

—James Bruggeman

Osborn, Sarah Haggar Wheaten (1714–1796)

Few people today have ever heard of Sarah Osborn, but by the end of her life in 1796, she had become one of the most respected female religious leaders of her time. Born in London in 1714 to devout Puritan parents, Benjamin and Susanna Haggar, she came to North America in 1723 with her family, eventually settling in NEWPORT, RHODE ISLAND. Her life was marked by recurring tragedy: She eloped in 1731 at the age of 17 with a sailor, Samuel Wheaten, who died two years later, leaving her with a one-year-old son to support; remarried a tailor, Henry Osborn, a widower with three children, who suffered a breakdown that left him unable to work; and toiled long hours as a schoolteacher and a seamstress in order to pay her family's bills. Despite her constant battle to achieve economic security, she remained so indigent that her name never appeared on Newport's tax lists. Her only child, Samuel, died in 1744 at the age of 12. Through everything, she suffered chronic bouts of illness.

Despite these tragedies, Osborn was so charismatic that many people in Newport sought her spiritual counsel. Inspired by the sermons of GILBERT TENNENT, during the revivals of the GREAT AWAKENING, she devoted the rest of her life to spreading her Calvinist faith. Reputed to be gifted in prayer, she became more popular than any of the ordained ministers in her town. During the winter of 1766–67 as many as 500 people—including more than 100 slaves—flocked to her house each week for prayer meetings. Although she remained poor, strangers from as far away as Canada and the West Indies sent money to defray her expenses, eager to help a woman who had become virtually a Protestant saint.

Under the cloak of anonymity Osborn published one of the earliest theological tracts written by an American woman: *The Nature, Certainty, and Evidence of True Christianity* (Boston, 1755). Like many CONGREGATIONALISTS, she kept a voluminous diary in which she examined her life for evidence of God's grace. Although the majority of her manuscripts have been lost, more than 1,500 pages of her diaries and letters have been preserved in various archives. After her death her pastor, Samuel Hopkins, published two edited volumes containing extracts from her writings: *Memoirs of the Life of Mrs. Sarah Osborn* (Worcester, Mass., 1799), and *Familiar Letters, Written by Mrs. Sarah Osborn and Miss Susanna Anthony, Late of Newport, Rhode Island* (Newport, 1807).

Further reading: Mary Beth Norton, ed., "'My Resting Reaping Times': Sarah Osborn's Defense of Her 'Unfeminine Activities'" (*Signs*, 2 (1976), 515–29); Charles E. Hambrick-Stowe, "The Spiritual Pilgrimage of Sarah Osborn (1714–1796)" *Church History*, 61 (1992), 408–21).

—Catherine A. Brekus

Ostenaco (1741?–1777)

Ostenaco, also known as Judd's Friend and as Outacite (meaning "mankiller"), was a prominent Cherokee leader and warrior in the mid-18th century. During the SEVEN YEARS' WAR he led more than 100 warriors against the French and their Indian allies. So great was Ostenaco's contribution that the governor of VIRGINIA, Robert Dinwiddie, invited him to ride in his coach in a parade. Unfortunately, Cherokee relations with the British colonists were rapidly deteriorating. Cherokee returning from campaigns were accused of harassing white settlements. Frontiersmen were accused of killing Cherokee to trade their scalps for the bounties that colonial governments had placed on enemy Creek warriors. A series of skirmishes erupted into war when in 1759 the governor of SOUTH CAROLINA arrested a Cherokee delegation on its way to CHARLESTON to make peace. The conflict revealed both sides' capacity to inflict heavy casualties and their vulnerability to attack. The Cherokee settlements in western NORTH CAROLINA were devastated, but the British frontier was pushed back more than 100 miles by Cherokee attacks.

Ostenaco, who was instrumental in the Cherokee war effort, hosted the British peace delegation and returned with it in 1762 to Williamsburg, Virginia, where he met a young Thomas Jefferson. Desiring to continue his political rise, Ostenaco seized the opportunity to lead a Cherokee delegation to Britain. A rival, Attakullakulla ("Little Carpenter"), had made the journey two decades earlier, which established his role as an intermediary between the British and Cherokee and thus secured his prominence. In Britain Ostenaco toured the leading attractions of the day, always under the gaze of thousands of spectators eager to catch a glimpse of the warrior whose escapades had been reported in the British press. He had an audience with King George III (1760–1820), who had financially supported the visitors' stay, as was the custom for visiting leaders of nations. Returning to North America, Ostenaco became a leading advocate of peaceful coexistence with the British, enjoying substantial prestige and later unsuccessfully opposing independent America's attempts to acquire Cherokee land.

Further reading: Tom Hatley, *The Dividing Paths: Cherokees and South Carolinians through the Era of Revolution* (New York: Oxford University Press, 1993).

—Troy O. Bickham

P

Parris, Samuel (1653–1720)

When nine-year-old Betty Parris began acting strangely in late 1691, her father, the Reverend Samuel Parris, at first believed she was the victim of a physical ailment. Soon, however, Parris determined that Betty and a rapidly growing list of "afflicted girls" were victims of a more sinister agent, the devil. By February 1692 what began as an isolated incident in the minister's household grew into the infamous Salem WITCHCRAFT trials, with Samuel Parris at the center of the controversy.

Born the son of a London cloth merchant, Samuel Parris began his adult life as a plantation owner in Barbados. Unable to secure a satisfactory living on the island, Parris moved to MASSACHUSETTS in 1680 hoping to make his fortune as a merchant. There he married and began a family, but his business interests soon failed. Parris turned to the ministry in the late 1680s and was settled as the new minister for Salem Village in 1689. The parish was deeply divided over Parris's appointment, reflecting larger social and economic rifts developing in the area. When investigators determined that the source of the original bewitchment was Tituba, the West Indian slave living in the Parris household, Parris began leading antiwitchcraft sermons and prayer sessions. By increasingly viewing the conflict as diabolical in nature, Parris transformed what might have been an isolated incident into a widespread frenzy pitting neighbor against neighbor. Satan, Parris suggested, was turning previously devout colonists into worldly men and women obsessed more with financial than spiritual rewards. Even the Puritan church was no refuge from the devil's work, according to Parris, as accusations of bewitchment spread from a few outsiders to prominent church members, including a former minister.

Nineteen executions and hundreds of arrests later, the Salem witch trials ended in October 1692. Only then did Parris's sermons display a sense of doubt about the righteousness of the divisions and factionalism the minister may not have created but certainly exacerbated. By 1693 Parris began to emphasize the biblical message of reconciliation, but it was too late to save his job. A formal apology to the congregation in 1694 gave Parris a few more years in the pulpit, but he was finally removed in 1697. Parris moved to various frontier towns in the early 18th century until his death in 1720.

Further reading: Paul Boyer and Stephen Nissenbaum, *Salem Possessed: The Social Origins of Witchcraft* (Cambridge, Mass.: Harvard University Press, 1974).

—Melanie Perreault

Parsons' Cause (1755–1765)

The Parsons' Cause was a dispute in VIRGINIA in 1755 over the salary provided by law to the clergy. It evolved into a debate over the authority of the Virginia assembly (HOUSE OF BURGESSES) to impose internal taxes. The dispute had its roots in the 1630s, when it had been agreed to pay clergy in TOBACCO. The church of Virginia required all people, whether members or not, to contribute to its support, and tobacco took the place of money as a medium of exchange. In 1753 the salary of £80 provided to clergy members was deemed insufficient to attract new clergy and to sustain the existing ministers, many of whom had families to support. The Virginia assembly raised the per annum salary to £100. On May 15, 1755, the clergy requested an increase in salary because the excessive issuance of treasury notes to meet the expenses of the SEVEN YEARS' WAR had caused inflation, thereby eroding the purchasing power of fixed salaries.

In the 1755 Twopenny Act the assembly allowed a rapidly depreciating currency to be substituted for tobacco in the payment of clergy salaries. According to the laws of England, no act of the assembly could supersede an earlier measure on the same subject that had received royal approval. However, the Twopenny Act did not include a suspending clause that would allow it to take effect after receiving royal consent. Many of the clergy were determined to refuse depreciated currency and to demand payment in tobacco instead. Led by Reverend John Camm, rector of the York-Hampton Parish, the clergy met in convention on November 24, 1755, and appealed to the Crown for relief. The House of Burgesses argued that the new law allowing payment in tobacco aided poor people on the frontier; the ministers responded that the Virginia assembly aimed to lessen the influence of the Crown and reduce the maintenance of the clergy. Most colonists supported the Twopenny Act, but the Crown disallowed it, thus permitting the clergy to sue for damages. In the most celebrated suit, *James Murry v. Fredericksville Parish,* the jury awarded damages of one cent.

Further reading: Glenn Curtis Smith, *The Parsons' Cause: Virginia 1755–65.* (Richmond, Va.: Richmond Press, 1939).

—Caryn E. Neumann

Paxton Boys (1763–1764)

The Paxton Boys mostly came from the Scots-Irish immigrant communities established along the PENNSYLVANIA frontier in the 1720s. Some had ties to local militia groups in Lancaster County and Northampton County, west and north of PHILADELPHIA, and many fought Indians during the 1750s when hostile DELAWARE and Shawnee attacked isolated frontier plantations that had been built on disputed territory claimed by both cultures. After the SEVEN YEARS' WAR Scots-Irish settlers feared the continued presence of NATIVE AMERICANS in the region and, making no distinction between allies and enemies, took out their anger on a peaceful Indian community nearby. The initial attack came on December 14, 1763, when a group of armed men from Paxton township in Lancaster County, Pennsylvania, marched on Conestoga Manor, killing and SCALPING six of the Christian Indians living on the small reserve of land. A few weeks after the original attack, 50 or 60 armed men on horseback attacked the surviving CONESTOGA Indians who had been placed under protective custody in the jailhouse at Lancaster.

The Pennsylvania governor and other Pennsylvania leaders, including Benjamin Franklin, condemned the actions of the Paxton Boys as being more "savage" than those of the Indians they hated. The colonial government did not criticize the brutal murder of Indian people but instead worried that poor white frontier inhabitants had challenged their authority and feared that they would continue to do so. Indeed, by early 1764 nearly 250 "Paxton Volunteers," as they called themselves, gathered and headed for Philadelphia intending to kill several hundred Indians under the protection of the Moravians and Pennsylvania government. Benjamin Franklin and a small militia force stopped the group in Germantown, just short of their goal, but a pamphlet war quickly ensued that explicated the grievances of the frontier inhabitants. Through satirical verse, cartoons, and pointed prose the largely Presbyterian Scots-Irish group questioned the loyalties, morality, and masculinity of politically powerful QUAKERS in the provincial assembly. Matthew Smith and James Gibson, the most vocal of these pamphlet authors, complained that the largely Quaker assembly had refused to help frontier settlers during the war with funds for a militia and protective FORTS. Instead, those in power had used public monies and private donations to assist Indians, such as the Delaware, who, with Quaker support, claimed rights to land in eastern Pennsylvania. Still, the Paxtons' ultimate complaints revolved around issues of relative political power and their own place within the BRITISH EMPIRE. They contended that frontier inhabitants in the western counties of Pennsylvania had less political representation in the provincial assembly than did the smaller eastern counties and that the legal justice system did not extend into their isolated communities. The Paxtons, demanding that the British treat them as equal subjects, took out their anxieties on the Conestoga Indians, who they thought did not deserve recognition or protection from the Pennsylvania government.

Whether or not the Paxton Boys' actions came from a nascent nationalism, the massacre and its aftermath set a precedent for Indian-white relations on the American frontier. After 1763 the level of "Indian-hating" dramatically increased. Other groups of frontier vigilantes, patterned on the Paxton Boys, attacked peaceful Indian communities in the Ohio Valley during the Revolutionary War. In turn, very few Native American groups allied themselves with colonists against Great Britain.

Further reading: Alden T. Vaughn, "Frontier Banditti and the Indians: The Paxton Boys' Legacy, 1763–1775" (*Pennsylvania History,* 51, 1984).

—Jane T. Merritt

Pelham, Peter (1695?–1751)

One of the most prolific printmakers of his generation, Peter Pelham was the only one to focus on separately published prints instead of book illustrations. Nearly as important is his legacy as an educator; his schools and assemblies helped to transform BOSTON from a provincial town into a leading American cultural center. Born in England, Pelham apprenticed to a mezzotint engraver. Mezzotint was a tool that enabled portrait engravers to use varying shades of gray to depict details in face and apparel using paintings as models. After framing and glazing, these prints usually hung in private homes. Pelham did engravings of many famous people, including members of the MONARCHY and members of the nobility.

Perhaps seeking to avoid disgrace or to escape competition, Pelham and his family immigrated to Boston about 1727. With few portraits available to copy, Pelham painted his own, including one of COTTON MATHER. Sold by subscription, the popular mezzotint was available for distribution four months after Mather's death in 1728. That same year Pelham issued mezzotints of clergymen, the governor, and a plan of Louisbourg, site of a key battle during a recent war, each of which sold hundreds of copies.

After JOHN SMIBERT's arrival in North America in 1730, demand declined for Pelham's paintings. However, Pelham and Smibert occasionally worked together, with Pelham making engravings of Smibert's paintings.

Unable to support himself and his growing family (after the death of his first wife, he married twice more), Pelham opened a dancing school in 1730 and began organizing concerts and musical assemblies in his home. While the PURITANS forbade musical instruments in worship settings, they permitted them in secular music, a distinction not lost upon the Anglican Pelham. He soon expanded his school to include reading, writing, and arithmetic. Pelham became a Mason in 1738, which widened his social connections, thus increasing the audience for his prints and the number of parents willing to send their children to his school. The Masons also hired him to make engravings of meeting notices, which boosted his income.

Pelham's son Henry became a portrait painter and miniature painter, while his stepson, John Singleton Copley, learned painting from Pelham. He died in Boston in December 1751.

—Victoria C. H. Resnick

Penn, William (1644–1718)

William Penn, a Quaker, was the founder of PENNSYLVANIA. He was born in England, the son of Admiral Sir William Penn and Margaret Jasper Vanderschuren, the daughter of a Rotterdam merchant. Penn studied at Chigwell Free Grammar School, then attended Christ Church College, Oxford, from which he was expelled in 1662 for criticizing the ANGLICAN CHURCH. He traveled in Europe, where he seemed to shed his unorthodox leanings, then returned to England in 1664 and studied law at Lincoln's Inn.

Penn assisted his father in business until 1667, when, while in Ireland supervising family properties, he adopted Quakerism. He quickly became a leading advocate of the Society of Friends (QUAKERS), using his acquaintances in Charles II's court, particularly his friendship with the king's brother, James, duke of York. He defended the Quaker faith against attacks by protagonists of other religions and was jailed for blasphemy and attending Friends meetings, which the English government considered illegal "conventicles." Penn campaigned against legal requirements to attend Anglican services, pay tithes to the established church, and take oaths, all of which Friends opposed. Through these efforts he engaged the larger principle of religious liberty. Penn also helped to set legal precedent in the landmark Penn-Meade trial of 1670, in which juries won the authority to reach verdicts contrary to the judge's instructions.

In the 1670s Penn achieved first-rank status in the Society of Friends, traveled to Holland, Germany, and parts of England on missionary visits, and became involved in colonization in North America, specifically in NEW JERSEY. Penn helped to draft the liberal West New Jersey Concessions and Agreements (1676), which gave broad powers to a popularly elected assembly. He inherited his father's fortune and landholdings in 1670, including a debt owed by Charles II, which by 1680 amounted, with interest, to £16,000. Penn negotiated with the Crown for about a year, obtaining a charter for Pennsylvania in March 1681. His reasons for founding the colony were both idealistic and financial. He had not been successful in winning religious liberty for Friends in England, and he thus built on his experience with New Jersey to conceive of a model society in America. He also needed a new source of funds, for he lived well beyond his means and could not collect rents from his English and Irish TENANTS. He hoped that sale of Pennsylvania lands and continuing income from quitrents would solve his financial problems.

Penn was hugely successful in promoting his colony through pamphlets such as *Some Account of the Province of Pennsylvania* (1681) and among the network of Quakers in England, Ireland, Scotland, and Europe. With advice from Algernon Sidney and several lawyers, he drafted the *Frame of Government* and *Laws Agreed upon in England* (1682). This constitution became more conservative with each draft but still included a popularly elected bicameral legislature and the right to trial by jury. Penn extended religious liberty to everyone who believed in one God, but only Christians could vote and hold political office. Land sales were brisk, and by 1682 Penn had more than 500 buyers. He carefully purchased the property from the Lenape Indians, thereby maintaining peaceful relations. He also obtained the three Lower Counties (DELAWARE) from James, duke of York, incorporating the Swedish, Dutch, and English residents into his government.

While Penn's "holy experiment" was much more successful during his lifetime than were colonies such as VIRGINIA and MASSACHUSETTS in establishing friendly relations with the NATIVE AMERICANS, largely because of the Quakers' pacifism, Pennsylvania quickly became part of the Atlantic slave system. SLAVERY had existed in the Delaware Valley under the Dutch and Swedes; with

Quaker settlement many wealthy Friends, including Penn, purchased Africans or brought slaves with them from the West Indies. Pennsylvania became enmeshed in the West Indies trade, exchanging foodstuffs, livestock, and lumber in return for West Indies sugar, molasses, and slaves. Many enslaved Africans lived and worked in PHILADELPHIA, where their estimated portion of the population peaked at 17 percent in the first decade of the 18th century, then declined. Although Pennsylvania had a less brutal regime than did plantation colonies to the south, its legislators created a caste society based on perceptions of race, including separate courts without juries for all blacks, whether slave or free.

William Penn lived in Pennsylvania for only four years, in 1682–84 and 1699–1701. Despite the colony's rapid demographic and economic growth, the proprietor quickly considered it a failure. When he was unable to collect quitrents, the cost of governing the province put him further in debt. He spent nine months in debtors' prison after the heirs of his steward, Philip Ford, won a judgment against him in 1707. Penn's monetary problems and long legal battle with Charles Calvert, Lord Baltimore, over the MARYLAND-Pennsylvania boundary (which was settled with the Mason-Dixon survey only in 1767) left his proprietorship constantly embattled. Most hurtful, perhaps, was the insubordination and bickering of Pennsylvania colonists, including its Quaker leadership, whom Penn had expected to create a model consensual society. When he suffered a debilitating stroke in 1712, his wife, Hannah, became acting proprietor. The proprietorship remained in the Penn family until the American Revolution.

Further reading: Jean R. Soderlund, ed., *William Penn and the Founding of Pennsylvania: A Documentary History* (Philadelphia: University of Pennsylvania Press, 1983); Gary B. Nash, *Quakers and Politics: Pennsylvania, 1681–1726* (Princeton, N.J.: Princeton University Press, 1968, 1997).

—Jean R. Soderlund

Pennsylvania

From settlement in the late 17th century as a haven for persecuted QUAKERS to its central place in American culture and American independence during the 18th century, Pennsylvania and its capital, PHILADELPHIA, played a crucial part in early American life.

Native Americans

The first inhabitants of the Pennsylvania region were Indians, who had been living in the area for centuries at the time of European settlement. The Lenape (DELAWARE), members of the ALGONQUIN linguistic stock, occupied much of the state's area. The Shawnee were another important Algonquian-speaking tribe who entered the region from the west in the 1690s. Both the Lenape and the Shawnee eventually came into conflict with the settlers, and many of them allied with the French in the SEVEN YEARS' WAR. The Susquehannock were an Iroquian-speaking group who lived along the Susquehanna River in Pennsylvania and MARYLAND. These three groups, in addition to the Nanticoke, Conoy, and CONESTOGA, constituted most of the approximately 15,000 natives in the region when WILLIAM PENN arrived.

Relations between NATIVE AMERICANS and white colonists in early Pennsylvania demonstrated that the two groups could peacefully coexist as long as Europeans maintained a commitment to fair dealings with the continent's original inhabitants. Following their high ideals, William Penn and his Quaker followers initially did not occupy Indian lands without purchasing them. Moreover, natives and colonists alike profited both from trade and from sharing TECHNOLOGY and knowledge. But in the 1730s, with thousands of new Scots-Irish immigrants aggressively seeking land on the frontier and not holding the Quakers' commitment to pacifism, conflict between natives and white people increased. The WALKING PURCHASE OF 1737 cheated Indians out of much of their lands and betrayed earlier Quaker ideals. Relations between Indians and colonists deteriorated, and various conflicts ensued, from the Seven Years' War to the 1763 slaughter of the Conestoga by the PAXTON BOYS.

Early Explorers

Many explorers visited Pennsylvania before William Penn commenced his Holy Experiment in the colony. Captain JOHN SMITH visited the Susquehannock Indians on the Susquehanna River in 1608. The following year, 1609, HENRY HUDSON, in service to the Dutch East India Company, entered Delaware Bay. In 1610 Captain Samuel Argall of VIRGINIA visited the Delaware Bay, naming it for the governor of Virginia, Lord de la Warr. The Dutch sailors Cornelis Hendricksen and Cornelis Jacobsen explored the region in, respectively, 1616 and 1623. In the early part of the 17th century, posts were established for fur trading with the Indians. Swedish explorers founded the first permanent settlement in 1637–38 at Wilmington, DELAWARE. Governor Johan Printz of New Sweden established his capital on Tinicum Island in present-day Pennsylvania. In 1655 Governor PETER STUYVESANT of NEW NETHERLAND captured New Sweden and incorporated it into the Dutch colony. In 1664 the English conquered the area in the name of the duke of York (later, King James II). Except for a brief period in 1673–74 when the Dutch exercised temporary control, the region remained under the duke of York's control until 1681.

William Penn, Quakerism, and Religious Toleration

Pennsylvania and its capital, Philadelphia, were the result of the vision and ideas of the most famous "American" Quaker, William Penn. The story of the establishment and settlement of Pennsylvania and its capital city is a familiar one, but it bears relating because so much of what Pennsylvania later became resulted directly from its founding. During the ENGLISH CIVIL WAR of the 1640s, a number of radical religious groups sprang up, each dedicated to remolding English society along the lines of its own religious vision. One of these was founded by George Fox and Margaret Fell and came to be known as the Society of Friends (Quakers). These Quakers, as the Friends were more commonly called, held a number of ideas that were considered heretical to the main body of PURITANS, who dominated England politically. Among these ideas was the belief that all people had an "inner light" that, when developed properly, allowed the individual to commune directly with God. The Quakers differed markedly from the New England Puritans in their belief that with God's help they could approach spiritual perfection. Furthermore, Quakers had little use for the notion of original sin, and they rejected the notion of predestination of a few "elect" people; Quakers believed that everyone could be saved. Friends also had little need for ministers because the individual could intimately know what God's word was, and their meetings were largely silent affairs punctuated by the spontaneous utterances of people who had been moved by the spirit of God.

The Quakers had a unique social vision that accompanied their religious views. They believed that all humans, regardless of GENDER and race, were equal in the sight of God (the institution of slavery would soon cause moral problems among the Friends), and they downplayed CLASS divisions. Quakers became known (and sometimes despised) for their pacifism, their refusal to swear oaths or to observe customs of social deference (like doffing their hats to their "superiors"), and the prominent role their society accorded women, even encouraging them to preach.

William Penn converted to Quakerism in the 1660s while in college at Oxford. In 1681 Penn received a huge land grant from King Charles II (1660–85), largely in payment of a debt that the king owed Penn's father. Penn began to plan carefully because as proprietor of this land grant he desired both to create a haven for Quakers and to realize a profit from land sale and rents. The settlers who eventually migrated to Penn's land were by no means all Quakers. Because Penn's only source of revenue was from the sale of land and the collection of rents, he promoted his colony aggressively throughout England, Ireland, and Germany. He even printed and distributed pamphlets in several languages extolling Pennsylvania's fertile ground. The response was overwhelming, and Penn threw the doors of his territory open to men and women of all nations.

This painting shows William Penn negotiating a treaty with Native Americans. *(Library of Congress)*

As a result, Pennsylvania became one of the most multicultural regions in the New World. Many who came were English, Irish, and Welsh Quakers, but others hailed from such countries as France, Holland, Denmark, Sweden, Scotland, and Germany. As a result, they represented diverse religious views. Religious denominations included Quakers, Anglicans, Mennonites, Amish, Moravians, Schwenkfelders, ROMAN CATHOLICS, PRESBYTERIANS, Methodists, JEWS, and LUTHERANS. Several thousand African slaves were also brought to Pennsylvania by 1730, despite protests to slavery by a few Quakers. Penn was not interested in a haven solely for Quakers, but rather a haven for peoples of various ethnic groups and religious persuasions. By 1700 approximately 30,000 persons were living in the colony. This number grew to roughly 300,000 by the American Revolution.

The visiting Dr. Alexander Hamilton depicted the heterogeneity of Philadelphia religious society when he wrote on June 8, 1744:

> I dined at a tavern with a very mixed company of different nations and religions. There were Scots, English, Dutch, Germans, and Irish; there were Roman Ca-

> tholics, Church men, Presbyterians, Quakers, Newlightmen, Methodists, Seventh day men, Moravians, Anabaptists, and one Jew. The whole company consisted of 25 planted round an oblong table in a great hall well stoked with flys. The company divided into committees in conversation; the prevailing topic was politicks and conjectures of a French war.

Hamilton's imagery is important because it provides a picture of people living in harmony in the face of significant religious and cultural differences. It is an imagery that largely mirrors historical reality in spite of friction between the Quaker assembly and the Anglican proprietors (William Penn's successors converted), some anti-Catholicism, and some discomfort over the increasing numbers of "Palatine Boors" from Germany. Furthermore, religion seems not to have been a major source of conflict. Indeed, the German immigrant GOTTLIEB MITTELBERGER was horrified at the plethora of religions in Philadelphia and even more horrified to find that "many pray neither in the morning nor in the evening, nor before or after meals. In the homes of such people are not to be found any devotional books, much less a Bible." The fact that there were only 18 churches in Philadelphia in 1776 (or one for every 2,200 people) lends support to Mittelberger's observations that many Pennsylvanians may not have been deeply religious.

Politics

When he arrived in 1682, William Penn brought with him a constitution for his new colony. A second constitution was enacted the following year, which established a bicameral legislature composed of a provincial council and a general assembly. Penn lost his colony between 1692 and 1694 due to his friendship with King James II, who was deposed during the GLORIOUS REVOLUTION of 1688. In the meantime. friction between the two houses of the legislature was growing. A popular movement led by DAVID LLOYD demanded greater powers for the assembly, some of which were granted by Markham's Frame of Government in 1696. Penn returned to Pennsylvania in 1699 and agreed to a revised form of government. The Charter of Privileges, which was enacted in 1701 and remained in effect until 1776, granted the assembly full legislative powers and gave Delaware (which was part of Pennsylvania until the American Revolution) a separate legislature of its own. Penn died in 1718, but constant tensions between the proprietors (Penn's descendants who gradually gave up Quakerism for Anglicanism) and the assembly (often dominated by Quakers) characterized Pennsylvania politics until the American Revolution. Another important political theme during the 18th century was the constant battle on the part of frontier peoples for greater representation in the government.

The Seven Years' War

Pennsylvania was relatively peaceful until the mid-18th century, when war broke out between the colonists and the French and Indians who opposed the westward expansionism of Pennsylvanians. The Seven Years' War was part of a larger imperial struggle between France and Great Britain over territory ranging from Europe to North America to Asia. In July 1755 British forces commanded by General EDWARD BRADDOCK were defeated near Fort Duquesne. Native Americans subsequently attacked the colonists, burning villages and killing settlers on the frontier and coming within 30 miles of Philadelphia itself. Eventually, the British emerged victorious, as confirmed by the 1763 TREATY OF PARIS. After the war Indians continued to resist European expansion. Pontiac's Rebellion ensued, which, in part, caused the British to issue the Proclamation of 1763 that supposedly limited the expansion of the colonists into Indian lands.

Economic Life

Colonial Pennsylvania boasted a varied and dynamic economic life. Aided by rich soils, the colony quickly became an important source of agricultural products, the surplus of which was sold as exports to Europe and the West Indies. Wheat became the most important crop, but corn and rye were also significant. Pennsylvanians also developed manufacturing. Sawmills and gristmills, SHIPBUILDING, iron production, PRINTING AND PUBLISHING, papermaking, tanning, and gun making were all important enterprises. The Conestoga wagon, soon to be revamped for westward expansion, was a product of the Lancaster region. By 1763 Philadelphia was perhaps the most vital economic center in North America. Like most port cities, it was an entrepôt through which passed foodstuffs bound for Europe and British manufactured goods to be sold in the backcountry.

Culture and Learning: Philadelphia and the American Enlightenment

Enlightenment SCIENCE exploded in those colonies that would make up the United States, particularly during the last generation before the American Revolution. By this time colonial accomplishments, although still overshadowed by those from abroad, were beginning to rise to the level of those to be found in European nations.

That American scientific accomplishments began to compare favorably with those of Europe was due to a number of factors, not the least of which was the fact that during the 18th century colonial society matured rapidly. It became more populous, city-oriented, interconnected, and wealthy, so that more people (Benjamin Franklin being the prime example) had leisure time to devote themselves to scientific inquiry. Institutions such as libraries, colleges, and learned societies, as well as the growth of printing presses, printed materials, and a more efficient postal system stimulated intellectual interchange among the colonists and a wider dissemination of innovative ideas. Furthermore, Americans responded favorably to the efforts of British institutions such as the Royal Society of London and individuals such as Peter Collinson to establish science in the colonies. Finally, by the 18th century the British colonists were much less concerned with physical survival and could turn their attention to understanding the universe instead of just attempting to live in it. Unlike many of the European philosophers, Enlightenment figures in the British colonies were working intellectuals; the colonists managed to do quite well despite the fact that they did not enjoy the patronage of king and enlightened nobles that many European intellectuals enjoyed.

From COTTON MATHER's emphasis on SMALLPOX inoculation in BOSTON to Alexander Garden's botany in SOUTH CAROLINA, from CADWALLADER COLDEN and JANE COLDEN's botany in NEW YORK to Thomas Jefferson's gadgets and ARCHITECTURE in Virginia, Enlightenment science influenced the 13 colonies in important ways. However, it was most strongly felt in Philadelphia, which became the center of the Enlightenment in the British North American colonies.

Philadelphia had its share of colonial scientific luminaries. The wealthy and erudite JAMES LOGAN, secretary to William Penn and lifelong defender of proprietary interests, amassed a large library of classical works and scientific treatises (he owned the first copy of Newton's *Principia Mathematica* known to exist in the colonies) and undertook many scientific studies of his own. He was a mathematician and worked on understanding the Moon's motion, prepared a treatise on optics, and even suggested some improvements on Huygen's method of treating lenses. He also published several papers in the Philosophical Transactions of the Royal Society of London, including studies on astronomy and lightning. Logan's most impressive scientific accomplishment came in the field of botany, in which, demonstrating the function of pollen in fertilizing maize, he explained the functions of the sexual organs of plants. Until his death Logan remained one of the colony's premier scientific minds and could be counted on to lend support to various scientific endeavors.

Other capable men joined Logan in this scientific milieu that existed in Philadelphia in the 18th century. Joseph Breintnall, Quaker merchant and member of Franklin's Junto, published papers on the aurora borealis and the effects of rattlesnake bites in the *Philosophical Transactions;* JOHN BARTRAM became the most significant botanist in the colonies, a difficult feat considering that many dabbled in botany; and Adam Kuhn studied botany with Carolus Linnaeus. The emphasis on botany and natural history was so great in Philadelphia that even William Young, an obscure young German man from Philadelphia, managed to get himself named botanist to the king and queen. The geographer Nicholas Scull produced a valuable map of Philadelphia and Pennsylvania, while THOMAS GODFREY, self-taught in mathematics and familiar with the Newtonian system after teaching himself Latin and borrowing Logan's copy of the *Principia Mathematica,* developed a better quadrant for measuring latitude at sea slightly before Hadley did. Finally, David Rittenhouse, like many American ARTISANS who became practical scientists, developed an accurate orrery later in the century, an important accomplishment in light of Brook Hindle's contention that they served as "monuments to the faith of the Enlightenment in the reasonableness of the world." Rittenhouse joined fellow Philadelphians Benjamin Franklin, William Penn, and Dr. John Morgan in becoming colonial Fellows of the Royal Society of London. These were by no means all of the important scientific contributions of the 18th century, but they indicate the extent to which scientific vigor grasped the minds of Philadelphians.

Of course, the foremost scientific mind in the colony belonged to Benjamin Franklin. Born to a candlemaker of modest means, Franklin began as an apprentice to his older brother in the printing business in Boston. Becoming restless, Franklin moved to Philadelphia, where he became a very successful printer, businessman, politician, and scientist. His demonstration, using kite and key, that lightning was electricity made him famous throughout the Western world. He retired from business at age 42 to devote his life to scholarly pursuits and public service. Franklin's life, in a very real sense, stood as a symbol for his age. He demonstrated that it was possible (if not usual) for a poor boy to rise above his station in life to become respected and revered, and he was typical of a large number of philosophers in Philadelphia. Indeed, many, like James Logan, were wealthy men in pursuit of knowledge, but Franklin represented the world of the artisan. A quick glance at the Junto (Leatherstocking Club) would be enough to indicate that common men as well as elites actively engaged in philosophical debate. It was possible for men like Franklin and Thomas Godfrey to make a name for themselves in the realm of science.

In their pursuit of knowledge and rational inquiry, Philadelphians revered usefulness above all else. There were two main reasons for this. First, Enlightenment figures throughout the Western world were reacting against Scholasticism, which, they believed, engendered much brainwork, sometimes without involvement in the everyday world. In this way the Enlightenment rejected what many believed to be wasted energy and inane speculation. Second, Philadelphians were still in the midst of building colonial society, and the practical aspects of that infused their intellectual approach to problems.

A tremendous purveyor of Enlightenment thought was found in Philadelphia's subscription libraries, which were open to the public. Franklin's library was opened in 1731, and in 1742 the Junior Library Company was formed. The Union Library Company followed, organized by craftsmen and tradesmen in 1747, and in 1757 the Amicable and Association Libraries opened. Over time these libraries were consolidated and finally absorbed by the Library Company of Philadelphia in 1769, making it, perhaps, the best library in the colonies. Despite their importance as innovative institutions, the subscription libraries were not the only voluntary associations that brought Enlightenment ideas to Philadelphia and disseminated them. Franklin's Junto was an important center of discussion and philosophical debate, especially during the 1730s and 1740s. The famous AMERICAN PHILOSOPHICAL SOCIETY eventually exerted even greater influence in the realm of Enlightenment thought than did the Junto.

Pennsylvania on the Edge of Revolution

By 1763 Pennsylvania was an established colony characterized by general religious toleration, a robust ECONOMY, ethnic and racial diversity, and a growing metropolis that was rapidly becoming the nation's dominant city. Over the next 20 years Pennsylvania was drawn into the vortex of revolution and new nationhood, emerging on the other side as the center of American political, economic, and cultural life. Birthplace of both the Declaration of Independence and the U.S. Constitution, Philadelphia took the lead in establishing the new nation.

Further reading: Joseph E. Illick, *Colonial Pennsylvania: A History* (New York: Scribner's, 1976); Gary B. Nash, *Quakers and Politics: Pennsylvania, 1681–1726* (Princeton, N.J.: Princeton University Press, 1968, 1997).

—Donald Duhadaway

Pequot

When Europeans arrived in southern New England, the Pequot inhabited what is now southern CONNECTICUT. These Indians lived primarily by horticulture, supplemented by hunting, gathering, and FISHING. By the 1630s they had developed into the dominant power in the southern Connecticut Valley and had established regular ties with English and Dutch traders. Their power stemmed partly from their involvement in the trade of purple and white shell beads called WAMPUM. Indians throughout the Northeast attributed both sacred and economic value to wampum. The Pequot lived near the source of the shells needed to produce wampum, and they spent much of each winter producing strings of the highly valued beads.

Efforts to monopolize the wampum trade antagonized the Dutch as well as neighboring Indians, including the Mohegan and NARRAGANSETT. The Pequot then tried to form an alliance with the MASSACHUSETTS Bay Colony, which was eyeing the land of the Connecticut Valley. Instead of accepting the Pequot overtures, the English demanded that the Pequot hand over the alleged killers of some English traders. Pequot refusal led to English vengeance. The English, along with Narragansett and Mohegan allies, attacked the Pequot. The PEQUOT WAR climaxed in a surprise attack against the Pequot at Fort Mystic in May 1637, killing up to 700 Pequot. Most of the dead were noncombatants, including many women and children. Many of the surviving Pequot were doled out to English and other Indians as servants. Some were sold into CARIBBEAN SLAVERY. In the Treaty of Hartford (1638) the English declared the Pequot tribe nonexistent.

Nevertheless, the Pequot survived. Despite the Treaty of Hartford, Connecticut recognized the existence of the Pequot and established towns with Pequot "governors." Under the close supervision of Connecticut, they eventually evolved into two separate political entities, an Eastern and Western, or Mashantucket, Pequot. From the Pequot War until KING PHILIP'S WAR, these communities participated in an integrated regional ECONOMY, selling services, wampum, and land to other Indians and colonists. This economy unraveled in the mid-1660s with the collapse of the FUR TRADE and a decline in the demand for wampum. The outbreak of King Philip's War in 1675 ended the delicate balance of power among New England's Indians and English that had rested upon this economy. Fortunately for the Pequot, they had allied themselves with the victorious English.

After the war and throughout the 18th century the Pequot, numbering at most a few hundred, successfully fought to retain lands. They did so despite a decline in their numbers caused partly by their participation in the SEVEN YEARS' WAR. However, efforts to fend off illegal land sales in the 19th century failed. Nevertheless, the Pequot survived, achieving federal recognition in 1983.

Further reading: Laurence M. Hauptman and James D. Wherry, eds., *The Pequots in Southern New England: The Fall and Rise of an American Indian Nation* (Norman: University of Oklahoma Press, 1990).

—James D. Drake

Pequot War (1637)

The Pequot War facilitated permanent English settlements in CONNECTICUT and led to the rise of the Mohegan at the expense of the PEQUOT. It also temporarily unified the factious English despite challenges against Puritan orthodoxy presented by colonists like ANNE MARBURY HUTCHINSON during the Antinomian controversy. The conflict centered on the Dutch and English efforts to take advantage of the trade rivalry between the NARRAGANSETT and Pequot. These tribes dominated much of southern New England because they controlled the supply of WAMPUM—valuable strings of beads produced from shells found mostly along the coast. Among Europeans the Dutch exercised the greatest influence in the region in the 1620s, with ties to both the Pequot and Narragansett. As parties of English splintered off from MASSACHUSETTS and expanded into the lower Connecticut River Valley in the 1630s, the Dutch tried to solidify their claim to the region's commerce by building a trading post and buying land. The Dutch could not, however, ease discontent within the tribes with whom they traded. Some of these communities had tributary relations with the Pequot and looked to the English as a way of severing these ties. Some signed separate trade agreements with the English or even ceded them land. Others, like the Narragansett, would, partially under the influence of English religious dissenter ROGER WILLIAMS, ally with the Massachusetts Bay Colony.

Hostilities arose because the English demanded that the Pequot hand over to Puritan justice the Indians whom they believed had killed Captain John Stone and some

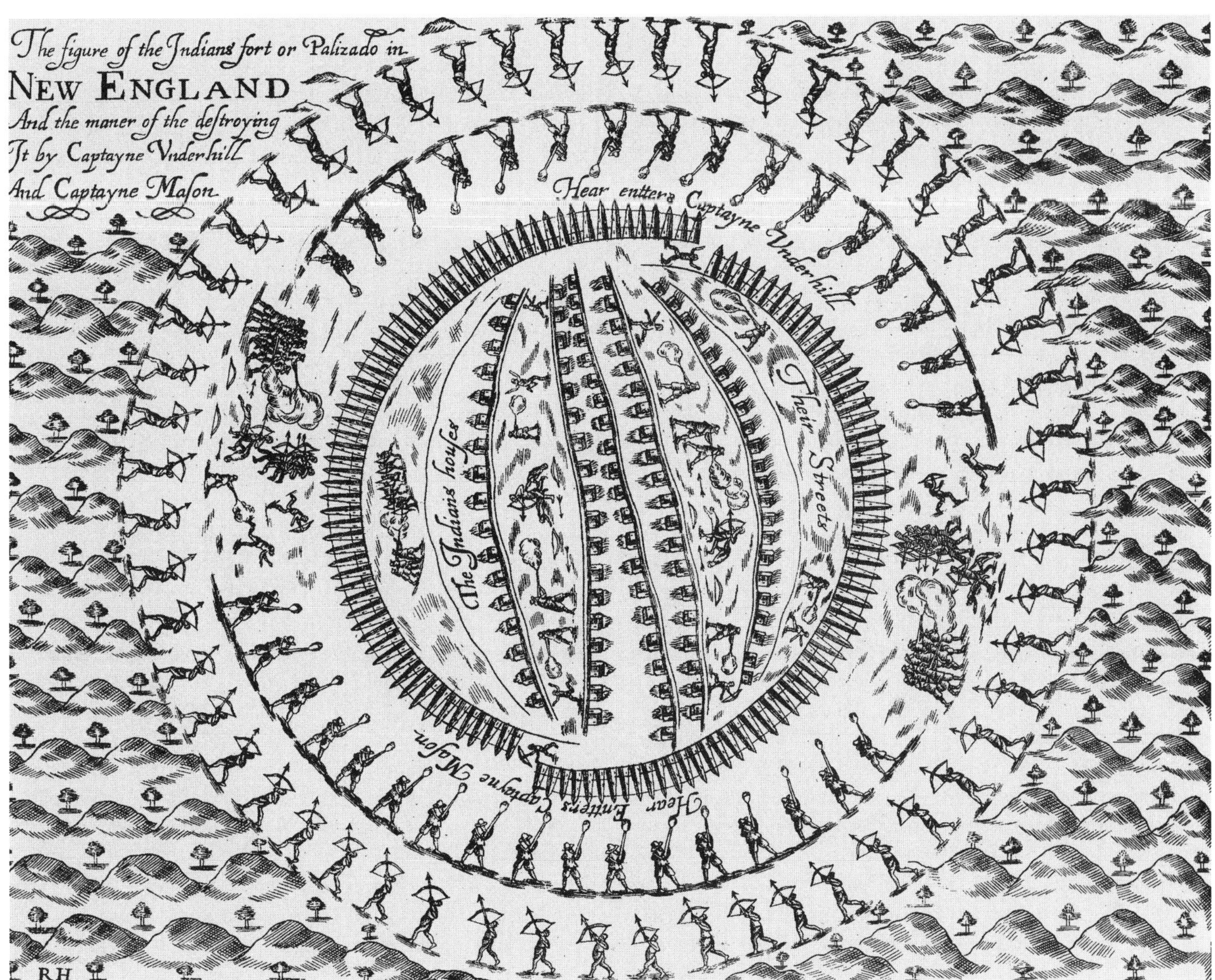

This engraving depicts the Pequot encampment under attack by Captain John Mason and his men. *(New York Public Library)*

members of his crew. The English subsequently demanded that the Pequot pay hefty indemnities and provide hostages to guarantee that they would comply with the colonists' desires. When the Pequot refused, the colonists sought vengeance. Together with their Narragansett and Mohegan allies, the English set out to subdue the Pequot, who, not coincidentally, occupied some of the most highly sought-after agricultural land in New England. Any hopes that the Pequot had of resisting were quashed in May 1637, when the English and their Indian allies attacked a palisaded Pequot village on the Mystic River. They surprised the village before dawn, and in the ensuing chaos the PURITANS torched the village. As for those Pequot men, women, and children who managed to flee the flames, Englishmen, to the horror of their Indian allies, shot them down with their muskets. By the end of the day up to 700 Pequot had died. Most were noncombatants. Over the next several months the English captured many of the Pequot who were not at the scene. They executed some of the men and doled out most women and children to colonists or other Indians as servants. They even sold some Pequot into CARIBBEAN SLAVERY. In the Treaty of Hartford (1638), which officially ended the war, the English declared the end of the Pequot nation.

The English and their Indian allies had contrasting views of the war and, particularly, the attack on Mystic River. The English, for the most part, saw the carnage as a sign of divine favor in their struggle against "savages." The Indians, on the other hand, even if they had allied with the English, had never witnessed warfare of the scope or scale that waged by the English at the Pequot village. Their culturally prescribed rules of war had in the past dictated low-casualty conflicts characterized by hit and run tactics —often with the aim of acquiring live captives. The torching of the village and shooting of inhabitants as they fled prompted the Narragansett to complain about "the manner of the Englishmen's fight . . . because it is too furious, and slays too many men."

Although the Indians were shocked at the conduct of the Pequot War, some benefited from its results. Before the war Uncas's Mohegan were linked to the Pequot by intermarriage and a tributary status. Uncas himself claimed to be the rightful leader by birth of both the Mohegan and Pequot. However, leadership of the Pequot was not entirely hereditary but stemmed partially from elections. In the first half of the 1630s, Uncas tried several times to depose the Pequot leader, Sassacus, only to fail repeatedly. When the English arrived looking to avenge John Stone's death, Uncas found a power that could tilt the political balance in his favor. The aftermath of the Pequot defeat in 1637 saw Uncas's emergence as the grand sachem of the Pequot and Mohegan. Uncas's power coincided with the sharp rise of English power in Connecticut. The number of colonists living there increased sixfold in the six years after the war.

Further reading: Alfred A. Cave, *The Pequot War* (Amherst: University of Massachusetts Press, 1996).

—James D. Drake

pewter

Pewter was a common metallic alloy for centuries, from late medieval Europe to the founding of the United States. The increasing affluence of urban peoples and the growing middle CLASS on both sides of the Atlantic made it possible for pewter to displace the wood, earthenware, and animal horn that previously had been made into vessels, utensils, and ornaments. As historian Ledlie Laughlin wrote, "From the settlement of Plymouth in 1620 until the founding of the Republic (or later), pewter was probably the commonest metal that entered into the lives of our colonial forebears." A skeptic might respond that iron—inexpensive, strong, durable, and heat resistant—was far more plentiful than pewter, being essential for structural hardware, tools with cutting edges, and objects used in and around fire.

All but the poorest households in British North America had spoons, dishes, and mugs made of pewter. One of the most typical pewter vessels was the porringer, a bowl with one or two flat decorative handles. In prosperous homes pewter appeared widely, including many vessels and utensils for serving FOOD and drink, candlesticks, oil lamps, shaving mugs, chamber pots, and ornamental wares. Taverns served beer in pewter mugs and tankards. Churches had pewter plates, cups, chalices, and baptismal bowls. Distillers made liquor in pewter worms (tubing).

Pewter is an alloy of mostly tin with, for common objects, a smaller amount of lead; for better items the remainder of the alloy was a combination of lead, copper, brass, antimony, or bismuth. Usually of a dull gray color, better quality pewter can approach the luster of silver. A soft alloy with a low melting point, pewter was relatively easy to cast and shape into objects domestic, commercial, and religious. Items worn or broken through years of daily use were easily melted and recast. With its high tin content, pewter does not convey a metallic taste to food and drink.

Most pewter goods in British North America came from England, as intended by a mercantilist economic policy that kept the colonies reliant on British manufacturing. Pewterers in North America were usually limited to melting worn or broken objects for recasting and finishing with a lathe, other cutting tools, or hammers. The costly investment in metal molds meant that the styles of objects changed slowly. Pewterers, among the most important ARTISANS in early North America, also took on other metal work, such as plumbing, and sold imported pewter and other goods. Pewter remained a common metal into the early 19th century, when consumers switched to newly available, more appealing materials, such as blue-on-white glazed pottery, glassware, and electroplated silver.

Further reading: Ledlie Irwin Laughlin, *Pewter in America: Its Makers and Their Marks* (Barre, Mass.: Barre Publishers, 1940, 1969).

—Dale Martin

Philadelphia

Philadelphia was the premier city in North America during the late colonial era. Much like Athens in ancient Greece, the City of Brotherly Love served as the political, economic, and cultural center of the colonies and the new nation. From its small beginnings in 1682 WILLIAM PENN played a dominant role in the evolution of Philadelphia. He named the city, chose its location, designed the street plan, and distributed the house lots. Penn's plans were quickly altered by the inhabitants, who ignored Penn's vision of a "greene countrie towne" dominated by large landowners living in big houses set on large lots and surrounded by orchards. Instead, Philadelphians congregated on small lots close to the Delaware River, the lifeline of the ECONOMY. Penn's plan for a central city square also had to be postponed because the city grew north and south along the Delaware River before expanding westward to the Schuylkill River. Still, the city maintained some of the outlines of Penn's original design, including large parks in its center. By the beginning of the 18th century Philadelphia assumed some of the characteristics of a congested urban area, with houses springing up in crowded alleys.

William Penn's decision to open his lands to peoples of all nationalities and religious beliefs and the subsequent influx of people ensured that 18th-century Philadelphia would become one of the most multicultural cities in the world. In the words of the Anglican minister William Smith, Philadelphians were "a people, thrown together from various quarters of the world, differing in all things—language, manners and sentiments." Although they normally managed to keep control of the assembly until the American Revolution, the QUAKERS became a minority in the city, and, according to Carl and Jessica Bridenbaugh, "after 1735 it is an anachronism to speak of Philadelphia as the Quaker city." Hundreds of thousands of German, Dutch, Swiss, English, Irish, Scots, and Scots-Irish immigrants landed at its port and either passed through or settled in Philadelphia during the 18th century. For example, in the half century preceding the American Revolution at least 70,000 Germans arrived in Philadelphia, 7,000 in 1739 alone, although most quickly moved through to the countryside. In 1763 Philadelphia contained approximately 22,000 residents, making it the largest city in British North America.

An organized city government began with the Philadelphia Charter of 1701, which created a municipal system based on an English model of a corporation. The key components of Philadelphia's self-perpetuating government were a 12-man council, eight aldermen, a recorder, and a mayor chosen from the aldermen for a one-year term. These officials passed ordinances, regulated trade, and acted as a judiciary. Members who served in the Philadelphia corporation held positions of great honor but increasingly saw their power eroded by the Philadelphia County government as well as the provincial assembly, which had the power to regulate cities.

Philadelphia's economy rested squarely on the foundation of commerce, and water dominated material life in the port city. The majority of Philadelphians depended, either directly or indirectly, on commerce with people scattered throughout the Atlantic world, from small farmers and storekeepers in the neighboring countryside to large manufacturers and MERCHANTS operating from the West Indies to Lisbon and London.

The hundreds of ships that annually docked at wharves lining the city's eastern edge formed the backbone of the economy. They disgorged molasses from the West Indies and manufactured goods from Europe, which were dispersed throughout the city and the surrounding countryside. The abundant grain and livestock products of the city's rich hinterlands, encompassing parts of PENNSYLVANIA, NEW JERSEY, DELAWARE, and MARYLAND, were loaded onto vessels sailing to Europe and the CARIBBEAN. Producing, transporting, and selling these commodities created a complex economy involving thousands of individuals. MARINERS sailed ships, stevedores moved cargoes, and carters and laborers transferred merchandise between boats and warehouses. Waggoners, farmers, and flatboat operators carried flour, bread, and other foodstuffs into the city and returned to the countryside ladened with shoes, textiles, and other processed goods. Coopers fashioned barrels to hold items bound for the sea, while shopkeepers and grocers peddled foreign and local merchandise in retail stores. Subsidiary sectors of the economy developed that provided jobs to workers in the construction of houses and ships, encouraged ARTISANS to fashion wares for local consumption, and stimulated the service roles played by keepers of boardinghouses, inns, and taverns as well as by smiths, farriers, wheelwrights, riggers, sailmakers, and chandlers who cared for horses, carts, and boats. All the while, merchants, clerks, and other tradesmen directed and organized the entire system.

People in these occupations were divided roughly into three "classes," or, in 18th-century terminology, "sorts."

The "lower sort" were unskilled laborers who worked with their hands cleaning chimneys, excavating cellars, draining swamps, hauling building materials, and stowing and unloading ship cargoes. Hundreds of sailors also belonged in this category because they shared with laborers a minimal living standard, low status, and limited occupational and economic mobility.

The "middle sort" was comprised mostly of artisans, people who fashioned items by hand. While most artisans belonged to this category, they were a somewhat amorphous group who were spread along the spectrum of wealth, ranging from impoverished apprentice shoemakers to affluent master carpenters. At the bottom end of the scale, where tailors, shoemakers, and coopers congregated, they had much in common with sailors and laborers, including low income, uncertain prospects of advancement, and, in most cases, exclusion from the ranks of property holders (and therefore from the ranks of voters before the Revolution). At the upper end were tanners, bakers, sugar-boilers, brewers, goldsmiths, and some construction contractors, although artisans rarely reached the pinnacle of the social hierarchy.

Many merchants and a few substantial shopkeepers belonged to the "upper sort." Of course, not all merchants were wealthy; some were grocers who lived no better than prosperous master craftsmen, but the pillars of the mercantile community sometimes earned fabulous fortunes, dressed in fashionable finery, and constructed marvelous mansions. Doctors, lawyers, clergymen, government officials, and other professionals also enjoyed high social status, even if their wealth rarely matched that of merchants.

Outside these occupational and social horizontal layers stood unfree people of two kinds. Indentured servants (mostly European migrants) were bound to individual masters, often for three or four years, and their liberties were greatly restricted while under indenture. African and African-American slaves were owned perpetually by another person, their human rights were abridged, and their position was hereditary. These unfree people worked in all areas of the city, from sailors to servants and caulkers to clerks.

Philadelphia's growing population often led to problems associated with urban centers. Early studies of the city, while recognizing the problem of poverty, indicated that society was fluid and that people could relatively easily work their way out of poverty, given the opportunities available in the growing city. More recent studies reveal that Philadelphia's poverty problem grew during the 18th century and that elite Philadelphians tried to relieve the problem privately by providing charity to the "industrious" poor. An early Quaker almshouse and the PENNSYLVANIA Hospital, a charity hospital that opened in 1752, were among many efforts to help the less fortunate. Meanwhile, public assistance to the needy likewise increased, and the Overseers of the Poor constructed an almshouse in 1767. However, these efforts fell short. Philadelphia, like other cities before and since, experienced poverty in the midst of plenty.

Founded on the notion of religious freedom, Pennsylvania, unlike most other British colonies, never adopted an officially sponsored state religion and was open to anyone who wanted to immigrate. Consequently, the colony's religious landscape was heterogeneous. Philadelphia was home to many different religious groups and was a microcosm of the European religious spectrum. Overwhelmingly Protestant but welcoming to ROMAN CATHOLICS and JEWS, Philadelphia was, from the beginning, religiously pluralistic and tolerant. Without a heavy hand of church or state, no institutions dictated religious conformity for the society at large.

During the early 18th century revivalism and spiritual awakening spread across Europe and throughout the colonies, including Pennsylvania, as spiritual leaders such as GEORGE WHITEFIELD, JONATHAN EDWARDS, JOHN WESLEY, and the German Pietists attracted large followings with their fear of recidivism and the wrath of God. Even a secular figure like Benjamin Franklin was not immune from the spiritual awakenings of the first half of the 18th century, and he turned out to hear George Whitefield when he visited Philadelphia.

Philadelphia was the home of the AMERICAN ENLIGHTENMENT. If William Penn was the dominant figure in molding the political and religious life of Pennsylvania, then Benjamin Franklin was the emblem of the Enlightenment. Writer and publisher, scientist and diplomat, philosopher and statesman, Franklin was the driving force behind Philadelphia's cultural and intellectual life until his death in 1790. As the home of Franklin, the Quaker City bore the fruits of his tremendous energy and intellect. Many of its inhabitants embraced both Franklin's scientific approach to knowledge and his deep commitment to improving his community. Philadelphians thus established the AMERICAN PHILOSOPHICAL SOCIETY, the College of Physicians, the first subscription libraries, and the University of Pennsylvania to advance philosophical and practical wisdom. They also supported a host of private and public measures designed to aid the needy, cure the sick, educate the children, clean and light the streets, combat fires, and regulate markets. Nor was Franklin alone: THOMAS GODFREY, JAMES LOGAN, and JOHN BARTRAM were among those who worked with Franklin to make Philadelphia the home of the American Enlightenment and the center of urban life in the colonies.

See also BOSTON; CHARLESTON; NEW YORK CITY; NEWPORT.

Further reading: Gary B. Nash, *First City: Philadelphia and the Forging of Historical Memory* (Philadelphia: University of Pennsylvania Press, 2001); Billy G. Smith, *The "Lower Sort:" Philadelphia's Laboring People, 1750–1800* (Ithaca, N.Y.: Cornell University Press, 1990); Russell F. Weigley, ed., *Philadelphia: A 300-Year History* (New York: Norton, 1982).

—Donald Duhadaway and Billy G. Smith

Pilgrims

A group of 41 Puritan Separatist CONGREGATIONALISTS, known as Pilgrims, were the backbone of the 102 English colonists who sailed to North America on the *Mayflower* in 1620 and established the PLYMOUTH Colony in New England. Puritans felt the Elizabethan church settlement failed adequately to purge the ANGLICAN CHURCH of its traditional Catholic organization and ceremonies. Instead of venerating pomp and ceremony, the Puritans embraced a fanatical piety embedded in the damnation of original sin, predestination, and salvation by faith. In the late 1500s the Puritans split into two groups, Non-Separatists and Separatists. Non-Separatists wanted to work within the Anglican Church for reform. Separatists, like the Pilgrims, adopted a more zealous doctrine, preaching that the established church was incapable of reformation. They consequently severed their local congregation, located in Scrooby, Nottinghamshire, from the Anglican Church.

The Pilgrims embraced Congregationalism, the idea that congregational independence, decentralized authority, and democratic control by elected leadership offered the best chance for salvation. The Pilgrims' idea of democracy included only male church elders. On a broader social scale the revolt of Puritan factions against the established church also reflected the 17th-century struggle of an emerging middle CLASS against absolute authority and privilege.

The Anglican Church persecuted Separatist congregations. The Ecclesiastical Commission of York imprisoned Scrooby separatists and fined others. William Brewster, WILLIAM BRADFORD, and John Robinson organized an unsuccessful attempt by the Scrooby congregation to leave England in 1607. Local authorities charged and jailed the Separatists for attempting an illegal exit from the country. By 1608 most of the Scrooby congregation arrived in Amsterdam, finally settling in Leiden in 1609.

The Pilgrims never completely adapted to the idea of becoming Dutch instead of remaining English. In 1617 they decided to end their voluntary exile and move to North America. In 1619 the Pilgrims' representatives, Deacon John Carver and Robert Cushman, obtained financial support from Thomas Weston and his group of adventurers. The Pilgrims agreed to form a joint-stock company with Weston's merchant investors. Their seven-year contract required the Pilgrims to establish a trading post in North America and made all property and profit the communal property of the company. The majority of the Leiden congregation rejected this proposal, and only a minority sailed to England to make final arrangements for the voyage to the New World.

After a 66-day voyage across the Atlantic, the *Mayflower* arrived off Cape Cod on November 11, 1620. The Pilgrims realized they were outside the domain of the original charter. To preserve order and establish control over any non-Congregationalist English "strangers" who might start their own settlement, they persuaded all 41 adult men on board to sign the MAYFLOWER COMPACT and agree to accept a democratically elected communal government. The *Mayflower* anchored in Plymouth Bay on December 16, 1620.

Plymouth Colony differed markedly from JAMESTOWN. Unlike Jamestown's male-dominated company of profit seekers, the *Mayflower* carried families. Of the 41 Pilgrims on board, there were 17 men, 10 women, and 14 children. The site chosen for Plymouth Colony was the abandoned village of the Patuxet that a plague had decimated in 1617. After an initial brutal winter that killed 44 settlers, the spring of 1621 brought contact with the local natives. Samoset, the first Indian to come to Plymouth Colony, spoke English he had learned from fishermen. He arranged the visit of MASSASSOIT, chief of the neighboring Wampanoag, who befriended the settlement. Plymouth Colony also found a friend in Tisquantum, or SQUANTO, the sole survivor of the Patuxet tribe. Squanto showed the colonists how, when, and what to plant in the old Patuxet fields near Plymouth. The Pilgrims also learned where to fish and hunt. In the fall of 1621 the settlement felt established enough to observe the first Thanksgiving day to offer thanks for their survival after the first winter's hardships. The colony became official in November 1621, when the *Fortune* brought 36 new settlers and a charter for Plymouth Plantation from the Council for New England.

Further reading: Crispin Gill, *Mayflower Remembered: A History of the Plymouth Pilgrims* (Newton Abbot: David & Charles, 1970).

—Tristan Traviolia

Pima revolt (1751)

The Pima Indian tribe of southern Arizona is centered along the middle Gila River. During Spanish rule the Arizona tribes were known collectively as the Pimerian, with the northerly tribes known as Pima Altas, or Upper Pima, while those farther south were referred to as Pima Bajas, or Lower Pima. For much of the early Spanish period, the Pima Indians remained outside the reach of Spanish colonial and mission control. Permanent contact between Europeans and the Pima began in 1687, when Jesuit missionary Eusebio Kino established a mission at Dolores in northern Sonora, Mexico. From this point the Spanish penetrated Pima lands. In 1694 Kino investigated the Gila River, and in 1697 the Spanish military and missionaries explored farther into Pima territory, baptizing nearly 100 Pima. Kino preached among the Pima until his death in 1711. Roman Catholic Friars continued conversion work with the Pima until the revolt.

Tribes in the Pima Altas region led the insurrection in 1751, a violent rebellion against Spanish economic, cultural, and religious persecution. Intending to depose the Spanish government, obliterate Spanish culture, and restore traditional ways among his people, Luis Oacpicagigua triggered the rebellion by slaying 18 Spaniards in his hometown of Saric in northern Sonora. He also sacked the mission at Tubutama. Most of the Pima did not participate in the rebellion, yet more than 100 Spanish missionaries and officials were killed before the rebellion was suppressed when the Spanish captured Oacpicagigua.

—James Jenks

Pinckney, Elizabeth Lucas (1722–1793)

An amateur horticulturist, Elizabeth Lucas was born in Antigua, the eldest daughter of George Lucas, a British army officer, and his wife, Anne. Elizabeth, nicknamed Eliza, was educated in England. As a teenager she settled in SOUTH CAROLINA with her parents. In 1738 Lieutenant Colonel Lucas was called back to active duty during the WAR OF JENKINS' EAR and left Eliza in charge of her invalid mother and the three family plantations in South Carolina.

She acted as the steward of her family's holdings and, with the encouragement of her father, experimented with various potential cash crops: INDIGO, ginger, alfalfa, and cotton. These endeavors were driven by her avid interest in horticulture as well as heavy debts on the Lucas family property of both land and slaves. By 1744 Eliza's indigo experiments were successful. That year the Lucas family plantation at Wappoo produced a crop of saleable indigo dye and sufficient seed to allow her to share with many of her neighboring plantation owners. Eliza's efforts in producing a viable indigo crop greatly benefited the ECONOMY of colonial South Carolina, especially as the demand for rice declined. Indigo became an important staple crop, second only to rice. The dye was eagerly sought by textile manufactures in Great Britain and Europe. By 1775 CHARLESTON was exporting more than 1 million pounds of indigo dye annually.

In the same year as her first successful indigo crop, Eliza married widower Charles Pinckney. She spent the next 12 years raising their children: Charles Cotesworth (1746–1825), Harriot (1748–1830), and Thomas (1750–1828). When her husband died suddenly in 1758, Eliza returned to the responsibility of running a plantation and a household, as she had done for her father. Her sons, educated in England, returned to South Carolina and eventually became leaders in the Revolutionary War. At the end of the war Charles Cotesworth was a South Carolina delegate to the Constitutional Convention and Thomas was elected governor of South Carolina. Harriot had married a local rice plantation owner, Daniel Horry.

GENDER prescriptions were somewhat less restrictive on women in colonial North America than was the case in the early 19th century. Eliza, thanks to the advantages of EDUCATION and CLASS, and with the encouragement of both her father and her husband, moved between the worlds of business and plantation management and that of wife and mother. Her legacy comes from both spheres. Her horticultural experiments led to the successful commercialization of indigo dye production. This crop was an important economic contributor to pre–Revolutionary War South Carolina. Her daughter, following her mother's example, managed her husband's estates following his death; her sons made important contributions to colonial South Carolina and later, early American politics. Eliza Lucas Pinckney died in PHILADELPHIA on May 26, 1793.

—Margo Krager

piracy

The crime of piracy was a constant threat in the colonial period. Pirates not only helped build the transatlantic empires of the Spanish, Dutch, French, and British but also preyed on them. The attitudes of royal officials and the usefulness of the pirates to ambitious colonials changed radically during the two centuries of colonization and settlement.

Elizabethan "Sea Dogs" like Sir Francis Drake and Sir Walter Raleigh were quasi legal pirates led by noblemen and court favorites of Queen Elizabeth I (1558–1603). Their preying on the SPANISH COLONIES and treasure fleets in the late 16th century simultaneously filled the English treasury and allowed the queen to disavow any knowledge of their activities. They not only brought in much needed hard currency but also had the experience and skill to defeat the Spanish Armada in 1588, initiating a period of English pride and maritime confidence.

By the mid-17th century the legend of the Elizabethan pirates had grown, producing a new generation of imitators based mainly in the CARIBBEAN. Centering around Jamaica, some of this new generation were veterans of the 1655 English parliamentary expedition sent to take the island. Soon, French, Dutch and English "buccaneers," named for the way they smoked meat, were preying mercilessly on Spanish fleets and towns in Central and South America. These buccaneers quickly gained a reputation for cruelty and ruthlessness.

Welshman Sir Henry Morgan (ca. 1635–88) rose through the ranks of Jamaican privateers to lead attacks on the Spanish towns of Puerto Principe, Cuba (1668), Maracaibo, Venezuela (1669), and Panama (1671). Morgan helped established the English presence in the Caribbean with the help of pirates. He was knighted by Charles II and made deputy governor of Jamaica in 1674, where he began the process of eradicating the pirates who had previously served with him. The exploits of Morgan, François L'Olonnais, and others were documented by Dutchman Alexander Olivier Exquemelin in the widely popular *History of the Buccaneers of America,* first published in Holland in 1681 and quickly translated and republished in several languages.

The period from the 1680s into the 1720s became known as the "Golden Age of Piracy," when the most renowned and famous of all pirates were active. Like the buccaneers chronicled in Exquemelin's book, pirates of this period were thoroughly documented in a contemporary publication, *A General History of the Pyrates* (1724), by Captain Charles Johnson. The *General History* is based on a variety of sources including hearsay, eyewitness testimony, newspaper accounts, court records, and published materials like execution sermons and trial transcripts. The otherwise unknown Johnson might have been a pseudonym for English novelist Daniel Defoe, according to some scholars. Whoever the author, Johnson's history provides much of the popular information and stories associated with the Golden Age's two distinct generations, the first during the 1690s and the second during the decade from 1715 to 1725.

There had been pirates and piracy along the North American coast since the founding of the colonies. The Pilgrim's first shipment of materials to England was taken by French pirates in 1621. BOSTON-based Dixey Bull raided the newly founded towns of coastal MASSACHUSETTS in 1631. Even so, these were only minor threats to the still developing trade routes. By the 1690s, however, trade routes were firmly established and lucrative markets were waiting for various goods. Britain had passed several Navigation Acts, which attempted to harness the unregulated trade of the colonial MERCHANTS, beginning in 1651 in order to receive the appropriate customs fees. At the same time, pirates were suddenly growing in number and boldness.

Many pirates, finding the Spanish in the Caribbean now heavily armed, struck out at new targets, notably the unprotected shipping in the Indian Ocean and the Red Sea, where convoys of Muslims making pilgrimages to Mecca provided easy targets. Pirate captain Thomas Tew of RHODE ISLAND arrived in NEWPORT in April 1694, his sloop *Amity* filled with gold, silver and ivory from the capture of an Indian treasure ship. English captain Henry Avery scored one of the largest prizes in history when he and his crew captured the *Fateh Muhammed* and the *Gunjsawai* in 1695.

The ports of Boston, Newport, NEW YORK CITY, PHILADELPHIA, and CHARLESTON welcomed pirates and provided them with safe harbors because pirates visiting these ports were quick to spend their share of treasure. This was the easiest, and sometimes only, source of hard cash in the English colonies. It was only natural that the ports welcomed pirates so that merchants could profit handsomely from trafficking with them. William Markham, PENNSYLVANIA's lieutenant governor from 1694 to 1699, had a reputation for being the pirates' "Steddy Friend." Governor Sir William Phips of Massachusetts was rumored to have invited pirates to Boston from Philadelphia. Rhode Island was widely considered "the chief refuge for pyrates" in New England. Governor Benjamin Fletcher of NEW YORK and merchant Frederick Philipse made fortunes from trading with the pirates based in Madagascar. Pirates were also tolerated in the coastal inlets and islands of the Carolinas.

The effect of this widespread freebooting was the loss of royal customs revenue and strained relations between the royal chartered companies and the local rulers of India and the East Indies. Vice admiralty courts were commissioned throughout the empire in 1696, and laws were passed "for the more effectual suppression of piracy." The famous captain William Kidd was commissioned to hunt down pirates in the Indian Ocean but allegedly turned pirate himself. His former patron, the earl of Bellomont, who was governor of Massachusetts at the time, arrested Kidd in 1699 in Boston and sent him to London as a sign of Bellomont's loyalty to the Crown. Kidd was tried, found guilty, and executed. A few years later, in 1704, Captain John Quelch, while attempting to return home with his spoils, was captured, tried, and executed in Boston for piracy. An all-out war against the pirates had begun.

The second generation of pirates arose when QUEEN ANNE'S WAR ended in 1713, leaving thousands of sailors unemployed. A large group gathered on New Providence and Nassau Islands in the Bahamas. The pirates gathered there became some of the most infamous and lasting pirates in history. This generation of pirates was indiscriminate, ruthless, and uncontrollable. Gathered together under Captain Benjamin Hornigold, they were divided by the general amnesty offered in 1716, which some accepted but many refused, sailing off to begin their own careers. Captain EDWARD TEACH, alias Blackbeard, terrorized the VIRGINIA and Carolina coasts, where he was hunted down. Captain STEDE BONNET, the gentleman turned pirate, vacillated between piracy and legitimate PRIVATEERING but ended up at the end of a noose. Captain Black Sam Bellamy and all his crew perished when their ship, the *Whydah Galley,* was wrecked in a storm off the coast of Cape Cod. Calico Jack Rackham and his famous female crew members Anne Bonney and Mary Read were sentenced to death in Port Royal, Jamaica, but only Rackham swung. Bonney and Read "pleaded their bellies" and because they were both pregnant escaped the hangman. The dozens of pirates of this period made for popular reading in the newspapers and pamphlets that were printed in Britain and the colonies. A pirate's execution brought out crowds in the thousands to hear the local minister, especially the Reverend COTTON MATHER in Boston, and to witness the gruesome spectacle.

Pirate crews often were comprised of MARINERS who were unemployed, criminals, or those otherwise dissatisfied with society's regulation. They commonly operated under a rough type of democracy, electing their captains and demoting leaders who failed to carry out the wishes of the crew. Pirates usually did not kill the crews of captured ships but, instead, offered them the opportunity to join in their illegal adventures. Indeed, the operation of pirate crews provides a window into the world of common people in the early Atlantic world.

By 1726 the last of this generation of pirates had been captured and punished. Regular shipping made them unnecessary and unwanted in the American ports. There were occasional pirates in the Atlantic waters after this date, but never again were they so organized and constant a presence as in the period from 1680 to 1730.

Further reading: David Cordingly, *Under the Black Flag* (New York: Random House, 1995); Hugh Rankin, *The Golden Age of Piracy* (Williamsburg, Va.: Colonial Williamsburg, 1969); Marcus Rediker, *Between the Devil and the Deep Blue Sea: Merchant Seamen, Pirates, and the Anglo-American Maritime World, 1700–1750* (Cambridge, U.K.: Cambridge University Press, 1987).

—Stephen C. O'Neill

plantation system

Export-oriented settlers in the southern colonies relied on a North American version of the New World plantation system. It was an economic and social system of LABOR relations in which a planter with capital invested in bound laborers, land, and buildings that constituted the means of production. In the 15th century the Portuguese forged a general model of the system using African slaves on the Cape Verde Islands off West Africa, subsequently introducing it into Brazil. In the New World it appeared in the CARIBBEAN in the 17th century, then spread in the Americas during the next two centuries. In most colonies of English North America, British and German indentured servants made up most of the unfree laborers in the 17th century. Planters purchased thousands of transported British criminals in the 18th century, but African slaves were imported in much greater numbers in the 18th century. By the 1730s the trend was clear: The richest planters owned labor forces composed almost entirely of black slaves, and society was organized primarily along racial lines in the Tidewater coastal region of the southern colonies. Masters exercised great personal power over slaves and servants in regard to their general treatment and corporal punishment, and a slave code and other legal apparatuses backed up their authority. By 1763 organized white militias maintained the system on a day-to-day basis. If servants or slaves threatened the planters' power, as occurred in BACON'S REBELLION, soldiers could be summoned from Britain.

The successful planter put together several economic elements, but only the shrewdest and most resolute men and women could arrange these elements to best advantage. The land was the important first decision: The best lands lay in the Tidewater region extending from the CHESAPEAKE BAY to GEORGIA and in the lower Mississippi Valley's NEW ORLEANS region. These bottomlands, sometimes partially cleared by NATIVE AMERICANS, typically were rich, well watered and well drained, and located near major rivers used to transport produce. It did not take much of the best land (250 to 500 acres) to support a highly profitable enterprise, but most of the finest land was quickly bought up by the richest of the earliest colonial families, some of them owning more than 100,000 acres. They monopolized large reserves for the support of future generations, because intensive plantation AGRICULTURE exhausted the soil.

The richest planters erected imposing estates. A mansion house usually was set near the crest of a natural levee, facing the river, often with formal gardens. Barns, separate kitchens, wells, privies, and other necessities were arranged not far from the "big house" in accord with drainage requirements. An overseer's house might also exist. Beyond these premises were located the slave quarters, where slave cabins, crude and lacking in comforts, were arranged in a block pattern. However, most plantations were far more humble.

The fields required highly specific cultivation according to a strictly regulated seasonal agenda to produce rice, TOBACCO, and INDIGO. Hydraulic techniques of flood control and knowledge of rice in AFRICA enabled slaves to establish that very profitable crop along the SOUTH CAROLINA and Georgia coasts. The African tradition of hoe agriculture, with which English ploughjoggers were unfamiliar, was necessary to maximize the production of the crop. The system was a capital-intensive response to rising consumer demand for excellent VIRGINIA quality smoking and snuff tobacco—especially in Europe and particularly in France—to strong demand in southern Europe for rice, and to the demand in all ports for high-quality indigo.

As a social unit the plantation system contained contradictions in all of its relations. Planters used violence to force an arbitrarily defined "race" of people to work and to submit as the planter kept most of the profits of their labor. The plantation was divided socially in another way: Patriarch, wife, and their children lived in the big house as a family, sharply withdrawn from the traditional village life that remained important for the English gentry. Their isolation intensified as the increasing shortage of land drove nonslaveholding whites out of the Tidewater. By contrast, the slave quarters formed a communal space with kin and unmarried people living in close quarters, often with two or more generations. The plantation system was riddled with weaknesses that redounded to the benefit of slaves. Most important was the ability of most slaves to resist dehumanization and play satisfying roles in the slave community. Many also engaged in subversive social relations with other laborers and free white farmers. As a result planters had to exercise unrelenting vigilance to maintain control of the slave population. In addition, most slaves and servants had family plots of waste lands assigned by the master, and much of the best produce of these plots (hogs, fowls, greens) was purchased by planters for their own CONSUMPTION. While indentured servants had hope of getting free and even prospering in some cases, slaves generally were without hope of purchasing or otherwise gaining their freedom.

The work of bound laborers was long and grueling. Tobacco and rice required germination, transplanting, and frequent worming and weeding, followed by preparing and curing the product for export. Other seasonal activities were interspersed in the schedule of the main crop: digging drainage ditches and laying by corn, fodder, firewood, and lumber.

See also MARYLAND; SLAVERY.

Further reading: Allan Kulikoff, *Tobacco and Slaves: The Development of Southern Cultures in the Chesapeake, 1680–1800* (Chapel Hill: University of North Carolina Press, 1986); Kulikoff, *From British Peasants to Colonial American Farmers* (Chapel Hill: University of North Carolina Press, 2000); Philip D. Morgan, *Slavery Counterpoint: Black Culture in the Eighteenth-Century Chesapeake and Lowcountry* (Chapel Hill: University of North Carolina Press, 1998).

—Thomas N. Ingersoll

Plymouth

When the PILGRIMS—members of the Leiden Separatist congregation and the nondissenting "Strangers"—onboard the *Mayflower* finally reached the MASSACHUSETTS coast, they saw, in Governor WILLIAM BRADFORD's words, "a hideous and desolate wilderness, full of wild beasts and wild men." The land where the English settlers began building Plymouth had already been cleared and cultivated years before by the Wampanoag Indians. Their village, Patuxet, was destroyed by DISEASE around 1617. The only survivor, Tisquantum, or SQUANTO, had been kidnapped and brought to England before the epidemic. When he returned he found the village gone. The Pilgrims viewed the epidemic that emptied the village as a providential sign that God wanted them to establish their own town there, but it was still a struggle for the Pilgrims to build Plymouth during the first winter. Bradford wrote, "they had now no friends to welcome them nor inns to entertain or refresh their weatherbeaten bodies; no houses or much less towns to repair to, to seek for succor."

Of the 102 passengers that traveled on the *Mayflower*, four died on the voyage, and another 44 did not survive to the following spring; after that, there was never another "starving time." The first "Thanksgiving" was celebrated in the fall of 1621. It was a harvest festival attended by the English and more than 90 of their Wampanoag allies, including their leader, MASSASOIT.

The first form of government, the MAYFLOWER COMPACT, had been agreed to because the Pilgrims found themselves north of their destination, VIRGINIA, and several passengers threatened to venture out on their own. The compact was necessary for everyone's survival. In 1621 the Pierce Patent was sent to Plymouth, then replaced by the Bradford Patent in 1630. Plymouth Colony never received a royal charter. The colony finally paid off the debts to its creditors in 1644 from the profits of fur trading. The colony joined Massachusetts, CONNECTICUT, and New Haven in the New England Confederation in 1643.

Plymouth's government was similar to that of the later New England colonies: an annually elected governor, assistants, and SUFFRAGE limited to freemen admitted to full church membership. Governor Bradford held the office for nearly 30 years, documenting much of it in his thoughtful and literate history *Of Plymouth Plantation*. Governor Thomas Prence, Bradford's successor, presided over two WITCHCRAFT trials (both women were acquitted) and was a relentless persecutor of QUAKERS, although Plymouth never executed any.

Plymouth enjoyed peaceful relations with the Wampanoag through the friendship of the sachem Massasoit. He died in 1660 and was succeeded by his sons Alexander (Wamsutta) and Philip (METACOM). Alexander died within a few years, leaving Philip as sachem of the Wampanoag.

Tensions had been increasing over the years as more English towns were established, steadily encroaching upon native lands. The resulting KING PHILIP'S WAR (1675–76) destroyed nearly half the English towns in New England, including several in Plymouth Colony. The war also destroyed the native tribes as a force in southern New England.

The town of Plymouth, the colony's seat of government, lacked a deep harbor and therefore never prospered as a major port, but it did support FISHING, SHIPBUILDING, and limited trading throughout the 17th and 18th centuries. In 1685 the colony was divided into three counties, Plymouth, Bristol, and Barnstable, when the colony was included in the short-lived DOMINION OF NEW ENGLAND. The "Old Colony," with a population of about 7,400, ceased to exist as a separate entity when it was annexed under a new charter to the Province of Massachusetts Bay in 1692, but its mythology and cultural importance outlived it and continue to grow.

Further reading: John Demos, *A Little Commonwealth* (New York: Oxford University Press, 1971); George D. Langdon, Jr., *Pilgrim Colony: A History of New Plymouth, 1620–1691* (New Haven, Conn.: Yale University Press, 1966).

—Stephen C. O'Neill

Pocahontas (1595?–1617)

Pocahontas was a nickname that translates roughly as "the willful one." Her proper names included Matoaka, possibly Amonute, Rebecca Rolfe, and Mrs. JOHN ROLFE. She was a POWHATAN–Renape diplomat, a cultural mediator, a favored daughter of Wahunsonakok (Powhatan) and, later, the wife of planter John Rolfe.

Whether by choice, accident, or her father's will, Matoaka crossed the boundary into English life to mediate relationships between the JAMESTOWN colonists and the Powhatan. The colony's secretary, William Strachey, noted 11-year-old Pocahontas's first appearance: "sometymes resorting to our Fort . . . gett [ing] the boyes [to go] forth with her into the markett place and make them wheele, falling on their hands turning their heeles upwards, whome she would follow, and wheele so her self naked as she was all the fort over." During JOHN SMITH'S CAPTIVITY by the Powhatan in December 1607, Pocahontas participated in Smith's mock execution, part of a ceremony that initiated him into the tribe and confirmed his role as werowance (subchief), thereby symbolically transforming Jamestown into a subject village under Powhatan's rule. Pocahontas ritually interceded on Smith's behalf during the ceremony ("when no intreaty could prevaile, got his head in her armes, and laid her own upon his to save him from death"), thereby becoming Smith's sponsor into tribal membership.

Perhaps because of her ties to Smith, Pocahontas assumed a special responsibility for English-Indian relations. During the starving months of 1608, after the English storehouses had burned down, Pocahontas and her attendants regularly brought the colonists FOOD "that saved many of their lives, that els[e] for all this [would] had starved." Pocahontas also served as an intermediary between Powhatan and Smith. In May 1608, after Smith raided several villages and took Indian hostages, Powhatan dispatched Pocahontas, who successfully negotiated their release. Pocahontas's mediation, however, could not prevent the outbreak of major hostilities between the two peoples, which occurred when Powhatan and Smith failed to agree upon an exchange of Indian corn for English goods. Stranded after a disgruntled Powhatan precipitously removed himself and his people from Werowocomoco when negotiations failed, Smith was saved by Pocahontas who, in defiance of her father's orders, secretly returned to warn him of an impending attack by her people.

After Smith's departure in 1609, Pocahontas disappeared from the colony. Secretary Strachey claimed that in 1610 she married Kocoum, a "pryvate Captayne" and supporter of Powhatan, but the marriage may have involved another of Powhatan's daughters, several of whom carried the same nickname. By 1613 Pocahontas was living with the Patawamake along the Potomoc River, where Captain Argall, leading an English expedition in search of trading partners, found her. Conspiring with the Patawamake headman, Iapazaws, Argall lured Pocahontas aboard his ship and forcibly took her as a hostage to Jamestown, where Governor Dale hoped she would persuade Powhatan to release the English hostages, swords, and firearms he had captured. Pocahontas refused to participate in the negotiations but, possibly irked by Powhatan's tough bargaining, accepted her stay on the English side of the cultural boundary. "If her father had loved her," Governor Dale recounted, "he would not value her lesse then old Swords, Peeces, or Axes: wherefore shee should still dwell with the Englishmen, who loved her." Even so, she was not an eager convert to English ways. Dale and Reverend Alexander Whitaker "laboured a long time" to induce Pocahontas to renounce "publickly her countrey Idolatry" and embrace the Christian faith, taking the baptismal name Rebecca.

John Rolfe, her suitor during the captivity, agonized over his decision to marry the now Christian Pocahontas. The colonists hitherto had rebuffed offers to marry Indian women because English sensibilities concerning civility, decorum, and the proper station of men and women were offended by Powhatan women's monopoly of agricultural work, the flexible division of LABOR in the Powhatan vil-

Native American princess Pocahontas in European dress *(Hulton/Archive)*

lages, and the sexual openness displayed by Powhatan of both genders. Rolfe finally surrendered to his passions, as he wrote Governor Dale, "for the good of the Plantacon, the honor of or Countrye, for the glorye of God, for myne owne salvacon." His marriage to Rebecca in 1614, therefore, was a significant cultural concession by the English to Indian ethnic sensitivities and resulted in an eight-year truce with the Powhatan. Despite the hope of some English writers that Rolfe and Rebecca would become the progenitors of a new, Christian American people, there was no accompanying rush by xenophobic English men to marry Indian women. The 18th-century VIRGINIA historian ROBERT BEVERLEY felt that the absence of widespread intermarriage was the single greatest cause of the inexorable conflict between the two peoples.

After three years in the colony and the birth of their son, Thomas, in 1615, the young couple was summoned to London by the directors of the Virginia Company to serve as advertisements of the company's successes. In 1616 the Rolfes sailed to England accompanied by Governor Dale, Rebecca's highborn Indian attendants, and Uttamatamakin (Tomocommo), Powhatan's representative, charged with ascertaining the fate of John Smith. During their seven-month stay the couple was received by London society "with festivall, state, and pompe," and feted to a whirlwind of celebrations, interviews, masques, and possibly audiences with Queen Anne and King James. In early 1617 Rebecca fell critically ill, possibly with tuberculosis or pneumonia, and Rolfe removed her to Brentford, where Smith called on her for the last time. Her final, bittersweet words to Smith perhaps reflected her stress and equivocation about returning to Virginia and facing the onerous task of persuading her countrymen to abandon their religious and cultural practices and accept English ways: "your Countriemen will lie much. . . . You did promise Powhatan what was yours should be his, and he the like to you; you called him father, being in his land a stranger, and by the same reason so must I to you. . . . I should call you father . . . and you shall call me child, and so I will be for ever and ever, your countrymen."

The Rolfes departed London in March 1617, reaching only Gravesend at the mouth of the Thames, where Pocahontas died. Rolfe left their son, Thomas, in the care and guardianship of Sir Lewis Stukly and returned to Virginia, where he served as a colonial officer and TOBACCO planter until he was killed by Pocahontas's countrymen during Opechancanough's attack of 1622. Thomas Rolfe, the son of John and Pocahontas, returned to Virginia as a young man in 1635 to reclaim his father's lands.

Further reading: Karen Ordahl Kuppermann, *Indians & English: Facing Off in Early America* (Ithaca, N.Y.: Cornell University Press, 2000); Robert S. Tilton, *Pocahontas: The Evolution of an American Narrative* (Cambridge, Mass.: Harvard University Press, 1994).

—James Bruggeman

Pontiac's Rebellion See volume III

Popé (1630?–1690?)

Little is known about the early life of Popé, the man who led the PUEBLO REVOLT of 1680. He was born in the Tewa-speaking village of San Juan around 1630. By that time Spanish colonizers had lived among the Pueblo for more than a generation, demanding labor and crops from the villages and suppressing traditional religious rites and ceremonies. As a young man Popé seems to have been a war chief in San Juan and would have been keenly aware of the risks of defying Spanish rule. Several other villages initiated rebellions during his youth, and the Spaniards crushed them all.

By the 1660s and 1670s, when drought and famine threatened the entire valley, Popé was perhaps the principal religious figure in his community. Through elaborate rituals, he openly appealed to the traditional Pueblo gods for rain and relief. Leaders in other villages did the same, and in 1675 Spanish authorities arrested them for WITCHCRAFT. Three were executed. Popé and 42 others were flogged in public, and they would have been sold into SLAVERY except that a large party of Pueblo warriors demanded their release. Once freed, Popé withdrew to Taos Pueblo and began quietly forging alliances that would lead to one of the most successful pan-Indian uprisings in North American history.

Popé's brilliant leadership depended on his gifts for explanation and organization. All the valley's troubles, he insisted, could be traced to the Spanish. The droughts, crop failures, famine, mysterious disease, and increasing Apache attacks were all consequences of the Spanish presence and the corresponding neglect of traditional religion. The Europeans' insatiable demand for land, LABOR, and tribute only compounded problems. The way to regain the blessings their ancestors had enjoyed, he explained, was to kill the Spaniards and erase their memory from the valley. To convey his message and coordinate the resistance, Popé tirelessly repeated his arguments and enlisted other native leaders throughout the Rio Grande Valley, forging a consensus that had been missing in earlier revolts. Not all villages participated, and some actively worked against him, but Popé secured enough support for a successful general uprising in August 1680.

With 500 Spaniards dead and the rest in retreat, Popé traveled throughout the valley calling for the destruction of all vestiges of Spanish culture and religion. Conflicts arose even amidst the celebrations. Many villagers insisted on retaining Spanish ANIMALS and crops. Moreover, the promised rains did not come, and the region endured another decade of drought. Local disagreements reemerged, and villagers began to question Popé's promises. He lost his position of leadership in San Juan and died sometime around 1690, after his hard-won consensus collapsed, but before the Spaniards returned to reconquer his people.

See also SPANISH COLONIES.

Further reading: Charles Wilson Hackett, ed., *Revolt of the Pueblo Indians* (Albuquerque: University of New Mexico Press, 1942); Joe S. Sando, *Popé, Architect of the First American Revolution* (Santa Fe: Clearlight Publishers, 1998).

—Brian DeLay

population trends

Between 1585 and 1763 the population of British North America increased enormously as growing numbers of Europeans and Africans replaced declining numbers of NATIVE AMERICANS. The best estimates are that the colonies contained approximately 4,600 people of European and African descent in 1630, a quarter million in 1700, and slightly more than 2 million on the eve of the Revolution.

Scholars disagree about the number of Indians who lived north of the Rio Grande before contact with Europeans. Estimates vary from 1 to 13 million inhabitants. Contact with Europeans had a disastrous impact on Native Americans. Common European childhood diseases, such as whooping cough, measles, and especially SMALLPOX, killed tens of thousands of Indians, who had not been previously exposed to these illnesses. Indeed, these diseases often killed Native Americans who had never even seen a white person, because the pathogens that caused these illnesses—often unknowingly carried by natives who had been infected through contact with whites—frequently preceded the arrival of Europeans.

The first English colonists at Roanoke, unaware that they carried pathogens to which the natives had no resistance, noted that Indians often became sick and died. English commercial anglers went ashore in present-day New England in the 1610s to dry their catch and trade with the natives; in the process, they passed diseases to the local peoples. By the time the PILGRIMS arrived in the area in 1620, DISEASE had killed so many native people that one English trader, noting the skeletons and abandoned wigwams that littered the landscape, called it a "new found Golgotha."

Disease, however, did not affect only those who died; it also devastated those who survived. When a large number of people in a community fell ill, the healthy often fled, hoping to avoid the contagion. If they went to another village, they unwittingly carried the disease with them. Disease on a large scale meant that no one was available to tend fires, carry water, prepare FOOD, or care for the sick. If crops were not harvested, the survival of the community after the epidemic was jeopardized. Women who survived disease were less likely to bear children, thereby affecting future generations. Indians in the interior of the country usually had sufficient time to renew their population before facing the onslaught of European settlers. However, East Coast natives sometimes found that the combination of population decline caused by diseases and the aggressive seizure of land by white settlers were too intense to survive.

Among European colonists population growth varied over time and space, although it generally increased rapidly due both to immigration and natural increase (the difference between the number of births and deaths). In New England, despite the 50 percent MORTALITY rate in the first few years among the Pilgrims, the population grew rapidly.

The arrival of migrants in family groups, the general good health of the region, and the widespread availability of land all encouraged high fertility and low mortality rates. It was not uncommon for settlers to survive into their 70s, much longer than their counterparts in the mother country. Many lived long enough to exert control over their adult children and to see their grandchildren—another rarity in England. In addition, waves of immigrants increased the number of inhabitants. From a population of 14,000 in 1640, the New England population multiplied to perhaps 87,000 by 1690. It continued to expand, albeit at a somewhat slower rate, during the 18th century.

In sharp contrast to New England, the white population of the Chesapeake area colonies did not increase rapidly in the early 17th century. Indeed, the English population actually declined during the initial decades of settlement. Between 1625 and 1640 15,000 people immigrated to VIRGINIA, yet only 8,000 whites lived in the colony in 1640. Unlike New England, where entire families immigrated, most immigrants to the Chesapeake area were single males arriving as indentured servants. The resulting GENDER imbalance, with males at times outnumbering females by seven to one, created very low birth rates. In addition, because large planters concentrated almost entirely on raising TOBACCO rather than foodstuffs, diets were often inadequate. Diseases like malaria, common in a hot, damp climate, as well as shallow wells poisoned by saltwater, also took a high toll on human life. Not until the end of the 17th century did the number of births exceed the number of deaths in the Chesapeake area colonies. One stabilizing factor in this period was the constant replenishment, both in settlers and in indentured servants, from England. Unlike New England, the British population of the Chesapeake area did not become self-reproducing until the 18th century, but the population then grew relatively rapidly until the War for Independence.

The Middle Colonies experienced enormous growth resulting from both natural increase and migration. While NEW YORK and NEW JERSEY had steady, although not spectacular, rates of population growth, PENNSYLVANIA, founded in 1681, contained the second largest population in British North America by 1770 and the largest white population by 1780. Much of Pennsylvania's demographic increase in the 18th century can be attributed to the influx of large numbers of German settlers, who by the 1750s accounted for a third of the colony's population. Their huge numbers, language, and observance of German customs caused some uneasiness among English colonists. Benjamin Franklin, for example, worried that Pennsylvania would soon become a "Colony of Aliens." Pennsylvania was also the destination of thousands of Scots, Irish, and Scots-Irish immigrants, most of whom headed for the frontier and the land available there.

The 18th-century black slave population of British North America was unique in that it was the only bound population in the New World that reproduced itself. However, this reproduction did not begin in the 17th century. Throughout the first half of the 17th century newly arrived African slaves suffered high mortality rates. Many died within five years after landing in the Chesapeake area as disease, inadequate diets, depression, and brutal working conditions took their toll. After the Middle Passage many Africans were in poor health on arriving in the colonies. The African population in the Chesapeake area was small in the early 17th century because planters invested in less expensive white indentured servants rather than African slaves. After 1675, as planters turned to purchasing African slaves, their population increased substantially. By the end of the first decades of the 18th century, slaves had formed sufficiently stable communities and marriages to enable them to reproduce their numbers. Their population was continually augmented by newly purchased slaves from abroad, as more than 250,000 blacks were brought into America between 1700 and 1775. Indeed, more Africans than Europeans arrived in British America in the 18th century.

The slave population in SOUTH CAROLINA exploded in the early 18th century, once planters found that rice was a profitable crop and that they could purchase slaves relatively inexpensively. In some rice cultivation areas blacks accounted for 80 to 90 percent of the inhabitants. Bond-

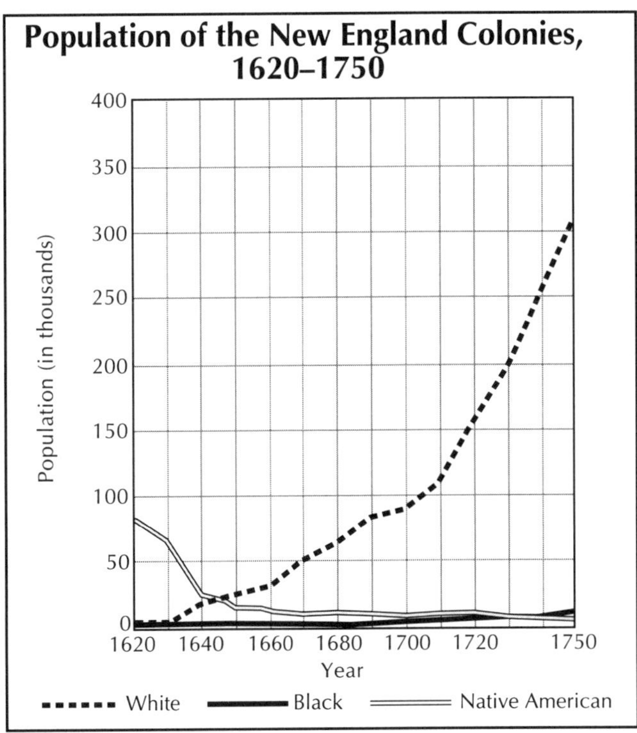

people were forced to labor in very hazardous conditions, detrimental to their health, on those plantations. The only advantage that some enjoyed was partial immunity to malaria.

By the 1730s AFRICAN AMERICANS made up about 15 percent of the population of NEW YORK CITY and accounted for about 8 percent of BOSTON's population. By the mid-18th century African Americans constituted one-third of the people living in the coastal areas stretching from the CHESAPEAKE BAY to GEORGIA. On the eve of the American Revolution one of every five colonists was black.

Further reading: Robert V. Wells, *Revolutions in Americans' Lives: A Demographic Perspective on the History of Americans, Their Families, and Their Society* (Westport, Conn.: Greenwood Press, 1982).

—Roger Carpenter

postal service

Mail was vital for colonists' economic, political, and social interactions. Correspondence connected the colonists with people throughout the colonies and with family and officials in Great Britain, Europe, and other parts of the world. The colonial postal service encouraged the distribution of information, raw materials, and finished goods within the colonies and abroad. Mail meant that colonists were less isolated socially and culturally and had more immediate access to news and information. As the postal service expanded, roads were improved and extended into remote areas, and industries were built on these routes, contributing to local economies.

Senders often wrote messages on scraps of paper, which they folded, sealed with wax, and addressed with the recipient's name and geographic location. Because postage stamps were not sold until the mid-19th century, recipients either paid for the mail that was sent to them (fees were based on the number of sheets and distance conveyed) or refused letters and packages. Such costs prevented many colonists from participating in the postal system. Enslaved AFRICAN AMERICANS were forbidden to write and lacked incomes to purchase paper and pens. Indentured servants also were mostly excluded from the postal system's benefits, as were poorer settlers and residents on the isolated frontiers in the South and West.

The primary colonial postal patrons were prominent, educated white men living in urban areas who could afford writing supplies and postal fees; some affluent colonial women also sent and received mail. These postal customers had reasons to use the postal system, such as engaging in political and commercial professions. Newspapers and advertisements were circulated by the mail, and some nefarious individuals used the postal system to commit such crimes as mail fraud or even to threaten people. Colonial leaders recorded their philosophical thoughts and concerns in correspondence, which has been preserved in archives and annotated for scholarly use.

Initially, colonists depended on travelers and MERCHANTS to transport letters and packages by walking or driving stagecoaches on land or sailing vessels on rivers and canals. NATIVE AMERICANS occasionally acted as messengers, and mail to and from Britain relied on ships. Because the British traditionally used pubs as mail drops, the general court of MASSACHUSETTS selected Richard Fairbanks's BOSTON tavern as the colonies' first central postal site in 1639. Colonists could both receive and send mail from Fairbanks's tavern. Inns served as additional postal sites, and surveyors designated post roads between the colonies, although delivery was often erratic, especially in remote regions where roads were often swampy.

King Charles II (1660–85) ordered Francis Lovelace and JOHN WINTHROP, the governors of NEW YORK and CONNECTICUT, to initiate a mail route between New York and Boston to encourage colonists to correspond frequently. In January 1673 the first post rider traveled for three weeks on this assignment, and his duties included carrying mail, looking for military deserters and runaway slaves, helping fellow travelers, and identifying useful river crossings. After eight months this postal service was terminated.

The British Crown granted funds to create a postal service in 1691. NEW JERSEY Governor ANDREW HAMILTON served as the first colonial deputy postmaster general. By 1737 Alexander Spotswood served in that position and appointed Benjamin Franklin as postmaster for PHILADELPHIA. Sixteen years later Franklin and William Hunter, the Williamsburg, VIRGINIA, postmaster, were named as joint postmasters general of the colonies. Franklin inspected post offices, established regular postal schedules, and initiated surveys of postal roads to determine shorter routes and expand services. In an effort to achieve more efficient delivery, he ordered post riders to TRAVEL at night between Philadelphia and New York.

Franklin also created the position of surveyor, a predecessor to the later Postal Inspection Service. He made the postal system profitable for the British. Colonists, however, were distressed by expensive postal rates, which they viewed as unfair taxation and monopolistic; Franklin attempted to explain that postal fees paid for services that were unrelated to the Stamp Tax of 1765. Because of his pro-Independence political views, however, the British Crown dismissed Franklin in 1774 despite his effective reforms and defense of postal costs. William Goddard created the Constitutional Post, a subscription postal system that colonial committees oversaw.

In July 1775 the Second Continental Congress established a Post Office Department and appointed Franklin as postmaster general. While many colonists sought independence from Great Britain, Franklin built the American postal service's foundation, which has remained essentially unchanged in the centuries since. Many modern postage stamps depict colonial figures and events, such as Christopher Columbus's arrival in the CARIBBEAN.

Further reading: Carl H. Scheele, *A Short History of the Mail Service* (Washington, D.C.: Smithsonian Institution Press, 1970).

—Elizabeth D. Schafer

Pott, John (1591–1642)

A physician, John Pott also served as governor of VIRGINIA. He was born in 1591 in Macclesfield, Cheshire, England, but little else is known about his early life. By age 30, he had become a doctor and had married Elizabeth (maiden name unknown). In early 1621 Pott was hired by the VIRGINIA COMPANY OF LONDON to serve as a physician in the colony as well as to sit on its governing council. By November Pott and his wife had arrived in JAMESTOWN. Within a decade he had increased his small estate to a plantation outside Jamestown nearing 2,000 acres, which he named "Harrop."

Pott's career in Virginia was defined by struggle against rampant DISEASE and equally troublesome faction-ridden politics. In August 1624 he was removed from the council, having been accused by his enemies of poisoning local NATIVE AMERICANS. He was restored, however, less than two years later after allied members of the council wrote to London complaining that Pott had been the victim of a smear campaign. The height of Pott's political career came in March 1629, when he was elected governor of the colony. His tenure was short-lived and generally uneventful. By the following March he had been replaced by Sir John Harvey. They clashed almost immediately. A few months later Pott was dismissed from the council and confined to his estate by orders of the governor. An enraged and armed Pott was said to have attacked Harvey, who put him in prison. In response Pott's wife and friends in the council called on the Privy Council in England to have him released, declaring that he had been mistreated. Harvey circumvented these requests by asking the king to pardon Pott, which he did. Within a year Pott had regained his lands, previously forfeited under the terms of the pardon. His animosity toward Harvey intensified as fellow planters grew incensed with Harvey's conduct. In 1635 Pott instigated a mini-rebellion. Sympathy for the planters was short-lived, and upon arriving in London to plead their case, Pott's brother Francis was arrested. The consequences for Pott are unknown, but by keeping a low profile thereafter he seems to have maintained his lands, which he passed to his brother upon his death in 1642.

—Troy O. Bickham

Powhatan (1540?–1618)

Wahunsonacock, or Powhatan, was the founder and supreme chieftain (Mamanatowick) of Tsenacommacah ("densely inhabited land"), a strong Tidewater ALGONQUIN empire, which he forged through conquest, intimidation, and diplomacy during the last quarter of the 16th century. Born into a matrilineal clan of werowances (leading chiefs), Wahunsonacock inherited six to eight village territories in the area of what is now Richmond, VIRGINIA, acquiring his English name—Powhatan—from the most prominent village. Exploiting the depopulation and instability caused by the ravages of European diseases and the effects of climatic change on Indian AGRICULTURE, Wahunsonacock extended his control over another 31 village territories, an accomplishment reflecting a preexisting trend among the coastal Algonquin groups toward greater political consolidation and territorial expansion. From his capital, Werowocomoco, Wahunsonacock ruled by placing sons, brothers, and kinsmen as werowances in the principal villages, thereby creating a chiefdom encompassing 8,000 square miles, probably the largest and most politically complex society east of the Appalachians before European settlement.

At the apogee of his powers, Wahunsonacock dealt confidently with the tiny, squabbling band of starving English who established JAMESTOWN in 1607. The Powhatan overlord sought to incorporate Jamestown into his network of subject villages and assimilate the English colonists into the Powhatan culture through intimidation, gifts of FOOD, and offers of intermarriage. Likewise, the English sought to transform the Powhatan into compliant allies, trading partners, and pious Christians through the enticements of European trade goods and, if necessary, displays of English firearms. Between 1607 and 1609 Wahunsonacock and JOHN SMITH scrutinized each other's intentions, tested each other's military strength, and struggled to understand each other's culture and language in order to find common ground upon which to coexist. The xenophobic English rebuffed Powhatan offers of social intimacy and kinship through intermarriage. Commercial propensities also blinded the English to the fact that the Powhatan gifts of food and assistance, upon which Jamestown desperately depended for its survival, were regarded by the Powhatan not as capitalist economic exchanges involving profit and loss, but rather as traditional Algonquin social exchanges entailing obligations of reciprocity whose goal was to bind together the two peoples. Similarly, the Powhatan were indifferent to Christianity, annoyed by the English refusal to sell them firearms, and insulted by the English insistence that the Powhatan give corn for whatever the English chose to offer.

At their critical and final meeting at Worowocomoco in January 1609, both Smith and Wahunsonacock realized that the price for peace based on trade and cultural assimilation was too great for each side to pay. Failing to find a mutually acceptable and voluntary mode of exchange, Smith began to extort desperately needed foodstuffs by intimidating Powhatan villages, taking hostages, and manhandling village werowances. Finally convinced that the English had come "to destroy my Countrie," Wahunsonacock was drawn, albeit reluctantly, into the first Anglo-Powhatan War. This cruel and bloody genocide raged on until 1613, when the capture and Christian conversion of Wahunsonacock's favored daughter, POCAHONTAS, and the destruction of Powhatan forces in the field forced the Powhatan chieftain to accept a humiliating peace treaty. By the conclusion of hostilities in 1614, the English, then under the command of SIR THOMAS DALE and Sir Gates, had wrested effective control of the James River Valley from the CHESAPEAKE BAY to the fall line near present-day Richmond.

Broken by defeat and weakened by age, Wahunsonacock retreated into domestic life, allowing leadership of the Powhatan peoples to slip to his relatives OPECHANCANOUGH and Opitchapam. "I am old," he admitted to John Smith during their crucial January 1609 encounter, "and ere long must die. . . . I knowe it is better to eat good meat, lie well, and sleep with my women and children, laugh and be merrie . . . then [to] be forced to flie . . . and be hunted." Grief-stricken by news of Pocahontas's death in England in 1617, the once great overlord waned into a shadow of his former greatness. Wahunsonacock died in April 1618, a sad supplicant to the English colonists who in 1607 he could so easily have destroyed.

Further reading: Karen Ordhal Kupperman, *Indians and English: Facing Off in Early America* (Ithaca, N.Y.: Cornell University Press, 2000).

—James Bruggeman

Powhatan Confederacy

The English settlers who established a colony at JAMESTOWN in 1607 faced Wahunsonacock, a powerful ALGONQUIN paramount chief. He controlled an 8,000-square-mile area from the fall line to CHESAPEAKE BAY and from the James River basin to just south of the Potomac River, an area encompassing more than 14,000 people and more than 30 tribal groups, including the Pamunkey, Appomatuc, Paspahegh, Kecoughtan, and the POWHATAN (Wahunsonacock's home group), from which the English derived their name for him and his confederacy. Known to its inhabitants as Tsenacommacah ("densely inhabited land"), this strong Tidewater Algonquin polity was among the most politically complex tribal societies east of the Appalachians at the time of European arrival.

The Powhatan tribes shared many cultural traits with other Algonquin-speaking peoples along the Atlantic coast, but Powhatan government and society under Wahunsonacock were more autocratic and aristocratic than some of the northern Algonquin groups. Other coastal Indian societies in the late 16th century, such as the Roanoke under WINGINA, were experiencing similar political consolidation, territorial expansion, and CLASS differentiation as chief matrilineages accumulated hereditary power, territory, and riches. Wahunsonacock ruled from his capital, Werowocomoco, by placing sons, brothers, and relatives as werowances (subchiefs) over the principal villages and then exacting, but also redistributing, tribute from the villages under their control. Wahunsonacock's authority was enhanced by the fact that he, his werowances, and his priests (*quiyoughquisocks*) were considered lesser gods (*quioccasuks*). His divinely enhanced power was tempered somewhat by his need to seek the advice and support of a council of priests and werowances. Furthermore, the powerful Chickahominy, while accepting Wahunsonacock as their overlord, ruled themselves through their own council. Just before his death in 1618, Wahunsonacock resumed the tradition of dual chiefdoms. He appointed as his successors an inside chief (Itoyatan), who dealt with the council and internal tribal affairs, and a war, or diplomatic, chief (OPECHANCANOUGH), who dealt with outsiders and external affairs.

The VIRGINIA colony's aristocratic leadership closely examined Powhatan society, hoping to find social and political demarcations that would mirror and thereby validate those of traditional English society. Although misinterpreting many features of Powhatan society, the English elite found much that met their approval. The Powhatan were a settled, agricultural people who lived in villages ruled by "kings" and a hereditary caste of the "better sort," who in turn were ruled by "emperor" Wahunsonacock. Other features displayed by these "civil savages" assured, but also disturbed, the English. The English happily perceived that Powhatan society was built around a core of religious values, beliefs, and practices focused on the worship of Okee, but, in English eyes, Powhatan religion was pagan, and the Powhatan would dwell in "darkness" until brought into the "light" of Christianity. Likewise, the Powhatan seemed to respect GENDER differences, honor marriage, and form ordered families, yet the English were incensed that Powhatan women bore sole responsibility for planting, cultivating, harvesting, and preserving crops, which in England was men's work. They clearly misunderstood the power and esteem that traditional matrilineal descent and women's monopoly of agricultural work provided Powhatan women. Although they saw the virtues of Powhatan society as a "living reproach to England," the English pointed to Powhatan paganism and the perceived exploitation of Indian women as justification for colonization. The xenophobic and insecure English leaders also were uncomfortable and abrasive around Indians and spurned Powhatan overtures of social intimacy, particularly intermarriage. The VIRGINIA colony's lower-class laborers and servants, on the other hand, were far less queasy with Powhatan ways, and in the early years they often deserted, sometimes en masse, to live among them.

During the early years of the Jamestown colony, the Powhatan and the English made mutual efforts to "civilize," dominate, and incorporate each other into their respective societies through military intimidation, political ritual, trade, negotiation, and religious persuasion. Both Powhatan and English staged displays of affectionate friendship alternating with acts of military aggression to persuade or intimidate in ways that the other deemed "civil." The Powhatan captured, adopted, and anointed JOHN SMITH as a werowance of Capahowasick, just as Captain Newport crowned a reluctant Wahunsonacock as a subsidiary monarch to James I. Smith and his successors conducted extensive but ultimately fruitless negotiations to find a mutually acceptable basis for trade of the Indian foodstuffs essential for English survival in return for the European manufactured goods and firearms coveted by the Powhatan. English clergy labored tirelessly among the Indians, even establishing a college to educate Powhatan children, but the proudly ethnocentric Powhatan, led by charismatic priests such as Nemattanew, tenaciously resisted English proselytizing. POCAHONTAS's conversion to Christianity and marriage to JOHN ROLFE in 1613 produced a temporary peace between the two peoples but only a trickle of converts, and many Powhatan who imitated her apostasy did so selectively, adopting only those Christian beliefs and practices that fit into their traditional religious worldview.

Aggressive proselytizing, the increasing expansion of English settlement on Indian lands, and the murder of Nemattanew by the English provoked Powhatan war chief Opechancanough into launching a devastating surprise attack on English settlements in 1622. The ensuing Anglo-Powhatan War ground on for a decade, resulting in a qualified victory for the Powhatans, who temporarily were able to preserve their way of life, yet their resistance tipped even sympathetic English authorities toward a long-standing policy in British America of expelling Indians from lands coveted by whites and segregating them from white colonists in what were to become the first Indian reservations.

English settlers, hungry for land on which to grow highly lucrative TOBACCO, continued to encroach on Powhatan lands. Opechancanough consequently led another desperate attack on the English plantations in 1644. This conflict ultimately ended in Opechancanough's murder while in English CAPTIVITY, and the Powhatan, in the words of the report of the Virginia assembly, were "so routed and dispersed that they are no longer a nation." DISEASE, warfare, and constant killings by white settlers reduced the Powhatan population from about 15,000 in 1607 to fewer than 2,000 in 1669. Murder and enslavement of Powhatan, both friendly and hostile, by English settlers during and after BACON'S REBELLION in 1675 further diminished Powhatan power, morale, and unity. By the middle of the 18th century the tattered remnants of the once mighty confederation, largely 700 to 1,000 Pamunkey and Mattaponi, were confined to two reservations, where they intermarried with fugitive white servants and runaway African slaves. Others were banished to the margins of white society, where they eked out a living as servants and day laborers.

The Powhatan survived European colonization. Today, members of the Accomac, Chickahominy, Nansemond, Potomac, Rappahannock, Werowocomoco, Nanticoke, and Wicocomoco bands are scattered throughout communities in Virginia and NEW JERSEY. The Powhatan-Renape band lives in the Delaware Valley of PENNSYLVANIA. Only the Mattaponi and Pamunkey retain the state reservation lands that are the legacy of Opechancanough's defeat.

Further reading: Frederic W. Gleach, *Powhatan's World and Colonial Virginia: A Conflict of Cultures* (Lincoln: University of Nebraska Press, 1997); Helen C. Rountree, *The Powhatan Indians of Virginia through Four Centuries* (Norman, Okla.: University of Oklahoma Press, 1990).

—James Bruggeman

praying towns

As part of its colonial charter, the MASSACHUSETTS BAY COMPANY was required by the English Crown to convert NATIVE AMERICANS to Christianity. Although the PURITANS had made permanent settlements in New England in the 1630s, they placed little priority initially on converting Indians. By the 1640s the Crown began to criticize Puritans for not fulfilling this part of their obligations. Building on the traditions of the Spanish Franciscan MISSIONS of Latin America and the French Jesuit mission villages in Canada, the English began to establish villages set apart from both English towns and Indian communities. Thomas Mayhew and JOHN ELIOT were two of the pioneers of these praying towns. Mayhew established a praying town on Martha's Vineyard, while Eliot established numerous villages throughout New England. While each town served a different population of Indians and had its own particular history, they all served the same fundamental purpose: to eradicate native religious and social practices that strayed from the English standard.

Unlike the JESUITS and Franciscans, these ministers were Protestant, not from a monastic order, and funded by the British Crown. Like the Jesuits and Franciscans, they served a religious and social function. To teach Indians about Christianity, they translated the Bible and prayer books into Indian languages. They also required that Indians abandon their non-Christian relatives, live in European-style homes, and give up traditional hunting and farming techniques for European-style AGRICULTURE. Indian men were required to cut their hair and take up farming, traditionally women's work among New England Indians. Women were expected to be subservient to their husbands, in accordance with English rather than Indian norms. On the surface the goal of the towns was to instruct the Indians well enough that the town might be considered a congregation, that is, a collection of "saints," or individuals accepted by God for salvation. This Puritan notion suggested the possibility that Indian praying towns might be considered equal with English congregations, yet the acceptance of these towns as congregations was relatively rare. Many historians have argued that the racism of the Puritans prevented them from fully accepting Christian Indians as religious equals, regardless of their willingness to abandon traditional dress, hairstyle, and social organization.

The English missionary effort suffered a severe blow in the wake of KING PHILIP'S WAR in 1676. Although the English eventually defeated their Wampanoag enemies with the help of praying town Indians, the event triggered fear and resentment of Indians among the colonists, and they dismantled most of the mission villages in New England. The remaining villagers were forced to return to their traditional communities or seek refuge among other tribes to the north.

Further reading: Neal Salisbury, *Manitou and Providence: Indians, Europeans, and the Making of New England, 1500–1643* (New York: Oxford University Press, 1982); George Tinker, *Missionary Conquest: The Gospel and Native American Cultural Genocide* (Minneapolis, Minn.: Fortress Press, 1993).

—Thomas J. Lappas

Presbyterians

Presbyterians are Protestants whose congregations are governed by elders ("presbyters") elected by their membership. These elders govern collectively, as a session, with some of them chosen as representatives to the local presbytery, the regional synod, and the national general assembly. Presbyterians trace their origins to 16th-century Geneva, where John Calvin instituted a rudimentary form of Presbyterianism. Their theological distinctions are summarized in the Westminster Confession (1647) and Shorter (1647) and Larger (1648) Catechisms. English Puritans were too divided to impose these tenets on the Church of England, but they were adopted by the Church of Scotland and later by breakaway denominations in Scotland as well as by daughter churches in America.

The first Presbyterian church in what became the United States was established in Hempstead, NEW YORK, in 1644, with others soon following in Newark (1667), PHILADELPHIA (1692), and elsewhere along the mid-Atlantic coast. Francis Makemie, a Scots-Irish missionary recognized as the father of American Presbyterianism, arrived in 1683. In 1706 he led in organizing the Presbytery of Philadelphia, serving as its first moderator; in 1716 this was reorganized as the Synod of Philadelphia. Most of its growth stemmed from the influx of Scots-Irish immigrants and the southward surge of New England Puritans. While the Scots-Irish generally stressed the centrality of doctrinal orthodoxy as defined by fidelity to the Westminster Confession, New Englanders generally urged the secondary status of all standards other than the Bible and emphasized the centrality of "experimental" (experiential) religion. Tensions between the two were temporarily eased by the Adopting Act of 1729, in which the synod embraced Westminster as its doctrinal standard while making room for those with scruples about nonessential aspects of Westminster's teaching.

These wings endured a painful separation during the GREAT AWAKENING. Experience-oriented Presbyterians, dubbed New Lights, welcomed the revival as God's work, while doctrine-oriented Presbyterians, dubbed Old Lights, saw New Light excesses as reason enough to reject it outright. At the synod's 1741 meeting the Old Lights revoked the Adopting Act and ousted most New Light ministers. Prorevival Presbyterianism now entered a period of accelerated growth; in 1745 New Lights organized the Synod of New York, and a year later they founded the College of New Jersey, Princeton University's predecessor, primarily to provide their congregations with well-educated pastors. Meanwhile, antirevival Presbyterianism experienced stagnation and numerical decline that eventually forced the Old Lights' reconciliation with the New Lights on the latter's terms. In 1758 their synods merged to form the Synod of New York and Philadelphia.

Further reading: Randall Balmer and John R. Fitzmier, *The Presbyterians* (Westport, Conn.: Greenwood Press, 1993); Leonard J. Trinterud, *The Forming of an American*

Tradition: A Reexamination of Colonial Presbyterianism (Philadelphia: Westminster Press, 1949).

—George W. Harper

Priber, Christian Gottlieb (1697–1744?)

Christian Gottlieb Priber was a utopian philosopher who advocated a radically different society while living among the CHEROKEE Indians. Despite contemporary and subsequent suspicions that he was a French agent or a French Jesuit, Christian Priber was, in fact, born in Zittau, Saxony, the son of Friedrich Priber, publican and linen merchant, and Anna Dorothea Bergmann. His early career saw him gain a doctorate in jurisprudence at Erfurt University, after which he returned to Zittau to practice law and to marry Christiane Dorothea Hoffman, with whom he had had five children by 1732. By 1735 Priber, who claimed to have fled persecution for his beliefs, was at CHARLESTON. A 500-mile journey over the Appalachians took him to Great Tellico, a principal town of the Cherokee. It was here, after learning the local language, altering his physical appearance to conform with local custom, and gaining the trust and affection of the local Cherokee, that he began (filled with fashionable contemporary notions about the "noble savage") to build what was described as his "Kingdom of Paradise." In this utopian state there was to be equality of the sexes, communal care of children, communal possession of all property (which was to be distributed strictly according to need), and a radically limited legal code. Priber's suggestion that the Cherokee begin to trade on equal terms with both the English and the French and his teaching the Cherokee the use of weights and measures to protect themselves from dishonest merchants annoyed the local English authorities. After several failed attempts to capture him, Priber was finally seized by a group of Creek in 1743, taken to Fort Frederica, and interrogated by JAMES OGLETHORPE. It was at Frederica that, in all likelihood, he died.

Further reading: Knox Mellon, Jr., "Christian Priber's Cherokee Kingdom of Paradise" (*Georgia Historical Quarterly*, 57 (1973), 319–33).

—Jonathan Wright

primogeniture and entail

Primogeniture and entail were ancient feudal rights transplanted to the colonies from England and designed to support and maintain a landed aristocracy of large estates. Primogeniture and entail of estates were found throughout the English colonies in North America but were most common in the Middle and Southern colonies. Primogeniture is the legal right of the first-born son to be the sole inheritor of an entire estate. The process of primogeniture was designed to keep a fiefdom intact and its owner responsible for the feudal services owed to a lord. Entail is the legal restriction of an estate to a grantee (owner) and certain of his direct descendants. An entailed estate could not be removed from the family or sold so long as lineal heirs meeting the proper requirements of the original grant were alive.

During the European Middle Ages and early modern period primogeniture, or the practice of willing all of a family's immovable goods to the eldest son, was the most common form of property inheritance. The popularity of primogeniture was in large part due to the problems inherent in partible inheritance, the system by which landed property was divided among all eligible heirs, resulting in diminution of patrimony over the course of a few generations. Because noble families worked to consolidate their power, they embraced the concept of primogeniture. The British so loved the concept that they applied it to noble titles as well as land. The impact of the system on the British peerage was considerable; younger sons of British peers became de facto commoners, thus preventing the type of rapid growth of the nobility that had taken place in other western European lands.

Among the New England colonies, only RHODE ISLAND continued the practice of primogeniture. The other colonies actively opposed the process of primogeniture, although in MASSACHUSETTS the eldest son was required to be willed a double share of an inheritance. The lasting effect of this practice was the continued division of lands and farms in New England until, by the 18th century, many sons could not support a family on the tiny plot of land they inherited. The difficulty of farming the poor lands in New England (except for the CONNECTICUT River Valley) coupled with smaller and smaller estates made these colonies unprofitable for large-scale AGRICULTURE. Consequently, many New Englanders engaged in other trades, such as SHIPBUILDING, FISHING, and mercantile trade.

Cultural and historical factors in the Middle and Southern colonies made the practice of primogeniture and entail more acceptable. NEW YORK had a tradition of large manors established by Dutch settlers. Large plantations in the Chesapeake area and Tidewater regions of the South favored the practice of maintaining a large estate rather than dividing it among heirs. The lifestyles of the southern aristocracy, made possible by the LABOR of thousands of slaves, were possible and profitable only when a plantation was left intact through successive generations. While large plantation owners like the Byrd and Carter families in VIRGINIA were few, their influence over colonial society was enormous.

The general opinion in the colonies, however, was that primogeniture and entail were not compatible with the growth of viable communities; also, they were viewed as unnecessary because there was a seemingly inexhaustible supply of "vacant" land. By the third generation in New England, those who faced unprofitable farms because of their small size sometimes saw the large frontier areas as an area of opportunity. This intensified the westward movement of colonists as they spread into the interior lands occupied by NATIVE AMERICANS. A similar phenomenon occurred in the Tidewater region when the soil of smaller farms was exhausted, forcing colonists to move toward the interior of the Carolinas and Virginia. By the time of the Revolution, sentiment was so against the use of primogeniture that it was generally abolished, while entail continued in some areas under limited circumstances.

Further reading: Kermit Hall, *The Magic Mirror: Law in American History* (New York: Oxford University Press, 1989); Carole Shammas, Marylynn Salmon, and Michel Dahlin, *Inheritance in America: From Colonial Times to the Present* (New Brunswick, N.J.: Rutgers University Press, 1987).

—Stephen C. O'Neill

Prince, Lucy Terry (1730–1821)

Lucy Terry Prince was probably the first black American poet. She holds this distinction for her only known poem, "Bars Fight," written in 1746, when she was 16 years old. It was occasioned by the death of two white families during a hostile encounter with NATIVE AMERICANS in Deerfield, MASSACHUSETTS. Her description is the fullest contemporary account of that struggle.

Lucy Terry was a victim of the slave trade. While we do not know where on the African continent she was born, she first appears in the historical record as Lucy Terry, slave of Ensign Ebenezer Wells of Deerfield. She was five when baptized during the GREAT AWAKENING, and she was admitted to the "fellowship of the church" at age 14.

Lucy Terry thrived in part because of New England's "benign paternalism." She was literate and a renowned storyteller. In 1756 she married a free black man twice her age, Abijah Prince. Although Prince owned land in a nearby town, they continued to live at Deerfield in a house near a place still known as Bijah's Brook. They began raising a family that eventually included six children. Meanwhile, Abijah Prince had been bequeathed 100 acres in Guilford, VERMONT. In the 1760s the family moved to the village of 2,000 inhabitants.

Lucy Terry Prince flourished in Vermont. She attempted, unsuccessfully, to persuade the Williams College board of trustees to admit her son, barred because of his color. On another occasion she brought a lawsuit against Colonel Eli Bronson, her neighbor, for falsely claiming part of her family's land. In extreme old age she rode horseback between Guilford and Bennington, 18 miles away. Lucy Terry Prince died in 1821 at the age of 91.

—Leslie Patrick

Princeton College

Princeton was one of nine colleges existing in the colonies before the Revolution. Following the English tradition, religious groups founded educational institutions in order to train students for the ministry and for state service. The schools were identified with specific denominations, restricted to males, and generally limited to upper-CLASS families. Their curricula were designed to strengthen the mental and moral powers of students through classical studies (Latin and Greek) and strict discipline. In the 18th century colleges differed more in their theological outlooks than in their approaches to academics.

The founders of the College of NEW JERSEY in 1746 were followers of Irish evangelist WILLIAM TENNENT, SR.'s, work at Log College. Members of the "New Light" wing of Presbyterians, they aimed to train ministers for the GREAT AWAKENING, causing a temporary schism in the church. The first president of the college, housed in New Brunswick, was Reverend Jonathan Dickinson. Reverend Aaron Burr presided over its second home in Newark, and in 1756 the College of New Jersey moved to ROBERT SMITH's Nassau Hall in Princeton. (It took its present name in 1896.) Princeton was the religious and educational center for Scots-Irish Presbyterians during the Great Awakening. The evangelical community attracted noted ministers JONATHAN EDWARDS and GEORGE WHITEFIELD. Aaron Burr led a religious revival at the college in 1757 that was accompanied by a lively literary culture. Although their goal was to train ministers, the Presbyterian educators at the College of New Jersey were also interested in worldly learning.

—Deborah C. Taylor

printing and publishing

SIR WILLIAM BERKELEY, governor of VIRGINIA for 38 years, wrote in 1671: "But I thank God, we have not free schools nor printing; and I hope we shall not have these hundred years." Despite his wish, printing thrived in colonial America.

In 1639, a century after the Spanish had established a printing press in Mexico City, printing began in British North America. The first press was established in Cambridge, MASSACHUSETTS, primarily for the use of HARVARD COLLEGE. The first printed item was *The Oath of a Free-Man,* a broadsheet containing an oath for all citizens of the Massachusetts Bay Colony; the first book was the *Bay*

Psalm Book (1639). While BOSTON became the primary center for printing, presses were established in PHILADELPHIA in 1685 and in NEW YORK CITY by 1693. By 1760 60 printers worked in the colonies.

While the presses in the SPANISH COLONIES printed primarily government documents and religious works, printers in British North America produced a wider collection of materials, including fiction, magazines, almanacs, and schoolbooks. Newspapers, however, were slow to develop in the British colonies. Demand for news was initially satisfied by English papers, which arrived frequently by ship; apparently, there was little interest in local news, because the settlers were more oriented toward their homeland than to their colonial neighbors. The growth of commerce and the possibility of advertising revenue helped the development of newspapers. In 1690 BENJAMIN HARRIS published his *Publick Occurences Both Foreign and Domestick,* the first American newspaper, which authorities banned after only one issue. There would not be another American newspaper until 1704, when John Campbell, the postmaster of the Boston post office, published the first continuous American newspaper, the *Boston News-Letter.* Campbell clipped items from incoming London newspapers and printed them as foreign news. Circulation never exceeded 300 copies, a small number that reflected the dullness of a newspaper in which the copy was cleared with either the governor or his secretary.

Independent JOURNALISM emerged with the establishment in 1721 of the *New England Courant* by James Franklin (the elder brother of Benjamin). While James Franklin's paper lasted only five years, it was extremely influential. Franklin began what has become known as "crusade" journalism when he attacked INCREASE MATHER and his son COTTON MATHER for supporting the idea of inoculating people with blood from recovered SMALLPOX patients. Franklin was bitingly nasty in his attacks until it became clear that the Mathers were right. This independent style of journalism attracted more readers, and by 1750 14 weekly newspapers appeared in the six most populous colonies.

Except for a few success stories, such as the Bradfords in New York, the Greens in Boston, and, most famously, Benjamin Franklin in Philadelphia, colonial printers usually were not prosperous. Most were hardworking ARTISANS who scraped by with whatever business they could find.

While men dominated printing, their widows occasionally inherited and maintained presses and thereby exerted considerable influence in early America. ANN SMITH FRANKLIN, the widow of James Franklin, became the first female printer in New England and successfully ran the printing business for several decades.

Further reading: William L. Joyce, ed., *Printing and Society in Early America* (Worcester, Mass.: American Antiquarian Society, 1983); Lawrence C. Wroth, *The Colonial Printer* (Charlottesville, Va.: Dominion Books, 1938, 1964).

—Kenneth Pearl

privateering

To the specie-poor English colonies, privateering commissions meant the possibility of fast cash and quick returns on investments despite the risks. The almost continual state of warfare among England, France, Holland, and Spain throughout the 17th and 18th centuries made privateering one of the most profitable ventures for enterprising colonial investors and provincial governors.

Securing a privateering commission from one of the colonial governors meant a ship flying under the English flag could legally seize enemy merchant vessels. The seized cargoes would be then be brought into port to be legally "condemned" before an admiralty court. This ensured that the Crown and the grantors of the commission would receive their entitled shares. The ship's owners and the captain, often a part owner himself, would receive 40 shares each, while each mariner would receive only one share. This seemingly small portion of the spoil was still often better than the small wages earned on board a Royal Navy or merchant ship. The shares, though small, still provided a powerful incentive, making privateer crews easy to obtain.

English "sea dogs" of the late 1500s developed this more tolerable version of PIRACY when England's rivalry with Spain became outright warfare. The need of the English for bases from which to attack Spanish shipping spurred both the creation and the demise of several colonial settlements like Roanoke, JAMESTOWN, and the Popham Colony in Maine. As more colonies were established, trade increased on the wide highway of the Atlantic Ocean, and privateering arose as the legal rationale for plundering a rival's supply lines.

During the wars British and colonial MERCHANTS faced depredations from foreign privateers, resulting in loss of profits and goods. Captain William Kidd of NEW YORK was granted a privateering commission in 1695 near the end of KING WILLIAM'S WAR (1688–97). He was sent to hunt for pirates in the Red Sea but turned pirate himself, according to the British authorities. Kidd, however, kept a privateer captain's 40 shares of the treasure when a pirate captain would receive only two shares. The poorly defined distinction between piracy and privateering, exemplified by Kidd's career, convinced British authorities that piracy had to be crushed and privateering brought under better control. QUEEN ANNE'S WAR (1702–13) employed thousands of privateers to prey on French and Spanish ships bound to and from their American colonies. The war's end forced many unemployed former privateers to turn to piracy.

Privateers were sleek, fast, often colonial-built ships that usually preyed on the slower and more cumbersome merchant vessels throughout the 17th and 18th centuries. Merchant ships typically sailed with only a few cannon and small crews because space for cargo was the top priority. Moreover, privateer crews, who would only get shares if they were successful, were far more motivated than the poorly paid crews onboard the merchant ships.

Among the North American colonies NEW YORK CITY and NEWPORT were the leading centers of privateering, although almost all ports were involved to some extent. The practice of privateering was most profitable during the wars, which provided the greatest incentives, patriotism, legal excuses, and highest returns on commissions. During KING GEORGE'S WAR, for example, captured prizes escalated to an estimated worth of £17,000,000. The SEVEN YEAR'S WAR saw more privateers than any earlier conflict, as English and American colonial vessels harried the French ships bound to and from the American colonies.The daring and skills learned by these American privateers would be put into effective action once again during the American Revolution and the War of 1812.

Further reading: James G. Lydon, *Pirates, Privateers and Profits* (Upper Saddle River, N.J.: Gregg Press, 1970).

—Stephen C. O'Neill

Proclamation of 1763 See volume III

Protestantism

Protestantism was born in 16th-century Europe, which had been primarily Catholic until that time (except for small clusters of JEWS throughout the continent and the Muslim Moors in Spain). The centuries of rule had taken their toll on the Catholic hierarchy, which by the 15th century seemed corrupt to many. It controlled vast property and wealth, its priests were sometimes immoral, and it demanded too much money from all ranks of society. Protestantism denied the authority and infallibility of the pope and advocated a "return" to the "true" church, with an emphasis on scripture.

Calvinism

Calvinism, based on the teachings of French religious leader John Calvin (1509–64), emphasized five principal tenets: the total depravity of humans, God's unconditional "election" of certain people to eternal salvation, Jesus Christ's atonement for human sins being limited only to the sins of the elect, the inability of the elect to refuse salvation, and their inability to fall from their state of grace. Calvinists believed that God's will was supreme and that the task of the elect on earth was to compel everyone to carry out God's will. No one on earth had any way of knowing who was predestined for salvation, but a blameless life was an indication that a person might be elected.

Calvinism flourished in the New World initially, especially among PURITANS, but by the end of the early 18th century it was in decline. The logic of predestination suggested that there was little point in leading a moral life, because the elect could not fall from grace. In addition, the seeming arbitrariness of predestination gradually lost its appeal in a society which emphasized rewards and success for merit and hard work.

Conflict with Catholicism

Protestants believed that ROMAN CATHOLICS were not true Christians. They denied the supremacy of the pope and despised the ritual of the Catholic service, believing that it obscured rather than revealed the true nature of God. Their first attempts were to reform Catholicism, not to destroy it. However, Martin Luther and others soon realized that they would have to leave the church rather than change it.

The Puritans who founded MASSACHUSETTS had no tolerance for Catholicism. Any Catholic found in the colony was banished; if he or she returned, the penalty was death. Most other 17th-century colonies also oppressed Roman Catholics to a greater or lesser degree. Exceptions were MARYLAND, founded as a Catholic colony in 1634, and PENNSYLVANIA, in which all peaceable worshipers of God were welcome. After the GLORIOUS REVOLUTION in England (1688), the Catholic Calvert family who had established Maryland was ousted, and the population became increasingly Anglican.

The French and Spanish explorers who settled Canada and the Southwest were Roman Catholics. The missionaries who sailed with them converted many Indians, both forcibly and voluntarily; part of the original Spanish mission to the New World was to convert "heathens" to the Catholic faith. Franciscan friars founded MISSIONS throughout the Rio Grande Valley between 1598 and 1630, and Jesuit Father Eusebio Francisco Kino (1654–1711) founded many missions in Arizona in the 1690s. In 1768 the JESUITS withdrew from North America.

Denominationalism

Denominationalism is a system of voluntary church affiliation. Rather than being coerced by the state to join a particular church, people who live under this system are free to choose a church of their own. It is up to the church to recruit new members without assistance from the state.

Some colonies, such as RHODE ISLAND and Pennsylvania, always operated under this system. In most colonies, however, the state enforced a system of either Anglicanism or Congregationalism. In spite of the first amendment to the Constitution, church and state were not separated in all states until 1833, when Congregationalism was officially disestablished in Massachusetts.

The many differing brands of Protestantism found among the population of the colonies, not to mention other faiths such as Catholicism, made denominationalism almost essential for survival in British America. Colonists in places such as NEW YORK soon realized that they could not bar Protestants from their rights as citizens simply because of the church at which they worshipped.

Protestantism and the English Reformation

The English Reformation differed from the Lutheran and Calvinist Reformation in continental Europe in an important respect: Its roots were political rather than theological. In fact, Henry VIII opposed Luther; he wrote a defense of the seven sacraments in 1521 for which the pope rewarded him with the title "Defender of the Faith."

King Henry VIII (1509–47) used the pope's refusal to grant him a divorce from Catherine of Aragon as his excuse to deny the supremacy of the church in England. In 1534 Henry created the Church of England, named himself as its supreme head, and granted his own divorce. The Church of England made no immediate attempt to change Catholic doctrine; apart from the denial of papal supremacy, Anglicanism and Catholicism seemed identical.

In 1547, when Edward VI became king, the Protestants took control of the government. They instituted significant changes to the church, removing images from churches, forbidding prayer to saints, and repealing the tradition of clerical celibacy. Thomas Cranmer, archbishop of Canterbury during this period, wrote the *Book of Common Prayer* and the Forty-two Articles, which stressed justification by faith and the supreme authority of the Bible.

Under Catholic Queen Mary (1553–58) many of these reforms were repealed, and Cranmer and dozens of other Protestant leaders were executed. When Queen Elizabeth (1558–1603) took the throne in 1558, she restored the Protestant reforms. In 1571 the Forty-two Articles were shortened to the Thirty-nine Articles, which were not quite radical enough to please many Puritans. Thus, the English Reformation did not go far enough for this minority, thousands of whom eventually sailed to North America to worship as they pleased.

Evangelical Protestantism

Evangelical Protestantism emphasizes individual conversion, the authority of the Bible, and moral and social reform. Evangelicalism began with Dutch theologian Jacob Arminius (1560–1609), who argued that each human being had the power to choose or refuse salvation. This directly contradicted the Calvinist doctrine of predestination.

The prominence of Evangelicalism in early North America began in 1726, when Dutch Reformed minister THEODORUS JACOBUS FRELINGHUYSEN of northern NEW JERSEY demanded that members of his congregation openly repent of their sins and admit their reliance on the Holy Spirit. Church membership grew, and others, notably WILLIAM TENNENT, SR., and his sons Gilbert, John, and William, followed Frelinghuysen's lead. In the 1720s and 1730s ministers who graduated from Tennent's Log College spread Evangelicalism further through the colonies.

Probably the most famous of all the evangelical ministers of the period is JONATHAN EDWARDS of Northampton, Massachusetts. Edwards believed in justification by faith, not in the Arminian creed of salvation by choice, and his dramatic, emotional sermons led to a great rise in church membership during the mid-1730s. Edwards published a book about the religious revival he helped to bring about that attracted the attention of GEORGE WHITEFIELD, who preached throughout 1739 and 1740 on the need for spiritual reawakening. The GREAT AWAKENING peaked with Whitefield's tour of the colonies. It was responsible for a temporary schism within the Presbyterian Church, for the conversion of many Puritan New England congregations into Baptist ones, and for a sudden rise in the number of Baptist congregations in VIRGINIA.

Lutheranism

Martin Luther argued that civil powers had a right to reform the church. This was an important tenet of Puritanism as it evolved in New England, where status as a church member meant status as a citizen. Luther denied that priests were any closer to God than were other Christians, because God spoke directly to all persons of faith. He held that only two sacraments—baptism and the Lord's Supper—could be justified on the basis of the New Testament. He believed in justification by faith, with faith being the unquestioning acceptance of God. Faith could not be earned; it was a gift from God.

Swedish Lutherans founded a settlement called New Sweden in the DELAWARE River Valley during the 1630s; the first Lutheran congregation in North America was established in Wilmington, Delaware, in 1638. By 1669 Lutherans had established churches in Albany and Manhattan. When Pennsylvania was established in the 1680s, Lutherans arrived in large numbers. Their common language and culture led them to join in worship with German Reformed congregations.

In 1742 HENRY MELCHIOR MUHLENBERG arrived in North America and formed the Lutheran Church's first

American governing body. Muhlenberg used this Pennsylvania Ministerium to return the Lutheran Church in North America to the teachings of Luther.

Puritanism

Puritanism had its roots in Calvinist doctrines of the depravity of humans and the supremacy of the will of God. Puritanism stressed the covenant between God and people and strict standards for church membership. Everyone was required to attend church, but only those who experienced conversion were entitled to be full church members and to have their children baptized. Only full church members could vote; Puritans trusted no one but the elect to decide on matters that affected the community.

New England was the stronghold of Puritanism. In the 1630s thousands of Puritans migrated to New England with the purpose of establishing a "New Jerusalem"—a modern city of God. In 1636 the Puritans established HARVARD COLLEGE across the river from BOSTON to ensure that their ministers would be educated. Ideally, the Puritan minister (always male) was better educated and informed about Scripture than his parishioners, but he was not an intermediary between them and God. Instead, a minister was considered a community leader and a teacher.

As the population of New England grew and the high standards for church membership ensured that membership rolls declined to the point of endangering the faith, Puritan leaders agreed to the "Halfway Covenant" of 1662. According to this covenant, the children of righteous Christians who were not church members were still eligible for baptism.

Quaker Doctrine

The Society of Friends (QUAKERS) followed the teachings of George Fox (1624–91). He rebelled against the strict Puritanism of his parents' home, from which he ran away in his youth. Fox believed that religion was something experienced in the head and the heart, not externally by repeating set prayers or listening to ordained clergymen. When Fox was 22, he believed he heard God speaking to him. He and his followers preached the doctrine that the enlightening power of the Holy Spirit was conferred directly on all people. Therefore, all members of a congregation were equal; there was no need for ordained clergy. In Quaker meetings any person who felt moved to speak of his or her reception of the Holy Spirit was encouraged to do so.

The doctrine that women and men were equal in the sight of God, both capable of receiving the "inner light" and equally deserving of attention when speaking in meetings, was unique to Quakers. Women held few positions of power in other Protestant denominations until the 20th century. Quakers did not accept the sacraments. They embraced pacifism and were the first denomination officially to condemn SLAVERY.

Quakers were the targets of Puritan persecution throughout New England, except in tolerant Rhode Island. They eventually found a welcome in Pennsylvania, the colony established by Quaker WILLIAM PENN in the 1680s.

Further reading: Martin E. Marty, *Pilgrims in Their Own Land: 500 Years of Religion in America* (New York: Penguin, 1985); Kenneth Silverman, *The Life and Times of Cotton Mather* (New York: Harper & Row, 1984).

—Stephanie Muntone

Protestant work ethic

In 1630 about 1,000 Puritans set sail for the American colonies intending to establish a community that would reflect and embody their religious views. Their beliefs centered not around the individual but on the community, and Puritans emphasized that people were bound together by reciprocal responsibilities and rights. One important aspect of Puritanism lay in their theory of work, associated with the Calvinist notion of a "calling" in which the LABOR of every person was equally valued. Hard work and discipline were for the glory of God. Therefore, idleness was equated with sin, while work was associated with obedience. Individuals worked not so much to increase their own material wealth as to improve the society. If a person grew wealthier, it was sometimes a sign of God's blessing. This emphasis on dedicated, continual labor had not characterized Western preindustrial societies, in which work routines were generally much more casual.

As 18th-century American culture began to stress individualism, ambition, and materialism, the Puritan emphasis on self-discipline and hard work for the sake of church and community slowly eroded. Increasingly, colonists viewed work and land as a means to acquire material goods.

In a secular sense, Benjamin Franklin is the quintessential representative of the Protestant work ethic. The 12th child of a BOSTON candle maker, Franklin began his life in poverty but managed to rise to a position of wealth and power. By the age of 23 Benjamin Franklin was a financial success, a self-made human being in material terms. In 1748 he launched *Poor Richard's Almanack,* a collection of common sense, wit, and, most of all, financial advice. One reason for the almanac's incredible success was its advice on how to gain wealth, including such aphorisms as "time is money" and "lost time is never found again." Hard work and frugality were primary values Franklin advocated, thus continuing, in a secular sense, the historical threads of the Protestant work ethic.

—Kate Werner

Pueblo

By A.D. 700 the ancestors of the Pueblo Indians had adopted irrigation AGRICULTURE, developed sophisticated basketry and pottery traditions, lived in multistory buildings, and practiced an elaborate ceremonial religion. In the 12th and 13th centuries they built massive structures at Chaco Canyon, Mesa Verde, and elsewhere. Sometime around 1300 they abandoned them, probably because of drought, soil exhaustion, and raids from enemy Indians. Most of the displaced inhabitants established similar but smaller villages in present-day NEW MEXICO and Arizona. Europeans later used the term *Pueblo* to refer simultaneously to the individual villages, the people who inhabited them, and the regional population of native village-dwellers as a whole.

Different Pueblo villages shared common building technologies and agriculture techniques, and each nourished a rich religious life that revolved around the kiva, or ceremonial lodge. While they settled, worked, and worshiped in similar ways, profound differences separated one community from another. Seven different languages were spoken among the Pueblo. These languages belonged to four entirely different language families and were subdivided into distinctive and often mutually unintelligible dialects. Villages in the relatively well-watered Rio Grande Valley were separated ecologically from Hopi and Zuni pueblos in the dry west. Each pueblo was a stubbornly autonomous unit, with distinctive cultural priorities and social organizations.

The first significant contact between Spaniards and Pueblo came in 1540, when explorer Francisco Coronado journeyed north from Mexico looking for cities of gold. The Spanish returned in 1598 to colonize the Rio Grande Valley, and they fiercely suppressed native resistance. Most notoriously, Spaniards brutally punished "rebels" in Acoma by destroying the pueblo itself, killing 800 of its residents, enslaving 500 women and children, and, in a great public ceremony, chopping off one foot from each of 80 surviving men.

Spanish colonists made demands on nearly every facet of Pueblo life. Villagers fulfilled Spanish needs through tributes of crops and manufactured goods and provided LABOR for innumerable public and private projects. Franciscans suppressed traditional Pueblo religion by raiding and burning kivas, confiscating ceremonial objects, and imprisoning native religious leaders. The burdens of colonization aggravated other, more familiar problems: In 1640 alone, drought and famine resulted in thousands of Pueblo deaths. Several pueblos revolted against Spanish rule unsuccessfully during the 17th century. Finally, under the leadership of Tewa medicine man POPÉ, a remarkable coalition of villages drove the Spaniards out of New Mexico altogether in the PUEBLO REVOLT of 1680.

When the Spaniards returned in 1692, individual pueblos resisted but without the same coordination. The Spanish had thoroughly reestablished themselves in the Rio Grande Valley by 1700. A great many Pueblo who had resisted the reconquest fled to live among the Apache, the NAVAJO, or with the distant Hopi, who had maintained their independence. For those who stayed, colonial rule was milder in the 18th century. Spanish authorities made fewer demands for labor and tribute, Franciscans interfered less in village life, and officials established new legal protections to safeguard Pueblo lands and property. While still distinct, Pueblo and Spanish worlds integrated more fully after the reconquest as the overall regional ECONOMY gradually improved for both peoples. Still, the Pueblo population reached its historical low point at midcentury. Spaniards estimated that there were 80,000 Pueblo Indians living in at least 134 villages in 1598. By 1750 there were hardly 8,000 Pueblo living in 40 villages. War, famine, flight, and especially DISEASE had utterly transformed the valley.

See also SPANISH COLONIES.

Further reading: Alfonzo Ortiz, ed., *Handbook of North American Indians*, vol. 9: *Southwest.* (Washington D.C.: Smithsonian Institution, 1979); Ramón A. Gutiérrez, *When Jesus Came the Corn Mothers Went Away: Marriage, Sexuality, and Power in New Mexico, 1500–1846* (Palo Alto: Calif.: Stanford University Press, 1991).

—Brian DeLay

Pueblo Revolt (1680)

Spanish colonists throughout NEW MEXICO awoke with alarm on August 10, 1680, to find that a previously deeply divided indigenous population had united in a massive and unprecedented revolt, which would ultimately drive Spaniards out of the colony for more than a decade. The PUEBLO had organized a unified surprise attack, in which rebels used knotted cord calendars to coordinate the attack among villages. Panicked Spaniards quickly retreated to Santa Fe, where Governor Antonio de Otermín tried to defend the city. He was forced to abandon the colony on September 21 and retreat 300 miles across the Rio Grande to El Paso, accompanied by all the Spaniards in the colony. By this time the Pueblo had killed more than 400 of 3,000 Hispanic residents living in the region. They also desecrated churches and killed 21 of the province's 33 Franciscans, torturing many in the process. Part of the wave of Indian revolts that swept northern New Spain in the 1680s (among them, revolts by the Suma, Concho, and Pima), this rebellion signaled that a population believed by the Spanish to be "pacified" was anything but.

The events of the summer of 1680 were rooted in 80 years of Spanish colonization that had left the Pueblo communities of the region in a dire state. European colonists had taken advantage of superior firepower and internal divisions in this ethnically diverse region to force Christianity on the indigenous peoples and to relocate many into Franciscan-ruled mission pueblos. The Pueblo Indians became the principal source of wealth for the Europeans, whose demands for LABOR and tribute sparked Indian revolts as early as the 1640s. Simultaneously, because of European pathogens, unregulated exploitation, and intertribal warfare, the Pueblo population fell from 60,000 in 1600 to 30,000 in the 1640s, and was again nearly halved, to 17,000, by 1680. Conflicts over defending Pueblo religious traditions also grew more acute as the colony expanded. Spanish attacks on religious rituals were interpreted by many as an assault on the very existence of the Pueblo community. In addition, the 1670s were a period of severe drought, famine, DISEASE, and intensified Apache raids on Pueblo communities. These factors contributed to a religious revival among many Pueblo, which the Spanish aggressively repressed. As sedentary agriculturalists, the Pueblo were not likely to flee the region, and so by this period a concerted revolt seemed their best option. In the weeks prior to August 10, a series of leaders, notably the famed leader POPÉ of the Tewa-speaking Pueblo community of San Juan, traveled the region, garnering support and planning the uprising.

It would be 12 years before a Spanish military force under Diego de Vargas could reconquer the Pueblo. Vargas took advantage of renewed internal divisions to defeat all the Pueblo towns by 1694. Only the Hopi Pueblo in modern-day Arizona were never again subdued. Having regained control, however, the Spanish acted more carefully than they had before the revolt. After 1700 they became more tolerant of Pueblo religious practices and made fewer demands on Pueblo labor. Nonetheless, the following decades continued to see considerable problems for the Pueblo community. Within decades the number of Europeans in the colony surpassed the remaining indigenous peoples, and the loss of land, religion, and customs that many had decried in 1680 accelerated. The number of Indian slaves and detribalized Indians gradually increased, and those seeking to live outside the reach of European hegemony found themselves under pressure not only from Europeans but also from the waves of migration from the Great Plains that followed French and English colonization to the north.

Further reading: Andrew L. Knaut, *The Pueblo Revolt of 1680: Conquest and Resistance in Seventeenth-Century New Mexico.* (Norman: University of Oklahoma Press, 1995).

—Alexander Dawson

Puritans

Puritanism has proved a particularly vexing concept to define. Scholars have variously denominated it a program to reform the English church, an intellectual construction compounded of covenant theology and Ramist logic, a particular subset of Protestant principles, a political program and the Anglo-American scion of the Calvinist church family. A few have even denied the term's utility, arguing that little distinguished "Puritans" from the mass of English Protestants. Puritanism is best understood, however, as primarily a religious sensibility centered around the protracted experience of conversion—the transforming encounter with the Holy Spirit grounded in God's Word as shaped by Reformed Protestant theology—that effected a triple transformation in those so regenerated, the Saints. Religiously, conversion transformed individuals from damnation to salvation, with the assurance that they would enjoy eternal life. Ecclesiastically, it impelled them to model churches on the Scripture's blueprint and emphasize the importance of discipline, that is, the procedures for securing the church's capacity to proscribe unregenerates from the sacraments. Sociologically, it energized believers to obey God's will, fashioning ministers, magistrates, and laity into a triumvirate zealous to build holy communities obedient to God's laws. Although Puritanism's specific doctrines, ecclesiastical arrangements, and liturgical practices changed over time, the dual imperatives to gain salvation through conversion and improve society's morals always characterized the movement.

Puritanism emerged among English Protestants unhappy that the Elizabethan Religious Settlement (1559) had arrested the Reformation before the Church of England had achieved the "perfection" of continental churches. From the 1560s to the 1580s Puritans assayed various means to conform their institution to Geneva's template, challenging episcopal demands that they retain "popish" practices in worship, filing bills in Parliament, and erecting clandestine presbyteries to edify ministers and impose proper discipline. All failed, withered by the opposition of Crown and church. In reaction, several hundred "Separatists" fled to the Netherlands, having concluded that the Church of England could never be made true; a portion of one such group founded PLYMOUTH Colony (1620).

More mainstream Puritans remained within the church, however, now concentrating on preaching for conversion and covenanting with like-minded persons to cleanse the church from within. By the 1620s networks of the self-proclaimed "godly" honeycombed the English parishes. When that decade brought Charles I's personal rule, depression in the cloth trade, and the ascendance of William Laud's Arminian faction, which imposed a non-Reformed liturgy and persecuted nonconformists, Puritans read these troubles as signs from God to establish his "City on a Hill" in New England. Between 1630 and 1640 some 15,000 migrated, effecting the First Puritan Reformation, the construction of the purified church and society that English conditions had forestalled. Institutionally, the City on a Hill featured a church stripped of Anglican ceremonies in which the congregation (not just the clergy) controlled the disciplinary apparatus and a government chartered by the king was charged (among other tasks) with protecting the church and securing moral order. After a generation of settlement, Puritans could well believe that they had fulfilled their mission to God.

Time's passage corroded their expectations. Population growth (which forced people in search of unclaimed land to quit town centers), the failure of children and grandchildren to own the covenant, the emergence of a counterculture averse to moral rigor, a heightening of contradictions within Reformed theology, natural disasters like SMALLPOX epidemics, and human-made disasters like war and England's new-found desire to govern its American possessions more jealously—all pressured the "New England Way." Conversion rates declined and raucous jollity increased while a host of spiritual plagues—BAPTISTS, QUAKERS, and witches—threatened the church's hegemony. Ministers marked the changes in the jeremiad, a rhetorical formula excoriating New Englanders for their sins and bemoaning the loss of piety, yet promising that God would renew his covenant should his people repent.

In a series of piecemeal innovations that collectively constituted the Second Puritan Reformation, Saints tried to accommodate their religious and moral program to the new conditions. The Halfway Covenant allowed baptizing the grandchildren of regenerates, thereby bringing a CLASS of potential outcasts under church government. Ceremonies renewing churches' original covenants sought to excite personal piety, as did calls to read the devotional tracts the nascent book trade made available with greater frequency. The Reforming Synod (1679–80) issued a comprehensive plan to redress the region's sins, while JEREMIADS implored magistrates to perform their godly duties. Northampton's Solomon Stoddard opened the Lord's Supper, previously restricted to Saints, to all churchgoers in an effort to increase the number of conversions. His fervent preaching, laced (atypically) with threats of damnation, resulted in five "refreshings," a forerunner of revivals, during which worship and new births soared. The Second Puritan Reformation reversed the decline in church membership and brought some of the worst moral excesses (like drunkenness) under control. However, in the end Puritanism as a religious movement succumbed (at least in MASSACHUSETTS) to the English state, which in 1691 issued the Bay Colony a new charter that made the governor a royal

A painting of early New England Puritans going to worship armed *(Library of Congress)*

appointee and mandated toleration for certain other Protestants, thereby subverting the holy commonwealth's political foundation. Reformed Protestant theology and its associated spirituality, however, flourished far into the 18th century.

Although Puritanism did not shape American religious development in its image, as some have claimed, it did affect colonial New England profoundly. Its ecclesiology grounded Congregational (and later Baptist) church government and contributed to the strength of popular political participation. The coordination of church and state to promote moral order effected a series of establishments that survived into the 19th century. Puritan mores dominated the region's cultural life, and the Saints' desire to instill God's word in their young as early as possible contributed to the highest literacy rates and only full-fledged public school system in early America. Puritan evangelical preaching and desire for conversion grounded a type of religious revivalism and, eventually, its greatest theorist, JONATHAN EDWARDS. Finally, the religious rhetoric perfected in the 17th century became a vehicle for revolution in the 18th as many New Englanders learned about the "Rights of Man" in the accents of God's Word.

Further reading: David D. Hall, *Worlds of Wonder, Days of Judgment* (New York: Knopf, 1989); Perry Miller, *The New England Mind: From Colony to Province*, vol. 2. (Cambridge, Mass.: Harvard University Press, 1953).

—Charles L. Cohen

Quakers (Society of Friends)

The Society of Friends, a religious denomination also known as the Quakers, dates from the late 1640s. It began as a radical movement that empowered individuals and encouraged disrespect for prevailing institutions. George Fox is typically identified as the founder of the movement, although others, especially Margaret Fell, also contributed to its creation. The Quakers believed that an educated ministry and a church hierarchy were detrimental to true religion, and instead urged the believer to look to the "light," or "seed," within. This divine spark was thought to be a part of Christ within each believer. Their detractors sometimes falsely accused the early Quakers of claiming actually to be Christ. Because their message encouraged people to act independently of established institutions, it offered answers to those who found the English civil wars, regicide, and increased radicalism of the 1640s unsettling. The early Quakers were imbued with the millennialism common in the era. They felt compelled to spread the news of the "inward light." An early group of converts, later known as the "first publishers of the truth," traveled throughout England gathering many converts. Any believer, having been convinced of the sect's message, could begin to preach publicly, and many of them did, including a large number of women. The movement spread from the north of England into London and from there throughout the countryside.

The response to the early Quakers was mixed. An official policy of religious toleration in the 1650s protected them to some extent from persecution and allowed the growth of the movement. After George Fox converted Margaret Askew Fell, wife of a justice of the peace in Lancashire, her home at Swarthmore Hall became central to the movement. Despite the convincement (discovery of truth) of someone of Fell's social standing, the Quaker message frightened conservatives, who saw it as socially leveling as well as heretical. The aggressive preaching style of the early Quakers, which included harangues aimed at passers-by and at congregations gathered for other sorts of worship services, earned them enmity from crowds as well as magistrates. Such peculiar practices as the refusal to swear an oath or to doff one's hat to a social superior were often greeted with suspicion. To defend their views and further their movement, the sect published many pamphlets. In 1655 James Nayler outraged conservatives by recreating Christ's entry into Jerusalem, riding into Bristol on an ass while his followers sang "Hosanna." Parliament tried Nayler for blasphemy and considered the death sentence but in the end ordered his mutilation, whipping, and imprisonment. Quaker convincements in the British Isles, however, may have reached 30,000, and traveling witnesses had begun to visit other parts of Europe, the Middle East, and the Americas.

The restoration of the Stuart MONARCHY in 1660 brought greater persecution. The Quakers, led by Fox and Fell, responded by developing new policies that would assuage some of the concerns of conservatives. They also organized the movement to sustain it over time. The Society of Friends as a distinctive organization with a structure of monthly, quarterly, and yearly meetings, a CLASS of recognized ministers (both male and female), and a generally accepted body of doctrines was born after 1660. The society embraced quietism, the plain style, and pacifism. It continued to grant a greater role and more authority to women than any other religious movement. Elite young men, some of them university trained, joined the movement. WILLIAM PENN, Robert Barclay, George Keith, and Isaac Pemberton were among those converted. The period from 1660 to 1680 was one of modest growth and consolidation. Persecution was heavy, especially initially, and the organization systematically collected accounts of sufferings. This literature of suffering, along with the journals of traveling Friends and doctrinal tracts, became staples of the Quaker library.

Quakers had been drawn to North America from the 1650s, and traveling witnesses had convinced colonists from Barbados to Maine. RHODE ISLAND boasted an especially active Quaker population. MASSACHUSETTS vigorously opposed the spread of Quakerism, banishing, whipping, and mutilating missionaries who visited there in the 1650s. Finally, it ordered banishment on pain of death, which led to the execution of four Quakers, including former BOSTON resident MARY DYER, between 1659 and 1661. The persecution was scaled back after Charles II ordered an end to the executions in 1661. A Quaker meeting was gathered in the town of Salem, and it continued to meet despite efforts to crush it. In 1672 George Fox toured Quaker meetings in the CARIBBEAN and North America. He, along with other members of the society, sought a colonial site to which British Quakers could migrate to escape persecution. As a result, a number of English Quakers were involved in the establishment of NEW JERSEY. This activity formed a prelude to the major Quaker colonization effort, PENNSYLVANIA.

William Penn, a convert to Quakerism, inherited a debt owed to his father by Charles II, who paid it by naming Penn the proprietor of a large tract in North America. Penn envisioned Pennsylvania as a moneymaking venture for himself (but like most proprietors he would be disappointed in this) and a haven for his co-religionists. In keeping with Quaker principles, he pursued a pacifistic policy with the Native American population, did not require military service of inhabitants, and permitted liberty of conscience. Many Quakers migrated to the colony after it was founded in 1681. The Society of Friends was a dominant force in Pennsylvania society and politics until Quaker men withdrew from politics in large numbers during the French and Indian Wars, or SEVEN YEARS' WAR.

Shortly after the founding of Pennsylvania, the society experienced a major controversy, known as the Keithean schism. Keith, a well-educated Scottish convert, was serving as a tutor in PHILADELPHIA when he proposed a series of reforms to the society. Had they been adopted, these reforms would have made the society more like other Christian churches of its day, with a confession of faith, tests for membership, and a greater reliance on the Bible. Although Keith did not prevail and eventually left the society to become an Anglican missionary and polemicist, the schism rocked early Pennsylvania and sent reverberations throughout the Atlantic Quaker community. A later schism that led to an orthodox (or evangelical) versus Hicksite split in the 19th century revolved around some similar issues.

The connections between Friends in Britain and North America fostered economic enterprises, and some Quakers grew rich as a result of their commercial activities. The image of the Quaker as hard-working, honest, and sober brought business to Friends, and later sociologist Max Weber would use the society as the primary example of how Protestant religion fostered economic development. These connections were maintained by a unique system of traveling ministers, individual Quakers who felt called to visit other communities of Friends. They traveled, usually in same-sex pairs, with a certificate granted by their original meeting and supplemented by testimonials from other meetings they visited. They traveled back and forth across the Atlantic, around the British Isles, and up and down the coast of North America. Women as well as men made these journeys, occasionally leaving young children at home to be tended by relatives while they went on tours that might last many months. These travelers and the journals they produced of their experiences helped to knit together a transatlantic Quaker community. They also reaffirmed the movement's commitment to spiritual equality.

By 1760 50,000 to 60,000 Quakers lived in the mainland North American colonies controlled by Britain; half resided around Philadelphia and in MARYLAND. All Friends met in local meetings for weekly worship. Monthly meetings for business handled disciplinary cases, granted permission to couples to marry, and produced certificates and testimonials in support of traveling Friends. A yearly meeting decided policies and handled the most contentious cases of discipline or dissent. By 1760 six yearly meetings met in North America, including meetings for New England, NEW YORK, Pennsylvania, New Jersey, Maryland, and VIRGINIA and NORTH CAROLINA. The Philadelphia yearly meeting (covering the regions of Pennsylvania and New Jersey) was the largest. The smaller meetings might look to the Philadelphia or London yearly meeting for guidance, but each meeting was officially autonomous. Just as the society used suasion to bring recalcitrant members into line, it used similar strategies to keep all Friends "united in the truth."

In Pennsylvania the Society of Friends learned to exercise power, an experience it had not had previously. The danger of becoming a powerful and complacent majority presented new challenges to the American branch of the Society of Friends. The society eventually became concerned about the need to police its own borders, and in the 1750s it began to disown members who married outside the meeting or engaged in other unacceptable activities. This period of renewed attention to the features that made the sect distinctive has been referred to as "the reformation of American Quakerism." It resulted in a decline in membership but also in a recommitment to the principles of the sect among the remaining members.

Because of its principled commitment to social justice, nonviolence, and honesty, the society experienced periodic reform movements intended to reaffirm the sect's commitment to its principles. The withdrawal from politics of Quaker men in the 1750s occurred after members decided that continued involvement required too great a compromise. The issue of SLAVERY was another area of concern, and Friends eventually opposed the traffic in human beings. Germantown Quakers petitioned against the practice as early as 1688, and agitation over the issue continued sporadically thereafter. In the 18th century reformer JOHN WOOLMAN led the way on this issue. Decision making by consensus was a slow process, but the ideal was to bring everyone along. Once the meetings had agreed to phase out first the SLAVE TRADE and later slavery, Quakers could be disowned for trading in slaves (after 1743) or for owning them (1770s). Quakers, especially ANTHONY BENEZET, formed the first antislavery society in 1775 and worked with British Friends to make antislavery an international cause.

See also PROTESTANTISM.

Further reading: Hugh Barbour and J. William Frost, *The Quakers* (New York: Greenwood Press, 1988); Barry Reay, *The Quakers and the English Revolution* (Hounslow, U.K.: Maurice Temple Smith Ltd., 1985).

—Carla Gardina Pestana

Queen Anne's War (1702–1713)

Queen Anne's War was the American counterpart of the European War of the Spanish Succession. The most important early battles entailed attempts by the British in SOUTH CAROLINA (1702) to capture Spanish ST. AUGUSTINE, FLORIDA, and the Spanish attempt to conquer CHARLESTON (1706). Both failed, at great cost to the attackers. In 1703 South Carolina governor James Moore successfully organized 1,500 Yamasee Indians to destroy the Spanish mission among the Apalachee Indians on the Chatahoochee River in West Florida; more than a thousand Apalachee were enslaved or resettled in Carolina.

In the North for the first four years of the war, pro-French Indians raided the NEW YORK and New England frontiers. Their surprise attack on Deerfield in February 1704 left the town uninhabited; 40 were killed and 111 captured. However, MASSACHUSETTS learned from the enemy: "flying columns" of militia relieved sieges of Lancaster, Haverhill, and a repopulated Deerfield, while one under Benjamin Church launched a successful raid against Grand Pré, a French outpost in Acadia (Nova Scotia).

The scale of war increased in 1707. Directed by Massachusetts governor JOSEPH DUDLEY, 1,000 volunteer New England troops, mainly drawn from his colony, unsuccessfully attacked Port Royal, the most important French base in Acadia. The following year Scottish merchant Samuel Vetch persuaded the British government to aid another Massachusetts attempt on Canada. The expedition of 1709 was a disaster because a diversionary strike by New York and the IROQUOIS never occurred. After raising troops and gathering supplies, the promised British force sailed to Portugal instead.

Britain did come through in 1711, when a huge expedition of 11,000 soldiers and sailors in 15 warships and 46 transports joined 1,500 colonials in an attempt to assault Quebec. However, with British pilots unable to navigate the treacherous St. Lawrence River, the force withdrew after eight transports and more than 800 men perished in a shipwreck. The New York diversionary force of 2,000 soldiers disbanded as well when they learned the news.

Queen Anne's War brought some success to the British in North America. The Peace of Utrecht gave Acadia, Newfoundland, and Hudson Bay to Britain. However, where Acadia ended and Canada began was never established, and the British mistrusted the ACADIANS until they deported them in 1755. Frontier warfare persisted into the 1720s and resumed in the 1740s along both the Carolina and northern frontiers.

Further reading: Philip S. Haffenden, *New England in the English Nation, 1689–1713* (Oxford, U.K.: Clarendon Press, 1974).

—William Pencak

R

race and racial conflict

Despite its common usage, the concept of "race" is elusive, slippery, and elastic. While scholars mostly now agree that race is not a valid human category, a belief in race and racial differences played a decisive and critically important role in the development of colonial North America's human interactions. Before British contact with the peoples who inhabited the African and North American continents, the term *race* was inconsistently applied to a variety of social groups now conceived of as nations or ethnic groups. Race in the British North American colonies was an idea that acquired strength once contact occurred. The term then assumed meanings that suited the interests of the colonizer, not the colonized; the enslaver, not the enslaved.

Africans and NATIVE AMERICANS did not invent the concept of race; Europeans did. The concept functioned to organize and mediate differences among groups of people who occupied overlapping territories. The term's content derived from relations of power that frequently resulted in conflict. Indeed, ideas of race and racial conflict are mutually dependent upon each other, and this was especially true in the British colonies of North America.

While most scholars have adopted the view that the concept of race is socially constructed, some historians have enlarged on this idea. For them, the concept of race is not fixed in time or space. Its meaning is historically specific as well as socially constructed. Historian Ira Berlin sums up this point: "Race, no less than class, is the product of history, and it only exists on the contested social terrain in which men and women struggle to control their destinies." The idea of race gave birth to the reality of racial conflict.

The concept of race has a long history that stretches back to well before British colonization of North America or the later enslavement of people who inhabited the African continent. Before contact with the indigenous peoples of North America, the English maintained simultaneous but contradictory views about Native Americans—that they were friendly and ingenuous on the one hand, but treacherous and savage on the other. The negative notions of race were used against Native Americans when white colonists demanded their land. Even in those instances in which initial contact had been relatively benign, conflict nearly always ensued.

British ideas about Africans constituting a distinct race were equally vague and imprecise before the middle of the 17th century, that is, before their participation in the SLAVE TRADE. The earliest exchanges suggest that Africans were considered both civil and hospitable. Once England became a major power in the slave trade, however, ideas about the racial inferiority of Africans crystallized. Although historians disagree about whether the slave trade resulted from ideas about race or from the economic necessity for an inexpensive and permanent LABOR force, the concept of race served as the foundation for the belief that people of African ancestry were ideally suited for slavery. Slave revolts and other forms of resistance to enslavement are the most blatant examples of Africans' opposition to, and hence conflict about, designations that resulted in what was intended to be permanent subjugation based on their "race."

Despite different and changing perceptions by Europeans of Africans and Native Americans, there was one characteristic in common: Each group came to be described in terms of its "color." It is, of course, possible to distinguish people by color. However, it was not the color in itself that determined a group's fate. Rather, color was used in conjunction with an assigned status, such as savage, slave, or civilized. Red, black, and white became insidious shorthand for designating status and power.

Given the circumstances that brought the British into contact with Native Americans and Africans, it was probable that conflict among the groups would ensue. Simply put, the English demanded land from Native Americans and labor from Africans. Although the primary contestants in British North America were the English against Native Americans and Africans, the latter two groups variously joined forces or fought against each other. The reasons that Native Americans and Africans fought each other during the colonial era, however, rarely included racial considerations of the sort that defined both of them as subjugated groups.

Ideas about race were important in the colonial era and have had a lasting influence on American history. Only rarely, however, have American historians considered how Africans and Native Americans thought about groups other than their own before they encountered the British. Historians have greater knowledge of European than non-European ideas about race, and with few exceptions have little understanding of or concern with the ways that non-Europeans conceived of themselves. Moreover, most American historians have been more concerned with the idea of race than with the conflicts it promotes, although racial conflict is more easily documented than are ideas about race. Their concerns suggest that the very definition of fields of historical inquiry in America is still dominated by unequal relations of power between Western and non-Western worldviews. Arguably, the enterprise of historical writing about race in America is itself a continuation of racial conflict by other means.

Further reading: Thomas F. Gossett, *Race: The History of an Idea in America* (New York: Schocken, 1967); Francis Jennings, *The Invasion of America: Indians, Colonialism, and the Cant of Conquest* (Chapel Hill: University of North Carolina, 1975); Winthrop D. Jordan, *White Over Black: American Attitudes Toward the Negro, 1550–1812* (Chapel Hill: University of North Carolina Press, 1968); Gary B. Nash, *Red, White & Black: The Peoples of Early North America* (Upper Saddle River, N.J.: Prentice Hall, 1974, 2000); Audrey Smedley, *Race in North America: Origin and Evolution of a Worldview* (Boulder, Colo.: Westview, 1993); Ian K. Steele, *Warpaths: Invasions of America* (New York: Oxford University Press, 1994); Alden T. Vaughan, *Roots of American Racism: Essays on the Colonial Experience* (New York: Oxford University Press, 1995).

—Leslie Patrick

Randolph, Edward (1632–1703)

Edward Randolph, an English colonial official, was born in Canterbury, England, the son of a physician. After some legal training and several minor government positions he was led toward a career in the American colonies by marriage into the family of Robert Tufton Mason, claimant to the proprietorship of NEW HAMPSHIRE. In 1676 Mason secured Randolph's appointment to carry a royal letter to BOSTON concerning Mason's claims and to bring back information on New England's condition and its people's loyalty to the Crown. On his return Randolph charged the MASSACHUSETTS government with abuse of its charter powers, tolerance of illegal trade, and tyranny over its neighbors. Later he proposed plans for royal intervention. His detailed reports were essential to the Crown's eventual 1684 annulment of the Massachusetts charter of government.

Randolph returned to Boston in 1679 as the king's collector of customs in New England. With a small group of colonists he identified as willing to collaborate with the Crown, he planned the new form of government, the DOMINION OF NEW ENGLAND, created in 1685 to replace the Puritan regime in Massachusetts. Within the dominion Randolph held office as councilor, secretary and register, deputy postmaster, surveyor of woods, and deputy auditor general. His sweeping proposals to regulate trade, reissue land titles, and further the cause of the ANGLICAN CHURCH were intensely unpopular. In April 1689 popular discontent exploded into revolt. Randolph and other members of the dominion government were seized and imprisoned before being sent back to England. There, he received new employment in October 1691 as surveyor general of customs throughout the American colonies.

Between 1692 and 1695 Randolph traveled to almost every eastern port between MAINE and NORTH CAROLINA, uncovering illegal trade and criticizing local officials. Back in England he worked with the customs commissioners and Parliament to enact a 1696 law that tightened London's regulation of colonial trade. Following another stay in North America he pressed unsuccessfully to bring all the American colonies under direct royal government. In 1702 he traveled once more to America—his 17th transatlantic voyage—and died in VIRGINIA.

Randolph represented a new kind of immigrant to North America, one of men who joined their own advancement to that of royal authority. He was exceptional in his unbending zeal, in his grasp of larger issues of policy, and in the rigor and accuracy of his countless letters and reports. No English official of his time played a larger role in extending royal authority in colonial America.

See also ACTS OF TRADE AND NAVIGATION; SIR EDMUND ANDROS; JOSEPH DUDLEY.

Further reading: Michael G. Hall, *Edward Randolph and the American Colonies, 1676–1703* (Chapel Hill: University of North Carolina Press, 1960).

—Richard R. Johnson

Red Shoes (1700?–1747)

Red Shoes (Shulush Homa) was a CHOCTAW Indian war leader whose actions precipitated the Choctaw Civil War (1746–50). Red Shoes grew up in a period of adjustment for the Choctaw. He was born around the time that the

French first arrived on the Gulf Coast to establish the LOUISIANA colony in 1699. Choctaw trade with France began immediately in order to acquire guns to counter the slave raids of their British-supplied native neighbors. Red Shoes rose to prominence in the 1720s and 1730s as the French paid Choctaw warriors to attack the CHICKASAW Indians, and he led others successfully in battle. In addition to gaining the respect and admiration of his fellow Choctaw for demonstrating his mastery over the spiritual powers necessary for success in war, Red Shoes also acquired numerous gifts from the French that further bolstered his authority. France rarely supplied enough manufactured goods for the Indian trade, though, and some Choctaw like Red Shoes sought merchandise from British settlements in the east.

In the 1730s Red Shoes and partisans from his western division (one of three political and geographic divisions among the Choctaw) journeyed to Carolina several times to establish a consistent trade with the British. British trade goods entered Choctaw towns intermittently in the 1730s and 1740s, but France viewed contact between Britain and the Choctaw as a threat. They sought to isolate Red Shoes by denying him the presents distributed to all Choctaw chiefs and war leaders at annual conferences. In addition, eastern division Choctaw chiefs resented Red Shoes's attempts to disrupt the relationship with France and to establish himself as a prominent leader.

At the urging of embittered chiefs in both the western and eastern divisions, and instigated further by France and Britain, Choctaw from those two divisions began fighting one another in 1746. Red Shoes and his followers killed three Frenchmen in August 1746, France placed a price on Red Shoes's head that same year, and an eastern division warrior killed him on June 23, 1747. The war that was started by competition over access to manufactured goods continued, however, resulting in the deaths of hundreds of Choctaw before ending in 1750.

Further reading: James Taylor Carson, *Searching for the Bright Path: The Mississippi Choctaws from Prehistory to Removal* (Lincoln: University of Nebraska Press, 1999); Richard White, *The Roots of Dependency: Subsistence, Environment, and Social Change among the Choctaws, Pawnees, and Navajos* (Lincoln: University of Nebraska Press, 1983).

—Greg O'Brien

redemptioners

The redemptioner system appeared in the early decades of the 18th century, a variation of INDENTURED SERVITUDE. It started as a means for German families to immigrate to the colonies but was used extensively by British immigrants, primarily Irish, traveling to PENNSYLVANIA. The system differed in significant ways from indentured servitude. Servants typically traveled to the colonies alone and exchanged the costs of their transportation for a period of LABOR service. While not all contracts were negotiated before embarking for the New World, most servants signed their indentures before their journey. Redemptioners immigrated more often in family units and typically paid some portion of the costs for TRAVEL to the colonies. Ship captains or MERCHANTS took whatever money they had, shipped the family members to the colonies, and, upon arrival in the New World, gave the passengers a specified amount of time to "redeem" the balance of payment. The fortunate ones could locate relatives or friends who would pay off the remaining debt.

By the mid-18th century it became increasingly difficult for immigrants to count on family and friends to redeem the cost of their passage. When the ship docked in the port, redemptioners began a frantic search to procure funds. In the early part of the century, when ships remained in port for long periods of time, immigrants might have as much as a month to make the necessary contacts to help pay the debt. Eventually, they were limited by law to 14 days. If they could not raise the balance, they were indentured to whomever would pay the amount necessary to satisfy the debt. The master paid the captain the cost, and the redemptioner served out the time until the debt was satisfied.

At times the process functioned smoothly. Lists of servants indentured to PHILADELPHIA masters reveal that redemptioners secured places within a week or two. For others, however, the search was frustrating. Announcements in the Philadelphia newspaper threatened that if redemptioners did not pay, they risked prosecution, and unlike indentured servants who traveled alone, redemptioners had to find places for all members of their family. If the market in servants was slow, "none would take a man with the encumbrances of a Wife or small Children."

Further reading: Marianne Wokeck, *Trade in Strangers: The Beginnings of Mass Migration to North America* (University Park: Pennsylvania State University Press, 1999).

—Sharon V. Salinger

religion, African-American

From 1585 to 1763 the religion of AFRICAN AMERICANS underwent a fundamental shift as traditional African faiths gradually gave way to a Protestant-based Christianity that used many features of African religions and became known as slave religion. Africans who were transported to the Americas as slaves came from complex and diverse religious backgrounds. While specific beliefs and practices varied, most West African societies held beliefs about a god or gods, an afterlife, and a spirit world. Most cultures also shared ancestral worship and certain moral injunctions, such as the condemnation of married women with children who committed adultery. Many slaves arrived in North America with a religious background deeply influenced by Islamic traditions.

The religious heritage of slaves transported from AFRICA was not passed on intact to subsequent generations. Documents left by whites reveal little about the religion of the first slaves except the ignorance that masters appear to have shared. This contemptuous attitude on the American continent toward African religions, as well as factors in the situation of bondage itself, produced an environment that created spiritual difficulties for many slaves. African religious practices were communally based, but newly purchased slaves usually did not share the language and culture of their fellow bondpeople. High MORTALITY rates and a lack of spiritual leadership likewise undermined communal religious experience. This was not alleviated until the slaves had an opportunity to form new communities and begin developing a new culture.

Several elements of African culture were preserved and eventually became a significant portion of the emerging African-American culture. For example, slaves often conducted burials according to African customs, which involved burying items with the dead. Conjuring, a practice involving communication with ancestral spirits, also survived as a common element in African-American culture. Archaeological excavations suggest that African practices such as healing, calling on ancestral spirits, and divination were practiced secretly and on a small scale. A minority of slaves maintained Islamic beliefs and practices they had embraced in Africa and continued to practice them in SLAVERY.

In the 17th century masters often distrusted the idea of Christianity among their slaves, voicing concerns that slaves who converted to Christianity would then consider themselves equal to their masters and in possession of a valid claim to freedom. Early ministers strove to counteract this idea by emphasizing that slaves would always be required to serve their masters and even included promises to do so in the baptismal ceremony of slaves. Evangelicals also attempted to persuade masters that a conversion to Christianity would render slaves more docile, obedient, and trustworthy. There is no conclusive evidence that their claims were fulfilled, and many masters remained hesitant and occasionally openly hostile toward Christianity in their slaves quarters, setting the stage for secret meetings and a movement toward a distinctly African-American Christianity.

A minority of slaves practiced their faith among whites in white churches. Olaudah Equiano and Phillis Wheatley produced LITERATURE heavily influenced by Christian themes. These slaves converted to a Christianity that had distinctive European roots, and they were often segregated and usually given a minimal role within the church. This did not change until intense efforts were practiced by Evangelicals in the GREAT AWAKENING, when large numbers of slaves converted to Christianity.

BAPTISTS began to actively seek slave converts during the 1760s, and Methodists began in the 1770s. As their ranks grew, black Christians formed their own congregations, chose their own pastors, and attended their own meetings. Their religion began to take on distinct African elements, including active worship with shouting and dancing, an emphasis on freedom, secret meetings, and call and response preaching, which eventually shaped slave religion.

Further reading: Ira Berlin, *Many Thousand Gone: The First Two Centuries of Slavery in North America* (Cambridge, Mass.: The Belknap Press of Harvard University Press, 1998); Albert J. Raboteau, *A Fire in the Bones: Reflections on African-American Religious History* (Boston: Beacon Press, 1995).

—Linda Kneeland

religion, Euro-American

When Europeans sailed west to explore and conquer the New World, one of their goals was to convert the natives to Christianity. For medieval Europeans, there was no separation between church and state. Religion was an important everyday concern, not just something celebrated once a week. Religion was also used as a weapon against minorities and a rationale for war.

Christianity is a worldwide religion of those who believe that Jesus Christ was the Messiah, the son of God who died for the sins of humankind. Because it is a missionary religion, Christianity has spread to practically every corner of the globe.

Except for small pockets of JEWS in urban areas throughout Europe and the Muslim Moors who invaded Spain, Europe was entirely Catholic throughout the Middle Ages. The Protestant Reformation of the 16th century came about because various Europeans felt that Catholicism had become corrupted; they attempted to force reforms that would "return" the church to "true" Christianity. This Protestant Reformation was one of the reasons for the 17th-century migration to North America and had a lasting effect on American religion.

The Protestant Reformation entailed the rejection of clerical authority as represented by the pope and the celibate orders of clergy. While ROMAN CATHOLICS held that

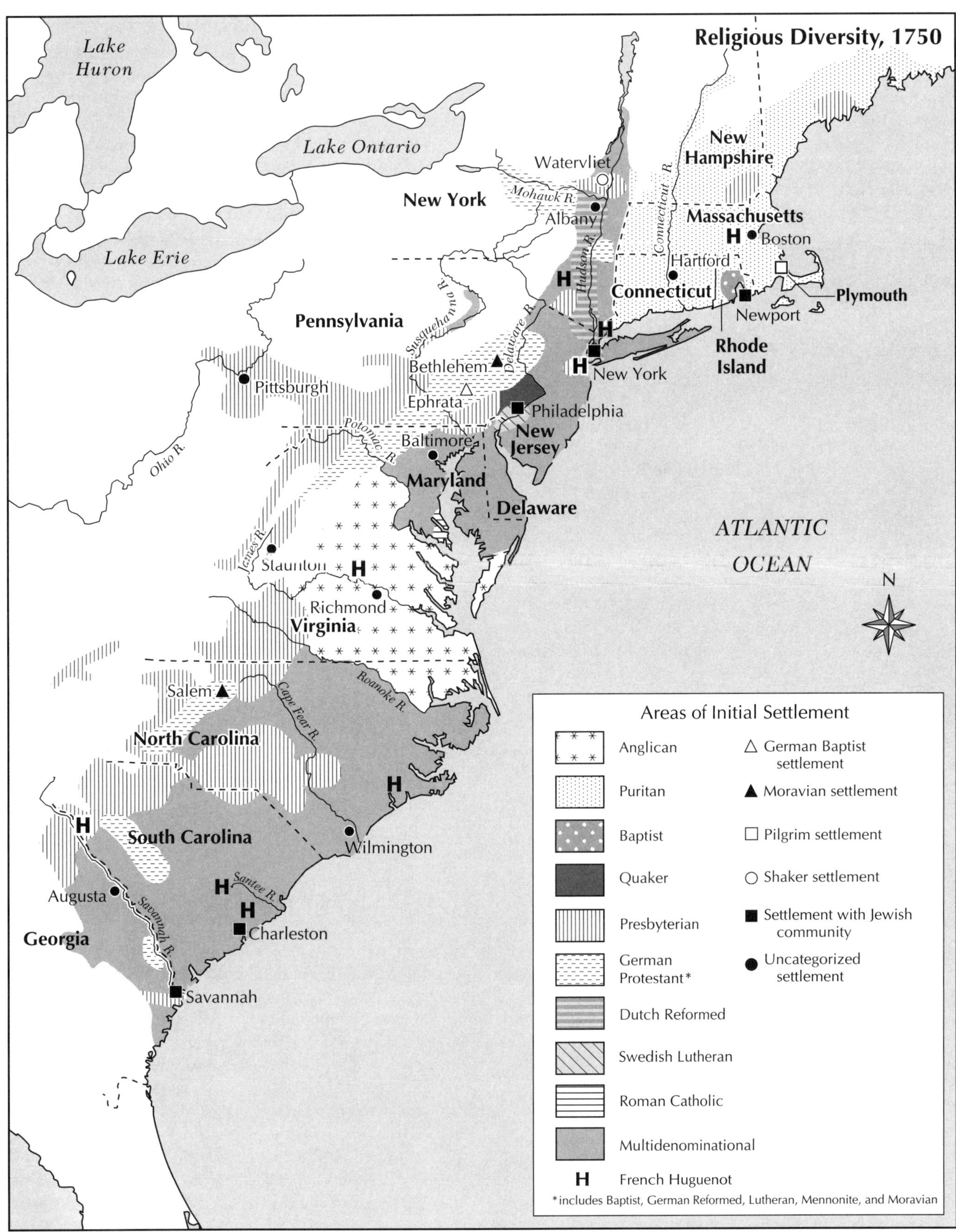
Religious Diversity, 1750
Lake Huron
Lake Ontario
Lake Erie
New York
Pennsylvania
New Hampshire
Massachusetts
Connecticut
Rhode Island
New Jersey
Maryland
Delaware
Virginia
North Carolina
South Carolina
Georgia
ATLANTIC OCEAN
Watervliet
Albany
Boston
Hartford
Plymouth
Newport
New York
Bethlehem
Ephrata
Pittsburgh
Philadelphia
Baltimore
Staunton
Richmond
Salem
Wilmington
Augusta
Charleston
Savannah
Mohawk R.
Hudson R.
Connecticut R.
Delaware R.
Susquehanna R.
Potomac R.
Ohio R.
James R.
Roanoke R.
Cape Fear R.
Santee R.
Savannah R.
N
Areas of Initial Settlement
Anglican
Puritan
Baptist
Quaker
Presbyterian
German Protestant*
Dutch Reformed
Swedish Lutheran
Roman Catholic
Multidenominational
French Huguenot
German Baptist settlement
Moravian settlement
Pilgrim settlement
Shaker settlement
Settlement with Jewish community
Uncategorized settlement
*includes Baptist, German Reformed, Lutheran, Mennonite, and Moravian

priests were intermediaries between God and the faithful, Protestants emphasized direct communication between God and an individual believer. This emphasis on the individual had its parallel in the 18th-century Enlightenment ideals of the importance of the individual.

The Reformation resulted in the establishment of numerous Protestant churches. Broadly speaking, followers of Martin Luther believed in justification by faith, while follower of Calvin believed that a chosen few were predestined for eternal salvation. In the North American colonies, Calvinist PURITANS established a stronghold in New England, German and Swedish LUTHERANS in the Middle Colonies, and Anglicans in the South. During the early 1700s a long period of religious revival began, inaugurating evangelical forms of PROTESTANTISM that would later become known as Fundamentalism.

The ANGLICAN CHURCH was born when the pope refused to grant King Henry VIII (1509–47) a divorce from Queen Catherine. Henry's solution was to deny the pope's supremacy over the king of England, to establish an English church with himself as its head, and to grant his own divorce. Anglicanism remains very similar to Catholicism in most respects apart from the supremacy of the pope and a celibate clergy.

Puritans who migrated to New England embraced the idea of "predestination," a Calvinist doctrine holding that God chose some human beings for eternal salvation. These "elect" could not fall from grace nor refuse to be saved. Their salvation did not depend on virtue; it was arbitrarily decided for them, nor could salvation be earned by excessive virtue. A blameless life was no more than a sign that a person might be among the elect. Congregationalism was a brand of Puritanism that vested authority in the hands of each congregation rather than in a church hierarchy. New England was the stronghold of Congregationalism; the punitive measures to which it resorted to uphold its rigid standards were, in part, responsible for its failure to establish itself throughout the rest of the colonies. MASSACHUSETTS and CONNECTICUT were the primary homes of Congregationalism. RHODE ISLAND, on the other hand, declared people of all faiths welcome in 1663; the colony contained hundreds of BAPTISTS and QUAKERS.

PENNSYLVANIA, founded by Quaker WILLIAM PENN in the 1680s, also preached and practiced religious tolerance. Pennsylvania quickly became home to people of such diverse faiths as Calvinism, Judaism, and Catholicism. New England generally resisted religious groups other than Puritans until after 1700, while the Middle Colonies welcomed all faiths.

MARYLAND was founded in 1634 as a Catholic colony and continued thereafter to have the highest percentage of Roman Catholics, although the colony grew more Anglican as time passed. In 1648 Catholic governor Calvert was driven from the colony and a Protestant named in his place. In 1689, with the GLORIOUS REVOLUTION in England, Protestants overthrew Maryland's Catholic government. Protestant-Catholic tussles in the colony continued until the colonies declared their independence.

The Anglican Church in North America was established in VIRGINIA. Church membership, attendance, and conformity were required by law. However, Virginia did not make a success of its attempt to establish the Anglican Church. In the early years of the 17th century mere survival was the most important consideration. Afterward, many factors combined to make it difficult for the church to play a major role in Virginia. The population was too widely scattered, there were no bishops, and economic prosperity was of much greater concern to many than spiritual well-being.

Anglicanism remained limited to the area around the CHESAPEAKE BAY for many years, but by the mid-18th century missionaries from the SOCIETY FOR THE PROPAGATION OF THE GOSPEL ensured that there were Anglican churches in all the thirteen colonies. American Anglicans pleaded for the English church to send bishops to the New World, but representatives of almost every other faith protested. Experience told them that bishops were far too likely to become politically powerful, and they wanted to weaken rather than strengthen English authority in the colonies. NORTH CAROLINA and GEORGIA were home to a diverse religious population. In 1758 Georgia officially established and supported the Anglican Church.

Deism is a belief in a logical God who created a rational universe. Deists believe that God was bound by the same physical laws and moral standards as his creatures. Although many believed in an afterlife as an incentive for good behavior on earth, Deists were skeptical of any element of religion that appeared to entail superstition. Deism was a philosophy more than it was a religion. Most deists in the American colonies were Anglicans or Protestants of other denominations.

Deist beliefs in the rationality of the universe, the perfectibility of humankind, and the supremacy of intellect rather than birth or titles all supported the revolutionary mood that swept the colonies after the SEVEN YEARS' WAR. Deism grew especially among urban ARTISANS and among intellectuals like Benjamin Franklin and Thomas Jefferson. Its insistence on rational thought also helped to secularize the United States, just as was the case in Europe.

During the early days of colonization the church and the state were unified. British Protestants, Swedish Lutherans, and Dutch Reformed all established small communities within which the church was supported by taxes and full church membership was required for citizenship. Only church members could vote, hold public office, and serve on juries.

However, this system was challenged by the arrival of thousands of immigrants of many faiths. Many Protestants, Jews, and Roman Catholics migrated west to escape religious persecution or to establish places in which they could worship as they chose, without state interference. The existence of so many faiths meant that toleration was often necessary to survival. Rhode Island was the first colony to guarantee religious tolerance in its charter of 1663. In the 1680s William Penn made it clear that Pennsylvania welcomed all peaceable worshipers of God—everyone was to be left alone to worship as he or she chose.

During the 18th century important political leaders in both Europe and North America concluded that people should be free to worship in any institution they chose, without fear of political pressure or oppression. Thomas Jefferson and James Madison worked together to try to weaken the Anglican church establishment in Virginia, arguing that officials of the government were no more theologians than they were physicists or mathematicians and thus were not competent to establish the rules by which people worshipped. In 1786 Jefferson wrote a Statute for Religious Freedom that, when passed, carried the case for religious freedom.

The first amendment to the Constitution guarantees the separation of church and state. The roots of this separation lie in the religious pluralism that was always a fact of life in the American colonies.

Further reading: Martin E. Marty, *Pilgrims in Their Own Land: 500 Years of Religion in America* (New York: Penguin, 1985); Clifton E. Olmstead, *History of Religion in the United States* (Englewood Cliffs, N.J.: Prentice-Hall, 1960).

—Stephanie Muntone

religion, Native American

Although anthropologists and archaeologists can only extrapolate precontact forms of worship from surviving artifacts and oral traditions, it is clear that American Indian peoples practiced a wide variety of religious rites and held myriad beliefs about religion and its relationship to the material world. For example, all tribes had creation stories that helped to link them to their physical ENVIRONMENT and the animal world and to explain the social structures of human societies. PUEBLO, NAVAHO, Mandan, and CHOCTAW all believed that their ancestors emerged from under the earth. New England Algonquin insisted that their predecessors had been formed from trees. The IROQUOIS and HURON told slightly different versions of the "world that was built on Turtle's back," in which Sky Woman fell or was pushed from the heavens into a vast ocean where different ANIMALS brought her mud to create the world. There, she gave birth to twin brothers and, through their conflicts and actions, life on earth began. This female creation story mirrored the matrilineal nature of Iroquois and Huron societies.

In general, the deity structure of Native American religions was polytheistic. Although highly developed native civilizations such as the Aztecs believed in a hierarchy of powerful gods, most tribes presumed that a pantheon of spirits, or manitous, possessed the animals, plants, and natural features of their landscape. Others believed that the spirits of their ancestors wandered the earth and potentially might assist or terrorize the living. Religious practices, then, involved the ritual appeasement or manipulation of these manitous for supernatural assistance in everyday life. After the first kill of a hunting expedition, the Algonquin often prepared ritual offerings and a great feast. They set out TOBACCO by a bear or deer carcass or blew smoke into the mouth of the dead animal, asking the spirits to refrain from interfering with their hunt. In the American Southwest Anasazi (and later Pueblo) implored katsina, or the cloud-spirits of their dead ancestors, to bring rain for their crops by offering gifts of prayer sticks, DANCE, and cornmeal. Aztecs performed elaborate rituals, including the sacrifice of captives to appease their war/sun god, Huitzilopochtli. In other words, gods and spirits were not necessarily benign; they required careful handling so they might act on the behalf of humans.

Most native societies had a priest, or shaman, CLASS who mediated for the gods and performed necessary rituals. They usually had knowledge of herbal remedies and performed curing ceremonies, connecting bodily health with spiritual well-being, but Indians also found ways to appeal directly to spirits. Sweat lodges or extreme privation sometimes induced much sought-after dreams and visions that made up the mainstay of individual spiritual experience.

When European nations colonized North America, traditional Native American religious practices came under pressure. Spanish, French, and English colonization efforts all included a religious component that influenced the development of Native American religious practices in the 16th, 17th, and 18th centuries. During the early 17th century Franciscans from Spain and JESUITS from France established Catholic MISSIONS among the Pueblo and Huron, respectively. Although not supported by a centralized church or by the British monarch, English Protestants also established mission communities, or PRAYING TOWNS, among the sedentary Algonquin tribes in New England during the 17th century. Native Americans often approached the introduction of Christianity by adapting selected elements of the new religion into customary practices, rather than replacing existing religious systems. For instance, Huron and Algonquin of the St. Lawrence River

This drawing shows an Algonquin shaman preparing his medicine *(Library of Congress)*

initially invited Jesuits to visit their villages because they recognized them as powerful holy men with access to the spirits. They hoped that the Jesuits might help to slow down or stop the devastation of SMALLPOX epidemics. However, the Huron also assumed that Jesuits might help them in war against their native enemies. As one historian put it, rather than converting to Christianity, the Huron, in a sense, converted Christ into a manitou. Even women, who had been central to traditional native religious life in the East, found ways to retain their power in a Christian context. For example, in the 17th century, Kateri Tekakwitha, an Iroquois woman, joined a female order of the Catholic Church in New France and practiced extreme mortification of the flesh through fasting and infliction of pain on herself. Before her death believers sought her blessing during times of crisis, and she is likely to become the first Native American saint.

Only a small percentage of NATIVE AMERICANS accepted Christianity. There were many examples of profound resistance. In 1680, after a century of contact with Franciscan friars and conversion to Catholicism, the Pueblo coordinated a revolt against Spanish rule. Especially angry at the suppression of katsina worship, the medicine men who had kept traditional religious practices alive in hidden kivas encouraged the Pueblo to kill Catholic priests and drive Spanish settlers away. By the 18th century, despite the proliferation of Protestant mission activities in the American Northeast, native religious REVITALIZATION MOVEMENTS gained momentum.

Further reading: Walter H. Capps, ed., *Seeing With a Native Eye: Essays on Native American Religion* (New York: HarperCollins, 1976); Ramón A. Gutiérrez, *When*

Jesus Came the Corn Mothers Went Away: Marriage, Sexuality, and Power in New Mexico, 1500–1846 (Palo Alto, Calif.: Stanford University Press, 1991); Ruth Murray Underhill, *Red Man's Religion: Beliefs and Practices of the Indians North of Mexico* (Chicago: University of Chicago Press, 1965).

—Jane T. Merritt

Rensselaerswyck

On the governing board of the DUTCH WEST INDIA COMPANY, Kiliean van Rensselaer, a diamond merchant, headed a faction that pushed for permanent settlement of the company's property, despite the continued failure of programs to establish small farms on Manhattan to supply company traders and ships. Van Rensselaer was a major proponent and one of the original recipients of a "patroonship" in 1629, a land grant contingent on his importation and settlement of 50 colonists within four years. The patroon controlled all of the land within the grant, leasing it to TENANTS, and had the power to appoint officials and magistrates within the settlements as well as charge fees for milling and other services performed at the patroon's facilities. After meeting company requirements, van Rensselaer received eight years' exemption from company duties, and his colonists obtained 10 years' exemption from taxes.

By 1635 Rensselaerswyck was the only one of the six original patroonships still in existence. The location along the Hudson River proved ideal for supplying company traders and took advantage of the nearby company garrison at Fort Orange. Despite a large capital expenditure and the dispatch of skilled indentured servants, horses, millstones, and tools from Holland, van Rensselaer had problems keeping people on his lands. Desperate, he even outfitted a private ship, the *Rensselaerswyck*, to transport colonists, but this proved too expensive to maintain. For their part, tenants were often dissatisfied with not owning land, and they frequently departed to obtain their own property elsewhere in America. When displeased with the company's management of trade with them, local tribes frequently made reprisal raids on Rensselaerswyck, a problem exacerbated by the colonists' illegal sale of ALCOHOL to the Indians.

By diversifying his well-placed settlement's ECONOMY away from total dependence on the FUR TRADE, van Rensselaer ensured its survival, although continued use of the lease system led to resentments on the part of the tenants, which, beginning in 1751, exploded into a series of antirent revolts that were put down violently in 1766. This situation was a major factor in the loyalty of many Rensselaerswyck tenants during the American Revolution, who often reacted in opposition to the politics of their landlords.

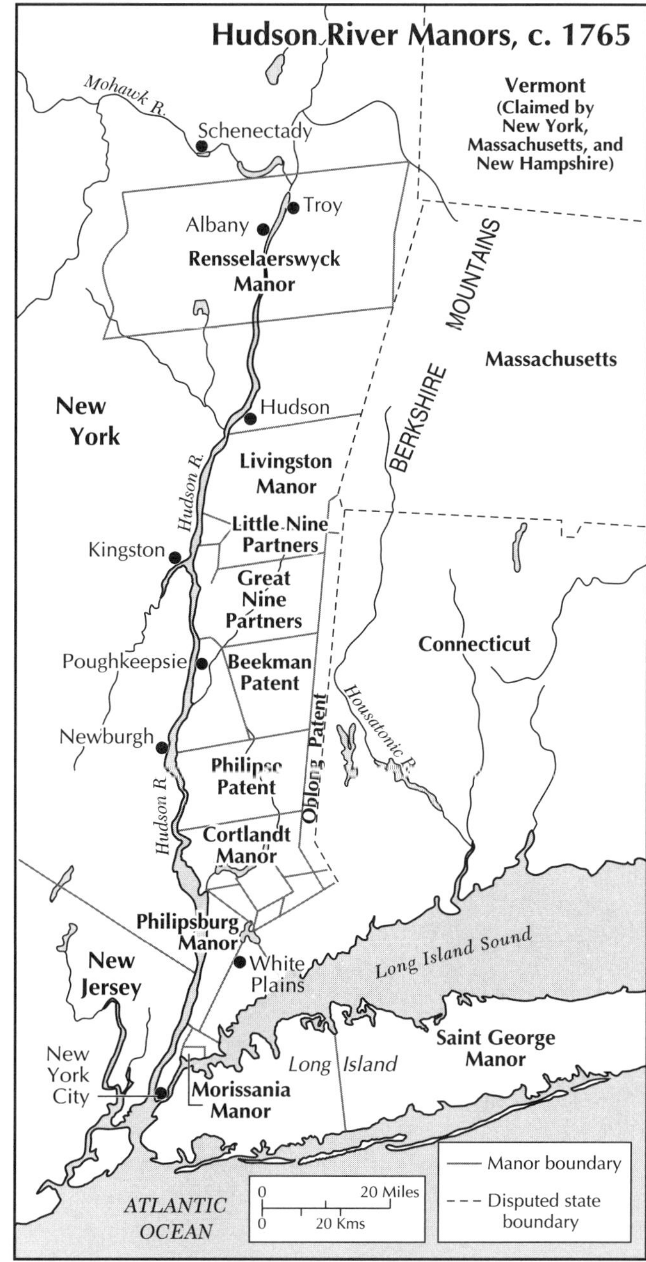

Further reading: Florence Van Rensselaer, *The Van Rensselaers in Holland and America* (New York, n.p., 1956).

—Margaret Sankey

revitalization movements

When one thinks of Native American revitalization movements, most often the Shawnee prophet Tenskwatawa, the religion of Handsome Lake at the turn of the 19th century, the Ghost Dance movement a hundred years later, and even the emergence of the Native American Church and its peyote culture in the 20th century come to mind, yet these nativistic movements that periodically revived Indian-centered religious practices had their origins on the upper Susquehanna River and the Ohio Valley in the middle of the 18th century among DELAWARE, Shawnee, and IROQUOIS peoples. Sometimes called the Indians' GREAT AWAKENING, these reform movements had common elements. They were led by a variety of prophets and reformers who often had visions that provided instructions for religious and social solutions to the contemporary crises faced by native communities. Spiritual leaders believed that the proliferation of DISEASE among Native populations and scarcity of game experienced in the colonial period were part of their god's punishment for bad behavior. Supposedly, Indians had become corrupt through their growing dependence on Euro-American economic systems, which caused a variety of social problems. To make the world right, Indians would have to abandon the vices that white people had introduced, especially the use of alcohol, and return to their past high moral standards.

In part a reaction to the introduction of Christianity and the increased missionary activities in the mid-Atlantic colonies, revivalists began to appear along the Susquehanna River by the 1750s. For instance, one Delaware woman in the Wyoming Valley, reacting to Presbyterian attempts to missionize, demanded that Indians separate themselves from white people. Still, even nativist reformers were influenced by Christian doctrine. They articulated a new theological structure of monotheism, claiming close ties to a supreme being rather than a pantheon of spirits. As they exhorted their followers to return to native religious practices, reformers began to define native moral behavior by reference to the immoral and hypocritical actions of white Christians, whom they blamed for problems within Indian communities. By the mid-18th century native spiritual leaders were less concerned with ritual manipulation and appeasement of gods and spirits and more preoccupied with questions of individual morality and sin. They admonished Indians to reform their behavior or face the hell that awaited them in the afterlife.

One of the most prominent nativist reformers of the colonial period was the Delaware prophet NEOLIN, whom the English called the Imposter. In the 1760s he advocated a radical separation from white society, rejecting Euro-American trade goods and alcohol. He introduced a series of new rituals and devotions that included a diet to purify the body—in essence, physically purging white ways from Indian society. Pontiac, inspired by Neolin's message, believed that the Indians' god would help him fight the English and translated revivalism into a militant resistance movement in his 1763 uprising. Indeed, by the late 18th century religious revivalism became an increasingly important part of pan-Indian resistance that marked the relationship between NATIVE AMERICANS and Euro-Americans. The revitalization movements represented an Indian-based solution to the social problems of colonialism.

Further reading: Gregory Evans Dowd, *A Spirited Resistance: The North American Indian Struggle for Unity, 1745–1815* (Baltimore: Johns Hopkins University Press, 1992).

—Jane T. Merritt

Rhode Island

Rhode Island retained a reputation for political and social eccentricity from the time of its founding until the 19th century. In the early 17th century approximately 10,000 NATIVE AMERICANS lived in the area of present-day Rhode Island. The majority (approximately 6,000) were NARRAGANSETT, who dominated the stretch of land from present-day Providence south along Narragansett Bay to South Kingston and Exeter. The Wampanoag Indians held the eastern shore, while the Nipmuc resided inland and the Niantic along the southern coast. All four groups depended on farming, FISHING, and hunting for subsistence. They remained an important presence in Rhode Island during the first decades of English settlement. In 1675, however, the Narragansett and Wampanoag joined forces in KING PHILIP'S WAR, a futile effort to harry English settlers out of the region. Famine and warfare decimated the combatants and their communities. After the war the remnants of the once-powerful Narragansett and Wampanoag tribes took refuge with the Niantic, who had remained neutral in the war, and formed a new Indian community, which eventually adopted the name Narragansett.

ROGER WILLIAMS, a radical and controversial English clergyman, founded the first English settlement in Rhode Island in 1636. Williams had immigrated to Salem, MASSACHUSETTS, in 1631, but he soon disturbed orthodox Puritan settlers by advocating religious toleration, separation of church and state, and negotiation for, rather than seizure of, Indian lands. Massachusetts Bay banished Williams in 1636, and he and his followers moved south to the head of Narragansett Bay, where they established the town of Providence. In the decade that followed two other small but noteworthy groups of Puritan dissenters settled near Narragansett Bay. ANNE MARBURY HUTCHINSON, who had been banished from Massachusetts Bay for preaching Antinomianism (the idea that works as well as faith contributed to salvation), arrived with her husband and a small group of followers in 1638. They purchased the island of Aquidneck from the Narragansett Indians and founded the town of Portsmouth; a schism within this community led to the founding of NEWPORT in 1639. SAMUEL GORTON, another

Puritan dissident, established Warwick in 1642–43. Other early English settlements in Rhode Island included Wickford (1637) and Pawtuxet (1638).

These early English settlements were insecure, as the settlers' title to their lands rested solely on Indian deeds. Neighboring colonies soon began to cast covetous eyes on Narragansett Bay. In 1643 Roger Williams journeyed to England to obtain a patent to the region. He returned in 1644 with a charter that united the disparate towns into a single colony named Rhode Island and secured settlers' titles to their lands. The towns formed a loose confederate government in 1647, but political problems continued to plague them. The other New England colonies—Massachusetts Bay, PLYMOUTH, CONNECTICUT, and New Haven—were reluctant to recognize Rhode Island's charter; meanwhile, WILLIAM CODDINGTON, founder of Newport, declared himself ruler for life of the island towns, causing a political schism within the colony. Roger Williams and John Clarke, an opponent of Coddington, traveled to England in 1651 and in 1654 succeeded in reestablishing the Rhode Island towns' confederate government. In 1663, following the restoration of the Stuart MONARCHY in England, Clarke secured a royal charter that guaranteed religious liberty and self-government and reaffirmed Rhode Island's territorial claims. This charter was among the most liberal granted to any of the English colonies in North America, and it served as the foundation of Rhode Island's government until long after the American Revolution; it was superseded only in 1843.

Rhode Island suffered severely from the political and military tumults of the late 17th century. Although the colony did not officially join in King Philip's War, many of the English settlements in Massachusetts and Connecticut were burned and most of the mainland settlers were obliged to take refuge in Rhode Island (Aquidneck). The Great Swamp Fight, one of the pivotal battles of the war, took place in December 1675 near present-day Kingston. A decade later James II's plan to consolidate the New England colonies in the DOMINION OF NEW ENGLAND (1686–9) under the leadership of SIR EDMUND ANDROS vexed Rhode Island settlers. The cycle of imperial wars that began in the 1680s and lasted, with intermissions, until the American Revolution frequently disrupted transatlantic trade, which was central to Rhode Island's ECONOMY.

The governorship of Samuel Cranston (1698–1727) ushered in an era of greater political stability. Cranston worked to establish internal political unity and improve Rhode Island's relations with the British imperial government. The most important political development of the 18th century, however, was the growing commercial rivalry between Providence and Newport. By the 1740s sectional parties formed under the leadership of Samuel Ward (Newport) and Stephen Hopkins (Providence) and competed for control of the legislature. Boundary settlements with Connecticut (1726–27) and Massachusetts (1746–47) allowed Rhode Island to annex Cumberland and several East Bay towns, including the port of Bristol.

Rhode Island's population grew steadily in the 18th century, from a modest 6,000 in 1698 to 18,000 in 1731 and 32,000 by midcentury. It was more racially and religiously diverse than the other New England colonies. In addition to the substantial Indian presence, there were a considerable number of African-American slaves who labored on dairy farms and cattle ranches in South County and in the Newport shipping industry. By 1760 AFRICAN AMERICANS composed roughly 20 percent of Newport's population and 17 percent of South Kingston's population. Most Rhode Island slaveholders owned only a handful of slaves, but a few operated large-scale plantations; some experimented with the task system (popular in SOUTH CAROLINA's rice-growing regions), under which slaves performed assigned agricultural tasks with minimal white supervision. Rhode Island's policy of religious toleration attracted many religious minorities, including QUAKERS (1657), JEWS (1658), and Huguenots (1686). In addition, one of the first American Baptist churches was constituted in Providence in 1639.

Rhode Island's economy rested jointly on AGRICULTURE and trade. The colony exported horses, salt fish, and other local products to the West Indies. Prosperous MERCHANTS also participated in the notorious "triangle trade": they exported rum to Africa, exchanged it for slaves, sold the slaves in the West Indies in exchange for molasses, and imported the molasses, which was distilled into rum. Merchants frequently disregarded the Navigation Acts; SMUGGLING was common throughout the 18th century. Most Rhode Islanders, however, reaped their living from agriculture rather than trade. Livestock, grain, and dairy products, raised for subsistence or local markets, were the principal crops. Some farmers also grew flax, hemp, low-grade TOBACCO, and green onions, and many manufactured barrel staves, shingles, clapboards, and other wood products. In spite of bounties, the fishing industry was only moderately successful.

Diverse, commercial Rhode Island devoted less energy to higher EDUCATION and intellectual life than did the stricter Puritan colonies. Several of Rhode Island's early leaders, including Williams, Coddington, and Gorton, argued that it was not necessary for ministers to be college educated, and relatively few Rhode Island boys attended college. The College of Rhode Island (Brown University) was not established until 1770. The Newport and Providence gentry founded literary, philosophical, and musical clubs in the 18th century, but most colonists had little schooling and slight access to high culture. The GREAT AWAKENING affected Rhode Island less profoundly than neighboring Connecticut, as the colony's religious life was already splintered among several Protestant denominations. It was the most liberal of the New England colonies but the least communitarian; a great social gap divided its urban merchants and seafarers from village farm families.

Further reading: Carl Bridenbaugh, *Fat Mutton and Liberty of Conscience: Society in Rhode Island, 1636–1690* (Providence: Brown University Press, 1974); Sydney V. James, *Colonial Rhode Island: A History* (New York: Scribner's, 1975).

—Darcy R. Fryer

Rittenhouse, David (1732–1796)

David Rittenhouse is perhaps most significant as the first celebrated American natural mechanical genius. Born near Germantown, PENNSYLVANIA, Rittenhouse acquired a set of books and tools from his uncle when he was a young man on his father's farm at Norriton. With these he educated himself in horology, astronomy, optics, instrument-making, and mathematics, during the course of which he achieved a mastery of Isaac Newton's epoch-making *Principia Mathematica* (1687). The achievements of Rittenhouse's early years were mainly in astronomy. His orreries (mechanical planetaria illustrating the movements of the planets and other celestial bodies) brought him considerable fame during the 1760s, inviting comparisons with Newton himself. Thomas Jefferson was even moved to rechristen the orrery a "Rittenhouse," such was the nationalistic pride he took in his fellow countryman's technical accomplishments. Rittenhouse's second major early contribution was his work observing the transit of Venus across the sun in 1769. To this end he built an observatory to house a new telescope of his own construction—the first by an American.

Rittenhouse continued to work in both mathematics and experimental SCIENCE and TECHNOLOGY throughout his life, but he also became involved in the practical political reorganization necessitated by the American Revolution. Although not generally known for strong ideological commitments, Rittenhouse signed the most radically democratic state constitution of the period, the Pennsylvania Constitution of 1776. During the War for Independence he oversaw saltpeter and cannon production and became president of the Council of Safety. Among numerous other offices, he taught natural philosophy at the University of Pennsylvania, succeeded Benjamin Franklin as president of the AMERICAN PHILOSOPHICAL SOCIETY, and, once more paralleling the career of Newton in England, became the first director of the United States Mint. Rittenhouse engaged in several projects involving boundary and river surveying, especially after the 1780s, and was, in general, an active advocate of useful knowledge and practical improvements (such as canal navigation and AGRICULTURE), despite the lack of success such projects typically met with in this era.

His considerable technical achievements, public service, and renowned moral character aside, Rittenhouse, despite his lack of formal education, commanded an apparently innate ability in astronomy, mathematics, and mechanical construction. Comparing him to Benjamin Franklin, the greatest American exemplar of autodidacticism (self-education), Thomas Jefferson said of Rittenhouse that among astronomers "in genius he must be the first, because he is self taught."

See also AMERICAN ENLIGHTENMENT.

Further reading: Brooke Hindle, *David Rittenhouse* (Princeton, N.J.: Princeton University Press, 1964).

—James Delbourgo

Rolfe, John (1585–1622)

A VIRGINIA settler and husband of POCAHONTAS, John Rolfe was born into a yeoman family in Heachem, Norfolk, England. He sailed for Virginia in 1609 in the *Sea Venture,* which was wrecked off Bermuda. Stranded for several months, where his first daughter was born, Rolfe and the castaways made their way to Virginia on two Bermuda-made pinnacles. In 1612, after the death of his wife and child, Rolfe began experimental trials in cultivating native Virginian and CARIBBEAN TOBACCO, which by 1617 yielded a leaf that "smoked pleasant, sweet, and strong," with high value relative to the cost of transporting it to England. Tobacco quickly became Virginia's chief export, spurring the rapid demographic and economic growth of the Chesapeake area colonies.

Rolfe fell in love with Pocahontas during her CAPTIVITY in Jamestown in 1613. After agonizing over union with a once "heathen Savage," Rolfe eventually married Pocahontas in 1614, with the blessings of POWHATAN and SIR THOMAS DALE (the leader of the Jamestown colony). The VIRGINIA COMPANY OF LONDON immediately touted their wedlock as an example of successful missionary efforts among the Powhatan, the willingness of the Indians to adopt English "civilized ways," and a new Anglo-Powhatan accord. To attract new settlers and fresh investments, the company in 1616 sent the Rolfes, their son Thomas (b. 1615), the priest Uttamatomakkin, and an entourage of fellow Powhatan on a promotional tour of England. While touring London, Rolfe sent an optimistic description of Virginia to Sir Robert Rich and King James I (1603–25); meanwhile, Uttamatomakkin was unimpressed by the king's unimposing physical presence and insulted by his stinginess. King James spurned an audience with Rolfe because, as a commoner, he had transgressed CLASS boundaries by marrying a member of the Powhatan aristocracy. Returning home to Virginia in March 1617, Pocahontas suffered a lung infection and died off Gravesend; she was interred in the nave of St. George's Church.

Deeply saddened, Rolfe left the sickly Thomas under the guardianship of Sir Lewis Stukly and returned to Virginia, where he resumed his office as the colony's secretary and recorder until 1619. In the same year Rolfe made note of Virginia's burgeoning market in indentured servants, the scandalous "buying and selling men and boies," that his tobacco experiments and the resulting boom had created. In 1619 he married Jane, the daughter of local magnate and councillor Captain William Pierce, who at the time owned Angelo, an African servant woman, among the first brought to Virginia in August 1619. In 1621 Rolfe was appointed to the council of state representing his home settlement, Bermuda Hundred. Bermuda Hundred and Rolfe's plantation *Varina* were destroyed during Opechancanough's uprising in 1622 and, probably with it, John Rolfe. Jane Rolfe and their baby Elizabeth somehow survived. Thomas Rolfe, the son of John and Pocahontas, came home to Virginia as a young man in 1635 and reclaimed his father's lands. Thomas married an Englishwoman, Jane Poythress, and their offspring became the ancestors of Virginia's great aristocratic families—the Blairs, Bollings, Randolphs, and Lewises.

—James Bruggeman

Roman Catholics

The number of Roman Catholic settlers in the British colonies was negligible compared to the SPANISH COLONIES and FRENCH COLONIES, where they constituted a majority. Of the approximately 2.5 million inhabitants of British North America at the time of the American Revolution, only about 1 percent can be identified as Roman Catholics. They were most numerous in MARYLAND and PENNSYLVANIA, where unique conditions of religious toleration were present, either temporarily or permanently.

Cecilius Calvert, the second lord Baltimore and a Catholic, intended to turn his colony of Maryland into a refuge for others of his faith when the first ships sailed for that colony in 1634. However, he also needed to attract enough settlers to make the enterprise a paying proposition, and, ultimately, Maryland enticed more Protestant than Catholic immigrants. In the early years of the colony all settlers were granted land on equal terms, and religious freedom prevailed, although the government was largely Catholic. When the ENGLISH CIVIL WAR broke out, however, Richard Ingle and his Protestant followers seized the Maryland government, and Roman Catholics were singled out for abuse. In the aftermath the Calverts were careful to appoint mostly Protestants to government posts, and they made sure legally to guarantee the religious rights of all the settlers. The 1649 Act Concerning Religion mandated punishments for those who attacked Christianity or violated anyone's rights to worship freely. Maryland's Roman Catholics were increasingly marginalized because of official preference for Protestants. In 1655 a Puritan-controlled council seized power, repealed the Act Concerning Religion, and disenfranchised all Roman Catholics. By 1658 the Calverts regained control but remained wary of alienating the Protestant majority.

The Protestant majority protested that they were being taxed for the benefit of a Catholic minority. The Anglicans in particular believed that their inability to grow in numbers resulted from government policy. These charges received increased attention in the wake of the GLORIOUS REVOLUTION in England, when the Maryland governors were accused of being Jacobites (supporters of the deposed James II) and of attempting to make Catholicism the established religion of the colony. Moreover, they charged that the Roman Catholics were in league with NATIVE AMERICANS in a plot to exterminate all Protestants.

A Protestant army under former Anglican minister John Coode seized the capital of ST. MARY'S CITY in 1689. They demanded a thoroughly Protestant government, removal of the Calvert proprietors, and conversion of Maryland into a royal colony. This was implemented in 1691, as well as an oath of allegiance that excluded Roman Catholics from voting and holding public office. Catholic Mass was permitted only in private homes. In 1702 the ANGLICAN CHURCH became the established church in Maryland. By the early 18th century the Calverts again regained control of the colony, although they, along with many other prominent Roman Catholics, converted to Anglicanism.

Laws were passed to limit immigration of additional Roman Catholics to Maryland. Lacking public support, Catholicism was maintained in secret. Wealthy Roman Catholics could afford to hold Mass in their private chapels and send their children abroad for EDUCATION in European Catholic institutions. Poor Roman Catholics were not so fortunate. For them, itinerant Jesuit missionaries provided what they could. In 1745 the JESUITS opened a secret elementary school at Bohemia Manor in Cecil County near the Pennsylvania border. The Catholic minority was kept under scrutiny because it was rumored that they favored the restoration of the Stuarts to the British throne. During the SEVEN YEARS' WAR Roman Catholics were double-taxed for not serving in the militia, from which they were legally excluded as suspected traitors. By 1763 Roman Catholics constituted only 9 percent of the population of Maryland.

In Pennsylvania Roman Catholics made up an even smaller percentage of the population (approximately 0.6

percent in 1760) than in Maryland, but they enjoyed greater religious freedom. This was due largely to the influence of WILLIAM PENN's belief in religious toleration and his close friendship with prominent Roman Catholics in England, especially King James II (1685–88). As in Maryland, the chief impediments to Catholic growth in Pennsylvania were the Glorious Revolution and the opposition of the Anglican Church. In 1693 Roman Catholics were excluded from holding public office by the requirement that they take an oath of allegiance. William Penn lost control of his colony during this period, but when he regained it he attempted to restore full religious liberty. That was not to be, for the British government insisted on Catholic exclusion from office.

Roman Catholics prospered, however, in the nonpublic sphere. QUAKERS assisted them in obtaining land for their churches, where, unlike in Maryland, they were free to worship openly. The Catholic population grew slowly, principally by immigration from Maryland and Germany. Many Roman Catholics married Protestants, attended Protestant churches, and modified a strict observance of Catholic practices. This was unavoidable given the scarcity of Catholic marriage partners, the shortage of priests, and the generally amicable relations with their neighbors. Jesuit missionaries from Maryland, who traveled secretly into Pennsylvania to minister to rural Roman Catholics, tried to keep the faith alive under difficult circumstances. By 1734 there was a Catholic church in PHILADELPHIA with a resident priest, and a second chapel was built in 1763.

Anglican clergymen frequently complained of Quaker toleration of Roman Catholics. They often interpreted their lack of proselytizing success in Pennsylvania as the result of an insidious Quaker-Catholic collaboration. As in Maryland, Roman Catholics came under careful scrutiny during times of crisis. After Penn died in 1718 and the conversion of his successors to Anglicanism, limitations were placed on the growing immigration into the colony of the Catholic Irish and German REDEMPTIONERS. Roman Catholics frequently were suspected of being a potential "fifth column" in wartime. During the Seven Years' War anti-Catholic fears reached a peak with attacks on a number of their churches and with the passage of the 1757 Militia Act that taxed Roman Catholics heavily and prohibited them from joining the militia and from owning guns or ammunition.

There were very few Roman Catholics in the other colonies of British North America. Notably, a Catholic governor of NEW YORK, Thomas Dongan, sponsored a bill of rights in 1683 that contained a guarantee of religious freedom. During the GLORIOUS REVOLUTION Jacob Leisler, a German Calvinist, overthrew Dongan's government and forced the Catholic clergy to flee. By 1693 the Church of England was the established religion of the colony, and Roman Catholics were restricted. Subsequent harsh legislation banning priests from the colony meant that few Roman Catholics remained in New York during the 18th century; many of them migrated to Pennsylvania.

Roman Catholics were much more numerous and influential in the Spanish and French colonies. The DOMINICANS, Jesuits, and Franciscans sent missionaries into Spanish FLORIDA, Texas, NEW MEXICO, and California. While converting thousands of NATIVE AMERICANS, the work of these Christians also sometimes had tragic results as the cultures of indigenous peoples were undermined and their populations decimated by European diseases. Spanish Catholicism remains an important religious force in the western United States today. Jesuit JACQUES MARQUETTE led the efforts to convert Indians in New France, especially in the continent's interior along the Mississippi River.

Further reading: James Hennesey, *American Catholics: A History of the Catholic Community in the United States* (New York: Oxford University Press, 1981).

—Joseph J. Casino

Rowlandson, Mary White (1637?–1711)

Author of the first published Indian CAPTIVITY narrative, Mary White Rowlandson was born in Somerset, England, to John White and Joan West White. The Whites immigrated to MASSACHUSETTS in 1639, eventually settling in Lancaster in 1653, where John White became one of the town's wealthiest landowners. In 1656 Mary White married Joseph Rowlandson, Harvard graduate and Lancaster's first minister. The Rowlandsons had four children, three of whom were living when NARRAGANSETT attacked the town on February 10, 1676, during KING PHILIP'S WAR.

Joseph Rowlandson was away in BOSTON petitioning for military reinforcements when Indians raided and burned their palisaded house, one of six in Lancaster built as a defense against Native American assault. Mary witnessed the death of several relatives before she and 23 others, including her children, a sister, and six nieces and nephews, were captured. Her youngest daughter, Sarah, died as a result of her wounds several days into their captivity.

Rowlandson became the prisoner of Quinnapin, the Narragansett sachem, and his chief wife, Weetamoo, King Philip's sister-in-law. During her captivity she bartered her sewing and knitting skills for FOOD and other supplies from her captors, including King Philip (METACOM). Historians estimate Rowlandson traveled 150 miles in 11 weeks before she was redeemed for £20 on May 2, 1676.

Rowlandson joined her husband in Boston and was soon reunited with her two remaining children, one of whom had also been ransomed and the other of whom had escaped. Called to a new church, Joseph moved the family to Wethersfield, CONNECTICUT, in 1677, where he died on November 24, 1678. Eight months later Mary married Captain Samuel Talcott, another Harvard graduate and community leader. Captain Talcott died on November 11, 1691; Mary died on January 5, 1710.

Rowlandson probably composed her text, *The Sovereignty & Goodness of God, Together with the Faithfulness of His Promises Displayed; Being a Narrative of the Captivity and Restauration of Mrs. Mary Rowlandson*, shortly after her release, but it was not published until 1682 in a first edition bracketed by an anonymous preface and her first husband's last sermon. Scholars agree that INCREASE MATHER penned the preface. The narrative quickly became a best-seller, and it has rarely been out of print since. Rowlandson constructed a powerful Puritan text of a Christian soul fortified by trial in the wilderness as well as the story of a survivor who ultimately negotiated the price of her own ransom. Her book became the prototype for the Indian captivity narrative.

Further reading: Kathryn Zabelle Derounian-Stodola and James Arthur Levernier, *The Indian Captivity Narrative, 1550–1900* (New York: Twayne, 1993); Rebecca Blevins Faery, "Mary Rowlandson" (*Legacy* 12:2 (1995), 121–32).

—Mary Murphy

Royal African Company

The Royal African Company, chartered by King Charles II (1660–85) in 1672, held the monopoly on England's slave traffic until 1698. Beginning in the late 1500s, a few English vessels had trafficked in slave cargo. However, England was a latecomer to the SLAVE TRADE, which had been dominated by Portuguese, Spanish, French, Dutch, and Danish importers. The first British experience with African slaves in its home territory occurred when colonists in JAMESTOWN, VIRGINIA, bought a few "negars" from a Dutch trading ship in 1619. The English colonies' involvement in SLAVERY was then haphazard until 1663, when Charles II, the restored Stuart king, chartered the Royal Adventurers Trading to AFRICA. The company floundered during the English–Dutch wars and was then replaced by the Royal African Company, which established FORTS along the coast of West Africa from which to launch raids upon or trade with local Africans to procure slaves. Although slaves were landed at several colonial ports in the Americas, the company concentrated its efforts on Jamaica and other British-controlled West Indian islands, sending an estimated yearly average of more than 100 ships carrying as many as 400 slaves each. In 1698 English MERCHANTS pressured Parliament to throw open the slave trade to individual entrepreneurs, ending the Royal African Company's monopoly. In 1731 the Royal African Company discontinued the commerce in slaves, replacing it with trade in ivory and gold, thereby avoiding the risk of having the cargo resist, fall ill, or die. However, by 1750 a new British slave company, the Merchants Trading to Africa, resumed the lucrative trade in human LABOR.

—Emma Lapsansky

royal colonies

Royal colonies were those under the direct and immediate authority of the British MONARCHY, ruled by governors appointed by the Crown. Except for RHODE ISLAND and CONNECTICUT, all of the original thirteen colonies began as chartered or proprietary colonies. However, most surrendered their charters and became royal colonies as they encountered various governmental problems. By the end of the colonial era, royal colonies had become the dominant form of colonial government.

Following the British political model, royal colonies had a similar three-part structure: a governor, legislature, and a judiciary. The Crown, on the recommendation of the Board of Trade and Plantations, named the governor. As the chief representative of the Crown, he was invested with wide powers to implement British laws. The governor also enjoyed the right to call and dissolve the legislature, to approve the choice of its speaker, and to initiate and veto its legislation.

The legislatures in most colonies existed as bicameral bodies. The upper house, representing the colonial elite, developed from the advisory council of the governor's wealthy appointees. The lower house (assembly) represented local interests in the law-making process; it was elected by the white male property owners. Judges usually were appointed and could be dismissed by governors, while the upper house acted as the highest colonial courts of appeal. Although initially the power of royal governors vis-à-vis the legislature was even greater than the British MONARCHY had in its relation with Parliament, the colonial assemblies after the GLORIOUS REVOLUTION steadily reduced the prerogatives of the governors, particularly in legislation and finances.

The experience of the royal colonies contributed significantly to the American political tradition, enriching it with ideas and institutions from Britain. At the same time, the development and transformation of these institutions in North America stimulated political trends and processes that ultimately helped create the War for Independence.

Further reading: Jack P. Greene, *The Quest for Power: The Lower Houses of Assembly in the Southern Royal*

Colonies, 1689–1776 (Chapel Hill: University of North Carolina Press, 1963).

—Peter Rainow

rum trade

The introduction of sugarcane and SLAVERY into the West Indies gave rise to the PLANTATION SYSTEM, which entailed the transport of more than 11 million Africans as slaves to the Americas and established the foundation for the Atlantic ECONOMY. Sugar (known as a cash crop because of its enormous initial profits) and its by-product rum (distilled from molasses) quickly became incredibly important commodities. As the productive capabilities of the sugar plantations increased, the price of sugar, molasses, and rum decreased. Inexpensive rum thus became the drink of choice in the Americas, especially among the lower classes, who mixed rum and water to produce grog. The demand for rum created a transatlantic trade in the commodity that centered not only on the West Indies, where the best quality rum came from, but also on New England. MERCHANTS in PENNSYLVANIA and especially New England established a lucrative rum trade with the West Indies, thereby earning sufficient credit to purchase consumer goods from England. Merchants throughout the Atlantic found rum to be a durable, desirable, and easily transportable commodity that served middlemen well.

The rum trade is best known as part of the "triangle trade": New Englanders purchased molasses in the West Indies, distilled it into rum in New England, carried it to West AFRICA to trade for slaves, then sold Africans in the West Indies and bought more molasses. The rum trade illustrates the ability of colonists to evade the Navigation Acts by which Britain hoped to create a tightly controlled mercantile system. North Americans became capable smugglers, trading illegally with the French, Dutch, and Spanish. They thereby circumvented the Molasses Act of 1733 and increased both their CONSUMPTION and production of rum. By the late 1760s more than 6 million gallons of molasses was imported annually into British North America, while approximately 5 million gallons of rum was produced yearly in 140 distilleries operating mainly in New England.

See also TRADE AND SHIPPING.

Further reading: John J. McCusker, *Rum and the American Revolution: The Rum Trade and the Balance of Payments of the Thirteen Continental Colonies* (New York: Garland, 1989).

—Ty M. Reese

Russian settlements

The primary Russian colony in North America was in present-day Alaska, but their interests extended southward along the west coast of North America. At the height of their North American colonization, the Russians made efforts to explore the Columbia River and established a fort 50 miles north of San Francisco. The movement to Alaska was part of the Russian eastward expansion. The period of Russian settlements is generally dated from 1741, beginning with explorations by Aleksei Chirikov and VITUS JONASSEN BERING. Russian fur traders found the region a good source for business, although the first permanent settlement was not established until 1784 as a private venture of Grigorii Shelikhov and Ivan Golikov on Kodiak Island. This enterprise evolved into the Russian American Company in 1799, with the czar as one of the stock owners. The leading characters of the early company were Nikolai Rezanov, the company head, and Alexander Baranov, who was eventually appointed governor. The colony expanded when New Archangel (Sitka) was founded in 1799.

Russian success in the control of the native populations varied, with their treatment of native peoples often being brutal. They sometimes held women and children hostage to compel ALEUT men to hunt sea otters. As the ANIMALS were decimated, the Russians forced Aleut to exploit new hunting grounds as far south as California. The Tlingit's resistance to the Russian advances was more successful. In 1802 they destroyed New Archangel before the Russians were able to gain a permanent foothold in the area. The Russians gained control of territory, but not Tlingit.

In 1867 Russia envisioned its future primarily in Asia and, believing the expansion of the United States to be almost unstoppable, it sold Alaska to the United States for $7.2 million.

Further reading: Raymond Henry Fisher, *Bering's Voyages: Whither and Why* (Seattle: University of Washington Press, 1977).

—Donald E. Heidenreich, Jr.

S

sachems

An ALGONQUIN term, *sachem* refers to leaders of the Algonquin Indians or IROQUOIS Indians who lived in northeastern North America. Indigenous peoples of this region typically were divided into family-based clans and villages. Sachems were generally the acknowledged leaders of a clan who oversaw intertribal diplomacy, village ceremonies, tribal councils, and warfare against rival tribes. Merit as a courageous warrior or skilled hunter was a common path to appointment as a sachem, while among some groups the position was hereditary. Among the Iroquois, however, women made the appointments.

European colonists often interpreted Indian sachems according to their own understanding of a powerful MONARCHY; in reality sachems possessed much more limited authority. Power was derived from consensus building and concern for the overall welfare of the tribe. Communal in nature, Algonquin and Iroquoian groups expected sachems to put concerns over family, clans, and villages first. Wisdom was associated with generosity and gift giving, in essence providing sachems with the ability to redistribute wealth, a characteristic of a communal society. Such redistribution also provided a tool for persuasion, vital for the tribal unanimity sachems relied on. Dreams also played a powerful role within many of these communities. Sachems were expected to aid in dream fulfillment for a tribal member, and occasionally they derived power from dream interpretation.

See also NATIVE AMERICANS.

Further reading: William C. Sturtevant, *Handbook of North American Indians: Northeast,* vol. 15. (Washington, D.C.: Smithsonian, 1978).

—James Jenks

St. Augustine (founded 1565)

Founded in 1565 by Don Pedro Menéndez de Aviles, St. Augustine, FLORIDA was the first permanently settled European city in the present-day United States. Although Spaniards were aware of Florida long before settling St. Augustine, the decision to settle came in reaction to French colonization attempts near present-day Jacksonville, Florida. The Spanish believed that a presence in Florida would provide military support for Spain's treasure-laden ships that traveled along the Gulf Stream.

Although St. Augustine never produced material wealth, it was frequently the center of military action. British privateer Francis Drake was the first European to attack the city when he nearly destroyed the outpost in 1586. In reaction to frequent attacks the Spanish constructed a large stone fort called the Castillo San Marcos and surrounded the city with earthen, wooden, and stone walls. Although fortified, the presidio was still attacked periodically. The most damaging assaults came in 1702 and 1740. Each time, a British force was sent to remove the Spanish from Florida, and each attempt ended in failure. Throughout the 18th century conquering St. Augustine remained a high priority for British officials in the colonies north of Florida. Thus, defense became St. Augustine's principal purpose.

Life inside the city gates was usually tied to the desires of the military and royal government. Without any significant economic activity, the residents of St. Augustine relied on annual payments from the government. In addition, the local climate and poor soils in the immediate vicinity made the maintenance of a nonmilitary ECONOMY difficult. Malnutrition, DISEASE, and Indian attack were other hazards the Spanish had to accept. Therefore, the city never attracted immigrants, families, or single women. Regardless of the poverty and misery, St. Augustine displayed certain signs of luxury.

More than 50 years before the British first purchased slaves in North America, African slaves were held in Spanish Florida. Because St. Augustine was the first European settlement in North America, it also housed the first slaves. Many of these slaves were owned by the government and came from other Spanish territories. Government slaves were often skilled laborers sent to build and maintain a city's defensive fortifications. Others belonged to a few wealthy residents and worked primarily as domestics.

From the outset the Spaniards found maintaining the colony a difficult task. While its population was never significant and the economy rarely improved, St. Augustine remained the central settlement in Spanish Florida. In 1763 the British took control of Florida following the SEVEN YEAR'S WAR. Twenty-one years later the Spanish regained St. Augustine after the British lost America's War for Independence. St. Augustine remained a part of the Spanish empire until the United States government took possession of Florida in 1819.

Further reading: Eugene Lyon, *The Enterprise of Florida: Pedro Menéndez de Avilés and the Spanish Conquest of 1565–1568* (Gainesville: University Presses of Florida, 1974).

—Shane Runyon

St. Mary's City

St. Mary's City was the first capital of MARYLAND and the fourth permanent North American English settlement. In 1632 King Charles I (1625–49) granted GEORGE CALVERT, the first lord Baltimore, land from the original VIRGINIA grant to create a colony. Calvert died soon thereafter, and his sons, Cecelius Calvert (the second lord Baltimore) and LEONARD CALVERT (Maryland's first governor) recruited both Catholic and Protestant settlers from various social classes.

Founded in 1634 when Leonard Calvert and 140 English settlers arrived on the pinnaces *Ark* and *Dove,* St. Mary's City was established as the nucleus of lord Baltimore's colony in the New World. St. Mary's City was a small village located on an inlet where the St. Mary's River flows into the Potomac River. Baltimore envisioned a hierarchical manorial system of landlords and TENANTS, which was common in England, and servants outnumbered gentlemen in St. Mary's City. Laborers composed a greater percentage of the workforce than did skilled workers.

A Catholic refuge promoting religious toleration, St. Mary's City served as the base for ROMAN CATHOLICS in the English colonies. Because of the city's proximity to the Atlantic Ocean, shipbuilders settled in St. Mary's City. The Woodland Indians, primarily the Piscataway, coexisted with the settlers of St. Mary's City, teaching them to plant TOBACCO. The natives, however, eventually emigrated from their land due to strife with colonists.

Tobacco growers farmed land surrounding St. Mary's City, and their plantations contained vast acreage worked by slaves. Both SLAVERY and INDENTURED SERVITUDE were common in St. Mary's City, with servants helping in homes as well as tending livestock and gardens. A Dutch ship brought 20 Africans to Maryland in 1619. Within four decades almost 400 Africans lived in the area. Because the Maryland colony thrived on its tobacco ECONOMY, a statehouse was built at St. Mary's City to serve as a court. Inns and taverns were erected, and such businesses as a printing shop were opened. Men outnumbered women six to one; unmarried women enjoyed rights to land, which was not common in England.

From 1645 to 1646 St. Mary's City was embroiled in Ingle's Rebellion. During the ENGLISH CIVIL WAR this Protestant uprising occurred in Maryland in an attempt to remove the colony's Catholic government. The rebellious forces seized and looted property in St. Mary's City, took prisoners, and caused Leonard Calvert and several hundred residents to flee. Calvert hired mercenary soldiers from Virginia to end the conflict. Some Protestants, such as William Claiborne, continued to wage attacks on St. Mary's City, but unsuccessfully. After the rebellion yeoman planters dominated St. Mary's City's economy. Some servants became landowners, and earlier unequal land and wealth distribution became more balanced.

In 1689 John Coode paralyzed the government in Maryland by seizing government records and preventing ships from departing St. Mary's City to England. Believing Coode's false accusations that Roman Catholics planned to massacre Protestants, England's rulers, William and Mary, appointed Lionel Copley the first royal governor in 1691. His successor, Francis Nicholson relocated the capital to Annapolis in 1695, and St. Mary's City was abandoned by many of its residents.

See also MARGARET REED BRENT.

Further reading: Gloria L. Main, *Tobacco Colony: Life in Early Maryland, 1650–1720* (Princeton, N.J.: Princeton University Press, 1982).

—Elizabeth D. Schafer

Sandys, George (1578–1644)

George Sandys was an important figure in the early VIRGINIA colony, and he became a renowned poet. The son of Edwin Sandys (archbishop of York) and his second wife, Cecily Wilford, he was educated at St. Peter's School, York, and Corpus Christi, Oxford, before entering the Middle Temple for legal training. By family arrangement he married Elizabeth Norton, his father's ward before 1603, but by 1606 the marriage had collapsed. To avoid this unhappy situation, Sandys embarked on a grand tour of the Near East. He wrote the popular *Relations of a Journey Begun Anno Dom. 1610* about his travels in the Ottoman Empire, Egypt, Jerusalem, and Italy, concentrating on the history, government, and religions of those areas and approaching them in a humanistic and scholarly way. Upon his return he became involved with the Virginia and Bermuda Companies through his elder brother, Sir Edwin Sandys, who named him to committees on the colony's government and TOBACCO production.

In 1621 he was elected resident treasurer of Virginia and embarked with the new governor, SIR FRANCIS WYATT, aboard the *George.* Sandys's four plantations sustained heavy losses as part of the 1622 attack by the Powhatan; in retaliation Sandys personally led a counterattack against the Tappanhannock. Sandys wrote promotional letters for the colony to attract settlers, sponsored small industries like silk, glass and iron production, and insisted that FOOD crops had to be grown along with tobacco to feed the colony's inhabitants. Returning to England in 1625, after the dissolution of the VIRGINIA COMPANY OF LONDON, Sandys won renown for his translations of Ovid's *Metamorphosis,* which contained many references to North America, and for his court poetry. He served on a Privy Council subcommittee for plantations and acted as the Virginia colony's legal agent during Wyatt's second term as governor. A firm exponent of the Virginia assembly and of self-government, Sandys continued to promote diversified AGRICULTURE and settlement until his death on his estates in Kent.

—Margaret Sankey

Savannah

The town of Savannah was laid out in 1733 18 miles from the Atlantic Ocean on a sandy bluff 50 feet above the Savannah River. The site was chosen partly because of its proximity to a local Indian village, partly because of its defensive merits, and partly to substantiate English claims to lands south of the Savannah River. Savannah was designed according to a precisely organized plan. Each town ward was centered on a square, following the fashion of contemporary Georgian Britain, with four public lots and 40 private lots making up the rest of the ward. The initial plan called for six squares, although as the city expanded in the early 19th century there were eventually to be 24 squares. In addition to the town lots, Savannah's plan called for garden plots of 50 acres to surround the town, where residents could grow FOOD. Early buildings were made of wood and did not last long in GEORGIA's humid climate.

After Georgia became a royal colony in 1752, Savannah's population grew rapidly, and new public and private brick buildings began to be built. By the 1760s the town's increasing economic independence meant it was able to import manufactured goods directly from Britain, sending rice and other staples in return. As a further sign of the increased importance of the town, slave ships from African ports began to TRAVEL directly to Savannah. However, although a number of free and enslaved Africans lived and worked there, Savannah never had a black majority population. Indeed, the various employment opportunities offered in the town meant it contained far more white working people than did surrounding rural areas. The town also had a number of elite residents. As the seat of colonial government, Savannah attracted MERCHANTS, politicians, and planters, and their lifestyles stood in stark contrast to the poverty of the majority of the town's population. Savannah was a cosmopolitan place where rich and poor, slave and free, and black and white interacted in a multitude of complex ways.

—Timothy James Lockley

scalping

In many Native American societies the removal of a scalp served as a symbol with military and religious significance. Although some scholars have suggested that Europeans introduced scalping to the Americas, archaeological and other evidence offers convincing proof that scalping was widespread throughout North America before the European arrival. While the particular rituals varied by tribal group, the ceremonial removal of a defeated enemy's scalp was a common feature of Indian warfare.

The scalplock, a long lock of hair typically located on the top of the head, was a source of pride for Indian men. While European visitors often derided the Indian men's apparent obsession with braiding, decorating, and occasional painting of their hair, they failed to recognize the religious significance of the scalplock. Especially for men, the scalplock represented the soul or spirit; elaborate dressings and styles were not so much signs of vanity as they were statements of spiritual power. By cutting off the scalplock, or even by grabbing the lock without actually severing it, the power of the individual's spirit was transferred from the victim to the conqueror. The removal of the scalp did not always coincide with actual death, but survivors were considered to be spiritually dead. The religious significance of scalping was evident in the elaborate rituals surrounding the cutting of the scalp and in the careful attention to its subsequent display. The scalps also served as visible evidence of a warrior's martial prowess. Public display of the trophies offered a daily reminder of the courage and skill of the possessor.

When Europeans arrived in the Americas, they displayed a mixture of fascination and repulsion over the practice of scalping. Visions of bloody scalps haunted terrified colonists on the frontier, who saw nothing but savagery in the ritual. Other accounts described in almost clinical detail the methods of removal and preservation. Colonial governments quickly set aside their supposed shock at scalping and encouraged the practice through the institution of scalp bounties. As early as the 1630s, authorities in New England offered money for the scalps of their Indian enemies. When the intercolonial wars between France and England broke out in the late 17th century, each side offered financial remuneration not only for Indian scalps but for European scalps as well. The bounties continued into the Revolutionary War despite the protests of some colonists that the practice was morally suspect and militarily ineffective. As Americans pushed westward in the 19th century, scalping continued to be a significant component of the Anglo-Indian conflict, especially in border regions.

Further reading: James Axtell, *The European and the Indian: Essays in the Ethnohistory of Colonial North America* (New York: Oxford University Press, 1981).

—Melanie Perreault

science

Early modern investigations of the natural world were not separated into specialized disciplines. The modern fields of mathematics, physics, chemistry, astronomy, and optics were encapsulated in "natural philosophy"; biology, geology, botany, zoology, and mineralogy belonged to "natural history." Moreover, natural studies were generally not thought to conflict with religion. Rather, all such studies were situated within a Protestant framework that cast them as celebrations of the wondrousness, yet also the rationality, of God's creation. Knowledge of nature was godly knowledge, which philosophers felt sure actively supported their religious views. This view of the fundamentally harmonious relation of physical to theological knowledge was often referred to as "physico-theology" or "natural theology," and would not be challenged directly until the evolutionary theories of Charles Darwin in the mid-19th century.

British-American society was emphatically decentralized, so natural studies lacked the support of powerful educational and research institutions and of monarchical or aristocratic patronage. Only a wealthy minority of colonial gentlemen possessed the financial independence and leisure to investigate nature systematically. Where sustained inquiries into nature did thrive, they did so more individualistically than in Europe. More significant than institutions like the BOSTON PHILOSOPHICAL SOCIETY (1683–1688) and the AMERICAN PHILOSOPHICAL SOCIETY (1768) was the vast and intricate web of personal correspondence throughout the colonies and especially across the Atlantic to centers of scientific activity in Britain. This was the vaunted "republic of letters" of the Enlightenment, which made possible the circulation of new ideas about the natural world, technologies for experimentation, and specimens for examination, as well as organizing and sustaining international efforts like the astronomical observations of the transit of Venus across the sun in 1769.

Natural history was the most popular mode of formal natural inquiry in British America. Descriptions of American flora and fauna in the 17th century, like Thomas Harriot's, were catalogs of natural commodities that English MERCHANTS wished to exploit for commercial profit. In the 18th century many colonial gentlemen and some ladies (among them JANE COLDEN) worked to classify plants within the less obviously utilitarian framework designed by Carolus Linnaeus, which distinguished species according to their sexual characteristics. Physiological experiments were also conducted along Linnaean lines, like JAMES LOGAN's on seed fertilization and Dr. John Mitchell's on male–female opossum anatomy, and numerous specimens were shipped back to the Royal Society. JOHN BARTRAM, whom Linnaeus heralded as "the greatest natural botanist in the world," lacked extensive formal EDUCATION but won precious British support for his botanical expeditions through the southern colonies and for cultivating and circulating innumerable plant specimens back to Britain. He was named King's Botanist in 1765.

In natural philosophy Aristotle's teachings shaped American curricula well into the 18th century, but these were eventually eclipsed by the new mechanical philosophy and experimental method introduced by what is now known as the Scientific Revolution. The transition from older textual accounts of nature to modern mathematical and experimental science was profoundly affected by local religious concerns. Charles Morton's *Compendium Physicae* introduced the new experimental philosophy at Harvard in 1687, although at Yale SAMUEL JOHNSON continued to study Aristotle's purely textual accounts into the 1710s. After reading Isaac Newton and JOHN LOCKE Johnson abandoned Aristotle and converted from Calvinism to Anglicanism, because the latter was more scientifically up-to-date. However, Johnson became alarmed at the potential for atheistic philosophies based on Newton and subsequently embraced the teachings of British divine John Hutchinson, who argued that the Bible provided a pious natural philosophy.

"Newtonianism," although widely invoked, was diverse in its applications and ambiguous in its implications. Beginning in the 1720s Isaac Greenwood and John Winthrop IV at Harvard taught an experimental version of Newtonianism with applications to practical mechanics. CADWALLADER COLDEN attempted to perfect Newton's theory of gravity in the 1740s, although religious friends like Samuel Johnson feared that his version of Newtonianism leaned in the direction of philosophical materialism, the view that the natural world sustains itself without any divine assistance. The most celebrated adaptation of Newton was Benjamin

Franklin's experimental work in electricity. Franklin's achievements exemplified the combination of hypothetical speculation, empirical testing, and close observation characteristic of natural philosophy in the Enlightenment. He explained better than any rival the action of positive and negative electrical charges in the Leyden Jar, was the first to prove the identity of lightning and electricity, and invented the lightning rod. Itinerant lecturers in the major cities gave spectacular demonstrations of his electrical system and thereby disseminated experimental methods through public culture.

Beyond the learned and the urban, a wealth of folk beliefs about "occult" operations in nature, many of them astrological, survived and coexisted with the new philosophies. From the 17th century New England clergymen had publicized Copernican astronomy to discredit what they branded as the ungodly folklore of astrology, but almanacs retained astrological advice on MEDICINE, AGRICULTURE, and weather-prediction throughout the colonial period, while comets, earthquakes, and similar natural phenomena remained both astrologically and providentially significant for many. The learned themselves pursued a mixture of new and arcane natural studies. Christian spiritualists transplanted from Germany to PENNSYLVANIA, like Johannes Kelpius and Christopher Witt, drew on alchemy, magic, and religious mysticism in their natural philosophy and medical practices. Ezra Stiles's interests included experimental philosophy, the Jewish Kabbala, and angelology (the systematic study of angels). Popular beliefs about WITCHCRAFT, magic, divining, and like practices, although increasingly marginalized, persisted well beyond the colonial period.

See also AMERICAN ENLIGHTENMENT; INCREASE MATHER; TECHNOLOGY.

Further reading: Herbert Leventhal, *In the Shadow of the Enlightenment: Occultism and Renaissance Science in Eighteenth-Century America* (New York: Oxford University Press, 1976); Raymond Phineas Stearns, *Science in the British Colonies of America* (Urbana: University of Illinois Press, 1970).

—James Delbourgo

Serra, Junípero (1713–1784)

A priest in the Franciscan Order of the Spanish Catholic Church, Junípero Serra was a driving force in the Spanish conquest, colonization, and missionization of modern-day Mexico and California. Born Miguel Jose Serra on the island of Mallorca, Spain, Serra entered the Franciscan Order of St. Francis of Assisi in Palma, Mallorca, and took a new first name, Junípero. Already established as a brilliant scholar and orator, Serra was appointed a professor of theology at age 24, and six years later he received a doctorate in philosophy as well as a professorship at the prestigious Lullian University in Palma. Despite his success in the pulpit and as a professor in Spain, he volunteered to serve the Franciscan MISSIONS in the Spanish New World. In 1750 Serra sailed to Vera Cruz, Mexico, then Baja California in New Spain. Upon landing and despite ill health from the voyage, Serra walked 200 miles from Vera Cruz to begin his mission work at the shrine of Our Lady of Guadalupe, near Mexico City. Serra spent the next 17 years involved in mission activities in New Spain, converting NATIVE AMERICANS to Christianity, preaching, and establishing a string of missions in north-central Mexico. Serra also aided in the foundation of Mexico City's College of San Fernando.

In 1767 the Franciscans were asked to take over the administration of Spanish missions in Alta California following the Jesuit expulsion. In 1769 Serra joined the Gaspar de Portolá expedition to Alta California to found missions at San Diego and Monterey, thereby establishing the Spanish claim to Alta California in the face of compet-

Junípero Serra *(Library of Congress)*

ing European powers and converting Native Americans to Christianity. The missions and their Franciscan administrators ushered in many processes enormously destructive to CALIFORNIA INDIANS. Epidemics, poor diet, strenuous work regimens, hostile Spanish soldiers, suppression of indigenous spirituality and social traditions, crowded living conditions, and the destruction of traditional life patterns created a MORTALITY rate of nearly 40 percent at many Alta California missions. Overall, the California Indian population fell by nearly half, from 320,000 to 170,000, during the Spanish occupation.

Serra spent the rest of his life in Alta California overseeing the establishment of eight additional missions along the California coast and more than 6,000 Indian baptisms. He died at the San Carlos Borromeo mission at Carmel, California, in 1784.

Further reading: Donna Genet, *Father Junipero Serra: Founder of California Missions* (New York: Enslow, 1996).

—James Jenks

Seven Years' War (French and Indian War) (1754–1763)

The French and Indian War ensured the dominance of English-speaking peoples over North America and set the stage for the American Revolutionary War (1775–83). At the end of the war France lost all of her lands in present-day Canada to Britain. With the French threat in North America eliminated, Britain and its colonies could wrangle over the nature of the imperial relationship. In addition, many of the men who would later lead the Americans in their struggle against the British, George Washington, Philip Schuyler, and Benjamin Franklin among them, rose to prominence during that conflict.

This war is known by a variety of names, reflecting three increasingly large dimensions of the conflict. As the French and Indian War, it began in 1754 in what is now western PENNSYLVANIA. A VIRGINIA force of some 400 troops under 22-year-old colonel George Washington was defeated and sent home by a French expedition about double its size. Both had arrived to secure the Ohio Valley, but instead of simply considering this one of many border incidents that had troubled colonial relations since the 17th century, the British government, alarmed that the French had constructed a chain of FORTS from Nova Scotia to the Gulf of Mexico since the end of KING GEORGE'S WAR in 1748, decided for the first time to begin a major war over a colonial dispute. In Europe the conflict is known as the Seven Years' War, because more general fighting broke out in 1756 that pitted Britain and Prussia against Russia (until 1762), France, Austria, and (beginning in 1762) Spain. Historian Lawrence Henry Gipson dubbed the conflict "The Great War for Empire" to call attention to the fact that the skirmish fought by Washington mushroomed into a world war fought on every inhabited continent then known, including Asia, Africa, and South America as well as Europe and North America.

The war's first major combat occurred in western Pennsylvania. In 1755 an expedition of more than 2,000 Virginians and British regulars commanded by General EDWARD BRADDOCK was ambushed and annihilated, with a loss of more than 800 of his men and only 39 of the French and Indians, just before it reached its intended goal of Fort Duquesne (present-day Pittsburgh). Pennsylvania, still ruled by the pacifist Quaker faction, had only grudgingly supplied FOOD and wagons to Braddock. NATIVE AMERICANS in western Pennsylvania had been forced off of their lands in the eastern part of the state during the previous 25 years through treaties the colony had negotiated with the IROQUOIS, whom the colony recognized as sovereign in the area. Consequently, following Braddock's defeat, the Indians launched a ferocious series of attacks that forced the line of European settlement eastward about 100 miles, behind the Susequehanna River. Raiding parties reached the environs of Reading and Bethlehem and came within 30 miles of the port city of PHILADELPHIA.

The British experienced minor victories and major setbacks for two years as they implemented an ambitious plan designed to drive the French from North America once and for all. The British planned to proceed along three fronts toward the center of French power at Quebec: from the west via Forts Duquesne, Niagara, and Oswego; from Louisbourg, the French fort at Cape Breton Island and down the St. Lawrence River from the east; and, after capturing the French Fort Carillon (Ticonderoga), through NEW YORK and up Lakes George and Champlain. However, until 1758, when a large expedition headed by the dying general John Forbes compelled the French to evacuate Fort Duquesne and when Jeffrey Amherst succeeded in conquering Louisbourg, the British enjoyed only minor successes while suffering major disasters. Only the 1755 conquest of Acadia in Nova Scotia—which led to the "ethnic cleansing" of the French ACADIANS ("Cajuns") and their dispersal as far away as LOUISIANA—and the conquest of Kittaning, the main base for Native American attacks in western Pennsylvania, provided relief.

When Sir William Pitt became prime minister in 1757, he realized British forces and resources would be spread thinly throughout the European continent and North America. Thus, he encouraged the raising of royal colonial regiments and funded the various colonies' war efforts to the tune of more than 1 million pounds sterling, perhaps a third of all Britain's expenses. However, the close association of British professional soldiers with colonial volunteers and civilians bred hostility on both sides. The British

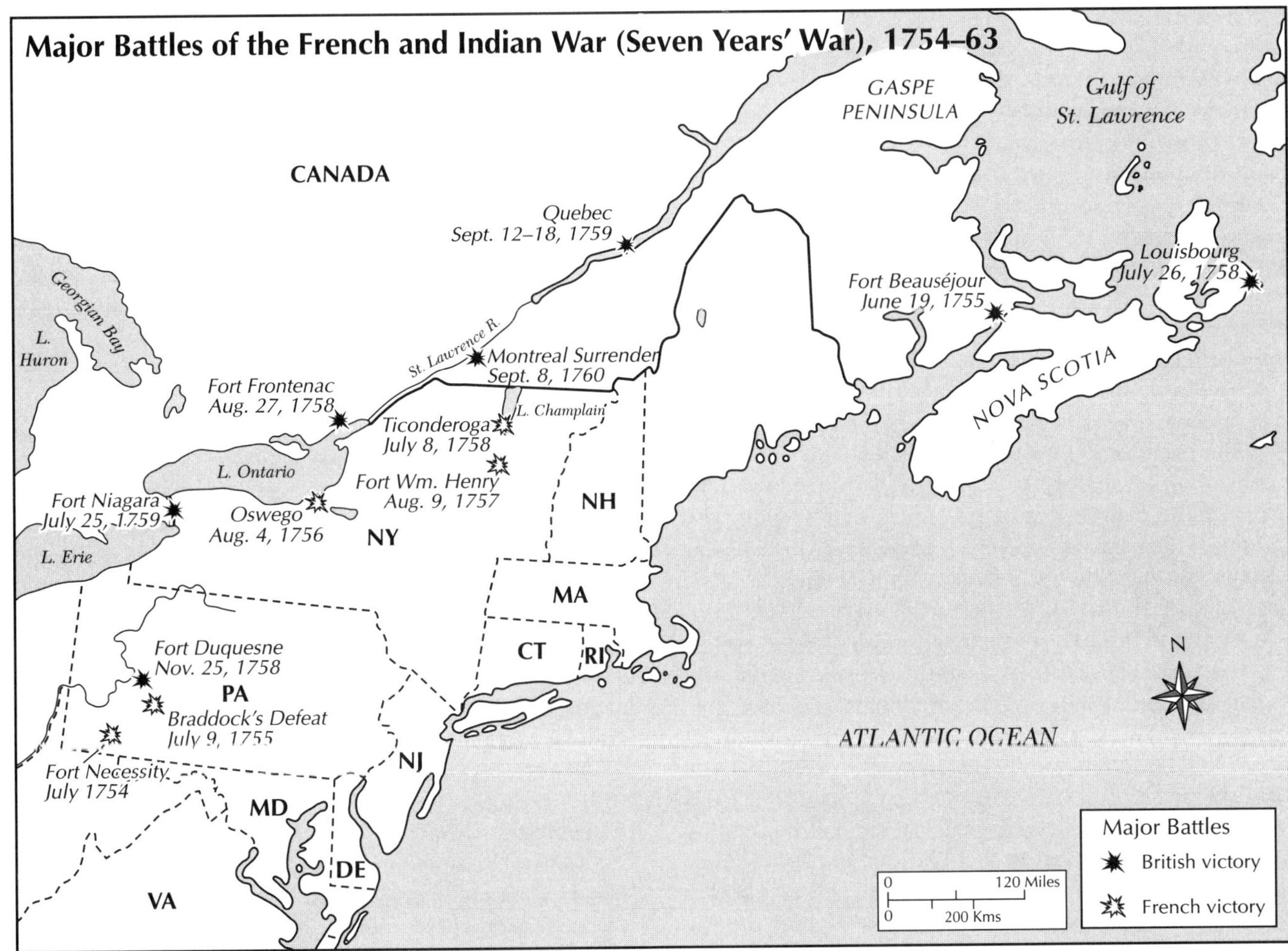

insisted on subordinating all colonial officers to Europeans, attempted to quarter troops in colonial cities to popular dismay, and, in general, relegated colonial soldiers, whom they treated contemptuously, to garrison duty and support work such as digging trenches. In turn, the colonists considered the British officers impossibly arrogant and their common soldiers badly behaved. The colonists insisted on choosing and following only their own officers and returning home each year to tend their farms and shops. MASSACHUSETTS, which provided the most soldiers—up to 8,000 per year—also was the most rambunctious; its troops mutinied 11 times. Other points of contention included American MERCHANTS trading with the enemy (the French West Indies sugar islands offered high prices for American foodstuffs) and the impressment of American MARINERS into the British navy.

The success of JAMES WOLFE in conquering Quebec in 1759 temporarily eclipsed past misunderstandings. Considered reckless, if not insane, by fellow British officers, Wolfe ascended the St. Lawrence with a force of 4,500 men, who seemed to be helplessly stuck before the high cliffs guarding Quebec. Suffering from DISEASE and fearing the onset of winter, which would trap their ships in the river's ice, Wolfe and his soldiers, in a last-ditch effort, climbed the cliffs and presented themselves on September 12 before the city walls on the Plains of Abraham. Instead of waiting for a relief force that was nearby, the French commander, Marquis de Montcalm, led his approximately equal force out of the city and onto the battlefield. Most of it consisted of poorly disciplined Canadian militia and Indians, no match in the open field for the British, but Montcalm, who had only contempt for Indians and nonprofessional soldiers, feared his troops would desert unless he fought immediately.

Although victory at Quebec appeared to have secured the British triumph, important operations remained. Amherst conquered Montreal the following year, and Colonel Henry Bouquet, who with Amherst's knowledge distributed SMALLPOX-infected blankets to Native Americans in a primitive version of germ warfare, temporarily pacified the Ohio Valley. The TREATY OF PARIS (1763), which ended the war, gave Canada and most of the territory in North America east of the Mississippi River (except for NEW ORLEANS and a vaguely defined West FLORIDA) to the British. Defying the royal Proclamation of 1763, British colonists poured into the west. Bouquet and the British army were again required, this time to defeat what has been called PONTIAC'S REBELLION (1763–5). It was actually a great intersocietal rebellion of Native Americans who increasingly were acquiring a common identity, even as white people were defining them collectively as racially inferior, suitable only for extermination or removal.

The futile British effort to curtail westward settlement was only one of many policies that made the Seven Years' War the necessary, if not sufficient, prelude to the American Revolution. Efforts to eliminate illegal trade with the West Indies, from which major American merchants such as John Hancock prospered, stemmed from British anger at colonial trading with the enemy during war and the avoidance of taxes through SMUGGLING. The Stamp Act of 1765 was designed in part so Americans might at least pay the ongoing expenses of the garrisons that Britain was planning for the frontier to prevent future Indian wars.

Perhaps most important, the war ended with two proud and confident victors who had vastly different conceptions of the BRITISH EMPIRE. Convinced that European Britons alone had won the war, the mother country put forth the novel theory that Parliament was sovereign and all colonial legislatures merely subordinate bodies. Pointing to their own substantial efforts during the war, the colonies rejoiced in an empire whose prime virtue was to protect the right to self-government that they had traditionally enjoyed, subject to a vague and loosely enforced British authority. As Britain rejoiced in becoming the world's greatest power, Americans looked forward to a destiny in which their population would continue to grow by leaps and bounds, and they would expand, as a people chosen by their Protestant God, throughout the continent. However, another world war, which developed out of the American Revolution, was required to decide which vision would prevail.

Further reading: Fred Anderson, *Crucible of War: The Seven Years War and the Fate of the British Empire in North America, 1754–1766* (New York: Knopf, 2000).

—William Pencak

Sewall, Samuel (1652–1730)

Puritan, magistrate, diarist, and jurist, Samuel Sewall presents the most complete historical portrait of a MASSACHUSETTS Puritan. Sewall was born in England in 1652 and immigrated with his family to Massachusetts in 1661. He attended HARVARD COLLEGE, class of 1671, and prepared for the ministry. His marriage to Hannah Hull, the daughter of wealthy merchant John Hull, provided a large enough dowry for Sewall to embark on a career in trade. He served several governmental offices. In 1692 he was named to the Salem Court of Oyer and Terminer to judge those accused of WITCHCRAFT, and he was appointed later that year as an associate justice of the Massachusetts Superior Court of Judicature. He served as chief justice of the court from 1718 to 1728 and as a member of the Massachusetts Provincial Council from 1691 to 1725.

Sewall's humanity comes across clearly through his writings. His diary is an encyclopedic account of BOSTON, of Massachusetts, and its people from 1676 to 1728. The diary records everything through Sewall's Puritan eyes: the righteous anger of God at his people during KING PHILIP'S WAR, his sometimes stormy friendships with INCREASE MATHER and COTTON MATHER, his large extended circle of family and friends (their births, marriages, and deaths), and even his old-age indignation at seeing young gentlemen in Boston wearing fashionable wigs. Sewall had a pronounced sense of compassion. He was the only judge of the Salem witches who publicly recanted his judgments and accepted guilt for sending them to their deaths. Sewall stood in front of the congregation of Boston's Old South Church in 1697 while the minister read aloud a prepared statement of repentance.

Sewall also wrote the first antislavery tract in American history, occasioned by "The Numerousness of Slaves at this day in the Province, and the Uneasiness of them under their Slavery." *The Selling of Joseph* was published as a pamphlet in 1700 and decried the practice of importing Africans to America as unlawful and immoral, likening it to the Biblical story of Joseph being sold into slavery in Egypt by his brothers. "It is certain," Sewall wrote, "that all men, as they are the Sons of Adam, are Coheirs; and have equal right unto Liberty, and all other outward Comforts of Life."

Further reading: M. Halsey Thomas, *The Diary of Samuel Sewall 1674–1729* (New York: Farrar, Straus, & Giroux, 1973).

—Stephen C. O'Neill

shamans

The term *shaman* traces its origin to Siberia, where the term describes individuals who cure people of illnesses and have some type of contact with the spiritual or metaphysical world. In North America anthropologists have adopted the term to refer to Native American healers and religious figures from many diverse nations, even when the shaman might play a different role in each society or derive his or her power from a different source. In most tribes a shaman was a religious figure who had the ability to cure illnesses using local flora, through rituals, or by properly interpreting a dream or vision. In some tribes the shaman was distinctly different from political or military figures, while in others political and spiritual power might be unified in one individual. Among the IROQUOIS individuals belonged to a particular MEDICINE society, each of which held certain sacred songs. By the 16th and 17th centuries these societies also used a variety of masks in healing ceremonies, which were in high demand due to the numerous European diseases that spread through Indian communities. Shamans, healers, and medicine societies were tested during the period of colonialism due to the epidemics, against which traditional medicines and rituals seemed ineffective.

Shamans were frequently the objects of derision by Christian missionaries, who often saw the shaman as an impediment to conversion at best and a helper of Satan at worst. When a shaman's power was undermined by his or her inability to cure, a Christian missionary might provide an alternative form of medicine or spiritual power. Indeed, many Indian people turned to missionaries and Christianity only after their traditional shamans seemed to have lost their power. While the shaman remains part of many Native American cultures today, during the colonial period seemingly incurable DISEASE and missionaries' persistent ridicule of their power challenged shamans throughout North America.

Further reading: James Axtell, *The Invasion Within: The Contest of Cultures in Colonial North America* (New York: Oxford University Press, 1985).

—Thomas J. Lappas

shipbuilding

The tall trees of the New England coast provided English colonists with their most valuable resource (after codfish) and the raw materials for the entire shipbuilding industry. A fleet of vessels was a necessity for the colonists to conduct regular transportation and trade with England and with other colonies. It was the one colonial industry that British officials never sought to regulate because ships were always required, especially in time of war, when the merchant fleet suffered losses by the enemy. Ships built and owned by colonial MERCHANTS also allowed them closer control over their commerce without being dependent on ships and merchants in the mother country.

Colonial shipbuilding began in MASSACHUSETTS in the 1640s, where there was the need, the resources, and a growing merchant community. Throughout the colonial period Massachusetts remained the center of shipbuilding activity, taking the early lead in volume of construction. Before the Revolution Massachusetts-made ships accounted for one-third of all American-built vessels. The most important shipyards clustered around BOSTON and along the Merrimack and North Rivers. The industry expanded along the coast of MAINE (then part of Massachusetts) and to other New England colonies. Ships made in Maine, Massachusetts, and CONNECTICUT ranged from small coastal sloops to larger oceangoing ships, characterized by sound design and solid construction.

Shipbuilding centers developed in other colonies during the early 18th century. PHILADELPHIA, soon after its founding, fostered the industry by welcoming shipbuilders. The Chesapeake region and SOUTH CAROLINA developed their own shipbuilding industry, albeit on a much smaller scale. Throughout the colonies shipbuilding added diversity to local business ventures, such as supplementing the TOBACCO trade in the Chesapeake area. Shipbuilding also contributed to the development of direct commerce with Europe, AFRICA, and the West Indies.

Shipbuilding employed hundreds of shipwrights and laborers, who often faced difficult and sometimes dangerous working conditions. They usually worked seasonally. Master shipwrights could become wealthy, while lesser-skilled ARTISANS and laborers sometimes struggled to eke out an existence.

Further reading: Joseph A. Goldenburg, *Shipbuilding in Colonial America* (Charlottesville: University Press of Virginia, 1976).

—Stephen C. O'Neill

Shippen, William, Jr. (1736–1808)

Son of William Shippen, Sr., a respected PHILADELPHIA physician and member of the Continental Congress, William was born in Philadelphia in 1736. He graduated from PRINCETON COLLEGE with highest honors in 1754 and began his medical studies immediately, first with his father, then in London and at the University of Edinburgh. After receiving his M.D. in 1761, Shippen spent six more months studying in Paris. While abroad he married Alice Lee, sister of Richard Henry Lee, future VIRGINIA delegate to the Continental Congress.

Upon returning to Philadelphia in 1762, Shippen began the first anatomy lectures and anatomy school in North America. Here, he added the dissection of human bodies to the traditional pictures and casts used for educational purposes, despite the sometimes violent protests of Philadelphians. When the medical school opened at the University of Pennsylvania, he became its first professor of anatomy and surgery and later taught midwifery to both medical students and women training as MIDWIVES. Shippen was also a founding member of the College of Physicians of Philadelphia, an attending physician at the

Pennsylvania Hospital, and an active member of the AMERICAN PHILOSOPHICAL SOCIETY for many years.

During the Revolutionary War Shippen served the Continental Army in several medically related capacities. Congress accepted his plans for the reorganization of the hospital department, appointing him director general of military hospitals in 1777, a position he held until January 3, 1781. Although later court-marshaled for suspected financial irregularities while serving in the army, he was exonerated.

While studying MEDICINE in Europe, Shippen realized the need for a medical school in America. His long career as a medical educator brought him recognition in both America and Europe. He died in Philadelphia in 1808.

—Anita DeClue

slave codes

SLAVERY preceded the emergence of slave codes in colonial North America. Initially, African-American workers' legal status was often ambiguous. Some were held in lifelong slavery, others were treated as indentured servants, and some acquired freedom through manumission or self-purchase. The earliest known reference to lifelong, hereditary black slavery occurs not in a law but in a 1640 VIRGINIA court decision. This indicates that colonial courts enforced local customs regarding African-American slavery before slavery was enshrined in law.

Slave codes developed haphazardly in the second half of the 17th century as the number of African and African-American workers in the American colonies grew. Slaves' activities were restricted: They were forbidden to carry guns, possess liquor, or own property. At the same time, lawmakers closed off possible avenues to freedom by legislating that conversion to Christianity did not justify manumission and that children followed the status of their mother. Laws against MISCEGENATION and interracial marriage separated the social worlds of African-American slaves and poor white settlers and put a premium on "whiteness." The southern gentry used slave laws as tools for social control; legislators aimed not only to restrict the movements of slaves but also to discourage poor white people from associating with them, lest the two groups cooperate in property crimes or political rebellion.

In 1705 the Virginia legislature codified several decades of legislation pertaining to slaves into a single, massive slave code. Other southern colonial legislatures used the Virginia code and, later, the SOUTH CAROLINA code as models for their own slave codes. (The northern colonies, which were less dependent on slavery, seldom codified their scattered slave legislation into formal slave codes.) Slave codes not only restricted slaves' economic and social activities but also defined their relationship to the law; slaves were generally forbidden to testify under oath and were subject to the death penalty for many offenses that were not capital crimes when committed by whites. Colonial legislatures often revised slave codes as social and political conditions changed. The South Carolina assembly, for example, issued a revised slave code in the wake of the STONO REBELLION of 1739.

Further reading: Leon Higginbotham, *In The Matter Of Color: Race and the American Legal Process in the Colonial Period* (New York: Oxford University Press, 1978); Robert Olwell, *Masters, Slaves, and Subjects: The Culture of Power in the South Carolina Low Country, 1740–1790* (Ithaca, N.Y.: Cornell University Press, 1998).

—Darcy R. Fryer

slave resistance

During the 17th and 18th centuries the emergence of SLAVERY as a legalized institution created a violent system of forced LABOR that spurred the social, economic, and political development of British North America. From the point of their enslavement, when they became property, to their life of endless labor throughout North America's plantations, cities, and farms, slaves did not passively accept their fate. African resistance to slavery by men and women of all ages occurred in a variety of aggressive and subtle ways. Through resistance, bondpeople played a significant role in negotiating the relationship between master and slave.

One of the initial ways that slaves resisted their enslavement occurred after they boarded the slave ships off the West African coast. The majority of ship revolts occurred at the beginning of the transatlantic crossing. At this early stage of the Middle Passage—the voyage of slaves from West AFRICA to the Americas—the coastline remained visible, inspiring some slaves to hope that a successful uprising would enable them to return home. Once the coastline disappeared, insurrections were less common because Africans were chained in the hold, and few had any knowledge about operating European-designed vessels. Even if they killed the crew, where could they go and how would they get there? While most ship revolts were not successful, they greatly worried ship captains and crew, who often used brutal measures to control their human cargo.

Africans continued to resist after arriving in the New World. Open revolt was extremely risky because white people responded immediately and brutally. All slave uprisings on the mainland North American continent ended in the death of rebels and sometimes their family and friends as well. Revolt often constituted an act of desperation, when no other solution seemed available and when a chance of success might be possible. Recently arrived Africans were most likely to resist slavery openly, although this does not mean that seasoned, CREOLE, or American-born slaves passively accepted their position. Most major slave revolts between 1585 and 1763 occurred in the West Indies and in Central and South America, in areas where black people significantly outnumbered white people and where distinct geographical features offered a possibility of success. These conditions existed more rarely in British North America, although slave revolts occurred there as well.

In 1712 a group of approximately 20 slaves and fellow conspirators started a fire in NEW YORK CITY, then waited to ambush the arriving firefighters. Their attack killed nine white people and injured others, but the revolt was quickly quashed. White people engaged in brutal retributions. Local authorities arrested 70 people for their alleged roles in the revolt. Twenty-five slaves were found guilty: 13 were taken to the gallows, six committed suicide before their sentences could be carried out, one starved to death, three were burned at the stake, and one was broken on the wheel. The colony of NEW YORK responded by legislating a very harsh slave code rivaling that of the southern colonies.

In 1739 along the Stono River in SOUTH CAROLINA, the most famous of America's pre–19th-century slave revolts occurred—the STONO REBELLION. A group of 20 slaves forcibly obtained arms and ammunition in the hopes of fleeing to Spanish FLORIDA. One motivation behind this centered on the Spanish king's 1733 declaration making Florida a refuge for runaway slaves. As the slaves started their journey, they attacked, plundered, and burned plantations while killing all the white people they encountered. They also recruited slaves to join them. They were soon engaged by a combination of South Carolinian militia and NATIVE AMERICANS who, because of their superior numbers and firepower, effectively ended the revolt by killing 30 slaves. The colony of South Carolina, greatly fearful that other revolts would follow, prohibited further slave imports and worked to greatly restrict the movement and interaction of slaves.

While slaves initiated the 1712 New York and 1739 Stono rebellions, the NEGRO PLOT OF 1741 in New York City illustrated growing racial and CLASS tensions. In New York, PHILADELPHIA, and other urban areas where masters owned and used slaves, extensive interaction occurred among slaves, indentured servants, and the developing white urban working class. The Negro Plot of 1741 involved not only slaves resisting a system that restricted their freedom as humans, but also the growing economic discrepancies between rich and poor. The plot began when Quack, a slave, was roughly refused entrance into the governor's home to see his wife, a slave cook. Quack, angered by the events that had occurred, went to Hughson's, a tavern frequented by slaves, indentured servants, and members of the working class, to vent his frustrations. Quack soon returned to the governor's home, but rather then visiting his wife he started a fire. As the blaze grew, it threatened the town; soon after, other fires burned throughout the city, causing the free citizens to believe that a slave conspiracy existed. Mobs quickly started to round up slaves, who were tried for conspiracy. In the end, punishments included hanging 17 black people and burning another 13 at the stake; four white people were sent to the gallows for their role in the conspiracy. Another 72 people were banished from the city.

While rebellions constituted the most concerted resistance against the institution of slavery, escape occurred on a continual basis and clearly demonstrated the desire of African slaves to resist bondage. Fleeing was less violent than open rebellion, and the punishment less harsh, even though it was still an activity that undermined the slave system. Among the problems for fugitive slaves was where they could flee to safety because the British colonies all endorsed slavery. In the 17th century some slaves fled to the frontier, although they met with a mixed reception from Native Americans. A few, especially in Florida, found refuge among Indians.

In the 18th century slaves born in North America, capable of speaking English and understanding Euro-American culture, were more likely than new arrivals to take to their heels. These fugitives often possessed the knowledge of where to go and how to get there. The group of slaves best able to disappear from the plantation or their master were those who already possessed or had acquired specialized skills, such as being a smith, which allowed them more easily to find employment in a new location. Cities, especially Philadelphia, New York, and CHARLESTON, were magnets for runaways seeking to blend into a relatively large free and slave population, where they might carve out new lives. Another option for runaway slaves was to escape North America altogether by going to sea as MARINERS. African and African-American "Black Jacks" thus traveled throughout the Atlantic world, and, as the Atlantic ECONOMY developed, an ever increasing number of sailors were needed.

While revolts and flight constituted visible signs of the determination and desire of slaves to resist their enslavement, bondpeople also engaged in more subtle forms of rebellion. Many masters complained of the "laziness" of their slaves, not realizing that their bondpeople were passively resisting their own exploitation. When slaves refused to work, or worked as little as possible, they hindered their master's ability to profit from their labor. In the same vein, slaves also broke tools, hoed plants instead of weeds, harmed domesticated ANIMALS, destroyed crops, burnt buildings, and stole food, liquor, and other commodities from their masters. These subtle forms of resistance decreased the efficiency and profitability of bondage and provided slaves with power to negotiate their relationship with their owner.

Slaves were not passive pawns who humbly accepted their enslavement. Instead, they employed various forms of resistance, from violent uprisings to nonviolent covert work slowdowns. While the threat of ship revolts and slave rebellions struck fear in the hearts of slave owners, more effective forms of resistance sometimes involved the everyday defiance of slavery.

Further reading: T. J. Davis, *A Rumor of Revolt: The "Great Negro Plot" in Colonial New York* (New York: Free Press, 1985); Gerald W. Mullin, *Flight and Rebellion: Slave Resistance in Eighteenth-Century Virginia* (New York: Oxford University Press, 1972); Billy G. Smith and Richard Wojtowicz, eds., *Blacks Who Stole Themselves: Advertisements for Runaways in the Pennsylvania Gazette, 1728–1790* (Philadelphia: University of Pennsylvania Press, 1989).

—Ty M. Reese

slavery

Slavery was the most exploitative and one of the most common forms of LABOR in the New World. Slavery was legal and prevalent throughout all the colonies in North and South America. It was based on a legal definition of a race of slaves, whose status was inherited solely by descent from their mothers and whose lives were subject to special laws or SLAVE CODES, concerning chattel property and the treatment of slaves by masters. Slaves were considered property rather than citizens, possessed virtually no legal rights, could not own property, and were subject to severe corporal and psychological punishments. African slavery on plantations, the dominant form, was adopted by various European colonizers of the West Indies in the 17th century to produce export crops. The Tidewater planters of the Chesapeake area colonies and Lower South imitated them and created slave societies by 1700, although the resulting social structure was quite different than in the West Indies. Slaves could outnumber whites by 10 times or more in the islands in the 18th century, but they composed only about two-fifths of the population of the southern colonies by 1776.

A slave society was defined as one in which a planter CLASS depended primarily on slave labor for basic production, and the entire social structure was oriented to keeping slaves in their place. It comprised two interlocking social formations: The slaves had a social life and maintained cultural ways in their quarters somewhat apart from the whites' dominant culture, but neither side was free of the influence of the other, and together they created a creolized society. All colonies in the Americas had at least some black and a few Indian slaves. They were not all slave societies, however, which were found only in certain geographic areas in some colonies by 1763. Slave societies existed in enclaves on the Atlantic coast of Brazil; the richest West Indian islands, especially the former Spanish possessions of English Jamaica and French Saint-Domingue; the coastal portions of southern continental colonies from GEORGIA to DELAWARE; the isolated NEW ORLEANS Parish in French LOUISIANA, and certain small areas in NEW JERSEY and RHODE ISLAND.

Ancient empires from the Sumerian to the Egyptian included slaves, but the capture of large numbers of "barbarians" enabled the ancient Greeks and Romans to create true slave societies, with many small slaveholders and some giant slave latifundia. Aristotle described his society as composed of a small group of natural masters, a poor majority of Greek men who owned no slaves, and a mass of slaves not fit to be citizens. Estimates are that the slaves of Greece at its height formed a third of the population. The final step in the development of ancient slavery was the codification of the law of slavery, carried out by the Christian Roman emperors.

Ancient slavery began to decline into tenantry and serfdom in the later Roman Empire, but some slaves existed in continental Europe in feudal times until the 15th century, most of European birth, many of them Slavs—thus our word *slave*. They were most numerous in certain towns in Italy and Spain. Vikings and Englishmen also carried on a trade in Irish slaves in medieval times. Then the Portuguese opened up the transoceanic African slave trade, importing the first large cargo of Africans to Lisbon in 1441. The best customers during the first century were Europeans, who had imported 275,000 slaves from Africa by 1600.

The African slave trade opened up the possibility of more structured racial slavery than in the past because of the separation of Africans from their homes and allies by an ocean. By contrast with ancient times, in Europe and the American colonies slavery could be defined racially as "black" and as an indefinitely inheritable status. The Spanish and Portuguese established the special status of black slaves in the Americas. They forcibly moved about 184,000 of them across the Atlantic between 1521 and 1640 to serve as a labor force working to produce staples in the New World. The sugar plantation district in Portuguese Brazil became the largest slave society in the world by 1763 and contained a population of 2,061,532 in 1800, with bondpeople constituting three-fourths of the total population in core regions. By contrast, the great period of Spanish colonial slavery did not begin until after 1763, the year reforms were initiated in Cuba that would make it a large slave society producing sugar to rival Brazil and Saint Domingue.

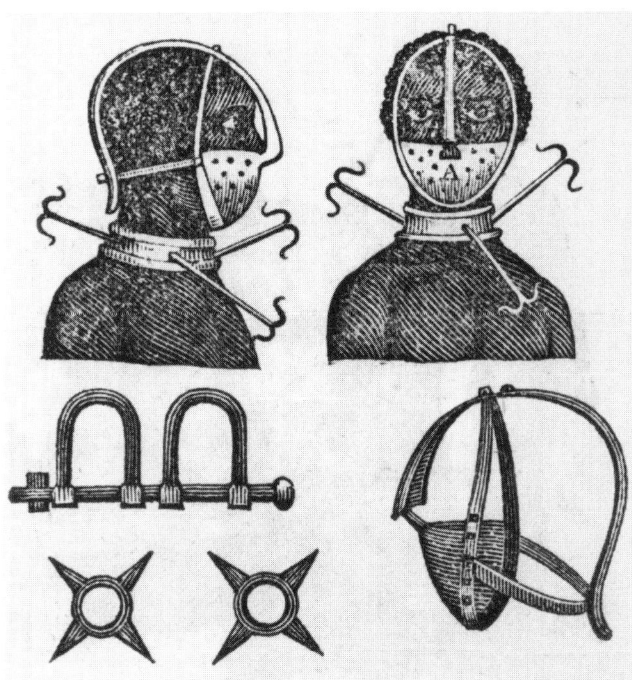

This engraving depicts an iron mask and collar used by some slaveholders to keep field workers from running away and to prevent them from eating crops such as sugarcane. *(Library of Congress)*

The vast majority of the some 11 million slaves brought to the New World during the era of the slave trade (the 15th through the 19th centuries) were carried to the Spanish, Portuguese, French, English, and Dutch colonies in the West Indies and South America. About 427,000 (or 4.5 percent of the total) arrived in the 13 North American colonies and the United States before prohibition of the African slave trade by the federal government in 1808. In 1763 more than 200,000 slaves had already been imported into the thirteen colonies.

The purpose of slavery was to gain profits for masters from the production of staples for export such as TOBACCO, rice, and INDIGO. It resulted in part from the planters' desire to replace or reduce their dependence on white indentured labor. In all North American colonies except in New England after 1660, British indentured servants were a principal component of the labor supply, but exploitation of them was limited in important ways. Indentured servants could not be reduced to slavery. Those who survived their servitude became free; some escaped their contracts and joined neighboring white societies; all were likely, once free, to be turbulently opposed to the restrictive land policies of the Tidewater planters. So eager were they for labor that the planters likely would have reduced white peoples to slavery, but English law, politics in Britain, and the class menace in the colonies represented by white indentured servants led planters to prefer exploiting a race of black slaves. The indentured continued to arrive until the 19th century, but black slaves became the dominant form of labor in the Tidewater region of the South, growing especially numerous during the late 16th and early 17th centuries.

At the time of English arrival in North America, some Native Americans owned a small number of Indian slaves who were neither regarded as a separate race nor intended to labor for their owners' profits. Their children might become respected members of the tribe. In England slavery was not sanctioned by law, nor did it exist there as a social condition. In the New World, however, British colonists, in part from observing slave societies in South America, simply assumed that dark-skinned heathens could be reduced to slaves. British colonists enslaved Indians, especially in the South, but their efforts mostly failed because Indians could too easily escape into neighboring native societies, because the process of capturing Indian slaves often incited wars, and because Indians were more susceptible than were Africans to European diseases. Colonists in all English colonies enslaved some Indians, mainly to export them for sale in the West Indies. At the time when the SOUTH CAROLINA lowcountry became a black slave society (1708), Indian slavery probably reached its peak, when 1,400 Indians constituted nearly a quarter of the slave force; they were mainly women and children because most men were exported for sale in the islands.

Africans became the preferred choice of white planters in the late 17th century for five major reasons. First, the color of Africans made them easier to identify and control, and the entire white population was supposed to police black Africans to minimize their resistance. Second, AFRICA was somewhat outside Europe's ECONOMY, so European slave traders could purchase and export many members of its workforce without concern about the consequences. Third, the supply of indentured servants from Great Britain declined at the end of the 17th century, just when the ROYAL AFRICAN COMPANY began making many more Africans available for sale to Americans. Fourth, some Africans enjoyed partial immunity to malaria, a major scourge of the southern colonies, so they were somewhat less likely to die during the dangerous "seasoning" of people arriving in the New World. Finally, unlike Britons, Africans were familiar with the cultivation of some of the principal export crops in the New World because they were also grown in Africa; they were also familiar with intensive hoe AGRICULTURE. In short, imported Africans offered planters several distinct advantages over indentured Britons: They could be defined as slaves by color and better policed, separated from their homeland, obtained in more steady supply, invested in with less risk, and exploited more profitably because of their superior agricultural skills.

Black slaves were available for sale in Africa because human bondage already existed there, although in a much different form than it was to assume in North America. African masters initially sold war captives, surplus laborers, and unruly slaves (mainly men) to passing traders. Not consciously part of the Atlantic slave trade, masters eventually funneled exiles into a network leading to coastal slave trading posts dominated by the various European powers. Over time a number of free Africans were also kidnapped into slavery, like the famous writer and abolitionist Olaudah Equiano (1745–97), son of a substantial West African slaveholder, kidnapped from his house and reduced to slavery in Virginia in about 1757. He compared African to American slavery in his 1789 autobiography, noting that in Africa masters and slaves performed similar work and a master's authority was no greater than that "which the head of a family possesses" among free people. Moreover, slavery in Africa was not racial and not regarded as indefinitely inheritable; it often permitted certain astute slaves considerable authority in African societies where property relations were most highly developed.

Scholars have debated the proposition that antiblack British cultural attitudes made Anglo-Americans look with special racial contempt on Africans—that is, that racism caused slavery. The other side in this debate insists that racism was primarily the result of slavery, that to satisfy their demand for labor planters would have enslaved white workers if they could, with no racial rationale. The basic decisions that led to a huge growth in the trade during the 18th century arose from shrewd investment in the best skilled workers available. English colonists simply assumed that blacks were slaves, as they had been in Latin American colonies for a century before the first cargo arrived—in Virginia in 1619—and gradually colonial assemblies passed laws to clarify the status of slaves as necessary. Christians were presumptively free, so an important law was to exempt slaves from the moral right to claim freedom if they converted to Christianity. Before any slave laws were passed in a colony, however, slaves existed as a minority of the population, even in the absence of laws. Racial ideas served primarily to justify black slavery after the fact.

Africans came from very diverse cultural origins. Over time the focus of the slave trade shifted steadily from West Africa to Central Africa. Hence every society in America had a special mix of African cultural influences, depending on when the slaves were imported, the nationality of the slave trader, specific tastes of planters for slaves of particular ethnic groups, and historical conditions in Africa. Most slaves imported to North America came directly from Africa or following brief stops on West Indian islands before transshipment to the mainland. The slave populations of the northern colonies were exceptions, composed primarily of West Indians carried to the continent and sold by their owners. In the South most slaves arrived directly from Africa. In North American slave societies slaves became self-reproducing populations by the middle of the 18th century, whereas they succumbed more readily to epidemic diseases in those places where the slave trade was more active and the DISEASE mix more dangerous, like the West Indies. By 1700 slave culture was a syncretic African mix created out of what they brought with them. By 1763, however, strong African culture remained among the newly arrived and older slaves, while a CREOLE (meaning born in America) population was creating new African-American cultural traditions. The latter were oriented primarily to their need to resist the unnatural human power relation by which masters degraded them.

Individual slave societies varied widely, shaped by a number of factors: the ratio of slaves to the white population; the GENDER ratio among slaves; the percentage of African-born and Creoles among slaves; the concentration of slaveholding as measured by the average plantation size; local environmental conditions; the degree of planter absenteeism; the degree of inequality among planters; the work regime based on the specific local export crop(s); the commercial wealth of the local Atlantic port; and the specific historical era in the imperial contest to control transatlantic commerce. Even so, generalizations about slave societies are possible. In comparison to West Indian and Brazilian societies, slave populations in British North America were relatively smaller; their gender ratio became more balanced over time; Creolization produced by natural reproduction was greater; slaveholding was less concentrated; natural provisions and cultivated foods were more abundant (enough to ship a surplus to the islands); the rate of planter absenteeism was much lower; while the "gang system" of labor prevailed in the Chesapeake area, similar to the islands, the individual "task system" characterized the Lower South; Atlantic ports were smaller and less rich than Caribbean ports; and slave populations increased later in North America and at a slower rate than in the islands. African slaves were abundantly available in English colonies in this era—if not cheap at £25–35—but North American planters had a financial motive to extend the value of their investments by encouraging the slave population to reproduce naturally by making them somewhat more comfortable in their daily conditions of life.

In all slave societies Africans recovered from the shock of the slave trade and attempted to form their own communities, but knowledge about the development of many of their intimate social relations in the slave quarters is limited by lack of evidence. The slave community, or "quarter," was usually based on the family unless planters deliberately created situations in which conjugal families could not develop. An unbalanced sex distribution existed to a pronounced degree in the early period, but by the early 1700s women slaves were sufficiently numerous for many families to form in most locations in North America. Extensive kinship ties within and between plantations developed, with many of the rights and obligations of kinship that were typical of Africa, as revealed in naming practices. Contrary to an older impressionistic view of chaotic family relations in the quarters, most slave families had two parental heads and were knit into extended networks for mutual support.

Slaves created their own rules of behavior and social status based on standards similar to those in free society. Although their homes and garden plots belonged to the master, slaves tended to become proprietarial about them. Slave societies established parallel cash economies by which some slaves could accumulate money, either by working for the master or someone else on the free day, Sunday, or by selling on the local domestic market the agricultural and artisanal produce of the soil, forests, and waterways. Masters and other whites purchased most of the pigs and fowls raised by slaves in their patches, the fish they caught, and the firewood and other items they gathered in their free time. As a result slaves might hold a significant portion of the local circulating currency in their possession. Slaves who engaged in local market activities were also more likely to come in contact with white people other than the master and his family. All of these status markers or networking advantages may have strongly affected individual slave status in the quarter. In rare cases it was the key to liberation because individual slaves tried to buy themselves when they had the money, a practice approved by some masters. Probably most slaves who were manumitted somehow earned it. By 1763, moreover, in some places the number of free blacks was becoming sufficient to enlarge their local population mainly by marriage and reproduction. The growth of this additional social layer must have enriched and complicated matters in the slave quarters where relatives of free blacks lived. An individual slave's status began with sex and age, became more specific based on the strength of a kinship network, but could also be shaped by customary relationships with the master and his family, other white people, free blacks, and Native Americans and may well have reflected personal wealth as well.

Cultural factors played an important role in the creation of African-American communities, although they are less useful in comparative analysis because of their variability, instability, and poor documentation. The syncretization of religious beliefs, languages, and productive arts by individuals from a variety of African backgrounds into something African American demonstrates the extraordinary adaptive capacity of human culture and its potential to facilitate rational social relations even in the

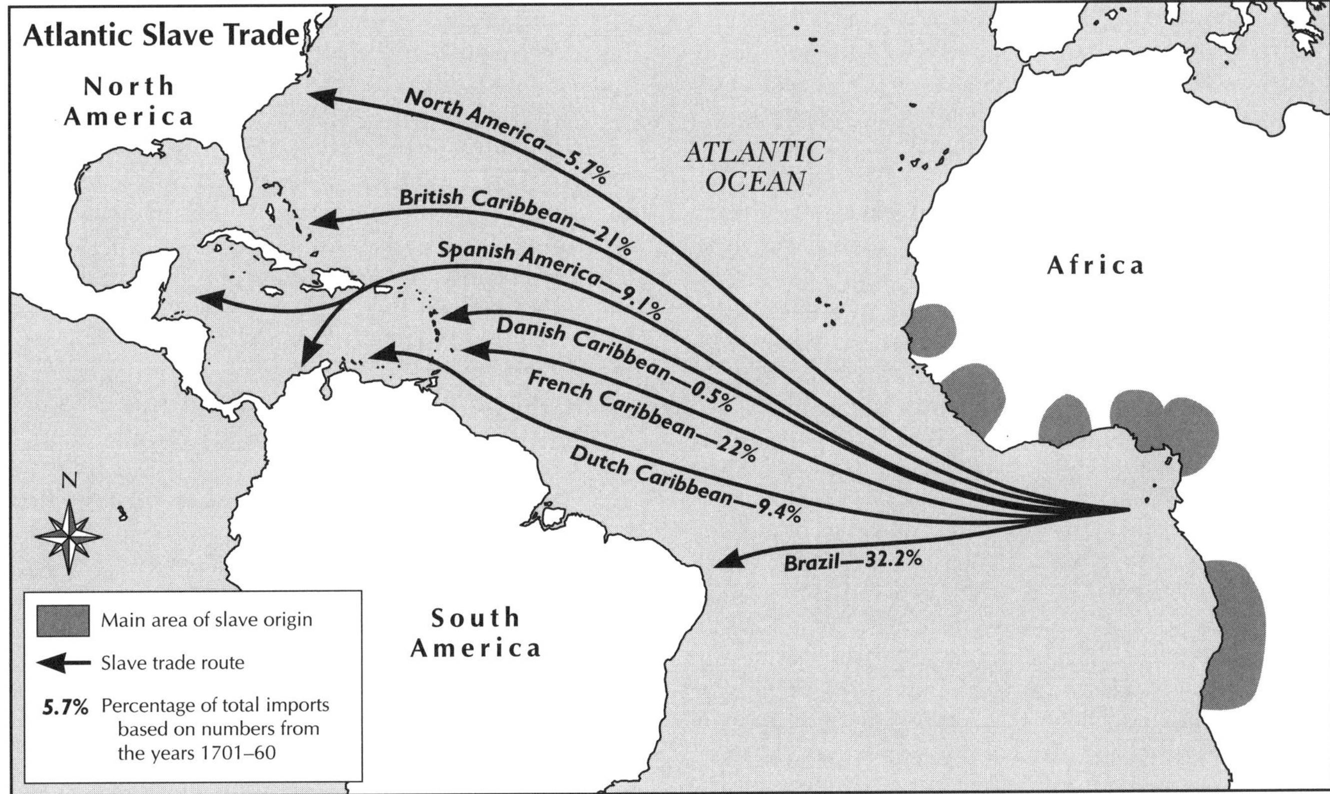

worst circumstances. Incessant and rapid cultural change provided individual slaves an opportunity to create a flexible cultural matrix in which to fashion a parallel society in the slave quarter, the community that enabled slaves to resist complete dehumanization. They did this in part by adapting elements of European culture to their own needs, in particular the English language they soon learned, into which they introduced many African words, meanings, speech patterns, and subversive intonations. Blacks also imported an abundance of medical lore, music, agricultural knowledge, and other elements that had great and lasting effect on the larger American culture.

One older historical interpretation indicates that slavery was most dehumanizing in English and Dutch slave societies, least so in Spanish and Portuguese slave societies, and somewhat in between in French plantation colonies. That model relied on comparing laws, the size of free black populations, and religious opportunities. Recently, historians have shown that slave laws and manumission rates were approximately the same in all the colonies before 1763; instead, the nature of slave religion is now playing an especially large role in debate. Roman Catholic priests routinely baptized virtually all slaves in Latin American and in the FRENCH COLONIES, perhaps following the basic catechism, perhaps not, depending on the volume of the slave trade. Beyond that, planters resisted further interference by clergy in their slave quarters, although slaves were usually permitted to attend church services. By contrast, Protestant clergy were more reluctant to baptize slaves, and masters in Protestant colonies were just as resistant as were Catholic masters to thorough Christianization of their slaves and equally fearful that it made them proud and rebellious.

A few historians have emphasized that some slaves in British North America responded along with many free people to the emotion-charged evangelism of the GREAT AWAKENING in the 1740s and 1750s. Others emphasize the continuing primary influence of African religious beliefs, at least in regions like Georgia's rice coast. Another view holds that the planters' policy was both to suppress African beliefs and practices and to prevent Christianization, so that by 1763 slaves were experiencing a religious "holocaust."

A final sociocultural factor that is still little understood and affects comparative analysis is the degree of racial intermixture in a given slave society. People of mixed racial parentage were called mulattoes disparagingly, and North American laws decreed banishment, imprisonment, or stiff fines for racial intermarriage, making the practice rare. The older cultural model holds that this pattern of hostility to racial intermixture and manumission was uniquely characteristic of the English and Dutch, but recent scholarship suggests that these policies were much the same in French, Spanish, and Portuguese colonies.

In 1763 the potential of the plantation slave system to spread in North America was limited only by the royal Proclamation of 1763 prohibiting colonial expansion beyond a line marked out along the Appalachian Mountain system and by the potential rebelliousness of the slaves. Many recent historians have described a slave culture deeply imbued with traditions of resistance to dehumanization. The power of masters, although decisive in the end, was limited by slave sabotage and rebellion. The 1720s and 1730s saw considerable plotting or outright rebellion. White South Carolina was terrified by the STONO REBELLION of 1739. Convinced that they had enough slaves by midcentury, the Tidewater planters frequently tried to limit the African slave trade because they saw it as a source of social unrest, but they were opposed by many young white men without slaves, who formed the majority of free people in all the colonies. Slavery in the southern colonies was depleting the soils in the coastal regions, and it was producing ambitious sons and daughters of slaveowners who were determined to develop the rich soils of the North American interior beyond the mountains. The Crown was of two incompatible minds, eager to protect the fur-producing areas west of the Proclamation Line but now increasingly dependent on the royal revenues arising from the slave trade itself and from slave-produced export staples. The final settlement of this issue would come with the War for Independence, for the slave system expanded into many new regions and created new states beyond the mountains after 1776.

Further reading: Ira Berlin, *Many Thousand Gone: The First Two Centuries of Slavery in North America* (Cambridge, Mass.: The Belknap Press of Harvard University Press, 1998); Allan Kulikoff, *Tobacco and Slaves: The Development of Southern Cultures in the Chesapeake, 1680–1800* (Chapel Hill: University of North Carolina Press, 1986); Edmund S. Morgan, *American Slavery, American Freedom: The Ordeal of Colonial Virginia* (New York: Norton, 1975); Philip Morgan, *Slave Counterpoint: Black Culture in the Eighteenth-Century Chesapeake and Lowcountry* (Chapel Hill: University of North Carolina Press, 1998); John Thornton, *Africa and Africans in the Making of the Atlantic World, 1400–1680* (Cambridge, U.K..: Cambridge University Press, 1992); Peter H. Wood, *Black Majority: Negroes in Colonial South Carolina from 1670 through the Stono Rebellion* (New York: Norton, 1974).

—Thomas N. Ingersoll

slaves See African Americans; slavery

slave trade

The transatlantic slave trade contributed immense wealth to the development of European states and their colonies, and it hardened the negative racial attitudes toward people of African ancestry, many of which endure to this day. The slave trade between Europe and AFRICA arose when it became clear that neither whites nor NATIVE AMERICANS would suffice as unfree laborers in the New World. This ensured that millions of Africans would be enslaved and that they would be greatly responsible for building the colonies and securing the wealth accumulated by American MERCHANTS, planters, and politicians.

The slave trade was a multifaceted process through which groups of African people were captured or bought, marched to the west coast, and imprisoned in FORTS (referred to as baracoons). There they would await the arrival of ships, in the holds of which they would be involuntarily transported, first to Europe between 1451 and 1575, and later, between 1526 and 1870, to the New World. Historians disagree about the aggregate number of Africans transported across the Atlantic. Their estimates range between 11 million and 20 million people, with women making up roughly a third of the total. Captives came primarily from the western areas of Africa, from present-day Angola in the south to Senegal in the north as well as from the west and west-central interior. Farmers, herders, fishermen, blacksmiths, weavers, potters, traders, artisans, artists, and religious figures were among the millions stolen from their homes.

The slave trade was an international enterprise, with Portugal, Spain, Holland, France, and England all carrying Africans to the Western Hemisphere. It began in the 1440s, well before the British North American colonies were established, and ended more than 400 years later, long after their independence. Portugal and Spain dominated the trade initially, but after 1670 England transported the largest number of Africans to the Western Hemisphere. The North American colonies received the smallest number of captives directly from Africa. Between 1601 and 1760 an estimated 140,192 Africans were transported to the British North American colonies. The vast majority of captives, nearly 3.5 million, arrived in the CARIBBEAN, Spanish America, and Brazil during these years. The 1619 arrival of 20 Africans at JAMESTOWN, VIRGINIA, is a useful example illustrating the slave trade's international character. The Africans had Spanish names and were sold to the English colony by a Dutch trader. This transaction marked the introduction of the international slave trade to mainland British North America.

Although the largest number of captives transported to North America during the colonial era arrived in MARYLAND and Virginia, all British colonies participated in the slave trade. By 1700 North American colonists were fully involved in and profiting from the slave trade, which, according to W. E. B. Du Bois, "was the very life of the colonies" and had "become an almost unquestioned axiom in British practical economics." New England shipbuilders, mid-Atlantic merchants, and southern planters transported, sold, and bought the African captives.

Often the slave trade is described as a triangle, the sides of which linked Europe, Africa, and the colonies of the Western Hemisphere. This static spatial description, however, fails to capture the complex interactions and negotiations that changed over time. Initially, European merchants financed voyages by investing in and outfitting ships and paying mariners, who sailed to the African continent with merchandise such as liquor, cloth, beads, iron, and guns to exchange for human beings. Captives were not especially valuable near the place of their abduction; close to home they might escape. Prudent captors moved pris-

This diagram, which shows a hold literally packed with human beings, gives some idea of conditions aboard a slave ship. *(Library of Congress)*

oners rapidly and sold them quickly if there were no compelling demands for their labor. Even if there was a great need for labor, it was often advantageous to sell local captives and buy slaves from some distance away. Either trade or raid would bring together individuals, otherwise unknown to one another, who would be forcibly removed from their homes, families, and ancestors.

Another method of acquiring captives resulted from trade organized by African elites, merchants, and warlords, although historians disagree about the extent to which Africans were fully aware of the likely fate of those they sold. For example, in 1700 the Asante state in modern-day Ghana began supplying slaves to traders in exchange for firearms, a practice that continued into the 19th century. On the other hand, some African states refused to participate in the nefarious practice. In 1516 the kingdom of Benin prohibited the export of all male slaves, a ban that continued until the 18th century. One African captive, Ottobah Cuguano from the Fante nation, summarized the dispute about African participation in the slave trade. He wrote that his countrymen "kidnapped and betrayed" him to be exiled into SLAVERY but added, "if there were no buyers there would be no sellers."

The captives were marched to the coast, shackled and malnourished, and there imprisoned to await their dreadful fate. Not all captives acquiesced. Some organized revolts while imprisoned in the coastal forts where traders awaited the arrival of the vessels for transport across the Atlantic. Others resisted shortly after being driven on board the vessels, when, according to historian Robin Blackburn, they realized "that they were in the hands of white men rather than being kept as part of the slave labour force on the coast."

The route to the Western Hemisphere, commonly referred to as the Middle Passage, was one of the most horrible and terrifying ordeals in human history. Olaudah Equiano, a captive who claimed to have been from Benin, vividly recounted what he and others suffered on the gruesome journey across the Atlantic. Men were chained in the hold of the ship, "which was so crowded that each had scarcely room to turn himself." The involuntary inhabitants produced "copious perspirations, so that the air soon became unfit for respiration, from a variety of loathsome smells." Captives also suffered from inadequate nutrition and rough handling by sailors. The ship's crew commonly subjected women, often kept on deck, to sexual indignities.

Men, women, and children perished or committed suicide during the journey that, depending on conditions, could take from two to four months. Dehydration was the major cause of death, although contagious diseases also took their toll. MORTALITY rates were considerable, given the conditions in which people were transported. Between

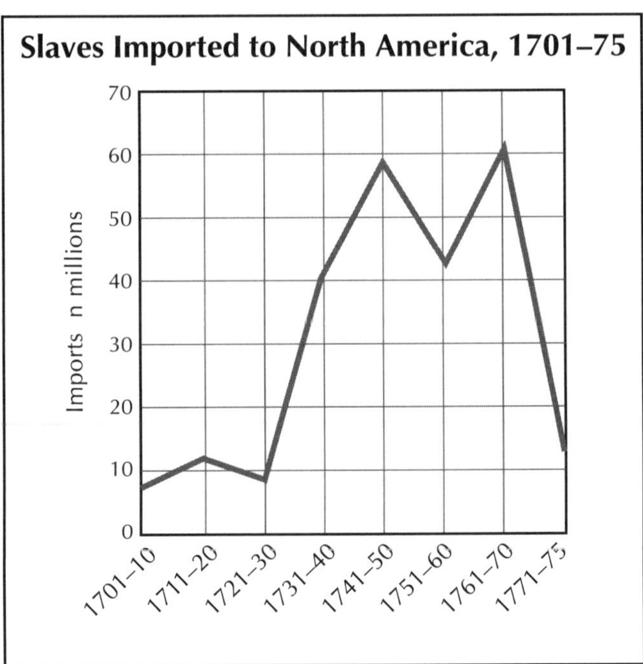

1500 and 1760 British ships left Africa with 1,662,000 captives and arrived in the Western Hemisphere with 1,252,000 men, women, and children, a loss of one in four captives. After 1750 mortality rates declined significantly due to increased knowledge about providing fresh water and preventing contagious diseases.

The slave trade was not without both defenders and detractors. Church and state justified the practice. Theological justification claimed that heathens would benefit from becoming slaves to Christians. Political theorists argued that the slave trade would bring savages to civilization. Opposition came from Africans, of course, and a very small number of white people. Unfortunately, there are very few written accounts from Africans who survived and undoubtedly opposed their CAPTIVITY, transport, and enslavement. More prevalent are the eyewitnesses' accounts of Africans throwing themselves overboard or starving themselves to death. The earliest protest by whites in British North America occurred in 1688 in Germantown, PENNSYLVANIA. Four men who had recently immigrated from Holland submitted a petition to the Society of Friends Monthly Meeting protesting that the slave trade, among other things, violated the Golden Rule. They were ignored.

Further reading: Robin Blackburn, *The Making of New World Slavery: From the Baroque to the Modern, 1792–1800* (London: Verso, 1997); Philip D. Curtin, *The Atlantic Slave Trade: A Census* (Madison: University of Wisconsin Press, 1969); David Eltis, *The Rise of African Slavery in the Americas* (Cambridge, U.K.: Cambridge

University Press, 2000); David Eltis, Stephen D. Behrendt, David Richardson, Herbert S. Klein, *The Trans-Atlantic Slave Trade: A Database on CD-ROM* (Cambridge, U.K.: Cambridge University Press, 2001); Herbert S. Klein, *The Atlantic Slave Trade* (Cambridge, U.K.: Cambridge University Press, 1999).

—Leslie Patrick

smallpox

Smallpox, a highly infectious and deadly viral DISEASE known in the West since antiquity, was among the most feared and deadliest diseases in colonial America. Carried to the CARIBBEAN and Mexico by Spanish conquistadores and to North America by French, Dutch, and British traders and explorers, smallpox decimated NATIVE AMERICANS, who had no immunity to European diseases. Smallpox also devastated colonial populations, appearing about once a generation, often killing one-10th of the inhabitants of an affected city, yet this disease was also one that the primitive medical SCIENCE of the era was increasingly able to understand and, to some extent, to control.

Smallpox was a major factor in the English colonists' success in establishing permanent settlements. Virgin soil epidemics (diseases introduced to people with no immunity) severely eroded the ability of Indians to counter colonial settlement and expansion. Epidemics in 1616, 1618, 1622, and 1633 resulted in native depopulation as high as 90 percent in some coastal areas of North America. Native populations suffered less in the continent's remote interior, although smallpox still spread to kill many Indians who had never encountered a European. Given the close living conditions and communal orientation of most natives, just a few contaminated individuals could easily spread the disease to an entire village. Indeed, Indian curing rituals, which often took place in crowded longhouses and involved sweating and fasting, further spread contagious diseases. Not only did ailments such as smallpox tragically reduce the Native American population, they also undermined Indian societies. For example, natives often were unable to explain such drastic misfortune; they sometimes blamed themselves or questioned their own spiritual beliefs. Among groups such as the IROQUOIS, the loss of so many people led to an increase in "mourning wars" against their Indian enemies—armed conflict intended in part to capture prisoners to "requicken" and replace tribal members lost to disease. Scholars disagree about the extent to which Europeans consciously waged biological warfare by spreading smallpox among Indians. Regardless, European disease fundamentally disrupted Native American culture and patterns of life, altered their relations with white people and other Indians, and undermined their ability to resist the European invasion.

Smallpox was endemic among many of the colonists, meaning that most young children of European ancestry contracted the disease, but more deadly smallpox epidemics also afflicted colonial population centers with alarming regularity. Sailors and immigrants brought the illness (along with measles, influenza, diphtheria, and typhus) into seaports, where crowded conditions aided its diffusion. Frequently the epidemics were isolated to specific geographical areas; sometimes they were more widespread, such as the contagion that ranged from NEW YORK to Canada in 1689 and 1690. Often smallpox struck a population already weakened by other diseases, such as the 1698–99 epidemic in CHARLESTON, where smallpox and YELLOW FEVER combined to kill at least 400 people.

Colonial physicians did not understand the cause of smallpox, but the symptoms were well known and certain measures were understood to be helpful. Both detaining ships outside the harbor when smallpox was suspected on board and isolating victims of the disease helped prevent its spread, yet there was little to do for the victims except to let the disease take its course. Throughout the colonial period many people believed that smallpox was God's punishment on a sinful populace, for which the only preventative was prayer.

During the smallpox epidemic of 1721–22 in BOSTON, the state of medical science advanced dramatically due primarily to the efforts of Reverend COTTON MATHER and Dr. ZABDIEL BOYLSTON to introduce inoculation. By this method, which had been practiced for centuries in China, Africa, and India, a healthy person was deliberately given a mild case of smallpox to produce lifetime immunity. Boylston's results were impressive: Those who submitted to his experiments were six times less likely to die than were those who contracted the disease naturally. Even so, improperly administered inoculation could and did spread the infection, and the controversy over the treatment of smallpox raged along with the disease throughout the colonial period.

Further reading: Henry R. Vietz, ed., *Smallpox in Colonial America* (New York: Arno Press, 1977); Neal Salisbury, *Manitou and Providence: Indians, Europeans, and the Making of New England, 1500–1643* (New York: Oxford University Press, 1982).

—Anthony Connors

Smibert, John (1688–1751)

Born in Scotland and apprenticed to a housepainter, from whom he learned to paint designs and decorate plaster ceilings, John Smibert became an important painter in colonial North America. He progressed to copying the works of the old masters, and he eventually attended ART school in

London. Twelve years of work in Scotland, Italy, and London followed; although he did several paintings of important people, Smibert never managed to compete with the most successful painters in Europe, receiving few commissions from the nobility.

In 1727 George Berkeley invited Smibert to join the faculty of a university to be established in Bermuda. Smibert arrived in NEWPORT, RHODE ISLAND, in 1729, where he remained for a few months before making what he thought would be a brief visit to BOSTON. When commissions poured in to his studio, he stayed and painted about 100 portraits in the next five years, including one of SAMUEL SEWALL. Smibert's most influential work, *The Bermuda Group,* honored Berkeley's expedition. Although a commissioned piece that took Smibert two years to complete, it proved impossible to deliver, and the painting remained in his studio, where it became his best-known work.

Smibert married the wealthy Mary Williams in 1730 and fathered four children. After painting religious leaders, MERCHANTS, and politicians, Smibert gradually moved into landscapes in the 1740s, when his sight began to fail. He also became an architect, designing Faneuil Hall, the first public market in Boston, and the Harvard chapel. Smibert influenced other painters, including ROBERT FEKE and John Singleton Copley. After his death Smibert's studio remained intact and became a place of artistic pilgrimage.

—Victoria C. H. Resnick

Smith, John (1580?–1631)

English explorer, colonizer, geographer, publicist, historian, and, unwittingly by adoption, the first Anglo-POWHATAN werowance (headman), John Smith was born in Willoughby, Lincolnshire, England into a yeoman family. He rose to gentleman status by dint of his enormous energy and self confidence, military experience, and common sense. As counselor and later president of the VIRGINIA colony's council from 1607 to 1609, Smith's aggressive, often ruthless, devotion to establishing and expanding England's precarious foothold at JAMESTOWN was critical to its survival in its early years. Much of what we know of Smith's career comes from his own recounting of events. Smith's writings, including *True Travels* (1630), *True Relations* (1608), and *Generall Historie* (1624), are colored by inconsistencies, self-promotion, and exaggerated accounts of his own exploits, yet their credibility has survived the critical examinations of historians, ethnologists, and geographers.

Smith left home at 16, when his father died, served an apprenticeship in horsemanship and the other arts of war under an Italian nobleman, but soon embarked on a series of "brave adventures" across Europe and the Levant. Like so many of his fellow leaders of England's Virginia enterprises, Smith joined volunteers to fight against Spain in France and the Low Countries for the cause of PROTESTANTISM and Dutch independence. After two years of service in the Low Countries ("that university of Warr"), Smith sailed the Mediterranean as a mariner on a merchant ship, but in 1600 the lure of military life drew him to join the Habsburg forces fighting the Ottoman Turks in Hungary. He claimed credit for two great Austrian victories and a series of single-handed duels with Turkish warriors—feats of bravery that earned Smith a coat of arms signifying the attainment of gentleman status and a pension from Prince Bathori of Transylvania. While fighting in Transylvania, Smith was captured by the Turks, enslaved, and sent to Istanbul to serve a young noblewoman, Charatza Tragabigzanda. After killing Charatza's brother, to whom he had been sent for safekeeping, Smith escaped the Ottoman Empire through Russia. He later boasted that these "Warres in Europe, Asia, and Affricca taught me how to subdue the wilde Salvages in Virginia."

After wandering eastern Europe and North Africa, Smith returned to England in 1605, where he involved himself in a scheme to colonize Guiana and, when that fell through, signed on to the VIRGINIA COMPANY OF LONDON's expedition to found a colony in Virginia. Smith's familiarity with foreign cultures, his purported elevation to gentleman status, and his military experience and disposition may account for his selection for leadership by the company directors, who were well aware of their colony's vulnerability to Spanish attack and potential Indian enmity, yet he was to prove to be a thorn in the company's side before, during, and after his career in Virginia.

Although he arrived in the colony as a prisoner accused of plotting mutiny midpassage, Smith eluded hanging and quickly became a dominating influence in the colony's governing council, to which company directors had secretly appointed him. Forever the upstart, Smith was regarded by some fellow colonists as "an Ambitious unworthy and vainglorious fellow." Relentlessly browbeating and bullying colonists into working diligently for the common good, Smith brought a degree of military discipline, industry, and political order, albeit intermittent, to the factious colony. With a heavy hand he bargained and bullied corn from the neighboring Powhatan Indians, preventing starvation in a colony incapable of raising its own food. Smith's forceful securing of FOOD and his dispersal of the colonists upriver away from the sickly lowlands of Jamestown staved off wholesale starvation and checked for a while the runaway morbidity in the colony.

Smith's explorations and descriptions of the CHESAPEAKE BAY area, as contained in *A True Relation* (1608) and *A Map of Virginia* (1612), added immensely to English knowledge of its geography and peoples. While exploring the Chickahominy in December 1607, Smith was captured

John Smith *(Library of Congress)*

by Powhatan's warriors and taken on a four-week ritual tour of Powhatan's domains, culminating in a three-day ceremony by which he was adopted as Powhatan's "sonne Nantaquoud" and made a werowance (subordinate chief), thereby transforming Jamestown, in Powhatan eyes, into an allied, subject village within the POWHATAN CONFEDERACY. Unaware of the Powhatan's true intentions and misunderstanding the ritual's meaning, Smith thought that Powhatan's 11-year-old daughter, Moatoka (POCAHONTAS), saved his life during the ceremony, thus giving rise to an American legend. He was released in friendship, but neither the proud Powhatan nor the xenophobic English could accept the social and political reciprocity of closer relationships between the two peoples—whether through trade, intermarriage, or religious conversion—without compromising their respective senses of dignity and ethnic identity. Nevertheless, the Powhatan never disavowed Smith's special status among them, a fact of which Pocahontas (by then Mrs. JOHN ROLFE) bitterly reminded Smith when he visited her in England.

The arrival in 1609 of a fleet of new settlers with a new charter and new government combined with the horrible burns he suffered as result of a gunpowder explosion forced Smith to relinquish the presidency of the council and return to England. For the next decade he petitioned the company for employment but was repeatedly ignored. In 1612 he further alienated his former employers by publishing *A Map of Virginia,* whose graphic layout enhanced his exploits and further diminished those of the company's managers and investors. In 1622 Smith allied himself with Sir Thomas Smyth and the earl of Warwick, who were wresting control of the company from Edwin Sandys and the earl of Southampton. *Smith's General Historie of Virginia* (1624), published at the height of the battle in Parliament and the royal courts, was directed toward swaying public opinion in favor of the Smyth-Warwick faction, whose machinations resulted ultimately in the dissolution of the Virginia Company and control of Virginia by the Crown.

Smith returned to North America in 1614 to explore the coast of New England under the auspices of the PLYMOUTH Company, whose merchant directors were interested in the region's prospects for settlement and trade. Based on this voyage, he wrote *A Description of New England* (1616), which contained a detailed map of the region. Smith's vigorous promotion of colonization in both Virginia and New England kept alive English imperial aspirations for North America in an era when nearby Ireland and the opulent Far East competed for England's attention, investment, and enterprise.

Further reading: Philip Barbour, ed., *The Complete Works of Captain John Smith (1580–1631),* 3 vols. (Chapel Hill: University of North Carolina Press, 1986); J. A. Leo Lemay, *The American Dream of Captain John Smith* (Charlottesville: University Press of Virginia, 1991).

—James Bruggeman

Smith, Robert (1722–1777)

Robert Smith was a notable architect who designed graceful Georgian buildings in the colonies. Born in Dalkeith Parish, Midlothian, Scotland, to a family of masons and builders, he apprenticed in these trades, then immigrated to America in the late 1740s. Proficient in woodworking, stone masonry, and contracting, he joined PHILADELPHIA's Carpenters' Company soon after his arrival and became the city's leading craftsman-architect. Acting as principal carpenter, his first major project was the construction of the 196-foot steeple of Christ Church, completed in 1754. As Philadelphia's "city house carpenter" from 1758 to 1761, Smith led the construction of St. Peter's as well as the Zion Lutheran Church, one of the largest churches in North America at the time. He also designed the elegant Carpenters' Hall, completed in 1773, and the Walnut Street

Prison, which, with its unique fireproof vaults, was his largest commission for design and execution. In 1770 Smith designed the first insane asylum in the colonies at Williamsburg, VIRGINIA. While his Georgian style public buildings in PENNSYLVANIA, Virginia, RHODE ISLAND, and NEW JERSEY were most notable, Smith also designed residences, among them Benjamin Franklin's house in Philadelphia.

Active in public affairs, Smith supported the crusade for independence and was a member of both the AMERICAN PHILOSOPHICAL SOCIETY and the Continental Congress. The city of Philadelphia appointed him regulator of party walls and partition fences, a desirable position equivalent to building inspector. Working as a military engineer during the American Revolution, Smith designed *cheveaux-de-frise,* underwater spiked barricades used in the DELAWARE River as a defense against British warships.

—Catherine Goetz

Smith, Venture (Broteer) (1729–1805)

Venture Smith, whose father named him Broteer, was born in AFRICA. In 1798 he published his autobiography, recounting his life in Guinea, enslavement in the colonies, and hard-earned success. Historians disagree about whether Smith thoroughly assimilated to colonial values or maintained African values.

At the age of eight Broteer was among 200 African captives who arrived in Barbados, where a steward bought him and renamed him "Venture." His third owner supplied a surname; thus Broteer, son of a Guinea prince, became Venture Smith, colonial slave. He lived variously in RHODE ISLAND, NEW YORK, and CONNECTICUT.

Smith planned for freedom during his 28 years of enslavement. A robust man, he labored unceasingly. At nine he was carding wool and pounding corn. Subsequently, he earned money to buy his freedom by cleaning shoes, hunting game, raising produce, cording wood, threshing grain, and FISHING. Like many black Americans, Smith did not surrender to SLAVERY. He and three indentured whites once stole his master's boat, intending to reach the Gulf of Mexico. When the conspirators fell out, the plan was abandoned. On another occasion Smith defended his wife, Meg, from a beating by her mistress, who turned her wrath on him. He defended himself and his wife without harming the mistress, only to be punished by his master.

In 1765 Smith purchased his freedom. He had been "sold three different times, made considerable money with seemingly nothing to derive it from, had been cheated out of a large sum of money, lost much by misfortunes and paid an enormous sum for my freedom."

Although Smith was free, his wife and children were not. He then toiled to buy their liberty. He chartered a 30-ton sloop, took on a crew, and plied the wood trade. He also fished for eels and lobsters, joined a whaling voyage, and raised watermelons for market. His labor paid off, although he had to work harder than white Americans simply to secure freedom for himself and his family. He purchased his wife for £40 and his daughter for £44, paid $400 to liberate his sons, and also redeemed three black friends from slavery.

Smith's family settled in Connecticut, where they had bought land, built a house, and hired "two black farmhands." He died at age 76.

Further reading: Robert E. Desrochers, Jr., "'Not Fade Away': The Narrative of Venture Smith, an African American in the Early Republic" (*The Journal of American History,* 1997, 40–66); Venture Smith, *A Narrative of the Life and Adventures of Venture A Native of Africa, But Resident Above Sixty Years in the United States of America* (1798; reprint, Middletown, Conn.: J. S. Stewart, 1897).

—Leslie Patrick

smuggling

Colonial merchants engaged in widespread smuggling as a means of avoiding taxes levied by the British Parliament. Crown official Edmund Randolph decried the flagrant violation of trade regulations by American merchants and loss of revenue to the Crown as early as 1676. Reporting in a pamphlet entitled "The present State of the Affairs in New England," Randolph charged that Americans "violate all the acts of trade and navigation, by which they have ingrossed the greatest part of the West India Trade, whereby his Majestie is damaged in his Customs above 100,000 £ yearly." While his figure is an exaggeration, many MERCHANTS in the colonies were certainly involved in some form of illegal smuggling. Americans saw wealth to be made by avoiding paying customs duties, regardless of the law.

The many inlets, coves, and islands along the Atlantic seaboard provided perfect locations for colonial smugglers of all varieties. The widely accepted process of smuggling in the American colonies helped create some of the largest fortunes. Frederick Philipse of NEW YORK was widely known to traffic with the pirate outpost on Madagascar in the Indian Ocean. John Hancock of MASSACHUSETTS, who inherited his uncle Thomas's fortune and shipping business at the age of 27, soon became one of the wealthiest men in the colonies, primarily from the profits of smuggling.

Apart from these two famous cases, it is uncertain to what extent smuggling was carried on by colonial merchants. There was no effective force to stop colonial smuggling altogether, and local customs officials could be bribed. Records, beyond the official complaints of Randolph, are not to be found. Two particular areas of smuggling that are known to have developed in the 1600s were the importation of European manufactured goods into the colonies and the West Indies trade of sugar, molasses, and rum. Passage of the Navigation Acts was designed to stop illegal trade by the colonies with any non-English merchants, particularly the Dutch. The acts were passed specifically for the benefit of the mother country but also, as in the case of the Molasses Act of 1733, for the benefit of a particular group. That act was passed for the Barbados sugar planters, who faced competition from colonists buying cheaper French and Spanish sugar in return for colonial foodstuffs. By the 1760s the acts passed to counter colonial smuggling began to be viewed as an attack on the rights and freedom of colonial merchants.

Further reading: John W. Tyler, *Smugglers and Patriots: Boston Merchants and the Advent of the American Revolution* (Boston: Northeastern University Press, 1986).

—Stephen C. O'Neill

society, British American

"What then is this American, this new man?," Hector St. John Crèvecoeur inquired in 1782. Twenty-two years earlier Benjamin Franklin questioned the whole idea of a "typical" American. The colonies, he explained, "were not only under different governors, but have different forms of government, different laws, different interests, and some of them different religious persuasions and different manners."

Crèvecoeur's question and Franklin's assessment described coexisting aspects of colonial British American society. Throughout most of the colonial period, British America consisted of several distinct societies. These cultures distinguished themselves through their demographic conditions, LABOR arrangements, economic structures, racial and GENDER roles, and political frameworks, yet, at the same time, the notion that a single "American" had emerged after the Revolution suggested that colonial America shared unifying characteristics that bound its diverse regions into a single culture. Franklin and Crèvecoeur were two of colonial America's most astute observers. An understanding of their competing perspectives contributes to an appreciation of colonial America's social complexity.

Within 10 years of JAMESTOWN's 1607 founding, the Chesapeake region had created a commercialized TOBACCO ECONOMY strong enough to shape the region's early social development. A young, male-dominated population of white planters, white and black indentured servants, and African slaves prepared the region's large plantations for extensive tobacco exportation. The conditions under which these men labored confirmed the planters' drive for profit. An inadequate FOOD supply, overworked laborers, and unhealthy water resulted in high MORTALITY rates and frequent political instability. These conditions, along with fluid racial categories, the lack of families, and an increasingly skewed distribution of wealth, encouraged personal autonomy and greed while discouraging social deference, traditional gender roles, and political stability. The planters' ongoing quest for land, moreover, not only strained relations among whites but antagonized relations with NATIVE AMERICANS. Major battles between settlers and Indians broke out in 1622, 1644, and 1675. Early VIRGINIA and MARYLAND thus stood in sharp contrast to society in England.

Chesapeake area settlers ameliorated these destabilizing conditions by approximating familiar metropolitan traditions. Throughout the 17th century the establishment of county courts and parishes, representative lawmaking assemblies, and widespread political participation provided the Chesapeake region with a sociopolitical framework coherent enough to moderate its destructive trends. White planters further contributed to this emerging stability by manipulating race and gender so as to define more rigidly a once ambiguous hierarchy of power. By perpetuating a racial distinction between white servitude and black SLAVERY through SLAVE CODES, white planters defused the CLASS tensions that fueled BACON'S REBELLION in 1676 and established the basis for a white supremacist ideology. Furthermore, the division of labor along gender lines, the regulation of white women's sexuality, and the condemnation of Native Americans' division of labor (Indian women managed fieldwork) similarly constructed once fluid gender expectations into less flexible gender roles. As more women arrived in the colony this evolving patriarchal norm exerted a social influence that contributed to the region's growing stability.

New England PURITANS established England's second large North American society in 1629. Although the MASSACHUSETTS Bay Colony and the Chesapeake region were outposts of the same metropolitan culture, the contrasts between these societies were striking. Most migration to New England occurred in a short burst of voyages lasting from 1630 to 1642. It landed about 4,000 white, Puritan, middle-class families in a healthy ENVIRONMENT replete with natural resources, even if the farmland was less rich than in other colonies. The economic quest for transatlantic profits through cod, timber, and fur exports initially yielded to modest family farms that closely replicated English traditions. Puritans employed servant labor rather than slaves, made the family rather than the plantation the central economic unit, and immediately adopted the patriarchal assumption (enforced by the practice of "coverture") that husbands controlled their wives' property and person. Puritans did not oppose material gain. Instead, they tempered commercial pursuits with values gleaned from covenant theology, familial stability, and the supposed moral benefits of hard work. Accordingly, they established a political system favoring religiously "elect" white men who monitored social behavior for signs of subversion. The banishment of ROGER WILLIAMS for transgressing Congregational theology and ANNE MARBURY HUTCHINSON for contradicting the gendered order suggest the magnitude of this vigilance. A low infant mortality rate, a nearly equal sex ratio, and a mixed economy supportive of an equitable wealth distribution allowed New England to evolve without the benefit of constant immigration. New England quickly became a fair approximation of England.

While the early Chesapeake region worked to impose stability on its evolving society, New England labored to preserve it. And while the Chesapeake area largely succeeded, New England generally failed. The theologically driven, socially homogeneous society that the founding generations forged bowed under the weight of several changes. New England became an aggressively commercial society defined less by its ministers' sermons than its MERCHANTS' ledgers. The anxiety inspired by a growing commercial elite manifested itself in events such as the Halfway Covenant (1662) and the Salem Witch Trials (1692). New Englanders' further challenged their founding ideals by abandoning their original towns for cities like BOSTON, NEWPORT, and New Haven, or for frontier communities. Migration and urbanization disrupted church organizations, strained traditional gender roles, and undermined the deferential attitudes once enforced by family, church, and community. Commercialization and internal migration, moreover, ushered in slavery and poverty. By the late 17th and early 18th centuries growing wealth from the cod, timber, and whale trades enabled a powerful minority of New Englanders to import slave labor. If New England slaveholders and those who fell into poverty were relatively few, their presence nevertheless reflects the larger changes unhinging New England from its original mission. As "peaceable kingdoms" of the 17th century diminished, New England started to look more like the rest of colonial British America.

The Middle Colonies—primarily NEW YORK and PENNSYLVANIA—emerged later in the century (1664 and 1681, respectively) and quickly assumed a unified sociocultural character. Like the Chesapeake region, the Middle Colonies exhibited materialistic and individualistic tendencies during their settlement years. Unlike the Chesapeake area, though, an influx of immigrants from Scotland, Ireland, and Germany channeled potentially disruptive social impulses into the development of colonial America's most stable and diverse economy. A healthy balance of family farms, merchant houses (especially among Pennsylvania QUAKERS), and shipping firms enabled this region to negotiate both local and transatlantic markets. Through the exportation of wheat and livestock, a local trade in iron, dairy products, and bread, and the provision of services including SHIPBUILDING and food processing, the Middle Colonies nurtured an economic culture that made it, according to one historian (referring to Pennsylvania), "the best poor man's country."

The Middle Colonies' economic progress was inextricably linked with the region's social development. As in New England, family labor dominated the Middle Colonies. Quaker families in particular advocated an arrangement whereby parental authority remained weak, the nuclear family prevailed, partible inheritance became common, and children left home at young ages to improve their material conditions. Tenancy and servitude, however, were also common features of the social landscape, and these institutions placed poorer immigrants in positions of extreme dependency. Despite tenant uprisings on New York's manorial estates in the 1740s, however, tenancy and servitude sometimes became stepping-stones to a freehold in the hinterland or artisanal independence in the city, rather than remaining a permanent condition.

However, opportunities for upward mobility were not ubiquitous. Slavery was a growing reality in the Middle Colonies. NEW YORK CITY and the manufacturing centers around PHILADELPHIA craved skilled slave labor. By 1746 30 percent of New York City's laborers were slaves. Slaveholders in the Middle Colonies never employed the brutal gang labor techniques used in the Chesapeake region, but slaves still suffered the cruelties of their condition. Slave codes mandated the same racial dichotomy that prevailed in the Chesapeake area, and violent resistance among disgruntled slaves remained an ongoing and often real threat. Colonial North America's first slave insurrection took place in New York in 1712. Servitude, tenancy, and slavery, moreover, fostered a differentiated social structure. In cities the wealthiest 10 percent owned more than 50 percent of the taxable wealth, with the bottom 30 percent owning less than 2 percent. Stratification was lower in rural areas, with a distribution of property more equal than in New England. Finally, government in the Middle Colonies reflected the antiauthoritarianism of the Quaker population by remaining weak, highly inclusive, and responsive to the needs of white males.

Planters from Barbados settled the Lower South in the 1680s. By the early 1700s the dominant sociocultural traits of the Lower South included a dedication to staple crops (rice and later INDIGO), an unhealthy environment, rapid demographic growth due to English, Scots, Ulster Scots, and GERMAN IMMIGRANTS, and a fierce commitment to slave labor. The logic behind staple AGRICULTURE required the importation of a slave population that in some counties dramatically exceeded that of whites (as high as 90 percent), a wealth disparity that made a select minority of planters the richest men in colonial North America, and unprecedented displays of conspicuous CONSUMPTION. The Lower South adopted a restrictive approach towards the black population, especially after the 1739 STONO REBELLION, but its stance towards other institutions, such as the family, was comparatively lax. White women in SOUTH CAROLINA, for example, routinely contradicted traditional gender norms. Married women were allowed to maintain an estate, and thus a measure of independence, separate from their husbands' holdings. This provision, in addition to the many slaves that white widows inherited, conferred unusual economic power upon southern women and perpetuated fluid gender norms inconsistent with the rest of colonial North America. If there was a culture that looked the most different from the metropolis of Britain, it was the Lower South.

The differences among these four colonial regions, stark as they seem, coexisted with four broad social developments that, throughout the 18th century, transcended distinctions among colonial societies and provided colonial British America a shared foundation upon which to negotiate their differences and build a unified, highly complex society. First, scattered pockets of slavery evolved into a comprehensive slave society that influenced life from New England to the Carolinas. Black slaves, unlike indentured servants, lacked formal rights, became cheaper and easier to obtain, and, unlike Native Americans, were initially reluctant to escape into an unfamiliar countryside. In 1640 the mainland colonies had about 1,000 slaves—about 2 percent of the European-American population. By 1780 they had well over 500,000—about 25 percent of the European-American population. The economic consequences of this transition catapulted the mainland colonies to a position of international significance. Its sociocultural consequences, however, were equally profound. Enslaved Africans negotiated incredible difficulties to establish an influential African-American society that pervaded the British mainland colonies. Slaves from the Carolinas to New England reconstructed family life to incorporate aspects of their African pasts into their colonial present. They conducted extralegal marriages, traveled widely to maintain kinship and friendship connections, and, in so doing, supported vibrant African-American communities. Slaves participated actively in public culture. Through music, marriage ceremonies, storytelling, and dancing, enslaved blacks preserved traditions while carving out a meaningful place within colonial America's growing public sphere. Slaves resisted the institution under which they labored through finely coordinated strategies. Whether it was slacking off work on the plantation, breaking field equipment, running away, or assaulting (and even murdering) whites, slaves honed a sense of community and shared culture unlike any other immigrants to America. Their suffering and strategies to manage that suffering forged a set of common ideals that influenced white societies throughout colonial British America.

Second, although historians have vigorously debated the extent of its impact, religious expression also shaped a discrete American society. As colonists took advantage of North America's comparatively tolerant religious environment to embrace dissenting Protestant ideals, they established social trends that resonated deeply throughout the colonies. Most visibly, congregational expansion after 1700—be it Baptist, Methodist, Lutheran, or Presbyterian—transformed America's physical space. Churches and meeting houses replete with bells and spires gradually "sacralized" the colonial landscape. This landscape, in turn, became the context for transcolonial evangelical revivals that grew especially intense in the 1740s, leading some historians to call this movement the GREAT AWAKENING. These periods of spiritual rapture encouraged colonists of all religious backgrounds and from all regions to balance traditional doctrinal loyalty with personal introspection. Colonial American religious development also granted women unique opportunities to assert their independence and authority. Although they could not be ordained, chair meetings (except Quakers), or hold office, women constituted a majority of church membership, and their numerical strength allowed them to influence hiring, policy, and church discipline.

A third factor influencing the convergence of a single American society involved consumer behavior. Throughout the 18th century, European-Americans, slaves, and Native Americans experienced important changes in their material lives. The diet of white Americans improved, incorporating finer cuts of meat, a wider variety of fruits and vegetables, and more herbs and spices. Slaves also developed more sophisticated diets as masters allotted them time to grow their own food, keep their own livestock, and do their own cooking in separate quarters. Sickness, drought, and dispossession of their land placed Native Americans in a different position. For them, diminished agricultural activity meant dependency on European-Americans for their food. In terms of CLOTHING, white colonists enjoyed both increasing imports from England and clothes made domestically. They could, especially after 1730, choose from a plethora of affordable fabrics and complement their outfits with distinctive hats, shoes, and underwear. Garments became status markers, and as wealthy merchants donned the finest silk shirts and French shoes, slaves, with their rough-cut shirts and threadbare pants, reflected the lowest rung of the sartorial ladder. Native Americans, in contrast, embraced a culturally diverse style of dress, incorporating European styles into traditional garb, often donning European shirts, leggings, and the traditional feathered headdress. Finally, with respect to HOUSING, whites enjoyed the major improvements. Homes grew in size and sophistication, and colonists decorated them with imported furniture, china, carpets, and drapery—items all made affordable by a "consumer revolution." While vernacular styles persisted, the rudiments of an early American ARCHITECTURE slowly cohered.

The final element driving the convergence of colonial America's separate societies involved the relegation of Native Americans to the most distant periphery of British America. Throughout the colonial period Indians and Europeans were engaged in an ongoing battle to shape their own economic and social destinies, and the object of that battle was invariably land. Major wars between Indians and whites included KING PHILIP'S WAR (1676), a battle in Deerfield, Massachusetts (1704), the Tuscarora War in NORTH CAROLINA (1712), and the Yamasee War in South Carolina (1715). During the SEVEN YEARS' WAR (1754–63) Indians were able to achieve substantial diplomatic leverage by playing French and English interests against each other. For groups like the CATAWBA in the South and the IROQUOIS in the North, these strategies proved temporarily beneficial. By the end of the Seven Years' War, however, as the Revolutionary Era approached, white Americans moved West with such force and rapidity that many Indians, who no longer enjoyed the diplomatic advantages that the English-French conflict conferred, disintegrated as coherent tribal entities. Some tribes, like the Mississippi Chickasaw and the FLORIDA Seminole, extended their autonomy, but they were the exceptions. The Oneida took refuge in camps, and the Iroquois Confederacy was dissolved. The marginalization of Native Americans throughout colonial North America unified the colonies in a relentless quest for land.

"What then is this American, this new man?" In light of these four developments, Crèvecoeur's question has added resonance. Franklin may have been correct in highlighting colonial America's bewildering diversity (his observation even rings true for contemporary North America), but the emergence of a slave society, the freedom to pursue individual spiritual enlightenment, the acquisition of similar consumer goods, and the elimination of Native Americans as legitimate competitors for America's most valuable resource all converged in the years before the Revolution to the forge the foundation of a distinctly American society.

Further reading: Jon Butler, *Becoming America: The Revolution Before 1776* (Cambridge, Mass.: Harvard University Press, 2000); Jack P. Greene, *Pursuits of Happiness: The Social Development of Early Modern British Colonies and the Formation of American Culture* (Chapel Hill: University of North Carolina Press, 1988); Alice Hanson Jones, *Wealth of a Nation to Be: The American Colonies on the Eve of the Revolution* (New York: Columbia University Press, 1980).

—James E. McWilliams

Society for the Propagation of the Gospel in Foreign Parts (SPG)

Founded in England in 1701 by royal charter, the Venerable Society for the Propagation of the Gospel in Foreign Parts was formed to strengthen the Church of England and convert non-Christian peoples in the British colonies. The charter provided for a governing board in London headed by the archbishop of Canterbury and comprised of numerous MERCHANTS. The society used both public and private contributions, focusing its activities in the 17th century primarily in British North America and the West Indies.

Between 1701 and 1783 the SPG sent more than 300 ordained clergy and 65 teachers to the 13 colonies and contributed to the construction of many churches and schools. Although only white men were sent from England, the society did support a few women teachers, Native American catechists, and at least two former slaves who were recruited as teachers in the colonies. The missionaries were instructed to live simply, stress loyalty to the monarch, evangelize dissenters, NATIVE AMERICANS, and slaves, minister to Protestants who had immigrated from other lands, and report regularly to London. The SPG also provided Bibles, prayerbooks, and religious monographs for church and college libraries.

While their missionary efforts were most successful among British colonists, SPG ministers also worked among 47 different Native American tribes, from the northern IROQUOIS to the southern Yamasee. The most successful missionary effort was among the Mohawk, begun in 1712 in response to a plea for Christian instruction from four Mohawk SACHEMS who presented their request to Queen Anne (1702–14) in London in 1710. Over the next 60 years many tribal members were baptized, the *Book of Common Prayer* and much of the Bible were translated into the Mohawk language, and native leaders were trained as catechists and teachers.

Christian instruction for African slaves was more problematic. Missionaries attempted to provide basic literacy instruction for slaves, contending that church members needed to be able to read to participate in the liturgy, but slaveholders often thwarted these efforts. Many blacks, however, were baptized and enrolled in local congregations. Schools for AFRICAN AMERICANS were also established, such as that taught by Huguenot convert Elias Neau in NEW YORK CITY from 1704–22. The school continued after his death and eventually formed the basis for black public schools after independence.

As revolutionary fervor increased, aside from notable exceptions, most SPG ministers upheld the loyalist cause. In 1783 the society withdrew its support from the newly formed United States. The correspondence between local SPG agents and the London office, available on microfilm, is a rich resource for colonial social history.

Further reading: Daniel O'Connor, et al., *Three Centuries of Mission: The United Society for the Propagation of the Gospel, 1702–2000* (New York: Continuum, 2000).

—Mary Sudman Donovan

South Carolina

The colony of South Carolina became one of the most important of the original 13 colonies, as it dominated the political and economic life of the Lower South.

Native Americans

Before the European invasion, various Indian groups, including the Cusabo, CATAWBA, Yamasee, and CHEROKEE, inhabited the area that would become South Carolina. When the first English colonists arrived in present-day North Carolina in 1585, the Catawba numbered among the many tribes who lived in the Piedmont region of North and South Carolina. During the next two centuries, European diseases decimated their population, while their independence, culture, and lands came under attack. Like many other NATIVE AMERICANS, they gradually became dependent on European goods, especially metal pots, arrow tips, knives, and guns. The Catawba and their neighbors initially killed deer and exchanged their skins for these articles, but, as the number of deer declined in their territory, the Catawba became the brokers in the trade between the English settlers and nearby Indians. Their position as merchants and their reputation as fierce warriors provided them with some protection from the excessive violence of the colonists. As neighboring tribes suffered even more severely from DISEASE and war, they often sought refuge with and were adopted into the Catawba, thereby forging new cultures. The SMALLPOX epidemics of the mid-18th century, along with the weakening deerskin trade, diminished the power of the Catawba.

When the Europeans arrived in North America, the Cherokee people dominated the Appalachian Mountains in present-day Georgia, Alabama, Tennessee, and North and South Carolina. They lost a great many people to the diseases contracted from Spanish explorers during the 16th century, but, unlike many Indians along the eastern seaboard, they had time to regain their population before engaging in sustained contact and trade with the English in the 17th century. In 1650, the Iroquoian-speaking Cherokee probably numbered about 22,000. Their numerous villages typically consisted of a small number of log cabins. Women and men commonly shared political and social power, and women were primarily responsible for the agricultural production and gathering of foods, while men engaged in hunting. Chiefs, chosen by each town, had a division of responsibilities between wartime and peacetime leaders.

The Cherokee began to engage in significant trade with English settlers by the late 17th century. Some Cherokee villages signed treaties with South Carolina settlers, and a number of Cherokee women married Europeans, especially traders. Like the Catawba, the Cherokee came to rely on metal goods and commerce with white settlers, which undermined their power and independence. Their CONSUMPTION of these commodities was so enormous that the Cherokee ceded large tracts of lands, from South Carolina to Tennessee, to British-American settlers in payment for their debts. The Cherokee were entangled in the complex political struggles among the British, French, and Spanish in the 18th century, and they often attempted to play one European power off against the other for their own benefit. During the SEVEN YEAR'S WAR, some Cherokee towns supported the French and attacked the Carolina backcountry in 1760, while many others fought with the British. Siding with the British during the American Revolution, the Cherokee eventually lost even more land and became subordinate to the new U.S. government.

Both the Spanish and the French many times attempted but failed to establish settlements in South Carolina in the 16th century. King Charles I of England claimed Carolina (named from the Latin name for "Charles") in 1629 by granting the region to Sir Robert Heath. However, he did not attempt to found settlements. After the Stuart Restoration, King Charles II, responding to the requests of a group of prominent politicians, granted the area to eight supporters whom he named the Lords Proprietors over Carolina. Their charter provided them with extensive power over the colony, and they promised political and religious freedom as well as land to settlers. When these promises failed to attract many colonists, Lord Anthony Ashley Cooper (subsequently earl of Shaftesbury) and the philosopher JOHN LOCKE wrote the Fundamental Constitutions of Carolina in 1669, which maintained feudal privileges but also granted some popular rights. Its purpose was to define a well-ordered, hierarchical colony, with counties of equal size, each of which was apportioned in equal parcels. The proprietors would own the largest number of parcels, the colonial aristocracy the next greatest number, and the least amount of land was reserved for less affluent settlers. Whites without property would enjoy no political rights, while black slaves were to be completely subject to their masters. Political power would rest primarily in the hands of the wealthy.

Settlers did not adopt the Fundamental Constitutions, and the colony developed along considerably different lines than envisioned by the authors of that document. Politically, the proprietors appointed the governor and half of the council, who essentially ruled the colony. The free men elected an assembly with very limited power. Meanwhile, northern and southern Carolina evolved into distinct societies. In NORTH CAROLINA (initially separate in 1712, then officially in 1729 when the king formally divided the region), freeholders used slave laborers and indentured servants to produce corn, TOBACCO, livestock, and naval stores. South Carolina's first permanent English settlement was at Albemarle Point, where immigrants from England and Barbados arrived in 1670. During the next 10 years, most new arrivals were white Barbadians and their black slaves. For the next few decades, South Carolina produced wood staves, corn, and livestock to trade with the sugar-producing island of Barbados, becoming, as one historian has called it, the "colony of a colony." In 1680, the colonists moved their capital to Charles Town (later CHARLESTON), which expanded rapidly and became the center of the colony's political, social, and cultural life. Roughly 5,000 colonists lived in South Carolina at the end of the 17th century, many of whom were Indians and black slaves. Although white settlers quickly established a slave society, many Africans and AFRICAN AMERICANS exercised at least some nominal freedoms and engaged in diverse occupations, at least during the final years of the 17th century.

Cultivated by black slaves familiar with the crop in their homeland, RICE was introduced into South Carolina about 1680, and within a quarter century, it quickly became the colony's most important export. The intense labor demands associated with rice production spurred an incredible expansion of slavery and the establishment of a harsh plantation regime that brutalized bound laborers. One result was that black inhabitants outnumbered white residents throughout most of the 18th century. In some marshy rice-producing areas, and especially when owners fled to Charleston during the summer to escape malaria and the heat, slaves accounted for more than three-quarters of the population. These conditions, combined with the continual importation of Africans, enabled slaves to blend traditions, religions, and languages from various parts of Africa to create a distinct culture. In 1739, when black bondpeople were more than twice as numerous as white residents in the colony, a group of 50 slaves staged the STONO REBELLION—the largest slave revolt in early North America. Hoping to escape to the freedom promised by the Spanish in FLORIDA, slaves attacked property and killed more than 20 whites before being defeated by the militia. In response, the colony's assembly passed the most severe slave code in mainland North America. Thereafter, slaves adopted subtler, less violent ways to resist their exploitation.

The early 18th century was a time of considerable difficulty. In 1715, the Yamasee attacked the colony, killing more than 400 settlers and causing the colonists to abandon half of their cultivated lands. Meanwhile, the growing number of pirates off the coast contributed to the unrest. Dissatisfied settlers complained about the proprietors' failure to protect them or to grant them additional lands. In 1719, the colonists engaged in a bloodless rebellion and received the protection of the Crown. The next year, the British sent Francis Nicholson to serve as the provincial royal governor. South Carolina became a royal colony in 1729 when the original proprietors' heirs sold their rights to the Crown.

The remainder of the colonial era was somewhat more peaceful and stable. INDIGO became the second most important product of South Carolina during the 1740s. In addition to African forced migrants, large numbers of Germans and Swiss arrived in the 1730s and 1740, while the Scotch-Irish moved southward from PENNSYLVANIA and VIRGINIA in the 1760s. Yet, the colony remained fractured in regional, economic, and social terms. Poorer farmers in the backcountry struggled against the powerful rice planters along the coast, and the latter ruled and continued to rule the region for decades.

Further reading: Philip D. Morgan, *Slavery Counterpoint: Black Culture in the Eighteenth-Century Chesapeake and Lowcountry* (Chapel Hill, University of North Carolina Press, 1998); Edward A. Pearson, "'A Countryside Full of Flames': A Reconsideration of the Stono Rebellion and Slave Rebelliousness in the Early Eighteenth-Century South Carolina Lowcountry," *Slavery & Abolition* 17 (1996): 22–50; M. Eugene Sirmans, *Colonial South Carolina: A Political History, 1663–1763* (Chapel Hill: University of North Carolina Press, 1966); Peter H. Wood, *Black Majority: Negroes in Colonial South Carolina from 1670 through the Stono Rebellion* (New York, W. W. Norton, 1974).

Spanish colonies

After a century of violent expansion Spain's American colonies were reaching maturity by 1585, as a society dominated by the drive for conquest was giving way to a formal colonial system. Some peripheral regions remained unconquered, but the major agricultural and mining centers of Spain's colonies had been in production for nearly 40 years. Colonial life was centered in the Viceroyalties of New Spain and Peru, both of which produced vast quantities of silver for the empire. By this date Spain's colonies were also typified by a series of religious, political, caste, and economic hierarchies. Never as rigid in practice as they appeared on paper, these hierarchies nonetheless succeeded in reserving the majority of wealth and privilege in colonial society to a small number of Europeans.

Historians often refer to the period before the 1580s as the "Conquest of Labor and Souls," referring to the fact that Spanish conquistadores had the dual mission of evangelizing indigenous peoples and extracting their LABOR and tribute. By the end of the 16th century these two endeavors were overshadowed by the desire to extract mineral and agricultural wealth from the colonies. Massive silver mines were discovered at Potosí (modern-day Bolivia) in 1545 and in Zacatecas and Guanajuato (modern-day Mexico) between 1548 and 1558. Often worked by forced Indian labor, Potosí was long the greatest silver mine in the world, but silver production from New Spain's mines as well grew to 50 million pesos per year from the 1560s to the 1620s. Although production fluctuated, silver exports from these mines expanded to more than 100 million pesos annually by the 1750s.

Over time AGRICULTURE became similarly crucial to the colonial endeavor. Native producers in Spain's colonies cultivated highly prized cochineal and indigo for the European market. Haciendas—agricultural estates based in part on the medieval idea of the seigneurial manor—also supplied both local and regional markets with foodstuffs and exported some goods to Europe. During the 17th century plantation agriculture also emerged in coastal Mexico and the CARIBBEAN. The plantations, often known as *ingenios,* were heavily capitalized, had significant investments in machinery and slaves, and produced for the international market. Plantation-grown sugar became the dominant export of the region in the 18th century, by which time Saint-Domingue (modern-day Haiti) and Jamaica (followed by the Portuguese colony of Brazil) became the largest sugar producers in the world. Cuban TOBACCO also became an important source of revenue for the Spanish Crown during the 18th century. By the 1740s the revenues from Cuban tobacco were more than four times the total income from New Spain.

Plantations and haciendas profoundly affected the demographics of the Americas, but they also produced lasting impacts on the ecosystem of the Americas. Oxen, mules, sheep, pigs, and horses, which were central to the development of agriculture by the late 16th century, also prompted environmental crises. With few natural predators and agricultural systems that were ill-suited to cope with their grazing patterns, European ANIMALS often turned fertile farmland into deserts. The Spanish plow had similar effects on the topsoil, leading to considerable erosion, particularly in those areas prone to torrential rainfall.

Spain's colonial empire was designed to concentrate as much power as possible in the hands of a clique directly responsible to the Crown. The Council of the Indies in Madrid sat at the apex of a pyramid that included the House of Trade, viceroys (the supreme authority in each colony, controlling the administration, the treasury, and military and religious issues), and a series of subordinate officials. Each viceroyalty was divided into *audiencias,* which were in turn divided into *corregimientos, alcaldías, mayores,* and *gobernaciones.* The only source of local authority, *cabildos* (town councils), were theoretically elected bodies, but powerful local families typically controlled them.

In spite of these efforts at control, the sheer size of the viceroyalties and their layers of administration produced a highly decentralized system largely centered on the *audiencias.* (New Spain alone comprised the Caribbean, modern-day Venezuela, Central America, Florida, Mexico, and the western United States, and its *audiencias* were in GUADALAJARA, Mexico, Guatemala, and Santo Domingo.) Members of the *audiencias* typically acted as a brake on viceregal authority, often taking conflicts with royal officials to the Council of the Indies and ensuring that Madrid was kept abreast of affairs in the colonies. Nonetheless, the great distances between the colonies and Madrid made effective control nearly impossible.

Often described as a rentier state, the Crown used its political authority and economic restrictions to draw as much revenue as possible from the colonies, while royal officials generally used their positions to amass individual wealth. Official trade with Europe was tightly controlled, and merchant guilds kept local markets deliberately understocked, amassing their wealth through bottlenecks, scarcity, and monopolies. After 1550 the Crown also used the fleet system, which limited trade to two trading fleets per year, one of which traveled to Veracruz and the other to Panama. This generated a series of distortions in the colonial ECONOMY that was typified by shortages, underdevelopment of essential economic sectors, and, by the late 17th century, an informal sector that was larger than the "official" economy. As time passed fewer Spanish goods were involved in the trade, which itself began to break down in the 1620s. By this time most colonial production was simply funneled through Spain to the more dynamic economies of western Europe. By the end of century the fleet system was in a state of collapse, and contraband trade flourished.

Reflecting their own poor dynastic fortunes, Habsburg interest in the colonies declined during the 17th century. The practice of selling colonial offices became widespread, eventually reaching as high as the appointment to viceroy. Appointments on *audiencias* were increasingly sold to *criollos* (Spaniards born in the colonies), expanding local autonomy within the empire. During this period much of the wealth generated in the colonies managed to remain there to pay for public works and administration, and an increasing array of products were made in the colonies to satisfy local demands. This trend was reversed however, after the death of the last Habsburg monarch at the end of the 17th century and the ascendance of the Bourbon dynasty. The period 1713–62 was characterized by efforts to curb abuses, make the empire function efficiently, and improve revenue collection. The 18th century likewise saw a loosening of restrictions on foreign traders in Spanish American ports, weakening the power of the traditional monopolies. The Crown also increasingly turned to registering ships for trade and abandoned the fleet system by the 1740s.

During the 17th and 18th centuries defense also became a central issue for the colonies. Pirate attacks on Spanish shipping and ports grew more frequent (although the bullion was captured only twice, in 1628 and 1656), and during the 1620s and 1630s the English established settlements in the Caribbean, claiming Jamaica in 1655. Likewise, the French established colonies on Martinique and Guadelupe and ultimately seized the western half of the island of Hispaniola, renaming it Saint-Domingue. Unable to stop these incursions, Spain was forced to recognize the claims of other European powers. PIRACY declined after the Treaty of Madrid between England and Spain in 1670, and with the Treaty of Ryswick in 1697 the Spanish recognized St. Domingue. Simultaneously, the Crown expanded the MISSIONS, presidios, and military colonies that ringed the northern frontier of New Spain, from California to Florida. In 1739 the need for defense also led to the creation of the Viceroyalty of New Granada, which included modern-day Venezuela, Colombia, Ecuador, and Panama.

As with the economy and political institutions, colonial society was defined by a series of hierarchies. Distinctions were made between *criollos* and *peninsulares* (Spaniards born in Spain), with most of the best positions in the colonies being reserved for the latter. European society was also divided among nobles, clerics, and commoners, with special privileges reserved for only the first two groups. Beyond this, the social hierarchy was based on the concept of *limpieza de sangre,* which organized society according to those whose ancestry could be traced most directly to the "Old Christians," Spaniards without any mixed ancestry. This system delineated those of pure Spanish ancestry as *gente de razón* (people of reason), and Indians and other caste categories as *gente sin razón* (people without reason). Over time Spaniards developed an increasingly complex set of social conventions to maintain their privilege, a task that was incredibly difficult in an increasingly multicultural society. By the 18th century the hierarchy included no less than 19 categories to describe people of mixed ancestry (among them, mestizo, castizo, and mulatto).

Spaniards migrated to the colonies at a rate of between 3,000 and 4,000 per year during the period 1585–1650. Immigration slowed after 1650, and by end of the 17th century only 500,000 Iberians had migrated to Spain's colonies. Along with the native-born Spaniards, Europeans represented about one-fourth of the population (almost 600,000) by the end of the 17th century. After recovering from the epidemics of the 16th and early 17th centuries, the population of the colonies began a long period of growth around 1650, reaching 9.4 million by the mid-18th century. Broken down into ethnic categories, by this time the population was 55 percent Indian, 23 percent Spaniard, 15 percent mixed ancestry (*castas*), and 6 percent black.

Approximately 80 percent of Latin Americans lived in rural areas, residing mostly in small hamlets. Most were poor, peasant holders or workers on haciendas, but rural areas also held a tiny middle strata that included small-scale landowners, lower-level bureaucrats, traders, mule drivers, and peddlers. The countryside included relatively few Europeans, as Spaniards tended overwhelmingly to live in cities and have their lands run by hired managers. Cities were the core of colonial life and were vertically organized, with rich Spaniards living in the center around a central plaza and increasingly poor and less ordered barrios spreading out from there. By the close of the 17th century Mexico City contained 200,000 inhabitants, and while preferable for Europeans, this setting was also ideal for many *castas* (one-third of the population of New Spain at the time). Within the fluid social setting of the cities, the caste system was fairly difficult to enforce; able and fortunate migrants could move up the social scale. The metropolis also experienced occasional riots and upheavals, typified by the 1692 uprising in Mexico City, when crowds, suffering from famine and a general economic crisis, destroyed much of the viceregal palace.

In Spanish society two related notions, honor and virtue, were the essential social codes that determined status. Although people of the lower castes were denied both qualities due to their low birth, in elite circles the concepts of masculine honor and feminine virtue played important roles in determining the place of individuals and their families in the social, political, and economic hierarchy. Women were expected to be chaste and pure and to model their lives on the Virgin Mary. Men were expected to defend themselves and their families from any taint of dishonor, ranging from cowardice to illegitimacy to marriages with people of lower rank. These GENDER codes reflected the profound importance of the Catholic Church in colonial society. Although of marginal importance in many indigenous cultures, the Catholic Church acted as one of the most important social, educational, and economic institutions in the colonies. In some cases, however, the social codes created through Roman Catholic ideology could be breached, especially in families that had the financial means to cover up indiscretions by petitioning for legitimacy through the court and church. Wealthy mestizos and MULATTOES might also "whiten" themselves by marrying up the caste ladder, a practice that was not uncommon in the region.

Women were not considered citizens in a political sense in Latin America, but Spanish customs created opportunities for some women. Spanish inheritance rules dictated that daughters were entitled to an equal share of their parents' estates and could continue to control their wealth after marriage. Women of means often conducted their own business, and wealthy widows sometimes became important landowners, MERCHANTS, and miners. Many young women also preferred the convents that proliferated in the colonial capitals to the vagaries of marriage. In convents they could conduct their affairs freely and live a life unencumbered by male authority. The Mexican Sor Juana Inés de la Cruz (1651–95) was perhaps the most famous woman to choose such a life during the colonial period. Born the illegitimate child of a modest provincial family, she was given patronage by the wife of a viceroy to enter a Carmelite convent at age 15. In the convent she produced an opus of poetry that ranks her among the best poets Mexico has ever produced.

Poor and rural women were also essential in the ECONOMY, as most poor families relied on female labor. Given the frequency with which males migrated for work, it was common in indigenous communities for women to play a crucial role in trade, local agriculture, religious observances, and even rebellions. Furthermore, for those Indian women who survived the epidemics of the 16th century, the opportunities to acquire property expanded, although in many cases their social position eroded as their traditional roles were devalued under colonialism. Indigenous women faced diminished prestige within the Christian nuclear family, and missionary activities tended to lead to an exaggeration of female subordination.

Those at the lowest levels of the hierarchy were perhaps most deeply affected by colonialism. In the area that was to become New Spain, the population plummeted in one of the worst demographic disasters in world history. The 50 million to 100 million Indians in 1492 fell drastically after 1500 due to epidemics and abuse by colonizers. In the Caribbean the population was completely wiped out by 1570, while in central Mexico it declined from as many as 25 million in 1500 to 1 million in 1605. Because of this crisis, the Crown began to resettle Indian populations and passed a series of laws designed to protect the Indian population from further decimation. The reforms of the 16th century made it illegal for non-Indians to reside or hold lands within a specified radius of an Indian village, except for royal officials and church functionaries. The first new Indian villages, called *congregaciones,* were founded in the 1550s, followed by others between 1593 and 1605. They were governed by traditional indigenous authorities (caciques) who ruled in conjunction with the royal officials known as *corregidores de indios.* Although charged with protecting Indian communities, these administrators were often their worst exploiters.

The *congregaciones* represented both positive and negative developments for indigenous peoples. On the positive side, they afforded mechanisms to defend indigenous communities against Spanish colonizers. Due to the protections afforded by the Crown, some land-owning Indian communities survived the colonial period. In more commercially active regions, such as Mexico's Bajío, NATIVE AMERICANS tended to be displaced from villages and became tenant farmers in spite of legal protections. However, in some regions, like Oaxaca, Indian villages successfully held on to their lands in the face of encroaching Spaniards. Far from using their legal protections to completely isolate themselves, in villages that maintained their land indigenous peoples often cultivated a mixture of wheat, maize, beans, and squash for domestic CONSUMPTION and local markets. They also produced other market goods, including pots, homespun cotton, wool, wooden items, and beeswax. Some even developed centers of silver working, weaving, and woodworking.

Native Americans in more remote regions often successfully continued their traditional cultures. These villages maintained solidarity through *cofradias,* religious organizations that funded local rituals and festivals. Religious life tended to preserve indigenous spiritual identities, even if local religious leaders shrouded their practices and beliefs in Catholic ritual. The synthesis between native religions and Catholic iconography encouraged a type of superficial conversion, most clearly seen in the syncretic Guadalupe-Tonantzin, who remains the most venerated religious icon in Mexico to the present.

On the negative side of the equation, in payment for defending indigenous rights the Crown demanded labor and tribute from Native Americans. Indian goods were taxed, and a head tax was exacted on all Indian adult males. Royal officials forced members of Indian communities to buy goods, mules, and clothes under a system known as the *repartimiento de mercancias.* Labor demands for public works, haciendas, and mines came through the *repartimiento* (taking the form of the *mita* in Peru), which obligated adult male Indians to work 45 days each year for the Crown. However, indigenous peoples quickly adopted strategies, ranging from buying their way out of the work requirement to taking flight. Their resistance was so successful that in most regions the *repartimiento* quickly

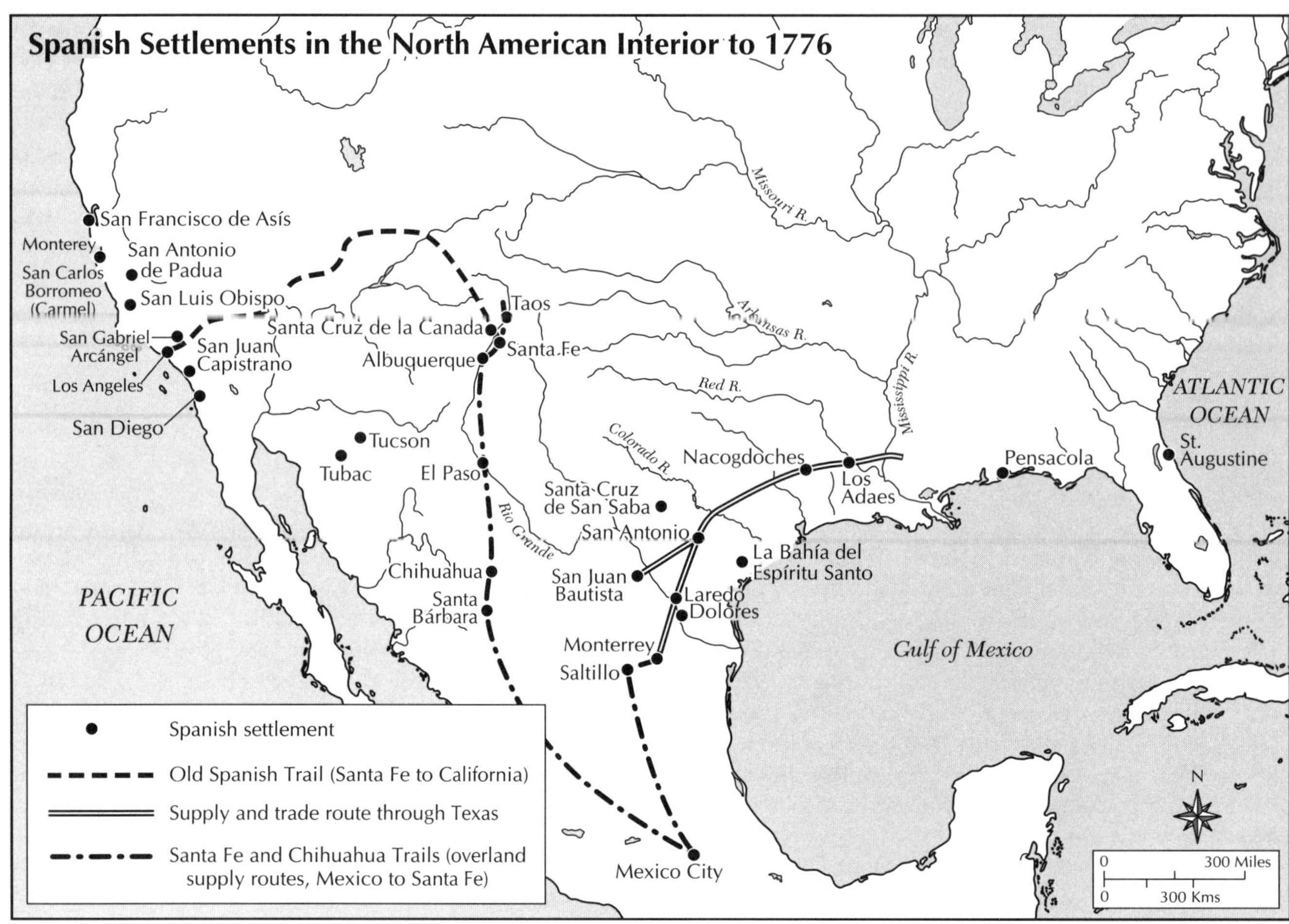

became unfeasible. Although it survived in Central America into the 19th century, by the end of the 16th century most mineworkers and agricultural laborers in New Spain were Indians hired as wage labor and retained through debt peonage.

The work of enslaved Africans was also essential to this system. The first African slaves arrived in the region in the early stages of conquest, with some even acting as conquistadores. By the 1570s slaves were being imported in significant numbers, arriving mostly from present-day Senegambia, Congo, and Angola, with their population reaching 75,000 by century's end. Initially, slaves mostly worked in urban areas but within a few decades constituted a key source of labor for mines and plantations. There were 3,700 slaves in Mexico's silver mines by 1570, representing about 45 percent of the labor force. By 1590 their number declined to 20 percent of the labor force (approximately 1,000 people), and they mostly worked in less dangerous jobs. SLAVERY in Mexico reached its height during the 1650s, when there were 35,000 African slaves in the colony. After this date slavery steadily declined in both Mexico and Peru as the plantation complexes of the Caribbean and Brazil came to dominate. Estimates of the numbers of slaves brought to the Americas by the end of the 18th century vary widely, but the total was about 8 million. Most of these slaves were taken to the Portuguese colony of Brazil or to French, Dutch, and British colonies in the Caribbean. Spanish colonies, including the mainland colonies of New Spain and Peru, along with their colonies in the Caribbean (notably Cuba), imported about 1 million slaves of the total.

The tempo and type of economic activity was decisive in determining the experience of slaves. In the Spanish colonies African slaves occupied a wide variety of jobs, in agriculture, domestic service, and in some cases even urban trades. Some slaves lived apart from their masters and even traveled as muleteers and sailors. By contrast, life for the millions who found themselves immersed in the plantation complex was horrific. Slave life on the plantations was characterized by short lifespans (as little as seven years for newly imported slaves), sex ratios seriously skewed in favor of men, linguistic diversity, and harsh labor conditions. Slaves born in the region rarely lived beyond their 30s, and those brought from AFRICA had even shorter lives. Prosperous plantations tended to be the worst, because the cost of replacing a slave was often lower than the cost of maintaining healthy workers. A typical plantation in Latin America had about 50 slaves, most of whom lived in communal barracks. Women worked in the fields alongside men but were excluded from more skilled jobs, making their escape from the backbreaking labor unlikely.

In other parts of the region manumission was an uncommon but realizable goal. Slave ARTISANS might use money earned from their trades to purchase freedom for themselves and others. Sex, consensual and forced, between white owners and slave women produced a growing mulatto population, some of whom were freed by their masters. By the end of 18th century there were 650,000 free black and mulatto people in Spanish America, more than twice the number of slaves. In the urban areas of Spanish America African slaves enjoyed an active communal life through their own *cofradias.* They preserved African social organizations, customs, languages, and religions, creating syncretic cultures that drew from African, European, and indigenous traditions. Escaped slave communities, known in Spanish as *palenques* and Portuguese as *quilombos,* also provided opportunities to undermine the dehumanizing practices of slavery and to challenge the institution of racial bondage. These communities flourished in the Caribbean, parts of Mexico, Central America, and Brazil. At least 35 existed in Brazil, some reaching several thousand members.

By the time of the SEVEN YEAR'S WAR, Spain's American colonies had been a mature system for 200 years. Although still central to the colonial enterprise, the extraction of silver was increasingly overshadowed by the rich plantation complex of the Caribbean. This was itself problematic for the empire, as a region that once had been the preserve of Spain alone was being contested by more prosperous and aggressive colonial competitors. Conquered by the British during the war, Havana was both a strategic and economically crucial lynchpin of the empire. All along the northern frontier as well, the empire was under siege, meaning that expanded militarization (and increased revenue to pay for it) would likely be the only way of preserving the colonies in the future. This was an ominous sign for the *casta,* indigenous, and African peoples throughout the region because growing quantities of their labor, tribute, and military service would be demanded in order to save the empire.

Further reading: D. A. Brading, *The First America: The Spanish Monarchy, Creole Patriots and the Liberal State* (Cambridge, U.K.: Cambridge University Press, 1991); Alfred Crosby, *The Colombian Exchange: Biological and Cultural Consequences of 1492* (Westport, Conn.: Greenwood, 1972); Nancy Farriss, *Maya Society under Colonial Rule: The Collective Enterprise of Survival* (Princeton, N.J.: Princeton University Press, 1984).

—Alexander Dawson

Spanish immigration

The first Spanish immigrants to arrive in the New World were the conquistadores. They had no interest in settling or farming but only in finding riches. A few, such as Hernán Cortés and Francisco Pizarro, were fabulously successful. Conquistadores paid for their own equipment and received permission for their expeditions from the Spanish MONARCHY in exchange for the "royal fifth," that is, one-fifth of the plunder confiscated by the conquistadores. While some of the conquistadores came from affluent families, few had much material wealth before their expeditions. The practice of primogeniture in Spain meant that younger sons and daughters inherited little. The New World thus offered an opportunity to acquire wealth and honor denied them in Spain. The majority of the conquistadores were young males who came from the working classes. They hoped to gain the title *hidalgo* (literally "son of someone"), the lowest rank of nobility.

Once the conquest ended a new type of Spanish immigrant began to arrive in the New World. They were educated and well connected with the mother country. Many of the new arrivals became royal officials or religious leaders. They often received the favor of the royal court, much to the despair of the earlier settlers. Many of the new arrivals saw their positions in the New World as a steppingstone to better things and never became permanent residents. ARTISANS, laborers, soldiers, and sailors also arrived to begin new lives in New Spain. Almost 40 percent of the immigrants came from Andalusia, a poor agricultural region in southern Spain. Many others came from various outposts of the Spanish empire, such as the Azores, the Cape Verde Islands, and the Canary Islands.

During the 16th century approximately 225,000 Spaniards moved to the New World. Another 200,000 had arrived by 1650. Despite the immigration, Spaniards never made up more than 2 percent of the population in New Spain. Few women went to New Spain in the early years. By the 1580s the proportion of women migrating to New Spain was nearly one in three, having increased from a ratio of one in 20 before 1519.

Although small in number, the *peninsulares,* people born on the Iberian peninsula, were the ruling class. They held the best positions in the government and the church. They outranked pure-blooded Spaniards born in New Spain, the *criollos.* Because relatively few women migrated to New Spain, Spanish men often married Indians or blacks, creating a generation of mestizos and MULATTOES.

Each succeeding generation became more racially diverse, with race an important determinant of social status.

Further reading: Michael C. Meyer and William L. Sherman, *The Course of Mexican History* (New York: Oxford University Press, 1999).

—Jeffrey D. Carlisle

spinsters

During the 17th century the term *spinster* came to mean not only a female spinner of wool, cotton, or linen, but also a never-married woman. The two meanings overlapped because many single women earned their living by spinning. Over the course of the 17th and 18th centuries *spinster* took on a derogatory meaning, England apparently leading the way in developing this connotation. Some scholars contend that spinsters, in addition to challenging prevailing models of womanhood that prescribed the proper role of an adult woman to be wife and mother, were seen as impediments to British mercantile and imperialist expansion, which required constant childbearing to reproduce the workforce.

While single women formed between 10 and 20 percent of the adult female population in Europe between 1250 and 1800, they were anomalies in the early North American colonies. For example, between 1619 and 1622 approximately 150 single English women came to VIRGINIA. By the end of 1622 every one of them had married. In 17th-century New England virtually all white women married as well. New England authorities deemed single people, both men and women, to be so potentially disruptive to social order that they were directed to live with "well governed families." Single women over the age of 23 earned the label *spinster.* If they were still unmarried at 26, they were called "thornbacks," an unflattering reference to a sea skate with sharp spines on its back and tail. Unmarried women were also more vulnerable to charges of WITCHCRAFT. By the 18th century spinsters were not seen as necessarily threatening to social order, but as objects of derision and scorn. Old maids were considered odd, ugly, ill-natured, nosy, and possessing undue curiosity, childlike credulity, absurd affectations, and spiteful natures.

In Europe spinsters or "maids" most commonly supported themselves as servants, but some also engaged in other wage labor, piece work, petty trading, or small shopkeeping. In 17th-century New England the apprenticeship system trained girls only for housewifery; there is no record of a mercantile establishment hiring a single woman until after KING PHILIP'S WAR. By the 18th century more single women found employment in the kinds of jobs available in Europe, traders were sometimes referred to as "she-merchants," and some single women worked in newspaper printing, teaching, and sewing. Even so, as was true across the Atlantic, these were usually poorly paid positions, with low status and little hope of economic security.

Further reading: Judith M. Bennett and Amy M. Froide, eds., *Singlewomen in the European Past, 1250–1800* (Philadelphia: University of Pennsylvania Press, 1999); Karin A. Wulf, *Not All Wives: Women of Colonial Philadelphia* (Ithaca, N.Y.: Cornell University Press, 2001).

—Mary Murphy

Squanto (1580?–1622)

One of the most pivotal figures in the history of English colonization of North America was Squanto, a Patuxet Indian. The Patuxet were an ALGONQUIN-speaking tribe who engaged in AGRICULTURE, hunting, and FISHING in the coastal region of what would become southern New England. Europeans visited the area with several exploratory ventures, most notably SAMUEL DE CHAMPLAIN in 1605 and JOHN SMITH in 1614, describing a land with a substantial population that offered potential for FUR TRADE and agricultural development. Details about Squanto's early life are sketchy, as are the events leading to his departure from the American mainland. One likely scenario offered by historians is that Thomas Hunt, an officer left in charge of the fishing operation in Smith's expedition, captured Squanto along with approximately 20 other NATIVE AMERICANS and attempted to sell them as slaves in Spain. Not surprisingly, Hunt's action served to embitter relations between Europeans and Native Americans in New England.

Not much is known about Squanto's life shortly after his capture, but in 1617 he was living in London in the household of John Slany, an employee of the Newfoundland Company. Through this association Squanto met Sir Ferdinando Gorges, who decided to send Squanto back to New England to act as an interpreter for a 1619 expedition. The New England Squanto encountered upon his return was already radically changed from the one he had left only years earlier. The most dramatic difference was in the native population, which had fallen victim to an epidemic of European DISEASE in 1616. The Patuxet were hit particularly hard, and the surviving members abandoned their village before Squanto arrived. Left without family or tribal ties, Squanto offered to serve as an interpreter for the Wampanoag Indians and the newly arrived English colony at PLYMOUTH in 1620. Along with Samoset, Squanto served as translator and intermediary between the Pilgrim settlers and MASSASOIT, the Wampanoag sachem.

Like many natives who worked (willingly or through force) as translators in the early colonial period, Squanto soon found himself caught between two worlds, with one foot in English culture and one ensconced in the Algonquin world. By helping the struggling PILGRIMS learn how to grow crops in the marginal New England soil, Squanto ensured their survival and established himself in a position of considerable authority within the English colony. In addition, as the primary interpreter between Massasoit and the Pilgrims, Squanto was central to the increasingly fractious political negotiations that took place after 1620. The balance was impossible to hold for long, however, and Squanto soon fell out of favor with Massasoit, in part due to his failed attempt to play each side off the other to elevate his own political and economic status. Increasingly dependent upon the English, in 1622 Squanto succumbed to the same diseases that had ravaged his people in the earlier epidemic.

Further reading: Kathleen J. Bragdon, *Native People of Southern New England, 1500–1650* (Norman: University of Oklahoma Press, 1996).

—Melanie Perreault

Standish, Myles (1584?–1656)

As the military commander of the PILGRIMS and the PLYMOUTH Colony, Captain Myles Standish was responsible for the colony's security. Standish claimed descent from the Roman Catholic family Standish and that his inheritance from the family had been "surreptitiously detained." He served in the continental wars in the Low Countries before joining the Pilgrim Separatists in London on their voyage to North America. He was one of the signers of the MAYFLOWER COMPACT. Standish's experiences on various campaigns apparently rendered him hardy enough to escape the "general sickness" of the first winter in Plymouth, which claimed the life of his first wife, Rose. He led several of the exploratory expeditions in and around Plymouth, including the 1622 offensive against the Massachusett Indians at Wessagusset.

Standish was derisively referred to as "Captaine Shrimp" by THOMAS MORTON of Merrymount. Standish had broken up the Merrymount trading settlement in 1628 and arrested Morton, sending him back to England. Standish remarried in 1623 or 1624 and helped established Duxbury, the first direct offshoot of the Plymouth church, which was incorporated as a town in 1637. Standish was also a chief negotiator with local natives, learning several dialects and helping to keep peaceful relations between them and the colonists. Henry Wadsworth Longfellow chose Standish as the hero of his 1858 poetic romance, *The Courtship of Miles Standish,* based on the story published in Timothy Alden's *A Collection of American Epitaphs and Inscriptions* (1814). Standish was depicted as a courageous, hot-tempered military man, unable to court Priscilla Mullins because of his lack of words and instead requesting his young friend JOHN ALDEN to court her on Standish's behalf. There is little evidence beyond oral tradition for the romance, but it was one of the most popular poems in 19th- and 20th-century America.

—Stephen C. O'Neill

Starbuck, Mary Coffin (1645–1717)

The youngest daughter of one of the earliest and most prominent settlers of Nantucket, Mary Coffin became an important proselytizer and the first recognized minister of the Society of Friends (QUAKERS) on the island. She was born February 20, 1645, in Haverhill, MASSACHUSETTS, to Tristram Coffin and Dionis Stevens, who moved the family to Nantucket in 1662. That same year Mary became the wife of Nathaniel Starbuck.

Mary's wealth and status afforded her a significant role in the community. Her husband, the wealthiest man on the island, operated a farm and served as a government official. Mary tended their 10 children (two died before reaching adulthood) and the households of her extended family after the deaths of both her and Nathaniel's mothers. Her most remembered role, though, is as a religious leader.

Literate and well-versed in the scriptures but apparently a member of no particular church, Mary joined a Calvinist "circle" attended by her in-laws and ultimately became its leader. In the 1690s, however, a rift in the community over land titles and the deaths of several prominent Nantucket leaders ushered in a new era, allowing Quaker missionaries to gain what at first seemed to be a weak foothold on the island. Mary became one of the earliest to be included among the converted.

That she had assumed a leadership role in her previous religious organization suggests that some similarities existed between the beliefs of that group and those of the Quakers. Most important for Mary was the Quaker support of equal status for women in religious activities, including ministering. By 1708 the Starbucks had begun holding Quaker meetings in their home, known as "Parliament House," and Mary, at age 63, had become an influential leader.

Women of the period typically played a large role in the religious EDUCATION of their children, and Mary was no exception. Although her children had reached adulthood by the time of her conversion, she still maintained significant influence over their lives. Only one of her children did not embrace Quakerism.

—Nicki Walker Carroll

Stono Rebellion (1739)

The Stono Rebellion was the largest slave revolt in British North America. It began on Sunday, September 9, 1739, when a group of roughly 20 slaves (the exact number is uncertain), led by a slave named "Jemmy," broke into Hutchenson's store near the Stono River in St. Paul's parish southwest of CHARLESTON. After beheading two storekeepers and seizing weapons at the store, the rebel band marched southward toward FLORIDA, where they expected to find freedom among the Spanish at ST. AUGUSTINE, who had promised liberty to black fugitives from Carolina. Beating drums and shouting "liberty," the rebels gathered more than 50 recruits along the way. The rebel "army" attacked and burned selected plantations and killed at least a score of white people before an armed posse of militiamen sent by Lieutenant Governor William Bull from SOUTH CAROLINA defeated the rebels in pitched battles at Stono, only 50 miles from Florida. Some of the rebels escaped, and several made their way to St. Augustine, where they became integrated into the large black community there and, joined by other runaways, fought on the side of the Spanish in the border war against their former masters. However, the main body of rebels was caught. In a fury of revenge and also in a calculated move to demonstrate white power, the militiamen shot, hanged, and "Gibbeted alive" the rebels. For weeks thereafter suspected (and real) rebels and black fugitives were captured and killed as Carolina authorities clamped down on SLAVE RESISTANCE of any kind.

The rebellion grew out of the changing structure of race relations and SLAVERY in South Carolina. As the black population came to outnumber the white people in the colony by almost a two-to-one ratio by 1739, and as the slave population increasingly was made up of direct "imports" from Africa, mostly young males from present-day Angola, white control over slaves became more tenuous. White people previously had relied on slaves to join in the defense against Indian attacks and Spanish incursions and entrusted acculturated slaves with large responsibilities as cowherders, boatmen, and planters. However, the demographic change, the emergence of a plantation ECONOMY, an epidemic raging among white inhabitants, and hostilities with the Spanish left the white people feeling exposed. A tighter slave code seemed in the offing as authorities sought to increase white vigilance and curtail black mobility. The first rumblings of the GREAT AWAKENING, with its egalitarian outreach to people of all classes and conditions, added to the social unrest. News of the start of a war between Spain and England made everyone in Carolina edgy, but the Spanish promise of liberty to fugitive slaves triggered the uprising. That some of the newly arrived Africans likely had military experience and that Jemmy and other slaves were attuned to local circumstances and knew the region's geography no doubt encouraged the rebels to act. The rebels' early success (which included almost capturing the lieutenant governor) attested to their ability and planning. Historians speculate that had the rebels made good their bid for freedom, the revolt would have spread and possibly threatened slavery in Carolina altogether.

The South Carolina authorities took no chances with any further erosion of white mastery. In 1740 the assembly enacted the most stringent slave code in the North American colonies, cut back on African importations, and moved against the Spanish and black fugitives in Florida. Ironically, even as the memory of the Stono Rebellion haunted planters, their need for field hands to work the rice plantations led them to resume importations of Africans, whose numbers and large concentrations in the Low Country reinforced African culture and contributed to a higher degree of slave cultural autonomy there than anywhere else in colonial North America. Under such circumstances resistance took more subtle forms rather than outright collective violence. No more Stono Rebellions occurred in the Carolinas or anywhere in the colonies thereafter, but the establishment of a free black colony at Fort Mose in Florida served as a haven for Carolina runaway slaves headed south. More important to the memory of Stono, slaves in South Carolina seized the moment of the American Revolutionary war to flee plantations and remind their masters that ownership of slaves did not mean mastery of them.

Further reading: Philip D. Morgan, *Slavery Counterpoint: Black Culture in the Eighteenth-Century Chesapeake and Lowcountry* (Chapel Hill: University of North Carolina Press, 1998); Edward A. Pearson, "'A Countryside Full of Flames': A Reconsideration of the Stono Rebellion and Slave Rebelliousness in the Early Eighteenth-Century South Carolina Lowcountry" (*Slavery & Abolition* 17 (1996), 22–50); John K. Thornton, "African Dimensions of the Stono Rebellion" *American Historical Review* 96 (1991), 1101–13); Peter H. Wood, *Black Majority: Negroes in Colonial South Carolina from 1670 through the Stono Rebellion* (New York: Norton, 1974).

—Randall M. Miller

Stuyvesant, Peter (1610?–1672)

Peter Stuyvesant served as the director general of the NEW NETHERLAND colony for 17 years, making his tenure the longest of any governor of colonial NEW YORK. Son of a Dutch Reformed minister in the Netherlands, Stuyvesant spent some time at university before becoming an employee of the DUTCH WEST INDIA COMPANY. His first foreign assignments were in the Dutch colony of Brazil. In 1638 he became the chief commercial officer on the CARIBBEAN island of Curaçao and within four years was promoted to the governor's chair. During his tenure in the West Indies, Stuyvesant lost part of his right leg in a military engagement. While recuperating in the Netherlands, the Dutch West India Company rewarded Stuyvesant for his valor and service by conferring on him its top post in the New Netherland colony.

Stuyvesant's iron determination met a formidable challenge in Holland's fledgling colony. In 1647 he arrived on Manhattan to find a village in shambles, largely the result of his predecessor's disastrous nine-year tenure. A choleric, industrious ruler, Stuyvesant immediately set about reforming the disorderly town, instituting new laws on sanitation, trade with NATIVE AMERICANS, vice, and ALCOHOL. Ordered by his superiors to share power with a council of prominent men chosen by the people, Stuyvesant instead hand-picked his Board of Nine Men and restricted their power, thus ensuring a strained relationship with his counselors for the rest of his term. He was less successful in forcing his will on the towns outside NEW AMSTERDAM. Before his arrival the English settlements on western Long Island had succeeded in procuring local self-government from the Dutch authorities. During Stuyvesant's watch, the Dutch towns on the island followed suit.

Stuyvesant also tried to hold back the tide of religious diversity in this polyglot colony. A devout Calvinist, the director general enforced the establishment of the Dutch Reformed congregation, the only church permitted to hold public services in New Netherland. While successfully restricting other Christian sects from public establishment, Stuyvesant tried to expel both JEWS and QUAKERS. He called the 23 Jewish refugees from Brazil who arrived in 1654 "hateful enemies and blasphemers of the name of Christ." He labeled the Quakers who landed in 1657 as "heretics, deceivers, and seducers." The directors of the West India Company overruled Stuyvesant's attempt to expel these groups, asserting that religious repression would discourage prospective settlers.

Stuyvesant dealt with outside threats as well. In 1655 he organized an expedition of 600 men to conquer the Swedish settlements on the Delaware. Stuyvesant's colony also defeated three major military challenges from the area's native population, but the most serious outside threat came from England. In 1650 Stuyvesant went to Hartford, CONNECTICUT, to hammer out the terms of a treaty that defined the borders between New Netherland and New England, yet when war erupted in Europe between England and Holland, New England resurrected its old claims and threatened to conquer New Netherland. In response to the English menace, Stuyvesant built a "high stockade" that ran east to west across the island and later became Wall Street. Surviving the first English-Dutch War, New Netherland experienced great growth and prosperity in the waning years of Dutch rule. The beaver trade reached its zenith, and the number of houses tripled in the last years of Stuyvesant's rule. During the second Dutch-English War, the English finally made good on their threat, sailing to the city in August 1664 and promising a continuation of Dutch trading and property rights. Despite Stuyvesant's strong objections, the inhabitants of the city, including his eldest son, urged him to surrender peacefully. Stuyvesant spent the next three years in Holland defending his reputation in light of the effortless British conquest. He returned to his farm, then situated in the British colony of New York, to live out the remaining years of his life. He died in February 1672 and is buried in the vault of St. Mark's-in-the-Bowery Church, the site of the chapel built by Stuyvesant on his farm.

Peter Stuyvesant *(Hulton/Archive)*

Further reading: Oliver A. Rink, *Holland on the Hudson: An Economic and Social History of Dutch New York* (Ithaca, N.Y.: Cornell University Press, 1986).

—Judy VanBuskirk

suffrage

British colonial suffrage laws were modeled on English laws but varied considerably from one colony to another. Political leaders tacitly assumed that only free white men would cast votes, although some jurisdictions occasionally permitted property-holding single women, NATIVE AMERI-

CANS, and free AFRICAN AMERICANS to vote. Suffrage laws became somewhat more uniform in the 18th century, as the American colonies increasingly reserved voting rights for Protestant men of European descent. SOUTH CAROLINA and VIRGINIA disenfranchised free African Americans in 1716 and 1723, respectively. Several colonies also disenfranchised ROMAN CATHOLICS and JEWS in the early 18th century; on the other hand, many colonies repealed suffrage restrictions they had previously placed on Protestant dissenters.

Among white men suffrage was restricted to free property holders. Indentured servants were sometimes permitted to vote in local elections but seldom in colony-wide elections. South Carolina, Virginia, NEW YORK, and PENNSYLVANIA explicitly disenfranchised indentured servants in the 18th century. Property requirements for voting were quite liberal, however: possession of a 40-shilling freehold or an estate worth £40 was a common requirement in the northern colonies, while the plantation colonies typically required voters to own 50 acres of land. By 18th-century European standards, American colonists enjoyed an exceptionally broad suffrage.

Although many adult white men enjoyed the right to vote, the value of the suffrage was limited. Several colonies instituted property qualifications for assembly candidates that were much higher than were those for voters; local elites dominated colonial legislatures from NEW HAMPSHIRE to GEORGIA. Consensus was an important political value in New England and parts of the plantation South, and many elections were not contested. For all these reasons, voter turnout was relatively low, typically between 20 and 40 percent of adult white men. Many voters attended polling places primarily in order to express fealty to political patrons or to enjoy the refreshments provided by the candidates.

—Darcy R. Fryer

Susquehannock War (1676)

The Susquehannock War of 1676 was one of many wars between NATIVE AMERICANS and European settlers that set the East Coast ablaze in 1675–7. The Susquehannock, who had been decimated by SMALLPOX and wars with the IROQUOIS, fled to MARYLAND and camped on Piscataway Creek near the fort occupied by the Piscataway Indians. The Susquehannock asked the governor to allow them to settle in Maryland because they had a treaty of peace and friendship with the colony. Worried about potential conflicts between the Susquehannock and the Piscataway, Maryland officials offered the Susquehannock land above the Potomac's Great Falls, a remote region that the Susquehannock found undesirable. In July 1675 trouble began. Murders and robberies in VIRGINIA and Maryland were attributed by colonists to the Susquehannock. In September Colonel John Washington of Virginia asked permission and cooperation from the Maryland council to attack the Susquehannock in Maryland. Both Maryland and Virginia raised 500 troops each to carry out orders that the Susquehannock "be forthwith forced off from the place they now are and remove themselves to the place they assured the last Assembly they would goe and seate themselves." Many local Indians joined the colonial forces.

The colonial commanders accused the Susquehannock of murders in both colonies, which they denied. Although the treaty with Maryland pledged eternal friendship with the Susquehannock, colonial forces murdered the Indian leaders and laid siege to their encampment. With only 100 warriors, the Susquehannock managed to resist for six weeks, killing between 50 and 100 colonists. Eventually, the Susquehannock escaped and fled into Virginia, where they raided settlements at the heads of the Rappahannock and York Rivers.

This tragedy was a triggering event of BACON'S REBELLION, in which Nathaniel Bacon and his followers attacked peaceful Indian allies and eventually challenged the Virginia government itself. In the process, many of the local Indian groups were exterminated.

Further reading: Helen C. Rountree and Thomas E. Davidson, *Eastern Shore Indians of Virginia and Maryland* (Charlottesville: University Press of Virginia, 1997).

—James F. Adomanis

Swedish colonies

The Swedish colony of Nya Sverige (New Sweden) on the Delaware River was the smallest of all European colonies in North America, with a population of only about 200 for most of its short duration (1638–55), but New Sweden was significant beyond its size and longitude in establishing patterns of population diversity and Indian relations unknown in most of the other colonies. The population included Swedes, Finns, Dutch, Germans, Poles, and English. From the start the colony's leaders purchased lands from the local Lenape and Susquehannock Indians rather than claiming land rights by "first discovery," as the Dutch and English had.

Peter Minuit led the first Swedish expedition and established Fort Christiana (now Wilmington, DELAWARE) in 1638 as an outpost of the New Sweden Company, a private company of Dutch and Swedish investors who expected to profit from trade in furs and TOBACCO. By 1641 the Swedish Crown had bought out the Dutch investors.

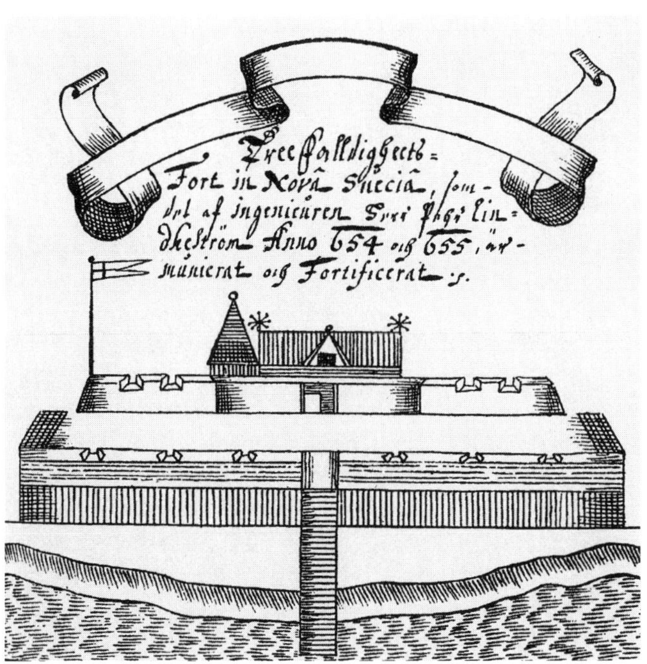

This woodcut shows Fort Christiana, the Swedes' main outpost on the Delaware River. *(Library of Congress)*

The colony began as a military and trading post but evolved into a successful trading and agricultural settlement under the governorship of Johan Printz (1643–53). Printz's daughter, Armgard, one of the first Swedish women to arrive in the colony, married her father's successor, Johan Papegoja, and achieved notoriety when she refused to accompany her husband back to Sweden.

Over an 18-year period 12 expeditions set out from Sweden for New Sweden; two of these never made it to the colony (one was seized by the Dutch, the other by the Spanish). Most immigrants were from areas then under the control of the Swedish Crown, which encompassed Finland and, during the Thirty Years' War (1618–48), extended over much of Poland and Prussia as well as some German towns. The earliest immigrants were mostly soldiers and other single men; some were convicted criminals who had chosen military service in New Sweden instead of death by hanging. Subsequent settlers included nobles, clergy, MERCHANTS, civil servants, peasants, and laborers. The final expedition in 1656 included 350 women, men, and children, most of them Finns or Swedes who had lived in Finland. Even before the ships sailed, New Sweden had surrendered to the Dutch, who controlled the region until the English took control in 1664 and again in 1674. After WILLIAM PENN became proprietor in 1681, he relied on Swedish traders and interpreters in his negotiations with the Lenape and other Indians. In 1697 the Swedish and Finnish population in the region numbered at least 1,200; many continued to speak the languages of their ancestors until well into the 18th century.

Further reading: C. A. Weslager, *New Sweden on the Delaware, 1638–1655* (Wilmington, Del.: Middle Atlantic Press, 1988).

—Alison Duncan Hirsch

T

taverns and inns

Two types of buildings were present in most colonial towns and villages—churches and taverns—and public drinking houses were far more common than public houses of worship. Although *tavern* was the term most commonly employed, *ordinary, inn,* and *public house* were used interchangeably.

Taverns assumed many forms. The City Tavern in PHILADELPHIA, for instance, was an elaborate affair, a two-story brick building measuring 50 feet by 46 feet. The building's appearance was especially fashionable because it was set back a considerable distance from the street. The bar and public meeting rooms filled the first floor, each extending for the entire length of the building. In these spaces patrons could find various colonial and British newspapers. Moveable screens provided flexibility for smaller, more private meetings. On the second floor were two clubrooms that could be altered to be one large space measuring nearly 50 feet in length. The second floor also contained a long room appropriate for gaming or, for the more genteel folks opposed to this sort of entertainment, the rooms could be used for meetings. Similarly, the Indian King, a converted Philadelphia mansion, consisted of 18 rooms, 14 with fireplaces, and stables for up to 100 horses.

These upper-end establishments attracted their clientele from society's elite and required experienced, worthy proprietors. One applicant to manage the City Tavern claimed to be qualified because he had kept a tavern in Dublin that "entertained noblemen and gentlemen." Proprietors of such large public houses had a wide range of functions. They cared for the rooms and stables, managed the kitchen, acted as host, greeted new arrivals, assisted with special events, and handled the funds. They also played supervisory roles over a staff that might include cooks and waiters, drivers, and wood carters. They were also responsible for the quality of the entertainments that ranged from FOOD and drink to conversation and diversions.

Taverns open for lower- and middling-status patrons varied enormously. Proprietors often converted houses into ordinaries by posting a sign, serving liquor, and setting up additional beds for guests. Interior spaces were undifferentiated; travelers might encounter sleeping accommodations in any room of the house. Benjamin Bullivant, who journeyed from MASSACHUSETTS, spent a sleepless night in a NEW JERSEY tavern because a group of privateers partied in the public room with "theyr girles." When the tavern was a single room, all activities took place in the same space. Waightstill Avery arrived at Powel's Tavern somewhere in NORTH CAROLINA, where he encountered a drunk assembly—the landlord, a neighbor, and two travelers—eating supper. "There being but one room in the house . . . I watched carefully all night, to keep them from falling over and spewing upon me."

Early Americans entered taverns for a variety of activities, all of which they lubricated generously with drink. Men gathered on a regular basis to transact business, argue about politics, or share a convivial pint with friends. Visitors staying at these establishments might witness a heated argument about the price of wheat in PENNSYLVANIA or the inspirational quality of a minister's sermon in BOSTON. The laboring classes exchanged news of the day, plotted political action, or drank among coworkers and friends. Customers who depended on rural taverns joined mixed company. If these inns were well situated on a main road, the patrons included local residents as well as travelers who needed a night's lodging, a warm fire in winter, and a cool drink in summer. Colonial militias practiced on the village green and then retired to the local tavern to quench their thirst and relive their feats.

Every colony established a legal code to control the behavior inside taverns. The North Carolina statute was typical: Taverns were required to have "good Wholesome, and cleanly Lodging and Dyet for Travellers and Stable, Fodder, and Corn, or Pasturage and Corn . . . for their horses." Massachusetts lawmakers concurred. Public houses were to be established primarily for the "receiving and refreshment of travaillers and strangers, and to serve the public occasions of such town or precinct." Laws also defined who could have access to taverns. Servants and slaves were prohibited from partaking of tavern services unless given explicit permission by their masters. All colonies passed laws making it illegal to sell alcoholic beverages to Indians, and the statutes placed MARINERS in a special category. Their time inside taverns was limited, and tavern keepers could not extend credit to them.

Local leaders determined what forms of alcoholic beverages were to be sold by which establishments. Pennsylvania, for example, designated some public houses for the sale of wine and beer, while others could offer the whole range of spirituous liquors. In addition, a "take out" trade developed that allowed retail establishments to sell larger quantities to be consumed off the tavern premises. In the 17th century all licenses specified what beverages could be sold. Most sold beer and cider. Some had permission to sell wine. The Bay Colony drew the finest distinctions among drink sellers. Richard Knot, for example, was granted a license to sell "strongwater at retail only to his own fishermen [belonging to his boat or concerned in the voyage]." In the first decades of the 18th century, as demands for particular drinks altered, some Boston tavern keepers stocked rum exclusively. Massachusetts magistrates also stipulated how distilled liquors were to be produced in an effort to protect their citizens from potentially lethal drink. In 1723–4 it was unlawful to distill rum or other strong liquors in lead pipes because it was "judged on good grounds to be unwholesome and hurtful."

All colonies set prices on provisions for horses and for food, drink, and lodging for humans, making it a crime to charge above the rates. Certain localities created very detailed price lists. Overnight rates in Hampshire County, Massachusetts, varied depending on whether the traveler insisted on clean sheets and whether a lodger was willing to share a bed and if so, with how many people. In Edgecomb County, North Carolina, sharing a bed with one other person was half the rate of having one's own bed. In Rowan County, North Carolina, additional savings were possible if travelers were willing to share the bed "with 2 or more" persons. It appears as if Hampshire County, Massachusetts's, lawmakers merely toyed with this idea; they crossed out the line "with 2 or more in the same bed each person." Gradually, in an attempt to protect the patrons, all colonies required that tavern keepers display the rates "in the common entertaining room."

As in England, operating a tavern in any of the North American colonies required a license. The process to obtain a license varied somewhat from colony to colony, but in the 17th century it was usually initiated by petitioning the office of the governor. The hopeful petitioner stated why he or she was a suitable candidate for selling alcoholic beverages and assured the governor that his or her house was well equipped to tend to the needs of travelers. By the 18th century the licensing procedures had moved from the provincial level exclusively to town or county. For example, a Boston petitioner continued to request a license from the selectmen who made their recommendations to the Court of General Sessions of the Peace. They then gave final approval. Committees annually visited "the taverns and houses of retailers" in Suffolk County towns to assess the quality of accommodations, furnishings, and provisions. They also determined whether the current tavern keepers were suitable for their employment and whether any of the towns might be in need of more taverns. Based on this annual tour, the selectmen presented their recommendations. They identified towns that required taverns and listed tavern licenses to be renewed or canceled. Similarly, Philadelphia residents petitioned the justices of the Court of Quarter Sessions, who passed on their recommendations to the governor. In some cases the petitioner was required to post a bond guaranteeing that the public would display good behavior inside the public house.

Regardless of their size or the quality of their food and drink, colonists conceded that their lives would be incomplete without access to taverns. Contemporaries who wrote about the tavern identified a far greater role than simply a place where colonists gathered to socialize. The public house was, according to a theorist of social relations, a space in which "the informal logic of actual life" could be discovered and reconstructed.

—Sharon V. Salinger

Teach, Edward ("Blackbeard") (unknown–1718)

"Come," spoke Captain Edward Teach, "let us make a Hell of [our] own, and try how long we can bear it." These words are attributed to the most well-known pirate of the "Golden Age of Piracy," known as Blackbeard. Originally from Bristol, England, Teach made his way to the West Indies by working aboard privateers during QUEEN ANNE'S WAR (1702–13). When hostilities ended many privateer crews found themselves suddenly unemployed. Providence Island in the Bahamas became a colony for these ex-privateers, and under the leadership of Captain Benjamin Hornigold, many turned to piracy in 1715 and 1716. Edward Teach, because of his cruelty and fearlessness, became a pirate captain by the spring of 1717. Hornigold accepted an amnesty from the Crown on returning to Providence Island, but Teach refused and began his piracy career in earnest, sailing his ship, the *Queen Anne's Revenge*, through the CARIBBEAN and then off the Carolina and VIRGINIA coasts.

Blackbeard sailed in consort at various times with other pirate captains STEDE BONNET and Charles Vane. Blackbeard and his crew met with Governor Charles Eden of NORTH CAROLINA to accept an amnesty in January 1718, but Blackbeard clearly had little intention of ceasing his piratical activities. There is evidence that Governor Eden and his secretary, Tobias Knight, were in league with the notorious pirate. In May 1718 Blackbeard, by now commanding a small flotilla of ships, blockaded CHARLESTON Harbor. SOUTH CAROLINA's governor and council had no choice but to pay off the pirates with medical supplies because of the colony's desperate position after several years of fighting the Tuscarora Indians. Blackbeard and his crew then established a base among the islands and inlets of North Carolina. Governor Alexander Spotswood of Virginia issued a proclamation against pirates, offering rewards for their capture or deaths. Lieutenant Robert Maynard of the Royal Navy soon trapped Blackbeard in Ocracoke Inlet, North Carolina. Maynard and Blackbeard and their crews engaged each other in fierce fighting, much of which was hand-to-hand. Blackbeard was eventually killed during the fighting. Lieutenant Maynard ordered the pirate's severed head to be hung from the bowsprit of the Royal Navy vessel. Blackbeard's surviving crew were arrested; many of them were tried and executed.

Although his career was relatively short, Blackbeard looms large in pirate lore, especially according to the descriptions of him in Captain Charles Johnson's *General History of the Pyrates.* His appearance was designed to strike fear in both his friends and his enemies. Blackbeard had a large, thick black beard and long hair, which he tied in small queues and to which he affixed lighted rope matches. The effect was to create a halo of smoke around his head and the smell of burning rope. Blackbeard was a fearsome sight, wearing a sling with three pistols, usually emboldened by rum, and often charging headlong into battle. Blackbeard, apart from his appearance as "Fury from Hell," also played politics in his dealings with the local governors and MERCHANTS, recklessly double-dealing with officials as he saw fit.

Further reading: Daniel Defoe, *A General History of the Pyrates* (Mineola, N.Y.: Dover, 1999); Robert C. Ritchie, *Captain Kidd and the War Against the Pirates* (Cambridge, Mass.: Harvard University Press, 1989).

—Stephen C. O'Neill

technology

Seventeenth-century English colonizers brought with them the technologies of a preindustrial, agricultural society, many of whose tools and techniques dated to the Middle Ages. Colonial North American technologies were defined by four main characteristics. They were based in handicrafts; tools, houses, and ships were built of wood (iron was too precious); instruments were individually handmade from start to finish (there was minimal division of labor); and ARTISANS drove production. NATIVE AMERICANS relied on canoes for transportation, traps for hunting, furs for CLOTHING, and wooden utensils. English settlers, meanwhile, wielded axes to clear woods for cultivating the land and raising livestock. These practices severely disrupted native land-use and local ecosystems, but there was also significant cross-cultural technological transfer. Natives taught Europeans new FISHING, hunting, and agricultural techniques, while Europeans taught natives new CRAFTS and traded guns and iron tools to them. Unlike later industrially manufactured goods, most crafts were practiced, and their products used, in the home. This domestic production force included women, servants, and slaves, who acquired many artisanal skills.

The colonists welcomed machines because LABOR was in chronically short supply. Water power drove sawmills for producing lumber (established in New England from the 1630s), the first "fulling" MILLS for cotton textiles in the late 1600s, and gristmills for turning grain into flour (especially important in the Middle Colonies after 1700). The king and later most colonies granted patents for inventions, a system with medieval origins that was codified by Parliament in 1623. Towns, meanwhile, offered rewards for the completion of practical projects for civic improvement (like waterworks), as occasionally did colonial legislatures. Probably the best known colonial invention was the lightning rod by Benjamin Franklin (1752), which anticipated the modern relation between SCIENCE and technology.

The most important overall factor in technological production was membership in the BRITISH EMPIRE. Colonial British America not only lacked a central government to fund and direct technological development but was deliberately maintained as a technological colony within Britain's system of trade and economics (known as MERCANTILISM). Parliamentary legislation prevented Americans from producing and exporting their own finished manufactures and exploited them instead as a source of raw material, such as lumber for SHIPBUILDING. Britain limited colonial production of certain goods to the initial stages; iron ore, for example, was mined and smelted in North America but sent across the Atlantic for refining. The colonies were producing one-seventh of the world's wrought and pig iron by the time of the Revolution, when boycotts of British goods and calls for manufacturing self-sufficiency finally loosened the mother country's technological stranglehold.

See also ACTS OF TRADE AND NAVIGATION; AGRICULTURE; ENVIRONMENT.

Further reading: Judith A. McGaw, ed., *Early American Technology: Making and Doing Things from the Colonial Era to 1850* (Chapel Hill: University of North Carolina Press, 1994).

—James Delbourgo

Teedyuscung (1709?–1763)

Teedyuscung, the son of a woman from the Toms River band of Lenape (DELAWARE Indians) and a colonist father, was born near Trenton, New Jersey, about 1709. He grew up along the Atlantic shore as a member of his mother's band, moving with them into the Forks of Delaware in eastern PENNSYLVANIA in 1733. This and several other northern Lenape bands had seasonally hunted in the area bounded by the Lehigh and upper Delaware Rivers known as the Forks since before 1600. This territory had long been a shared resource zone used by the four Native American groups surrounding this region: the Susquehannock, Lenape, Munsee, and Lenope. In 1737 the Pennsylvania colonial government purchased much of the region in a fraudulent land deal known as the WALKING PURCHASE OF 1737, a treaty that Teedyuscung signed as a young adult.

Although converted to Christianity and baptized by the Moravians as "Gideon," Teedyuscung rarely interacted with other converted Indians. Continually opposing the authority of the IROQUOIS over his people, he mastered the art of Indian diplomacy and claimed to represent several groups of natives in the buffer zone along the NEW YORK–Pennsylvania border. He acted as a cultural broker with colonial authorities. Teedyuscung allied with the British during the SEVEN YEARS' WAR. In his later life he falsely assumed the role of "speaker" for many native groups.

Further reading: Anthony F. C. Wallace, *King of the Delawares: Teedyuscung, 1700–1763* (Philadelphia: University of Pennsylvania Press, 1949).

—Marshall Joseph Becker

tenants

From the late 16th through the late 18th centuries the English moved from a feudal system to one of private landholding. The men who worked hardest for that change appropriated land and made it less available to others. Many people found themselves forced to rent land because they could not pay the fees associated with these changes. From roughly 1585 to 1763 (and beyond) English landowners tightened their grip on arable land, political power, and capital, increasingly defined those who did not own land as "the poor," and excluded these landless men from politics. Many tenants found themselves thrown into grinding, landless misery after failing to pay rents because of death, DISEASE, injury, poor harvests, or bad weather. While land practices changed in England, most of the rest of Europe maintained a system in which most people leased land for short periods of time (one to five years), paid high rent (upwards of 70 percent of their harvests), and stood well outside the world of political power.

The promise of land in the New World lured poor migrants from places like Scotland, England, Wales, Ireland, France, and Germany. They hoped to get what they could not have at home—land—and to become independent householders. Some early colonial landowners aspired to amass huge estates to create a manorial system that resembled landed estates in Europe. They succeeded in places like NEW YORK's Hudson Valley and in MARYLAND. The availability of land in the New World made tenancy less desirable for anyone who could afford to buy it. By the end of the 17th century land sales directly to farmers made land ownership more common in America than in Europe. Even landlords in the Hudson Valley and in Maryland had to entice prospective tenants with low rent (typically 10 percent to 25 percent of their harvests) and long leases (from 60 years to two generations). Still, tenancy attracted primarily those people too poor to buy land.

Tenants throughout North America followed traditional agricultural production practices, and they tended to live frugally. Most built utilitarian houses, barns, fences, and other buildings from the lumber they harvested when they cleared wilderness. Landlords often required tenants to pay rent with a specific crop, such as wheat, but most tenants grew a variety of crops to minimize risk. If one crop failed, they could still survive off the others. In northern colonies they grew wheat, corn, oats, barley, vegetables, and cultivated some fruit trees. In the south some tried to grow TOBACCO as a cash crop. Most farmers also kept a few cattle, pigs, sheep, and chickens for FOOD and sometimes cows for milk. While men in the household worked in the fields and cared for some of the ANIMALS, their wives and daughters typically kept a vegetable and fruit garden near the house, made and repaired clothes, churned butter, cooked all the meals, and cared for the children and some of the animals. Women also worked in the fields during periods of intense labor, such as planting and harvesting. Indeed, everyone on the farm contributed to a household's success.

Tenants did not enjoy the same kinds of independence as freeholders. Many landlords restricted their access to markets and MILLS off the manor and demanded that tenants sell surplus goods to landowners first. Some tenants found their status kept them from participating in politics because nearly all of the colonies required adult males to own a certain amount of property to qualify for SUFFRAGE. Thus, they could neither vote, serve on juries, nor hold political office. As in the Old World, tenants in the New World found themselves on the outside of political power.

Tenancy increased in 18th-century British North America as population growth fueled by immigration and natural increase created more crowded conditions in many colonies, like in New England. In VIRGINIA landed tycoons kept as much as half the land in the colony off the market by requiring that rich men will their estates to only one son. At the same time, more and more people moved into the Middle Colonies, where tenancy had a foothold in the 17th century. These migrants found that available land was in short supply because landlords refused to sell it or sold it at highly inflated prices. They had little choice but to become tenants. By 1763, even in places like MASSACHUSETTS and PENNSYLVANIA where most people had owned land, tenancy was on the rise throughout British North America.

Further reading: Allan Kulikoff, *From British Peasants to Colonial American Farmers* (Chapel Hill: University of North Carolina Press, 2000).

—Thomas J. Humphrey

Tennent, Gilbert (1703–1764)

Presbyterian minister and a leader of the GREAT AWAKENING, Gilbert Tennent was born in Vinnescash, County Armagh, Ireland, on February 5, 1703. He was the first child of William Tennent, Sr. (1673–1746), a University of Edinburgh–educated Scots-Irish Presbyterian clergyman, and Katherine Kennedy, whose father was a well-known Presbyterian minister. Gilbert Tennent came to North America with his parents in 1718. While William Tennent, Sr., served congregations in NEW YORK and PENNSYLVANIA, he educated his oldest son so thoroughly that in 1725 Gilbert Tennent received the degree of Master of Arts from YALE COLLEGE despite his lack of a baccalaureate degree. A moving religious experience in 1723 led Gilbert Tennent into the ministry. The PHILADELPHIA Presbytery licensed him in 1725 and in 1726 ordained and installed him in New Brunswick, NEW JERSEY. He served that and neighboring congregations until 1743.

During the 1730s and early 1740s Tennent was one of the most active "New Light" revivalists during the Great Awakening. He preached the necessity of "experiential religion" to his own congregation and sometimes intruded, uninvited, into others as well. When the English evangelist GEORGE WHITEFIELD arrived in North America in 1739, Tennent introduced him to his colleagues. He accompanied Whitefield on a preaching mission in the Middle Colonies in 1740 and to New England in 1741. Extremely censorious toward "Old Light" associates whom he suspected were not sufficiently spiritual, Tennent condemned them harshly in a sermon titled *The Danger of an Unconverted Ministry*.

The alleged enthusiastic and disorderly ministry of the Presbyterian New Lights led to their expulsion from the Synod of Philadelphia. Under Tennent's leadership they formed the New Brunswick Presbytery and joined with northern colleagues to form the Synod of New York. In 1743 Gilbert Tennent left New Brunswick to serve Whitefield's Philadelphia followers, who formed the Second Presbyterian Church. There he tempered his ministry, preaching to other congregations only when asked, and spoke no longer extemporaneously but from a manuscript. He explained that his new congregation needed EDUCATION, not exhortation. Tennent's father, William Tennent, Sr., had established the "Log College" in the valley of the Neshaminy Creek in southeastern Pennsylvania, where he educated numerous Presbyterian ministers. After it closed in the early 1740s, Gilbert Tennent and others founded a college at Elizabethtown that became Princeton University. From 1746 until his death he served as a trustee of the new institution. In 1753 he went with SAMUEL DAVIES on a two-year fund-raising tour for the college. Tennent's later mod-

Gilbert Tennent *(Library of Congress)*

eration enabled him to assist in the PRESBYTERIANS' reunion in 1758.

Little information about Tennent's family life has survived. His first wife died in 1740, and he married Cornelia De Peyster Clarkson in 1742. She died in 1753. His third wife, whom he married sometime before 1762, was Sara Spoffard, with whom he had three children. Tennent's health declined during his last two years. He died in 1764 and was buried under the center aisle of his church.

Further reading: Milton J. Coalter, Jr., *Gilbert Tennent, Son of Thunder: A Case Study of Continental Pietism's Impact on the First Great Awakening in the Middle Colonies* (New York: Greenwood Press, 1986).

—John B. Frantz

Tennent, William, Jr. (1705–1777)

Presbyterian minister William Tennent, Jr., was born on June 3, 1705, in County Armagh, Ireland. He was the second child of WILLIAM TENNENT, SR., clergyman and educator, and Katherine Kennedy, daughter of the prominent Presbyterian minister Gilbert Kennedy. His parents were Scots-Irish. In 1718 Tennent, Jr., moved to North America with his family. He was educated at what was called the "Log College" that his father founded in the Neshaminy area of southeastern Pennsylvania, primarily for the preparation of Presbyterian clergy. He studied also under the supervision of his older brother, GILBERT TENNENT, who served congregations in and around New Brunswick, NEW JERSEY.

The PHILADELPHIA Presbytery ordained and installed Tennent, as minister of the Freehold, New Jersey, congregation, where he succeeded his deceased brother, John (1706–32). He held this position until his death in 1777. Throughout his ministry he was faithful to his calling, visiting his parishioners frequently and preaching regularly to his congregation and to others who invited him. His moderately Calvinistic sermons were well received. He served as a trustee of the Presbyterian College of New Jersey, later Princeton University, and resisted vigorously Royal Governor William Franklin's attempt to transform it into a public institution. During the GREAT AWAKENING of the 1730s and 1740s, William Tennent, Jr., was a "New Light" who participated in religious revivals. He accompanied Samuel Blair and John Rowland on evangelistic tours to MARYLAND and VIRGINIA. When the Presbyterian Church split, he became an important member of the New Light New Brunswick Presbytery and Synod of NEW YORK.

Because he concentrated so intently on his ministry, he neglected personal matters. A dishonest manager mishandled his land and caused him to fall into debt. Too busy for romance, a friend advised that a wife could manage his finances effectively and provide "conjugal enjoyment." The friend introduced him to Catherine van Burgh Noble, whom he married in 1738. They had six children. He died in 1777 and was buried beneath the floor of his church in Freehold.

—John B. Frantz

Tennent, William, Sr. (1673–1746)

Presbyterian minister and educator William Tennent was born in 1673, probably in Scotland, to John Tennent, Jr., an Edinburgh merchant, and Sarah Hume, from a powerful Scottish border clan. In 1695 Tennent earned a Master of Arts degree from the University of Edinburgh. He was licensed by a Scottish presbytery and served briefly as a chaplain to Lady Anne, the duchess of Hamilton. By 1701 he had moved to Ireland and was received by the Synod of Ulster. Nevertheless, in 1704 he was ordained by the Church of Ireland (Anglican).

Tennent's dissatisfaction with his situation in Ireland caused him to emigrate with his wife and five children to North America in 1718, where he renounced Anglicanism and became a member of the Presbyterian Synod of PHILADELPHIA. He served congregations in East Chester and Bedford, NEW YORK, until 1726, when he moved to Bucks County, PENNSYLVANIA, and served congregations at Bensalem, New Town, and Neshaminy. At Neshaminy he made his most significant contribution.

Not only did he preach an evangelical Calvinism, but he educated others to follow his example. Having received a classical EDUCATION at Edinburgh, he taught young men, including his four sons, Hebrew, Greek, Latin, and theology. Initially he taught students in his home. In 1735, however, he constructed a building that opponents called contemptuously the "Log College." Almost all of Tennent's students became Presbyterian ministers who led the GREAT AWAKENING in the Middle Colonies. The Log College they had attended was a model for academies that they established. Increasingly infirm, Tennent began to curtail his activities in 1742. The "Log College" had closed by the time of his death in 1746.

Details about Tennent's personal life are scarce. In 1702 he married Katherine Kennedy, daughter of a prominent Irish Presbyterian minister. Because of the expenses involved in feeding and HOUSING many of his students as well as in raising four sons and a daughter, he usually struggled with indigence.

Further reading: Mary A. Tennent, *Light in Darkness: The Story of William Tennent, Sr., and the Log College* (Greensboro, N.C.: Greensboro Printing Co., 1971).

—John B. Frantz

theater

Theater had a dim reputation in 17th-century British America. Many American towns and colonies outlawed dramatic productions because supposedly they were associated with promiscuity, drunkenness, and other vices. Colonists who staged amateur productions, such as the three VIRGINIA men who were prosecuted for staging a play in 1665 or the group of Harvard students who produced *Gustavus Vasa* in 1690, often ran into trouble with authorities. In contrast, New France (Quebec) supported frequent theatrical productions from the 1640s onward. Religious plays were particularly popular and formed part of the curriculum at Jesuit and Ursuline schools. In the West both Spanish colonists and NATIVE AMERICANS staged religious dramas for their communities.

The geography of colonial theatrical productions changed markedly in the early 18th century. Infighting between religious and civil authorities in New France led the colony's bishop to outlaw public theater (including school productions) by 1699. Subsequent French colonial productions were few and amateurish. On the other hand, the British colonies became more interested in theater as the influence of PURITANS and other religious dissenters waned. A professional theater opened in Williamsburg, Virginia, in 1717, only to close six years later. NEW YORK CITY acquired a theater in 1733, CHARLESTON in 1735. By the Revolutionary era several American cities had permanent professional theaters.

British colonial theater was an offshoot of English and Irish provincial theater; American colonists made few innovations in the genre. Young, unsuccessful, and impoverished actors immigrated to the colonies to jumpstart their careers. John Moody, an Irish actor, founded a theater company in Jamaica in 1745, and in 1749 Thomas Keane and Walter Murray organized a professional theater troupe in PHILADELPHIA. The members performed a repertoire of dramas by Shakespeare, Addison, Dryden, Fielding, and other English playwrights in Philadelphia, New York, and Virginia. Theater was a popular diversion in colonial cities (except Puritan BOSTON), but the quality of colonial theatrical productions was quite poor. Not until after the Revolution did British-Americans develop an independent theatrical tradition characterized by distinctively American settings and themes.

Further reading: George O. Seilhamer, *History of the American Theatre, Before the Revolution,* vol. 1 (New York: Greenwood Press, 1968).

—Darcy R. Fryer

Theus, Jeremiah (1719?–1774)

Jeremiah Theus, a colonial artist, was the son of a Swiss Protestant immigrant to Orangeburgh, SOUTH CAROLINA. He moved to CHARLESTON in 1740, where he lived for more than 30 years, marrying twice and fathering nine children. He first advertised his services as a sign and coach painter but soon managed to establish a business as a portrait artist. Early in his career Theus ran an ART school, where he taught painting "in every branch." It is not known where he acquired his skills.

His painting style remained somewhat static throughout his career, with the quality of his work only occasionally matching that of his metropolitan contemporaries. Traveling throughout the Lower South, Theus painted hundreds of portraits of the region's wealthy planter and merchant CLASS, including Gabriel Manigault, Colonel Daniel Heyward, and Elias Ball. His prodigious output makes him one of colonial America's most important artists. Theus also contributed to one of Charleston's most impressive buildings, St. Michael's Church, where he used his skills to gild the interior and the steeple. The substantial income he received from his various pursuits made him a member of Charleston's elite. He maintained substantial properties in the town, owned four slaves, and was an active participant in the South Carolina Society—a charitable club founded by Huguenots and subsequently populated by wealthy ARTISANS and MERCHANTS. When he died in 1774, he left an estate worth thousands of pounds sterling and was eulogized in the local newspaper as having been a "very ingenious and honest man."

—Emma Hart

tobacco

The production of tobacco was a significant component of the colonial ECONOMY. The demands of that production encouraged the growth of INDENTURED SERVITUDE and SLAVERY in the Chesapeake area colonies as well as the expansion of white colonists onto Indian lands.

Many NATIVE AMERICANS cultivated *tabacum* and *rustica,* two of 60 species of the genus *Nicotiana* of the Solanaceae, or nightshade, family. They ingested it by chewing, snuffing, and drinking, and even with enemas, but mostly by smoking. Tobacco was used for medicinal, ceremonial (especially peacemaking), and religious purposes. Practice and belief varied, but hallucinations (induced by strong nicotine content or mixing with other substances) were widely construed as representing communication with spirits occupying tobacco plants.

Europeans initially viewed tobacco medicinally, especially after Spanish physician Nicholas Monardes rated it a panacea in 1571. CONSUMPTION increased as availability rose and prices fell. English imports, 25,000 pounds in 1603, reached 38,000,000 by 1700; meanwhile prices declined from 40 pence per pound in 1618 to 1 pence by the 1660s. Mass consumption, with 25 percent of adults smoking a pipeful each day, appeared in England by the 1670s and in much of Europe by 1750. Pipes were favored initially (although Iberians, like Native South Americans, preferred cigars), but snuff became more common in the 18th century. Consumption was not restricted by CLASS, race, or GENDER, although 18th-century elites incorporated tobacco into genteel rituals, while others used "sot weed" for their own hallucinogenic and recreational purposes.

Tobacco was cultivated in Amazon settlements and Guiana from 1609, Bermuda and VIRGINIA from 1612, and MARYLAND from 1634, and the CARIBBEAN colonies St. Kitts, Barbados, Providence Island, Nevis, Antigua, and Montserrat were founded on tobacco. From the mid-17th century island production declined in favor of cotton, INDIGO, and especially sugar.

The Chesapeake region became the New World's largest producer, exporting more than 100 million pounds in 1771. Tobacco proved so profitable after JOHN ROLFE's experiments in JAMESTOWN beginning in 1612, Virginians dedicated their efforts almost totally to producing tobacco and failed to grow sufficient food, thereby contributing to the colony's near collapse. Despite falling prices and wartime disruptions, tobacco remained fundamental to the Chesapeake economy and society: "our meat, drinke, cloathing and monies," according to Reverend Hugh Jones in 1699.

Cultivation required about 50 acres of land per worker, accounting for rapid but scattered settlement. Although LABOR intensive, the crop yielded little economy of scale, and small farms remained common in the Chesapeake area. From the 1680s the supply of indentured servants

This engraving shows tobacco leaves being pressed, cured, and packed by slaves. *(Hulton/Archive)*

declined, and larger planters amassed sufficient capital to buy slaves. Chesapeake area slaves increased rapidly, from 1,708 in 1660 to 189,000 in 1760, rising from 5 percent to 38 percent of the population. From the 1660s law and custom forged greater distance between the races, and this allowed development of semiautonomous African-American community, culture, and resistance. A slaveholding plantocracy appeared by the 1690s, consolidating its wealth dynastically. It developed a genteel "tobacco culture" that emerged from a consignment system of direct market and social relationships with British MERCHANTS. Material inequality rose (70 percent of white householders owned land in 1660, but only 50 percent by 1760), yet white racial solidarity increased as Euro-Americans envisioned themselves as part of a superior race. Wider access to markets, credit, and imported goods (including slaves) through Scottish merchants in the Chesapeake region raised standards of living among most white people after 1730, creating a more stable white society.

Further reading: Lois Green Carr, Russell R. Menard, and Lorena Walsh, *Robert Cole's World: Agriculture and Society in Early Maryland* (Chapel Hill: University of North Carolina Press, 1991); Jordan Goodman, *Tobacco in History: The Cultures of Dependence* (New York: Routledge, 1993); Allan Kulikoff, *Tobacco and Slaves: The Development of Southern Cultures in the Chesapeake, 1680–1800* (Chapel Hill: University of North Carolina Press, 1986).

—Steven Sarson

Tomochichi (1650?–1739)

Tomochichi was the chief, or *mico,* of the Yamacraw tribe whose village was adjacent to John and MARY BUSOMWORTH MUSGROVE's trading post, later to be the site of the town of SAVANNAH. Tomochichi was born in the mid-17th century and during his CHILDHOOD lived in the Creek town of Coweta. The Yamacraw were a small, isolated group who had been expelled from the main Creek lands some years earlier. Tomochichi believed that his people were best served by a close trading relationship with the English, first in Carolina, later in GEORGIA. The English provided them with weapons for defense and with trade goods. When JAMES OGLETHORPE landed on Savannah bluff in February 1733, Tomochichi was quick to forge an alliance with the assistance of the half-Creek, half-English Mary Musgrove. He summoned the Creek to meet with Oglethorpe and arranged for the first land concessions in Georgia to the English. His friendship with Oglethorpe ensured that the infant colony received supplies, advice, and technological aid from NATIVE AMERICANS. When Oglethorpe returned to England in 1734, he took Tomochichi with him, presenting him to King George II (1727–60) and the Georgia trustees and gaining favorable publicity for the colony in the process. On his death in 1739, Tomochichi was accorded a formal burial by Oglethorpe; his tomb still stands under a monument in one of Savannah's squares.

—Timothy James Lockley

trade and shipping

Trade was the foundation of the early American ECONOMY, with commercial ties extending in many directions. Colonists established exchange with NATIVE AMERICANS that ranged from casual to well-developed enterprises. Settlers also participated in transatlantic trade, primarily with England and the West Indies. In addition, an internal trade network developed involving both backcountry and coastal communities. Over time the nature and extent of these networks changed, reflecting the growth and development of colonial America.

Before the arrival of Europeans, Native Americans engaged extensively in trade with one another, and archaeologists have found evidence that goods sometimes were transported across the continent. Most items traded were items of luxury rather than necessity. European colonists were often very interested in trading with natives because animal furs and pelts gained high prices in the Old World. JAMESTOWN residents traded metal pots, fishhooks, and traps for foodstuffs and furs. MASSACHUSETTS settlers exchanged iron tools, cloth, firearms, and liquor for furs. In the Middle Colonies Indians sold fish, pelts, and venison at town markets.

In the Carolinas traders bought deerskins from the WESTO, Creek, and CHEROKEE Indians. This trade proved significant, accounting for 18 percent of Carolina's total export earnings before 1749 and remaining at roughly 10 percent until 1775. Carolinians also engaged in trading Indian slaves. Between 1690 and 1710 perhaps 12,000 Indians were exported from the Carolinas to the northern colonies and the CARIBBEAN. This trade increased tensions between settlers and nearby Indians, set off a series of wars, and disrupted the deerskin exchange. As a result, Carolinians abandoned this SLAVE TRADE by the 1720s.

Over time the FUR TRADE became highly organized and one of the most valuable enterprises in the British and French colonies. Some tribes, acting as intermediaries, collected furs from Indians hunting as far west as the Great Lakes. The furs were then traded to colonial MERCHANTS and exported to Europe. As fur-bearing ANIMALS in some areas grew scarce, trade gradually shifted northward. The HUDSON'S BAY COMPANY, established in 1670, focused its operation on fur-rich areas in northern Canada.

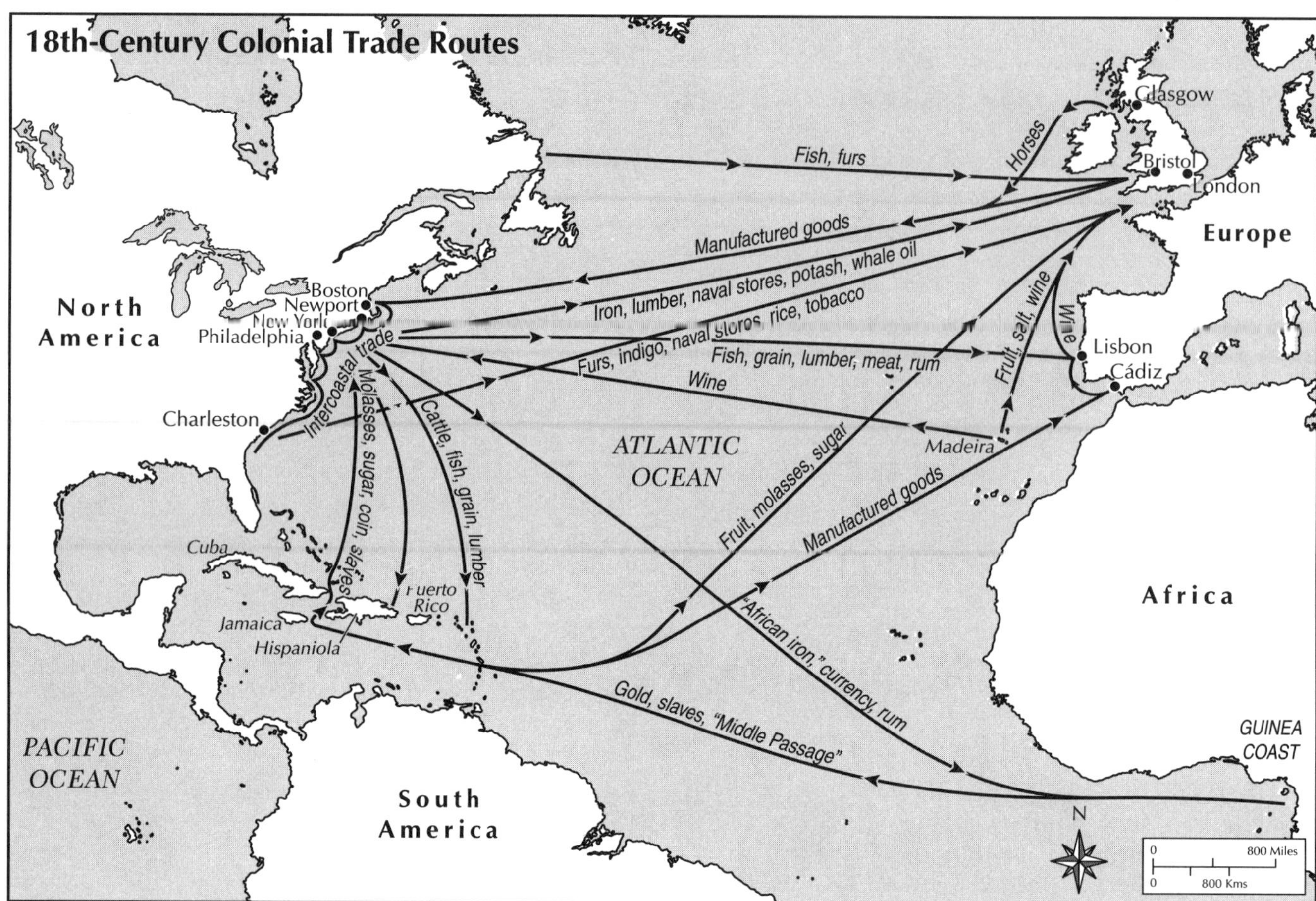

Colonists also engaged in transatlantic trade. In the early years of settlement planters and merchants in VIRGINIA exported TOBACCO to England. New Englanders shipped grain and lumber to the West Indies and fish to southern Europe. In exchange colonists imported such goods as molasses, coffee, salt, and wine.

Beginning in the 1650s, Parliament began to issue a series of acts to control trade within the empire. They required that certain enumerated commodities be shipped only to England, on English ships with British (including colonial) crews. Although these policies restricted some aspects of colonial trade, they also protected and stimulated many commercial enterprises. Colonists had a guaranteed market for many of their exports. Their SHIPBUILDING industry also profited; by the mid-18th century nearly one-third of all British ships were American made. Moreover, many policies were often evaded by colonists and not strictly enforced by Parliament.

The American colonies formed an important link in the transatlantic trade that saw goods flow to and from colonial North America, the West Indies, and England. American merchants shipped furs, naval stores, tobacco, rice, and INDIGO to England. They exported grains, fish, lumber, and livestock to the West Indies. In return colonists imported manufactured products from England and slaves and molasses from the West Indies. Through this route most black slaves were brought to the British mainland colonies.

Between 1619 and 1760 approximately 400,000 slaves were brought to the thirteen colonies. British slave-trade companies supplied the bulk of the slaves, but American merchants, most of them based in RHODE ISLAND, organized the sale of slaves in the colonies. During the 18th century Rhode Island merchants controlled 60 to 90 percent of North America's trade in African slaves.

The colonies also developed internal trade networks. Backcountry farmers sold surplus grain and fresh vegetables to coastal communities. Rice and tobacco from the southern colonies were shipped north and exchanged for meat and grain. By 1760 roughly 30 percent of the total tonnage of colonial ships was destined for other American mainland ports.

These various trade connections combined to stimulate growth and development. The populations of port cities like BOSTON, NEW YORK CITY, and PHILADELPHIA increased, as did job possibilities for merchants, shopkeepers, shipbuilders, ARTISANS, and others in trade-related industries. This intercolonial trade likewise promoted the development of roads and interactions among colonists.

The changing dynamics of trade with England reflect the maturing of colonial America. During the early 17th century the value of exports far exceeded the value of imports, reflecting the relatively low standard of living consistent with early settlement. By the early 18th century the value of imports from Britain was greater than exports to the mother country; this trend continued throughout the century. This transformation in trade indicates the changing consumption patterns of North America before the Revolution.

See also ACTS OF TRADE AND NAVIGATION.

Further reading: John J. McCusker and Russell M. Menard, *The Economy of British America, 1607–1789* (Chapel Hill: University of North Carolina Press, 1985).

—Virginia Jelatis

travel

Early Americans traveled primarily for work. Judges moved from town to town to preside at circuit courts. Ministers, who were responsible for more than one congregation or had no fixed place, traveled to folks eager to hear them preach. Peddlers took to the roads to sell their wares, and traders moved around in the colonial interior to exchange goods with Indians. Occasionally, travel was motivated by an official function. WILLIAM BYRD II journeyed with a small group to mark the boundary between Carolina and VIRGINIA. Colonial leaders met with NATIVE AMERICANS to negotiate treaties and form trading partnerships. Representatives left home for meetings of the assembly.

Water transportation offered the easiest, cheapest, and most favored form of travel. PENNSYLVANIA farmers avoided the bumpy wagon ride by loading their grain onto shallops and relying on the network of rivers to move their produce to market. Southern planters transported their TOBACCO from their farms to the docks of JAMESTOWN or CHARLESTON for shipping to European or British markets. Because tobacco was bulky and fragile, they avoided the jostling from uneven roads and depended upon inland waterways to carry their crop to eastern ports. According to one source, "it was easier and less traumatic in good weather to sail from London to Boston than to reach Charleston from Massachusetts by horse."

Taverns were the first hotels and motels in early America. By law they were required to provide nourishment and lodging for humans and horses. The 1692 MASSACHUSETTS law was typical: "The ancient, true and principal use of Inns . . . is for the Receipt, Relief and Lodging of Travellers and Strangers, and the Refreshment of persons upon lawful Business." Colonial authorities tried spacing taverns at convenient distances; if an individual wished to open a tavern, claiming that they were conveniently located on a well-traveled road offered the most compelling argument. Because people used both land and water transportation, public houses in the Middle and New England colonies were located on public roads and ferry landings. Very few taverns existed in the Chesapeake region, Lower South, and western regions of the colonies. While surveying the Virginia-Carolina border, William Byrd and his party were forced to camp for much of their journey. Travelers in these regions often had to impose upon private homes for lodging. Virginia law acknowledged the inadequate number of taverns by requiring plantation owners to furnish lodging for passers-by.

Travel for most colonists was uncommon. The vast majority of early Americans rarely ventured beyond home, church, and fields, with an occasional trip to market. Only wealthy individuals had the luxury of travel for leisure. Dr. Alexander Hamilton, for example, journeyed from his home in Annapolis, MARYLAND, to New England and back seeking a cure for his ill health. Sons of elite planters or New England leaders often crossed the Atlantic for a European tour or for advanced EDUCATION. Elites moved from their city homes to their country dwellings to escape the summer epidemics.

If travel was unusual for most colonists, it was even rarer for women. SARAH KEMBLE KNIGHT, who journeyed from BOSTON in 1704, complained bitterly about having to stay in taverns, but she was unable to avoid them altogether. At Mr. Havens's inn she was disturbed all night by "the Clamor of some of the Town topers in the next room, Who were entred into a strong debate." Women did venture inside the tavern. However, respectable women preferred to avoid the discomfort and the risk to their reputations.

The mode of transportation was related to an individual's social and economic status. The earliest settlers moved around primarily on foot. Once horses were introduced, only poorer members of society continued to walk. When Benjamin Franklin moved from Boston to PHILADELPHIA, he followed a typical pattern. He started his journey by sea and then walked from Amboy to Burlington, NEW JERSEY.

Stagecoaches improved travel markedly. They first appeared in 1752, covering the 50 miles between Burlington and Amboy, New Jersey. From these points ferries connected travelers with Philadelphia and NEW YORK CITY. Another stage route linked these two port cities in 1766. If the weather cooperated, travelers could expect to make the trip in two days. One year later stagecoach service was established between Boston and Providence. Soon after, the stagecoaches connected Salem with Boston and Boston with Portsmouth, NEW HAMPSHIRE. The reliability of the stagecoach increased the amount of travel in the colonies.

—Sharon V. Salinger

Treaty of Paris (1763)

The 1763 Treaty of Paris, signed on February 10 of that year, officially ended the SEVEN YEARS' WAR. This war was the last of four wars between France and Britain (and various allies on both sides) concerned, in part, with who would control the Atlantic world and parts of Asia. This war featured Britain and Prussia against France, Spain, Austria, and Russia. The three earlier conflicts resolved little in the New World, but the Seven Years' War permanently altered the course of North American history in Britain's favor. France forfeited nearly all its claims to territory on the North American mainland, except the FISHING islands of St. Pierre and Miquelon south of Newfoundland. France ceded its claims to Canada and to all lands east of the Mississippi River. France retained the sugarcane rich West Indies islands of Martinique and Guadeloupe, as well as Marie-Galante and Désirade. The results of a secret treaty between France and Spain made the previous year, in which France ceded the LOUISIANA territory (west of the Mississippi River) and NEW ORLEANS to Spain, were also approved. Cuba, which the British had seized during the war, was returned to Spain. After 1763 the British claimed all territory east of the Mississippi River on mainland North America except New Orleans. Of course, NATIVE AMERICANS inhabited much of the land claimed by Britain, and Pontiac led a pan-Indian resistance to colonial attempts to occupy their lands.

—Doug Baker

Turell, Jane Colman (1708–1735)

Born into a BOSTON Congregationalist family, Jane Colman was precocious, memorizing scripture and reciting the catechism at an early age. Her minister father, Benjamin, to whom she remained close all her life, encouraged her intellectual development, praising her couplets and hymn lyrics and engaging in epistolary dialogues to improve her writing skills. Poor health resulted in a sedentary CHILDHOOD, and by the age of 18 she had read every volume in her father's library, frequently staying up all night with a book.

At 19 Jane Colman married Ebenezer Turell, a Harvard-educated minister, and they moved to Medford, MASSACHUSETTS. Turell continued to write after her marriage, reading daily and setting aside time each month to compose. The Turells had four children, only one of whom survived infancy. The stress of repeated pregnancies, in addition to her poor health, probably hastened Turell's early death.

Women who pursued literary activities in early America stepped outside the usual female role. Even her supportive father reminded Turell not to prioritize writing over her traditional duties; Turell admitted that she found this difficult. She never sought publication, instead distributing her work privately among friends and family. Although Turell wrote in a variety of ways and on many topics, the only writings that remain are the ones that Ebenezer Turell chose to publish with his memoir. He destroyed her humorous essays so that all would know she prioritized religion, morality, and childbearing.

See also ANNE DUDLEY BRADSTREET.

—Victoria C. H. Resnick

Tuscarora

During much of the colonial period the Tuscarora Indians inhabited the region of western NORTH CAROLINA known as the Piedmont. Linguistically, they were distantly related to the Five Nation IROQUOIS of upstate NEW YORK. At some point in the pre-Columbian period they had separated from them and relocated in the South, where they engaged in a mixed ECONOMY of hunting, gathering, and AGRICULTURE. The Five Nations (Seneca, Cayuga, Onondaga, Oneida, and Mohawk) occupied a very powerful position in the East, and the Tuscarora maintained an alliance with them through much of the colonial period. The Iroquois frequently traveled to the South on raids against their joint enemies, the CATAWBA. The Tuscarora, speaking an Iroquoian language and knowledgeable about the Piedmont region, were a valuable ally to the Five Nations.

During the colonial period the Tuscarora became heavily involved in trade with the British. By the 1700s Indian nations were jockeying for position with the Europeans to receive the best and highest quantity of trade goods. This issue, as well as British encroachment on Tuscarora lands, made the Piedmont a tremendously volatile place. Furthermore, British colonists seeking Indian slaves paid the Tuscarora's enemies handsomely to raid their villages and capture them. In retaliation for this and other offenses, the Tuscarora killed an English trader and attacked the English settlers' plantations in an event known as the TUSCARORA WAR (1711–13).

The North Carolina colonists received help from SOUTH CAROLINA, which sent troops to defend the colony. The joint force from the Carolinas routed the Tuscarora, driving them into the interior. After suffering hundreds of casualties, the Tuscaroras assessed their situation and arranged to move northward to join their allies among the Five Nations Iroquois. Although the Tuscarora had been negotiating with the Five Nations before the war, their recent losses made their situation desperate, and they moved into the region occupied by the Oneida. In the early 1720s the Iroquois officially accepted the Tuscarora as the Sixth Nation, giving them the right to speak in the confederacy's councils. After the 1720s the Iroquois as a whole suffered from a gradual loss of autonomy. With the Tuscarora's fortune tied to the confederacy, they suffered when the SEVEN YEARS' WAR ended with the French departure from North America. Without the need for an Indian ally against their French and Indian foes, the British took greater license in encroaching upon Iroquois lands in upstate New York.

Further reading: Daniel Richter, *The Ordeal of the Longhouse: The Peoples of the Iroquois League in the Era of European Colonization* (Chapel Hill: University of North Carolina Press, 1992).

—Thomas J. Lappas

Tuscarora War (1711–1713)

The Tuscarora War was a conflict in a region now encompassed in the state of NORTH CAROLINA between the English settlers of the Carolinas and their NATIVE AMERICAN allies and the TUSCARORA Indians. The area to the west of the coastal plain in the American South, called the Piedmont, had been the site of numerous skirmishes between the Tuscarora, settlers from VIRGINIA and the Carolinas, and other Indian tribes. By the early 18th century most tribes in the Southeast had become heavily dependent on European trade goods such as guns, metal cooking utensils, and metal tips for arrows. As the Indians became increasingly dependent on their European neighbors for trade, the English settlers grew more desirous of Indian lands in the Piedmont. For the Tuscarora this was extremely problematic, as they were the easternmost tribe in the Piedmont. As Carolina settlers were encroaching upon their lands, they were also using the Tuscarora's enemies to raid their towns, capturing Tuscarora villagers and selling them to the Carolina planters as slaves. Devastated by these events, the Tuscarora sought council with their allies, the Five Nation IROQUOIS from upstate NEW YORK, who shared many of the Tuscarora's enemies and with whom they were linguistically related.

During a council with the Iroquois in 1710, the Tuscarora asked the Five Nations to allow them to live in Iroquoia (the upstate New York territory occupied by the Iroquois Confederacy) to escape the frequent abuse by their neighbors. However, while negotiations were underway, the Tuscarora at home captured and killed a British trader named John Lawson. After the murder the Tuscarora swept through the Carolina plantations in violent retaliation for the incursions on their land. North Carolina, fearful of further attacks, solicited help from their SOUTH CAROLINA neighbors. The South Carolinians forged a two-pronged attack, one led by John Barnwell, the other by James Moore, Jr. Made up of settlers as well as some Shuteree, Sugaree, and Cheraw enemies of the Tuscarora, the war parties fell upon the Tuscarora, killing many of them and capturing others, who were then forced into SLAVERY in the South. Those who escaped fled to the Oneida, one of the eastern members of the Iroquois Confederacy, where they found refuge. The Tuscarora lived in the Susquehanna Valley of New York and eventually became the Sixth Nation of the Iroquois Confederacy in the early 1720s. The war remained in the minds of many Tuscarora, who, with their new allies, continued to raid the southern tribes in the next decades.

Further reading: James Merrell, *The Indians' New World: The Catawbas and their Neighbors from European Contact through the Era of Removal* (New York, Norton, 1989).

—Thomas J. Lappas

V

Van Rensselaer, Maria Van Cortlandt (1645–1689)

Maria Van Cortlandt Van Rensselaer was a tenacious woman who administered one of the major land grants in the NEW YORK colony for more than 12 years until her son could inherit it. Born in NEW AMSTERDAM in 1645, Maria Van Cortlandt married Jeremias Van Rensselaer, the director of the patroonship of RENSSELAERSWYCK, when she was 16 years old. After 12 years of marriage, her husband died, leaving her with six young children and a disputed claim on the 1-million-acre estate.

With no adult children to assume her husband's responsibilities, Maria Van Rensselaer managed the patroonship for slightly more than 10 years. She negotiated land deals, collected rents, administered an extensive payroll, oversaw the construction of houses, and marketed beavers, planks of wood, grain, butter, peas, cattle, and horses to NEW YORK CITY, BOSTON, the West Indies, and various Indian groups. This prodigious activity yielded little profit, a source of great concern to family members in North America and in Holland who benefited from the proceeds of the patroonship.

While sorting through complex tax matters, title claims, and the debts incurred by her husband's family, Van Renssalaer also contended with challenges to her son's right to inherit control of the patroonship. Family members in Holland as well as in-laws in America tried to control the estate or to expropriate large pieces of territory. Maria Van Rensselaer prevailed over the Livingstons, the Schuylers, and the Dutch Van Rensselaers to see her son come into his inheritance with a clear patent from the English royal governor in 1685. She had little time to savor the quiet life she so craved, dying just two years after her son's patrimony was secured.

Her letters from this period survive and chronicle the bad harvests, calculating politicians, grasping relatives, and irate TENANTS with which this physically frail woman had to contend. In one of those letters, she described herself as a "sorrowful widow who with God's help . . . seeks to bring up her children and tries to satisfy every one, which in the sorrowful state in which I am at present often makes me sigh." Despite setbacks, Maria Van Rensselaer managed to keep her "colony" intact for more than a decade.

Further reading: A. J. F. Van Laer, ed., *Correspondence of Maria Van Rensselaer, 1669–1689* (Albany: The University of the State of New York, 1935).

—Judy VanBuskirk

Vargas Zapata y Luján Ponce de León, Diego de

See De Vargas, Diego

Vermont

Originally inhabited by the Abenaki tribe, the area that would become Vermont was first explored by Europeans in 1609, when it was claimed for France by the SAMUEL DE CHAMPLAIN expedition. French settlers occupied Isle La Motte in 1666, an area claimed by both the French and the Dutch under vague and largely unsurveyed land grants. By 1724 a number of Dutch squatters, fleeing the NEW YORK tenant system, had settled on the Hoosic River, many believing themselves to be in French Canada. Although the 1763 Treaty of Paris placed the entire region in British hands, negating the French and Dutch claims, it introduced new problems as the colonies of both New York and NEW HAMPSHIRE issued land titles in the area to speculators. By 1764 more than 20 townships were sponsored by New Hampshire speculators, leading to New York efforts to dislodge them. Some settlers, like Ethan Allen and his family, took advantage of the situation and bought New Hampshire grants while using force to drive off the New Yorkers. In 1777 Vermont declared itself independent and remained a separate republic until 1791, when the federal government reached an acceptable compromise over the New York grants, and Vermont joined the union as the 14th state.

Further reading: Jan Albers, *Hands on the Land: A History of the Vermont Landscape* (Cambridge, Mass.: MIT Press, 2000).

—Margaret Sankey

Virginia

Virginia was the first permanent English settlement in North America. Two earlier British colonization attempts, at Roanoke Island in present day NORTH CAROLINA and at Newfoundland, ended in disaster. Still, James I hoped to give the English a foothold in the New World and provide a bulwark against Spanish settlements in the CARIBBEAN. In 1606 he granted the VIRGINIA COMPANY OF LONDON, a joint-stock company formed to speculate in American lands, a patent to an enormous region of southern North America, stretching from the CHESAPEAKE BAY to the Pacific coast. In May 1607 the Virginia Company founded a settlement at JAMESTOWN on the James River, which flows into the mouth of Chesapeake Bay.

Virginia Company entrepreneurs cherished grandiose visions of the colony's potential, both as a tool for Christianizing and "civilizing" local NATIVE AMERICANS and, still more importantly, as a supplier of precious metals, furs, and other valuable raw materials, but the colony floundered because the Virginia Company settlers refused to perform the agricultural and other LABOR necessary to support themselves. They neither farmed, fished, hunted, nor gathered; observers reported that men died of sheer "idleness." The Jamestown settlement was organized as a military expedition, and the Virginia Company's servants likely expected to live off the land and endure high death rates. The English settlers may also have suffered from pellagra, a nutritional DISEASE that leads to apathy and anorexia, or from dysentery resulting from drinking polluted water from the James River. Whatever the cause, however, the first years of the Jamestown settlement were a bitter tragedy of violence, MORTALITY, disappointed hopes, and squandered opportunities.

The Native Americans who lived along the Chesapeake Bay viewed the English settlement ambivalently. At the beginning of the 17th century approximately 20,000 Native Americans lived in the Chesapeake region. The region's preeminent political power was the POWHATAN CONFEDERACY, a diplomatic league of 32 ALGONQUIN-speaking tribes founded by POWHATAN's father in the 16th century. Powhatan, who led the confederacy when the English arrived, hoped to establish a lucrative trade with the new settlers; indeed, he gave them maize to help them through the first difficult winters in Virginia. However, in 1609 the English settlers, who had grown dependent on the crops supplied by Powhatan's people, began to raid Native American communities for FOOD. In an illogical burst of anger, the English killed the Indians who had been supporting them and destroyed their crops. Powhatan retaliated by trying to starve the English settlers out, resulting in catastrophic mortality.

The Virginia Company did not accept defeat; it shipped many new immigrants and livestock to Virginia to revive the faltering colony. Moreover, it launched a vigorous war against the Powhatan Confederacy. By 1613 the Virginia Company colonists dominated the region between the James and York Rivers, and in 1614 Powhatan reluctantly accepted a peace treaty. Virginia's disastrous early years were followed by a decade of unsteady growth in which several important precedents were set. In 1612 JOHN ROLFE began experimenting with a hybrid strain of TOBACCO that was particularly well suited to the Virginia climate, and for the first time Virginia Company speculators began to see a return on their investments. The introduction of tobacco profoundly affected Virginia's social and economic structure. It was a highly labor-intensive crop and so, in order to recruit sufficient labor, the Virginia Company established the headright system in 1616. It granted a specified number of acres to each immigrant or the person who paid the immigrant's passage encouraged immigration (by families and single women as well as men); some wealthy colonists amassed substantial plantations by importing indentured servants from England and collecting their headrights. African slaves were first brought to the colony in 1619, but early planters relied mainly on the labor of white indentured servants. In 1619, too, the Virginia Company convened the HOUSE OF BURGESSES, the first representative assembly in colonial North America.

Nevertheless, the Virginia colony remained highly unstable. A series of typhus and dysentery epidemics washed over the settlement between 1617 and 1624; by 1624 more than 85 percent of the colonists who had immigrated to Virginia since 1607 were dead. Meanwhile, Powhatan's successor, OPECHANCANOUGH, marshaled anti-English forces with the Powhatan Confederacy and on Good Friday, March 22, 1622, launched a surprise attack on the Jamestown settlement, killing nearly 350 people, a quarter of Virginia's English population. This attack initiated a destructive 10-year war, but the English Crown did not wait until the war's end to reorganize the colony's government. In 1624 the Crown revoked the Virginia Company's charter and made Virginia a royal colony.

The first decades of royal rule were a prosperous period for the English colony in spite of the continuing problems of disease, famine, and war. By 1640 Virginia's English population had risen to 10,000, while the region's Native American population had declined to an equal number. In 1645 the English settlers finally captured Opechancanough; his execution marked the eclipse of the Powhatan Confederacy, whose power declined steadily

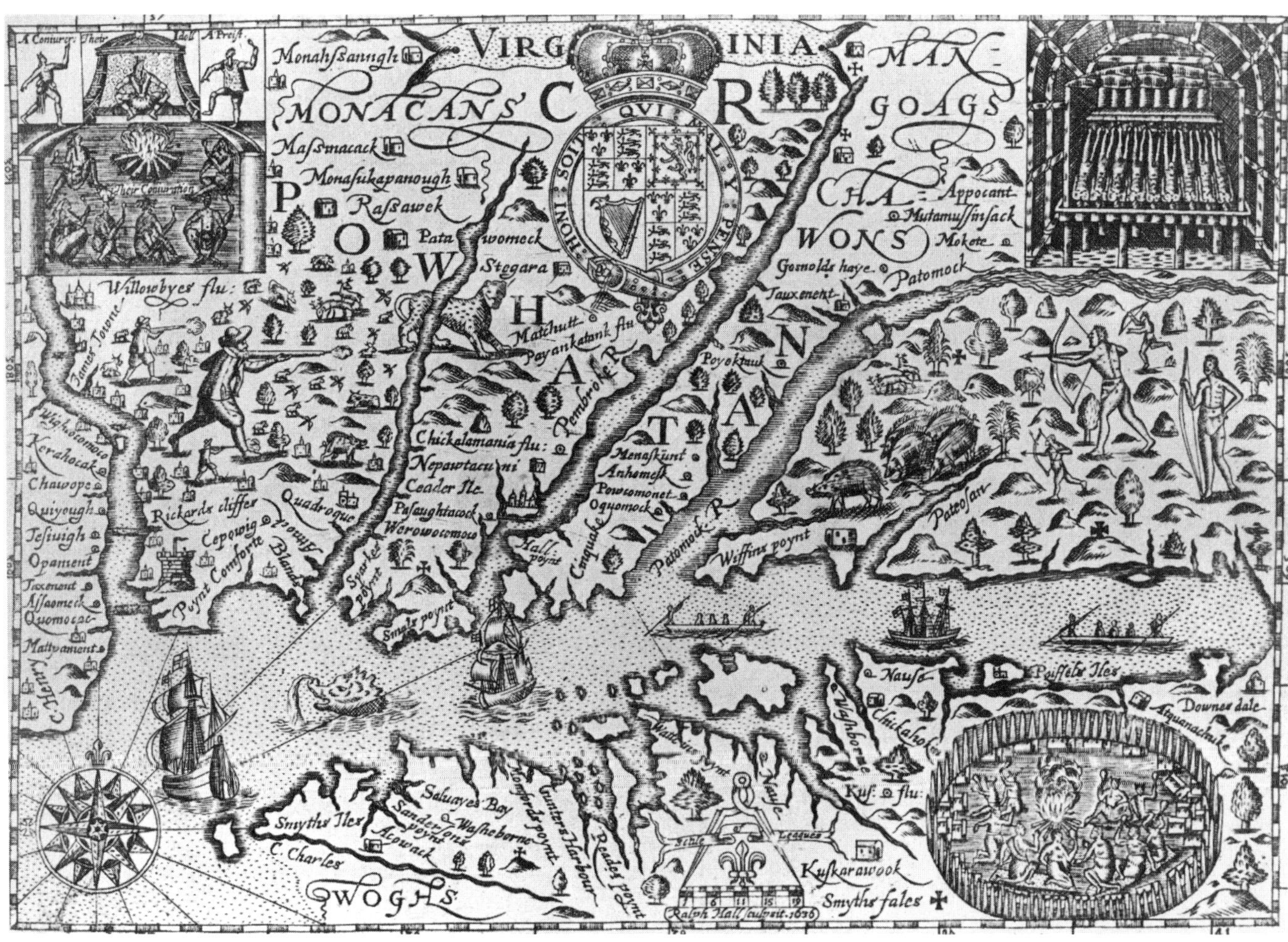

An engraving of a map of Virginia by Ralph Hall *(Hulton/Archive)*

thereafter. Although the English had conquered Virginia, settlers continued to live in squalid conditions; even the wealthiest planters occupied rough houses of one or two rooms. At least three-quarters of immigrants arrived as indentured servants, having bartered their labor for a number of years (usually between four and seven) in exchange for passage to Virginia. Most indentured servants were single young men; the colony's GENDER ratio was highly imbalanced throughout the 17th century. Free women married quickly (men who courted female indentured servants sometimes offered to buy their freedom), and the high mortality rate enabled planters' widows to amass substantial estates, making them prizes on the marriage market. Tobacco remained the principal crop; soil exhaustion pushed English settlers farther and farther into what had once been Indian territory.

In the 1670s long-simmering social tensions erupted in a violent episode that became known as BACON'S REBELLION. The Susquehannock Indians, who lived along the upper Potomac River, opposed white settlers' encroachment on their land. In response Nathaniel Bacon led frontier planters and landless settlers on raids of Indian villages, killing many natives. Virginia governor SIR WILLIAM BERKELEY tried to suppress Bacon's raids to preserve social order, but his opposition exacerbated a second axis of conflict: that between the established Virginia gentry and restless freedmen (former indentured servants), who embraced Bacon as their champion. In the spring of 1676 Bacon's troops looted and burned Jamestown. The rebellion collapsed quickly after Bacon's death in October. Nevertheless, it profoundly frightened the planter gentry and probably spurred the transition to slave labor in the colony in the late 17th and early 18th centuries.

Virginia planters adopted slave labor for several other reasons. By the late 17th century economic conditions in England had begun to improve, stemming the flow of indentured servants to British North America. At the same time Virginia's demographic regime stabilized so that the majority of European and African immigrants now survived their first few years in the colony. Slaves cost more than indentured servants; it was not cost effective to purchase slaves unless most of them survived longer than a typical indentured servant's term of four to seven years. Around the 1670s, however, it became clear that slaves were a better long-term investment. In addition, the supply of slaves increased and their price declined. The wealthiest planters consequently began to switch from servant to slave labor. Social tensions contributed to their choice; the supply of good land available to ex-servants was decreasing, and established planters did not want to expand the pool of restless freedmen, laborers, and squatters who threatened their hegemony. By 1700 slaves probably outnumbered indentured servants. Virginia planters did not make the transition from servant to slave labor all at once, however. White indentured servants continued to labor beside African and African-American slaves on Chesapeake area plantations well into the 18th century.

This important transition to SLAVERY was accompanied by the expansion and codification of Virginia's black code. Initially, slavery was regulated by local custom rather than law; many mid-17th century African laborers held an ambiguous status between servant and slave, and quite a few eventually obtained their freedom. In the 1660s, however, the House of Burgesses began to pass laws defining slaves' status as property and blocking off potential paths to freedom: Children of slave mothers were deemed to be slaves; conversion to Christianity did not justify emancipation; the murder of a slave by his or her master did not constitute a felony; slaves could not own firearms. Wealthy planters probably hoped to co-opt the political support of poorer white people by attaching political value to "whiteness"; the concepts of black slavery and white liberty became intricately entangled in the minds of 18th-century white Virginians. In 1705 the Burgesses' restrictive laws were collected in a comprehensive Virginia Slave Code. By then the vast majority of Africans and AFRICAN AMERICANS living in Virginia were held as slaves.

Between 1700 and 1770 approximately 80,000 slaves were imported to Virginia and MARYLAND. Most grew tobacco on properties that ranged in size from small farms, where a handful of slaves and servants labored beside the white family, to sprawling, villagelike plantations worked by 100 or more slaves. Eighteenth-century Virginia slaves were healthier and longer-lived than their counterparts in the Caribbean and South America due to better nutrition, a less extreme work regime, and a less deadly disease ENVIRONMENT. By the 1730s the Virginia slave population had begun to grow by natural increase; it was the first slave population in the Americas to do so. Over the course of the 18th century slaves created a syncretic African-American culture, fusing social and religious traditions from several regions of AFRICA with European influences. MUSIC, DANCE, funeral rites, naming patterns, and CREOLE dialects that blended vocabulary and grammatical patterns from various African and European languages all played a pivotal role in early African-American culture. In the 1760s and 1770s many African-American slaves converted to Christianity and began to fuse Christian beliefs and customs with African religious traditions to form a distinctive mode of Afro-Christianity. African-American culture also influenced white Virginians' material culture, accents, musical tastes, and cuisine.

Virginia was not only the oldest of Britain's mainland North American colonies but also the most populous. After the early years its population grew steadily from 18,700 people in 1650 to 58,600 in 1700 and 340,000 in 1763. Slaves constituted slightly more than a quarter of Virginia's population in 1700 and more than 40 percent by 1760. The colony's white social structure included large planters who owned 20 or more slaves and from one to several plantations; small planters who owned fewer than 20 slaves and one small-scale plantation; backcountry and tenant farmers who grew tobacco and cereal crops on small farms, relying primarily on family rather than slave labor; and indentured servants. ARTISANS and shopkeepers congregated in small towns such as Williamsburg, but in spite of the House of Burgesses's attempts to encourage the creation of towns, Virginia remained overwhelmingly rural throughout the colonial period. The county was the principal unit of local government; in the absence of towns, colonists congregated at court days, militia musters, and rural stores and taverns. In 18th-century Virginia about 60 percent of adult white men held enough land to qualify for the vote. This was an unusually broad SUFFRAGE by European standards. Large planters monopolized the House of Burgesses, which soon superseded the governor's council in political influence.

Eighteenth-century Virginia was a firmly hierarchical society. The Tidewater gentry exercised power not only through political and judicial service but also through patronage and material display. In contrast to 17th-century planters, who often lived in small, bare houses, their 18th-century counterparts constructed elegant Georgian mansions on their estates. Weddings, funerals, and other lifecycle events were celebrated with elaborate banquets and parties that could last as long as three days. Churchgoing was another important occasion for social display; the local elite congregated in the churchyard and made a regal entrance just before the service began. Large planters often marketed tobacco, obtained consumer goods, and did business for smaller neighboring planters, thus drawing them into semidependent relationships. It was also customary for political candidates (mostly large planters) to "treat" voters (mostly small landowners) with liberal allowances of FOOD and ALCOHOL on election days, effectively purchasing their votes not with money but with promises of hospitality and patronage. The social status of the Tidewater gentry within the larger BRITISH EMPIRE remained ambiguous, however. In spite of the enormous influence they exercised in Virginia, many of them struggled with a perennial sense of cultural inferiority to the British gentry they sought to emulate.

The backcountry's social structure differed considerably from that of the Tidewater region. Although many wealthy planters speculated in backcountry lands, few actually lived in that region, nor were there many slaves in the colonial Virginia backcountry, because most backcountry farmers could not afford to purchase them. After the 1720s new immigrants, many of them German and Scots-Irish, flooded into the Virginia Piedmont; by the 1750s European settlement had reached the edge of the Appalachian Mountains. The new immigrants raised livestock and grew cereal crops and low-grade tobacco on the rich Piedmont soil. Some enjoyed a comfortable standard of living, although they never approached the Tidewater gentry in wealth or political influence; the poorest were squatters, who led a precarious existence without legal title to their land. In the wake of the SEVEN YEARS' WAR the British government attempted to relieve tensions between white settlers and Native Americans in the Ohio Valley by issuing the Proclamation of 1763, which forbade white settlement west of the Appalachians. Many frontier settlers resisted this decree, which contributed to Virginians' growing resentment of British colonial rule.

Virginia's early intellectual and religious life was relatively calm and undistinguished. Because Virginia was a royal colony, the ANGLICAN CHURCH was established as the colony's official church, and all taxpayers contributed to its support. Most white Virginians adhered to the Anglican Church, at least nominally, but the Chesapeake region lacked the religious fervor of the Puritan and Quaker colonies. Anglican clergymen—mostly ENGLISH IMMIGRANTS—exercised little social authority. New backcountry settlements often lacked churches; itinerant ministers performed marriages and baptisms, although many couples cohabited without marrying. The educational situation was similarly bleak. In the 17th century schools were few and far between; wealthy planters sent their children to England for schooling, others simply did without formal EDUCATION. In the 18th century many planter parents hired private tutors for their children or sent them to small local schools, but offspring of poorer families enjoyed little chance to study. The COLLEGE OF WILLIAM AND MARY was established at Williamsburg (soon to be the new capital of Virginia) in 1693. The college's elegant buildings introduced the Virginia gentry to the architectural principles of Christopher Wren and inspired a spate of mansion construction, but the college's academic standards were initially low. Careful parents sent their sons to northern institutions to protect them from the dissipations of Williamsburg.

The character of Virginia's religious life changed dramatically during THE GREAT AWAKENING, a wave of evangelical religious revivals that spread throughout the mainland British colonies in the mid-18th century. The Great Awakening reached the Virginia Piedmont in the mid-1740s, but its full effect was not felt until the 1760s. Every layer of Virginia society, from rich planters to slaves, responded to evangelical preaching. The BAPTISTS and METHODISTS, the two leading evangelical denominations, grew rapidly; the revivals also reshaped and invigorated Scots-Irish Presbyterian congregations. Intriguingly, evangelical PROTESTANTISM attracted many African-American slaves to Christianity for the first time. Slaves attended revivals, preached, and joined Baptist and Methodist congregations; for a few decades in the late 18th century many Virginians belonged to interracial churches. (In the early 19th century most of these congregations splintered into separate African-American and white meetings.) The Great Awakening utterly transformed Virginia society in the decades before the American Revolution. Indeed, the revivalists' preaching style and their emphasis on challenging established authority may have prepared Virginians to embrace the Revolutionary rhetoric of liberty. As the largest and oldest mainland colony, Virginia was often in the spotlight and played a leading role in early Revolutionary protests.

Further reading: Kathleen M. Brown, *Good Wives, Nasty Wenches, and Anxious Patriarchs: Gender, Race, and Power in Colonial Virginia* (Chapel Hill: University of North Carolina Press, 1996); Rhys Isaac, *The Transformation of Virginia, 1740–1790* (New York: Norton, 1982); Edmund S. Morgan, *American Slavery, American Freedom: The Ordeal of Colonial Virginia* (New York: Norton, 1975); Philip Morgan, *Slave Counterpoint: Black Culture in the Eighteenth-Century Chesapeake and Lowcountry* (Chapel Hill: University of North Carolina Press, 1998); Darrett B. Rutman and Anita H. Rutman, *A Place in Time: Middlesex County, Virginia, 1650–1750* (New York: Norton, 1984).

—Darcy R. Fryer

Virginia Company of London (1606–1624)

Responding to a petition to private individuals with connections of family and interest in Raleigh's and Gilbert's earlier colonies, James I promulgated a charter in 1606 authorizing new English colonies in America under the aegis of two joint-stock companies: the Virginia Company of London, whose grant allowed them to plant colonies

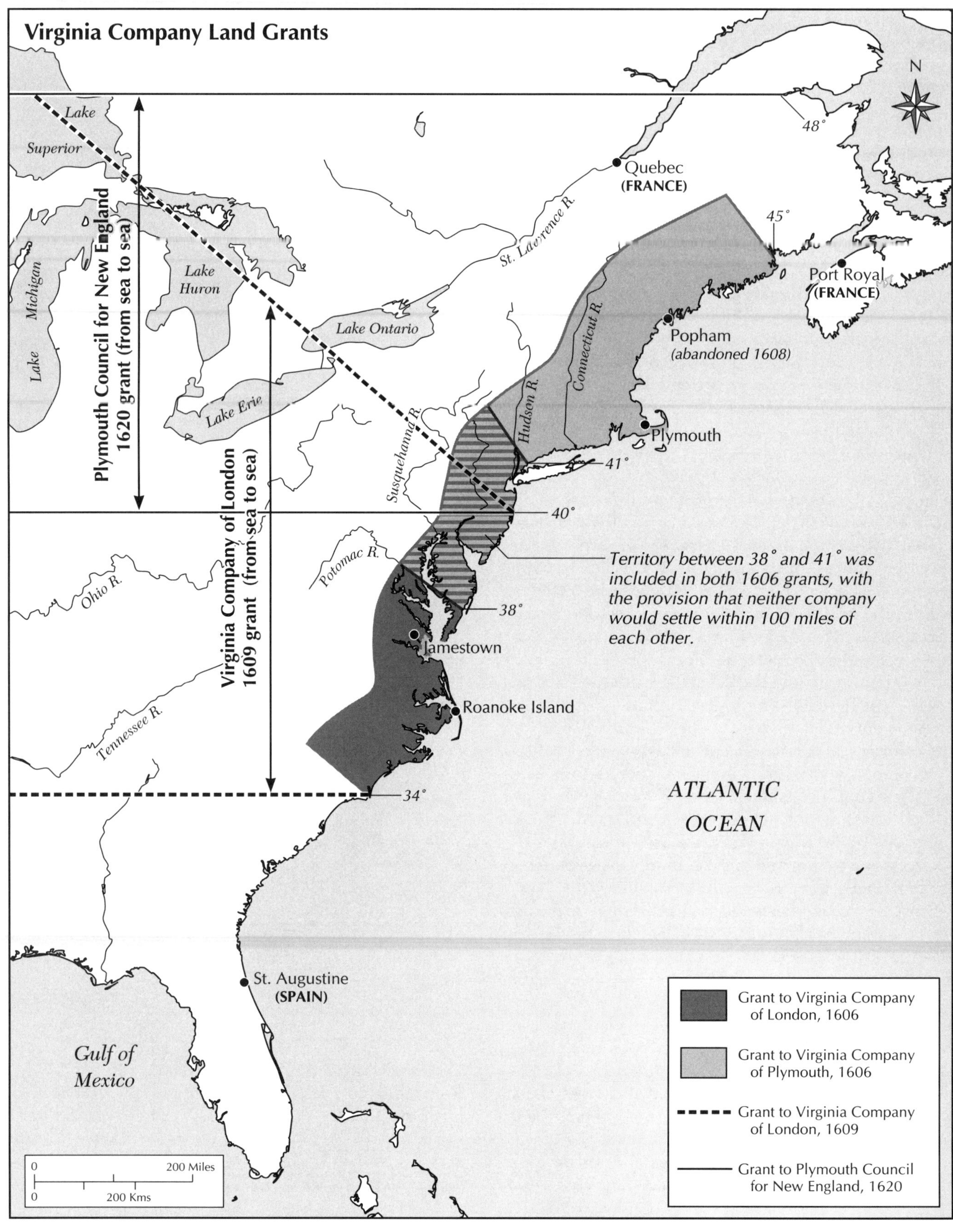

Virginia Company Land Grants
N
Lake Superior
Lake Michigan
Lake Huron
Lake Ontario
Lake Erie
Plymouth Council for New England 1620 grant (from sea to sea)
Virginia Company of London 1609 grant (from sea to sea)
Quebec
(FRANCE)
St. Lawrence R.
48°
45°
Port Royal
(FRANCE)
Popham
(abandoned 1608)
Connecticut R.
Hudson R.
Susquehanna R.
Plymouth
41°
40°
Potomac R.
Ohio R.
Territory between 38° and 41° was included in both 1606 grants, with the provision that neither company would settle within 100 miles of each other.
38°
Jamestown
Roanoke Island
Tennessee R.
34°
ATLANTIC OCEAN
St. Augustine
(SPAIN)
Gulf of Mexico
0 200 Miles
0 200 Kms
Grant to Virginia Company of London, 1606
Grant to Virginia Company of Plymouth, 1606
Grant to Virginia Company of London, 1609
Grant to Plymouth Council for New England, 1620

from present-day NORTH CAROLINA to Long Island, and the Virginia Company of PLYMOUTH, with colonization rights extending over the New England area.

The Virginia Company of London was primarily a business venture whose goal was to realize a profit, although the company's appeals for investors were couched in terms of broader national and religious interests. A factional cross-section of the English aristocracy capitalized and led the Virginia Company of London, which established the JAMESTOWN colony in 1607. The "ancient companies" and the great London MERCHANTS, especially Sir Thomas Smith, who served as the company's treasurer, brought to the enterprise their experience of trading with Russia and the Levant. The Rich family, particularly Sir Robert Rich, the second earl of Warwick, aspired to realize the old dream of a PRIVATEERING base in the New World from which to strike at Spain and its treasure fleets. Many landed gentry, eventually championed by Sir Edwin Sandys, invested heavily in the company, hoping that lucrative returns would shore up their incomes, which, heavily dependent on fixed rents, were being rapidly eroded by inflation. Meanwhile, humanitarians and clergy among the founders would assist the unemployed poor who were flooding London by making them indentured servants to work the company plantation. They also aspired to make the Virginia Indians "civilized" and acquire Christian allies and customers for English-made trade goods, the demand for which would stimulate the English domestic ECONOMY. These conflicting goals and interests bred division, suspicion, and intrigue that undermined the cooperation needed to solve the immense problems of debt and insolvency entailed by the expense of sustaining the Jamestown colony until it could become profitable.

Peopling, governing, capitalizing, and making profitable the Jamestown colony was an experiment without precedent, except perhaps the failed Roanoke colony and the brutal English colonization of Celtic Ireland, models that boded ill for English-Indian relations. Unable to find a lucrative export, misruled and beset by DISEASE, unable to feed itself or to keep peace with the POWHATAN Indians, Jamestown floundered, forcing company officials down a path of repeated, but ultimately futile, reforms. The company secured a second charter in 1609 that limited royal control of its affairs, brought the colony under the control of "one able and absolute Governor," and permitted public sale of stock. Its third charter in 1612 gave control of the financially promising Somers Isles (Bermuda) and allowed fundraising through a public lottery. Dissatisfied with the management of the London merchants, smaller stockholders in 1619 initiated another round of reform and eventually ousted treasurer Sir Thomas Smith, replacing him with Sir Edwin Sandys.

Sandys recruited more than 3,500 settlers for Virginia, many of whom were the unemployed poor forced into INDENTURED SERVITUDE. The company made land grants to private individuals in return for quitrents and established "particular plantations" farmed by TENANTS along the James River, further encroaching on Indian lands. Bowing to stockholder unease over burgeoning and exclusive TOBACCO production, Sandys encouraged the production of commodities such as iron, potash, and lumber. The company set up a representative assembly that quickly became a means for the wealthiest colonists to control the LABOR of tenants and servants, maintain their own power, and subvert the company's will, especially its discouraging of tobacco cultivation. The failure of the reforms to produce profits and the Powhatan uprising in 1622 accelerated internal dissension among the stockholders, causing Charles I to dissolve the company in 1624 and declare Virginia a royal colony.

Further reading: Edmund S. Morgan, *American Slavery; American Freedom: The Ordeal of Colonial Virginia* (New York: Norton, 1975).

—James Bruggeman

W

wage and price controls

Most 17th-century European states and towns instituted wage and price controls to regulate the local economy. Both the traditional concept of the "moral economy" (an economy regulated by social principles rather than market forces) and the newer theory of MERCANTILISM (the idea that the state should regulate commerce in order to foster its own power) promoted the use of such controls. Moreover, early modern Europeans generally assumed that prices and wages should remain stable over time. Colonists often quibbled over the details of wage and price controls, but both the governors and the governed favored economic regulation.

The English Statute of Artificers (1562) provided a model for colonial regulations of laborers' hours and wages. It was often difficult to adapt statutory law to local conditions, however, so in most cases justices of the peace actually set maximum and minimum wages. The scarcity of labor in the American colonies tended to drive wages up, to the consternation of those who believed that the real value of work varied little from one place to another. Wages in the American colonies remained higher than wages for comparable work in England, but colonial courts nevertheless indicted some laborers for accepting "excessive" wages. Local officials also regulated the fees that millers, tavern keepers, ferry owners, gravediggers, and other essential community functionaries were permitted to charge.

The quintessential price control was the assize of bread, which specified the proper size, quality, and price of a loaf of bread. Local officials regulated the price of other essential goods, such as meat, leather, bricks, and nails, as they thought necessary. Shipping costs naturally drove up the price of many imported goods, but colonists were initially reluctant to make allowances for this; in the early 17th century BOSTON merchant Thomas Keayne was prosecuted for incorporating shipping costs into the price of imported nails. Indeed, colonial courts vigorously punished individuals who violated the doctrine of the moral economy. Colonial governments also outlawed market manipulations such as "engrossing" (creating a monopoly) and "forestalling" (buying up the entire stock of a particular commodity) to drive up the costs of goods.

Local economic regulations fell into decline in the mid-18th century. A new generation of economic theorists questioned the value of commercial regulation, while an increasingly diverse and mobile population questioned the concept of a moral economy structured to promote community welfare. Nevertheless, popular support for economic regulation occasionally resurfaced in wartime or during periods of rapid inflation. In the midst of Revolutionary boycotts in 1774, the Continental Congress called on colonial governments to punish price gougers.

Further reading: John J. McCusker and Russell R. Menard, *The Economy of British America, 1607–1789* (Chapel Hill: University of North Carolina Press, 1985).

—Darcy R. Fryer

Walking Purchase of 1737

In the mid-1730s the Lenape Indians (called DELAWARE by Euro-Americans) still owned much of Bucks County and the Lehigh Valley in eastern PENNSYLVANIA. As proprietors of Pennsylvania, Thomas and John Penn (the sons of WILLIAM PENN) and their agent, JAMES LOGAN, conspired to remove the Delaware from these lands. Logan argued that a copy of a deed dated 1686 proved that the Lenape had sold all lands that could be walked in a day and a half north of the previous boundary in Bucks County. Nutimus, a Delaware elder, denied that the deed included his land between Tohickon Creek and the Lehigh River. When the IROQUOIS of NEW YORK sided with the proprietors, the Delaware acquiesced.

In preparation for the "walk" James Logan directed men to clear a path so the "walkers" could move swiftly.

From Wrightstown on the morning of September 19, 1737, three young settlers, Solomon Jennings, James Yeats, and Edward Marshall, accompanied by two Delaware observers, walked north at a very rapid pace. They covered much more ground than Nutimus, Lapowinsa, and other native leaders expected. In the afternoon, when the walkers crossed the Lehigh River, the Indian observers departed. Lapowinsa refused to send others, objecting that the Penns had "got all the best land, and they might go to the Devil for the bad." The walkers slept overnight near Hockendauqua, Lapowinsa's town. The Delaware refused to allow the Euro-Americans to enter the town because they were holding a religious ceremony. The walkers passed Kittatinny (or Blue) Mountain before lunch on September 20, 1737, then continued to a point near present-day Jim Thorpe. After a total of 18 hours only one man completed the entire 64 miles. James Logan drew the boundary there, extending the line northeast to the Delaware River, and set off 10 square miles near Hockendauqua for a reservation called the Indian Tract Manor.

In the 1740s and 1750s the Penns sold lands in the area of the Walking Purchase to growing numbers of European settlers. Some natives stayed in the region, while others moved west to the Susquehanna and Ohio Valleys. In 1755 many Delaware allied with the French to push out the colonists during the SEVEN YEARS' WAR. The British and colonists defeated the French in 1763, but not the Delaware. Conflict between NATIVE AMERICANS and settlers continued in the area through the American Revolution.

Further reading: Francis Jennings, *The Ambiguous Iroquois Empire* (New York: Norton, 1984).

—Jean R. Soderlund

Walter, Thomas (1696–1725)

Thomas Walter composed religious music in early America. Born in Roxbury, MASSACHUSETTS, the son of a minister, Thomas Walter was the grandson of INCREASE MATHER. Although his family tried to shield him from the world, Walter was precocious and earned a reputation for brilliance and conviviality. Despite early association with theological radicals, Walter was ordained in 1718 and installed as assistant pastor to his conservative father. He married Rebekah Belcher on Christmas Day, 1718, and they had one daughter.

In 1719 Walter entered a public dialogue with the theologian John Checkley, debating the order and government of the church. Walter sought to improve the quality of congregational singing at this time, compiling songbooks and preaching sermons on the importance of MUSIC in worship. In 1721 he published his best-known hymnal, *Grounds and Rules of Musick Explained; or, an Introduction to the Art of Singing By Note, Fittest to the meanest capacity.* This text contained hymns in three parts and emphasized simple technique. Walter's connection to the Mathers, one of the most influential families in colonial New England, meant that his work drew particular attention. This hymnal went through eight editions by 1764, and a few songs remain in use today.

Walter volunteered to be vaccinated for SMALLPOX, which Increase Mather supported. He nearly died when someone threw a bomb into the room where he lay recovering after the inoculation. Shortly afterward Walter contracted consumption and died after a lengthy and painful illness.

—Victoria C. H. Resnick

wampum

Wampum, or *wampumpeag*, were manufactured strings of purple and white whelk and clam shells found in the Narragansett Bay and Long Island Sound regions of New England. ALGONQUIN Indians worked the shells by grinding and drilling them into small tubular pieces, polishing them, and stringing them together to fashion belts and rectangular matlike pieces.

Before European arrival belts and sections of wampum were sacred objects among New England Indians, denoting the power and prestige of their holders. Wampum usually adorned only SACHEMS or other prominent persons to evince rank and dignity; ordinary natives rarely possessed or accumulated much. It was exchanged during rituals and used as payment of tribute between peoples, as dowry, and as signs of friendship and diplomatic relations. In their designs wampum belts could also mark special events or occasions, acting as a type of mnemonic or commemorative device recording local history. Wampum thus functioned as both a symbol of personal or tribal identity and as a medium in the culture of gift exchange that marked both inter- and intragroup interactions among New England peoples.

The coming of European colonists transformed the meaning and usage of wampum. Discovering its immense value among many of the peoples they encountered and realizing its potential to facilitate trade and amity with them, first Dutch and later English settlers attempted to corner its manufacture in the 17th century by establishing relations with the Mohegan, NARRAGANSETT, and PEQUOT, who controlled the coastal areas of Long Island Sound, where true wampum shells were found. These natives obtained metal drillbits from Europeans to replace stone varieties, and wampum production grew far beyond earlier levels. Wampum began to lose much of its formal ceremonial meaning and to take on characteristics of currency. It was used to purchase goods or services. An exchange rate was computed in English money, and a market in counterfeit shells emerged. Wampum ownership became more common among ordinary Indians, and native peoples from other regions who previously had not participated in its exchange were increasingly drawn into a nascent wampum ECONOMY. Historians have referred to the transformation of wampum shells from sacred and symbolic objects to commodities and versions of money under European influence as the "wampum revolution."

Further reading: William Cronon, *Changes in the Land: Indians, Colonists, and the Ecology of New England* (New York: Hill & Wang, 1983); Neal Salisbury, *Manitou and Providence: Indians, Europeans, and the Making of New England, 1500–1643* (New York: Oxford University Press, 1982).

—Bradley Scott Schrager

war and warfare

Organized violence to achieve a particular end existed in North America long before the arrival of Europeans, but the colonists introduced new motives for and methods of warfare that resulted, when combined with Native American traditions, in a blend of the two that is distinctly American. During the colonial period wars were fought between different groups of NATIVE AMERICANS, between colonists from European nations and Native Americans, and between rival colonists, although there is a good deal of overlap in these categories.

Conflicts among Native Americans along the East Coast usually did not entail a large loss of life. Instead, small groups might be killed or captured for adoption into tribes. Wars between Native Americans were transformed by the introduction of new weapons, especially firearms. The adoption of the horse by the Plains peoples transformed their ways of war, which would become a major factor as Europeans, and later white Americans, spread west. European colonization also introduced a new motive for inter–Native American warfare—access to trade with the new arrivals.

Wars between colonists and Native Americans tended toward raids and reprisals. Europeans were frustrated by the unwillingness of their foes to stand and fight, while Native Americans were mystified by European concepts of battlefield discipline. The colonists turned to such tactics as the destruction of crops and homes when they could not bring their enemies to battle. As they were often unable or unwilling to differentiate between different groups of Native Americans, they tended to strike whatever group was handy, even if that group was friendly. Native Americans generally came from a raiding tradition of warfare that involved striking at isolated outposts and killing or capturing the entire population. Both sides tended to view the other's methods as barbaric and inhuman.

Wars were also common among colonists of rival European powers as they struggled to control the Atlantic World. A series of four major struggles between the British and French resulted in the end of French claims to mainland North America. While these wars were closely related to conflicts on the European continent, they assumed a different character. North America was ill suited to European open-field tactics. It lacked many open fields where linear tactics could be applied (the battle on the Plains of Abraham outside Quebec in 1759 is a notable exception). Despite their reluctance to adopt supposedly "barbaric" methods, colonists combined their European traditions with Native American techniques. This blending was aided by the recruiting by both England and France of substantial numbers of Native American allies. The French more often adopted their allies' tactics, while the English stuck closer to their traditions and used Native Americans as auxiliaries.

Whether involved in the great struggle for continental domination and empire or the smaller but no less violent disputes on the colonial frontier, warfare was an important part of the Native American and colonial experiences. From these experiences came a blend of European and Native American styles of fighting—a uniquely American way of war.

See also BACON'S REBELLION; DUTCH-INDIAN WARS; FORTS; FORT NECESSITY; KING PHILIP'S WAR; PEQUOT WAR; SEVEN YEARS' WAR; WAR OF JENKINS' EAR.

Further reading: Fred Anderson, *Crucible of War: The Seven Years War and the Fate of the British Empire in North America, 1754–1766* (New York: Knopf, 2000); Robert Utley and Wilcomb Washburn, *Indian Wars* (New York: American Heritage, 1977).

—Grant Weller

Ward, Nancy (1738?–1824)

Nancy Ward was an influential CHEROKEE leader. Biographical details are uncertain because of the lack of written records. According to legend, she was born about 1738 at Chota in eastern Tennessee. First named Nan'yehi, she married a Cherokee warrior whom she accompanied to battles. When her husband was killed at the 1755 Battle of Taliwa, Ward seized his gun and forced the enemy to retreat. After that action she was called Ghigau, or "Beloved Woman," the highest courtesy title given to Cherokee women. In the Cherokee's matrilineal society Ward gained power, privileges, and responsibilities, including voting rights in the General Council. She married

Bryant Ward, a white trader, in the 1750s, but he abandoned her to return to his family in SOUTH CAROLINA.

Serving as an ambassador, Ward negotiated peace with white people who settled on Cherokee lands despite the royal Proclamation of 1763, which recognized NATIVE AMERICANS' land rights. Ward interceded in 1776, when she learned of Cherokee plans to raid white settlements on the Holston and Watauga Rivers, warning white people and saving a white woman captive. Ward learned to weave cloth and tend livestock, part of the transformation of GENDER roles among the Cherokee as women began to work cloth while men farmed. The first Cherokee to own cows and slaves, Ward introduced dairy husbandry to supplement their diet.

Ward protected the Cherokee's interests during peace talks with John Sevier in 1781. Four years later she negotiated on behalf of the Cherokee for the Treaty of Hopewell, the first treaty discussed with representatives of the United States. Aware that white people wanted Cherokee lands, Ward worried about the fate of her tribe. Gradually Native American women's political power waned, but Ward insisted on voicing her opinions. At the 1808 Women's Council that she led, Ward emphasized that the Cherokee should not sell more land to whites. Nine years later she advised the Cherokee to wage war to preserve their territory.

After her tribal lands were sold in 1819, Ward relocated to an inn she managed near the Ocoee River. She died in 1824, five years before women were denied voting and office rights by the Cherokee constitution and 14 years before the southern Cherokee were forcibly removed to western reservations.

Further reading: Paula Gunn Allen, *The Sacred Hoop: Recovering the Feminine in American Indian Traditions* (Boston: Beacon Press, 1992).

—Elizabeth D. Schafer

War of Jenkins' Ear (1739–1743)

The War of Jenkins' Ear began in 1739 and involved the international ambitions of Britain and Spain. Although the fighting did not begin in earnest until 1740, the event that led to the conflict occurred nearly 10 years earlier. In 1731 Captain Juan de Leon Fandino, a Spanish naval officer, boarded a British vessel off Havana's coast. Fandino accused British captain Robert Jenkins of SMUGGLING. During the search an argument ensued, and in the heat of the altercation Fandino sliced off Jenkins's ear. Throwing the ear at Jenkins, Fandino reportedly exclaimed "Take this to your king and tell him if he were here I would do the same."

As tensions increased between the British and Spanish in North America, Jenkins returned to London with ear in hand. Addressing Parliament, Jenkins described his altercation with the Spanish sailor and, to prove his point of Spanish savagery, produced the preserved ear. Although the Jenkins incident was one of numerous altercations along the North American frontier, his ear became a rallying cry for aggressive action. As Parliamentarians protested Spain's belligerency on the coast, further developments near FLORIDA increased tensions. When the British established GEORGIA, SLAVERY was prohibited. This prohibition was supposed to create a buffer zone between British SOUTH CAROLINA's slaves and Spanish Florida's offer of asylum to those who successfully ran away. Despite their best efforts, British planters could not stop escaped slaves from reaching freedom in Florida. FORT MOSE continued to threaten the peace in South Carolina, and in 1739 Britain declared war against Spain, supposedly for Jenkins' ear but more important because of the threat of slave unrest.

In the fall of 1739 slaves in Stono, South Carolina, revolted. For those involved the ultimate goal was passage to ST. AUGUSTINE and freedom. Fort Mose, once an abstract threat to British control, became an immediate concern for the very survival of Britain's southern colonies. Hoping to drive the Spanish from Florida, Georgia founder and general JAMES OGLETHORPE led troops on a mission to take St. Augustine in the spring of 1740. Although the British destroyed numerous frontier outposts, including Fort Mose, they could not remove the Spanish from St. Augustine. As the British advanced the residents of St. Augustine sought protection in the city's large stone fort. While the Spaniards waited for reinforcements to arrive, Oglethorpe shelled the city. The fort, however, proved impenetrable to the British attack; the British ultimately left Florida in defeat on July 4, 1740.

—Shane Runyon

Warren, Mary Cole (1653–1697?)

Mary Cole was born at the family TOBACCO farm, St. Clement's Manor, in MARYLAND to prosperous English Roman Catholic immigrants Robert and Rebecca Cole. The first daughter of five children, Mary learned to read the Bible and to sew. Like many Maryland children of the 17th century, Mary became an orphan when her mother died in 1642 and her father a year later. While many orphans suffered abuse or neglect at the hands of strangers, Mary was more fortunate in that Robert had both inventoried his possessions and chosen guardians to provide materially and spiritually for his offspring. Neighbor Luke Gardiner raised the children and sent Mary to live for a short time with her grandmother in England. Following the custom of the day, daughters received movable property from estates, and, accordingly, Mary inherited 11 cattle, a feather bed with sheets, an iron pot, an 18-gallon copper kettle, and a spice mortar when she came of age. By 1673 she had married tobacco planter and innkeeper Ignatius Warren of Newtown Hundred. Mary then disappears from the historical record. It is not known if Mary had any children, and it is believed that she died, aged about 45, before Ignatius went bankrupt.

See also WOMEN'S STATUS AND RIGHTS.

Further reading: Lois Green Carr, Russell R. Menard and Lorena S. Walsh, *Robert Cole's World: Agriculture and Society in Early Maryland* (Chapel Hill: University of North Carolina Press, 1991).

—Caryn E. Neumann

Weiser, Johann Conrad (1696–1760)

Johann Conrad Weiser helped maintain the alliance between the IROQUOIS Indians and the British. He was born November 2, 1696, in Affstät, Württemberg, in present-day Germany. Responding to the constant warfare and destruction of their homeland and following the death of his mother, in 1710 Weiser's family heeded the advertisements of the British colonies and joined other migrants from the Palatinate to the New World. After several months in NEW YORK CITY the Weiser family moved to upstate NEW YORK, joining other Palatines in the Schoharie Valley. When Conrad was 16, he lived in a village of Mohawk. By the end of his visit he had learned to speak Iroquoian fluently, had begun to understand Native American culture, and had developed what would become lifelong friendships. In 1729 Weiser moved from Schoharie and settled in the Tulpehocken Valley of western Berks County, PENNSYLVANIA, where he joined other German migrants and established a prosperous farm. In religious matters he was an active member of the local German Lutheran church and, during a time of personal spiritual crisis, spent time among the religious community at Ephrata. Like many other prosperous farmers and tradesmen, Weiser speculated in land after his arrival in Berks County. Through his investments he cultivated a relationship with the proprietary government that proved mutually beneficial.

His experience with NATIVE AMERICANS as a youth was advantageous for both the Pennsylvania government and the regional Indian confederacies. In 1731 Weiser accompanied Shikellamy, a chieftain of the Oneida, to PHILADELPHIA for negotiations with provincial officials, serving as translator for both parties. Over time Weiser became renowned for his skill at mediating between the agents of the Penn family and the area tribes, earning the name "Holder of the Heavens" for his services. Through his efforts the province was able to maintain peaceful relations with the Native Americans throughout much of the 18th century. On several occasions he assisted with the negotiations for land purchases, as in the notorious WALKING PURCHASE OF 1737 with the DELAWARE Indians. His diplomatic skills extended beyond Pennsylvania, as his efforts also improved Native American relations with MARYLAND and VIRGINIA. His last great act was at Easton in 1758, when he persuaded Native Americans of the Ohio Valley to sever ties with the French. By the time of his death in 1760, Weiser had also succeeded in mediating relations between German and English interests in Pennsylvania as well as among white settlers and the Native Americans.

See also DAVID ZEISBERGER.

Further reading: James H. Merrell, *Into the American Woods: Negotiators on the Pennsylvania Frontier* (New York: Norton, 1999); Paul A. W. Wallace, *Conrad Weiser, 1696–1760: Friend of Colonist and Mohawk* (Philadelphia: University of Pennsylvania Press, 1945).

—Karen Guenther

Wesley, John (1703–1791)

John Wesley was born in 1703 in Epworth, Lincolnshire. The son of an Anglican rector, Wesley was educated at Christ Church College, Oxford, and was ordained as an Anglican priest in 1725. While at Oxford, Wesley, together with his brother Charles and GEORGE WHITEFIELD, formed a "Holy Club" known as the Oxford Methodists to discuss spiritual issues. Although Wesley gained a reputation for piety and came to the notice of the GEORGIA trustees as a result, his time at Oxford seems only to have deepened his sense of spiritual inadequacy. However, when the trustees offered him the chance to be a missionary to the Indians while acting as the minister in SAVANNAH, Wesley accepted.

Wesley arrived in North America in February 1736 in the throes of a spiritual crisis but determined to bring a new religious discipline to Savannah. Even at this young age, Wesley's implementation of Anglicanism was more rigorous than that of many other ministers. While his sober habits and his willingness to hold regular services in Savannah earned him the initial respect of colonists, Wesley eventually fell foul of his own stern morality. Like his brother Charles, who had taken the post as minister in Frederica farther south, John found that Georgians did not enjoy having their numerous faults and moral failings repeatedly pointed out to them. Charles returned to England after only six months, but John remained in Georgia for nearly two years.

His strict moral code earned Wesley the animosity of Savannah's citizenry, but his personal failings brought Wesley's downfall in the colony. Wesley had formed an attach-

John Wesley *(Library of Congress)*

ment to Sophia Hopkey, niece of Thomas Causton, who managed the trustees' store and was one of the most powerful and influential men in Savannah. Many, including JAMES OGLETHORPE and Causton, believed that the pair would marry. However, when Sophia rejected a marriage proposal from Wesley and wed another man instead, Wesley reacted by singling out the newlyweds for criticism. After Sophia missed several church services, Wesley felt justified in denying her Holy Communion. The decision caused an uproar and led to a defamation suit from Sophia's husband, John Williamson. Under this threat of court action, Wesley fled Savannah in 1737.

Despite claiming later that his time in Georgia had been a success, it is clear that Wesley failed to have a significant impact in colonial America. However, shortly after his return to London in 1738 Wesley underwent a religious conversion experience and embarked on a nationwide evangelical revival. Until his death in 1791 Wesley shaped religious revivalism in England and North America and the future of the Methodist faith.

See also GREAT AWAKENING.

Further reading: David T. Morgan "John Wesley's Sojourn In Georgia Revisited" (*Georgia Historical Quarterly,* 1980, pp. 253–62).

—Timothy James Lockley

West Indies See Caribbean

Westo

The Westo were a native people of the Middle Atlantic and Southeast region during the middle and late 17th century. They played a significant role in the early stages of European colonial incursion into North America, acting both as partners to the expansionary English colony of Carolina as well as feared enemies of Spanish FLORIDA and the native peoples within its orbit of MISSIONS and towns. The Westo are best known as allies of early English settlers of Carolina, with whom they formed a tenuous partnership in the 1670s that featured trade in firearms and English goods, Indian slaving, and mutual defense. Contemporary descriptions of them survive in reports and narratives by English colonial agents, like Dr. Henry Woodward, who spent much time among them as the representative of Carolina.

The exact identification of the Westo has caused confusion among historians because of migrations between the Chesapeake region and the Lower South as far as central GEORGIA. Their ethnohistory remains mysterious; some scholars have suggested an Iroquoian connection that places their origins in the Northeast, others a Yuchean background that implies southern roots. Because the Westo ranged across a southeastern imperial landscape contested by both Spaniards and English, European documents concerning them include incongruous mentions and conflicting information. English settlers in the Chesapeake area knew the Westo initially by the name Recohockrians, a people of the James River region with whom they had several confrontations in the 1650s. Spaniards in Florida first met the group through native refugees fleeing the raids staged by Westo, armed with English guns, deep into the Southeast in the early 1660s. Spaniards called the Westo *chichimecos,* a term the Spanish also used in other New World settings to denote fierce and uncontrollable Indians who threatened Spanish and native settlements.

The English in Carolina during the 1670s sought powerful native partners to help support their fledgling colony, and the Westo, described by one correspondent as "bold and warlike," fit their requirements. For most of that decade Westo served as the primary native allies of Carolina, providing Englishmen with the Indian slaves, deerskins, and defensive protection that fueled that settlement's expansion. Indeed, English officials and traders often seemed quite wary of their Westo partners, fearful that they might turn upon Carolina. Correspondents spoke of the arrangement between Westo and Carolinians in terms that belied the power of the natives and the weakness of the colony; one admitted that "if trade were not permitted the Westos . . . they would cut all [our] throats."

Disputes between English traders and the Westo escalated in the late 1670s, and Carolinians moved to destroy their native partners, who now seemed less likely to submit to the colonial arrangement. The motivation for the Westo War of 1680 originated with planters and traders who dominated the Indian trade; the lords proprietors of Carolina saw the campaign from England as ill-advised and charged local leaders with putting personal gain before the welfare of the colony. Despite those objections, Carolinians along with newly allied Savannah Indians attacked the Westo. By 1683 correspondents claimed there were "not fifty Westos left alive, and those scattered," and the Savannah had usurped the role of primary native allies of Carolina, a station clearly as fraught with peril as opportunity.

Further reading: Verner Crane, *The Southern Frontier* (New York: Norton, 1981); J. Leitch Wright, Jr., *The Only Land They Knew: American Indians in the Old South* (Lincoln: University of Nebraska Press, 1981).

—Bradley Scott Schrager

Wetamo (unknown–1676)

Wetamo was an influential leader whose life reflects the increasing tensions between NATIVE AMERICANS and English colonists. Born to a distinguished Native American family, Wetamo took Wamsutta, the son of the Wampanoag leader and the older brother of METACOM, for her husband. Following her husband's mysterious 1664 death while in English custody, Wetamo became the sachem of the Wampanoag town of Pocasset, a position of authority that placed more than 300 warriors under her guidance and made her a political power in her own right. She also embarked upon a second marriage to Petananuet, the sachem of a smaller Wampanoag community. This relationship became a casualty of the split among the Native Americans when Metacom's War erupted in 1675. Her husband cast his lot with the English, while Wetamo, who had tried to keep the peace, joined with Metacom. Because of family ties to Metacom, she had firmly opposed concessions of land and authority to the English. The war went badly for Wetamo's side, and in the summer of 1675 she fled to the safety of the neutral NARRAGANSETT. According to New England Indian ethics, the Narragansett were obliged to honor a request for refuge, but the English interpreted Wetamo's arrival as a hostile act and invaded Narragansett territory. Wetamo resumed fighting with her new husband, Quanopin, one of the Narragansett leaders. Together the two successfully invaded the town of Lancaster, MASSACHUSETTS. With Wetamo proving to be a formidable foe, the English sought her defeat for military reasons but also because the lands that Wetamo held would pay for the cost of the war. In 1676, with the English in hot pursuit, the newly widowed Wetamo fled through a field and tried to cross a river in the area of PLYMOUTH. She drowned. When the English discovered her body a few days later, they cut off her head and placed it on a pole at Taunton.

See also WOMEN'S STATUS AND RIGHTS.

Further reading: Carol J. Berkin, *First Generations: Women in Colonial America* (New York: Hill & Wang, 1996).

—Caryn E. Neumann

Wheelock, Eleazar (1711–1779)

A leading exponent of the GREAT AWAKENING, Wheelock trained Native American missionaries and founded DARTMOUTH COLLEGE. Born to a prosperous farm family in Windham, CONNECTICUT, Wheelock graduated from YALE COLLEGE in 1733 and two years later settled into a pastorate at Lebanon, Connecticut. He preached widely in his home state and in neighboring MASSACHUSETTS. Interested in the conversion of NATIVE AMERICANS to Christianity, Wheelock in 1754 entered the missionary field by starting a school for Indian youths. The school would remove Native American children from what Wheelock viewed as the destructive influence of their parents, and he aimed to train the young men as missionaries to their own people. Not surprisingly, recruitment of Native Americans always proved a challenge, but Wheelock filled the seats by attracting white students. This new institution, known as Moor's Indian Charity School, was established in Lebanon, Connecticut. Because all the Native Americans were charity students and only about a third of the white scholars paid tuition, Wheelock supported his school by raising funds through various means, including targeting missionary societies of Great Britain and their American branches.

Among Wheelock's more prominent students were Samson Occom, a Mohegan, and Joseph Brant, a Mohawk. Wheelock hoped to produce students who would convert their people, but the school's record in Indian EDUCATION was mixed at best, and much of Wheelock's energy was devoted to fundraising.

Further adding to his woes, the number of Indian students dwindled steadily, with many of the students complaining that the school required more labor than studying. Wheelock eventually had to concentrate on recruiting Indian students from Canada after the

IROQUOIS completely rejected his overtures and other Native Americans expressed reluctance to send their children to work with him. Occom traveled to England to raise funds but later complained that Wheelock's school resembled *Alba Mater* ("White Mother") rather than *Alma Mater.* At no time had Indians outnumbered white people at the school. In 1769 the school moved with 30 students to Hanover, NEW HAMPSHIRE and became Dartmouth College. Despite its goal of Native American education, Dartmouth produced only three Native American graduates in the 18th century.

Further reading: Colin G. Calloway, ed., *The World Turned Upside Down: Indian Voices from Early America* (Boston: Bedford/St. Martin's, 1994).

—Caryn E. Neumann

Wheelwright, John (1592?–1679)

The founder of Exeter, NEW HAMPSHIRE, John Wheelwright was a minister who became involved in religious controversy in early MASSACHUSETTS. He was born in Lincolnshire, England, the son of Robert Wheelwright and Katherine Mawer. A large landowner, Robert Wheelwright had the means not only to send his son to Sidney Sussex College, Cambridge, but also to leave him a substantial estate. After receiving a B.A. in 1615 and an M.A. in 1618, Wheelwright was ordained a priest and became vicar at Bilsby. A critic of the Church of England, Wheelwright lost his Bilsby living in 1632. Following the death of his first wife, Marie Storre, Wheelwright married Mary Hutchinson, a union that eventually led to an alliance with his new sister-in-law, ANNE MARBURY HUTCHINSON.

In 1636 Wheelwright and his family joined the Puritan migration to Massachusetts, where he quickly became involved in the controversy surrounding his sister-in-law. Anne Hutchinson accused the clergy of the colony, except JOHN COTTON and Wheelwright, of preaching a covenant of works. Hutchinson and her supporters promoted the appointment of her brother-in-law as a minister for the congregation in BOSTON. After a powerful minority in the congregation, led by former governor JOHN WINTHROP, blocked the appointment, Wheelwright accepted a position in Mount Wollaston.

Wheelwright, however, could not steer clear of controversy. He accepted an opportunity to give a Fast Day sermon in Boston in early 1637. Wheelwright outraged many when he argued, as had Anne Hutchinson, that too many church members knew Christ only through the good works they performed rather than acknowledging that justification came through faith alone. The province's General Court found Wheelwright guilty of sedition and banished him to New Hampshire shortly before they likewise banished his sister-in-law.

In 1644, after receiving conciliatory letters from Wheelwright, the General Court lifted his banishment. In the mid-1650s he sailed to England but returned to Massachusetts shortly after the restoration of Charles II. He became pastor at a church in Salisbury and died there in 1679. Wheelwright remains a significant figure largely because of his alliance with Anne Hutchinson, an accomplished woman who challenged a patriarchal culture.

Further reading: John Heard, *John Wheelwright, 1592–1679* (Boston: Houghton Mifflin, 1930).

—Larry Gragg

White, Andrew (1579–1656)

Known as the "Apostle of Maryland," Andrew White was a missionary to Indians and often involved in religious controversy. Born in England, he studied in France and took vows there as a Roman Catholic priest in 1605. He returned to England, where priests were prosecuted following the Gunpowder Plot. Banished, White fled to Belgium, where he became a Jesuit. He returned to London in 1612, then alternated between missionary work in that city and teaching positions on the European continent for 21 years.

In 1633 White wrote a promotional tract encouraging settlers to move to MARYLAND; he also wrote a version in Latin for the Jesuit leaders. Cecil Calvert approved both the terms that White offered to would-be settlers and his glowing descriptions of the land. In November 1633 White and two other JESUITS accompanied the first Maryland colonists. He wrote several widely circulated accounts of the voyage, EXPLORATION, and settlement, in Latin and English, describing the local vegetation and geography, using wry humor, and including information on the Indians of the area. White devoted much of his time as a missionary to Indians and to learning their languages. In 1640 he baptized Chief Chitomachon of the Canoy, along with several other important members of the tribe. Accounts of this episode appeared throughout Jesuit LITERATURE and inspired other priests to go as missionaries to the New World.

During political struggles in Maryland White was captured and sent in chains to England on charges of being a Roman Catholic priest. Acquitted because he had been forced to return to England, he fled to Belgium and started a never-completed history of Maryland. After his 1650 return to England White repeatedly requested to be allowed to visit Maryland but was refused; he died in England.

—Victoria C. H. Resnick

Whitefield, George (1714–1770)

George Whitefield was the itinerant evangelist whose preaching spread the religious revival known as the GREAT AWAKENING throughout British America. From his native Britain he made several voyages to North America, preaching to open-air crowds from MASSACHUSETTS to GEORGIA to proclaim a message of spiritual rebirth and personal salvation.

Born in Gloucester, England, Whitefield attended Pembroke College, Oxford. There he met Charles and JOHN WESLEY and joined the "Holy Club," a group of men who followed John Wesley's method of focused scriptural study and prayer. One evening as he studied, he suddenly felt an overwhelming sense of God's presence, pardon, and love—a spiritual rebirth. This experience transformed his religious life and became the central core of his preaching. His description of this conversion, *A Short Account of God's Dealings with the Reverend Mr. George Whitefield* (Philadelphia, 1740), was widely sold in Britain and America.

Whitefield was ordained a deacon in the Church of England in 1736, and two years later he followed the Wesley brothers to Georgia. Although they had left by the time that Whitefield arrived, he became active in the new colony, preaching and starting schools in SAVANNAH and outlying settlements. After four months Whitefield returned to England to raise funds to establish an orphanage in Georgia.

George Whitefield *(Library of Congress)*

On January 14, 1739, Bishop Martin Benson ordained Whitefield an Anglican priest. However, his evangelistic emphasis on spiritual rebirth and his collecting money for personal causes angered the established clergy, and Church of England pulpits generally were closed to him. He preached in public halls and outdoors, with crowds growing as his oratorical fame spread.

Returning to North America in 1739 with funds and supplies for the Georgia orphanage, he spent most of this visit as an itinerant evangelist, preaching at stops from PHILADELPHIA southward along the East Coast. Arriving in Georgia in January 1740, he opened the orphanage (Bethesda) and settled many orphans there, although angering some people by wresting the children from families already pledged to care for them. In CHARLESTON Whitefield became involved in a preaching duel with the Church of England commissary, Reverend Alexander Garden. Both men's attacks were subsequently published, adding to the enmity between Anglicans and Whitefield.

The remainder of his life followed a similar pattern. He made six more visits to North America, generally collecting funds for the orphanage and visiting the major urban centers from BOSTON to Savannah. Often he traveled on horseback, preaching daily to crowds gathered in open fields. His eloquent voice and uncanny ability to speak to the needs of his audience inspired and enthused the crowds. He was clear about his own mission: He had come to plant; others would water and reap the harvest. Skillfully using advertising techniques, he provided newspapers with his itinerary and articles on his preaching campaigns in Britain. He steadily produced printed works and corresponded with a network of evangelical clergymen, sending them notices of his latest publications and sermons. Even opposition from major church leaders expanded into pamphlets that attracted notoriety.

His message was consistent. God was spreading across the Atlantic world a "GREAT AWAKENING" to the power of spiritual rebirth. Diligent biblical study was the means by which individuals might appropriate that new birth for themselves; its reality would become evident in amended lives. In this he remained theologically a Calvinist, stressing that though no one had the certainty of God's "election" (salvation), the proclamation of God's love should be made available to all.

Recent scholars stress the importance of Whitefield's work in enabling revolutionary discourse. His travels throughout the colonies and his refusal to be identified with a particular church or sect provided a unifying vocabulary. The effectiveness of his preaching in arousing individual action inspired a later generation of patriot orators. His message of individual empowerment and his castigation of religious leaders who had abandoned their ecclesiastical responsibilities gave courage to common people who would later hold governors, even the king himself, accountable for their misdeeds.

Whitefield died in Newburyport, Massachusetts, in the midst of a revival journey through New England. His collected works were published after his death.

Further reading: Frank Lambert, *"Pedlar in Divinity": George Whitefield and the Transatlantic Revivals* (Princeton: Princeton University Press, 1994).

—Mary Sudman Donovan

Wigglesworth, Edward (1693–1765)

Edward Wigglesworth was born in Malden, MASSACHUSETTS, the son of MICHAEL WIGGLESWORTH, a Puritan minister and author of the popular 1662 poems *The Day of Doom* and *Sybel Sparhawk.* He was educated at Boston Latin School and HARVARD COLLEGE, graduating from the latter in 1710. After a decade of preaching at several churches and teaching at Boston Latin School, Wigglesworth became Harvard's first Hollis Professor of Divinity in 1721. Nine years later he received a doctorate in divinity from Edinburgh University in Scotland. Following the death of his first wife, Sarah Leverett, he married Rebecca Coolidge. The couple had four children.

Wigglesworth remained at Harvard for the rest of his life, twice declining the rectorship of YALE COLLEGE. Despite increasing deafness, he had a distinguished career as an educator and theologian. He also served several years as a commissioner for London's Society for Propagating the Gospel among Indians. The mid-18th-century evangelical movement known as the GREAT AWAKENING posed a particular challenge to "Old Light" theologians like Wigglesworth. Intensely critical of itinerant ministers like the famed Englishmen GEORGE WHITEFIELD, Wigglesworth charged that such men caused considerable religious disorder with their emphasis upon emotion and enthusiasm, views he published in *A Letter to the Reverend Mr. George Whitefield* (1745).

Although he railed against the "New Light" ministers, Wigglesworth was willing to reconsider his own religious views, and an examination of his published sermons and pamphlets reveals a shift away from predestination, the notion that God arbitrarily determined one's salvation. Over time he began to embrace Arminian beliefs, acknowledging the free will of individuals and the importance of good works in assuring salvation. This is most evident in a work he published very late in life, *The Doctrine of Reprobation* (1763). Wigglesworth was also involved in an important public policy debate. In 1720 he published a number of letters in opposition to a proposed land bank scheme to improve farmers' access to credit, a proposal Wigglesworth believed would lead to crippling indebtedness. Despite his opposition, Massachusetts instituted a land bank two decades later. Still, Wigglesworth's was an important voice in the religious and secular controversies in 18th-century Massachusetts.

Further reading: Perry Miller, *The New England Mind: From Colony to Province* (Cambridge, Mass.: Harvard University Press, 1953).

—Larry Gragg

Wigglesworth, Michael (1631–1705)

Michael Wigglesworth was a popular religious poet who warned the PURITANS to follow their God. Born in England, he immigrated with his family in 1638, settling in New Haven, CONNECTICUT. CHILDHOOD illness left him physically unwell for the rest of his life. Wigglesworth was educated at HARVARD COLLEGE and taught there briefly.

In 1654 he moved to Malden, MASSACHUSETTS, to serve as minister. He preached there for several years without being ordained. Wigglesworth's diary from this time describes his confusion, illnesses, sexual desires, and doubts about his calling. Marriage to a cousin, Mary Reyner, in 1656 and the birth of a daughter helped ease his mind, as did living with his mother and sister. At last ordained in 1657, ill health frequently necessitated the hiring of substitute preachers.

The 1659 death of his wife and troubles with his parish in 1661 led Wigglesworth to write "The Day of Doom." This lengthy poem vividly describes the horrors of Judgment Day for the community according to Puritan doctrine, using familiar scriptural passages and millennial fears. Written in common meter and using an internal rhyme scheme, it is easy to memorize, as many did; for more than a century, "The Day of Doom" was the most popular poem in New England.

Profits from this work permitted Wigglesworth to visit Bermuda, where he studied medicine and attempted to regain his health. He returned to Malden a year later to find that his congregation had hired a replacement, so he became the town doctor. Wigglesworth continued writing; his best known work from this period, "Meat Out of the Eater" (1669), emphasizes the instruction of individual souls, arguing that affliction is a purifying experience.

In 1679 Wigglesworth scandalized Malden by marrying his much younger housekeeper and subsequently fathering six children; he married a third time in 1791. His health and spirits improved, and in 1686 Wigglesworth returned to the pulpit, remaining there until his death.

Further reading: David D. Hall, *Worlds of Wonder, Days of Judgment* (New York: Knopf, 1989).

—Victoria C. H. Resnick

Willard, Samuel (1640–1707)

Part of the second generation of New England PURITANS, Samuel Willard promoted and defended orthodoxy in an era of change. Born in Concord, MASSACHUSETTS, to Simon and Mary Willard, Samuel entered HARVARD COLLEGE in 1655. In 1663 he began preaching at Groton. A year later Samuel wed Abigail Sherman, who bore him six children. Widowed in 1676, Willard married Eunice Tyng in 1679 and fathered 14 more children. When Groton was destroyed in 1675 during KING PHILIP'S WAR, Willard moved to BOSTON and soon joined the South Church. After a brief span as copastor, Willard became a full minister in the church in 1678.

A conservative, Willard championed the New England theocracy and did much to obstruct the inroads of BAPTISTS and QUAKERS. He saw Antinomianism as a distortion of the essential elements of Christianity, such as revelation, and in his preachings he sought to preserve the balance of divine sovereignty and human responsibility. His major concern was to devise a system by which checks and balances would preserve the cause of orthodoxy. To protect the faith, Willard tried to halt the excesses of the 1692 Salem witch trials by urging caution in the accusing individuals and by arguing that greater evidence than suspected WITCHCRAFT was needed for prosecutions. Unable to stop the hysteria at Salem, Willard sought to atone for the hangings by arranging a day of humiliation. A prolific author, he produced 50 works, including *Covenant Keeping* (1682), an exploration of the key elements of Puritanism, *Heavenly Merchandise* (1686), an examination of the meaning of truth, and *A Compleat Book of Divinity* (1726), a full statement of the Puritan synthesis. Always interested in strengthening orthodoxy, Willard helped secure a charter for Harvard College that would protect the interests of Puritanism. In 1701 he became the president of the college. Shortly before his death Willard prepared a number of sermons on the sacraments that elaborated upon traditional views. Among other points, he argued that the second commandment established the ministry, and therefore public maintenance of the church (opposed by Quakers) was not a human choice but a divine order.

Further reading: Seymour Van Dyken, *Samuel Willard 1640–1707: Preacher of Orthodoxy in an Era of Change* (Grand Rapids, Mich.: Eerdmans, 1972).

—Caryn E. Neumann

Williams, Roger (1603?–1683)

The founder of the RHODE ISLAND colony, Roger Williams was an advocate for the cause of religious liberty in colonial New England. Likely born in 1603, Williams spent the majority of his life embroiled in controversy and exile. After graduating from Pembroke College of Cambridge University (1627), Williams accepted an Anglican post as the private chaplain of William Masham. During his tenure in this position, Williams aligned with the Puritan efforts to reform the Church of England. With the threat of persecution looming for such dissenters and nonconformists, Williams followed his friend JOHN WINTHROP to the New World, landing at Nantasket, MASSACHUSETTS, on February 5, 1631. Initially excited about the arrival of the young minister, the Massachusetts Bay Colony soon lost interest in Williams due to his tendencies toward separatism—a movement of strict CONGREGATIONALISTS who questioned the piety of the established New England churches. Convinced of the illegitimacy of an established church, Williams entered a polemical war with JOHN COTTON over the issue of religious liberty. This controversy culminated in Williams's banishment from Massachusetts Bay on October 9, 1635.

After a difficult winter in the New England wilderness, Williams entered an agreement with the NARRAGANSETT to occupy a tract of land at the headwaters of Narragansett Bay. With the aid of Native American allies, Williams established the settlement of Providence, which soon became a haven for other exiles, such as ANNE MARBURY HUTCHINSON and SAMUEL GORTON. Shortly after settling at Providence, Williams assisted in founding the first Baptist church in North America (1638). Even though his adherence to the Baptist faith ended in 1639, his affiliation with Baptist principles fostered his friendship and cooperation with John Clarke, who founded a Baptist congregation at NEWPORT, Rhode Island. Hoping to secure the right to freedom of worship, Williams returned to England in 1643 to seek a charter for his fledgling colony. After a brief yet intense struggle, Williams successfully petitioned for a royal charter in March 1644 (although it was not officially signed until 1663).

With the colony's charter granted, Williams again turned his attention toward the dangers of established religion. His *Queries of Highest Consideration* (1644) addressed the hesitancy of other dissenters toward religious liberty. Williams followed this collection of 12 questions with *The Bloudy Tenent of Persecution, for Cause of Con-*

Exiled by the Massachusetts Bay Colony for his radical religious views, Roger Williams found asylum among the Narragansett Indians in what became the colony of Rhode Island. Shown is *Roger Williams and the Narragansett Indians,* an engraving by J. C. Armytage and A. H. Wray. *(Library of Congress)*

science (1644), which was received with much criticism, including public burning in London. These volumes, along with *The Bloudy Tenent Yet More Bloudy: By Mr Cottons Endeavor to Wash it White in the Blood of the Lambe* (1652) and *The Examiner Defended* (1652), relate Williams's arguments against the establishment of religion and for religious liberty.

In addition to striving for religious freedom, Williams labored on behalf of NATIVE AMERICANS both politically and religiously. In the political realm he questioned the right of the Europeans to seize Indian lands. When the Massachusetts Bay Colony banished Williams, he turned to his Native American allies, in particular the Narragansett chiefs CANONICUS and MIANTONOMO, for land. Not only did Williams believe the Native Americans owned North America, he also supported their right to worship as they pleased, as evidenced in *Christenings Make Not Christians* (1645), in which he argues against forced conversions. His interaction with Native Americans prompted Williams to publish *A Key into the Language of America* (1643). Largely due to the influence of this volume, Williams often served, albeit not always successfully, as a mediator between the colonists and the various tribes.

Further reading: Edwin S. Gaustad, *Liberty of Conscience: Roger Williams in America* (Valley Forge, Pa.: Judson Press, 1999).

—Richard A. Bailey

Wingina (Pemisapan) (unknown–1586)

Wingina was an ALGONQUIN overlord of the Albemarle and Pamlico Sound (NORTH CAROLINA) area during Raleigh's first two expeditions to establish the first English colony in America. Ruling the Roanoke Algonquin from his principal town, Dasamonquepeuc, on the mainland immediately across the sound from the Roanoke Island colony, Wingina was informally allied through kinship with the werowances of the neighboring Weapemeoc and Choanoke tribes. Wingina ruled Roanoke Island itself through his brother, the werowance Granganimeo, who hospitably greeted and feasted Philip Amadas and Arthur Barlowe, the two MARINERS dispatched by Raleigh in 1584 to reconnoiter sites for his proposed colony. When Richard Grenville's expedition arrived to establish a colony in 1584, Wingina immediately directed his people to plant crops and set fish weirs for the English in return for their trade goods. From these first friendly encounters, the English mistakenly concluded that the Indians would, in Thomas Harriot's words, come to "honour, obey, feare, and love" them.

His "love" of English trade goods and "fear" of their seemingly supernatural powers shaped Wingina's initial friendly but cautious policy toward the English. His proximity to the Roanoke colony allowed Wingina to become the intermediary for coveted English goods, which he funneled into the already existent intertribal trade networks, thereby enhancing his influence over neighboring tribes. The absence of women and children among the English and the spreading devastation of European DISEASE induced a fearful belief in Wingina—who himself became "so grievously sick that he was like to die"—that the English had risen from the dead and could kill people from a great distance with invisible bullets. Fear quickly overcame love.

Grenville's burning of the Secotan town of Aquascogok in retaliation for the theft of a silver cup and Ralph Lane's armed extortion of scarce POWHATAN foodstuffs throughout the winter of 1585–86 convinced Wingina that the English meant to deal with his people in a violent, military manner. After the deaths of Granganimeo and his "savage father" Esenore in April 1586 silenced the most powerful pro-English voices on Wingina's council, Wingina signaled a new policy of resistance by changing his name to Pemisapan. The Roanoke and the neighboring tribes withdrew from the English, broke their fish weirs, refused to plant corn for them, and eventually formulated a plot to kill Ralph Lane and the colonists. Raiding Esenore's memorial service, Lane took Skiko, the Secotan werowance's son, hostage. When Skiko eventually revealed the details of Wingina's plot, Lane and 25 armed Englishmen raided Dasemunkepeuc. Wounded in the ensuing fight, Wingina escaped. Lane's Irish servant boy pursued the werowance into the forest, emerging shortly thereafter "with Pemisapan's head in his hand." The murder of Wingina left the Roanoke temporarily leaderless but implacably hostile to the English.

Further reading: Karen Ordahl Kupperman, *Roanoke: The Abandoned Colony* (Totowa, N.J.: Rowman & Allanheld, 1984).

—James Bruggeman

Winthrop, John (1588–1649)

No other single figure is so completely identified with the Puritan movement that founded the MASSACHUSETTS Bay colony as is John Winthrop. A firm believer in the godly commonwealth of "visible saints," Winthrop was the leading figure in Massachusetts for 19 years. His history of the colony, written in the form of annals, provides a closely detailed account of the first two decades.

John Winthrop was the son of Adam Winthrop, a lawyer and the lord of the manor of Groton, and his second wife, Anne Browne, the daughter of a trader. Winthrop attended Trinity College, Cambridge, but left without taking a degree. He then became an attorney himself, being admitted to both Gray's Inn (1613) and the Inner Temple (1628), received the lordship of the manor of Groton from his father (1619), and was appointed an attorney for the Court of Wards and Liveries in London (1626). Winthrop had become a devout Puritan while still at Cambridge, and suffered along with other PURITANS in England during the restrictive era of Archbishop Laud. Winthrop decided to emigrate with his family to New England when Charles I granted a charter incorporating the governor and company of the Massachusetts Bay, and he was quickly drawn into a leadership position.

Winthrop's Puritan ideology was stated clearly in "A Model of Christian Charity," a secular sermon he delivered aboard the *Arbella,* flagship of the first fleet of Puritan immigrants in 1630. "We shall be as a city upon a hill," he warned his fellow emigrants, so that if they should fail to build their new Jerusalem properly, the entire world would see their disgrace. Winthrop helped to establish BOSTON in September of 1630 as the capital of a Puritan commonwealth. Winthrop, like most other English settlers, argued that the Puritans of Massachusetts had a legal right to the land despite the Native American inhabitants. It was, to English thinking, a vacant land "which we took peaceably, built a house upon it, and so it hath continued in our peaceable possession ever since," land the settlers had "taken and possessed as *vacuum domicilium* [which] gives us a sufficient title against all men."

Far from wanting a democracy for Massachusetts, Winthrop attempted to transfer the English concept of

CLASS to the colony. He reluctantly gave in to the pressure from the freemen of the colony to have more control of and say in the government. Political dissensions arose between Winthrop and his rival, THOMAS DUDLEY, in 1636, the same time that the Antinomian crisis of ANNE MARBURY HUTCHINSON threatened the colony. Winthrop proved successful in defending the colony's actions against her, denouncing Hutchinson, whom he called "a woman of ready wit and bold spirit." Hutchinson and her followers were banished despite the support of Governor Henry Vane and Reverend JOHN COTTON. At the same time as the Hutchinson controversy, Winthrop was accused of being too lenient with ROGER WILLIAMS; Winthrop was suspected of harboring and assisting Williams both before and after his exile from the Bay Colony.

In the same year that the Massachusetts General Court divided itself into two houses of deputies and magistrates in 1643, Winthrop finally saw realized his goal of a protective league among the New England colonies of Massachusetts, PLYMOUTH, CONNECTICUT, and New Haven, with the notable exception of RHODE ISLAND. Winthrop, however, still followed an individual course when he privately assisted the French Acadian official La Tour against his rival D'Aulnay, despite the protests of the confederation commissioners. Winthrop was singled out for impeachment in 1645 as an example of the magistrates attempting to take too much power away from the freemen. He was acquitted and delivered a secular sermon on the acceptance of liberty as instituted by God.

John Winthrop *(Library of Congress)*

Winthrop was a sometimes vain and arrogant Puritan, often at odds with those around him and deeply stung by any criticism of his actions, but he was aware of these faults and communicated them through his journal and published writings. Winthrop was also the foremost defender of Massachusetts against all perceived foes, whether other religious adherents, Crown officials, or NATIVE AMERICANS. He thought the colony should be spiritually and secularly combined in a "Godly" Puritan commonwealth.

Further reading: Richard S. Dunn, James Savage, and Laetitia Yeandle, eds., *The Journal of John Winthrop, 1630–1649* (Cambridge, Mass.: The Belknap Press of Harvard University Press, 1996); Edmund S. Morgan, *The Puritan Dilemma: The Story of John Winthrop* (New York: HarperCollins, 1958).

—Stephen C. O'Neill

Wistar, Caspar (1696–1752)

Caspar Wistar (Hans Caspar Wüster) became a colonial leader and glass manufacturer. He was born in February 1696 in Waldhilsbach, a small village in the Palatinate, in present-day Germany. The first-born son of a forester or hunter, Wistar received little formal EDUCATION. Instead, he worked for his father, hunting and fowling, until he was 17, when he began a four-year hunting apprenticeship. In 1717 the "Lord of all Lords inspired" Wistar to TRAVEL to PENNSYLVANIA.

Wistar was one of 100,000 German-speaking immigrants who arrived in British North America during the 18th century. Unlike many of these immigrants, he avoided INDENTURED SERVITUDE because he could pay for most of his transportation costs. On his arrival Wistar worked briefly for a soap maker and then apprenticed as a brass button maker. Four years after his voyage he purchased a prime city lot in PHILADELPHIA and set up shop as a brazier and a merchant. In addition to buttons, he sold dry goods, hardware, made-to-order long rifles, and German-language LITERATURE. In 1726, after joining the Society of Friends (QUAKERS), Wistar married Catherine Jansen, the daughter of prominent Quakers in Germantown. By the early 1730s he was speculating in backcountry land. In the process he provided credit to his fellow German-speaking immigrants squatting on the land, aided the Penn family in clearing land titles, and earned tremendous profits. In 1738, relying on knowledge from his forestry background and skilled European glassblowers, Wistar established the United Glass Company in Salem County, New Jersey, the business for which he is best known. In each of his enterprises Wistar succeeded by creatively adapting his European knowledge to his American circumstances. He also made shrewd use of his ethnic identity to craft a position as mediator between GERMAN IMMIGRANTS and their Anglo-American neighbors. When he died in 1752, Wistar, who still considered himself primarily a brass button maker, left his widow and his six adult children a large estate valued at 26,000 Pennsylvania pounds.

Further reading: Marianne S. Wokeck, *Trade in Strangers: The Beginnings of Mass Migration to North America* (University Park: Pennsylvania State University Press, 1999).

—Rosalind J. Beiler

witchcraft

The widespread belief in witches and witchcraft was transported to the colonies from Europe. Colonists, especially in MASSACHUSETTS and CONNECTICUT, believed in a very real devil and very real witches. It was common belief that some women and men signed the devil's book, thereby gaining power over their neighbors through sorcery. Many colonial communities had a "wise" woman or man, someone who had a store of folk knowledge and traditional MEDICINE, and these people often faced the possibility of persecution. Single women were particularly vulnerable to accusations of witchcraft, in part because they lacked much power and in part because some widows had inherited land and wealth from their husbands, placing them in an unusual situation in 17th-century New England.

Suspected witches in Europe were executed on a vast scale in both Protestant and Catholic countries. The English colonies in America copied Europe, but on a much smaller, more personal scale. Many authorities, particularly the PURITANS, took the Biblical command "Thou shall not suffer a witch to live" literally. The New England colonies witnessed 57 trials for witchcraft between 1647 and 1691, although only a few cases were tried in NEW YORK and VIRGINIA. Witchcraft cases began to occur sporadically in the colonies during the 1640s. The handful of accusations, indictments, and trials for witchcraft in Virginia and New York resulted in only one conviction, in 1655. The convicted Virginia warlock (male witch) was sentenced to 10 lashes and banishment. Authorities in Connecticut and Massachusetts, however, were more zealous, executing at least 14 people found guilty of witchcraft. The cases of witchcraft before 1692 were usually characterized by reasonably fair legal proceedings and a skeptical attitude. Even in the New England colonies, more than 70 percent of those brought to trial for witchcraft were acquitted. Trials in New England for offenses other than witchcraft usually ended in acquittal only 10 percent of the time.

The "supernatural" element of witchcraft cases made them popular topics for gossip and publishing. One particular case in BOSTON, that of the widow Glover (a Gaelic-speaking Irish Catholic) who was executed in 1688, attracted the attention of the Puritan reverend COTTON MATHER. He published a detailed account of the case, complete with descriptions of the symptoms of possession, the following year in his *Memorable Providences Relating to Witchcraft and Possessions.* He warned the people of Massachusetts of the threat of a witchcraft epidemic as punishment for running away from their former religious conviction. Mather's prediction soon came true.

The outbreak of the infamous witchcraft hysteria in Salem Village, Massachusetts, began in January 1692. A group of local girls gathered in the home of Reverend SAMUEL PARRIS, the minister of the parish. They listened to stories told by Tituba, a slave of the Parris household who was originally from Barbados. The girls joined Tituba in rituals, then, fearful of being caught after acting possessed, accused Tituba of being a witch. Tituba in turn accused two other women of being witches. Events spiraled out of control as various factors, long-standing feuds, jealousies, and family rivalries made the situation more serious. The group of girls, the "afflicted children," began accusing dozens of people, until finally more than 200 were arrested and jailed on charges of witchcraft.

Governor Sir William Phips, arriving home in Boston with Reverend INCREASE MATHER (Cotton's father) and the second Massachusetts charter in May, commissioned a special Court of Oyer and Terminer, hoping to put an end to the hysteria. The court began to try several of the accused witches, relying heavily on eyewitness testimony and "spectral evidence," which manifested its presence in the fits of screaming and frenzied behavior of the girls. The court initially found all accused witches guilty and convinced many to confess to escape the gallows by identifying other witches. Most who maintained their innocence were convicted and sentenced to death.

Indictments during the hysteria ranged from a few social outcasts to prominent and wealthy colonists, including MERCHANTS and even a minister. Seventy-five percent of those accused of witchcraft were married or widowed women between the ages of 40 and 60 years old, while most of the accusers were single adolescent girls between 11 and 20. Fourteen women and five men were convicted and executed by hanging. One older man, Giles Corey, was pressed to death by stones for not entering a plea of guilty or not guilty at his trial; his final words reportedly were "more weight." One man and three women died in jail.

This engraving depicts a Salem witchcraft trial. *(Library of Congress)*

Legal proceedings against 156 people from 24 towns had been initiated by the end of September. Several leading ministers, notably Increase Mather, began to doubt the legality of the proceedings in Salem, especially the use of the spectral evidence. Governor Phips, whose wife was among the accused, suspended the proceedings and dismissed the court. General pardons were soon issued. When the newly created Massachusetts Superior Court of Judicature (with many of the Salem court's judges) convened in January, spectral evidence was not admitted. The remaining cases were quickly acquitted and the hysteria subsided. Many jurors publicly apologized for their verdicts four years later, and in 1714 the Massachusetts legislature officially exonerated the victims.

The Salem witchcraft hysteria was the final and largest outbreak of witchcraft in the colonies. Isolated accusations would occasionally appear afterwards, in Virginia in 1706 and in PHILADELPHIA as late as 1787 (where one woman was killed), but nothing came close to the scale or the religious intensity that surrounded the Salem trials. Skepticism marked legal proceedings against witches after 1692. The lessons of Salem had apparently been learned.

Further reading: Paul Boyer and Stephen Nissenbaum, *Salem Possessed: The Social Origins of Witchcraft* (Cambridge, Mass.: Harvard University Press, 1974); John Demos, *Entertaining Satan: Witchcraft and the Culture of Early New England* (New York: Oxford University Press, 1982).

—Stephen C. O'Neill

Wolfe, James (1727–1759)

James Wolfe was the British general who captured Louisbourg and Quebec during the SEVEN YEARS' WAR, thereby helping to ensure a British victory in that conflict. Wolfe was born in Westerham, England, the elder son of General Edward Wolfe. At the age of 14, James joined the British army, in which he served with honor during the War of the Austrian Succession (1740–48) and against the Scottish pretender to the throne, Charles Edward Stuart, in 1746. Early in the Seven Years' War Wolfe was serving as a brigadier general under Major General Jeffrey Amherst when he captured the French fort at Louisbourg, Nova Scotia, in July 1758. In failing health Wolfe returned to

England, where the British political leader William Pitt promoted him to the rank of major general and returned him to Canada to lead the expedition against the French at Quebec. In June 1759 Wolfe led about 9,000 troops up the St. Lawrence River and camped on the river island of Orleans, across from Quebec. Built on a high bluff overlooking the river, the city was easy to defend. General Marquis de Montcalm, the French commander, kept his troops inside the fortress city. As a result Wolfe ordered a frontal assault east of the city on July 31, but the French repelled it. For more than a month the British siege of Quebec lingered. Finally, on September 12, Wolfe surprised Montcalm by secretly moving 5,000 soldiers up the river and onto the Plains of Abraham west of the city. Montcalm realized that he must either face the British in an open battle outside the city or be cut off by land and river. The next day the British defeated the French, and the city surrendered a few days later. However, Wolfe died of a third wound suffered in the battle, his career cut short at the age of 32. This victory essentially won the war for the British in North America, although Montreal did not fall for another year. The TREATY OF PARIS officially ended the war in 1763.

Further reading: Christopher Hibbert, *Wolfe at Quebec* (New York: Cooper Square Press, 1999).

—Doug Baker

wolves

"The wolves in Carolina are very numerous, and more destructive than [other] animal[s]," wrote naturalist MARK CATESBY in 1743. "They go in droves by night, and hunt deer like hounds, with dismal yelling cries." This was the ALGONQUIN park wolf, *Canis lupus lycaon* (sometimes called the eastern wolf and thought by many modern taxonomists to be related to the red wolf), a canid that once inhabited the broadest range of any North American subspecies. When the first Europeans arrived the range of the Algonquin wolf stretched from Hudson Bay south along the eastern seaboard to FLORIDA and west as far as eastern Minnesota, where it likely intermixed with another subspecies, the Minnesota wolf (*Canis lupus nubilus*). Today the Algonquin wolf remains confined to parts of Ontario, Quebec, and possibly northern Minnesota (although taxonomists debate the status of these wolves). Morphological and physiological measurements of extant skull specimens from the eastern seaboard demonstrate that it, like the red wolf, was smaller than most other North American subspecies.

With its "dismal yelling cries" echoing in the North American wilderness, the very wilderness that European colonists sought to transform into cultivated farmland, it should not be surprising that these settlers had essentially exterminated the wolf in the East by the 19th century. In England, homeland of many colonists, wolves had been hunted to extinction nearly a century earlier, during the reign of Henry VII (1485–1509). In Scotland wolves survived until 1743, while in Ireland populations of the animal lasted until the 1770s. In North America part of the motivation for exterminating wolves was economic. In 1610 VIRGINIA colonists brought cattle from the West Indies, while other settlers raised sheep. Legislation against killing livestock in the early years sought to ensure that the ANIMALS proliferated, but "sheep for a few years suffered greatly from the ravages of wolves," wrote one observer, and stock never reached anticipated numbers. A 1638 letter by colonist Edmund Browne succinctly explained, "Our greatest enemies are our wolves."

Colonists reacted swiftly and relentlessly against "marauding companies" of wolves. MASSACHUSETTS Bay Colony, for example, offered bounties to colonists for dead wolves throughout the 1630s and 1640s; in exchange for a severed wolf head (which constables later buried after cutting off its ears and tongue), NATIVE AMERICANS received corn and wine. In May 1645 Massachusetts Bay colonists formed a committee to "consider . . . the best ways and means to destroy the wolves which are such ravenous cruel creatures." Three years later BOSTON bought dogs "for the destruction of wolves." Similar legislation appeared in the New PLYMOUTH and Virginia colonies, where Native Americans brought in wolf heads as tribute to their new colonial masters. In 1640 RHODE ISLAND witnessed the birth of professional wolf hunters whom they paid "thirty shillings a head for every one killed." ROGER WILLIAMS led a "grand hunt" to "extirpate" the wolves of Rhode Island, but he met with limited success as wolves "continued to be a source of annoyance."

The threat of wolves in North America was more than economic, however. Eighteenth-century theologian COTTON MATHER preached to colonists that they needed to turn America's "howling wilderness" into a "fruitful field." Similarly, in 1756 John Adams wrote that once the "whole [North American] continent [had been] one of continued dismal wilderness, the haunt of wolves and bears and more savage men," but after the tilling and killing of this wilderness it had been made the "magnificent habitations of rational and civilized people." Religious pilgrims to the New World often viewed the wilderness as a place without God, and wolves, symbolic of such wilderness, were targeted as animals that needed to be extirpated. In this sense, wolf killing should be understood as part of the "errand into the wilderness." This need to extirpate wolves, moreover, later became part of the migration of white settlers into the American West, where they hunted wolves to near extinction.

Further reading: Rick McIntyre, ed., *War Against the Wolf: America's Campaign to Exterminate the Wolf* (Stillwater, Minn.: Voyageur Press, 1995).

—Brett L. Walker

women's status and rights

The status of women in the British North American colonies varied significantly according to the ethnic group and CLASS to which they belonged. Religion, region, and maturity of the colonial settlement also had an impact on women's lives.

Within European settlements English law, custom, and religion established distinct yet flexible boundaries between the roles of women and men. Men were dominant in politics and society as well as within families; they were responsible for the financial support and protection of their wives and children. Women had a constricted public role, and within the household they contributed unpaid LABOR and promised obedience to their husbands.

The GENDER ideology of early modern England contained the contradictory constructs of women's inferiority, on the one hand, and capability, on the other. The English, like other Europeans, believed that men and women had different natures, with males assuming central, dominant, and positive characteristics and females portrayed with marginal, subordinate, and negative traits. Europeans believed that women were intellectually and morally inferior to men, less able to control their passions, and more likely (as in the case of Eve) to make compacts with Satan. While females were weaker physically and mentally, their openness to the devil's deception gave them powers that men feared and sought to control.

English common law contained both the means of subordinating women and recognition of their potential strength. Under the concept of unity of person, a woman and a man became a single entity upon marriage. The husband received legal authority to act for both—to sell, buy, transfer, and bequeath property, control earnings, sue and be sued, make contracts, and act as guardian of the children. The wife, as a married woman, held the legal status called *feme covert;* she could take none of these actions independent of her husband. She did retain the right to dower, the use of one-third of the couple's real estate upon her husband's death.

If her husband became incapacitated or was absent for a long time, a woman was often expected to manage his affairs—to become a "deputy husband," as historian Laurel T. Ulrich has explained. Courts recognized the authority of women in such situations to make contracts and to carry on business regardless of whether they had a formal power of attorney. Thus, English common law placed married women in an inferior position but recognized their ability to manage family business. It further confirmed women's capacity in the *feme sole* status accorded unmarried women. *Femes soles* retained or, in the case of widows, regained the property rights that married women lost. Thus, they could legally establish businesses and support themselves and their families.

Among Eastern Woodlands Indians the lack of private ownership of land worked to women's benefit. The tribe as a whole claimed ownership rights, not individual members or families. Kinship groups, or extended families, formed the basis of Native American society and government. The heads of kinship groups chose the band's primary leaders (called SACHEMS) who, with advice, assigned fields for planting, decided where and when to hunt, managed trade and diplomacy, and judged whether to go to war. Among ALGONQUIN-speaking people the heads of extended families were usually men, as were the sachems they chose. However, in IROQUOIS culture women served as clan leaders, taking a share of political power. Iroquois society was matrilineal, with family membership passing from mother to children, and matrilocal, as the husband left his family upon marriage to live with his wife's family. A woman divorced her husband by setting his possessions outside the door; a man could divorce his wife by removing his belongings from her family's longhouse. Women elders could not speak publicly at tribal councils or serve as sachems, but they chose these political leaders and advised them on such matters as waging war.

While the family lives of slave women are difficult to reconstruct from the existing records, scholars have argued that they exercised more power within their families than did white women. As slaves, black men did not possess the economic means to provide them a foundation for claims of authority over their wives. In addition, many husbands and wives lived apart, on separate plantations in the South or in separate households in the North, further encouraging the independence of slave women. Bound women, like free women, undertook both productive and reproductive work. In addition, slave women were liable to sexual exploitation by their masters.

Work

In general, women's work roles differed from those of men and varied by class, ethnic origin, and individual need or opportunity. Except in far northern New England, where the growing season was short, East Coast Indians had a mixed economy of AGRICULTURE, gathering, FISHING, and hunting. Native American women were responsible for raising corn, squash, beans, and (where possible) TOBACCO. They also gathered nuts and fruit, built houses, made CLOTHING, took care of the children, and prepared meals, while men cleared land, hunted, fished, and protected the town from enemies. This gender division of labor was somewhat different than that of the English, who believed free women should avoid field work and thus considered Indian women's agricultural labor too onerous.

English women were primarily responsible for domestic tasks, whether they supervised servants and slaves or performed these necessary, productive chores themselves. Their workplace encompassed the house and yard. They prepared and served meals, baked bread, cared for children, built fires, carried water and waste, cleaned the house and furnishings, washed and ironed laundry, gardened, tended poultry, milked cows, and made clothing and other household articles. Some women specialized in one or more activities and traded surplus production with neighbors and shopkeepers. Women in established rural communities were more likely to produce textiles and dairy products than either frontier women, who with their husbands were too busy meeting the challenges of establishing farms, or urban women, who lacked space for spinning wheels, looms, or livestock and could readily purchase manufactured goods and foodstuffs at the market.

Colonial women took responsibility for a large part of medical care, delivering babies, treating wounds and illnesses, and administering drugs. Literate mothers taught their own children to read, and in New England towns some women opened dame schools for young girls and boys. Women throughout the provinces transmitted skills to young women in the "art, trade, and mystery" of housewifery or a specific craft such as weaving. In the ministry and law, women did not have access to formal professional training, in college or apprenticeships. They did often assist their husbands in trades and took control of businesses after their deaths. Women thus worked in shoemaking, cabinetmaking, brewing, printing, and similar CRAFTS; some ran shops, taverns, and inns.

On plantations and farms, where most women lived in colonial British America, their work varied widely by class, ethnicity, and stage of settlement. Under normal circumstances a British colonial farm woman expected to escape heavy fieldwork, except at harvest, just as her husband avoided domestic chores. However, many women and girls worked side by side with men in the fields. Immigrants to 17th-century VIRGINIA and MARYLAND included female indentured servants, who paid for the cost of their transportation by tending a master's tobacco for four or more years. In NEW JERSEY and PENNSYLVANIA servant women from England, Ireland, Scotland, and Germany spent at least part of their labor in the fields. Indeed, German farm women, whether free or bound, customarily tended and harvested crops.

Enslaved African and Native American women worked in many occupations. In areas like the Chesapeake and the Carolinas, with labor-intensive staple crops, most spent long hours performing hard physical labor raising tobacco, corn, and rice. Masters differentiated between men and women in the assignment of tasks other than ordinary fieldwork. Only men had the opportunity to become drivers and ARTISANS. Slave women, usually those too old or too young for fieldwork, served as nurses, cooks, and spinners. Both women and men performed domestic service. At the same time, female slaves were responsible for the household needs of their own families, including laundry, FOOD preparation, and sewing. In the northern colonies enslaved women engaged in a wide variety of tasks, as these colonies lacked staple crops that consumed huge amounts of agricultural labor.

Inheritance Practices

According to English common law and colonial statutes, a widow had the right of dower to one-third of the couple's real estate for use during her life. The children or other heirs, if adults, received the other two-thirds immediately and the widow's third at her death. If the husband left a will, he was obligated to grant his wife dower (otherwise she could contest the will), but he was free to distribute his personal estate as he saw fit. In regard to the rights of sons and daughters, English common law specified primogeniture, with the eldest son normally receiving all of the real estate. Most colonial parents divided their estates more evenly, attempting to provide all of their children with a start in life, whether a farm, college tuition, an apprenticeship, livestock, or cash. Sons more often received real estate, while daughters received personalty such as slaves, household furniture, or money.

Historians have measured the degree to which husbands adhered to the legal guidelines in making bequests to their wives. Lois Green Carr and Lorena S. Walsh discovered how men in 17th-century Maryland often gave their wives responsibility for managing their entire estates, including the children's share, despite the fact that widows quickly remarried and thereby ceded control of the property to their new mates. Early Maryland society was highly unstable and fragmented, with high MORTALITY and disrupted kinship networks. Husbands chose, perhaps because in their minds they had little alternative, to give greater authority to their wives than was customary in England.

In northern colonies, in contrast, more testators lived long enough to see sons reach maturity. They gave less authority to their widows and sometimes adopted a practice that was rare in the Chesapeake area: They devised all of their real estate to one or more sons and made the heirs responsible for supporting their mother. Instead of receiving her dower right of one-third of the real estate for life, the widow obtained possession of a room; the right to pass through the house to and from her room; and firewood, food, use of a horse, and a small amount of cash paid annually.

Ethnicity as well as demographic conditions influenced men's testamentary practices. In NEW YORK during the first generations after the English conquest, Dutch colonists retained the tradition of community property within marriage, that is, that the wife and husband held property jointly. Dying husbands left most or all of their possessions to their wives, who kept control during their widowhood. Sons and daughters, even if mature at the death of their father, had to wait until their mother died or remarried before receiving their inheritance. At that point the children obtained equal portions, with daughters as well as sons receiving real estate.

THE
LADY's LAW:
OR, A
TREATISE
OF
Feme Coverts:
CONTAINING
All the Laws and Statutes relating to WOMEN, under feveral HEADS:
VIZ.

I. Of Difcents of Lands to Females, Coparceners, &c.
II. Of Confummation of Marriage, ftealing of Women, Rapes, Polygamy.
III. Of the Laws of Procreation of Children; and of Baftards or fpurious Iffue.
IV. Of the Privileges of *Feme Coverts*, and their Power with refpect to their Husband, and all others.
V. Of Husband and Wife, in what Actions they are to join.
VI. Of Eftates Tail, Jointures and Settlements, real and perfonal in Women.
VII. Of what the Wife is entitled to of the Husband's, and Things belonging to the Wife, the Husband gains Poffeffion of by Marriage.
VIII. Of Private Contracts by the Wife, Alimony, feparate Maintenance, Divorces, Elopement, &c.

The SECOND EDITION.

To which is added,
Judge HIDE's very remarkable Argument in the *Exchequer-Chamber*, *Term. Trin.* 15 *Car.* 2. In the Cafe of *Manby* and *Scot*, whether, and in what Cafes, the Husband is bound by the Contract of his Wife:
And Select *Precedents* of *Conveyances* in all CASES concerning Feme Coverts.

In the *SAVOY*:
Printed by E. and R. NUTT, and R. GOSLING, (Affigns of *E. Sayer*, Efq;) for *H. L.* and Sold by C. CORBETT, at *Addifon*'s Head, and E. LITTLETON, at the *Mitre*, both againft St. *Dunftan*'s Church in *Fleetftreet*. 1737.

Shown here is the title page of a 1737 work on the legal status of women that was imported to Virginia from Britain. *(Hulton/Archive)*

Religion

The degree to which a woman could take part in religious affairs depended on her faith. In Native American communities women occasionally served as SHAMANS (priests). Indian religions often recognized both female and male characteristics in their deities. Christianity, which dominated the British settlements, was more patriarchal. In all Christian denominations women stood equal with men in the eyes of God, but the extent to which they could participate in decision making and the ministry varied widely.

Among New England PURITANS women sat separately from the men, could not speak except to sing hymns, and were allowed no leadership role. Their status improved little over the colonial period and, in fact, probably deteriorated after 1650 as they became an increasing proportion of members. Puritan women challenged these restrictions in a variety of ways. Most often they used their influence, or informal authority, to sway the church fathers. Although men alone had the right to cast votes and sign petitions for new churches, women spurred the establishment of new congregations by convincing their husbands of the need. Women of Rowley, MASSACHUSETTS, in 1674 successfully opposed the ordination of their young minister, Jeremiah Shepard, at least in part because he was disrespectful to female members. Other women challenged the 17th-century Puritan order more dramatically, expressing publicly their less-than-orthodox beliefs. Most famous was ANNE MARBURY HUTCHINSON, who in 1637 was tried for defaming ministers. She defended herself well and nearly escaped conviction but then shocked her judges by announcing that God had told her that they would be destroyed. Hutchinson was banished from the commonwealth and settled in RHODE ISLAND with family and supporters.

The ANGLICAN CHURCH also expected women to accept a subordinate role, as only men could preach, administer the sacraments, and serve on the vestry boards that were in charge of all parish business, including aid to the poor, sick, and elderly. Like Puritans, however, Anglican women wielded informal authority that emanated from their responsibility for religious practice in their families, supervising preparations for burials and marriages, most of which took place at home.

QUAKERS, on the other hand, believed that revelation did not end with the Bible and that the "inner light" could bring new understanding, which revealed that women should serve as ministers, missionaries, and leaders of the church. Quakers also denied any continuing significance of the fall of Adam and Eve, arguing that equality of women and men returned with spiritual rebirth. In their own separate monthly meetings for business, Quaker women made disciplinary decisions concerning women and girls, supervised marriages, and provided relief to the poor. While women Friends lacked complete equality with the men, because most women's meetings technically were required to seek the men's permission before disowning anyone, the men's meetings apparently always approved the women's decisions.

Women and Community

When women exercised authority in colonial British society, they did so primarily among women and girls. Middle-aged and elderly women took responsibility for the female half of the population. They observed the actions of the community's young women—not just their own daughters and granddaughters—to guard against sexual offenses and disorderly marriages. If a young girl showed signs of departing from the straight and narrow, they warned her of the consequences of sin. In the Society of Friends, women's meetings dealt most frequently with unsupervised weddings, marriages to non-Friends, fornication before marriage, and bastardy; these constituted the misdeeds of most female offenders. In Puritan New England, although elder women lacked the institutionalized power of the Quaker meetings, they took responsibility for the behavior and well-being of younger women. Everywhere in colonial British America women were barred from serving as justices or members of juries. Nevertheless, they counseled, reprimanded, and aided girls and young women who were victims or accused of crimes.

By law the woman held most accountable for reporting sexual misconduct was the midwife, a respected and mature member of the female community. She had such official and semiofficial functions as testifying in court as to whether an unmarried mother had named an infant's father during labor, reporting whether an infant was born prematurely or at full term, verifying birth dates, and examining female prisoners to determine whether they were truly pregnant or just claiming that condition to avoid punishment. More important to nurturing a community of women, however, was the midwife's role in orchestrating the activity that brought women together and excluded men—childbirth. During the colonial period professional MIDWIVES presided over most births, which a group of female relatives and neighbors also attended. Childbirth, or "travail," as the English colonists called it, was imbued with female ritual and tradition, including special bed linen, food, and paraphernalia such as the "midwife's stool."

Although elder women carried weight as the guardians of younger women and girls, they lacked political power and thus were subject, like all women, to the judgment and domination of men. In fact, elder women were most at risk of being charged with WITCHCRAFT, defined legally as making a compact or conversing with Satan. The colonists, like their Old World contemporaries, believed that God and the devil both influenced everyday events. Weak individuals, especially women, could be recruited by Satan to perform evil deeds against God's people. In the British colonies the New England governments prosecuted the great majority of witchcraft cases; this was partly the result of the centrality of religion in society. Also important was the fact that elder women, the people most at risk, were much more numerous in the Puritan colonies than elsewhere during the 17th century, when witchcraft hysteria peaked. According to historian Carol Karlsen, between 1620 and 1725 about 350 New Englanders, mostly women, faced accusations of witchcraft. The most famous episode occurred in Salem, Massachusetts, in 1692, when almost 200 people were accused and 20 persons executed for conspiring with the devil.

Gender differences also existed in the prosecution of other kinds of crime. Women were convicted of murder, theft, fraud, and assault, but at rates much lower than men. The prosecution of women most often stemmed from sexual crimes, especially fornication. A double standard existed in English law granting property rights in the chastity of women to husbands and fathers. A woman's sexual purity was valued as property, belonging to her father before marriage and her husband after, but wives and mothers had no similar rights in the chastity of men. Thus, adultery committed by a woman was considered more serious than that committed by a man. The 1648 Massachusetts legal code, for example, defined adultery, which was punishable by death, as illicit sexual relations involving a married woman. If a married man and a single woman had intercourse, they committed fornication, which was not a capital crime. In practice, magistrates reduced the charges of most people accused of adultery, and just a few were put to death for the crime. The same was true in the case of rape, which was also a capital offense in the Bay colony. Women had difficulty proving that they had not consented to the act. Men of higher status were likely to escape punishment, while white servants and black people received harsh punishment for attacks on white women. Consistent with the double standard, rapes were considered trespasses on the property rights of the assaulted woman's husband or father.

Before 1763, then, the conflicting concepts of women's capability and inferiority defined gender relations in British North America. English custom and law and Protestant theology held women responsible for guaranteeing the smooth operation of households, representing and protecting their families in the absence of husbands, and maintaining God's providence over the community, but required their subordination to men. Indian women held a higher status in their communities, as NATIVE AMERICANS respected women as full participants in the ECONOMY and in land ownership. Iroquois and some Algonquin-speaking groups practiced matrilineal descent and recognized women's leadership in politics and society. Most African-American women in pre-1763 British America were slaves, as the emancipation movement expanded only after that date. As slaves, women had little control over their work and family and were less likely than men to escape their bonds.

Further reading: Marylynn Salmon, *Women and the Law of Property in Early America* (Chapel Hill: University of North Carolina Press, 1986); Laurel Thatcher Ulrich, *Good Wives: Image and Reality in the Lives of Women in Northern New England, 1650–1750* (New York: Knopf, 1982).

—Jean R. Soderlund

Wood, William (flourished 1629–1635)

William Wood arrived in the MASSACHUSETTS Bay region in 1629 as an agent of English PURITANS who were interested in learning more about North America before they made the decision to migrate. Settling in an area that would become Lynn, he surveyed the region from Dorcester to the Merrimack River, taking extensive notes on the region's Indian inhabitants, including their physical appearance and economic habits, as well as the region's topography and natural resources. Wood was also an enthusiastic entrepreneur who traveled widely up and down the coast in support of Massachusetts's early FISHING ventures and burgeoning trade with the natives.

When he returned to England in 1633, Wood became particularly well known for a book that he published in London in 1639 called *New England's Prospect: A True, Lively, and Experimental Description of that Part of America commonly called New England.* He wrote, "To enter into a serious discourse concerning the natural disposition of these Indians might procure admiration from the people of any civilized nations, in regard of their civility and good natures." *New England's Prospect* also included a rare map of the New England coast, entitled "The South Part of New England, as it is planted this yeare, 1634," which became a very accurate guide for many migrants. Together, Wood's account and map played an important role in fueling the great migration of Puritan families to the Massachusetts Bay Colony.

—James E. McWilliams

Woolman, John (1720–1772)

John Woolman was born to a prosperous Quaker farm family in Burlington County, NEW JERSEY. He became a shopkeeper, tailor, and schoolteacher rather than follow his father's occupation of farming. He focused early in his life on spiritual matters, becoming a Quaker lay minister at age 22.

Influenced by Quaker theology that God's spirit, or the "inner light," could enter everyone regardless of ethnicity or gender, Woolman devoted his life to eradicating SLAVERY. He first indicated his concern when, in his early 20s, his employer asked him to write a bill of sale for an enslaved woman. Although slaveholding was common in his neighborhood, Woolman became committed to the antislavery cause during a 1746 ministerial journey to MARYLAND, VIRGINIA, and NORTH CAROLINA. Upon his return home he wrote *Some Considerations on the Keeping of Negroes; Recommended to the Professors of Christianity of Every Denomination* (1754) but delayed submitting it to the PHILADELPHIA Yearly Meeting overseers of the press because he expected opposition from prominent slaveholding Friends who served on the committee. The essay gently reminded masters of the rule "not to do that to another which . . . we would not have done to us," then warned prophetically of God's wrath if owners refused to free their slaves. This essay, along with the 1754 epistle of the Philadelphia Yearly Meeting that he probably assisted ANTHONY BENEZET in drafting, swayed Quaker opinion against the SLAVE TRADE and later slavery itself.

From 1746 to 1772 Woolman made numerous journeys throughout the mainland British colonies and collaborated with Benezet and other abolitionists to strengthen Friends' discipline against black bondage. He served on a Philadelphia Yearly Meeting committee to visit every Quaker slave owner in the DELAWARE Valley. He cut back his retail business when it became too time consuming, stopped wearing dyed CLOTHING because of the use of slave LABOR in producing dyes, and sometimes traveled by foot on his ministerial journeys. He tried to live simply because he recognized that luxury for some demanded the exploitation of others. In 1762 Woolman published *Considerations on Keeping Negroes: Part Second,* then recommended monetary restitution to former slaves or their heirs in his remarkable essay *A Plea for the Poor* (1793), published posthumously.

In his *Journal* (1774) and essays Woolman addressed many issues, including EDUCATION, violence and war, injustice toward Indians, and the sinfulness of greed and ostentation. He was particularly insightful in linking the expropriation of Indians, "the offspring of those ancient possessors of the country (in whose eyes we appear as newcomers)," with the oppression of slaves, particularly through the sale of rum made from West Indies sugarcane. The focus of his energies and his enduring legacy remained unequivocal opposition to slavery. In 1772 Woolman died of SMALLPOX at York while visiting England and thus witnessed neither the Quaker prohibition of slave ownership in the mid-1770s nor the gradual emancipation movement in the northern United States.

See also ABOLITIONISM; QUAKERS.

Further reading: Phillips P. Moulton, ed., *The Journal and Major Essays of John Woolman* (New York: Oxford University Press, 1971).

—Jean R. Soderlund

Wyatt, Sir Francis (1588–1644)

Sir Francis Wyatt served as governor of Virginia from 1621 to 1626 and again from 1639 to 1641. During Wyatt's first term in office, in 1624, Parliament revoked the Virginia Company's charter, thus making him the colony's first royal governor. Wyatt was an able administrator and guided the colony through some of its most difficult trials, including an Indian rebellion in 1622 and the plague of 1622–23, both of which claimed thousands of colonists' lives. Wyatt was also an outspoken advocate for the colony, and he openly criticized company officials for their unreasonable demands and general ignorance of conditions in the colony. He also made repeated appeals to the king for the restoration of Virginia's charter rights, an effort that eventually bore fruit in 1639. Wyatt's second term, largely taken up with matters of TOBACCO regulation, was cut short by the outbreak of the ENGLISH CIVIL WAR in 1641. Charles I, desiring a more compliant representative in Virginia, removed Wyatt in favor of SIR WILLIAM BERKELEY.

Further reading: Wesley Frank Craven, *The Southern Colonies in the Seventeenth Century, 1607–1689* (Baton Rouge: University of Louisiana Press, 1949).

—Kenneth A. Deitreich

Yale, Elihu (1649–1721)

Born in BOSTON to American colonists who returned to England in 1651, Elihu Yale was educated in London. In 1670 he went to India in the service of the East India Company in Madras (now Chennai) and rose to the position of governor of the company at Fort St. George in 1682. His work contributed to the consolidation of British power on the subcontinent. A financial scandal within his administration caused his removal as governor in 1692. He returned to England in 1699, having amassed a large fortune from his private trading ventures, and became a high sheriff in 1704. Yale was a generous donor to schools, churches, and missionary societies. In 1718 COTTON MATHER wrote him suggesting the need for a benefactor after whom the Collegiate School of Saybrook, CONNECTICUT, might be named. Yale responded with a gift of nine bales of East India Company goods, which the college sold for 562 British pounds to buy books and erect its new building at New Haven. In 1718 the school was renamed YALE COLLEGE. This was the largest private gift to a college up to that time.

—Deborah C. Taylor

Yale College

The "Collegiate School within his Majesties Colony of Connecticot" was founded in 1701 by a group of ministers, including COTTON MATHER, the influential Puritan theologian and writer. Designed to maintain order and tradition, early American colleges followed the English system of training young upper-CLASS men for the ministry and for service to the state. Ministers taught theological and classical studies accompanied by strict discipline. The first classes were held at the home of Rector Abraham Pierson in Killingworth, CONNECTICUT, then moved to Saybrook in 1707. In 1716 the Collegiate School moved to its permanent home in New Haven. Two years later the college was renamed in honor of ELIHU YALE, who responded to a request for donations from Mather. Yale, born in BOSTON and educated in England, was a wealthy East India Company trader, British civil servant, and philanthropist. He sent nine bales of East India Company goods to New Haven that the college then sold for 562 British pounds to buy books and buildings. In 1731 George Berkeley donated books and his RHODE ISLAND farm to provide further support for the school. The present charter for Yale College, now University, was drawn up in 1745.

—Deborah C. Taylor

Yeardley, Sir George 1587–1627)

George Yeardley served as an early governor of VIRGINIA, and he arranged the purchase of the first African slaves in British North America. Born in the Southwark borough of London, England, the son of Ralph Yeardley and Rhoda Marston, Yeardley became a ward of Sir Henry Peyton, his godfather, after his parents died in 1601. Peyton arranged a military apprenticeship, which Yeardley served in the Netherlands. Attaining the rank of captain, he sailed for Virginia in 1609. Delayed by shipwreck, he did not arrive until May 1610. Yeardley served various officials in a military capacity until 1616, when he became deputy governor to Thomas West, baron De La Warr. West spent most of his time in England, leaving Yeardley to govern Virginia until Samuel Argall replaced him on May 15, 1617.

Yeardley returned to England, when he married Temperance Flowerdieu. On November 18, 1618, he was appointed governor of Virginia for a three-year term and knighted by King James I (1603–25) on November 22. Yeardley returned to Virginia to institute a new government that included an assembly comprised of his council and eight elected burgesses. The Virginia Company instructed Yeardley to distribute land to individuals, which, combined with the growth of TOBACCO cultivation, created demand for laborers. Yeardley worked to bring English indentured servants to the colony while governor. He also organized buying the first African slaves in British North America in

1619 as well as purchasing brides for the colony's predominantly male settlers. He became wealthy and one of the largest owners of servants in Virginia. Yeardley died after being reappointed governor.

Further reading: Edmund S. Morgan, *American Slavery, American Freedom: The Ordeal of Colonial Virginia* (New York: Norton, 1975).

—Eugene VanSickle

yellow fever

One of the most horrific diseases to plague the coastal cities of colonial America was yellow fever. Considered a common CHILDHOOD DISEASE in AFRICA, the yellow fever virus came to the New World on slave ships along with the *Aëdes aegypti* mosquito —the insect vector required for transmission. This mosquito preferred living in urban environments, breeding in water-filled artificial containers provided for them by their human hosts. Once infected by this winged vector, patients often suffered high fevers, pains in head, back, and legs, nausea and vomiting, and acute exhaustion. The most serious cases displayed the classic signs of yellow fever: jaundice, black vomit (partially digested blood), and liver or kidney failure. Eventually, many patients slipped into comas, dying from a series of organ failures, internal bleeding, and shock. Survivors, however, enjoyed immunity for life.

Medical historians believe the first yellow fever outbreak in the colonies occurred in the summer of 1693, when the British fleet carried it from Barbados to the port city of BOSTON. The *Aëdes aegypti* survived in the water barrels on board ship and kept the infection in circulation by biting nonimmune soldiers and sailors. Although colonial officials instituted a strict quarantine, yellow fever spread into the city. The Native American population, already decimated by other foreign diseases, lived well inland and were thus spared from another new deadly epidemic. Although unaware of how the disease was spread, officials noted that the fever abruptly ended with the advent of cold weather.

Other colonial cities along the eastern seaboard also suffered from yellow fever epidemics. NEW YORK CITY suffered epidemics in 1702 and then on three occasions in the 1740s—1743, 1745, and 1748. In the mid-Atlantic region PHILADELPHIA lost one in six citizens in its 1699 epidemic. It again suffered in 1741, 1747, and 1762. CHARLESTON, a semitropical port city where mosquitoes thrived, endured more epidemics than northern cities. Yellow fever attacked there at least seven times in less than 50 years. The first epidemic struck in 1699, but others followed it in 1703, 1728, 1732, 1739, 1745, and 1748. During the epidemics of the 1740s, West Indian and southern colonial physicians noted that few African slaves sickened or died. They asserted "black" immunity quite erroneously because few American-born slaves experienced yellow fever as a childhood disease, especially in northern seaport towns. After 1748 only Philadelphia in the summer of 1762 had confirmed cases of yellow fever until the 1790s. When yellow fever returned to Philadelphia in 1793, it killed more than 4,000 people and brought the nation's capital to a standstill.

Further reading: John Duffy, *Epidemics in Colonial America* (Baton Rouge: Louisiana State University Press, 1953, 1971).

—Anita DeClue

Youngs, John (1623–1698)

A political agitator and power broker on Long Island, John Youngs was born in April 1623 in Southwold, England, to Joan Herrington Youngs and the Reverend John Youngs, a Puritan minister. His teen years were spent on the move as his family secretly left England, settled briefly in MASSACHUSETTS and CONNECTICUT, and then crossed the Long Island Sound to found the town of Southold on eastern Long Island. Living on land claimed by both Dutch and English, Youngs looked for direction at first from the colony of New Haven and later from Connecticut. The New England colonies enlisted Youngs in 1655 to command a vessel of observation in the Long Island Sound that monitored a group of NARRAGANSETT who threatened to attack the Montauk on Long Island. Eight years later Youngs marched with a band of English raiders who swept Long Island "making a great uproar with colors flying, drums beating, and trumpets sounding" to inform the Dutch population that Long Island belonged to the English. Captain Youngs in particular was singled out by the Dutch as the man who threatened to burn a Dutch village to the ground. In 1664 Youngs participated in the English conquest of NEW NETHERLAND.

With the Dutch obstacle eliminated, Youngs began anew his campaign to place Long Island within the colony of Connecticut, whose religious and ethnic composition and representative government were undoubtedly more appealing to Youngs and his constituents. Nevertheless, Long Island became part of the new colony of NEW YORK and remained so even after Youngs used the brief Dutch reconquest of 1673 and the GLORIOUS REVOLUTION of 1689 to swing the island back to Connecticut.

Youngs served his community as magistrate, deputy, high sheriff, boundary commissioner, and colonel of the militia. He was a member of the panel of judges that convicted Jacob Leisler of treason. Youngs spent his last 12 years on the governor's council and died in 1698.

—Judy VanBuskirk

Z

Zeisberger, David (1721–1808)

Born in Moravia, David Zeisberger joined the PENNSYLVANIA Moravian community in 1739 and trained as a missionary. He spent most of his life as a missionary to NATIVE AMERICANS. Blessed with extraordinary linguistic skills, he learned to speak many Indian languages, including Mohawk, Onondaga, and DELAWARE, and was adopted into the Onondaga IROQUOIS nation. Zeisberger served as an interpreter for Moravian church officials during their visits to the Indian nations of Pennsylvania and NEW YORK. In 1763 he accompanied 125 Delaware converts who had been ordered to PHILADELPHIA by the governor. One convert had been accused of murder, and the PAXTON BOYS had threatened to kill all the converts. The accused was acquitted in 1764, and the surviving Moravian Delaware and their missionaries were released from protective custody in 1765.

As a missionary Zeisberger followed the Moravian Church's guidelines. Male and female converts, in the role of assistants, helped run the MISSIONS, approving new residents and new candidates for baptism and communion. Women assistants were responsible for ministering to female converts. Zeisberger made it very clear that race was not important, culture was. There were "white Indians" (white Americans who had been captured, usually as children, by Native Americans) at his missions, and he always referred to them and treated them as Indians. One of his own white Moravian assistants married an Indian convert, was adopted into her nation, and consequently "became" an Indian to Zeisberger. Zeisberger's only requirement for conversion was religious conversion; he left all other social constructs alone. Zeisberger's greatest accomplishments occurred after the Revolution, when he founded several villages in Ohio.

Further reading: Earl P. Olmstead, *David Zeisberger: A Life Among the Indians* (Kent, Ohio: Kent State University Press, 1997).

Zenger, John Peter (1697–1746)

John Peter Zenger, a journalist and printer, was involved in an important political court case that had implications for freedom of the press in early America. He was born in the German Palatinate and came to North America in 1710 with a group of refugees sponsored by NEW YORK's incoming governor, Robert Hunter. Zenger was apprenticed to New York printer WILLIAM BRADFORD. In 1719 he set up a printing shop in MARYLAND, but by 1723 he was back in New York working for Bradford. After 1726 he tried, with little success, to compete with his former master. In 1732 and 1733 he joined with LEWIS MORRIS and a group of dissident New York politicians who were trying to end the tenure of that colony's new governor, William Cosby. In 1733 Zenger became the printer and publisher of the *New-York Weekly Journal,* which competed with Bradford's *New-York Gazette* and which featured political satire and criticism of Cosby. James Alexander, a lawyer and ally of Morris's, was the real editor of the newspaper. Zenger printed furiously critical essays of Alexander, Morris, and their associates as well as texts borrowed from English "opposition" authors opposed to the Whig hegemony of Robert Walpole. This development illustrates the increasing attractiveness to American political thinkers of "Commonwealth" or republican political ideas, a phenomenon that continued into the Revolutionary era. Cosby and his allies at first tried to ignore Zenger's jibes, then to ridicule and intimidate their authors, and finally to suppress them. Issues of the *Weekly Journal* were publicly burned, and in late 1734 Zenger was charged with seditious libel against the government. When the case came to trial in 1735 Cosby and New York's chief justice, James DeLancey, tried to rig the proceedings by disbarring Zenger's attorney, Alexander, and by manipulating the jury selection process. They were frustrated by Alexander's old friend ANDREW HAMILTON, a PHILADELPHIA lawyer, who persuaded a jury—over the state's strong objections and to the dismay of DeLancey—that public statements that were "true" could not be libelous. Zenger was acquitted, and, after a brief period as a symbolic hero, he spent the rest of his life as a relatively obscure printer and publisher. For a long time it was believed that his trial was a landmark in the evolution of American libel and free speech jurisprudence, but scholars have largely abandoned that interpretation. Instead, they recognize the Zenger case as an early and important example of the "political trial" in America.

Further reading: Stanley N. Katz, ed., *A Brief Narrative of the Case and Trial of John Peter Zenger: Printer of the New York Weekly Journal* (Cambridge, Mass.: Harvard University Press, 1972); Leonard W. Levy, *Emergence of a Free Press* (New York: Oxford University Press, 1985).

—Wayne Bodle

Chronology

1606–1700
Dutch monopolize slave trade.

1606
Virginia Companies of London and Plymouth receive patents to colonize lands in North America.

1607
English settlement established at Jamestown.

1608
Champlain founds Quebec.

1613–14
Rolfe experiments with tobacco and marries Pocahontas.

1616–21
European diseases decimate Native American population in New England.

1617
Tobacco first shipped from Virginia.

1619
Africans arrive and are sold in Virginia.

House of Burgesses, the first elected colonial legislature, meets in Virginia.

1620
Pilgrims adopt Mayflower Compact and land at Plymouth.

1622
Opechancanough and Powhatan tribes attack Virginia settlements.

1624
Dutch colonize mouth of Hudson River.

British king assumes control of Virginia.

1626
Minuit establishes New Amsterdam.

1630
Puritan migration to Massachusetts Bay begins.

1632
Lord Baltimore (George Calvert) receives land grant to establish Maryland.

1633–34
New England Native Americans again attacked by European diseases.

1635
Williams is banished to Rhode Island.

Virginia's Council deports Governor John Harvey, thereby challenging the power of officials appointed by the Crown.

1636
Hutchinson is banished from the Massachusetts Bay Colony.

Williams founds Providence.

Hooker establishes Hartford.

1637
New England colonists wage war against the Pequot Indians.

1638
Minuit founds New Sweden.

1640s
New England merchants begin their engagement in the African slave trade.
Virginia forbids black residents to carry guns.

1642–49
English Civil War halts the great Puritan migration to New England.

1643
Massachusetts, Plymouth, Connecticut, and New Haven establish the first intercolonial union, the United Colonies of New England.

1644
Opechancanough's second attack on colonial Virginians.

1650–1670
Judicial and legislative decisions in the Chesapeake colonies harden racial differences.

1651
Parliament passes the first Navigation Act.

1659–61
Puritans execute four Quakers in Boston.

1660
Charles II restored to the English throne.
Parliament passes new Navigation Act.

1662
Half-Way Covenant is introduced in New England.

1663
Eight proprietors receive the first Carolina charter.

1664
English capture New Netherland and rename it New York.
Royal grant of the Jersey lands to proprietors.

1665
New Jersey becomes a separate colony.

1670
First permanent English settlement in South Carolina.

1673–85
French expand into Mississippi Valley.

1675–76
King Philip's War is fought in New England.

1677
The Laws, Concessions and Agreements for West New Jersey provide for the most democratic government of any colony.

1676
Bacon's Rebellion begins in Virginia.

1680–1700
Transition from white indentured servants to black slave laborers begins in Chesapeake.

1680
Charleston established.
Pueblo Revolt in New Mexico.

1681
William Penn receives Pennsylvania charter.

1682
La Salle explores the Mississippi River and claims Louisiana for France.

1684
Massachusetts charter is revoked.

1685–1715
Stagnation takes hold in the tobacco market.

1686
Dominion of New England is established.

1688–89
Glorious Revolution occurs in England.

1689
Leisler's Rebellion breaks out in New York.
Overthrow of Governor Andros in New England takes place.
As a result of the Glorious Revolution, royal governors are removed in Massachusetts, New York, and Maryland.

1689–97
King William's War is fought.

1691
Leisler is executed in New York.

1692
Witchcraft hysteria occurs in Salem; 19 people are executed.

1696
Parliament creates Board of Trade.

1699
French establish Louisiana.

1700
Spanish install first mission in Arizona.

1701
First colonial unicameral legislature meets in Pennsylvania.
Iroquois establish a policy of neutrality among European nations.

1702–13
Queen Anne's War is fought.

1704
The first colonial newspaper, the *Boston News-Letter*, is published.

1705
Virginia adopts a comprehensive slave code.

1707
English–Scottish union creates kingdom of Great Britain.

1712
Slaves revolt in New York City.

1713
Peace of Utrecht ends Queen Anne's War.
Scots-Irish and German immigration to North America begins.

1715–30
Volume of African slave trade doubles.

1715
Yamasee War devastates South Carolina.

1716
Spanish begin to colonize Texas.

1718
French establish New Orleans.

1720s
Black population begins to increase naturally.

1721
Smallpox variolation (inoculation) is introduced in Boston.

1732
Georgia charter is granted by Parliament.

1733
Molasses Act is passed.

1734–36
Great Awakening begins in Northampton, Massachusetts.

1735
Zenger is acquitted of seditious libel in New York.

1739
Slaves revolt in Stono, South Carolina, occurs.
Whitefield's first American visit spreads the Great Awakening.

1740s
Indigo becomes a major crop in the Lower South.

1741
Slave conspiracy in New York City takes place.

1744–48
King George's War is fought.

1747
Benjamin Franklin publishes the first *Poor Richard's Almanack*.
A major riot in Boston breaks out against impressment by the Royal Navy.

1754
The first congress of all the colonies meets at Albany and agrees on a Plan of Union (which the British government rejects).

1755
Braddock is defeated by the Indians and their French allies.
British exile Acadians from Nova Scotia.

1756–63
Seven Years' War is fought.

1758
British seize Fort Duquesne, Fortress Louisbourg, and Fort Frontenac.

1759
Wolfe dies while defeating the French at Quebec.

1760–61
Cherokee War is fought against the colonists in South Carolina.

1760
French Canada surrenders to the British.

Africans account for 20 percent of the inhabitants in the colonies.

1760s
Economic depression occurs in many colonies.

Spanish found California mission system.

1763
Treaty of Paris ends Seven Years' War.

Proclamation of 1763 legally limits westward expansion of colonists.

Documents

Governor John Winthrop, "Model of Christian Charity" (1630)

The Winthrop Papers (Boston: Massachusetts Historical Society), Vol. 2, pp. 282–295

1. For the persons, we are a Company professing ourselves fellow members of Christ. . .

2. for the work we have in hand, it is by mutual consent through a special overruling providence, and more than an ordinary approbation of the Churches of Christ to seek out a place of Cohabitation and Consortship under a due form of Government both civil and ecclesiastical. . . .

3. The end is to improve our lives to do more service to the Lord the comfort and increase of the body of christ whereof we are members that ourselves and posterity may be the better preserved from the Common corruptions of this evil world. . . .

4. for the means whereby this must be effected, they are 2fold, a Conformity with the work and end we aim at, these we see are extraordinary, therefore we must not content ourselves with usual ordinary means whatsoever we did or ought to have done when we lived in England, the same must we do and more also where we go: That which the most in their Churches maintain as a truth in profession only, we must bring into familiar and constant practice, as in this duty of love we must love brotherly without dissimulation, we must love one another with a pure heart fervently we must bear one another's burdens, we must not look only on our own things, but also on the things of our brethren, neither must we think that the lord will bear with such failings at our hands as he doth from those among whom we have lived. . . .

. . . [F]or we must Consider that we shall be as a City upon a Hill, the eyes of all people are upon us; so that if we shall deal falsely with our god in this work we have undertaken and so caused him to withdraw his present help from us, we shall be made a story and a by-word through the world, we shall open the mouths of enemies to speak evil of the ways of god and all professors for God's sake; we shall shame the faces of many of gods worthy servants, and cause their prayers to be turned into Curses upon us till we be consumed out of the good land whether we are going.

John Mason's Account of the Puritan-Pequot War (1637)

David J. Rothman and Sheila M. Rothman, eds. *Sources of the American Social Tradition* (New York: Basic Books, 1975), pp. 32–35

To the Honourable the General Court of Connecticut

Honoured Gentlemen, . . .

In the Beginning of May 1637 there were sent out by Connecticut Colony Ninety Men under the Command of Capt. John Mason against the Pequots, with Onkos an Indian Sachem living at Mohegan, who was newly revolted from the Pequots. . . .

In the Morning, we awaking and seeing it very light, supposing it had been day, and so we might have lost our Opportunity, having purposed to make our Assault before Day; rowsed the Men with all expedition, and briefly commended ourselves and Design to God, thinking immediately to go to the Assault; the Indians shewing us a Path, told us that it led directly to the Fort. . . . Then Capt. Underhill came up, who marched in the Rear; and commending ourselves to God, divided our Men: There being two Entrances into the Fort, intending to enter both at once: Captain Mason leading up to that on the North East Side; who approaching within one Rod, heard a Dog bark and an Indian crying Owanux! Owanux! Which is Englishmen! Englishmen! We called up our Forces with all expedition, gave Fire upon them through the Pallizado; the Indians being in a dead indeed their last Sleep: Then we wheeling off fell upon the main Entrance, which was blocked up with Bushes about Breast high, over which the Captain passed, intending to make good the Entrance, encouraging the rest to follow. Lieutenant Seeley endeavoured to enter; but being somewhat cumbred, stepped back and pulled out the Bushes and so entred, and with him about sixteen Men: We had formerly concluded to destroy them by the Sword and save the Plunder.

Whereupon Captain Mason seeing no Indians, entred a Wigwam; where he was beset wit many Indians, waiting all opportunities to lay Hands on him, but could not prevail. At length William Heydon espying the Breach in the Wigwam, supposing some English might be there, entred; but in his Entrance fell over a dead Indian; but speedily recovering himself, the Indians some fled, others crept under their Beds: The Captain going out of the Wigwam saw many Indians in the Lane or Street; he making towards them, they fled, were pursued to the End of the Lane, where they were met by Edward Pattison, Thomas Barber, with some others; where seven of them were Slain, as they said. The Captain facing about, Marched a slow pace up the Lane he came down, perceiving himself very much out of Breath; and coming to the other End near the Place where he first entered, saw two Soldiers standing close to the Pallizado with their Swords pointed to the Ground: The Captain told them that We should never kill them after that manner: The Captain also said, We must Burn them; and immediately stepping into the Wigwam where he had been before, brought out a Firebrand, and putting it into the Matts with which they were covered, set the Wigwams on Fire. Lieutenant Thomas Bull and Nicholas Omsted beholding, came up; and when it was thoroughly kindled, the Indians ran as Men most dreadfully Amazed.

And indeed such a dreadful Terror did the Almighty let fall upon their Spirits, that they would fly from us and run into the very Flames, where many of them perished. And when the Fort was thoroughly Fired, Command was given, that all should fall off and surround the Fort; which was readily attended by all; only one Arthur Smith being so wounded that he could not move out of the Place, who was happily espied by Lieutenant Bull, and by him rescued. . . .

Thus were they now at their Wits End, who not many Hours before exalted themselves in their great Pride, threatning and resolving the utter Ruin and Destruction of all English, Exulting and Rejoycing with Songs and Dances: But God was above them, who laughed his Enemies and the Enemies of his People to Scorn, making them as a fiery Oven: Thus were the Stout Hearted spoiled, having slept their last Sleep, and none of their Men could find their Hands: Thus did the Lord judge among the Heathen, filling the Place with dead Bodies!

And here we may see the just Judgment of God, in sending even the very Night before this Assault, One hundred and fifty Men from their other Fort, to join with them of that Place, who were designed as some of themselves reported to go forth against the English, at that very Instant when this heavy Stroak came upon them where they perished with their Fellows. So that the Mischief they intended to us, came upon their own Plate: They were taken in their own snare, and we through Mercy escaped. And thus in little more than one Hour's space was their impregnable Fort with themselves utterly Destroyed, to the Number of six or seven Hundred, as some of themselves confessed. There were only seven taken captive, and about seven escaped.

Of the English, there were two Slain outright, and about twenty Wounded: Some Fainted by reason of the sharpness of the Weather, it being a cool Morning, and the want of such Comforts and Necessaries as were needful in such a Case. . . .

And was not the Finger of God in all this? . . . What shall I say: God was pleased to hide us in the Hollow of his Hand; I still remember a Speech of Mr. Hooker at our going abroad; That they should be Bread for us. And thus when the Lord turned the Captivity of his People, and turned the Wheel upon their Enemies; we were like Men in a Dream; then was our Mouth filled with Laughter, and our Tongues with Singing; thus we may say the Lord hath done great Things for us among the Heathen, whereof we are glad. Praise ye the Lord!

Chrestien LeCler, "A Micmac Indian Responds to the French," (ca. 1677)

Chrestien LeCler, *New Relation of Gaspesia, with the Customs and Religion of the Gaspesian Indians,* ed. and trans. William F. Ganong (Toronto: Champlain Society, 1910), pp. 104–106

I am greatly astonished that the French have so little cleverness, as they seem to exhibit in the manner of which thou hast just told me on their behalf, in the effort to persuade us to convert our poles, our barks, and our wigwams into those houses of stone and of wood which are tall and lofty, according to their account, as these trees. Very well! But why now, . . . do men of five to six feet in height need houses which are sixty to eighty? For, in fact, as thou knowest very well thyself, Patriarch—do we not find in our own all the conveniences and the advantages that you have with yours, such as reposing, drinking, sleeping, eating, and amusing ourselves with our friends when we wish? This is not all, . . . my brother, hast thou as much ingenuity and cleverness as the Indians, who carry their houses and their wigwams with them so that they may lodge wheresoever they please, independently of any seignior whatsoever? Thou art not as bold nor as stout as we, because when thou goest on a voyage thou canst not carry upon they shoulders thy buildings and thy edifices. Therefore it is necessary that thou preparest as many lodgings as thou makest changes of residence, or else thou lodgest in a hired house which does not belong to thee. As for us, we find ourselves secure from all these inconveniences, and we can always say, more truly than thou, that we are at home everywhere, because we set up our wigwams with ease wheresoever we go, and without asking permission of anybody. Thou reproachest us, very inappropriately, that our country is a little hell in contrast with France, which thou comparest to a terrestrial paradise, inasmuch as it yields thee, so thou sayest, every kind of provision in abundance. Thou sayest of us also that we are the most miserable and most unhappy of all men, living without religion, without manners, without honour, without social order, and, in a word, without any rules, like the beasts in our woods and our forests, lacking bread, wine, and a thousand other comforts which thou hast in superfluity in Europe. Well, my brother, if thou dost not yet know the real feelings with our Indians have towards thy country and towards all thy nation, it is proper that I inform thee at once. I beg thee now to believe that, all miserable as we seem in thine eyes, we consider ourselves nevertheless much happier than thou in this, that we are very content with the little that we have; and believe also once for all, I pray, that thou deceivest thyself greatly if thou thinkest to persuade us that thy country is better than ours. For if France, as thou sayest, is a little terrestrial paradise, art thou sensible to leave it? And why abandon wives, children, relatives, and friends? Why risk thy life and thy property every year, and why venture thyself with such risk, in any season whatsoever, to the storms and tempests of the sea in order to come to a strange and barbarous country which thou considerest the poorest and least fortunate of the world? Besides, since we are wholly convinced of the contrary, we scarcely take the trouble to go to France, because we fear, with good reason, lest we find little satisfaction there, seeing, in our own experience, that those who are natives thereof leave it every year in order to enrich themselves on our shores. We believe, further, that you are also incomparably poorer than we, and that you are only simple journeymen, valets, servants, and slaves, all masters and grand captains though you may appear, seeing that you glory in our old rags and in our miserable suits of beaver which can no longer be of use to us, and that you find among us, in the fishery for cod which you make in these parts, the wherewithal to comfort your misery and the poverty which oppresses you. As to us, we find all our riches and all our conveniences among ourselves, without trouble and without exposing our lives to the dangers in which you find yourselves constantly through your long voyages. And, whilst feeling compassion for you in the sweetness of our repose, we wonder at the anxieties and cares which you give yourselves night and day in order to load your ship. We see also that all your people live, as a rule, only upon cod which you catch among us. It is everlastingly nothing but cod—cod in the morning, cod at midday, cod at evening, and always cod, until things come to such a pass that if you wish some good morsels, it is at our expense; and you are obliged to have recourse to the Indians, who you despise so much, and to beg them to go a-hunting that you may be regaled. Now tell me this one little thing, if thou hast any sense: Which of these two is the wisest and happiest—he who labours without ceasing and only obtains, and that with great trouble, enough to live on, or he who rests in comfort and finds all that he needs in the pleasure of hunting and fishing? It is true, . . . that we have not always had the use of bread and of wine which your France produces; but, in fact, before the arrival of the French in these parts, did not the Gaspesians live much longer than now? And if we have not any longer among us any of those old men of a hundred and thirty to forty years, it is only because we are gradually adopting your manner of living, for experience is making it very plain that those of us live longest who, despising your bread, your wine, and your brandy, are content with their natural food of beaver, of moose, of waterfowl, and fish, in accord with the custom of our ancestors and of all the Gaspesian nation. Learn now, my brother, once for all, because I must open to thee my heart: there is no Indian who does not consider himself infinitely more happy and more powerful than the French.

Nathaniel Bacon's Charges Against the Virginia Governor (1676)

Nathaniel Bacon, "Declaration of Nathaniel Bacon in the Name of the People of Virginia, July 30, 1676, " in *The Southern Colonies*, Vol. 3, part 2 of *Foundations of Colonial America: A Documentary History*, ed. W. Keith Kavenagh (New York: Chelsea House, 1973), pp. 1,783–1,784

1. For having, upon spacious pretences of public works, raised great unjust taxes upon the commonalty for the advancement of private favorites and other sinister ends, but no visible effects in any measure adequate; for not having, during this long time of his government, in any measure advanced this hopeful colony either by fortifications, towns, or trade.

2. For having abused and rendered contemptible the magistrates of justice by advancing to places of judicature scandalous and ignorant favorites.

3. For having wronged his Majesty's prerogative and interest by assuming monopoly of the beaver trade and for having in it unjust gain betrayed and sold his Majesty's country and the lives of his loyal subjects to the barbarous heathen.

4. For having protected, favored, and emboldened the Indians against his Majesty's loyal subjects, never contriving, requiring, or appointing any due or proper means of satisfaction for their many invasions, robberies, and murders committed upon us.

5. For having, when the army of English was just upon the track of those Indians, who now in all places, burn, spoil, murder, and when we might with ease have destroyed them who then were in open hostility, for then having expressly countermanded and sent back our army by passing his word for the peaceable demeanor of the said Indians, who immediately prosecuted their evil intentions, committing horrid murders and robberies in all places, being protected by the said engagement and word past of him the said Sir William Berkeley, having ruined and laid desolate a great part of his majesty's country, and have now drawn themselves into such obscure and remote places and are by their success so emboldened and confirmed by their confederacy so strengthened that the cries of blood are in all places, and the terror and consternation of people so great, are now become not only a difficult but a formidable enemy who might at first with ease have been destroyed.

6. And lately, when upon the loud outcries of blood, the assembly had, with all care, raised and framed an army for the preventing of further mischief and safe-guard of this his Majesty's colony.

7. For having, with only the privacy of some few favorites without acquainting the people, only by the alteration of a figure, forged a commission, by we know not what hand, not only without but even against the consent of the people, for the raising and effecting civil war and destruction, which being happily and without bloodshed prevented; for having the second time attempted the same, thereby calling down our forces from the defense of the frontiers and most weakly exposed places.

8. For the prevention of civil mischief and ruin amongst ourselves while the barbarous enemy in all places did invade, murder, and spoil us, his Majesty's most faithful subjects.

Of this and the aforesaid articles we accuse Sir William Berkeley as guilty of each and every one of the same, and as one who traitorously attempted, violated, and injured his Majesty's interest here by a loss of a great part of this his colony and many of his faithful loyal subjects by him betrayed and in a barbarous and shameful manner exposed to the incursions and murder of the heathen. And we do further declare these the ensuing persons in this list to have been wicked and pernicious councillors, confederates, aiders, and assisters against the commonalty in these our civil commotions.

Sir Henry Chichley Nicholas Spencer
Lt. Col. Christopher Wormeley Joseph Bridger
Phillip Ludwell William Claiburne, Jr.
Ri: Lee Thomas Hawkins
Thomas Ballard William Sherwood
William Cole John Page Clerke
Richard Whitacre John Cluffe Clerk
John West, Hubert Farrell, Thomas Reade, Math. Kempe

And we do further demand that the said Sir William Berkeley with all the persons on this list be forthwith delivered up or surrender themselves within four days after the notice hereof, or otherwise we declare as follows.

That in whatsoever place, house, or ship, any of the said persons shall reside, be hid, or protected, we declare the owners, masters, or inhabitants of the said places to be confederates and traitors to the people and the estates of them is also of all the aforesaid persons to be confiscated. And this we, the commons of Virginia, do declare, desiring a firm union amongst ourselves that we may jointly and with one accord defend ourselves against the common enemy. And let not the faults of the guilty be the reproach of the innocent, or the faults or crimes of the oppressors divide and separate us who have suffered by their oppressions.

These are, therefore, in his Majesty's name, to command you forthwith to seize the persons above mentioned as traitors to the King and country and them to bring to Middle Plantation and there to secure them until further order, and, in case of opposition, if you want any further assistance you are forthwith to demand it in the name of the people in all countries of Virginia.

Nathaniel Bacon
General by consent of the people.

Jonathan Edwards, "Sinners in the Hands of an Angry God" (1741)

Samuel Austin, ed. *The Works of President Edwards*, 6 vols. (Worcester, Mass.: Isaiah Thomas, 1808), Vol. 2, pp. 72–79

. . . This that you have heard is the case of every one of you that are out of Christ. That world of misery, that lake of burning brimstone, is extended abroad under you. There is the dreadful pit of glowing flames of the wrath of God; there is hell's wide gaping mouth open; and you have nothing to stand upon, nor any thing to take hold of; there is nothing between you and hell but the air; 'tis only the power and mere pleasure of God that hold you up.

You probably are not sensible of this; you find you are kept out of hell, but don't see the hand of God in it, but look at other things, as the good state of your bodily constitution, your care of your own life, and the means you use for your own preservation. But indeed these things are nothing; if God should withdraw his hand, they would avail no more to keep you from falling, than the thin air to hold up a person that is suspended in it.

Your wickedness makes you as it were heavy as lead, and to tend downwards with great weight and pressure towards hell; and, if God should let you go, you would immediately sink, and swiftly descend and plunge into the bottomless gulf; and your healthy constitution, and your own care and prudence, and best contrivance, and all your righteousness, would have no more influence to uphold you and keep you out of hell, than a spider's web would have to stop a falling rock. . . .

The God that holds you over the pit of hell, much as one holds a spider or some loathsome insect over the fire, abhors you, and is dreadfully provoked. His wrath towards you burns like fire; he looks upon you as worthy of nothing else but to be cast into the fire. He is of purer eyes than to bear you his sight; you are ten thousand times as abominable in his eyes as the most hateful, venomous serpent is in ours. You have offended him infinitely more than ever a stubborn rebel did his prince, and yet 'tis nothing but his hand that holds you from falling into the fire every moment. . . .

O sinner! Consider the fearful danger you are in! 'Tis a great furnace of wrath, a wide and bottomless pit, full of fire and of wrath that you are held over in the hand of that God whose wrath is provoked and incensed as much against you as against many of the damned in hell. You hang by a slender thread, with the flames of Divine wrath flashing about it, and ready every moment to singe it and burn it asunder. . . .

It would be dreadful to suffer this fierceness and wrath of Almighty God one moment; but you must suffer it to all eternity. There will be no end to this exquisite, horrible, misery. . . .

How dreadful is the state of those that are daily and hourly in danger of this great wrath and infinite misery! But this is the dismal case of every soul in this congregation that has not been born again, however moral and strict, sober and religious, they may otherwise be. Oh! that you would consider it, whether you be young or old!

Gottlieb Mittelberger's Account of Immigration (1750)

Gottlieb Mittelberger, *Journey to Pennsylvania*, eds. Oscar Handlin and John Clive (Cambridge, Mass.: Belknap Press of Harvard University Press, 1960)

When the ships have weighed anchor for the last time, usually off Cowes in Old England, then both the long sea voyage and misery begin in earnest. For from there the ships often take eight, nine, ten, or twelve weeks sailing to Philadelphia, if the wind is unfavorable. But even given the most favorable winds, the voyage takes seven weeks.

During the journey the ship is full of pitiful signs of distress—smells, fumes, horrors, vomiting, various kinds of sea sickness, fever, dysentery, headaches, heat, constipation, boils, scurvy, cancer, mouth-rot, and similar afflictions, all of them caused by the age and the highly-salted state of the food, especially of the meat, as well as by the very bad and filthy water, which brings about the miserable destruction and death of many. Add to all that shortage of food, hunger, thirst, frost, heat, dampness, fear, misery, vexation, and lamentation as well as other troubles. Thus, for example, there are so many lice, especially on the sick people, that they have to be scraped off the bodies. All this misery reaches its climax when in addition to everything else one must also suffer through two to three days and nights of storm, with everyone convinced that the ship with all aboard is bound to sink. In such misery all the people on board pray and cry pitifully together. . . .

Among those who are in good health impatience sometimes grows so great and bitter that one person begins to curse the other, or himself and the day of his birth, and people sometimes come close to murdering one another. Misery and malice are readily associated, so that people begin to cheat and steal from one another. And then one always blames the other for having undertaken the voyage. Often the children cry out against their parents, husbands against wives and wives against husbands, brothers against sisters, friends and acquaintances against one another.

But most of all they cry out against the thieves of human beings! Many groan and exclaim: "Oh! If only I were back at home, even lying in my pig-sty!" Or they call out: "Ah, dear God, if I only once again had a piece of good bread or a good fresh drop of water." Many people whimper, sigh, and cry out pitifully for home. . . .

When at last after the long and difficult voyage the ships finally approach land, when one gets to see the headlands for the sight of which the people on board had longed so passionately, then everyone crawls from below to the deck, in order to look at the land from afar. And people cry for joy, pray and sing praises and thanks to God. The glimpse of land revives the passengers, especially those who are half-dead of illness. Their spirits, however weak they had become, leap up, triumph, and rejoice within them. . . .

When the ships finally arrive in Philadelphia after the long voyage only those are let off who can pay their sea freight or can give good security. The others, who lack the money to pay, have to remain on board until they are purchased and until their purchasers can thus pry them loose from the ship. In this whole process the sick are the worst off, for the healthy are preferred and are more readily paid for. The miserable people who are ill must often still remain at sea and in sight of the city for another two or three weeks—which in many cases means death. Yet many of them, were they able to pay their debts and to leave the ships at once, might escape with their lives. . . .

This is how the commerce in human beings on board ships takes place. Every day Englishmen, Dutchmen, and High Germans come from Philadelphia and other places, some of them very far away, sometime twenty or thirty or forty hours' journey, and go on board the newly arrived vessel that has brought people from Europe and offers them for sale. From among the healthy they pick those suitable for the purposes for which they require them. Then they negotiate with them as to the length of the period for which they will go into service in order to pay off their passage, the whole amount of which they generally still owe. When an agreement has been reached, adult persons by written contract bind themselves to serve for three, four, five or six years, according to their health and age. The very young, between the ages of ten and fifteen, have to serve until they are twenty-one however.

Many parents in order to pay their fares in this way and get off the ship must barter and sell their children as if they were cattle. Since the fathers and mothers often do not know where or to what masters their children are to be sent, it frequently happens that after leaving the vessel, parents and children do not see each other for years on end, or even for the rest of their lives.

Mary Jemison's Account of Her Capture by the Iroquois (1755)

James E. Seaver, *A Narrative of the Life of Mrs. Mary Jemison* (n.p., 1824)

. . . Our family, as usual, was busily employed about their common business. Father was shaving an axe-helve at the side of the house; mother was making preparations for breakfast;—my two oldest brothers were at work near the barn; and the little ones, with myself, and the woman and her three children, were in the house.

Breakfast was not yet ready, when we were alarmed by the discharge of a number of guns, that seemed to be near. Mother and the women before mentioned, almost fainted at the report, and every one trembled with fear. . . .

. . . They first secured my father, and then rushed into the house, and without the least resistance made prisoners of my mother, Robert, Matthew, Betsey, the woman and her three children, and myself, and then commenced plundering. . . .

The party that took us consisted of six Indians and four Frenchmen, who immediately commenced plundering, as I just observed, and took what they considered most valuable; consisting principally of bread, meal and meat. Having taken as much provision as they could carry, they set out with their prisoners in great haste, for fear of detection, and soon entered the woods. . . .

Early the next morning the Indians and Frenchmen that we had left the night before, came to us; but our friends were left behind. It is impossible for any one to form a correct idea of what my feelings were at the sight of those savages, whom I supposed had murdered my parents and brothers, sister and friends, and left them in the swamp to be devoured by wild beasts! But what could I do?. . . .

My suspicions as to the fate of my parents proved too true; for soon after I left them they were killed and scalped, together with Robert, Matthew, Betsey, and the woman and her two children, and mangled in the most shocking manner . . . .

After a hard day's march we encamped in a thicket, where the Indians made a shelter of boughs, and then built a good fire to warm and dry our benumbed limbs and clothing; for it had rained some through the day. . . .

In the course of the night they made me to understand that they should not have killed the family if the whites had not pursued them. . . .

At the place where we halted, the Indians combed the hair of the young man, the boy and myself, and then painted our faces and hair red, in the finest Indian style. We were then conducted into the fort, where we received a little bread and were then shut up and left to tarry alone through the night. . . .

The morning at length arrived, and our masters came early and let us out of the house. . . .

. . . [I]t was not long before I was in some measure relieved by the appearance of two pleasant looking squaws of the Seneca tribe, who came and examined me attentively for a short time, and then went out. After a few minutes absence they returned with my former masters, who gave me to them to dispose of as they pleased. . . .

At night we arrived at a small Seneca Indian town, at the mouth of a small river, that was called by the Indians, in the Seneca language, She-nan-jee. . . .

Having made fast to the shore, the Squaws left me in the canoe while they went to their wigwam or house in the town, and returned with a suit of Indian clothing, all new, and very clean and nice. My clothes, though whole and good when I was taken, were now torn in pieces, so that I was almost naked. They first undressed me and threw my rags into the river; then washed me clean and dressed me in the new suit they had just brought, in complete Indian style; and then led me home and seated me in the center of their wigwam.

I had been in that situation but a few minutes, before all the Squaws in the town came in to see me. I was soon surrounded by them, and they immediately set up a most dismal howling, crying bitterly, and wringing their hands in all the agonies of grief for a deceased relative. . . .

"Of our brother! Alas! He is dead—he has gone; he will never return! Friendless he died on the field of the slain, where his bones are yet lying unburied! Oh, who will mourn his sad fate? No tears dropped around him; oh no! No tears of his sisters were there!. . .

. . . His spirit has seen our distress, and sent us a helper whom with pleasure we greet. Dickewamis has come: then let us receive her with joy! She is handsome and pleasant! Oh! She is our sister, and gladly we welcome her here. In the place of our brother she stands in our tribe. With care we will guard her from trouble; and may she be happy till her spirit shall leave us."

In the course of that ceremony, from mourning they became serene—joy sparkled in their countenances, and they seemed to rejoice over me as over a long lost child. I was made welcome amongst them as a sister to the two Squaws before mentioned, and was called Dickewamis; which being interpreted, signifies a pretty girl, a handsome girl, or a pleasant, good thing. That is the name by which I have ever since been called by the Indians.

I afterwards learned that the ceremony I at the time passed through, was that of adoption. The two squaws had lost a brother in Washington's war, sometime in the year before, and in consequence of his death went up to Fort Pitt, on the day on which I arrived there, in order to receive a prisoner or an enemy's scalp, to supply their loss.

. . . If they receive a prisoner, it is at their option either to satiate their vengeance by taking his life in the most cruel manner they can conceive of; or, to receive and adopt him into the family, in the place of him whom they have lost. All the prisoners that are taken in battle and carried to the encampment or town by the Indians, are given to the bereaved families, till their number is made good.

Olaudah Equiano's Account his Capture and Enslavement (1757)

Olaudah Equiano, *The Life of Olaudah Equiano, or Gustavus Vassa the African Written by Himself* (London:1789; reprint, New York: Negro Universities Press, 1969)

One day, when all our people were gone to their works as usual, and only I and my dear sister were left to mind the house, two men and a woman got over our walls, and seized us both, and they stopped our mouths, and ran off with us into the nearest wood. Here they tied our hands, and continued to carry us as far as they could, till night came on, when we reached a small house, where the robbers halted for refreshment, and spent the night. We were then unbound, but were unable to take any food; and being quite overpowered by fatigue and grief, our only relief was some sleep, which allayed our misfortune for a short time. The next morning we left the house, and continued travelling all the day. . . . When we went to rest the following night they offered us some victuals; but we refused it; and the only comfort we had was in being in one another's arms all that night, and bathing each other with our tears. But alas! we were soon deprived of even the small comfort of weeping together. The next day proved a day of greater sorrow than I had yet experienced; for my sister and I were then separated, while we lay clasped in each other's arms. It was in vain that we besought them not to part us; she was torn from me, and immediately carried away, while I was left in a state of distraction not to be described. I cried and grieved continually; and for several days I did not eat anything but what they forced into my mouth. . . .

The first object which saluted my eyes when I arrived at the coast was the sea, and a slave ship, which was then riding at anchor, and waiting for its cargo. These filled me with astonishment, which was soon converted into terror when I was carried on board. . . . I was now persuaded that I had gotten into a world of bad spirits, and that they were going to kill me. Their complexions too differing so much from ours, their long hair, and the language they spoke, (which was very different from any I had ever heard) united to confirm me in this belief. . . . When I looked round the ship too and saw a large furnace of copper boiling, and a multitude of black people of every description chained together, every one of their countenances expressing dejection and sorrow, I no longer doubted of my fate; and, quite overpowered with horror and anguish, I fell motionless on the deck and fainted. When I recovered a little I found some black people about me, who I believed were some of those who brought me on board, and had been receiving their pay; they talked to me in order to cheer me, but all in vain. I asked them if we were not to be eaten by those white men with horrible looks, red faces, and loose hair. They told me I was not. . . . Soon after this the blacks who brought me on board went off, and left me abandoned to despair. I now saw myself deprived of all chance of returning to my native country, or even the least glimpse of hope of gaining the shore, which I now considered as friendly; and I even wished for my former slavery in preference to my present situation, which was filled with horrors of every kind, still heightened by my ignorance of what I was to undergo. I was not long suffered to indulge my grief; I was soon put down under the decks, and there I received such a salutation in my nostrils as I had never experienced in my life: so that, with the loathsomeness of the stench, and crying together, I became so sick and low that I was not able to eat, nor had I the least desire to taste anything. I now wished for the last friend, death, to relieve me; but soon to my grief, two of the white men offered me eatables; and, on my refusing to eat, one of them held me fast by the hands, and laid me across I think the windlass, and tied my feet, while the other flogged me severely. I had never experienced any thing of this kind before; and although, not being used to the water, I naturally feared that element the first time I saw it, yet nevertheless, could I have got over the nettings, I would have jumped over the side, but I could not; and, besides, the crew used to watch us very closely who were not chained down to the decks, lest we should leap into the water: and I have seen some of these poor African prisoners most severely cut for attempting to do so, and hourly whipped for not eating. This indeed was often the case with myself. In a little time after, amongst the poor chained men, I found some of my own nation, which in a small degree gave ease to my mind. I inquired of these what was to be done with us; they gave me to understand we were to be carried to these white people's country to work for them. I then was a little revived, and thought, if it were no worse than working, my situation was not so desperate: but still I feared I should be put to death, the white people looked and acted, as I thought, in so savage a manner; for I had never seen among any people such instances of brutal cruelty; and this not only shewn towards us blacks, but also to some whites themselves. One white man in particular I saw, when we were permitted to be on deck, flogged so unmercifully with a large rope near the foremast that he died in consequence of it; and they tossed him over the side as they would have done a brute. This made me fear these people the more; and I expected nothing less than to be treated in the same manner. I could not help expressing my fears and apprehensions to some of my countrymen: I asked them if these people had no country, but lived in this hollow place (ship): they told me they did not, but came from a distant one. "Then," said I, "how comes it in all our country we never heard of them?" They told me because they lived so very far off. I then asked where were their women? had they any like themselves? I was told them had "and why" said I, "do we not see them?" they answered, because they were left behind. I asked how the vessel could go? they told me they could not tell; but that there were cloths put upon the masts by the help of ropes I saw, and then the vessel went on and the white men had some spell or magic they put in the water when they liked in order to stop the vessel. I was exceedingly amazed at this account, and really thought they were spirits. I therefore wished much to be from amongst them, for I expected they would sacrifice me: but my wishes were vain. . .

At last we came in sight of the island of Barbadoes, at which the whites on board gave a great shout, and made many signs of joy to us. We did not know what to think of this; but as the vessel drew nearer we plainly saw the harbour, and other ships of different kinds and sizes; and we soon anchored amongst them off Bridge Town. Many merchants and planters now came on board, though it was in the evening. They put us in separate parcels, and examined us attentively. They also made us jump, and pointed to the land, signifying we were to go there. We thought by this we should be eaten by these ugly men as they appeared to us; and, when soon after we were all put down under the decks again, there was much dread and trembling among us, and nothing but bitter cries to be heard all the night from these apprehensions, insomuch that at last the white people got some old slaves from the land to pacify us. They told us we were not to be eaten, but to work, and were soon to go on land, where we should see many of our country people. This report eased us much; and sure enough, soon after we were landed, there came to us Africans of all languages. We were conducted immediately to the merchant's yard, where we were all pent up together like so many sheep in a fold, without regard of sex or age. As every object was new to me every thing I saw filled me with surprise. What struck me first was that the houses were built with stories, and in every other respect different from those in Africa; but I was still more astonished on seeing people on horseback. I did not know what this could mean; and indeed I thought these people were full of nothing but magical arts. . . . We were not many days in the merchant's custody before we were sold after their usual manner, which is this: On a signal given (as the beat of a drum), the buyers rush at once into the yard where the slaves are confined, and make choice of that parcel they like best. The noise and clamour with which this is attended, and the eagerness visible in the countenances of the buyers, serve not a little to increase the apprehensions of the terrified Africans, who may well be supposed to consider them as the ministers of that destruction to which they think themselves devoted. In this manner, without scruple, I remember in the vessel in which I was brought over, in the men's apartment, there were several brothers, who, in the sale, were sold in different lots; and it was very moving on this occasion to see and hear their cries at parting. . . .

While I was thus employed by my master I was often a witness to cruelties of every kind, which were exercised on my unhappy fellow slaves. I used frequently to have different cargoes of new negroes in my care for sale; and it was almost a constant practice with our clerks, and other whites, to commit violent depredations on the chastity of the female slaves; and these I was, though with reluctance, obliged to submit to at all times, being unable to help them. When we have had some of these slaves on board my master's vessels to carry them to other islands, or to America, I have known our mates to commit these acts most shamefully, to the disgrace, not of Christians only, but of men. I have even known them to gratify their brutal passion with females not ten years old;. . . . And yet in Montserrat I have seen a negro man staked to the ground, and cut most shockingly, and then his ears cut off bit by bit, because he had been connected with a white woman who was a common prostitute: as if it were no crime in the whites to rob an innocent African girl of her virtue; but most heinous in a black man only to gratify a passion of nature, where the temptation was offered by one of a different colour, though the most abandoned woman of her species. Another negro man was half hanged, and then burnt, for attempting to poison a cruel overseer. Thus by repeated cruelties are the wretched first urged to despair, and then murdered, because they still retain so much of human nature about them as to wish to put an end to their misery, and retaliate their tyrants!

Bibliography

Alexander, James A. *A Brief Narrative of the Case and Trial of John Peter Zenger.* Cambridge, Mass.: Harvard University Press, 1969.

Allen, Paula Gunn. *The Sacred Hoop: Recovering the Feminine in American Indian Traditions,* revised edition. Boston: Beacon Press, 1992.

Anderson, Fred. *A People's Army: Massachusetts Soldiers and Society in the Seven Years' War.* Chapel Hill.: University of North Carolina Press, 1984.

———. *Crucible of War: The Seven Years War and the Fate of the British Empire in North America, 1754–1766.* New York: Knopf, 2000.

Axtell, James. *The European and the Indian: Essays in the Ethnohistory of Colonial North America.* New York: Oxford University Press, 1981.

———. *The Invasion Within: The Contest of Cultures in Colonial North America.* New York: Oxford University Press, 1985.

Bailyn, Bernard. *New England Merchants in the Seventeenth Century.* Cambridge, Mass.: Harvard University Press, 1980.

———. *Origins of American Politics.* New York: Knopf, 1970.

———. *The Peopling of British North America: An Introduction.* New York: Knopf, 1986.

Bancroft, Hubert H. *History of Alaska 1730–1885.* San Francisco: University of California Press, 1986.

Barbour, Hugh and J. William Frost. *The Quakers.* New York: Greenwood Press, 1988.

Barbour, Philip, ed. *The Complete Works of Captain John Smith (1580–1631),* 3 vols. Chapel Hill: University of North Carolina Press, 1986.

Bellesiles, Michael A. *Arming America: The Origins of a National Gun Culture.* New York: Knopf, 2000.

Berkin, Carol J. *First Generations: Women in Colonial America.* New York: Hill & Wang, 1996.

Berlin, Ira. *Many Thousand Gone: The first Two Centuries of Slavery in North America.* Cambridge, Mass.: The Belknap Press of Harvard University Press, 1998.

Blackburn, Robin. *The Making of New World Slavery: From the Baroque to the Modern, 1792–1800.* London: Verso, 1997.

Bolster, W. Jeffrey. *Black Jacks: African American Seamen in the Age of Sail.* Cambridge, Mass.: Harvard University Press, 1997.

Bonomi, Patricia U. *Under the Cope of Heaven: Religion, Society, and Politics in Colonial America.* New York: Oxford University Press, 1986.

Boyer, Paul, and Stephen Nissenbaum. *Salem Possessed: The Social Origins of Witchcraft.* Cambridge, Mass.: Harvard University Press, 1974.

Brading, D. A. *The First America: The Spanish Monarchy, Creole Patriots and the Liberal State.* Cambridge, U.K.: Cambridge University Press, 1991.

Bragdon, Kathleen J. *Native People of Southern New England, 1500–1650.* Norman: University of Oklahoma Press, 1996.

Braund, Kathryn E. Holland. *Deerskins & Duffels: Creek Indian Trade with Anglo-America, 1685–1815.* Lincoln and London: University of Nebraska Press, 1993.

Breen, T. H., and Stephen Innes. *"Myne Owne Ground": Race and Freedom on Virginia's Eastern Shore, 1640–1676.* New York: Oxford University Press, 1980.

Brown, Kathleen M. *Good Wives, Nasty Wenches, and Anxious Patriarchs: Gender, Race, and Power in Colonial Virginia.* Chapel Hill: University of North Carolina Press, 1996.

Brown, Milton W. *American Art to 1900: Painting, Sculpture, Architecture.* New York: H. N. Abrams, 1977.

Bushman, Richard L. *From Puritan to Yankee: Character and the Social Order in Connecticut, 1690–1765.* Cambridge, Mass.: Harvard University Pess, 1967.

———. *The Refinement of America: Persons, Houses, Cities.* New York: Vintage Books, 1992.

Butler, Jon. *Becoming America: The Revolution Before 1776.* Cambridge, Mass.: Harvard University Press, 2000.

Capps, Walter H., ed. *Seeing With a Native Eye: Essays on Native American Religion.* New York: HarperCollins, 1976.

Carney, Judith A. *Black Rice: The African Origins of Rice Cultivation in the Americas.* Cambridge, Mass.: Harvard University Press, 2001.

Carr, Lois Green, Russell R. Menard, and Lorena Walsh. *Robert Cole's World: Agriculture and Society in Early Maryland.* Chapel Hill: University of North Carolina Press, 1991.

Carson, Cary, Ronald Hoffman, and Peter J. Albert, eds. *Of Consuming Interests: The Style of Life in the Eighteenth Century.* Charlottesville and London: University Press of Virginia for the United States Capital Historical Society, 1994.

Cave, Alfred A. *The Pequot War.* Amherst: University of Massachusetts Press, 1996.

Chase, Gilbert. *America's Music: From the Pilgrims to the Present.* Urbana: University of Illinois Press, 1987.

Corkran, David H. *The Creek Frontier, 1540–1783.* Norman: University of Oklahoma Press, 1967.

Crane, Elaine Forman. *A Dependent People: Newport, Rhode Island in the Revolutionary Era.* New York: Fordham University Press, 1985.

———. *Ebb Tide in New England: Women, Seaports, and Social Change, 1630–1800.* Boston: Northeastern University Press, 1998.

Cray, Robert E., Jr. *Paupers and Poor Relief in New York City and its Environs, 1700–1830.* Philadelphia: Temple University Press, 1988.

Creel, Margaret Washington. *A Peculiar People: Slave Religion and Community Culture Among the Gullah.* New York: New York University Press, 1988.

Cronon, William. *Changes in the Land: Indians, Colonists, and the Ecology of New England.* New York: Hill & Wang, 1983.

Crosby, Alfred W. *The Columbian Exchange: Biological and Cultural Consequences of 1492.* Westport, Conn.: Greenwood, 1972.

Davis, Harold E. *The Fledgling Province: Social And Cultural Life In Colonial Georgia, 1733–1776.* Chapel Hill: University of North Carolina Press, 1976.

Davis, T. J. *A Rumor of Revolt: The "Great Negro Plot" in Colonial New York.* New York: The Free Press, 1985.

Dayton, Cornelia Hughes. *Women Before the Bar: Gender, Law, and Society in Connecticut, 1639–1789.* Chapel Hill: University of North Carolina Press, 1995.

Demos, John. *The Unredeemed Captive: A Family Story from Early America.* New York: Knopf, 1994.

Dickason, Olive Patricia. *Canada's First Nations: A History of Founding Peoples from Earliest Times.* Norman: University of Oklahoma Press, 1992.

Dowd, Gregory Evans. *A Spirited Resistance: The North American Indian Struggle for Unity, 1745–1815.* Baltimore and London: Johns Hopkins University Press, 1992.

Drake, James D. *King Philip's War: Civil War in New England, 1675–1676.* Amherst: University of Massachusetts Press, 1999.

Duffy, John. *Epidemics in Colonial America.* Baton Rouge: Louisiana State University Press, 1953, reprinted 1971.

Eccles, William J. *The French in North America, 1500–1783.* East Lansing: Michigan State University Press, 1998.

Ekirch, A. Roger. *Bound for America: The Transportation of British Convicts to the Colonies, 1718–1775.* New York: Oxford University Press, 1987.

Eltis, David. *The Rise of African Slavery in the Americas.* Cambridge, U.K.: Cambridge University Press, 2000.

Galenson, David. *White Servitude in Colonial America.* New York: Cambridge University Press, 1984.

Gaustad, Edwin Scott. *The Great Awakening in New England.* New York: Harper & Row, 1957.

Gilje, Paul A. *Rioting in America.* Bloomington: University of Indiana Press, 1996.

Goodfriend, Joyce D. *Before the Melting Pot.* Princeton, N. J.: Princeton University Press, 1994.

Greene, Jack P. *Negotiated Authorities: Essays in Colonial Political and Constitutional History.* Charlottesville and London: University of Virginia Press, 1994.

Guelzo, A. C. *Edwards on the Will: A Century of American Theological Debate.* Middletown, Conn.: Wesleyan University Press, 1989.

Gutiérrez, Ramón A. *When Jesus Came the Corn Mothers Went Away: Marriage, Sexuality, and Power in New Mexico, 1500–1846.* Palo Alto: Stanford University Press, 1991.

Hall, David D. *Worlds of Wonder, Days of Judgment.* New York: Knopf, 1989.

Hall, Gwendolyn Midlo. *Africans in Colonial Louisiana: The Development of Afro-Creole Culture in the Eighteenth Century.* Baton Rouge: Louisiana State University Press, 1992.

Hall, Kermit. *The Magic Mirror: Law in American History.* New York: Oxford University Press, 1989.

Hatley, Tom. *The Dividing Paths: Cherokees and South Carolinians through the Era of Revolution.* Oxford, U.K.: Oxford University Press, 1993.

Higginbotham, Leon. *In the Matter of Color: Race and the American Legal Process in the Colonial Period.* New York: Oxford University Press, 1978.

Hodges, Graham Russell. *Root and Branch: African Americans in New York and East Jersey, 1613–1863.* Chapel Hill: University of North Carolina Press, 1999.

Hurt, R. Douglas. *Indian Agriculture in America: Prehistory to the Present.* Lawrence: University of Kansas Press, 1987.

Ingersoll, Thomas N. *Mamon and Manon in Early New Orleans: The First Slave Society in the Deep South, 1718–1819.* Knoxville: University of Tennessee Press, 1999.

Jennings, Francis. *The Ambiguous Iroquois Empire.* New York: Norton, 1984.

Kammen, Michael. *Colonial New York: A History.* New York: Oxford University Press, 1975.

Karlsen, Carol F. *The Devil in the Shape of a Woman: Witchcraft in Colonial New England.* New York: Norton, 1987.

Klepp, Susan E., and Billy G. Smith, eds. *The Infortunate: The Voyage and Adventures of William Moraley, an Indentured Servant.* University Park: Pennsylvania State University, 1992.

Knaut, Andrew L. *The Pueblo Revolt of 1680: Conquest and Resistance in Seventeenth Century New Mexico.* Norman: University of Oklahoma Press, 1995.

Kulikoff, Allan. *From British Peasants to Colonial American Farmers.* Chapel Hill: University of North Carolina Press, 2000.

———. *Tobacco and Slaves: The Development of Southern Cultures in the Chesapeake, 1680–1800.* Chapel Hill: University of North Carolina Press, 1986.

Kupperman, Karen Ordhal. *Indians and English: Facing Off in Early America.* Ithaca, N.Y.: Cornell University Press, 2000.

———. *Roanoke: The Abandoned Colony.* Totowa, N.J.: Rowman & Allanheld, 1984.

Lepore, Jill. *The Name of War: King Philip's War and the Origins of American Identity.* New York: Knopf, 1998.

Linebaugh, Peter, and Marcus Rediker. *The Many-Headed Hydra: Sailors, Slaves, Commoners, and the Hidden History of the Revolutionary Atlantic.* Boston: Beacon Press, 2000.

Lockridge, Kenneth A. *The Diary, and Life, of William Byrd II of Virginia, 1674–1744.* Chapel Hill: University of North Carolina Press, 1987.

Main, Gloria L. *Tobacco Colony: Life in Early Maryland, 1650–1720.* Princeton, N.J.: Princeton University Press, 1982.

McCusker, John J., and Russell R. Menard. *The Economy of British America, 1607–1789.* Chapel Hill: University of North Carolina Press, 1985.

McGaw, Judith A., ed. *Early American Technology: Making and Doing Things from the Colonial Era to 1850.* Chapel Hill: University of North Carolina Press, 1994.

Merrell, James H. *Into the American Woods: Negotiators on the Pennsylvania Frontier.* New York: Norton, 1999.

Morgan, Edmund S. *American Slavery, American Freedom: The Ordeal of Colonial Virginia.* New York: Norton, 1975.

Morgan, Philip D. *Slavery Counterpoint: Black Culture in the Eighteenth-Century Chesapeake and Lowcountry.* Chapel Hill: University of North Carolina Press, 1998.

Nash, Gary B. *Forging Freedom: The Formation of Philadelphia's Black Community, 1720–1840.* Cambridge, Mass.: Harvard University Press, 1988.

———. *Quakers and Politics: Pennsylvania, 1681–1726.* 1968, Reprint, Princeton, N.J.: Princeton University Press, 1997.

———. *The Urban Crucible: Social Change, Political Consciousness, and the Origins of the American Revolution.* Cambridge, Mass.: Harvard University Press, 1979.

Norton, Mary Beth. *Founding Mothers & Fathers: Gendered Power and the Forming of American Society.* New York: Vintage Books, 1997.

Pestana, Carla Gardina. *Quakers and Baptists in Colonial Massachusetts.* New York: Cambridge University Press, 1991.

Rediker, Marcus. *Between the Devil and the Deep Blue Sea: Merchant Seamen, Pirates, and the Anglo-American Maritime World, 1700–1750.* Cambridge, U.K.: Cambridge University Press, 1987.

Richter, Daniel K. *The Ordeal of the Longhouse: The Peoples of the Iroquois League in the Era of European Colonization.* Chapel Hill: University of North Carolina Press, 1992.

Rountree, Helen C. *The Powhatan Indians of Virginia through Four Centuries.* Norman: University of Oklahoma Press, 1990.

Salinger, Sharon V. *"To Serve Well and Faithfully": Labor and Indentured Servants in Pennsylvania, 1682–1800.* Bowie, Md.: Heritage Books, 2000.

Salisbury, Neal. *Manitou and Providence: Indians, Europeans, and the Making of New England, 1500–1643.* New York: Oxford University Press, 1982.

Salmon, Marylynn. *Women and the Law of Property in Early America.* Chapel Hill: University of North Carolina Press, 1986.

Sando, Joe S. *Popé, Architect of the First American Revolution.* Santa Fe, N.Mex.: Clearlight Publishers, 1998.

Schultz, Ronald. *The Republic of Labor: Philadelphia Artisans and the Politics of Class, 1720–1830.* New York: Oxford University Press, 1993.

Slaughter, Thomas P. *The Natures of John and William Batram, 1734–1777.* New York: Knopf, 1996.

Sleeper-Smith, Susan. *Indian Women and French Men.* Amherst: University of Massachusetts Press, 2001.

Smith, Billy G. *The "Lower Sort:" Philadelphia's Laboring People, 1750–1800.* Ithaca, N.Y.: Cornell University Press, 1990.

Smith, Billy G. and Richard Wojtowicz, eds. *Blacks Who Stole Themselves: Advertisements for Runaways in the Pennsylvania Gazette, 1728–1790.* Philadelphia: University of Pennsylvania Press, 1989.

Smith, William, Jr. *History of the Province of New York,* 2 vols. Cambridge, Mass.: Harvard University Press, 1972.

Thornton, John. *Africa and Africans in the Making of the Atlantic World, 1400–1680.* Cambridge, U.K.: Cambridge University Press, 1992.

Ulrich, Laurel Thatcher. *Good Wives: Image and Reality in the Lives of Women in Northern New England, 1650–1750.* New York: Knopf, 1982.

Wallace, Anthony F. C. *The Death and Rebirth of the Seneca.* New York: Knopf, 1970.

Weber, David J. *The Spanish Frontier in North America.* New Haven, Conn.: Yale University Press, 1992.

Wells, Robert V. *Revolutions in Americans' Lives: A Demographic Perspective on the History of Americans, Their Families, and Their Society.* Westport, Conn.: Greenwood Press, 1982.

White, Richard. *The Middle Ground: Indians, Empires, and Republics in the Great Lake Region, 1650–1815.* New York: Cambridge University Press, 1991.

Wokeck, Marianne. *Trade in Strangers: The Beginnings of Mass Migration to North America.* University Park: Pennsylvania State University Press, 1999.

Wood, Betty. *Slavery in Colonial Georgia.* Athens, Ga.: University of Georgia Press, 1983.

Wood, Peter H. *Black Majority: Negroes in Colonial South Carolina from 1670 through the Stono Rebellion.* New York: Norton, 1974.

Wulf, Karin A. *Not All Wives: Women of Colonial Philadelphia.* Ithaca, N.Y.: Cornell University Press, 2001.

Index

Boldface page numbers denote extensive treatment of a topic. *Italic* page numbers refer to illustrations; *c* refers to the Chronology; and *m* indicates a map.

D

K

L

M

S

T